Critical Race Theory

Critical Race Theory

THE KEY WRITINGS
That Formed the Movement

Edited by

KIMBERLÉ CRENSHAW,

NEIL GOTANDA, GARY PELLER, AND

KENDALL THOMAS

The New Press · New York

Page v constitutes an extension of this copyright page.

Requests for permission to reproduce selections from this book should
be made through our website: https://thenewpress.com/contact.

Published in the United States by The New Ptess, New York, 1996
Distributed by Two Rivers Distribution

ISBN 978-1-56584-270-0 (hc.)
ISBN 978-1-56584-271-7 (pbk.)
CIP data available.

The New Press publishes books that promote and enrich public discussion and
understanding of the issues vital to our democracy and to a more equitable world.
These books are made possible by the enthusiasm of our readers; the support of a
committed group of donors, large and small; the collaboration of our many partners in the
independent media and the not-for-profit sector; booksellers, who often hand-sell
New Press books; librarians; and above all by our authors.

www.thenewpress.com

Book design by Charles Nix

Printed in the United States of America

20

CONTENTS

Foreword   xi

Introduction   xiii

PART 1. INTELLECTUAL PRECURSORS: EARLY CRITICISM
OF CONVENTIONAL CIVIL RIGHTS DISCOURSE

Derrick A. Bell, Jr.
Serving Two Masters: Integration Ideals and Client Interests   5
in School Desegregation Litigation

Derrick A. Bell, Jr.
Brown v. Board of Education and the Interest Convergence Dilemma   20

Alan David Freeman
Legitimizing Racial Discrimination through Antidiscrimination Law: A Critical Review   29
of Supreme Court Doctrine

Richard Delgado
The Imperial Scholar: Reflections on a Review of Civil Rights Literature   46

PART 2. CRITICAL RACE THEORY AND CRITICAL LEGAL STUDIES:
CONTESTATION AND COALITION

Mari Matsuda
Looking to the Bottom: Critical Legal Studies and Reparations   63

Harlon L. Dalton
The Clouded Prism: Minority Critique of the Critical Legal Studies Movement   80

Anthony E. Cook
Beyond Critical Legal Studies: The Reconstructive Theology of Dr. Martin   85
Luther King, Jr.

Kimberlé Williams Crenshaw
Race, Reform, and Retrenchment: Transformation and Legitimation in Anti-   103
discrimination Law

PART 3. TOWARD A CRITICAL CULTURAL PLURALISM: PROGRESSIVE ALTERNATIVES TO MAINSTREAM CIVIL RIGHTS IDEOLOGY

Gary Peller
Race-Consciousness   127

Duncan Kennedy
A Cultural Pluralist Case for Affirmative Action in Legal Academia   159

Gerald Torres and Kathryn Milun
Translating "Yonnondio" by Precedent and Evidence: The Mashpee Indian Case   177

Patricia J. Williams
Metro Broadcasting, Inc. v. FCC: Regrouping In Singular Times   191

PART 4. CRITICAL RACE THEORY AND LEGAL DOCTRINE

Lani Guinier
Groups, Representation, and Race-Conscious Districting: A Case of the Emperor's Clothes   205

Charles R. Lawrence, III
The Id, the Ego, and Equal Protection: Reckoning With Unconscious Racism   235

Neil Gotanda
A Critique Of "Our Constitution Is Color-Blind"   257

Cheryl I. Harris
Whiteness as Property   276

Linda Greene
Race in the Twenty-First Century: Equality through Law?   292

Derrick A. Bell, Jr.
Racial Realism   302

PART 5. THE SEARCH FOR AN OPPOSITIONAL VOICE

John O. Calmore
Critical Race Theory, Archie Shepp, and Fire Music: Securing an Authentic Intellectual Life in a Multicultural World   315

Taunya Lovell Banks
Two Life Stories: Reflections of One Black Woman Law Professor   329

Charles R. Lawrence, III
The Word and the River: Pedagogy as Scholarship as Struggle   336

PART 6. THE INTERSECTION OF RACE AND GENDER

Kimberlé Williams Crenshaw
  Mapping the Margins: Intersectionality, Identity Politics, and Violence   357
  Against Women of Color

Dorothy E. Roberts
  Punishing Drug Addicts Who Have Babies: Women of Color, Equality,   384
  and the Right of Privacy

Regina Austin
  Sapphire Bound!   426

PART 7. RACE AND POSTMODERNISM

Jayne Chong-Soon Lee
  Navigating the Topology of Race   441

Richard Thompson Ford
  The Boundaries of Race: Political Geography in Legal Analysis   449

Kendall Thomas
  Rouge et Noir Reread: A Popular Constitutional History of the Angelo   465
  Herndon Case

PERMISSIONS

Foreword

CRITICAL Race Theory is the most exciting development in contemporary legal studies. This comprehensive movement in thought and life—created primarily, though not exclusively, by progressive intellectuals of color—compels us to confront critically the most explosive issue in American civilization: the historical centrality and complicity of law in upholding white supremacy (and concomitant hierarchies of gender, class, and sexual orientation). The pioneering works of the late, visionary legal scholar Robert Cover and the distinguished judge and pioneering historian A. Leon Higginbotham, Jr., were prophetic voices in the legal wilderness a few decades ago. But their focus on the fundamental role of race in the formation of American law was marginalized in the American legal academy. Hence, the doings and sufferings of indigenous people, Latin-, Asian-, and African-Americans remained, for the most part, hidden in American legal education. When Derrick Bell, Jr., began to question the basic assumptions of the law's treatment of people of color in the leading law reviews—the essays that open this collection—he was virtually the lone dissenter in the arena of legal scholarship.

The genesis of Critical Race Theory as a scholarly and politically committed movement in law is historic. Critical Race Theorists have, for the first time, examined the entire ediface of contemporary legal thought and doctrine from the viewpoint of law's role in the construction and maintenance of social domination and subordination. In the process, they not only challenged the basic assumptions and presuppositions of the prevailing paradigms among mainstream liberals and conservatives in the legal academy, but also confronted the relative silence of legal radicals—namely critical legal studies writers—who "deconstructed" liberalism, yet seldom addressed the role of deepseated racism in American life. These pages reflect the complex set of inquiries that Critical Race Theorists have pursued in the process of mounting an intellectual and political opposition to the prevailing ideology of contemporary American law: What does it mean to engage in theoretical activity at this downbeat moment in American society and culture? How do we candidly incorporate experiences of intense alienaton and subordination into the subtle way of "doing " theory in American academy? What are the new constructive frameworks that result from the radical critiques of the prevailing paradigms in United States legal education? What is our vocation as oppositional intellectuals who choose to stay in a legal academy of which we do not feel fully a part? How can liberation-minded scholars of color engage with white radical intellectuals without falling into the pitfalls of coalitions between such groups in the sixties?

In short, Critical Race Theory is an intellectual movement that is both particular to our postmodern (and conservative) times and part of a long tradition of human resistance and liberation. On the one hand, the movement highlights a creative—and tension-ridden—fusion of theoretical self-reflection, formal innovation, radical politics, existential evaluation, reconstructive experimentation, and vocational anguish. But like all bold attempts to reinterpret and remake the world to reveal silenced suffering and to relieve social misery, Critical Race Theorists put forward novel readings of a hidden past that disclose the flagrant shortcomings of the treacherous present in the light of unrealized—though not unrealizable—possibilities for human freedom and equality.

Reading these pages, one cannot help but conclude that this had been a barbaric century for the legal academy, which has, wittingly or not, constructed for the justificatory framework for shameful social practices that continue to this day. Critical Race Theory is a gasp of emanicipatory hope that law can serve liberation rather than domination.

Cornel West
Harvard University

INTRODUCTION

THIS volume offers a representative, though by no means exhaustive, compilation of the growing body of legal scholarship known as Critical Race Theory (CRT). As we conceive it, Critical Race Theory embraces a movement of left scholars, most of them scholars of color, situated in law schools, whose work challenges the ways in which race and racial power are constructed and represented in American legal culture and, more generally, in American society as a whole. In assembling and editing these essays, we have tried both to provide a sense of the intellectual genesis of this project and to map the main methodological directions that Critical Race Theory has taken since its inception. Toward these ends, the essays in the first few parts are arranged roughly in the chronological order of their publication. The remaining parts, however, are devoted to the most important methodological strands of Critical Race Theory today. We have chosen to present the substance of the original essays rather than small portions of a greater number of works, in the interest of providing the reader with texts that retain as much of their complexity, context, and nuance as possible.

As these writings demonstrate, there is no canonical set of doctrines or methodologies to which we all subscribe. Although Critical Race scholarship differs in object, argument, accent, and emphasis, it is nevertheless unified by two common interests. The first is to understand how a regime of white supremacy and its subordination of people of color have been created and maintained in America, and, in particular, to examine the relationship between that social structure and professed ideals such as "the rule of law" and "equal protection." The second is a desire not merely to understand the vexed bond between law and racial power but to *change* it. The essays gathered here thus share an ethical commitment to human liberation—even if we reject conventional notions of what such a conception means, and though we often disagree, even among ourselves, over its specific direction.

This ethical aspiration finds its most obvious concrete expression in the pursuit of engaged, even adversarial, scholarship. The writings in this collaboration may be read as contributions to what Edward Said has called "antithetical knowledge," the development of counter-accounts of social reality by subversive and subaltern elements of the reigning order. Critical Race Theory—like the Critical Legal Studies movement with which we are often allied—rejects the prevailing orthodoxy that scholarship should be or could be "neutral" and "objective." We believe that legal scholarship about race in America can never be written from a distance of detachment or with an attitude of objectivity. To the extent that racial power is exercised legally and ideologically, legal scholarship about race is an important site for the construction of that power, and thus is always a factor, if "only" ideologically, in the economy of racial power itself. To use a phrase from the existentialist tradition, there is "no exit"—no scholarly perch outside the social dynamics of racial power from which merely to observe and analyze. Scholarship—the formal production, identification, and organization of what will be called "knowledge"—is inevitably political. Each of the texts in this volume seeks in its own way not simply to explicate but also to intervene in the ideological contestation of race in America, and to create new, oppositionist accounts of race.

The aspect of our work which most markedly distinguishes it from conventional liberal and conservative legal scholarship about race and inequality is a deep dissatisfaction with traditional civil rights discourse. As several of the authors in this collection demonstrate, the reigning contemporary American ideologies about race were built in the sixties and seventies around an implicit social compact. This compact held that racial power and racial justice would be understood in very particular ways. Racial justice was embraced in the American mainstream in terms that excluded radical or fundamental challenges to status quo institutional practices in American society by treating the exercise of racial power as rare and aberrational rather than as systemic and ingrained. The construction of "racism" from what Alan Freeman terms the "perpetrator perspective" restrictively conceived racism as an intentional, albeit irrational, deviation by a conscious wrongdoer from otherwise neutral, rational, and just ways of distributing jobs, power, prestige, and wealth. The adoption of this perspective allowed a broad cultural mainstream both explicitly to acknowledge the fact of racism and, simultaneously, to insist on its irregular occurrence and limited significance. As Freeman concludes, liberal race reform thus served to legitimize the basic myths of American meritocracy.

In Gary Peller's depiction, this mainstream civil rights discourse on "race relations" was constructed in this way partly as a defense against the more radical ideologies of racial liberation presented by the Black Nationalist and Black Consciousness movements of the sixties and early seventies, and their less visible but intellectually subversive scholarly presentations by people such as James Turner, now a teacher in black studies at Cornell. In the construction of "racism" as the irrational and backward bias of believing that someone's race is important, the American cultural mainstream neatly linked the black left to the white racist right: according to this quickly coalesced consensus, because race-consciousness characterized both white supremacists and black nationalists, it followed that both were racists. The resulting "center" of cultural common sense thus rested on the exclusion of virtually the entire domain of progressive thinking about race within colored communities. With its explicit embrace of race-consciousness, Critical Race Theory aims to reexamine the terms by which race and racism have been negotiated in American consciousness, and to recover and revitalize the radical tradition of race-consciousness among African-Americans and other peoples of color—a tradition that was discarded when integration, assimilation and the ideal of color-blindness became the official norms of racial enlightenment.

The image of a "traditional civil rights discourse" refers to the constellation of ideas about racial power and social transformation that were constructed partly by, and partly as a defense against, the mass mobilization of social energy and popular imagination in the civil rights movements of the late fifties and sixties. To those who participated in the civil rights movements firsthand—say, as part of the street and body politics engaged in by Reverend Martin Luther King, Jr.'s cadres in town after town across the South—the fact that they were part of a deeply subversive movement of mass resistance and social transformation was obvious. Our opposition to traditional civil rights discourse is neither a criticism of the civil rights movement nor an attempt to diminish its significance. On the contrary, as Anthony Cook's radical reading of King's theology and social theory makes explicit, we draw much of our inspiration and sense of direction from that courageous, brilliantly conceived, spiritually inspired, and ultimately transformative mass action.

Of course, colored people made important social gains through civil rights reform, as did American society generally: in fact, but for the civil rights movements' victories against racial exclusion, this volume and the Critical Race Theory movement generally could not have been taught at mainstream law schools. The law's incorporation of what several authors here call "formal equality" (the prohibition against explicit racial exclusion, like "whites only" signs) marks a decidedly progressive moment in U.S. political and social history. However, the fact that civil rights advocates met with some success in the nation's courts and legislatures ought not obscure the central role the American legal order played in the deradicalization of racial liberation movements. Along with the suppression of explicit white racism (the widely celebrated aim of civil rights reform), the dominant legal conception of racism as a discrete and identifiable act of "prejudice based on skin color" placed virtually the entire range of everyday social practices in America—social practices developed and maintained throughout the period of formal American apartheid—beyond the scope of critical examination or legal remediation.

The affirmative action debate, which is discussed in several essays in this volume, provides a vivid example of what we mean. From its inception, mainstream legal thinking in the U.S. has been characterized by a curiously constricted understanding of race and power. Within this cramped conception of racial domination, the evil of racism exists when—and only when—one can point to specific, discrete acts of racial discrimination, which is in turn narrowly defined as decision-making based on the irrational and irrelevant attribute of race. Given this essentially negative, indeed, dismissive view of racial identity and its social meanings, it was not surprising that mainstream legal thought came to embrace the ideal of "color-blindness" as the dominant moral compass of social enlightenment about race. Mainstream legal argument regarding "race relations" typically defended its position by appropriating Dr. King's injunction that a person should be judged "by the content of his character rather than the color of his skin" and wedding it to the regnant ideologies of equal opportunity and American meritocracy. Faced with this state of affairs, liberal proponents of affirmative action in legal and policy arenas—who had just successfully won the formal adoption of basic antidiscrimination norms—soon found themselves in a completely defensive ideological posture. Affirmative action requires the use of race as a socially significant category of perception and representation, but the deepest elements of mainstream civil rights ideology had come to identify such race-consciousness as racism itself. Indeed, the problem here was not simply political and strategic: the predominant legal representation of racism as the mere recognition of race matched the "personal" views of many liberals themselves, creating for them a contradiction in their hearts as well as their words.

Liberal antidiscrimination proponents proposed various ways to reconcile this contradiction: they characterized affirmative action as a merely "exceptional" remedy for past injustice, a temporary tool to be used only until equal opportunity is achieved or a default mechanism for reaching discrimination that could not be proved directly. Separate but related liberal defenses of affirmative action hold that its beneficiaries have suffered from "deprived" backgrounds that require limited special consideration in the otherwise fully rational and unbiased competition for social goods, or that affirmative action promotes social "diversity," a value which in the liberal vision is independent of, perhaps even at odds with, equality of opportunity or meritocracy.

The poverty of the liberal imagination is belied by the very fact that liberal theories of affirmative action are framed in such defensive terms, and so clearly shaped by the felt need to justify this perceived departure from purportedly objective findings of "merit" (or the lack thereof). These apologetic strategies testify to the deeper ways civil rights reformism has helped to legitimize the very social practices—in employment offices and admissions departments—that were originally targeted for reform. By constructing "discrimination" as a deviation from otherwise legitimate selection processes, liberal race rhetoric affirms the underlying ideology of just desserts, even as it reluctantly tolerates limited exceptions to meritocratic mythology. Despite their disagreements about affirmative action, liberals and conservatives who embrace dominant civil rights discourse treat the category of merit itself as neutral and impersonal, outside of social power and unconnected to systems of racial privilege. Rather than engaging in a broad-scale inquiry into why jobs, wealth, education, and power are distributed as they are, mainstream civil rights discourse suggests that once the irrational biases of race-consciousness are eradicated, everyone will be treated fairly, as equal competitors in a regime of equal opportunity.

What we find most amazing about this ideological structure in retrospect is how very little actual social change was imagined to be required by "the civil rights revolution." One might have expected a huge controversy over the dramatic social transformation necessary to eradicate the regime of American apartheid. By and large, however, the very same whites who administered explicit policies of segregation and racial domination kept their jobs as decision makers in employment offices of companies, admissions offices of schools, lending offices of banks, and so on. In institution after institution, progressive reformers found themselves struggling over the implementation of integrationist policy with the former administrators of segregation who soon regrouped as an old guard "concerned" over the deterioration of "standards."

The continuity of institutional authority between the segregationist and civil rights regimes is only part of the story. Even more dramatic, the same criteria for defining "qualifications" and "merit" used during the period of explicit racial exclusion continued to be used, so long as they were not directly "racial." Racism was identified only with the outright formal exclusion of people of color; it was simply assumed that the whole rest of the culture, and the de facto segregation of schools, work places, and neighborhoods, would remain the same. The sheer taken-for-grantedness of this way of thinking would pose a formidable and practically insurmountable obstacle. Having rejected race-consciousness in toto, there was no conceptual basis from which to identify the cultural and ethnic character of mainstream American institutions; they were thus deemed to be racially and culturally neutral. As a consequence, the deeply transformative potential of the civil rights movement's interrogation of racial power was successfully aborted as a piece of mainstream American ideology.

Within the predominantly white law school culture where most of the authors represented in this volume spend professional time, the law's "embrace" of civil rights in the Warren Court era is proclaimed as the very hallmark of justice under the rule of law. In our view, the "legislation" of the civil rights movement and its "integration" into the mainstream commonsense assumptions in the late sixties and early seventies were premised on a tragically narrow and conservative picture of the goals of racial justice and the domains of racial power. In the balance of this introduction, we describe as matters both of institutional politics and intellectual inquiry how we have come to these kinds of conclusions.

In his essay on the Angelo Herndon case, Kendall Thomas describes and pursues a central project of Critical Race scholarship: the use of critical historical method to show that the contemporary structure of civil rights rhetoric is not the natural or inevitable meaning of racial justice but, instead, a collection of strategies and discourses born of and deployed in particular political, cultural, and institutional conflicts and negotiations. Our goal here is similar. We hope to situate the strategies and discourses of Critical Race Theory within the broader intellectual and social currents from which we write, as well as within the specific work place and institutional positions where we are located and from which we struggle.

The emergence of Critical Race Theory in the eighties, we believe, marks an important point in the history of racial politics in the legal academy and, we hope, in the broader conversation about race and racism in the nation as a whole. As we experienced it, mostly as law students or beginning law professors, the boundaries of "acceptable" race discourse had become suddenly narrowed, in the years from the late sixties to the late seventies and early eighties, both in legal institutions and in American culture more generally. In the law schools we attended, there were definite liberal and conservative camps of scholars and students. While the debate in which these camps engaged were clearly important—for example, how the law should define and identify illegal racial power—the reigning discourse seemed, at least to us, ideologically impoverished and technocratic.

In constitutional law, for example, it was well settled that government-sanctioned racial discrimination was prohibited, and that legally enforced segregation constituted such discrimination. That victory was secured in *Brown v. Board of Education* and its progeny. In the language of the Fourteenth Amendment, race is a "suspect classification" which demands judicial strict scrutiny. "Race relations" thus represent an exception to the general deference that mainstream constitutional theory accords democratically elected institutions. Racial classifications violate the equal protection clause unless they both serve a compelling governmental interest and further, are no broader than necessary to achieve that goal. Within the conceptual boundaries of these legal doctrines, mainstream scholars debated whether discrimination should be defined only as intentional government action . . . or whether the tort-like "de facto" test should be used when government actions had predictable, racially skewed results . . . or whether the racial categories implicit in affirmative action policy should be legally equivalent to those used to burden people of color and therefore also be subject to strict scrutiny . . . and then whether remedying past social discrimination was a sufficiently compelling and determinate goal to survive strict scrutiny . . . and so on.

In all these debates we identified, of course, with the liberals against the intent requirement established in *Washington v. Davis*, the affirmative action limitations of *Bakke* (and later *Croson*), the curtailment of the "state action" doctrine resulting in the limitation of sites where constitutional antidiscrimination norms would apply, and so on. Yet the whole discourse seemed to assume away the fundamental problem of racial subordination whose examination was at the center of the work so many of us had spent our college years pursuing in Afro-American studies departments, community mobilizations, student activism, and the like.

The fact that affirmative action was seen as

such a "dilemma" or a "necessary evil" was one symptom of the ultimately conservative character of even "liberal" mainstream race discourse. More generally, though, liberals and conservatives seemed to see the issues of race and law from within the same structure of analysis—namely, a policy that legal rationality could identify and eradicate the biases of race-consciousness in social decision-making. Liberals and conservatives as a general matter differed over the degree to which racial bias was a fact of American life: liberals argued that bias was widespread where conservatives insisted it was not; liberals supported a disparate effects test for identifying discrimination, where conservatives advocated a more restricted intent requirement; liberals wanted an expanded state action requirement, whereas conservatives wanted a narrow one. The respective visions of the two factions differed only in scope: they defined and constructed "racism" the same way, as the opposite of color-blindness.

In any event, however compelling the liberal vision of achieving racial justice through legal reform overseen by a sympathetic judiciary may have been in the sixties and early seventies, the breakdown of the national consensus for the use of law as an instrument for racial redistribution rendered the vision far less capable of appearing even merely pragmatic. By the late seventies, traditional civil rights lawyers found themselves fighting, and losing, rearguard attacks on the limited victories they had only just achieved in the prior decade, particularly with respect to affirmative action and legal requirements for the kinds of evidence required to prove illicit discrimination. An increasingly conservative judiciary made it clear that the age of ever expanding progressive law reform was over.

At the same time that these events were unfolding, a predominantly white left emerged on the law school scene in the late seventies, a development which played a central role in the genesis of Critical Race Theory. Organized by a collection of neo-Marxist intellectuals, former New Left activists, ex-counter-culturalists, and other varieties of oppositionists in law schools, the Conference on Critical Legal Studies established itself as a network of openly leftist law teachers, students, and practitioners committed to exposing and challenging the ways American law served to legitimize an oppressive social order. Like the later experience of Critical Race writers vis-à-vis race scholarship, "crits" found themselves frustrated with the presuppositions of the conventional scholarly legal discourse: they opposed not only conservative legal work but also the dominant liberal varieties. Crits contended that liberal and conservative legal scholarship operated in the narrow ideological channel within which law was understood as qualitatively different from politics. The faith of liberal lawyers in the gradual reform of American law through the victory of the superior rationality of progressive ideas depended on a belief in the central ideological myth of the law/politics distinction, namely, that legal institutions employ a rational, apolitical, and neutral discourse with which to mediate the exercise of social power. This, in essence, is the role of law as understood by liberal political theory. Yet politics was embedded in the very doctrinal categories with which law organized and represented social reality. Thus the deeply political character of law was obscured in one way by the obsession of mainstream legal scholarship with technical discussions about standing, jurisdiction and procedure; and the political character of judicial decision-making was denied in another way through the reigning assumptions that legal decision-making was—or could be—determined by preexisting legal rules, standards, and policies, all of which were applied according to professional craft standards encapsulated in the idea of "reasoned elaboration." Law was, in the conventional wisdom, distinguished from politics because politics was open-ended, subjective, discretionary, and ideological, whereas law was determinate, objective, bounded, and neutral.

This conception of law as rational, apolitical, and technical operated as an institutional regulative principle, defining what was legitimate and illegitimate to pursue in legal scholarship, and symbolically defining the professional, businesslike culture of day-to-day life in mainstream law schools. This generally centrist legal culture characterized the entire post-war period in legal education, with virtually no organized dissent. Its intellectual and ideological premises had not been seriously challenged since the Legal Realist movement of the twenties and thirties—a body of scholarship that mainstream scholars ritually honored for the critique of the "formalism" of turn-of-the-century legal discourse but marginalized as having "gone too far" in its critique of the very possibility of a rule of law. Writing during the so-called liberty of contract period (characterized by the Supreme Court's invalidation of labor reform legislation on the grounds that it violated the "liberty" of workers and owners to contract with each other over terms of employment) the legal realists set out to show that the purportedly neutral and objective legal interpretation of the period was really based on politics, on what Oliver Wendell Holmes called the "hidden and often inarticulate judgments of social policy."

The crits unearthed much of the Legal Realist work that mainstream legal scholars had ignored for decades, and they found the intellectual and theoretical basis for launching a full-scale critique of the role of law in helping to rationalize an unjust social order. While the Realist critique of American law's pretensions to neutrality and rationality was geared to ward the right-wing libertarianism of an "Old Order" of jurists, crits redirected it at the depoliticized and technocratic assumptions of legal education and scholarship in the seventies. Moreover, in the sixties tradition from which many of them had come, they extended the intellectual and ideological conflict they engendered to the law school culture to which it was linked.

By the late seventies, Critical Legal Studies existed in a swirl of formative energy, cultural insurgency, and organizing momentum: It had established itself as a politically, philosophically, and methodologically eclectic but intellectually sophisticated and ideologically left movement in legal academia, and its conferences had begun to attract hundreds of progressive law teachers, students, and lawyers; even mainstream law reviews were featuring critical work that reinterpreted whole doctrinal areas of law from an explicitly ideological motivation. Moreover, in viewing law schools as work-places, and thus as organizing sites for political resistance, "CLSers" actively recruited students and left-leaning law teachers from around the country to engage in the construction of left legal scholarship and law school transformation. CLS quickly became the organizing hub for a huge burst of left legal scholarly production and for various oppositional political challenges in law school institutional life. Several left scholars of color identified with the movement, and, most important for the eventual genesis of Critical Race Theory a few years later, CLS succeeded in at least one aspect of its frontal assault on the depoliticized character of legal education. By the late seventies, explicitly right-wing legal scholarship had developed its own critique of the conventional assumptions, just as the national mood turned to the right with the election of Ronald Reagan. The law school as an institution was, by then, an obvious site for ideological contestation as the apolitical pretensions of the "nonideological" center began to disintegrate.

Critical Race Theory emerged in the interstices of this political and institutional dynamic. Critical Race Theory thus represents an attempt to inhabit and expand the space between two very different intellectual and ideological formations. Critical Race Theory sought to stage a simultaneous encounter with the exhausted vision of reformist civil rights scholarship, on the one hand, and the emergent critique of left legal scholarship on the other. Critical Race Theory's engagement with the discourse of civil rights reform stemmed directly from our lived experience as students and teachers in the nation's law schools. We both saw and suffered the concrete consequences that followed from liberal legal thinkers' failure to address the constrictive role that racial ideology plays in the composition and culture of American institutions, including the American law school. Our engagement with progressive-left legal academics stemmed from our sense that their focus on legal ideology, legal scholarship and the politics of the American law school provided a language and a practice for viewing the institutions in which we studied and worked both as sites of and targets for our developing critique of law, racism, and social power.

In identifying the liberal civil rights tradition and the Critical Legal Studies movement as key factors in the emergence of Critical Race Theory, we do not mean to offer an oversimplified genealogy in which Critical Race Theory appears as a simple hybrid of the two. We view liberal civil rights scholarship and the work of the critical legal theorists not so much as rudimentary components of Critical Race Theory, but as elements in the conditions of its possibility. In short, we intend to evoke a particular atmosphere in which progressive scholars of color struggled to piece together an intellectual identity and a political practice that would take the form both of a left intervention into race discourse and a race intervention into left discourse. To better capture the dynamics of these trajectories, we now turn to two key institutional events in the development of Critical Race Theory as a movement. The first is the student protest, boycott, and organization of an alternative course on race and law at Harvard Law School in 1981—an event that highlights the significance of Derrick Bell and the Critical Legal Studies movement to the ultimate development of Critical Race Theory, and symbolizes Critical Race Theory's oppositional posture vis-à-vis the liberal mainstream. The second is the 1987 Critical Legal Studies National Conference on silence and race, which marked the genesis of an intellectually distinctive critical account of race on terms set forth by race-conscious scholars of color, and the terms of contestation and coalition with CLS.

As Richard Delgado states in "The Imperial Scholar," quite bluntly, the study of civil rights and antidiscrimination law in the mainstream law schools in which we found ourselves in the eighties was dominated by a group consisting almost entirely of white male constitutional law professors. Derrick Bell was one of the few exceptions; he went to Harvard after a distinguished record as a litigator in the civil rights movement, becoming one of only two African-American professors on the large Harvard faculty. In his course and book *Race, and Racism and American Law,* Bell developed and taught legal doctrine from a race-conscious viewpoint. Implicitly repudiating the reigning idea of the color-blindness of law, pedagogy, and scholarship, he used racial politics rather than the formal structure of legal doctrine as the organizing concept for scholarly study.

It is important to understand the centrality of Bell's coursebook and his opposition to the traditional liberal approach to racism for the eventual development of the Critical Race Theory movement. A symbol of his influence is his inclusion as the first page of his book of a photograph of Thomas Smith and John Carlos accepting their Olympic trophies at the 1968 Mexico City Summer Games. In the foreground are balding white men in suits, apparently Olympic officials of some kind; rising behind them are Smith and Carlos, standing on the raised platforms in sleek warmup suits, at the height of their competitive achievement. In one hand, the victorious athletes hold their gold and silver medals; Smith and Carlos defiantly hold their other hand over their heads in the clinched fist of the Black Power salute. This symbolic action, staged during the playing of the National Anthem, spawned an enormous controversy in the United States; patriots charged that Smith and Carlos embarrassed the country and privileged their racial identity over their more important identity as Americans.

To those of us who were then law students and beginning law teachers, Bell's inclusion of the Smith-Carlos photograph as a visual introduction to his law school casebook suggested a link between his work and the Black Power movements that most of us "really" identified with, whose political insights and aspirations went far beyond what could be articulated in the reigning language of the legal profession and the legal studies we were pursuing. Although we could not then fully articulate the nature and basis of this connection, we were able to recognize that Derrick Bell's position within legal study bore a family resemblance to the oppositional stance that Smith and Carlos had taken in Mexico City. Just as Carlos and Smith participated on behalf of their nation in the Olympic competition, Bell had chosen to enter the arena of American legal scholarship instead of eschewing it and taking the path of total separation. Similarly, just as Carlos and Smith refused to allow American nationalism to subsume their racial identity, Bell insisted on placing race at the center of his intellectual inquiry rather than marginalizing it as a sub-classification under the formal rubric of this or that legal doctrine. In a subtle way, Bell's position within the legal academy—an arena that defined itself within the conventional legal discourse as neutral to race—was akin to putting up his fist in the black power salute.

As his articles in the first part of this volume demonstrate, Bell provided some of the earliest theoretical alternatives to the dominant civil rights vision we have described. In the face of the hegemony of racial integration as the ideal of reform in the seventies, he argued in "Serving Two Masters," the essay that opens this collection, that the exclusive focus on the goal of school integration responded to the ideals of elite liberal public interest lawyers rather than to the actual interests of black communities and children. In "The Interest-Convergence Dilemma," Bell sketched a full-scale structural theory to account for the ebb and flow of civil rights reform in America, according to the political machinations of whites themselves.

In 1980, Bell left Harvard to become dean of the University of Oregon Law School and one of the first African-Americans to head a mainstream American law school. Student activists, particularly students of color, demanded that Harvard hire a teacher of color to replace him and to teach his courses in constitutional law and minority issues. The liberal white Harvard administration responded to student protests, demonstrations, rallies and sit-ins—including a takeover of the Dean's office—by asserting that there were no qualified black scholars who merited Harvard's interest. Harvard's response was structured around two points produced from within liberal race discourse which Critical Race Theory would ultimately contest. First, they asked why the students wouldn't prefer an excellent white professor over a mediocre black one—that is, at a conceptual level, they posited the particular liberal epistemology that associated color-blindness with intellectual merit. Second, the Harvard administration, skeptical about the pedagogical value of a course devoted to racial topics, asserted that no special course was needed when "those issues" were already covered in classes devoted to constitutional law and employment discrimination thus, to our minds, failing to comprehend the significance of Bell's projects. Instead, Jack Greenberg and Julius Chambers, both important and distinguished civil rights litigators, were hired to teach a three-week mini-course on civil rights litigation.

It was in the midst of this kind of institutional struggle, played out in one form or another at mainstream law schools around the country, that many of us now writing in the Critical Race Theory genre began to elaborate what we took to be the limitations of traditional race analysis and argument. After all, in a context such as Harvard, administrators saw themselves as racially enlightened: they were liberals who were against racial discrimination—indeed, Harvard wanted to honor a heroic litigator of the school desegregation era with a visiting professorship. Clearly, the cool, technocratic and business-like culture of mainstream law schools was hostile at all points to raw "prejudice"—these were not institutions in which a hardcore, "Bull Conner" type racist would receive a warm welcome. Although those of us who were agitating for hiring teachers of color knew we didn't accept the kinds of justifications the Harvard administrators offered, we also knew that we lacked an adequate critical vocabulary for articulating exactly what we found wrong in their arguments. It was out of this intellectual void that the impetus for a new conceptual approach to race and law was based. Our critique of ideas like "color-blindness," "formal legal equality," and "integrationism" are linked to their institutional manifestations as a rhetoric of power in the schools we attended and the work-places we now occupy.

In the local Harvard confrontation, student organizers decided to boycott the mini-course offered by the administration and organized instead "The Alternative Course," a student-led continuation of Bell's course which focused on

American law through the prism of race. Taught by scholars of color from other schools who were each asked to speak about topics loosely organized to trace the chapters of Bell's *Race, Racism and American Law* book, the course simultaneously provided the means to develop a framework to understand law and racial power and to contest Harvard's deployment of meritocratic mythology as an instance of that very power.

The Alternative Course was in many ways the first institutionalized expression of Critical Race Theory. With the aid of outside funding and sympathetic Harvard teachers (many of them white crits who provided encouragement, strategic advice, and independent study credit to enable students to attend the classes) the course brought together a critical mass of scholars and students, and focused on the need to develop an alternative account of racial power and its relation to law and antidiscrimination reform. Among the guest speakers were Charles Lawrence, Linda Greene, Neil Gotanda, and Richard Delgado, all of whom were already in law teaching. Mari Matsuda, then a graduate law student, was a participant in the Alternative Course, and Kimberlé Crenshaw one of its main organizers.

The Alternative Course is a useful point to mark the genesis of Critical Race Theory for many reasons. First, it was one of the earliest attempts to bring scholars of color together to address the law's treatment of race from a self-consciously critical perspective. There had been some race-conscious organizing in law schools in the preceding years. For example, within the Association of American Law Schools, (AALS) the professional association of law teachers, a minority section had been established which Ralph Smith of the University of Pennsylvania and Denise Carty-Bennia of Northeastern University used as a vehicle for intellectual development. However, the AALS group neither provided a basis for sustained dialogue, nor openly identified itself within the profession as intellectually oppositional and politically left-progressive. Recognizing these inherent institutional limitations, legal academics of color created an informal network of support for law students and teachers of color, whose existence was enormously important in developing a critical mass of law teachers of color. These were efforts, though, that carried no direct implications for scholarship and theory.

Second, the Alternative Course exemplified another important feature of the Critical Race Theory movement, namely, the view—shared with the Critical Legal Studies movement—that it is politically meaningful to contest the terrain and terms of dominant legal discourse. In one sense, the importance of mainstream law school discourse to Critical Race Theorists flows from the view that power is implicated in, say, the privileging of certain topics and viewpoints as worthy of being curricular entries at mainstream law schools. The idea here, in essence, is that knowledge and politics are inevitably intertwined. As an influential site for indoctrination and propagation, the ideology of law schools helps in turn to shape and give substance to the broader legal and social ideologies about race and legitimacy. In another sense, the focus on the law school and legal scholarship as a terrain worth contesting is based on a view of law schools in left terms as work-places in which we find ourselves as part of a productive enterprise, the "production of knowledge." This perspective helps to explain an important difference with earlier conceptions of race reform, which looked to law schools and other legal institutions as places to gather tools to deploy in political struggles that occurred "out there" in the South, the ghetto, or some other place besides law schools or courtrooms themselves. Against this view, we take racial power to be at stake across the social plane—not merely in the places where people of color are concentrated but also in the institutions where their position is normalized and given legitimation. The Alternative Course reflected—as well as helped to create—the sense that it was meaningful to build an oppositional community of left scholars of color within the mainstream legal academy.

Finally, the Alternative Course embodied one of the key markers of Critical Race Theory—the way in which our intellectual trajectories are rooted in a dissatisfaction with and opposition to liberal mainstream discourses about race such as those presented by the Harvard administration.

We turn now to the Critical Legal Studies conferences of the mid-eighties and the general engagement with the white left in and outside of the legal academy both of which were crucial in the development of the Critical Race Theory project. If the Alternative Course symbolizes the trajectory of Critical Race Theory as a left intervention in conventional race discourse, then the Critical Legal Studies Conferences during the mid-eighties can be equally useful in situating Critical Race Theory as a race-conscious intervention on the left.

At its inception in the late 70s, Critical Legal Studies (CLS) was basically a white and largely male academic organization. By the mid-eighties, there was a small cadre of scholars of color who frequented CLS conferences and summer camps. Most were generally conversant with Critical Legal Theory and sympathetic to the progressive sensibilities of Critical Legal Studies as a whole. Unlike the law school mainstream, this cadre was far from deterred by CLS critique of liberal legalism. While many in the legal community were, to put it mildly, deeply disturbed by the CLS assault against such ideological mainstays as the rule of the law, to scholars of color who drew on a history of colored communities' struggle against formal and institutional racism, the crits' contention that law was neither apolitical, neutral, nor determinate hardly seemed controversial. Indeed, we believed that this critical perspective formed the basic building blocks of any serious attempt to understand the relationship between law and white supremacy. However, while the emerging "race crits" shared this starting position with CLS, significant differences between us became increasingly apparent during a series of conferences in the mid-eighties.

Our discussions during the conferences revealed that while we shared with crits the belief that legal consciousness functioned to legitimize social power in the United States, race crits also understood that race and racism likewise functioned as central pillars of hegemonic power. Because CLS scholars had not, by and large, developed and incorporated a critique of racial power into their analysis, their practices, politics and theories regarding race tended to be unsatisfying and sometimes indistinguishable from those of the dominant institutions they were otherwise contesting. As race moved from the margins to the center of discourse within Critical Legal Studies—or, as some would say, Critical Legal Studies took the race turn— institutional and theoretical disjunctures between critical legal studies and the emerging scholarship on race eventually manifested themselves as central themes within Critical Race Theory.

One of the most significant institutional manifestations of CLS's underdeveloped critique of racial power occurred during the 1986 CLS conference. The 1986 conference, organized by a group of women who worked in feminist legal theory, marked the zenith of the feminist turn within CLS. Having placed feminism and its critique of patriarchy squarely within the discourse of and about CLS, the "fem-crit" conference organizers asked scholars of color to facilitate several concurrently held discussions about race. Drawing on a central CLS tenet that power is not, ultimately, "out there," but in the very institutions and relationships that shape our lives, the handful of scholars of color attending this conference designed the workshop to uncover and discuss various dimensions of racial power as manifested within Critical Legal Studies. Though the practice of uncovering and contesting power within law school institutions was a standard feature of CLS politics, the attempt to situate this practice within CLS as a "white" institution drew a surprisingly defensive response. The pitched and heated exchange that erupted in response to our query, "what is it about the whiteness of CLS that discourages participation by people of color?" revealed that CLS's hip, cutting edge irreverence toward establishment practices could easily disintegrate into handwringing hysteria when brought back "home." Of course, not all crits were resistant to this dialogue and it is only fair to point out that those who did find the query to be unnecessarily adversarial probably held a good faith belief that CLS marked a sphere of activity completely distinct from both

law schools and society at large. Since "we" were joined as allies rather than adversaries within the law school arena, crits troubled by our workshop no doubt believed that critical energies would be best directed at tearing down institutional practices at our workplace rather than bringing these disruptive interventions "home." But feminists had already problematized the conceptualization of "home" that seemed to ground this view, revealing such spaces to be a site of hierarchy and power as well. Moreover, as the race crits experienced it, despite some points of convergence, some of the racial dynamics of CLS as an institution were not entirely distinct from the law school cultures "we" had set out to transform.

Another point of conflict and difference between white crits and scholars of color revolved around the widely debated critique of rights. According to other scholars of color at the 1987 conference, another dimension of the failure of CLS to reflect the lived experience of people of color could be glimpsed in the CLS critique of rights. Crits tended to view the idea of legal "rights" as one of the ways that law helps to legitimize the social world by representing it as rationally mediated by the rule of law. Crits also saw legal rights—like those against racial discrimination—as indeterminate and capable of contradictory meanings, and as embodying an alienated way of thinking about social relations.

Crits of color agreed to varying degrees with some dimensions of the critique—for instance, that rights discourse was indeterminate. Yet we sharply differed with critics over the normative implications of this observation. To the emerging race crits, rights discourse held a social and transformative value in the context of racial subordination that transcended the narrower question of whether reliance on rights could alone bring about any determinate results. Race crits realized that the very notion of a subordinate people exercising rights was an important dimension of Black empowerment during the civil rights movement, significant not simply because of the occasional legal victories that were garnered, but because of the transformative dimension of African-Americans re-imagining themselves as full, rights-bearing citizens within the American political imagination. We wanted to acknowledge the centrality of rights discourse even as we recognized that the use of rights language was not without risks. The debate that ensued in light of this different orientation engendered an important CRT theme: the absolute centrality of history and context in any attempt to theorize the relationship between race and legal discourse.

A third ideological difference emerged in a series of critiques of early attempts by scholars of color to articulate how law reflects and produces racial power. Most of these critiques were articulated at the next 1987 CLS conference, "The Sounds of Silence," sponsored by Los Angeles area law schools. Although the terms of the debate were not fully clear, and at the time, there were few key words or concepts on which our analysis could then focus, we have come to articulate the central criticism by crits to be that of "racialism". By racialism, we refer to theoretical accounts of racial power that explain legal and political decisions which are adverse to people of color as mere reflections of underlying white interest. To phrase this critical model in more contemporary terms, we might say that racialism is to power what essentialism is to identity—a narrow, and frequently unsatisfying theory in which complex phenomena are reduced to and presented as a simple reflection of some underlying "facts." Specifically, the "sin" of racialism is that it presumes that racial interests or racial identity exists somewhere outside of or prior to law and is merely reflected in subsequent legal decisions adverse to nonwhites.

Such an approach struck crits as far too instrumental to be a useful account of race and power. During the eighties, crits had been debating the issue of "instrumentalist" and "irrationalist" accounts of law; most agreed with the problematic character of what came to be called "vulgar Marxism." Briefly stated, in traditional Marxist analysis, law appears as merely an instrument of class interests that are rooted outside of law in some "concrete social reality." In sum, law is merely an "ideological reflection" of some class interest rooted elsewhere. Many critics—echoing the late sixties New Left—

sought to distinguish themselves from these "instrumentalist" accounts on the grounds that they embodied a constricted view of the range and sites of the production of social power, and hence of politics. By defining class in terms of one's position in the material production process, and viewing law and all other "superstructural" phenomena as merely reflections of interests rooted in social class identification, vulgar Marxism, crits argued, ignored the ways that law and other merely "superstructural" arenas helped to constitute the very interests that law was supposed merely to reflect. Crits such as Freeman, Duncan Kennedy, and Karl Klare (to name a few) developed non-instrumentalist accounts of law and its relationship to power that focused on legal discourse as a crucial site for the production of ideology and the perpetuation of social power. First, Critical Legal theorists developed a genealogical account of the relationship between law and social interests. Noting the degree, for example, to which political struggles in the U.S. are conducted in the language and logic of the law, crits argued that social interests, and the weight they are accorded, do not exist in advance of or outside the law, but depend on legal institutions and ideology for both their content and form. Second, the crits provided a detailed inventory of the ideological practices by which the legal order actively seeks to persuade those who are subject to it that the law's uneven distribution of social power is nonetheless "just." Third, in their account of legal consciousness, critical legal theorists demonstrated the precise mechanisms by which legal institutions and ideology obscure and thus legitimize their productive, constitutive social role. The crits argued that the law does not passively adjudicate questions of social power; rather, the law is an active instance of the very power politics it purports to avoid and stand above. In brief, the crits revealed in often dizzying detail the cunning complexity of legal texts which traditional Marxists simply dismissed as "capitalist ideology."

One consequence of this particular intellectual genealogy is that in their engagement with orthodox and scientistic forms of Marxist thought on the left, CLS scholars had already developed a critique of the kinds of instrumentalist analyses that were presented in the language of race. To critics of racialism, prevailing theorizations of race and law seemed to represent law as an instrumental reflection of racial interests in much the same way that vulgar Marxists saw the legal arena as reflecting class interests. Just as the white left had learned, by the eighties, that a one-dimensional class account was too simplistic for legal analysis, they interpreted racialist accounts as analogous to class reductionism.

To be sure, some of the foundational essays of CRT could be vulnerable to such a critique, particularly when read apart from the context and conditions of their production. Yet, when read as interventions against a liberal legalist tradition that viewed law as an apolitical mediator of racial conflict, it becomes clear that by articulating a structural relationship between law and white supremacy, these essays dislodged an entrenched pattern of viewing racial outcomes as merely the random consequences of aracial legal processes. These early essays thus constituted a critical first step in identifying the operation of racial power within discursive traditions that had been widely accepted as neutral and apolitical. By legitimizing the use of race as a theoretical fulcrum and focus in legal scholarship, so-called racialist accounts of racism and the law grounded the subsequent development of Critical Race Theory in much the same way that Marxism's introduction of class structure and struggle into classical political economy grounded subsequent critiques of social hierarchy and power.

At the same time, the critique of racialism did help clarify what was "critical" about our race project. As we noted earlier, their dissatisfaction with the narrow instrumentalist view of law had moved CLS scholars to elaborate a theory of the constitutive form of legal ideology. The crits challenged the understanding of social and political interests that instrumentalist portrayals of law had viewed as simply given. The crits' more dynamic and dialectical model revealed the constitutive force of law, the ways legal institutions constructed the very social interests and relations that cruder instrumentalist accounts of law thought it merely regulated and ratified. For our purposes, the chief theoretical advantage of this anatomy of the constitutive dimensions of law was that it made it possible to argue that the legal system is not simply or mainly a biased referee of social and political conflict whose origins and effects occur elsewhere. On this account, the law is shown to be thoroughly involved in constructing the rules of the game, in selecting the eligible players, and in choosing the field on which the game must be played.

Drawing on these premises, we began to think of our project as uncovering how law was a constitutive element of race itself: in other words, how law *constructed* race. Racial power, in our view, was not simply—or even primarily—a product of biased decision-making on the part of judges, but instead, the sum total of the pervasive ways in which law shapes and is shaped by ""race relations" across the social plane. Laws produced racial power not simply through narrowing the scope of, say, of antidiscrimination remedies, nor through racially-biased decision-making, but instead, through myriad legal rules, many of them having nothing to do with rules against discrimination, that continued to reproduce the structures and practices of racial domination. In short, we accepted the crit emphasis on how law produces and is the product of social power and we cross-cut this theme with an effort to understand this dynamic in the context of race and racism. With such an analysis in hand, critical race theory allows us to better understand how racial power can be produced even from within a liberal discourse that is relatively autonomous from organized vectors of racial power.

If the foregoing critique clarified at least one dimension of our project that grew from a shared theoretical investment with CLS, it also revealed subtle, but crucial theoretical divergences between CLS and CRT. Despite the sophistication of the crits' understanding of how law constituted social interests and legal identity, they were, for the most part, unable to transpose these insights into an analysis of racial power and law. Our point here is not that the crits committed the typical Marxist error of subsuming race under class. Rather, our dissatisfaction with CLS stemmed from its failure to come to terms with the particularity of race, and with the specifically racial character of "social interests" in the racialized state. For some, their lack of critical thinking about race was a reflection of intellectual interest. With respect to other crits, however, our divergence produced a much sharper conflict. While we were straining to strengthen our understanding of racial power, it appeared to us that some crits were deploying racialist critiques from a position on race that was close if not identical to the liberalism we were otherwise joined in opposing. To be sure, these crits positioned themselves in a discourse far removed from liberalism—a certain postmodern critique of identity. Yet the upshot of their position seemed to be the same: an abiding skepticism, if not outright disdain, toward any theoretical or political project organized around the concept of race. Where classical liberalism argued that race was irrelevant to public policy, these crits argued that race simply didn't exist. The position is one that we have come to call "vulgar anti-essentialism." By this we seek to capture the claims made by some critical theorists that since racial categories are not "real" or "natural" but instead socially constructed, it is theoretical and politically absurd to center race as a category of analysis or as a basis for political action. This suggested to us that underlying at least some of the critiques from the left was not simply a question about the *way* we represented racial power, but instead, a more fundamental attack on the very possibility of our project. In short, this position constituted an attack on "color-consciousness" which differed from the conservative assault only in its rhetorical politics.

Many of us did, of course, accept the more complicated notions of power and identity implicated by both the anti-instrumentalist and anti-essentialist positions. Yet in our view, neither was inconsistent with the project of mapping the domain of law and racial power. It was obvious to many of us that although race was, to use the term, socially constructed (the idea of biological race is "false"), race was nonetheless "real" in the sense that there is a material dimension and weight to the experience of being "raced" in American society, a materiality that in significant ways has been produced and sustained by law. Thus, we understood our project as an effort to construct a race-conscious and at the same time anti-essentialist account of the processes by which law participates in "race-ing" American society.

Perhaps prophetically, the conference was also occasioned by a prototype of an assault launched against critical race theory from a position firmly situated within the very paradigm we sought to criticize. The highlight of the 1987 conference was a plenary in which numerous scholars of color articulated how institutional practices and intellectual paradigms functioned to silence insurgent voices of people of color. Responding to the critique, another scholar of color shared with the audience his impression that the absence of much of minority scholarship was attributable to its poor quality, and to the lack of productivity of minority scholars. Scholars of color were urged to stop complaining and simply to write. Of course, the discussion that followed was animated. But more important than what was said was what was assumed—namely, that the arena of academic discourse was functionally open to any scholar of merit who sought to enter it. Yet the very point that the speakers were trying to reveal (perhaps too subtly, in retrospect) was that the notions of merit that were so glibly employed to determine access and status within the intellectual arena were themselves repositories of racial power. This exchange, and the subsequent incarnation of this conflict in the pages of the *Harvard Law Review*—provides one of the clearest points of demarcation between critical and liberal race discourses.

The 1986 and 1987 CLS conferences thus marked significant points of alignment and departure, and should be considered the final step in the preliminary development of CRT as a distinctively progressive critique of legal discourse on race. As a political and intellectual matter, the upshot of this engagement with CLS can best be characterized as "coalition." We see CLS and CRT as aligned—in radical left opposition to mainstream legal discourse. But CRT is also different from CLS—our focus on race means that we have addressed quite different concerns, with distinct methodologies and traditions that we honor.

We have argued that the institutional and ideological antecedents of CRT can be usefully grounded in two historical sites: the Harvard boycott, and the CLS conferences of the mid-eighties. These roughly parallel the duality of CRT as both a progressive intervention in race discourse and a race intervention on the left. Yet, while we have identified these moments and will trace the trajectory of these themes into the writings that appear in this volume, it would be remiss for us to leave the impression that CRT subsequently developed as a disembodied, abstracted, and autonomous intellectual formation. In the first place, we believe that this image of scholarship is simply false—intellectual work is always situated, reflective to varying degrees of the cultural, historical, and institutional conditions of its production. Second and most importantly, this view of scholarship obscures the shared difficulties that insurgent scholars must negotiate and the importance of developing collective strategies to write about racial power from within the institutions central to its reproduction. A thorough mapping of Critical Race Theory, then, must include a discussion of the role of community-building among the intellectuals who are associated with it, particularly in light of the challenging conditions under which insurgent scholarship is produced.

During the mid-eighties, many of us met in smaller groups, before and after larger law school conferences and conventions, first at the fringes of and then as a caucus within Critical Legal Studies meetings, and so on. Shared experiences at the margins of liberal institutional policies and critical legal studies provided some basis for a collective identity. Yet the process of recognizing ourselves as a group with a distinct intellectual project was gradual. Our ad hoc meetings prior to and during various conferences provided an occasional opportunity to discuss our views; however, the key formative event was the founding of the Critical Race Theory workshop. Principally organized by Kimberlé Crenshaw, Neil Gotanda, and Stephanie Phillips, the workshop drew together thirty five law scholars who responded to a call to synthesize a theory that, while grounded in critical theory, was responsive to the realities of racial politics in America. Indeed, the organizers coined the term "Critical Race Theory" to make it clear that our work locates itself in intersection of critical theory and race, racism and the law. To be sure, while we have emphasized throughout the liberal and critical poles against which Critical Race Theory developed, in experience, such dialectical relations produce less of a sharp break, and more of a creative and contestatory engagement with both traditions. This is true not only of the content of Critical Race Theory, but is true as well of the workshop's participants. Indeed, both liberal race theorists and critical legal theorists have been deeply engaged in critical race discourse. For example, among the range of scholars who were attracted to the workshop and who contributed to the development of Critical Race Theory were scholars who had written squarely within the liberal paradigm. The workshop itself was underwritten by a grant provided by David Trubek, a founding member of the Critical Legal Studies Conference and a law professor at the University of Wisconsin, Madison. Finally, as this volume attests, we consider the work of members of CLS conference to represent a crucial contribution to the Critical Race Theory literature.

In the opening pages of this introduction, we argued that Critical Race Theory does not simply seek to understand the complex condominia of law, racial ideology, and political power. We believe that our work can provide a useful theoretical vocabulary for the practice of progressive racial politics in contemporary America. The need for an oppositional vision of racial justice becomes particularly acute in light of the Supreme Court's radical movement toward a jurisprudence which not only accepts but affirms the current racial regime.

As this volume goes to press, the U.S. Supreme Court has issued a series of decisions which effectively repeal the ideological "settlement" struck during the civil rights era. In *Adarand Constructors* v. *Pena,* the Supreme Court extended its 1989 decision in *City of Richmond* v. *J.A. Croson* to categorically require strict judicial scrutiny whenever government, at any level, considers race in its decisionmaking process. In the last few years, the Supreme Court had all but foreclosed the adoption of race-conscious responses to racial inequity by state and local governments. In a cramped conception of the scope of national power under the Fourteenth Amendment, the *Adarand* Court has pressed further and formally forbidden even the federal government from taking race explicitly into account in addressing societal-wide discrimination. In *Missouri* v. *Jenkins,* the Supreme Court held that racially-concentrated public schools could no longer be deemed presumptively unconstitutional, even in the presence of a history of formal segregation. As to any continuing racial segregation in these schools, the *Jenkins* opinion concluded that the courts could not address the problem of racial concentration if it could plausibly be said that a public school district was making a "good faith" effort to achieve desegregation "to the extent practicable". The court has thus effectively mandated the withdrawal of the federal judiciary from continued involvement in the effort to achieve racial desegregation in the nation's public schools. Finally, in *Miller* v. *Johnson,* the Supreme Court retreated from its longstanding enforcement of the historic Voting Rights Act, erecting rigid new barriers to the federal government's effort to increase the participation and representation of racial minorities in the political process.

Reading these decisions, one cannot help but notice the degree to which they deploy traditional liberal racial principles. The current Court has effectively conscripted liberal theories of race and racism to wage a conservative attack on governmental efforts to address the persistence of societal-wide racial discrimination. This harsh reality confirms the need for a critical theory of racial power and an image of racial justice which reject classical liberal visions of race as well as conservative visions of equal citizenship.

We believe that core concepts from Critical Race Theory can be productively used to expose the irreducibly political character of the current Court's general hostility toward policies which would take race into account in redressing historic and contemporary patterns of racial discrimination. We might, for example, draw on Critical Race Theory's deconstruction of color-blindness to show that the current Supreme Court's expressed hostility toward race-consciousness must be deemed a form of race-consciousness in and of itself. As Neil Gotanda has cogently argued, one cannot heed the newly installed constitutional rule that forbids race-conscious approaches to racial discrimination without always first taking race into account. Similarly, Critical Race Theory helps us understand how race-consciousness implicitly informs the current Court's paradoxical insistence that the norm of color-blindness requires a voting rights regime which effectively deprives racial minorities of political advantages that are accorded to other organized social interests.

Critical Race Theory indicates how and why the contemporary "jurisprudence of color-blindness" is not only the expression of a particular color-consciousness, but the product of a deeply politicized choice. The current Court would have us believe that these decisions are the product of an ineluctable legal logic. Critical Race Theory tells us rather that the Court's rulings with respect to race may more plausibly be deemed a result of a tactical political choice among competing doctrinal possibilities, any one of which could have been legally defensible. The appeal to color-blindness can thus be said to serve as part of an ideological strategy by which the current Court obscures its active role in sustaining hierarchies of racial power. We believe that Critical Race Theory offers a valuable conceptual compass for mapping the doctrinal mystifications which the current Court has developed to camouflage its conservative agenda.

The preceding discussion has focused on the possible uses to which Critical Race Theory might be put in understanding and intervening in the politics of racial jurisprudence. However, since discussions about race and rights in the U.S. have always overrun the narrow institutional confines of the law, we want to conclude this introduction to Critical Race Theory by suggesting some of the implications our work as legal scholars holds for broader national conversations about racial politics. In our history of the development of Critical Race Theory, we have highlighted the ways in which our work is a record of our engagement with what we saw as limitations of liberal, leftist and racialist accounts of racial power in law. The similar limitations of recent liberal defenses of affirmative action, left-liberal discourses on globalization, and racialist responses to post-civil rights retrenchment suggest that Critical Race Theory may provide new and much needed ways to think about (and challenge) the contemporary politics of racial domination.

We turn first to the vexed question of liberal discourse in the current national disputations regarding affirmative action. Earlier in this introduction we noted how the liberal defense of affirmative action has been stymied from its inception by a decidedly ambivalent attitude toward the matters of race and racial power. To be sure, liberals are generally willing to concede that racism continues to be an ""obvious and boring fact" of American life (as the liberal pundit Michael Kinsley rather remarkably put it in a recent article). What liberal proponents of affirmative action seem unwilling to do is to move toward a direct critique of the hidden racial dimensions of the meritocratic mythology that their conservative opponents have so deftly used to control the terms of the current debate.

This ambivalence toward race-consciousness is best understood as a symptom of liberalism's continued investment in meritocratic ideology and its unacknowledged resistance to reaching any deep understanding of the myriad ways racism continues to limit the realization of goals such as equal opportunity. This liberal ambivalence is particularly manifested in today's debates, particularly about affirmative action. But it is also reflected in the lukewarm liberal defense of the Great Society programs of the 1960s and other policies which were adopted to address contradictions between American ideals and historical realities. Like the Harvard Law School administration's response to the demand for a course focused on race and the law, the liberal position reflects an abiding uncertainty about the value of such projects, and a lingering, wistful sense that if we could just agree to abandon race-consciousness, racism and racial power would somehow recede from the American political imagination.

Critical Race Theory is instructive here in that it uncovers the ongoing dynamics of racialized power, and its embeddedness in practices and values which have been shorn of any explicit, formal manifestations of racism. Critical Race Theory thus provides a basis for understanding affirmative action as something other than "racial preference" (a notion whose implicit premise is that affirmative action represents a deviation from an otherwise non-racial neutrality). Critical Race Theory understands that, claims to the contrary notwithstanding, distributions of power and resources which were racially determined before the advent of affirmative action would continue to be so if affirmative action is abandoned. Our critiques of racial power reveal how certain conceptions of merit function not as a neutral basis for distributing resources and opportunity, but rather as a repository of hidden, race-specific preferences for those who have the power to determine the meaning and consequences of "merit." We have shown that the putatively neutral baseline from which affirmative action is said to represent a deviation is in fact a mechanism for perpetuating the distribution of rights, privileges, and opportunity established under a regime of uncontested white supremacy. Critical Race Theory recognizes accordingly that a return to that so-called neutral baseline would mean a return to an unjust system of racial power. Finally, Critical Race Theory fully comprehends that the aim of affirmative action is to create enough exceptions to white privilege to make the mythology of equal opportunity seem at least plausible. In fact, a defense of affirmative action premised upon CRT rather than liberal ambivalence would neither apologize for affirmative action nor assume it to be a fully adequate political response to the persistence of white supremacy. Rather, Critical Race Theory supports affirmative action as a limited approach which has achieved a meaningful, if modest measure of racial justice.

A second discussion to which we believe Critical Race Theory might bring a useful perspective is liberal and left debate in the U.S. over the proliferation of economic, political, social relations across national borders which has come to be known as globalization. Like Critical Legal Studies in the mid-1980s, the left-liberal approach to globalization has yet to generate an adequate account of the connections between racial power and political economy in the New World Order. Instead, generalized references to the "North" and "South" figure as a metaphorical substitute for serious and sustained attention to the racial and ethnic character of the massive distributive transformations that globalization has set in motion. Abstract allusions to "rich" and "poor" nations simply fail to yield an adequate vocabulary for analyzing the precise processes that produce globalized racial stratification. As the Nigerian scholar Claude Ake has argued, globalization enacts a "hierarchization of the world" and the "crystallizing of a domination". While that domination may be essentially *constituted* by economic power, it is essentially *legitimized* by racial power or, to use Ake's term, by ideologies of "political ethnicity." Critical Race Theory would thus focus on the degree to which the effects of globalization in the (so-called) Third World demand analysis as an instance of what Arjun Makhijani calls "economic apartheid."

This general indifference to questions of racial ideology and power also informs liberal and left efforts to explain the political significance of global economic processes within the U.S. For the most part, liberal and left analysis of this question has focused on the impact of globalization on U.S. class structure and politics. To the extent these debates *do* consider the role of race in the age of globalization, they do so only in the context of conversations about the "cultural pathologies" of the "underclass" (in liberal circles), or (on the left) in terms of a "class" of subordinated racial groups whose

vulnerable economic position is the product of past, but not current, dynamics of racial power. The particularities of race and its persistent presence as an explicit rationalization of structural stratification in the current economy seem hardly to warrant discussion. One would think that the racial composition of the communities which have been chosen to bear the sharp edge of economic dislocation is altogether irrelevant. However, even a cursory review of current national discourses about public education, unemployment, education, immigration and welfare reform (to take a few examples) demonstrates the degree to which questions of race and racial ideology stand at the very center of today's debates. These developments defy explanation in terms of liberal accounts of poverty and social equality, on the one hand, or leftist formulations about the historical class relations between labor and capital, on the other.

A CRT-grounded response to these developments would intersect contemporary critical discourses concerning the domestic social transformations wrought by globalization and critical theories of race and power to better understand the "racial economy" of this transition. This CRT-informed investigation of the "South in the North" would examine the way a certain brand of racial politics has been mobilized to buffer the massive upward distribution of resources and opportunity within the United States, or explore the way racial ideologies have been used to justify relatively open border policies toward our Northern neighbors, even as we close off our borders to those from the South. Just as Critical Race Theory introduced racial ideology as a necessary component of hegemony in the wake of the Critical Legal Studies emphasis on legal consciousness, so too must contemporary social theory fully incorporate notions of racial power as a way of understanding (and contesting) changing economic relations.

A third and final aspect of contemporary politics on which Critical Race Theory might be brought to bear is the struggle within communities of color over the future direction of anti-racist politics. The difficulties critical race scholars faced in attempting to push the analysis of law and racial politics beyond the narrow boundaries of racialism may all be seen at work in contemporary political debates among people of color. The emergence of powerful voices of racialism is particularly evident within the African American community, in which contemporary racial crisis is frequently represented as a reflection of unmediated white power. Although the message of racialist politics speaks to a broad range of disaffected African-Americans, it is also the source of debilitating contradictions within black political life. Indeed, as a mode of political analysis and action, racialism has ironically facilitated ideological attacks on black America that are now simplistically represented as coming from "out there"—that is, from outside the African-American community.

To take one example, racialists rightly identify the right-wing decisions of the current Supreme Court as part of the panoply of assaults directed against black Americans. What they all too often fail to note is that this same racialist politics helped secure the radical right's crucial fifth vote on the Supreme Court, in the person of Clarence Thomas. At the time of his nomination, Thomas had left little doubt about his political commitments. Despite a clearly manifested ideological agenda from which one could fully predict his role in consolidating the conservative wing of the Supreme Court, Thomas was nonetheless able to garner crucial support across the spectrum of African-American political formations. Narrow notions of racial solidarity led African-Americans to rally behind a figure who, though black, had been and would continue to be an eager participant in the evisceration of the post-civil rights coalition.

Another dimension of the racialism that led black Americans to support the Thomas nomination was deeply gendered in its determination. The erroneous view that racial interests would be advanced by the appointment of *any African-American to the Supreme Court* was compounded by a misguided racialist belief that questions of gender power were irrelevant (if not antagonistic) to the interests of the "larger" black American community. During our earlier discussion of racialism, we argued that one of the chief problems with the racialist account of

social power and struggle lies in the tendency to "essentialize" the racial communities with which it represents the social world. In black racialist circles, the felt necessity to articulate a stable vision of group identity and interest has underwritten a "representational politics" in which the experience of one segment of black America is taken to be representative of black experience *tout court*. As a result, black racialism yields a flat, fixed image of racial identity, experience and interest, which fails to capture the complex, constantly changing realities of racial domination in the contemporary U.S.

The concrete implications of this crude essentialism became painfully apparent in the subordinating gender politics to which black racialist support for the Thomas nomination gave rise. As Kimberlé Crenshaw has argued, the black racialist account proffers a vision of racism which portrays racial power primarily through its impact on African-American males. Because it is unwilling or unable to apprehend the ways in which racial identities are lived within and through gendered identities, racial essentialism renders the particular experiences of black females invisible. Black racialist politics thus effectively denies the struggle against racialized gender oppression a place on its anti-racist agenda. A final recent example will suffice to show how black America continues to be held hostage to racialism's essentialist politics. Although much of the rhetoric supporting a proposed "Million Man March" is grounded in the need for a black American response to Supreme Court decisions, the March's proponents not only fail to problematize the racialist politics that installed Clarence Thomas, but effectively reproduce those politics by promoting gender exclusivity, with its concomitant subordination of the irreducibly gendered dimensions of black women's racial oppression.

Because there is no currently viable alternative to an ambivalent liberal vision of race, on the one hand, and an inadequate vision of racialism, on the other, many progressive voices in the black community tend to gravitate toward the racialist view. For all its faults, racialism at least acknowledges the persistence of racism (albeit in an essentialist and exclusionary way).

Without a counter vision of race that does not fall into the nebulous world of liberal ambivalence and apology, the dangers of racialist politics for communities of color will continue to go unheeded, even in light of the deep contradictions that such politics produces.

Historians of American racial politics may rightly remember the final years of the twentieth century as the "Age of Repudiation." All the evidence suggests that the 1990s mark the rejection of the always fragile civil rights consensus and the renunciation of by federal, state and city authorities (indeed, of the American people themselves) that government not only can but must play an active role in identifying and eradicating racial injustice. The ideological offensive against civil rights reform (not to mention deeper social change) has consolidated what we have called a new common sense regarding race and racism in the United States. Although the new racial common sense defies both reason and contemporary reality, this fact has not deterred makers of public policy and public opinion in the post-reform era from using it to justify their indifference or outright hostility toward those who continue to struggle for racial justice and multicultural democracy in the United States. In the 1980s, the architects of the new racial common sense provided an ideological foundation for dismantling many of the key reforms and programs adopted during the civil rights period. In the 1990s, the apologists for racial reaction have deepened and extended their attack to include the very principle of racial antidiscrimination. Emboldened by the successes of the 1980s, right-wing legal academics such as Richard A. Epstein now openly decry laws forbidding racial discrimination on the grounds that they are economically inefficient and morally indefensible. And in a deliberate distortion of the 1954 *Brown* decision, Supreme Court Justice Clarence Thomas has cynically described the *Brown* court's historically-based claim that racial segregation was "inherently" unequal as itself an example of white racism. The power of new racial common sense may be seen, too, in the felt necessity of Democratic President Bill Clinton to qualify his already compromised defense of affirmative action with a neo-liberal nod toward the "angry white males" who, against all the evidence, have positioned themselves as the chief "victims" of contemporary racial politics.

The task of *Critical Race Theory* is to remind its readers how deeply issues of racial ideology and power continue to matter in American life. Questioning regnant visions of racial meaning and racial power, critical race theorists seek to fashion a set of tools for thinking about race that avoids the traps of racial thinking. Critical Race Theory understands that racial power is produced by and experienced within numerous vectors of social life. Critical Race Theory recognizes, too, that political interventions which overlook the multiple ways in which people of color are situated (and resituated) as communities, subcommunities, and individuals will do little to promote effective resistance to, and counter-mobilization against, today's newly empowered right. It is our hope that the writings collected here will prove to be a useful critical compass for negotiating the treacherous terrain of American racial politics in the coming century.

Part One

INTELLECTUAL PRECURSORS: EARLY CRITICISM OF CONVENTIONAL CIVIL RIGHTS DISCOURSE

One

INTELLECTUAL PRECURSORS: EARLY CRITIQUE OF CONVENTIONAL CIVIL RIGHTS DISCOURSE

We begin with two of Derrick Bell's essays from the late 1970s. The first, "Serving Two Masters," appropriately sets the stage for the eventual development of Critical Race Theory. Perhaps there is no more sacred text for what we have described as the liberal civil rights consensus than the Supreme Court's opinion in *Brown v. Board of Education*. In fact, by the mid-1970s, when Bell was writing, the norms of racial integration had become so powerful that they were taken to define the difference between being enlightened and being backward. In other words, only racists—both black and white—could possibly oppose *Brown*. Bell was already a notable figure as one of the first African-Americans to be tenured at Harvard Law School; it was thus dramatic that he would take on the liberal ideology of the mainstream civil rights movement by criticizing the effect of the enforcement of *Brown* on the black community. As Bell argued, the *Brown* strategy was being pursued by "public interest" lawyers who were driven by a commitment to integration as the appropriate solution to black childrens' educational needs. The problem, according to Bell, was that the lawyers' commitment to integration often flew in the face of what was best for the African-American communities they legally represented, or what those communities themselves desired. For a black scholar to pose values

of a "quality education" against "integration" in the 1970s, he risked being branded, at best, an apologist for segregated education, and at worst, an accomplice to racist resistance to integration. As Bell illustrates, however, one need not share any sympathies with segregationists to question the utility of a singular focus on integrating schools. All that was necessary was a race-conscious perspective that focused on the effect of integration on the black community. That change in perspective is the intellectual starting point of Critical Race Theory.

Bell's second essay, "The Interest-Convergence Dilemma," reflects an early attempt to sketch out a structural theory of what he implicitly suggested in "Serving Two Masters"—that law is an undependable ally in the struggle for racial liberation. According to Bell, the traditional liberal image of law as the neutral, impersonal mediator of group conflict masks its function in producing and insulating white dominance. Legal decisions reflect the balance of racial power and any anxiety that exists in the larger social order. From this initial starting point, Bell develops a provocative, overtly instrumental account of the ebb and flow of legal decisions about race which explicitly ties each important stage of civil rights reform to the long-term interests of whites.

Alan Freeman is a founding member of the

Conference on Critical Legal Studies. His article "Legitimizing Racial Discrimination through Antidiscrimination Law" is both a classic example of a Critical Legal Studies approach and an important intellectual precursor to Critical Race Theory. Freeman focuses on *Brown* and the other important civil rights decisions of the Supreme Court during the 1960s and 1970s. He identifies tensions in the civil rights doctrine between cases that identify discrimination through the "perpetrator perspective", on the one hand, and through the "victim perspective," on the other. In direct challenge to the reigning idea of civil rights discourse as a rational and neutral development of uncontroversial norms of justice, Freeman presents the Supreme Court doctrine as evoking two competing, and starkly contrasting, ideologies for representing "racism": the narrower, perpetrator perspective he argues, has been privileged over the more expansive vision. In contrast to Bell's instrumental approach—within which doctrinal developments are seen to reflect fairly directly the relative balance of social interests—Freeman contends that legal doctrine must be understood as part of an ideological narrative about how race is understood, a narrative that can legitimate racial power by representing it as neutral and objective. As he argues, the legal adoption of the perpetrator perspective is part of an ideological process through which forms of racial power that do not register on the perpetrator framework get implicitly represented as "not racism" and, thus, are pushed beyond the scope of remediation.

Under the dominant understanding of civil rights in the late 1970s and early 1980s, enlightened people were not committed simply to *Brown* but to a particular understanding of the insignificance of race in all sorts of realms, including perhaps most particularly, intellectual work. An unstated assumption was that the race of a scholar didn't matter, just the merit of his or her ideas. Richard Delgado dramatically shattered that silent assumption with the publication of "The Imperial Scholar" in 1984. Delgado conducted an empirical analysis of civil rights commentary in the scholarly literature and found that the legal literature consisted of white scholars writing for and citing each other, a closed circle of civil rights experts from which scholars of color were excluded. Like Bell and Freeman, Delgado signaled an early and important break with the reigning antipathy toward race-consciousness in conventional civil rights discourse; he openly and explicitly charged that the race of a scholar matters to perspective and ideology.

Part One

INTELLECTUAL PRECURSORS:
EARLY CRITICISM OF CONVENTIONAL
CIVIL RIGHTS DISCOURSE

SERVING TWO MASTERS: INTEGRATION
IDEALS AND CLIENT INTERESTS IN
SCHOOL DESEGREGATION LITIGATION
Derrick A. Bell, Jr.

In the name of equity, we ... seek dramatic improvement in the quality of the education available to our children. Any steps to achieve desegregation must be reviewed in light of the black community's interest in improved pupil performance as the primary characteristic of educational equity. We define educational equity as the absence of discriminatory pupil placement and improved performance for all children who have been the objects of discrimination. We think it neither necessary, nor proper to endure the dislocations of desegregation without reasonable assurances that our children will instructionally profit.

—*Coalition of black community groups in Boston*[1]

THE espousal of educational improvement as the appropriate goal of school desegregation efforts is out of phase with the current state of the law. Largely through the efforts of civil rights lawyers, most courts have come to construe *Brown v. Board of Education*[2] as mandating "equal educational opportunities" through school desegregation plans aimed at achieving racial balance, whether or not those plans will improve the education received by the children affected. To the extent that "instructional profit" accurately defines the school priorities of black parents in Boston and elsewhere, questions of professional responsibility are raised that can no longer be ignored.

How should the term "client" be defined in school desegregation cases that are litigated for decades, determine critically important constitutional rights for thousands of minority children, and usually involve major restructuring of a public school system? How should civil rights attorneys represent the often diverse interests of clients and class in school suits? Do they owe any special obligation to class members who emphasize educational quality and probably cannot obtain counsel to advocate their divergent views? Do the political, organizational, and even philosophical complexities of school desegregation litigation justify a higher standard of professional responsibility on the part of civil rights lawyers to their clients or more diligent oversight of the lawyer-client relationship by the bench and bar?

As is so often the case, a crisis of events motivates this long-overdue inquiry. The great crusade to desegregate the public schools has faltered. There is increasing opposition to desegregation at local and national levels (not all of which can now be simply condemned as "racist"), while the once-vigorous support of federal courts is on the decline. New barriers have arisen—inflation makes the attainment of racial balance more expensive, the growth of black populations in urban areas renders it more difficult, an increasing number of social science studies question the validity of its educational assumptions.

Civil rights lawyers dismiss these new obstacles as legally irrelevant. Having achieved so much by courageous persistence, they have not waivered in their determination to implement *Brown* using racial balance measures developed in the hard-fought legal battles of the last two decades. This stance involves great risk for clients whose educational interests may no longer accord with the integration ideals of their attorneys. Indeed, muffled but increasing criticism of "unconditional integration" policies by vocal minorities in black communities is not limited to Boston. Now that traditional racial balance remedies are becoming increasingly difficult to achieve or maintain, there is tardy concern that racial balance may not be the relief actually desired by the victims of segregated schools.

This article will review the development of school desegregation litigation and the unique lawyer-client relationship that has evolved out of it. It will not be the first such inquiry; during the era of "massive resistance," southern states charged that this relationship violated professional canons of conduct. A majority of the Supreme Court rejected those challenges, creating in the process constitutional protection for conduct that, under the circumstances, would contravene basic precepts of professional behavior. The potential for ethical problems in these constitutionally protected lawyer-client relationships was recognized by the American Bar Association's *Code of Professional Responsibility*, but it is difficult to provide standards for the attorney and protection for the client where the source of the conflict is the attorney's ideals. The magnitude of the difficulty is more accurately gauged in a much older code that warns: "No servant can serve two masters: for either he will hate the one, and love the other; or else he will hold to one, and despise the other."

I. School Litigation:
A Behind-the-Scenes View

A. The Strategy

Although *Brown* was not a test case with a result determined in advance, the legal decisions that undermined and finally swept away the "separate but equal" doctrine of *Plessy v. Ferguson*[3] were far from fortuitous. Their genesis can be found in the volumes of reported cases stretching back to the mid-nineteenth century, cases in which every conceivable aspect of segregated schools was challenged. By the early thirties, the NAACP, with the support of a foundation grant, had organized a concerted program of le-

gal attacks on racial segregation. In October 1934, Vice-Dean Charles H. Houston of the Howard University Law School was retained by the NAACP to direct this campaign. According to the NAACP annual report for 1934, "the campaign [was] a carefully planned one to secure decisions, rulings and public opinion on the broad principle instead of being devoted to merely miscellaneous cases." These strategies were intended to eliminate racial segregation, not merely in the public schools but throughout society. The public schools were chosen because they presented a far more compelling symbol of the evils of segregation and a far more vulnerable target than segregated railroad cars, restaurants, or restrooms. Initially, the NAACP's school litigation was aimed at the most blatant inequalities in facilities and teacher salaries. The next target was the obvious inequality in higher education evidenced by the almost total absence of public graduate and professional schools for blacks in the South.

Thurgood Marshall succeeded Houston in 1938 and became director-counsel of the NAACP Legal Defense and Educational Fund (LDF) when it became a separate entity in 1939. Jack Greenberg, who succeeded Marshall in 1961, recalled that the legal program "built precedent," treating each case in a context of jurisprudential development rather than as an isolated private lawsuit. Of course, it was not possible to plan the program with precision: "How and when plaintiffs sought relief and the often unpredictable course of litigation were frequently as influential as any blueprint in determining the sequence of cases, the precise issues they posed, and their outcome." But as lawyer-publisher Loren Miller observed of *Brown* and the four other school cases decided with it, "There was more to this carefully stage-managed selection of cases for review than meets the naked eye."

In 1955, the Supreme Court rejected the NAACP's request for a general order requiring desegregation in all school districts, issued the famous "all deliberate speed" mandate, and returned the matter to the district courts.[4] It quickly became apparent that most school districts would not comply with *Brown* voluntarily;

rather, they retained counsel and determined to resist compliance as long as possible.

By the late fifties, the realization by black parents and local branches of the NAACP that litigation would be required, together with the snail's pace at which most of the school cases progressed, brought about a steady growth in the size of school desegregation dockets. Because of their limited resources, the NAACP and LDF adopted the following general pattern for initiating school suits: A local attorney would respond to the request of a NAACP branch to address its members concerning their rights under the *Brown* decision; those interested in joining a suit as named plaintiffs would sign retainers authorizing the local attorney and members of the NAACP staff to represent them in a school desegregation class action. Subsequently, depending on the facts of the case and the availability of counsel to prepare the papers, a suit would be filed. In most instances, the actual complaint was drafted or at least approved by a member of the national legal staff. With few exceptions, local attorneys were not considered expert in school desegregation litigation and so served mainly as a liaison between the national staff lawyers and the local community.

Named plaintiffs, of course, retained the right to drop out of the case at any time. They did not seek to exercise "control" over the litigation, and during the early years there was no reason for them to do so. Suits were filed, school boards resisted the suits, and civil rights attorneys tried to overcome the resistance. Obtaining compliance with *Brown* as soon as possible was the goal of clients as well as attorneys. In most cases, though, that goal would not be realized before the named plaintiffs had graduated or left the school system.

The civil rights lawyers would not settle for anything less than a desegregated system. While the situation did not arise in the early years, it was generally made clear to potential plaintiffs that the NAACP was not interested in settling the litigation in return for school board promises to provide better segregated schools.[5] Black parents generally felt that the victory in *Brown* entitled the civil rights lawyers to determine the

basis of compliance. There was no doubt that perpetuating segregated schools was unacceptable, and the civil rights lawyers' strong opposition to such schools had the full support of the named plaintiffs and the class they represented. Charges to the contrary initiated by several Southern states were malevolent in intent and premature in timing.

B. The Theory

The rights vindicated in school litigation literally did not exist prior to 1954. Despite hundreds of judicial opinions, these rights have yet to be clearly defined. This is not surprising. Desegregation efforts aimed at lunchrooms, beaches, transportation, and other public facilities were designed merely to gain access to those facilities. Any actual racial "mixing" has been essentially fortuitous; it was hardly part of the rights protected (to eat, travel, or swim on a nonracial basis). The strategy of school desegregation is much different: the actual presence of white children is said to be essential to the right in both its philosophical and pragmatic dimensions. In essence, the arguments are that blacks must gain access to white schools because "equal educational opportunity" means integrated schools, and because only school integration will make certain that black children will receive the same education as white children. This theory of school desegregation, however, fails to encompass the complexity of achieving equal educational opportunity for children to whom it so long has been denied.

The NAACP and the LDF, responsible for virtually all school desegregation suits, usually seek to establish a racial population at each school that, within a range of 10 to 15 percent, reflects the percentage of whites and blacks in the district. However, in a growing number of the largest urban districts, the school system is predominantly black. The resistance of most white parents to sending their children to a predominantly black school, combined with the accessibility of a suburban residence or a private school to all but the poorest, renders implementation of such plans extremely difficult. Although many whites undoubtedly perceive a majority-black school as ipso facto a poor school, the schools can be improved and white attitudes changed. All too little attention has been given to making black schools educationally effective; furthermore, the disinclination of white parents to send their children to black schools has not been lessened by charges made over a long period of time by civil rights groups that black schools are educationally bankrupt and unconstitutional per se. NAACP policies nevertheless call for maximizing racial balance within the district as an immediate goal while supporting litigation that will eventually require the consolidation of predominantly white surrounding districts.

The basic civil rights position that *Brown* requires maximum feasible desegregation has been accepted by the courts and successfully implemented in smaller school districts throughout the country. The major resistance to further progress has occurred in the large urban areas of both the South and North, where racially isolated neighborhoods make school integration impossible without major commitments to the transportation of students, often over long distances. The use of the school bus is not a new phenomenon in American education, but the transportation of students over long distances to schools where their parents do not believe they will receive a good education has, predictably, created strong opposition in white and even in black communities.

The busing issue has served to make concrete what many parents long have sensed and what new research has suggested: court orders mandating racial balance may be (depending on the circumstances) educationally advantageous, irrelevant, or even *disadvantageous*. Nevertheless, civil rights lawyers continue to argue, without regard to the educational effect of such assignments, that black children are entitled to integrated schools. This position might well have shocked many of the justices who decided *Brown*, and it hardly encourages those judges asked to undertake the destruction and resurrection of school systems in our large cities, which this reading of *Brown* has come to require.

Troubled by the resistance and disruptions caused by busing over long distances, those judges have increasingly rejected such an inter-

pretation of *Brown*. They have established new standards that limit relief across district lines,[6] which reject busing for intradistrict desegregation "when the time or distance of travel is so great as to either risk the health of children or significantly impinge on the educational process." Litigation in the large cities has dragged on for years and often culminated in decisions that approve the continued assignment of large numbers of black children to predominantly black schools.

II. LAWYER-CLIENT CONFLICTS: SOURCES AND RATIONALE

A. Civil Rights Rigidity Surveyed

Having convinced themselves that *Brown* stands for desegregation, and not for education, the established civil rights organizations steadfastly refuse to recognize reverses in the school desegregation campaign—reverses that, to some extent, have been precipitated by their rigidity. They seem to be reluctant to evaluate objectively the high risks inherent in a continuation of current policies.

I. THE BOSTON CASE

The Boston school litigation provides an instructive example of what, I fear, is a widespread situation. Early in 1975, I was invited by representatives of Boston's black community groups to meet them and NAACP lawyers over plans for Phase II of Boston's desegregation effort. Implementation of the 1974 plan had met with violent resistance that received nationwide attention. Even in the lulls between the violent incidents, it is unlikely that much in the way of effective instruction was occurring at many of the schools. NAACP lawyers had retained experts whose proposals for the 1975–76 school year would have required even more busing between black and lower-class white communities. The black representatives were ambivalent about the busing plans: they did not wish to back away after years of effort to desegregate Boston's schools, but they wished to place greater emphasis on upgrading the schools' educational quality, to maintain existing assignments at schools which were already integrated, and to minimize busing to the poorest and most violent white districts. In response to a proposal filed by the Boston School Committee, they sent a lengthy statement of their position directly to District Judge W. Arthur Garrity.

At the meeting I attended, black representatives hoped to convince the lawyers to incorporate their educational priorities into the plaintiffs' Phase II desegregation plan. The lawyers assigned by the NAACP to the Boston case listened respectfully to the views of the black community group, but they made clear that a long line of court decisions would limit the degree to which those educational priorities could be incorporated into the desegregation plan the lawyers were preparing to file. That plan contained far more busing to balance the racial populations of the schools than was eventually approved by the federal court. Acting on the recommendations of appointed masters, Judge Garrity adopted several provisions designed to improve the quality of the notoriously poor Boston schools. However, these provisions were more the product of judicial initiative than of civil rights advocacy.

2. THE DETROIT CASE

The determination of NAACP officials to achieve racial balance was also tested in the Detroit school case. Having failed in efforts to obtain an interdistrict metropolitan remedy in Detroit,[7] the NAACP set out to achieve a unitary system in a school district that was over 70 percent black. The district court rejected an NAACP plan designed to require every school to reflect (within a range of 15 percent in either direction) the ratio of whites to blacks in the school district as a whole, and it approved a desegregation plan that emphasized educational reform rather than racial balance. The NAACP general counsel, Nathaniel R. Jones, reportedly called the decision "an abomination" and "a rape of the constitutional rights of black children," and he indicated his intention to appeal immediately.

3. THE ATLANTA CASE

Prior to Detroit, the most open confrontation between NAACP views of school integration and those of local blacks who favored plans oriented toward improving educational quality occurred in Atlanta. There, a group of plaintiffs became discouraged by the difficulty of achieving meaningful desegregation in a district which had gone from 32 percent black in 1952 to 82 percent black in 1974. Lawyers for the local NAACP branch, who had gained control of the litigation, worked out a compromise plan with the Atlanta school board that called for full faculty and employee desegregation, but for only limited pupil desegregation. In exchange, the school board promised to hire a number of blacks in top administrative positions, including a black superintendent of schools.

The federal court approved the plan. The court's approval was apparently influenced by petitions favoring the plan's adoption, which were signed by several thousand members of the plaintiffs' class. Nevertheless, the national NAACP office and LDF lawyers were horrified by the compromise. The NAACP ousted the Atlanta branch president who had supported the compromise; then, acting on behalf of some local blacks who shared their views, LDF lawyers filed an appeal in the Atlanta case. The appeal also raised a number of procedural issues concerning the lack of notice and the refusal of the district court to grant hearings on the compromise plan. These issues gave the Fifth Circuit an opportunity to remand the case to the district court without reaching the merits of the settlement agreement. Undaunted, LDF lawyers again attacked the plan for failing to require busing of whites into the predominantly black schools, in which a majority of the students in the system were enrolled. However, the district court's finding that the system had achieved unitary status was upheld by the same Fifth Circuit panel.

As in Detroit, NAACP opposition to the Atlanta compromise plan was not deterred by the fact that local leaders, including black school board members, supported the settlement. Defending the compromise plan, Dr. Benjamin E. Mays, one of the most respected black educators in the country, stated:

We have never argued that the Atlanta Compromise Plan is the best plan nor have we encouraged any other school system to adopt it. This plan is the most viable plan for Atlanta—a city school system that is 82 percent Black and 18 percent white and is continuing to lose whites each year to five counties that are more than 90 percent white.

More importantly, Black people must not resign themselves to the pessimistic view that a nonintegrated school cannot provide Black children with an excellent educational setting. Instead, Black people, while working to implement *Brown*, should recognize that integration alone does not provide a quality education, and that much of the substance of quality education can be provided to Black children in the interim.[8]

B. *Alternatives to the Rigidity of Racial Balance*

Dr. May's thoughtful statement belies the claim that *Brown* can be implemented only by the immediate racial balancing of school populations. Nevertheless, civil rights groups refuse to recognize what courts in Boston, Detroit, and Atlanta have now made obvious: where racial balance is not feasible because of population concentrations, political boundaries, or even educational considerations, there is adequate legal precedent for court-ordered remedies that emphasize educational improvement rather than racial balance.

The plans adopted in these cases were formulated without the support—indeed, often over the objection—of the NAACP and other civil rights groups. They are intended to upgrade educational quality, and like racial balance, they may have that effect; but neither the NAACP nor the court-fashioned remedies are sufficiently directed at the real evil of pre-*Brown* public schools: the state-supported subordination of blacks in every aspect of the educational process. Racial separation is only the most obvious manifestation of this subordination. Providing unequal and inadequate school resources and excluding black parents from meaningful participation in school policymaking are at least as damaging to black children as enforced separation.

Whether based on racial balance precedents or compensatory education theories, remedies that fail to attack all policies of racial subordination almost guarantee that the basic evil of segregated schools will survive and flourish, even in those systems where racially balanced

schools can be achieved. Low academic performance and large numbers of disciplinary and expulsion cases are only two of the predictable outcomes in integrated schools where the racial subordination of blacks is reasserted in, if anything, a more damaging form.

Although some of the remedies fashioned by the courts themselves have been responsive to the problem of racial subordination, plaintiffs and courts seeking to implement such remedies are not assisted by counsel representing plaintiff classes. Much more effective remedies for racial subordination in the schools could be obtained if the creative energies of the civil rights litigation groups could be brought into line with the needs and desires of their clients.

C. *The Organization and Its Ideals*

Civil rights lawyers have long experience, unquestioned commitment, and the ability to organize programs that have helped to bring about profound changes in the last two decades. Why, one might ask, have they been so unwilling to recognize the increasing futility of "total desegregation," and, more important, the increasing number of defections within the black community? A few major factors that underlie this unwillingness can be identified.

I. RACIAL BALANCE AS A SYMBOL

For many civil rights workers, success in obtaining racially balanced schools seems to have become a symbol of the nation's commitment to equal opportunity—not only in education, but in housing, employment, and other fields where the effects of racial discrimination are still present. As Dean Ernest Campbell has observed, "[T]he busing issue has acquired meanings that seem to have little relevance for the education of children in any direct sense."[9] In his view, proponents of racial balance fear that the failure to establish busing as a major tool for desegregation will signify the end of an era of expanding civil rights. For them the busing debate symbolizes a major test of the country's continued commitment to civil rights progress. Any retreat on busing will be construed as an abandonment of this commitment and a return to segregation. Indeed, Dr. Campbell has suggested that some leaders see busing as a major test of black political strength. Under a kind of domestic domino theory, these leaders fear that failure on the busing issue would trigger a string of defeats, ending a long line of "major judicial and administrative decisions that substantially expanded the civil rights and personal opportunities of blacks in the post–World War II period." [10]

2. CLIENTS AND CONTRIBUTORS

The hard-line position of established civil rights groups on school desegregation is explained in part by pragmatic considerations. These organizations are supported by middle-class blacks and whites who believe fervently in integration. At their socioeconomic level, integration has worked well, and they are certain that once whites and blacks at lower economic levels are successfully mixed in the schools, integration also will work well at those levels. Many of these supporters either reject or fail to understand suggestions that alternatives to integrated schools should be considered, particularly in majority-black districts. They will be understandably reluctant to provide financial support for policies they think unsound, possibly illegal, and certainly disquieting. The rise and decline of the Congress of Racial Equality (CORE) provides a stark reminder of the fate of civil rights organizations relying on white support while espousing black self-reliance. . . .

School expert Ron Edmonds contends that civil rights attorneys often do not represent their clients' best interests in desegregation litigation because "they answer to a minuscule constituency while serving a massive clientele." [11] Edmonds distinguishes the clients of civil rights attorneys (the persons on whose behalf suit is filed) from their "constituents" (those to whom the attorney must answer for his actions). He suggests that in class action school desegregation cases the mass of lower-class black parents and children are merely clients. To define constituents, Edmonds asks, "[To] what class of Americans does the civil rights attorney feel he must answer for his professional conduct?" The answer can be determined by identifying those with whom the civil rights attorney confers as

he defines the goals of the litigation; he concludes that those who currently have access to the civil rights attorney are whites and middle-class blacks who advocate integration and categorically oppose majority black schools.

Edmonds suggests that, more than other professionals, the civil rights attorney labors in a closed setting isolated from most of his clients. No matter how numerous, the attorney's clients cannot become constituents unless they have access to him before or during the legal process. The result is the pursuit of metropolitan desegregation without sufficient regard for the probable instructional consequences for black children. In sum, he charges, "A class action suit serving only those who pay the attorney fee has the effect of permitting the fee paying minority to impose its will on the majority of the class on whose behalf suit is presumably brought."

3. CLIENT-COUNSEL MERGER

The position of the established civil rights groups obviates any need to determine whether a continued policy of maximum racial balance conforms with the wishes of even a minority of the class. This position represents an extraordinary view of the lawyer's role. Not only does it assume a perpetual retainer authorizing a lifelong effort to obtain racially balanced schools; it also fails to reflect any significant change in representational policy from a decade ago—when virtually all blacks assumed that integration was the best means of achieving a quality education for black children—to the present time, when many black parents are disenchanted with the educational results of integration.

This malady may afflict many idealistic lawyers who seek, through the class action device, to bring about judicial intervention affecting large segments of the community. The class action provides the vehicle for bringing about a major advance toward an idealistic goal. At the same time, prosecuting and winning the big case provides strong reinforcement of the attorney's sense of his or her abilities and professionalism. Dr. Andrew Watson has suggested that "[c]lass actions . . . have the capacity to provide large sources of narcissistic gratification and this may be one of the reasons why they are such a popular form of litigation in legal aid and poverty law clinics." The psychological motivations that influence the lawyer in taking on "a fiercer dragon" through the class action may also underlie the tendency to direct the suit toward the goals of the lawyer rather than the client.

III. Civil Rights Litigation and the Regulation of Professional Ethics
A. NAACP v. Button

The questions of legal ethics raised by the lawyer-client relationship in civil rights litigation are not new. The Supreme Court's 1963 treatment of these questions in *NAACP v. Button*,[12] however, needs to be examined in light of the emergence of lawyer-client conflicts, which are far more serious than the premature speculations of a segregationist legislature.

1. THE CHALLENGE

As the implementation of *Brown* began, southern officials looking for every possible means to eliminate the threat of integrated schools soon realized that the NAACP's procedure for obtaining clients for litigation resembled the traditionally unethical practices of barratry, and running and capping. Attempting to exploit this resemblance, a majority of southern states enacted laws defining NAACP litigation practices as unlawful. In Virginia, though unethical and unprofessional conduct by attorneys had been regulated by statute since 1849, NAACP legal activities had been carried on openly for many years. No attempt was made to use these regulations to proscribe NAACP activities until 1956. In that year, during an extra session "called to resist school integration," the Virginia legislature amended its criminal statues barring running and capping to forbid the solicitation of legal business by "an agent for an individual or organization which retains a lawyer in connection with an action to which it is not a party and in which it has no pecuniary right or liability." An attorney accepting employment from such an organization was subject to disbarment. The NAACP sued to restrain enforcement of

these new provisions, claiming that the statute was unconstitutional. The Virginia Supreme Court of Appeals found that the statute's purpose "was to strengthen the existing statutes to further control the evils of solicitation of legal business." The court held that the statute's expanded definition of improper solicitation of legal business did not violate the Constitution in proscribing many of the legal activities of civil rights groups such as the NAACP.

2. THE SUPREME COURT RESPONSE

The U.S. Supreme Court reversed, holding that the state statute as construed and applied abridged the First Amendment rights of NAACP members. Justice William Brennan, writing for the majority, reasoned that "the activities of the NAACP, its affiliates and legal staff shown on this record are modes of expression and association protected by the First and Fourteenth Amendments which Virginia may not prohibit, under its power to regulate the legal profession, as improper solicitation of legal business. . . . "[13] Justice Brennan placed great weight on the importance of litigation to the NAACP's civil rights program. He noted (with obvious approval) that blacks rely on the courts to gain objectives which are not available through the ballot box and said: "We cannot close our eyes to the fact that the militant Negro civil rights movement has engendered the intense resentment and opposition of the politically dominant white community of Virginia; litigation assisted by the NAACP has been bitterly fought."[14]

The court deemed NAACP's litigation activities "a form of political expression" protected by the First Amendment.[15] Justice Brennan conceded that Virginia had a valid interest in regulating the traditionally illegal practices of barratry, maintenance, and champerty, but noted that the malicious intent which constituted the essence of these common law offenses was absent here. He also reasoned that because the NAACP's efforts served the public rather than a private interest, and because no monetary stakes were involved, "there is no danger that the attorney will desert or subvert the paramount interests of his client to enrich himself or an outside sponsor. And the aims and interests of NAACP have not been shown to conflict with those of its members and nonmember Negro litigants...."[16]

To meet Virginia's criticism that the Court was creating a special law to protect the NAACP, the majority found the NAACP's activities "constitutionally irrelevant to the ground of our decision."[17] Even so, Justice William Douglas noted in a concurring opinion that the Virginia law prohibiting activities by lay groups was aimed directly at NAACP activities as part "of the general plan of massive resistance to the integration of the schools."[18]

Although the issue was raised by the state, the majority did not decide whether Virginia could constitutionally prohibit the NAACP from controlling the course of the litigation sponsored, perhaps because the NAACP consistently denied that it exercised such control. Justice Byron White, concurring in part and dissenting in part, cautioned:

> If we had before us, which we do not, a narrowly drawn statute proscribing only the actual day-to-day management and dictation of the tactics, strategy and conduct of litigation by a lay entity such as the NAACP, the issue would be considerably different, at least for me; for in my opinion neither the practice of law by such an organization nor its management of the litigation of its members or others is constitutionally protected.[19]

Justice White feared that the majority opinion would also strike down such a narrowly drawn statute.

3. JUSTICE HARLAN'S DISSENT
Joined by Justices Tom Clark and Potter Stewart, Justice Harlan expressed the view that the Virginia statute was valid. In support of his conclusion, Harlan carefully reviewed the record and found that NAACP policy required what he considered serious departures from ethical professional conduct. First, NAACP attorneys were required to follow policy directives promulgated by the national board of directors or lose their right to compensation. Second, these directives to staff lawyers covered many subjects relating to the form and substance of litigation. Third, the NAACP not only advocated litiga-

tion and waited for prospective litigants to come forward but also, in several instances and particularly in school cases, "specific directions were given as to the types of prospective plaintiffs to be sought, and staff lawyers brought blank forms to meetings for the purpose of obtaining signatures authorizing the prosecution of litigation in the name of the signer."[20] Fourth, the retainer forms signed by prospective litigants sometimes did not contain the names of the attorneys retained, and often when the forms specified certain attorneys as counsel, additional attorneys were brought into the action without the plaintiff's consent. Justice Harlan observed that several named plaintiffs had testified that they had no personal dealings with the lawyers handling their cases and were not aware until long after the event that suits had been filed in their names. Taken together, Harlan felt these incidents justified the corrective measures taken by the State of Virginia.

Justice Harlan was not impressed by the fact that the suits were not brought for pecuniary gain. The NAACP attorneys did not donate their services, and the litigating activities did not fall into the accepted category of aid to indigents. However, he deemed more important than the avoidance of improper pecuniary gain the concern shared by the profession, courts, and legislatures that outside influences not interfere with the uniquely personal relationship between lawyer and client. In Justice Harlan's view, when an attorney is employed by an association or corporation to represent a client, two problems arise:

> The lawyer becomes then subject to the control of a body that is not itself a litigant and that, unlike the lawyers it employs, is not subject to strict professional discipline as an officer of the court. In addition, the lawyer necessarily finds himself with a divided allegiance—to his employer and to his client—which may prevent full compliance with his basic professional obligations.[21]

He conceded that "[t]he NAACP may be no more than the sum of the efforts and views infused in it by its members," but he added a prophetic warning that "the totality of the separate interests of the members and others whose causes the petitioner champions, even in the field of race relations, may far exceed in scope and variety that body's views of policy, as embodied in litigating strategy and tactics." [22]

Justice Harlan recognized that it might be in the association's interest to maintain an all-out, frontal attack on segregation, even sacrificing small points in some cases for the major points that might win other cases. Yet he foresaw that

it is not impossible that after authorizing action in his behalf, a Negro parent, concerned that a continued frontal attack could result in schools closed for years, might prefer to wait with his fellows a longer time for good-faith efforts by the local school board than is permitted by the centrally determined policy of the NAACP. Or he might see a greater prospect of success through discussions with local school authorities than through the litigation deemed necessary by the Association. The parent, of course, is free to withdraw his authorization, but is his lawyer, retained and paid by petitioner and subject to its directions on matters of policy, able to advise the parent with that undivided allegiance that is the hallmark of the attorney-client relation? I am afraid not. [23]

4. *NAACP V. BUTTON* IN RETROSPECT

The characterizations of the facts in *Button* by both the majority and the dissenters contain much that is accurate. As the majority found, the NAACP did not "solicit" litigants but rather systematically advised black parents of their rights under *Brown* and collected retainer signatures of those willing to join the proposed suits. The litigation was designed to serve the public interest rather than to enrich the litigators. Not all the plaintiffs were indigent, but few could afford to finance litigation intended to change the deep-seated racial policies of public school systems.

On the other hand, Justice Harlan was certainly correct in suggesting that the retainer process was often performed in a perfunctory manner, and that plaintiffs had little contact with their attorneys. Plaintiffs frequently learned that suit had been filed and kept abreast of its progress through the public media. Although a plaintiff could withdraw from the suit at any time, he could not influence the primary goals of the litigation. Except in rare instances, policy decisions were made by the attorneys,

often in conjunction with the organizational leadership and without consultation with the client.

The *Button* majority obviously felt that the potential for abuse of clients' rights in this procedure was overshadowed by the fact that Virginia enacted the statute to protect the citadel of segregation rather than the sanctity of the lawyer-client relationship. As the majority pointed out, litigation was the only means by which blacks throughout the South could effectuate the school desegregation mandate of *Brown.* The theoretical possibility of abuse of client rights seemed a rather slender risk when compared with the real threat to integration posed by this most dangerous weapon in Virginia's arsenal of "massive resistance." . . .

B. *The ABA Response*

Button's recognition of First Amendment rights in the conduct of litigation led to subsequent decisions broadening the rights of other lay groups to obtain legal representation for their members. In so doing, these decisions posed new problems for the organized bar. The American Bar Association, faced with the reality of group practice, which it had long resisted, has attempted to adopt guidelines for practitioners; but the applicable provisions of its new *Code of Professional Responsibility* provide only broad and uncertain guidance on the issues of control of litigation and conflict of interest as they affect civil rights lawyers.

The *Code of Professional Responsibility* again and again admonishes the lawyer "to disregard the desires of others that might impair his free judgment." But the suggestions assume the classical commercial conflict or a third-party intermediary clearly hostile to the client. Even when the *Code* seems to recognize more subtle "economic, political or social pressures," the protection needed by civil rights clients is not provided, and the suggested remedy, withdrawal from representation of the client, is hardly desirable if the client has no available alternatives.

The market-system mentality of the drafters of the *Code* surfaces in another provision which suggests that problems of control are less likely to exist where the lawyer "is compensated directly by his client." Solving the problems of control by relying on the elimination of compensation from a source other than the client was rejected in *Button*. All that remains is the warning that a person or group furnishing lawyers "may be far more concerned with establishment or extension of legal principles than in the immediate protection of the rights of the lawyer's individual client."

The *Code* approach, urging the lawyer to "constantly guard against erosion of his professional freedom" and requiring that the "decline to accept direction of his professional judgment from any layman," is simply the wrong answer to the right question in civil rights offices, where basic organizational policies such as the goals of school desegregation are often designed by lawyers and then adopted by the board or other leadership group. The NAACP's reliance on litigation requires that lawyers play a major role in basic policy decisions. Admonitions that the lawyer make no important decisions without consulting the client, and that the client be fully informed of all relevant considerations, are, of course, appropriate; but they are difficult to enforce in the context of complex, long-term school desegregation litigation, in which the original plaintiffs may have left the system and the members of the class whose interests are at stake are numerous, generally uninformed, and—if aware of the issues—divided in their views.

Current ABA standards thus appear to conform with *Button* and its progeny in permitting the representation typically provided by civil rights groups. They are a serious attempt to come to grips with and provide specific guidance on the issues of outside influence and client primacy which so concerned Justice Harlan. However, they provide little help where, as in school desegregation litigation, the influence of attorney and organization are mutually supportive, and both are so committed to what they perceive as the long-range good of their clients, that they do not sense the growing conflict between those goals and the client's current interests. Given the cries of protest and the charges of racially motivated persecution that would probably greet any ABA effort to address

this problem more specifically, it is not surprising that the conflict—which, in any event, will neither embarrass the profession ethically nor threaten it economically—has not received a high priority for further attention.

Idealism, though perhaps rarer than greed, is harder to control. Justice Harlan accurately prophesied the excesses of derailed benevolence, but a retreat from the group representational concepts set out in *Button* would be a disaster, not an improvement. State legislatures are less likely than the ABA to draft standards that effectively guide practitioners and protect clients. Even well-intentioned and carefully drawn standards might hinder rather than facilitate the always-difficult task of achieving social change through legal action. Furthermore, too-stringent rules could encourage officials in some states to institute groundless disciplinary proceedings against lawyers in school cases, which in many areas are hardly more popular today than they were during the era of massive resistance.

Client involvement in school litigation is more likely to increase if civil rights lawyers themselves come to realize that the special status accorded them by the courts and the bar demands in return an extraordinary display of ethical sensitivity and self-restraint. The "divided allegiance" between client and employer which Justice Harlan feared would interfere with the civil rights lawyer's "full compliance with his basic professional obligation"[24] has developed in a far more idealistic and thus a far more dangerous form. For it is more the civil rights lawyers' commitment to an integrated society than any policy directives or pressures from their employers that leads to their assumptions of client acceptance and their condemnations of all dissent.

IV. The Class Action Barrier to Expression of Dissent

EVEN if civil rights lawyers were highly responsive to the wishes of the named plaintiffs in school desegregation suits, a major source of lawyer-client conflict would remain. In most such suits, the plaintiffs bring a class action on behalf of all similarly situated black students and parents; the final judgment will be binding on all members of the class. As black disenchantment with racial balance remedies grows, the strongest opposition to civil rights litigation strategy may come from unnamed class members. However, even when black groups opposed to racial balance remedies overcome their ambivalence and obtain counsel willing to advocate their positions in court, judicial interpretations of the federal class action rule make it difficult for dissident members of the class to gain a hearing in pending school litigation.

Ironically, the interpretations of Rule 23 of the Federal Rules of Civil Procedure which now hinder dissent derive from early school desegregation cases in which the courts sought to further plaintiffs' efforts to gain compliance with *Brown*. Typical of the early solicitude for plaintiffs in school desegregation cases was *Potts v. Flax*.[25] Defendants maintained at trial that the suit was not a class action because neither of the two plaintiffs had affirmatively indicated that they sought class relief. The district court found first that the suit properly presented the question of the constitutionality of defendant's dual school system. The court then determined that although the suit was instituted only by individuals, the right sued upon was a class right—the right to a termination of the systemwide policy of racial segregation in the schools—and thus affected every black child in the school district. The Fifth Circuit, approving the lower court's reasoning, doubted that relief formally confined to specific black children either could be granted or could be so limited in its effect. Viewing the suit as basically an attack on the unconstitutional practice of racial discrimination, the court held that the appropriate relief was an order that it be discontinued. Moreover, the court suggested, "to require a school system to admit the specific successful plaintiff Negro child while others, having no such protection, were required to attend schools in a racially segregated system, would be for the court to contribute actively to the *class* discrimination."

At one time, expressions of disinterest and even disapproval of civil rights litigation by portions of the class may have been motivated by fear and by threats of physical and economic intimidation. Yet events in Atlanta, Detroit, and Boston provide the basis for judicial notice that many black parents oppose total reliance on racial balance remedies to cure the effects of school segregation. As one federal court of appeals judge has put it, "Almost predictably, changing circumstances during those years of litigation have dissolved the initial unity of the plaintiffs' position."[26] Black parents who prefer alternative remedies are poorly served by the routine approval of plaintiffs' requests for class status in school desegregation litigation.

Basic principles of equity require courts to develop greater sensitivity to the growing disagreement in black communities over the nature of school relief. Existing class action rules provide ample authority for broadening representation in school cases to reflect the fact that views of the black community are no longer monolithic. One aspect of class action status requiring closer scrutiny is whether the representation provided by plaintiffs will "fairly and adequately protect the interests of the class." Because every person is entitled to be adequately represented when his rights and duties are being adjudicated, it is incumbent upon the courts to ensure the fairness of proceedings that will bind absent class members. The failure to exercise such care may violate due process rights guaranteed by the Fifth and Fourteenth Amendments.

These problems can be avoided if, instead of routinely assuming that school desegregation plaintiffs adequately represent the class, courts will carefully apply the standard tests for determining the validity of class action allegations and the standard procedures for protecting the interests of unnamed class members. . . .

The failure to monitor carefully class status in accordance with the class action rules can frustrate the purposes of those rules and intensify the danger of attorney-client conflict inherent in class action litigation. To a measurable degree, the conflict can be traced to the civil rights lawyer's idealism and commitment to school integration. Such motivations do not become "unprofessional" because they are subjected to psychological scrutiny; rather, they help to explain the drive that enables the civil rights lawyer to survive discouragement and defeat and to renew the challenge for change. However, when challenges are made on behalf of large classes unable to speak effectively for themselves, courts should not refrain from making those inquiries under the federal rules which cannot fail, when properly undertaken, to strengthen the position of the class, the representative, and the counsel who serve them both.

V. The Resolution of Lawyer-Client Conflicts

THERE is nothing revolutionary in any of the suggestions in this article. They are controversial only to the extent that they suggest that some civil rights lawyers, like their more candid poverty law colleagues, are making decisions, setting priorities, and undertaking responsibilities that should be determined by their clients and shaped by the community. It is essential that lawyers "lawyer" and not attempt to lead clients and class. Commitment renders restraint more, not less, difficult, and the inability of black clients to pay handsome fees for legal services can cause their lawyers, unconsciously perhaps, to adopt an attitude of "we know what's best" in determining legal strategy. Unfortunately, clients are all too willing to turn everything over to the lawyers. In school cases, perhaps more than in any other civil rights field, the attorney must be more than a litigator. The willingness to innovate, organize, and negotiate—and the ability to perform each with skill and persistence—are of crucial importance. In this process of overall representation, the apparent—and sometimes real—conflicts of interest between lawyer and client can be resolved.

Finally, commitment to an integrated society should not be allowed to interfere with the ability to represent effectively parents who favor education-oriented remedies. Those civil rights lawyers, regardless of race, whose commitment to integration is buoyed by doubts about the effectiveness of predominantly black schools should reconsider seriously the propriety of representing blacks, at least in those school cases involving heavily minority districts.

This seemingly harsh suggestion is dictated by practical as well as professional considerations. Lacking more viable alternatives, the black community has turned to the courts. After several decades of frustration, the legal system, for a number of complex reasons, responded. Law and lawyers have received perhaps too much credit for that response. The quest for symbolic manifestations of new rights and the search for new legal theories have too often failed to prompt an assessment of the economic and political conditions that so influence the progress and outcome of any social reform improvement.

In school desegregation blacks have a just cause, but this cause can be undermined as well as furthered by litigation. A test case can be an important means of calling attention to perceived injustice; more important, school litigation presents opportunities for improving the weak economic and political position that renders the black community vulnerable to the specific injustices the litigation is intended to correct. Litigation can and should serve lawyer and client as a community-organizing tool, an educational forum, a means of obtaining data, a method of exercising political leverage, and a rallying point for public support.

However, even when directed by the most resourceful attorneys, civil rights litigation remains an unpredictable vehicle for gaining benefits, such as quality schooling, which a great many whites do not enjoy. The risks involved in such efforts increase dramatically when civil rights attorneys, for idealistic or other reasons, fail to consider continually the limits imposed by the social and political circumstances under which clients must function even if the case is won. In the closest of lawyer-client relationships this continual reexamination can be difficult; it becomes much harder where much of the representation takes place hundreds of miles from the site of the litigation.

Leroy Clark has written that the black community's belief in the efficacy of litigation inhibited the development of techniques involving popular participation and control, that might have advanced school desegregation in the South. He feels that civil rights lawyers were partly responsible for this unwise reliance on the law. They had studied "cases" in which the conflict involved easily identifiable adversaries, a limited number of variables, and issues that courts could resolve in a manageable way. A lawyer seeking social change, Clark advises, must "make clear that the major social and economic obstacles are not easily amenable to the legal process and that vigilance and continued activity by the disadvantaged are the crucial elements in social change." For reasons quite similar to those which enabled blacks to win in *Brown* in 1954 and caused them to lose in *Plessy* in 1896, even successful school litigation will bring little meaningful change unless there is continuing pressure for implementation from the black community. The problem of unjust laws, as Gary Bellow has noted, is almost invariably a problem of distribution of political and economic power. The rules merely reflect a series of choices by the society made in response to these distributions. " '[R]ule' change, without a political base to support it, just doesn't produce any substantial result because rules are not self-executing: they require an enforcement mechanism."[26]

In the last analysis, blacks must provide an enforcement mechanism that will give educational content to the constitutional right recognized in *Brown*. Simply placing black children in "white" schools will seldom suffice. Lawyers in school cases who fail to obtain judicial relief that reasonably promises to improve the education of black children serve poorly both their clients and their cause.

In 1935, W. E. B. Du Bois, in the course of a national debate over the education of blacks—a debate that has not been significantly altered by *Brown*—expressed simply but eloquently the message of the coalition of black community groups in Boston with which this article began:

[T]he Negro needs neither segregated schools nor mixed schools. What he needs is Education. What he must remember is that there is no magic, either in mixed schools or in segregated schools. A mixed school with poor and unsympathetic teachers, with hostile public opinion, and no teaching of truth concerning black folk, is bad. A segregated school with ignorant placeholders, inadequate equip-

ment, poor salaries, and wretched housing, is equally bad. Other things being equal, the mixed school is the broader, more natural basis for the education of all youth. It gives wider contacts; it inspires greater self-confidence; and suppresses the inferiority complex. But other things seldom are equal, and in that case, Sympathy, Knowledge, and the Truth, outweigh all that the mixed school can offer.[27]

Du Bois spoke neither for the integrationalist nor the separatist, but for poor black parents unable to choose, as can the well-to-do of both races, which schools will educate their children. Effective representation of these parents and their children presents a still unmet challenge for all lawyers committed to civil rights.

NOTES

1. Freedom House Institute on Schools and Education, *Critique of the Boston School Committee Plan, 1975*, at 2. This fifteen-page document was prepared, signed, and submitted in February 1975 directly to federal judge W. Arthur Garrity by almost two dozen of Boston's black community leaders. The statement was a critique of a desegregation plan filed by the Boston School Committee in the Boston school case: *Morgan v. Hennigan*, 379 F. Supp. 410 (D. Mass.), aff'd sub nom. *Morgan v. Kerrigan*, 509 F.2d 580 (1st Cir. 1974), cert, denied, 421 U.S. 953 (1975); *Morgan v. Kerrigan*, 388 F. Supp. 581 (D. Mass.), aff'd, 509 F.2d 599 (1st Cir. 1975); *Morgan v. Kerrigan*, 401 F. Supp. 216 (D. Mass. 1975), aff'd No. 75–1184 (1st Cir., Jan. 14, 1976). It was written during two all-day sessions sponsored by the Freedom House Institute, a community house in Boston's black Roxbury area. Judge Garrity had solicited comments on the school committee's plan from community groups. Those who prepared this statement did so on behalf of the Coordinated Social Services Council, a confederation of forty-six public and private agencies serving minority groups in the Boston area. The cover letter was signed by Otto and Muriel Snowden, codirectors of Freedom House, Inc., and two of the most respected leaders in the Roxbury community. They advised Judge Garrity that the statement "represents the thinking of a sizable number of knowledgeable people in the Black community, and we respectfully urge your serious consideration of the points raised." . . .

Plaintiffs' counsel in the Boston school case expressed sympathy with the black community leaders' emphasis on educational improvement, but contended that the law required giving priority to the desegregation process. Few of the group's concerns were reflected in the plaintiffs' proposed desegregation plan rejected by the court. See *Morgan v. Kerrigan*, 401 F. Supp. 216. 229 (D. Mass. 1975), aff'd No. 75–1181 (1st Cir., Jan 14, 1976).

2. 347 U.S. 483 (1954).

3. 163 U.S. 537 (1896).

4. *Brown v. Board of Education* 349 U.S. 294 (1955) (*Brown II*).

5. I can recall a personal instance. While working on the James Meredith litigation in Jackson, Mississippi, in 1961, at a time when the very idea of school desegregation in Mississippi was dismissed as "foolishness" even by some civil rights lawyers, I was visited by a small group of parents and leaders of the black community in rural Leake County, Mississippi. They explained that they needed legal help because the school board had closed the black elementary school in their area even though the school had been built during the thirties with private funds and was maintained, in part, by the efforts of the black community. Closing of the school necessitated busing black children across the county to another black school. In addition, the community had lost the benefit of the school for a meeting place and community center. The group wanted to sue the school board to have their school reopened. I recall informing the group that both LDF and NAACP had abandoned efforts to make separate schools equal, but if they wished to desegregate the whole school system, we could probably provide legal assistance. The group recognized as well as I did that there were only a few black attorneys in Mississippi who would represent the group, and that those attorneys would represent them only if a civil rights organization provided financial support. Sometime later, the group contacted me and indicated they were ready to go ahead with a school desegregation suit. It was filed in 1963, one of the first in the state. . . .

6. In *Milliken v. Bradley*, 418 U.S., 717, 745 (1974), the Supreme Court held (5–4) that desegregation remedies must stop at the boundary of the school district unless it can be shown that deliberately segregative actions were "a substantial cause of inter-district segregation": "Before the boundaries of separate and autonomous school districts may be set aside by consolidating the separate units for remedial purposes or by imposing a cross-district remedy, it must first be shown that there has been a constitutional violation within one district that produces a significant segregative effect in another district." *Id.* at 744–45. The court so held despite the fact that the only effective desegregation plan was a metropolitan area plan. The majority opinion, severely criticized by the dissenting justices, has also been attacked by legal writers.

7. See *Milliken v. Bradley*, 418 U.S. 717 (1974).

8. Mays, "Comment: Atlanta—Living with *Brown* Twenty Years Later, 3 *Black L. J.* 184, 190, 191–92 (1974).

9. Campbell, "Defining and Attaining Equal Educational Opportunity in a Pluralistic Society," 26 *Vanderbilt L. Rev.* 461, 478 (1973).

10. *Id.*

11. Edmonds, "Advocating Integrity: A Critique of the Civil Rights Attorney in Class Action Desegregation Suits," 3 *Black L. J.* 176, 178 (1974). . . .

12. *371 U.S. 415 (1963).*

13. *Id.* at 428–29.

14. *Id.* at 435 (footnotes omitted).

15. *Id.* at 429.

16. *Id.* at 443.

17. *Id.* at 444–45.

18. *Id.* at 445.

19. *Id.* at 447.

20. *Id.* at 450.

21. *Id.* at 460.

22. *Id.* at 462.

23. *Id.*

24. *Id.* at 415, 460–62 (Harlan, J., dissenting).

25. 313 F. 2d 284 (5th Cir. 1963).

26. *Calhoun v. Cook*, 522 F. 2d 717, 718 (5th Cir. 1975) (Clark, J.).

27. Du Bois, "Does the Negro Need Separate Schools?," 4 *J. Negro Educ.* 328, 335 (1935).

BROWN V. BOARD OF EDUCATION AND
THE INTEREST CONVERGENCE
DILEMMA

Derrick A. Bell, Jr.

IN 1954, the Supreme Court handed down
the landmark decision *Brown v. Board of
Education*[1] in which the court ordered the end
of state-mandated racial segregation of public
schools. Now, more than twenty-five years after
that dramatic decision, it is clear that *Brown* will
not be forgotten. It has triggered a revolution in
civil rights law and in the political leverage
available to blacks in and out of court. As Judge
Robert L. Carter put it, *Brown* transformed
blacks from beggars pleading for decent treatment to citizens demanding equal treatment
under the law as their constitutionally recognized right.[2]

Yet today most black children attend public
schools that are both racially isolated and inferior.[3] Demographic patterns, white flight, and
the inability of the courts to effect the necessary
degree of social reform render further progress
in implementing *Brown* almost impossible. The
late Alexander Bickel warned that *Brown* would
not be overturned but, for a whole array of
reasons, "may be headed for—dread word—
irrelevance."[4] Bickel's prediction is premature
in law where the *Brown* decision remains viable,
but it may be an accurate assessment of its
current practical value to millions of black children who have not experienced the decision's
promise of equal educational opportunity.

Shortly after *Brown*, Herbert Wechsler rendered a sharp and nagging criticism of the
decision.[5] Though he welcomed its result, he
criticized its lack of a principled basis. Wechsler's views have since been persuasively refuted,[6]
yet within them lie ideas that may help to
explain both the disappointment of *Brown* and
also what can be done to renew its promise.

In this comment, I plan to take a new look at
Wechsler within the context of the subsequent
desegregation campaign. By doing so, I hope to
offer an explanation of why school desegregation has in large part failed and what can be
done to bring about change.

I. Professor Wechsler's Search for Neutral Principles in Brown

THE year was 1959, five years after the
Supreme Court's decision in *Brown*. If
there was anything the hard-pressed partisans
of the case did not need, it was more criticism
of a decision ignored by the President, condemned by much of Congress, and resisted
wherever it was sought to be enforced.[7] Certainly, civil rights adherents did not welcome
adding to the growing list of critics the name
of Professor Herbert Wechsler, an outstanding
lawyer, a frequent advocate for civil rights
causes, and a scholar of prestige and influence.[8]
Nevertheless, Wechsler chose that time and
an invitation to deliver Harvard Law School's
Oliver Wendell Holmes Lecture as the occasion
to raise new questions about the legal appropriateness and principled shortcomings of *Brown*
and several other major civil rights decisions.[9]

Here was an attack that could not be dismissed as after-the-fact faultfinding by a conservative academician using his intellect to further a preference for keeping blacks in their
"separate but equal" place. Wechsler began by
saying that he had welcomed the result in
Brown; he noted that he had joined with the
NAACP's Charles Houston in litigating civil
rights cases in the Supreme Court.[10] He added
that he was not offended because the court
failed to uphold earlier decisions approving segregated schools; nor was he persuaded by the
argument that the issue should have been left
to Congress because the court's judgment might
not be honored.[11]

Wechsler did not align himself with the "realists," who "perceive in law only the element of
fiat, in whose conception of the legal cosmos
reason has no meaning or no place,"[12] nor with
the "formalists," who "frankly or covertly make
the test of virtue in interpretation whether its
result in the immediate decision seems to hinder
or advance the interests or the values they support."[13] Wechsler instead saw the need for
criteria of decision that could be framed and
tested as an exercise of reason and not merely
adopted as an act of willfulness or will. He
believed, in short, that courts could engage in a

"principal appraisal" of legislative actions that exceeded a fixed "historical meaning" of constitutional provisions without, as Judge Learned Hand feared, becoming "a third legislative chamber."[14] Courts, Wechsler argued, "must be genuinely principled, resting with respect to every step that is involved in reaching judgment on analysis and reasons quite transcending the immediate result that is achieved."[15] Applying these standards, which included constitutional and statutory interpretation, the subtle guidance provided by history, and appropriate but not slavish fidelity to precedent, Wechsler found difficulty with Supreme Court decisions where principled reasoning was, in his view, either deficient or, in some instances, nonexistent.[16] He included the *Brown* opinion in the latter category.

Wechsler reviewed and rejected the possibility that *Brown* was based on a declaration that the Fourteenth Amendment barred all racial lines in legislation.[17] He also doubted that the opinion relied upon a factual determination that segregation caused injury to black children, since evidence as to such harm was both inadequate and conflicting.[18] Rather, Wechsler concluded, the court in *Brown* must have rested its holding on the view that "racial segregation is, *in principle,* a denial of equality to the minority against whom it is directed; that is, the group that is not dominant politically and, therefore, does not make the choice involved."[19] Yet Wechsler found this argument untenable as well, because, among other difficulties, it seemed to require an inquiry into the motives of the legislature, a practice generally foreclosed to the courts.[20]

After dismissing these arguments, Wechsler then asserted that the legal issue in state-imposed segregation cases was not one of discrimination at all but, rather, of associational rights: "the denial by the state of freedom to associate, a denial that impinges in the same way on any groups or races that may be involved."[21] Wechsler reasoned that "if the freedom of association is denied by segregation, integration forces an association upon those for whom it is unpleasant or repugnant."[22] Concluding with a question that has challenged legal scholars, and

Wechsler asked, "Given a situation where the state must practically choose between denying the association to those individuals who wish it or imposing it on those who would avoid it, is there a basis in neutral principles for holding that the Constitution demands that the claims for association should prevail?"[23]

In suggesting that there was a basis in neutral principles for holding that the Constitution supports a claim by blacks for an associational right, Wechsler confessed that he had not yet written an opinion supporting such a holding. "To write it is for me the challenge of the school-segregation cases."[24]

II. The Search for a Neutral Principle: Racial Equality and Interest Convergence

SCHOLARS who accepted Wechsler's challenge had little difficulty finding a neutral principle on which the *Brown* decision could be based. Indeed, from the hindsight of a quarter century of the greatest racial consciousness-raising the country has ever known, much of Wechsler's concern seems hard to imagine. To doubt that racial segregation is harmful to blacks, and to suggest that what blacks really sought was the right to associate with whites, is to believe in a world that does not exist now and could not possibly have existed then. Charles Black, therefore, correctly viewed racial equality as the neutral principle that underlay the *Brown* opinion.[25] In Black's view, Wechsler's question "is awkwardly simple,"[26] and he states his response in the form of a syllogism. Black's major premise is that "the equal protection clause of the fourteenth amendment should be read as saying that the Negro race, as such, is not to be significantly disadvantaged by the laws of the states."[27] His minor premise is that "segregation is a massive intentional disadvantaging of the Negro race, as such, by state law."[28] The conclusion, then, is that the equal protection clause clearly bars racial segregation because segregation harms blacks and benefits whites in ways too numerous and obvious to require citation.[29]

Logically, the argument is persuasive, and

Black has no trouble urging that "[w]hen the directive of equality cannot be followed without displeasing the white[s], then something that can be called a 'freedom' of the white[s] must be impaired."[30] It is precisely here, though, that many whites part company with Professor Black. Whites may agree in the abstract that blacks are citizens and are entitled to constitutional protection against racial discrimination, but few are willing to recognize that racial segregation is much more than a series of quaint customs that can be remedied effectively without altering the status of whites. The extent of this unwillingness is illustrated by the controversy over affirmative action programs, particularly those where identifiable whites must step aside for blacks they deem less qualified or less deserving. Whites simply cannot envision the personal responsibility and the potential sacrifice inherent in Black's conclusion that true equality for blacks will require the surrender of racism-granted privileges for whites.

This sober assessment of reality raises concern about the ultimate import of Black's theory. On a normative level, as a description of how the world *ought* to be, the notion of racial equality appears to be the proper basis on which *Brown* rests, and Wechsler's framing of the problem in terms of associational rights thus seems misplaced. Yet on a positivistic level—how the world *is*—it is clear that racial equality is not deemed legitimate by large segments of the American people, at least to the extent it threatens to impair the societal status of whites. Hence, Wechsler's search for a guiding principle in the context of associational rights retains merit in the positivistic sphere, because it suggests a deeper truth about the subordination of law to interest group politics with a racial configuration.

Although no such subordination is apparent in *Brown*, it is possible to discern in more recent school decisions the outline of a principle, applied without direct acknowledgment, that could serve as the positivistic expression of the neutral statement of general applicability sought by Wechsler. Its elements rely as much on political history as legal precedent and emphasize the world as it is rather than how we might

want it to be. Translated from judicial activity in racial cases both before and after *Brown*, this principle of "interest convergence" provides: The interest of blacks in achieving racial equality will be accommodated only when it converges with the interests of whites. However, the Fourteenth Amendment, standing alone, will not authorize a judicial remedy providing effective racial equality for blacks where the remedy sought threatens the superior societal status of middle- and upper-class whites.

It follows that the availability of Fourteenth Amendment protection in racial cases may not actually be determined by the character of harm suffered by blacks or the quantum of liability proved against whites. Racial remedies may instead be the outward manifestations of unspoken and perhaps subconscious judicial conclusions that the remedies, if granted, will secure, advance, or at least not harm societal interests deemed important by middle- and upper-class whites. Racial justice—or its appearance—may, from time to time, be counted among the interests deemed important by the courts and by society's policymakers.

In assessing how this principle can accommodate both the *Brown* decision and the subsequent development of school desegregation law, it is necessary to remember that the issue of school segregation and the harm it inflicted on black children did not first come to the court's attention in the *Brown* litigation: blacks had been attacking the validity of these policies for one hundred years.[31] Yet, prior to *Brown*, black claims that segregated public schools were inferior had been met by orders requiring merely that facilities be made equal.[32] What accounted, then, for the sudden shift in 1954 away from the separate but equal doctrine and toward a commitment to desegregation?

I contend that the decision in *Brown* to break with the court's long-held position on these issues cannot be understood without some consideration of the decision's value to whites, not simply those concerned about the immorality of racial inequality, but also those whites in policymaking positions able to see the economic and political advances at home and abroad that would follow abandonment of segregation.

First, the decision helped to provide immediate credibility to America's struggle with communist countries to win the hearts and minds of emerging third world people. At least this argument was advanced by lawyers for both the NAACP and the federal government.[33] The point was not lost on the news media. *Time* magazine, for example, predicted that the international impact of *Brown* would be scarcely less important than its effect on the education of black children: "In many countries, where U.S. prestige and leadership have been damaged by the fact of U.S. segregation, it will come as a timely reassertion of the basic American principle that 'all men are created equal.' "[34]

Second, *Brown* offered much needed reassurance to American blacks that the precepts of equality and freedom so heralded during World War II might yet be given meaning at home. Returning black veterans faced not only continuing discrimination but also violent attacks in the South which rivaled those that took place at the conclusion of World War I.[35] Their disillusionment and anger were poignantly expressed by the black actor, Paul Robeson, who in 1949 declared, "It is unthinkable . . . that American Negroes would go to war on behalf of those who have oppressed us for generations . . . against a country [the Soviet Union] which in one generation has raised our people to the full human dignity of mankind."[36] It is not impossible to imagine that fear of the spread of such sentiment influenced subsequent racial decisions made by the courts.

Finally, there were whites who realized that the South could make the transition from a rural plantation society to the sunbelt with all its potential and profit only when it ended its struggle to remain divided by state-sponsored segregation.[37] Thus, segregation was viewed as a barrier to further industrialization in the South.

These points may seem insufficient proof of self-interest leverage to produce a decision as important as *Brown.* They are cited, however, to help assess—and not to diminish—the Supreme Court's most important statement on the principle of racial equality. Here, as in the abolition of slavery, there were whites for whom recogni-

tion of the racial equality principle was sufficient motivation. As with abolition, though, the number who would act on morality alone was insufficient to bring about the desired racial reform.[38]

Thus, for those whites who sought an end to desegregation on moral grounds or for the pragmatic reasons outlined above, *Brown* appeared to be a welcome break with the past. When segregation was finally condemned by the Supreme Court, however, the outcry was nevertheless great, especially among poorer whites who feared loss of control over their public schools and other facilities. Their fear of loss was intensified by the sense that they had been betrayed. They relied, as had generations before them, on the expectation that white elites would maintain lower-class whites in a societal status superior to that designated for blacks.[39] In fact, there is evidence that segregated schools and facilities were initially established by legislatures at the insistence of the white working class.[40] Today, little has changed: many poorer whites oppose social reform as "welfare programs for blacks" although, ironically, they have employment, education, and social service needs that differ from those of poor blacks by a margin that, without a racial scorecard, is difficult to measure.[41]

Unfortunately, poorer whites are now not alone in their opposition to school desegregation as well as to other attempts to improve the societal status of blacks: recent decisions, most notably by the Supreme Court, indicate that the convergence of black and white interests that led to *Brown* in 1954 and influenced the character of its enforcement has begun to fade. In *Swann v. Charlotte-Mecklenburg Board of Education,*[42] Chief Justice Warren Burger spoke of the "reconciliation of competing values" in desegregation cases.[43] If there was any doubt that "competing values" referred to the conflicting interests of blacks seeking desegregation and whites who prefer to retain existing school policies, then the uncertainty was dispelled by *Milliken v. Bradley,*[44] and *Dayton Board of Education v. Brinkman (Dayton I).*[45] In both cases, the court elevated the concept of "local autonomy" to a "vital national tradition."[46] "No single tradition in public education is more deeply rooted than local control over the operation of schools; local autonomy has long been thought essential both to the maintenance of community concern and support for public schools and to quality of the educational process."[47] Local control, however, may result in the maintenance of a status quo that will preserve superior educational opportunities and facilities for whites at the expense of blacks. As one commentator has suggested, "It is implausible to assume that school boards guilty of substantial violations in the past will take the interests of black school children to heart."[48]

As a result of its change in attitudes, the court has increasingly erected barriers to achieving the forms of racial balance relief it earlier had approved.[49] Plaintiffs must now prove that the complained-of segregation was the result of discriminatory actions intentionally and individuously conducted or authorized by school officials.[50] It is not enough that segregation was the "natural and foreseeable" consequence of their policies.[51] Even when this difficult standard of proof is met, moreover, courts must carefully limit the relief granted to the harm actually proved.[52] Judicial second thoughts about racial balance plans with broad-range busing components, the very plans that civil rights lawyers have come to rely on, is clearly evident in these new proof standards.

There is, however, continuing if unpredictable concern in the Supreme Court about school boards whose policies reveal long-term adherence to overt racial discrimination. In many cases, trial courts exposed to exhaustive testimony regarding the failure of school officials to desegregate or to provide substantial equality of schooling for minority children become convinced that school boards are violating *Brown*. Thus far, unstable Supreme Court majorities have upheld broad desegregation plans ordered by these judges,[53] but the reservations expressed by concurring justices[54] and the vigor of those justices who dissent[55] caution against optimism in this still controversial area of civil rights law.[56]

At the very least, these decisions reflect a substantial and growing divergence in the interests of whites and blacks. The result could prove to be the realization of Wechsler's legitimate fear that, if there is not a change of course, the purported entitlement of whites not to associate with blacks in public schools may yet eclipse the hope and the promise of *Brown*.

III. INTEREST CONVERGENCE REMEDIES UNDER BROWN

FURTHER progress to fulfill the mandate of *Brown* is possible to the extent that the divergence of racial interests can be avoided or minimized. Whites in policymaking positions, including those who sit on federal courts, can take no comfort in the conditions of dozens of inner-city school systems where the great majority of nonwhite children attend classes that are as segregated and ineffective as those so roundly condemned by Chief Justice Warren in the *Brown* opinion. Nor do poorer whites gain from their opposition to the improvement of educational opportunities for blacks: as noted earlier, the needs of the two groups differ little.[57] Hence, over time, all will reap the benefits from a concerted effort toward achieving racial equality.

The question still remains as to the surest way to reach the goal of educational effectiveness for both blacks and whites. I believe that the most widely used programs mandated by the courts—"antidefiance, racial balance" plans—may in some cases be inferior to plans focusing on "educational components," including the creation and development of "model" all-black schools. A short history of the use of the antidefiance strategy would be helpful at this point.

By the end of the fifties, it was apparent that compliance with the *Brown* mandate to desegregate the public schools would not come easily or soon. In the seventeen border states and the District of Columbia, fewer than two hundred thousand blacks were actually attending classes with white children.[58] The states in the deep South had not begun even token desegregation,[59] and it would take Supreme Court action to reverse the years-long effort of the Prince Edward County School Board in Virginia to abolish rather than desegregate its public schools.[60] Supreme Court orders[61] and presidential action had already been required to enable a handful of black students to attend Central High School in Little Rock, Arkansas.[62] Opposition to *Brown* was clearly increasing; its supporters were clearly on the defensive, as was the Supreme Court itself.

For blacks, the goal in school desegregation suits remained the effective use of the *Brown* mandate to eliminate state-sanctioned segregation. These efforts received unexpected help from the excesses of the massive resistance movement that led courts to justify relief under *Brown* as a reaffirmation of the supremacy of the judiciary on issues of constitutional interpetation. Brown, in the view of many, might not have been a wise or proper decision, but violent and prolonged opposition to its implementation posed an even greater danger to the federal system.

The Supreme Court quickly recognized this additional basis on which to ground school desegregation orders. "As this case reaches us," the court began its dramatic opinion in *Cooper v. Aaron,*[63] "it raises questions of the highest importance to the maintenance of our federal system of government."[64] Reaching back to *Marbury v. Madison,*[65] the court reaffirmed Chief Justice John Marshall's statement that "[i]t is emphatically the province and duty of the judicial department to say what the law is."[66] There were few opponents to this stand, and Professor Wechsler was emphatically not one of them. His criticism of *Brown* concluded with a denial that he intended to offer "comfort to anyone who claims legitimacy in defiance of the courts."[67] Those who accept the benefits of our constitutional system, Wechsler felt, cannot deny its allegiance when a special burden is imposed. Defiance of court orders, he asserted, constituted the "ultimate negation of all neutral principles."[68]

For some time, then, the danger to federalism posed by the secessionist-oriented resistance of southern state and local officials provided courts with an independent basis for supporting school desegregation efforts.[69] In the lower federal courts, the perceived threat to judicial status was often quite personal. Surely, I was not the only civil rights attorney who received a favorable decision in a school desegregation case less by legal precedent than because a federal judge, initially hostile to those precendents, my clients, and their lawyer, became incensed with school board litigation tactics that exhibited as little respect for the court as they did for the constitutional rights of black children.

There was a problem with school desegregation decisions framed in this antidefiance form which was less discernible then than now. While a prerequisite to the provision of equal educational opportunity, condemnation of school board evasion was far from synonymous with that long-promised goal. Certainly, it was cause for celebration when the court recognized that some pupil assignment schemes,[70] "freedom-of-choice" plans,[71] and similar "desegregation plans" were in fact designed to retain constitutionally condemned dual school systems. When the court, in obvious frustration with the slow pace of school desegregation, announced in 1968 what Justice Lewis Powell later termed "the *Green/Swann* doctrine of 'affirmative duty,'"[72] which placed on school boards the duty to disestablish their dual school systems, the decisions were welcomed as substantial victories by civil rights lawyers. Yet the remedies set forth in the major school cases following *Brown*—balancing the student and teacher populations by race in each school, eliminating single-race schools, redrawing school attendance lines, and transporting students to achieve racial balance[73]—have not in themselves guaranteed black children better schooling than they received in the pre-*Brown* era. Such racial balance measures have often altered the racial appearance of dual school systems without eliminating racial discrimination. Plans relying on racial balance to foreclose evasion have not eliminated the need for further orders protecting black children against discriminatory policies, including resegregation within desegregated schools,[74] the loss of black faculty and administrators,[75] suspensions and expulsions at much higher rates than white students,[76] and varying forms of racial harassment ranging from exclusion from extracurricular activities[77] to physical violence.[78] Antidefiance remedies, then, while effective in forcing alterations in school system structure, often encourage and seldom shield black children from discriminatory retaliation.

The educational benefits that have resulted from the mandatory assignment of black and white children to the same schools are also debatable.[79] If benefits did exist, they have begun to dissipate as whites flee in alarming numbers from school districts ordered to implement mandatory reassignment plans.[80] In response, civil rights lawyers sought to include entire metropolitan areas within mandatory reassignment plans in order to encompass mainly white suburban school districts, where so many white parents sought sanctuary for their children.[81]

Thus, the antidefiance strategy was brought full circle from a mechanism for preventing evasion by school officials of *Brown*'s antisegregation mandate to one aimed at creating a discrimination-free environment. This approach to the implementation of *Brown*, however, has become increasingly ineffective; indeed, it has in some cases been educationally destructive. A preferable method is to focus on obtaining real educational effectiveness, which may entail the improvement of presently desegregated schools as well as the creation or preservation of model black schools.

Civil rights lawyers do not oppose such relief, but they clearly consider it secondary to the racial balance remedies authorized in the *Swann*[82] and *Keyes*[83] cases. Those who espouse alternative remedies are deemed to act out of suspect motives. *Brown* is law, and racial balance plans are the only means of complying with the decision. The position reflects courage, but it ignores the frequent and often complete failure of programs that concentrate solely on achieving a racial balance.

Desegregation remedies that do not integrate may seem a step backward toward the *Plessy* "separate but equal" era. Some black educators, however, see major educational benefits in schools where black children, parents, and teachers can utilize the real cultural strengths of the black community to overcome the many barriers to educational achievement.[84] As Laurence Tribe has argued, "[J]udicial rejection of the 'separate but equal' talisman seems to have been accompanied by a potentially troublesome lack of sympathy for racial separateness as a possible expression of group solidarity."[85]

This is not to suggest that educationally oriented remedies can be developed and adopted without resistance. Policies necessary to obtain effective schools threaten the self-interest of teacher unions and others with vested interests in the status quo. However, successful magnet schools may provide a lesson that effective schools for blacks must be a primary goal rather than a secondary result of integration. Many white parents recognize a value in integrated schooling for their children, but they quite properly view integration as merely one component of an effective education. To the extent that civil rights advocates also accept this reasonable sense of priority, some greater racial interest conformity should be possible.

Is this what the *Brown* opinion meant by "equal educational opportunity?" Chief Justice Warren said the court could not "turn the clock back to 1868 when the [Fourteenth] Amendment was adopted, or even to 1896 when *Plessy v. Ferguson* was written."[86] The change in racial circumstances since 1954 rivals or surpasses all that occurred during the period that preceded it. If the decision that was at least a catalyst for that change is to remain viable, those who rely on it must exhibit the dynamic awareness of all the legal and political considerations that influenced those who wrote it.

Professor Wechsler warned us early on that there was more to *Brown* than met the eye. At one point, he observed that the opinion is "often read with less fidelity by those who praise it than by those by whom it is condemned."[87] Most of us ignored that observation openly and quietly raised a question about the sincerity of the observer. Criticism, as we in the movement for minority rights have every reason to learn, is a synonym for neither cowardice or capitulation. It may instead bring awareness, always the first step toward overcoming still another barrier in the struggle for racial equality.

NOTES

1. 347 U.S. 483 (1954).

2. Carter, "The Warren Court and Desegregation," in D. Bell, ed., *Race, Racism and American Law*, 456–61 (1973).

3. See Bell, Book Review, 92 *Harv. L. Rev.* 1826, 1826 n. 6 (1979). See also C. Jencks, *Inequality*, 25–28 (1972).

4. A. Bickel, *The Supreme Court and the Idea of Progress* 151 (1970).

5. Wechsler, "Toward Neutral Principles of Constitutional Law," 73 *Har. L. Rev.*, 1 (1959); the lecture was later published in a collection of selected essays. H. Wechsler, *Principles, Politics, and Fundamental Law*, 3 (1961).

6. See e.g., Black, "The Lawfulness of the Segregation Decisions," 69 *Yale L. J.*, 421 (1960); Heyman, "The Chief Justice, Racial Segregation, and the Friendly Critics," 49 *Calif. L. Rev.*, 104 (1961); Pollack, "Racial Discriminiation and Judicial Integrity: A Reply to Professor Wechsler," 108 *U. Pa. L. Rev.*, 1 (1959).

7. The legal campaign that culminated in the *Brown* decision is discussed in great depth in R. Kluger, *Simple Justice* (1976). The subsequent fifteen years are reviewed in S. Wasby, A. D'Amato, and R. Metrailer, *Desegregation from Brown to Alexander* (1977).

8. Wechsler is the Harlan Fiske Stone Professor of Constitutional Law Emeritus at the Columbia University Law School. His work is reviewed in 78 *Colum. L. Rev.*, 969 (1978) (issue dedicated in Professor Wechsler's honor upon his retirement).

9. See Wechsler, *supra* note 5, at 31–35.

10. Wechsler recalled that Houston, who was black, "did not suffer more than I in knowing that we had to go to Union Station to lunch together during the recess"; *id.* at 34.

11. *Id.* at 31–32.

12. *Id.* at 11.

13. *Id.*

14. *Id.* at 16.

15. *Id.* at 15.

16. *Id.* at 19.

17. *Id.* at 32.

18. *Id.* at 32–33.

19. *Id.* at 33 (emphasis added).

20. *Id.* at 33–34.

21. *Id.* at 34.

22. *Id.*

23. *Id.*

24. *Id.*

25. See Black, *supra* note 6, at 428–29.

26. *Id.* at 423.

27. *Id.*

28. *Id.*

29. *Id.* at 425–26.

30. *Id.* at 429.

31. See, e.g. *Roberts v. City of Boston*, 59 Mass. (5 Cush.) 198 (1850).

32. The cases are collected in Larson, "The New Law of Race Relations," 1969. *Wis. L. Rev.*, 470, 482, 483 n. 27; Leflar and Davis, "Segregation in the Public Schools—1953," 67 *Harv. L. Rev.*, 377, 430–35 (1954).

33. See Bell, "Racial Remediation: An Historical Perspective on Current Conditions," 52 *Notre Dame Law.*, 5, 12 (1976).

34. *Id.* at 12 n. 31.

35. C. Vann Woodward, *The Strange Career of Jim Crow*, 114 (3d rev. ed. 1974): I. Franklin, *From Slavery to Freedom*, 428–86 (2d ed. 1967).

36. D. Butler, "Paul Robeson," 137 (1976) (unwritten speech before the Partisans of Peace, World Peace Congress in Paris).

37. Professor Robert Higgs argued that the "region's economic development increasingly undermined the foundations of its traditional racial relations"; Higgs, "Race and Economy in the South, 1890–1950," in R. Haws, ed. *The Age of Segregation*, 89–90 (1978). Sociologists Frances Fox Piven and Richard Cloward have also drawn a connection between this economic growth and the support for the civil rights movement in the forties and fifties, when various white elites in business, philanthropy, and government began to speak out against racial discrimination. F. Piven and R. Cloward, *Regulating The Poor*, 229–30 (1971); see also F. Piven and R. Cloward, *Poor People's Movements*, 189–94 (1977).

38. President Abraham Lincoln, for example, acknowledged the moral evil in slavery. In his famous letter to publisher Horace Greeley, however, he promised to free all, some, or none of the slaves, depending on which policy would most help save the Union: M. Roe, ed., *Speeches and Letters of Abraham Lincoln, 1832–65*, at 194–95.

39. See Piven and Cloward, *Poor People's Movements*, 187 (1977), and, generally, Bell, *supra* note 33.

40. See Woodward, *supra* note 35, at 6.

41. Robert Heilbronner suggests that this country's failure to address social issues including poverty, public health,

housing, and prison reform as effectively as many European countries is due to the tendency of whites to view reform efforts as "programs to 'subsidize' Negroes. . . . In such cases the fear and resentment of the Negro takes precedence over the social problem itself. The result, unfortunately, is that the entire society suffers from the results of a failure to correct social evils whose ill effects refuse to obey the rules of segregation"; Heilbronner, "The Roots of Social Neglect in the United States," in E. Rostow, ed., *Is Law Dead?*, 288, 296 (1971).

42. 402 U.S. 1 (1971).

43. *Id.* at 31.

44. 418 U.S. 717 (1974) (limits power of federal courts to treat a primarily black urban school district and largely white suburban districts as a single unit in mandating desegregation).

45. 433 U.S. 406 (1977) (desegregation orders affecting pupil assignments should seek only the racial mix that would have existed absent the constitutional violation).

46. *Id.* at 410, 418 U.S. at 741–742.

47. 418 U.S. at 741.

48. The Supreme Court, 1978 Term, 93 *Harv. L. Rev.*, 60, 130 (1979).

49. See generally Fiss, "School Desegregation: The Uncertain Path of the Law," 4 *Philosophy and Pub. Aff.* 3 (1974); Kanner, "From Denver to Dayton: The Development of a Theory of Equal Protection Remedies," 72 *NW. U. L. Rev.*, 382 (1977).

50. *Dayton Bd. of Educ. v. Brinkman (Dayton I)*, 433 U.S. 406 (1977).

51. *Columbus Bd. of Educ. v. Penick*, 99 S. Ct. 2941, 2950 (1979).

52. *Austin Independent School Dist. v. United States*, 429 U.S. 990, 991 (1976) (Powell, J., concurring).

53. *Dayton Bd. of Educ. v. Brinkman (Dayton II)*, 99 S. Ct. 2917 (1979); *Columbus Bd. of Educ. v. Penick*, 99 S. Ct. 2941 (1979).

54. See *Columbus Bd. of Educ. v. Penick*, 99 S. Ct. 2941, 2952 (1979) (Burger, C. J., concurring); *id.* at 2983 (Stewart J., concurring).

55. See *id.* at 2952 (Rehnquist, J., dissenting); *id.* at 2988 (Powell, J., dissenting). See also *Dayton Bd. of Educ. v. Brinkman (Dayton II)*, 99 S. Ct. 2971, 2983 (1979) (Stewart, J., dissenting).

56. The court faces another difficult challenge in the 1979 term when it reviews whether the racial balance plan in Dallas, Texas, goes far enough in eliminating one-race schools in a large district that is now 65 percent black and Hispanic. *Tasby v. Estes*, 572 F. 2d 1010 (5th Cir. 1978), *cert. granted sub nom. Estes v. Metropolitan Branches of Dallas NAACP*, 440 U.S. 906 (1979).

57. See p. 21 *supra*.

58. P. Bergman, *The Chronological History of the Negro in America*, 561 (1969).

59. *Id.* at 561–62.

60. *Griffin v. County School Bd.*, 372 U.S. 218 (1964).

61. *Cooper v. Aaron*, 358 U.S. 1 (1958).

62. P. Bergman, *supra* note 58, at 555–56, 561–62.

63. 358 U.S. 1 (1958).

64. *Id.* at 4.

65. 5 U.S. (1 Cranch) 137, 177 (1803).

66. 358 U.S. at 18.

67. Wechsler, *supra* note 5, at 35.

68. *Id.*

69. See, e.g., *Goss v. Board of Educ.*, 373 U.S. 683 (1963) (struck down "minority to majority" transfer plans enabling resegregation of schools); *Bush v. New Orleans Parish School Bd.*, 188 F. Supp. 916 (E. D. La.), *aff'd*, 365 U.S. 569 (1961) (invalidation of state "interposition acts"); *Pointdexter v. Louisiana Financial Comm'n.*, 275 F. Supp. 833 (E. D. La. 1967), *aff'd per curiam*, 389 U.S. 215 (1968) ("tuition grants" for children attending private schools voided).

70. These plans, requiring black children to run a gauntlet of administrative proceedings to obtain assignment to a white school, were at first judicially approved. See *Covington v. Edwards*, 264 F. 2d 780 (4th Cir.), *cert. denied*, 361 U.S. 840 (1959); *Shuttlesworth v. Birmingham Bd. of Educ.*, 162 F. Supp. 372 (N. D. Ala.), *aff'd*, 358 U.S. 101 (1958).

71. *Green v. County School Bd.*, 391 U.S. 430 (1968) (practice of "free choice"—enabling each student to choose whether to attend a black or white school—struck down).

72. *Keyes v. School Dist. No. 1*, 413 U.S. 189, 224 (1973) (Powell, J., concurring in part and dissenting in part).

73. See, e.g., *Swann v. Charlotte-Mecklenburg Bd. of Educ.*, 402 U.S. 1 (1976); *Green v. County School Bd.*, 391 U.S. 430 (1968).

74. See, e.g., *Jackson v. Marvell School Dist. No. 22*, 425 F. 2d 211 (8th Circ. 1970). There were also efforts to segregate students within desegregated schools by the use of standardized tests and achievement scores. See *Singleton v. Jackson Mun. Separate School Dist.*, 419 F. 2d 1211 (5th Cir.), *rev'd per curiam*, 396 U.S. 290 (1970); *Hobson v. Hansen*, 269 F. Supp. 401 (D. D. Cir. 1967), *aff'd sub nom. Smuck v. Hobson*, 408 F 2d 175 (D. C. Cir. 1969).

75. See, e.g., *Chambers v. Hendersonville City Bd. of Educ.*, 364 F. 2d 189 (4th Cir. 1966). For a discussion of the wholesale dismissal and demotion of black teachers in the wake of school desegregation orders, see materials compiled in 2 N. Dorsen, P. Bender, B. Neuborne, and S. Law, *Enerson, Haber, and Dorsen's Political and Civil Rights in the United States*, 679–80 (4th ed. 1979).

76. *Hawkins v. Coleman*, 376 F. Supp. 1330 (N. D. Tex. 1974); *Dunn v. Tyler Independent School Dist.*, 327 F. Supp. 528 (E. D. Tex. 1971), *aff'd in part and rev'd in part*, 460 F. 2d 137 (5th Cir. 1972).

77. *Floyd v. Trice*, 490 F. 2d 1154 (8th Cir. 1974); *Augustus v. School Bd.*, 361 F. Supp. 383 (N. D. Fla. 1973), *modified*, 307 F. 2d 152 (5th Cir. 1975).

78. For a recent example, see the account of racial violence resulting from desegregation in Boston, in Husoch, "Boston: The Problem That Won't Go Away," *New York Times*, Nov. 25, 1979, SS 6 (Magazine), at 32.

79. See N. St. John, *School Desegregation*, 16–41 (1975).

80. See D. Armor, "White Flight, Demographic Transition, and the Future of School Desegregation" (1978) (Rand Paper Series, the Rand Corp.); J. Colemen, S. Kelly, and J. Moore, "Trends in School Segregation, 1968–1973" (1975) (Urban Institute Paper). But see Pettigrew and Green, "School Desegregation in Large Cities: A Critique of the Coleman 'White Flight' Thesis," 46 *Harv. Educ. Rev.*, 1 (1976); Rossell, "School Desegregation and White Flight," 90 *Pol. Sci. Q.* 675 (1975), R. Farley, "School Integration and White Flight" (1975) (Population Studies Center, U. Mich.).

81. See, e.g., *Milliken v. Bradley*, 418 U.S. 717 (1974). In Los Angeles, where the court ordered reassignment of sixty-five thousand students in grades four through eight, 30–50 percent of the twenty-two thousand white students scheduled for mandatory busing boycotted the public schools or enrolled elsewhere: U.S. Commission on Civil Rights, *Desegregation of the Nation's Public Schools: A Status Report*, 51 (1979).

82. *Swann v. Charlotte-Mecklenburg Bd. of Educ.*, 402 U.S. 1 (1971).

83. *Keyes v. School Dist. No. 1*, 413 U. S. 189 (1973).

84. S. Lightfoot, *Worlds Apart*, 172 (1978). For a discussion of the Lightfoot theory, see Bell, *supra* note 3, at 1838.

85. L. Tribe, *American Constitutional Law*, §16–15, at 1022 (1978) (footnote omitted).

86. *Brown v. Board of Educ.*, 347 U. S. 483, 492 (1954).

87. Wechsler, *supra* note 5, at 32.

LEGITIMIZING RACIAL DISCRIMINATION THROUGH ANTIDISCRIMINATION LAW: A CRITICAL REVIEW OF SUPREME COURT DOCTRINE

Alan David Freeman

I. THE PERPETRATOR PERSPECTIVE

THE concept of "racial discrimination" may be approached from the perspective of either its victim or its perpetrator. From the victim's perspective, racial discrimination describes those conditions of actual social existence as a member of a perpetual underclass. This perspective includes both the objective conditions of life (lack of jobs, lack of money, lack of housing) and the consciousness associated with those objective conditions (lack of choice and lack of human individuality in being forever perceived as a member of a group rather than as an individual). The perpetrator perspective sees racial discrimination not as conditions but as actions, or series of actions, inflicted on the victim by the perpetrator. The focus is more on what particular perpetrators have done or are doing to some victims than on the overall life situation of the victim class.

The victim, or "condition,"[1] conception of racial discrimination suggests that the problem will not be solved until the conditions associated with it have been eliminated. To remedy the condition of racial discrimination would demand affirmative efforts to change the condition. The remedial dimension of the perpetrator perspective, however, is negative. The task is merely to neutralize the inappropriate conduct of the perpetrator.

In its core concept of the "violation," antidiscrimination law is hopelessly embedded in the perpetrator perspective. Its central tenet, the "antidiscrimination principle," is the prohibition of race-dependent decisions that disadvantage members of minority groups, and its principal task has been to select from the maze of human behaviors those particular practices that violate the principle, outlaw the identified practices, and neutralize their specific effects. Antidiscrimination law has thus been ultimately indifferent to the condition of the victim; its demands are satisfied if it can be said that the "violation" has been remedied.

The perpetrator perspective presupposes a world composed of atomistic individuals whose actions are outside of and apart from the social fabric and without historical continuity. From this perspective, the law views racial discrimination not as a social phenomenon but merely as the misguided conduct of particular actors. It is a world in which, but for the conduct of these misguided ones, the system of equality of opportunity would work to provide a distribution of the good things in life without racial disparities, and a world in which deprivations that did correlate with race would be "deserved" by those deprived on grounds of insufficient "merit." It is a world in which such things as "vested rights," "objective selection systems," and "adventitious decisions" (all of which serve to prevent victims from experiencing any change in conditions) are matters of fate, having nothing to do with the problem of racial discrimination.

Central to the perpetrator perspective are the twin notions of "fault" and "causation." Under the fault idea, the task of antidiscrimination law is to separate from the masses of society those blameworthy individuals who are violating the otherwise shared norm. The fault idea is reflected in the assertion that only "intentional" discrimination violates the antidiscrimination principle.[2] In its pure form, intentional discrimination is conduct accompanied by a purposeful desire to produce discriminatory results. One can thus evade responsibility for ostensibly discriminatory conduct by showing that the action was taken for a good reason or for no reason at all.

The fault concept gives rise to a complacency about one's own moral status; it creates a class of "innocents" who need not feel any personal responsibility for the conditions associated with discrimination, and who therefore feel great resentment when called upon to bear any burdens in connection with remedying violations. This resentment accounts for much of the ferocity surrounding the debate about so-called reverse discrimination, for being called on to bear burdens ordinarily imposed only upon the guilty involves an apparently unjustified stigmatization of those led by the fault notion to believe in their own innocence.

Operating along with fault, the causation requirement serves to distinguish those conditions that the law will address from the totality of conditions that a victim perceives to be associated with discrimination. These dual requirements place on the victim the nearly impossible burden of isolating the particular conditions of discrimination produced by and mechanically linked to the behavior of an identified blameworthy perpetrator, regardless of whether other conditions of discrimination, caused by other perpetrators, would have to be remedied for the outcome of the case to make any difference at all. The causation principle makes it clear that some objective instances of discrimination are to be regarded as mere accidents, or "caused," if at all, by the behavior of ancestral demons whose responsibility cannot follow their successors in interest over time. The causation principle also operates to place beyond the law discriminatory conduct (action taken with a purpose to discriminate under the fault principle) that is not linked to any discernible "discriminatory effect."

The perpetrator perspective has been and still is the only formal conception of a violation in antidiscrimination law. Strict adherence to that form, however, would have made even illusory progress in the quest for racial justice impossible. The challenge for the law, therefore, was to develop, through the usual legal techniques of verbal manipulation, ways of breaking out of the formal constraints of the perpetrator perspective while maintaining ostensible adherence to the form itself. This was done by separating violation from remedy, and doing through remedy what was inappropriate in cases involving only identification of violations. However, since one of the principal tenets of the perpetrator perspective is that remedy and violation must be coextensive, it was necessary both to state this tenet and violate it—no mean task even for masters of verbal gamesmanship. For a while, the remedial doctrines seemingly undermined the hegemony of the perpetrator form, threatening to replace it with a victim perspective. In the end, however, form triumphed, and the perpetrator perspective, always dominant in identifying violations, was firmly reasserted in the context of remedies as well.

II. 1954–1965: THE ERA OF UNCERTAINTY, OR THE JURISPRUDENCE OF VIOLATIONS

IN the first era of modern antidiscrimination law, commencing with the Supreme Court's decision in *Brown v. Board of Education (Brown I)*, there was little occasion to consider the limits of the perpetrator perspective. For the most part, the Court concerned itself with identifying violations rather than with remedying them, and it was therefore able to remain within the perpetrator perspective tradition of merely declaring the illegality of specific practices. Although it was obvious that school desegregation was going to require something more than a statement of illegality, the Court in its subsequent opinion in *Brown v. Board of Education (Brown II)* chose to relegate the problem to lower courts, leaving ambiguous the scope of the remedial obligation.

The *Brown I* opinion offers no clear statement of the perpetrator perspective, however; rather, it contains within its inscrutable text a number of possible antidiscrimination principles that "explain" the result in the case.

A. Brown v. Board of Education

There are a number of different ways of looking at *Brown*, all of which permeate the subsequent evolution of antidiscrimination law. I shall discuss five such: the color-blind constitution theory; the equality of educational opportunity theory; the white oppression of blacks theory; the freedom of association theory; and the integrated society theory.

I. COLOR-BLIND CONSTITUTION

To explain *Brown* by invoking the slogan that the "Constitution is color-blind"[3] reflects a means-oriented view of the equal protection clause. On this view, the failure of school segregation was the governments use of an irrational classification—race. This approach, however, does not explain why it was irrational to classify

people by race if the purpose was to prevent blacks and whites from going to school together. How else could one rationally achieve segregation by race in public schools? One answer is that the purpose itself is illegitimate, that it is no business of government to seek to segregate by race in public schools. If that is the answer, however, the color-blind constitution theory is not a means-oriented approach at all, but rather one that collapses into substantial equal protection. If that is the case, however, one must consider not legislative rationality, but, as I suggested above, particular relationships between blacks and whites in the context of American history.

A ploy that avoids the quick collapse into substantive equal protection is to bootstrap the means-oriented principle into its own substantive principle. This is done by starting with the means-oriented assumption that racial classifications are almost always unrelated to *any* valid governmental purpose ("purpose" here being the wholly abstract world of possible purposes). Since such classifications are likely to be irrational, they should be treated as "suspect," and subjected to "strict scrutiny," which they will survive only if found to satisfy a "compelling governmental interest." If the degree of scrutiny is so strict and the possibility of a sufficiently compelling governmental interest so remote that the rule operates as a virtual per se rule, we then seem to have a means-oriented principle that explains the *Brown* case.

The problem with this second formulation of the color-blind theory is that it still contains a substantive assumption: to wit, racial classifications are almost always unrelated to any valid governmental purpose. As an abstract matter, this is hardly intuitively obvious. One could easily envision a society in which racial or other ethnic classifications are unrelated to any pattern of oppression or domination of one group by another and, on the contrary, promote feelings of group identity. Thus, the initial assumption cannot be made except in the context of a particular historical situation, and the source of the assumption that underlies the color-blind theory can easily be found in American history by taking a brief glance at relationships between whites and blacks. Accordingly, the color-blind theory must originate in a notion of substantive equal protection.

Despite this fact, the color-blind theory has tended to become a reified abstraction, to gain a life of its own, and finally to turn back on its origins. Thus, a pure form of the color-blind theory would outlaw any use of racial classifications no matter what the context, thereby providing easy answers to questions like whether a black community can refuse to participate in an integration plan or whether black students at a public university can establish their own housing units from which whites are excluded. The answers remain easy only so long as the theory remains divorced from its origins in the actuality of black-white relations. By abstracting racial discrimination into a myth world where all problems of race or ethnicity are fungible, the color-blind theory turns around and denies concrete demands of blacks with the argument that to yield to such demands would be impossible since every other ethnic group would be entitled to make the same demand.

The color-blind theory has never become the law; the Supreme Court has in fact explicitly upheld the remedial use of racial classifications on a number of occasions. Nevertheless, the theory does share certain features with something that *is* part of the law—the perpetrator perspective. Among these features is the emphasis on negating specific invalid practices rather than affirmatively remedying conditions, with a consequent inability to deal with ostensibly neutral practices. In addition, the color-blind theory exerts an insistent pressure on antidiscrimination law to produce special justifications for deviations from its norm, as well as to limit their duration in order to facilitate a quick return to the comfortable, abstract world of color-blindness.

2. EQUALITY OF EDUCATIONAL OPPORTUNITY
Brown can also be viewed as a case concerned with equality of educational opportunity. This approach corresponds with the fundamental right concept of equal protection. Under this view, *Brown* did not merely outlaw segregation in public schools; it also guaranteed that black

children would have an affirmative right to a quality of education comparable to that received by white children. The court's opinion stressed the importance of education, calling it the "very foundation of good citizenship"[4] and "a principal instrument in awakening the child to cultural values, in preparing him for later professional training, and in helping him to adjust normally to his environment." The court added that where a state undertakes to provide public education, it "is a right which must be made available to all on equal terms."

By way of hindsight, the case stood for both more and less than a guarantee of equal educational quality. It came to stand for more insofar as its holding was quickly extended to other forms of state-imposed segregation; yet it came to stand for a great deal less insofar as black children today have neither an affirmative right to receive an integrated education nor a right to equality of resources for their schools—which, ironically, was a litigable claim under the regime of de jure segregation. While there is no way to prove "objectively" what the opinion in *Brown* meant with respect to a right to educational equality, both a claim for equal resources and a claim for the choice of an integrated education can be supported from the text of the opinion. The court assumed for its opinion that the black and white schools in the cases under review "have been equalized, or are being equalized, with respect to buildings, curricula, qualifications and salaries of teachers, and other 'tangible factors.'"[5] With respect to the fact of integration, the court quoted a finding of one of the lower courts: "Segregation of white and colored children in public schools has a detrimental effect upon the colored children. The impact is greater when it has the sanction of the law; for the policy of separating the races is usually interpreted as denoting the inferiority of the negro group."[6] To the extent the text suggests that the detrimental effect, with its attendant denotation of inferiority, would persist even in the absence of state sanction, the case may be read as addressing not the *practice* but the *fact* of racial separation.

Were the court to have recognized affirmative claims to resources or integrated classrooms, it would have adopted explicitly a victim perspective on racial discrimination. Essential to this perspective is the conferral upon the members of the formerly oppressed group a choice that is real and not merely theoretical with respect to conditions over which they had no control under the regime of oppression. Instead, though, under the perpetrator perspective, the court recognizes only the right of the black children to attend schools that are not intentionally segregated by the jurisdiction that runs them. This right, it is argued, is all that *Brown* stands for anyway, since all the case did was outlaw de jure segregation.

3. WHITE OPPRESSION OF BLACKS

On this view, the *Brown* case was a straightforward declaration that segregation was unlawful because it was an instance of majoritarian oppression of black people, a mechanism for maintaining blacks as a perpetual underclass. This approach, which begins and ends with historical fact instead of trying to find a neutral abstraction from which one can deduce the invalidity of segregation, was eloquently stated by Charles Black in 1960:

> First, the equal protection clause of the fourteenth amendment should be read as saying that the Negro race, as such, is not to be significantly disadvantaged by the laws of the states. Secondly, segregation is a massive intentional disadvantaging of the Negro race, as such, by state law. There is no subtlety at all. Yet I cannot disabuse myself of the idea that that is really all there is to the segregation cases.

That this was the "explanation" for the "segregation cases" was self-evident to Black on the basis both of American history and of his own boyhood experience in Texas. The striking feature of his approach is that it makes sense not as the presentation of another "neutral principle" that can be separated from its factual context and given a life of its own but, rather, as a method for taking a hard look at the truth and describing it as one knows it to be. It is the same method that the Supreme Court used, in a more candid opinion than *Brown*, to outlaw Virginia's criminal miscegenation statute:

> There is patently no legitimate overriding purpose independent of invidious racial discrimination which justifies this classification. The fact that Virginia prohibits only interracial marriages involving white persons demonstrates that the racial classifications must stand on their own justification, as measures designed to maintain White Supremacy.[7]

As method, the white oppression of blacks approach would ask in each case whether the particular conditions complained of, viewed in their social and historical context, are a manifestation of racial oppression. Such an approach would reflect adoption of the victim perspective. It is not an approach congenial to a system of law that wishes to rationalize continued discrimination just as much as it wants to outlaw it. That goal, if it is to be accomplished through a practice that can be convincingly described as "law," requires a gap between social reality and legal intervention, with that gap mediated by an abstract, objective principle against which particular instances of discrimination can be tested and upheld or struck down depending on the results.

Regarded as a principle, Charles Black's formulation is ambiguous, however, and can lead just as easily to a perpetrator perspective. One can argue that he said nothing more than that "southern" segregation is illegal, that the violation is simply the practice of intentional, de jure segregation. So formulated, the principle does not speak to the problem of remedying that practice, nor does it indicate which other practices or conditions might be regarded as sufficiently similar to "southern" segregation to be deemed unlawful. That the version of substantive equal protection described by Black is the explanation for *Brown* seems obvious, but it took some years to transform his method into an abstraction, largely under the influence of the color-blind theory.

4. FREEDOM OF ASSOCIATION

The freedom of association view sees *Brown* not as an equal protection case at all but, rather, as a case dealing with people's due process right to associate with one another free of state interference. While it is clear that this was not the actual rationale of the *Brown* opinion, as the court specifically eschewed reliance on any due

process theory and later cases specifically rejected the freedom of association viewpoint, it
nevertheless seems worth discussing. For one
thing, the freedom of association theory may be
a more accurate explanation of the limits of
Brown in its historical context; for another, it
exemplifies the rationalization that serves to
legitimize discrimination and therefore provides
an early model for the contemporary perpetrator
perspective. Also, it is still a living principle,
although one operating in a narrow context,
that does serve to explain some contemporary
decisions. Finally, the theory shares some significant features with the color-blind theory,
and it further exposes the abstract worldview
associated with color-blindness.

The freedom of association theory is as much
a statement about the right to discriminate as it
is about the right not to be discriminated
against. All that it outlaws is state action; the
autonomous individual remains free to discriminate, or not, according to personal preference.
Racial discrimination is thus wrenched from its
social fabric and becomes a mere question of
private, individual taste. This theory serves to
explain a few Supreme Court interventions
against racial discrimination during the otherwise racist hegemony of *Plessy v. Ferguson.* Yet
it also sheds light on *Brown,* since the ethical
norm reflected in national antidiscrimination
law at the time of the *Brown* decision was
one that recognized the legitimacy of private
discrimination. Because of the constraints of
the state action principle, there was nothing
illegal, as a matter of *national* law, about blatant
and explicit discrimination in employment,
housing, or public accommodations, so long as
such practices were "private." The freedom of
association theory legitimizes that tolerance of
racial discrimination by transforming it into a
freedom to discriminate. It thus speaks directly
to the needs of an era that had not yet fully
developed even the perpetrator perspective, in-
asmuch as only one perpetrator—the state—
could be held accountable for racial discrimination.

On its own terms, the theory became moot
with the subsequent demise of the state action
doctrine through legislation and constitutional

decisions expanding the list of responsible perpetrators. It serves to explain only those contemporary decisions that do affirm a right to
discriminate in the limited areas that are still
beyond the reach of the perpetrator principle.
However, the presence of even those few areas
of permissible discrimination does keep alive
the idea that racial discrimination is ethically
proper, as long as it is restricted to private life.

Where it does apply, the freedom of association theory implies a notion of racial equivalence
similar to the color-blind theory's idea that
blacks and whites have equal grounds for complaint about instances of racial discrimination.
In this sense, the two theories share a
worldview—the abstract utopia where racial
discrimination has never existed and where,
ironically, both theories would probably be irrelevant. The only way that discriminations by
whites against blacks can become ethically
equivalent to discriminations by blacks against
whites is to presuppose that there is no actual
problem of racial discrimination. It is just like
saying today that the principles of freedom of
association and color-blindness govern relationships between long- and short-earlobed people.

5. THE INTEGRATED SOCIETY

This view is not so much another way of explaining the *Brown* decision as it is an additional perspective from which to regard all of
the other theories and explanations. It begins
with the assumption that a decision such as
Brown, which merely outlaws a particular practice, nevertheless implies that the practice is
being outlawed in order to achieve a desired
end state in which conditions associated with
the outlawed practice will no longer be evident.
If particular practices are to be outlawed as
deviations from a norm, then the norm must
include within it a vision of society in which
there would not be such deviations. It should
then be possible to test current conditions
against the desired end state to decide whether
progress is being made. The end state usually
associated with antidiscrimination law is some
version of the "integrated society." This ambiguous phase, however, contains within it a number of possibilities as to the content of the end

state, the extent to which it has already been achieved, and whose interest is served by achieving it.

The most complete version of the integrated society can be found in a science fiction story in which it is the year 2200 and everybody is a creamy shade of beige. Race has not merely become irrelevant but has disappeared altogether under the guiding hand of genetic entropy. A second and slightly less extreme version of the utopia posits a society in which racial identification is still possible, but no longer relevant to anyone's thinking or generalizations about anyone else. In this world of racial irrelevance, the sensory data employed in making a racial identification, though still available, would have returned to the domain of other similar human identification data in such a way as to obliterate the cultural concept of race. Race would have become functionally equivalent to eye color in contemporary society. In yet a third version of the integrated society, racial identification persists as a cultural unifying force for each group, equivalent to an idealized model of religious tolerance. Each group respects the diverse character of every other group, and there are no patterns of domination or oppression between different groups.

Each of these visions of the future reflects the achievement of a casteless, if not classless, society in which there is no hierarchy of status corresponding with racial identification. The essential defect in the color-blind theory of racial discrimination is that it presupposes the attainment of one of these futures. It is a doctrine that both declares racial characteristics irrelevant and prevents any affirmative steps to achieve the condition of racial irrelevance. The freedom of association theory, to the extent that it is antidiscrimination at all, also presupposes an already-existing future, but it is the tolerance model that it contemplates.

These theories are not alone in presupposing the goal that one is purportedly working toward. Suppose one were to visit the future society of racial irrelevance and discover conditions that in any other society might be regarded as corresponding with a pattern of racial discrimination. Among such conditions might be that one race seems to have a hugely disproportionate share of the worst houses, the most demeaning jobs, and the least control over societal resources. For such conditions to be fair and accepted as legitimate by the disfavored race in future society, they would have to be perceived as produced by accidental, impartial, or neutral phenomena utterly dissociated from any racist practice. Otherwise the future society would fail to meet its claim of racial irrelevance and would not be a future society at all.

Any theory of antidiscrimination law which legitimizes as nondiscriminatory substantial disproportionate burdens borne by one race is effectively claiming that its distributional rules are already the ones that would exist in future society. From the perspective of a victim in present society, where plenty of explicitly racist practices prevail, the predictable and legitimate demand is that those ostensibly neutral rules demonstrate themselves to be the ones that would in fact exist in future society. The legitimacy of the demand is underscored by the fact that those very rules appealed to by the beneficiaries to legitimize the conditions of the victims were created by and are maintained by the dominant race. From the perpetrator perspective, however, those practices not conceded to be racist are held constant; they are presumed consistent with the ethics of future society, and the victims are asked to prove that such is not the case. This is a core difference between the victim and perpetrator perspectives.

A vision of the future also bears on the question of who will benefit from the attainment of the integrated society. To introduce this issue more precisely, one might ask whether the integrated society is an end in itself or just a symbolic measure of the actual liberation of an oppressed racial group from the conditions of oppression. To say that the integrated society is an end in itself, apart from the interest of the oppressed group in its own liberation, is basically to say that the goal is in the interest of society at large or in the interest of the dominant group as well as of the oppressed one. It is hardly controversial to contend that integration is for everyone's benefit, or even that it is in some sense for the benefit of the dominant group.[8] However, problems arise when interests diverge and the dominant group's desire for integration supersedes the victim group's demand for relief.

Although rarely litigated, this issue did arise in *Otero v. New York City Housing Authority.*[9] The Second Circuit there upheld in principle the notion of a benign "integration quota" to be imposed on black residents of a housing project so as to limit their numbers; the purpose of such a quota is to keep the number of black people below the level at which, according to social scientists, a "tipping point" will be reached and the white majority, presumably motivated by racism, will leave the area. The net result of this approach is both to keep the black group as a small minority within the project and to deny the benefit to blacks otherwise eligible for it, all for the sake of producing an "integrated result." In such a situation, it is really unclear whose interests the integrated result serves.

The potential conflict of interest raised by the integration quota problem is a powerful metaphor for some of the deeper problems of antidiscrimination law. Such a quota admits a token number of black people to a more desirable condition of existence, thereby illustrating progress toward the integrated society, while making sure that they remain outnumbered by the whites so as to be powerless and nonthreatening. At the same time, the deprivation imposed on those blacks who are denied admission is rationalized as being in everybody's interest since an integrated society is the goal to be attained.

B. Post-Brown *Developments*
The remainder of the era of uncertainty offered almost no occasions for resolving any of the ambiguities of *Brown* or for exposing the difference between the perpetrator and victim perspectives. Instead, the major task for that era, which put off the question of remedy, was to increase the list of perpetrators against whom antidiscrimination law might be directed. Strict adherence to the perpetrator form makes results irrelevant, a concern with results violates the form. For a time, in the next era of antidiscrimi-

nation law, the Supreme Court violated the form—even as it pretended not to do so—to produce some results. In the third and present era, the court returns to strict adherence, pretending never to have deviated from it, while pretending to have produced some results in the interim.

III. 1965–1974: THE ERA OF CONTRADICTION, OR THE JURISPRUDENCE OF REMEDY

A. An Overview
A growing tension between the concepts of violation and remedy characterized the second era of modern antidiscrimination law. While the form of the law, with one possible exception, remained squarely within the perpetrator perspective, its content began to create expectations associated with the victim perspective. The perpetrator perspective remained the basic model for a violation, without which there could be no occasion for remedy. Given that finding, however, remedial doctrine took over, and, in so doing, subtly changed the concept of violation by addressing itself to substantive conditions beyond the scope of the original violation.

One problem case is the "no results" situation. Suppose that for many years a community maintained a blatant de jure system of school segregation according to race which was finally declared unconstitutional. Further suppose that despite the ruling of unconstitutionality, no remedial efforts occurred or were required for a number of years, with the result that when those efforts were finally undertaken, the resultant school system looked like one that was still substantially segregated. Why? Because the new basis of school assignment, neighborhood, for example, while itself not a manifestation of discriminatory purpose, nevertheless amplified an existing pattern of pervasive discrimination.

The problem here is embarrassment; it is difficult to call these schools "desegregated" because there has been substantially no change since the era of explicit segregation. To cover the embarrassment requires some integrated schools even though, under the perpetrator perspective, there is no affirmative right to have

such schools, nor is it the condition of segregation (as opposed to the practice) that is the
violation. By going after the conditions, ostensibly in order to remedy the original violation,
the victim perspective is incorporated, and one
wonders whether the very same conditions are
equally remediable elsewhere regardless of the
remote presence of a no-longer-existent violation.

Another example is the case of the ostensibly
neutral and rational practice. Suppose an employer for years simply refused to hire any black
workers at all, then suddenly, in response to
recently enacted antidiscrimination law, adopts
an aptitude test for prospective employees that
just happens to exclude all black applicants.
There is an inescapable inference that the employer is trying to do implicitly what can no
longer be done explicitly, but there is no plausible evidentiary link between the prior *practice*
and the current one. If one wants either to
remedy what looks like a continuation of the
earlier violation or to avoid the no results dilemma, the neutral practice must be the target
of inquiry. At that point, however, the analysis
again shifts to the victim perspective, demanding that the neutral practices–producing
conditions of discrimination at the very least
justify themselves in terms of their own claims
to rationality. Here again the plausible contention arises that the very same practices, as
well as a lot of similar ones, should be required
to justify themselves wherever they appear.

The patterns illustrated by these typical cases,
occurring either singly or in combination, are
characteristic of the era of contradiction. The
following sections will describe the appearance
and operation of these patterns in two substantive areas: education and employment.

B. Employment: The Griggs Case

Griggs v. Duke Power Co., the Supreme Court's
first substantive decision under Title VII of the
Civil Rights Act of 1964, is as close as the court
has ever come to formally adopting the victim
perspective; it is the centerpiece of the era of
contradiction. One tribute to its importance is
the amount of effort currently being made to
repudiate it. While the actual decision in *Griggs*

may be explained in at least two ways that are
consistent with the perpetrator principle, the
case seems to go beyond that perspective to the
extent that it requires neutral practices to justify
themselves, radically alters the concept of "intention" in antidiscrimination cases, and implies
a demand for results through affirmative action.

The court posed the issue in *Griggs* as

> whether an employer is prohibited by the Civil
> Rights Act of 1964, Title VII, from requiring a
> high school education or passing of a standardized
> general intelligence test as a condition of employ-
> ment in or transfer to jobs when (a) neither stan-
> dard is shown to be significantly related to success-
> ful job performance, (b) both requirements operate
> to disqualify Negroes at a substantially higher rate
> than white applicants, and (c) the jobs in question
> formerly had been filled only by white employees
> as part of a longstanding practice of giving prefer-
> ence to whites.[10]

A unanimous court, speaking through Chief
Justice Warren Burger, answered that question
in the affirmative.

That the case was rooted firmly in the perpetrator perspective may be inferred from the behavior of the employer in the case. Prior to July
1965, the employer had blatantly discriminated
against black workers, permitting them to work
in only one of its five departments, where the
highest-paying job paid less than the lowest-
paying job in any of the other four departments.
In 1965, the employer abandoned its policy of explicit discrimination. In the same year, however,
the employer added a high school diploma requirement for transfer out of the previously
"black" department and a requirement that a
person had to "register satisfactory scores on two
professionally developed aptitude tests, as well as
. . . have a high school education" for placement
in any department except the previously "black"
one. These newly imposed requirements operated to limit severely the opportunities available
to black employees and applicants. Thus, the
case posed the problem of the "ostensibly neutral
practice" introduced as a substitute for blatant
racial discrimination and achieving substantially
the same results.

By making its rationale dependent on the
prior explicit discrimination, the court could

have stayed within the perpetrator perspective—
but doing so would have been somewhat disin-
genuous. For one thing, the prior discriminatory
conduct in *Griggs* was legal when it occurred
and could not by itself have given rise to a
violation. Moreover, to have made the illegality
of the test and diploma requirements dependent
upon the prior discrimination would have
meant that, absent such a history, the very same
practices would be valid, however disproportionate their impact. In any event, the court
chose to sever its rationale from any dependence
on the prior discrimination, and in so doing left
the perpetrator perspective as explaining at most
why—but not how—the court intervened in
Griggs.

Alternatively, the court in *Griggs* might have
remained closer to the perpetrator perspective,
while not clearly within it, by straying no further
than it had in *Gaston County v. United States.*[11]
On this view, the tests and diploma requirements were not violations in and of themselves
but, rather, only to the extent that they penalized blacks for the inferior educations they had
received in segregated schools. Some language
in *Griggs* even supports this view: "Basic intelligence must have the means of articulation to
manifest itself fairly in a testing process. Because they are Negroes, petitioners have long received inferior education in segregated schools
and this Court expressly recognized these differences in *Gaston County v. United States....* "[12]
Had this rationale emerged as the dominant
one in *Griggs,* the case would have been just
another school desegregation case, with the formal violation not the employee selection procedures invalidated but the preexisting system of
de jure segregated schools. The *Gaston County*
rationale, however, while supportive of the result in *Griggs,* could not be easily transferred to
the *Griggs* circumstances.

A straightforward application of *Gaston
County* to *Griggs* would have invalidated all test
and diploma requirements until the day when
black applicants no longer suffered the residual
effects of inferior education. However, while
the court was willing to say that all citizens
could vote regardless of literacy, they were not
equally willing to say that all applicants should

be hired regardless of qualifications. The court
clearly needed a rationale that would describe
the instances where tests or other job qualifications could be validly applied even against
black applicants who had suffered inferior educations. To develop such standards, the court
had to take a look at tests on their merits.
Almost inadvertently, then, the opinion
switched from blaming the victim to scrutinizing the neutral practices themselves with respect
to their claims of rationality. At that point,
the background of segregated schools became
irrelevant, since standards addressed solely to
the merits of the neutral practices limit the
issue to whether, under Title VII, a particular
employee selection procedure that disproportionately excludes black applicants is valid, regardless of the educational experience of the
applicants.

Thus, the central rationale of *Griggs* is that
selection procedures, even ostensibly neutral
ones, which disadvantage minority applicants
are not valid unless they can demonstrate themselves to be rational: "The Act proscribes not
only overt discrimination but also practices that
are fair in form, but discriminatory in operation.
The touchstone is business necessity. If an employment practice which operates to exclude
Negroes cannot be shown to be related to job
performance, the practice is prohibited." The
standard of rationality set by the court seemed
to be a tough one, demanding a showing of job-
relatedness, the removal of "artificial, arbitrary,
and unnecessary barriers," and standards that
"measure the person for the job and not the
person in the abstract." In short, the opinion
amounts to a demand that the myth of a meritocratic scheme of equality of opportunity be
transformed into a reality.

Thus for the first time the court held that a
neutral practice, not purposefully discriminatory, that nevertheless failed to admit blacks to
jobs had to justify itself or else be declared
invalid. Although the opinion was decided under Title VII, its logic did not seem easily
confined. The Court even took one general
swipe at the workings of meritocracy: "The
facts of this case demonstrate the inadequacy of
broad and general testing devices as well as the

infirmity of using diplomas or degrees as fixed measures of capability. History is filled with examples of men and women who rendered highly effective performance without the conventional badges of accomplishment in terms of certificates, diplomas, or degrees."[13]

Since the case was concerned not with remedy but with the meaning of "violation" under Title VII, it seemed reasonable to conclude that a discriminatory practice under Title VII would also be a discriminatory practice under the Fourteenth Amendment in areas not subject to Title VII. Read this way, the case becomes a generalized demand that all objective selection procedures under the coverage of some antidiscrimination law be required to justify themselves as consistent with the notion of equality of opportunity. *Griggs* in no way contradicts the meritocratic model but, rather, assumes that it can be made to work, that those who are deserving can be objectively separated from those who are not.

In addition to legitimizing the assertion of an affirmative claim directed at a systemic practice, *Griggs* changed the notion of "intentional" in antidiscrimination law. This aspect of the opinion derives from the Court's severance of its rationale from the prior discriminatory practices of the defendant employer. The opinion makes it clear that "good intent or absence of discriminatory intent does not redeem employment procedures or testing mechanisms that operate as 'built-in headwinds' for minority groups," and that "Congress directed the thrust of the Act to the *consequences* of employment practices, not simply the motivation." Under the notion of "intention" that emerges from the opinion, then, one is intentionally discriminating if one continues to use a practice or maintains a condition that disadvantages a minority group without being able to justify the rationality of the practice or condition. This idea, too, did not seem easily confined within the employment area to tests alone, nor easily within the employment area at all.

When applied to ostensibly rational practices, the *Griggs* notion of intention merely demands a showing of rationality. When applied to nonrational practices, such as school or voter dis-

tricting, jurisdictional boundaries, or zoning decisions, all of which are inherently arbitrary, the *Griggs* notion becomes a demand for results and, therefore, an adoption of the victim perspective. If, for example, there are a number of ways to divide a community into districts for school assignment purposes, and the one currently employed produces a great deal of racial concentration in schools, to perpetuate the existing scheme with the knowledge of the racial concentration produced becomes intentional discrimination—unless there is a sufficiently good reason for having chosen that scheme. To follow out the analogy to *Griggs*, such a reason would have to be one that tells the black children, who are confined to schools segregated in fact, why it is *legitimate* that they be so confined. Absent such a reason, the children would have the right to a redistricting that did not produce racial concentration.

The third outstanding feature of *Griggs* is that it virtually coerces employers (and others affected by its rationale) into adoption of affirmative action programs. The *Griggs* rationale, with its attendant demand for justification, is not even triggered unless the practice complained of produces a disproportionate impact on a minority group. A potential defendant who wishes to avoid litigation, or who wishes to avoid the adoption of different or more cumbersome selection procedures, need only negate the disproportionate impact by adopting different procedures for the minority groups disproportionately excluded. While such an approach in no way legitimizes the original procedure under the rationale of *Griggs*, it does at least neutralize its illegitimacy by offering an alternative. Thus, *Griggs* implicitly offers a choice: either make the meritocracy work on its own terms or make up for its flaws through affirmative efforts. That choice also suggests a way of looking at the so-called reverse discrimination issue.[14]

C. *Education Revisited:* Swann, Wright, *and* Keyes

In education, the era of contradiction most thoroughly realized itself in three cases decided during the three years following the *Griggs* decision: *Swann v. Charlotte-Mecklenburg Boara of Education, Wright v. Council of Emporia,* and *Keyes v. School District 1.* Each of these cases may be explained by, and remains formally within, the perpetrator perspective, but each, especially when read in light of *Griggs,* creates expectations more consistent with the victim perspective.

All three cases involved explicit findings of de jure segregation. *Swann* and *Wright* involved southern school systems in which the de jure systems were preexisting and remote in time from the actual conditions being litigated; *Keyes* involved a northern city—Denver—where the district court had found de jure segregation in one part of the city. In addition, all three cases involved challenges to neutral practices that operated to produce racially concentrated schools. In *Swann* and *Keyes,* the practice was the neighborhood school; in *Wright,* it was deconsolidation of a combined city-county school system.

In each case, the court retained formal adherence to the perpetrator perspective by "linking" the current condition under attack to the actual de jure violation. Thus, in *Swann,* while invoking the magic phrase that the "nature of the violation determines the scope of the remedy," the court proceeded to show how by inference alone one could conclude either that the prior system of segregation produced segregated neighborhoods, which in turn produced the current condition of segregation, or that the residential segregation led to school siting decisions that continued to produce racial concentration, despite the abolition of de jure segregation. Having linked the current condition to the past violation, the court was able to conclude that although a prescription of racial balance is not ordinarily within the authority of a federal district court, both an "awareness of the racial composition of the whole school system" and the use of mathematical ratios were appropriate to remedy the current violation.

In *Wright,* the court could have tied its reasoning to the perpetrator perspective, since the city involved had decided to sever its relationship with the county school system only two weeks after a federal court had ordered pairing

of schools. That severance would have changed the racial composition of the system from 66 percent black and 34 percent white to 72 percent black and 28 percent white (county) and 52 percent black and 48 percent white (city). While stressing the factual history and emphasizing that the case involved desegregation rather than lack of racial balance, the court nevertheless based its decision on the *effect* of deconsolidation: "Thus, we have focused upon the effect—not the purpose or motivation—of a school board's action in determining whether it is permissible method of dismantling a dual system. The existence of a permissible purpose cannot sustain an action that has an impermissible effect." [15]

In *Keyes,* the court made a similar effort to tie the condition of segregation to the identified violation. The court held that proof of a violation with respect to one area of a city, plus racial concentration elsewhere in the system, raised by evidentiary inference (prior similar acts or causal spread) a prima facie case of de jure segregation throughout the system. The school board was thereupon obligated to show that the racial concentration elsewhere was not adventitious, a burden that was not met by a neighborhood school assignment policy.

In all three cases, the court permitted challenges to neutral practices that produced racial concentration in schools. In none of the cases did it demand proof that the original violation caused the challenged racial concentration. In fact, by indulging in causation analysis at least as plausible as that utilized by the court, one might easily conclude that the real villain in all three cases was discrimination in housing, which produced segregated residential patterns. In both *Swann* and *Keyes,* racially concentrated neighborhoods produced the racially concentrated schools; in *Wright,* the relative racial composition of county and city produced the result. Thus regarded, the cases suggest that the de jure segregation merely served as a backdrop for challenges to *conditions* of segregation produced by generalized patterns of discrimination. They further suggest that those same conditions should be equally subject to attack whereever they can be ascribed to patterns of discrimination, which would be anywhere other than the future society.

This conclusion gains much greater force from the fact that the three cases followed the decision in *Griggs*—for two aspects of *Griggs* explain the results in *Swann*, *Wright*, and *Keyes* much more convincingly than the formal reasoning used in those opinions. One is the notion that ostensibly neutral practices producing racially disproportionate results must justify themselves or be regarded as violations. Alternatively, by employing the *Griggs* corollary, one might conclude that the "intentional" violation in the three cases was adherence to a practice (the neighborhood schools) or a decision (the deconsolidation) that produced results associated with segregation. Under this view, retention of the practice in the face of its known results becomes a prima facie case of discrimination, again giving rise to a demand for rational justification. Under either approach, the rational justification would have to be one that not only explains the action taken but also makes the condition of discrimination legitimate. Neither the neighborhood school assignments in *Swann* and *Keyes* nor the deconsolidation in *Wright* satisfied those requirements.

Thus, by the end of the era of contradiction, the court, while remaining within the perpetrator perspective, had nevertheless managed to offer to black people expectations of proportional racial political power, a working system of equality of opportunity, if not actual jobs, and integrated schools. In the next era, these expectations were systematically defeated and only the perpetrator perspective was preserved.

IV. 1974– ?: THE ERA OF
RATIONALIZATION, OR THE
JURISPRUDENCE OF CURE

A. An Overview

The typical approach of the era of rationalization is to "declare that the war is over," to make the problem of racial discrimination go away by announcing that it has been solved. This approach takes many forms. Its simplest and most direct version is the declaration that, despite the discriminatory appearance of current conditions, the actual violation has already been cured, or is being remedied, regardless of whether the remedy prescribed can be expected to alleviate the condition. A more sophisticated approach is to declare that what looks like a violation, based on expectations derived from the era of contradiction, is not a violation at all.

Central to the era of rationalization is the pretense—associated with the color-blind theory of racial discrimination—that but for an occasional aberrational practice, future society is already here and functioning. The contradictions implicit in the earlier cases are thus resolved largely by pretending they were never there. This resolution has in turn facilitated a quick and easy return to the comfortable and neat world of the perpetrator perspective. As a result, the actual conditions of racial powerlessness, poverty, and unemployment can be regarded as no more than conditions— not as racial discrimination. Those conditions can then be rationalized by treating them as historical accidents or products of a malevolent fate, or, even worse, by blaming the victims as inadequate to function in the good society.

B. Education

The era of rationalization began in the same substantive area as modern antidiscrimination law—school desegregation. In *Milliken v. Bradley (Milliken I)*, the court for the first time applied antidiscrimination law to rationalize a segregated result in a case where a constitutional violation had been found to exist. Despite extensive de jure segregation in the City of Detroit, the court refused to approve a remedy that would consolidate Detroit schools with those of surrounding suburbs for the purpose of achieving an integrated result. In so holding, the Court rendered irrelevant the district court's conclusion that absent such a remedy, the schools of Detroit would become all black within a few years. Coupled with the decision a year earlier in *San Antonio Independent School District v. Rodriguez*, which rejected a claim of resource equalization among school districts without regard to ability to pay, the message of *Milliken I* is stark and clear: if whites can find a way to leave the inner city, they may legally insulate their finances and schools from the demands of blacks for racial equality. The only additional requirement for that sense of security is the availability of easily manipulated restrictive land-use practices, which the court has graciously provided in other cases.

To achieve this result, the court had to emphasize the form of *Swann* and *Keyes* over their substance, make results irrelevant, refuse to recognize the implications of *Griggs*, and renew its insistence on proof of causation. Citing *Swann*, the court pointed out that "[t]he controlling principle consistently expounded in our holdings is that the scope of the remedy is determined by the nature and extent of the constitutional violation." The district court's mistake had been in proceeding on the erroneous assumption that "[t]he Detroit schools could not be truly desegregated . . . unless the racial composition of the student body of each school substantially reflected the racial composition of the population of the metropolitan area as a whole." That the district court so assumed is hardly surprising, however, if one reads *Swann* and *Keyes* in light of *Griggs*'s concept of intentional violation or its treatment of neutral practices. Even if one takes a narrower view and simply analogizes the neighborhood school policy, which seemed to be the real cause of the segregation in *Swann* and *Keyes*, to the district boundaries in *Milliken*, the district court's assumption again seems sensible.

It is not clear why the court thought district boundaries were sacrosanct while neighborhood school assignments were not. The court offered no comparative judgment, merely announcing that the boundary lines were a manifestation of the sacred principle of local autonomy: "No single tradition in public education is more deeply rooted than local control over the operation of schools; local autonomy has long been thought essential both to the maintenance of community concern and support for public schools and to the quality of the educational process." Yet it was not even the principle of

local autonomy that the court was exalting in *Milliken*; it was the precise fact of the district boundaries existing in the Detroit metropolitan area that served to facilitate the operation of virtually all-white suburban schools. The principle of local autonomy may be a fine one as applied to an area of relative equality; in the usual suburb-city context where it is invoked, however, "local autonomy" is a code word for rationalizing and protecting the prior appropriation of financial resources, environmental amenity, and, in this case, racial homogeneity. In short, it is a principle of vested rights.

Moreover, the local autonomy discussion, although central to the historical meaning of *Milliken I*, was not even relevant to the rationale of the case. Since the court refused to advance the implicit thrust of *Griggs-Swann-Keyes*, which would have made the conditions of racial concentration produced by the boundary lines at least a prima facie violation, there was no occasion to demand that the boundary lines be justified as either rational or innocently nonrational. The only practice deemed to be a violation at all was the de jure segregation of the City of Detroit. Here, the crucial step toward the result was to narrow the concept of violation. To accomplish that step, the court had to return to the secure world of the perpetrator perspective:

> Before the boundaries of separate and autonomous school districts may be set aside by consolidating the separate units for remedial purposes or by imposing a cross-district remedy, it must first be shown that there has been a constitutional violation within one district that produces a significant segregative effect in another district. Specifically, it must be shown that racially discriminatory acts of the state or local school districts, or of a single school district have been a substantial cause of inter-district segregation. Thus an inter-district remedy might be in order where the racially discriminatory acts of one or more school districts caused racial segregation in an adjacent district, or where district lines have been deliberately drawn on the basis of race. In such circumstances an inter-district remedy would be appropriate to eliminate the interdistrict segregation directly caused by the constitutional violation.[16]

Under the strict causation requirements of *Milliken I*, the law does not offer a feeble presumption that the extensive ghettoization of the City of Detroit in relation to its surrounding suburbs has anything to do with racial discrimination. Having rejected the implications of *Swann* and *Keyes*—that results mattered, and that school desegregation remedies would be used to counter the effects of residential segregation—the Court insured that residential racial concentration will be subject to scrutiny, if at all, only in the difficult-to-litigate and virtually impossible-to-remedy domain of housing discrimination. Under the combined force of *Rodriguez* and *Milliken,* black city residents are thus worse off in terms of legal theory than they were under the "separate but equal" doctrine of pre-*Brown* southern school litigation, where a claim of equivalent resources for black schools was at least legally cognizable. And even if it makes sense within the narrow world of the perpetrator perspective to say that school desegregation should not be a remedy for housing discrimination, the effect of *Milliken I* is far worse than neutral with respect to housing. By offering the lure of suburban isolation, the decision invites white flight, thereby stimulating even greater racial concentration in housing.

That the Supreme Court had become indifferent to results became clear two years after *Milliken I.* In *Pasadena City Board of Education v. Spangler,* the court completed the task of rationalizing into obscurity the remaining victim perspective implications of *Swann* and *Keyes. Pasadena* involved a single jurisdiction that had been previously adjudged to have maintained segregated schools. The court-ordered remedial plan, which went into effect for the 1970–71 school year, mandated a set of pupil assignment practices that would ensure that no school in the system had a majority of minority students. The remedial plan produced that result for only one year, however, and by 1974, five of the thirty-two schools in the system again had black majorities. The Court attributed this change to a "normal pattern of human migration [that] had resulted in some changes in the demographics of Pasadena's residential patterns," and decided that despite the maldistribution in fact, Pasadena had achieved a unitary school system within the meaning of *Swann.*

Whether or not the actual behavior that produced the demographic changes in *Pasadena* should be deemed white flight, the message of the case on that point is as clear as it was in *Milliken I.* If the only obligation imposed by desegregation is to produce racially balanced schools for a year, intrajurisdictional white flight becomes as attractive an escape as the interjurisdictional variety offered by *Milliken I.* In another sense, however, *Pasadena* was just a logical corollary of *Milliken I.* If the court had ordered further racial balance in Pasadena's schools, it would likely have accomplished no more than to stimulate further the kind of white flight already legitimized by *Milliken I.*

Pasadena marks the full restoration of the perpetrator perspective in school desegregation cases, with the substance of *Swann* subdued by its form. If it was a concern for lack of results that permitted the victim perspective to creep into the jurisprudence at all, it is a brazen indifference to results that has facilitated the current doctrinal restoration. Only from the perpetrator perspective does it make sense to say that segregated schools are "caused" by the "badness" of particular actors, that the ephemeral negation of the conditions associated with that "badness" neutralizes the "badness" itself, and that the reappearance of the very same conditions is as irrelevant as if it were to occur in future society.

C. Employment

If *Griggs* was the most important case of the era of contradiction, the only one offering a genuine threat to the hegemony of the perpetrator perspective, then the major task of the era of rationalization must be the obliteration of *Griggs.* And so it is in the area of employment that one finds the case likely to become the centerpiece of the era of rationalization: *Washington v. Davis.* While not quite obliterating *Griggs,* the court has so undermined it that it has ceased to be a credible threat. This overall result has been achieved in three discrete steps: *Griggs's* apparent implications for all of antidiscrimination law have been squelched by limiting its doctrine to Title VII; its forceful assault on the system of equality of opportunity from within the structure of Title VII has been blunted by softening the scrutiny required; and its apparent application to analogous Title VII problems has been denied by refusing to extend it to the other major substantive area where it had been applied by the lower courts for some time—seniority. The first two of these steps appear in *Washington v. Davis;* the third required an additional case.

As noted above, *Griggs* was apparently significant for other than Title VII cases insofar as it found that neutral practices producing racially disproportionate results would have to be justified; that, for the purposes of antidiscrimination law, intent would mean no more than voluntary conduct producing racially disproportionate results; and that the best way to avoid or at least defer the impact of the first two was to initiate a voluntary affirmative action program. In *Washington v. Davis,* the court explicitly rejected the first two implications, thereby removing any suggestion of obligation from the third and relegating it to the easier world of voluntary tokenism.

Washington v. Davis involved a test that purported to measure verbal ability, vocabulary, reading, and comprehension. The test was challenged in its role as a criterion for admission to the training program for District of Columbia police officers. Given a failure rate that was four times as high for blacks as for whites, the plaintiffs asserted, in an action commenced before Title VII became applicable to governmental employment, that the test was prima facie unconstitutional. The court held that absent direct or inferential proof that the test was employed with a design to produce racially disproportionate results, the disproportionate failure rate was not itself significant enough to create a prima facie case and that there was no requirement that the test demonstrate any rationality at all. Using an intriguing kind of inside-out reasoning, the court quickly rebutted the commonsense notion that racial discrimination under the Fifth or Fourteenth Amend-

ments meant the same thing as racial discrimination under Title VII. Justice Byron White's terse offering was, "[w]e have never held that the constitutional standard for adjudicating claims of invidious racial discrimination is identical to the standards applicable under Title VII, and we decline to do so today."

To support its position, the court offered a "parade of horribles" argument that would be embarrassing in a first-year law class: "A [contrary] rule ... would raise serious questions about, and perhaps invalidate, a whole range of tax, welfare, public service, regulatory, and licensing statutes that may be more burdensome to the poor and the average black than to the more affluent white."[17]

Thus, with quiet efficiency, the court eliminated all extra-Title VII implications of *Griggs.* The alternative holding of *Washington v. Davis* went a step further, softening the severe scrutiny thought to be required by *Griggs* to the point where *Griggs* is no longer much of a threat even in Title VII cases. *Griggs* itself had never reached the question of degree of rationality demanded from the tests, since the case offered a strong inference of purposeful discrimination, and since the employer declined to offer any proof concerning the validity of the test. *Griggs,* however, did use strong language in its insistence on job-relatedness, business necessity, and the elimination of "built-in headwinds" to minority employment. In addition, it cited with approval the tough stance on job-relatedness taken by the Equal Employment Opportunity Commission (EEOC) and paid homage to the EEOC as deserving of deference in its administrative interpretations of the statute. This strict insistence on proof of job-relatedness seemed doctrinally secure as late as 1975, when the court in *Albemarle Paper Co. v. Moody* insisted on genuine proof of job-relatedness and again relied on the EEOC guidelines.

In three respects, the court in *Washington v. Davis* dropped any pretense of strictness with respect to job-relatedness and simultaneously abandoned its posture of deference to the EEOC: the test was ultimately validated by nothing more than intuitive generalization.

There may have been evidence that the challenged test correlated, with some degree of significance, with another test given to trainees at the end of the training program, but there was no evidence that either the entrance test or the final test in any way related to qualities or abilities relevant to being a police officer. In fact, there was no proof that the test given at the end of the training program measured anything taught in that program, even assuming that the program was related to future performance as a police officer. The most that was established was that the test correlated with another test, which in itself is hardly surprising. However, that other test may or may not measure something, which something, even if measured, may or may not have anything to do with the job for which the training program is supposed to prepare those who pass the initial test. In this context, the court's conclusion, shared with the district court, that "some minimum verbal and communicative skill would be very useful, if not essential, to satisfactory progress in the training regimen" seems little more than an assumption of the desired conclusion.

V. CONCLUSION

IN this article, I have attempted to describe, with an emphasis on what I have called the "victim perspective," the major developments in antidiscrimination law from the *Brown* case through the present. I do not think the "why" of this development can be answered with reference to legal doctrine, nor do I think that it is satisfactory merely to invoke the rules that would be appropriate in a future color-blind society. Despite any implications to the contrary, the preceding pages have not been a critique of the Burger Court, at least not in the sense that I hold that institution responsible for failing to legislate the victim perspective into being. I do believe that the decisions of the era of contradiction created expectations that were subsequently frustrated by Burger Court decisions, but I cannot regard the court as autonomous and separate from the society that orches-trates it, and I therefore cannot regard that one institution as the villain of the tale.

NOTES

1. I concede an irony in, but nevertheless will adhere to, my use of "victim perspective." If the real point of the victim perspective is to talk about conditions rather than practices, why talk about victims? Because both are true. In the context of race, "victim" means a current member of the group that was historically victimized by actual perpetrators or a class of perpetrators. Victims are people who continue to experience or are ostensibly tied to the historical experience of actual oppression or victimization, whether or not individual perpetrators, or their specific successors in interest, can be identified now. The victim perspective is intended to describe the expectations of an actual human being who is a current member of the historical victim class—expectations created by an official change of moral stance toward members of the victim group. Those expectations, I suggest, include changes in conditions.

2. On the ideology of fault, see Pashukanis, "The General Theory of Law and Marxism," in *Soviet Legal Philosophy*, III, 216–21, trans. H. Babb (1951). The fault notion as applied to racial discrimination today is, I believe, related to the assumption of fifties liberals that such discrimination was largely a southern problem. I can recall distinctly the response of my own naively liberal consciousness, as I was sitting in a fifth grade classroom at an all-white elementary school in New York City in 1954, to the announcement that the Supreme Court had outlawed racial segregation in schools: "The law is going to make those bad southerners behave; the land of opportunity is just around the corner."

3. The color-blind theory was first given explicit voice in 1896: "Our Constitution is color-blind, and neither knows nor tolerates classes among citizens"; *Plessy v. Ferguson*, 163 U.S. 537, 559 (1896) (Harlan, J., dissenting).

4. 347 U.S. at 493.

5. *Id.* at 492.

6. *Id.* at 494 (quoting "a finding in the Kansas case").

7. *Loving v. Virginia*, 388 U.S. 1, 11 (1967).

8. See, e.g., *Trafficante v. Metropolitan Life Ins. Co.*, 409 U.S. 205 (1972); cf. Hegel, *The Phenomenology of Mind*, 228–40, trans. J. Baillie (1968) (1st ed. Bamberg 1807).

9. 484 F.2d 1122 (2d. Cir. 1973)

10. 401 U.S. at 425–26.

11. In *Gaston County*, "because of the inferior education received by Negroes . . . this court barred . . . a literacy test for voter registration on the ground that the test would abridge the right to vote indirectly on account of race. Congress did not intend by Title VII, however, to guarantee a job to every person regardless of qualifications."

12. *Id.* at 430.

13. *Id.* at 425–26.

14. For example, one might justify the adoption of a minority admissions program of the sort at issue in *Bakke* not by claiming to compensate those admitted or by touting the affirmative utilitarian benefits to be gained for society at large but, rather, by simply showing that the existing selection procedure is a prima facie violation under *Griggs* with respect to those disproportionately excluded, that although the procedure cannot be demonstrated to be sufficiently rational, it cannot be replaced without great administrative cost, and that the minority admissions program serves to neutralize for a time the worst effects of an admittedly defective scheme, insofar as that scheme would otherwise operate to exclude those who have been the historical targets of blatant discrimination.

The key to this argument is, of course, the potential applicability of the *Griggs* notion of violation to the existing selection program. Once that potentiality has been neutralized, or greatly reduced, as by limiting the coverage of the *Griggs* rule, or by insisting on a prior adjudication of violation, the argument is easily brushed aside.

15. 407 U.S. at 462.

16. 418 U.S. at 444–45.

17. 476 U.S. at 248.

THE IMPERIAL SCHOLAR: REFLECTIONS ON A REVIEW OF CIVIL RIGHTS LITERATURE
*Richard Delgado**

I. CIVIL RIGHTS SCHOLARSHIP— IDENTIFYING A TRADITION

WHEN I began teaching law in the mid-seventies, I was told by a number of well-meaning senior colleagues to "play things straight" in my scholarship—to establish a reputation as a scholar in some mainstream legal area and not get too caught up in civil rights or other "ethnic" subjects. Being young, impressionable, and anxious to succeed, I took their advice to heart and, for the first six years of my career, produced a steady stream of articles, book reviews, and the like, impeccably traditional in substance and form. The dangers my friends warned me about were averted; the benefits accrued. Tenure securely in hand, I turned my attention to civil rights law and scholarship.

Realizing I had a great deal of catching up to do, I asked my research assistant to compile a list of the twenty or so leading law review articles on civil rights. I gave him the criteria you would expect: frequent citation by courts and commentators; publication in a major law review; theoretical rather than practical focus, and so on. When he submitted the list, I noticed that each of the authors was white. Each was also male. I checked his work myself, with the same result. Further, a review of the footnotes of these articles disclosed a second remarkable coincidence: the works cited were also written by authors who were themselves white and male. I was puzzled. I knew that there are about one hundred black, twenty-five Hispanic, and ten Native American law professors teaching at American law schools.[1] Many of them are

* Charles Inglis Thomson Professor of Law, University of Colorado. J.D., University of California, Berkeley (1974). The reader who wishes to read an updated version of this article should see "The Imperial Scholar Revisited: How to Marginalize Outside Writing, Ten Years Later," 140 *Pa. L. Rev.*, 1349 (1992).

writing in areas about which they care deeply—antidiscrimination law, the equality principle, and affirmative action. Much of that scholarship, however, seems to have been consigned to oblivion.[2] Courts rarely cite it, and the legal scholars whose work *really* counts almost never do. The important work is published in eight or ten law reviews and is written by a small group of professors who teach in the major law schools.[3]

Most of this latter work, to be sure, seems strongly supportive of minority rights. It is all the more curious that these authors, the giants in the field, only infrequently cite a minority scholar. My assistant and I prepared an informal sociogram, a pictorial representation of who-cites-whom in the civil rights literature. It is fascinating. Paul Brest cites Laurence Tribe; Laurence Tribe cites Paul Brest and Owen Fiss; Owen Fiss cites Bruce Ackerman, who cites Paul Brest and Frank Michelman, who cites Owen Fiss and Laurence Tribe and Kenneth Karst. . . .

It does not matter where one enters this universe; one comes to the same result: an inner circle of about a dozen white, male writers who comment on, take polite issue with, extol, criticize, and expand on each other's ideas.[4] It is something like an elaborate minuet.

The failure to acknowledge minority scholarship extends even to nonlegal propositions and assertions of fact. W. E. B. Du Bois, deceased black historian, receives an occasional citation.[5] Aside from him, little else rates a mention. Higginbotham's monumental *In the Matter of Color*[6] might as well not exist; the same is true of the work of Kenneth Clark,[7] black psychologist and past president of the American Psychological Association, and of Alvin Poussaint,[8] Harvard Medical School professor and authority on the psychological impact of race. One searches in vain for references to the powerful book by physicians Grier and Cobbs, *Black Rage*,[9] or to Frantz Fanon's *The Wretched of the Earth*[10] or even to writings of or about Martin Luther King, Jr.,[11] Cesar Chavez,[12] and Malcolm X.[13] When the inner-circle writers need an authority for a factual or social-scientific proposition about race, they generally cite reports of the U. S. Commission on Civil Rights[14] or else each other.[15]

A single anecdote may help to illustrate what I mean. Recently, a law professor who writes about civil rights showed me, for my edification, a draft of an article of his. It is, on the whole, an excellent article: it extols the value of a principle I will call "equal personhood"—the notion, implicit in several constitutional provisions and much case law, that each human being, regardless of race, creed, or color, is entitled to be treated with equal respect. To treat someone as an outsider, a nonmember of human society, violates this principle and devalues the self-worth of the person so excluded.

I have no quarrel with this premise, but, on reading the hundred-plus footnotes of the article, I noticed that its author failed to cite black or minority scholars, an exclusion from the community of kindred souls as glaring as any condemned in the paper. I pointed this out to the author, citing as illustration a passage in which he asserted that unequal treatment can cause a person to suffer a withered self-concept. Having just written an article on a related subject,[16] I was more or less steeped in withered self-concepts; I knew who the major authorities were in that area.

The professor's authority for the proposition about withered self-concepts was Frank Michelman, writing in the *Harvard Law Review*. I pointed out that although Michelman may be a superb scholar and teacher, he probably has relatively little first-hand knowledge about withered self-concepts. I suggested that the professor add references to such works as Kenneth Clark's *Dark Ghetto*[17] and Grier and Cobbs' *Black Rage*,[18] and he agreed to do so. To justify his selection of Michelman for the proposition about withered self-concept, the author explained that Michelman's statement was "so elegant."

Could inelegance of expression explain the absence of minority scholarship from the text and footnotes of leading law review articles about civil rights? Elegance is, without question, a virtue in writing, in conversation, or in anything else in life. If minority scholars write inelegantly and Frank Michelman elegantly, then it would not be surprising if the latter were read and cited more frequently, and the former less so. However, minority legal scholars seem to have less trouble being recognized and taken seriously in areas of scholarship other than civil rights theory.[19] If elegance is a problem for minority scholars, it seems mainly to be so in the core area of civil rights: affirmative action, the equality principle, and the theoretical foundations of race relations law.

In 1971, Judge Skelly Wright wrote an article entitled, "Professor Bickel, the Scholarly Tradition, and the Supreme Court."[20] Judge Wright took a group of scholars to task for their bloodless carping at the Warren Court's decisions in the areas of racial justice and human rights. He accused the group of missing the central point in these decisions—their moral clarity and passion for justice—and labeled the group's excessive preoccupation with procedure and institutional role, and its insistence that the court justify every element of a decision under general principles of universal application a "scholarly tradition."[21]

I think I have discovered a second scholarly tradition. It consists of white scholars' systematic occupation of, and exclusion of minority scholars from, the central areas of civil rights scholarship. The mainstream writers tend to acknowledge only each other's work. It is even possible that, consciously or not, they resist entry by minority scholars into the field,[22] perhaps counseling them, as I was counseled, to establish their reputations in other areas of law. I believe that this "scholarly tradition" exists mainly in civil rights; nonwhite scholars in other fields of law seem to confront no such tradition.[23]

II. DEFECTS IN IMPERIAL SCHOLARSHIP

TO this point, I have been making an empirical claim. A person who disagreed with my thesis could attempt to show that some white inner-circle authors do cite nonwhite scholars appropriately, perhaps by introducing a sociogram of his or her own. My examination of the literature in the field, while admittedly not a scientific study, leads me to believe that this is a vain task. A second response would assert that the exclusion of minority viewpoints from white scholarship about civil rights is, as they say, harmless error; it doesn't matter *who* advocates freedom and equality, so long as they are advocated by someone.

In one sense, this assertion echoes the holding of *Trafficante v. Metropolitan Life Insurance Co.*,[24] which gave white tenants standing to challenge a building owner's racially discriminatory renting practices on the grounds that these rendered the building a white ghetto and deprived the tenants of interracial contacts. Everyone, not just minorities, has an interest in achieving a racially just society, so why should not anyone be free to advocate it in print? Does a contrary policy not deny free speech and constitute a gratuitous rejection of a helping hand?

Put in simple terms, what difference does it make if the scholarship about the rights of group A is written by members of group B? Although Derrick Bell, Jr., raised this question in a footnote,[25] no one seems to have addressed it directly. There are, however, legal doctrines and case law that may suggest answers by way of analogy. Relevant doctrines include standing,[26] real party in interest,[27] and *jus tertii*[28]—doctrines that in general insist that B does not belong in court if he or she is attempting, without good reason, to assert the rights of or redress the injuries to A. We also have rules pertaining to joinder of parties,[29] intervention,[30] and representation in class suits,[31] all of which serve to assure that the appropriate parties are before the court. On a more general level, our political and legal values contain an antipaternalistic principle that forbids B from asserting A's interest if A is a competent human being of adult years, capable of independently deciding upon and asserting that interest.

Abstracting from these principles, it is possible to compile an a priori list of reasons why we might look with concern on a situation in which the scholarship about group A is written by members of group B. First, members of group

B may be ineffective advocates of the rights and interests of persons in group A. They may lack information; more important, perhaps, they may lack passion, or their passion may be misdirected. The B's scholarship may tend to be sentimental, diffusing passion in useless directions or wasting time on unproductive breast-beating. Second, while the Bs might advocate effectively, they might advocate the wrong things. Their agenda may differ from that of the As[32]; they may pull their punches with respect to remedies, especially where remedying A's situation entails uncomfortable consequences for B. Despite the best of intentions, Bs may have stereotypes embedded deep in their psyches that distort their thinking, causing them to balance interests in ways inimical to As. Finally, domination by members of group B may paralyze members of group A, causing the As to forget how to flex their legal muscles for themselves.

A careful reading of the inner-circle articles suggests that many of the above-mentioned problems and pitfalls are not simply hypothetical but do in fact occur. A number of the authors were unaware of basic facts about the situation in which minority persons live or ways in which they see the world. From the viewpoint of a minority member, the assertions and arguments made by nonminority authors were sometimes so naive as to seem incomprehensible—hardly worthy of serious consideration. For example, some writers took seriously the reductio ad absurdum argument about an infinitude of minorities (If blacks and Hispanics, why not Belgians, Swedes, and Italians? What about an individual who is one-half black, or three-quarters Hispanic?),[33] or worried about whether a white citizen forced to associate with blacks has his or her freedom of association violated as much as does a black compelled to attend segregated schools.[34] One author reasoned that *Carolene Products* "footnote four" analysis is no longer fully applicable to American blacks, because they have ceased to be an insular minority in need of heightened judicial protection.[35] Another placed the burden on proponents of preferential admissions to show that no nonracial alternative exists, because to-day's minority may become tomorrow's majority and vice versa.[36]

In addition to factual ignorance or naiveté, some of the writing suffered from a failure of empathy, an inability to share the values, desires, and perspectives of the population whose rights are under consideration. In his article, "Serving Two Masters: Integration Ideals and Client Interests in School Desegregation Litigation,"[37] Derrick Bell, Jr., pointed out that litigators in school desegregation cases have often seemed unaware of what their clients really wanted, or have pursued one remedy (for example, integration) out of ideological commitment, even though the client wanted something different (for example, better schools).[38] A similar distancing of the scholar from the community he writes about was visible in the civil rights commentaries. The authors in the core group tended to be very concerned about *procedure.* Many of the articles were devoted, in various measures, to scholarly discussions of the standard of judicial review that should be applied in different types of civil rights suits.[39] Others were concerned with the relationship between federal and state authority in antidiscrimination law, or with the respective competence of a particular decision-maker to recognize and redress racial discrimination.[40] One could easily conclude that the question of who goes to court, what court they go to, and with what standard of review are the burning issues of American race-relations law. Perhaps the emphasis on procedure and judicial role is harmless, just a peculiar kink lawyers get in law school; but, as I will argue later in this essay, there is more to it than that.[41]

Other peculiarities of perspective surfaced in connection with choosing a principle on which to base (or oppose) affirmative action. Measures to increase minority representation in education and the workforce have been justified in three broad ways: reparations (or retribution),[42] social utility,[43] or distributive justice.[44] The reparations argument emphasizes that white society has mistreated blacks, Native Americans, and Hispanics, and that it now must make amends for that mistreatment. Utility-based arguments justify affirmative action on the grounds that increased representation of minorities will be useful to society. The distributive justice rationale says that there is a certain amount of wealth available and argues that everyone is entitled to a minimum share of it. Many of the minority scholars emphasize the reparations argument and stress the inherent cost to whites; the authors of the inner-circle articles generally make the case on the grounds of utility or distributive justice.[45]

Emphasizing utility or distributive justice as the justification for affirmative action has a number of significant consequences. It enables the writer to concentrate on the present and the future, and to overlook the past. There is no need to dwell on unpleasant matters like lynch mobs, segregated bathrooms, Bracero programs, migrant farm labor camps, race-based immigration laws, or professional schools that, until recently, were lily-white. The past becomes irrelevant; one just asks where things are now and where we ought to go from here, a straightforward social-engineering inquiry of the sort that law professors are familiar with and good at. However, just as the adoption of either of the two present-oriented perspectives renders the investigation comfortably safe, it robs affirmative action programs of their moral force in favor of a sterile theory of fairness or utility.[46] No doubt, there is a great social utility to affirmative action, but to base it solely on that ground ignores the *right* of minority communities to be made whole and the *obligation* of the majority to render them whole. Moreover, what if the utility calculus changes in the future, so that the programs no longer appear "useful" to the majority?[47] Can society then ignore those who still suffer the effects of past discrimination?

Distributive justice is a somewhat less objectionable ground for justifying affirmative action, but it too ignores history and makes for a rather weak, pallid case. It also invites the neutral-principles response:[48] If the idea is to start playing fair now, how can we achieve fairness by discriminating against whites? Moreover, the remedies espoused under both the social utility and distributive justice rationales are often justified because they have been voluntarily created

by legislatures, employers, or schools.[49] A "we-they" analysis, espoused by several of the commentators,[50] justifies a disadvantage that *we* (the majority) want to impose on ourselves to favor *them* (the minority). This type of thinking, however, leaves the choice of remedy and the time frame for that remedy in the hands of the majority; it converts affirmative action into a benefit, not a right. It neglects the possibility that a disadvantaged minority may have a moral claim to a particular remedy.

The inner-circle commentators rarely deal with issues of guilt and reparation. When they do, it is often to attach responsibility to a scapegoat, someone of another time or place, and almost certainly of another social class than that of the writer. These writers tend to focus on intentional and determinable *acts* of discrimination inflicted on the victim by some perpetrator and to ignore the more pervasive and invidious forms of discriminatory *conditions* inherent in our society. This "perpetrator" perspective[51] deflects attention from the victim-class, the blacks, Native Americans, Chicanos, and Puerto Ricans who lead blighted lives for reasons directly traceable to social and institutional injustice.

A corollary of this perspective is that racism need not be remedied by means that encroach too much on middle- or upper-class prerogatives.[52] If racial inequality is mainly the fault of the isolated redneck, outmoded ritual violence, or even long-abrogated governmental actions, then remedies that would encroach on simple "conditions" of life—middle-class housing patterns, for example, or the autonomy of local school boards—are unnecessary.[53] Many persons of minority race see racism as including institutional components that extend far beyond lynch mobs, segregated schools, or epithets such as "nigger" or "spick."[54] Self-interest, mixed with inexperience, may make it difficult for the privileged white male writer to adopt this perspective or to face up to its implications.

The uniformity of life experience of the inner circle of writers may color not only the way they conceptualize and frame problems of race, but also the solutions or remedies they devise.[55] Remedies pursued at "all deliberate speed"[56] or couched in terms of vague targets and goals entered the law when the legal system turned in earnest to problems of race. Their appearance is probably related to a utility-based perspective that ignores past injustices and simply seeks to engineer a solution with the most utility to society as a whole and the minimal amount of disruption. If the issue is not one of simple injustice requiring immediate correction but, rather, merely an unfortunate and abstractly created problem requiring remedy, that leisurely treatment is not surprising.

Moreover, regardless of the scope and time frame of racial remedies, their costs are generally imposed disproportionately on minorities and lower-class whites.[57] Most university affirmative action programs, for example, pit minorities against each other and against low-income whites. The programs generate hostility among these groups,[58] while exempting from such unpleasantness the high-achieving white product of a private prep school and Ivy League college,[59] who can remain aloof from these battles. There is an alternative—an overhaul of the admissions process and a rethinking of the criteria that make a person a deserving law student and future lawyer. It would be possible to devise admission standards that would result in a proportionate number of minorities, whites, and women gaining admission. Minority commentators have suggested such an approach,[60] but it has been often ignored and never instituted.

Despite the potential bias of mainstream scholarship, it might be argued that law review writing is basically harmless. The reviews are almost never read by anyone outside a narrow readership and rarely have an impact on the real world. Since the genre is essentially innocuous, why get excited if the authors of certain articles play by odd rules?

The game is not harmless. Courts do cite law review articles;[61] judges, even when they do not rely on an article expressly, may still read and be informed by it. What courts do clearly matters in our society. Moreover, what law professors say in their elegant articles contributes to a legal climate, a culture. Their ideas are read and discussed by legislators, political scientists, and

their own students. They affect what goes on in courts, law classrooms, and legislative chambers. Ideologies—perspectives, ways of looking at the world—are powerful. They limit discourse. They also enable the dominant class to maintain and justify its own ascendancy. Law professors at the top universities are part of this dominant class, and their writings contribute to the ideologies that this class creates and subscribes to. These writings are not harmless; they have clout.

My conclusion to this point is that there is a second scholarly tradition, that it consists of the exclusion of minority writing about key issues of race law, and that this exclusion does matter; the tradition causes blunting, skewings, and omissions in the literature dealing with race, racism, and American law. What accounts for, what sustains this tradition? Can it be defended or justified?

III. Imperial Scholarship— Explaining the Tradition

STUDIED indifference to minority writing on issues of race would be justified if the writing were second-rate, inelegant, unscholarly, or unimaginative. As was mentioned earlier, though, minority writers have had little trouble gaining recognition outside the core areas of civil rights.[62] Poor quality of the writing therefore seems an unlikely explanation. It could also be argued that minority authors who write about racial issues are not objective, that passion and anger render them unfit to reason rigorously or express themselves clearly, while white authors are above self-interest and thus capable of thinking and writing objectively. Yet this too seems implausible, for it presupposes that white writers have no vested interest in the status quo. Moreover, common experience suggests that most persons, including minorities, perform better, not worse, at tasks they care deeply about. Even if minority authors were offering one-sided views, their suggestions are at least data, material that deserves mention for what it discloses; one would not expect such telling data to be completely ignored. When discussing women's issues, white male elite writers more often seem to cite at least some white female writers (such as Kay, Weitzman, and Ginsberg).[63] These women write with passion and commitment, qualities that evidently do not render them unfit to be taken seriously. Lack of objectivity on the part of minority authors, then, seems an inadequate explanation for their treatment at the hands of leading white scholars.

In explaining the strange absence of minority scholarship from the text and footnotes of the central arenas of legal scholarship dealing with civil rights, I reject conscious malevolence or crass indifference. I think the explanation lies at the level of unconscious action and choice.[64] It may be that the explanation lies in a need to remain in *control*, to make sure that legal change occurs, but not too fast. The desire to shape events is a powerful human motive, one that could easily account for much of the exclusionary scholarship I have noted. The moment one makes such a statement, however, one is reminded that it is these same liberal authors who often have been the strongest supporters of affirmative action in their own university communities, and who have often been prepared to take chances (as they see it) to advance the goal of an integrated society. Perhaps the two behaviors can be reconciled by observing that the liberal professor may be pleased to have minority students and colleagues serve as figureheads, ambassadors of good will, and future community leaders, but not necessarily happy with the thought of a minority colleague who might go galloping off in a new direction.

Once, early in my career, I coauthored a law review article about Mexican-Americans (as they were called then) as a legally cognizable class, one that can sue in its own name for injuries to its members.[65] This was in the mid-seventies when the results of Chicano activism were just reaching the courts. At that time, a few decisions, notably *Lopez Tijerina v. Henry*,[66] had held that Chicanos could not sue collectively because of problems with class definition.[67] Some Chicanos speak Spanish, some do not; some have Spanish surnames, some do not; some trace their ancestors to Mexico, some do not. Chicanos were thus held too amorphous a group to be permitted to sue for class-based relief.[68] My article explained several valid ways of getting around the class-definition problem and gave several reasons why this should happen. Shortly after the article appeared, I received a long letter from a white litigator at a public interest law firm that concerns itself with the legal problems of Mexican-Americans. The letter told me, in clear, terse language, of the disservice I had done to the cause of Chicano legal rights. Its essence was that the writer's organization had been successfully finessing the class-definition problem, and my article had instead focused attention on it, making matters worse. I suffered terrible remorse until the Supreme Court decided in the following term that Mexican-Americans are a legally cognizable class for the purpose of civil rights suits.[69]

Had the litigator, a former professor at a major law school, simply made a mistake in judgment? Or was there more behind the letter and its insistence that I stay out of the picture and leave things to persons who know better? I think many civil rights activists and scholars derive a sense of personal satisfaction from being at the forefront of a powerful social movement.[70] Command and influence are heady things; it takes an alert person to realize when to step back, to know when his or her efforts have begun to interfere with the intended beneficiaries' effective engagement in their own affairs. The inner-circle authors' strong identification with their own role may prevent them from understanding when it is time for them to begin to leave it behind.

Another closely related motive is fear. Most of the white scholars who make up the inner circle spent some of their formative years of teaching during the late sixties and early seventies when a number of extraordinary things were happening in our society. Lawyers, and especially law professors, are deeply committed to the rule of law, but during those years the rule of law seemed to mean relatively little: events were out of control, and law seemed powerless to stop the popular tides that surged—the civil rights movement, inner-city riots, draft resistance. The professors who now dominate legal scholarship and dictate legal styles saw what the excesses of passion can do. Perhaps, scarcely knowing it, they came to emphasize scholarship that is controlled, incremental, and seemingly nonideological, and to resist that of a more tempestuous, change-oriented nature.[71] The fear of losing control would explain a number of things—the emphasis on procedure and role, the downplaying of substance.[72] It would explain inattention to the reparations argument[73] and avoidance of issues of guilt and complicity.[74] It would explain the treatment of racism and discrimination as vestigial aberrant behavior not connected by any common thread, much less as illustrating an implied social compact.[75] It would explain the lack of citation to minority writers, who have drawn attention to some of the thornier problems and conflicts in the area of race relations.[76]

Whatever the explanation of the phenomenon, it has not gone unnoticed. Derrick Bell, Jr., once observed that the exclusion of minority participants from litigation and scholarship about black issues reminds him of traditional families of former years in which parents would tell their children, "Keep quiet. We are talking about you, not to you."[77]

What should be done? As a beginning, minority students and teachers should raise insistently and often the unsatisfactory quality of the scholarship being produced by the inner circle—its biases, omissions, and errors. Its presuppositions and worldviews should be made explicit and challenged. That feedback will increase the likelihood that when a well-wishing white scholar writes about minority problems, he or she will give minority viewpoints and literature the full consideration due. That consideration may help the author avoid the types of substantive error catalogued earlier.[78]

While no one could object if sensitive white scholars contribute occasional articles and useful proposals (after all, there are many more of the mainstream scholars), must these scholars make a career of it? The time has come for white liberal authors who write in the field of civil rights to redirect their efforts and to encourage their colleagues to do so as well. There are many other important subjects that could and

should engage their formidable talents. As these scholars stand aside, nature will take its course; I am reasonably certain that the gap will quickly be filled by talented and innovative minority writers and commentators. The dominant scholars should affirmatively encourage their minority colleagues to move in this direction, as well as simply to make the change possible.

Only such a transformation will end the incongruity of one group's maintenance of a failed ideology for another, an irony that Judge Wyzanski saw as clearly as anyone:

> To leave non-whites at the mercy of whites in the presentation of non-white claims which are admittedly adverse to the whites would be a mockery of democracy. Suppression, intentional or otherwise, of the presentation of non-white claims cannot be tolerated in our society.... In presenting non-white issues non-whites cannot, against their will, be relegated to white spokesmen, mimicking black men. The day of the minstrel show is over.[79]

The day of the minstrel show is, indeed, over.

NOTES

1. A directory of minority law professors listed 133 black law professors, 22 Spanish-surnamed professors, and 4 American Indian professors for 1979–80. Section on Minority Groups (D. Bell, ed.) Association of American Law Schools, *1979–80 Directory of Minority Law Faculty Members* (1980), hereinafter cited as *1979–80 Directory.* The 1981–82 edition of this directory listed 198 black law professors, 20 Chicano and Puerto Rican law professors, and 15 American Indian professors. These figures do not include administrators, librarians, or professors not on tenure tracks.

2. See Bell, "*Bakke,* Minority Admissions and the Usual Price of Racial Remedies," 67 Calif. L. Rev., 3, 4 n. 2 (1979) (listing minority scholarship overlooked by the Supreme Court in *Bakke,* including articles by Mildred Ravenell, Ralph Smith, Derrick Bell, Cruz Reynoso, Leo Romero, and Richard Delgado). See also D. Bell, Jr., *Race, Racism and American Law* (2d ed. 1980), the footnotes of which contain extensive reference to articles and books by minority legal scholars.

3. The following are frequently cited authors, together with representative articles: Ackerman, "Integration for Subsidized Housing and the Question of Racial Occupancy Controls," 26 *Stan. L. Rev.,* 245 (1974); Bickel, "The Supreme Court, 1960 Term—Foreword: The Passive Virtues," *Harv. L. Rev.,* 40 (1961); Bittker, "The Case of the Checker-Board Ordinance: An Experiment in Race Relations," 71 *Yale L. J.,* 1387 (1962); Black, "The Lawfulness of

the Segregation Decisions," 69 *Yale L. J.*, 421 (1960); Blasi, "*Bakke* As Precedent: Does Mr. Justice Powell Have a Theory?" 67 *Calif. L. Rev.*, 21 (1979); Brest, "The Supreme Court, 1976 Term—Foreword: In Defense of the Antidiscrimination Principle," 90 *Harv. L. Rev.*, 1 (1976); Cox, "The Supreme Court, 1966 Term—Foreword: Constitutional Adjudication and the Promotion of Human Rights," 80 *Harv. L. Rev.*, 91 (1966); Eisenberg, "Disproportionate Impact and Illicit Motive: Theories of Constitutional Adjudication," 52 *N.Y.U. L. Rev.*, 36 (1977); Ely, "The Constitutionality of Reverse Racial Discrimination," 41 *U. Chi. L. Rev.*, 723 (1974); Fiss, "The Supreme Court, 1978 Term—Foreword: The Forms of Justice," 93 *Harv. L. Rev.*, 1 (1979); Graglia, "Special Admission of the 'Culturally Deprived' to Law School," 119 *U. Pa. L. Rev.*, 351 (1970); Greenawalt, "Judicial Scrutiny of 'Benign' Racial Preferences in Law School Admissions," 75 *Colum. L. Rev.*, 559 (1975); Gunther, "The Supreme Court, 1971 Term—Foreword: In Search of Evolving Doctrine on a Changing Court: A Model for a Newer Equal Protection," 86 *Harv. L. Rev.*, 1 (1972); Hellerstein, "The Benign Quota, Equal Protection, and 'The Rule in Shelley's Case,' " 17 *Rutgers L. Rev.*, 531 (1963); Henkin, "*Shelley v. Kramer*: Notes for a Revised Opinion," 110 *U. Pa. L. Rev.*, 473 (1962); Horowitz, "Unseparate but Unequal—The Emerging Fourteenth Amendment Issue in Public School Education," 13 *UCLA L. Rev.*, 1147 (1966); Kaplan, "Equal Justice in an Unequal World: Equality for the Negro—The Problem of Special Treatment," 61 *NW. U. L. Rev.*, 363 (1966); Karst, "The Supreme Court, 1977 Term—Foreword: Equal Citizenship under the Fourteenth Amendment," 91 *Harv. L. Rev.*, 1 (1977); Karst and Horowitz, "Affirmative Action and Equal Protection," 60 *Va. L. Rev.*, 955 (1974); Michelman, "The Supreme Court, 1968 Term—Foreword: On Protecting the Poor through the Fourteenth Amendment," 83 *Harv. L. Rev.*, 7 (1969); O'Neil, "Racial Preference and Higher Education: The Larger Context," 60 *Va. L. Rev.*, 925 (1974); Pollak, "Racial Discrimination and Judicial Integrity: A Reply to Professor Wechsler," 108 *U. Pa. L. Rev.*, 1 (1959); Sandalow, "Racial Preferences in Higher Education: Political Responsibilities and the Judicial Role," 42 *U. Chi. L. Rev.*, 653 (1975); St. Antoine, "Color Blindness But Not Myopia: A New Look at State Action, Equal Protection, and 'Private' Racial Discrimination," 59 *Mich. L. Rev.*, 993 (1961); Tribe, "Perspectives on *Bakke*: Equal Protection, Procedural Fairness, or Structural Justice?," 92 *Harv. L. Rev.*, 864 (1979); Van Alstyne, "Rites of Passage: Race, the Supreme Court, and the Constitution," 46 *U. Chi. L. Rev.*, 775 (1979); Van Alstyne and Karst, "State Action," 14 *Stan. L. Rev.*, 3 (1961); Wechsler, "Toward Neutral Principles of Constitutional Law," 73 *Harv. L. Rev.*, 1 (1959). The list contains articles published during the last twenty-four years; an adjustment has been made for recency of publication; relatively recent articles were included in the list even though they had received fewer citations than older articles. Not all authors have been active at a given time.

4. Cf. Bell, "Price of Racial Remedies," *supra* note 2, at 3–4, 6 (discussion of dominant role of white professors in the minority admissions debate).

5. See, e.g., Bittker, *supra* note 3, at 1416 n. 15 (citing Du Bois, "Does the Negro Need Separate Schools?," 4 *J. Negro Educ.*, 328, 331 (1935).

6. L. Higginbotham, *In the Matter of Color* (1978).

7. K. Clark, *Dark Ghetto* (1965); K. Clark, *Prejudice and Your Child* (1955).

8. J. Comer and A. Poussaint, *Black Child Care* (1975).

9. W. Grier and P. Cobbs, *Black Rage* (1968).

10. F. Fanon, *The Wretched of the Earth*, trans. C. Farrington (1966).

11. E.g., M. L. King, Jr., *Why We Can't Wait* (1964), *Strength to Love* (1963), *Where Do We Go From Here: Chaos or Community?* (1968).

12. E.g., J. Levy, *Cesar Chavez: Autobiography of La Causa* (1975); P. Mathiessen, *Sal Si Puedes: Cesar Chavez and the New American Revolution* (1969).

13. A. Haley and Malcolm X, *The Autobiography of Malcolm X* (1964).

14. See, e.g., U.S. Commission on Civil Rights, *Report on Housing* (1961), cited in Kaplan, *supra* note 3, at 397 n. 67; U.S. Commission on Civil Rights, *Report on Education* (1961), cited in Kaplan, *supra* note 3, at 399 n. 75.

15. See *supra* notes 3–4 and accompanying text. This situation may be contrasted with that which prevails in social science research. It is my own experience that in this other body of scholarly writing, minority status constitutes virtually a presumption of expertise: blacks writing about the black community and Chicanos about the Chicano community are accepted as equal (perhaps more than equal) partners; indeed, ethnic studies departments sometimes resist hiring Caucasian faculty members out of the belief that they are generally less qualified for the position than candidates who are members of the minority group in question (telephone interview with Michael Olivas, director, Institute on Law and Higher Education, University of Houston, Sept. 14, 1983).

Why the ready acceptance of minority scholars in social science research dealing with minority issues when minority legal scholars receive quite different treatment? Social science research may be less threatening to the status quo than legal research; much social science research is descriptive rather than change-oriented. Also, social science research may be peripheral to fundamental reallocations of power and decision-making authority; in contrast, legal scholarship may portend drastic changes in the status quo. See *infra* notes 61–76 and accompanying text.

16. Delgado, "Words That Wound: A Tort Action for Racial Insults, Epithets, and Name Calling," 17 *Harv. C. R.—C. L. L. Rev.*, 133 (1982).

17. Clark, *Dark Ghetto* (1965).

18. Grier and Cobbs, *supra* note 9.

19. Articles and books by Harry Edwards and William Gould on labor law are widely cited in that field. For

example, Gould, "Labor Arbitration of Grievances Involving Racial Discrimination," 119 *U. Pa. L. Rev.*, 40 (1969), has been cited in seven cases and thirty-four law review articles: see *Shepard's Law Citations* (1979 and Sept. 1983). Similarly, Edwards, "Emerging Duty to Bargain in the Public Sector," 71 *Mich. L. Rev.*, 885 (1973), has been cited in forty-one cases and thirty law review articles: see *Shepard's Law Review Citations* (1979 and Sept. 1983). Henry McGee's articles and casebook on housing law are considered major works in the field. My own work is cited in such sundry places as M. Franklin and R. Rabin, *Cases and Materials on Tort Law and Alternatives*, 300 (3rd ed. 1983); J. Nowak, R. Rotunda, and J. Young, *Constitutional Law*, 944 (2d ed. 1983); R. Perkins, *Criminal Law*, 1074 (1982); M. Shapiro and R. Spece, Jr., *Cases, Materials and Problems on Bioethics and Law*, 18, 55, 174, 278, 308, 451; L. Tribe, *American Constitutional Law*, § 15–8, at 912 n. 12 (1978).

20. 84 *Harv. L. Rev.*, 769 (1971).

21. *Id.* at 776–77 (tradition pursued by "self-appointed scholastic mandarins"); *id.* at 784, 789–92, 803 (further criticism of "scholarly tradition").

22. See *infra* notes 64–70, 77, and accompanying text.

23. See *supra* note 19 and accompanying text.

24. 409 U.S. 205 (1972).

25. Bell, "Price of Racial Remedies," *supra* note 2, at 4 n. 2.

26. See J. Cound, J. Friedenthal and A. Miller, *Civil Procedure: Cases and Materials*, 523 (3d ed. 1980). See generally Davis, "Standing: Taxpayers and Others," 35 *U. Chi. L. Rev.*, 601 (1968) (discussing relationship between standing and plaintiff interests in constitutional challenges to government expenditures by taxpayers).

27. See Cound, *supra* note 26, at 522–26; see also *Fed. R. Civ. P.*, 17(a).

28. See 11 AM, JUR. 2d *Bills and Notes* § 655 (1963).

29. See Cound, *supra* note 26, at 522–53; see also *Fed. R. Civ. P.*, 18, 19.

30. See Cound, *supra* note 26, at 625–42; see also *Fed. R. Civ. P.*, 24.

31. See Cound, *supra* note 26, at 561–601; see also *Fed. R. Civ. P.*, 23(a)(4).

32. For a discussion of the conflict between the traditional civil rights lawyer, the black litigants, and the white liberal financial supporters, see Clark, "The Lawyer in the Civil Rights Movement—Catalytic Agent or Counterrevolutionary?," 19 *U. Kans. L. Rev.*, 459, 469 (1971).

33. Graglia, *supra* note 3, at 352; Van Alystyne, *supra* note 3, at 804–7.

34. Wechsler, *supra* note 3, at 34.

35. Fiss, *supra* note 3, at 7.

36. O'Neil, *supra* note 3, at 933–34; cf. *supra* note 33 and accompanying text.

37. 85 *Yale L. J.*, 470 (1976) [the essay is included in this volume—ED.].

38. See *id.* at 471–72, 482–87.

39. See, e.g., Ely, *supra* note 3, at 727; Fiss, *supra* note 3, at 7; Greenawalt, *supra* note 3, at 559; O'Neil, *supra* note 3, at 927; Tribe, *supra* note 3, at 865–67.

40. See, e.g., Gunther, *supra* note 3, at 43–46; Tribe, *supra* note 3, at 876–77; Wechsler, *supra* note 3.

41. See *infra* text accompanying note 72.

42. See, e.g., D. Bell, Jr., *Race, Racism, and American Law*, 44–47 (2d ed. 1980).

43. See, e.g., Karst and Horowitz, *supra* note 3, at 964–66.

44. See, e.g., Michelman, *supra* note 3, at 13.

45. Compare, e.g., D. Bell, Jr., *supra* note 42, at 44–47 ("Reparations for Racism"); Bell, "*Brown v. Board of Education* and the Interest Convergence Dilemma," 93 *Harv. L. Rev.*, 518, 523 (1980) [the essay is included in this volume—ED.] (it follows that the "availability of fourteenth amendment protection in racial cases may not actually be determined by the character of harm suffered by blacks or the quantum of liability proved against whites." Instead, racial remedies may be the "outward manifestation of unspoken . . . judicial conclusions that the remedies, if granted, will secure, advance, or at least not harm societal interests deemed important by middle and upper class whites.") Also, Burns, "Law and Race in America," in *The Politics of Law*, 82 (D. Kairys, ed. 1982) (historical examples of racially disparate treatment) with Brest, *supra* note 3, at 49–51 (rejecting group-based reparations and distributive justice); Ely, *supra* note 3, at 723 (concern with utility, curing society of the sickness of racism); Karst and Horowitz, *supra* note 3, at 964–66 (utility); Michelman, *supra* note 3, at 13 (distributive justice); Sandalow, *supra* note 3, at 673–74 (utility); and Van Alstyne, *supra* note 3, at 803–10 (social disutility; affirmative action will lead to competition and resentment among racial minorities). But see Black, "Civil Rights in Times of Economic Stress—Jurisprudential and Philosophic Aspects," 1976 *U. Ill. L. F.*, 559, 566 (1981); Black, *supra* note 3 (Black, a nonminority author, derives duty to redress racial discrimination from society's past misconduct toward blacks); Wasserstrom, "Racism, Sexism, and Preferential Treatment: An Approach to the Topics," 24 *UCLA L. Rev.*, 581, 615–22 (1977) (nonminority author argues for affirmative action to correct injustices grounded in history and contemporary reality).

46. In some guises, utility-based justifications are also demeaning. In law school admissions, for example, majority persons may be admitted as a matter of right, while minorities are admitted because their presence will contribute to "diversity." Diversity means that the minority admittees have different skin color, different life experiences, and bring different perspectives, for example perspectives on police conduct, to the classroom. The assumption is that such diversity is educationally valuable to the majority.

However, such an admissions program may well be perceived as treating the minority admittee as an ornament, a curiosity, one who brings an element of the piquant to the lives of white professors and students. Do not women treated in this manner complain, rightly, for the same reasons?

47. Cf. Graglia, *supra* note 3, at 361 (affirmative admission of minorities doomed to fail; programs will only lead to frustration and failure and so are not socially useful).

48. See Gaglia, *supra* note 3, at 352; Van Alstyne, *supra* note 3, at 809–10. For a discussion of the neutral principles theory, see generally Wechsler, *supra* note 3.

49. See, e.g., Ely, *supra* note 3, at 732–40 ("we-they" analysis shows that discrimination of majority against itself is benign, thus permissible).

50. *Id.* at 732–38; Greenawalt, *supra* note 3, at 569–76; see also Brest, *supra* note 3, at 16–17 ("benign" racial discrimination benefitting minority at expense of society at large).

51. The term "perpetrator" perspective is used in Freeman, "Antidiscrimination Law: A Critical Review," in D. Kairys, ed., *The Politics of Law*, 96, 98–99; (1982); Freeman, "Legitimizing Racial Discrimination through Antidiscrimination Law: A Critical Review of Supreme Court Doctrine," 62 *Minn. L. Rev.*, 1049, 1052–54 (1978). The perpetrator perspective has been embraced by authors in varying forms and to varying degrees. See, e.g., Brest, *supra* note 3, at 2 (discussing the antidiscrimination principle that lies at the core of most state and federal civil rights legislation: "By definition the antidiscrimination principle applies only to race-dependent decisions and their effects"; *id.* at 5); Eisenberg, *supra* note 3, at 132–55 (motive analysis: to offer protection, the court must be convinced that the decisionmaker's motives are illicit).

52. See *supra* sources cited in note 51; Bell, "Price of Racial Remedies," *supra* note 2, at 7–12, 19.

53. For a discussion of the resistance of whites to any policy requiring them to pay for racial wrongs they did not themselves commit, see Bell, "Price of Racial Remedies," *supra* note 2, at 3–4, 12, 16.

54. On institutional racism, see Wasserstrom, *supra* note 45, at 596–603.

55. Such persons rarely, if ever, experience group-based harm or confront social institutions that are systematically biased against them; all injurious treatment that comes their way is individually based and comparatively infrequent. Why should not this same picture apply to minorities, who are simply subject to a somewhat more incessant version of it?

56. *Brown v. Board of Educ.*, 349 U.S. 294, 300–1 (1955). For a critique of the *Brown* remedy, see Wasserstrom, *supra* note 45, at 599–600; see also Bell, "Price of Racial Remedies," supra note 2, at 11–12 (discussing the way mainstream whites may support nondiscrimination in theory, but avoid or even oppose remediation).

57. See Bell, "Price of Racial Remedies," supra note 2.

58. *Id.* at 14–16, 19 (resistance of working-class whites to affirmative action programs); Van Alstyne, *supra* note 3, at 803–10 (affirmative action leads to competition and resentment among racial minorities).

59. See Bell, "Price of Racial Remedies," supra note 2, at 14.

60. E.g., Romero, Delgado, and Reynoso, "The Legal Education of Chicano Students: A Study in Mutual Accommodation and Cultural Conflict," 5 *N.M. L. Rev.*, 177, 188–90 (1975). For a discussion of the need for more broad-based admission criteria, see Bell, "Price of Racial Remedies," supra note 2, at 17.

61. See, e.g., *Regents of Univ. of Cal. v. Bakke*, 438 U.S. 265, 288 n. 25 (1978) (citing ten law review articles by white male authors).

62. See *supra* note 19 and accompanying text.

63. See, e.g., L. Tribe, *supra* note 19, § 16–27, at 1072 n. 16, § 16–28, at 1075 n. 4–5; Karst, *supra* note 3, at 11 n. 56, 55 n. 306, 56 n. 310, 57 n. 320.

64. See Blumer, "Race Prejudice as a Sense of Group Position," 1 *Pac. L. J.* 3, 4 (1958) (racial prejudice inhering in a collective sense of group position); Brest, *supra* note 3, at 14–15 (discussing "unconscious racially selective indifference"); Lawrence, "Book Review," 35 *Stan. L. Rev.*, 831, 841–43 (1983) ("Ideology as an Unconscious Defense Mechanism").

65. Delgado and Palacios, "Mexican-Americans as a Legally Cognizable Class under Rule 23 and the Equal Protection Clause," 50 *Notre Dame Law.*, 393 (1975).

66. 48 F.R.D. 274 (D.N.M. 1969), *appeal dismissed*, 398 U.S. 916 (1970), discussed in Delgado and Palacios, *supra* note 65, at 398–404; see also *id.* at 398 n. 43 (examples of cases holding that Mexican-Americans are not a race for equal protection purposes).

67. All suits must be brought in the name of an individual or a well-defined group. See, e.g., *Tijerina*, 48 F.R.D. at 276–78, discussed in Delgado and Palacios, *supra* note 65, at 399–401.

68. *Tijerina*, 48 F.R.D. at 276–77.

69. *Castaneda v. Partida*, 430 U.S. 482, 494–96 (1977); see also *Keyes v. School Dist. No. 1*, 413 U.S. 189, 197 (1973), discussed in Delgado and Palacios, *supra* note 65, at 396.

70. Cf. V. Countryman and T. Finman, *The Lawyer in Modern Society*, 577–84 (1966) (in the early sixties, lawyers for southern black clients were difficult to find); *id.* at 584–87 (fear of verbal disapproval, adverse publicity, loss of prestige, and loss of clients may deter lawyers from accepting unpopular clients); Lawrence, *supra* note 64, at 842–43 (psychology of white leader confronted with fact of racism).

71. See sources cited *supra* note 3; cf. *supra* text accompanying note 63, where it was observed that some inner-circle writers do cite feminist writers, even though the work of many feminist writers shows passion and commitment; any apparent differences in these observations are reconcilable. On a general level, feminist literature may be less threatening to establishment male writers than militant minority literature because the latter, unlike the former, is identified with a movement that at times in its history has embraced violence or civil disobedience. Upon close examination, the difference in treatment of feminist and minority literature may be illusory. The more radical feminist writers, such as Catharine MacKinnon or Susan Brownmiller, seem to be cited less often than the more mainstream feminist authors, such as those mentioned in the text accompanying note 63. Like much minority literature, the generation of more radical feminists propose far-reaching changes in the ways in which society is constituted. The more mainstream feminists tend to be more assimilationist in their proposals: in contrast to the more radical, they are primarily concerned with expanding women's role within the existing societal framework. The writing of this latter group may thus strike a sympathetic chord with inner-circle writers, while the work of the more radical group may be ignored for reasons similar to those which explain the treatment of minority writers discussed in this article.

72. See *supra* notes 39–41 and accompanying text.

73. See *supra* notes 44–45 and accompanying text.

74. See *supra* notes 45–48 and 51–71 and accompanying text.

75. See *supra* notes 51–55 and accompanying text.

76. Minority writers have focused on difficult problems overlooked by mainstream writers include Bell, "Price of Remedies," *supra* note 2, at 12 (discussion of mainstream opposition to any means to achieve racial equality that burdens the white majority); Bell, "Serving Two Masters: In-

tegration Ideals and Client Interests in School Desegregation Litigation", 85 *Yale L. J.*, 470 (1976) (conflicts between the goals of minority clients and their lawyers); Bell, "In Defense of Minority Admissions Programs: A Reply to Professor Graglia", 119 *U. Pa. L. Rev.*, 364 (1970) (criticism of the abandonment of efforts undertaken to remedy past racial injustices); Ravenell, "DeFunis and Bakke . . . The Voice Not Heard," 21 *How. L. J.*, 128 (1978) (proposal for achieving racial diversity in professional schools); Romero, Delgado, and Reynoso, *supra* note 60 (attention to the shortage of minority professionals and the need to alleviate that shortage); Smith, "Reflections on a Landmark: Small Preliminary Observations on the Development and Significance of the *University of California v. Allan Bakke*," 21 *How. L. J.*, 72 (1978) (proposal to revamp current professional school admissions procedures to compensate for minority deprivation). See generally "Symposium, A Step Toward Equality: Affirmative Action and Equal Opportunity," 4 *Black L. J.*, 211 (1974).

77. Bell, "Price of Racial Remedies," *supra* note 2, at 4; see also R. Wilkins, *A Man's Life*, 216–17 (1982) (author, a black, attended a high-level political strategy session of "White Brahmins" engaged in planning country's civil rights policy; expressed anger that minority representatives, except himself, were not present); Lawrence, *supra* note 64, at 846 ("Because virtually an entire community of thinkers share the privileged positions, the need for justifications, and the resulting distorted perceptions, those perceptions are mutually confirming and appear undistorted.").

78. See *supra* text accompanying notes 33–60.

79. *Western Addition Community Org. v. NLRB*, 485 F. 2d 917, 940 (D.C. Cir. 1973) (Wyzanski, J., dissenting), *rev'd*, 420 U.S. 50 (1975).

Part Two

CRITICAL RACE THEORY AND CRITICAL LEGAL STUDIES: CONTESTATION AND COALITION

Two

CRITICAL RACE THEORY AND CRITICAL LEGAL STUDIES: CONTESTATION AND COALITION

The articles in this section reflect some of the diverse ways that critical race scholars have engaged with the leftist movement known as Critical Legal Studies. Founded in 1976, the Conference on Critical Legal Studies (CLS) is the name of a group of law teachers, students, and some practitioners ("crits," "CLSers"), who are loosely organized as leftist intellectuals and activists. Like Critical Race Theory, CLS includes a wide diversity of methodology and approach. As these articles indicate, most critical race theorists acknowledge a close connection with CLS, particularly in terms of the critical methodology employed in examining legal discourse. At the same time, the articles reflect an extended set of intellectual and theoretical disagreements between CLS and the emerging Critical Race Theory movement.

Harlon Dalton's "The Clouded Prism" echoes Richard Delgado's complaints about liberal constitutional law scholars. Dalton contends that CLSers have also engaged in exclusionary or exploitive conduct with respect to minority scholars. He argues that any coalition between white scholars and scholars of color must deal with the divergent cultural backgrounds that each is bringing to the dialogue. Dalton's work is notable for quite bluntly expressing some of the traditional problems that progressive people

of color have encountered when they have engaged white leftists. Written at the inception of Critical Race Theory as an organized movement, Dalton challenges white leftists to make this coalition different than those of the past.

In "The Reconstructive Theology of Dr. Martin Luther King, Jr.," Anthony Cook criticizes CLS work for failing to move beyond critique to reconstruction. He first provides a useful introduction to, and summary of, CLS jurisprudential work. He argues that the CLS critique of liberalism is correct but incomplete because it is not grounded in the experiences of people struggling against oppression. Cook argues that reconstructive efforts require more than simply the application of thought; but rather, they need an experiential basis for commitment in the world. He relates the predicament of CLS in the difficulty of moving beyond critique to the issues that King faced as he strategized on various fronts about how to resist white racial power. Weaving together jurisprudence, political theory, and a description of the historic role of theology in black community life, Cook points to King's image of the "organic intellectual" as the basis for understanding the role that progressive scholars of color can play, as well as to King's image of the "Beloved Community" as the normative orientation for critical and reconstructive work.

Mari Matsuda's article is an attempt to find useful common ground between interests of progressive scholars of color and critics. According to Matsuda, CLS has developed effective critiques of dominant legal ideology, but it has become abstract and theoretical, divorced from any grounding in real-world experience. She suggests the jurisprudential method of "looking to the bottom" to improve upon the work of Critical Legal Studies. In turn, she argues that CLS has a great deal to contribute to the reconstructive work of scholars of color. Using the possibility of a legal claim of reparations for Japanese-American victims of the American policy of detention during World War II as an extended concrete example, Matsuda shows how ideas developed through critical thinking about law help to imagine the basis for ways to articulate the interests of people of color.

Kimberlé Crenshaw's article "Race, Reform, and Retrenchment" is an important window into the intellectual issue that provided the framework for the first several years of engagement and contestation between white crits and progressive scholars of color—the issue of "rights." CLS writers had developed a critique of the concept of legal rights on the grounds that rights are necessarily indeterminate and contradictory (one person's right is another's duty) and that thinking in terms of rights embodied an alienated way of thinking about the social world (in terms of unrelated individuals approaching each other as rights-bearing units). Much CLS work claimed that the idea of "rights" was part of the legitimation function of liberal legal ideology in presenting the world as equal and free because everyone "has their rights." Crenshaw traces the ways that the civil rights gains of the 1960s were curtailed in the 1970s and 1980s. She criticizes the neoconservative commitment to formal equality for being contradictory and for denying the continuing realities of racial power. While agreeing with much of the CLS approach, she criticizes CLS work for failing to engage with the actual experience of people of color and the reality of race consciousness as an element of social power. In particular, Crewnshaw argues that the left's critique of rights ignores the particular role that the struggle for rights has played in black liberation politics and the practical possibilities given the mainstream ideologies against which civil rights proponents worked. Finally, using strands of postmodern analysis, she develops a theoretical frame for understanding the relation between legal doctrine and the exercise of racial power. She concludes by sketching the need for reform ideologies that are sensitive both to the dangers of cooptation and of utopianism.

Part Two

CRITICAL RACE THEORY AND CRITICAL LEGAL STUDIES: CONTESTATION AND COALITION

LOOKING TO THE BOTTOM: CRITICAL LEGAL STUDIES AND REPARATIONS
Mari Matsuda

INTRODUCTION

WHEN you are on trial for conspiracy to overthrow the government for having taught the deconstruction of law, your lawyer will want black people on your jury. Why? Because black jurors are more likely to understand what your lawyer will argue—that people in power sometimes abuse law to achieve their own ends, and that the prosecution's claim to neutral application of legal principles is false.[1] This article discusses the similar perspectives and goals of people of color and critical legal scholars. It also suggests that the failure of the two groups to develop an alliance is tied to weaknesses of the Critical Legal Studies movement.

The central problem facing critical legal scholars, and indeed all thoughtful legal scholars, is the search for a normative source. Arthur Leff, in an oft-cited article, asked, "[W]ho among us ... ought to be able to declare 'law' that ought to be obeyed?"[2] Although postrealist legal thinkers—left, right, and center—are often ready to proffer a specific perspective, they also conclude that no external, universally accepted normative source exists to resolve conflicts of value. Critical legal scholars disparage traditional sources of norms such as the market system, the pluralist tradition, and classical liberalism, yet they hesitate to proclaim new sources of norms. "Speak, God,"[3] the cry goes forth, but as yet no voice has answered—at least not in the pages of the law reviews.

This article suggests that those who have experienced discrimination speak with a special voice to which we should listen. Looking to the bottom—adopting the perspective of those who have seen and felt the falsity of the liberal promise—can assist critical scholars in the task of fathoming the phenomenology of law and defining the elements of justice.

The method of looking to the bottom is analogous to but different from the method of legal philosophers such as Rawls[4] and Ackerman,[5] who have proposed moral theories that call for special attention to the needs of the least advantaged. What is suggested here is not abstract consideration of the position of the least advantaged; the imagination of the academic philosopher cannot recreate the experience of life on the bottom. Instead we must look to what Gramsci called "organic intellectuals,"[6] grassroots philosophers who are uniquely able to relate theory to the concrete experience of oppression.[7] The technique of imagining oneself black and poor in some hypothetical world is less effective than studying the actual experience of black poverty and listening to those who have done so. When notions of right and wrong, justice and injustice, are examined not from an abstract position but from the position of groups who have suffered through history, moral relativism recedes and identifiable normative priorities emerge. This article, then, suggests a new epistemological source for critical scholars: the actual experience, history, culture, and intellectual tradition of people of color in America. Looking to the bottom for ideas about law will tap a valuable source previously over-looked by legal philosophers. . . .

I. CRITICAL LEGAL STUDIES AND THE MINORITY SCHOLAR

It is evident that all reforms have their beginning with ideas and that for a time they have to rely solely on the tongue and pen for progress. . . .

—Frederick Douglass[8]

THE movement known as Critical Legal Studies is characterized by skepticism toward the liberal vision of the rule of law, by a focus on the role of legal ideas in capturing human consciousness, by agreement that fundamental change is required to attain a just society, and by a utopian conception of a world more communal and less hierarchical than the one we know now.

This movement is attractive to minority scholars because its central descriptive message—that legal ideals are manipulable, and that law serves to legitimate existing maldistributions of wealth and power—rings true for anyone who has experienced life in nonwhite America. Frederick Douglass realized this truth about law before Oliver Wendell Holmes ever picked up a pen.

The sophistication of CLS description is also attractive and useful to minority scholars. It is one thing to suspect that law is indeterminate, but it is quite another to grasp exactly how that indeterminacy works in specific contexts. In particular, the development of the concepts of the relative autonomy of law[9] and of legal consciousness[10] has reached unprecedented heights in critical legal scholarship. Knowing when doctrine sticks, when it doesn't, and why—and suggesting why knowing why is important—are major intellectual contributions of the CLS movement. Long before CLS discovered the thought of Antonio Gramsci, Frederick Douglass said, "Find out just what any people will quietly submit to and you have found out the exact measure of injustice and wrong which will be imposed upon them."[11] The additional contribution of CLS is the detailed study of legal consciousness in a myriad of technical legal contexts.[12]

This descriptive work of critical legal scholars is liberating. To those who believe that law is a cage within which radical social transformation is impossible, the critical legal scholar can respond with the sophisticated confidence born of a significant body of scholarship. This is why we read Duncan Kennedy as well as Frederick Douglass. CLS is a legitimation process for outsiders.

The Critical Legal Studies movement's prescriptive power is also valuable to people of color. The willingness at least to consider the utopian prospect and the passionate criticism of existing conditions of racism and poverty attract nonwhite readers to CLS. Moreover, an elevated understanding of the traditional legal concepts of neutral principles and rights helps to protect victims of oppression from the unsophisticated rights-thinking that can be a seductive trap for those on the bottom. . . .

II. THE CRITIQUE OF CRITICAL LEGAL STUDIES

. . .

STANDARD critique: "Incoherency," as used here, is the expression of extreme skepticism that law can produce determinate results free from reference to value, politics, or historical conditions. While no CLS scholar suggests pure incoherency, the highly developed method of "trashing," or exposing standard liberal legalisms as incoherent, emphasizes the indeterminate elements of law.

Incoherency, critics contend, is an inadequate and inaccurate description of law which fails to account for the lawyer's experience that, given a specific doctrinal query, certain outcomes are inevitable and technically correct as a matter of law, even when such results challenge existing power. Those who characterize the law as incoherent are also criticized for portraying those who use legal doctrine, legal principles, and liberal theory for positive social ends as co-opted fools or cynical instrumentalists. Looking to the bottom can help to form a response to the critique of the incoherency description.

. . .

The dissonance of combining deep criticism of law with an aspirational vision of law is part of the experience of people of color. These people have used duality as a strength, and have developed strategies for resolving this dissonance through the process of appropriation and transformation. W. E. B. Du Bois noted long ago the resiliency of the consciousness of "Black Folk."[13] The consciousness he described includes both mainstream American consciousness and the consciousness of the outsider. Applying the double consciousness concept to rights rhetoric allows us to see that the victim of racism can have a mainstream consciousness of the Bill of Rights as well as a victim's consciousness. These two viewpoints can combine powerfully to create a radical constitutionalism that is true to the radical roots of this country. The strands of republicanism that legal historians are reviving with the feather-brush care of an archaeologist are alive and well in the constitutional discourse of nonwhite America.

Frederick Douglass's interpretive work is an example of dual conceptions. Garrisonian abolitionists in the 1840s argued that the Constitution was a corrupt document that endorsed slavery. As a Garrison protégé, Douglass at first accepted this interpretation and its corollary, that reformist political action was an ineffectual means to abolish slavery. Douglass later split from the Garrisonians and argued that the Constitution, including the Preamble and the Bill of Rights, contained a ringing indictment of slavery.

Douglass stated in his widely disseminated writings and public lectures that slavery was unconstitutional, un-American, and inconsistent with the basic values necessary for the survival of the nation. Douglass's skill in transforming the standard text of American political life into a blueprint for fundamental social change is instructive: he chose to believe in the Constitution but refused to accept a racist Constitution. In his hands, the document grew to become greater than some of its drafters had intended. Douglass's reconstructed Constitution inspired his black readers to endure the tremendous personal costs of resistance. Martin Luther King, Jr.'s reconstructed Constitution produced the same effect in the twentieth century.

This ability to adopt and transform standard texts and mainstream consciousness is an important contribution of those on the bottom. Black Americans, the paradigmatic victim group of our history, have turned the Bible and the Constitution into texts of liberation, just as John Coltrane transformed the popular song "My Favorite Things" into a jazz fugue of extraordinary power.[14] This and other examples of the tendency to trope, appropriate, "signify," and otherwise draw transformative power out of the dry wells of ordinary discourse is discussed by Henry Louis Gates in his important article on black language and literary theory, "The Blackness of Blackness: A Critique of the Sign and the Signifying Monkey." Gates sees this transforming skill in jazz composition, in black English, in the black church, and in black writers' adaptive uses of standard literary forms. This transformative skill, Gates suggests is a direct result of the experience of oppression.

Those who lack material wealth or political power still have access to thought and language, and their development of those tools will differ from that of the more privileged. Erlene Stetson realized this distinction when, in her essay on black women poets, she wrote, "[C]reativity has often been a survival tactic."[15] Studying the centuries-old tradition of American black women's poetry reveals, according to Stetson, three major elements: "a compelling quest for identity, a subversive perception of reality, and subterfuge and ambivalence as creative strategies."[16] In poetry, the most concentrated form of language, black women have employed words to criticize and transform existing assumptions. Poetry to black women has never been merely aesthetic: it has, first and foremost, been a tool of social change.[17] Gwendolyn Brooks opened one 1949 sonnet: "First fight. Then fiddle."[18]

Black musicians see fiddling as part of the fight. Objecting to the detransformation of black jazz for white audiences and also to the commodification of black musicians,[19] be-bop artists such as Thelonious Monk vowed to "create something they can't steal because they can't play it."[20] Black musicians resist co-option by asserting their moral claim to the jazz form.[21]

The black artists' fight to establish progressive language and music is relevant to the legal theorist because the fight over the body and soul of American law is part of the same struggle. The law, as critical scholars recognize, consists of language, ideals, signs, and structures that have material and moral consequences. Transforming this kind of system into one's own has a long tradition in the black community. . . .

Nonwhite lawyers have passionately invoked legal doctrine, legal ideals, and liberal theory in the struggle against racism. Their success is attributable in part to the passionate response that conventional legalisms can at times elicit. These lawyers recited the Bill of Rights and demanded their participatory share of the American polity. At the same time, however, they maintained disrespect for claims of legality that accompanied oppressive acts. Such lawyers needed no reminder that the Constitution is merely a piece of paper in the face of the monopoly on violence and capital possessed by those who intend to keep things just the way they are.

How could anyone believe both of the following statements? (1) I have a right to participate equally in society with any other person; (2) Rights are whatever people in power say they are. One of the primary lessons CLS can learn from the experience of the bottom is that one can believe in both of those statements simultaneously, and that it may well be necessary to do so.

This duality is evident in the thought of those Japanese-Americans who have described their bitterness and outrage at being incarcerated by their own government during World War II. They acknowledge that they were powerless to resist the government's repressive actions; the Constitution, they found, offered no protection from the guns of military police or from the orders of racist generals. Yet the victims nevertheless maintained their belief in constitutional democracy.

From behind barbed wire in America's concentration camps, many young *nisei* (second-generation Japanese-Americans) volunteered to fight in World War II. They spilled their blood on the beaches of Italy and in the forests of France because of their faith in American constitutionalism and their demand for recognition as citizens.[22] It is important to understand how claims to equality, procedural fairness, and political participation prove so compelling that human beings are willing to die for them.

Consistent with the tradition of belief in constitutional principles, *sansei* (third-generation Japanese-American) lawyers who are successfully battling to delegitimize the infamous Korematsu decision,[23] base their arguments upon the Bill of Rights.[24] CLS theorists might ask, "Have such rights-based, legalistic claims so muddled the thinking of Japanese-Americans that they can no longer conceive of radical social change?" Such a question evokes two responses. First, the memory of the internment—the separated families, the infants lost to lack of medical care, the machine-gun towers, the primitive facilities, and smell of horse manure in the racetrack holding camps—remains a part of Japanese-American consciousness. Such recollections prod a mainstream liberal organization such as the Japanese Americans Citizens League (JACL), the Japanese-American equivalent of the NAACP, to rise in vigorous protest at any hint of government bigotry. During the Iranian hostage crisis, for example, JACL members were among the few to condemn the persecution of Iranians in America. Today they support the Big Mountain People facing relocation from their homeland, and they oppose federal immigration authorities, proposals for a Louisiana detention camp for suspected "undesirable" aliens. This active involvement with unpopular issues indicates a radicalizing influence of the internment experience, one that enables Japanese-Americans to resist co-option.

An alternative response questions the assumption that rights rhetoric is co-opting. If trust in the Constitution sustains Japanese-Americans in their uphill battle against racist oppression, then the Constitution for them has become a radical document. Their consciousness—legal consciousness, if you will—of the ultimate legitimacy of their fight against racism allows them to hold unpopular and ultimately transformative opinions with confidence, and to risk retribution from powerful opponents.

Critical legal scholars have recognized the lockgrip of legal consciousness as a primary impediment to radical social change, just as they have recognized that constitutional interpretation in the traditional sense is simply not possible. The nonwhite tradition of constitutional interpretation, one that draws upon the experience of suffering racism and read's the Constitution as a text of liberation, suggests a critical response to the limited mainstream version of legal consciousness.

The desire for a rule of law which is determinate and committed to the end of oppression exists, it is said, within all of us. The minority experience of dual consciousness accommodates both the idea of legal indeterminacy as well as the core belief in a liberating law that transcends indeterminacy. . . .

The strength CLS can derive from the experience of people of color is the realization that apparent logical inconsistency in intellectual argument is not inconsistency in the real world. Intellectual arguments may be paradoxical; real experiences cannot be. "Love it or leave it" is not a valid critique of CLS, for the criticism, transformation, and validation of law are all part of the same project. . . .

III. REPARATIONS AS A CRITICAL LEGALISM: AN EXAMPLE OF LAW DERIVED FROM THE BOTTOM

THE challenge facing critical legal scholars is the development of new norms and new laws that will achieve and maintain their utopian vision. Following the methodology suggested in Parts I and II of this article, this part suggests a new, reconstructed legalism that attempts to meet that challenge. Reparations is a legal concept generated from the bottom. It arises not from abstraction but from experience. This discussion begins by summarizing the factual basis for two reparations claims that are presently under consideration by the United States government. Whether this concept of reparations is consistent with standard liberal legal[25] thought is then considered, with emphasis on the minority perspective. This

part concludes with a consideration of the power of a theory of reparations to withstand corruption.

A. Japanese-American Claims for Redress
Japanese-Americans have organized the redress movement to obtain compensation for their internment during World War II. This internment, now recognized as a constitutional violation,[26] was initiated without any reasonable cause to believe the Japanese-Americans posed a threat to national security,[27] as recently revealed documents confirm.[28] The government's own conclusion that Japanese-Americans were loyal citizens was withheld from the Supreme Court in an act of fraud so egregious that federal judges have seen fit to use the extraordinary writ of *error corum nobis* to set aside the convictions of internment resisters some forty years after the fact.[29]

The internment was the result of racist hysteria fueled in part by the vicious Hearst newspapers and the long-standing resentment of Japanese-Americans' modest economic success on the West Coast. Many interned families lost homes and possessions in bargain-basement evacuation sales, while others lost property in racially motivated escheat trials promoted by the California government. Farm families that had spent generations reclaiming unusable land lost the fruits of their toil. Even more devastating than the loss of property was the loss of opportunity: many of the *issei,* or first-generation immigrants, were deprived of their most productive years, the period when their hard work, experience, and careful investments might have yielded the financial security that many were never able to achieve after internment. *Nisei* internees report the end of promising careers, businesses and educational opportunities as a result of their incarceration.

Internees endured physical suffering during the dusty desert days and freezing nights.[30] Families were crammed into tiny one-room, tar-papered units, and they shared communal toilet and dining facilities, making normal family living impossible. Food supplies were erratic. Special meals and facilities required for infants, diabetics, and others with medical needs were nonexistent; inadequate health facilities could not address problems suffered by a camp population ranging from newborns to the frail elderly. Death and permanent injury resulted from lack of medical care.[31]

These physical and economic deprivations, though significant, were not the greatest harms inflicted upon internees. These victims have expressed their greatest bitterness and anger over the betrayal by a government they supported and believed in. The Japanese-Americans on the West Coast were predominantly assimilationist.[32] They shared the tastes and aspirations of the non-Japanese. The *nisei*, in particular, excelled academically, fully absorbing the rhetoric of American liberal ideals. They followed baseball and big bands, and considered themselves full-fledged Americans; many disparaged and ridiculed Japan. The shock of the un-American label to those who knew no other culture wounded deeply.

The *nisei* struggled to reconcile patriotism with the fact of internment. One woman recalls planning a Fourth of July program while imprisoned at the Fresno fair grounds:

> [W]e decided to recite the Gettysburg Address as a verse choir. We had an artist draw a big picture of Abraham Lincoln with an American flag behind him. Some people had tears in their eyes; some people shook their heads and said it was so ridiculous to have that kind of thing recited in a camp. It didn't make sense, but it was our hearts' cry. We wanted so much to believe that this was a government by the people and for the people and that there was freedom and justice.[33]

These betrayed Americans have made it their cause to seek redress for the illegal evacuation and incarceration. . . .

B. The Native Hawaiian Claim for Reparations
Native Hawaiians are also seeking reparations from the United States for the overthrow of native Hawaiian rule and loss of native lands. Native Hawaiians are unique among indigenous Americans in that, prior to annexation, they lived under a Western-style constitutional government, whose sovereignty was recognized internationally as well as by the United States. That sovereignty ceased, however, with the

overthrow of the Hawaiian monarchy—an overthrow in which the United States participated. The Hawaiians' claim for loss of their government as well as of their land forms a unique basis for reparations.

The Hawaiians were descended from Polynesian voyagers who settled in the Hawaiian Islands and established a communal, agrarian society governed by a regime of custom and ruled by hierarchical leadership. The Hawaiian leaders, who governed the islands for over a thousand years before the arrival of Captain Cook, proved adept at responding to the influx of outside influence during the nineteenth-century period of Pacific exploration and trade. King Kamehameha used Western military devices to consolidate control of the islands, and his royal descendants instituted a Western-style constitutional monarchy in order to establish Hawaiian sovereignty in Western eyes. The major international powers, including the United States, formally recognized Hawaiian sovereignty.

The Hawaiian monarchy quickly adopted Western laws and acquired Western tastes in royal accoutrements. The missionary-educated native Hawaiian population, while sometimes critical of royal expenditures and the favors granted to Western advisers, generally supported the monarchy. Commoners in particular favored those monarchs who promoted Hawaiian culture and nationalism.

However, white Americans, a growing economic presence in the islands, began to resent the Hawaiian leadership. These planters, merchants, and traders desired annexation by the United States. They accused the Hawaiian monarchy of incompetence, waste, and anti-democratic rule. Dissatisfaction came to a head in 1893, when a handful of foreigners and white subjects of the kingdom carried out a revolution.

Native Hawaiians, the overwhelming majority of the population, together with white loyalists, opposed the quest for annexation. U.S. government representatives, however, saw the threatened revolution as an apportunity to wrest the islands from indigenous control. United States Minister for Hawaii John L. Stevens had written earlier to the State Department, "The

Hawaiian pear is now fully ripe, and this is the golden hour for the United States to pluck it."[34]

The self-appointed revolutionaries were a small band of poorly armed merchants and planters; alone, they were no match for Queen Liliuokalani's military forces. However, Stevens landed U.S. troops on the islands to secure the queen's surrender. The queen, desiring to avoid bloodshed and trusting that the U.S. government would adhere to its treaties respecting Hawaiian sovereignty, temporarily surrendered and appealed to the President to restore her to the throne. Stevens later asserted that his intent had been merely to protect American citizens in Hawaii. His correspondence, however, made no pretense that his goal was anything other than an overthrow of the monarchy.

Newly installed President Grover Cleveland dispatched an emissary to investigate the U.S. involvement. He determined that the takeover was indeed a a result of U.S. military intervention against the will of the majority of Hawaiian citizens, in violation of international law and American foreign policy. The government's commitment to legality, however, faltered in the face of powerful political considerations, including strategic and economic benefits, which favored annexation. The Hawaiian government was never restored to power, and after a five-year congressional standoff between anti-imperialists and annexationists, Hawaii became a U.S. territory in 1898.

Native Hawaiians never voted in any plebiscite on either the overthrow or annexation. In fact, the highly literate and politically astute Hawaiians overwhelmingly supported their native government and mourned the U.S. takeover.

In the process of the takeover, the United States obtained vast acreages of land that had belonged to the Kingdom and had been held in trust for the Hawaiian people. Some of this land remains in federal hands today, as vast military bases, national parks, and open spaces. The remainder was returned to the State of Hawaii, which agreed to hold the land in trust for the native Hawaiian people. The state, however, has never complied with the trust mandate: proceeds from trust land are commingled with other revenue, not targeted to benefit the indigenous Hawaiian community. While the state's own legislative auditor recognizes the state's questionable record of upholding trust responsibilities, courts have ruled that individual Hawaiians lack standing to sue for these violations.

Many native Hawaiians seek reparations for the overthrow of the Hawaiian government and loss of land. They request a formal recognition of the illegal destruction of Hawaiian sovereignty and an apology from the United States; they also seek resumption of Hawaiian rule, return of at least part of the lands presently held by the federal and state governments, and monetary compensation. In one survey of Hawaiian opinion, a majority of respondents favored reparations in the form of land and programs benefiting Hawaiians collectively, as well as individual monetary awards.

Non-Hawaiian opponents of reparations argue that the American takeover was a historical inevitability, and that present-day taxpayers are not responsible for the wrongdoing of government officials a century ago. Yet the recent judicial and congressional recognition of moral and legal obligations for treaty violations and uncompensated expropriation of the land of Native North Americans has encouraged Hawaiians to press their claims. A study commission established by Congress, with commissioners appointed by a Republican administration, concluded that reparations were not due the Hawaiians. A minority of the commissioners, however, filed a strong dissenting report.

The Native Hawaiian and Japanese-American claims for reparations each represent emerging norms and social movements generated from the bottom. Sympathetic academics can now develop the concept. The following section attempts to use CLS methodology in conjunction with the method of looking to the bottom to develop a theory of reparations.

C. Reparations Claims within the Context of Liberal-Legalism

This section considers standard objections to reparations and suggests critical responses that can be strengthened by looking to the bottom.

I. STANDARD DOCTRINAL OBJECTIONS TO REPARATIONS

. . .

a. Identification of victims and perpetrators. The problem of specific identification of wrongdoers and victims is a common objection to reparations. This reservation reflects a penchant for horizontal and vertical logic in legal doctrine. Privity, standing, and nexus are typical conceptual expressions of this compulsion for close and ordered relations between individual disputants. Reparations challenges this rigid order by suggesting new connections between victims and perpetrators.

The standard legal claim resembles:

Plaintiff A (individual victim)

v.

Defendant B (perpetrator of recent wrongdoing)

In contrast, a claim in reparations looks like this:

Plaintiff Class A (victim group members)

v.

Defendant Class B (perpetrator descendants and current beneficiaries of past injustice)

Several components of the standard legal claim are not part of the second illustration. First, the horizontal, intragroup connections are absent: not all members of the victim group are similarly situated. Some are rich, some poor, some feel betrayed, others do not; some are easily identifiable as group members, others have weak claims to membership. Camp internees, for example, include the all-American veteran carrying deep psychological scars from internment, the wealthy retired capitalist who recovered easily from internment, and anti-American protestors. Native Hawaiians have intermarried and assimilated so that native ancestry is found both among those who continue to live within the

Hawaiian culture and those who left it long ago. Non-Hawaiian loyalist citizens of the Hawaiian kingdom also lost land, status, and power in the U.S. takeover, yet proof of past loyalty seems an unworkable and awkward criterion for victim identification.

Similarly, of those taxpayers who must pay the reparations, some are direct descendants of perpetrators while others are merely guilty by association. Under a reparations doctrine, the working-class whites whose ancestors never harbored any prejudice or ill will toward the victim group are taxed equally with the perpetrators' direct descendants for the sins of the past.

However, looking to the bottom helps to refute the standard objections to reparations. In response to the problem of horizontal connection among victims and perpetrators, a victim would note that because the experience of discrimination against the group is real, the connections must exist. The hierarchical relationship that places white people over people of color was promoted by the specific wrongs of the past: the destruction of Hawaiian sovereignty and the internment of Japanese-Americans are tied to the idea of white dominance and nonwhite difference. Each specific act of oppression against a minority group reinforces, entrenches, and promotes the assumption that nonwhites are different and properly treated as different.

Victims necessarily think of themselves as a group, because they are treated and survive as a group. The wealthy black person still comes up against the color line; the educated Japanese still comes up against the assumption of Asian inferiority. The wrongs of the past cut into the heart of the privileged as well as the suffering.[35]

The continuing group damage engendered by past wrongs ties victim group members together, satisfying the horizontal unity sought by the legal mind. Indigenous Hawaiians, for example, are on the bottom of every demographic indicator of social survival: they have lower birth weights, higher infant mortality, and, if they survive, higher rates of disease, illiteracy, imprisonment, alcoholism, suicide, and homelessness. Hawaiians realize their forgotten status in their own land. Poor and rich, Democrat and Republican, commoner and royalty—native Hawaiians largely agree that they have been robbed.

Japanese-Americans, as well, bear the continued burdens of racism. Though on the whole successful by standard indicators, many former internees still have not recovered from the economic setback of the evacuation. The Japanese-American elderly frequently live below the poverty line. Even those who are younger and more affluent continue to face various forms of discrimination. University administrators are under attack for excluding Japanese-American applicants on the basis of a myth that Asians are "overrepresented" in the professions.

The myth of Asian success fails to confront the crucial question of costs of conventional success. Japanese-Americans are often over-educated for the jobs they hold, and, like white women, they frequently report that they must be twice as good in order to receive half the recognition. Many whites hold stereotypes of Japanese as "passive" or "good with numbers," and they resent Japanese who exhibit assertiveness or verbal skills. Japanese-Americans are often passed over for leadership positions and are patronized by whites, who are surprised to find out, for example, that an educated Japanese-surnamed person can write well-crafted English prose. Exploring the experience of Japanese-American life shows that the surface success has had significant internal costs. Japanese-Americans live with the suppressed rage of knowing that their success comes at greater personal cost and in the face of pervasive discrimination.

Added to this subtle bigotry is the overt racism of epithets, slurs, and stereotypes pervading popular discourse, which are revived every December 7 by ignorant Americans who have not yet learned to distinguish between Japanese-Americans and Japanese nationals. Finally, the recent upsurge of physical attacks on Asians increases the threat of racist violence. In short, the experience of the Hawaiians and Japanese-Americans as members of a victim group is raw, close, and real.

A horizontal connection exists as well within the perpetrator group. Members of the dominant class continue to benefit from the wrongs of the past and the presumptions of inferiority imposed upon victims. They may decry this legacy and harbor no racist thoughts of their own, but they cannot avoid their privileged status.

Any nonnative resident of Hawaii, for example, benefits from the loss of Hawaiian sovereignty and the demise of the Hawaiian landownership. If Hawaiians had not lost their land, others would not be living on it; if the Hawaiians had not been pushed to the bottom of the socioeconomic pile, nonnatives would not hold as many positions of power and influence. Beneficiaries—who are not required to prove their intelligence, responsibility, and worth to the same extent that victim group members must—are protected by a subtle magic they may not notice because they have never experienced life without it. In addition, the abundance of material comforts in this nation has resulted in part from the labor of the nonwhite workers— a group that includes black slaves, Chinese railroad workers, Chicano miners, and legions of today's undocumented toilers in factory and field—who have been relegated to some of the hardest, most dangerous, and least compensated work. One cannot be detached from privilege while enjoying the benefits of this country's high standard of living; in that sense, we are all part of the beneficiary class. Victims and perpetrators belong to groups that, as a matter of history, are logically treated in the collective sense of reparations rather than the individual sense of the typical legal claimant. Looking to the bottom, we can expand our narrow vision of what a legal relationship should look like, addressing the historical reality before us.

b. Linkage between act and present claim. The linkage of victims and perpetrators for acts occurring in the immediate past is another trait of standard legal claims. Concepts such as the time bar, proximate cause, and laches ensure that claims are fresh, capable of factual determination, and reasonably connected in time and space to the acts of an individual wrongdoer. These rules promote efficiency by allowing people to go about their business without waiting for the ax of the long-gone past to fall. They also satisfy a sense of fairness: the sins of the past should not forever burden the innocent generations of the future, nor should the consequences of one false step create disproportionate fault into eternity.

At what point should we lay to rest the sins of the past and concede to these classical legal doctrines? Traditional discourse limits these doctrines through standard exceptions. Plaintiffs operating under a disability are not required to press their claims until the disability is removed; a continuing wrong does not start the clock running under a statute of limitation until the wrong culminates in an act of finality; fraud in concealing the availability of, or grounds for, an action is another standard exception. All of these exceptions apply to claims for reparations. Indeed, the need for reparations arises precisely because it takes a nation so long to recognize historical wrongs against those on the bottom. Thus, something other than a rigid conception of timeliness is required.

Reparations claims are based on continuing stigma and economic harm. The wounds are fresh and the action timely given ongoing discrimination. Furthermore, the injuries suffered—deprivation of land, resources, educational opportunity, personhood, and political recognition—are disabilities that have precluded successful presentation of the claim at an earlier time. Outright fraud and factual misrepresentation have also delayed presentation of claims.

The question of causal connection in tort law is typically bifurcated into actual and legal, or proximate cause. On the question of whether the wrongs of the past actually caused any harm, the record is available to a finder of fact and will show the requisite but-for causation. The more significant causation question concerns whether the wrong and the harm are so closely connected that the imposition of damages is fair. In the case of reparations, the vertical gap of time is particularly troublesome. Even mainstream jurists, however, recognize that the proximate cause question is essentially political. They have suggested that more egregious wrongs, such as intentional torts, justify reach-

ing across wider gulfs of time and space to connect act and injury. Proximate cause analysis is typically reduced to consideration of the innocence of the victim, the culpability of the wrongdoer, the foreseeability and magnitude of the harm, and the weight of the broad social goals of fair compensation, deterrence and retribution.

An act of racism against a powerless victim is a classic case justifying imposition of a proximate causal connection. The typical reparations claim involves powerless victims in no way capable of contributing to the illegal acts. These situations involve the gross imbalance of moral claim between the innocent and guilty to which the law is peculiarly sensitive.

In determining foreseeability, the classical legal mind typically considers whether a reasonable person contemplating the consequences of a particular act would have imagined the harm that in fact occurred. It would have required no clairvoyant skill to predict the harm that would befall Hawaiians from the loss of their nation and land or the Japanese-Americans taken abruptly from their homes to the desert relocation centers. What a reasonable person would have predicted would occur did in fact occur, thus satisfying one classic test for proximate causal connection.

Deterrence is particularly advanced by reparations doctrine. The very process of determining the validity of claims will force collective examination of the historical record. The discovery and acknowledgment of past wrongs will educate us and help us to avoid repeating the same errors. Acknowledging and paying for the wrong of the World War II relocation, for example, would help us to analyze current proposals for preventive detention. Victim-consciousness, including an acute awareness of threats to freedom, could become part of mainstream consciousness.

The reparations concept also serves the goal of retribution. The decision to award reparations is an act of contrition and humility that can ease victims' bitterness and alienation. A classic legal justification for imposing public liability—avoiding the chaos of individual, private revenge-seeking—is advanced, thereby strengthening the social order.

Still, opponents might argue that some outer limit is required lest claims trace back to the beginning of time, requiring compensation for such past events as the Norman Conquest. The victim's perspective provides an alternative time bar. The outer limit should be the ability to identify a victim class that continues to suffer a stigmatized position enhanced or promoted by the wrongful act in question. Thus, in a European context, the Norman Conquest would not be compensable, because those victims no longer constitute an identifiable and disadvantaged class, while the conquest of identifiable indigenous groups that continue to suffer a degraded position, such as the Sami people of Scandinavia, might be.

c. Relief. Finally, the impossibility of a fair damage assessment is a standard doctrinal objection to reparations. How can we attach a monetary figure to the loss of a right? Amorphous ideas such as sovereignty, dignity, personhood, and liberty are incapable of uniform valuation. We risk undervaluing the right to avoid bankrupting the government, or, conversely, overvaluing it in relation to actual economic losses.

This objection should carry little weight. Judges and juries calculate nonquantifiable damages all the time. As Richard Delgado points out, the refusal to formulate compensation for racial hate messages is in itself racist,[36] given a tort law system that calculates damages for loss of such intangibles as privacy, reputation, and mental tranquility. Similarly, the selective choice to refuse to quantify damages for reparations claimants is suspect.

Damages are also inappropriate, it is charged, because distribution might include the undeserving. In other contexts, however, courts tolerate inexact distribution. The cy pres doctrine in trust law and commercial law, for example, allows such inexactitude. If named trust beneficiaries are absent, a court will determine alternative beneficiaries. The problem of identification is not a sufficient reason to abandon other legal goals and obligations. The courts will attempt to achieve the goals of the law to the extent possible, accepting a certain level of misallocation. If actual victims of a rate-making violation cannot be identified, the court may award damages to the next best class. Similarly, in price-fixing cases, a future price rollback is an appropriate remedy even though some victims have ended their market participation and some beneficiaries are newcomers to the market. Exactitude is less important than other social goals of the law. Better a windfall to nonvictims than to wrongdoers; better rough justice than no justice at all.

A requirement of scientific precision in reparations claims would set a higher standard for reparations claimants. Minorities have often sought to disassociate from the negative stereotypes attributed to their group, only to find that others refuse to think of them as individuals. To be then deprived of benefits because they lack sufficient evidence of group coherency is a double insult.

Group members themselves are in the best position to identify those entitled to relief. Deference to victims respects their rights to personhood and self-determination. Some native Hawaiians, for example, have suggested that a willingness to take an oath of loyalty to the Hawaiian government could be a prerequisite to membership in the beneficiary class. . . .

CLS method reveals the flexibility of legal doctrine and invites new consciousness of what law can be. This method complements the demands for reparations made by those on the bottom. Given the doctrinal basis for reparations thus revealed, the question becomes one of whether, given our conception of justice and our social goals, we wish to exercise that doctrinal option. The following section considers the concept of reparations from the standpoint of restructured liberal ideals and from the standpoint of critical legal thought, with both views informed by non-white experience.

d. "Traneing":[37] *Reparations as transformed liberalism.* . . . The preceding section suggests the doctrinal door for reparations; the next question is whether we should open that door. Just as John Coltrane could "trane" standard melodies into sounds so unique that no mainstream musician could ever appropriate them, radical lawyers hope to transform standard constitutionalism into something their own that no mainstream attorney can exploit. This section considers the transformation of standard liberal and constitutional values to include reparations. Also considered is whether such a transformed consciousness has true critical power, or whether it is fair game for reappropriation.

2. THE REFRAIN OF REPARATIONS WITHIN THE VICTIMS' CONSTITUTION

In interpreting the Constitution and distilling its values, those on the bottom have found the inspiration for a new order. Constitutional interpretation, whether originalist, intentionalist, or pluralist, is expanded by considering the version of the document supported by people of color at Concord, Appamatox, Anzio, and Selma.

For those Americans, the constitutional promise of liberty holds special meaning. Liberty, viewed from the bottom, has encompassed physical liberty from constraint of the person. It has encompassed life itself—freedom from life-threatening abuse as well as the right to seek the nurturance and livelihood human beings need for survival. Liberty has meant personhood and participation—the recognition of one's existence as a human being, free and equal, with power and control over the political processes that govern one's life. The promise of liberty, for those on the bottom, has meant freedom from public and private racism, freedom from inequalities of wealth distribution, and freedom from domination by dynasties. This interpretation of liberty, implicit in the founding document of this nation, is the interpretation that has convinced so many on the bottom to work for, rather than against, the Constitution. That so many have believed in this version of the Constitution, and fought to establish and preserve the union on the basis of that belief, lends historical support to the victim's interpretation.

This interpretation supports a doctrine of reparations. Reparations recognizes the personhood of victims. Lack of legal redress for racist acts is an injury often more serious than the acts themselves, because it signifies the political nonpersonhood of victims. The grant of reparations declares: "You exist. Your experience of deprivation is real. You are entitled to compensation for that deprivation. This nation and its laws acknowledge you."

This recognition is an important prerequisite to the victim's political participation. Classic democratic theory holds that broad participation invigorates and informs the process of governance, and yet the United States tolerates one of the lowest voter participation rates of all the nominally democratic countries. Affirming the legitimacy of victims' claims could bring back into the polity those who had concluded that this government has nothing to offer them. This in turn would bring new legitimacy to the government. The price of a continuing failure to recognize the experience of those at the bottom is the social dislocation and violence that follow when outsiders conclude they can gain nothing by participating in existing governmental processes. Further, discrimination that is officially condoned or ignored can lead to increasingly violent attacks on the victims of that discrimination. All of us, in this sense, are victims: we suffer from the deep divisions between races, the bitter prejudices maintained by both victim and perpetrator groups, and the inability to form community which comes when old wounds go unsalved.

Reparations also begins to address the substantive barriers to liberty. Money for education, housing, medical care, food, job training, cultural preservation, recreation and other pressing needs of victim communities will raise the standard of living of victim groups, promoting their survival and participation. In addition, the transferral of resources alleviates in part the destabilizing inequities in wealth distribution. . . .

3. INTO THE CAGE: THE CRITICAL CHOICE TO ADOPT THE CONCEPT OF REPARATIONS

Ishmael Reed captured the outsider's wary approach to mainstream consciousness in his poem "Dualism: In ralph ellison's invisible man":

i am outside of history. i wish i had some
    peanuts, it looks hungry there in its cage.
i am inside of history. its hungrier than i
    thot.[38]

. . . Reparations is a "critical legalism," a legal concept that has transformative power and avoids the traps of individualism, neutrality, and indeterminancy which plague many mainstream concepts of rights or legal principles. Reparations avoids standard liberal pitfalls because, first, it is a concept directed at remedying wrongs committed against the powerless. Unlike "free speech" or "due process," payment for past injustice is a one-way value: those on the bottom—minority group members, political outsiders, the exploited—will receive reparations.

Second, reparations doctrine supports group rights rather than individual rights and thus escapes some of the ideological traps of traditional rights thinking.

Finally, reparations is at its heart transformative. It recognizes the crimes of the powerful against the powerless. It condemns exploitation and adopts a vision of a more just world. The reparations concept has the aspirational, affirming, idealistic attraction of rights rhetoric, without the weak backbone. While rights rhetoric turns to dust time and again, reparations theory, should we accept and internalize it, may prove more dependable.

This progressive tilt of reparations, however, can mask lurking dangers. Some detect a certain commodifying vulgarity in throwing money at injured people. Richard Abel raises this point in his objection to tort damages for accidental property damage or for negligent infliction of emotional distress. Reparations, one could argue, promotes the idea that everyone has a price, that every wound is salved by cash, that success merely means more money.

The practical shortage of resources in the injured communities weighs against this risk of commodification. Monetary grants will not compensate for the terrible losses sustained. No sum can make up for loss of freedom or sovereignty. The award serves a largely symbolic function, much as the passing of a pig in a Pacific island apology ceremony. The judgment states: "Something terrible has happened for which we are responsible. While no amount can compensate for your loss, we offer here a symbol of our deep regret and our continuing obligation."

Resistance to commodification is important.

If reparations are viewed as an equivalent exchange for past wrongs, continuing claims are terminated. Any obligation to victim groups would end, because their injury is transformed into a commodity and the price paid. A reparations claim would become a dangerous gamble for victims, and a welcome *res judicata* opportunity for perpetrators. One generation could sell away their claim at bargain-basement prices, to the detriment of future generations, in an effort to cash in at the earliest opportunity. Commodification must be resisted if reparations is to be more than a coercive quit-claim mechanism.

A related and indeed troubling objection to reparations comes from looking to the bottom. Some thoughtful victim group members are inclined to reject reparations because of the political reality that any reparations award will come only when those in power decide it is appropriate. Hayden Burgess, a native Hawaiian nationalist lawyer, suggests that any award of cash reparations is inadequate, for it ignores the Hawaiian's primary need—restoration of the Hawaiian government and removal of the U.S. presence in Hawaii. Rather than a top-down model of reparations granted by the United States, Burgess prefers negotiations between the Hawaiians and the United States as equals, perhaps mediated by a neutral third party in an international forum, to determine an appropriate remedy for the overthrow of the Hawaiian government. Burgess suggests that self-determination for the Hawaiian people is guaranteed by international law, and that self-determination includes the right to negotiate with the United States for the return of the Hawaiian Islands. Reparations, on the other hand, would merely enforce the role of the United States as lawgiver and patron.

Reparations awards, in this view, portray the government as benign and contrite. Reparations buys off protest, assuages white guilt, and throws responsibility for continued racism upon the victims. "We paid you, why are you still having problems? It must be in your genes."

To avoid this corruption, victims must define the remedies, and the obligation of reparations must continue until all vestiges of past injustice are dead and buried. Reparations is not, then, equivalent to a standard legal judgment: it is the formal acknowledgment of historical wrong, the recognition of continuing injury, and the commitment to redress, looking always to victims for guidance.

Finally, there is the difficult problem of the effect of reparations to one group upon other victim groups that remain uncompensated. Just as affirmative action in employment and college admission—a form of reparations—may negatively affect the white underclass, monetary reparations to one victim group may result in a new group slipping to the bottom.

Reparations will result in a new form of disadvantage only if they are made outside of a broader consciousness that always looks to the needs of the bottom. A critical theory of reparations recognizes economic as well as racial injustice. It looks to human experience to guide compensation to those in need. Such an approach would view each reparations award to a successful claimant group as a step forward in the long journey toward substantive equality. Thus, progressive Hawaiians view awards already made to Native Americans on the mainland United States not as a chunk taken out of a limited fund, leaving less for Hawaiians, but as a symbol of the possibility of reparations for Hawaiians as well. The arguments that victims will have to make and perpetrators will have to accept before any reparations are awarded will raise consciousnesses about the obligation and need to correct past wrongs. Each separate commitment to the concept of reparations thus internalizes new norms and moves us closer to the end of all forms of victimization.

A theory of reparations formulated in consideration of both a victim's consciousness and the insights of critical legal theorists provides a critical legalism, moving us away from repression and toward community. . . .

NOTES

1. For example, the prosecution in Angela Davis's trial alleged that she had participated in a bizarre prison escape and murder conspiracy. Defending against the felony charges, she and her attorneys educated the jury about the reality of government oppression of blacks, in particular blacks who are communists. In her extended two-hour opening statement to the jury, Davis spoke about her political activities in "the struggle for Black liberation and for the rights of all working people—Chicano, Puerto Rican, Indian, Asian and white." She also spoke of her antiwar and prison rights activities, and the government spy campaign directed against her, contrasting her highly visible political activities with the lack of evidence of criminal acts. The jury acquitted her. See B. Aptheker, *The Morning Breaks: The Trial of Angela Davis* (1975); A. Davis, *Angela Davis, An Autobiography* (1974).

2. A. Leff, "Unspeakable Ethics, Unnatural Law," *Duke L. J.* 1229, 1233 (1979).

3. Unger, *Knowledge and Politics,* 295 (1975). The allusion in the text is to the well-known conclusion of Leff's article (*supra* note 2, at 1249):

> Nevertheless:
> Napalming babies is bad.
> Starving the poor is wicked.
> Buying and selling each other is depraved.
> Those who stood up to and died resisting Hitler, Stalin, Amin, and
> Pol Pot—and General Custer too—have earned salvation.
> Those who acquiesced deserve to be damned.
> There is in the world such a thing as evil.
> [All together now:] Sez who?
> God help us.

4. See J. Rawls, *A Theory of Justice* (1971). . . .

5. See B. Ackerman, *Social Justice in the Liberal State,* 238–39 (1980) (dialogue between hypothetical disadvantaged and advantaged persons on the principle of equal sacrifice).

6. A. Gramsci, "The Intellectuals," in *Selections from the Prison Notebooks,* 5 (1971); see also, C. West, *Prophesy of Deliverance,* 121–22 (1982) (discussion of the application of the organic intellectual model to black American culture).

7. The jurisprudential value of informing abstract reason with concrete experience has been recognized by feminists. See, e.g., MacKinnon, "Feminism, Marxism, Method and the State: An Agenda for Theory (Parts 1 and 2)," 7 *Signs: J. of Women in Culture & Society,* 515 (1982) and 8 *Signs: J. of Women in Culture & Society,* 635 (1983).

8. Our Position in the Present Presidential Canvass," Sept. 10, 1852, reprinted in 2 P. Foner, *The Life and Writings of Frederick Douglass,* 213 (1950).

9. As used here, the "relative autonomy of law" refers to a description of law as connected to but not wholly dependent upon historical, economic, and political realities. In contrast to the view of law as completely reflexive, "relative autonomy" attempts to account for the occasional development of law in seeming contradiction to existing material conditions.

10. "Legal consciousness" refers to ideas about law that control human behavior from within rather than from

without. In contrast to the phenomenon of people obeying law because they are forced to, or because they lack the means to alter existing power structures, legal consciousness suggests that people sometimes internalize legal norms and become mentally unable to imagine and act on other legal possibilities. Ed Greer suggests Gramsci's example of a factory worker who internalizes the concept of private property and thus does not believe it possible for workers to take over the factory. See Greer, "Antonio Gramsci and 'Legal Hegemony,'" in D. Kairys, ed., *The Politics of Law: A Progressive Critique*, 305 (1982); see also Kennedy, "Toward an Historical Understanding of Legal Consciousness: The Case of Classical Legal Thought in America, 1850–1940," in S. Spitzer, ed., 3 *Research in Law and Sociology*, 23 (1980). Kennedy defines legal consciousness as: "the particular form of consciousness that characterizes the legal profession as a social group, at a particular moment. The main peculiarity of this consciousness is that it contains a vast number of legal rules, arguments, and theories, a great deal of information about the institutional workings of the legal process, and the constellation of ideals and goals current in the profession at a given moment." . . .

11. F. Douglass, "Speech at Rochester (July 5, 1852)," reprinted in W. Martin, *The Mind of Frederick Douglass*, 175 (1984). . . .

12. See, e.g., Klare, "Critical Theory and Labor Relations Law," in *The Politics of Law*, *supra* note 10, at 65; Gabel and Feinman, "Contract Law As Ideology," in *id.* at 172.

13. W. E. B. Du Bois, *The Souls of Black Folk* (1969).

14. See Gates, "The Blackness of Blackness: A Critique of the Sign and the Signifying Monkey," H. Gates, ed., in *Black Literature and Literary Theory*, 285, 291 ("Repeating a form and then inverting it through a process of variation is central to jazz—a stellar example is John Coltrane's rendition of 'My Favorite Things,' compared to Julie Andrews's vapid version").

15. E. Stetson, *Black sister* 90 (1981) at xvii. . . .

16. *Id.* The black female poet's task, as Erlene Stetson identifies it, is analogous to the task of the critical theorist. Stetson states: "These poets have brought to their quest a perception of reality that is subconscious and subversive. It is a perception rising out of their disenchantment with the emptiness of American life. It recognizes that the appearance is not reality, but only a partial and ineffective semblance of reality. And finally it is a perception of reality as unified and dialectic rather than fragmented and disjunctive. Subterfuge and ambivalence arise as active strategies for living and for creating art where more direct means for survival and self-expression have been denied." . . .

17. The two central questions Erlene Stetson identifies for black women poets are: "How do we assert and maintain our identities in a world that prefers to believe we do not exist? How do we balance and contain our rage so that we can express both our warmth and love and our anger and pain?" E. Stetson, *supra* note 15, at xvii.

18. G. Brooks, "The 'Womanhood' section of Annie Allen" (1949), quoted in E. Stetson, *supra* note 15, at xix.

19. Archie Shepp said: "Give me leave to state this unequivocal fact: jazz is the product of the whites. . . . It is the progeny of the blacks—my kinsmen. By this I mean: you own the music, we make it"; 32 *Down Beat Music* 11 (Dec. 16, 1965), quoted in R. Backus, *Fire Music* 1 (1976). Backus's work explores the commodification of black musicians, such as Ornette Coleman, by repeating their own words: "In jazz, the Negro is the product. On the 28th of February, 1963, I was staying at 278 East 10th Street. . . . When I got there, I saw lots of stuff on the street. I said Oh, . . . somebody's passed in my building. The closer I got, I could see it was my own stuff. The marshal had chopped the door down and put all my shit out on the streets. And I was only one month behind in rent. So when I realized I couldn't pay $97.50 for an apartment, and I had six records out . . . [t]hat is when I realized I was in the wrong business"; *id.* at 44–45. . . .

20. T. Monk, as quoted by Mary Lou Williams. Hentoff, "Hear Me Talkin' to You," 340–41 (1955), reprinted in R. Backus, *supra* note 19, at 37.

21. See R. Backus, *supra* note 19, at 86. "[W]e see jazz as one of the most meaningful social, aesthetic contributions to America," explains Archie Shepp. "[I]t is anti-war . . . it is for Cuba; it is for the liberation of all people. That is the nature of jazz. That's not far-fetched. Why is that so? Because jazz is a music itself born out of oppression, born out of the enslavement of my people."

22. Captain/Chaplain George Aki wrote in a dedication to those who died: "They were ordinary youths wanting to live, but they became 'extraordinary' as they dared to choose to come forth from the concentration camps to fight for the land that incarcerated them and their families. And they became heroes because they dared to take the first step to become 'equals' with others in American society.

"And we know that they sincerely desired to return home when their work was done. But they died, not in their homeland, but alone, in agony, in a strange land . . . ignorant of the legacy that their passing would create. . . . They attained the stature of giants as they fought and secured human rights, justice, and equality not only for themselves and their families but for all who were oppressed"; C. Tanaka, *Go For Broke: A Pictorial History of the Japanese-American 100th Infantry Batalion and the 442d Regimental Combat Team*, iii (1982). *Nisei* veterans frequently repeated this kind of rhetoric to explain why they fought.

23. *Korematsu v. United States*, 323 U.S. 214 (1944). For a recent critique of the *Korematsu* decision, see Yamamoto, "*Korematsu* Revisited—Correcting the Injustice of Extraordinary Government Excess and Lax Judicial Review: Time for a Better Acommodation of National Security Concerns and Civil Liberties," 25 *Santa Clara L. Rev.*, 1 (1986).

24. See *Korematsu v. United States*, 584 F. Supp. 1406 (N.D. Cal. 1984) (vacating the conviction of Fred Kore-

matsu because of the manifest injustice resulting from the government's deliberate withholding of relevant information in the original judicial proceedings). Fred Korematsu's exoneration was the result of a Writ of Error Corum Nobis, written by *sansei* attorneys, and filed with the U.S. District Court for the Northern District of California, January 19, 1983 (No. CR 27630W). See Yamamoto, *supra* note 23. See also D. Minami, "Coram Nobis and Redress," in R. Daniels, S. Taylor and H. Kitano. eds., *Japanese Americans: From Relocation to Redress* (1986). The decisions to defy the evacuation orders were based upon a deeply held belief in the principles of American democracy and the obligation to challenge injustice. See Hosokawa, *JACL in Quest of Justice,* 175–78 (1982); "The Japanese American Coram Nobis Cases: Exposing the Myth of Disloyalty," 13 *N.Y.U. Rev. of L. & Soc. Change* 199 (winter 1984–85).

25. "Liberal legalism," as used here, refers to both the ideology of liberalism (exemplified by individual rights, procedural fairness, equality, and liberty) and the corollative commitment to legalism (an appeal to legal reasoning and the rule of law as somehow logical, coherent, and determinant). The question presented in this section is whether, ascribing for the moment at least some moral and descriptive validity to a liberal concept of law, it is possible to derive reparations for Native Hawaiians and Japanese-Americans from such law; cf. Klare, "Law Making as Praxis," 40 *Telos,* 123, 132 n. 28 (1979): "I mean by 'liberal legalism' the particular historical incarnation of legalism, 'the ethical attitude that holds moral conduct to be a matter of rule following,' which characteristically serves as the institutional and philosophical foundation of the legitimacy of the legal order in capitalist societies. Its essential features are the commitment to general 'democratically' promulgated rules, the equal treatment of all citizens before the law, and the radical separation of morals, politics and personality from judicial action.

"Liberal legalist jurisprudence and its institutions are closely related to the classical liberal political tradition, exemplified in the work of Hobbes, Locke and Hume. The metaphysical underpinnings of liberal legalism are supplied by the central themes of that tradition: the notion that values are subjective and derive from personal desire, and that therefore ethical discourse is conducted profitably only in instrumental terms; the view that society is an artificial aggregation of autonomous individuals; the separation in political philosophy between public and private interest, between state and civil society; and a commitment to a formal or procedural rather than a substantive conception of justice."

26. Contemporary constitutional scholars are in virtual agreement that the *Korematsu* decision is "bad law" according to conventional legal analysis and moral theory: see, for example, Yamamoto, Takahata, "The Case of Korematsu v. United States: Could It Be Justified Today?" 6 *Hawaii L. Rev.,* 109 (1984); Rostow, "The Japanese American Cases—A Disaster," 54 *Yale L. J.,* 489 (1945). John Tateishi quotes Senator Sam Ervin as calling the relocation

"the single most blatant violation of the Constitution in our history"; J. Tateishi, *And Justice For All: An Oral History of the Japanese American Detention Camps,* xvi (1984). This view eventually came to be shared by Chief Justice Earl Warren, who, as governor of California, had supported evacuation. In his memoirs, quoted in R. Wilson and B. Hosokawa, *East to America: A History of the Japanese in the United States,"* 291 (1980), Warren wrote, I have since deeply regretted the removal order and my own testimony advocating it. . . . Whenever I thought of the innocent little children who were torn from home, school friends, and congenial surroundings, I was conscience-stricken. It was wrong to react so impulsively. . . . It demonstrates the cruelty of war when fear, get-tough military psychology, propaganda and racial antagonism combine. . . ." [. . .]

27. General DeWitt, whose final report on the evacuation was heavily relied on by the *Korematsu* majority in upholding the constitutionality of the evacuation orders, cited the fact that no Japanese-American had yet committed an act of sabotage as a "disturbing and confirming indication that such action will be taken." J. Tateishi, *supra* note 26, at xv. After all, as then-California Attorney General Earl Warren reasoned, Pearl Harbor had been a well-timed surprise; *id.* at xv-xvi. Justice Frank Murphy cites that "amazing statement" from the final report in a footnote to his dissenting opinion in *Korematsu,* 323 U.S. at 241, n. 15. His opinion uses the final report extensively to demonstrate the obvious racial discrimination in the orders.

Ironically, Japanese in Hawaii, who retained stronger cultural ties to Japan, were not interned because their labor was vital to the economy, and because Hawaii lacked the racist sentiments of the West Coast; *id.* at xvii.

28. See Yamamoto, *supra* note 26, at 2. Materials recently obtained through Freedom of Information Act requests "revealed two extraordinary facts: first, government intelligence services unequivocally informed the highest officials of the military and of the War and Justice Departments that the West Coast Japanese as a group posed no serious danger to the war effort, and that no need for mass evacuation existed; and second, that the Supreme Court was deliberately misled about the "military necessity" that formed the basis of the *Korematsu* decision." Yamamoto notes the concurrence of the lower federal courts on this point. See *Horhi v. United States,* No. 84–5460, slip op. (D.C. Cir. 1986); *Korematsu v. United States (Korematsu II),* 584 F. Supp. 1406 (N.D. Cal. 1984).

29. See *Korematsu II, supra* note 28, and *Hirabayashi v. United States (Hirabayashi II),* 627 F. Supp. 1445 (W.D. Wash. 1986); see also, Irons, "In Re Hirabayashi," *The Nation,* Mar. 1, 1986, at 229.

30. An internment victim recalls: "Up at Manzanar it's 100 degrees during the day, but at night it's cold as hell. . . . You had a dust storm come through. You get a half an inch of dust. . . . Used to come from underneath the floor. The floor used to have at least half an inch openings;" J. Tateishi, *supra* note 26, at 95. Internees were held at racetracks,

stables, and fair grounds while permanent detention centers were built. Jerry Enomoto testified to the conditions at the holding camps: "Evacuees ate communally, showered communally, defecated communally.... [N]o partitions had been built between toilets.... [T]he stench became oppressive in the summer heat, especially in stables which had been merely scraped out and no floors put in"; N. Kittrie, *The Tree of Liberty*, 615 (1986).

31. One man recalls the death of his wife and twin daughters at childbirth: "And so they worked on her and then all I can remember is telling, you know, help me, help me. Through junior high school in the rough neighborhood and everything like that, I could always protect her physically; but I just stood there holding her hand you know, holding on to her, and she just drained away.... I don't know what happened to the babies.... Whether it was carelessness. Or that it was something that was going to happen. I know for a fact that the twins were born and the camp did not have facilities.... years later I found out one of the twins had lived twenty-four hours"; J. Tateishi, *supra* note 26, at 96. Mabel Ota tells of her father's death from a diabetic coma, misdiagnosed as melancholia and treated with electroshock therapy; *id.* at 111. Another woman recalls being shipped to Arkansas with her two-week-old infant, who had pneumonia: "We were supposed to be on a medical train. There was only one doctor ... and his wife couldn't even get hot water for the baby's formula"; *id.* at 126–27. The same woman lost a mother-in-law to cancer. There were no facilities for cancer treatment in camp; *id.* at 131. Dr. Ota reported "suicides ... shortened lives ... heart disease and cancers, the depressive states, all brought on by the terrible consequences of the Evacuation," in an August 28, 1981, letter to the editor of *The Rafu Shimpo*, a Japanese-American community newspaper. A nurse recalls shortages of supplies and staff, leading to "a lot of unnecessary deaths in camp. You wouldn't believe it. It's just that there were not enough people to watch the patients...." J. Tateishi, *supra* note 26, at 150. Women died in childbirth because no surgeons were available to perform cesareans when necessary, and untrained staff inadvertently killed patients, as in one case of mercury poisoning from a broken thermometer; *id.* Yoshiye Togasaki, the first Japanese woman graduate of Johns Hopkins Medical School, recalls treating the sick in the camps without the necessary vaccines, sanitary facilities, or medications; *id.* at 224–25. Mabel Ota reports dismay at finding her diabetic father eating a camp meal of bread, potatoes, and spaghetti; *id.* at 111. One mother describes leaving behind her three-year-old with measles. "It was easier for me because he was asleep. I don't know. But when I thought about how he might wake up and be in a strange place, with strange people, I just really broke down and cried. I cried all morning over it, but there was nothing we could do but leave him. He stayed at general hospital and joined us at Manzanar in three weeks"; *id.* at 24. In some cases, families were forced by the government to institutionalize handicapped relatives who had been cared for at home before relocation; *id.* at 8.

32. Attorney Minoru Yasui, for example, described his father's assimilated status: "Masuo Yasuo Yasui was a member of the local Rotary Club, a member of the board of the Apple Grower's Association, a pillar of the local Methodist Church ... a friend and neighbor of the local bank president, the most prominent lawyer in town, the editor of the local newspaper, and all the 'important people' in Hood River, Oregon"; J. Tateishi, *supra* note 26, at 64. Internment victim Helen Murao recalls, "as children, we went to school as the only Japanese family ... our peer associations were not with Japanese people at all, so this [internment] was my first experience among Japanese people"; *id.* at 44.

33. J. Tateishi, *supra* note 26, at 14.

34. President Grover Cleveland's Special Message to Congress, Dec. 18, 1893, 26 *Cong. Rec.*, 309.

35. Oral accounts of the internment are the same across economic classes of Japanese-Americans. In one such account, the mother begins by describing her six-year-old son's food poisoning and her desperate attempts to obtain medical care for him. He was taken to a hospital outside the internment camp, but the mother was not allowed inside the hospital. The next day the parents wanted to call the hospital, but military officials refused. Three internees threatened violence, and finally permission was granted to make the call. The mother succeeded in getting to the hospital to retrieve her child. She then describes what followed: "Here's this little six-year-old kid; he was lying on his side and just crying, but silently, you couldn't hear him. I asked him what was the matter and he just threw his arms around me and held on to me. And he said, 'Oh, take me back to camp. They were going to let me die last night.' I said, 'What are you talking about?' And he said, 'Well, the nurse said, "Let this little Jap die, don't even go near him.",' And to this day he remembers that. He's forty-five years old now, but he still remembers that"; J. Tateishi, *supra* note 26, at 218.

36. See generally, Delgado, "Words That Wound: A Tort Action for Racial Insults, Epithets, and Name-Calling," 17 *Harv. C.R.-C.L. L. Rev.*, 133 (1982).

37. "Traneing" is a verb derived from the name of jazz musician John Coltrane; it means, roughly, doing what John Coltrane does. As used here, it refers to the ability to take something ordinary and limited, and to transform it into something extraordinary and unlimited in its potential for promoting the human spirit.

38. As quoted in Gates, *supra* note 14, at 316.

THE CLOUDED PRISM: MINORITY CRITIQUE OF THE CRITICAL LEGAL STUDIES MOVEMENT

Harlon L. Dalton

I'D like to begin by discussing some remarks that Bob Gordon made in a sensitive essay entitled "New Developments in Legal Theory."[1] . . . Professor Gordon begins by assaying the relationship between theorists and practitioners, or, more precisely, the tendency of people who attend Critical Legal Studies conferences to sort themselves into two categories—theorists and practitioners. As you listen to the passage, I want you to substitute mentally the phrase "people of color" for the term "practitioners." I ask this of you for two reasons. First, most minority scholars are, by virtue of our life circumstances, practitioners in one way or another, people committed to pursuing an active program to change the situation of our people. (I will return to this point in a moment.) Second, it seems to me that in any event the position of "practitioners" and that of people of color, vis-à-vis the tastemakers of CLS, are much the same.

After acknowledging the practitioner/theorist split, Gordon observes: "It is not—not at all—that the 'practitioners' are against theory." (Remember, "practitioners" equals "people of color.")

> They are hungry for theory that would help make sense of their practices; that would order them meaningfully into larger patterns of historical change or structures of social action; that would help to resolve the perpetual dilemma of whether it is or is not a contradiction in terms to be a "radical lawyer," whether one is inevitably corrupted by the medium in which one works, whether one's victories are in the long run defeats or one's defeats victories; or that would suggest what tactics, in the boundless ocean of meanness and constraint that surrounds us, to try next.[2]

I want to affirm that Gordon's is a fair and accurate description both of practitioners and of people of color. We hunger for theory. But, as Gordon goes on to point out, there is the lingering and widespread suspicion within the CLS movement that the theorists do not hun-

ger for praxis. And it is this absence of a positive program on the part of many in CLS (with some quite notable exceptions), and indeed the disdain for program by some,[3] that is one of the central difficulties that people of color have with the Critical Legal Studies movement. I think that this difficulty is rooted in biography, in specific history, in what Cornel West refers to as "genealogy." . . .

The black, brown, red, and yellow folks who have circled around CLS's door in fluctuating numbers for the last ten years [are] always invited in for tea, but rarely invited to stay for supper, lest we use the wrong intellectual fork. No matter how smart or bookish we were, we could not retreat from the sights, sounds, and smells of the communities from which we came. We learned from life as well as from books; we learned about injustice, social cruelty, political hypocrisy, and sanctioned terrorism from the mouths of our mothers and fathers and from our very own experiences. Books sometimes confirmed that reality; more often they misrepresented or were indifferent to our reality. And from the beginning we learned, not as an article of political faith but rather as a simple fact of life, that our fate and that of all persons of similar hue were inseparably intertwined. That fundamental connectedness, together with our distinctive subcultures, nourished and sustained us, created in us an unshakable sense of community. The lucky ones among us reveled in that community, fed on it; others of us resented it, or tried to hide from it. But escape was not possible, for the community was within us and we were branded forever.

Part of the reality of that community, at least in our time and space, was that "the life of the mind" as an overriding and singular commitment was not possible. Not only would "putting on airs" not win us many friends, but neither would it position us to influence people. As Malcolm X used to ask, "What do you call a black man with a Ph.D.?" And, as every person of color in this room knows, the answer is "nigger." A thoroughgoing familiarity with Foucault, Derrida, Habermas, and Gramsci will not save us from "the fishy stare on the bus." And so, whether out of social concern or self-preservation, we learned from the start to harness our brains to the problems of the day. We felt the freedom to play with mind puzzles only after the practical intellectual work of the day was done.

I think that the genealogical differences between classic CLSers on the one hand, and us pretenders, on the other, helps to explain why CLS patriarchs (again with some notable exceptions) feel no need to articulate a positive program, and in some cases even glory in the absence of one, whereas people of color cannot be satisfied unless and until a program emerges. Similarly, the quite distinct social circumstance of white males has led to a "rights critique" that is oblivious to, and potentially disruptive of, the interests of people of color. . . .

The failure or refusal to develop a positive program and the dismissive critique of rights discourse are perhaps the most significant theoretical divides between classic CLS and progressive people of color. There are, however, other points of tension that exist wholly apart from any particular theoretical concern. . . . Two thoughts come primarily to mind: one is our sense of having been silenced by CLS, and the second is our sense of having been appropriated or used.

How have we been silenced? One way . . . is the existence of high barriers to entry into discussion.[4] I am not familiar with the CLS version of "talking that talk" and "it don't mean a thing if it ain't got that swing," but there's a sense in which if you don't talk that talk, you won't be heard. . . .

Fortunately, there are several signs that this mental lockstep is breaking down. . . . As the kinetic discussion at the plenary session of this conference demonstrated,[5] there is a fair amount of discontent with the trap of prescribed language.

A second silencing mechanism. . . is especially insidious. My favorite form of it is: "I don't want to be made to feel like a guilty white male." This conversation-stopper has really sapped the energy of the caring people—white, black, brown, and yellow—who worked hardest at putting together this conference. And it has threatened to derail those of us who were never too sure we were welcome on this train in the first place.

A third silencing mechanism, the one mentioned most frequently at the minority caucus is, I think, the simplest: exclusion from all dialogue that matters. As John Powell put it, "I feel spoken for and I feel spoken about, but rarely do I feel spoken to." . . .

To see this phenomenon in action we need look no further than the way in which this conference was initially planned. White folk decided to have a conference about the concerns of colored folk and set an agenda that focused solely on what CLS could do for us. It apparently did not occur to the original organizers that the objects of the conference might also serve in a more creative, more constructive, more personal, and less reified role. Nor did it occur to them, as best I can tell, that a central focus of any such conference should be what we can do for CLS. In what way is the work of CLS impoverished by our absence from the dinner table? We do have a hell of a lot to offer.

For example, I take it that everyone drawn to CLS is interested in specifying in concrete terms the dichotomy between autonomy and community. If so, talk to us. Talk *to* us. Listen to us—we have lots to say, out of the depths of our own experiences. For many of us, our sense of community is a strength, a resource, something we struggle to hang on to, sometimes in the most peculiar ways, especially when the pull of autonomy is strongest. The day that I am awarded tenure, should that happy event occur, any pleasure that I experience will be more than offset by the extreme panic that I'm sure will set in: I will worry that I have been propelled (or, more honestly, that I have wittingly, selfishly and self-destructively propelled myself) two steps further away from so much that has nurtured me for so long. Even for those of us who have reveled in the sense of connectedness that, paradoxically, racial oppression has conferred upon us, there is a kicker: we don't have any choice in the matter. We can't choose to be a part of the community; we can't choose not to

be a part of the community. It's not like deciding whether to go to CLS summer camp this
year.

Not only do we have much to offer that
persons with a different genealogy cannot otherwise apprehend, but what we have to offer is
important, as bell hooks so beautifully demonstrated. With creativity and an open mind, "we
can," she informs us, "use information from the
margin to transform how we think about the
whole."[6]

Let me turn briefly to the other tension
between classical CLSers and us pretenders,
which is not specifically rooted in differences
over theory: the feeling or fear of many people
of color that even as we are being silenced or
ignored, our concerns are being appropriated.
Let me offer just one simple anecdote to illustrate. A couple of days ago I described to a once
lost, now found friend, Trina Grillo, an article
I had recently read that was in the form of a
dialogue between Duncan Kennedy and Peter
Gabel. The piece, entitled "Roll Over Beethoven,"[7] uses as an epigraph the chorus of Chuck
Berry's song of the same name:

Roll over Beethoven
Tell Tchaikovsky the news.
I got the rockin' pneumonia
Need a shot of rhythm and blues.

Trina's response was characteristically passionate, funny, and insightful. Her second reaction
was, "Gee, isn't it appropriate that they would
identify themselves as rock stars."; her first reaction had been, "How dare they appropriate our
music in that way?"

That remark instantly resonated for me, but
it was a bit of a surprise coming from Trina;
when I first met her in college twenty-two years
ago, she terrorized me into paying attention to
Bob Dylan, despite my loudly voiced protest
that I didn't want to listen to any music "by
that white boy" who, in any event, "can't even
sing." Trina disarmed me by agreeing with
both of my assessments, but pronouncing them
irrelevant. And I learned that she was right:
Dylan can't sing but he sure can preach, and he
may be white but he is universal as well.

So it seemed unlikely that Trina was ob-

jecting in principle to white folks listening to
Chuck Berry, and as we talked it became clear
that her concern, and mine, was deeper and
more specific. The employment, or "deployment" if you prefer, of "Roll Over Beethoven"
as the title and epigraph for a dialogue between
two classic CLSers suggested a deep concern
for the needs of black folk and a heightened
sensitivity to our culture and history. Yet nothing in the fifty-plus pages that followed the
Chuck Berry chorus fulfilled that promise. Nor
indeed did the piece provide "a shot of rhythm
and blues"—Mantovani perhaps . . . or at best
Windham Hill.

Let me end on a somewhat more positive
note. At the minority caucus, we discussed not
only our alienation from CLS but also our
attraction to it. The latter subject produced a
quite rich and full conversation. As Kimberlé
Crenshaw observed, one of the nice things
about dealing with CLSers is that you don't
have to start from scratch in a conversation.
You can start at step five or so, and then have
an argument. We are not unmindful of the fact
that there are, within the CLS literature and in
practice as well, instances of concern for the
needs of people of color,[8] albeit usually without
recourse to our own "take" on those needs.
Questions of race aside, there is some terrific
writing in the now-quite-voluminous CLS literature. . . . And there are many wonderful people among the members of the conference, a list
that overlaps but is not necessarily coextensive
with the list of folks I like to read. Furthermore,
there are some quite wonderful scholars and
human beings among the people who classify
themselves as "fellow travelers," the category in
which most progressive people of color place
ourselves. . . .

Finally, I am quite drawn, intellectually and
spiritually, to the work of many "femcrits."
Indeed, the only reason I did not place some of
them on my illustrative list of CLS favorites is
that I'm not sure of the extent to which they
have been included as part of the CLS family
by those with the power to recognize kinship.[9]
That said, I suspect that one of the likely
outcomes of this conference will be a deepening
of solidarity between people of color and others

in the fellow traveler category, and between people of color and femcrits. More broadly, I hope that this conference results in a sense of deepened solidarity among all of us here, regardless of race or gender, who have on occasion felt silenced, or at least stifled, who have felt devalued or undervalued, who have felt a bit manipulated, or at least pulled along in a direction we weren't sure we wanted to follow.[9]

NOTES

1. Gordon, "New Developments in Legal Theory," in D. Kairys, ed., *The Politics of Law: A Progressive Critique* (1982).

2. *Id.* at 281.

3. I am not unmindful of the concern expressed by many critical legal theorists that until and unless we have successfully jettisoned our dominant belief systems, any attempt to formulate a positive program will likely (inevitably?) reintroduce the very patterns of domination and alienation that we seek to escape.

I am likewise aware of the related conviction that the best way (the only way?) to break out of the straitjacket of "liberal legal consciousness" is to concentrate on delegitimating—"trashing," if you prefer—its conceptual underpinnings. Indeed, I share the concern that we risk undermining ourselves by moving ahead with a positive program before the critique has adequately altered our consciousness. I also recognize the utility and even necessity of delegitimation. I am convinced, however, that the movement can and must proceed on two tracks simultaneously. Despite the risk of replicating the tried and untrue path, we must create even as we reenvision. In my view, negative critique and positive program are, or at least can be, symbiotic; the former launches the latter and keeps it on course, whereas the latter saves the former from petulance and self-parody.

4. The conference's opening plenary session was entitled "Thinking About Race in America." The panelists Rodolfo Acuna (professor of Chicano studies at California State University at Northridge), bell hooks (assistant professor of English, African, and Afro-American studies at Yale), and Cornel West (associate professor of philosophy of religion at the Yale Divinity School), gave powerful, mind-expanding presentations, each in his or her own quite distinctive voice. During the question and answer period, bell hooks took the occasion to ask her colleague and friend Cornel West a question: "Why do you insist on using all that meta-language when you know it serves to put distance between you and the very people you're talking about?" The ensuing intellectual donnybrook was the most lively and broadly participatory session of the conference.

5. I refer here to the reaction to bell hooks' critique of meta-language. *See supra* note 4 and accompanying text.

6. To illustrate this point, hooks at the conference drew upon the work of Rollo May. She discussed how May, in his book *The Courage to Create* (1975), described his attempt to understand how children who are abandoned by their parents cope. May, after interviewing a number of subjects, noted a marked discrepancy between the responses of children from privileged circumstances and those of children born into the underclass. The latter were much more successful at coping with abandonment in a healthy and constructive way.

Hooks observed that many, if not most, scholars would assume that this puzzling disparity was somehow explained by the unfathomable "pathology of the ghetto" and would therefore either trim the sample to exclude "atypical" households, or drop a footnote acknowledging the mystery of it all. May did neither; instead he explored further the results "from the margin" and discovered that the difference between the two groups lay in the extent to which the children knew and understood early on that abandonment might be their fate. In the privileged families, discord and dissolution were never discussed, and the truth was squelched and covered over. By contrast, underclass parents leveled with their kids about the precarious state of the family. The children, therefore, had a jump on coming to grips with their eventual abandonment and, more importantly, did not deeply resent their parents for keeping them in the dark.

The moral drawn by hooks from this story is that May's decision to take seriously the people at the margin of society taught him something of benefit to the whole, a lesson that likely would have escaped him had he focused solely on the center. hooks illustrates this same phenomenon in a different context in her own book, *Feminist Theory From Margin to Center* (1984), especially in chapter one.

7. Gabel and Kennedy, "Roll Over Beethoven," 36 *Stan. L. Rev.*, 1 (1984).

8. A notable example in the literature is Alan Freeman's "Legitimizing Racial Discrimination through Antidiscrimination Law: A Critical Review of Supreme Court Doctrine," 62 *Minn. L. Rev.* 1049 (1978) [the essay is included in this volume—ED.]. A notable example in practice is the decision to devote this conference to racism as a phenomenon. Notwithstanding my criticisms about the way the conference was put together and the anticipatory pouting of various powers that be, the simple decision to have the conference at all is commendable, and of enormous benefit in these parlous times.

9. It was suggested to me, following my remarks, that my implicit recognition of the prevailing statusarchy serves, in a real sense, to perpetuate it. Upon reflection, I'm inclined to agree. I should have realized that in order to transcend, one sometimes has to transcend.

10. During the plenary session on the last day of the conference, it was suggested that white males had felt silenced by my remarks. I was instantly reminded of my own response, at age seven or so, to a playmate whose mother had recently died. "I know how you feel," I said knowingly. "We just buried my favorite turtle after it softened to death."

It was also suggested that an attempt had been made to "kill the father." Insofar as the comment was meant to evoke Freud, I will charitably let it pass. There is, however, a sense in which the speaker was right. I do think that the time has come to say goodbye to bwana, the Great White Father. However, I, for one, have no taste for blood. The smart ruler, upon sensing that an aroused populace has taken to the streets in the direction of the palace, will dash to the front of the crowd, baton in hand, and proclaim the whole thing a victory parade. Far from wanting to kill the father, I want the person inside that role to take his rightful place as my brother. Older brother, perhaps, in the ways of the world we would reenvision together if not in the ways of the one we presently inhabit—wiser even. But brother, nonetheless.

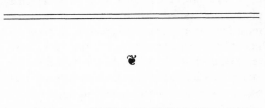

BEYOND CRITICAL LEGAL STUDIES: THE RECONSTRUCTIVE THEOLOGY OF DR. MARTIN LUTHER KING, JR.

Anthony E. Cook

IN recent years, criticism of the Critical Legal Studies movement by minority legal scholars has intensified the controversy surrounding this body of nontraditional scholarship. Although initially inspired by the zeal with which CLS's adherents questioned the legitimacy and exposed the oppressiveness of legal ideology, some minority scholars are troubled by CLS's reluctance to acknowledge the unique relationship between law and the history of American racism. These scholars assert that CLS's critique of the liberal state, and this critique's implicit constructive vision, fail to appreciate the role the state can play in neutralizing and eradicating ubiquitous racial oppression. Furthermore, minority scholars have criticized the failure of the CLS movement to acquaint itself with the history and perspective of those who have, in different contexts, endured the problems of most concern to CLS—problems associated with hierarchy, powerlessness, and legitimating ideologies.

Given this context, this article has two goals. First, by focusing on the African-American church and its role in the struggle for African-American liberation, I hope to foster a greater knowledge of, and appreciation for, the concrete experiences of the powerless and oppressed. I contend that such knowledge and appreciation is indispensable to CLS's primary project of deconstruction. Second, I wish to point out the particular relevance of the critical theology of Dr. Martin Luther King, Jr., for the increasing numbers of legal scholars who have begun to look to religion as a potential source for alternative conceptions of community. As the towering organic intellectual of twentieth-century American life, King integrated theory, experience, and transformative struggle to create a rich and effective form of critical activity.

In his attempt to reconcile the contradictions of various theological perspectives, King undertook a project similar to that of CLS—to understand the hegemony of repressive ideologies and to deconstruct the limits they appear to set on the possibilities of change. Moreover, King was deeply committed to the reconstruction of a social reality based on a radically different assessment of human potential, a vision he often referred to as the "Beloved Community." As a result, a closer examination of King's intellectual odyssey may provide valuable insight to those CLS scholars interested in not merely explicating an unjust social order, but in reconstructing a just community. . . .

I. THE LIMITS OF THE CLS PROJECT

A. The Project and the Problem

. . .

CLS has unabashedly challenged the accepted values of classical liberalism by undermining the interpretations of private property, individual rights, equality of opportunity, meritocracy, and governmental power which have sustained and reproduced oppressive hierarchies of wealth and power. Although liberalism purports to effect a neutral reconciliation between individual freedom and the collective constraints needed to preserve that freedom, CLS suggests that such neutrality is inherently illusory. Through structured argumentation based on manipulable legal categories, the legal system legitimates a status quo characterized by vast inequalities of wealth and power.

. . . One of the goals of the CLS project is to understand why people acquiesce in the social systems that oppress them. CLS asks how the backdrop values, which are in fact indeterminate, find their way into mass consciousness as conventional wisdom, thereby limiting the range of acceptable—or even conceivable— social arrangements. CLS scholars purport to show that our social-political world, from which law is inseparable, is of our own making. . . . We can choose to structure our institutions in hierarchy and dominance, and limit our understanding of others and ourselves to the distorted roles and images generated by social rules and laws, or we can choose to alleviate the alienation and loneliness that stifle our societal needs and impulses, by restructuring those institutions and practices which distance us from others and cause us to perceive others with trepidation and suspicion. None of what we now experience and blindly accept is carved in stone. If we despair over our present social order—and CLS believes that many of us do, whether we realize it or not—we can "hew out of the mountain of despair a stone of hope."[1]

But how do we begin this reconstructive enterprise? What use do we make of our new-found liberation? If we are free to define collectively our existence and to transcend our present context, are we any better equipped to act than before? How do we know that the community to which we aspire is better than the social order we transcend? How do we know that a world of love, understanding, and mutual trust awaits us, rather than a world of greater oppression and alienation, filled with the uncertainties born of the knowledge that all that separates civility from brutality is our faith in the goodness of humankind? In short, what values and concerns will guide us in this reconstructive moment?

The failure to address these important questions constitutes the most significant shortcoming of the CLS project, which is in part explained by the fact that the "answers" can only develop, tentatively and in fits and starts, through the concrete experiences of struggle and survival. Yet CLS consistently deemphasizes the individual and institutional experiences of those who are subjugated. Thus CLS's theoretical deconstruction of liberalism fails to explain—or even ask—why subordinated individuals, those most disadvantaged by hierarchies of wealth and power, place such faith in the liberal state.

There are at least three possible explanations for this faith on the part of subordinated peoples. The first possibility is false consciousness: the rhetoric of liberalism has duped those at the bottom of the social and economic hierarchy. Liberalism's protestations of equality, fairness, and neutrality have convinced them that their disadvantages are somehow just, perhaps because other results have given them advantages in the past or may do so in the future. The second possibility is denial: people want to believe that the system is working as it claims,

although they know it is not. Continued faith in the disproven values of neutrality and objectivity may allow us to avoid the onerous reality that life is what we make of it—no more and no less. Finally, individuals may suffer from neither false consciousness nor denial, but may simply be ostracized or marginalized, limited by the existential constraints of enslavement, apartheid, intimidation, or poverty, which make meaningful social struggle difficult if not impossible.[2]

The kind of deconstruction to which CLS is methodologically committed—what I characterize as "theoretical deconstruction with a limited experiential deconstruction"—may indeed liberate the first grouping, people duped by the rhetoric of liberalism. Such individuals have not perceived the contradictions of their belief systems and have not confronted the harsh realities of their existence. Thoughtful discussion and examination may liberate them from the mental constructs that limit their self-actualization.

People in the second grouping do not suffer from false consciousness. Although theoretical deconstruction can serve as a catalyst to generate a sense of empowerment, these people are most in need of constructive goals of social struggle and practical strategies of mobilization. They lack a sense of community with those who share their feelings and who are willing to engage in various forms of collective social struggle to transform existing conditions. The knowledge that they are not alone in their pain and isolation is often enough to shake these people from the stupor of their self-denial and encourage them both to formulate the goals of social struggle and to adopt viable strategies for securing those goals.

People in the third grouping suffer neither from false consciousness nor self-denial; rather, the dominant powers' use of various methods of coercion and social control simply does not provide much space for substantive struggle. Critical activity must focus here on alleviating these existential constraints as well as on exposing the role of ideology in maintaining them.

Theorists in search of alternative foundations

for human community, those seeking to replace one kind of faith with another, must embrace a form of critical activity that deals with the problems of those suffering from false consciousness, denial, and existential subjugation. By themselves, theoretical deconstruction and an experiential deconstruction preoccupied with the oppression of liberalism cannot achieve this objective. Although theoretical deconstruction is important, the ultimate goal of critical theory should be the reconstruction of community from the debris of theoretical deconstruction, a project capable of reaching each of the groupings outlined above. I suggest . . . that the prophetic Christianity of Dr. Martin Luther King, Jr., as well as the most enabling assumptions of liberal theory provide sturdy ground for this reconstructive endeavor. . . .

B. Critical Legal Studies and Reconstructive Vision

. . . In this section, I examine the relationship between a limited conception of deconstruction and the deficient reconstructive project found in the CLS critique.

I. CRITICAL LEGAL STUDIES: A SUMMARY

> What happens is people start translating their political feelings into unconscionability arguments or right-to-privacy arguments without realizing that there is a weird dissociation taking place. . . . Without even knowing it, they start talking as if "we" were rights-bearing citizens who are "allowed" to do this or that by something called "the state," which is a passivizing illusion—actually a hallucination that establishes the presumptive political legitimacy of the status quo.[3]

Many CLS scholars see the liberal conception of community as heavily dependent on the faith that the state can and does set community-defining boundaries that establish the limits of collective action through the neutral application of objective and determinate principles. Although sovereignty is theoretically vested in "the people," the specific nature and conditions of that sovereignty are the subject of a "legal" text and subject to the interpretation of a "judicial aristocracy" of federal judges. CLS asks,

"On what grounds can the people be legitimately robbed of this sovereignty?" One response is that the courts must enforce the boundaries articulated by the Constitution that define the spheres of privacy within which the collective cannot intrude. This enforcement requires a delicate balance between individual rights and duties. The apparatus of liberal rights mediates the relationship between ourselves and others whose cooperation both threatens, and is indispensable to, our survival. Under liberal theory, the process of mediation requires the establishment of private spheres of autonomy into which others are not permitted to intrude. A liberal discourse of abstract rights and duties purports to map out the borders of these private spheres of autonomy and to set the conditions under which they may justifiably be disregarded.

The most troubling aspect of this story of neutrality and dispassionate adjudication is that those in power draw the line between public and private so as to preserve the distributions of wealth and power which limit transformative change and preserve hierarchies directly or indirectly benefiting them. How does CLS respond to this problem? One way is by showing the inherent indeterminacy of line-drawing. . . . Another way is by offering an alternative vision of community, a new way of drawing the lines between rights and duties. CLS has not done very much of this, although its negative critique implies such a vision, and its analysis occasionally supports such alternatives.

The alternative vision begins with a different conception of the self. Because liberal theory is thought to legitimize its social order by deducing it from specific conceptions of human nature, some have thought it necessary to posit a different conception of human nature in order to deduce a different conception of community, one that transcends the limitations of liberalism. This alternative conception of human nature rejects the conceptions offered by classical and contemporary liberal theory. It implies that liberal theory has mistaken the symptoms of the individual's condition for its causes. That is, what Thomas Hobbes and John Locke describe as "natural" merely reflects the individual's alienation from his true nature.

The individual is not, by nature, an autonomous and acquisitive being who desires to dominate others and appropriate property. Rather, her alienation and loneliness are socially produced. Individuals long for a genuine connection with others, a mutual acknowledgment of their humanity and need for empowerment. However, socially imposed roles temper their desires for connection with fears of rejection. The regime of liberal rights establishes many of these roles through the distribution of abstract rights and duties that distance us from ourselves and from others whom we long to experience in more meaningful ways than our present social existence permits.

We are lonely because our relationships with each other are distorted by these abstractions, and thus the potential for genuine connection is always limited by the socially contrived roles we adopt. Landlord/tenant, employer/laborer, professor/student, bank teller/customer, and judge/lawyer are all roles that distance us, diminish our intersubjectivity, and decrease the likelihood of a sustained sense of community. The liberal state, however, provides us with an alternative community that really is no community at all: to mediate the threat posed by others to ourselves, the state fosters an illusion of a community consisting of rights-bearing citizens said to be equal before the law and thus members of a community of equals.

This is problematic because at one level we perceive others as the bearers of rights, as equals in a community of equals, while at a different level—that of the market for instance—we perceive others as a threat, something to be dominated or neutralized in the acquisitive world of "dog eat dog." The day-to-day realities of our private loneliness and alienation belie the image of our communitarian existence as equal political citizens.

The illusory liberal community is held together by the manipulation of political symbols by elites through their access to the mass media, and by our utter need to believe in community, even when it is utterly absent. That is, we long for community so desperately that a chief executive's invasion of a small island, bombing of an African country, and general rhetoric of

American patriotism shape our conception of community and fill the emptiness we experience daily.

Given the pervasive sense of alienation which characterizes individuals' interactions with others, then, they place great faith in the capacity of the state to define the nature of community. Part of that definition consists of the state's ability to articulate and enforce neutral boundaries defining the liberal equality of individuals—their equal freedom within private spheres of autonomy protecting them from the arbitrary incursion of private and collective forces.

When a careful "trashing" of legal doctrine reveals, however, that all things are infused with both public and private qualities, there no longer exists any supposed objective criterion by which to logically characterize all things as either public or private. Under the weight of this analysis, the private / public dichotomy collapses and with it the artificial limitations imposed upon the possibilities of collective action needed to create alternative forms of community. We need not maintain faith in a state . . . proven incapable of objectively mediating the contradiction between public and private life.

The prescription of some, therefore, is to eliminate the state as we know it and, along with it, the artificially generated social roles that limit the possibilities of our communitarian impulses. In short, some call for a type of decentralized socialism . . .

> where one need not hide behind the private for either protection or self-aggrandizement. Communities where relationships might be just "us, you and me, and the rest of us," deciding for ourselves what we want, without the alienating third of the state. In that setting . . . we might even make group decisions about reproduction, replacing our pervasive alienation and fear of one another with something more like mutual trust, or love.[4]

. . . The implications for social struggle are clear. Activist lawyers must recognize that every time they "bring a case and win a right, that right is integrated within an ideological framework that has as its ultimate aim the maintenance of collective passivity. That doesn't mean you don't bring the case—it means you keep your eye on power and not on rights." By focusing on the role of law as power, critics constantly remind us that the liberal discourse of rights is "just one among many systems of meaning that people construct in order to deal with one of the most threatening aspects of social existence: the danger posed by other people, whose cooperation is indispensable to us."[5]

Therefore, nothing about law or our present social order is sacrosanct or compelled by forces independent of our own capacities to envision and construct alternative forms of community. Deconstruction that demonstrates the indeterminacy both of legal doctrine and of the political assumptions undergirding legal doctrine emphasizes that the kind of community in which we live remains a matter of choice—the important question being who will make those choices.

2. CRITICAL LEGAL STUDIES: A CRITIQUE

The CLS emphasis on the legitimating role of liberalism and the dynamics of power is accurate but dangerously incomplete. It is incomplete for several reasons. First, theoretical deconstruction does not tell the complete story: we need to know the full range of conditions that lead people to believe, or act as if they believe, that authority is legitimate. . . .

Second, . . . we must realize that there are some liberating as well as legitimating aspects of the line-drawing or boundary-setting enterprise that we critique. Democratic socialism, the American Revolution, the African-American civil rights movement, and other social movements were based, in part, on the liberating dimensions of liberal theory. Failing to recognize this, some scholars unwittingly fall into an overly simplistic analysis of the problem and its possible solutions. When we appreciate the liberating dimension of ideology, revealed by experiential deconstruction, we might conclude that there are many dimensions of the present system that are good and quite enabling.

Thus, although I share critical methods, I question the conclusions of CLS. The CLS critique rightly points out that we need not accept oppressive institutions and practices as unalterable expressions of truth, because the premises on which they are based are contradictory and indeterminate at best. The critique suggests, therefore, that we are free to envision and construct alternative forms of community which represent a more accurate or at least more plausible conception of human nature—one believed to be fundamentally good, which may replace "our pervasive alienation and fear of one another with something more like mutual trust."[6] . . . From this optimistic view, one might envision a quite oppressive community emerging—one in which groups, behind the guise of love and mutual dependency, legitimate behavior that is [even] more oppressive. . . . Thus, when CLS proponents argue that liberalism's public/private dichotomy undermines a society's transformative potential, we should also ask, "How and when does it advance those efforts?" Indeed, if CLS's primary concern is one of legitimation and power, it is important to ask under what conditions the liberal discourse of rights may be strategically delegitimizing and substantively empowering.

The third problem with the CLS critique is that it threatens to conflate the unique histories of the various forms of alienation and oppression engendered by the subconscious acceptance and assimilation of liberal ideology. The experiences of racism and sexism—to name but two—are certainly related to the way individuals experience liberalism as oppressive but cannot be reduced to that experience. Therefore, exploration of the various histories of oppression, often ignored by CLS's . . . account, . . . can provide an essential basis for any reconstructed community.

Finally, deconstruction should ultimately lead to a reconstructive vision, which will involve some line-drawing and boundary-setting. CLS should not only explain why liberalism's boundary-setting is problematic; it must also suggest how to redraw those boundaries to satisfy other goals.

. . . I believe CLS too often falls victim to a myopic preoccupation with the limited role of theoretical deconstruction and a too narrowly tailored experiential deconstruction that focuses exclusively on how individuals experience liberalism. Hegemonic ideologies are never maintained by logical consistency alone; knowledge of how people experience oppression, or knowledge of the full range of conditions under which they remain oppressed, exposes new problems and possibilities. When one begins to contemplate how alternative visions of community might look and be implemented, one must consider carefully the view from the bottom[7]—not simply what oppressors say but how the oppressed respond to what they say.... The view from the bottom may offer insights into why individuals accept their subordinate status in society despite the illogic and inconsistency of the dominant ideology.

It may also provide the basis and catalyst for transformative social change. This is the case with African-American prophetic religion. ...

II. KING'S CRITICAL THEOLOGY

THE difference between the writings and works of Martin Luther King, Jr., and much CLS thought can be seen in King's understanding of the possibilities and limitations of theoretical deconstruction, his use of experiential deconstruction, his articulation of an alternative vision of community, and his development of strategies to realize that vision. King's demonstration of the theoretical indeterminacy of political and religious theories reinforcing oppression drew on a knowledge of the specific histories and experiences of oppression. This engagement with history guided his theoretical project and informed his struggles to reform American society. With the benefit of both theoretical and experiential deconstruction, he committed his life to mobilizing people of conscience into organizations and movements capable of transforming the theories, institutions, and practices of oppression that his critiques exposed as incoherent, historically situated, and indeterminate. This project required a normative vision of community encapsulated in his conception of the "Beloved Community."

A. King as an Organic Intellectual

Because King appreciated the dialectic of theory and the broad-based confrontational strate-

gies of socially transformative action, King stands as the paradigmatic organic intellectual of twentieth-century American life. His method and practice offer direction to progressive scholars concerned about the exclusionary, repressive, and noncommunal dimensions of American life.

Gramsci's conception of the organic intellectual provides a useful framework for understanding the thought of King and what it has to offer CLS. The organic intellectual brings philosophy to the masses, not for the merely instrumental purposes of unifying them, "but precisely in order to construct an intellectual-moral bloc which can make politically possible the intellectual progress of the mass and not only of small intellectual groups."[8] Gramsci's organic intellectual struggles to transform those who are oppressed as a means of transforming the conditions under which they are oppressed. Gramsci understands domination in terms of both coercion and consent, the latter constituting what he refers to as "hegemony." Under his formulation, hegemony consists, then, of "[t]he 'spontaneous' consent given by the great masses of the population to the general direction imposed on social life by the dominant fundamental group."[9] Gramsci argues that "this consent is 'historically' caused by the prestige (and consequent confidence) which the dominant group enjoys because of its position and function in the world of production." Thus, oppression is not only physical and psychological but also cultural.

King, like Gramsci's organic intellectual, empowered his community through a practical effort to bridge the gap between theory and lived experience.... First, he used theoretical deconstruction to free the mind to envision alternative conceptions of community. Second, he employed experiential deconstruction to understand the liberating dimensions of legitimating ideologies such as liberalism and Christianity, dimensions easily ignored by the abstract, ahistorical, and potentially misleading critiques that rely exclusively on theoretical deconstruction. Third, he used the insights gleaned from the first two activities to postulate an alternative social vision intended to transform the conditions of oppression under which people struggle. Drawing from the best of liberalism and the best of Christianity, King forged a vision of community that transcended the limitations of each and built upon the accomplishments of both. Finally, he created and implemented strategies to mobilize people to secure that alternative vision. I refer to this multidimensional critical activity as "philosophical praxis." . . .

King filtered his theoretical deconstruction of hegemonic theologies through his knowledge of the history and experience of oppression, and thereby made that theoretical deconstruction richer, more contextual, and ready to engage the existential realities of oppression. The interplay between King's theoretical and experiential deconstruction is best illustrated by reference to the African-American church—the institution providing the organic link between philosophy and the masses, theory and praxis. . . .

B. The Role of the African-American Church in the American Slave Experience

African-American religion was vital to the community-building enterprise necessitated by the social disintegration and chaos of the American slavery experience. Confronted by practices of social control that suppressed their West African heritage, language, and traditions, Africans were expected to conform to a community created by their slavemasters. Slavemasters attempted to refashion the African's identity through the eradication of collective memory. In the void created by the socially imposed atomization of the African community, the African-American church served both to legitimate and delegitimate the moral authority of a slaveowning society.

I. THE ROLE OF RELIGION IN THE LEGITIMATION OF AUTHORITY

Slavemasters believed Christianity had a stabilizing and disciplining influence on the slave's disposition, and they thought it would foster consent by Africans to the legal and extralegal devices of slavery. The conservative evangelicalism [10] of slave society was premised on five basic assumptions. The first was the fallen nature of human beings, the pervasiveness of human

depravity and sin. The second was contrition, a period of mourning characterized by feelings of personal guilt and sorrow for sins. The third was conversion, an intensely personal experience with God in which the burdens of sin are lifted and the soul cleansed and made fit for the Kingdom of God. The fourth was the separation of believers, the sometimes physical but most times psychological separation of the community of believers from sinful worldly concerns and pursuits. And the last was the separation of church and state, the extreme deference to the existing social order and dependence on the state for the laws and rules necessary to constrain the sinful nature of earthly beings.

These features of conservative evangelicalism were considered rooted in an infallible scripture representing the untainted word of God; they legitimated slavemasters' authority in several ways. Southern evangelicals elaborated the scriptural justifications for slavery and invoked the will of God to reconcile slaves to their subordinate status. Slavery could not be sin, they reasoned, because God sanctioned it in His infallible Word. Evangelicals frequently cited the Old Testament story of Noah's son, Ham, whose progeny God supposedly condemned to a legacy of servitude for his indiscretion. These and other scriptural evidences were, to the evangelicals, conclusive proof of God's authorization of the enslavement of Africans.

Having provided the moral justification for slavery through scripture, evangelicals constructed an argument designed so as to avert any effort by the Church to transform the institution. Because the scripture supported slavery, and secular authority established and protected it under state law, the Church, mindful of its commitment to the separation of church and state, could not condemn slavery. Because slavery did not constitute sin, God's law did not contradict the civil law: slavery fell under the latter, and the scriptures dictated obedience to secular authority.

Moreover, conservative evangelicalism dictated that because God would deal with the evil of Southern slavery and apartheid in His own way and time, the eradication of those institutions should await His divine deliverance as

evidenced by the changed hearts and minds of women and men. Thus, patience and the implicit acceptance of one's subordinate status were exalted as the highest of Christian virtues.
. . .

2. THE ROLE OF RELIGION IN THE DELEGITIMATION OF AUTHORITY

Although the use of religion as an instrument of social control often necessitated oversight by white masters, strict enforcement was not maintained, and slaves often met separately for religious services, including weekly and Sunday-evening services. It was within the freedom provided for religious worship that Africans began to assert some control over how the void created by the disintegration of their historical identity and community would be filled. In this small space of freedom, an alternative conception of community was defined and the history of a new American people began to emerge. African-American religion and its primary vehicle of expression, the African-American church, supplied the needed catalyst for the reconstruction of community destroyed by slavery.

To the surprise and fear of many whites, slaves transformed an ideology intended to reconcile them to a subordinate status into a manifesto of their God-given equality. This deconstruction was both revolutionary and pragmatic in nature. The Africans' appropriation of conservative evangelicalism as a bulwark against the degradation and countless microaggressions of slavery proved that there were alternate interpretations of the text that supposedly justified their subjugation. Slaves demonstrated that scripture was subject to an alternative interpretation that called for the eradication of the very social structure evangelicals sought to legitimate. In short, slaves deconstructed ideology through their struggles against oppression.

Although slavemasters and evangelicals attempted to limit the transmission of counter-hegemonic interpretations of scripture, their efforts met with limited success. African gospel preachers and slaves who learned to read against their masters' wishes (and, many times, against state law as well) were determined to read the Bible in light of their own experiences. Many

slaves realized that the message of submission, docility, and absolute obedience to the master was a distorted picture of the Bible's eternal truths.

Many slaves found in Christianity, and particularly in Jesus, a call to revolutionary action. They read of a Jesus who proclaimed that God had anointed him to "preach the gospel to the poor; . . . to preach deliverance to the captives, and . . . to set at liberty them that are bruised"; who commanded those who would follow him to care for "the least of these": the hungry, naked, sick, and those in prison; who entered Jerusalem to the revolutionary cry of Hosannah; and who defiantly asserted "[t]hink not that I am come to send peace on earth: I came not to send peace, but a sword." Denmark Vessey and Nat Turner, for example, recognized the revolutionary potential of Christianity: "since God is on our side, we strike for freedom, confident in his protection."[11] The Reverend Henry Highland Garnet contended: "To such degradation [as slavery] it is sinful in the extreme for you to make voluntary submission. . . . Brethren arise, arise! Strike for your lives and liberties. Now is the day and the hour. . . . Rather die freemen than live to be slaves."[12]

Those unwilling to act on the revolutionary impulses of the Bible found scriptural support for a more patient and pragmatic opposition to slavery which still fostered and preserved a healthy sense of self-worth. Conservative evangelicalism taught that slavery was a divinely ordained practice instituted by the master race for the benefit of morally deficient Africans; but slaves read of Moses, the Hebrew children, and God's mighty deliverance from the hardships of Egyptian slavery. The story provided proof of God's intolerance of American slavery and His intention someday to divide the Red Sea of Southern oppression and lead His people out of Pharaoh's land.

Against the formidable oppression of slavery, segregation, and contemporary forms of subjugation, this deconstructed, pragmatic evangelicalism provided the means by which African-Americans could survive their daily travails. Its emphasis on personal faith nurtured a forward-looking people who could sing with conviction the words "I'm so glad, that trouble won't last always."[13] Its emphasis on love bolstered a sense of self-esteem diminished by the debilitating and degrading practices of a culture that relegated them to the status of objects. It nurtured an inward-looking people who could sing with reassurance the words "The trumpet sounds within my soul. I know I ain't got long to stay here."[14] . . .

The disparity between what slaves read and heard from their own preachers, on the one hand, and the practices of whites in the slave system, on the other, had two important consequences. First, it preserved and enhanced the self-esteem of the slaves; the realization that some whites were not faithful to the Word provided them with a sense of moral superiority: even in slavery, slaves could be the light unto the sinner's path. Second, it provided a standard against which they could measure whites individually, rather than collectively by their social status as master race. It provided a framework for understanding the differences between cruel white overseers and whites who worked on the underground railroad to freedom. Even when the institutions of oppression seemed most intractable, understanding their oppression as the sin of unfaithful whites maintained for the Africans a sense of sanity and hope tempered only by the revolutionary focus on power and immediate liberation. In short, the appropriation of Christian ideology by the African-Americans provided the basis for their survival through slavery's many brutalities and indignities.

Although this appropriation helped to restore the dignity of the African slave, it also had paradoxical effects. Pragmatic evangelicalism admirably served the cause of survival but its eschatological and inward orientation simultaneously served the function of social control. It saved black Christians from a debilitating hatred that, if permitted to fester, would have created a pervasive sense of despair and hopelessness that would have substantially impaired the moral will to survive. However, it also promoted as virtues patience and tolerance of the social institutions of oppression. Viewing morality in terms of individual character thus undermined the possibilities of a sustained

Christian radicalism against what was perhaps the most debilitating and sustained system of subordination known to the modern world—American slavery.

3. THE ROLE OF RELIGION IN THE SHAPING OF ALTERNATIVE CONCEPTIONS OF COMMUNITY

The revolutionary and pragmatic faith drawn from conservative evangelicalism represented the beginnings of what Cornel West has called "prophetic Christianity."[15] It drew heavily on the interplay between the individualist orientation of pragmatic Christianity and the collectivist orientation of revolutionary Christianity, encouraging an intensely personal relationship with God while nurturing the possibilities of collective defiance and transformation.

The African-American church rejected white Christianity's claim that the law and order of an oppressive secular authority were necessary to constrain the evil proclivities of human nature. Many slaves never accepted the view that slavery was justified because the human nature of Africans necessitated African enslavement and white superiority. For these slaves, the spiritual freedom and sense of equality that accompanied the conversion of the soul threw into question the morality of the social order in which they lived. One student of this period writes:

> Contradicting a system that valued him like a beast for his labor, conversion experientially confirmed the slave's value as a human person, indeed attested to his ultimate worth as one of the chosen of God.
> . . . [M]eetings encouraged participants to include references to individual misfortunes and problems in their prayers and songs, so that they might be shared by all. This type of consolation . . . [was] the answer to the crucial need of individuals for community.[16]

The religious experience of conversion was central to the belief system of slaves. The process of conversion in African-American religion involved a period of sustained mourning in which the contrite sinner would assemble with worshipers in prayer for as many successive meetings as required to "bring the sinner through"— a phrase used to express the sinner's completion of a rite of passage from the alienated existence of sinner to the bonds of Christian fellowship and community. The process of conversion often resulted in a cataclysmic seizure of the person by the Holy Spirit which catapulted all into a rapture of ecstatic joy and praise. The experience was collectively cathartic. In the slave community, uninhibited shouting and praise temporarily obliterated secular distinctions in status between the slaves. It was a process in which personalities disintegrated by the social chaos of oppression found meaning and commonality by fusing with others in a collective act of self-affirmation and even defiance.

The prophetic Christianity that resulted from this synthesis between revolutionary and pragmatic Christianity offered the alternative conception of community which would inspire King to develop his notion of a "Beloved Community" and struggle to transform American society. King's objective to rebuild community from the social death of slavery and segregation paralleled the conversion experience in slavery. A sense of individual self-worth was essential to any social struggle; segregation laws and impoverished conditions that diminished self-worth had to be challenged and abolished. Although the ideal was to break down the barriers of hatred and misunderstanding which prevented individuals from seeing and respecting the God-given humanity of all, King knew that only collective action and organized defiance could achieve the destruction of such barriers. Redistribution of wealth and power through the collectively cathartic experience of social conversion was a necessary part of this conception of community. Law and the power of the state would have to assist in the obliteration and amelioration of many of the secular distinctions founded on race, class, and gender which were created and reinforced by public and private forces.

C. King and Theoretical Deconstruction

I. DECONSTRUCTING FIRST PRINCIPLES: THE INCOHERENCY CRITIQUE

During the Birmingham demonstrations of 1963, the white clergy criticized King for the breach of law and order precipitated by his "untimely," nonviolent direct action protests to desegregate the city. In his famous "Letter from Birmingham City Jail,"[17] King responded that he had

> almost reached the regrettable conclusion that the Negro's great stumbling block in the stride toward freedom is not the White Citizen's Counciler or the Ku Klux Klanner, but the white moderate who is more devoted to "order" than to justice; . . . who paternalistically feels that he can set the timetable for another man's freedom. . . . I had hoped that the white moderate would understand that law and order exist for the purpose of establishing justice, and that when they fail to do this they become dangerously structured dams that block the flow of social progress.[18]

King examined and exposed the mutual dependence of order and freedom. He understood that the primary difference between the two was that a belief in the primacy of order assumed that human nature was fundamentally evil and in need of restraint, while a belief in the primacy of freedom assumed that it was fundamentally good and capable of autonomy. The privileging of order over freedom assumed that the latter was only possible within the constraints imposed by sovereign authority; otherwise, civil society would degenerate into a Hobbesian war of all against all. . . . The white clergy of Birmingham privileged the conception of human nature as fundamentally evil over the conception of human nature as fundamentally good. Thus, the ordinances and injunctions prohibiting demonstrations in the city were necessary restraints on freedom needed to maintain order in the face of the human capacity for evil.

King's incoherency critique exposed the white clergy's preference of order over freedom and evil over good, and it demonstrated that this preference lacked an objective foundation. The hierarchy could easily be inverted. If freedom presupposes order, as the white clergy contended, it is no less true that order presupposes freedom: for if humans are not also capable of substantial good, no social order is possible, because individuals would by definition be ungovernable. In this way, the social order supposedly necessitated by human evil presupposes the freedom and human goodness it denies.

2. DECONSTRUCTING FIRST PRINCIPLES: THE UNIVERSALITY CRITIQUE

Even if the privileging of order over freedom and the conception of human nature as fundamentally evil over its opposite conception were not seen as incoherent, King realized that these privileged conceptions need not be accepted as universally valid. They might be viewed as historically contingent and conditioned, and thus subject to change if individuals are willing to engage in transformative struggles to alter the conditions under which these conceptions appear coherent.

The evangelicalism of Dr. George Washington Davis, King's professor of theology at Crozer Seminary, and the social gospel of Walter Rauschenbusch[19] gave King the theological perspectives to challenge conservative evangelicalism's conception of human nature and its debilitating dichotomy between the spiritual and the secular, as well as between order and freedom. Evangelical liberalism turned conservative evangelicalism's conception of human nature on its head and called into question the universality of that theology's assumptions. Evangelical liberalism posited the goodness of human nature, as reflected in and resulting from human moral reasoning, and it conjectured that evil institutions had limited people's efforts to pursue the ideal of the Kingdom of Value, what King would later call the "Beloved Community."

Evangelical liberalism, from its theory of human nature, deduced a new role for the Church and for Christians. Given intrinsic human goodness, social institutions could and should be transformed to reflect more accurately the ideals of universal kinship and cooperation. An infallible scripture reflecting the static will of God could not justify social institutions like slavery and segregation. In addition, oppressive institutions could no longer seek justification by invoking the need to restrain the evil nature of persons; such institutions were themselves the source of evil and thus in need of reform.

A second important source of King's universality critique is the social gospel of Walter Rauschenbusch. Consistent with evangelical liberalism, Rauschenbusch saw humans as intrinsically good. Evil, he argued, was the product of an evil society; in America's case, the greed and selfish individualism of a spawning industrialism trampled the Christian values of kinship and love, created gross inequities of wealth, and relegated thousands to abject poverty. Rauschenbusch called for the abandonment of capitalism and the creation of a new social order that would socialize economic resources and allow people to inhabit a sinless Christian commonwealth based on love, cooperation, and solidarity.

By closing the chasm between the individual and the society, between religion and ethics, and between spirituality and everyday existence, Rauschenbusch avoided the limitations of conservative evangelicalism. Social justice constituted the telos of the Christian faith in his view, and he evaluated Christian discipleship in terms of its commitment to this moral end. Thus, unlike the dichotomy of conservative evangelicalism, there was a necessary relationship between the sacred and the secular, the Church and social issues. Evidence of a person's love for God, he contended, must be the fruits of love for suffering humanity. Such love necessitated the conversion of all social institutions and practices that maintain and reproduce poverty, racial oppression, and other social ills. The social gospel turned Christian attention from the glories of the kingdom to come to the injustices of the kingdom at hand. It premised individual salvation on the transformation of the world's evil social institutions.

Evangelical liberalism and the social gospel repudiated the traditional conception of human nature; they replaced that traditional conception with an antithetical view and reached a different conclusion about the relationships between church and state as well as between Christians and the evil world in which they lived. King used these two strands of theology to challenge the view of human nature which counseled

African-Americans to be patient in the face of oppression.

3. DECONSTRUCTING FIRST PRINCIPLES: THE INDETERMINACY CRITIQUE

In addition to challenging conservative evangelicalism by positing an alternative conception of human nature, King argued that even if conservative evangelicalism's conception of human nature were valid, that conception would not necessitate any one vision of community. For example, when white ministers claimed that the civil rights protests resulted in a loss of law and order in Birmingham, and that King was primarily responsible for the tension and deteriorated relations that then pervaded the community, King responded with an indeterminacy critique. Conservative evangelicalism assumed that scripture required the Church's deference to the authority of the state ordained by God; but King pointed out that order must serve the end of justice. Even assuming that we each must defer to the state, King maintained, we must respect the law of God:

> A just law is a man-made code that squares with the moral law or the law of God. An unjust law is a code that is out of harmony with the moral law . . . not rooted in eternal and natural law. Any law that uplifts human personality is just. Any law that degrades human personality is unjust. All segregation statutes are unjust because segregation distorts the soul and damages the personality. It gives the segregator a false sense of superiority, and the segregated a false sense of inferiority. . . . So segregation is not only politically, economically and sociologically unsound, but it is morally wrong and sinful.

King held that disobeying human law, even unjust law, must be done out of love and with a willingness to suffer the penalty for its breach. Through this unjust suffering, the transgressor evidences the highest respect for law and order while remaining true to his higher Christian duty.

King realized that even when first principles were accepted, they did not mechanically determine specific visions of community: how we live in community remains a matter of choice that implicated a host of competing values. What,

then, could be deduced from the presupposition that human nature is fundamentally evil and deference to the laws of social order essential? Segregationists deduced that King should cease all protests because they were illegal activities, and that he should accept African-American subjugation as the best of all possible worlds. Moderates deduced that King should cease all protests and pursue more peaceful and orderly avenues for desegregating the city—a goal surely to be achieved in due time. For King, it meant respecting the law and the need for social order through a willingness to suffer the penalty for breaching unjust laws. Each deduction is logical, although none are compelled. What one finds persuasive largely depends on other values related to human potential and social relations, power, and community.

4. SYNTHESIZING FIRST PRINCIPLES

The incoherency, universality, and indeterminacy critiques gave King the intellectual freedom to posit a radically different conception of human nature, one that focused more on reconstructive struggle than theoretical deconstruction. Although initially he rejected conservative evangelicalism and its pessimistic view of human nature, King later realized that the optimistic view of human nature upon which evangelical liberalism and the social gospel constructed their utopias posed significant dangers. The indeterminacy critique suggested, and historical experience made clear, that evil and oppression could follow as easily from an optimistic faith in human nature as from a more orthodox conception of human depravity.

Evangelical liberalism stressed the power of human reason to discern the moral good of life, and it possessed an inexorable optimism concerning human capacity for goodness. However, the more King "observed the tragedies of history and man's shameful inclination to choose the low road," the more he came to see the "depths and strength of sin." His experiences convinced him that evangelical "liberalism had been all too sentimental concerning human nature and that it leaned toward a false idealism"—one that failed to see that "reason is darkened by sin" and "is little more than an instrument to justify man's defensive ways of thinking."

At the other extreme from evangelical liberalism was the neo-orthodoxy of Karl Barth, which emphasized the intractable nature of sin and evil and the relative futility of utopian aspirations.[20] Barth maintained that many of the social injustices of the world were necessary evils which could only be rectified by the apocalyptic return of the Kingdom of God. Although he recognized the insights of neo-orthodoxy, King could not fully accept this view—it cast too dark a shadow upon the possibilities of social change.

King searched for a philosophical middle ground that saw human nature as a struggle between good and evil, a philosophy that conceded humanity's finiteness yet acted on the faith that God could use finite creatures to establish a Beloved Community based on love and justice. He found this philosophical common ground in a Christian existentialism influenced by his study of Søren Kierkegaard, Friedrich Nietzsche, Karl Jaspers, Martin Heidegger, and Jean-Paul Sartre.

Like the existentialists, King believed that liberalism failed to give serious consideration to humanity's finite freedom—our existential estrangement in an evil world from our essential nature of goodness as creatures of God. King described as "perilous" the assumption by some liberal theologians that sin was but a mere "lag of nature that can be progressively eliminated as man climbs the evolutionary ladder." For King, the estrangement from perfection was fundamental: the individual was always in the process of becoming and could never fully realize the ideal of the Beloved Community in history. Nevertheless, he believed that the struggle to actualize the ideal in history could transform social relations. Only the struggle to achieve the Beloved Community allows us to experience our essential nature and to change our limited knowledge and understanding of the world.

. . . King's use of theory to deconstruct oppressive and hegemonic theologies was guided by the historic mission of the African-American church to rebuild community from the socially imposed amnesia and atomization of slavery and segregation. Seeing the individual as incorrigibly evil would make societal reform impossible. Similarly, viewing the individual as purely good would make coerced societal reform unnecessary because reasoned deliberation could simply usher in the Beloved Community. Instead, King understood that individuals were both good and evil, and that mind must be met with mind and power with power.

D. King and Experiential Deconstruction

The incoherency, universality, and indeterminacy critiques illustrate the open-ended character of organizing principles. Such critiques supply the intellectual courage to think differently. They demystify theories of their natural law-like image and free the mind to envision new conceptions of community. But this alone is insufficient; because these critiques are abstract and ahistorical they do not provide the rich historical contextuality essential to an understanding of the actual operation of power. . . . They may miss conditions of great importance that explain legitimacy in ways that logic and reason cannot. Furthermore, experiential deconstruction may provide insights into the ways in which marginalized groups transform powerless conditions into powerful possibilities, thereby informing a broader reconstructive vision than previously existed.

. . . King realized that very few African-Americans probably ever believed that the assumptions of conservative evangelicalism logically compelled their submission to authority. Their submission was not based on consent to a social order they believed to be legitimate; rather, coercion and its constant threat of death, injury, humiliation, or impoverishment compelled their submission. Individuals may have fully agreed with King's incoherency, universality, and indeterminacy critiques, and yet been constrained by existential limitations that made collective struggle to attain alternative conceptions of community difficult if not impossible. King eloquently describes these existential limitations through experiential deconstruction:

[W]hen you have seen vicious mobs lynch your mothers and fathers at will and drown your sisters and brothers at whim; when you have seen hate-filled policemen curse, kick, brutalize and even kill your black brothers and sisters with impunity; when you see the vast majority of your twenty million Negro brothers smothering in an airtight cage of poverty in the midst of an affluent society; . . . when you take a cross-country drive and find it necessary to sleep night after night in the uncomfortable corners of your automobile because no motel will accept you; when you are humiliated day in and day out by nagging signs reading "white" and "colored"; when your first name becomes "nigger" and your middle name becomes "boy" (however old you are) and your last name becomes "John," and when your wife and mother are never given the respected title "Mrs."; when you are harried by day and haunted by night by the fact that you are a Negro, living constantly at tiptoe stance never quite knowing what to expect next, and plagued with inner fears and outer resentments; when you are forever fighting a degenerating sense of "nobodiness"; then you will understand why we find it difficult to wait.

King saw the world and evaluated the theories marshaled in support of it through the lens of these experiences of oppression. These experiences necessitated his eclectic appropriation of various theologies and philosophies, which he constantly revised in light of his growing understanding of the problems of American life. King drew inspiration and instruction from the history of African-American religion and the Church for dealing with these existential limitations. The history and experiences of African-Americans under oppression taught King several valuable lessons. First, submission to illegitimate authority did not derive exclusively from a hegemonic ideology like conservative evangelicalism or political liberalism; public and private brute force and coercion played a significant role in maintaining submission. Second, far from being duped by the political and religious ideologies intended to oppress them, African-Americans had often successfully turned those ideologies on their heads and used them as instruments of survival and liberation. Third, within the space created by the interplay of coercion and hegemony, African-Americans articulated and implemented conceptions of community important to broader visions of a reconstructed society.

King's Christian existentialism was significantly informed by experiential deconstruction, the past and present experiences of Afri-

can-American people. The tension between pragmatic and revolutionary evangelicalism suggested a profoundly personal relationship between the individual and God, with implications for the community as a whole. King maintained that although God was indeed working to change the sinful hearts and minds of white oppressors, collective organization through nonviolent direct action would be His instrument of salvation. King saw this as an empowering synthesis of the Old Testament's concern for justice and the New Testament's emphasis on love. "Greater love has no man than this, that a man lay down his life for his friends."[21] Justice and love were inseparable: it was a necessary expression of one's love for God, then, to lead souls blinded by the darkness of sin to the light, to raise consciousness, and to challenge the injustice anywhere that threatened justice everywhere.

King's synthesis of pragmatic and revolutionary evangelicalism was most powerfully expressed in his "Letter from Birmingham City Jail." Conservative evangelicalism's dichotomy between the spiritual and the secular caused many religious leaders, as it had in the days of slavery, to continue to oppose any interpretation of Christianity demanding that equality before God in the spiritual realm also be embodied in the legal and social relations defining the secular realm. These leaders still offered patience as a panacea for the pain of persecution and the joys of an afterlife as an answer for the sufferings of this life. If integration was the will of God, He and not humans would change people's hearts in His own way and time. Be patient, they urged, and wait on the Lord.[22] King discerned the hegemonic role of this theology and boldly challenged the injustice to which it gave rise wherever he encountered it. To those who urged that nonviolent, direct action was "unwise and untimely," King sharply retorted:

We know through painful experience that freedom is never voluntarily given by the oppressor; it must be demanded by the oppressed. Frankly, I have never yet engaged in a direct action movement that was "well-timed," according to the timetable of those who have not suffered unduly from the disease of segregation. For years now I have heard the words "Wait!" It rings in the ear of every Negro with a piercing familiarity. This "Wait" has almost always meant "Never." . . . We must come to see with the distinguished jurist of yesterday, that "justice too long delayed is justice denied."[23]

King expressed his great disappointment with this otherworldly orientation of the white Church:

> In the midst of blatant injustices inflicted upon the Negro, I have watched white churches stand on the sideline and merely mouth pious irrelevancies and sanctimonious trivialities. In the midst of a mighty struggle to rid our nation of racial and economic injustice, I have heard so many ministers say, "Those are social issues with which the gospel has no real concern," and I have watched so many churches commit themselves to a completely otherworldly religion which made a strange distinction between body and soul, the sacred and the secular.[24]

Thus, King spent his life leading African-Americans into direct confrontation with oppressive institutions and practices. Through direct action the African-American community exposed the contradictions and violence endemic to American society. In this way, the civil rights movement King led was itself a powerful form of experiential deconstruction, one that provided fertile ground for a new vision of community in America.

E. King and the Reconstructive Vision of Community

King's reconstructive vision emanated from the interplay of theory and experience, and from the synthesis of rights and duties. Rights represent the pragmatic, individualist orientation focusing on formal equality before the law in the political context; duties represent the collectivist, revolutionary orientation focusing on justified coercion by the collective to implement alternative conceptions of community. . . . King's reconstructive vision of the Beloved Community synthesizes both dimensions of this traditional dichotomy. . . . King used the insights of theoretical and experiential deconstruction . . . to posit a reconstructive vision in which rights limited duties in a socially conscious and egalitarian manner rather than in a manner that preserved a status quo permeated with hierarchy and inequality.

I. PRAGMATIC RIGHTS AND REVOLUTIONARY DUTY

Many of the communal and cooperative dimensions of King's theory of the state depended on the optimistic view of human nature posited by evangelical liberalism and the social gospel. Individuals could harness the powers of the state to usher in a Beloved Community here on earth. Conversely, King understood the limitations and dangers of this optimism—that the reality of sin and evil must never be forgotten. This awareness was captured in his commitment to a Christian existentialism that posited a human nature fragmented by an alienated and anxiety-filled existence which severely circumscribed one's ability to know, much less change, the world. Under this existentialist view, individual rights represent a hedge against our imperfect attempts to reconcile our existential and essential selves, and they extend far beyond the traditional litany of liberties and rights against the state espoused by classical and contemporary liberalism. These rights were "inherent rights that are God-given and not simply privileges extended by the state."[25] For King, the rights of life, liberty, and the pursuit of happiness meant that "all individuals everywhere should have 'three meals a day for their bodies, education and culture for their minds, and dignity, equality and freedom for their spirits.' "[26] This required that the state affirmatively create the institutions necessary to realize these natural rights.

Unlike some CLS scholars, King understood the importance of a system of individual rights. CLS proponents have urged that rights are incoherent and indeterminate reifications of concrete experiences—reifications, moreover, that obfuscate, through the manipulation of abstract categories, disempowering social relations. King, on the other hand, understood that the oppressed could make rights determinate in practice: although "law tends to declare rights—it does not deliver them. A catalyst is needed to breathe life experience into a judicial decision."[27] For King, the catalyst was persistent social struggle to transform the oppressiveness of one's existential condition into ever-closer approximations of the ideal. The hierarchies of race, gender, and class define those conditions, and the struggle for substantive rights closes the gap between the latter and the ideal of the Beloved Community. Under the pressures of social struggle, the oppressed can alter rights to better reflect the exigencies of social reality—a reality itself more fully understood by those engaged in transformative struggle.

King's Beloved Community accepted and expanded the liberal tradition of rights. King realized that the liberal vision, notwithstanding its limits, contained important insights into the human condition. For those deprived of basic freedoms and subjected to arbitrary acts of state authority, the enforcement of formal rights was revolutionary. African-Americans understood the importance of formal liberal rights, and they demanded the full enforcement of such rights in order to challenge and rectify historical practices that had objectified and subsumed their existence.

Although conservatives contended that the emphasis on rights disrupted the gradual moral evolution that would ultimately change white sentiment, King contended that "[j]udicial decrees may not change the heart, but they can restrain the heartless."[28] On the other hand, although radicals contended that such rights were mere tokens that created a false sense of security masking continued violence, King understood that the strict enforcement of the rule of law was essential to any struggle for social justice, whether that struggle was moderate or radical in its sentiment and goals. Freedom of dissent and protest; freedom from arbitrary searches, seizures, and detention; and freedom to organize and associate with those of common purpose were necessary rights that no movement for social reconstruction could take for granted.

Furthermore, King saw the initial emphasis on civil rights, . . . as a necessary struggle for the collective self-respect and dignity of a people whose subordination was, in part, maintained by laws reproducing and reinforcing feelings of inadequacy and inferiority. The civil rights struggle attempted to lift the veil of shame and degradation from the eyes of a people who could then glimpse the possibilities of their personhood and achieve that potential through varied forms of social struggle. King's

richer conception of rights provided limitations on collective action while broadening the scope of personal duty to permit movement toward a more socially conscious community.

King's conception of duty complemented his conception of rights; it called for individual action, but action consistent with a more humane and contextual rule of law. Although clearly inspired by the revolutionary tradition, King's conception was not as consuming as that of the revolutionary Christians. The orientation toward duty of revolutionary Christianity required individuals to see themselves as part of some larger and similarly situated community. Each had a personal duty that ran to the community at large, thereby subordinating personal welfare to the welfare of the community. One's duty to God could only be understood by reference to one's duty to others, and one's duty to others obligated the individual to be his brother's and sister's keeper, to meet power with power in the struggle for justice.

King, too, called for the immediate transformation of American institutions and practices, but he rejected the use of violence in this transformative struggle. He refused to place the goal of a reconstructed community above the means used to achieve it. Moreover, he believed that nonviolent direct action and mass civil disobedience could secure the revolutionary end of dismantling Jim Crow and winning the war against poverty. Through nonviolent direct action, one could be both moral and revolutionary. It provided oppressors the opportunity to redeem themselves voluntarily from a sinful past while providing the coercive dimension of a disruptive and crisis-packed boycott, march, or protest to urge them along.

In this way, King balanced pragmatic and revolutionary Christianity as well as rights and duties. King's prophetic Christianity recognized the importance of both rights and duty as a practical matter. Rights were prerequisites to survival; nonviolent civil disobedience was the heart of duty. Duty was consistent with rights because, through civil disobedience, one could simultaneously demonstrate respect for the rule of law in preserving social order while opposing laws supportive of unjust social orders. Thus, King envisioned a rule of law rooted in experience and responsive to the conditions of oppression that denied the humanity of so many.

. . .

III. Summary and Conclusion

. . . In conclusion, I believe the postmodern preoccupation with deconstruction is but a precursor to serious reflection on how we should live in community. Critics—scholars, activists, organizers, and citizens—must turn their attention and energies to reconstructive theorizing and struggle. Although theoretical deconstruction provides some with the intellectual freedom to think and act, the more contextual experiential deconstruction discussed in this article illustrates that what we see as plausible solutions to our oppressed existence will largely depend on what we perceive as the problem. In this regard, our assessment of the problems can be no better than the lenses through which we examine those problems. I have argued that those lenses must reflect the different histories and experiences that constitute our community. The process must be deliberative, participatory, and respectful of difference and diversity.

Experiential deconstruction tells us that we should pay more attention to the specific kind of community we envision with reference to the specific experiences of oppression which characterize our histories. We must question how that alternative community will better protect African-Americans and others from the subjugation of racism, bigotry, sexism, and grave inequalities of wealth and power. This can only be achieved through the detailed examination of American institutions and the systematic development of alternative institutions designed to rectify present oppression and injustice.

In this regard, King was ahead of his time, and although there is much we can learn from a study of his life and thought, his assassination in 1968 prevented him from fully developing his alternative vision of community. That task is ours. It is often said that the hottest places in hell are reserved for those who in times of moral crisis remain neutral. Let us not fall victim to the paralysis of neutral analysis. Instead, we must meet and talk together, appreciating our respective histories and experiences of alienation and oppression. We must talk specifically about

the kind of community we would fashion and how the rules, laws, and rituals defining the roles we adopt can be mutually empowering and facilitative of a community of equals. We must talk specifically about how we should organize, protest, agitate, and struggle to achieve our objectives, realizing that we are perennially engaged in a dialectic in which the program shapes our practices, which in turn refine and redefine our program. With such mutual respect and openness to each others' pain, suffering, and faith, we must work out more fully and struggle toward King's ideal of the Beloved Community and thereby hew from our mountain of despair a stone of hope.

NOTES

1. "I Have a Dream," address by Dr. Martin Luther King, Jr., at the march on Washington, D.C. for civil rights (Aug. 28, 1963), reprinted in *A Testament of Hope: The Essential Writings of Martin Luther King, Jr.*, 217, 219 (1986).

2. These "possibilities" are not mutually exclusive groupings of the oppressed. This is a fluid typology, with individuals sometimes moving in and out of each grouping, and often occupying more than one at a time. My point is that critical activity must account for all three possibilities and the different problems associated with each.

3. Gabel and Kennedy, "Roll Over Beethoven," 36 *Stan. L. Rev.*, 1, 26 (1984).

4. Freeman and Mensch, "The Public Private Distinction in American Law and Life," 36 *Buffalo L. Rev.*, 237, 256–57 (1987) (footnote omitted).

5. Robert Gordon, for example, suggests that an ideal means of scrutinizing "belief-structures" is to demonstrate their historical contingency. *See* Gordon, *New Developments in Legal Theory*, in The Politics of Law (D. Kairys ed. 1982) at 281, 289. Gordon's demonstration of contingency is a response to the problem of "reification," the process of allowing the structures we ourselves have built to mediate relations among us so as to make us see ourselves as performing abstract roles in a play that is produced by no human agency. . . . It is a way people have of manufacturing necessity: they build structures, then act as if (and genuinely come to believe that) the sturctures they have built are determind by history, human nature, economic law. *Id.* at 289.

6. *Id.* at 257.

7. See Matsuda, "Looking to the Bottom: Critical Legal Studies and Reparations," 22 *Harv. C.R.–C.L. L. Rev.*, 323 (1987).

8. Q. Hoare and G. Smith, eds. *Selections from the Prison Notebooks of Antonio Gramsci*, 332–33 (1971).

9. *Id.* at 12.

10. I understand conservative evangelicalism to be an eclectic blend of Calvinist dogma and the spiritualism of the eighteenth-century Great Awakening. Historians of Christian evangelicalism have noted its emphasis on individualism, an emphasis traced to the sixteenth-century Protestant Reformation and vividly seen in the rebellion of Martin Luther against the hierarchy of the Roman Catholic Church and in the universalization of the Lutheran faith by John Calvin. See, for example, L. Gasper, *The Fundamentalist Movement*, 126 (1963) (arguing that "fundamentalism must not be regarded as an aberration in Protestantism," and that "the kind of individualism which the Reformation encouraged, and revivalism [the Great Awakening] in America solidified, is one of the main characteristics of fundamentalism"). It should be noted that Gasper is characterizing the early history and Calvinist underpinnings of fundamentalism, described above as conservative evangelicalism.

The antihierarchical and individualist tendencies of Protestantism prefigured the secular individualism that characterized the liberalism of Hobbes and Locke much later. By the eighteenth-century Great Awakening, Calvinism had adapted to the demands of the modern world and stood ready to provide the theological vehicle for American slave religion. Gasper describes the influence of Calvinism as follows: "Calvin's ideals for all Christians were 'thrift, industry and sobriety,' which permitted men to prosper economically without fear of being regarded as tainted by the sin of avarice," *id.* at 4. But see M. Novak, *The Spirit of Democratic Capitalism* (1982) (arguing that the theological foundations of capitalism are fundamentally democratic).

11. Raboteau, "The Black Experience in American Evangelicalism: The Meaning of Slavery," in L. Sweet, ed., *The Evangelical Tradition in America*, 181, 190 (1984).

12. *Id.* (emphasis in original, footnote omitted), quoting Garnet, "An Address to the Slaves of the United States of America" (1843), reprinted in S. Stuckey, *The Ideological Origins of Black Nationalism*, 165, 168–72 (1972).

13. "Hush, Hush, Somebody's Calling My Name," in *Songs of Zion*, 125 (1981).

14. "Steel Away to Jesus," *Id. at 180.*

15. *See* C. West, *Prophesy Deliverance!*, 15 (1982). West, an African-American philosopher, describes prophetic Christianity as having a "transcendent God before whom all persons are equal[,] thus endow[ing] the well-being and ultimate salvation of each with equal value and significance"; *id.* at 16. He calls "this radical egalitarian idea the Christian principle of the self-realization of individuality within community"; *id.* (emphasis in original).

16. Raboteau, *supra* note 11, at 193–94 (emphasis in original).

17. King referred to Birmingham as America's most segregated city. It was certainly among the most visibly violent against African-Americans in the country. Police dogs, waterhoses, cattleprods, and unmerciful brutality were used against demonstrators, and many, including King, were jailed over the long period of protest. In his "Letter from Birmingham City Jail," King responded to an open letter from a group of eight "liberal" white clergymen which chastised King for fomenting the widely publicized "direct campaigns" in the city rather than relying exclusively on legal remedies through the courts. [. . .]

18. King, "Letter from Birmingham City Jail" (1963), reprinted in *A Testament of Hope, supra* note 1, at 295.

19. The major theological assumption that inspired the Social Gospel movement was that "salvation had a social and individual dimension and that social institutions had to be 'saved.' " [. . .] The Church had to concern itself, not only with individual morality, but also with social justice and social structures. [. . .]

20. See, e.g., K. Barth, *The Epistle to the Romans*, 167, trans. E. Hoskyns, (1933). Barth argues that the reality of death is the "supreme law" of the temporal world, and that the inhabitants of this "world of death" are necessarily "men of sin." Barth further argues that "[s]in is that by which man as we know him is defined, for we know nothing of sinless men. Sin is power—sovereign power. By it men are controlled"; *id.* For a brief summary of how Barth fits into larger trends in modern religious thought, see F. Baumer, *Modern European Thought: Continuity and Change in Ideas 1600–1950*, at 444–45 (1977).

21. John 15:13 (King James Version).

22. One white clergyman admonished King for his "untimely" Birmingham demonstrations by pointing out that "[a]ll Christians know that the colored people will receive equal rights eventually, but it is possible that you are in too great of a religious hurry. It has taken Christianity almost two thousand years to accomplish what it has. The teachings of Christ take time to come to earth."

23. King, "Letter From Birmingham City Jail" (1963), reprinted in *A Testament of Hope, supra* note 1, at 292 (emphasis added).

24. *Id.* at 299.

25. K. Smith and I. Zepp, *Search for the Beloved Community: The Thinking of Martin Luthur King, Jr. (1986) at 127.*

26. *Id.,* quoting King, "Nobel Prize Acceptance Speech," reprinted in *Negro Hist. Bull.*, May 1968, at 21. [. . .]

27. M. King, "The Time for Freedom Has Come" (1961), reprinted in *A Testament of Hope, supra* note 1 at 160, 165.

28. M. King, "The Ethical Demands for Integration" (1963), reprinted in *A Testament of Hope, supra* note 1, at 117, 124; see also M. King, "The American Dream" (1961), reprinted in *A Testament of Hope, supra* note 1, at 208, 213 ("It may be true that the law can't make a man love me, but it can keep him from lynching me, and I think that's pretty important also.").

RACE, REFORM, AND RETRENCHMENT:
TRANSFORMATION AND LEGITIMATION
IN ANTIDISCRIMINATION LAW
Kimberlé Williams Crenshaw

I. INTRODUCTION

IN 1984, President Ronald Reagan signed a
bill that created the Martin Luther King,
Jr. Federal Holiday Commission.[1] The commission was charged with the responsibility of
issuing guidelines for states and localities to
follow in preparing their observances of King's
birthday. The commission's task would not be
easy. Although King's birthday had come to
symbolize the massive social movement that
grew out of African-Americans' efforts to end
the long history of racial oppression in
America,[2] the first official observance of the
holiday would take place in the face of at least
two disturbing obstacles: first, a constant, if not
increasing, socioeconomic disparity between the
races,[3] and second, a hostile administration devoted to changing the path of civil rights reforms which many believe responsible for most
of the movement's progress.[4]

The commission, though, was presented with
a more essential difficulty: a focus on the continuing disparities between blacks and whites
might call not for celebration but for strident
criticism of America's failure to make good on
its promise of racial equality. Yet such criticism
would overlook the progress that has been
made, progress that the holiday itself represents.
The commission apparently resolved this dilemma by calling for a celebration of progress
toward racial equality while urging continued
commitment to this ideal. This effort to reconcile the celebration of an ideal with conditions
that bespeak its continuing denial was given the
ironic, but altogether appropriate title "Living
the Dream."[5] The "Living the Dream" directive
aptly illustrates Derrick Bell's observation that
"[m]ost Americans, black and white, view the
civil rights crusade as a long, slow, but always
upward pull that must, given the basic precepts of the country and the commitment of
its people to equality and liberty, eventually
end in the full enjoyment by blacks of all rights

and privileges of citizenship enjoyed by
whites."[6]

Commentators on both the right and the left,
however, have begun to cast doubt upon the
continuing vitality of this shopworn theme. The
position of the New Right, articulated by members of the Reagan administration and by neoconservative scholars such as Thomas Sowell, is
that the goal of the civil rights movement—the
extension of formal equality to all Americans
regardless of color—has already been achieved,
hence the vision of a continuing struggle under
the banner of civil rights is inappropriate. The
position of the new left, presented in the work
of scholars associated with the conference on
Critical Legal Studies, also challenges the perception that the civil rights struggle represents
a long, steady march toward social transformation. CLS scholars do not significantly disagree
with the goal of racial equality, but assert only
the basic counterproductivity of seeking that
objective through the use of legal rights. Indeed,
CLS scholars claim that even engaging in rights
discourse is incompatible with a broader strategy of social change. They view the extension
of rights, although perhaps energizing political
struggle or producing apparent victories in the
short run, as ultimately legitimating the very
racial inequality and oppression that such extension purports to remedy. This article challenges
both the New Left and New Right critiques of
the civil rights movement. . . .

II. THE NEW RIGHT ATTACKS: CIVIL RIGHTS AS "POLITICS"

A. The Neoconservative Offensive

The Reagan administration arrived in Washington in 1981 with an agenda that was profoundly hostile to the civil rights policies of the
previous two decades. The principal basis of its
hostility was a formalistic, color-blind view of
civil rights that had developed in the neoconservative "think tanks" during the seventies. Neoconservative doctrine singles out race-specific
civil rights policies as one of the most significant
threats to the democratic political system.
Emphasizing the need for strictly color-blind
policies, this view calls for the repeal of affirmative action and other race-specific remedial

policies, urges an end to class-based remedies, and calls for the administration to limit remedies to what it calls "actual victims" of discrimination.

A number of early episodes sent a clear message that the Reagan administration would be inhospitable to the civil rights policies adopted by earlier administrations. For example, the Civil Rights Division of the Justice Department, under Deputy Attorney General William Bradford Reynolds, abruptly changed sides in several cases.[7] Other serious attacks on the civil rights constituency included Reagan's attempt to fire members of the U.S. Commission on Civil Rights, the administration's opposition to the 1982 amendment of the Voting Rights Act, and Reagan's veto of the Civil Rights Restoration Act.

These fervent attempts to change the direction of civil rights law generated speculation that the Reagan administration was antiblack and ideologically opposed to civil rights. Yet the administration denied that any racial animus motivated its campaign. Far from viewing themselves as opponents of civil rights, Reagan, Reynolds, and others in the administration apparently saw themselves as "true" civil rights advocates seeking to restore the original meaning of civil rights.

Neoconservative scholar Thomas Sowell perhaps best articulates the philosophy underlying the New Right policies on race and law. Sowell presents the neoconservative struggle against prevailing civil rights policies as nothing less than an attempt to restore law to its rightful place and to prevent the descent of American society into fascism.[8] Sowell suggests that the growing popularity of white hate groups is evidence of the instability wrought by improvident civil rights policies. To Sowell, the growth of antiblack sentiment is an understandable reaction to a vision that has threatened to undermine democratic institutions, delegitimize the court system, and demoralize the American people.

The culprit in this epic struggle is a political view that Sowell has dubbed "the civil rights vision"; according to him, this view developed as the leaders of the civil rights movement shifted the movement's original focus on equal treatment under the law to a demand for equal results notwithstanding genuine differences in ability, thereby delegitimizing the movement's claim in a democratic society. The civil rights vision has nothing to do with the achievement of civil rights today, according to Sowell, because in reality "the battle for civil rights was fought and won—at great cost—many years ago."[9] Sowell's central criticism is that the visionaries have attempted to infuse the law with their own political interpretation, which Sowell characterizes as separate from and alien to the true meaning of civil rights. He argues that although these visionaries have struggled and sacrificed in the name of civil rights, they nonetheless merit censure for undermining the stability of American society through their politicization of the law.

Sowell singles out the judiciary for especially harsh criticism. Judges, according to Sowell, have ignored the original understanding of Title VII of the Civil Rights Act of 1964 and imposed their own political views instead: "The perversions of the law by federal judges . . . have been especially brazen."[10] Judges, he asserts, have participated in a process by which "law, plain honesty and democracy itself [have been] sacrificed on the altar of missionary self-righteousness."[11] Sowell cautions that when judges allow law to be overridden by politics, the threat of fascism looms ever large: if judges reduce the law to a question of who has the power and whose ox is gored, they can hardly disclaim responsibility or be morally superior when others respond in kind.[12] . . .

B. A Critique of the Critique: The Indeterminacy of Civil Rights Discourse

Given the seriousness of his accusations, particularly those against the judiciary, one would expect Sowell's proof of subversion to be substantial. His repeated accusations that the true law has been subverted raise expectations that he will eventually identify some determinate, clearly discernible version of that law. Sowell's true law would presumably stand apart from the politics of race, yet control it, without being influenced by inappropriate political factors. Sowell's only "proof" that the law has been subverted, however, rests on his assumption that such subversion is self-evident. In the context of voting, for example, Sowell declares simply: "the right to vote is a civil right. The right to win is not. Equal treatment does not mean equal results."[13]

Sowell fails to substantiate his accusations because he cannot tell us what the real law is or whether it ever existed as he claims. He simply embraces language from antidiscrimination texts, imports his own meaning of its purpose, and ignores contradictory purposes and interpretations. Here Sowell, apparently without realizing it, merely embraces one aspect of a tension that runs throughout antidiscrimination law—the tension between equality as a process and equality as a result.

This basic conflict has given rise to two distinct rhetorical visions in the body of antidiscrimination law: I term these the expansive view and the restrictive view. The expansive view stresses equality as a result, and it looks to real consequences for African-Americans. It interprets the objective of antidiscrimination law as the eradication of the substantive conditions of black subordination, and it attempts to enlist the institutional power of the courts to further the national goal of eradicating the effects of racial oppression.

The restrictive vision, which exists side by side with this expansive view, treats equality as a process, downplaying the significance of actual outcomes. The primary objective of antidiscrimination law, according to this vision, is to prevent future wrongdoing rather than to redress present manifestations of past injustice. "Wrongdoing," moreover, is seen primarily as isolated actions against individuals rather than as a social policy against an entire group. Nor does the restrictive view contemplate the courts' playing a role in redressing harms from America's racist past, as opposed to merely policing society in order to eliminate a narrow set of proscribed discriminatory practices. Moreover, even when injustice is found, efforts to redress it must be balanced against and limited by competing interests of white workers—even when those interests were actually created by

the subordination of blacks. The innocence of whites weighs more heavily than do either the past wrongs committed upon blacks or the benefits that whites derived from those wrongs. In sum, the restrictive view seeks to proscribe only certain kinds of subordinating acts, and then only when other interests are not overly burdened.

Although the tension between the expansive and restrictive vision is present throughout antidiscrimination law, Sowell dismisses the full complexity of the problem by simply declaring that equal process is completely unrelated to equal results. Yet it is not nearly as clear as Sowell suggests that the right to vote, for instance, has nothing to do with winning; no measure of a process's effectiveness can be wholly separated from the purpose for which it was initiated. Sowell implicitly acknowledges that voting is related to some notion of actual representation; having done so, he cannot completely sever that process from its admitted purpose. Depending on how one views society, democracy, and the historic significance of racial disenfranchisement, the "appropriate" relationship between voting and representation can be defined to require anything from representation at large to full proportional representation. Sowell's attempt to sever voting from winning merely raises the question of process and results; it does not answer it.

As the expansive and restrictive views of antidiscrimination law reveal, there simply is no self-evident interpretation of civil rights inherent in the terms themselves. Instead, specific interpretations proceed largely from the worldview of the interpreter. For example, to believe, as Sowell does, that color-blind policies represent the only legitimate and effective means of ensuring a racially equitable society, one would have to assume not only that there is only one "proper role" for law but also that such a racially equitable society already exists. In this world, once law had performed its "proper" function of assuring equality of process, then differences in outcomes between groups would not reflect past discrimination but rather real differences between groups competing for social rewards. Unimpeded by irrational prejudices against identifiable groups and unfettered by government-imposed preferences, competition would ensure that any group stratification would reflect only the cumulative effects of employers' rational decisions to hire the best workers for the least cost; the deprivations and oppression of the past would somehow be expunged from the present. Only in such a society, where all other social functions operate in a nondiscriminatory way, would equality of process constitute equality of opportunity.

This belief in color-blindness and equal process, however, would make no sense at all in a society in which identifiable groups had actually been treated differently historically and in which the effects of this difference in treatment continued into the present. If employers were thought to have been influenced by factors other than the actual performance of each job applicant, it would be absurd to rely on their decisions as evidence of true market valuations. Arguments that differences in economic status cannot be redressed, or that they are legitimate because they reflect cultural rather than racial inferiority, would have to be rejected; cultural disadvantages themselves would be seen as the consequence of historical discrimination. One could not look at outcomes as a fair measure of merit, since one would recognize that not everyone had been given an "equal" start. It would be apparent that institutions had embraced discriminatory policies in order to produce disparate results, so it would be necessary to rely on results to indicate whether these discriminatory policies have been successfully dismantled.

These two visions of society correspond closely to those held by Sowell and the civil rights visionaries. In each vision, all arguments about what the law is in fact are premised upon what the law should be, given a particular world-view. The conflict is not, as Sowell has suggested, between the true meaning of the law and a bastardized version, but rather between two different interpretations of society. Thus, though they attempt to lay claim to an apolitical perch from which to accuse civil rights visionaries of subverting the law to politics, the neoconservatives as well rely on their own political interpretations to give meaning to their respective concepts of rights and oppression. Law

itself does not dictate which of various visions will be adopted as an interpretive base. The choice between various visions and the values that lie within them is not guided by any determinate organizing principle. Consequently, Sowell has no basis from which to argue that color-conscious, result-oriented remedies are political perversions of the law, but that his preference, color-blind, process-oriented remedies are not.

C. The Constituency's Dilemma

The passage of civil rights legislation nurtured the impression that the United States had moved decisively to end the oppression of blacks. The fanfare surrounding the passage of these acts, however, created an expectation that the legislation would not and could not fulfill. The law accommodated and obscured contradictions that led to conflict, countervision, and the current vacuousness of antidiscrimination law.

Because antidiscrimination law contains both the expansive and the restrictive view, equality of opportunity can refer to either. This uncertainty means that the societal adoption of racial equality rhetoric does not itself entail a commitment to end racial inequality. Indeed, to the extent that antidiscrimination law is believed to embrace color-blindness, equal opportunity rhetoric constitutes a formidable obstacle to efforts to alleviate conditions of white supremacy. As Alfred Blumrosen observes, "it [is] clear that a 'color-blind' society built upon the subordination of persons of one color [is] a society which [cannot] correct that subordination because it [can] never recognize it."[14] In sum, the very terms used to proclaim victory contain within them the seeds of defeat. To demand "equality of opportunity" is to demand nothing specific because "equality of opportunity" has assimilated both the demand and the object against which the demand is made—it is to participate in an abstracted discourse that carries the moral force of the movement as well as the stability of the institutions and interests that the movement opposed.

Society's adoption of the ambivalent rhetoric of equal opportunity law has made it that much more difficult for black people to name their reality. There is no longer a perpetrator, a clearly identifiable discriminator. Company Z can be an equal opportunity employer even though Company Z has no blacks or any other minorities in its employ. Practically speaking, all companies can now be equal opportunity employers by proclamation alone. Society has embraced the rhetoric of equal opportunity without fulfilling its promise; creating a break with the past has formed the basis for the neoconservative claim that present inequities cannot be the result of discriminatory practices because this society no longer discriminates against blacks.

Equal opportunity law may have also undermined the fragile consensus against white supremacy. To the extent that the objective of racial equality was seen as lifting formal barriers imposed against participation by blacks, the reforms appear to have succeeded. Today, the claim that equal opportunity does not yet exist for black America may fall upon deaf ears—ears deafened by repeated declarations that equal opportunity exists. Even Alfred Blumrosen—himself a civil rights visionary—demonstrates how the rhetoric of formal racial equality, by bringing about the collapse of overt obstacles, convinced people that things have changed significantly:

> The public sympathy for the plight of black Americans circa 1965 cannot be recreated, because the condition of black American[s] in 1985 is so much improved, as a result of the 1964 legislation. The success of the Civil Rights Act contained the seeds of its loss of public support. Racism alone simply will no longer do as an explanation for the current condition of depressed minorities. The rhetoric of the sixties sounds hollow to Americans of the eighties because it is hollow.[15]

Blumrosen and others may be correct in pointing out that many things have changed under the political, legal, and moral force of the civil rights movement. Formal barriers have constituted a major aspect of the historic subordination of African-Americans. . . . The elimination of those barriers was meaningful. Indeed, equal opportunity rhetoric gains its power from the fact that people can point to real changes that accompanied its advent. . . . However, what at first appears an unambiguous commit-

ment to antidiscrimination conceals within it many conflicting and contradictory interests. In antidiscrimination law, the conflicting interests actually reinforce existing social arrangements, moderated to the extent necessary to balance the civil rights challenge with the many interests still privileged over it.

The recognition on the part of civil rights advocates that deeper institutional changes are required has come just as the formal changes have begun to convince people that enough has been done. Indeed, recent cases illustrate that the judiciary's commitment to racial equality has waned considerably. These doctrinal and procedural developments, taken along with the overall political climate, indicate that the policy of redressing discrimination no longer has the high priority it once had. . . .

The flagging commitment of the courts and of many whites to fighting discrimination may not be the only deleterious effect of the civil rights reforms. The lasting harm must be measured by the extent to which limited gains hamper efforts of African-Americans to name their reality and to remain capable of engaging in collective action in the future. The danger of adopting equal opportunity rhetoric on its face is that the constituency incorporates legal and philosophical concepts that have an uneven history and an unpredictable trajectory. If the civil rights constituency allows its own political consciousness to be completely replaced by the ambiguous discourse of antidiscrimination law, it will be difficult for this constituency to defend its genuine interests against those whose interests are supported by opposing visions that also employ the same discourse. The struggle, it seems, is to maintain a contextualized, specified worldview that reflects the experience of blacks. The question remains whether engaging in legal reform precludes this possibility.

III. THE NEW LEFT ATTACK: THE HEGEMONIC FUNCTION OF LEGAL RIGHTS DISCOURSE

VARIOUS scholars connected with the CLS movement have offered critical analyses of law and legal reform which provide a broad framework for explaining how legal reforms help to mask and legitimate continuing racial inequality. The critics present law as a series of ideological constructs that operate to support existing social arrangements by convincing people that things are both inevitable and basically fair. Legal reform, therefore, cannot serve as a means for fundamentally restructuring society. This theory, however, is a general one, and its utility is limited in the context of civil rights by its insufficient attention to racial domination. Removed from the reality of oppression and its overwhelming constraints, the critics cannot fairly understand the choices that the civil rights movement confronted or, still less, recommend solutions to its current problems.

A. The Critical Vision

In broadest terms, CLS scholars have attempted to analyze legal ideology and discourse as . . . social artifacts that operate to recreate and legitimate American society. In order to discover the contingent character of the law, CLS scholars unpack legal doctrine to reveal both its internal inconsistencies (generally by exposing the incoherence of legal arguments) and its external inconsistencies (often by laying bare the inherently paradoxical and political worldviews embedded within legal doctrine). Having thus exposed the inadequacies of legal doctrine, CLS scholars go on to examine the political character of the choices that were made in the doctrine's name. This inquiry exposes the ways in which legal ideology has helped to create, support, and legitimate America's present class structure.

I. THE ROLE OF LEGAL IDEOLOGY

Critical scholars derive their vision of legal ideology in part from the work of Antonio Gramsci, an Italian neo-Marxist theorist who developed an approach to understanding domination which transcends some of the limitations of traditional Marxist accounts. In examining domination as a combination of physical coercion and ideological control, Gramsci articulated the concept of hegemony, the means by which a system of attitudes and beliefs, permeating both popular consciousness and the ideology of elites, reinforces existing social arrange-

ments and convinces the dominated classes that the existing order is inevitable. After observing the ability of the Italian system to withstand aggressive challenges in the years preceding the ascent of fascism, Gramsci concluded that "when the State trembled a sturdy structure of civil society was at once revealed. The State was only an outer ditch, behind which there stood a powerful system of fortresses and earthworks. . . ."[16]

Some CLS scholars place great emphasis on understanding the "fortifying earthworks" of American society. The concept of hegemony allows these scholars to explain the continued legitimacy of American society by revealing how legal consciousness induces people to accept or consent to their own oppression. Legal historian Robert Gordon, for example, declares that one should look

> not only at the undeniably numerous, specific ways in which the legal system functions to screw poor people . . . but rather at all the ways in which the system seems at first glance basically uncontroversial, neutral, acceptable. This is Antonio Gramsci's notion of "hegemony," i.e., that the most effective kind of domination takes place when both the dominant and dominated classes believe that the existing order, with perhaps some marginal changes, is satisfactory, or at least represents the most that anyone could expect, because things pretty much have to be the way they are.[17]

According to Gordon, Gramsci directs our attention to the many thoughts and beliefs that people have adopted which limit their ability "even to imagine that life could be different and better."[18]

Although society's structures of thought have been constructed by elites out of a universe of possibilities, people reify these structures and clothe them with the illusion of necessity. Law is an essential feature in the illusion of necessity because it embodies and reinforces ideological assumptions about human relations which people accept as natural or even immutable. People act out their lives, mediate conflicts, and even perceive themselves with reference to the law. By accepting the bounds of law and ordering their lives according to its categories and relations, people think that they are confirming reality—the way things must be. Yet by accepting the worldview implicit in the law, people are also bound by its conceptual limitations. Thus, conflict and antagonism are contained: the legitimacy of the entire order is never seriously questioned.

Relating this idea to the limitations of antidiscrimination law, Alan Freeman argues that the legal reforms that grew out of the civil rights movement were severely limited by the ideological constraints embedded within the law and dictated by "needs basic to the preservation of the class structure."[19] These ideological pillars supporting the class structure were at once repositories of racial domination and obstacles to the fundamental reordering of society. For example, Freeman argues, formal equality, combined with the fact that American law does not formally recognize any difference based on wealth, precluded most remedies that would have required the redistribution of wealth. Yet economic exploitation and poverty have been central features of racial domination, and poverty is its long-term result. A legal strategy that does not include redistribution of wealth cannot remedy one of the most significant aspects of racial domination. Similarly, the myths of "vested rights" and "equality of opportunity" were necessary to protect the legitimacy of the dominant order, thus they constituted insuperable barriers to the quest for significant redistributive reform. Freeman's central argument is that the severe limitations of legal reform were dictated by the legitimating role of legal discourse. If law functions to reinforce a worldview holding that things should be the way they are, then law cannot provide an effective means to challenge the present order.

Some critics see the destructive role of rights rhetoric as another symptom of the law's legitimating function. Mark Tushnet has offered a four-tiered critique of rights:

(1) Once one identifies what counts as a right in a specific setting, it invariably turns out that the right is unstable; significant but relatively small changes in the social setting can make it difficult to sustain the claim that a right remains implicated. (2) The claim that a right is implicated in some settings produces no determinate conse-

quences. (3) The concept of rights falsely converts into an empty abstraction (reifies) real experiences that we ought to value for their own sake. (4) The use of rights in contemporary discourse impedes advances by progressive social forces. . . .[20]

Tushnet's first and second arguments crystallize the doctrinal dilemmas faced by the civil rights community. Antidiscrimination doctrine does not itself provide determinate results. To give rights meaning, people must specify the world; they must create a picture of "what is" that grounds their normative interpretation.

Tushnet's third and fourth arguments spell out pragmatic reasons to approach rights with caution. According to Tushnet, the language of rights undermines efforts to change things by absorbing real demands, experiences, and concerns into a vacuous and indeterminate discourse. The discourse abstracts real experiences and clouds the ability of those who invoke rights rhetoric to think concretely about real confrontations and real circumstances.

According to Tushnet, the danger that arises from being swept into legal rights discourse is that people lose sight of their real objectives. Their visions and thoughts of the possible become trapped within the ideological limitations of the law. . . . Peter Gabel suggests that the belief in rights and in the state serves a hegemonic function through willed delusion:

[B]elief in the state is a flight from the immediate alienation of concrete existence into a split-off sphere of people's minds in which they imagine themselves to be a part of an imaginary political community—"citizens of the United States of America." And it's this collective projection and internalization of an imaginary political authority that is the basis of the legitimation of hierarchy. It's the mass-psychological foundation of democratic consent. Hegemony is reinforced through this "state abstaraction" because people believe in and react passively to a mere illusion of political consensus. [The critics] assert that these abstractions blind people to the contingent nature of human existence. When people act as if these illusions are real, they actually recreate their own oppressive world moment by moment.[21]

2. TRANSFORMATION IN THE CRITICAL VISION

The vision of change that CLS scholars express flows directly from their focus on ideology as the major obstacle that separates the actual from the possible. Because it is ideology that prevents people from conceiving of—and hence from implementing—a freer social condition, these critics propose the exposure of ideology as the logical first step toward social transformation. . . .

   Viewing the structures of legal thought as central to the perception of the world as necessary and the status quo as legitimate, they believe it is crucial to demonstrate the contingency of legal ideology. Once false necessity or contingency is revealed, these critics suggest, people will be able to remake their world in a different way.

B. A Critique of the Critique: The Problem of Context

CLS scholars offer an analysis that is useful in understanding the limited transformative potential of antidiscrimination rhetoric. There are difficulties, however, in attempting to use CLS themes and ideas to understand the civil rights movement and to describe what alternatives the civil rights constituency could have pursued, or might now pursue. While these scholars claim that their project is concerned with domination, few have made more than a token effort to address racial domination specifically, and their work does not seem grounded in the reality of the racially oppressed.

   This deficiency is especially apparent in critiques that relate to racial issues. CLS scholars have criticized mainstream legal ideology for its tendency to portray American society as basically fair, and thereby to legitimate the oppressive policies that have been directed toward racial minorities. Yet these scholars do not sufficiently account for the effects or the causes of the oppression that they routinely acknowledge. The result is that CLS literature exhibits the same proclivities that mainstream scholarship does—it seldom speaks to or about black people.

   The failure of the CLS scholars to address racism in their analysis also renders their critique of rights and their overall analysis of law in America incomplete. Specifically, this failure leads to an inability to appreciate fully the

transformative significance of the civil rights movement in mobilizing black Americans and generating new demands. Further, the failure to consider the reality of those most oppressed by American institutions means that the CLS account of the hegemonic nature of legal thought overlooks a crucial dimension of American life—the ideological role of racism itself. Gordon, Freeman, Tushnet, and Gabel fail to analyze racism as an ideological pillar upholding American society, or as the principal basis for black oppression. These and other critics' failure to analyze the hegemonic role of racism also renders their prescriptive analysis unrealistic. . . . CLS scholars often appear to view the trashing of legal ideology "as the only path that might lead to a liberated future." Yet if trashing is the only path that might lead to a liberated future, black people are unlikely to make it to the CLS promised land.

   The commitment of CLS scholars to trashing is premised on a notion that people are mystified by liberal legal ideology and consequently cannot remake their world until they see how contingent such ideology is. However, this version of domination by consent does not present a realistic picture of racial domination. Coercion explains much more about racial domination than does ideologically induced consent.[22] Black people do not create their oppressive worlds moment to moment but rather are coerced into living in worlds created and maintained by others; moreover, the ideological source of this coercion is not liberal legal consciousness but racism. If racism is just as important as (if not more important than) liberal legal ideology in explaining the persistence of white supremacy, then the CLS scholars' single-minded effort to deconstruct liberal legal ideology will be futile.

   Finally, in addition to exaggerating the role of liberal legal consciousness and underestimating that of coercion, CLS scholars also disregard the transformative potential that liberalism offers. Although liberal legal ideology may indeed function to mystify, it remains receptive to some aspirations that are central to black demands; it may also perform an important function in combating the experience of being excluded and oppressed.[23] This receptivity to black aspirations is crucial, given the hostile social world that racism creates. The most troubling aspect of the critical program, therefore, is that trashing rights consciousness may have the unintended consequences of disempowering the racially oppressed while leaving white supremacy basically untouched. . . .

C. Questioning the Transformative View: Some Doubts about Trashing

The critics product is of limited utility to blacks in its present form. The implications for blacks of trashing liberal legal ideology are troubling, even though it may be proper to assail belief structures that obscure liberating possibilities. Trashing legal ideology seems to tell us repeatedly what has already been established—that legal discourse is unstable and relatively indeterminate. Furthermore, trashing offers no idea of how to avoid the negative consequences of engaging in reformist discourse or how to work around such consequences. Even if we imagine the wrong world when we think in terms of legal discourse, we must nevertheless exist in a present world, where legal protection has at times been a blessing—albeit a mixed one. The fundamental problem is that although CLS scholars criticize law because it functions to legitimate existing institutional arrangements, it is precisely this legitimating function that has made law receptive to certain demands in this area.

The CLS emphasis on deconstruction as the vehicle for liberation leads to the conclusion that engaging in legal discourse should be avoided because it reinforces not only the discourse itself but also the society and the world that it embodies. Yet CLS scholars offer little beyond this observation: their focus on delegitimating rights rhetoric seems to suggest that once rights rhetoric has been discarded, there exists a more productive strategy for change, one that does not reinforce existing patterns of domination.

Unfortunately, no such strategy has yet been articulated, and it is difficult to imagine that racial minorities will ever be able to discover one. As Frances Fox Piven and Richard Clo-ward point out in their excellent account of the civil rights movement, popular struggles are a reflection of institutionally determined logic and a challenge to that logic. People can demand change only in ways that reflect the logic of the institutions they are challenging.[24] Demands for change that do not reflect the institutional logic—that is, demands that do not engage and subsequently reinforce the dominant ideology—will probably be ineffective.

The possibility for ideological change is created through the very process of legitimation, which is triggered by crisis. Powerless people can sometimes trigger such a crisis by challenging an institution internally, that is, by using its own logic against it.[25] Such crisis occurs when powerless people force open and politicize a contradiction between the dominant ideology and their reality. The political consequences of maintaining the contradictions may sometimes force an adjustment—an attempt to close the gap or to make things appear fair. Yet, because the adjustment is triggered by the political consequences of the contradiction, circumstances will be adjusted only to the extent necessary to smooth the apparent contradiction.

This approach to understanding legitimation and change is applicable to the civil rights movement. Because blacks were challenging their exclusion from political society, the only claims that were likely to achieve recognition were those which reflected American society's institutional logic—legal rights ideology. Civil rights protestors, articulating their formal demands through legal rights ideology, exposed a series of contradictions, the most important being the promised privileges of American citizenship and the practice of absolute racial subordination. Rather than using the contradictions to suggest that American citizenship was itself illegitimate or false, civil rights protestors proceeded as if American citizenship were real and demanded to exercise the "rights" that citizenship entailed. By seeking to restructure reality to reflect American mythology, blacks relied upon and ultimately benefited from politically inspired efforts to resolve the contradictions by granting formal rights. Although it is the need to maintain legitimacy which presents powerless

groups with the opportunity to wrest concessions from the dominant order, it is the very
accomplishment of legitimacy that forecloses
greater possibilities. In sum, the potential for
change is both created and limited by legitimation.

The central issue that CLS scholars fail to
address, then, is how to avoid the "legitimating"
effects of reform if engaging in reformist discourse is the only effective way to challenge the
legitimacy of the social order. Perhaps the only
situation in which powerless people may receive
any favorable response is where there is a political or ideological need to restore an image of
fairness that has somehow been tarnished. Most
efforts to change an oppressive situation are
bound to adopt the dominant discourse to some
degree. On the other hand, Peter Gabel may
well be right in observing that the reforms
which come from such demands are likely to
transform a given situation only to the extent
necessary to legitimate those elements of the
situation that "must" remain unchanged. Thus,
it might just be the case that oppression means
"being between a rock and a hard place"—in
other words, that there are risks and dangers
involved both in engaging in the dominant
discourse and in failing to do so. What subordinated people need is an analysis that can inform
them about how the risks can be minimized
and how the rocks and the very hard places can
be negotiated.

IV. The Context Defined: Racist Ideology and Hegemony

THE failure of the CLS scholars to consider race in their account of law and
legitimacy is not a minor oversight: race-
consciousness is central not only to the domination of blacks but also to whites' acceptance of
the legitimacy of hierarchy and their identity
with elite interest. Exposing the centrality of
race-consciousness is crucial to identifying and
delegitimating beliefs that present hierarchy as
inevitable and fair. Moreover, exposing the centrality of race-consciousness shows how the options of blacks in American society have been
limited, and how the use of rights rhetoric has

emancipated blacks from some manifestations
of racial domination.

A realignment of the CLS project to incorporate race-consciousness must begin with beliefs
about blacks in American society, and how
these beliefs legitimize racial coercion. My
purpose here is to examines the deep-rooted
problem of racist ideology—or white race-
consciousness—and to suggest how this form
of consciousness legitimates prevailing injustices
and constrains the development of new solutions that would benefit black Americans. . . .

A. The Hegemonic Role of Racism: Establishing the Other in American Ideology

Throughout American history, the subordination of blacks was rationalized by a series of
stereotypes and beliefs that made their conditions appear logical and natural. Historically,
white supremacy has been premised upon various political, scientific, and religious theories,
each of which relies on racial characterizations
and stereotypes about blacks which have coalesced into an extensive legitimating ideology.
Today, it is probably not controversial to say
that these stereotypes were developed primarily
to rationalize the oppression of blacks. What is
overlooked, however, is the extent to which
these stereotypes serve a hegemonic function by
perpetuating a mythology about both blacks and
whites even today, reinforcing an illusion of a
white community that cuts across ethnic, gender, and class lines.

As presented by CLS scholars, hegemonic
rule succeeds to the extent that the ruling class
worldview establishes the appearance of a unity
of interests between the dominant class and
the dominated. Throughout American history,
racism has identified the interests of subordinated whites with those of society's white elite.
Racism does not support the dominant order
simply because all whites want to maintain their
privilege at the expense of blacks, or because
blacks sometimes serve as convenient political
scapegoats; rather, the very existence of a clearly
subordinated Other group is contrasted with
the norm in a way that reinforces identification
with the dominant group. Racism helps to cre-

ate an illusion of unity through the oppositional force of a symbolic "other."[26] The establishment of an Other creates a bond, a burgeoning common identity of all nonstigmatized parties—whose identity and interests are defined in opposition to the other.

According to the philosophy of Jacques Derrida, a structure of polarized categories is characteristic of Western thought:

> Western thought . . . has always been structured in terms of dichotomies or polarities: good vs. evil, being vs. nothingness, presence vs. absence, truth vs. error, identity vs. difference, mind vs. matter, man vs. woman, soul vs. body, life vs. death, nature vs. culture, speech vs. writing. These polar opposites do not, however, stand as independent and equal entities. The second term in each pair is considered the negative, corrupt, undersirable version of the first, a fall away from it. . . . In other words, the two terms are not simply opposed in their meanings, but are arranged in a hierarchical order which gives the first term priority. . . .[27]

Racist ideology replicates this pattern of arranging oppositional categories in a hierarchical order; historically, whites have represented the dominant element in the antinomy, while blacks came to be seen as separate and subordinate. This hierarchy is reflected in the list below; note how each traditional negative image of blacks correlates with a counterimage of whites:

Historical oppositional dualities

White Images	Black Images
industrious	lazy
intelligent	unintelligent
moral	immoral
knowledgeable	ignorant
enabling culture	disabling culture
law-abiding	criminal
responsible	shiftless
virtuous/pious	lascivious

The oppositional dynamic exemplified in this list was created and maintained through an elaborate and systematic process. Laws and customs helped to create "races" out of a broad range of human traits. In the process of creating races, the categories came to be filled with meaning: whites were characterized one way and associated with normatively positive charac-

teristics, whereas blacks were characterized another way and became associated with the subordinate, even aberrational characteristics. The operation of this dynamic, along with the important political role of racial oppositionalism, can be illustrated through a few brief historical references.

Edmund Morgan provides vivid illustration of how slaveholders from the seventeenth century onward created and politicized racial categories in order to maintain the support of nonslaveholding whites. Morgan recounts how the planters "lump[ed] Indians, mulattoes, and Negroes in a single slave class," and how these categories became "an essential, if unacknowledged, ingredient of the republican ideology that enabled Virginians to lead the nation."[28] Having accepted a common interest with slaveholders in keeping blacks subordinated, even those whites who had material reasons to object to the dominance of the slaveholding class could challenge the regime only so far. The power of race-consciousness convinced whites to support a system that was opposed to their own economic interests. As George Fredrickson put it, "racial privilege could and did serve as a compensation for class disadvantage."[29]

Domination through race-consciousness continued throughout the post-Reconstruction period. Historian C. Vann Woodward has argued that the ruling plantocracy was able to undermine the progressive accomplishments of the Populist movement by stirring up antiblack sentiment among poor white farmers; racism was articulated as the "broader ground for a new democracy."[30] As racism formed the new base for a broader notion of democracy, class differences were mediated through reference to a racial community of equality.[31] A tragic example of the success of such race-conscious political manipulation is the career of Tom Watson, the leader of the progressive Populist movement of the 1890s. Watson, in his attempts to educate the masses of poor farmers about the destructive role of race-based politics, repeatedly told black and white audiences: "You are made to hate each other because upon that hatred is rested the keystone of the arch of financial despotism which enslaves you both. You are deceived and blinded that you may not see how this race antagonism perpetuates a monetary system which beggars you both."[32] Yet by 1906, Watson had joined the movement to disenfranchise blacks; according to Woodward, Watson had "persuaded himself that only after the Negro was eliminated from politics could Populist principles gain a hearing. In other words, the white men would have to unite before they could divide."[33]

White race-consciousness also played a role in the nascent labor movement in the North. Labor historian Herbert Hill has demonstrated that unions of virtually all trades excluded black workers from their ranks and often entirely barred black employment in certain fields. Immigrant labor unions were particularly adamant about keeping out black workers; indeed, it was precisely in order to assimilate into the American mainstream that immigrant laborers adopted these exclusionary policies.[34]

The political and ideological role that race-consciousness continues to play is suggested by racial polarization in contemporary presidential politics. Several political commentators have suggested that many whites supported Ronald Reagan in the belief that he would correct a perceived policy imbalance that unjustly benefited blacks, and some argue further that Reagan made a direct racist appeal to white voters. ... Reagan received nearly 70 percent of the white vote, whereas 90 percent of black voters cast their ballots for Mondale. Similarly, the vast majority of blacks—82 percent—disapproved of Reagan's performance, whereas only 32 percent of whites did.

Even the Democratic party, which has traditionally relied on blacks as its most loyal constituency, has responded to this apparent racial polarization by seeking to distance itself from black interests. Although some have argued that the racial polarization demonstrated in the 1984 election does not represent a trend of white defections from the Democratic party, it is significant that, whatever the cause of the party's inability to attract white votes, Democratic leaders have expressed a willingness to moderate the party's stand on key racial issues in an effort to recapture the white vote.[35]

B. The Role of Race Consciousness in a System of Formal Equality

The previous section has emphasized the continuity of white race-consciousness over the course of American history. This section, by contrast, focuses on the partial transformation of the functioning of race-consciousness which occurred with the transition from Jim Crow to formal equality in race law.

Prior to the civil rights reforms, blacks were formally subordinated by the state. Blacks experienced being the "other" in two aspects of oppression, which I shall designate as symbolic and material.[36] Symbolic subordination refers to the formal denial of social and political equality to all blacks, regardless of their accomplishments. Segregation and other forms of social exclusion—separate restrooms, drinking fountains, entrances, parks, cemeteries, and dining facilities—reinforced a racist ideology that blacks were simply inferior to whites and were therefore not included in the vision of America as a community of equals.

Material subordination, on the other hand, refers to the ways that discrimination and exclusion economically subordinated blacks to whites and subordinated the life chances of blacks to those of whites on almost every level. This subordination occurs when blacks are paid less for the same work, when segregation limits access to decent housing, and where poverty, anxiety, poor health care, and crime create a life expectancy for blacks that is five to six years shorter than for whites.

Symbolic subordination often created material disadvantage by reinforcing race-consciousness in everything from employment to education. In fact, symbolic and material subordination were generally not thought of separately: separate facilities were usually inferior facilities, and limited job categorization almost invariably brought lower pay and harder work. Despite the pervasiveness of racism, however, there existed even before the civil rights movement a class of blacks who were educationally, economically, and professionally equal—if not superior—to many whites; yet even these blacks suffered social and political exclusion as well.

It is also significant that not all separation resulted in inferior institutions. School segregation—although often presented as the epitome of symbolic and material subordination—did not always bring about inferior education. It is not separation per se that made segregation subordinating; rather, this result is more properly attributable to the fact that it was enforced and supported by state power, and accompanied by the explicit belief in African-American inferiority.[37]

The response to the civil rights movement was the removal of most formal barriers and symbolic manifestations of subordination. Thus, "whites only" notices and other obvious indicators of the social policy of racial subordination disappeared—at least in the public sphere. The disappearance of these symbols of subordination reflected the acceptance of the rhetoric of formal equality, signaling the demise of white supremacy rhetoric as expressing America's normative vision. In other words, it could no longer be said that blacks were not included as equals in the American political vision.

Removal of these public manifestations of subordination was a significant gain for all blacks, although some benefited more than others. The eradication of formal barriers meant more to those whose oppression was primarily symbolic than to those who suffered lasting material disadvantage. Yet despite these disparate results, it would be absurd to suggest that no benefits came from these formal reforms, especially in regard to racial policies, such as segregation, that were partly material but largely symbolic. Thus, to say that the reforms were "merely symbolic" is to say a great deal: these legal reforms and the formal extension of "citizenship" were large achievements precisely because much of what characterized black oppression was symbolic and formal.

Yet the attainment of formal equality is not the end of the story. Racial hierarchy cannot be cured by the move to facial race-neutrality in the laws that structure the economic, political, and social lives of black people. White race-consciousness, in a new but nonetheless virulent form, plays an important, perhaps crucial, role in the new regime that has legitimated the

deteriorating day-to-day material conditions of the majority of blacks.

The end of Jim Crow has been accompanied by the demise of an explicit ideology of white supremacy. The white norm, however, has not disappeared; it has only been submerged in popular consciousness. It continues in an unspoken form as a statement of the positive social norm, legitimating the continuing domination of those who do not meet it. Nor have the negative stereotypes associated with blacks been eradicated. The rationalizations once used to legitimate black subordination based on a belief in racial inferiority have now been reemployed to legitimate the domination of blacks through reference to an assumed cultural inferiority.

Thomas Sowell, for example, suggests that underclass blacks are economically depressed because they have not adopted the values of hard work and discipline. He further implies that blacks have not pursued the need to attain skills and marketable education, and have not learned to make the sacrifices necessary for success. Instead, he charges, blacks view demands for special treatment as a means for achieving what other groups have achieved through hard work and the abandonment of racial politics.

Sowell applies the same stereotypes to the mass of blacks that white supremacists had applied in the past, but bases these modern stereotypes on notions of "culture" rather than genetics. Sowell characterizes underclass blacks as victims of self-imposed ignorance, lack of direction, and poor work attitudes: culture, not race, now accounts for this Otherness. Except for vestigial pockets of historical racism, any possible connection between past racial subordination and the present situation has been severed by the formal repudiation of the old race-conscious policies. The same dualities that historically have been used to legitimate racial subordination in the name of genetic inferiority have now been adopted by Sowell as a means for explaining the subordinated status of blacks today in terms of cultural inferiority.[37]

Moreover, Sowell's explanation of blacks' subordinated status also illustrates the treatment of the now-unspoken white stereotypes as the positive social norm. His assertion that the absence of certain attributes accounts for the continued subordination of blacks implies that it is the presence of these attributes that explains the continued advantage of whites. The only difference between this argument and the older oppositional dynamic is this: whereas the latter explained black subordination through reference to the ideology of white supremacy, the former explains black subordination through reference to an unspoken social norm. That norm—although no longer explicitly white supremacist—nevertheless, remains a white norm.

White race-consciousness, which includes the modern belief in cultural inferiority, furthers black subordination by justifying all the forms of unofficial racial discrimination, injury, and neglect that flourish in a society only formally dedicated to equality. Indeed, in ways more subtle, white race-consciousness reinforces and is reinforced by the myth of equal opportunity which explains and justifies broader class hierarchies.

Race-consciousness also reinforces whites' sense that American society truly is meritocratic, and thus it helps to prevent them from questioning the basic legitimacy of the free market. Believing both that blacks are inferior and that the economy impartially rewards the superior over the inferior, whites see that most blacks are indeed worse off than whites are, which reinforces their sense that the market is operating "fairly and impartially"; those who logically should be on the bottom are on the bottom. This strengthening of whites' belief in the system in turn reinforces their beliefs that blacks are indeed inferior. After all, equal opportunity is the rule, and the market is an impartial judge; if blacks are on the bottom, it must reflect their relative inferiority. Racist ideology thus operates in conjunction with the class components of legal ideology to reinforce the status quo, both in terms of class and race.

To bring a fundamental challenge to the way things are, whites would have to question not just their own subordinate status but also both the economic and the racial myths that justify the status quo. Racism, combined with equal opportunity mythology, provides a rationaliza-

tion for racial oppression, making it difficult for whites to see the black situation as illegitimate or unnecessary. If whites believe that blacks, because they are unambitious or inferior, get what they deserve, it becomes that much harder to convince whites that something is wrong with the entire system. Similarly, a challenge to the legitimacy of continued racial inequality would force whites to confront myths about equality of opportunity which justify for them whatever measure of economic success they may have attained.

Thus, although CLS scholars have suggested that legal consciousness plays a central role in legitimating hierarchy in America, the otherness dynamic enthroned within the maintenance and perpetuation of white race-consciousness seems to be at least as important as legal consciousness in supporting the dominant order. Like legal consciousness, race-consciousness makes it difficult—at least for whites—to imagine the world differently. It also creates the desire for identification with privileged elites. By focusing on a distinct, subordinate Other, whites include themselves in the dominant circle—an arena in which most hold not real power but only their privileged racial identity. Consider the case of a dirt-poor, southern white shown participating in a Ku Klux Klan rally in the movie *Resurgence,* who declared; "Every morning, I wake up and thank God I'm white."[38] For this person, and for others like him, race-consciousness—manifested by his refusal even to associate with blacks—provides a powerful explanation of why he fails to challenge the current social order.

C. Rights Discourse as a Challenge to the Oppositional Dynamic

The oppositional dynamic, premised upon maintaining blacks as an excluded and subordinated Other, initially created an ideological and political structure of formal inequality against which rights rhetoric proved to be the most effective weapon. Although rights rhetoric may ultimately have absorbed the civil rights challenge and legitimated continued subordination, the otherness dynamic provides a fuller understanding of how the very transformation afforded by legal reform itself has contributed to the ideological and political legitimation of the continuing subordination of blacks.

Rights discourse provided the ideological mechanisms through which the conflicts of federalism, the power of the presidency, and the legitimacy of the courts could be orchestrated against Jim Crow. Movement leaders used these tactics to force open a conflict between whites, which eventually benefited black people. Casting racial issues in the moral and legal rights rhetoric of the prevailing ideology helped to create the political controversy without which the state's coercive function would not have been enlisted to aid blacks.

Merely critiquing the ideology from without or making demands in language outside the rights discourse would have accomplished little. Rather, blacks gained by using a powerful combination of direct action, mass protest, and individual acts of resistance, along with appeals, both to public opinion and to the court, that were couched in the language of the prevailing legal consciousness. The result was a series of ideological and political crises in which civil rights activists and lawyers induced the federal government to aid blacks and triggered efforts to legitimate and reinforce the authority of the law in ways that benefited blacks. Merely insisting that blacks be integrated or speaking in the language of "needs" would have endangered the lives of those who were already taking risks—and with no reasonable chance of success. President Eisenhower, for example, would not have sent federal troops to Little Rock simply at the behest of protesters demanding that black schoolchildren receive an equal education. Instead, the successful manipulation of legal rhetoric led to a crisis of federal power that ultimately benefited blacks.

Some critics of legal reform movements seem to overlook the fact that state power has made a significant difference—sometimes between life and death—in the efforts of black people to transform their world. Attempts to harness the power of the state through the appropriate rhetorical and legal incantations should be appreciated as intensely powerful and calculated political acts. In the context of white supremacy,

engaging in rights discourse should be seen as an act of self-defense. This was particularly true once the movement had mobilized people to challenge the system of oppression, because the state could not assume a position of neutrality regarding black people; either the coercive mechanism of the state had to be used to support white supremacy, or it had to be used to dismantle it. We know now, with hindsight, that it did both.[39]

Blacks did use rights rhetoric to mobilize state power to their benefit against symbolic oppression through formal inequality and, to some extent, against material deprivation in the form of private, informal exclusion of the middle class from jobs and housing. Yet today the same legal reforms play a role in providing an ideological framework that makes the present conditions facing underclass blacks appear fair and reasonable. However, the eradication of barriers has created a new dilemma for those victims of racial oppression who are not in a position to benefit from the move to formal equality. The race neutrality of the legal system creates the illusion that racism is no longer the primary factor responsible for the condition of the black underclass; instead, as we have seen, class disparities appear to be the consequence of individual and group merit within a supposed system of equal opportunity. Moreover, the fact that some blacks are economically successful gives credence both to the assertion that opportunities exist and to the backlash attitude that blacks have "gotten too far." Psychologically, for blacks who have not made it, the lack of an explanation for their underclass status may result in self-blame and other self-destructive attitudes.

Another consequence of the formal reforms may be the loss of collectivity among blacks.[40] The removal of formal barriers created new opportunities for some blacks which were not shared by various other classes of African-Americans; as blacks moved into different spheres, the experience of being black in America became fragmented and multifaceted, and the different contexts presented opportunities to experience racism in different ways. The social, economic, and even residential distance between the various classes may complicate efforts to unite behind issues as a racial group. Although "whites only" signs may have been crude and debilitating, they at least presented a readily discernible target around which to organize. Now, the targets are obscure and diffuse, and this difference may create doubt among some blacks as to whether there is enough similarity between their own life experiences and those of other blacks to warrant collective political action.

Formal equality significantly transformed the black experience in America. With society's embrace of formal equality came the eradication of symbolic domination and the suppression of white supremacy as the norm of society. Future generations of black Americans would no longer be explicitly regarded as America's second-class citizens. Yet the transformation of the oppositional dynamic—achieved through the suppression of racial norms and stereotypes, and the recasting of racial inferiority into assumptions of cultural inferiority—creates several difficulties for the civil rights constituency. The removal of formal barriers, although symbolically significant to all and materially significant to some, will do little to alter the hierarchical relationship between blacks and whites until the way in which white race-consciousness perpetuates norms that legitimate black subordination is revealed. This is not to say that white norms alone account for the conditions of the black underclass; it is, instead, an acknowledgment that until the distinct racial nature of class ideology is itself revealed and debunked, nothing can be done about the underlying structural problems that account for the disparities. The narrow focus of racial exclusion—that is, the belief that racial exclusion is illegitimate only where the "whites only" signs are explicit—coupled with strong assumptions about equal opportunity, makes it difficult to move the discussion of racism beyond the societal self-satisfaction engendered by the appearance of neutral norms and formal inclusion.

D. Self-Conscious Ideological Struggle

Rights have been important. They may have legitimated racial inequality, but they have also been the means by which oppressed groups have secured both entry as formal equals into the dominant order and also the survival of their movement in the face of private and state repression. The dual role of legal change creates a dilemma for black reformers. As long as race-consciousness thrives, blacks will often have to rely on rights rhetoric when it is necessary to protect their interests; but the very reforms brought about by appeals to legal ideology seem to undermine the ability to move forward toward a broader vision of racial equality. In the quest for racial justice, winning and losing have been part of the same experience.

CLS scholars are correct in observing that engaging in rights discourse has helped to deradicalize and co-opt the challenge. Yet they fail to acknowledge the limited range of options presented to blacks in a context where they were deemed Other and the unlikelihood that specific demands for inclusion and equality would be heard if articulated in other terms. This abbreviated list of options is itself contingent upon the ideological power of white race-consciousness and the continuing role of black Americans as Other. Future efforts to address racial domination and class hierarchy must consider the continuing ideology of white race-consciousness by uncovering the oppositional dynamic and by chipping away at its premises. Central to this project is the task of revealing the contingency of race and exploring the connection between white race-consciousness and the other myths that legitimate both class and race hierarchies. CLS scholars and others whose agendas include challenging hierarchy and legitimation must not overlook the importance of revealing the contingency of race.

Optimally, the deconstruction of white race-consciousness might lead to a liberated future for both black and whites. Yet until whites recognize the hegemonic function of racism and turn their efforts toward neutralizing it, African-American people must develop pragmatic political strategies—self-conscious ideological struggle—to minimize the costs of liberal reform while maximizing its utility. A primary step in engaging in self-conscious ideological struggle must be to transcend the oppositional dynamic in which blacks are cast simply and solely as whites' subordinate Other.

The dual role that rights have played makes strategizing a difficult task. Black people can afford neither to resign themselves to, nor to attack frontally, the legitimacy and incoherence of the dominant ideology. The subordinate position of blacks in this society makes it unlikely that African-Americans will realize gains through the kind of direct challenge to the legitimacy of American liberal ideology that is now being waged by CLS scholars. On the other hand, delegitimating race-consciousness would be directly relevant to black needs, and this strategy will sometimes require the pragmatic use of liberal ideology.

This vision is consistent with the views forwarded by theoreticians such as Frances Fox Piven and Richard Cloward, Antonio Gramsci, and Roberto Unger. Piven and Cloward observe that oppressed people sometimes advance by creating ideological and political crisis, but that the form of the crisis-producing challenge must reflect the institutional logic of the system. The use of rights rhetoric during the civil rights movement created such a crisis by presenting and manipulating the dominant ideology in a new and transformative way. Challenges and demands made from outside the institutional logic would have accomplished little, because blacks, as the subordinate Other, were already perceived as being outside the mainstream. The struggle of blacks, like that of all subordinated groups, is a struggle for inclusion, an attempt to manipulate elements of the dominant ideology in order to transform the experience of domination. It is a struggle to create a new status quo through the ideological and political tools that are available.

Gramsci called this struggle a "war of position" and he regarded it as the most appropriate strategy for change in Western societies. According to Gramsci, direct challenges to the dominant class accomplish little if ideology plays such a central role in establishing authority that the legitimacy of the dominant regime is not challenged. Joseph Femia, interpreting Gramsci, writes: "the dominant ideology in modern capitalist societies is highly institution-

alized and widely internalized. It follows that a concentration on frontal attack, on direct assault against the bourgeois state ('war of movement' or 'war of manoeuvre') can result only in disappointment and defeat."[41] Consequently, the challenge in such societies is to create a counter-hegemony by maneuvering within and expanding the dominant ideology to embrace the potential for change. . . .

V. CONCLUSION

FOR blacks, the task at hand is to devise ways to wage ideological and political struggle while minimizing the costs of engaging in an inherently legitimating discourse. A clearer understanding of the space we occupy in the American political consciousness is a necessary prerequisite to the development of pragmatic strategies for political and economic survival. In this regard, the most serious challenge for blacks is to minimize the political and cultural cost of engaging in an inevitably co-optive process in order to secure material benefits. Because our present predicament gives us few options, we must create conditions for the maintenance of a distinct political thought that is informed by the actual conditions of black people. Unlike the civil rights vision, this new approach should not be defined and thereby limited by the possibilities of dominant political discourse; rather, it should maintain a distinctly progressive outlook that focuses on the needs of the African-American community.

NOTES

1. Act of Aug. 27, 1984, Pub. L. No. 98–399, 98 Stat. 1473. President Reagan's signing is reported in 20 *Weekly Comp. Pres. Doc.* 1192 (Sept. 3, 1984).

2. I shall use "African-American" and "black" interchangeably. . . . The naming of Americans of African descent has had political overtones throughout history. See W. E. B. Du Bois, 2 *The Seventh Son*, 12–13 (1971) (arguing that the "N" in Negro was always capitalized until, in defense of slavery, the use of the lower case "N" became the custom in "recognition" of Blacks' status as property; that the usage was defended as a "description of the color of a people"; and that the capitalization of other ethnic and national origin designations made the failure to capitalize "Negro" an insult). "African-American" is now preferred by some because it is both culturally more specific and histori-

cally more expansive than the traditional terms that narrowly categorize us as America's Other. . . .

3. Continuing disparities exist between African-Americans and whites in virtually every measurable category. In 1986, the African-American poverty rate stood at 31 percent, compared with 11 percent for whites; see Williams, "Urban League Says Blacks Suffered Loss over Decade," *New York Times,* Jan. 15, 1988, A10:1. "[B]lack median income is 57 percent that of whites, a decline of about four percentage points since the early 1970's"; Bernstein, "20 Years After the Kerner Report: Three Societies, All Separate," *New York Times,* Feb. 29, 1988, B8:2. Between 1981 and 1985, black unemployment averaged 17 percent, compared to 7.3 percent for whites; see National Urban League, *The State of Black America 1986,* 15 (1986). In 1986, approximately 44 percent of all black children lived in poverty; see Lauter and May, "A Saga of Triumph, a Return to Poverty: Black Middle Class Has Grown but Poor Multiply," *Los Angeles Times,* April 2, 1988, 1. 16:1. Blacks comprise 60 percent of the urban underclass in the United States; *id.* at 16:3.

The African-American socioeconomic position in American society has actually declined in the last two decades. Average annual family income for African-Americans dropped 9 percent from the seventies to the eighties, see Williams, *supra,* A10:1. Since 1969, the proportion of black men between 25 and 55 earning less than $5000 a year rose from 8 to 20 percent; see Lauter and May, *supra.* African-American enrollment in universities and colleges is also on the decline; see Williams, *supra,* A10:2.

The decline in the African-American socioeconomic position has been paralleled by an increase in overt racial hostility. See generally U.S. Commission on Civil Rights, *Intimidation and Violence: Racial and Religious Bigotry in America* (1983). In addition to well-publicized incidents of racial violence like the Howard Beach attack. . . and the lynching of Michael Donald, . . . racial unrest has risen dramatically on university campuses; see Wilkerson, "Campus Blacks Feel Racism's Nuances," *New York Times,* April 17, 1988, 1.1:3.

For a comprehensive analysis of the conditions afflicting the black urban underclass, see W. Wilson, *The Truly Disadvantaged: The Inner City, the Underclass, and Public Policy* (1987).

4. The principal civil rights reforms are the Civil Rights Act of 1964, Pub. L. No. 88–352, 78 Stat. 243 (codified as amended at 42 U.S.C. ss 2000(e)-2000(h)(6) (1982)); the Voting Rights Act of 1965, Pub. L. No. 89–110, 79 Stat. 437 (codified as amended at 42 U.S.C. ss 1971–1974 (1982)); U.S. CONST. amends. XIII-XV; 42 U.S.C. ss 1981, 1983, 1985 (1982); Exec. Order No. 11,246, 3 C.F.R. 339 (1964–1965 comp.); and the Equal Employment Opportunity Commission regulations, 29 C.F.R. ss 1600–1691 (1987).

See ACLU, *In Contempt of Congress and the Courts—The Reagan Civil Rights Record* (1984); Chambers, "Racial Justice in the 1980's," 8 *Campbell L. Rev.,* 29, 31–34 (1985); Devins, "Closing the Classroom Door to Civil Rights," 11 *Hum. Rts.,* 26 (1984); Selig, "The Reagan Justice Department and Civil Rights: What Went Wrong," 1985 *U. Ill. L. Rev.,* 785; Wolvovitz and Lobel, "The Enforcement of Civil Rights Statutes: The Reagan Administration's Record," 9 *Black L. J.,* 252 (1986); see also Hernandez, Weiss, and Smith, "How Different Is the World of 1984 from the World of 1964?," 37 *Rutgers L. Rev.,* 755, 757–60 (1985).

Some scholars have been critical of the overall development of civil rights law over the past decade, positing that we have reached the end of the "Second Reconstruction"; see generally D. Bell, *And We Are Not Saved* (1987); Bell, "The Supreme Court, 1984 Term—Foreword: The Civil Rights Chronicles," 99 *Harv. L. Rev.,* 4 (1985).

5. Martin Luther King, Jr., Federal Holiday Commission, *Living the Dream* (1986).

6. D. Bell, *Race, Racism and American Law* (2d ed. 1981).

7. The most notorious was *Bob Jones University v. United States,* 461 U.S. 574 (1983), in which the Reagan administration refused to argue a case, initiated by the Justice Department during the previous administration, that sought to maintain the Internal Revenue Service policy of denying tax-exempt status to schools that discriminated on the basis of race. The Supreme Court denied the Justice Department's request for a dismissal, and appointed a private attorney to argue the case. . . .

8. See T. Sowell, *Civil Rights: Rhetoric or Reality?,* 116 (1984).

9. *Id.* at 109.

10. See T. Sowell, *supra* note 8, at 120. This I also take to be the import of Walter Williams's misleading reference to Thurgood Marshall's remark, "You guys have been practicing discrimination for years. Now it is our turn"; Williams, "Discrimination in Public Policy," in I *Selected Affirmative Action Topics in Employment and Business Set Asides: A Consultation/Hearing of the United States Commission on Civil Rights* 10 (March 6–7, 1985) (quoting W. Douglas, *The Court Years 1939–1975: The Autobiography of William O. Douglas,* 149 (1980)).

11. T. Sowell, *supra* note 8, at 119.

12. *Id.*

13. *Id.* at 109.

14. A. Blumrosen, "Twenty Years of Title VII, An Overview," 16 (April 18, 1983), unpublished manuscript on file at the Harvard Law Library (emphasis added).

15. *Id.* at 13.

16. *Selections From the Prison Notebooks of Antonio Gramsci,* 238, Q. Hoare and G. Smith, trans. (1971).

17. Gordon, "New Developments in Legal Theory," in D. Kairys, ed., *The Politics of Law: A Progressive Critique,* 286 (1982).

18. *Id.* at 287 (emphasis in original).

19. See Freeman, "Antidiscrimination Law: A Critical Review," in *The Politics of Law, supra* note 17, at 96.

20. Tushnet, "An Essay on Rights," 62 *Tex. L. Rev.*, 1363–64 (1984). For a different rendition of the critique of rights which is centered in psychoanalytic theory, see Gabel, "The Phenomenology of Rights-Consciousness and the Pact of the Withdrawn Selves," 62 *Tex. L. Rev.*, 1563 (1984).

21. Gabel and Kennedy, "Roll Over Beethoven," 36 *Stan. L. Rev.*, 1, 29 (1984) (emphasis added). In this piece, the authors acknowledge that the critique of rights is itself in danger of becoming reified. See *id.* at 36–37. Elsewhere, Kennedy has advocated "working at the slow transformation of rights rhetoric, at dereifying it, rather than simply junking it"; Kennedy, "Critical Labor Law Theory: A Comment," 4 *Indus. Rel. L. J.*, 503, 506 (1981). "Embedded in the rights notion," Kennedy observes, "is a liberating accomplishment of our culture: the affirmation of free human subjectivity against the constraints of group life, along with the paradoxical countervision of a group life that creates and nurtures individuals capable of freedom"; *id.*

22. The term "coercion" is used here to describe all nonconsensual forms of domination—that is, all forces external to the individual or group that maintain that individual or group's position in society's hierarchy. As such, it refers to everything from baton-wielding police officers to court injunctions to "whites only" signs. More importantly, it also refers to more subtle forms of exterior domination, such as the institutionalized oppositional dynamic—the vision of "normative whiteness" that pervades current forms of race-consciousness.

23. The degree to which rights-consciousness has been receptive to black aspirations is probably the most overlooked aspect in the critique of rights. This may be attributed to critics' limited understanding of nonmaterial manifestations of racial domination. Although critics argue that rights-consciousness only creates an illusion of community which produces alienation..., this analysis tends to underestimate the extent to which blacks' exclusion from the illusion creates its own experience of alienation. Thus, although critics have acknowledged the pragmatic value of rights rhetoric, ... they have not recognized the legitimacy of black demands for inclusion in the social illusion and the consequent utility of rights discourse in articulating such demands.

24. Strikes, for example, are a reflection of the logic of the work institution. It only makes sense for employed workers to use strikes as a tactic. Unemployed workers, of course, cannot use the strike to press their grievances.

25. Conversely, groups that do not engage the institutional logic are unlikely to create such a crisis; indeed, they are routinely infiltrated, isolated, and destroyed. Compare, for example, the history of the NAACP with that of the Black Panthers. One should not infer from the fact that the Panthers have ceased to exist whereas the NAACP has not that insurgent groups are not essential to reform. Indeed, it is their insurgency that ultimately benefits more moderate groups. Both moderate and radical groups, however, face similar limitations: although they can create a crisis that

forces an institutional response, no oppressed group can control the response. Institutions can respond with either repression or conciliation; often they respond with both. Thus, even enlisting the dominant, legitimating ideology in struggle does not guarantee protection against violent repression.

Indeed, the degree of violence and repression that an oppressed group must endure to wrest even moderate reforms from the dominant class is a measure of its subordinate status in society. Consider, for example, how much real suffering people had to endure during the civil rights movement before even moderate concessions were made. The injustice of racial oppression is succinctly characterized by the fact that thousands of lives were risked, and some lost, to secure for blacks the most basic rights that whites were routinely granted. ...

26. The notion of blacks as a subordinated Other in Western culture has been a major theme in scholarship exploring the cultural and sociological structure of racism. See Trost, "Western Metaphysical Dualism as an Element in Racism," in J. Hodge, D. Struckmann, and L. Trost, eds., *Cultural Bases of Racism and Group Oppression* 49 (1975) (arguing that black and white are seen as paired antinomies, and that there is a hierarchy within the antinomies, with Caucasians and Western culture constituting the preferred or higher antinomy). Frantz Fanon has summarized the attitude of the West toward blackness as a projection of Western anxiety concerning the Other in terms of skin color: "In Europe, the black man is the symbol of Evil. ... The torturer is the black man, Satan is black, one talks of shadow, when one is dirty one is black—whether one is thinking of physical dirtiness or moral dirtiness. It would be astonishing, if the trouble were taken to bring them all together, to see the vast number of expressions that make the black man the equivalent of sin. In Europe, whether concretely or symbolically, the black man stands for the bad side of the character. As long as one cannot understand this fact one is doomed to talk in circles about the 'black problem.' Blackness, darkness, shadow, shades, night, the labyrinths of the earth, abysmal depths, blacken someone's reputation; and on the other side, the bright look of innocence, the white dove of peace, magical, heavenly light"; F. Fanon, *Black Skins, White Masks*, 188–89 (1967); see S. Gilman, *Difference and Pathology: Stereotypes of Sexuality, Race, and Sadness*, 30 (1985) (arguing that the notion that "blacks are the antithesis of the mirage of whiteness, the ideal of European aesthetic values, strikes the reader as an extension of some 'real,' perceived difference to which the qualities of 'good' and 'bad' have been erroneously applied. But the very concept of color is a quality of Otherness, not of reality."); Isaacs, "Blackness and Whiteness," *Encounter*, 8 (Aug. 1963); see also W. Jordan, *White Over Black: American Attitudes Toward the Negro, 1650–1712* (1968) (discussing how sixteenth- and seventeenth-century English writers used the concept that blacks were the Europeans' polar opposites in order to establish an elaborate hierarchy to classify other colored people in the world). Others who have used the concept of Otherness as a framework for

examining black/white relations include C. Degler, *Neither Black Nor White: Slavery and Race Relations in Brazil and The United States* (1971), and Copeland, "The Negro as a Contrast Conception," in E. Thompson, ed., *Race Relations and the Race Problem: A Definition and An Analysis*, 152–79 (1939). . . .

27. J. Derrida, *Dissemination*, viii, trans. B. Johnson (1981) (emphasis in original).

28. E. Morgan, *American Slavery—American Freedom*, 386 (1975).

29. G. Fredrickson, *White Supremacy: A Comparative Study in American and South African History*, (1981).

30. C. Vann Woodward, *The Strange Career of Jim Crow*, 76 (1958).

31. One might argue that the fact that many poor whites were simultaneously disenfranchised cuts against the idea that racist ideology was the glue that organized and held whites together across class lines. In reality, the ability to exclude lower-class whites was achieved politically, via racist rhetoric.

32. *Id.* at 44–45.

33. *Id.* at 73–74.

34. "The historical record reveals that the embrace of white supremacy as ideology and as practice was a strategy for assimilation by European working class immigrants, the white ethnics who were to constitute a major part of the membership and leadership of organized labor in the United States"; . . . Hill, "Race and Ethnicity in Organized Labor: The Historical Sources of Restrictions to Affirmative Action," *J. Intergroup Rel.*, 6 (winter 1984). Even today, unions that are supposed to represent the "consciousness of the working class" often still fail to represent the interests of the black American worker. For an account of the racist history of the AFL-CIO, see Hill, "The AFL-CIO and the Black Worker: Twenty-Five Years After the Merger," *J. Intergroup Rel.*, 5 (Sept. 1982).

35. This effort to minimize black influence reflects what Derrick Bell, Jr., has called the principle of "involuntary sacrifice"; see D. Bell, *Race, Racism, and Americal Law*, U 1.8, at 29–30. . . . Bell asserts that throughout American history, Black interests have been sacrificed when necessary to reestablish the bonds of the white community, "so that identifiably different groups of whites may settle a dispute and establish or reestablish their relationship"; *id.* at 30.

36. These two manifestations of racial subordination are not mutually exclusive. In fact, it only makes sense to separate various aspects of racial oppression in this post–civil rights era in order to understand how the movement changed some social norms and reinforced others. Most blacks probably did not experience or perceive their oppression as reflecting two separate structures.

37. Socially, many blacks lived in a society comparable in many ways to that of the white elites. Hardly strangers to debutante balls, country clubs, and vacations abroad, these blacks lived lives of which many whites only dreamed. Nevertheless, despite their material wealth, upper-middle-class blacks were still members of a subordinated group. Where rights and privileges were distributed on the basis of race, even a distinguished African-American had to take a back seat to each white—no matter how poor, ignorant, or uneducated the white might be. . . .

38. Sowell exemplifies what may be the worst development of the civil rights movement—that some blacks who have benefited the most from the formal gestures of equality now identify with those who attempt to affirm the legitimacy of oppressing other blacks. Clearly, this legitimation and desertion by some blacks has been politically damaging and may undermine future efforts to organize.

39. *Resurgence* (Skylight Pictures, Emancipation Arts, Sept. 1981).

40. Consider, for example, the possible police responses to students who violated local ordinances by sitting in at segregated lunch counters and demanding service. Government officials could have ordered the students arrested, thereby upholding the segregation policy, or they could have ignored them, which would have incidentally supported the students' efforts. Both tactics were followed throughout the course of the movement. Because officials sometimes had a degree of choice in the matter, and courts had the ultimate power to review the legitimacy of the laws and the officials' actions, black protesters' use of rights rhetoric can be seen as an effort to defend themselves against arrest or conviction for violating the norms of white supremacy.

41. J. Femai, *Gramsci's Political Thought: Hegemony, Consciousness, and the Revolutionary Process* 51 (1981).

Part Three

TOWARD A CRITICAL CULTURAL PLURALISM: PROGRESSIVE ALTERNATIVES TO MAINSTREAM CIVIL RIGHTS IDEOLOGY

Three

TOWARD CRITICAL CULTURAL PLURALISM: PROGRESSIVE ALTERNATIVES TO MAINSTREAM CIVIL RIGHTS IDEOLOGY

The articles in this section are linked through their shared opposition to the ideology of color-blindness and their shared commitment to progressive forms of pluralism. In diverse ways, they each confront the ethical consequences of acknowledging rather than denying cultural difference.

In his article, "Race-Consciousness," Gary Peller traces the roots of contemporary ideologies about race to the 1960s collision between integrationist and black nationalist interpretations of racial domination. Peller argues that the victory of integrationism, based on a coalition of liberal whites and moderate and conservative blacks, included a discourse for rejecting black nationalists as reverse racists; addressing himself primarily to other white progressives, he urges the adoption of a new, progressive form of race-consciousness as the framework for understanding racial justice. In Peller's argument, race defined historically constructed and distinct communities whose interactions should be conceived in terms of nation-to-nation relations rather than in terms of the integrationist, color-blind model of race which he ascribes to the mainstream liberal conception of racial justice.

Duncan Kennedy is also a founder of CLS, and probably the movement's best-known figure. In this essay, "A Cultural Pluralist Case

for Affirmative Action in Legal Academia," Kennedy, like Peller, writes explicitly as a white leftist. Utilizing Randall Kennedy's attack on race-conscious scholarship as an example of "color-blind meritocratic fundamentalism," and using the context of hiring in law schools as the setting for his theoretical speculation, Kennedy develops a critique of each element of conservative race ideology. He proposes that law schools engage in large-scale affirmative action hiring on grounds of the justice of political and cultural pluralism and responds to objections that might be lodged from within color-blind race ideology.

Gerald Torres and Kathryn Milun focus on the way that cultural difference can make social realities invisible. In the Mashpee Indian case, one issue was whether a group of Native Americans on Cape Cod constitute a "tribe." The essay demonstrates the dissonance between legal definitions, on the one hand, and Native Americans' own conceptions of social organization and community continuity, on the other. The authors use this example to develop an extended analysis of how legal categories help to construct social reality and, thus, work as important political symbols.

In "Regrouping in Singular Times," Patricia Williams takes on the task of articulating the possibilities of a legal discourse that would embrace the norms of multiculturalism. She uses the Supreme Court's opinions in *Metro Broadcasting*, a case upholding the constitutionality of race-consciousness in awarding broadcast licenses, as a vehicle for developing a pluralist and group-based understanding of legal justice.

Closely analyzing the language and imagery used by the justices, she describes the competing visions of equality which conservatives and progressives promote. Williams concludes that legal discourse can and should adapt to comprehend the reality of a multicultural society.

Part Three

TOWARD A CRITICAL CULTURAL PLURALISM: PROGRESSIVE ALTERNATIVES TO MAINSTREAM CIVIL RIGHTS IDEOLOGY

RACE-CONSCIOUSNESS
Gary Peller

The entire civil rights struggle needs a new interpretation, a broader interpretation. We need to look at this civil rights thing from another angle—from the inside as well as from the outside. To those of us whose philosophy is black nationalism, the only way you can get involved in the civil rights struggle is to give it a new interpretation. The old interpretation excluded us. It kept us out.

—Malcolm X, 1963.[1]

. . . The commitment to a race-conscious perspective by many critical race theorists is dramatic because explicit race-consciousness has been considered taboo for at least fifteen years in mainstream American politics, and for far longer within the particular conventions of law and legal scholarship. Instead, race has been understood through a set of beliefs—what I call "integrationist" ideology—which locates racial oppression in the social structure of prejudice and stereotype based on skin color, and which identifies progress with the transcendence of a racial consciousness about the world. In 1963, when Malcolm X asserted that this conventional interpretation of civil rights excluded black nationalists, he could not have foreseen that nationalist activism would revitalize and transform the struggle against racial oppression in the late sixties and early seventies, only to be relegated once more to the cultural margins and the desperate streets in the eighties.

But he did identify the basic racial compromise that the incorporation of "the civil rights struggle" into mainstream American culture

would eventually embody: along with the suppression of white racism, which was the widely celebrated aim of civil rights reform, the dominant conception of racial justice was framed in a way which required that black nationalists be equated with white supremacists, and that race consciousness on the part of either whites or blacks be marginalized as beyond the good sense of enlightened American culture.

In this essay, I want to explore the ideological roots of this particular political moment—in which the repudiation of race-consciousness defines conventional civil rights thinking—by contrasting integrationist and black nationalist images of racial injustice, and by comparing the ways in which white and black communities have understood race. My argument, in summary form, is that the boundaries of today's dominant rhetoric about race were set in the late sixties and early seventies, in the context of an intense cultural clash between black nationalists on one side, and integrationists (white and black) on the other. Current mainstream race-reform discourse reflects the resolution of that conflict through a tacit, enlightened consensus that integrationism—understood as the replacement of prejudice and discrimination with reason and neutrality—is the proper way to conceive of racial justice, and that the price of the national commitment to suppress white supremacists would be the rejection of race-consciousness among African Americans. . . .

The conflict between nationalists and integrationists in the late sixties and early seventies represented a critical juncture in American race relations. At that time, black nationalism arguably had overtaken integrationism as the dominant ideology of racial liberation among African-Americans, while virtually all liberal and progressive whites embraced a theory of integration as the ultimate definition of racial justice. Although there has been some refinement since this historical moment—particularly with the development of a national commitment to a limited form of "cultural pluralism"[2]—the basic boundaries of contemporary mainstream thinking about race were set in the early seventies when a loose coalition of "moderate" African-Americans joined with liberal and progressive whites to resist—and equate—black nationalists and white supremacists. . . .

It is now time to rethink the ways that racial justice has been understood in dominant discourse for the past several decades. Serious limits to the integrationalist vision existed from the beginning; the fact that support for substantively reformist programs such as affirmative action is articulated in the defensive rhetoric of "remedy" or "diversity," posed as counterbalancing factors to "lack of merit," is only one manifestation of the deeper ways that civil rights reformism has worked to legitimate the very social relations that originally were to be reformed. . . .

I. THE ANALYTICS AND ASSUMPTIONS OF INTEGRATIONISM

A SEGREGATED school system isn't necessarily the same situation that exists in an all-white neighborhood. A school system in an all-white neighborhood is not a segregated school system. The only time it's segregated is when it is in a community other than white, but at the same time is controlled by whites. So my understanding of a segregated school system—or a segregated community, or a segregated school—is a school that's controlled by people other than those who go there. . . . On the other hand, if we can get an all-black school, one that we can control, staff it ourselves with the type of teacher who has our good at heart, with the type of book that has many of the missing ingredients that have produced this inferiority complex in our people, then we don't feel that an all-black school is necessarily a segregated school. It's only segregated when it's controlled by someone from outside. I hope I'm making

my point. I just can't see why, if white people can go to a classroom with no negroes present and it doesn't affect the academic diet they're receiving, an all-black classroom can be affected by the absence of white children. . . . So, in my opinion, what the integrationists are saying when they say that whites and blacks must go to school together, is that the whites are so much superior that just their presence in a black classroom balances it out. I can't go along with that.[3]

—Malcolm X, 1963

Today the story of the civil rights struggle is commonly told in linear fashion, as if progress in race relations followed a teleological evolution—from an ignorant time, when racial status was taken to signify real and meaningful differences between people, to the present enlightened time, when race properly is understood in mainstream culture not to make a difference except as vestiges of unfortunate historical oppression or in terms of a vague and largely privatized "ethnic heritage." This sense of linear evolution has lent an aura of inevitability to the story, as if progression from the racial caste system of American slavery to the widespread acceptance of integration and the transcendence of race consciousness as the unquestioned goals of social progress were historically determined. The process has been neither linear nor inevitable: the institution of racial integration as a social norm results from a cultural struggle—played out in various theaters of social power—over the meaning of racial domination and racial justice in America. The sense of integrationism as the inevitable means to achieve racial enlightenment reflects both the institutionalization of a particular understanding of what racism means and the marginalization not only of white supremacists but also of the opposing analysis, which was represented in the sixties by Malcolm X and other black nationalists. . . .

A. The Analytic Components of Integrationism

The goal of racial integration has taken many forms and has been supported by various worldviews. At one time, the idea of racial integration represented a powerful, spiritually rooted social resistance movement that threatened to destabilize the status quo of American institutional life in profound ways. Under the banner of integrationism, hundreds of thousands of people mobilized to challenge the political, economic, and cultural power relations in cities and towns across the country, employing tactics that included mass protest, economic boycotts, civil disobedience, sit-ins, and strikes.[4] There is, therefore, nothing intrinsic to the concept of racial integration which demands that it be understood in the way I am about to describe it. What I want to capture here is the general cultural sense—which became dominant in the sixties and seventies—of what racism consists of and how to overcome it.

From this perspective, integrationism should be understood to comprise a set of attitudes and beliefs for perceiving the meaning of racist domination and for identifying the goals of racial justice. The concepts of prejudice, discrimination, and segregation are the key structural elements of this ideology. Each idea embodies a different manifestation of what is seen as the central aspect of racism—the distortion of reason through the prism of myth and ignorance.

In the integrationist perspective, racism is rooted in consciousness, in the cognitive process that attributes social significance to the arbitrary fact of skin color. The mental side of racism is accordingly represented either as "prejudice," the prejudging of a person according to mythological stereotypes, or as "bias," the process of being influenced by subjective factors. The key image here is of irrationalism: the problem with prejudice is that it obscures the work of reason by clouding perception with beliefs rooted in superstition.[5] The paradigmatic manifestation is the white supremacist myth structure that asserts natural, biological differences between blacks and whites—the familiar identification of whites with the qualities of intelligence, industriousness, and piousness, and the corresponding association of blacks with the qualities of dullness, laziness, and lustfulness.[6] The opposite of the ignorance that appears as racism is knowledge—knowledge gleaned from actual interracial experience rather than mythologies of stereotype.

In the integrationist ideology, racism achieves social form when the distortion of prejudice in consciousness subsequently translates into practice. Here racism manifests itself in the practice of "discrimination," the disparate treatment of whites and blacks, which the irrational attribution of difference is supposed to justify. The paradigmatic practice of racism in its systematic, social form was the Jim Crow system of de jure segregation, which institutionalized racial apartheid on the basis of an ideology of white supremacy.[7] And just as "prejudice" is implicitly contrasted with knowledge, "discrimination" is contrasted with neutrality, the social practice of equal treatment.

The solution to segregation, then, is integration, understood as a social vision opposed to racism, in each realm in which racism manifests itself. Within consciousness, integration means overcoming prejudice based on skin color; therefore, reflecting one dimension of integrationist ideology, people began to understand themselves as possible racists to the extent they believed in irrational images of people based on skin-color stereotypes. The ideal was to transcend stereotypes in favor of treating people as individuals free from racial group identification.[8]

At the level of practice, the integrationist cure for discrimination is equal treatment according to neutral norms; and at the institutional level, integrationism obviously means an end to the social system of racial segregation. In sum, the cure for racism would be equal treatment on an individual level and integration on an institutional level. In any event, integrationists believed the two would go hand in hand. Once neutrality replaced discrimination, equal opportunity would lead to integrated institutions; experience in integrated institutions would, in turn, replace the ignorance of racism with the knowledge that actual contact provides. This deep link between racism and ignorance, on the one hand, and integration and knowledge, on the other, helps to explain the initial focus of integrationists on public education: children who attended integrated schools would learn the truth about each others' unique individuality before they came to believe stereotypes rooted in ignorance. And by attending the same schools, children would have equal opportunity at the various roles in American social life.[9]

The integrationists' diagnosis of the distortions of the white supremacy ideology focuses on the failure of white supremacists to recognize the universal characteristics shared by whites and blacks. According to the integrationists, white racists perceive the world through a false structure of "same" and "other" which utilizes a concept of blacks as Other and denies that the attributes characteristic of whites exist in blacks. Thus, the rationality and piousness that supposedly characterize whites are, in racist ideology, denied to blacks. The integrationist proposes to correct this situation by distributing these characteristics across race lines: blacks can be rational and pious, while whites can be emotional and lustful. In other words, according to integrationist ideology, racists make the mistake of "essentializing" racial categories and believing that there is some necessary, intrinsic relationship between race and particular social characteristics. Integrationists are committed to the view that race makes no real difference between people, except as unfortunate historical vestiges of irrational discrimination. In an extreme form of the integrationist picture, the hope is that when contact occurs between different groups in society not only race but all "ethnic identity will become a thing of the past."[10]

B. Race, Universal Reason, and Liberal Progress
Of course, this is a very abstracted model of what I mean by the "ideology of integrationism"; I assume that these general ideas about race are so familiar that simply evoking them calls to mind the fuller meaning of integrationism in mainstream American culture. At the same time, though, it is important to grasp the integrationist worldview at this level of generality. Integrationists comprehend racism at a high level of abstraction, in part because they wish to transcend the bias of particularity which they see as the root of racist consciousness. Integrationism, in short, links up with a broader set of liberal images—images that connect truth, universalism, and progress. . . .

A commitment to a type of universalism, as well as an association of universalism with truth and particularism with ignorance, forms the infrastructure of American integrationist consciousness. Within this frame for organizing social perception, controversy revolves around how to categorize particular social practices—as rational and neutral, or as irrational and biased. Liberals and conservatives can be distinguished by how far they believe the realms of bias or neutrality extend. . . . But to both liberals and conservatives, racism consists of a form of distortion that could be superseded by an aracial arena of social understanding. Once we remove prejudice, reason will take its place; once we remove discrimination, neutrality will take its place; and once we remove segregation, integration will take its place.[11]

One way that integrationism's universalizing character manifests itself in perception is that diverse social phenomena begin to appear the same, because they are all viewed through the same analytic lens. From within this structure for cataloging and organizing thinking about social life, racism becomes equivalent to other forms of prejudice and discrimination based on irrational stereotype. Social domination based on race, gender, sexual preference, religion, age, national origin, language, and physical disability, or appearance can all be categorized as the same phenomena, because they all represent bias—understood as a deviation from a neutral rational standard. Similarly, the fact that relations between Anglos and African-Americans, Asians, and Hispanics are all perceived as presenting the issues of "discrimination against racial minorities" in legal and political discourse reflects the same structure of abstraction. From this structure, it begins to appear that the social subordination of various groups does not have a complex, particular, and historical context, but rather is a formal, numeric problem of the relations of majorities to minorities, unified under the concept "discrimination."

Moreover, given this universalist dimension to integrationist thinking, it is plausible to conceive of a category of "reverse racism," which is really not "reverse" at all. Since racism means a deviation from a universal norm of objectivity, it can be practiced by anyone, and anyone can be its victim, regardless of their particular historical circumstances or power relations. Thus, within the integrationist ideology, a black person who stereotypes whites is racist in the "same" way as a white person who harbors prejudice against blacks; and blacks who discriminate against whites are guilty of the same kind of racism as whites who discriminate against blacks. Anyone can engage in racism, because we can identify racism from a vantage point of race neutrality, of not making someone's race count for anything. In short, the symmetry of the integrationist picture is rooted in the idea that racism consists of possessing a race-consciousness about the world, in thinking that race should make a difference in social relations.

Finally, given the idea of immutability common to categories of "discrimination," the story of the struggle against racism can be related in a way that follows the basic script of liberal progress more generally. Race-consciousness is associated with status-based social coercion, in which individuals are treated in a particular way because of the arbitrary fact of their membership in a social group they did not choose. The transcendence of race-consciousness represents a social movement toward the freedom of the individual to choose group identification. Like classical images of common law, the vision underlying integrationist ideology is of American culture purifying itself by overcoming the distortions of various kinds of prejudice in favor of the increasing rationalization of institutional forms, which, free of coercive social power, in turn provides greater individual liberty to choose. Freedom from racial discrimination is but one instance of the historical move from status to contract, from caste to individual liberty. Individualism and universalism are thereby linked together.

The aims of racial integration seem self-evident because they are one part of a web of meaning that constitutes the dominant ideology of social progress itself. The meaning of race has been grafted onto other central cultural images of progress, so that the transition from segregation to integration and from race-consciousness to race neutrality mirrors move-ments from myth to enlightenment, from ignorance to knowledge, from superstition to reason, from the primitive to the civilized, from religion to secularism, and, most important, the historical self-understanding of liberal society as representing the movement from status to individual liberty.[12] . . .

C. Integration and Legitimation

. . . The image of transcending racial consciousness forms a large part of the deep appeal that the integrationist vision has for many of us. This vision seems to reflect, at the ideological level, the occasional glimpses we attain in personal relations of a deep shared identity as fellow human beings in what are often the very best moments of social life. . . .

However, this universalism also marks the narrowing limits of integrationist ideology. . . . As I have described it, integrationism is organized around an image of reason and neutrality which represents the transcendence of bias and prejudice. The liberal discourse of race represented by integrationism actually contains within itself two distinct ways to perceive social practices. On the one hand, the possibility of bias and prejudice constitutes a language of critique and reform that provides a framework to articulate what needs to be changed in society; on the other, this liberal discourse also constitutes a narrative of legitimation, a language for concluding that particular social practices are fair because they are objective and unbiased. This second aspect of liberal discourses embodies a conception of a realm of social life outside the influence of racial history and politics.

Take, for example, the debate about affirmative action. In this context, race-consciousness is employed by those interested in race reform. The familiar "dilemma" surrounding affirmative action is that it requires the use of race as a socially significant category, despite the fact that the deepest aims of integrationist ideology point toward the transcendence of race consciousness.

The dominant discourse about affirmative action reflects the core categories of the liberal theory of race, which I have described. The issues in the affirmative action debate are organized around the same structural opposition between reason and bias. Here, the category of "merit" represents the universal, impersonal side of integrationist perception; the use of race-conscious means to distribute social goods is problematic because it represents a deviation from the impersonality of merit. Thus, liberal support of affirmative action has always been defensive because its proponents themselves experience it, at least in part, as dissonant with their most fundamental convictions. Affirmative action has been characterized as merely an exceptional remedy for past injustice, rather than an affirmative right rooted in present social circumstances. It has been characterized as temporary and necessary only to achieve integration, at which time equal opportunity can take over. And affirmative action has been defended on the grounds that its beneficiaries have suffered from a "deprived" background, so that putting a thumb on the minorities' side of the scales of social decision-making helps to even out the otherwise rationalized competition for social goods.[13]

Alternatively, affirmative action has been defended on the grounds of promoting diversity, an approach that challenges the notion of merit as the sole basis on which to distribute social opportunities. According to this justification, merit is only one value to be vindicated in determining admission to various institutions. Alongside merit is the value of having a racially diversified society, a justification that can be used to counterbalance merit as a criterion.

Whether articulated in terms of remedy or diversity, this discourse assumes that minority applicants are less qualified on neutral, impersonal, and objective criteria. Thus, to integrate institutions, we must compromise meritocratic standards either temporarily, in order to break the cycles of institutional life that racial domination entailed, or permanently, by diffusing merit with other ends such as diversity. Today, conservative integrationists preach a principled commitment to color-blindness in institutional practices, even if it results in segregated institutions, and liberal integrationists advocate limited, effects-oriented race-consciousness in order to ensure that some integration actually

takes place. Yet from within the discourse through which they perceive the issues, both commit to the premise that the category of merit itself is neutral, impersonal, and somehow developed outside the economy of social power—with its significant currency of race, class, and gender—that marks American social life.

Given integrationists' view of the pervasive nature of American racism, at least in the recent past, it is conceivable that they might have demanded a radical transformation of social practices before they assumed the existence of merit-based decision-making. Instead, though, integrationists assumed that fair, impersonal criteria simply would be what remained once the distortion of race-consciousness was removed. One manifestation of this assumption was that the purportedly broad social transformation reflected in the national struggle against racism resulted in hardly any change in administrative personnel. The transformation from a Jim Crow to an integrationist racial regime was thought to require only a change in the rules of social decision-making. Yet the same whites who once carried out the formal program of American apartheid actually kept their jobs as the decision-makers charged with evaluating merit in the employment offices of companies and in the admissions offices of schools in the postsegregation world. In institution after institution, progressive reformists have found themselves struggling over the implementation of racial integration with the former administrators of racial segregation, many of whom soon constituted an old guard "concerned" over the deterioration of "standards." . . .

Even more dramatic than the continuity of personnel (since the particular people in power eventually age, retire, and die), the same criteria that defined the "standards" during the period of explicit racism continue to be used, as long as they cannot be linked "directly" to racial factors. Within liberal integrationism, racism, seen to consist of a deviation from neutral, impersonal norms, focused on the exclusion of people of color, with the idea that all the rest of the cultural practices of formerly segregated institutions would stay the same. From within the integrationist ideology of neutral standards, no conceptual base existed from which integrationists could question whether "standards," definitions of "merit," and the other myriad features of the day-to-day aspects of institutional life constructed or maintained during segregation might have reflected deeper aspects of a culture within which the explicit exclusion of blacks seemed uncontroversial. And integrationists, organizing their perception of racial justice around images of objectivity, rationality, and neutrality, never considered whether this language for distinguishing the worthy from the unworthy itself might serve to help justify racial domination—if not to its victims then at least to white beneficiaries who need to believe that their social positions result from something more than the brute fact of social power and racial domination.

Liberal integrationist ideology is structured so that some social practices are taken out of the economy of race relations and understood to be undistorted by racial power. To be sure, there is no analytically necessary point from within the terms of the integrationist view of race at which the line between racial discrimination and neutral meritocracy must be drawn. One can imagine that the very definition of what constitutes the qualifications to attend law school, to work as a police officer, to own a home, to live in a particular neighborhood, or to have a particular income could be challenged as either directly rooted in the distortions of race-consciousness or more indirectly dependent on a rhetoric through which the powerful generally justify their share of the distribution of social benefits. And, in some contexts, reform within the integrationist tradition followed this path. But integrationism also labels the distribution of social goods as impersonal and neutral once we remove "distortions" such as race-consciousness. Integrationists tend to understand racism as a particular, identifiable deviation from an otherwise rational decision-making process that itself is not based in the history of social struggle between groups and worldviews. This narrow image of the domain of racial power characterizes the tendency of liberal integrationism to become part of a self-

justifying ideology of privilege and status. The realm of "neutral" social practices from which to identify bias and deviation constitutes a whole realm of institutional characteristics removed from critical view as historical, contingent, and rooted in the particularities of culture—which itself is a manifestation of group power, of politics.

D. Integrationism in Social Form: Public Schools

. . . Integrationist assumptions do not manifest themselves solely in self-conscious legal and political argument about race; instead, they provide the filter for how we experience, perceive, and construct a broad range of social relations and institutional practices. Seeing integrationism as the "race" component of a wider cultural ideology reflects our sense that a wide array of social practices and programs for reform "hang" together—not as implicated by analytic necessity, but nevertheless recognizable as a particular discourse in our culture.

Consider the program for reform of southern public schools in which integrationism played a central part in the sixties. Public education, at least in the South, embodied the most realized attempt to institutionalize the cultural assumptions of the liberal enlightenment ideology underlying integrationism. Integrationists put tremendous energy and effort into the struggle over southern schools. Here, the universalism of liberal race ideology appeared as a commitment to centralism in institutional culture and a corresponding opposition to local control. Moreover, the terms of the cultural compromise, reflected in the national embrace of integrationism, were clearest: in liberal education reform, the definition of what constitutes enlightened good sense was drawn in negative contrast to an image of the "backward" and ignorant whites who opposed the racial integration of southern public schools, and whose lack of enlightenment was further symbolized by their embrace of the "mythologies" of fundamentalist religion. Liberal integrationism entailed a trade-off of this "redneck" culture with African-American culture: in consideration for the suppression of white, southern working-class culture in schools, blacks were expected to accede to the suppression of African-American culture as well. Instead, school life would be characterized by the particular culture of technocracy and professionalism, presented as the aracial, neutral face of "quality" in education, and as the transcendence of localism and particularity.

Racial integration of southern schools represented only one aspect of the liberal reform of public education, though. Roughly simultaneous with the constitutional prohibition of racial segregation in public education, school prayer was also declared an unconstitutional violation of the norm of state neutrality. There was a deep link between these two major reforms: the logic of the joint rejection of school segregation and school prayer was contained in the sense that each reform reflected a progressive move from ignorance and parochialism to enlightenment and equality, from the particular and biased to the universal and objective. Just as school segregation represented the bias of the primitive beliefs of white supremacists, school prayer represented the bias of local, primitive religious beliefs. Just as school segregation formed one manifestation of the social face of racial discrimination, compulsory school prayer was the social face of religious intolerance, of discrimination according to theology. And just as school integration substituted universal and neutral norms for the particularities of white supremacist myth, the ban on school prayer substituted a neutral secular discourse for the particularities of religious belief.

The similarity in the way that segregation and prayer were understood is one manifestation of the deep connections between integrationism as an ideology and centralism as an institutional norm. Today's culture of public education is marked by a commitment in institutional life to the same kind of universalizing that integrationism reflects in ideological form. Along with the banning of the perceived local biases of segregationism and religion, a great centralization of curriculum and administration has occurred. The advanced degrees of administrators, the prevalent professional status of school board members, the implementation of standardized tests on a widespread basis, the

exclusion of religion from schools, and the near-universal replacement of corporal punishment ("paddling" in the southern vernacular) with therapeutic or contractual counseling approaches to student discipline—these all reflect the attempt to substitute a standardized national culture of public school administration for the perceived repression (rooted in parochialism) of the former institutional culture of southern schools. There is no analytic reason for the simultaneous occurrence of all these changes in the culture of the public schools: racial integration has been just one part of a more general sanitization of southern public education. The formerly maternal relationship between teacher and student has been replaced by the cool of professional distance; graduate schools teaching expertly tested methods of instruction replaced traditional training of teachers through contact with older faculty. The decentralization of curricula now exists only as a formality: public education has, for all practical purposes except funding, been nationalized. The standardized test and the cultural commitment to the No. 2 pencil are the lived, institutionalized rituals that reflect the commitment to impersonality and objectivity at the ideological level.

In educational discourse, professionalism plays the same symbolic role as merit, as a neutral alternative to irrational bias. Liberal reformers of public education in the late fifties and sixties associated professionalism with centralism, understanding that both provide a way to oppose local parochialism: "The public interest is almost invariably better served by leaving professional questions to the professionals."[14] Likewise, "local control results in the same kind of intellectual parochialism that characterizes schools in totalitarian countries."[15] Professionalism is the legitimizing rhetoric of public school administration.

Centralism and professionalism became responsive images to the liberal perception of the previous problems with public education—the idea that localism and parochialism compromised neutrality and objectivity. The underlying assumption was that once public education eradicated the influences of locality and bias, it would achieve a neutral, acultural form that, precisely because of its impersonality, would treat everyone alike.

This brings us back to the Malcolm X quote that introduces this section. In his view, the problem with school "segregation" was not the failure to integrate black and white children but, rather, the dynamics of power and control which formed the historical context of racial separation. Whereas liberals experienced integrationism as a progressive rejection of local bias and parochialism in favor of the impersonality of centralized authority, Malcolm X asserted that the very goal of the struggle against racism was to achieve local control, to liberate community institutions from outside colonial rule. While the dominant culture translated the demand for local control as the "states' rights" discourse of southern racism and the religious dogma of southern fundamentalists, Malcolm X associated local control with racial liberation. And while integrationists understood public school integration to be the institutional synonym for racial justice, Malcolm X asserted that integration was a manifestation of white supremacist ideology. To grasp how he could understand racial liberation in terms so diametrically opposed to the mainstream discourse of liberal integrationism, it makes sense to turn now to the alternative ideology of race developed by Malcolm X and other black nationalists.

II. THE BLACK NATIONALIST CRITIQUE

THUS, within the black community there are two separate challenges to the traditional integration policy that has long constituted the major objective of established negro leadership. There is the general skepticism that the negro, even after having transformed himself into a white black-man, will enjoy full acceptance in American society; and there is the longer-range doubt that even should complete integration somehow be achieved, it would prove to be really desirable, for its price may be the total absorption and disappearance of the race—a sort of painless genocide.

Understandably, it is the black masses who have most vociferously articulated these dangers of assimilation, for they have watched with alarm as the more fortunate among their ranks have gradually risen to the top only to be promptly "integrated" off into the white community—absorbed into another culture, often with undisguised contempt for all that had previously constituted their racial and cultural heritage. Also, it was the black masses who first perceived that integration actually increases the white community's control over the black community by destroying institutions, and by absorbing black leadership and coinciding its interests with those of the white community. ... Such injurious if unintended, side effects of integration have been felt in almost every layer of the black community.[16]

Like integrationism, black nationalism among African-Americans has taken various forms and has been associated with divergent worldviews.[17] The long tradition dates back to antebellum proposals by Martin Delany and others to colonize parts of Africa as a homeland for American blacks.[18] Some form of nationalism was manifest in Booker T. Washington's self-help and separatist ideas of black advancement.[19] Black nationalism in its modern, urban form can be traced among the poor to the organizing efforts of Marcus Garvey in the thirties,[20] and of the black Muslims since,[21] and among the middle class to W. E. B. Du Bois's critique of the National Association for the Advancement of Colored People's policy of integrationism in the thirties.[22] There is little doubt, however, that black nationalism had its most complete and sophisticated theoretical development, as well as its greatest mass appeal, during the sixties and early seventies, when it was articulated as an alternative worldview to integrationism and as part of a program of radical social transformation by, among others, Malcolm X,[23] Eldridge Cleaver,[24] Stokely Carmichael,[25] Imamu Baraka,[26] Harold Cruse,[27] the Black Panthers,[28] and quickly expanding factions of the Student Nonviolent Coordinating Committee (SNCC) and the Congress of Racial Equality (CORE).[29] ...

A. Black Power

The black nationalist position received its first modern wave of sustained mass exposure in

1966 when Willie Ricks and Stokely Carmichael began using the term "black power" during the March Against Fear in Mississippi.[30] Tension between integrationist and nationalist approaches had already mounted within and between various civil rights organizations. But the high-profile and polarized controversy over the term "black power" transformed what had been largely an underground conflict into a full-scale, highly charged public debate over the fundamental direction and conception of the civil rights movement.[31]

The mainstream reactions to the idea of comprehending the civil rights movement as a struggle for black power reflect the discourse associated with the marginalization of nationalist race-consciousness in the dominant cultural rhetoric. Both black and white integrationists equated black power with white supremacy. Hubert Humphrey responded by "reject[ing] calls for racism, whether they come from a throat that is white or one that is black."[32] Roy Wilkins charged that "no matter how endlessly they try to explain it, the term 'Black Power' means anti-white power," and he characterized black power as "a reverse Mississippi, a reverse Hitler, a reverse Ku Klux Klan."[33] *Time* magazine and Kenneth Clark each referred to black power as a "racist philosophy,"[34] and *Crisis,* the publication of NAACP, called black power advocates "black neo-segregationists" and "advocates of apartheid."[35] In fact, the virulent and extreme denunciation of black power symbolized the unity of what would quickly become the new center of American consciousness about race.

The integrationists saw two problems with black power. First, the concept assumed that power should be distributed on a racial basis, thereby assuming that American society should be thought of in terms of separate white and black communities. Black power thus violated both the integrationist principle of transcending race-consciousness at the ideological level and the integrationist program to end the segregation of whites and blacks at the institutional and community level.

Second, the idea of black power troubled

integrationists because it assumed that power, rather than reason or merit, determined the distribution of social resources and opportunities. It was not simply the theory of black power that engendered the charged reaction but, rather, the resistance—which the black power movement, for a time, embodied—to the reigning liberal idea of progress through reasoned discussion and deliberation. The clenched fist of the black power salute and the militaristic affectation of many black nationalist groups were the overt physical manifestations of this dimension of the movement.

Through the ideological filters of integrationism, black nationalism and white supremacy appear essentially the same because both are rooted in race-consciousness, in the idea that race matters to one's perception and experience of the world. Integrationists saw nationalists as regressive because, in the integrationist view, progress meant transcending race as a basis of social decision-making and in the long term, replacing power with reason as the basis for the distribution of resources. With the establishment of integrationism as the mainstream ideology of American good sense, nationalism became marginalized as an extremist and backward worldview, as the irrational correlate in the black community to the never-say-die segregationists of the white community. . . .

The mainstream reactions to black nationalism were so vociferous not because the black power movement presented any real threat of racial domination by blacks but, rather, because black nationalism embodied a profound rejection of the reigning ideology for understanding the distribution of power and privilege in American society. Just as integrationism became the mainstream discourse for racial justice—to the extent that it could be articulated in the terms of a deep cultural self-identity of enlightenment-through-evolution toward rationality and objectivity—the nationalist analysis of racial justice became threatening, in part, because it challenged the universalist assumptions underlying these images of progress. These images were challenged as themselves elements of a particular ideology of power and of the particular culture of whites.

B. *Nationalism as a Critique of Universalism*

Integrationists by and large never comprehended the analysis of racial domination presented by black nationalists. From their universalist view of racism as a distortion of an otherwise aracial rationality, integrationists interpreted the race consciousness of black nationalists as the mark of racism; they never considered the nationalist position as a competing, alternative, and systematic analysis of the meaning of racial domination. Thus, when black nationalists declared that integration was "a subterfuge for white supremacy"[36] and even represented "a form of painless genocide,"[37] integrationists literally could not understand what they were talking about. The black nationalist worldview was based on a fundamentally different set of beliefs and perceptual categories through which reforms that looked progressive to integrationists looked regressive to nationalists.

The contrast between the integrationist commitment to centralization and expertise in public education, on the one hand, and Malcolm X's discourse of local, community control, on the other, was only one manifestation of the deep and thoroughgoing opposition between integrationists and nationalists on the more basic issue of the meaning of race in America. Where integrationists understood race through the prism of universalism—from within which race-consciousness appeared arbitrary, irrational, and symmetrically evil whether practiced by whites or blacks—nationalists viewed race in the particular context of American history: racial identity was seen as a central basis for comprehending the significance of various social relations as they are actually lived and experienced, and the meaning of race was anything but symmetrical. The opposition between centralism and local control that distinguished integrationist and nationalist rhetoric about schools had its philosophical correlates in the opposition between timeless—as opposed to historicist—views about identity and group-consciousness, between the discourse of impersonal professionalism and ideas of organic community, and most generally between the assumptions of "universalism" and the assertions of qualitative cultural differences encompassed in the idea of "nationalism."

These basic differences are reflected in the very idea that African Americans comprise a "nation." This starting point is commonly associated with separatism in general, and with the demand for a separate nation as a homeland for American blacks in particular. But while at least some geographic separation has often characterized nationalist programs,[38] and while the idea of a formal nation-state has been advocated by several nationalist groups,[39] there is, as I see it, no necessary relation between nationalism as a way to understand race relations and a formal demand for geographic separation.

Instead, the image of African-Americans as a "nation within a nation,"[40] should be understood as a symbol of the core assertion that race-consciousness constitutes African-Americans as a distinct social community in much the same way that national self-identity operates to establish the terms of recognition and identity in "regular" nations. In contrast to the integrationist premise that blacks and whites are essentially the same, the idea of race as the organizing basis for group-consciousness asserts that blacks and whites are different, in the sense of coming from different communities, neighborhoods, churches, families, and histories, and of being in various ways foreigners to each other.[41] And in contrast to the white supremacist ideology of natural, essential racial characteristics, the image of nationhood locates differences between whites and blacks in social history, in the temporal context in which all national identity must come into being. As Dr. C. Munford put it:

> It is different from other emergent nations only in that it consists of forcibly transplanted colonial subjects who have acquired cohesive identity in the course of centuries of struggle against enslavement, cultural alienation, and the spiritual cannibalism of white racism. This common history which the Black people of America share is manifested in a concrete national culture with a peculiar

"spiritual complexion," or psychological temperament. Though the Black nation expresses its thoughts, emotions, and aspirations in the same tongue as American whites, the different conditions of existence ... have, from generation to generation, welded the bonds of a national experience as different from that of white existence as day is from night. And what differentiates nations from one another are dissimilar conditions of life.[42]

The depth of identification of self and recognition of others implicit in the idea of nationhood based on generations of "dissimilar conditions of life" marks a vision of community that cannot be captured in the liberal dichotomies of either liberty/coercion or reason/myth. The public assertion of spiritual cohesion represented by black nationhood contested the liberal belief in a boundary between public objectivity and private sentiment underlying the link between universality and individualism. Nationhood, understood as a historically created community, assumes that social bonds of identity, recognition, and solidarity can be liberating and fulfilling outside the family.

In this way, nationalists articulated what might be seen as a "historicized" view of social relations. In opposition to the universal vantage point from which integrationists identified bias and prejudice, nationalists presented the time-bound, messy, and inherently particular social relations between nations as the central ground from which to perceive race. In opposition to the essentializing of race in which white supremacists engaged, nationalists located the meaning of race in history, in the social structures that people—rather than God or some objectified nature—have created.

Again, the commitment to a historical view means that there is no objective or natural necessity to the way that groups, identifies, and social meanings have been structured. Because the structure of race relations is a social creation, it could have been constructed differently in the past and could still be changed in the future. However, the nationalist view—a voluntary, willed association—contrasts with the liberal image of group identity either as an irrational status or as a matter of choice. The idea of a nationalist base of social identity is that we are,

in a sense, thrown into history, with aspects of social reality already structured to limit some possibilities while making others available. Rather than imagining that people simply exist as autonomous individuals who create social relations with acts of private will, Munford, for example, saw African-Americans in terms of traditions and communities that provide the historical context for individual identity. From a nationalist perspective, the fact that African-Americans compose a socially created community, in terms of a contingent history, does not mean that the existing community should be rejected because it represents either a distortion to be transcended or results from a domination that must be erased. Against the liberal image that group identity and status are opposed to the possibility of individual freedom, the nationalist perspective sees in historical structures the very basis for social meaning.[43]

C. The Nationalist Interpretation of School Integration

"Integration" as a goal speaks to the problem of blackness, not only in an unrealistic way but also in a despicable way. It is based on complete acceptance of the fact that in order to have a decent house or education, black people must move into a white neighborhood, or send their children to a white school. This reinforces, among both black and white, the idea that "white" is automatically superior and "black" is by definition inferior. For this reason, "integration" is a subterfuge for the maintenance of white supremacy. . . . The goal is not to take black children out of the black community and expose them to white middle-class values; the goal is to build and strengthen the black community. . . . "Integration" also means that black people must give up their identity, deny their heritage. . . . The fact is that integration, as traditionally articulated, would abolish the black community. The fact is that what must be abolished is not the black community but the dependent colonial status that has been inflicted on it.

—Stokely Carmichael, 1967.[44]

The conception that African-Americans created "a concrete national culture" and constitute an integral, historically created national community within the structure of American social relations is crucial to understanding the divergent ways that nationalists and integrationists understand racial domination. Compare, for example, the different ways that nationalists and integrationists interpreted public school integration.

Nationalists believed that school integration was undesirable for two main reasons. First, integration of black and white schools entailed the abolition of one of the few organized institutions in the black community. School integration therefore contributed an even greater loss of social power: blacks lost the ability to control and shape their children's education. As Malcolm X described community control, it is necessary in order to create the curriculum, textbooks, and general content of educational life in a way that responds to the needs and wishes of the black community. By conceiving of African-Americans in nationalist terms, black nationalists focused attention on the impact of race reform on the community as a whole and evaluated integration according to whether the black community was made stronger or weaker. As Stokely Carmichael and Charles Hamilton stated: "[T]he racial and cultural personality of the black community must be preserved and the community must win its freedom while preserving its cultural integrity. . . . This is the essential difference between integration as it is currently practiced and the concept of Black Power."[45]

Second, nationalists asserted that school integration meant the adaptation of blacks to white norms—to quote Carmichael, integration entailed, "taking black children out of the black community and exposing them to white middle-class values." Of course, there was no analytically intrinsic content to the idea of integration which mandated that school integration proceed on the basis of white cultural norms—just as there was nothing intrinsic to the concept of integration that entailed Robert Browne's image of "the Negro . . . transform[ing] himself into a white black-man."[46] Yet Carmichael and Browne highlighted an aspect of American racial integration which is buried in the mainstream ideology of neutrality and universalism but central to the black nationalists' analysis—a consideration of the cultural terms on which

integration in social institutions would proceed. According to Harold Cruse, the commitment to integration embodied absorption into white culture through a failure to recognize the integrity of the black culture created in conditions of domination:

> [T]he Negro working class has been roped in and tied to the chariot of racial integration driven by the Negro middle class. In this drive for integration the Negro working class is being told in a thousand ways that it must give up its ethnicity and become human, universal, full-fledged American. Within the context of this forced alliance of class claims there can be no room for Negro art . . . or art institutions . . . because all of this is self-segregation which hangs up "our" drive for integration.[47]

In fact, "[t]he integrationist philosophy sees Negro ghettoes as products of racial segregation that should not even exist. Hence, nothing in the traditions of ghettoes are worth preserving even when the ghettos do exist in actuality. This is typical integrationist logic on all things social."[48]

In more general terms, this understanding of integrationism as based on a vision of a "universal, full-fledged American" underlies the sense expressed by Carmichael and Browne that integration entailed the abolition of the black community. Because integrationists had no conceptual category with which to comprehend African-Americans as a separate national group, they by and large ignored the possibility of understanding racial justice in terms of the transfer of resources and power to the black community as an entity. Hence, rather than providing the material means for improving the housing, schools, cultural life, and economy of black neighborhoods, nationalists saw mainstream race reform as entailing "progress" only through blacks moving into historically white neighborhoods, attending historically white schools, participating in white cultural activities, and working in white-owned and white-controlled economic enterprises. "Even if such a program were possible, its result would be, not to develop the black community as a functional and honorable segment of the total society, with its own cultural identity, life patterns, and institutions, but to abolish it—the final solution to the Negro problem."[49] . . .

The correlate of the nationalist critique, that school integration meant not only the loss of an important institution in the black community but also the assimilation of blacks into white cultural practices, likewise was invisible to integrationists. Just as integrationists saw as a form of reverse prejudice the race-consciousness of the nationalist focus on the need for black institutional life, they also failed to comprehend the idea that racially integrated schools might prioritize and propagate white culture. Instead, the images of expertise and professionalism that became the ideology of public education signified for integrationists the institutional face of the commitment to reason and impersonality at a philosophical level. In school integration, its supporters believed that black children would be integrated into the aracial culture of quality education. The clinical computer printouts, reflecting the cognitive achievement level gleaned from standardized tests in statistical, percentile terms, symbolized the impersonality—hence cultural neutrality—of the liberal reform of public education.

But where integrationists saw school integration in terms of transcending the bias at the root of segregation in favor of an "objectively" defined "quality education," nationalists saw that process as assimilating black children to white middle-class norms. The nationalist perspective characterized the norms that constituted the neutral, impersonal, aracial, professional character of school integration as particular cultural assumptions of a specific economic class of whites. The vision of integration as a form of "painless genocide," then, stemmed from an analysis of integration as meaning not the liberation of the black community from racial domination but, instead, the transcendence of the black community itself in favor of "neutral" social practices; these could only be identified as historically situated and culturally particular from the outside, by those for whom their supposed universality is experienced as a particular form of Otherness.[50]

One can imagine a form of school integration that would have entailed a consideration of the integrity of African-American culture as well as a recognition of the cultural assumptions of dominant public school practices. Nothing in the simple area of racial integration necessitated that it be linked with universalist assumptions, but the nationalist analysis did correlate well with the ways that integrationism proceeded. The dismantling of dual school systems in reality meant closing black schools and integrating black children into white school programs. . . . Perhaps more telling, in light of the nationalist critique of integration as a "subterfuge for white supremacy," even where integration has been "successful" it has largely meant resegregation within the walls of formally integrated schools. On the purported basis of intelligence rather than race, the process of "tracking" utilizes various "objective" tests to segregate school children according to "cognitive ability." In school district after school district, the slower tracks disproportionately comprised of black children and faster tracks disproportionately of whites.[51]

The nationalist critique of integration highlights the ideological background against which this manner of conducting racial integration could seem plausible. Within the integrationist vision, once race-consciousness (and other "biases") are removed, then neutral, objective social practices remain. Thus, the logic of conducting school integration by closing black schools and firing black teachers and principals was premised on the ability to identity "quality" schools, teachers, and administrators in a neutral, objective way. In these neutral terms, black schools were closed because they were inferior as a result of discrimination between white and black institutions under segregation; similarly, tracking supposedly measures an acultural, objective mental process called "cognitive ability." Signifying the transcendence of race as a meaningful social category, integrationists rationalize the disproportionate representation of black children in decaying schools and slower educational tracks not as the manifestation of black inferiority but instead as the result of poverty—articulated bureaucratically as "low socioeconomic status" or, in the acronym, "low SES."[52] Just as integrationists failed to recognize the cultural achievements of black schools, and saw them, as Harold Cruse noted, simply as "products of racial segregation that should not even exist,"[53] they also failed to recognize the cultural specificity of white schools, which were instead seen only as "superior" education. The intense reaction on the part of liberals to black nationalist movements for community control of schools and for the establishment of separate and autonomous Afro-American Studies departments reflected the depth of the challenge that nationalism posed to the dominant cultural ideology that linked rationality, enlightenment, and progress with racial integration.

For a brief period in the late sixties and early seventies, issues of educational public policy crystallized the dramatic opposition between the nationalist ideology of cultural difference and organic community, on the one hand, and the integrationist ideology of universal reason and neutral institutions, on the other. In terms of community support and interest, nationalists produced their greatest organizational successes in the arenas of public schools and university politics. For low-income people of color, the nationalist approach to education unified popular movements for community control over schools in urban communities such as Harlem and Ocean Hill–Brownsville in New York City, and Adams-Morgan in Washington, D.C. In the middle class, nationalist activism took the form of demands for the establishment of Afro-American Studies departments in predominantly white colleges and universities across the country.[54] In each dimension, "the movement toward community control [is] a profound rejection of the core of liberal ideology," because liberal integrationism assumes that society is the "aggregation of independent individuals, rather than an organic compact of groups." Nationalists asserted that educational reform cannot be understood in terms of a "quality" education neutral as to race; rather, they said, it must be examined in terms of how schools serve the needs of an organic community held together by bonds of a particular racial culture and history. They therefore challenged the fundamental philosophical ideologies that "knowledge" itself represents some acultural achievement and

that schools could be evaluated according to some aracial standard based on how well they impart the neutral educational commodity of knowledge and reason. "[T]he word 'better' can only be taken to mean better according to some secular standards, and it is precisely those standards that are now rejected."[55]

The equation of integration with assimilation—as drawn by Stokely Carmichael, Robert Browne, Harold Cruse, and many other nationalists—constituted the most threatening aspect of the nationalist critique. Here the rejection of universalism took the form not only of an assertion that African-Americans constitute a distinct community, a "nation" but, conversely, that white Americans also constitute an historically identifiable group within the structure of American race relations. . . .

D. Nationalism as a Critique of Liberalism
It is necessary for us to develop a new frame of reference that transcends the limits of white concepts. It is necessary for us to develop and maintain a total intellectual offensive against the false universality of white concepts, whether they are expressed by author William Styron or U.S. Senator Daniel Patrick Moynihan. By and large, reality has been conceptualized in terms of the narrow viewpoint of the small minority of whites who live in Europe and North America. We must abandon the partial frame of reference of our oppressors and create new concepts that will release our reality, the reality of the overwhelming majority of men and women on this globe. We must say to the white world that there are things in the world that are not dreamt of in your history and your sociology and your philosophy.[56]

—Lenore Bennett, 1972

The alternative nationalist worldview embodied in the critique of public school integration manifested itself not only in an analysis of particular institutional practices, but also in a critique of each component of the integrationist worldview. At a more general and abstract level of nationalist analysis, the repudiation of the dominant ideology of public education corresponded to a thoroughgoing critique of the epistemological assumptions of liberalism as a whole. Black nationalists depicted the ideas of rationality, neutrality, and objectivity, which integrationists associated with the transcendence of bias and prejudice, as the particular cultural rhetoric of "the small minority of white men who live in Europe and North America." According to nationalists in the sixties, these traditional categories of liberal and enlightenment thought do not constitute an aracial or culturally neutral standard that measures social progress in overcoming partiality, parochialism, and bias; rather, they are simply elements in the dominant worldview of white elites.

The rejection of prevailing scholarly standards and methodologies represented one dimension of the challenge to the philosophical assumptions underlying liberal integrationism. Black nationalist scholars in the field of sociology, for instance, began to critique the social science norms of objectivity and value-neutrality as well as to draw a link between those general assumptions about the nature of intellectual and academic inquiry and the particular concepts that justified racial domination. Nationalist sociologists argued that American scholarly norms constituted a form of "academic colonialism" in which the discourse of universality and neutrality is embodied in assumptions about the superiority of white cultural practices and the corresponding inferiority of African-American culture.[57] According to one line of attack, the mind/body dichotomy implicit in the distinction between intellectual and manual work, and the tradition of distinguishing scholarship as a specialized activity in the mental realm, represented an attempt at class rationalization—the elevation of mental activity symbolized the superior entitlement of the leisure class to the distribution of goods in society.[58]

Black nationalist sociologists further criticized the idea of impartiality and the notion that there is a sharp dichotomy between the detachment that marks good research skills and the emotionalism that constitutes a form of bias. These sociologists contended that those research norms which require a lack of empathy and existential connection with the subjects of sociological studies reflect a particular value-orientation that ultimately helps to legitimate

conditions of racial hierarchy. According to black nationalist academics, the relationship between the "objective" researcher and his or her research subject mirrors the relationship between dominant and suppressed cultural group. The researcher represents, vis-à-vis the social groups under study, the same rhetoric of rationality and objectivity that the powerful use to justify their domination generally.[59]

Many black sociologists also sought to demonstrate a systematic bias in the ways that mainstream sociological research was conducted, arguing that white culture represented the implicit standard in empirical research, and that black cultural practices were represented as "deviations."[60] Similarly, nationalist sociologists criticized the analytical categories of prejudice and discrimination as based on a false image of reason and neutrality which embodied white cultural norms; and they concluded that integration as understood in mainstream sociological analysis was premised on the annihilation of black culture through its assimilation into white American culture.[61] ...

In general, the radical critique launched by black nationalist sociologists and cultural critics claimed that objective reason or knowledge could not exist because one's position in the social structure of race relations influenced what one would call "knowledge" or "rationality." The cultural differences between blacks and whites could not be studied through a neutral frame of reference because any frame of reference assumed the perspective of either the oppressed or the oppressor, either African-Americans or whites, either the sociologist or the subject. Nor were cultural differences limited to particular social practices such as religious activity or artistic production; instead, they were infused more generally into how people perceive reality and experience the world. There could be no neutral theory of knowledge: knowledge was itself a function of the ability of the powerful to impose their own views, to differentiate between knowledge and myth, reason and emotion, and objectivity and subjectivity. In the historicizing perspective of black nationalists, though, knowledge was necessarily a social construct. Understanding what society deemed worthy of calling "knowledge" depends on a prior inquiry into a social situation. Culture precedes epistemology.

This kind of generalized challenge to reigning cultural assumptions also characterized black nationalist perspectives on the debate about affirmative action. Rather than perceiving a conflict between "objective" merit and the goal of racial integration, the nationalist approach challenged the objectivity of the category of "merit" by viewing it in terms of the particular social practices by which whites historically distributed social goods. In the nationalist worldview, integrationist debates about affirmative action are a "subterfuge" for white supremacy: the debates focus on white cultural mores, present them as universal and objective, and then utilize them to characterize blacks as not "qualified."

A contemporary example of this process can be found in legal education. In law schools throughout the country, admissions, hiring, and tenure debates proceed on the basis of standards of academic and scholarly merit which were constructed in a period when African-Americans were excluded from mainstream law schools and when the very law to be studied itself sanctioned white supremicism. The notion that racism was limited only to the exclusion of blacks from law schools, and was not a part of the infrastructure for thinking about and constructing "qualifications," is emblematic of the limiting assumptions that nationalists perceived as underlying integrationism. The concepts of "merit" and "qualifications" have a function only in relation to existing social practices; black nationalists insisted that the existing social practices should not be taken as the standard, since those practices were created by a culture that considered it normal to exclude blacks—that is, a culture itself in need of transformation.

For example, imagine a legal challenge to the disproportionate racial impact of the Law School Admission Test (LSAT). The use of the LSAT might be justified based on the functional correlation with performance in law school, but such a functional defense views the status quo of legal education as the standard. Nationalists would argue that there is no intrinsic necessity to the current ways that law schools conduct legal education, and they would emphasize the genealogy of existing law school practices in terms of their roots in white culture. To be sure, the status quo of legal education itself might be justified by a functional relation to existing legal practice, but that merely pushes the controversy to another level—the nature of existing legal culture. And that is exactly what a challenge to the LSAT's exclusionary aspects contests, the way that the legal profession is currently constituted as a reflection of white culture.

In short, the nationalist approach emphasized and criticized the self-justifying character of meritocratic assumptions about qualifications. Once we consider the possibility that existing social practices might reflect the domination of particular racial groups, those practices can no longer provide a neutral ground from which to defend existing definitions either of qualifications or of merit as functionally correlated with necessary social roles.

E. Power, Subordination, and Colonialism

The assertion of nationhood on the part of African-Americans also comprised a declaration of alien-nation between races, an assertion that white culture is experienced as Other to blacks. Integrationists saw the transcendence of the structure of racism as replacing the same/Other image of white supremacists with expansion of sameness to blacks; nationalists conceived of the relations as Other to Other.

Integrationists located the roots of racism in consciousness, in the cognitive distortion of stereotype and prejudice. In contrast, the nationalist perception of whites and blacks as occupying different national spaces entailed a view of racial domination as located in the particular power relations between black and white communities, in the exteriors of social life rather than the interiors of consciousness. Given the focus on social context rather than consciousness, the "cure" for racial domination could not be centered on education and interracial contact to dispel stereotypes; instead, it depended on the transformation of power relations between black and white communities, or, in other words, on the achievement of "black power."

Similarly, since racism referred to the particular power relations between black and white communities, there was no center of comparison from which to equate racial identity with other forms of identity, or the domination of African-Americans with discrimination against other groups. The significance of race in terms of social relations and the self-identity of people was seen by black nationalists to have a particular weight and depth that could not be comprehended if one abstracted it from historical context and flattened out racial domination into one of many structurally equivalent forms of "discrimination." Nationalists asserted that a group identity that centers around race was not structurally the same as the "ethnic heritage" that every American has, because, in our social history, race has acquired a particular significance and centrality that is qualitatively different than the differences, say, between Italian-Americans and Polish-Americans.[62]

In contrast to the integrationist image of discrimination as the social practice of racism, the nationalist image was subordination, the hierarchy of the white community over the black community. Rather than conceive of race reform in terms of affirmative action aimed at integrating formerly white institutions, nationalists sought to strengthen and develop institutions in the black community which would serve African-Americans. Thus, nationalists tended to see racial justice in terms of reparations,[63] or foreign "aid" from developed countries to the third world.[64] This is why Malcolm X distinguished "segregation" from racial separation. According to his analysis, segregation amounted to a form of racial domination, in which the black community was not only separate from the white but also ruled by the white community. As he saw it, if the power relations were changed, the meaning of the separation would be dramatically different.

In contrast to the integrationist image of

segregation as a systematic form of racism, black nationalists developed an analysis that relied primarily on an image of whites and blacks constituting separate national communities. The systematic nature of American racism was described not as segregation, but as a form of colonialism.[65] According to Harold Cruse's description, it was "domestic colonialism": "instead of establishing a colonial empire in Africa, [the United States] brought the colonial system home and installed it in the southern states. . . . Emancipation elevated [the negro] only to the position of a semi-dependent man, not to that of an equal or independent being."[66] In the nationalist analysis, African-Americans exist in a "neocolonial" relationship with whites, as a colonized people "dispersed" throughout North America:

> Black Power must be viewed as a projection of sovereignty, an embryonic sovereignty that black people can focus on and through which they can make distinctions between themselves and others, between themselves and their enemies—in short, the white mother country of America and the black colony dispersed throughout the continent on absentee-owned land, making Afro-America a decentralized colony. Black Power says to black people that it is possible to build a national organization on someone else's land.[67]

Comprehending the relations between blacks and whites on a colonial model, sixties nationalists asserted that even black control of the black community would be insufficient if it merely meant that blacks would administer the same structural power relations that previously existed between white and black communities. The metaphor of colonialism thus symbolically placed sixties nationalists outside the bounds of the pluralist wing of integrationism by suggesting that the racial diversification of existing American institutions and social patterns might simply be another form of the colonial relationship. A radical transformation of the status quo institutional practices would be needed before identifiable black and white communities could relate on a just basis.[68]

The colonialism metaphor unified the nationalist analysis by capturing, in one image, the totalizing sense of alienation between whites and blacks which the rejection of common nationality represented; it also captured the structural and systematic power exercised by the white community as well as the conviction that group solidarity was necessarily to change existing power relations. It also provided the rhetoric for a critical analysis of relations within the black community between economic classes. Nationalists deploying a neo-colonialism analysis accounted for opposition to their position within the black community as the effects of "indirect rule," within which an elite was created among the colonized class to administer and mediate on behalf of colonial interests. According to many black nationalists, the black middle class played this role in America, and class differences with the black poor and working class accounted for the middle classes' support of integration.[69]

This orientation around colonialism connected various projects in the sixties and early seventies, including movements for community control over schools; for black political, economic, and police control over black neighborhoods; for race-conscious economic cooperation among African-Americans; for race-conscious reparations from the white community to African-American communities; for the establishment and control of Afro-American Studies departments in universities; for the preservation and transformation of black colleges and universities; and for cultural autonomy in arts, music, literature, and intellectual life. . . .

III. The Confrontation Over Race in the 1960s

THE borders of contemporary political and legal discourse about race were formed in the cultural crisis that militant black nationalism engendered when it was first articulated on a mass scale in the late sixties. Although there was nothing intrinsic in the concept of racial integration demanding that it be understood according to the universalist ideology I have described, and although there was no reason that African-American racial consciousness had to be equated with the race-consciousness of white supremacists, this way of thinking about race was produced in part to justify the rejection of black nationalism. . . .

Integrationism was supported by a wide range of those who denounced the "black power" slogan—a coalition between black, predominantly middle-class moderates, and white, predominantly middle- and upper-class liberals and progressives. Understanding themselves as specifically opposed to race-consciousness, integrationists needed to reject black nationalists because of the threat that they posed to the cultural self-identity of both the black middle-class moderates and the white upper-class liberals. The commitment to a universalist vision of racial justice reflected the shared ambiguities that these two groups had about their own racial identities. The upshot of their implicit coalition was that they constructed and embraced a conservative race ideology that helped to contain the issue of racial liberation—together with other disruptive challenges to the assumptions of everyday institutional life, such as the feminist movement—by perceiving all of these challenges as part of a single discourse, unified around an idea of "discrimination." This integrationist ideology served both to recognize racial power as a formal matter and yet to set boundaries for its critique. . . .

A. The Transformed Meaning of Black Nationalism

One important aspect of the confrontation between nationalism and integrationism in the sixties was that after decades of marginality within the African-American community, nationalism achieved mass appeal and arguably overtook integrationism as the dominant ideology of racial liberation. Black nationalism in the sixties represented both the reappearance of a long tradition that began at least as early as Martin Delany in the 1850s—a tradition that had been obscured by the unity created by integrationist-oriented leadership from the mid-fifties to the mid-sixties—and also embodied a reinterpretation of the nationalist ideology. This reinterpretation dramatically severed the associations between nationalism and accomodationism, a link dating back to the confluence, under Booker T. Washington's leadership, of separatist organizing and accomodationist relations with white domination.

According to Harold Cruse, "American Negro history is basically a history of the conflict
between integrationist and nationalist forces
in politics, economics and culture, no matter
what leaders are involved and what slogans are
used. . . ."[70] The reappearance of nationalism
in the sixties reflected a long-standing conflict
within the African-American community that
the brief unity around Martin Luther King,
Jr.'s leadership had temporarily obscured. What
made the struggle between black nationalists
and black integrationists particularly significant
in the sixties was not its continuity but its
changed cultural meaning: integrationism and
nationalism traditionally have been the stark
choices the African-American community associated with racial politics, but that does not
mean that the two ideologies were always understood in the same way.

In addition to the conflict over nationalist
and integrationist conceptions of race, the issue
of "accomodationism" versus resistance embodies another central dimension of African-American racial discourse.[71] The degree of resistance
and opposition associated with either integrationism or nationalism was an independently
important cultural issue—with its own history
of conflict—in the perception of each stance.

Although the black nationalist stance was
unmistakably identified with a commitment to
militancy—and eventually with violent revolution—by the late sixties and early seventies,
there was no necessary historic or analytic connection between black nationalism and the desire to confront and resist the white power
structure. To the contrary, virtually every other
significant black nationalist movement in
American history bore marks of accomodationism. Early-nineteenth-century colonization
movements were framed in a historical context
in which African-American support for "back-
to-Africa" programs were linked closely to those
white supremacists who supported colonization
as a means to deport black people from North
America.[72] In contrast to the colonists, the
abolitionist-, civil rights-, and integrationist-
influenced rhetoric of, say, Frederick Douglass
appeared far more militant and oppositionist.
Similarly, Du Bois based his critique of the self-

help, racial solidarity and separatism rhetoric of
Booker T. Washington on the way in which
Washington's approach amounted to a "submission" and a "surrender" to the Jim Crow social
structure rather than a challenge to that structure.[73] Du Bois's differences with Garvey centered on the same issue, although Garvey was
clearly more militant and confrontational than
Washington.[74] By the time that the integrationists' momentum increased in the forties and
fifties, black nationalism—represented mainly
by the socially and religiously conservative
dogma of the Nation of Islam—had achieved
the role of a kind of "traditionalism." Thus, in
the early years of the civil rights movement,
nationalist approaches—organized in the cultural margins of the black community—seemed
to many civil rights activists to imply an accommodation to the racial apartheid structure of
white society through a retreat to the "isolation"
of the black community.[75] In generational
terms, this meant that nationalist appeals to
young civil rights workers were likely experienced as the conservative voice of an older
generation saying, "don't make waves" and
"stick with your own people," in contrast to
the sense within the civil rights movement of
building a drive for resistance to and confrontation with the white power structure.

This symbolic association of nationalism with
accommodation and integrationism with resistance in the cultural perception of the basic
choices helps to account for how Martin Luther
King, Jr., could simultaneously represent the
militant, confrontation-oriented aspirations of
black activists and speak in the rhetoric of
integrationism, moralism, and civil rights.
When King began in Montgomery, one could
divide civil rights activists and groups according
to whether they supported a legalist, litigation-
oriented strategy of race reform or the approach
of direct action and confrontation. As an early
leader of mass direct action, King began his
career representing the militant, non-accomo-
dationist wing of the civil rights movement, a
faction whose strategies embodied the nationalist belief that racial solidarity and assertions of
group power were the means to attain racial
liberation. Thus, even while nationalist ideology

was most marginalized in the black community during the fifties and early sixties, one can detect aspects of nationalism within the integrationist civil rights movement itself. The historic opposition between nationalism and integrationism was reproduced in the conflict between the factions advocating legalism and direct action in the civil rights movement.

Prior to the resurgence of nationalist ideology in the mid-sixties, this tension within the civil rights movement was understood to encompass only the strategic question of the degree of militancy. The decision to turn back the marchers at the Petus Bridge in Selma became the cultural symbol of a split between black activists over how far to extend confrontational organizing. But, in retrospect, this argument over tactics can be seen to have contained the seeds of the later, more explicit opposition between nationalism and integrationism. For a time in the early sixties, in fact, the two tendencies merged in cultural perception. Militant, confrontational integrationists such as Robert Williams who advocated "armed self-defense" became associated with militant, confrontational nationalists like Malcolm X. It was possible to perceive as similar individuals and groups with such ultimately opposing and inconsistent ideologies because the issue of militancy versus accommodation embodied central cultural significance in ways that both transcended, and eventually subsumed, the split between nationalist and integrationist positions. It is therefore no coincidence that the most direct action—oriented groups under the civil rights umbrella, SNCC and CORE, would eventually renounce the civil rights analytics of prejudice, discrimination, and segregation in favor of the nationalist analytics of power, subordination, and colonialism.[76] ...

The widespread invocation of the colonialism model to describe race relations exemplifies how sixties-era black nationalists linked nationalism and social struggle, and thus how they symbolically broke the traditional association of separatism with accommodation. Previous nationalist movements, even militant Garveyism, always could be associated with the degradation of accomodationism to the extent that they seemed to accept American racial segregation. Rather than oppose the power dynamics between white and black communities in the United States, the separatist proposals—for a return to Africa (Delany and Garvey), the creation of a separate land base in the United States (like the Nation of Islam, the Republic of New Africa), or the various proposals for the creation of a separate black economic base (Du Bois, the Nation of Islam, Washington)—all carried a sense of retreat from mainstream American life into isolation and nonconfrontation. In contrast, the articulation of the relations between blacks and whites as neocolonialist served as a bridge between the aspirations for community power that were always at least implicit in the nationalist ideology of racial solidarity and self-help, on the one hand, and the militancy and confrontationism that had been the province of direct action integrationists, on the other. Rather than representing a fantasy of separation or isolation from whites, the colonialism metaphor presented nationalists as engaged in the struggle for power in the United States: it posed the problem facing African-Americans as the form that relations between white and black communities took instead of the fact that there were relations at all. The colonialist analysis located the solution not in a retreat from the United States but, rather, in a struggle to transform relations of subordination within America. Unlike the conservative aspects of earlier manifestations of black nationalism, the colonialist analysis comprehended the imposition of an external power structure on the African-American community and, accordingly, provided a symbolic mediation of the tendency for self-blame that a nationalist emphasis on self-help and personal discipline might otherwise imply.

In the sixties, black nationalists began to conceive of their project not as geographic separation from whites, but rather as the dismantling of the power relations between white and black communities. Instead of the choices appearing as either integration and assimilation, on the one hand, or total geographic separation, on the other, sixties-era nationalists, led most notably by Malcolm X, developed a "third way" that combined militant engagement with the white power structure and the racial solidarity and antiassimilationism traditionally associated with nationalism.[77] . . .

By the late fifties, King had united virtually the entire black community behind a program of confrontational direct action aimed at the achievement of integration, but the situation had changed by the late sixties. Nationalists claimed the symbolic ground of militancy. They developed a sophisticated critique of dominant American culture and power relations which at least rhetorically connected African-Americans to the Africans and Asians who were achieving independence from colonial rule; further, they utilized a class-based neocolonialist analysis to identify black integrationists with "moderate" and "assimilationist" middle-class accommodation to the white power structure. . . .

Nationalism upset the confidence that the black middle class had held since the turn of the century in the achievement of civil rights and integration into dominant American institutions—a goal that, to them, had seemed a real possibility. Nationalist ideology threatened the self-identity of the black middle class as society's elite who symbolized the achievement possible when blacks are accorded opportunity. Nationalists also undermined the black middle class conception that their role in racial liberation was to help the "brothers and sisters" left behind to "escape" the ghetto and join mainstream institutions. In the nationalist analysis, though, the very success of the black middle class in American society might undermine individual identity and betray the aspirations of the black community, because it reflected gains granted by a white power structure in exchange for black administration of white interests. This rhetoric called to mind the shame of the long history of accomodationism by black middle-class leaders and thus generated a kind of group anxiety. Integrationism—in the particular, universalist form that it took in the sixties—responded to this anxiety by denying that the status to which the black middle class aspired was racially identifiable as a particularly white world, rather than a realm of universal, culturally neutral social practice.

Similarly, the very predominance and strength of the integrationist civil rights tradition engendered a correlate anxiety for nationalists, an anxiety that extreme and polar expressions of black separatism helped to resolve. According to Harold Cruse, the particular violence and hateful rhetoric that came to characterize black nationalist discourse by the end of the sixties was rooted in a psychological attempt to overcome the ways that blacks had been conditioned historically to depend on whites in the realm of political action. In order to overcome the deeply ingrained interracialism that had characterized progressive coalitions for several decades, Cruse asserts that black nationalists had to muster hatred "to avoid the necessity of apologizing to whites for excluding them." Thus, just as black integrationists gravitated toward a particularly universalist interpretation of racial justice in order to resolve the anxiety that nationalists raised about their self-identity, so black nationalists gravitated toward particularly extreme interpretations in order to overcome their anxiety about their own relation to whites. Given these cultural postures, each group tended to confirm the suspicions of the other. The more universalist the integrationist ideology became, the more nationalists saw an apologia for assimilation into the white world and a corresponding betrayal of the black community; and the more hateful the nationalist ideology became, the more integrationists saw the same bitterness and parochialism that they saw in white supremacists.

B. Black Nationalism and Whites

The marginalization from mainstream discourse which black nationalists ultimately met reflects several historical factors. One important feature of this marginalization was the state repression that groups like the Black Panthers faced; another was the way in which the increasingly extremist and revolutionary rhetoric and social actions on the part of both the black and the white left began to appear more and more fantastic as time went on. Furthermore, limitations in ideology often led to a rigid, otherworldly revolutionary dogma gleaned from a conglomeration of Marx, Lenin, Mao, Frantz

Fanon, and others—which took on an extremist, righteous tone that began to assimilate anyone who had a job to the "white" power structure. This approach alienated masses of African-Americans and others who were not prepared to engage in an armed guerilla campaign in America. In addition, just as the economic health of black communities deteriorated during the "recession" of the early seventies and the associated cutback in federal spending, the black middle class expanded with the advent of integrationism as a national policy and, by and large, abandoned traditionally black neighborhoods. By the mid-seventies, successes in struggles for political influence in or control of many cities, combined with the national commitment to "cultural diversity," began to echo features of the nationalist program as mainstream American institutions seemed to accommodate a diffused and limited version of black race-consciousness—developments that all tended to obscure the nationalist position as a sharp alternative to integration.

Whatever else "caused" the decline of nationalism, however, there can be no question that its near-total rejection by whites played a critical factor in its exclusion from mainstream discourse. As indicated above, the overt analytic framework for this reaction was the identification of race-consciousness with the evil of racism and the consequent perception of black nationalists as racists. . . .

Various factors partially explain why white liberals and progressives in particular rejected nationalism as a way to analyze race relations. First, unlike the long tradition of progressive black nationalism in African-American communities, the only whites who explicitly perceived race as a significant feature of group identity were white supremacists—a group historically comprised of a loose cultural coalition of southern well-to-do whites and major segments of the white working class across the country. . . . Moreover, because black nationalism before the sixties was largely separatist and isolationist, whites consequently had little or no contact with the different tradition of race-consciousness among African-Americans. . . . Against this historical background of nonen-

gagement with and ignorance of the black nationalist tradition, black nationalism confronted white integrationists in the sixties through the militant rhetoric first of Malcolm X, and then of the proponents of black power. Although the particular form that nationalist rhetoric took in the sixties was largely responsive to the struggle between integrationists and nationalists within the black community, an obviously significant factor in the white response was the rejection and repudiation that whites experienced from black nationalists. . . .

Black nationalism caused great anxiety and turmoil for whites, in part because of the violence that nationalists symbolized, and in part because nationalism represented whites as constituting a community with particular cultural norms. As whites articulated their rejection of black nationalists, they complained of "reverse racism" because they experienced the nationalist depiction of a white culture as the same kind of essentializing and stereotyping that white racists used in describing black culture. To be sure, much nationalist rhetoric was reductionist with respect to the complexity of group relations within the white community; but through the identification of racial identity and group-consciousness as central to the structure of American social relations, the black nationalists of the sixties also identified the particular aspect of avoidance and denial which white support of black liberation assumed—the commitment by whites to deny the centrality of race as a historically constructed, powerful factor in the social structure of American life. Understanding racism as a form of "discrimination" from an assumed neutral norm was the cognitive face of a widespread cultural flight from white self-identity. Whites resolved the anxiety that nationalists raised by denying that blacks or whites had any identifiable culture at all. It made no sense to think of institutional practices in racial terms, because no culture was tied to race anyway—so it came to be, paradoxically, that for whites integrationism actually constituted an indirect defense of status quo social practices. The resurgence of ethnic group-consciousness among whites during the seventies, although in part a liberating attempt to reclaim cultural authenticity in the face of the mainstream culture of neutrality, was also in part a reflection of this same dynamic. Being Polish, Italian, or Irish meant, to a degree, not being simply white.

The broad effect of this particular resolution of the "race" issue within mainstream discourse was that the very whites who might otherwise have been allies of black nationalists during the sixties were motivated, in terms of their own cultural identity, to avoid racial identification altogether. Without the development of white race-consciousness, no significant group of whites either understood themselves as struggling to transform the white community itself in terms of race relations or as supporting African-Americans as a people, a nation. In terms of national policy, tremendous energy was committed to the centralized policy of integration, but little attention was paid to the integrity and health of black neighborhoods and institutions. Integration of dominant institutions, rather than reparations from one community to another, became the paradigm for racial enlightenment. . . .

IV. CONCLUSION

THE embrace of integrationism as the dominant ethos of race discourse is the symbolic face of the new cultural "center" that was created in the context of the various ruptures of American society in the sixties. Relative to this center, black "militants" and white "rednecks" were defined together as extremists; comprehending racism as a form of "discrimination" meant that race could be understood as just another example of the range of arbitrary social characteristics—like gender, physical handicap, or sexual preference—that right-thinking people should learn to ignore. For the cultural centrists, the concept of overcoming bias became the way to comprehend all the various challenges to mainstream culture in the sixties—movements by women, the poor, gays and lesbians, blacks, and young antiwar and leftist counterculturists—as together representing the basic idea that bias should be overcome in favor of objectivity and neutrality.

From the "outside," it was apparent that this "reasonable" and "enlightened" cultural center had a distinctly white, upper-middle-class, and Protestant flavor—a correlate in the cultural sphere to what Unitarianism, or maybe Presbyterianism, represents in the religious sphere. The culture that seemed to descend upon public schools throughout the South in the late sixties and seventies, for example, constituted more than the new policy of racial integration or a stricter separation of church and state. Its norms of professionalism, impersonality, and centralism were experienced in the South—by both blacks and whites—as imposed from the outside, vaguely from the upper-middle-class, white Northeast.

However, that character of the center was invisible from within it; instead, for the whites who embraced integrationism, the realm of social practices and attitudes they associated with racially integrated institutions was taken as culturally neutral and objective. The fact that everyday public school culture in integrated schools was essentially a white culture never really occurred to a whole range of otherwise decent and committed white liberals. For the middle-class black moderates who aligned with whites in constructing and supporting the integrationist ideology, the racial character of "integrated" institutions must have been more apparent, and yet its very obviousness made the embrace of universalist imagery all the more important to their self-respect.

Whatever the intentions and psychocultural needs of black and white integrationists in the past, it should now be apparent that the exclusion of a nationalist approach to racial justice from mainstream discourse has been a cultural and political mistake that has constrained the boundaries of racial politics. Instead of comprehending racial justice in terms of the relations of distinct, historically defined communities, the embrace of integrationism has signified the broad cultural attempt not to think in terms of race at all. Integrationists filter discussion of the wide disparities between African-American and white communities through the nonracial language of poverty and class, and avoid altogether any consideration of the racial implications of the institutional practices of "integrated" arenas of social life.

Moreover, the construction of race reform as overcoming bias at the level of consciousness, overcoming discrimination at the practice level, and achieving integration at the institutional level has meant that tremendous social resources and personal energy have been expended on integrating formerly white schools, workplaces, neighborhoods, and attitudes. This program, such as it is, has had some success in improving the lives of specific people and in transforming the climate of overt racial domination that pervaded American society thirty years ago. Yet it has been pursued to the exclusion of a commitment to the vitality of the black community as a whole and to the economic and cultural health of black neighborhoods, schools, economic enterprises, and individuals.

It is frustrating to reconsider the long history of American race relations from this perspective. One gets the sense that if, at any number of points in American history, a nationalist program of race reform had been adopted, African-Americans in virtually every urban center would not be concentrated in disintegrating housing, would not be sending their children to learn a nationally prescribed curriculum in underfunded, overcrowded schools and to play in parks and on streets alongside drug dealers and gang warriors, and would not be working at the bottom of the economic hierarchy (if they are lucky enough to have a job at all). If community-to-community reparations had been made (as promised), if there had actually been a massive transfer of economic resources from the white to the black community in the forties, then the kind of black economic cooperatives and black-run schools, newspapers, and cultural institutions advocated by Du Bois would likely exist today as foundations for healthy African-American neighborhoods. Alternatively, if a similar program had been adopted in the sixties, one can imagine that black neighborhoods would be by and large healthy, cosmopolitan parts of the urban scene rather than ghettos of hopelessness and frustration. In the integrationist ideology, as Harold Cruse observed, black communities should not

even exist because they are vestiges of segregation; it was therefore inconceivable to devote resources to their health rather than to programs like urban renewal plans of the late sixties premised on their destruction. . . .

NOTES

1. Malcolm X, *Malcolm X Speaks*, 31 (1965).

2. For example, the institutionalization of Black History Month as an element of official American culture.

3. Malcolm X, *By Any Means Necessary: Speeches, Interviews and a Letter*, 16–17 (1970).

4. There is now a substantial body of work describing the early years of the direct action civil rights movement. I have found most useful R. Blumberg, *Civil Rights: The 1960s Freedom Struggle* (1984); T. Branch, *Parting the Waters: America in the King Years, 1954–1963* (1988) (focusing on King and the Southern Christian Legal Conference) R. Brisbane, *Black Activism: Racial Revolution in the United States, 1954–1970* (1974); T. Brooks, *Walls Come Tumbling Down: A History of the Civil Rights Movement, 1940–1970* (1974); C. Carson, *In Struggle: SNCC and the Black Awakening of the 1960's* (1981); D. Garrow, *Bearing the Cross: Martin Luther King, Jr., and the Southern Christian Leadership Conference* (1986); A. Meier and E. Rudwick, *C.O.R.E., A Study of the Civil Rights Movement, 1942–1968* (1973); A. Morris, *The Origins of the Civil Rights Movement: Black Communities Organizing for Change* (1984); B. Muse, *The American Negro Revolution: From Nonviolence to Black Power* (1968); H. Sitkoff, *Struggle for Black Equality, 1954–1980* (1981); E. Stoper, *The Student Non-Violent Coordinating Committee: The Growth of Radicalism in a Civil Rights Organization* (1989); R. Weisbrot, *Freedom Bound: A History of America's Civil Rights Movement* (1990); H. Zinn, *SNCC: The New Abolitionists* (1965); Colaiaco, "Martin Luther King, Jr., and the Paradox of Nonviolent Direct Action," 47 *Phylon*, 16 (1986).

5. The classic text embodying this perspective is G. Allport, *The Nature of Prejudice* (1954). The comprehension of racism as embodied in the area of prejudice has had wide influence in academic study. See R. Blauner, *Racial Oppression in America*, 19 (1972) ("The analysis of race by social scientists has been shaped by an underlying assumption that the concern with color in human society is ultimately irrational or nonrational."). For works employing this concept of prejudice, see O. Cox, *Race Relations: Elements and Social Dynamics*, 21–40, 226–41 (1976); T. Cross, *The Black Power Imperative: Racial Inequality and the Politics of Nonviolence*, 83–136 (1984); R. Daniels and H. Kitano, *American Racism: Exploration of the Nature of Prejudice* (1970); J. Jones, *Prejudice and Racism* (1972); G. Myrdal, *An American Dilemma: The Negro Problem and Modern Democracy*, 106–12 (1944); R. Park, *Race and Culture* 231–43 (1950); F. Lapides and D. Burrous, eds., *Racism: A Casebook*

(1971); Blumer, "Race Prejudice as a Sense of Group Position," *Pac. Soc. Rev.*, 1 (spring 1958); Lusky, "The Stereotype: The Hard Core of Racism," 13 *Buffalo L. Rev.*, 450 (1964).

6. See M. Cassity, *Legacy of Fear: American Race Relations to 1900*, at 32–63 (1985); S. Drake, *Black Folk: Here and There*, 28–30 (1987) (explaining the origin and perpetuation of the stereotype of "the Negro"); G. Frederickson, *The Black Image in the White Mind: The Debate in Afro-American Character and Destiny, 1817–1914*, at 53–58, 275–82 (1972); R. Horsman, *Race and Manifest Destiny: The Origins of American Racial Anglo-Saxonism*, 43–61, 116–57 (1981); W. Jordan, *White Over Black: American Attitudes toward the Negro, 1550–1812* (1968); I. Newby, *Jim Crow's Defense: Anti-Negro Thought in America 1900–1930* (1968); C. Vann Woodward, *The Strange Career of Jim Crow*, 56–95 (1958).

7. See G. Frederickson, *White Supremacy* (1981); Woodward, *supra* note 6. The classic study is J. Dollard, *Caste and Class in a Southern Town* (1949). See generally Alkalimat, "The Ideology of Black Social Science," in J. Ladner, ed., *The Death of White Sociology*, 173, 175 (1973) (linking prejudice, discrimination, and segregation as key elements of restrictive "white" ideology about racism).

8. See Fein, "Community Schools and Social Theory: The Limits of Universalism," in H. Levin, ed., *Community Control of Schools*, 76, 91 (1970). According to Leonard Fein: "[T]he central tenet of liberals, when dealing with race, has been to assert its irrelevance. The argument has been that color is an accidental characteristic, which, in the truly rational liberated social order, ceases to have any empirical correlates. . . . The main thrust of the civil rights movement has been therefore, in the direction of persuading white America to become color-blind. The corollary of the liberal ethic that white people ought not to pay attention to the blackness of Negroes was the proposition that Negroes ought not to pay attention to their own blackness."

James Farmer tells a story indicating the extreme manifestation of the colorblindness affliction, at least among some whites. A twenty-year-old white CORE worker was mugged in her apartment. She described the assailant with great detail to the police, including height, weight, eyes, teeth, and clothing, but she didn't mention the fact that he was black "for fear of indicating prejudice;" J. Farmer, *Freedom—When?*, 85 (1965). As Farmer makes clear, this analysis of racism and prejudice was extremely individualistic; the error of prejudice was taken to be reaching conclusions about people on the basis of any group association at all.

9. See T. Cross, *supra* note 5, at 609–10. According to Cross, "Integration is indispensible to shattering racial stereotypes. . . . Only in day-to-day contact with blacks will whites learn that blacks are not less intelligent, less honest, or less human than whites. Through time, integrated living and integrated education are the most forceful weapons for breaking the stubborn and enduring mental habit of defining people's traits according to their race."

10. T. Shibutani and K. Kwan, *Ethnic Stratification: A Comparative Approach*, 589 (1965). Shibutani and Kwan

argue that "Human beings throughout the world are fundamentally alike. . . . Hence, whenever social distance is reduced, individuals recognize their resemblances. The basic differences between ethnic groups are cultural, and conventional norms serve as masks to cover the similarities. Whenever men interact informally, the common human nature comes through. It would appear, then, that it is only a matter of time before a more enlightened citizenry will realize this. Then, there will be a realignment of group loyalties, and ethnic identity will become a thing of the past."

11. See R. Blauner, *supra* note 5, at 266–67 ("The Liberal wants to judge a man in terms of his individual uniqueness and his universal humanity, not in terms of 'accidental' features like skin color. Universalism thus goes hand in hand with individualism, and in the area of race the two join in the ideal of 'color blindness.' ").

12. The link between images of universalism and progress in liberal ideology are well summarized by Robert Nisbet: "To regard all evil as a persistence or revival of the past has been a favorite conceit of liberals nourished by the idea of Progress. . . . Present evils could safely be regarded as regrettable evidences of incomplete emancipation from the past—from tribalism, from agrarianism, religion, localism, and the like. In one form or another, the theory of cultural lag has been the secular approach to the problem of evil;" R. Nisbet, *Community and Power* (1962), at 214.

13. The "cultural deprivation" analysis was especially prevalent in the sixties. See, for example, N. Glazer and D. Moynihan, *Beyond the Melting Pot* (1963), at 53 (arguing that lower-class problems are so great and the line dividing lower from middle class so thin that the "middle-class Negro" cannot deal with them); E. Liebow, *Tally's Corner: A Study of Negro Streetcorner Men*, 208–22 (1966) (concluding that black male street culture is not distinct from white culture but is merely a shadow system of values); C. Silberman, *Crisis in Black and White*, 249–307 (1964) (arguing that an "overall poverty of environment" accounts for the problems in slum schools and the poor educational performance of Negro children). Silberman later repudiated the position in C. Silberman, *Crisis in the Classroom: The Remaking of American Education*, 81 (1970). For one of many criticisms of the "cultural deprivation" approach as racist, see K. Clark, *Dark Ghetto*, and *Dilemmas of Power*, 129–53 (1965).

14. M. Lieberman, *The Future of Public Education*, 60 (1960).

15. *Id.* at 38.

16. Browne, "A Case for Separation," in R. Browne and B. Rustin, eds., *Separation or Integration: Which Way for America: A Dialogue*, 7–15 (1968).

17. For the best general histories of black nationalism, see R. Allen, *A Guide to Black Power in America: An Historical Analysis* (1970); R. Carlisle, *The Roots of Black Nationalism* (1975); H. Cruse, *The Crisis of the Negro Intellectual;* (1967); H. Cruse, *Rebellion or Revolution?*, 48–97, 193–

258 (1968); T. Draper, *The Rediscovery of Black Nationalism* (1969); W. Moses, *The Golden Age of Black Nationalism, 1850–1925* (1978); A. Pinkney, *Red, Black and Green: Black Nationalism in the United States* (1976); J. Bracey, Jr., A. Meier, and E. Rudwick, eds., *Black Nationalism in America* (1970) (a documentary history). Although I utilize different frames of reference, my analysis of competing African-American traditions has been influenced by Cornell West's excellent study; see C. West, *Prophesy Deliverance!: An Afro-American Revolutionary Christianity* (1982).

18. For Delany's views of American race relations, see M. Delany, *The Condition, Elevation, Emigration and Destiny of the Colored People of the United States*, 159–73 (1852) ("[T]hat there are circumstances under which emigration is absolutely necessary to [our] political elevation cannot be disputed. . . . We desire the civilization and enlightenment of Africa.") Recently, a body of scholarly work has considered Delany's significance in terms of the black nationalist tradition. See T. Draper, *supra* note 7, at 21–41; C. Griffith, *The African Dream: Martin R. Delany and the Emergence of Pan-African Thought* (1975); A. Pinkney, *supra* note 17, at 23–27; V. Ullman, *Martin R. Delany: The Beginnings of Black Nationalism* (1971).

Prior to Delany, Paul Cuffe had called for repatriation of blacks to Africa, petitioned Congress for assistance in 1814, and actually resettled thirty-eight blacks to Sierra Leone in 1815. See also S. Harris, *Paul Cuffe: Black America and the African Return* 62–65 (1972); W. Alexander, *Memoir of Captain Paul Cuffee, A Man of Colour: To Which is Subjoined the Epistle of the Society of Sierre Leone, in Africa & C.* (1811). Congress funded the American Colonization Society, founded by whites to resettle free blacks to Africa, in 1819. The society purchased land on the west coast of Africa and began what became, in 1847, the country of Liberia. The society had an explicit white supremacist ideology and was opposed by most African-Americans, although it claimed to have resettled thirteen thousand blacks prior to the Civil War. Delany, among other black leaders, refused to cooperate with the American Colonization Society, denouncing its leaders as "arrant hypocrites." E. Redkey, *Black Exodus*, 18–21 (1969). See R. Carlisle, *supra* note 17 (summaries of antebellum emigration proposals and efforts); T. Draper, *supra* note 17, at 14–33; A. Pinkney, *supra* note 17, at 19–23. Delany's nationalism was explicitly opposed to the ideology of constitutional civil rights, and he and Frederick Douglass had public disagreements. See Delany, "I Have No Hopes in This Country," quoted in T. Wagstaff, *Black Power: The Radical Response to White America,* 43 (1969).

An important advocate of emigration to Africa during the late nineteenth and early twentieth century was Bishop Henry Turner. See T. Draper, *supra* note 17, at 43–47; A. Pinkney, *supra* note 17, at 28–36; M. Ponton, *The Life and Times of Henry M. Turner* (1970).

19. According to Harold Cruse, Booker T. Washington is a central figure in the tradition of black nationalism in the United States: "Black Power is militant Booker T-ism"; H. Cruse, *Rebellion or Revolution?, supra* note 17, at 201. For Washington's analysis of racial progress, including his philosophy of economic self-improvement, see B. Washington, *Future of the American Negro* (1899); B. Washington, *Up from Slavery* (1901); see also A. Meier, *Negro Thought in America, 1880–1915; Racial Ideologies in the Age of Booker T. Washington* (1963). The leading biography of Washington is the two-volume work by Louis Harlan, *Booker T. Washington: The Wizard of Tuskegee*, 1901–1915 (1983). Documents concerning Washington are exhaustively collected in L. Harlan and R. Smock, eds., *The Booker T. Washington Papers* (1972–89) (14 vols.).

20. The most effective early-twentieth-century black nationalist leader, Marcus Garvey, a Jamaican emigrant to the United States, founded the Universal Negro Improvement Association (UNIA). The UNIA advocated black unity, a mass migration to Africa, and the liberation and unification of Africa as a homeland for all black people. Garvey urged the immediate organization of all-black businesses and established UNIA-operated cooperatives, including the Black Star Line steamship company. Garvey also started *Negro World*. Critical of the NAACP's focus on politics and civil rights and disparaging of its intellectual leader, W. E. B. Du Bois, Garvey attacked NAACP activists as race traitors. The UNIA attracted a half-million people at its height in the twenties, almost entirely from the poor of the urban ghettos, with chapters in cities across the United States and abroad. For the best studies of Garvey, see E. Cronon, *Black Moses: The Story of Marcus Garvey and the Universal Negro Improvement Association* (1955) (focusing on Garvey's shortcomings as a leader); A. Garvey, *Garvey and Garveyism* (1970) (a description of Garvey and the movement by his widow); T. Martin, *Race First: the Ideological and Organizational Struggles of Marcus Garvey and the Negro Improvement Association* (1976) (arguing that Garvey was a revolutionary and the greatest black figure of the century); T. Vincent, *Black Power and the Garvey Movement* (1971) (contending that Garvey was the direct forerunner of sixties nationalists). The religious component of Garveyism is analyzed in R. Burkett, *Garveyism As A Civil Religious Movement: The Institutionalization of a Black Civil Religion* (1978). For a collection of Garvey's pre-1925 views, see A. Garvey, ed., *Philosophy and Opinions of Marcus Garvey,* 2 vols. (1968); see also R. Hill, ed., *Marcus Garvey and Universal Negro Improvement Association,* 2 vols. (1983) (collection of documents relating to the Garvey movement).

21. For diverse views of the Muslims, see E. Essien-Udom, *Black Nationalism: A Search for an Identity in America* (1962); C. Lincoln, *The Black Muslims in America* (1962); E. Muhammad, *Message to the Black Man in America* (1965); A. Pinkney, *supra* note 17, at 155–64. For an analysis that connects the Nation of Islam to Booker T. Washington, see H. Cruse, *Rebellion or Revolution?, supra* note 17, at 211. Cruse writes that:

"[The] Nation of Islam was nothing but a form of Booker T. Washington's economic self-help, black unity, bourgeois hard work, law abiding, vocational training, stay-out-of-the-civil-rights-struggle agitation, separate-from-the-white-man, etc., etc., morality. The only difference was that Elijah Muhammad added the potent factor of the Muslim religion to a race, economic, and social philosophy of which the first prophet was none other than Booker T. Washington. Elijah also added an element of 'hate Whitey' ideology which Washington, of course, would never have accepted."

22. See Du Bois, "Postscript: The N.A.A.C.P. and Race Segregation," 41 *Crisis*, 52, 53 (1934); W. E. B. Du Bois, *Dusk of Dawn—Autobiography*, 193, 199 (1940). For a discussion of the significance of Du Bois's shift in ideology, see H. Cruse, *Plural But Equal: A Critical Study of Blacks and Minorities and America's Plural Society*, 80–101 (1987); H. Cruse, *The Crisis of the Negro Intellectual*, supra note 17, at 175–77, 330–36, 558–65; M. Marable, W. E. B. Du Bois: *Black Radical Democrat*, 140–42 (1986); J. White, *Black Leadership in America, 1895–1968*, at 52–61 (1985).

23. See Malcolm X with A. Haley, *The Autobiography of Malcolm X* (1965); Malcolm X, *By Any Means Necessary*, supra note 3; *Malcolm X Speaks*, supra note 1; P. Goldman, *The Death and Life of Malcolm X* (1973).

24. See E. Cleaver, *Post-Prison Writings and Speeches*, R. Scheer ed., (1969); E. Cleaver, *Soul on Ice* (1968).

25. See S. Carmichael and C. Hamilton, *Black Power: The Politics of Liberation in America* (1967) (Carmichael, a former chairperson of SNCC, is now known as Kwame Toure).

26. See Baraka, "The Pan-African Party and the Black Nation," *Black Scholar* (Mar. 1971), 24; I. Baraka, *Raise, Race, Rays, Raze* (1971).

27. See H. Cruse, *The Crisis of the Negro Intellectual*, supra note 17; *Rebellion or Revolution?* supra note 17.

28. See P. Foner, ed., *The Black Panthers Speak* (1970); H. Rap Brown, *Die Nigger Die!* (1969); G. Jackson, *Soledad Brother: the Prison Letters of George Jackson* (1970); G. Marine, *The Black Panthers* (1969); H. Newton, *To Die for the People: The Writings of Huey P. Newton* (1972); B. Seale, *Seize the Time: The Story of the Black Panther Party and Huey P. Newton* (1970). The founding platform and program of the Black Panther Party is reprinted in E. Greer, ed., *Black Liberation Politics: A Reader*, 380–82 (1971).

29. See C. Carson, *supra* note 4, at 50–55, 66–71 (describing the nationalist turn within SNCC); A. Meier and E. Rudwick, *supra* note 4, at 431 (describing the nationalist turn within CORE).

For general histories of black nationalism in the sixties, see R. Allen, *supra* note 17, at 18–74, 108–239; T. Draper, *supra* note 17, at 86–167; H. Haines, *Black Radicals and the Civil Rights Mainstream: 1954–1970*, at 57–76 (1988); A. Pinkney, *supra* note 17, at 76–219; R. Weisbrot, *supra* note 4, at 222–61; Turner, "Black Nationalism: The Inevitable Response," *Black World* (Jan. 1971), 4.

30. The March Against Fear was begun as a solitary march across Mississippi by James Meredith to protest the slaying of Medgar Evers. After Meredith was shot by a would-be assassin, the leaders of SCLC, SNCC, CORE, the NAACP, and the Urban League got together in Memphis to plan to continue the march symbolically on Mere-

dith's behalf. The Urban League and the NAACP eventually refused to participate in opposition to the manner in which the march's manifesto sharply criticized the slow pace of civil rights reform of the federal government. See D. Garrow, *supra* note 4, at 475–97; V. Harding, *The Other American Revolution*, 185–87 (1980); R. Weisbrot, *supra* note 4, at 193–221; J. White, *supra* note 22, at 139–43.

31. The term "black power" first gained publicity when Richard Wright so entitled his autobiographical reflections on Africa. R. Wright, *Black Power: A Record of Reactions in a Land of Pathos* (1954). It initially was used as a political slogan, without much notoriety, by Representative Adam Clayton Powell in 1966, during Howard University commencement exercises. See H. Cruse, *Rebellion or Revolution?*, *supra* note 17, at 207. However, it was not until Ricks and Carmichael began using the slogan during the March Against Fear that it gained mass appeal. The slogan originated as part of the competition between the King/SCLC faction and the SNCC faction of the march's organizers. Tension between the civil rights groups dated back at least to the 1961 Albany campaign, where SNCC organizers attempted to mobilize the black community en masse to resist the racial structure of the city as a whole, and where disagreements arose between SNCC organizers and the SCLC as to the militancy of nonviolent tactics, whether to violate federal court orders against marches, and more generally whether the civil rights campaign should be focused on building community strength or on persuading the federal government to grant civil rights; see C. Carson, *supra* note 4, at 56–65, 83–95; A. Morris, *supra* note 4, at 239–50; R. Weisbrot, *supra* note 4, at 30–38, 130–43.

By the 1963 March on Washington, the ideology of the groups had substantially diverged, with the SCLC leadership supporting the passage of the civil rights bill and cooperation with the Kennedy administration and John Lewis of SNCC prepared to deliver a scathing attack on the government and on the slow pace of race reform, including opposition to the Civil Rights Act as "too little, too late"; See R. Allen, *supra* note 17, at 20–21; T. Branch, *supra* note 4, at 869–70, 873–74, 878–80; D. Garrow, *supra* note 4, at 281–83; R. Weisbrot, *supra* note 4, at 76–83.

At the March Against Fear, the rift opened around the question of nonviolence, and, reflecting the beginnings of nationalist sentiment among the SNCC/CORE organizers, around the issue of whether to permit white participation in the march. Symbolically, the positions were represented by competing crowd chants, with the SCLC organizers trying to get the crowd to chant "freedom now" while the SNCC organizers were challenging with "black power." For descriptions of this context of the march, see C. Carson, *supra* note 4, at 209–10; D. Garrow, *supra* note 4, at 475–97; M. L. King, *Where Do We Go from Here: Chaos or Community?*, 31–32 (1967); R. Weisbrot, *supra* note 4, 193–221.

To be sure, the slogan "black power" did not itself have a necessary nationalist meaning; in fact, a virtual cottage industry was created around attempts to define its meaning, and many of its exponents were clearly integrationist. For examples of the substantial writing devoted to defining and evaluating "black power," see S. Carmichael and C.

Hamilton, *supra* note 25; E. Peeks, *The Long Struggle for Black Power* (1971); R. Scott and W. Brockriede, eds., *The Rhetoric of Black Power* (1969); N. Wright, *Black Power and Urban Unrest: Creative Possibilities* (1967); F. Barbour, ed., *The Black Power Revolt* (1968); Bennett, "Of Time, Space, and Revolution," *Ebony* (Aug. 1969), 24, 31–44; "Black Power: A Discussion," *Partisan Rev.* (spring 1968), 195 (symposium); Bloice, "Black Labor is Black Power," *Black Scholar* (Oct. 1970), 2; Lasch, "The Trouble with Black Power," 10 *N.Y. Rev. Books* (Feb. 29, 1968), 10; Onwachi, "Identity and Black Power," *Negro Dig.* (Mar. 1967), 16; Relyea, "Black Power as an Urban Ideology," *Educ. Dig.* (Feb. 1970), 35, 46–49; "Symposium on Black Power," *New South* (summer 1966).

For general commentaries on the black power controversy, see R. Allen, *supra* note 17; T. Draper, *supra* note 16, at 118–31; H. Haines, *supra* note 29, at 57–70; V. Harding, *supra* note 30, at 177–200; B. Muse, *supra* note 4, at 243–44; F. Powledge, *Black Power, White Resistance: Notes on the New Civil War* (1967).

The Black Power Conference called by Adam Clayton Powell and held in Newark in 1967 reflected the broad disagreements among those characterizing themselves as black power activists; see R. Allen, *supra* note 17, at 132–61; V. Harding, *supra* note 30, at 194–95; Stone, "The National Conference on Black Power," in *The Black Power Revolt*, 189. Further evidence of the elasticity of the slogan is produced by a recent book by Theodore Cross, *supra* note 5, who uses the concept of "black power" as an organizing idea for a clearly integrationist-oriented, antinationalist argument. Nevertheless, it is clear that for most, the black power slogan represented the beginning of repudiation of integrationist/civil rights ideology in favor of some form of nationalism; see A. Pinkney, *supra* note 17, at 64 ("The introduction of the concept of black power was the beginning of the current spread of nationalist sentiment among Afro-Americans, and signaled the decline of integration as the dominant thrust of the black movement"); T. Wagstaff, *Black Power: The Radical Response to White America*, 103 (1969) ("The Black Power Movement is a conscious attempt to harness the emotional power of Black Nationalism to a practical program for the elimination of racial oppression in America"); R. Weisbrot, *supra* note 4, at 169–70, 236–56.

32. Address by Hubert Humphrey, 57th Annual NAACP Convention (July 6, 1966), reprinted in Scott and Brockriede, eds., *The Rhetoric of Black Power*, *supra* note 31, at 65, 71.

33. Wilkins, "Whither 'Black Power?'" 73 *Crisis*, 353–54 (1966) (excerpts from keynote address delivered at the NAACP 57th Annual Convention, July 5, 1966), reprinted in *Black Protest Thought in the Twentieth Century*, (A. Meier, E. Ruelwick and F. Broderick eds. 1971) at 596–98.

34. C. Carson, *supra* note 4, at 22.

35. "The Black Neo-Segregationists" (editorial), 74 *Crisis* 439–40 (1967) reprinted in *Black Protest Thought in Twentieth Century*, *supra* note 33, at 598–604.

36. S. Carmichael and C. Hamilton, *supra* note 25, at 54.

37. Browne, "A Case for Separation," *supra* note 16 at 7.

38. See *supra* notes 18 and 20, and *infra* note 39.

39. This program characterized the early colonization efforts, as well as Garvey's Back to Africa movement and the Black Muslims' program. See *supra* note 20. See also the "Republic of New Africa" movement's proposal that the states of Mississippi, Louisiana, Alabama, Georgia, and South Carolina be ceded by the U.S. government for the creation of an independent black nation, along with the payment of $200 billion in reparations. R. Brisbane, *supra* note 4, at 183–85; A. Pinkney, *supra* note 17, at 125–26; Sherrill, "Birth of a (Black) Nation," *Esquire* (Jan. 1969), 70, 72.

40. The phrase originated with Martin Delany, M. Delany, *supra* note 18, at 203. Delany has been called "the first major Negro nationalist," see L. Bennett, *Before the Mayflower: A History of the Negro in America, 1619–1966*, at 137 (1966).

41. The idea that African-Americans have created a distinct culture that is not reducible to class or Americanism has been a controversial notion in the fields of sociology and anthropology. For example, it was long the dominant view that African-Americans have no ethnic culture, but instead that "the Negro is only an American and nothing else. He has no values and culture to guard and protect." N. Glazer and D. Moynihan, *supra* note 9, at 53. For other writers articulating the same idea, see E. Frazier, *The Negro in the United States*, 680–81 (rev. ed. 1957); G. Myrdal, *supra* note 5, at 928 ("In practically all of its divergencies, American Negro culture is not something independent of general American culture. It is a distorted development, or a pathological condition of American culture"); R. Park, *supra* note 5; K. Stampp, *The Peculiar Institution: Slavery in the Ante-Bellum South*, vii (1956) ("slaves were merely ordinary human beings . . . innately Negroes are, after all, only white men with black skins, nothing more, nothing less").

For criticism of this tradition in social science, see R. Blauner, *supra* note 5, at 124–55; R. Ellison, "An American Dilemma: A Review," in *Shadow and Act*, 303–17 (1964); R. Staples, *supra* note 24, at 6–9; W. Wilson, *supra* note 5, at 143; Alkalimat, *supra* note 7; Ladner, "Introduction," in *The Death of White Sociology*, *supra* note 7, at xxiii.

For discussions of the need to analyze a unique African-American culture, see L. Bennett, *supra* note 5, at 1–43, 293–312; A. Gayle, ed., *The Black Aesthetic* (1971); H. Gates, ed., *Black Literature and Literary Theory* (1984); J. Blackwell, *The Black Community: Diversity and Unity* (1985); J. Hale-Benson, *Black Children: Their Roots, Culture, and Learning Styles* (1982); C. Keil, *Urban Blues* (1966); T. Kochman, *Black and White Styles in Conflict* (1982); J. Ladner, *Tomorrow's Tomorrow: The Black Woman* (1971); A. Pinkney, *Black Americans* (1969); R. Staples, *supra* note 24; Baraka, "A Black Value System," *Black Scholar* (Nov. 1969), 54–60; Foster, "Toward a Definition of Black Referents," in A. Dixon and B. Foster, eds., *Beyond Black and White* (1971); Jones, "The Need for a Cultural Base to Civil Rights and Power Movements," in Barbour, ed., *The Black Power Revolt*, 119 (1968).

Black nationalist descriptions of the character of African-American culture have roughly divided between an emphasis on African roots in the Pan-Africanism tradition; see, for example, Baraka, *supra,* and the description of a unique Afro-American culture and community, in (e.g.), H. Cruse, *Rebellion or Revolution?, supra* note 17, at 48–138.

42. Turner, *supra* note 29, at 7–8, quoting an address by C. Munford, "Black National Revolution in America," Utah State University (May 1970).

43. Along with C. Munford and James Turner, Harold Cruse's conception of black nationalism exemplifies the historicist perspective that I believe marked the intellectual and theoretical advances made in the black nationalist position in the sixties. See H. Cruse, *The Crisis of the Negro Intellectual, supra* note 17, at 20–44, 544–65; H. Cruse, *Rebellion or Revolution?, supra* note 17, at 48–138, 193–258 (1968); Cruse, "The Fire This Time?," *N.Y. Rev. of Books* (May 8, 1969), 13–18.

44. S. Carmichael and C. Hamilton, *supra* note 25, at 54–55.

45. *Id.* at 55.

46. *Id.*

47. H. Cruse, *The Crisis of the Negro Intellectual, supra* note 17 at 283.

48. *Id.* at 234.

49. S. Carmichael, *Stokely Speaks,* 39 (1971); see also H. Cruse, *Rebellion or Revolution?, supra* note 17, at 72 (the trend toward integrationism has "favored the eradication of the Negro community as a symbol of segregation"); *id.* at 33–67 (criticizing integrationism in the arts as entailing destruction of African American cultural forms in favor of an already despiritualized and deadened European tradition).

50. See, for example, Crenshaw, "Foreword," *supra* note 4, at 2–6 (describing typical law school classes as assuming white perspective under the guise of "perspectivelessness"); Davidson, "The Furious Passage of the Black Graduate Student," in *The Death of White Sociology, supra* note 7, at 23 (describing graduate education as based on white norms); Hamilton, "An Advocate of Black Power Defines It," in *Rhetoric The Black Power, supra* note 31, at 190–91 (discussing ways that black-controlled schools would be reorganized to reflect the culture of the black community); T. Miller, *supra* note 6 (describing the cultural alienation of black students from predominantly white colleges).

For more general discussions of the idea that dominant images of neutrality and objectivity reflect white, European culture, see Jones, "The Need for a Cultural Base," *supra* note 41; Chrisman, in Borbour, *The Black Power Revolt* (1968), at 2–6; M. Gordon, *supra* note 9, at 9 (the central images of American culture are the expressions of white Anglo-Saxon Protestant ethnic consciousness).

51. For discussions of the racial impact of student classification schemes, see T. Cross, *supra* note 5, at 488–95, 668;

J. Oakes, *Keeping Track: How Schools Structure Inequality* (1985); Kirp, "Schools as Sorters: The Constitutional and Policy Implications of Student Classifications," 121 *U. Pa. L. Rev.,* 705 (1973).

52. See R. Staples, *Introduction to Black Sociology* (1976), at 36–8 (poverty has come to replace race as explanation for disparate black performance in schools); Peller, *supra* note 38, at 74–75 (same).

53. H. Cruse, *The Crisis of the Negro Intellectual, supra* note 17, at 283.

54. The best-known movement for community control influenced by the Black Power Movement occurred in the Ocean Hill–Brownsville area of Brooklyn, New York, where the city agreed to the establishment of an experimental school district over which local parents would have authority; when the local committee requested the transfer of several teachers to schools outside their neighborhood, the teachers' union went on strike citywide, and relations in New York—in particular between Jews and African Americans—reached high levels of hostility. For an account of the Ocean Hill–Brownsville movement, see Mayer, "The Full and Sometimes Very Surprising Story of Ocean Hill, the Teachers' Union and the Teacher Strikes of 1968," *New York Times* (Feb. 2, 1969), magazine, at 18. For accounts of other movements, see also Lauter, "The Short, Happy Life of the Adams-Morgan Community School Project," 38 *Harv. Educ. Rev.,* 235 (1968) (detailing the origin of the Adams-Morgan project in Washington, D.C., and the ensuing difficulties inherent in such projects); Epstein, "The Politics of School Decentralization," 10 *N.Y. Rev. Books* (June 1968), 26–32 (describing movements in Washington, D.C., and East Harlem).

55. Fein, *supra* note 9, at 94.

56. L. Bennett, *supra* note 5, at 35–36.

57. See Alkalimat, *supra* note 7, at 188 (criticizing the conventional social science assumption that "society evolves to be a higher level based on more universalistic rational standards of operation"); Davidson, *supra* note 50, at 27–42; Hare, "The Challenge of a Black Scholar," in *The Death of White Sociology, supra* note 7, at 67–78; Forsythe, "Radical Sociology and Blacks," in *id.* at 213 (criticizing mainstream sociology's "ideology of objectivity"). See also Cruse, "Black and White: Outlines of the Next Stage," *Black World* (Jan. 1971), at 19 (emphasizing the centrality of culture as a unifying concept for black studies and arguing that black studies should mean the construction of new interpretive paradigms related to black culture, rather than simply focusing existing scholarly assumptions on black subjects); Cruse, "Part 2: Black and White: Outlines of the Next Stage," *Black World* (March 1971), at 4, 13 (criticizing the "liberal consensus" of mainstream scholarship for "reflecting a 'universalist' stance in interpretation").

58. Hare, *supra* note 57, 68–69, citing T. Veblen, *The Theory of the Leisure Class* (1934).

59. See Ladner, "Tomorrow's Tomorrow: The Black Woman," in *The Death of White Sociology, supra* note 7, at 414, 420–21. Ladner writes: "[T]he relationship between the researcher and his subjects . . . resembles that of the oppressor and the oppressed, because it is the oppressor who defines the problem, the nature of the research, and to some extent, the quality of the interaction between him and his subjects. . . . [White sociologists'] inability to understand the nature and effects of neo-colonialism in the same manner as black people is rooted in the inherent bias of the social sciences. The basic concepts and tools of white Western society are permeated by this partiality in the conceptual framework of the oppressor. . . . Simply put, the slave and his master do not view and respond to the world in the same way. . . . George Washington and George Washington's slaves lived different realities. And if we extend that insight to all the dimensions of white American history we will realize that blacks lived at a different time and a different reality in this country. And the terrifying implications of all this is that there is another time, another reality, another America," *id.* quoting L. Bennett, *supra* note 5, at 39.

60. Murray, "White Norms, Black Deviation," in *The Death of White Sociology, supra* note 7, at 96.

61. Alkalimat, *supra* note 7, at 175–81.

62. See H. Cruse, *Plural But Equal, supra* note 22, at 53–58, 280–86, 362–70 (criticizing the conjunction of racial status with gender, immigrant and minority status).

63. For descriptions of the movements for reparations in the late sixties and seventies, see R. Lecky and H. Wright, eds., *Black Manifesto: Religion, Racism, and Reparations*, 1–2 (1969) (collection of views from the religious community on the reparations controversy); D. Bell, *And We are Not Saved, supra* note 6, at 123–39 (hypothetical discussion of the broad social changes that serious racial reparations might have effected); R. Brisbane, *supra* note 4, at 186–90 (discussing James Forman's Black Manifesto movement for reparations). For a recent work linking race-consciousness and a program of reparations, see Matsuda, *Looking to the Bottom*, in this collection. For analyses of the legal dimensions of black nationalist demands for reparations, see B. Bittker, *The Case for Black Reparations* (1973); Hughes, "Reparations for Blacks?," 43 *N.Y.U. L. Rev.*, 1063 (1968).

64. H. Cruse, *The Crisis of the Negro Intellectual, supra* note 17, at 91.

65. The term was first used in a comprehensive analysis of the situation of African-Americans by Cruse, "Revolutionary Nationalism and the Afro-American," *Two Studies on the Left*, 12–13 (1962). See also H. Cruse, "An Afro-American's Cultural Views," in *Rebellion or Revolution?, supra* note 17, at 48–67 (first published in *Presence Africaine*, Dec. 1957–Jan. 1958, 31); Cruse, "Negro Nationalism's New Wave," *New Leader* (Mar. 19, 1962), 16. By the mid-sixties, the neocolonial analogy was widely used by black nationalists; see, for example, Alkalimat, *supra* note 7, at

183–88; R. Allen, *Black Awakening in Capitalist America: An Analytic History*, 5–17 (1969); J. Blackwell, *supra* note 41, at 12–14; J. Boggs and G. Boggs, *Revolution and Evolution in the Twentieth Century* (1974); S. Carmichael and C. Hamilton, *supra* note 25, at 2–56; E. Cleaver, *Post-Prison Writings and Speeches, supra* note 24, at 57–72; H. Newton, *Essays from the Minister of Defense Huey Newton*, 2–10 (1968); A. Pinkney, *supra* note 17, at 8–13; R. Staples, *supra* note 24, at 13–14; W. Tabb, *The Political Economy of the Black Ghetto* (1970); "The Black Panther Party Platform and Program," in *Black Liberation Politics, supra* note 28. See also O'Dell, "A Special Variety of Colonialism, *Freedomways* (winter 1967), 1. Robert Blauner summarizes the analysis of black communities through the colonialist metaphor by focusing on four elements of colonization: (1) the colonized subjects enter the system involuntarily; (2) the subjects' indigenous culture is transformed or destroyed; (3) the subjects are managed or controlled by those outside their own ethnic status; and (4) racism prevails or the group is oppressed psychologically and socially by an outside group that conceives of itself as superior. Black communities are an example of the colonization process in that they are controlled politically, economically, and administratively from the outside, distinguishing them from the voluntary ethnic business and social communities of the Poles, Jews, Italians, and Irish. R. Blauner, *supra* note 5, at 83–89.

66. H. Cruse, *Rebellion or Revolution?, supra* note 17, at 76.

67. E. Cleaver, *Post-Prison Writings and Speeches, supra* note 24, at 57–72.

68. Stokely Carmichael pointed to the colonialist relationship as an explanation of the apparent similarity between the material conditions of African-Americans in diverse cities: "The American city, in essence, is going to be populated by the peoples of the Third World, while the white middle classes will flee to the suburbs. Now the black people do not control, nor do we own, the resources—we do not control the land, the houses or the stores. These are all owned by whites who live outside the community. These are very real colonies, in the sense that they are capital and cheap labor exploited by those who live outside the cities. . . . It does not seem that the men who control the power and resources of the United States ever sat down and designed those black enclaves, and formally articulated the terms of their dependent and colonial status. . . . Indeed, if the ghettos had been formally and deliberately planned instead of growing spontaneously and inevitably from the racist functionings of the various institutions that combine to make the society, it would be somehow less frightening—one could understand their similarity as being artificially and consciously imposed, rather than the result of identical patterns of white racism which repeat themselves in cities as far apart as Boston and Watts. . . ." S. Carmichael, *supra* note 49, at 86–87.

69. As Cruse saw it, the black middle class was frightened of the masses, dependent on the white power structure,

and ambivalent about their own identity; consequently, the installation of the black bourgeoisie as administrators of the black community did not necessarily serve the community's interests: "The tragedy of the black bourgeoisie in America is not that it simply 'sells out,' since all bourgeois classes are prone to compromise their sovereignty during a crisis. It is rather that no class the world over sells out so cheaply as the American black bourgeoisie, whose nation, the richest in the world, wastes billions overseas buying the fickle friendship of unworthy allies"; H. Cruse, *The Crisis of the Negro Intellectual, supra* note 17, at 91. See also R. Staples, *supra* note 52, at 205. Robert Staples notes the structurally different interests of the black middle class and predicts: "[T]he emergence of a class of Black petty bourgeoisie who will undertake the exploitation of the Black masses that is now done directly by the White colonial power structure. Hence, we shall witness large numbers of Blacks being elected to public office, programs created to develop a Black capitalist class, and Black functionaries replacing Whites in the role of colonial mediating positions such as teachers, social workers, policemen, etc." *id.* (citing Cleaver, "The Crisis of the Black Bourgeoisie," *Black Scholar* (Jan. 1973), 2–11.

70. H. Cruse, *The Crisis of the Negro Intellectual* (1967), at 564.

71. For discussion of the centrality of the idea of accomodationism in black politics, see Chrisman, "The Formation of a Revolutionary Black Culture,"*Black Scholar* (June 1970); G. Myrdal, *supra* note 5, at 721–27; Huggins, "Afro-Americans," in J. Higham, ed., *Ethnic Leadership in America*, 93–98 (1978); E. Ladd, *Negro Political Leadership in the South* (1966).

72. An early colonization effort was undertaken by Paul Cuffe in 1815, who arranged for a small expedition of black colonists to Africa, which inspired the creation of the American Colonization Society, a white-controlled group whose purpose was to relocate free blacks to Africa because they were, "a dangerous and useless part of the community"; H. Aptheker, ed., 1 *A Documentary History of the Negro People in the United States*, 71 (1951). See R. Allen, *supra* note 17, at 76–77. For a general description of white deportationists, and an analysis of the "ideological failure of colonization" focused on its associations with racist whites, see R. Carlisle, *supra* note 17, at 10–12, 24–30.

73. In criticizing Washington's famous Atlanta Compromise—where Washington advocated that, "[i]n all things purely social we can be as separate as the five fingers, and yet one as the hand in all things essential to mutual progress"—W. E. B. Du Bois, *The Souls of Black Folk* (1903), at 42, concluded that "Mr. Washington represents in Negro thought the old attitude of adjustment and submission . . . [which] practically accepts the alleged inferiority of the Negro races." *Id.* at 50. See generally *id.* at 41–59.

74. See T. Martin, *supra* note 20, at 297–99 (describing Du Bois's attempt to link Garvey with the accomodationism of Washington). While this was Du Bois's interpretation of Garveyism, Garvey painted the opposite picture: see J. White, *supra* note 22, at 61, 89–95; T. Martin, *supra* note 20, at 297–99; H. Cruse, *Rebellion or Revolution?, supra* note 17, at 86 ("The rise of Garvey nationalism meant that the NAACP became the accomodationists, and the nationalists became the militants").

75. See, for example, J. Johnson, *Negro Americans, What Now?* 35–40 (1934) ("[T]he outcome of voluntary isolation would be a permanent secondary status . . . I do not believe we should ever be willing to pay such a price for security and peace"); Bunche, "A Critical Analysis of the Tactics and Programs of Minority Groups," 4 *J. Negro Educ.*, 308, 312 (1935) ("Because of the seeming hopelessness of the fight to win equal rights for many minority racial groups, some of the leadership of such groups has often espoused a 'defeatist' philosophy, which takes the form of racial separatism"); Farmer, "We Cannot Destroy Segregation with a Weapon of Segregation" (editorial), *Equality* (Nov. 1944), 2 ("Garveyism [and other nationalisms] . . . are not liberating the Negro people; they are further enslaving their minds under the yoke of caste"); White, "Segregation: A Symposium," 41 *Crisis*, 80, 81 (1934) (responding to Du Bois's calls for voluntary self-segregation, White, then executive secretary of the NAACP, argued that "no Negro who respects himself and his race can accept these segregated systems without at least some inward protest"); R. Staples, *supra* note 52, at 301 ("[Garveyism] was an escapist philosophy"); *id.* at 302 ("Muslims did not engage in political action and insulated themselves from both the culture and everyday life of the Black community"; footnote omitted); R. Weisbrot, *supra* note 4, at 31 (direct actionists advised by elders to be cautious).

76. The community-organizing militancy of the direct action factions of the civil rights movement in the fifties and early sixties, and the later critique of nonviolence as a means to achieve integration, can be seen to have reflected a submerged form of nationalist ideology itself, to be made explicit by the mid-sixties when CORE and SNCC adopted formal nationalist programs and when, in 1967, Rap Brown, Stokely Carmichael, and James Foreman joined the Black Panthers, see C. Carson, *supra* note 4, at 196–207; H. Haines, *supra* note 29, at 57–75; A. Meier and E. Rudick, *supra* note 4, at 17–18.

77. See R. Staples, *supra* note 52, at 291–93; Turner, *supra* note 29, at 7–8; Scott and Brockriede, eds., *The Rhetoric of Black Power, supra* note 31, at 4–5.

❧

A CULTURAL PLURALIST CASE FOR AFFIRMATIVE ACTION IN LEGAL ACADEMIA

Duncan Kennedy

THIS article is about affirmative action in legal academia. It argues for a large expansion of our current commitment to cultural diversity on the ground that law schools are political institutions. For that reason, they should abide by the general democratic principle that people should be represented in the institutions that have power over their lives. Further, large-scale affirmative action would improve the quality and increase the value of legal scholarship.

My goal is to develop in the specific context of law school affirmative action the conception of "race-consciousness" which Gary Peller describes and advocates in his essay of the same name [included in this volume—ED.]. We need to be able to talk about the political and cultural relations of the various groups that compose our society without falling into racialism, essentialism, or a concept of the "nation" tied to the idea of sovereignty. We need to conceptualize groups in a "postmodern" way, recognizing their reality in our lives without losing sight of the partial, unstable, contradictory character of group existence.

I present my argument in the form of a dialogue with our society's dominant way of understanding race and merit in academia, which I call "color-blind meritocratic fundamentalism." I use Randall Kennedy's article "Racial Critiques of Legal Academia" as a principal representative of this point of view.[1] Throughout, I will be responding to Kennedy's general understanding of how we should organize legal academic life in a situation of racial and cultural division, rather than to his specific attacks on works of race-conscious scholarship.

I think the articles that Kennedy discusses, as well as the others in the genre of Critical Race Theory, represent the most exciting recent development in American legal scholarship. On some issues, I agree with Kennedy's criticisms, but overall I see the articles as developing positions that I share, and I don't find his article convincing as a refutation of them. I think it's best to leave it to the authors to debate him point by point. I am more interested in working out a left-wing (white ruling-class male academic) take on the underlying questions than I am in discussing whether his article is "fair."
. . .

I. COLOR-BLIND MERITOCRATIC FUNDAMENTALISM

MY attitude toward meritocracy grows from my experience as a white male ruling-class child who got good grades, gained admission to one elite institution after another, and then landed a job and eventually tenure at Harvard Law School. I belong to a group (only partly generationally defined) that, since some point in childhood, has felt alienated within this lived experience of working for success according to the criteria of merit which these elite institutions administer.

This alienation had and has two facets. First, there is a pervasive skepticism about the "standards" according to which we have achieved success. Always subject to the charge that we are simultaneously biting the hand that feeds us and soiling the nest, we just don't believe that it is real "merit" that institutions measure, anywhere in the system; success is a function of particular knacks, some socially desirable (being "smart") and some not (sucking up)—and of nothing more grandiose. This is not rejection of the idea that some work is better than other work. It is rejection of the institutional mechanisms that currently produce such judgments of the individuals who manage the institutions and of the substantive outcomes.

The second facet is a sense of shame and guilt at living in unjust, segregated racial privilege, combined with a sense of loss from the way we have been diminished by isolation from what the subordinated cultural communities of the U.S. might have contributed to our lives, intellectual, political, and personal. I might add that the members of this wholly hypothetical group have not done much (but not nothing, either) about the situation.

These attitudes were held by a scattering of people within elite institutions, and we had little contact with people outside that milieu. The experience on which the reaction was and is based is limited. It's hard to know whether the attitudes are really right. It's hard to know whether there is any workable alternative to the actual system.

During the sixties, these attitudes fed into the much larger complex of the New Left, the Movement, and the women's movement. The participants came from many different sectors of society. They were male and female, white and black, upper-middle-, middle-, and—to a limited extent—working- class. The whole thing was over before the deep differences among them were worked into anything like coherence. It remains an open question just how the antimeritocratic alienation I have described dovetails or doesn't with the attitudes of people who come from disadvantaged or nonelite backgrounds.

When political alliance and real communication between black and white and male and female radicals fell apart in the seventies, the project of working out a critique of meritocracy split apart too. However, before that happened there was a counterattack, associated with the general reaction against sixties' militancy and specifically addressed to the various contradictory radical critiques that had gained some currency. This reaction, which I call "fundamentalism," won the day: it became one of the ideological legitimaters of society's retreat from messing around with established institutions.

Color-blind meritocratic fundamentalism is a set of ideas about race and merit. Like other substructures within the consciousness of a time, it is no more than one of many fragments out of which people construct their personal philosophies. It is intrinsically neither right nor left, male nor female, black nor white. Fundamentalism has a long history within American liberalism, and within orthodox Marxism, as well as within the conservative tradition.

A. Fundamentalism as a System of Ideas
Fundamentalism consists of a set of tenets. Each is a slogan with appeal of its own; they

are rarely presented all together. Believers deploy them one by one as the argument may require. Some tenets are about knowledge and others about the social value of individuals and their work.

1(a). Knowledge:
  i. Attributes of the product rather than of the producer determine the value of purported contributions to knowledge.
  ii. In judging the value of a product, the race, sex, class, and indeed all the other personal attributes of the producer are irrelevant (derived from [i]).

Kennedy identifies these tenets with "the ethos of modern science." The scientific ideal is linked to an image of how intellectual work is done.

1(b). The production of knowledge:
  i. We produce work by individual application of talent to inert matter.
  ii. The value of the work is a function of the quality of the individual talent that produced it rather than of the inert matter of experience out of which the individual formed it (derived from [i]).

Fundamentalism includes the complex of liberal attitudes toward race that Peller calls "integrationism," but which seems to me better called color-blindness. Kennedy's article displays better than any recent document I know of the way meritocracy and color-blindness can be made mutually supportive.

For our purposes here, the important tenets of color-blindness are as follows:

2(a). "Prejudice" and "discrimination" are defined in opposition to "assessment of individuals on their merits":
  i. Merit is a matter of individual traits or products.
  ii. People are treated irrationally and unjustly—in short, they are discriminated against—when their merit is assessed according to their status rather than ac-

cording to the value of their traits or products (derived from [i]).

2(b). Racial discrimination as stereotyping:

    i. There is no reason to believe that race in any of its various socially constructed meanings is an attribute biologically linked to any particular meritorious or discreditable intellectual, psychological, or social traits of any kind.

    ii. Racial discrimination is irrational and unjust because it denies the individual what is due him or her under the society's agreed standards of merit (derived from [i]).

From these two sets of tenets, the fundamentalist moves easily to propositions about the proper institutional organization of academic (and other) rewards and opportunities.

3. The institutional organization of the production of knowledge:

    i. Academic institutions should strive to maximize the production of valuable knowledge and also to reward and empower individual merit.

    ii. Institutions distributing honor and opportunity should therefore do so according to criteria that are blind to race, sex, class, and all other particularities of the individual except the one particularity of having produced work of value (derived from [i] plus 1 and 2).

B. Color-Blind Meritocracy and Affirmative Action

Fundamentalism does not preclude adopting affirmative action programs so long as we recognize that they conflict with meritocratic allocation, and that the sacrifice of meritocratic to race-based outcomes is a social cost or loss. In this view, though, versions of affirmative action which obscure the cost by distorting standards in favor of minorities end up compounding it. They go beyond departure from merit in particular cases to endanger the integrity of the general system of unbiased judgment of value.

The political and cultural arguments for affirmative action I put forward in the next sec-

tion are consistent with fundamentalism in that they openly abandon the use of color-blind criteria, rather than distorting them in order to achieve desirable results. They do not treat race as an index of merit in the sense of making it a source of honor in and of itself, nor do they presume that minority scholars are, by virtue of their skin color, "better" scholars.

There remains an important area of disagreement. Fundamentalism treats a color-blind meritocratic system as the ideal. Kennedy's article, for example, concedes (even affirms) that our actual system departs very far from the ideal, but it urges that we should therefore redouble our commitment to purifying it:

> It is true ... that there are many nonracial and ameritocratic considerations that frequently enter into evaluations of a scholar's work. The proper response to that reality, however, is not to scrap the meritocratic ideal. The proper response is to abjure all practices that exploit the trappings of meritocracy to advance interests ... that have nothing to do with the intellectual characteristics of the subject being judged.[2]

If the concern is with racial justice, then loyalty to meritocracy suggests two paths. First, according to Kennedy, "there is nothing necessarily wrong with race-conscious affirmative action"[3] if one has a good reason for it, but the reasons he imagines include neither cultural diversity as an intellectual desideratum nor the recognition of the cultural and ideological relativity of the standards that faculty members apply in distributing jobs and honors.

> [O]ne might fear that without a sufficient number of minority professors a school will be beset by an intolerable degree of discord or believe that an institution ought to make amends for its past wrongs or insist upon taking extraordinary measures in order to integrate all socially significant institutions in American life.[4]

Second, Kennedy favors attacking the underlying social conditions, particularly the class stratification, that reduce the pool of minority applicants.

The point about affirmative action seen as peace-making, reparations, or integration for its own sake, and also about increasing the pool of minority applicants, is that all of them allow us

to preserve a sharp boundary between meritocratic decision and race-based decision.

> I simply do not want race-conscious decision-
> making to be naturalized into our general pattern
> of academic evaluation. I do not want race-con-
> scious decision-making to lose its status as a devi-
> ant mode of judging people or the work they
> produce. I do not want race-conscious decision-
> making to be assimilated into our conception of
> meritocracy.

The political and cultural cases for affirmative
action propose to do each of these things.

II. THE POLITICAL AND CULTURAL ARGUMENTS FOR AFFIRMATIVE ACTION

A. The Political Case

I favor large-scale race-based affirmative action,
using quotas if they are necessary to produce
results. The first basis for this view is that
law school teaching positions are a small but
significant part of the wealth of the United
States. They are also a small but significant part
of the political apparatus of the United States,
by which I mean that the knowledge that law
teachers produce is intrinsically political and
actually effective in our political system. In
short, legal knowledge is ideological.

A second basic idea is that we should be
a culturally pluralist society that deliberately
structures institutions so that communities and
social classes share wealth and power. The sharing of wealth and power which occurs automatically, so to speak, through the melting pot,
the market, and meritocracy are not enough,
according to this notion. At a minimum, cultural pluralism means that we should structure
the competition of racial and ethnic communities and social classes in markets and bureaucracies, and in the political system, in such a way
that no community or class is systematically
subordinated.

From these two ideas, I draw the conclusion
that, completely independently of "merit" as
we currently determine it,[5] there should be
a substantial representation of all numerically
significant minority communities on American
law faculties. The analogy is to the right to vote,
which we refuse to distribute on the basis of
merit, and to the right of free speech, which we
refuse to limit to those who deserve to speak or
whose speech has merit. The value at stake is
community rather than individual empowerment. In the case of affirmative action, as in
those of voting and free speech, the goal is
political and prior to the achievement of enlightenment or the reward of "merit" as determined by existing institutions.

Race is, at present, a rough but adequate
proxy for connection to a subordinated community, one that avoids institutional judgments
about the cultural identity of particular candidates. I would use it for this reason only—not
because race is itself an index of merit—and in
spite of its culturally constructed character and
the arbitrariness involved in using it as a pre-
dicter of the traits of any particular individual.
My argument is thus addressed to only one
of the multiple forms of group subordination,
though it could be extended to gender, sexual
preference, social class, and ethnicity within the
"white community."

The political argument includes the idea that
minority communities can't compete effectively
for wealth and power without intelligentsias
that produce the kinds of knowledge, especially
political or ideological knowledge, that will help
them get what they want. To do this, they need
or at least could use some number of legal
academic jobs. It also includes the idea that
cultural diversity and cultural development are
good in themselves, even when they do not lead
to increased power for subordinated communities in markets and political systems.

The political case is complicated by the fact
that when law faculties distribute jobs in legal
academia, they do more than distribute wealth
and the power to participate in politics through
the production of ideology. They also distribute
power to influence who will participate in the
future, because those they choose will vote on
those decisions. In deciding who to hire or
promote according to color-blind criteria, law
faculties make culturally and ideologically contingent judgments about what candidates are
most promising or deserving, and about who
should make these very judgments in the future.
Given the ideological and cultural character of
these choices, and their (limited but significant)

political impact, white males have no more business monopolizing the process of distributing the benefits than they have monopolizing the benefits themselves. . . .

It would seem to me a problem (requiring tradeoffs) if the implementation of this view would be unfair to individual whites excluded from teaching jobs, or if it would lead to a decline in the quality of legal scholarship. But I believe that massive affirmative action would not be unfair to excluded whites, and that it would improve the quality of legal scholarship as I assess it. It would also, I think, have a beneficial effect on the quality of life by undermining the fetishistic, neurotic, and just plain irrational attitude toward "standards" and merit-based "entitlement" that prevails in legal academia. . . .

B. Affirmative Action and White Entitlements
Suppose a law faculty adopts this version of affirmative action because it hopes to improve the quality of legal academic work, as well as because it is politically more just. When the faculty prefers a minority job applicant over a white, even though the present system would give the job to the white, it does so in part because it thinks that in the long run this approach will improve scholarship and teaching. We are treating race as a credential (as a proxy for culture and community) because we anticipate terrific work from some of these applicants, work that we don't think we can get from the whites they are favored over. The reason we don't expect it from them is that we believe that work from authors with ties to subordinated communities is likely to have different excellent qualities than work from inside the dominant community.

Are the excluded whites "entitled" to prevent this improvement in scholarship? I would say they are not. Even if all the color-blind criteria of academic promise that we can think of favor a white candidate, he or she lacks something we want in some substantial number of those we will hire. He or she has less promise of doing work with the particular strengths likely to derive from connection to a subordinated cultural community.

The white male law-teaching applicant whose résumé and interviews would get him the job, were it not for affirmative action, has indeed accomplished something and will not be rewarded for it with the job. Yet if he understands in advance that the terms of the competition are such that he is competing against other white males for a limited number of slots which a politically just system makes available to people who have had his advantages, then I don't think he has any reason to complain when a job he would have gotten under a different (less just) system goes to a minority applicant. However, the excluded white candidates do not have as strong a claim as assumed above.

First, those who win out in the existing system have no claim to be "the best," even according to the color-blind criteria, because the underlying systems of race and class as well as the system of testing excludes so many potential competitors from the very beginning. The competition in which our teaching applicants and tenure candidates win out is restricted, with only a tiny number of notable exceptions, to people born within a certain race-class distance of those positions. At every step, the differences in educational resources and the testing process screen out millions of people who might be able to do the job of law professor better than those who end up getting it. As against those excluded from the competition by race and class as well as the vagaries of the testing system, those who win out have only a very limited claim of entitlement.

Second, the "standards" that law schools apply in hiring assistant professors and promoting them to tenure are at best very rough proxies for accomplishment as we assess it after the fact. People who get good grades and have prestigious clerkships often turn out to be duds as legal scholars and teachers, by the standards of those who appointed them; people with less impressive résumés often turn out to be terrific scholars and teachers. People who get tenure on the basis of an article that looks good to the tenure committee (and those of the faculty who read it) often never produce anything of comparable quality again. "Entitlements" based on these rough proxies are worthy of only limited respect. The white males who would be displaced to make way for large numbers of minority scholars would be hurt, but not in a way that would be unfair, given the importance of the goals to be achieved.

Third, law school faculties apply a pedestrian, often philistine cultural standard in judging white male résumés, interviews, and presentations at the entry level, and white male teaching and tenure work at the promotion level. They administer this pedestrian, philistine standard with an unconscious but unmistakable moderate-conservative to moderate-liberal bias. They serve it up, moreover, with a powerful seasoning of old-boyism and arbitrary clique preference as between white males. This doesn't mean a more pluralist academy would necessarily do better or produce more political diversity. It does mean for me that there is an element of laughable exaggeration in the claims often made for the meritocratic purity of existing arrangements. The people who would win out in this system were it not for affirmative action have weak claims of unfairness, because they are not so wonderful, even by comparison with other white males, that they can regard themselves as innocent victims.

There is no trade-off between racial justice and legal academic quality. Indeed, both goals point in the same direction. There is no claim of entitlement against these goals even for candidates who are plausibly the best by every color-blind criterion. The actual candidates likely to be rejected have claims weakened by exclusion of competitors, especially competitors from the groups that would gain by affirmative action. Their claims are further weakened by the fact that their accomplishments are mere proxies for legal academic merit, and by the low cultural quality and arbitrary subjectivism of the screening system that would otherwise have delivered them the goods. . . .

This proposal obviously contemplates race-conscious decision-making as a routine, non-deviant mode, a more or less permanent norm in distributing legal academic jobs. A "racial distinctiveness" theory—actually, cultural distinctiveness—combined with race-conscious decision-making is "assimilated into our con-

ception of meritocracy," which is just what Kennedy's article urges us to avoid at all costs. The position is problematic as well as controversial, because it relies on the idea of cultural subordination, rather than on the more familiar fundamentalist ideas of prejudice and discrimination.

III. The Cultural Subordination Thesis

THE issue is whether there is enough cultural distinctiveness, and enough subordination and exclusion, that we must treat representation in academia as a political question, and that we can expect major intellectual gains from doing so.[6] The argument thus far has been largely hypothetical. Even if one accepted the value of the notions of culture and ideology, one might deny that, in the actual conditions of the United States in 1990, cultural and ideological differences are significant. Or one might merely deny that they are large enough that we need to structure law schools so as to take them into account.[7]

The cultural pluralist position, to the contrary, rests on a whole complex of ideas about American society. I am going to introduce them in highly schematic form. Together they define a variant of the "nationalist" ideology.

A. Premises of Cultural Pluralism

Groups exist in a sense that goes beyond individuals with similar traits. People act together, in the strong sense of working out common goals and then engaging in a cooperative process of trying to achieve them. Just as important, they engage in discussion and mutual criticism both about the goals and about what group members are doing (or not doing) to achieve them. This is true of small task-oriented groups (for example, family members getting the car packed for a trip) and also of large, diffuse groups, such as "the black community" or a law faculty.

An important human reality is the experience of defining oneself as "a member of a group" in this strong sense of sharing goals and a discursive practice. Another important experience is being treated by others as a group member. One's interlocutor interprets what one says and does as derived from a shared project. We all constantly identify groups and their members, assuming that we need to do so in order to understand other people and to predict what they will do.

Communities are more than mere statistical groupings of individuals with particular traits but less than self-organized groups. Membership presupposes interaction, but the interaction may be sporadic, routine, alienated. A community is a historically specific collection of people with a common past, and a future that will take place on the basis of what has gone before. That basis can be reinterpreted but not obliterated. We are stuck, at any given moment, in the communities we started or ended in, and that is never "just anywhere." Wherever it is, it is both more inert than a self-organized group and less demanding. The crucial idea is that communities are made up of living individuals but have an element of transindividual stability and particularity; to be a member is to be situated, and you can be situated only in one or two places at a time. Membership is limiting as well as empowering.

Communities have cultures. This means that individuals have traits that are neither genetically determined nor voluntarily chosen; rather, they are consciously and unconsciously taught through community life. Community life forms customs and habits, capacities to produce linguistic and other performances, and individual understandings of good and bad, true and false, worthy and unworthy. Culture is first of all a product of community. People living in different groups possess different understandings of value as well as exhibiting different capacities and behavior traits (kinship, cooking, dress). As I am using the term "culture," though, it is a characteristic of an individual as well. You can break all your ties to a community yet remain a person with that community's cultural identity.

A large part of the population of the United States lives in racial and ethnic communities that have a measure of cultural distinctiveness. The distinctiveness comes in part from the origins—in Africa, Asia, Europe, and Latin America—of the different groups that live here. However, the cultures of particular communities have been dramatically transformed by the experience of immigration, forced transportation, or annexation, as well as by the heterogeneous cultural life of this country. Each group has combined its culture of origin with its peculiar circumstances in the United States to produce a distinct set of behaviors, attitudes, beliefs, and values.

The racial and ethnic communities of the United States are in constant contact with one another. This contact is asymmetrical: there is a dominant cultural community that is less influenced by, and less conscious of, the subordinated groups than they are influenced by, and conscious of, it. As a result, it is hard to identify any aspect of the cultures of subordinated groups that might be relevant to academic production which has not been influenced by contact with the dominant culture.

The boundaries of cultural communities are blurred by the presence of large numbers of people who can trace their family history back into a subordinated community, but who now regard themselves, and are regarded by others, as situated in a culturally intermediate space or as assimilated to the dominant culture. There are millions of people for whom the "authenticity" of having always belonged to a relatively homogeneous community with an un-self-consciously shared ethos is simply impossible. Most of those likely to benefit by a program of culturally conscious distribution of academic power and opportunity come from these intermediate, multicultural positions. (The existence of this group may make it more likely that we could actually succeed in implementing cultural diversity.)

Though communities are different in ways that are best understood through the nonhierarchical, neutral idea of culture (some groups do things one way, value one set of things, while other groups do it in different ways), some differences are not like that. Americans pursue their collective and individual projects in a situation of group domination and group subordination. By this I mean that we can compare "how well" different groups have done with regard to income, housing, health, education, local and national political power, and access to cultural resources. The groups are not so different that they define these things in radically different ways, or that some groups are just not interested in them. With respect to these common measures of equality and inequality, we all recognize that some groups are enormously better off than others.

The experiences of youth within a particular community or on the border between communities equip individuals with resources for competition in markets and bureaucracies. Different communities have different access to wealth and power with which to endow their members. The rules of competition in markets and bureaucracies are structured in ways (both formal and informal) that benefit people from different communities regardless of the resources they bring as individuals to the competition.

Some of these advantages are overtly or covertly correlated to the community membership of the people competing. Historically, the white community imposed systematic race-based discrimination, outright job and housing segregation, and rules that excluded racial minorities and women from directly exercising political power. In the current situation, particular cultural groups control or dominate some markets and bureaucracies, and these groups exercise the enormous range of discretionary choice which is inevitable in ways that favor dominant over subordinated communities. Racial and gender discrimination still direct the flow of opportunities and thereby affect the shares groups achieve.

The notions of domination and subordination are meant to indicate that we cannot understand social phenomena through a model in which everyone in the society has innate or individual qualities and individual preferences they bring into a neutrally structured competitive process that correlates their rewards with their social contributions. There are patterns to the characteristics of the individuals society produces: they are identifiably members of the particular communities they grew up in, and their fortunes depend on that fact.

Differences of fortune result from themselves in a circular process. To speak of domination is to say that the group and individual exercise of power given by resources occurs in a competitive struggle in which better-off communities manage over time to reproduce their advantage by winning enough in each game to reconstitute their stakes. Even the rules of the game are produced by the game, in the sense that power to compete is also power to modify the rules. The dominant communities are those with the most resources and rewards, those which manage to influence the rules defining the game to their advantage, and those which, over time, manage to reproduce or improve their top-dog position through competitive struggle.

The game is cooperative as well as competitive. In order to be rewarded, members of different communities have to cooperate across ethnic lines in producing goods and services. There are all kinds of influences and concrete alliances formed, and there are areas and moments when community identity is for the most part submerged in the collective aspects of tasks. Within the communities, there are divisions that are best understood in class terms, and other cross-cutting divisions that represent the community's participation in national life (region, gender, religion, and so on). Power and resistance to power pervade the structure.

Though there is a self-conscious ruling class at the top of this structure, neither the class nor the structure fully controls the outcomes and impacts of the game on the communities whose members play it. All the players are functions of the game, and the game is a function of the players. There is no "outside position." Communities themselves change internally and through collision with other communities, but the process involves as much fate, drift, and chance mutation to it as it does mechanical necessity or self-organized group will. Communities can disperse or assimilate and then reform, and they can die out or be killed.

American racial and ethnic communities have intelligentsias, linked in overlapping patterns to a national intelligentsia and to each other. By an intelligentsia, I mean a "knowledge class" working in education, the arts, social work, the law, religion, the media, therapy, consulting, and myriad spin-offs such as charitable foundations, for-profit research ventures, and the like. Intelligentsia members perform multiple functions beyond their formal job descriptions. In self-organizing groups or individually, some of them work at defining their community's identity (its cultural distinctiveness) or lack thereof, its interests in both competition and cooperation with other communities, and its possible strategies.

National, racial, and ethnic intelligentsias are internally divided along ideological lines. One national ideological axis runs from radical to liberal to moderate to conservative to right-wing; another runs from traditional to modern to postmodern; yet another from science to social science to humanities to arts. There are also a wide range of ideological debates within particular intelligentsias, for example about their relationship to the national community.

An ideology, in the sense in which I am using it, is a set of contested ideas which provides a "partisan" interpretation (descriptive and normative) of a field of social conflict. The social conflict could be between capital and labor, farmers and banks, men and women, gays and straights, North and South, native-born and foreign-born, export industries and import industries, and so on. The concepts that describe and justify the positions of the conflicting groups can be drawn from almost anywhere, from philosophy to economics to religion to biology; within the fields that we use ideologically, complex systems of contested ideas both reflect and influence social conflict.

Ideologists choose their ideas, in the sense that there is no consensus either in their favor or against them. Many people may think a particular system is objectively right and many others that it is objectively wrong, or it may be seen as posing a question that one can resolve only by a leap of faith. The most basic critique of the ideologist is that she has chosen her ideas to fit her partisan allegiance, and therefore lacks allegiance to "truth." In the conception of ideology I am using, this must always be recognized as a possibility. People do sometimes distort their intellectual work to serve causes or interests they adhere to. At the same time, though, we have to recognize that where there is social

conflict and contested interpretations of that conflict, there is no intellectual space outside of ideology. Intelligentsia virtue consists not in "objectivity" or "neutrality," which are impossible once there is ideological division, but in the attempt to empower an audience to judge for itself.

It follows, then, that being an "ideologist" doesn't mean being closed-minded, or uninterested in questioning fundamental assumptions, or being blind to evidence that contradicts those assumptions. In this sense of the term, one is in the position of the ideologist just by virtue of having, at any given moment, made choices between contested views which influence the intellectual work one does (and are influenced by it). "Moderates" are ideologists because, when they call themselves that, they implicitly appeal to a controversial critique of "ideologues." (This is the ideology of moderation.)

Members of minority intelligentsias are linked to their cultural communities in various ways, and divided from them as well, usually by social class, income, intelligentsia interests, and links to the national intelligentsia and culture which are different from those of the "masses." A basic ideological conflict is over how to describe and evaluate the courses of conduct that intelligentsia members adopt in this situation. There are ideologies of assimilation and of authenticity, of group accommodation and of group resistance, of individual self-realization and of collective obligation, and so forth.

The existence of ethnic intelligentsias, their size, and the power they produce for communities all depend on access to resources, as does their ability to contribute to national intellectual-political life. One index of a community's cultural subordination is its dependence on others to produce knowledge in areas where it would seem, at least superficially, that community interests will be affected by what that knowledge is. Another is the inability of its intelligentsia to influence the national intelligentsia and, indirectly, the American mass-culture audience on issues of importance to the community.

The above definition of cultural subordination is patently ideological. The conceptual scheme proposed is only one of many available to describe and judge the status of an intelligentsia, and within each scheme there is a well developed critique of its rivals.

B. What Might Be Gained Through Large-Scale Affirmative Action

Against this background, I would deny the existence of a "black point of view" or a "black voice" in any essentialist (or racialist) sense. Yet that doesn't answer the particular questions that are relevant to the political and cultural arguments for large-scale affirmative action. The first of these is whether minority communities would get, from a much larger minority legal intelligentsia, a scholarly output that would better serve their diverse political, social, and economic interests than does what they get from an overwhelmingly white legal intelligentsia. The second is whether the legal academic community as a whole would get a more valuable total corpus of scholarship.

I see two likely changes in this regard. A much larger minority intelligentsia should produce more scholarship about the legal issues that have impact on minority communities. The subject matter of scholarship is determined at present by the unregulated "interest" of academics; what we decide to write about just "flows naturally" from our backgrounds, education, and individual peculiarities. I think it is obvious that some significant proportion of minority intellectuals would be led in this way to write about minority legal issues

The precedent for this is the creation of modern civil rights law by black lawyers who devised the litigation strategy of the National Association for the Advancement of Colored People. It would be far-fetched to argue that the race of these lawyers was irrelevant to their choice of subject matter, or that the black civil rights cause would have evolved in the same way had all the lawyers involved been white.

Along with more scholarship on minority issues, there should be more scholarship on the implications for minorities of any issue currently under debate. In other words, Hispanic scholars working on the purest of corporate law ques-

tions within the most unquestionably Anglo scholarly paradigm are still, I think, more likely than white scholars to devote, over the long run, some time to thinking about the implications of law in their chosen technical area for the Hispanic communities.

The second anticipated change is crucial to my argument. Along with a quantitative change in the focus of scholarship, it seems likely that an increase in minority scholarship would change the framework of ideological conflict within which discussions of the issues involving race (and other subjects) take place. I do not mean to say that there is a black (or other minority) ideology; rather, the point is that there are historic, already established debates within the minority intelligentsias that are obviously relevant to law, but they have been largely absent from legal scholarship.

Here are some examples of debates in the black intellectual community that have only begun to get played out and transformed in law: between nationalists and integrationists,[8] between progressives and conservatives,[9] between those who see current racism as a more or less important determinant of current black social conditions,[10] and between black feminists and traditionalists.[11] The nationalist versus integrationist and gender debates are now for the first time beginning to get a hearing as a result of the presence of more minorities in the legal academy.[12] There are similar debates in the other minority communities.[13] . . .

There is nothing that *precludes* white scholars from making the contributions anticipated from scholars of color. An outsider may learn about a culture and its debates and produce work about or even "within" them that is "better" than anything an insider has produced. There are advantages as well as disadvantages to outsider status, and everyone in a multicultural society is simultaneously inside and outside. There is nothing to guarantee that minority scholars will choose or be able to make those contributions. They may squander their resources, or decide to do work that is indistinguishable in subject matter and approach from that of white scholars. However, their track record, with and without affirmative action, has been good enough, easily, even as tokens, to sustain a prediction of excellence to come.

C. The Political Case in the Context of Cultural Subordination

Through scholarship focusing on their own concerns and through ideological debate played out in the legal arena, minority communities (through their intelligentsias) develop themselves internally, assimilate for their own purposes the resources of the culture at large, and build power for the competitive struggle with other groups. The power to create this kind of knowledge is political power; thus, it should be shared by all groups within the community affected.

This argument has two levels. First, both the choice and the application of academic standards have strikingly contingent cultural and ideological dimensions. Law faculties distribute political resources (jobs) through a process that is political in fact if not in name. One group (white males of the dominant culture) largely monopolizes this distribution process, and, perhaps not so surprisingly, also largely monopolizes the benefits (jobs). This outcome is politically illegitimate. Second, supposing that you disagree with what I have just said, and you believe that standards are and should be apolitical, your position is itself ideological. Law faculties shouldn't make the ideological choice between color-blind meritocracy and some form of race-conscious power-sharing without a substantial participation of minorities in making the decision.

I. CULTURAL AND IDEOLOGICAL DIMENSIONS OF ACADEMIC STANDARDS

There are different questions we ask when assessing an academic work. There is the question of truth or falsity, understood to be a question susceptible of answers that, when argued out, will produce a broad consensus. Then there are questions of "originality" and questions of "interest" or "value."

My experience has been that work in law (like, I assume, some work in physics) is some-

times wrong or untrue in a quite strong sense. I am convinced that when the error is pointed out just about everyone will agree that it was an error. I don't think the kinds of cultural differences that can plausibly be asserted to characterize American society have much impact on these judgments. This is sometimes true as well of questions of originality, interest and value.

Judgments of originality are obviously more contested. And judgments of whether the problem addressed was "interesting" or "valuable" seem to me very strongly influenced by the politics of academic life. Different people in a field often have very different ideas about which true, original work is interesting. Though the judges have a strong sense that they know what they mean by interest, and that they are not making "merely" subjective judgments, they also concede that the standard is difficult to apply.

More important for our purposes, they will generally concede that interest or value can be judged only by reference to a particular research tradition or scholarly paradigm, usually one among many that might have won dominance in the field. Yet conclusions at the level of what is valuable or interesting are very often dispositive in deciding which of two articles is better.

Once we acknowledge the possible existence of different research traditions, or collective scholarly projects, we have to acknowledge that the white male occupants of faculty positions have more than the power to decide which performances are better. They have also had the power to create the traditions or projects within which they will make these judgments. It seems obvious that these traditions or projects are culturally and ideologically specific products.

The projects themselves, as well as the judgments of originality, interest, and value they ground (not the narrow judgments of truth and falsity) would almost certainly change if people of excluded cultures and excluded ideologies were allocated power and opportunity to create research traditions and scholarly projects of their own, or to participate in those ongoing. If this were done, there would be a gradual reevaluation of existing legal scholarship. Some currently low-ranked work would gain esteem, and some high-ranked work would lose it. There are no meta-criteria of merit that determine which among culturally and ideologically specific research traditions or scholarly paradigms is "better" or "truer." Judgments of merit are inevitably culturally and ideologically contingent because they are inevitably paradigm-dependent. . . . The fundamentalist has to deal with the claim that choices to allocate scholarly opportunity are grounded in power, rather than merit, and function to reproduce the very distribution of power they reflect. The power is that of white, mainly male academics, mainly of "moderate" ideology, to impose their standards. They hold, and have held for many generations, the positions to which society has allocated authority to distribute this kind of opportunity. And they have distributed it to themselves.

As with the cultural case, there is nothing to guarantee that a larger minority legal intelligentsia would use the resources of law schools in ways that I would find politically constructive. More jobs might just widen the gap between scholars of color and their communities, and the hiring process might select those least likely, for class and ideological reasons, to pursue the project of empowerment. If that happened, those for whom empowerment is the goal would have to think of something else. . . .

IV. Do Race-Based Criteria of Scholarly Judgment "Derogate Individuality"?

THIS section turns to Randall Kennedy's claim that race-conscious decision-making "derogates from individuality." This argument is typical of fundamentalist thinking as it might apply to a culturally and politically based affirmative action program. (As noted above, Kennedy is sympathetic to affirmative action, though on other grounds.)

Kennedy's article makes the familiar argument that racial categorization is dangerous per se, because it can be and is used for racist purposes. I recognize that this is a danger, but I think its degree has to be assessed case by case. In most situations, it is easy to distinguish between racist and antiracist use of racial categories. Facially neutral categories can accomplish almost anything a confirmed racist would want. Whether we do better on balance by using race explicitly in institutional decision-making or by finding other ways to achieve racial objectives isn't a question to which we will ever find a decisive empirical answer. I advocate pervasive use of race-conscious decision-making because I don't think we can deal with the problem of subordination without confronting it directly, or that we can fully achieve the value of cultural pluralism without self-consciously designing our institutions with that in mind.

I don't think Kennedy's contrary position is just a matter of a different empirical-intuitive assessment of the probabilities of "misuse" or "socially destructive" application. Rather, it is tied to the general fundamentalist conception of prejudice and discrimination as subspecies of the evil of stereotyping. The intense fundamentalist preoccupation with stereotyping is, in turn, closely tied to what strikes me as the fetishizing of "individual merit." In Kennedy's article, there are a few paragraphs about the bad consequences of racial classification,[14] but the theme that pervades the whole article is that "racial generalizations, whether positive or negative, derogate from the individuality of persons insofar as their unique characteristics are submerged in the image of the group to which they are deemed to belong."

"Derogation from individuality" occurs whenever there is a failure to distinguish between the "will" of the individual and his or her merely "social," "accidental," "ascribed", or "inherited" characteristics. It occurs equally whenever we fail to distinguish the act of "will" from the materials, likewise merely given, on which the individual works:

> "[N]either one's racial status nor the experience one suffers as a result of that status is capable of translating itself into art, a point applicable as well to scholarship, the "art" of academicians. An experience is simply inert—something that happened. That something only becomes know-

able in a public way through an act of will: interpretation."[15]

Kennedy's article is a brief against allowing "race-conscious decision-making to be assimilated into our conception of meritocracy" because to do so would be unfair to "the individual," whether white or black, who is denied recognition of his or her "merit" in the sense of "accomplishment" (attainment or achievement).

This argument depends on our ability to separate people from their context: "As I define the term, 'merit' stands for achieved honor by some standard that is indifferent to the social identity of a given author." Judgments that are colored by "social identity" are "ameritocratic." Social identity gets in the way when we allow our judgment to be distorted by the skin color or ethnic experience of the person in question, and also when we allow personal relationships to influence us. . . .

The cultural and ideological aspects of my achievements (accomplishments, attainments) aren't separable, for purposes of other's judgment, from the effects of my "individuality" or of my "will." So there's nothing wrong, nothing "derogatory," in judging my work or my promise in a way that is race-conscious and sensitive to my ideological commitments. (Of course, the judgment may be incorrect, and it may be prejudiced.) Third, the judgment process, whose integrity Kennedy's article wants above all to preserve, is always already corrupted by the ideological and cultural factors he wants to exclude. We avoid this only if we deliberately impoverish and trivialize judgment by excluding those very aspects of individuals and their works which legal academics should care most about.

. . .

A. "Individuality" Cannot Be Distinguished from Culture and Ideology

In deciding to hire or promote, it is not unfair to judge the individual on the basis of the social characteristic of connection to a cultural community, because the individual cannot be separated from his or her culture in the way that Kennedy's article requires. The "individual" simply doesn't exist in that way. It is quite reasonable, and I have no cause to complain, if

you expect different things of me, predict different things of me, and make different interpretations and hence different evaluative judgments of what I say, because you know something of my cultural context.

It doesn't derogate from my individuality that you "do this to me." There just isn't "work I do," nor a "me" you can evaluate or about whom you can make reasonable predictions, that isn't embedded in culture. All I can do in response is to reserve the right to argue when I feel that the stereotypes you apply distort your perceptions of my meaning or my capacity.

Second, I wouldn't want my legal scholarship to be evaluated in a color-blind way. Because we do our scholarly work in a context of culturally specific meanings, we are limited as individuals in what we can do and express, even in what we can be understood to say. Yet we are also empowered to do things that are intelligible only because we do them in the particular context. I know that Randy Kennedy is a black American intellectual writing in 1989, so I get much more out of his article than I could if I had to guess at who had written it and when and where.

In an earlier article, "On Cussing Out White Liberals," Kennedy described a style of black protest and critiqued it.[16] "Racial Critiques of Legal Academia" has much the same agenda. I read both articles as written in the cussing-out-black-militants genre, in which a progressive integrationist black author takes black radicals to task. I suspect that I don't pick up on all the subtleties, but because I have a notion that this genre exists, the article has a whole level of coherence for me that it would not otherwise have.

An important rhetorical move in cussing is to begin with denunciations of white racism adequate to refute in advance the accusation of Uncle Tomism. Then comes the central pitch: the militants are using unsubstantiated accusations of white racist discrimination and white cultural bias as lame excuses for their own and the minority community's failure to live up to neutral standards of excellence. All the hot but in the end contentless talk about racial identity is just posturing.

Writers in this genre typically charge that black militant posturing diverts attention from the real problems of minority performance, and that it lays a spurious claim to special treatment from white institutions—a claim that white liberals are all too willing to accept. That acceptance is condescending, because the liberals won't openly apply to what the militants say the same standards of sensible discourse that they apply among themselves or to their white adversaries. This reflects both white liberal wimpiness and an underlying white racist belief that sloppy militant rhetoric is the best that can be expected from black (and Hispanic and Asian) folk.

Kennedy's article falls into the trickiest subspecies of this genre, the one that is concerned with the "academic study of academia." The basic move in this subgenre is to apply the standards the militants are criticizing to the militants' own critique. Neutral standards of scholarly excellence show that the attack on neutral standards of scholarly excellence lacks scholarly excellence. This type of argument can cut to the quick because of the history of racial stereotyping of minorities as intellectually inferior, and because mainstream postsixties political thought dismisses radical minority intellectuals as hysterical second-raters or racists.

I don't think it derogatory to assess Kennedy's article as a performance in this specific genre. The article is more interesting, and also it seems to me better in some ways and worse in others when read as coming from a racial (cultural) and ideological position. The "individual" who wrote it is more accessible when we understand the literary materials he was working with. The danger is that we will confuse the "voice" of the genre with the actual author, whose individuality, as I suggested above, is ungraspable. If we confused the person with the genre in this case, it would be difficult to understand how Randy Kennedy could have written the following:

> In the forties, fifties and early sixties, against the backdrop of laws that used racial distinctions to exclude Negroes from opportunities available to white citizens, it seemed that racial subjugation could be overcome by mandating the application

of race-blind law. In retrospect, however, it appears that the concept of race-blindness was simply a proxy for the fundamental demand that racial subjugation be eradicated. This demand, which matured over time in the face of myriad sorts of opposition, focused upon the condition of racial subjugation; its target was not only procedures that overtly excluded Negroes on the basis of race, but also the self-perpetuating dynamics of subordination that had survived the demise of American apartheid. The opponents of affirmative action have stripped the historical context from the demand of race-blind law. They have fashioned this demand into a new totem and insist on deference to it no matter what its effects upon the very group the fourteenth amendment was created to protect.[17]

Because you know that I am a white American intellectual writing in the nineties, there are a million things I can say in this article without saying them, because you will infer them from this cultural context; and there are a million things you will read in which I didn't mean to be there. I see the interdependence, the inseparability of my individuality and my context as inevitable and also as something to be embraced. Likewise my simultaneous limitation and empowerment by the fact of working in a context. My individuality is not "derogated" when I am judged and when I communicate in a context, though there is bitter with the sweet. The same is true of ideology.

B. Rational Meritocratic Judgment Cannot Be Culturally and Ideologically Neutral

The flipside is that there is no evaluation aimed at getting at what I value in my own work which won't be contingent on your cultural identity. What I am trying to achieve in my work is a contribution to a cultural situation in which I am implicated and culturally specific. This is equally true of the people whose judgment I most value. If I can't be judged outside of my context, they can't judge me outside of their context. This means that no matter how favorable the judgment, I can't take it as "objective." Yet it also means I can criticize critiques and reject their condemnation as "distorted." I don't have to claim or to abandon either universality or context-dependence. I can switch back and forth between the two perspectives, though without any "metalevel" assurance that I'm ever getting it right. All of the above applies to my ideological as well as to my cultural context.

There are a million misunderstandings, based on racial, ideological, national, and temporal stereotypes, to which Randy Kennedy and I are subject because you read us in this context. And because you know what you know of the context, there are good readings of our texts that you may discern against our will. There is nothing we can do about this, except argue on our own behalf.

The argument may involve racism. I see racism as more than "inaccurate stereotyping." It is "neurotic" in the same sense that the fetishizing of merit is; it is insisting on the stereotype's truth because you want or need it to be true, in the face of evidence that the group or a particular member is completely different from what you expected. The racist, whether white or black, won't let you be other than what he or she wants you to be, and that is something bad. However, if you accept that you have a cultural identity, the attack on it can't be dismissed as "just" irrational, in the way it could if all cultural communities were the same, or if the differences between them made no difference.

It might be true that the racist is making a correct negative judgment about something that really is a part of you, but that there is little or nothing you can do about, or it might be true because cultural communities are different, and you have characteristics that are derived from your cultural community. The hatred you encounter is wrong or crazy, as hatred; but there might be, somewhere mixed in with it, a valid negative judgment of your group identity. If you don't think that's so, then even after you have rejected and condemned the crazy hatred dimension, you have to defend the communal aspect of your being on the "merits."

Against this background, it seems to me legitimate and useful for Richard Delgado to attempt an explicitly race-conscious assessment of the white liberal constitutional law scholarship of the seventies and eighties. "Scholars should . . . evaluat[e] other scholars as individuals, without prejudgment, no matter what their

hue,"[18] as Kennedy's article suggests, in the sense of avoiding stereotyping like the plague; but Kennedy's article urges us (somewhat ambiguously) to "keep racial generalizations in their place, including those that are largely accurate."[19]

I don't agree with this if it means that we can't try to figure out whether, for example, a distaste for the "reparations" argument for affirmative action is a characteristic trait of a particular white liberal mode of constitutional law analysis. I see nothing wrong with trying to connect such a trait to the unconscious motives of white liberal scholars as a culturally and ideologically distinct group, or with condemning it as a "defect." It is, for me, not a question of the legitimacy of a type of analysis but of the plausibility of a particular interpretation.

In short, it is legitimate for Delgado to argue for a "linkage of White scholars' racial background to the qualities in their work that he perceives as shortcomings,"[20] so long as he makes his case. Kennedy's article poses a false alternative:

> [T]he point is that distance or nearness to a given subject—"outsiderness" or "insiderness"—are simply social conditions; they provide opportunities that intellectuals are free to use or squander, but they do not in themselves determine the intellectual quality of scholarly productions—that depends on what a particular scholar makes of his or her materials, regardless of his or her social position.[21]

Cultural and ideological situations are neither "simply social conditions" (in the sense of "inert matter") nor attributes that "determine . . . intellectual quality." They are betwixt and between: they are "formative" rather than "inert" or "determining." And this is the premise of Kennedy's own article, the first section of which is "The Cultural Context of Racial Critiques."

In that section, the article argues that the racial critiques "share an intellectual kinship with several well-known and influential intellectual traditions." We learn that we can't "understand" the racial critiques except in the context of "the ongoing effort by intellectuals of color to control the public image of minority groups." In the sections entitled, "The Racial

Exclusion Claim as a Form of Politics" and "The Politics of Publicity," Kennedy's article assesses the arguments of Bell, Delgado, and Matsuda as the arguments of scholars of color. Their claims have "an outer facet addressed principally to whites and an inner facet addressed principally to minorities."

He then proceeds to analyze the bad motives (guilt-tripping white liberals and cheerleading for minorities) behind their arguments in a way that seems indistinguishable from what Delgado did with the white liberal constitutional law scholars. His attribution of motives is a complex inference from their texts, but also from his knowledge that they are scholars of color who are writing in the radical intellectual tradition he has identified and pursuing a particular political (ideological) project.

Imagine that Kennedy's article shows up in the file of Professor Bell, Matsuda, or Delgado when one of them is being considered for a lateral appointment. The article would certainly be read as an assessment of the "merit" of their scholarship but hardly as applying a "standard that is indifferent to the social identity of a given author." Wouldn't it, using Kennedy's criterion, "derogate from [their] individuality ... insofar as their unique characteristics are submerged in the image of the group to which they are deemed to belong"? Indeed, one might argue that the article "stereotypes" them as "militants of color" in order to cuss them out for the sins of the Black Panthers and the black sociology movement of the sixties.

Of course, it is not unimaginable that any of the racial critique articles could have been written by a white. In that case, it seems likely that Kennedy's article would have leveled many of the same criticisms against the white author, but omitted some and added others. Kennedy's article asserts that "some observers do not have much confidence in the abilities, or perhaps even the capacities, of minority intellectuals. . . . [T]hey lack the sense that those with whom they disagree are their intellectual equals." If Bell, Matsuda, or Delgado were white, Kennedy might critique the "merit" of their discussions of minority scholarship through the observation that "[s]ometimes observers display their low-

ered expectations . . . by more generously praising work by minorities than they would praise similar work by whites."

My point is not to censure Kennedy's article for "race-conscious" assessment of merit; it is, rather, that if one wants to take work like theirs seriously, as he does, it just is not possible to make the rigid separation he proposes between the authors' merely accidental or inherited aspects and their "will" or "achievement" as "individuals." Kennedy is wrong to claim that the cultural background (race) and ideological affiliations of an author "have nothing to do with the intellectual characteristics of the subject being judged."[22]

Since it is legal scholarship and law teaching that is in question, culture and ideology (mediated through intellectual paradigms and research projects) permeate the subject being judged. It is about how our culturally diverse and ideologically divided society should be organized. We can achieve color-blind neutrality and ideological neutrality only if we refuse to assess these aspects. Kennedy's article proposes (his own practice to the contrary notwithstanding) to judge the work without considering its subject and purpose. This is an evasion of politics.[23] . . .

V. CONCLUSION

IF there is a conceptual theme to this article, it is that of "positionality," or "situatedness." The individual in his or her culture, the individual as a practitioner of an ideology, the individual in relation to his or her own neurotic structures, is always somewhere, has always just been somewhere else, and is empowered and limited by being in that spot on the way from some other spot. Communities are like that too, though in a complicated way. One of the things that defines a community's position—its situation, and the specific possibilities that go with it—is its history of collective accomplishment. Another is its history of crimes against humanity. It seems unlikely that there are communities without such histories.

The crime of slavery is deep in the past of white America. Ever since slavery, though, in each succeeding decade after the Emancipation Proclamation, we have added new crimes until it sometimes seems that the weight of commission and omission lies so heavily on nonwhite America that there just isn't anything that anyone can do about it. All anyone can hope is to be out of the way of the whirlwind, both the big one and all the little ones played out in day-to-day life.

The bad history also creates opportunities that other communities don't have, or have in different ways. It would be quite something to build a multicultural society on the basis of what has happened here, where we have neither a consensual foundation in history nor a myth of human benevolence to make it all seem natural. An American multicultural society will arise out of guilt, anger, mistrust, cynicism, bitter conflict, and a great deal of confusion and contradiction—if it arises at all—and it would be, to my mind, the more wonderful for it.

Of course, the specific proposal put forth above, for a kind of cultural proportional representation in the exercise of ideological power through legal academia, would be a very small step in that direction. As is true of any very specific proposal that can be implemented right now by small numbers of people holding local power, it is a drop in the bucket. However, the minute we imagine it as a government policy applied in a consistent way across the whole range of situations to which it is arguably applicable, it loses most of its appeal. First, none of us local powerholders could do much to bring it about, and, second, taking the proposal seriously as state policy might lead to all kinds of disastrous unintended side effects.

This has been a proposal for drops in the bucket, not for the reorganization of state power. If it made a trivial contribution at vast social cost, we could abandon it as we adopted it, faculty by faculty, decision by decision. If it worked, the "kerplunk" of drops falling in nearby empty buckets might cause others to prick up their ears. In any case, legal academics can and should exercise their power to govern themselves in accordance with the ideals of democracy and intellectual integrity—ideals

that white supremacy compromises all around us.

NOTES

1. R. Kennedy, "Racial Critiques of Legal Academia," 102 *Harv. L. Rev.*, 1745 (1989).

2. *Id.* at 1807.

3. *Id.*

4. *Id.*

5. "Independently of 'merit' " means regardless of whether the candidates in question would be hired or promoted if the law schools applied their current standards without taking affirmative action goals into account. I put the word "merit" in quotation marks because, in my twenty years as a law school faculty member, I have quite consistently found myself voting "on the merits," without regard to affirmative action, for minority teaching candidates who did not get the job and against white candidates who did. This means that I disagree with my own school's institutional application of the merit standard before we even get to questions of affirmative action. Extensive indirect exposure to hiring and promotion decisions at a range of other schools suggests to me that they are not different. I would say that most law school faculties give too much weight to paper credentials, overvalue old-boy connections, make bad intuitive judgments based on interviews, and tend to misevaluate the substantive quality of presentations and written work when applying formally color-blind standards.

6. The tone of Kennedy's article is unrelentingly hostile to the "racial distinctiveness" thesis but surprisingly unhelpful in assessing it. He writes as if it must mean either that there is a single minority or black or Hispanic "voice," or that anything any minority person says is said in a minority voice. He suggests (note the irony) that we should develop a definition of what a meritorious black voice is, and then apply color-blind criteria in judging whether candidates have it, or that we should just abandon the idea altogether. See R. Kennedy, *supra* note 1, at 1802–3. As indicated in the text following this note, the issue seems to me a good deal more complicated than his position makes it seem.

7. Randall Kennedy—like, I think, most others of his camp, is not willing to go that far. At a number of points, his article recognizes, tentatively, one might even say grudgingly, that the groups that make up our society have differing characteristics, and that under some circumstances it might make sense to take them into account: "[E]ven taking into account class, gender, and other divisions, there might remain an irreducible link of commonality in the experience of people of color: rich or poor, male or female, learned or ignorant, all people of color are to some degree 'outsiders' in a society that is intensely color-conscious and in which the hegemony of whites is overwhelming;" *id.* at 1784. Further: "I do not maintain that no appreciable differences exist in the prevailing opinions and

sensibilities of various racial groups. Nor do I maintain that it is improper ever to make decisions based on racial generalizations;" *id.* at 1816 (footnote omitted). See also *id.* at 1805 n. 271 (noting that in some cases the "fact of being black—like that of being tall, being able to see, or simply being alive—may help one to accomplish something admirable"). There is black literature, music, film, in the sense of contributions of individuals who happen to be black (*id.* at 1758–59), but no "black art" in a stronger sense (*id.* at 1803 and n. 262). There are patterns of behavior and particular opinions (for example, opposition to the death penalty; *id.* at 1816) that characterize one ethnic subculture more than another. It is even true that "racial and other ascriptive loyalties continue to organize a great deal of social, political and intellectual life throughout the world; in many areas such loyalties have intensified;" *id.* at 1782, (emphasis added, footnote omitted). When talking about the production of academic knowledge, the article places the burden of proof on the person who would assert that membership in a defined community is associated with a particular way of knowing or with particular intellectual strengths or weaknesses. The crucial question in the debate about standards is: "But what, as a function of race, is 'special' or 'distinct' about the scholarship of minority legal academics? Does it differ discernibly in ways attributable to race from work produced by white scholars? If so, in what ways and to what degree is the work of colored intellectuals different from or better than the work of whites? . . . [A]t least with respect to legal scholarship, [Matsuda] fails to show the newness of the 'new knowledge' and the difference that distinguishes the 'different voices;'" *id.* at 1778–79. It seems to me unlikely that we will get far by trying to resolve the substantive dispute by the placement of the burden of proof. If we take the idea of proof seriously, then whoever bears the burden will lose. The decision to allocate the burden to one side or the other is no less ideological than a decision on the merits.

8. I am referring here to the century-and-a-half-long discussion about the character of African-American identity and its implications for strategy. The debate involves famous pairs, among them Martin Delany, see *The Condition, Elevation, Emigration, and Destiny of the Colored People of the United States* (1852); and Frederick Douglass, see *My Bondage and My Freedom* (1855); Booker T. Washington, see *The Future of the American Negro* (1899); and W. E. B. Du Bois, see *The Souls of Black Folk* (1903); on Marcus Garvey, see E. Cronon, *Black Moses: The Story Marcus Garvey and the Universal Negro Improvement Association* (1957); and the later W. E. B. Du Bois, see *Dusk of Dawn: An Essay Toward an Autobiography of a Race Concept* (1940); E. Franklin Frazier, see *Black Bourgeoisie* (1957); and Harold Cruse, see *The Crisis of the Negro Intellectual* (1967); Malcolm X see with A. Haley, *The Autobiography of Malcolm X* (1965), and Martin Luther King, Jr., see J. Washington, ed., *A Testament of Hope: The Essential Writings of Martin Luther King, Jr.*, (1986). This list is just an appetizer. The primary and secondary literatures are enormous. A valuable summary and reinterpretation is C. West, "The Four Traditions of Response," in *Prophesy Deliverance!: An Afro-Ameri-*

can Revolutionary Christianity, 69 (1982). See also R. Allen, *Black Awakening in Capitalist America: An Analytic History* (1969). For an extensive collection of sources, see Peller, *supra* note 1.

9. See T. Sowell, *Markets and Minorities* (1981) and *Race and Economics* (1975). For a progressive critique of Sowell, see K. Crenshaw, "Race, Reform and Retrenchment," 101 *Harv. L. Rev.*, 1331, 1339–46 (1988) [the essay is included in this volume—ED].

10. See W. Wilson, *The Truly Disadvantaged: The Inner City, the Underclass, and Public Policy* (1987), and *The Declining Significance of Race?: A Dialogue among Black and White Social Scientists* (1978); see R. Kennedy, *supra* note 1, 3 at 1814 n. 296.

11. For a classic statement of the conflict, see Z. N. Hurston, *Their Eyes Were Watching God* (1937). See generally P. Giddings, *When and Where I Enter: The Impact of Black Women on Race and Sex in America* (1984); b. hooks, *Ain't I a Woman: Black Women and Feminism* (1981); see also L. Rainwater and W. Yancey, *The Moynihan Report and the Politics of Controversy* (1967); H. Cheatham and J. Stewart, *Black Families: Interdisciplinary Perspectives* (1990).

12. Derrick Bell's point of view has always contained elements of nationalism—particularly his writing on school desegregation. Bell, "Serving Two Masters: Integration Ideals and Client Interests in School Desegregation Litigation," 85 *Yale L. J.* 470 (1976) (educational improvement for blacks must take precedence over failed integration policies) [the essay is included in this volume—ED]; Bell, "The Burden of *Brown* on Blacks: History-Based Observations on a Landmark Decision," 7 *N.C. Cent. L. J.*, 25, 26 (1975) (recognizing *Brown*'s limitations and arguing that it should be used as "critical leverage for a wide range of [continuing] efforts" by black communities to improve education for blacks). The debate is internal to Bell's book *And We Are Not Saved*, *supra* note 4. With the publication of the articles cited in *supra* notes 4 and 5, and the response in R. Kennedy, *supra* note 1, the issue seems finally to have its own momentum within legal scholarship. On black feminism in law, see K. Crenshaw, "Demarginalizing the Intersection of Race and Sex: A Black Feminist Critique of Antidiscrimination Doctrine, Feminist Theory and Antiracist Politics," 1989 *U. Chi. Legal Forum*, 139; Harris, "Rose and Essentialism in Feminist Legal Theory," 42 *Standard Law Review* 581 (1990).

13. For example, compare R. Rodriguez, *Hunger of Memory: The Education of Richard Rodriguez* (1982) with A. Mirandé, *Gringo Justice* (1987).

14. These include his remarks on the use of the racial distinctiveness thesis by the Nazis, among others. *See supra* note 1, at 1789, n. 197. He also discusses the possibility that using race as an "intellectual credential" will backfire and harm minorities. *See id.* at 1796.

15. R. Kennedy, *supra* note 1, at 1804 (citing R. Ellison, *Shadow and Act* 146 (1972)).

16. *Nation*, September 4, 1982, at 169.

17. R. Kennedy, "Persuasion and Distrust: A Comment on the Affirmative Action Debate," 89 *Harvard Law Review* 1685 (1976), at 1335-36.

18. R. Kennedy, *supra* note 1, at 1796; *see also* "Argument as Character," 40 *Stanford Law Review* 869 (1988).

19. *Id.* at 1796.

20. R. Kennedy, *supra* note 1 at 1793. (commenting on Delgado, "Imperial Scholar: Reflections on a Review of Civil Rights Literature," 132 *University of Pennsylvania Law Review* 561 (1984).

21. R. Kennedy, *supra* note 1, at 1795.

22. R. Kennedy, *supra* note 1, at 1807.

23. Kennedy remonstrates that he does not seek to evade politics. He quotes Lionel Trilling with approval: "[O]ur fate, for better or worse, is political. It is therefore not a happy fate, even if it has an heroic sound, but there is no escape from it, and the only possibility of enduring it is to force into our definition of politics every human activity and every subtlety of human activity. There are manifest dangers in doing this, but greater dangers in not doing it;" *id.* at 1787 n. 191, quoting L. Trilling, *The Liberal Imagination*, 96 (1950).

❦

TRANSLATING "YONNONDIO" BY PRECEDENT AND EVIDENCE: THE MASHPEE INDIAN CASE

Gerald Torres and Kathryn Milun

I.

A song, a poem of itself—the word itself a dirge,
Amid the wilds, the rocks, the storm and wintry
*   night,*
To me such misty, strange tableaux the syllables
*   calling up . . .*

—Walt Whitman, "Yonnondio"

. . . When Walt Whitman wrote his poem "Yonnondio" for the collection *Leaves of Grass*, he added the following parenthetical explanation under the title: "The sense of the word is lament for the aborigines. It is an Iroquois term; and has been used for a personal name."[1] In fact, "Yonnondio" also is the title of a long narrative poem by William H. C. Hosmer, published in 1844, with the subtitle "Warriors of the Genesee: A Tale of the Seventeenth Century."[2] That poem, Hosmer wrote, is a description of "the memorable attempt of the Marquis de Nonville, under pretext of preventing an interruption of the French trade, to plant the standard of Louis XIV in the beautiful country of the Senecas."[3] In a note following the poem itself, Hosmer explained that "Yonnondio" was a title originally given by the Five Nations to M. de Montmagny, but became a style of address in their treaties, by which succeeding Governor Generals of New France were designated."[4]

It is easy to understand that Whitman took "Yonnondio" to signify "Lament for the Aborigines"; if "Yonnondio" is indeed the word the Iroquois used to address the state, then as Whitman says in his poem, its mere mention "is itself a dirge." For the Iroquois, "Yonnondio" itself took on new meaning as the relation to which it referred shifted. Even as the word became a greeting, its meaning was different for the Iroquois than for the French and other Europeans with whom the Iroquois had contact. This cascade of meanings reflects the highly volatile system of relations produced by contact between the Iroquois and the various Europeans intent on "opening up" or "claiming" the "New World." . . .

The telling of stories plays an important role in the work of courts. Within a society, there are specific places where most of the activities that make up social life within the society simultaneously are represented, contested, and inverted. Courts are such places: like mirrors, they reflect where we are, from a space where we are not. Law, the mechanism through which courts carry out this mirroring function, has a curious way of recording a culture's practices of telling and listening to its stories. Such stories enter legal discourse in an illustrative, even exemplary fashion.

"Yonnondio"—the address, the salutation— became a medium through which contending Indian and European cultures interacted. The evolving meaning of this salutation reflected changing relations of power as the Indians' early contact with European explorers themselves evolved into contact with the states represented by those explorers. Likewise, the land claim suits filed by various tribes during the seventies served as a channel through which some Indians attempted to communicate with the state—this time through the medium of courts. In order for the state to hear these claims, however, these Indians were forced to speak in a formalized idiom of the language of the state—the idiom of legal discourse. This paper analyzes one such land claim suit, *Mashpee Tribe v. Town of Mashpee*[5] and the formalized address that it incorporated. What happens, we ask, when such claims receive a legal hearing? We suggest that first they must be translated by means of examples that law can follow (precedent), and examples that law can hear (evidence).

We should suspect that the legal coding through which such translation is conducted highlights a problem inherent in the postmodern condition—the confrontation between irreconcilable systems of meaning produced by two contending cultures. The postmodern condition is a crisis of faith in the grand stories that have justified our history and legitimized our knowledge. The very idea of what we can know is unstable. The crisis in the law which emerged with the Legal Realists and the attempts to reconstitute formalism—as the basis for survival of the "rule of law"—also reflect our postmodern condition. In the case of the Mashpee, the systems of meaning are irreconcilable: the politics of historical domination reduced the Mashpee to having to petition their "guardian" to allow them to exist, and the history of that domination has determined in large measure the ways the Mashpee must structure their petitions. The conflict between these systems of meaning—that of the Mashpee and that of the state—is really the question of how can we "know" which history is most "true."

Yet the difficulty facing the Mashpee in this case is not just that they cannot find the proper "language" with which to tell their story or capture the essence of the examples which would prove their claims. The problem with conflicting systems of meaning is that there is a history and social practice reflected and contained within the language chosen. To require a particular way of telling a story not only strips away nuances of meaning, but also elevates a particular version of events to a noncontingent status. More than that, however, when particular versions of events are rendered unintelligible, the corresponding counterexamples those versions represent lose their legitimacy: they come unglued from both the cultural structure that grounds them and the legal structure that would validate them. The existence of untranslatable examples renders unreadable the entire code of which they are a part, while simultaneously legitimizing the resulting ignorance. This essay examines the nature of that ignorance.

"Ignorant," of course, merely means uninformed. The central problem addressed by this essay is whether the limitations of the legal idiom permit one party truly to inform the other, or conversely, whether the dimension of power hidden in the idiomatic structure of legal storytelling forecloses one version in favor of another. Note that this essay is not the story of "different voices."

When you are powerless, you don't just speak differently. A lot, you don't speak. Your speech is not just differently articulated, it is silenced—eliminated, gone. You aren't just deprived of a language with which to articulate your distinctiveness, although you are; you are deprived of a life out of which articulation might come.[6]

The law does not permit the Mashpee's story to be particularized and yet to remain legally intelligible. By imposing specific "ethnolegal" categories such as "tribe" on the Mashpee, law universalizes their story; this universalizing process eliminates differences the dominant culture perceives as destabilizing. Criticism of the imposition of cultural-legal categories on subcultures should not, however, be used to fetishize the idea of difference. Instead, the inability of the law to hear, or equally to weight, culturally divergent versions of "the truth" should be examined to help us understand how social knowledge is constructed.

Similarly, a recounting of the Mashpee's travails in their attempt to tell their story does not yield an object lesson in the open texture of American pluralism. Some versions of reality are foreclosed, plain and simple. The legal boundaries made apparent in the Mashpee's story require that they remain frozen in time: cultural evolution itself is prohibited for the Mashpee.

This essay examines the nature of "telling" within the confines of litigation. What constitutes proof and what constitutes authority? What are the pragmatics of "legal" storytelling? Pragmatics in this context might be analyzed best in terms of a game. Any game must have rules to determine what is an acceptable move, but the rules do not determine all available moves. Although the total content of acceptable moves is not predetermined, the universe of potentially permissible moves is limited necessarily by the structure of the game. All language, but especially technical language, is a kind of game. What rules govern discourse in the legal idiom? What kind of knowledge is transmitted? "[W]hat must one say in order to be heard, what must one listen to in order to speak, and what role must one play . . . to be the object of a narrative[?]"[7]

By highlighting the peculiar nature of legal discourse and comparing it to other ways of telling and reading the Mashpee's history, we can explore and make concrete the roles of power and politics in legal rationality. The Mashpee case is especially well suited to this investigation because it casts so starkly the problem of law as an artifact of culture and power. . . . The choices contained in the structure of law applied to the Mashpee case permitted only a limited kind of cultural vision, one from the perspective of the dominant culture. A pluralistic conception of justice may require the incorporation of those conflicting views, but law, in this instance, may not be where justice is found.

II.

A. Looking Back at Indians and Indians Looking Back: The Case

In 1976 in *Mashpee Tribe v. Town of Mashpee*,[8] the Indian community at Mashpee on Cape Cod sued to recover tribal lands alienated from them over the last two centuries in violation of the Indian Non-Intercourse Act of 1790.[9] The Non-Intercourse Act prohibits the transfer of Indian tribal land to non-Indians without approval of the federal government. The tribe claimed its land had been taken from it, between 1834 and 1870, without the required federal consent: according to the Mashpee, the Commonwealth of Massachusetts had permitted the land to be sold to non-Indians and had transferred common Indian lands to the Town of Mashpee. The defendant, Town of Mashpee, answered by denying that the plaintiffs, Mashpee, were a tribe. Therefore, they were outside the protection of the act and were without standing to sue.

As a result, the Mashpee first had to prove that they were indeed a "tribe"; a forty-day trial ensued on that threshold issue. The Mashpee were required to demonstrate their tribal existence in accordance with a definition adopted by the United States Supreme Court at the turn of the century in *Montoya v. United States:* "By a 'tribe' we understand a body of Indians of the same or a similar race, united in a community under one leadership or government, and inhabiting a particular though sometimes ill-defined territory. . . ." This is a very narrow and particular definition.

Judge Skinner agreed to allow expert testimony from various social scientists regarding the definition of "Indian tribe." By the closing days of the trial, however, the judge had become frustrated with the lack of consensus as to a definition. . . . In the end, he instructed the jury that the Mashpee had to meet the requirements of Montoya—rooted in notions of racial purity, authoritarian leadership, and consistent territorial occupancy—in order to establish their tribal identity, despite the fact that Montoya itself did not address the Non-Intercourse Act.

The case providing the key definition, *Montoya,* involved a company whose livestock had been taken by a group of Indians. The company sued the United States and the tribe to which the group allegedly belonged under the Indian Depredation Act.[10] This act provided compensation to persons whose property was destroyed by Indians belonging to a tribe. The theory underlying tribal liability is that the tribe should be responsible for the actions of its members; the issue in *Montoya* was whether the wrongdoers were still part of the tribe. The court found they were not.

Beyond reflecting archaic notions of tribal existence in general, the *Montoya* requirements incorporated specific perceptions regarding race, leadership, community, and territory which were entirely alien to Mashpee culture. The testimony revealed the *Montoya* criteria as generalized ethnological categories that failed to capture the specifics of what it means to belong to the Mashpee people. Because of this disjunction between the ethnolegal categories and the Mashpee's lived experience, the tribe's testimony and evidence never quite "signified" within the idiom established by the precedent. After forty days of testimony, the jury came up with the following "irrational" decision: The Mashpee were not a tribe in 1790, were a tribe in 1834 and 1842, but again were not a tribe in 1869 and 1870. The jury's finding was "irrational" because the judge had instructed them that if they concluded that the Mashpee had ever

relinquished their tribal status they could not regain it. Based on the jury's findings, the trial court dismissed the Mashpee's claim.

The Mashpee immediately challenged the trial court's dismissal on several grounds. The tribe argued that the jury verdict presumed it had disbanded voluntarily at some point—a presumption the tribe alleged had never been proven. Further, the tribe alleged that the verdict was entirely inconsistent with the trial court's instruction that once the jury found tribal existence ceased at a given time, it could not find the tribe existed again at a later date. The First Circuit rejected the Mashpee's assignment of error and affirmed the trial court's decision to dismiss their claim. The United States Supreme Court subsequently denied the tribe's petition for certiorari, allowing the First Circuit's decision to stand.

III.

A. The Baked and the Half-Baked . . .
Whether the Mashpee are legally a tribe is, of course, only half the question. That the Mashpee existed as a recognized people occupying a recognizable territory for well over three hundred years is a well-documented fact. In order to ascertain the meaning of that existence, however, an observer must ask not only what categories are used to describe it but also whether the categories adopted by the observer carry the same meaning to the observed.

The earliest structure used for communal Mashpee functions—a colonial-style building that came to be known as "the Old Meetinghouse"—was built in 1684.[11] The meetinghouse was built by a white man, Shearjashub Bourne, as a place where the Mashpee could conduct their Christian worship. Shearjashub's father, Richard Bourne, had preached to the Mashpee and oversaw their conversion to Christianity almost a generation earlier. The Bourne family's early interest in the Mashpee later proved propitious: the elder Bourne arranged for a deed to be issued to the Mashpee to "protect" their interest in the land they occupied. Confirmation of this deed by the General Court of Plymouth Colony in 1671 served as the foundation for including "Mashpee Plantation" within the protection of the Massachusetts Bay Colony. As part of the colony, the Mashpee were assured that their spiritual interests, as defined by their Christian overseers, as well as their temporal interests, would receive official attention. However, the impact of introducing the symbology of property deeds into the Mashpee's cultural structure reverberates to this day. Whether the introduction of European notions of private ownership into Mashpee society can be separated from either the protection the colonial overseers claim actually was intended or from the Mashpee's ultimate undoing, is of course, central to the meaning of "ownership."

Colonial oversight quickly became a burden. In 1760, the Mashpee appealed directly to King George III for relief from their British overlords. In 1763, their petition was granted: The Mashpee Plantation received a new legal designation, granting the "proprietors the right to elect their own overseers."[12] This change in the tribe's relationship with its newly arrived white neighbors did not last long, however. With the coming of the Colonies' war against England and the founding of the Commonwealth of Massachusetts, all previous protections of Mashpee land predicated on British rule quickly were repealed, and the tribe was subjected to a new set of overseers with even more onerous authority than its colonial lords had held. The new protectors were granted "oppressive powers over the inhabitants, including the right to lease their lands, to sell timber from their forests, and to hire out their children to labor."[13]

During this time, the Mashpee were on their way toward becoming the mélange of "racial types" that ultimately would bring about their legal demise two hundred years later. Colonists had taken Mashpee wives, many of whom were widows whose husbands had died fighting against the British. The Wampanoags, another southern Massachusetts tribe that suffered terrible defeat in wars with the European colonists, had retreated and had been taken in by the Mashpee; Hessian soldiers had intermarried with the Mashpee; runaway slaves took refuge with the tribe and married Mashpee Indians. The Mashpee became members of a "mixed" race, and the names some of the Mashpee

carried reflected this mixture. What was clear to the Mashpee, if not to outside observers, was that this mixing did not dilute their tribal status because they defined themselves not according to racial type but rather by membership in their community. In an essay on the Mashpee in *The Predicament of Culture*,[14] Professor Clifford explained that despite the racial mixing that had historically occurred in the Mashpee community, since the tribe did not measure tribal membership according to "blood," Indian identity remained paramount. In fact, the openness to outsiders who wished to become part of the tribal community was part of the community values that contributed to tribal identity. Thus, the Mashpee were being penalized for maintaining their aboriginal traditions because they did not conform to the prevailing "racial" definition of community and society.

In 1833, a series of events began that culminated in the partial restoration of traditional Mashpee "rights." William Apes, an Indian preacher who claimed to be descended from King Philip, a Wampanoag chief, stirred the Mashpee to petition their overseers and the governor of Massachusetts for relief from the depredation visited upon them. What offended Apes was the appropriation of the Mashpee's worshiping ground by white Christians. In response to the imposition of a white Christian minister on their congregation, they had abandoned the meetinghouse in favor of an outdoor service conducted by a fellow Indian. The petition Apes helped to draft began, "we, as a Tribe, will rule ourselves, and have the right to do so, for all men are born free and equal, says the Constitution of the country."[15] What is particularly important about this challenge is that it asserted independence within the context of the laws of the State of Massachusetts. The governor rejected this appeal, and the Mashpee's attempt at unilateral enforcement of their claims resulted in the arrest and conviction of Apes.[16]

The appeal of Apes's conviction, however, produced a partial restoration of the tribe's right of self-governance and full restoration of its right to religious self-determination, for the tribe was returned to its meetinghouse. When the white former minister tried to intervene, he was removed forcibly and a new lock was installed on the meetinghouse doors. By 1840, the Mashpee's right to worship was secured.[17]

Control of the land remained a critical issue for the Mashpee. By late in the seventeenth century, the area surrounding the homes and land of the "South Sea Indians" had been consolidated and organized into a permanent Indian plantation. The Mashpee's relationship to this land, however, remained legally problematic for the commonwealth: in 1842, Massachusetts determined that the land was to be divided among individual Mashpee tribe members, but their power over it was closely circumscribed—they could sell it only to other members of the tribe. The "plantation" could tax the land, but the land could not be taken for nonpayment of those taxes. In 1859, a measure was proposed to permit the Mashpee to sell land to outsiders and to make the Mashpee "full citizens" of the commonwealth. This proposal was rejected by the tribe's governing council. In 1870, however, the Mashpee were "granted" rights to alienate their property as "full-fledged citizens," and their land was organized by fiat into the town of Mashpee.

It was the land that had moved out of Indian control, eleven thousand acres of undeveloped land estimated to be worth fifty million dollars, that the Mashpee Wampanoag Tribal Council sued to reclaim in 1976. Some of the land had been lost in the intervening years, and more was in danger of being lost or reduced to nonexclusive occupancy. The council based its claim on the Non-Intercourse Act, which prohibits the alienation of Indian lands without federal approval. The act applies to transactions between Indians and non-Indians, and, despite its inherent paternalism, serves to protect tribal integrity.

However, the Non-Intercourse Act applied only if the Mashpee had retained their "tribal identity" (defined, however, by the white man's rules of the game) from the mid-seventeenth century until they filed their land claim action in 1976. In order to fall within the scope of the act's protection, the Mashpee had to prove first that they were indeed a "tribe," and that their

status as such had not changed throughout this period. If the Mashpee were no longer a "tribe" (or if they never had constituted a "tribe" in the first place), the protection provided by the act evaporated. If, however, the Indians retained their tribal status, then the transactions that resulted in the loss of their village were invalid. At the very heart of the dispute was whether the Mashpee were "legally" a people and thus entitled to legal protection.

Many of the facts underlying the Mashpee's suit were not disputed. What the parties fought about was the meaning of "what happened." Seen from the perspective of the Mashpee, the facts that defined the Indians as a tribe also invalidated the transactions divesting them of their lands. From the perspective of the property owners in the town, however, those same acts proved that the Mashpee no longer existed as a separate people. How, then, is an appropriate perspective to be chosen? As told by the defendants, the Mashpee's story was one about "a small, mixed community fighting for equality and citizenship while abandoning, by choice or coercion, most of its aboriginal heritage."[18]

Using the same evidence, the plaintiffs told a very different story. It was the story of cultural survival: "[T]he residents of Mashpee had managed to keep alive a core of Indian identity over three centuries against enormous odds. They had done so in supple, sometimes surreptitious ways, always attempting to control, not reject, outside influences."[19] Which of the two conflicting perspectives is the "proper" one from which to assess the facts underlying the Mashpee's claim? The answers provided by the courts that considered their claims exemplify both the use and abuse of examples in American law. As the next section illustrates, the exemplary nature of legal argument is bounded by the rules that control the substantive demonstration of the issues in dispute, as well as by the authoritative use of previously decided cases. Demonstration and authority are two ways in which examples are used to structure legal understanding. Yet the choice of examples is not a neutral process; it always involves adoption of a substantive perspective. The abuse of example arises when the substantive perspective that is authoritatively adopted is treated as though it arose naturally.

IV.

. . . A. Exempli Gratia

Two closely related kinds of examples seem to be at work in legal discourse. First, there is the authoritative example—that which determines whether or not one may proceed toward obtaining a legal remedy for a perceived injustice. Precedent, even in the context of our statutory age, is the cardinal manifestation of the authoritative example. A statute such as the Non-Intercourse Act may be a source of law, but courts, using a variety of common law techniques, ultimately determine the meaning of that statute. The role of authoritative examples thus is twofold, specifying the outer limits of a particular legal pronouncement and, at the same time, establishing a foundation for subsequent interpretations of those limits. This bifurcated function allows legal authority to appear as though it were timeless. The example from the past is merged with a new example from the present: linearity is redefined as simultaneity. The past is always present in the form of the authoritative example. Precedents accumulate as a "present body of law," but the fact of accumulation leaves the body forever present yet forever incomplete.

The second kind of example at work in legal discourse might be labeled "explanatory." An explanatory example is a statement or exhibit, either real or interpretive, taken as evidence of the sufficiency of a legal claim. In contrast to authoritative examples, which govern whether or not a particular legal claim can be pursued at all, explanatory examples "flesh out" legal claims, giving them substance within the confines established by the controlling authoritative example. Explanatory examples must be constructed to showcase the reality being tested by a given legal claim in terms recognized by the governing authoritative examples. Explanatory examples may both give meaning to the facts that underlie a legal claim and provide a basis for distinguishing that claim from apparently relevant, but undesirable, authoritative examples.

There are, of course, rules governing the use of either type of example. The essence of these rules is the predictive power they yield. Their predictive value resides in their power to inform legal actors how a given dispute will be resolved. However, the rules themselves are absolutely determinative only of the actual dispute to which they are applied—hence, their predictive potential necessarily involves something of a gamble. When seeking an authoritative example, an attorney or a judge always must determine at the outset whether the facts of some previously resolved dispute are sufficiently similar to the controversy at issue to dictate how the parties to that controversy ought to be treated. In order to make such a determination, the judge or attorney must closely examine the factual setting of the prior case—the legal precedent serving as authoritative example—for similarity, difference, and importance relative to the present dispute.

In a system that uses previously decided cases as the foundation for authoritative statements, at least two questions of fact are central to resolving a given dispute. First, what facts may be recognized as proof of the legal claim? Second, what facts are recognized as legally determinative in the search for an authoritative example—in short, what facts count in this search? Determining which facts are critical and which interpretation of the facts is most like the authoritative interpretation is a continuing process. The translation of the raw material of life into legally cognizable claims is at the heart of the lawyer's art, but like any other extremely stylized art form, the artist's creativity is constrained by the structure of the project.

The centrality of the meaning of facts, in the sense of "what happened," recurs constantly. From precedent we get two additional kinds of examples: first, the example of authoritative fact patterns, and second, the example of authoritative interpretations of those fact patterns. Judicial opinions typically begin with a statement of the facts in dispute. The statement usually presages the conclusion, but the precedential import of the facts changes as the meaning of the case changes over time. The simple conclusion that a court reached may not be the proposition for which the case is cited. The conclusory factual statement ultimately loses its mooring in the specific case. Thus, which facts are authoritative will change as the case is made to fit into an evolving system of relations that gives it meaning. In cases in which different courts try to answer the same legal question, creating or discovering a set of authoritative interpretations lies at the heart of the attorney's task. These interpretations must be used to frame the raw material of a given case so as to suggest it is sufficiently similar to previous cases or to some articulated statutory standard in order to justify a court's listening to the claim and subsequently granting the desired relief. . . .

Intuitively, one assumes that everything potentially helpful to telling the story behind a given legal claim ought to be allowed as part of the explanation. The reality of the legal process requires, however, that the story be told in accordance with a set of rules developed to protect the integrity of a subsequent decision as precedent or authoritative example. Further, the rules that limit notions of relevance to the authoritative commands also guide the structuring of the presentation.

B. The Rules of the Game: Telling a "Relevant" Story

The rules governing how one tells a story in court are supposed to protect the court from wasting its time by listening to immaterial information or testimony that might confuse or prejudice the ultimate decision-makers about what they are supposed to be deciding. These rules turn on the legal concept of "relevance."

Typically, a legal claim is composed of elements that must each be proven independently. "Relevant" evidence is a statement or exhibit that tends to demonstrate the relationship between a factual assertion and a particular element of a legal claim. According to the *Federal Rules of Evidence,* " 'Relevant evidence' means evidence having any tendency to make the existence of any fact that is of consequence to the determination of the action more probable or less probable than it would be without the evidence." [20] Thus relevance, the foundation for

rules permitting the introduction of evidence, controls and is controlled by the existence of other facts, which themselves are controlled by the substantive standard or statute being litigated. Relevance is the guide, but the question remains: Relevant to what? Treating relevance as though it were a neutral analytic category takes our attention away from the substantive standard being disputed because it requires the judge making the relevance determination to treat the substantive standard as a given. In cases like *Mashpee,* the underlying standard is often the heart of the dispute. Reread the definition. Relevance is a probability determination. The judge is to ask herself, "If I let this evidence in, will it add any probitive value to the facts we already know?" This inquiry begs the question of whether the "facts" already admitted are those that ought to be in.

The legal concept of relevance empowers a court to approve or disapprove certain narrative elements of a party's story. A court's evidentiary rulings, however, do not control truth but, rather, translate it into the terms of the substantive statute or standard at issue. The truth value of a particular fact within the confines of legal discourse, therefore, is directly related to whether it explicates the substantive claim being adjudicated. The issue being litigated is the measure of truth. Remember Judge Skinner's frustration at the testimony of the various "experts" concerning the definition of "tribe"; he had fully expected to consider some "objective" or, at minimum, generally accepted, definition of this ethnolegal category. Finding no agreement, Judge Skinner turned to a legal standard that was completely acontextual (as well as profoundly ethnocentric) by using *Montoya* to assess the Mashpee's claim to tribal status. Judge Skinner translated, via *Montoya,* the lived experience of the Mashpee into an objective, acontextual legal category.

The process of legal storytelling and relevance determination is more like a gathering of material for an index than the telling of a classic narrative. Facts are assembled to tell a story whose conclusion is determined by others. Each fact must point to the next, in not a temporal sense but, rather, only in the sense dictated by the substantive standard being litigated. The determinations of relevance—what can be admitted as evidence—locate the court as the indexer, the one who determines significance. The story told by the parties must point back constantly to the story told by the court and the precedents, which, of course, are merely the stories deemed acceptable by previous courts. By structuring legal storytelling in this way, questions of power, perspective, and value are evaded.

So what kind of story can be told within the confines of legal discourse? Let us turn to the story of the Mashpee Indians and listen to the story they tell about themselves and the story that is told about them, and then decide which story makes more sense.

C. Law Looks: Documentary Evidence

. . . In response to the Mashpee's claims, attorneys for the Town of Mashpee argued that the tribe lacked racial purity, and that it failed to retain a sufficient degree of self-government. It exercised little if any "sovereignty" over specific territory; it maintained no perceptibly coherent sense of "community," and therefore was not a tribe as defined by the Supreme Court in *Montoya*. The defense's main witness, Francis Hutchins, a historian, offered five days of exhaustive testimony. Although he and the Mashpee referred to more or less the same documents, his positivistic account of the Mashpee's history left no room to suggest that certain land deeds in fact reflected white, rather than Indian, notions of landownership. The very acceptance by the court and the witnesses of the symbology of deeds presupposed a certain structure for the Mashpee story. This structure, framed with the European indicia of ownership, was asserted by the defense as the only basis for the tribe's claims. In doing so, defendant's counsel translated the tribe's claims into terms foreign to the Mashpee. This rhetorical move stripped the land claim of nuances that deeds could not replace. The deeds not only reconstituted the tribe's basic claim but also temporalized it; deeds set it apart from the evolving tradition of the Indians' relationship to their physical surroundings, and, at once, both elevated and debased their relationship to the land.

With regard to political leadership, the defendants' historian found scant historical traces of Indian government at Mashpee. The court apparently did not recognize any irony in the defense's attack on the Mashpee's claim of "self-government." According to the defendants, the Mashpee could be "self-governed" only if the tribe adopted political forms susceptible to documentary proof. Unfortunately, the tribe did not see fit to create that kind of proof of its political existence, since the court was asking for evidence of the type of political life that white Europeans, but not the Mashpee, recognized as legitimate. The Mashpee tried to point out what was "appearing" as a "lack" or "gap" in the defendants' account of their history was something that they simply would not have recorded in written form. Within the idiom of documentary evidence as written record, because the Mashpee Indian culture is rooted in large measure on the passing of an oral record, their history could only signify silence. The commonplace view, replicated in the process of legal proof, is that "facts" only have meaning to the extent that they represent something "real." The stories that members of the Mashpee tribe told were stories that legal ears could not hear. Thus, the legal requirements of relevance rendered the Indian storytellers mute and the culture they portrayed invisible. The tragedy of power was manifest in the legally mute and invisible culture of those Mashpee Indians who stood before the court trying to prove that they existed.

V.

. . .

We are doubtless deluding ourselves with a dream when we think that equality and fraternity will someday reign among human beings without compromising their diversity. . . . For one cannot truly enjoy the other, identifying with him, and yet at the same time remain different.[21]

. . . What were the underlying structures or categories guiding the determination of what evidence in the Mashpee trial was deemed "material"—that is, within the confines of the legally defined dispute? In order to construct an answer, it is necessary to examine two other problems underlying the materiality of the evidence offered by the defense. First, in claiming blood as a measure of identity, the defense argued (to the all-white jury) that "black intermarriage made the Mashpees' proper racial identification black instead of Indian."[22] Because of the racial composition of the community, that the jury would be composed exclusively of white people virtually was guaranteed by the voir dire in which prospective jurors were asked whether they were themselves Indian, had any known Indian relatives, or had ever been identified with organizations involved in "Indian causes." White intermarriage was mentioned only in passing.

Second, "the trial court instructed the jury that the tribe could terminate through social or cultural assimilation of '*English forms*' and '*English labels.*'"[23] The court interpreted Mashpee adaptation to the dominant culture, necessary for their survival as an independent people, as proof that the tribe had surrendered its identity. This interpretation incorporates a dominant motif in the theory and practice of modern American pluralism. Ethnic distinctiveness often must be sacrificed in exchange for social and economic security.

In their appeal to the United States Court of Appeals for the First Circuit,[24] the Mashpee argued that "integration and assimilation have expressly been held insufficient to destroy tribal rights."[25] Notions of social and cultural assimilation, such as those upon which the defense relied, impute reified social standards to Indian communities which deny not only their right to historical change but also the reality of their paradoxical continued existence. If the Mashpee only could be "Indians" by fitting into the definitions relied upon by the court and the defense, then their lived experience was devalued to the extent it did not conform. Moreover, by arguing that the Mashpee had been assimilated into the dominant culture merely because they had adopted some forms of that culture meant that the Mashpee could not change, even if they determined that some cultural adaptation was necessary to their own cultural survival.

Thus, the story of the Mashpee and their Otherness can be told in several ways. Whether that story could be told in a way that is legally relevant, while still encompassing the multiple paradoxes of the general inquiry, remains the central problem.

At least one version of the Mashpee story begins with the rise of "Indian consciousness" in the late sixties and seventies, which resulted in compelling political expression, partially through established legal mechanisms and institutions. Among the manifestations of this consciousness were the Indian land claim suits of the seventies.[26] These legal attacks on what were believed to be secure land titles were devastatingly upsetting to white landowners largely because they had the potential to undercut more than a century of settled expectations and redistribute power in a material way. The suits sought to shift control over the most basic material resource, land. What made the Mashpee's challenge particularly disconcerting to the white landowners was that it was conducted according to rules now-frightened, non-Indian landowners felt compelled to respect—a lawsuit.

The Mashpee's story might begin another way. From the founding of the plantation for South Sea Indians and the Village of Mashpee until the mid-sixties, the area now known as the Town of Mashpee was controlled by people who identified themselves as Mashpee Wampanoag Indians. The Indian people of Mashpee exercised all the political power normally associated with Massachusetts's municipalities, including control over land use and permits for public activities. How the Mashpee actually described themselves was immaterial to their exercise of power. The normal disputes that arose out of the conduct of municipal affairs were, in effect, family squabbles. Even if some Mashpee did not approve of how others were acting, the integrity of the group remained unchallenged.

Circumstances drastically changed, however, in the mid-sixties. An influx of non-Indians who were not incorporated into the Mashpee people shifted the balance of political power in the town. With a change of political power in the community from Indian to non-Indian came changes in the material conditions of life in Mashpee. Land formerly open to the community was posted by its new private owners; seaside resort developments were planned where only unspoiled woods and shoreline existed before. These changes were unsettling to the long-term Indian residents of Mashpee, who turned to the Non-Intercourse Act as a means of halting development and restructuring political power in their town.

The story might begin yet another way. In 1901 in *Montoya v. United States,* the United States Supreme Court declared: "By a 'tribe' we understand a body of Indians of the same or similar race, united in a community under one leadership or government, and inhabiting a particular, though sometimes ill-defined territory...."[27] The *Montoya* definition of "tribe" was crucial to the Mashpee's claim, since the Non-Intercourse Act—the legal heart of their land claim suit—protected only "tribes" from the depredations of unscrupulous or unwise land deals. Rather than proving tribal identity in their own terms, the Mashpee were forced to present themselves in terms adopted by *Montoya* and subsequent cases.[28] More important, there was little authority on the definition of a tribe. A group of Indians could be described legally as a "tribe" or a "band," or as a "tribe" for some purposes but not for others. The structure of the narrative required by the precedent—as "fact-denuded rule"—privileged the definition adopted by *Montoya.*

The privileged *Montoya* narrative rested not merely on the foundation of rules governing both authoritative (fact-denuded) and explanatory (fact-filled) examples; the legal narrative was privileged because the rules governing the construction of the storytelling encompassed a complete perspective. Those rules—rules of evidence—give preference to documentary evidence over "mere" recollection of the tribe's members. Recorded memory relies less on the memory of the teller. The elevation of documentary evidence over oral recollection effectively debased the Mashpee's foundation of self-knowledge—their way of looking at, and knowing, themselves.

More important than just controlling the telling of stories in legal discourse, the rules also project reified social relations. The material social relations of the Mashpee that cannot be called up through documentary evidence had to be made to fit the model of Indian society projected by the rules. The relations must be translated into the form established by the rules to be comprehended by legal discourse, regardless of whether the self-constructed reality of the Mashpee corresponds to the legal model. Worse, these reified social relations are projected upon a background of settled expectations that run directly counter to the claims the Mashpee made. In order for their legal claim to make "sense," it had to be phrased within a strictly legal context, and that context had to include the justification for displacing two centuries of "the way things are."

In the context of this lawsuit, once "tribe" became exclusively a legal construct, it embodied all of the subsidiary or provisional social meanings that gave it life within a pseudo-objective legal form. By entering the universe of legal discourse, the term "tribe," in the context of the Non-Intercourse Act, had no meaning for the internal perspective of people claiming that status. Instead, "tribe" means a group of indigenous people who have structured their existence in such a way that outsiders, specifically legal experts, would say the grouping is a "tribe." Thus, the legal notion of "tribe" contains within it projected ethnological categories as well as political categories.

A tribe is incapable of legal self-definition; instead, it must point to something that will then point back and lead others to declare that the tribe is indeed what it claims to be. That "something" functions as an indexical sign—in other words, the information the sign supplies does not dispose of the legal identity but merely suggests where an answer may be found. The "things" that the Indians must point to in order to establish they form a tribe are the authoritative examples discussed earlier.

These authoritative examples are index-like in nature because they define the significance of other signs. Land can function as such a sign. The land is a constituent element of the tribe itself. Without the requisite documentation, the land is only a part of the tribe's cultural self-definition; legally, though, it is meaningless. A tribe can point to the land it occupies and controls as a sign that it exists. Thus, although the land becomes part of what constitutes tribal existence, it is a signal that the law can ignore.

But if a tribe is still capable of constituting itself outside of the legal process, what need is there for legal recognition? The law polices the boundaries between contending cultures and provides one possible foundation for the integrity of subordinate cultures. As has been illustrated, law also can be culturally subversive. For example, the indexical value of land in establishing identity is completely different than the legal value of land inscribed in deeds. The latter is legally recognized as ownership, carrying with it all the legal freight that "ownership" implies. The former may have constitutive power, but it appears to signify nothing when translated into the idiom of legal discourse. In this way, the law can undermine the foundational significance of land for a particular culture.

A deed signifies ownership. In the discourse of law, ownership of some interest is the most important relationship to land which one can have. Yet, according ownership this role occludes the important constitutive power specific land has for people and communities. We see this tension everywhere—in the "penny auctions" of the recent farm crisis and in the land claim suits brought by Indians.

The importance of community identity looms as large as the importance of "ownership" for any individual proprietor. The elevation to a dominant position of one aspect of a complex relationship reflects the power inherent in legal discourse to corrupt meaning, as well as the role of legal translation in that process.

VI. CONCLUSION

HEGEL once wrote that the relationship between the individual and the community can be looked at in only two ways: "[E]ither we start from the substantiality of the ethical order [such as, the traditions and laws of a given commu-

nity], or else we proceed atomistically and build on the basis of single individuals."[29]

Regulation of the interaction of groups within a polity that has taken the individual as a foundation of its moral and political order assumes a special poignancy where cultures conflict irreconcilably. Law provides no place of grace, because what is at issue is the definition of the polity. To grant subgroups a special status or alterative basis for defining themselves calls into question the "substantiality of the ethical order" that defines "rights" in terms of individuals; yet structuring the debate in this way, as illustrated above, merely means that the proponents of the preservation of aboriginal claims ultimately will lose. It does no good to claim otherwise, unless the basis for the aboriginal claims can be reconstructed on the basis of group identity. The preservation of an alternative order is a direct challenge to the plenary power of Congress and to any notions of sovereignty other than a dependent sovereignty so constricted that it cannot deflect countervailing normative visions of community. The law, as it has been narrowly conceived in this essay, creates at most a space where politics may be practiced; but in itself it is an ineffective form of politics, especially for those who would change the prevailing order.

As was argued in an earlier essay, the hope for the development of alternative cultural norms lies in the creation of a real cultural pluralism. A "real cultural pluralism" is one that, within the context of a democratic polity, respects the cultural foundations for differently conceived notions of the "good" and provides a social space for such conceptions to take on material form. The material aspects of a culture's existence should not be underestimated. Without the concrete capacity to reproduce itself, a culture must wither and disappear. With the disappearance of each culture, the range of possible futures available to individual persons must also wither and decline.

Our culture enables us to make sense of our lives and determines, to a large extent, which life choices we make. And those choices must make sense according to the stories our culture tells about us:

> We decide how to lead our lives by situating ourselves in certain cultural narratives, by adopting roles that have struck us as worthwhile ones, as ones worth living. . . . [Yet] [o]ur upbringing isn't something that can just be erased—it is, and always remains a constitutive part of who we are. Cultural membership affects our very sense of personal identity and capacity.[30]

Rather than wash individuals clean of any differentiating characteristics as a logical step prior to the assignment of rights, the recognition of cultural identity as an irreducible component of personal identity requires that we ask how group membership ought to be taken into account. Importantly, this recognition requires us to ask how group membership determines the capacity of the individual, who is the concern of liberal theory, to make "worthwhile choices." If the failure to respect a cultural grouping results in a limitation of the individual's capacity for self-determination, then the political choice leading to that end is indefensible on liberal grounds.

The Hegelian characterization of the tension between the individual and community presumes a single polity. The question it cannot answer is whether a truly culturally pluralistic, liberal, democratic system is feasible. Are we willing to have truly independent cultural enclaves that define their own polity or create their own normative definition of community? The acceptance of such a possibility generates the potential for alternative cultural spheres in which the future may be imagined in a variety of ways, including rejection of the enlightenment project that lies at the heart of liberal democratic theory. If that liberal faith is abandoned, what is the basis for mediating disputes between cultures? Without a reexamination of the foundation for liberal rights, the attempt to remake the argument for aboriginal claims from the perspective of liberal theory is fundamentally misguided.

Before these questions can be answered, remember that cultures have a material and intersubjective dimension. The debate about aboriginal claims in late-twentieth-century America cannot be limited to the realm of liberal democratic theory, but the debate also must include a critique of the material conditions in which Indian life reproduces itself. Cultural identity is integral to individual self-identity. To maximize the range of life choices and to preserve the capacity for individual integrity requires, in the context of aboriginal claims, that the cultural integrity of tribes be maintained. The law as presently structured allows no clear way to achieve that end. In fact, the reality of Indian life is, in a real sense, untranslatable. This untranslatability has a material dimension. Land claims have not a true aboriginal foundation but, rather, a legal mooring in the state, a mooring subject to change and reevaluation. The developmental priorities are set not by Indians but by others. The very theory of Indian sovereignty is debased by the plenary power of Congress.

The tragedy, of course, is that the failure is not merely a failure of theory. The reservation system was badly conceived, but it never was truly intended to provide a foundation for potentially competing powers. The reservations were designed to pacify, not to compensate. The loss that Indians have suffered is material both in the damage to real people and in the destruction of cultures. What has been ruined may be irretrievable, and the continuing loss inexorable. To the extent cultures are destroyed or rendered incapable of self-expression, we are destroying individuals in disservice to what are ostensibly our own underlying values. We have two choices—pluralism materially redefined or the cultural assimilation implied in pluralism as we know it. Yet, as one observer has noted, "Protecting people's cultural community and facilitating their assimilation into another culture are not equally legitimate options."[31]

NOTES

1. W. Whitman, "Yonnondio," in *Leaves of Grass* 524 (S. Bradley and H. Blodgett eds. 1958).

2. W. Hosmer, *Yonnondio, or Warriors of the Genesee: A Tale of the Seventeenth Century* (1844).

3. *Id.* at v.

4. *Id.* at 218.

5. 447 F Supp. 940 (D. Mass. 1978), aff'd sub nom. *Mashpee Tribe v. New Seabury Corp.*, 592 F. 2d 575 (1st Cir.), cert. denied, 444 U.S. 866 (1979).

6. C. MacKinnon, *Feminism Unmodified: Discourses on Life and Law* 39 (1987) (articulation of feminism as a critique of the gendered system of social heirarchy and social power).

7. J.-F. Lyotard, *The Postmodern Condition: A Report on Knowledge* (G. Bennington and B. Massumi trans. 1984), at 21.

8. 447 F. Supp. 940 (D. Mass. 1978), aff'd. sub nom. *Mashpee Tribe v. New Seabury Corp.*, 592 F.2d 575 (1st Cir.), *cert. denied,* 444 U.S. 866 (1979).

9. 25 U.S.C. 177 (1988) (derived from Act of June 30, 1834, ch. 161, 12, 4 Stat. 730).

10. Indian Depredation Act, ch. 538, 26 Stat. 851 (1891).

11. P. Brodeur, *Restitution: The Land Claims of the Mashpee, Pasamaquoddy, and Penobscot Indians of New England* (1985), at 11.

12. *Id.* at 15.

13. *Id.*

14. J. Clifford, *Predicament of Culture* 289 (1988).

15. P. Brodeur, *supra* note 11, at 17.

16. *Id.*

17. *Id.* at 18.

18. J. Clifford, *supra* note 14, at 302.

19. *Id.*

20. Fed. R. Evid. 401.

21. C. Lévi-Strauss, *The View From Afar* 24 (J. Neugroschel and P. Hosstrans. 1985).

22. Petition for Certiorari to the United States Court of Appeals for the First Circuit at 11, *Mashpee Tribe v. New*

Seabury Corp., 592 F. 2d 575 (1st Cir.) (No. 79–62), *cert. denied,* 444 U.S. 866 (1979).

23. *Id.* at 15–16 (emphasis added).

24. *Mashpee Tribe,* 592 F. 2d at 575.

25. *The Kansas Indians,* 72 U.S. (5 Wall.) 737, 756–57 (1867).

26. There is an interesting parallel to the Indian land claim suits in the emergence of Mexican-American political consciousness of the fifties, sixties, and seventies. See generally, M. Garcia, *Mexican Americans: Leadership, Ideology, and Identity, 1930–1960* (1989). Quite apart from the development of "Chicano" consciousness was the "Hispano-Indio" movement of New Mexico. With much less success, that movement attempted to enforce land claims which antedated the formal jurisdiction of the United States over that territory.

27. 180 U.S. 261 (1901).

28. At the time the Mashpee's claim was tried, two Supreme Court opinions cited *Montoya* as an appropriate source for the legal definition of "tribe." See *United States v. Chavez,* 290 U.S. 357, 364 (1933); *United States v. Candelaria,* 271 U.S. 432, 442 (1926).

29. Kymlicka, "Liberalism, Individualism, and Minority Rights," in A. Hutchinson and L. Green, eds., *Law and the Community,* 181 (1989), quoting G. F. Hegel, *Philosophy of Right,* T. M. Knox, ed., 261 (1942), discussing the liberal dilemma facing the Canadians in their attempt to redefine the federal government's relationship to Native peoples.

30. Kymlicka, *supra* note 29, ct 190, 193.

31. *Id.,* at 194.

METRO BROADCASTING, INC. v. FCC: REGROUPING IN SINGULAR TIMES

Patricia J. Williams

THE Supreme Court decision in *Metro Broadcasting, Inc. v. FCC,* which upheld limited preference programs to increase the number of minority owners of broadcast stations, was Justice William Brennan's last majority opinion before his retirement. Because his departure signals a significant shift in the balance of power on the court, some might perceive this case as the last hurrah of a dying liberal order. I believe, however, that this case represents an important element in a schema of vital civil guarantees that must be maintained and even expanded. This comment assesses the significance of *Metro Broadcasting* not merely as a nostalgic look backward, but also as the vehicle for greater comprehension of the significance of and necessity for group claims within our legal system. In addition, this comment considers the costs of pitting individual rights against group interests at a moment in our history when the groupings race and class intersect in such a way that race increasingly defines class, and such that the property interests of large numbers of white individuals are understood to be in irreconcilable tension with the collective dispossession of large numbers of people of color.

I. THE REAL ISSUES AT STAKE

ONE of the major issues in *Metro Broadcasting* was whether and to what extent the FCC's desire to promote racial and ethnic pluralism in programming is served by its choice to diversify broadcast ownership. Applying a standard of review that required the FCC's diversity program to be substantially related to an important governmental interest, the majority held that broadcast diversity was such an interest. According to the majority, although no necessary connection exists between ownership and diverse programming, both congressional and FCC findings strongly suggested that diversity would be promoted by increasing the representation of groups currently underrepre-

sented among owners. The dissenters, adhering to a standard of strict scrutiny, attacked the majority's use of the substantial relation test as a dangerous validation of racial classifications and challenged the notion that broadcast diversity was a compelling governmental interest. Moreover, the dissenters argued that without some guarantee that any particular minority station owner would structure programming differently than a nonminority owner, the FCC's use of race and ethnicity as factors in its licensing decisions could not be considered "narrowly tailored" enough to meet the declared interest in diversity. Although the majority and the dissenters framed the issue in terms of disagreement about the standard of review, their underlying characterizations of the facts and weighing of the evidence were so polarized that the split probably would have remained even had they agreed on this doctrinal issue. The conflict underlying the opinions is revealed by the subtly nuanced and infinitely slippery vocabulary employed by each side. There was a covert adjectival war taking place in *Metro Broadcasting,* in which words were inflated like balloons in order to make the issue of diversity large or trivial, compelling or merely important, natural or momentary, grandly futuristic or of the local past.

The intensity of these divisions is rooted in profound differences in political philosophy about the nature of group identity, individualism, and the role of the market. Justice Brennan's analysis placed issues on a historical continuum that looks both backward, to our divided and ruthlessly co-optive past, and forward, to our long-term interest in the cooperative diversification of our airwaves and our lives. The dissenters' insistence, on the other hand, on a "guaranteed" link between diversity in ownership and diversity in programming arises from a highly individualistic notion of discriminatory action in which a court can consider little history beyond the limited confines of an arm's-length commercially motivated bargain between neutrally feathered equals.

Similarly, the majority and the dissenters differed in their understandings of the very meaning of "necessity" in their respective descriptions of racial categorization as a means to desired ends. For the dissenters, the term referred to an abstracted and absolute requirement of racial neutrality in the word of law; for the majority, it referred to the historically contextualized objective of media diversity, the achievement of which was constrained by a relative lack of alternative. Beyond that, the starting points of each differed: for the majority, its sense of "narrowly tailoring" race-conscious efforts to eradicate discrimination had as its referential backdrop a larger social context, while for the dissenters, the sense of the menacing, unbounded "enormity" of the very same measures arose out of their singular focus on a methodological individualism. . . .

I would like to reframe some of the issues from a perspective that does not assume that simply because a problem such as discrimination is "societal" it is irremediable, or that because a problem is individualized or privatized it is therefore effectively bounded. Whether racial imbalances are called societal or found to be the result of individualized injury, in either case there are overlooked (or underestimated) ways of looking at the problem which could provide both more latitude for courts and a clearer appreciation of the nuanced gradations that characterize judicial responses such as those in *Metro Broadcasting*.

II. Diversity and the Recognition of Groups

BROADCASTING diversity is often portrayed as an attempt to propagate special-interest markets or to ghettoize audiences into "mass appeal," on the one hand, and minority markets, on the other. Its implications, however, are more complex; a real notion of diversity includes a concept of multiculturalism. This entails a view of a market in which there are not merely isolated interest groups, of which the "mass market" may be one, but in which "mass" accurately reflects the complicated variety of many peoples and connotes "interactive" and "accommodative" rather than "dominant" or even just "majoritarian."

This perspective embodies the historical con-

notations of the quest for diversity and the underlying intersection of race and culture. In particular, although it is true that there is no guaranteed relation between race and taste in television and radio fare, the seeming simplicity of this statement deserves some qualification. For example, the literal biological truth that blacks (or members of any other racial or ethnic groups) are not born with genetic inclination for "things black" is often used to obscure the fact that "black" (like most racial or ethnic classification) also defines a culture. Blackness as culture (perhaps more easily understood as such in the designation "African-American")[1] usually evokes a shared heritage of language patterns, habits, history, and experience.

Although all the cultures named by the FCC are exceedingly diverse, the most generalizable experience is that of battling cultural suppression if not obliteration, as well as discrimination and exclusion from the larger society.[2] If we cannot conclude absolutely that the victims of racial oppression are always the best architects of its cure, we must nevertheless assume that the best insight and inspiration for its amelioration will come from those most immediately and negatively affected. This allowance is not merely a concession in a random contest of cultures; it is a recognition central to the checking and balancing, the fine line of restraint, that distinguishes a fluidly majoritarian society from a singularly tyrannical one.

This notion of blackness as a culture, for example, and the recognition that this culture may be consistently suppressed or denigrated under the guise of neutral "mass" entertainment, may be difficult for people who identify themselves as part of the dominant culture to understand. The parallelism of "whiteness" as culture—or as any kind of unified experience—is not immediately apparent. While I remain convinced that there is a culture of whiteness in the United States, I appreciate the extent to which its contours are vaguely or even negatively discerned, so that its assertion is most clearly delineated as "not other," and most specifically as "not black." For the many Americans for whom minority cultures are themselves peripheral, I suspect that a realization that there exists a culture of whiteness is occasioned only rarely. Perhaps the argument is more easily understood as a matter of ethnic heritage; perhaps it is easier to look at immigrant communities of those whom we now call "whites" in order to recapture the extent to which acculturation in the United States is assimilationist in a deeply color-coded sense. It is easy to forget, for example, that the first waves of Italian, Portuguese, Greek, Jewish, and Middle-Eastern immigrants to this country were frequently considered nonwhites and suffered widespread discrimination.

It is therefore telling to note the degree to which we as Americans celebrate simultaneously our unity as a nation and the "Ellis Island" tradition of our variety. In the drive to achieve the unity to which our national mythology aspires, we frequently suppress, if not undo, the richness of our diversity by reconceptualizing any manifestation of it as a kind of un-American disunity. I think we do this by consistently, if unconsciously, underestimating ourselves as a distinct national culture and even denying outright the possibility of our power as a consuming, assimilationist force. We tend to universalize the characteristics commonly, if romantically, attributed to middle-class America—individualism, self-interest, self-assertion—so that the very force of our desire to embrace one another becomes an impediment to the necessary recognition that "we" are not the world.[3] . . .

III. DIVERSITY AND BROADCASTING

GIVEN the existence of minority cultures—and not just of minority individuals—the attempt by the *Metro Broadcasting* dissenters to disclaim any relation between programming and ownership becomes rooted in paradox. The dissenting opinions contest any relation between the multiculturalism of programming and the racial or ethnic background of station owners; yet there clearly is some relation between programming and the beliefs of an owner. Just as clearly, there is some relation between one's heritage and one's beliefs.

Underlying the dissenters' attempted disavowal of the connection between ownership and broadcasting content is a paradigm in which the class characteristics of good ownership are assumed to transcend racial, ethnic, or other forms of identity. As a friend of mine is fond of saying, middle-class status is nothing more than the inner conquest of any perceived racial or ethnic identity at all. The complete "young urban professional" (or the accomplished businessperson) is one who has achieved a certain tweedy neutrality of dress, speech, mannerism, and desire. Although there is facetiousness in this depiction, there is certainly nothing too unfamiliar in it: it merely updates and caricatures the model of the rational man who dutifully delays gratification, acts in perfect self-interest, lives with one finger on the pulse of market appetite, patterns a lifestyle upon strong if shifting trends, and under no circumstances wears anything louder than oxblood, loden, or slate.

Ironically, such an identity is not an expression of individuality; it is, rather, fashion, a collective aesthetic, a species of mass behavior wrapped in the discourse of self-interest. This deeply embedded notion of the rational market actor is in fact a conformed identity, so normalized that we seem to have lost the ability to see it as such. Nor is this identity really racially or ethnically neutral. For all the brilliant cultural mixtures in art, music, and film which America has given the world, middle- and upperclassness remains deeply steeped in Western European traditions and dominated by strong Protestant values. To this day, 95 percent of all corporate executives, including communications executives, are white males, "a figure that hasn't changed since 1979."[4] As the *Metro Broadcasting* majority observed, "in 1986, [minorities] owned just 2.1 percent of the more than 11,000 radio and television stations in the United States. Moreover, . . . as late entrants who often have been able to obtain only the less valuable stations, many minority broadcasters serve geographically limited markets with relatively small audiences."[5]

Furthermore, in an era of infomercials, the media is increasingly used simply to spread (rather than exchange) information about markets (rather than ideas). Television and radio undoubtedly enable people to shop faster and better; it is easier than ever before to stay informed about a wide range of consumer goods and services. Yet even as these media replace libraries (the traditional bastions of our culture), they do not seem to be serving the same interests or function as libraries: they are not being geared for the sort of browsing in which there is no commercial stake. Although electronically conveyed knowledge indeed may be cheaper and easier to obtain in one sense, I wonder about a larger question: the degree to which information itself needs a patron or sponsor to be conveyed in the first place. Our modern-day patrons are no longer popes and princes; they are corporations and philanthropies. The degree to which advertising alone purveys and censors information seriously threatens genuine freedom of information. The degree to which the major media, the culture creators in our society, are owned by a very few or are subsidiaries of each other's financial interests must be confronted as a skewing of the way in which cultural information is collected and distributed.

Thus, executives in the communications industry exercise a power that is not merely concentrated but also propagandistic. They make far-reaching choices in a way that few others in our society can. They project their images of the world out into it. They do not merely represent—they also recreate themselves and their vision of the world as desirable, salable. What they reproduce is not neutral, not without consequence. To pretend (as we all do from time to time) that film or television, for example, is a neutral vessel, or contentless, mindless, or unpersuasive, is sheer denial. It is, for better and frequently for worse, one of the major forces in the shaping of our national vision, a chief architect of the modern American sense of identity.

Even assuming that profit-seeking behavior explains all or that materialism is itself a kind of culture, if the United States is to be anything more than a loose society of mercenaries— of suppliers and demanders, of vendors and consumers—then it must recognize that other forms of group culture and identity exist. We must respect the dynamic power of these groups and cherish their contributions to our civic lives rather than pretend they do not exist as a way of avoiding argument about their accommodation. We must also be on guard against either privileging in our law a supposedly neutral "mass" culture that is in fact highly specific and historically contingent or legitimating a supposedly neutral ethic of individualism which is really a corporate group identity, radically constraining any sense of individuality, and silently advancing the claims of that group identity.

This is not to say that all women or blacks or men see the world in the same way or only according to their cultures. I do not believe that a "pure" black or feminist or cultural identity of any sort exists, any more than I think culture is biological. I am arguing against a perceived monolithism of "universal" culture which disguises our overlapping variety, and which locates nonwhites as "separate," "Other," even "separatist" cultures or—as in the context of *Metro Broadcasting*—that argues about whether such cultures even exist.

The point then is not that whites cannot program for blacks, or that blacks would not watch programming aimed at Hispanic audiences. And the point is not, for example, whether white actors can convincingly portray Asian characters, as was so reductively maintained by the producers in the recent debate over the ill-fated Broadway version of *Miss Saigon*,[6] or whether a black actor should be able to play the lead in Shakespeare's *Richard III*. I do maintain that a certain institutional skewing has taken place if, within a supposedly diverse society, it is only whites who represent Asians,[7] only men who play women, or only children who fill black roles. It would suggest a profound social imbalance if only North Americans compose the intellectual canon of South American history. And if rape occurs mostly to women, it seems peculiar to reserve control over the standards for its remediation exclusively to men. In fact, it is precisely these sorts of disrespectful exclusions that signal the most visible sites of oppression in any society.

In our society, the most obvious means of

tearing down such exclusions is dispersion of ownership. Participation in ownership of anything, but most particularly of broadcast stations or other tools of mass communication, is the gateway to our greatest power as Americans. Ownership enables one not merely to sell to others or to offer oneself to the call of the market; it also provides the opportunity to propagate oneself in the marketplace of cultural images. Participation in the privileges of ownership thus involves more than the power to manipulate property itself; it lends an ability to express oneself through property as an instrument of one's interests. We think of freedom of expression as something creative, innovative, each word like a birth of something new and different—but it is also the power to manipulate one's resources to sanction what is not pleasing. The property of the communications industry is all about the production of ideas, images, and cultural representations, but it also selectively silences even as it creates. Like all artistic expression, it is a crafting process of production and negation, in the same way that a painting may involve choices to include yellow and blue while leaving out red and green.

When one translates this understanding of ownership into the context of broadcast diversification, the issue becomes not only what is sanctioned but also who is sanctioning. It is not that minorities live in wholly separate worlds, enclaves walled in by barriers of language, flavors, and music; minorities are not languishing on electronically underserved islands, starving for the rap-marimba beat of a feminist Korean-speaking radio DJ whom only similar Others can understand. Nevertheless, a feminist Korean DJ is more likely to sanction insulting images of herself and more likely to choose to propagate images of herself which humanize her and her interests. Likewise, it is not that white owners cannot be persuaded not to rerun old *Amos 'n' Andy* shows, in which white actors in blackface portrayed blacks in derogatory if comic ways and which reiterated the exclusive (until recently) image of blacks in the media. Rather, it is much easier—and very likely not even necessary—to persuade Bill Cosby, for example, to choose to run programming that challenges

and variegates the perpetual image of blacks as foolish and deviant.

In fact, I think that Bill Cosby's very success—as owner, producer, writer, and actor—in delivering an image of at least a certain middle-class segment of imagistic blackness into the realm of the "normal," rather than the deviant, has run him up against yet an even more complex (if instructive) level of cultural co-optation. As *The Cosby Show*'s warm, even smarmy appeal has made it a staple in homes around the country, black cultural inflections that were initially quite conspicuous (speech patterns, the undercurrent of jazz music, the role of Hillman College as the fictional black alma mater of the Huxtables, hairstyles ranging from dreadlocks to "high-top fades") have become normalized and invisible.

Moreover, the process of normalizing has exaggerated the extent to which the black middle class and white middle class are not merely derivative, but identical, so that *The Cosby Show* has been described as little more than a portrayal of blacks costumed in cultural whiteface. Although this "whitening" of its appeal is refined into the language of "sameness," the process devalues and even robs the program of its black content.

Thus, as black cultural contributions are absorbed into mainstream culture, they actually come to be seen as exclusively white cultural property, with no sense of the rich multiculturalism actually at work. Ultimately, the minority set-aside policies at issue in *Metro Broadcasting* must address this consuming, unconscious power as well. It is not enough to have one Bill Cosby or two Oprah Winfreys if overall power is so concentrated in one community that it remains inconceivable that power could have any other source.

IV. BENIGN, BENIGHTED, AND
BEWILDERED

ONE basis for resisting this kind of analysis, I recognize, is the question of whether an expanded consideration—both of injury to groups, rather than simply to individuals, and of remediation that extends beyond the limited life circumstances of a single litigant—is a matter for the courts at all. The reflexive referral of all but the most privatized controversies to the legislature obscures the fact that even the narrowest contract or property dispute is never really as private as theory would have it. Courts always have to consider social ramifications that are rarely limited to the named parties, whether that consideration is of "policy" (the contemporaneous society of those similarly situated) or whether the consideration is funneled into issues of "precedent" (the prior or subsequent society of others).

Indeed, I think we must begin to appreciate the extent to which courts actually deal in and perpetuate not merely individual property interests but also property interests that govern, silence, and empower significant groups of us as citizens. One device by which courts have traditionally limited challenges to the social status quo is the consideration of cases and controversies constrained within a paradigm of private contract law. This insistence amounts to considering all litigation from within a contractarian paradigm that fragments the social contract into a series of little contracts. In the context of cases about civil liberties, this can be downright destructive.

As citizens, we tend to think of raw Hobbesian economic interest as being separate from the shrine in which our civil liberties, our freedom, and our humanity reside. Yet, as lawyers, we learn this is not so. Our liberty was always and is increasingly complex and contradictory, a symbology framed not just by economic notions in some general sense but also by specific contractarian ideas of commodification and bipolar exchange. The subjectivity of our civil and political selves is simultaneously objectified by our most distanced, arm's-length transactions.

This results in a twisted conception of freedom in which the notion of ourselves as "free" becomes transformed into that of "free agent." With this shift, another occurs: we no longer see freedom's inverse as "domination," but rather only as the inverse of free agency. Thus, those who by one set of criteria are living in states of cultural, economic, or physical subjugation may be redescribed as "inefficient wealth maximizers," mere depoliticized shoppers who are irrational and undeserving by either choice or resistance. A model of constitutional jurisprudence based on this contractarian vision therefore fails to anticipate the situation in which an aggregate of private transactions in a society begins to conflict with express social guarantees: those express protections or ideals are robbed of their force as law and become situated as "external," implicit interference.

Courts' ability to consider these matters is actually not as murky and unmanageable as the dissenters in *Metro Broadcasting* suggested. The impression that such matters are unmanageable is in fact built by a variety of rhetorical images; the dissenters waged a deflationary war on the value of diversity itself and on any evidence that diversity is a good, necessary, or considered goal. The *Metro Broadcasting* dissenters labeled the notion of societal [...] discrimination "amorphous"[8] and "reflexive";[9] actual legislative history was deemed too paltry;[10] congressional and agency findings were judged to be without a demonstrable "factual basis."[11] The attempt to defend historically vulnerable interests was reduced to the privileging of "viewpoints";[12] cultural identity was turned into racial "stereotypes,"[13] and the judicial responsibility to check the tyranny of any majority was abdicated out of a hypothesized fear of advancing or benefiting special groups.[14]

Beyond this devaluation of the interests at stake, the dissents are peppered with inexplicably inverted agency, demonstrating that any language of reform may be turned inside out by conflating it with historical tropes of negativity, even as its substance is being relentlessly dehistoricized. Whereas segregation and group exclusion were once thought of as the stigmata of inferiority, now, according to the dissenters, it is the very identification of blacks and other racial minorities as groups which is stigmatizing—no matter that the project is inclusion. The South African government is cited to demonstrate the truism that "policies of racial separation and preference are almost always justified as benign, even when it is clear to any sensible observer that they are not"[15]—tempting me to some easy inversions of my own: in the United

States, policies of racial inclusion and community are almost always vilified as harmful even when it is clear to any sensible observer that they are not.

It is not only the dissenters, however, whose language could stand reform. In the charged context of dismantling a system of favoritism that "favored" whites and "disfavored" blacks, the majority glibly reversed the vocabulary of preference so that it was blacks who were favored and whites automatically disfavored. The casual ahistoricism of this reversal implies a causal link between the inclusion of blacks and the oppression of whites. To give an example that would be extreme were it not asked so often, a student recently demanded of me, "Don't you think affirmative action is what creates a David Duke?"[16] Blacks are positioned in this query as responsible for the bitterest backlash against them, an eerie repeat of the responses (one being the founding of the Ku Klux Klan) to black gains, having nothing to do with affirmative action, during Reconstruction.

In fact, affirmative action and minority setaside programs are vastly more complicated than this "you're in, I'm out" conception suggests. Nothing in this rigid win/lose dichotomy permits the notion that everyone could end up a beneficiary, that expansion rather than substitution might be possible, and that the favoring of multiple cultures is an enhancement of the total rather than a sweepingly reflexive act of favoritism for anything other than the monolithic purity of an all-white nation.

This particular evocation, of a corrupt system of favoritism seesawing between "the deserving" and "the preferred," caters to an assumption that those who are included by the grace of affirmative action systems are therefore undeserving. I want to underscore that I do mean that it "caters to," rather than creates, an assumption of inferiority—for the assumption of inferiority has a life that precedes and, unfortunately, will probably outlive affirmative action programs. The subtlety of this distinction has terrified even some few blacks into distorting historic assumptions of blacks as inferior into the weird acceptance of their exclusion as its cure. Sitting on university admissions committees, for example, I have seen black candidates who write on their applications comments such as, "Don't admit me if you have to lower your standards." I have never seen the same acutely self-conscious disavowals from students who are admitted because they meet some geographical criterion—such as living in Wyoming, or France, or some other underrepresented area—or who are older reentry students, or football heroes, or alumni children. I think this is so because these latter inclusionary categories are thought to indicate group life experiences, whether we call them cultures or not, that "enrich" rather than "lower."

The question, then, becomes not how to undo inclusionary affirmative action programs but, rather, how to undo the stigma of inferiority which resides not merely in the label or designation of race, but which, according to our national symbology, is actually embodied in black presence. If it were truly as simple as erasing labels, then perhaps enough White-Out in our cases and codes would eliminate the problem once and for all. However, it is the ferocious mythology of blackness (or Otherness) as the embodiment of inferiority which persists whether blacks are inside or outside particular institutions and regardless of how they perform. . . .

In the same vein, the majority employs the halfhearted ambiguity of "benign racial classification"[17] in place of what might be more forcefully described as the principle of antidiscrimination. Furthermore, antidiscrimination and diversity are polarized in the dissents, so that it is no longer possible formally to recognize diversity without its being—not merely risking being—discriminatory. The quest for inclusion becomes transformed into the exact equivalent of that which would exclude: the slogan "separate but equal" is called up as the exact equivalent of the newly minted "unequal but benign."[18] In only twenty-five years, blacks and Bull Connor have become relativized in this soupy moral economy. The focused and meaningful inquiry of strict scrutiny has become a needle's eye through which minority interests are too inherently suspect to pass. Racial and ethnic identification as that against which one ought not discriminate has been twisted; now those very same racial and ethnic classifications are what discriminate. The infinite convertibility of terms is, I suppose, what makes the commerce of American rhetoric so very fascinating; but these linguistic flip-flops disguise an immense stasis of power, and they derail the will to undo it.

Furthermore, the complication of this rhetoric, an ironic result of the judicial desire to simplify, seems to have resulted in an odd and risky quest by the *Metro Broadcasting* dissenters to be rid not only of any undue power to discriminate negatively but also of the very ability to be discriminating in any sensitive, curious, or moral way. As I have written elsewhere, the idea that an egalitarian society can be achieved or maintained through the mechanism of blind neutrality is fallacious. Racial discrimination is powerful precisely because of its frequent invisibility, its felt neutrality. After all, the original sense of discrimination was one of discernment, of refinement, of choice, of value judgment— the courteous deflection to the noble rather than to the base. It is this complicated social milieu that must be remembered as the backdrop to what both the majority and dissenters refer to as "preferences" in this case. Racism inscribes culture with generalized preferences and routinized notions of propriety. It is aspiration as much as condemnation; it is an aesthetic. It empowers the mere familiarity and comfort of the status quo by labeling that status quo as "natural." If we are to reach the deep roots of this legacy, antidiscrimination must be a commitment to undo not merely the words of forced division but also the consequences of oppressive acts. As in the old saw about the two horses given "equal" opportunity to run a race, but one of whom has a stone in its shoe, the failure to take into account history and context can radically alter whether mere neutrality can be deemed just.

One consequence of a quietly racist aesthetic in which the status quo is naturalized is that any change will be felt as unnatural and thus as extremely unsettling. The costs of doing anything to alter the known, even when those alterations are matters of both social and self-

preservation, are inflated to terrifying proportions. It is not surprising, therefore, that the *Metro Broadcasting* dissenters turned any express judicial consideration of even the merest whisper of institutional adjustment into a slippery slope of misfortune. The ubiquity of racism is made menacing in its enormity, the recognition of it as a social problem held out as a threat, as a hedge against doing anything at all about it. Rather than being allowed to feel good about tackling it at some level, we are threatened relentlessly with the clatter of domino theories: this small concession now, hisses the amicus brief filed by the solicitor general's office, but what next? Do you really want those preferences in "virtually any business"?[19] (And would you want a preference moving in next door to you? To say nothing of marrying your sister?) That the *Metro Broadcasting* majority resisted such fear-mongering is a hopeful sign. Indeed, it is my hope that this case represents a renewed willingness to consider the costs of limiting judicial scrutiny by an account of humanity which is isolated from history, accident, and inextricable contiguity.

V. Conclusion

THE majority opinion in *Metro Broadcasting* marks an important step toward a recognition of multiculturalism and of the need to take active steps to nurture such diversity. If the holding in this case does not guarantee that minority owners will change programming in any constructive way, it does at least increase the likelihood.[20] Although the dissenters implicitly insisted on a guarantee that there be some relation, a necessary connection, such a strict guarantee can never be gained without expense to the freedoms provided by the First Amendment. Even diversity of employment at levels other than ownership is largely at the will and whimsy of those owners. If cultural diversity is, as even the dissenters acknowledge, an acceptable social goal, then alternative, creative means for its encouragement must be employed. That relation is fostered by making more frequent and enhancing the opportunities for minority owners and producers, who are more likely to hire minority writers, sponsor programs designed to serve the needs and interests of minority communities, and, perhaps most important, bring multiculturalism to mainstream programming.

Beyond the limited context of broadcasting, what I hope will be enduring about this opinion is the respect it gives to these pronounced social recognitions of the desirability of diversity in all aspects of our economy and of multiculturalism in our lives. A (probably too) concrete illustration may indicate the reconceptualization of equality that is so urgently needed. Imagine a glass half full (or half empty) of blue marbles. Their very hard-edged, discrete, yet identical nature makes it possible for the community of blue marbles to say to one another with perfect consistency both "we are all the same" and, if a few roll away and are lost in a sidewalk grate, "that's just their experience, fate, choice, bad luck." If, on the other hand, one imagines a glass full of soap bubbles, with shifting permeable boundaries, expanding and contracting in size like a living organism, then it is not possible for the collective bubbles to describe themselves as "all the same." Furthermore, if one of the bubbles bursts, it cannot be isolated as a singular phenomenon. It will be felt as a tremor, a realignment, a reclustering among all.

Marbles and soap bubbles are my crude way of elucidating competing conceptions of how to guarantee what we call "equal opportunity." One conception envisions that all citizens are equal, with very little variation from life to life or from lifetime to lifetime; even when there is differentiation among some, the remainder are not implicated in any necessary way.

The other conception holds that no one of us is the same, and that although we can be grouped according to our similarities, difference and similarity are not exclusive categories but, instead, are continually evolving. Equal opportunity is not only about assuming the circumstances of hypothetically indistinguishable individuals; it is also about accommodating the living, shifting fortunes of those who are very differently situated. What happens to one may be the repercussive history that repeats itself in the futures of us all.

NOTES

1. I use "black" throughout this comment in order to explore the connotation in the terms actually used by the FCC in this debate. Nevertheless, just as the shift in parlance from "negro" to "black," in its time, reinforced an empowering process of self-identification, I think the recent trend away from "black" and toward "African-American" is an effective way of evoking the specific cultural dimension of that identity.

2. I hope that readers will resist the temptation to reduce this struggle to protect one's culture and beliefs into an understanding of all-black culture, for example, as merely a "culture of resistance." To be extremely explicit, battling discrimination, although a generalizable group experience, is not the same as or the whole of what I am calling "culture."

3. This tendency pervades American scholarship. As Sacvan Bercovitch has observed: "The historians from George Bancroft to Daniel Boorstin who described the United States as a country without an ideology were speaking for a system of values so deeply ingrained they could assume it was simply common sense. The cultural commentators from Oliver Wendell Holmes to Louis Hartz who saw nothing in America but an expanding middle class were speaking for a way of life so completely internalized that its members could define America, tautologically, by excluding from it all Americans who were not middle class. The scholars who for two centuries have debated the nature of America's uniqueness have been arguing from within a certain long-nourished, richly endowed dominant culture, one that made the ritual terms of its ascendance—individualism, progress, and the American Way—appear no less self-evident, no less true to sacred and natural law, than the once eternal truths of hierarchy, providence, and the Catholic Church"; Bercovitch, "Afterword," in S. Bercovitch and M. Jehlen, eds., *Ideology and Classic American Literature* 418, 420 (1986).

4. Mann, "The Shatterproof Ceiling," *Washington Post* (Aug. 17, 1990), D3:5.

5. 110 S. Ct. at 3003 (citation omitted). Of the top twenty-four media giants, "approximately two-thirds ... are either closely held or still controlled by members of the originating family who retain large blocks of stock.... The control groups of the media giants are also brought into close relationships with the mainstream of the corporate community through boards of directors and social links. In the cases of NBC and the Group W television and cable systems, their respective parents, GE and Westinghouse, are themselves mainstream corporate giants, with boards of directors that are dominated by corporate and banking executives", E. Herman and N. Chomsky, *Manufacturing Consent*, 8 (1988).

6. *Miss Saigon* producer Cameron Mackintosh called the boycott by Actor's Equity "a disturbing violation of the

principles of artistic integrity and freedom," Rosenfeld, "No 'Miss Saigon' for Broadway," *Washington Post* (Aug. 9, 1990) D3:1. Actress Ellen Holly, on the other hand, points out that although Jonathan Pryce, the white actor whose role was at stake in the controversy, may have been an innocent victim, "he is not a victim of David Henry Hwang, B. D. Wong and the Asian-American theatrical community that, quite correctly, raised a question about his employment here. Rather, he is a victim of a long and profoundly frustrating history in America in which, decade after decade, the ideal world we all long for has functioned so that whites are free to play everything under the sun while black, Hispanic and Asian actors are not only restricted to their own category, but forced to surrender roles *in their own category* that a white desires"; Holly, "Why the Furor Over 'Miss Saigon' Won't Fade," *New York Times* (Aug. 26, 1990) 2. 7:2 (emphasis in original).

7. In the *Miss Saigon* controversy, casting director Vincent Liff said that "he was not able to find an Asian actor suitable for the role, one of more or less the right age who could act and sing." Rothstein, "Equity Panel Head Criticizes 'Saigon' Producer," *New York Times* (Aug. 16, 1990) C15:1. Of course, evaluation of this statement boils down to whether one believes that there really is not a single qualified Asian actor to be found anywhere in the whole United States. I do not believe it. And if one does believe that there are willing and qualified candidates, then the issue is reoriented from one of racial or other qualification to one of institutional resistance disguised as artistic taste. It was this resistance to which the attempted boycott by Actor's Equity spoke. Chuck Patterson, head of the Committee on Racial Equality of Actor's Equity, met with producers of the play and "asked for the opportunity for Asian-Americans to compete; they said absolutely not. . . . Equity is willing to admit that Jonathan Pryce is an actor of enormous talent. . . . But there are also Asian-American actors of enormous talent, and for a producer to say he can't find an Asian-American to play the role is absolutely racist"; *id.*

8. 110 S. Ct. at 3035 (O'Connor, J., dissenting).

9. *Id.* at 3039.

10. See *id.*

11. *Id.* at 3042 (O'Connor, J., dissenting).

12. *Id.* at 3035 (O'Connor, J., dissenting).

13. *Id.* at 3029.

14. See *id.* at 3035.

15. *Id.* at 3046 (Kennedy, J., dissenting).

16. David Duke is the former Ku Klux Klan leader who recently lost a race for U.S. Senator from Louisiana—but only narrowly, with 60 percent of the white vote and, according to one estimate, 70 percent of the white male vote.

17. 110 s. ct. at 3008–09.

18. *Id.* at 3047 (Kennedy, J., dissenting).

19. Brief for the United States as Amicus Curiae Supporting Respondent Shurberg Broadcasting of Hartford, Inc., at 18, *Metro Broadcasting* (No. 89–700).

20. It is possible, for example, but simply seems unlikely that a black producer would make a movie like *Mississippi Burning* in which, in a complete reversal of history, the civil rights movement becomes an epic saga of heroic FBI agents rushing to the South to save helpless blacks. It is possible, too, certainly, but I think extremely unlikely that a black director could have summoned up the same degree of unflappably cynical market "neutrality" in rationalizing this story line as did white director Alan Parker: "Because it's a movie, I felt it *had* to be fictionalized. The two heroes in the story had to be white. That is a reflection of our society as much as of the film industry. At this point in time, it could not have been made in any other way;" Holly, *supra* note 6 (emphasis in original).

❦

Part Four

CRITICAL RACE THEORY
AND LEGAL DOCTRINE

Four

CRITICAL RACE THEORY AND LEGAL DOCTRINE

Although many of the essays in this collection consider law in one way or another, we chose for this section articles that specifically focus on the connection between issues of race and specific doctrinal categories of legal analysis.

In "The Emperor's Clothes," Lani Guinier analyzes the biases of our present winner-take-all system for deciding political representation. Gaunier describes how the electoral influence of minority groups can be systematically curtailed—or broadened—within the norms of democratic theory. Drawing on her experience as a voting rights litigator for the NAACP Legal Defense Fund, she argues for a form of cumulative voting as the norm for protecting minority rights in a democratic decision-making structure.

In "The Id, the Ego, and Equal Protection: Reckoning With Unconscious Racism" Charles R. Lawrence, III, dissects the discriminatory "purpose" or "intent" requirement in equal protection jurisprudence. Lawrence shows that the vision of racial discrimination that informs this doctrine ignores the problem of unconscious racism, which is no less harmful to its victims than intentionally racist acts. Lawrence urges a shift in equal protection analysis away from the subjective intention of those charged with racial discrimination. To this end, Lawrence proposes adoption of a "cultural meaning" test that would consider a challenged practice or policy based on a broader social understanding about relations of racial power.

Neil Gotanda's study of the image of a "color-blind Constitution" traces the various uses to which race has been used in American legal ideology, as well as the diverse things that race has been used to signify. Gotanda argues that color-blind constitutionalism has worked to legitimate and perpetuate racial subordination by repressing the ways in which racial power shapes social relations. Connecting issues of racial and religious domination, Gotanda points to the Supreme Court's doctrine of religious liberty as an alternative way for constitutional law to comprehend racial difference.

In "Whiteness as Property," Cheryl Harris shows how the traditional and conventional legal category of "property" can be used to shed light on the various ways that race distributes power in America. She first shows that the various forms of racial privilege enjoyed by whites correspond to the traditional conceptions of property interests. She then shows how the property conception renders the affirmative action debate quite different than traditional discourse over qualifications and fairness.

In concluding this chapter, Linda Greene and Derrick Bell explicitly pose the same issue: in Greene's words, "whether meaningful equality can be obtained for African-Americans through law." Each author is pessimistic. Concentrating on the Supreme Court's trilogy of conservative civil rights decisions in 1989, Greene develops the outlines of a reinterpretation of civil rights doctrine which would significantly restrict the opportunity to achieve racial redress through discrimination law. Greene predicts that the Supreme Court will continue on its current course and suggests that people of color consider other avenues of social change.

Finally, Derrick Bell poses the development of a "Racial Realism," modeled after the Legal Realist movement of the 1930s and 1940s. According to Bell, it is time to demystify the possibilities of black progress through legal change and realistically to face the static position of blacks in America. Bell calls for a strategizing based on the foreseeable reality of subordination in place of an empty theorizing about a legally enforced equality that, in his view, will never happen.

Part Four

CRITICAL RACE THEORY
AND LEGAL DOCTRINE

GROUPS, REPRESENTATION, AND RACE-
CONSCIOUS DISTRICTING: A CASE OF
THE EMPEROR'S CLOTHES

Lani Guinier

I

NOW that the first round of reapportionment has been accomplished, there is
need to talk "one man, one vote" a little less and
to talk a little more of "political equity" and of
functional components of effective representation. *A mathematically equal vote that is politically
worthless because of gerrymandering or winner-
take-all districting is as deceiving as "the emperor's
clothes."*[1]

With voices pitched in the high decibel
range, critics of race-conscious districting[2] are
blasting the Voting Rights Act[3] and its 1982
amendments. A recent *Wall Street Journal* headline declares that voting is now "rigged by
race."[4] Ethnic activists, the writer asserts, are
collaborating with GOP operatives in an unholy
political alliance to herd minorities into their
own convoluted urban districts in order to improve GOP prospects in white-majority suburban areas.[5] According to such critics, this is a
"political one-night stand" made possible by
misguided federal courts and Department of
Justice officials construing the 1982 act to create
districts in which minorities are the majority,
the newest form of "racial packaging."[6]

My students inform me that Cokie Roberts,
as part of ABC's election-night coverage, dramatically illustrated the concerns of critics when
she traced on a map of the Chicago area the
"earmuff" district, allegedly carved out of two
noncontiguous Chicago neighborhoods joined
by a narrow rod to maximize the possibility that

the Latino residents would be able to elect a
representative of their choice to Congress.[7] And
in June 1993, the Supreme Court discovered a
new constitutional right enabling white voters
in North Carolina to challenge, based on its
odd and irregular shape, a "highway" district
that narrowly tracks the path of an interstate,
creating a swatch of voters on either side of the
highway from one end of the state to the other.[8]
This 54 percent black district, the most integrated in the state, elected Melvin Watt, one of
the first two blacks elected to Congress from
that state in this century.[9]

The Voting Rights Act codified the right of
protected minority groups to an equal opportunity to elect candidates of their choice, although
its language disclaims the rights to racial representation by members of the racial group in
direct proportion to population.[10] The critics
now claim this is special and unwarranted protection for racial and language minority
groups.[11] In the name of liberal individualism,
these critics assert that the statue effected a
radical transformation in the allocation and nature of representation.[12]

Although race-conscious districting[13] is their
apparent target, these critics have fixed their
aim on a deeper message—that pressing claims
of racial identity and racial disadvantage diminishes democracy. We all lose, the theory goes,
when some of us identify in racial or ethnic
group terms.[14]

In my view, critics of race-conscious districting have misdirected their fire. Their emperor has no clothes: their dissatisfaction with
racial group representation ignores the essentially group nature of political participation. In
this regard, the critics fail to confront directly
the group nature of representation itself, espe-

cially in a system of geographic districting. Perhaps unwittingly, they also reveal a bias toward the representation of a particular racial group rather than their discomfort with group representation itself.[15] In a society as deeply cleaved by issues of racial identity as ours, there is no one race. In the presence of such racial differences, a system of representation that fails to provide group representation loses legitimacy.[16]

Yet these critics have, in fact, accurately identified a problem with a system of representation based on winner-take-all territorial districts. There is in fact an emperor wearing his clothes, but not as they describe. Rather than expressing a fundamental failure of democratic theory based on group representation per se, the critics have identified a problem with one particular solution. It is districting in general—not race-conscious districting in particular—that is the problem.

Winner-take-all territorial districting imperfectly distributes representation based on group attributes and disproportionately rewards those who win the representational lottery. Territorial districting uses an aggregating rule that inevitably groups people by virtue of some set of externally observed characteristics, such as geographic proximity or racial identity. In addition, the winner-take-all principle inevitably wastes some votes. The dominant group within the district gets all the power; the votes of supporters of nondominant groups or of disaffected voters within the dominant group are wasted. Their votes lose significance because they are consistently cast for political losers.

The essential unfairness of districting is a result, therefore, of two assumptions: first, that a majority of voters within a given geographic community can be configured to constitute a "group"; and second, that incumbent politicians, federal courts, or some other independent set of actors can fairly determine which group to privilege by giving it all the power within the district. When either of these assumptions is inaccurate, as is most often the case, the districting is necessarily unfair.

Another effect of these assumptions is gerrymandering, which results from the arbitrary allocation of disproportionate political power to one group.[17] Districting breeds gerrymandering as a means of allocating group benefits; the operative principle is deciding whose votes get wasted. Whether it is racially or politically motivated, gerrymandering is the inevitable by-product of an electoral system that aggregates people by virtue of assumptions about their group characteristics and then inflates the winning group's power by allowing it to represent all voters in a regional unit.

Given a system of winner-take-all territorial districts and working within the limitations of this particular election method, the courts have sought to achieve political fairness for racial minorities. As a result, there is some truth to the assertion that minority groups, unlike other voters, enjoy a special representational relationship under the Voting Rights Act's amendments of 1982 to remedy their continued exclusion from effective political participation in some jurisdictions. However, the proper response is not to deny minority voters that protection. The answer should be to extend that special relationship to all voters by endorsing the equal opportunity to vote for a winning candidate as a universal principle of political fairness.

I use the phrase "one-vote, one-value" to describe the principle of political fairness that as many votes as possible should count in the election of representatives.[18] One-vote, one-value is realized when everyone's vote counts toward someone's election. The only system with the potential to realize this principle for all voters is one in which the unit of representation is political rather than regional, and the aggregating rule is proportionality rather than winner-take-all. Semiproportional systems, such as cumulative voting, can approximate the one-vote, one-value principle by minimizing the problem of wasted votes.

One-vote, one-value systems transcend the gerrymandering problem because each vote has an equal worth independent of decisions made by the voters themselves. These systems revive the connections between voting and representation, whether the participant consciously associates with a group of voters or chooses to participate on a fiercely individual basis. Candidates are elected in proportion to the intensity of their political support within the electorate itself rather than as a result of decisions made by incumbent politicians or federal courts once every ten years.[19]

My project in this paper is to defend the representation of racial groups while reconsidering whether race-conscious districting is the most effective way of representing these groups or their interests.[20] My claim is that racial group representation is important, but it is only imperfectly realized through an electoral system based on territorial districting or through the limited concept of racially "descriptive" representation.[21] . . .

For many liberal reformers, the "one person, one vote" principle is politically fair because its ideal of universal suffrage incorporates the respect due and the responsibilities owed to each citizen in a democracy.[22] One-person, one-vote cases attempt to equalize the purely formal opportunity to cast a ballot through a system of population-based apportionment.[23] Under this rationale, each district contains approximately the same number of people; each person within the district has the same opportunity to vote for someone to represent the district; and each district representative represents the same number of constituents.

The one-person, one-vote principle thus assures all voters the right to cast a theoretically equal ballot. In this section, I argue that this theoretical possibility is unlikely to be realized in an electoral system using winner-take-all districts. I further suggest that neither groups of voters nor individuals are fairly represented under such a system.

There are two issues at stake. One raises the question of whether voting is constitutionally protected because it implicates individual rights. If voting is an individual right, the second question asks whether the one-person, one-vote principles that operate within the confines of geographic districts adequately protect the right to vote. I concede that voting has garnered its highest constitutional protection when presented as an individual rights issue, but the widespread use of winner-take-all districts un-

dermines the validity of this characterization. The fact that constitutional rules about voting evolved within a system of regional representation suggests that posing the problem as one of individual rather than group rights has been a distraction. I claim that the heavy reliance on one-person, one-vote jurisprudence to develop a theory of democracy fails both as a theory and as an adequate doctrinal protection of either individual or group rights.

A. One-Person, One-Vote, and the Limits of Liberal Individualism

In this subsection, I examine the assumption that the allocation of representatives through winner-take-all districting is a form of representation of individuals. The heart of this assumption is that citizenship is the ultimate reflection of individual dignity and autonomy, and that voting is the means for individual citizens to realize this personal and social standing. Under this theory, voters realize the fullest meaning of citizenship by the individual act of voting for representatives who, once elected, participate on the voters' behalf in the process of self-government.[24] Indeed the very terminology employed in the Supreme Court's one-person, one-vote constitutional principle suggests that voting is an individual right.[25] For these reasons, some assume that the right at stake is the individual right to an equally weighted vote or an equally powerful vote.[26]

The assumption is that constitutional protection for voting is exclusively about protecting an individual right, not necessarily about ensuring equal voting rights. At first, the connection between the two concepts seems plausible because every citizen has the right to vote, and because every citizen has the right to an equally weighted vote. Yet the one-person, one-vote principle of voting is primarily about equal, not individual, representation.[27] Under this equality norm, the right to "fair and effective representation" subsumes concerns about equal voting and equal access. As the Supreme Court stated in one of its early reapportionment cases, the principle of equal representation for equal numbers of people is "designed to prevent debasement of voting power and diminution of access to elected representatives."[28] Implicit in this equality norm is the moral proposition that every citizen has the right to equal legislative influence. This means an equal opportunity to influence legislative policy.

The assumption that voting is an individual right is also unnecessary for the view that voting rights are a means of political empowerment. One-person, one-vote rules emerged in response to claims about population-based malapportionment and about the right of the majority of people to elect a proportionate share of representatives.[29] In announcing this principle, the Supreme Court recognized that the growing urban majority of the sixties would never command its fair share of legislative power unless the court intervened. In conjunction with concern about both a fair share of power and developments in the law of minority vote dilution, the court also adopted an instrumental view of voting: people would participate when and if they thought their vote mattered. Under this empowerment norm, the primary purpose of voting rights is to empower citizens to participate in the political process.[30]

I take the position that the right of the individual to participate politically is a right best realized in association with other individuals, in other words, as a group. As Justice Lewis Powell recognized, "[t]he concept of 'representation' necessarily applies to groups; groups of voters elect representatives, individual voters do not."[31] This is a bottom-up view of representation in which voters are empowered by their collective participation in the process of self-government. Under this view, voters engage in collective action to choose someone to represent their interests within the governing body. The representative is charged with influencing policy on behalf of constituents' collective interests.

However, the court's jurisprudence does not consistently express a bottom-up view of representation within either the equality or the empowerment norms.[32] On occasion, though, the court implicitly assumes the value of collective participation and influence in opinions that do not articulate the bottom-up view. For example, the court's discussion in Reynolds v. Sims of a fair share of representation for population majorities suggests that by equalizing the number of people for whom each representative is responsible, the election of a single individual can fairly represent what are in essence collect interests.[33] Another example is Baker v. Carr, where the plaintiffs' original complaint alleged a systematic plan to "discriminate against a geographical class of persons."[34]

The bottom-up view of representation is reflected in some of the court's early language about the importance of having a voice—meaning a public policy vote—in the process of self-government.[35] It also is the basis for the court's 1986 decision in Davis v. Bandemer that political gerrymandering claims are justiciable.[36] In his plurality opinion for the court in Davis, Justice White suggests that the policy decision to represent groups fairly already had been made in the context of racial minorities.[37]

Of course, one could counter that representation is essentially a process of providing individual constituents with individual service, and that it is therefore an individual right. This is a top-down view of representation in which the representative reaches back to his or her district to return government benefits to district constituents. In this sense, equalizing the number of constituents equalizes access for individuals, not groups of individuals. Representation becomes the formal opportunity to receive one's fair share of government benefits or to have access to one's representative for individual constituency service. Voting creates "a personal value," or a symbolic statement of belonging, by the mere act of casting a ballot.[38] A vote is meaningful because it is counted, whether or not it actually affects the outcome.

While this top-down view might rest on the assumption that the right to representation is an individual right, it does not mesh well with the assumption that the right to vote is an individual right. Indeed, a voter need not vote at all to be represented under this understanding. Actually casting a vote is less important than establishing voting status. Representation becomes the process of initiating a relationship in which one need not ever participate except by moving into the district. Even nonvoters are represented vicariously by choices made on their behalf.

Proponents of the philosophy of individualism attempt to use the one-person, one-vote principle to locate voting in the status of individual or constituent. They rely on the fact that every individual has the opportunity to cast a potentially winning vote or to be represented vicariously by one who does. This approach camouflages the group nature of voting by emphasizing the personal aspects of representation.

Consistent with their prevailing political philosophy of individualism, some members of the court have struggled mightily using one-person, one-vote rules to avoid the concept of group representation.[39] However, even when its nexus to group activity remains disguised, the principle of one-person, one-vote is as consistent with group as it is with individual representation. Similarly, the one-person, one-vote principle is consistent with semiproportional representation systems. Even if voters each were awarded five votes to plump as they choose, the one-person, one-vote principle would be satisfied, since each voter would have the same voting power or voting weight.

I argue that despite the efforts of some members of the court to characterize representation as an exclusively individual notion, the concept of group representation became unavoidable for two reasons. The first, which I develop in Section II, is that the concept of group voting was necessary to understand the political unfairness of excluding racial minorities in a racially polarized constituency. The second, to which I now turn, is that the one-person, one-vote principle was conceived and articulated within a construction of constituencies based on geography. It is districting itself that merges individual representation with the representation of groups of individuals. Thus, it always has been necessary to acknowledge, at least implicitly, the relationship between districts and interests. . . .

B. Group Representation and Territorial Districting

In this subsection, I argue that because of our explicit and implicit recognition of constituencies of geography, we have never actually employed a system of individual representation. Indeed, the use of geographic results as the basis for establishing representational constituencies is at its very heart a system of group-based representation. Moreover, even where districts comply with one-person, one-vote principles, such districts dilute the voting strength both of individuals and of groups.

The concept of representation necessarily applies to groups: groups of voters elect representatives, individuals do not.[40] Representation is more than the individual relationship between constituent and elected representative. Because representation is primarily about political influence, not about political service, bottom-up representation becomes the essential link to a genuine voice in the process of self-government. Districting is a form of group-interest representation, albeit an imperfectly realized one.

Districting, by definition, assumes that each voter is a " 'member' of a 'group' comprised of all the voters in her district."[41] As Justice Potter Stewart noted, "The very fact of geographic districting . . . carries with it an acceptance of the idea of legislative representation of regional needs and interests."[42] Regardless of whether other justices of the Warren Court ever consciously adopted the idea of interest representation, in working within territorial districts they assumed that interests reflect where people live.

The view that geography approximates political interests is not a new idea. Indeed, the idea that geographic units reflect a common or group identity is part of the historical explanation for the winner-take-all system of districts. The American system of winner-take-all districts was adapted from the system in Britain prior to 1832, which in turn can be traced to feudal origins. The feudal tradition helped to define the law of the franchise on the theory that "it was the land, and not men which should be represented."[43] It was the community, in theory, that was represented, and therefore the qualification for voting was corporative, with the franchise varying between communities. Functional groupings, not individuals, were the basic units of representation.[44]

The British system also created a link between political representation and geographically based interests. Elected representatives were not seen as representatives of individual constituencies; they were merely members of Parliament who represented all of Britain. The parliamentary system of representation had evolved in Britain because of feudal duties and obligations; the lord and his vassals were literally tied to the land, and representation in Parliament was actually part of the lord's feudal service to the king. Similarly, inhabitants of the medieval town were not separate, for representational purposes, from the town itself: the town was a political association, and the status of its inhabitants was defined by the rights of the group to which they belonged, namely the town. This link between political representation and economic or geographic ties was later carried over to the United States during the colonial period.

By the late eighteenth century, towns were directly represented in the American colonial legislatures by representatives with explicit instructions to represent the towns' interests. The relevance of town representation is that colonial towns "exercised power as a group, as a group they had rights, as a group they had powers."[45] Representation by geographical groups became the norm, in part because there was often no practical distinction between occupational and territorial representation.[46]

Indeed, the word "representation" originated as a term used by medieval jurists to describe the personification of collectivities; the spokesperson for a community was its embodiment, the bearer of its representative personhood.[47] Even in its modern form, representation often connotes the activity of furthering the interests of an abstraction rather than of an individual.[48] Although many liberal theorists of American democracy espouse the importance of representation of the rational individual, this claim is at odds with the historical roots of an electoral system that relies on regional rather than political units of representation.

It is also at odds with the practice of districting. The process of geographic districting collects people into units of representation by virtue of certain group characteristics or assumptions about shared characteristics within geographical communities. Geographic districting grounds the representational relationship in the opportunity to vote for a candidate to represent the interests of voters within a regionally defined political unit. It is assumed

that those voters who share the homogeneous characteristics that give the district its "identity" (its dominant political, regional, or racial affiliation) are in fact represented. Because all voters share at least a common regional identity—they all live within the district's geographic walls—all voters are therefore assumed to be represented without regard to their actual choice of a candidate.

However, the geographic unit is not necessarily politically homogeneous or of one mind as to who should represent it. In any contested election, some voters will vote for someone other than the winning candidate. These votes do not lead to the election of any candidate. Although these voters reside in equally populated districts, they have not chosen someone to represent their interests. Their theoretically equal votes are, as a practical matter, wasted in that the casting of their vote did not lead to the selection of their representative. The term "wasted votes," therefore, refers to votes cast for a candidate who does not win. In addition, I use the term to refer to votes cast for someone who does not need the votes to win. . . .

Constituents do not consciously choose to become members of this group, since very few people move somewhere in recognition of their likely voting efficacy within particular election subdistricts. Similarly, when they move, few people know in advance the particular elected officials by whom they are likely to be represented. In other words, voters do not move to an election district; they move to a neighborhood or community.

I am suggesting that constituents within a geographically districted group may be there involuntarily, without sharing the same interests as other community residents, and despite preexisting hierarchical relationships. In this way, membership in the territorial constituency is like membership in a family, with the former imposed by residence and the latter by kinship. Like family, geographic districts may not reflect conscious choice; as "compulsory constituencies," though, they nevertheless reflect ties that bind.

Moreover, even if this factual assumption is incorrect, voters who might move based on the likelihood that they will reside within a specific election district are not acting rationally. This is because the imperative of the one-person, one-vote rule mandates continual redistricting.[49] Even motivated voters can rely on existing district configurations for only limited lengths of time.

The level of mathematical equality now required by the courts[50] makes it hard to claim that many election districts are neighborhoods. The upshot of absolute population equality as the basis for representation is that equipopulous districts are more important than districts that preserve communities of interests or leave neighborhoods intact. In this respect, districting under the one-person, one-vote rule is arbitrary. Indeed, this was Justice Stewart's complaint when he accused the Supreme Court of privileging the personal right to vote over the efforts of local government to represent regional needs, communities of interest, or political subunits.[51]

Districting justifies the representation of this artificial group using a theory of virtual representation.[52] "Virtual" representation works like "constructive" in "constructive possession": it means "as if" or "pretended" representation.[53] In contrast to direct representation or bottom-up representation, virtual representation relies on three concepts: indirect representation, representation of similar interests elsewhere, and top-down representation. While the theory of virtual representation theoretically could be justified by any one of these concepts, the three assumptions generally are interrelated. Each of these assumptions is critical to the validity of virtual representation.

First, virtual representation assumes that the district winner indirectly represents the district losers. For this to hold true, the election winner must do an adequate job of representing all those who reside within the district, including his or her political opponents. This assumption is based on the golden-rule principle that the winner will not tyrannize the losers because the winner may become the loser in the next election. The winner realizes the value of political stability, so she will also represent the losers. Thus, in the long run, the losers' votes are not permanently wasted, because they operate to hold the winners in check.

The second assumption of virtual representation is that the district losers technically are represented by similarly situated voters elsewhere in the political system. In this assumption, voters are represented when other voters—who are like them—vote in other districts and succeed in electing their candidate of choice. This reasoning assumes that similarly situated voters are fungible—in other words, that they are essentially indistinguishable on some critical threshold issue—and that groups "district voters" by characteristics they share with "nondistrict voters." Because of these group characteristics, district losers are vicariously represented by winners in other districts for whom they would have voted had they been given the chance. As a result, the second assumption sees voters as represented based on certain "group" characteristics that can be externally predetermined for a ten-year period (between census counts) at the time of reapportionment, and can be measured jurisdictionwide, rather than districtwide.[54] Again, the district losers' votes technically are not wasted because these losers are represented by someone, albeit not someone for whom they voted.

The third virtual representation assumption is that the district itself is a cognizable group that is represented ultimately as a community of the whole. This incorporates the proposition that a district has some independent existence apart from the discrete individuals who form an electoral majority. This is the historical claim that the district itself has a political or group identity.

This argument relies on a top-down view of representation. Living in Pennsylvania, I am represented by two U. S. senators even if I am under eighteen years old, mentally incompetent, or disenfranchised based on noncitizenship or a criminal conviction. The assumption is that the district, and hence all its residents, are serviced whenever anyone is elected to represent the district. The key element of representation is equal access to the elected representative who is available to each constituent as a result of her status as a district resident. Each of the voters within the district is represented—those who voted for a losing candidate as well as those who did not or could not vote. Because voting is primarily symbolic of personal status within a coherent community, virtual representation argues that no one's vote is wasted.

Every voter in a district is presumed to be represented simply because her territorial constituency is represented. The voter within a territorial constituency is represented because she has someone to turn to in case of personal constituency service needs. She is presumed to be represented even if she did not vote for the winning candidate. The fact that she wasted her vote is ignored, because she is nevertheless "geographically" present within the political subdivision. No stock is placed in the fact that she did not vote for the representative. She is simply represented through the direct representation of her needs and her geographic nexus to the representative's supporters.

If districting is to be justified by virtual representation, the entire theory of districting depends upon the juxtaposition of territorial constituencies and interest constituencies. Drawing district boundaries presumably defines communities of interest. District lines determine a set of associations between the voter and a particular representative, as well as among the voters themselves. It is only because voters within a particular district are deemed unlikely to have opposing interests that the notion of a personal relationship between the voter and the representative can survive. Voters are presumed fungible. The representative otherwise would be unable to service disparate personal needs without compromising the interests of other constituents.

These virtual representation assumptions are related to two somewhat inconsistent premises of liberal individualism. One is the value of majority rule. The district majority governs with legitimacy, because the district is a coalition of shifting "factions" whose multiplicity of interests will keep any one from dominating. The factions demonstrate that the district is not homogeneous, but the winner will virtually represent the losers because the losers are not permanent; the winner may be the loser in

the next election. The first premise of liberal individualism thus shares the first premise of virtual representation. It posits that individuals who vote for losing candidates are adequately represented by the winning candidate and have as much opportunity to influence that candidate as do other voters in the district.

The second premise is that representation is primarily a personal relationship between the representative and her constituents. In this context, the representative does not know how a particular constituent voted and will service her needs in the hopes of recruiting or sustaining her allegiance. Adherents of the personal relationship perspective do not deny that the representative is more likely to represent faithfully the interests of those who voted for her; they simply suggest that the needs of each constituent also will be met because a district constituency establishes a relationship between the voter and her personal representative without regard to the voter's actual electoral preference.

However, this premise, unlike the majority-rule premise, is based on a view of relative homogeneity within the district. Because the district constituents have similar needs and interests, it is possible for one representative adequately to service all constituents. If the constituency has such common interests, one would expect a relatively unanimous constituency. By contrast, the majority-rule assumption relies on a more fractured constituency to balance the majority's urge to dominate. The personal relationship perspective and the majority-rule premise are, therefore, in some tension. They define voting by reference to competing notions of fungibility and personal access, on the one hand, and distinct interests, on the other.

As a consequence, the virtual representation assumptions do not fit neatly within a one-dimensional view of representation based on liberal individualism. In fact, the rational individual who serves as the focal point of individualism would often take actions that are wholly inconsistent with virtual representation. The most apparent inconsistency is the idea that one's interests can be effectively represented by someone whom the voter, when given the choice, rationally determined does not reflect her interests. There is something distinctly un-liberal in the view that indirect representation of interests is preferable to direct representation of groups or interests as defined by the voters themselves. If the voter who goes to the polls is represented by the person against whom he or she votes, then the representation of the major-ity of the people becomes a representation of the whole people. The voter is defined not by a rational individual choice but by the majority's choice.

Another inconsistency is the notion that the voter will be motivated to participate when she will be adequately represented by whoever is elected. Voting will simply become a habit, a civic duty, although it yields no direct results. In such a scenario, the rational individual would choose not to vote because of the small likeli-hood of casting the decisive vote.

Yet another inconsistency is produced by the virtual representation assumption that wasted votes—those cast for a losing candidate—do not reflect the absence of representation because the territory defines the community, the group, and its interests. This view suggests that mere geographical subdivisions have interests distinct from those of the people who inhabit them. Because individualism posits that the rational individual will act in her own self-interest, this external determination of the interests repre-sented is inconsistent with individualism.

Perhaps most inconsistent with the theory of autonomous, rational individuals is virtual representation's notion of fungibility. Virtual representation, explicitly in the second assump-tion and implicitly in the third, assumes that individuals are interchangeable based on some externally observed characteristics. Accordingly, individual choice is subordinated to the choices made by the majority, and the individual must allow someone in another district to act on her behalf.

In these often-unstated but related ways, districting conflates the view that territorial constituencies virtually represent discrete indi-viduals who reside therein with the view that territorial constituencies group like-minded voters. Related to each of the virtual representa-tion assumptions, therefore, is the corollary that

we can use proxies, in this case geography, for determining voter interests. Such proxies merge voters' own definitions of their interests with the self-interest of political incumbents or with the interests of a homogeneous territorial dis-trict majority. The use of such proxies reveals the fundamentally group-based nature of repre-sentation—a feature that is inherent in, but inadequately recognized by, our contemporary system of representation.

For example, where representation is only virtual rather than direct, those who vote for the losing candidate may find that their interests are not represented at all. The constituency is presumed to be a group based on a single choice—the decision where to reside. This one choice may not be a real choice for some; for others it may not satisfactorily carry all the weight being assigned. Alternatively, the as-sumption that the geographic constituency is not dominated by a highly organized majority may simply be wrong as a matter of fact.

It is important to recognize, therefore, that the districting debate is not only about repre-senting groups; it may also be about represent-ing groups or individuals unfairly. If voting reflects the voter's conscious choice rather than simply representing the voter's state of belong-ing, then winner-take-all districting in fact wastes votes both of individuals and of groups. First, it makes certain that there are political losers in each district. Those who vote—as individuals or as a group—for the losing candi-date do not obtain any direct political represen-tation. They did not initiate, and they cannot alone terminate, the representational relation-ship. In response, an individual rights advocate might argue that the individual who votes for a losing candidate is adequately represented by the winning candidate and has "as much oppor-tunity to influence that candidate as other voters in the district."[55] This, of course, makes sense only if one assumes both that election results count for very little, and that representation is exclusively about individual access to represen-tatives chosen by others.[56]

In response, districts could be made more homogeneous in order to reduce the number of wasted votes. However, this alternative demonstrates the second way in which winner-take-all districting wastes votes. When more people vote for the winning candidate than is necessary to carry the district, their votes are technically wasted because they were unnecessary to provide an electoral margin within the district, and they could have been used to provide the necessary electoral margin for a like-minded partisan in another district. In other words, packing voters in homogeneous districts wastes votes because it dilutes their overall voting strength jurisdictionwide.

The third way in which districting wastes votes becomes apparent if we consider voting broadly. I have suggested that voting is not simply about winning elections; the purpose of voting is to influence public policy. Accordingly, I have elsewhere proposed a concept, which I labeled "proportionate interest representation," to describe the importance of an equal opportunity to influence public policy, not just to cast a ballot.[57] This concept reflects both the equality and empowerment norms that I discussed earlier, because the right to cast an equally powerful vote subsumes the right to participate directly in the choice of representatives who then presumably enjoy an equal opportunity to influence legislative policy.

If voting is understood as a means of exercising policy influence, districting tends to limit that influence. Winner-take-all districting gives the district majority all the power. It creates an incentive, therefore, to seek electoral control of a district. However, electoral control of a district may isolate minority partisans from potential allies in other districts. In this way, districting wastes votes because it forces minorities to concentrate their strength within a few electoral districts and thereby isolates them from potential legislative allies.

For example, race-conscious districting attempts to provide disadvantaged racial groups the equal opportunity to participate by drawing geographic districts in which the majority are minorities (a "majority minority district"). Proponents of this strategy assume that electoral control—becoming a district majority—works as a proxy for interest, but creating majority black districts also means creating majority

white districts in which the electoral success of white legislators is not dependent upon black votes. In this way, race-conscious districting may simply reproduce within the legislature the disadvantaged numerical and racial isolation that the majority minority district attempted to cure at the electoral level.

Where blacks and whites are geographically separate, race-conscious districting isolates blacks from potential white allies—for example, white women—who are not geographically concentrated. It "wastes" the votes of white liberals who may be submerged within white, Republican districts. As a consequence, districting may suppress the development of cross-racial legislative coalition-building. Because majority black districts are necessarily accompanied by majority white districts, black representatives may be disenfranchised in the governing body. In this third sense, districting wastes votes because it fails to ensure legislative influence.

The wasted-vote phenomenon makes gerrymandering inevitable. Because winner-take-all districting awards disproportionate power to electoral majorities, it inflates the advantage of district control. This inflated power quotient drives the apportionment process and leads some, myself included, to conclude that on some level all districting is gerrymandering. Gerrymandering is inherent in the districting process, which in essence is the process of distributing wasted votes.

Where incumbent politicians seek safe districts to ensure their reelection, they may be inclined to gerrymander, that is, to waste the votes for their likely opponent; where political or racial partisans seek legislative control, they may be inclined to gerrymander, that is, to pack the minority party or minority race into a few districts to diminish their overall influence. Alternatively, they may fracture the likely supporters of the minority party or minority race, spreading out their votes among a number of districts and ensuring that they do not comprise an electoral majority in any district. These votes are counted, but they are essentially irrelevant in influencing the electoral or governing process.

The gerrymandering phenomenon illustrates once again the group nature of districting. Gerrymandering depends on assumptions about voters' likely behavior based on externally observed or supposed group characteristics or perceived common interests. Although the use of electoral districting has been defended with arguments based on the virtues of individual representation, assumptions about the nature of groups likely form the theoretical underpinnings of the election method.

I have tried to show that district representation weakens the connection between the voters' votes and the voters' representative by wasting votes. Unless all the voters in the district vote for the winning candidate, some of their votes are wasted. In addition, if a candidate only needs 51 percent of the votes to win, but the district is homogeneous and electorally noncompetitive, then all votes for the winning candidate over 51 percent are also technically wasted. The point is that the voter is deemed to be represented whether she votes for the losing candidate, is an unnecessary part of the winning candidate's victory margin, or fails to vote at all.

The concept of wasted voting reveals the one-dimensional quality of the virtual representation assumptions. Yet wasted voting is only one of the ways that district representation minimizes the connection between voting and representation. The winner-take-all aspect of territorial constituencies also tends to overrepresent the winning party and to deny the losing party a voice on behalf of their specific interests in the legislative forum where public policy is finally fashioned. In addition, territorial constituencies both submerge and subsume the concept of group representation. They also subsume individual definitions of relevant group identity in favor of individual residential decisions.

The artificial nature of these geographic associations suggests the limitations of the view that individual representation is the cornerstone of the right to vote. Territorial constituencies do not realize individual autonomy for at least three reasons. First, many people do not exercise real choice in deciding their place of residence.[58] Second, even where residential decisions are conscious and discretionary, they do not capture the range or salience of interests which voters may hold. Third, the one-person, one-vote requirement of equipopulous districting makes districting even more artificial. If the major constraint on the drawing of district lines is the number of people within each district, district lines cannot conform to naturally occurring areas of common interest. When incumbents exercise enormous control over the districting process, including the custody of census data and the access to computer technology, communities of interest may become mere reelection opportunities. This is the threat to functional interest representation that various justices have predicted over the years in their dissents to strict population equality principles. . . .

II.

IN this section, I argue that race is as effective as geography in functioning as a political proxy; neither, though, is as effective as allowing voters the opportunity to make their own local choices about the nature and salience of their interests. Semiproportional systems permit shifting coalitions to form based on voters' own determinations of their interests or their group identity. In other words, geography and race rely on representational assumptions about group association but do not suggest the necessity, standing alone, of either representing or defining group interests a particular way. Modified at-large systems, such as cumulative voting, could be viewed as preferable alternatives that allow members of racial groups, politically cohesive groups, and strategically motivated individuals to be both self-defined and represented, while minimizing the problem of wasted votes for all voters.

Race in this country has defined individual identities, opportunities, frames of reference, and relationships. Where race has been of historical importance and continues to play a significant role, racial group membership often serves as a political proxy for shared experience and common interests. At least to the extent that an overwhelming majority of group members experience a common "group identity,"[59] those who are group members are more likely to represent similar interests.[60] Group members also may share common cultural styles or operating assumptions.[61]

Group members also are more likely to be perceived by their constituents as representing them. This definition of representatives as descriptive likeness or racial compatriot has a psychological component. Just as the flag stands for the nation, the presence of racial group members symbolizes inclusion of a previously excluded group. The symbolic role results both from the personal characteristics of the racial group member and from the assumption that, because of those characteristics, the racial group member has had experiences in common with her constituents. As Hanna Pitkin writes in her groundbreaking work on representation, "We tend to assume that people's characteristics are a guide to the actions they will take, and we are concerned with the characteristics of our legislators for just this reason."[62] Thus, many racial minorities do not feel represented unless members of their racial group are physically present in the legislature.

As a result, traditional voting rights advocates comfortably rely on race as a proxy for interests. For example, in conventional voting rights litigation, election contests between black and white candidates help to define the degree of racial polarization, that is, the degree to which blacks and whites vote differently. The idea is that the outcome would be different if elections were held only in one community or the other. The assumption of difference extends explicitly to the specific candidate elected, and implicitly to the issues that candidate, once elected, would emphasize.

The assumption of this difference between races rests in part on the claim that where black candidates enjoy protection from electoral competition with whites, black voters can ratify their choices to hold their representatives accountable. In this way, the association between race and interests is modified to the extent that voters are given a meaningful choice in both initiating and terminating a representational relationship. Voting rights advocates assume that minority group sponsorship is critical.[63] It is only where minority voters exercise electoral

control or have a meaningful opportunity to retire their representative that race functions as a representational proxy. Thus, majority black single-member districts take advantage of segregated housing patterns to use geography as a proxy for racial choice, racial control, and racial representation.

I argued in Section I that the one-person, one-vote cases, with their focus on equalizing individual access through equalizing population, conceal the group nature of representation of districting. . . . Race-conscious districting confronts the group nature of representation more directly: it attempts to minimize the wasted-vote problem for minority voters whose preferred candidates—because of racial bloc voting by the majority—experience consistent defeat at the polls. Where voting is racially polarized, white voters and black voters vote differently. Where blacks are a numerical minority, racial bloc voting means that the political choices of blacks rarely are successful. To remedy this problem of being a permanent loser, black political activists and voting rights litigants have sought majority black districts in which the electoral choices of a majority of blacks determined the electoral winner.[64]

Nevertheless, some commentators challenge race-conscious districting on the grounds that special protection throughout the political process for the rights of minority groups is unnecessary as long as individual minority group members have a fair chance to participate formally by voting in an election.[65] For these commentators, race-conscious districting is illegitimate because the right to vote is individual, not group-based.[66] Relying again on assumptions about fungibility and access, these observers challenge the right of minority groups to representative or responsive government.

Given the prominence of racial group identities, I am not persuaded by this criticism to abandon the concept of group representation. I am aware of, but not in accord with, those critics of race-conscious districting who object on moral grounds to the drawing of districts along racial lines. Representation is a bottom-up process that ideally recognizes the importance of influencing public policy decisions on behalf of constituency interests. Accordingly, we cannot define political fairness merely as electoral fairness guaranteeing nonbiased conditions of voting eligibility and equally counted votes. Nor do I think the only issues are whether blacks have special claims for protection or whether whites can or should represent blacks, although I think they can and do.[67]

Yet, in making the argument that racial groups deserve representation, I do not rely primarily on the political, sociological, or cultural claims involved in racial group identity, or even on the historic context of group disenfranchisement. My principal argument rests on the distinction within the political process between a claim for group rights and a claim for group representation. I argue for the latter, based on the historic evidence that representation within territorial districts is implicitly about recognition of group interests, not just individual access. However, the future of such group representation—like the future of the group itself—lies less inside geographic boundaries and more within the cultural and political community forged by group consciousness and group identity. Empowerment—for a group as well as for an individual—comes from active assertion of self-defined interests. A group is represented where it has the opportunity to speak out, not just to be spoken for.

The argument for recognition of group interests makes three assumptions about representation. First, legislators should represent unanimous, not divided, constituencies.[68] Second, each voter's vote should count toward the election of a representative. Third, the unit of representation should be psychological, cultural, and/or political, rather than territorial. In other words, groups should be represented, but in ways that permit automatic, self-defined apportionment based on shifting political or cultural affiliation and interests. This would enable voters to form voluntary affiliative districts without the need for prior authorization or formal recognition of the group as one that deserves special treatment. Because such group identity would be affiliative and interest-based, group representation would encourage both coalition-building among racial and political factions and

grassroots political organization around issues, not just around individual candidacies.

If the decision to represent groups already has been made in the adoption of geographic districting, then group representation based on racial group association or historical oppression becomes less problematic. Whatever the alleged flaws in racial group representation, it is racial representation within a system of geographic districts that must be analyzed. One white Democratic congressman who represents a largely minority constituency is quoted as saying: "I'm torn about it. I do not believe you have to be of the exact same ethnic group to do a good job in representing that community. But, in the end, I think it's that community's choice."[69] Thus, it is important to emphasize the connection between choice, accountability, and group identification. Whoever represents minority interests (just as whoever represents majority interests) should be directly, not merely virtually, accountable to those interests.

However, some critics of race-conscious districting might attempt to distinguish race from geography as a useful political proxy. Such critics claim that the geographic association, unlike race, is temporal, individualistic, and discretionary, at least for some people. There are two problems with this purported distinction. First, geography is neither discretionary nor individualized for members of disadvantaged racial groups. Rather, it reflects the very essence of limitations on choice based on group identity. Race-conscious districting can capture racial communities of interest precisely because residential ghettos are often the result of racial discrimination. As Professor Pamela Karlan writes, residential segregation reflects racial discrimination in both the private and public housing markets.[70] Because residential segregation by definition results from the absence of choice, race-conscious districting "can serve as a proxy for a bundle of distinct political interests."[71]

A second problem is that this criticism applies only to race-conscious representation executed within a system of fixed district boundaries. Indeed, the concern can be avoided almost entirely where the voters themselves define their own interests using alternative, modified at-large systems of representation. Representation based on voluntary interest constituencies would unhitch racial group representation from arbitrary, involuntary assignments.

The voluntary interest constituencies would be comparable to Professor Iris Marion Young's model of a "highly visible" social group with emotional, historical, and social salience defined by a sense of group identity, not just shared attributes.[72] According to Young, groups exist only in relation to other groups.[73] The social processes of affinity and differentiation produce groups. Yet group differentiation is not necessarily oppressive nor homogeneous; it is created by multiple, cross-cutting, and shifting differences.

The group differentiation of racial minorities is a function of historical oppression, shared experience, and present inequality. Territorial configurations may track this phenomenon to the extent that disadvantaged racial groups are concentrated in substandard housing in urban ghettos, but differentiation by race cuts across geographic lines in many cases. Some racial group members share a group-consciousness without sharing group space; others are dispersed in small barrios throughout the jurisdiction. Still others may technically be group members in terms of their racial origin or current residence but not in terms of their racial identity.

In addition, group differentiation by race subsumes gender, age, and class differences. A racial group that is politically cohesive on civil rights or welfare policy may have some members with interests that are not shared throughout the group. On these issues, the racial group members may have more in common with group members of another race living outside of their immediate geographic area. In other words, racial groups are not monolithic, nor are they necessarily cohesive.

Race in conjunction with geography is a useful but limited proxy for defining the interests of those sharing a particular racial identity. However, it is the assumption that a territorial district can accurately approximate a fixed racial group identity—and not the assumption of a

racial group identity itself—that is problematic. Race-conscious districting, as opposed to racial group representation, may be rigidly essentialist, presumptuously isolating, or politically divisive. For example, different groups may share the same residential space but not the same racial identity. A districting strategy requires these groups to compete for political power through the ability to elect only one representative.

Yet strategies for race-conscious districting respond to important deficits in a non-race-conscious geographic districting process. Proponents of racial group representation confront on the jurisdictionwide level the unfairness of the indirect, virtual representation claims. In justifying race-conscious districting, voting rights activists appropriately employ the concept of racial group identity.[74] They can demonstrate that members of the racial group have distinctive interests that are often ignored by elected officials who suffer no adverse consequences at the polls.[75] In this way, the activists challenge the view that voters are fungible, especially where minority group voters are consistent losers as a result of racial bloc voting by the jurisdiction majority.

Based on complaints about the way that virtual assumptions operate at the macro level to dilute minority voting strength, race-conscious strategies seek to control small, majority minority districts. By making the minority a district majority, race-conscious districting seeks to exercise the prerogatives of majority rule on behalf of a jurisdictionwide minority. While they challenge the fairness of jurisdictionwide virtual representation of minority voters by the majority, though, proponents of race-conscious districts replicate many of the same fairness problems at the micro level.

The same assumptions about virtual representation that were the object of challenge at the macrolevel are now reproduced within subdistricts that the racial minority controls. The majority minority subdistrict operates on the same winner-take-all, majority-rule principles. Even as an imperfect geometric "fractal"[76] of a larger jurisdictionwide majority, it carries with it the assumptions of virtual representation to justify the minority group's domination. As a consequence, race-conscious districting raises in microcosm the theoretical questions I raised in Section I about districting itself.

An illustration of this fractal problem is a 1992 New York City congressional plan that included a Brooklyn-Queens district to represent the interests of a Latino minority.[77] This district concentrated Latinos in a new Twelfth Congressional District.[78] Several Latino activists filed as candidates in the Democratic primary; so did Representative Stephen Solarz, a white incumbent whose previous district was consolidated within one-fifth of the new "Latino" district.[79]

The entry of a well-financed, nine-term incumbent from a largely Jewish section of Brooklyn shifted the political expectations. The primary, which had been expected to focus on issues of interest to a poor Latino constituency, turned into a debate over whether a minority group could be represented by someone of a different ethnicity. According to a Latino community organizer, "The community is saying, 'Why is it that this Jewish person who has always represented other interests than ours, comes in now saying he's going to be our savior?' "[80] This complaint—that the white incumbent should not enter the race—rested on a complex, but misinformed, understanding of group representation.

The group is deemed represented where it has electoral control over the winner. The organizer's concern was that the 16 percent white minority in the district—not the Latino majority—could have electoral control by consolidating their votes and converting their minority status into a plurality win. Since there were at least four Latino candidates, the white candidate would most likely win if the Latino vote were split, even though Latinos are 55 percent of the district's voting-age population. If the Latino majority was disaggregated into factions supporting different Latino candidates, it could have been white voters who chose the representative for the new district.

Latino activists complained that this did not give their community the choice they deserved: "The whole idea was to give our community some degree of choice, Latinos or non-Latinos

who have some connection with the community. . . . [The well-financed white incumbent] doesn't fit that bill at all."[81] The white candidate answered, "The other candidates fear that I'll win, which somewhat belies their notion that the purpose of this district was to empower the people to make a choice."[82]

The nature of this controversy was captured by a *New York Times* headline that appeared before the primary: DOES POLITICS OF FAIRNESS MEAN ONLY THOSE FROM MINORITIES SHOULD APPLY?[83] I propose restating the problem as follows: Does politics of fairness mean that self-defined groups are best represented by territorial districts, even those they ostensibly control? So stated, the question shifts the issue from the candidate to the constituency. By asking this new question, we can see the three incongruous assumptions inherent in racial control of territorial constituencies.

The first assumption is that because they represent a majority of the district population, the 55 percent Latino voting-age population is appropriately empowered to represent the entire district, although 8 percent of the district is black, 21 percent Asian, and 16 percent white.[84] This assumption parallels the first virtual representation assumption: the district losers will be represented indirectly by majority winners.

Race-conscious districting is arguably necessary because the jurisdictionwide majority is organized racially and permanently.[85] This argument suggests that there is nothing inherently wrong with the principles of indirect representation underlying winner-take-all majoritarianism, except where the majority operates based on its prejudices. As long as the current pattern of racial bloc voting continues, the minority cannot become part of the jurisdictionwide governing coalition. Thus, "special" smaller majorities are warranted.

The second assumption is that a Latino majority in this district will choose a representative for all Latinos in the jurisdiction. This tracks the second vicarious representation assumption that similarly situated voters can represent each other. Because Latino interests are underrepresented in other winner-take-all congressional districts, their interests in the city as a whole are now fairly represented by virtue of their electoral control over this one district. Conversely, the Asian, black, and white minorities in this one district are vicariously represented by their electoral control over other districts in the city.

Thus, Latinos who do not live in the district are virtually represented by choices made by the Latinos who do live in the district. Race-conscious districting only approximates the diversity of voter identities in the jurisdiction as a whole, but not necessarily in each district.

With the second assumption, the race-conscious districting approach does not challenge political representation based on geography; it simply suggests that specific groups should dominate specific districts in proportion to their overall statewide or jurisdictionwide percentage. Here, the claim is that political fairness is measured by a jurisdictionwide baseline rather than by reference to a critique of group rights or majority domination more generally. Majority domination is acceptable as long as each group gets a chance to be represented somewhere in the jurisdiction by its own localized majority.

The third assumption is that the Twelfth Congressional District is a minority district without regard to the actual intra- or interminority conflict within the district. The third assumption presumes political cohesion based on the fiction that the district has an identity independent of the actual constituents. It also presumes equal access for constituency service within the district and relies on the claim that a minority identity ensures a minority ideology. Minority group interests will define the district identity and anyone who represents it.

The Asian, black, and white minorities are presumed to be represented because of their choice to live near Latinos. Stated differently, because Latinos are not as residentially segregated as other racial groups, they can represent the interests of their multicultural neighborhood as a whole. Their neighbors' interests are represented both for personal constituency service and for their territorially defined common interests.

The third assumption is related to the top-down view of representation. Like the virtual representation view that the district has an independent identity, the Twelfth Congressional District is a "Latino District." As a so-called minority district, it has an identity independent of the actual tensions present, the level of political cohesion, or the political participation rates of its constituents. In this way, race-conscious districting incorporates a static, somewhat monolithic, view of representation that, after the initial drawing of a majority minority district, diminishes the subsequent importance of broad authority from a consenting group of participants.

For example, Latinos within the district arguably are represented by any one of the four Latino candidates, even where a majority of the Latino residents vote for a losing candidate. The issue of choice is submerged within a presumption of ethnic solidarity in the majority Latino population district, even if Representative Solarz did not compete. This is because the district is a Latino district, and the elected representative will therefore service all constituents equally, especially other Latinos.[86]

Yet a top-down view of representation does not encourage broad-based political participation among the direct constituency. Nonvoters are represented equally with voters. Because representation is viewed primarily as a means of distributing constituency service and benefits and is primarily based on a common group identity, there is little incentive actively to monitor the public policy positions the representative takes within the governing body. Under this top-down view, elections serve not to initiate an interactive relationship, but to ratify an open-ended one.

In this way, the assumption of "minority district as independent identity" ignores issues of multiple, cross-cutting, and shifting differences. This is an empowerment strategy designed primarily to increase the proportion of minority group legislators. Because of the success of individual minority group members, the group as a whole is empowered. However, empowerment is not based on assumptions about phenotypic representation; voters also must be directly given the opportunity and the information necessary to define their interests for themselves.

These three assumptions, of course, invite the criticism that race-conscious districting arbitrarily reduces voters to their ethnic or racial identity and then only represents that characteristic in a way that isolates or balkanizes the population. However, the real complaint is not with the race-consciousness of the districting, but with the districting process itself: the race-conscious districting assumptions simply replay the same virtual representation assumptions that are used to justify territorial constituencies in the first place.

Thus, the race-conscious districting assumptions are neither unique nor necessarily contextual. For example, the winning candidate might be the one Latina who appeals to all the different ethnic and racial groups within the district, winning with a 5 percent plurality of Latino support and a solid majority of white, black, and Asian votes. Although this individual might be Latina in identity, she would not in fact be elected directly by Latinos to represent their interests.

In fact, the successful candidate was Nydia Velazquez, a former representative of Puerto Rico to New York, who polled 33 percent of the vote, compared to 27 percent for Mr. Solarz. According to the *New York Times*, Ms. Velazquez's margin of victory came from overwhelming Latino support in Brooklyn and from strong support from the black community.[87] She reportedly benefited from the endorsement by the city's black mayor, David Dinkins, and from the "firestorm" of criticism that erupted when Mr. Solarz decided to run in the newly drawn district.[88]

One might argue, then, that Ms. Velazquez's election affirmed the second and third assumptions of virtual representation. Because Latinos supported her within the Twelfth District, Latinos throughout New York City are now vicariously represented even though they could not vote for her. In addition, Ms. Velazquez's black support confirmed the viability of the third assumption that the Twelfth District is a bona

fide "minority district." The first virtual representation assumption is not directly implicated by the election because it depends upon postelection behavior of the elected representative.

Four other Latino candidates competed in the primary. Elizabeth Colon polled 26 percent; Ruben Franco polled 8 percent; Eric Ruano Melendez and Rafael Mendez each received 3 percent of the vote.[89] Although I do not have the actual precinct totals, these figures do not rebut the possibility that a majority of Latino voters (especially those living in Queens), actually preferred someone other than Ms. Velazquez. Similarly, they do not deny the possibility that blacks, who are only 8 percent of the district, may have supported Ms. Velazquez, but Asians and whites may have preferred someone else.[90]

Because Asians, at 21 percent, are the second-largest group in the district, it may not be appropriate to presume that interminority political cohesion extends to all of the district's minority voters. The other aspect of the third assumption—that this is a genuine Latino district—is also not clear, since a majority of Latinos may have preferred someone other than Ms. Velazquez.

The validity of the first assumption, that the electoral majority will now indirectly represent all the electoral minorities, also remains to be seen. It is currently a theoretical claim based on the operation of golden-rule reciprocity in conjunction with other assumptions about the individual nature of voting and representation. The district's political reality, however, may defy the theory that the district minority—those who wasted their votes—will act as a potent political check on a shifting district majority. For example, I noted the possibility that the election returns suggest distinct group interests among and within the Asian, black, and white district community. The votes of these subgroups may, as a practical matter, become permanently wasted.

Indeed, over the ten-year term of the district, the Latino majority may act cohesively and return the Latina incumbent to office. Reelection of the incumbent may occur with decreasing turnout as a percentage of all the district's population, but with increasing support among those who do vote simply because she is the incumbent. This is consistent with evidence that minority candidacies generate relatively high voter turnout the first time a viable minority candidate competes. Turnout, however, tends to go down when constituents realize that the election of a single minority incumbent changes very little of their day-to-day lives.

Nevertheless, the fact that the Latina is now an incumbent gives her tremendous resource advantages over any future opponents. Some may argue that her continued reelection reduces polarization within the district, as the other non-Latina voters see Ms. Velazquez work on their behalf. On the other hand, her predictable reelection success may exacerbate rather than reduce intergroup conflict. The district's complicated racial, ethnic, and linguistic mix is not reflected in the ethnic or racial group membership of its representative. The fact that the district winner in a multiethnic district has a psychological, cultural, and sociological connection primarily to one ethnic or racial group may alienate other groups over time.

If Asians, for example, feel consigned to permanent minority status within the minority district, they may bide their time until redistricting in the year 2000, when the legislature decides how many minority districts should be created and who should control them. The fight to be "the group" who gets the district, and with it all the power, pits minorities against each other. The fact that some members of the other minority groups in the Twelfth District can only cast wasted votes for ten years encourages each group ultimately to think in terms of its own moral, historical, and pragmatic claims to exclusive or primary district representation. Where representation becomes the lottery of competing oppression, no one wins.

Only the second assumption, at least on the psychological level of vicarious representation, is solidly supported by the election of Ms. Velazquez. This is based on evidence that those minority group members who do not vote for group members nevertheless feel "represented" by them. This phenomenon reflects the contin-

ued vitality of racial group identity. Many group members feel most represented by one of their own.

Even if the second vicarious representation assumption is true, one could maintain that people are represented without regard for whom they choose to vote simply because of where they choose to live or who they are. Latinos in Queens living a few blocks outside the Twelfth District, who cannot vote for Ms. Velazquez, will continue to "waste" their votes within the districts in which they reside. Their votes, which under some other district configuration might help elect an additional, or simply a different, Latino, are submerged within their non-Latino district.

Because their votes will be wasted, nondistrict Latinos are not encouraged to participate directly in the process of self-government. The process of voting itself may become meaningless. Districting ignores this problem with wasted votes by embracing group representation based on territorial contiguity and indirect representation.

Because geographic districting wastes votes, neither minority groups nor majority voters are fairly represented. Districting fails to deliver on its virtual representation assumptions, even where districts are drawn to maximize minority voting strength. Districting is not justified by the individual representation value because each voter's vote does not count to the greatest extent possible toward the election of a representative. Districting is not supported by the group representation value because legislators do not represent unanimous constituencies, and they therefore find it either hard to govern or easy to excuse unaccountability. The tensions— between values of individual and group representation; between direct and indirect representation; between top-down and bottom-up representation; and between wasted and effective votes—permeate virtual representation, even within race-conscious geographic districting.

For this reason, modified at-large systems used in corporate governance, such as cumulative voting, should be considered.[91] Under a modified at-large system, each voter is given the same number of votes as open seats, and the voter may plump or cumulate her votes to reflect the intensity of her preferences. Depending on the exclusion threshold,[92] politically cohesive minority groups are assured representation if they vote strategically.[93] Similarly, all voters have the potential to form voluntary constituencies based on their own assessment of their interests. As a consequence, semiproportional systems such as cumulative voting give more voters, not just racial minorities, the opportunity to vote for a winning candidate.

Racial group interests become those self-identified, voluntary constituencies which choose to combine because of like minds, not like bodies. Legitimate interest constituencies are formed among groups of individuals who share similar opinions or identities. These interest constituencies are less fixed than under territorial districting. Nevertheless, racial minority groups may still choose collectively to elect representatives—however, the minority voters' choices are now based on their conception of identity, which may be defined in racial terms because it is either racially apparent, racially derived, or a function of historical treatment by the numerically superior racial majority.[94]

Thus, even if voting is thought to be a concept of individual autonomy, the recognition of voluntary choices to affiliate or form associations minimizes wasted voting while transcending "artificial groups" based solely on residence or race. On the other hand, if voting is seen as a group representation concept, representation systems should minimize wasted votes in order to realize maximum influence and empowerment. Under either view of voting and representation, a semiproportional system is preferable because it minimizes wasted votes and defines voting behavior based on choices exercised by the voters themselves.

Additionally, if racial group identity is a value that deserves representation, territorial constituencies are an imperfect proxy. If racial group membership is thought to be affiliative yet involuntary in the sense that history, culture, and social pressures combine to define one's membership, it is equally important to provide openings within the political process for self-

defined group representation. Territorial constituencies do not do this, because they fail to maximize opportunities for group political empowerment and individual group members' participation and self-expression.

As a result, whether representation is considered essentially an individual or a group activity, the principle of one-vote, one-value is necessary to protect voters' interests. Everybody's vote should count for somebody's election. Voters are directly represented only if they actively choose who represents their interests.

In this sense, I am arguing for a more expansive account of the representational relationship for all voters. In order to achieve political equality and political fairness, an electoral system should give voters the direct opportunity to initiate and terminate their own representational relationship. It is not enough that some voters choose for everyone or that everyone has an equal chance to be the only electoral winner or electoral loser. Voting should become a positive-sum experience in which all voters actively participate in selecting their representative.

On the assumption that each participant should enjoy an equal opportunity both to participate and to influence, the concept of one-vote, one-value describes the idea that each voter should elect someone to represent her interests. This new view of the representational relationship draws on the concepts of equal opportunity to participate and equal opportunity to elect representatives of one's choice, concepts that are embodied in the Voting Rights Act amendments of 1982.[95] It arguably would expand the statutory view of the representational relationship in a way that benefits all voters.[96]

The courts, however, have been hesitant to employ a one-vote, one-value system as a remedy under the Voting Rights Act. In Granville County, North Carolina, black voters challenged the at-large method of electing the county commission.[97] Blacks, who comprised 44 percent of the county's population, had never been able to elect any person to the five-member commission.[98] The defendant-commissioners conceded that black voters were not represented on the county's at-large commission.[99] They also admitted that if the county were districted, and if two additional commissioner seats were added, blacks would be able to elect one of seven commissioners, giving the 44 percent black population "electoral control" over 14 percent of the commission.[100] The single-member districting remedy failed to capture much of the black community, which was dispersed throughout the county.

The plaintiffs proposed, and the district court approved, retention of the staggered-term, at-large method of election with a threshold-lowering, semiproportional modification that allowed voters to cast only three votes for the five open seats.[101] When the modified system was employed, three blacks were elected to the seven-person commission.[102]

The Fourth Circuit in *McGhee v. Granville* reversed and restricted the relief granted based on a narrow definition of the causal relationship between what the plaintiffs challenged and the available relief.[103] The court ruled that single-member districts were the only appropriate remedy. Since the plaintiffs challenged at-large elections, which prevented black candidates from getting elected, the exclusive remedy was to create single-member districts in which black candidates were likely to get elected. Even if all or many black voters did not reside in the newly configured majority black districts, their remedy was limited to the "virtual" representation they received from districts that enjoy black electoral success.

By articulating its analysis of vote dilution exclusively in terms of single-member districts, the courts have tended to promulgate single-member districts as a talismanic liability and remedial threshold.[104] At the same time that courts have moved closer to a single-member district, black electoral success standard, they have clearly established "descriptive" proportional representation as the ceiling.[105] The court in *Thornburg v. Gingles,* for example, reversed a finding of dilution in District 23, where it appeared that black voters enjoyed "proportionate" representation because a black was consistently elected over a twelve-year period.[106] The court did not discuss the fact that black voters in the district had to employ "bullet voting" to elect the black candidate and thus forfeited their chance to influence which whites would be elected.[107] Nor did the court address the evidence that the black who was elected was actually chosen by the white voters and had to "sail trim"[108] his legislative positions accordingly.[109]

Despite judicial reluctance to adopt alternative remedies, the principle of one-vote, one-value satisfies the representational needs of voters in two ways that districting does not. First, it extracts the unfairness of wasted votes from winner-take-all solutions. Votes that would have been wasted in a winner-take-all system are redistributed to voluntary constituencies consistent with the actual level of their political support. Second, it allows voters to choose their representational identity. Rather than imposing a group identity on a given geographic constituency, this system gives voters the opportunity to associate with the identity that fits their own view of psychological, cultural, and historical reality. Thus, racial and other politically cohesive groups could be represented in proportion to their actual strength in the electorate rather than in proportion to their geographic concentration. As a result of political organization, voter education, and strategic voting, any politically cohesive group that is numerous enough to meet the local threshold of representation could mobilize to gain representation.

Ultimately, what the one-vote, one-value principle does is to transform the unit of representation from a territorial or racial constituency to a political or psychological one. This affirms Iris Young's view of the social group as one based on self- and historical-identification, and it rejects representational groups based simply on the joint possession of externally observable attributes or the choice of a residence.[110]

One-vote, one-value makes the assumption that each voter should enjoy the same opportunity to influence political outcomes. No one is entitled to absolutely equal influence; but by the same token, no one is entitled to grossly disproportionate influence or a monopoly on control. The majority should enjoy a majority of the power, but the minority should also enjoy some power too. Thus, one-vote, one-value measures opportunities for fair participation using a baseline of actual participation and real political strength.

The principle of one-vote, one-value, as realized through cumulative voting, also restores the link between representation and voting by ensuring that legislators represent unanimous, not divided, constituencies. Representation becomes the process of bottom-up empowerment based on self-defined expressions of interest. Moreover, assuming that voters vote strategically, votes are not wasted either by voting for losing candidates or by packing voters into safe districts. The legislative body can reflect fairly the range of opinions and interests within the public at large, including racial minorities who can be represented based on their electoral strength. Gerrymandering becomes unnecessary and can no longer be used to enhance the disproportionate power of incumbents to ensure their own reelection or to exaggerate the political control of the party in power. Finally, local political organizations may be given the space and the possibility of success. Such parties can fill the needs for political mobilization, voter education, and legislative monitoring, which largely go unfilled in our current system.

Thus, by restoring the link between representation and voting, alternative election systems encourage voter participation. They also can broaden the range of debate by allowing local political organizations to emerge and interest-based political coalitions to form. These coalitions would not be limited to neighborhood communities of interest, certain racial groups, or particular elections; rather, they would contain dynamic possibilities for regional, reciprocal, or cross-racial political cohesion. The race-conscious context of districting might be retained, but only on an election-by-election, issue-by-issue, voter-by-voter basis. . . .

In balancing the fears of balkanization against observations about existing alienation, I conclude that exclusiveness is a greater evil than controversy, that passivity does not equal contentment, and that differences need not be permanently enshrined in the electoral configuration. Modified at-large election systems encourage continuous redistricting by the voters themselves based on the way they cast their

votes in each election. Whatever differences emerge, therefore, are those chosen by the voters rather than imposed externally on the voters based on assumptions about demographic characteristics or incumbent self-interest. These voter-generated differences may infuse the process with new ideas; diversity of viewpoint can be enlightening. Finally, the modified at-large system may simply reflect a necessary transition phase from power politics to principled politics. Whether it succeeds in that respect, it at least has the benefit of infusing the process with more legitimacy from the perspective of previously disenfranchised groups.[111]

I do not mean to denigrate concerns that the proliferation of political interest constituencies may undermine consensus, exacerbate tension, and destabilize the political system. These concerns reflect a preference for conflict resolution that camouflages rather than identifies political differences. My preference, however, is first to recognize salient differences, and then to work with those differences to achieve positive-sum solutions. My idea is that politics need not be a zero-sum game in which those who win, win it all. My idea is that where everyone can win something, genuine consensus is possible.

There is, in addition, a concern with one-vote, one-value principles that I have not previously considered. In my focus on wasted votes, I have not yet examined the effect of one-vote, one-value approaches on communities with large numbers of noncitizens, age-ineligible citizens, or people with other conditions that disable them from voting. For example, concerns about the representation of noncitizens are prominent in the Latino community;[112] concerns about the disproportionate number of young citizens are also relevant to the black community.[113] Thus, each of those communities has a special profile in terms of the number of people who are represented ultimately by each voting member of the community. This is a virtual representation problem within the electorate itself.

Since districting is based on population rather than on turnout or registration rates, people who do not vote at all are nevertheless represented. This idea is encompassed by the third virtual representation assumption—that the district identity is independent, yet consuming, of all constituents. Even if one cannot vote, one's interests are presumably represented by those who can. For minority communities whose population is in greater need of government service, access to representatives based on population may be more fair than access to representatives based on turnout. A voluntary interest constituency composed of like-minded voters devalues the interests of elements within the constituency who cannot or do not vote.

Of course, the same criticism can be leveled at safe districting. Although its population base extends top-down representational access to nonvoters, these constituents are stuck with whomever the majority of district voters choose. In others words, safe districting assumes that nonvoters and voters are fungible in that the voters indirectly represent the interests of the nonvoters. Accordingly, children are only indirectly represented by the representatives chosen by adults on their behalf.

Admittedly, changing the structure of electoral units is an incomplete solution even to those problems on which I have previously focused. Because of its potential disruption, it is also a solution worth considering only where the existing election system unfairly distributes political power in a way that is itself disruptive or illegitimate. As for the problem of differential participation rates, I can speculate about three possible responses. First, like districting systems, one-vote, one-value election systems require some subdistricting. Except in very small cities or towns, some multimember subdistricts would be required both to reduce the complexity of the ballot and to promote access for local communities of interest. In New York City, for example, boroughs might be appropriate multimember districts for boroughwide cumulative voting. This might accommodate the concern that representatives have a local constituency for whom they are responsible without regard to who actually voted for them.

Second, although interest representation based on one-vote, one-value does not directly protect nonvoters any better than do districts, it does create an environment in which they, as well as voters, are encouraged to participate directly. By "participation" I mean the broad range of bottom-up activity relating to the political process. I specifically disavow an emphasis exclusively on election-day voting. Because semiproportional systems rely on voluntary interest group constituencies, they reward local political organizing efforts more than systems with predetermined constituencies. Representation is earned in proportion to political activity and actual turnout rather than fixed population or majoritarian aggregating rules. This means that local political organizations, with an activated grass roots base, can actually win elections.

Nonvoters can participate in the organizing and monitoring effects of local political organizations and thus actively assert their own interests. Nonvoters can participate in all the pre- and post-election-day activities of the political organization. In this way, one-vote, one-value encourages representation directly of interests, not just of voters. Nonvoters can directly support a local organization that articulates their interests rather than passively rely on the presumption that they benefit from choices made by those who virtually vote their interests.

Third, the commitment to consensus politics implicit in the one-vote, one-value approach benefits voters and nonvoters, majorities and minorities. It infuses the process with receptivity to new ideas. It promotes a new definition of stability based on inclusiveness, not quietude. It creates positive-sum possibilities rather than limiting participation to winners and inevitable losers. With its focus on coalition-building and consensus, it does not assume that conflict is better suppressed than voiced; nor does it assume that politics need always be zero-sum.

One-vote, one-value represents a new vision of political participation. It assumes that empowerment comes from opportunities for the active assertion of one's own interests—speaking out, not just being spoken for. One-vote, one-value attempts to mediate directly the tension between individual and group representation that characterizes the districting process at each level. Thus it is more fair both to individuals and to groups.

III. Conclusion

THE controversy over racial group representation offers us an opportunity to reexamine the political fairness of our district-based electoral system. I posit that a system is procedurally fair only to the extent that it gives each participant an equal opportunity to influence outcomes. I call this principle one-vote, one-value. This is a measure of procedural, not substantive, legitimacy. According to this principle, outcomes are relevant only to the extent that they enable us to measure degrees of input, not to the extent they achieve some objective, substantive notion of distributive justice.

The challenge to racial group representation is actually a criticism of a different kind of group representation—representation based on homogeneous geographic constituencies. Race-conscious districting is simply one expression of a larger reality, winner-take-all districting. Both justify wasting votes with often-unstated assumptions about the group characteristics of district voters. In other words, the criticism of racial group representation is, at bottom, a criticism of winner-take-all districting in which the district boundaries and the incumbent politicians define the interests of the entire district constituency.

I conclude that group representation is as American as winner-take-all districting; that the two are conflated in criticisms of race-conscious districting; and that consideration of alternative means of representing racial groups can shift the debate about political fairness. By directly confronting the problem of wasted voting, we may make the system more legitimate from the perspective of previously disenfranchised groups and more fairly representative of issue-based groups that previously have been aggregated and silenced within the majority.

I have proposed a new view of the representational relationship that is more protective of all voters' ability and more conducive to all voters' initiative to choose directly who represents them. By critically examining certain fundamental assumptions about representation, I hope to revive our political imagination. "Change the way people think," said South

African civil rights martyr Steven Biko, "and things will never be the same."[114] Or as Professor Robert Dixon declared almost twenty-five years ago:

> [N]ow that the first round of reapportionment has been accomplished, there is need to talk "one man–one vote" a little less and to talk a little more of "political equity," and of functional components of effective representation. *A mathematically equal vote which is politically worthless because of gerrymandering or winner-take-all districting is as deceiving as "emperor's clothes."*[113]

NOTES

1. R. Dixon, Jr., *Democratic Representation: Reapportionment in Law and Politics*, 22 (1968) (emphasis added).

2. I use the phrase "race-conscious districting" to describe the practice of consolidating the number of minority group members in a single or a few winner-take-all subdistricts. Yet, in a racially polarized environment, the process of districting is inevitably race-conscious. See Guinier, "The Representation of Minority Interests: The Question of Single-Member Districts," 14 *Cardozo L. Rev.*, 1135, 1135 n. 2 (1993) (arguing that winner-take-all districts ultimately enable one group or another to dominate, meaning there is a racial consequence to the demographic constitution of all racially mixed districts if voting is racially polarized).

3. 42 U.S.C. ss 1971–1974 (1988).

4. J. Sleeper, "Rigging the Vote by Race," *Wall Street J.* (Aug. 4, 1992), A14. Sleeper admits he has taken many of the ideas about the Voting Rights Act from A. Thernstrom, *Whose Votes Count?* (1987).

5. Sleeper, *supra* note 4, at A14.

6. *Id.*

7. See ABC News Special, "The '92 Vote" (ABC television broadcast, Nov. 3, 1992), available in LEXIS, CMPGN Library, ABCNEW File. It may be worth noting for the record that Ms. Roberts' mother, Lindey Boggs, was arguably "redistricted" out of a seat in Congress in response to a successful lawsuit under the Voting Rights Act. See *Major v. Treen*, 574 F. Supp. 325 (E.D. LA, 1983).

8. See *Shaw v. Reno*, 113 S.Ct. 2816, 2828 (1993) ("For these reasons, we conclude that a plaintiff challenging a reapportionment statute under the Equal Protection Clause may state a claim by alleging that the legislation, though race-neutral on its face, rationally cannot be understood as anything other than an effort to separate voters into different jurisdictions on the basis of race, and that the separation lacks sufficient justification").

9. Major Garrett, "Frosh Planning to Clean House," *Washington Times* (Nov. 22, 1992), A1, available in LEXIS, Nexis Library, WTIMES File; see Kenneth J. Cooper,

"New Member Seen Boosting Urban Caucus," *Washington Post* (Nov. 13, 1992), A11. I use the term "integrated" to describe a racial composition close to 50 percent black and 50 percent white.

10. See 42 U.S.C. s 1973(b) (1988) (prohibiting representation where racial groups are given "less opportunity than other members of the electorate to participate").

11. See, for example, Thernstrom, *supra* note 4, at 237–38 (arguing that efforts to compensate for every potential source of inequality can only lead to a covert system of reserved seats comparable to India's system for caste representation).

12. See J. Sleeper, *The Closest of Strangers*, 159 (1990) ("Liberals and black civil rights activists thus shifted from demanding equality of individual opportunity which entails color-blind respect for a person's merits and rights beneath the skin, to demanding equality of condition, which submerges individual dignity beneath a color-based emphasis on the putative 'rights' of historically deprived ethnic groups").

13. See *supra* note 2.

14. See Sleeper, *supra* note 4, at A14.

15. This is essentially the argument that there is a dominant "culture of whiteness" that is a unifying—even if unconscious—experience for some and an exclusionary experience for those who are not white. See P. J. Williams, *"Metro Broadcasting, Inc. v. FCC:* Regrouping in Singular Times," 104 *Harv. L. Rev.*, 525, 529–31 (1990) [the essay is included in this volume—ED.].

16. By "legitimacy" I mean the perception that the process is fair, even from the perspective of adversely affected parties.

17. By this definition, the majority in *Shaw* misuses the term "gerrymandering" to describe a 54 percent black district that, as the majority concedes, was drawn to remedy a century of racial exclusion, and that, as the majority also acknowledges, did not arbitrarily enhance or diminish the political power of any group; see *Shaw v. Reno*, 113 S.Ct. 2816, 2824, 2832 (1993) (mentioning North Carolina's checkered race relations past and noting that the plaintiffs did not claim that the redistricting would lead to the dilution of the European-American vote). Calling the district a "racial gerrymander" is simply inaccurate since it does not "arbitrarily allocate disproportionate political power" to any group. As the majority recognizes, all districting takes race into account; *id.* at 2826. Thus, this district, by its very terms, did nothing more than take race into account to create a racially competitive or racially integrated district. Its offense, to the extent the court identifies the nature of the new constitutional injury, was that its "bizarre" shape was aesthetically unappealing to white voters and "stigmatizing" to black voters; *id.* at 2824–25. Although Justice O'Connor thundered against "political apartheid," the claim that the district separated voters by race is not supported by

the district's own racial composition, which is the most integrated district in the state; *id.* at 2827; see *supra* note 9.

In terms of aesthetics, O'Connor is quite correct that drawn on a map, the shape of the district is "bizarre"; *id.* However, the relevant inquiry is not the district's shape but its feel; does it reflect an effort to connect voters who have a relevant community of interests? Cf. *Cillard v. Baldwin County Bd. of Educ.*, 686 F. Supp. 1459 (M.D. Ala., 1988) (concluding that a district is sufficiently compact if it has a "sense of community"). The evidence in this case and others demonstrates that blacks in North Carolina are politically cohesive. Thus, the evidence of persistent racial bloc voting and racial appeals in North Carolina means that it is not an assumption, but a fact, that blacks function as a racial as well as a political group. To call this fact a racial stereotype takes all meaning from the term, which is about prejudging, not observing.

18. See U. P. Auerbach, "The Reapportionment Cases: One Person, One-Vote—One Vote, One-Value," 1964 *Sup. Ct. Rev.*, 1, 55, 56. "One-vote, one-value" means each voter should enjoy the opportunity to vote for someone who gets elected. Each voter should be able to choose, by the way she casts her votes, who represents her.

19. A recent example is Chilton County, Alabama, where the first Republican and the first black were elected to the county commission when the county implemented a modified at-large system of election using cumulative voting. J. Yardley, "1 Voter, 7 Votes? County Boosts Minority Clout," *Atlanta J. and Const.* (Oct. 23, 1992), G5. Because the balance of power on the commission is now closely divided between white Republicans and white Democrats, even if voting is racially polarized the black Democrat may become an influential swing vote.

20. By "representation of racial groups," I do not mean to suggest that only members of a group can represent its interests, that members of a group are necessarily racially similar, or that racial group members are necessarily homogeneous in thinking or interest.

21. Descriptive representation defines representation as based solely on representative physical characteristics or representative identity. It does not envision an interactive or a dynamic view of the representational relationship.

22. See S. Levinson, "Gerrymandering and the Brooding Omnipresence of Proportional Representation: Why Won't It Go Away?" 33 *UCLA L. Rev.*, 257, 263 (1985) ("The liberal side is manifested by [Chief Justice Warren's] statement that '[t]he right to vote freely for the candidate of one's choice is the essence of a democratic society, and any restrictions on that right strike at the heart of representative government,'" quoting *Reynolds v. Sims*, 377 U.S. 533, 555 (1964)).

23. See for example, *Wesberry v. Sanders*, 376 U.S. 1, 18 (1964) ("While it may not be possible to draw congressional districts with mathematical precision, that is no excuse for ignoring our Constitution's plain objective of making equal

representation for equal numbers of people the fundamental goal for the House of Representatives").

24. For the liberal, "the ultimate unit is not class, estate, rank or interest, but the independent, rational man. . . . The people are a mass, an entity, and, ideally, act as one. Yet they achieve that unity of action by a series of individual acts of mind stimulated by common discussion"; S. H. Beer, "The Representation of Interests in British Government: Historical Background," 51 *Am. Pol. Sci. Rev.*, 613, 634 (1957). However, even those who argue that it is the individual who is being represented concede that the individual's vote is influenced by group affiliations. See, for example, Auerbach, *supra* note 18, at 55, 56. The right to vote also bears purely symbolic significance. See J. N. Shklar, *American Citizenship: The Quest For Inclusion*, 27 (1991) (arguing that civic significance comes from having the right to vote, not from actually casting a ballot).

25. The court has described voting rights as "individual and personal in nature"; *Reynolds*, 377 U.S. at 561. The court continued, "Legislators represent people, not trees or acres. Legislators are elected by voters, not farms or cities or economic interests"; *id.* at 562.

26. John Low-Beer has distinguished the right to an equally weighted vote, which is implicated in reapportionment cases, from the right to an equally meaningful vote, which is implicated in gerrymandering cases; J. R. Low-Beer, "The Constitutional Imperative of Proportional Representation," 94 *Yale L. J.*, 163, 164 n. 3 (1984); cf. *Reynolds*, 377 U.S. at 578 (defining the "equal-population principle" as the standard for equal weighting); *Terry v. Adams*, 345 U.S. 461, 484 (1953) (finding that, "an empty vote cast after the real decisions are made" did not provide a meaningful right to vote). The equal population principle is, however, an imperfect approximation of equally weighted voting because district size is based on population, rather than on voting age population or registered voters; cf. *Mahan v. Howell*, 410 U.S. 315, 322 (1973) ("[P]opulation alone has been the sole criterion of constitutionality in congressional redistricting under Art. I, s 2."). If one-person, one-vote is satisfied by such population-based reapportionment, I would argue that this principle views representation as equal access to a representative, whether the voter voted for the representative or even voted at all. I have argued elsewhere that equality weighted voting really means an equal opportunity to influence the processes of government; see Guinier, "No Two Seats: The Elusive Quest for Political Equality," 77 *Virginia Law Review* 1413, at 1422. Under this view, the right to fair and effective representation subsumes both equally weighted voting and equally powerful voting.

27. Fair and effective representation envisions an equality norm—the right of all citizens to equal treatment as citizens in a democracy. In addition, the equality norm says that every person has an equal right to government services. An equal right to government services is not the same as a right to equal government services. In this sense, I am equating the right to services with a right to access to the benefits of government.

28. *Kirkpatrick v. Preisler*, 394 U.S. 526, 531 (1969).

29. The Supreme Court developed its one-person, one-vote jurisprudence in response to the disproportionate power exercised by a political minority; see *Gray v. Sanders*, 372 U.S. 368, 379 (1963) (expressing dissatisfaction with an electoral system that gives disproportionate weight to rural votes and to votes from less populous counties). The court found a constitutional right to population-based apportionment on the theory that the majority of the population should have a majority voice in the legislature; cf. *Reynolds v. Sims*, 377 U.S. 533, 565 (1964) (noting that denying the majority of the right to control the legislature would far surpass the dangers of any possible denial of minority rights). Of course, minority interests should also be represented. In fact, concern with representing group interests was a major theme of Justice Stewart's famous dissent in *Lucas v. Forty-Fourth General Assembly*, 377 U.S. 713, 744–65 (1964) (Stewart, J., dissenting). Stewart's group interests were determined by the state, not by the individual voter, in part because he perceived federalism concerns to be the missing element in the requirement of strict population equality; *id.* at 744–45. Stewart's repeated references to the legitimacy of group interests as recognized by the state, *id.* at 748–49, 759, 765, reflect, however, an implicit faith in state government to provide a voice to minority interests.

Some argue, however, that the one-person, one-vote principle was designed primarily to restore a competing principle—majority rule or majority legislative power; see Gordon E. Baker, "The Unfinished Reapportionment Revolution," in Bernard Grofman, ed., *Political Gerrymandering and the Courts*, 11, 14 (1990) (asserting that the outcome of an insistence on voter equality is "conditioned majoritarianism"). Yet majority rule need not mean that a simple majority inexorably prevails. Even if it does, there is a big difference between the majority winning legislative power and the majority controlling all the legislative power. I have argued elsewhere that winner-take-all majority rule is often fundamentally at odds with traditional notions of democracy; see Guinier, *supra* note 26, at 1441–43 (arguing that winner-take-all majority rule based on a prejudiced majority is itself illegitimate).

30. The empowerment norm is also explicated in the Voting Rights Act of 1965, as amended in 1982; see 52 U.S.C. s 1971(b) (1988) (protecting voting rights for racial minorities against intimidation, threats, or coercion). As such, the act is informed by the goals and strategies of the civil rights movement, which pushed for its passage in 1965, and which has been successful in extending and amending the Act in 1970, 1975, and 1982. The empowerment norm views political participation and the right to participate throughout the political process as critical to democratic legitimacy. In other words, it is not enough that people get certain formal or symbolic rights. What is critical is that citizens are given the opportunity and incentive to exercise those rights to promote their interests. What legitimates representative government is the fact that citizens knowingly choose who represents them and that citizens have the

opportunity not only to elect but to retire those who do not represent them effectively.

31. *Davis v. Bandemer,* 478 U.S. 109, 167 (1986) (Powell, J., concurring and dissenting).

32. Compare *Thornburg v. Gingles,* 478 U.S. 30, 77 (1986) (employing a top-down view to conclude that the presence of minority representatives would undercut a voting rights challenge) with *Davis,* 478 U.S. at 132 (implying a bottom-up approach by emphasizing the right to influence the political process rather than the right simply to win elections).

33. See *Reynolds,* 377 U.S. at 576 (holding that the right to equal representation ensures "adequate overall legislative representation to all of the state's citizens").

34. *Baker v. Carr,* 369 U.S. 186, 273 (1962) (Frankfurter, J., dissenting) (emphasis added). The dissenting opinions acknowledge the claim that the distribution of electoral strength among geographic units reflects a legislative judgment about the representation of interests; see, for example, *id.* at 334 (Harlan, J., dissenting).

35. See, for example, *Reynolds,* 377 U.S. at 555 ("The right to vote freely for the candidate of one's choice is of the essence of a democratic society. . . ."); see also *Terry v. Adams,* 345 U.S. 461 (1953) (arguing that a county's white primary system "strip[ped] Negroes of every vestige of influence in selecting the officials who control the local county matters").

36. See *Davis,* 478 U.S. at 124.

37. See *id.* at 125 and n. 9 (explaining that the racial gerrymandering cases established the objective of fair and adequate group representation). Justice O'Connor's majority opinion in *Shaw v. Reno,* 113 S.Ct. 2816 (1993), however, may suggest that the court will revisit this policy decision. As Justice Stevens suggests in dissent, the only group no longer entitled to fair representation now may be African-Americans; see *id.* at 2844–45 (Stevens, J., dissenting). If Justice Stevens' observation proves correct, such a "perverse" consequence would not eliminate the concept of group representation, which would still be available for "Polish Americans, or for Republicans"; *id.*

38. Cf. *Reynolds,* 377 U.S. at 567 ("To the extent that a citizen's right to vote is debased, he is that much less a citizen"). This is the equal shares—as opposed to the equal probability of casting a decisive vote—condition of political equity; see J. W. Still, "Political Equality and Election Systems," 91 *Ethics,* 375, 378–79 (1981).

39. See, for example, *Whitcomb v. Chavis,* 403 U.S. 124, 154–55 (holding that the simple fact that one interest group is outvoted and consequently unrepresented in the legislature of its own provides no basis for invoking constitutional remedies where . . . there is no indication that this segment of the population is being denied access to the political system").

40. In asserting the prominence of group identity and the necessity of collective action to political organization and efficiency, I do not set out a theory of group rights. Nor do I yet define the parameters of group representation. Group status could mean a collection of people with identifiable characteristics. It could also mean a collection of people with common interests. In this paper I simply pose the preliminary issue that the concept of representation necessarily applies to the representation of a group. Once I pass this threshold question, I will need to explore the next set of questions, one of which will certainly be: What is a group?

There is in addition an important caveat to the claim here that the concept of representation necessarily applies to groups. I am not assigning value to groups over individuals. Individuals as the ultimate objects of concern do not disappear from view. Indeed, I attempt to recognize the individual by empowering each voter to choose her district, that is, her temporary group affiliation. Indeed, by advocating the benefits of modified at-large elections, I seek to put in the hands of the voters the degree to which they want their race or other demographic characteristic to be represented, that is, the degree to which their group's status is salient or relevant.

41. J. Low-Beer, *supra* note 26, at 176 n. 63; the Supreme Court has recognized the impact that districting has on opposing groups. "It is not only obvious, but absolutely unavoidable, that the location and shape of districts may well determine the political complexion of the area. *District lines are rarely neutral phenomena.* They can well determine what district will be predominantly Democratic or predominantly Republican, or make a close race likely. Redistricting may pit incumbents against one another or make very difficult the election of the most experienced legislator. *The reality is that districting inevitably has and is intended to have substantial political consequences*"; *Gaffney v. Cummings,* 412 U.S. 735, 753 (1973) (emphasis added).

42. *Lucas v. Forty-Fourth General Assembly,* 377 U.S. 713, 75. (1964) (Stewart, J., dissenting.

43. A. F. Pollard, *The Evolution of Parliament* 164 (2d ed. 1926).

43. Beer, *supra* note 24, at 618. In contrast to this Whig view, liberals assumed that representation was of individuals rather than of "corporate bodies" or interests and could best be realized by equal electoral districts; *id.* at 629–30. However, while liberals in America had a pronounced suspicion of interests, their fear was based primarily on the representation of special interests; *id.* at 631. As I argue, though, the liberal claim that rule by the majority would defeat special interests is in fact informed by Old Whig theories of virtual representation.

44. See G. E. Baker, *The Reapportionment Revolution: Representation, Political Power, and the Supreme Court,* 16 (1966) ("In view of this English background, it is not surprising that representation in colonial America was originally based on localities"). This "representation by town"

was illustrated in 1787 when the delegates gathered to create the United States Constitution and the smaller states were reluctant to yield their accustomed equality of status; *id.* at 16–18.

45. See G. E. Frug, "The City as a Legal Concept," 93 *Harv. L. Rev.*, 1057, 1083 (1980) at 1098.

46. P. H. Douglas, "Occupational versus Proportional Representation," 29 *Am. J. Soc.* 129, 132 (1923).

47. H. F. Pitkin, "Introduction: The Concept of Representation," in *id* at 1, 2.

48. *Id.*, at 14.

49. *See* Mark T. Quinlivan, comment, "One Person, One Person Revisited: The Impending Necessity of Judicial Intervention in the Realm of Voter Registration," *U. Pa. L. Rev.* 2361, 2383 (1989) (explaining that the Supreme Court would probably view decennial redistricting as a minimum requirement under the one-person, one-vote rule).

50. See *Karcher v. Daggett*, 462 U.S. 725, 728 (1983) (holding that a congressional reapportionment plan with a maximum deviation of 0.7 percent was unconstitutional). But cf. *Gaffney v. Cummings*, 412 U.S. 735, 751 (1973) (establishing a lower standard for state and local plans and allowing a maximum deviation of 7.8 percent from mathematical equality).

51. See *Lucas*, 377 U.S. at 750 (Stewart, J., dissenting) ("The Court today declines to give any recognition to these [local] considerations and countless others, tangible and intangible. . . .").

52. The concept of virtual representation describes how nonvoters or losing voters are represented in legislatures; see J. P. Reid, *The Concept of Representation in the Age of the American Revolution*, 50 (1989). The English used this theory to explain how the American colonists were represented in Parliament; *id.*

53. See letter from F. Michelman, Professor of Law, Harvard University, to Lani Guinier, Associate Professor of Law, University of Pennsylvania (Aug. 26, 1991) (on file with author) ("Virtual representation is a species of the genus disfranchisement. You are virtually represented when you are disfranchised—not procedurally counted either in the assembly or in the electoral constituency—and the excuse for the disfranchisement is some theory about how someone else will act on your behalf or in your interest.").

54. See *United Jewish Orgs. v. Carey*, 430 U.S. 144, 166 n. 24 (1977) ("[T]he white voter who as a result of the 1974 plan is in a district more likely to return a nonwhite representative will be represented . . . by legislators elected from majority white districts"); *Karcher v. Daggett*, 462 U.S. 725, 759–60 n. 25 (1983) (Stevens, J., concurring) "([I]f the plaintiffs' challenge is based on a particular district or districts, the State may be able to show that the group's voting strength is not diluted in the State as a whole.");

Connor v. Finch, 431 U.S. 407, 427 (1977) (Blackmun, J., concurring in part and concurring in the judgment) ("Districts that disfavor a minority group in one part of the State may be counterbalanced by favorable districts elsewhere").

55. *Davis v. Bandemer*, 478 U.S. 109, 132 (1986), but see *id.* at 169–70 n. 7 (Powell, J., concurring and dissenting) (arguing that the plurality's finding that a "losing" voter will be adequately represented was a "leap" from the conclusion that a redistricting plan is not unconstitutional merely because it makes it harder for a group to elect its own candidate).

56. See *id.* (stating that, "the plurality apparently believes that effects on election results are of little import, as long as the losers have some access to their representatives").

57. See Guinier, "The Triumph of Tokenism: The Voting Rights Act and the Theory of Black Electoral Success," 89 *Mich. L. Rev.*, 1077, 1081–91 (1991), at 1136–44.

58. People with low incomes are relegated to living in deteriorating neighborhoods, while affluent and middle-class residential areas are generally not accessible to them; see for example, Housing and Urban Development Secretary Henry Cisneros's remarks on "The Changing Federal Role in Urban Policy" at a Progressive Policy Institute Conference, Reuter Transcript Rep., Apr. 19, 1993, available in LEXIS, Nexis Library, Wires File (noting that poverty is, "geographically isolated, economically depressed, [and] racially segregated," and that cities "have become warehouses of our poorest"); see also "Destabilized Suburbs: Officials Confront the Shortcomings of Section 8," 7 *Cent. Pa. Bus. J.*, 18 (Sept. 1992) (observing that families receiving subsidized housing are concentrated in "Section 8 corridor" in Cook County, Illinois).

59. By group identity, I mean the tendency to self-identify as a group member and to perceive one's group membership as a salient feature in relationships with group and nongroup members. In another context, Gerald Torres has suggested that this concept is captured by the question, "Does your cultural grouping determine the narrative structure through which you organize your life?" See G. Torres and K. Milun, "Translating Yonnondio by Precedent and Evidence: The Mashpee Indian Case," 1990 *Duke L. J.*, 625, 657–58 [the article is included in this volume—ED.].

60. Studies of black and female politicians do show that they have somewhat different agendas; see R. P. Browning et al., "Racial Politics in American Cities: Blacks and Hispanics in the U.S." in *Political Mobilization, Power and Prospects* (1990); see also R. W. Apple, Jr., "Steady Local Gains by Women Fuel More Runs for High Office," *New York Times* (May 24, 1992), 4.5 (reporting on a survey of approximately half of all state legislators which found that, "even when men and women shared the same party affiliation and ideology, women were much more likely to expend their energies on health care, children's and family questions and women's rights issues"); G. Ifill, "Female Lawmakers Wrestle with New Public Attitude on 'Women's' Issues," *New York Times* (Nov. 18, 1991), B7 (describing a study done

by the Center for American Women and Politics at Rutgers University which found huge gaps between male and female legislators over issues involving women's rights, health care, and children).

61. See Apple, *supra* note 60, at 4.5 (citing a survey that women public officials tend more than their male counterparts of the same party and ideology to involve private citizens in the governmental process, to focus on needs of the poor, and to conduct public business in the open rather than behind closed doors).

62. H. F. Pitkin, *The Concept of Representation*, 186–190 (1977), at 890.

63. See E. E. Shockley, "Note, Voting Rights Act Section 2: Racially Polarized Voting and the Minority Community's Representative of Choice," 89 *Mich. L. Rev.*, 1038, 1061–62 (1991) (explaining that in determining the relevance of a candidate's race, the "best [judicial] approach relies on sponsorship: the minority community's 'representative of choice' can only be a candidate who was sponsored by that community," and that such an approach "will satisfy proponents of a focus on civil inclusion").

64. Cf. S. Issacharoff, "Polarized Voting and the Political Process: The Transformation of Voting Rights Jurisprudence," 90 *Mich. L. Rev.*, 1833, 1856 (1992) ("[T]he increased number of minority elected officials is most directly attributable to the successes of redistricting and reapportionment litigation and the resulting creation of more minority-dominated electoral districts").

65. Cf. J. F. Blumstein, "Defining and Proving Race Discrimination Perspectives on the Purpose vs. Results Approach from the Voting Rights Act," 69 *Va. L. Rev.*, 633, 636 (1983) (concluding that while minorities have the right to ballot access, there is no corresponding entitlement to racial group representation).

66. *Id.* at 712 n. 378; see also M. Rosenfeld, "Affirmative Action, Justice, and Equalities: A Philosophical and Constitutional Appraisal," 46 *Ohio St. L. J.*, 845, 912 (1985) ("The right to vote is a paradigmatic individual right. Each individual has only one vote, and absent any discrimination or unfair procedures, no group of voters has a right to complain that its candidate lost").

67. This particular concern is primarily hypothetical. Blacks are very unlikely to be elected from any majority white districts, and all majority black congressional districts now elect black officeholders; B. Grofman and L. Handley, "The Impact of the Voting Rights Act on Black Representation in Southern State Legislatures," 16 *Legis. Stud. Q.*, 111, 117 (1991).

68. Unanimous constituencies are those in which all voters agree on a basic definition of their interests. A unanimous constituency lets the voters choose which interest is salient and should be promoted. In a divided constituency, it is the legislator whose choice is important as she attempts to strike a balance among her supporters.

Unanimous constituencies focus on the role of the voter; divided constituencies adopt a trustee view of representation. The former is a bottom-up view of representation; the latter is top-down.

The bottom-up view of unanimous constituencies assumes that voters, not legislators, should be empowered to make legislative choices, at least initially, for several reasons. First, it adopts a delegate or agency view of representation that suggests legislators represent the parts in order to avoid viewpoint monopoly. By encouraging the active assertion of diverse perspectives, the legislative process is infused with more and different ideas. This discourages monolithic control of legislative agendas by assuring the active representation of unanimous, issue-oriented constituencies. The second assumption is that compromise should occur openly after an election, as part of the deliberative process of legislative debate, rather than behind closed doors, where office seekers pre-"position" themselves to camouflage mutually inconsistent or divergent philosophies. In this sense, it reflects a more participatory view of fairness as the balancing of perspectives rather than as the absence of a viewpoint.

Second, it assumes that issue-based rather than candidate-based constituencies will be mobilized to participate throughout the political process, not just on election day. In this way it responds to the increasing levels of alienation and passivity within the electorate; cf. B. Neuborne, "Of Sausage Factories and Syllogism Machines: Formalism, Realism, and Exclusionary Selection Techniques," 67 *N.Y.U. L. Rev.*, 419 (1992) (noting that allowing jurors to be excluded from juries because of their race leads the community to lose faith in the jury system).

69. R. Brownstein, "Minority Quotas in Elections?," *L.A. Times*, Aug. 28, 1991, at A1, A15.

70. P. S. Karlan, "Maps and Misreadings: The Role of Geographic Compactness in Racial Vote Dilution Litigation," 24 *Harv. C.R.-C.L.L. Rev.*, 173, 177 (1989); see also *Whitcomb v. Chavis*, 403 U.S. 124, 131 n. 8 (1971) (defining a ghetto as a residential area with a defined racial population of lower than average socioeconomic status, *"whose residence in the area is often the result of a social, legal, or economic restriction or custom"*; emphasis added); *Wright v. Rockefeller*, 376 U.S. 52, 59 (1964) (Douglas, J., dissenting) ("Neighborhoods in our larger cities often contain members of only one race; and those who draw the lines of Congressional Districts cannot be expected to disregard neighborhoods in an effort to make each district a multiracial one").

71. Karlan, *supra* note 70, at 177.

72. I. M. Young, *Justice and the Politics of Difference*, 43–46 (1990) (arguing that "highly visible" groups—those who identify with a certain social status and have a common history produced by that status—are different from "mere" 'combinations of people'—such as voluntary clubs—which are defined by shared attributes).

73. *Id.* at 43.

74. See F. R. Parker, "Racial Gerrymandering and Legislative Reapportionment," in C. Davidson, ed., *Minority Vote Dilution* 85, 112 (1984) (concluding that the use of race-conscious remedies is "benign and beneficial to the minority community because it enhances their voting strength").

75. Cf. C. Davidson, "Minority Vote Dilution: An Overview," in *Minority Vote Dilution, supra* note 73, at 1, 10 (arguing that elected officials are often unaware of the extent of minority support and therefore respond to strong pressure from white voters).

76. A fractal is a set of jagged curves or surfaces that has, "the same index of jaggedness when examined at any level of minuteness or abstraction"; see L. Weinberg, "The Federal-State Conflict of Laws: 'Actual' Conflicts," 70 *Tex. L. Rev.*, 1743, 1777 n. 120 (1992). Pamela Karlan suggested the analogy to fractal geometry.

77. See A. Mitchell, "In Politics, There Is Only One Language," *New York Times* (July 19, 1992), A29.

78. M. B. W. Tabor, "Loyalty and Labor," *New York Times* (Sept. 17, 1992), B6.

79. S. Roberts, "Does Politics of Fairness Mean Only Those from Minorities Should Apply?" *New York Times* (July 27, 1992), B4.

80. Mitchell, *supra* note 77, at A29 (quoting David Santiago).

81. *Id.* (quoting Angelo Falcon, president of the Institute for Puerto Rican Policy).

82. Roberts, *supra* note 79, at B4 (quoting Rep. Steven J. Solarz). Others suggest that politics, not principles of choice, motivated Solarz's decision: "When his polls showed he couldn't win against any incumbent," he ran in an open district created to enhance the power of Latino residents; *id.* (quoting Fernando Ferrer, president of the Bronx Borough). Still others suggested that Solarz had an unfair advantage based not on his ethnic background but his financial foreground: "It's not a question of what background he is. It's the color of his money," said Herman Badillo, the city's first Latino congressman; *id.*

83. *Id.*

84. Mitchell, *supra* note 77, at AZ90.

85. The assumption is that race-conscious districting is necessary to remedy race-conscious exclusion. The exclusion is demonstrated by the unwillingness of the majority to include the minority in its governing coalition. Evidence of this premise is provided by patterns of racially polarized voting; see Guinier, "No Two Seats: The Elusive Quest for Political Equality," 77 *Va. L. Rev.* 1413, at 1441 (explaining that virtual representation assumes that, "[t]he 51% will look out for the 49% minority as their proxy" because majority self-interest is consistent with the common good; yet, where a permanent and homogeneous majority consistently exercises all the power, that fixed majority loses incentive to

look out for or cooperate with the minority, because minority political support is unnecessary).

86. This virtual representation assumption is also reflected in psychological or filial terms used to describe a common cultural or ethnic heritage. Even where all members of the racial group did not actively support a racial group member, they each are nevertheless represented by someone who is a "role model," a source of pride, and a "sister" or "brother."

87. Tabor, *supra* note 78, at B6.

88. See L. Gruson, "For Solarz, A Career Ends in Grief and Relief," *New York Times* (Oct. 7, 1992), B3 (attributing Ms. Velazquez's 1869–vote margin primarily to criticism of Solarz's decision to run in a "Hispanic district"; "New York: The Race for the House," *New York Times* (Sept. 16, 1992), B8 (listing the final election returns from the Democratic primary for the 12th district). Incidentally, Ms. Velazquez was heavily outspent; Solarz spent $2 million in the race, about $220 for each of the 9138 votes he won; A. Mitchell, "Rep. Solarz Loses in a New District," *New York Times* (Sept. 16, 1992), A1 (noting that Solarz had a "campaign fund of $2 million, more than all the other candidates combined").

89. "Tuesday's Primary Results," *New York Times* (Sept. 17, 1992), B6.

90. See Tabor, *supra* note 78, at B6 (suggesting that Elizabeth Colon weakened Mr. Solarz by drawing Asian and white votes).

91. Under a cumulative voting mechanism, the shareholders of a corporation can multiply the number of votes they are entitled to cast by the number of directors on the ballot and then distribute these votes however they wish. For example, a shareholder could cast all of her votes for only one director in one race and forgo voting in the other elections; see *Revised Model Business Corp.* Act s7.28 (1984). See generally A. T. Cole, Jr., "Legal and Mathematical Aspects of Cumulative Voting," 2 *S.C.L.Q.*, 225 (1949) (describing the cumulative voting process and analyzing a formula for calculating the maximum number of shares needed to elect a single or multiple director(s) under a cumulative voting arrangement); A. Glazer et al., "Cumulative Voting in Corporate Elections: Introducing Strategy into the Equation," 35 *S.C.L. Rev.*, 295 (1984) (providing a modified formula for maximizing director representation where shareholders vote in blocs).

In raising the idea of alternative remedies, I am not advocating a grand moral theory of representation; rather, I introduce the idea of cumulative voting primarily as a means of broadening the debate about solutions to the continuing problem of racial discrimination and polarization in the political process. I do not believe that cumulative voting is a panacea; nor do I suggest that it should be imposed on nonconsenting jurisdictions nationwide, or that it should be considered in the absence of evidence that existing electoral arrangements are operating unfairly.

92. The exclusion threshold is the minimum number of minority group members required to guarantee representation in a cumulative voting system; see Guinier, *supra* note 85, at 1483 n. 250.

93. The following formula determines the minimum number of voters needed to guarantee the election of one representative: $(V/R + 1) + 1$. See Cole, *supra* note 91, at 229. In this formula, V equals the total number of voters, and R equals the number of representatives to be elected. A minority group may assure itself of representation by having this number of voters plump their votes for a single candidate. In "No Two Seats," I suggested the following example of a jurisdiction that is to elect 10 representatives: "[I]n a jurisdiction with 1000 voters, 250 of whom are black, a modified at-large plan would use a threshold of exclusion of 1/11th based on the formula of one divided by one plus the number of open seats, plus one. This means that 1/11th of the voters could not be denied representation. The threshold exclusion would work out to be 91 voters (91 is 1/11th of 1000, plus 1). Here, there are 250 black voters. Blacks are more than 2/11ths, but short of 3/11ths, of the population.

If all voters had 10 votes and could plump them any way they wished, any candidate supported intensely (meaning receiving all 10 votes), by 91 voters, would get elected; Guinier, *supra* note 85, at 1466. Thus, by voting strategically and plumping their votes behind a single candidate, blacks in the scenario above could assure themselves of representation. If 182 black voters black voters plumped their votes evenly behind two candidates, they could assure themselves of representation by two candidates.

94. An interest constituency need not be racially homogeneous from a physiological standpoint. In other words, interests may be racially identifiable in that members of a particular racial group are more likely to hold certain views. However, not all members of the group are assumed to agree on all issues for the group to form an interest constituency. In addition, nongroup members may be part of the interest group to the extent that they identify with the group's primary agenda. In this sense, an interest constituency is defined by racial identification, not by racial origin. In this sense, an interest constituency is defined by racial identification, not by racial origin. Blacks in the United States are an obvious minority interest group, despite the presence of a range of ideologies and class status. Whites in South Africa are also a minority interest, although their choice to self-define is a function of their historical treatment of—not by—the numerically superior racial majority; see generally L. Thompson and A. Prior, *South African Politics*, 108–80 (1982).

95. See 42 U.S.C. s 1973(b) (1988) (prohibiting practices that give minority groups, "less opportunity than other members of the electorate to participate in the political process and to elect representatives of their choice").

96. Again, I do not argue that the 1982 amendments mandate this view. Especially in light of the Supreme Court's interpretation of the term "voting" in *Presley v. Etowah County Commission*, 112 S.Ct. 820 (1992), legislative action may be necessary in the context of a s 5 to reassert congressional intent about the scope of voting. At this point, I am simply suggesting an approach to curing political unfairness that builds on the themes that have been the subject of the debate surrounding the 1965 act and especially its 1982 amendments: How can we ensure political equality and meaningful opportunities to participate for a group that has historically been excluded from the franchise without reinforcing the polarization the act is designed to remedy?

97. *McGhee v. Granville County*, 860 F. 2d 110, 112 (4th Cir. 1988).

98. *Id.* at 113.

99. *Id.*

100. *Id.* at 114.

101. *Id.*

102. *Id.* at 114–15 n. 5.

103. See *id.* at 118 (holding that if vote dilution is established, "the appropriate remedy is to restructure the districting system to eradicate, to the maximum extent possible *by that means*, the dilution proximately caused by that system; it is not to eradicate the dilution by altering other 'electoral laws, practices, and structures' that were not actually challenged by the claim as made"; emphasis in original).

104. See, for example, *McNeil v. Springfield*, 851 F. 2d 937, 939, 942–43 (7th Cir. 1988) (holding, as a threshold requirement, that a minority must "demonstrate that it is sufficiently large and geographically compact to constitute a majority in a single-member district" (quoting *Thornburg v. Gingles*, 478 U.S. 30, 50 (1986), *cert. denied*, 490 U.S. 1031 (1989)).

105. See *Thornburg*, 478 U.S. at 77 (finding that the presence of minority representation would be inconsistent with an allegation of vote dilution); see also *supra* note 22.

106. *Thornburg*, 478 U.S. at 77.

107. Bullet voting is a technique employed in at-large election whereby a politically cohesive minority strategically concentrates its voting strength; Guinier, *supra* note 85, at 1142 n. 307. By voluntarily abnegating the right to vote for a full slate of candidates and casting instead only one ballot for the "black" candidate, the minority bloc can increase the probability of electing their favored candidate; see *id.* Bullet voting "forces a minority to limit its vote while the majority exercises control over the full state"; *id.*

108. "Sail-trimming" refers to the phenomenon where blacks elected from majority-white multimember districts "defer to other blacks to introduce and promote controversial legislation that would affect black constituents"; *id.* at 1104 n. 18.

109. White voters in District 23 thus elected all the legislative representatives; without some white crossover

voting, the black candidate would not have received enough support, even with bullet voting by blacks.

110. Young, *supra* note 110, at 72.

111. For example, where local county governments, such as Chilton County, Alabama, have adopted a modified at-large election system, new interest constituencies have been recognized. For the first time this century, white Republicans and a black Democrat were elected to the county school board and county commission. However, the process of self-government has not broken down. In a county that is about one-sixth black, three white Republicans, three white Democrats, and one black Democrat now sit on the school board and the commission. With the balance of power held so closely between Republican and Democratic commissioners, the black representative can be an influential swing vote.

112. See *Garza v. County of Los Angeles*, 918 F. 2d 763 (9th Cir. 1990), *cert. denied*, 111 S.Ct. 681 (1991).

113. Recognition of this fact was behind the development of the 65 percent rule. See *United Jewish Orgs. v. Carey*, 430 U.S. 144, 164 (1977) (noting that blacks generally constitute a smaller proportion of the voting-age population than of the total population).

114. D. Myers, "America's Social Recession," *Chicago Tribune* (July 30, 1992), 1.27.

115. Dixon, *supra* note 1, at 22 (emphasis added).

THE ID, THE EGO, AND EQUAL PROTECTION
RECKONING WITH UNCONSCIOUS RACISM

Charles R. Lawrence III

PROLOGUE

IT is 1948. I am sitting in a kindergarten classroom at the Dalton School, a fashionable and progressive New York City private school. My parents, both products of a segregated Mississippi school system, have come to New York to attend graduate and professional school. They have enrolled me and my sisters here at Dalton to avoid sending us to the public school in our neighborhood where the vast majority of the students are black and poor. They want us to escape the ravages of segregation, New York style.

It is circle time in the five-year-old group, and the teacher is reading us a book. As she reads, she passes the book around the circle so that each of us can see the illustrations. The book's title is *Little Black Sambo*. Looking back, I remember only one part of the story, one illustration: Little Black Sambo is running around a stack of pancakes with a tiger chasing him. He is very black and has a minstrel's white mouth. His hair is tied up in many pigtails, each pigtail tied with a different color ribbon. I have seen the picture before the book reaches my place in the circle. I have heard the teacher read the "comical" text describing Sambo's plight and have heard the laughter of my classmates. There is a knot in the pit of my stomach. I feel panic and shame. I do not have the words to articulate my feelings—words like "stereotype" and "stigma" that might help cathart the shame and place it outside of me where it began. But I am slowly realizing that, as the only black child in the circle, I have some kinship with the tragic and ugly hero of this story—that my classmates are laughing at me as well as at him. I wish I could laugh along with my friends. I wish I could disappear.

I am in a vacant lot next to my house with

black friends from the neighborhood. We are listening to *Amos 'n' Andy* on a small radio and laughing uproariously. My father comes out and turns off the radio. He reminds me that he disapproves of this show that pokes fun at Negroes. I feel bad—less from my father's reprimand than from a sense that I have betrayed him and myself, that I have joined my classmates in laughing at us.

I am certain that my kindergarten teacher was not intentionally racist in choosing *Little Black Sambo*. I knew even then, from a child's intuitive sense, that she was a good, well-meaning person. A less benign combination of racial mockery and profit motivated the white men who produced the radio show and played the roles of Amos and Andy. But we who had joined their conspiracy by works our laughter had not intended to demean our race.

A dozen years later I am a student at Haverford College. Again, I am a token black presence in a white world. A companion whose face and name I can't remember seeks to compliment me by saying, "I don't think of you as a Negro." I understand his benign intention and accept the compliment. But the knot is in my stomach again. Once again, I have betrayed myself.

This happened to me more than a few times. Each time my interlocutor was a good, liberal, white person who intended to express feelings of shared humanity. I did not yet understand the racist implications of the way in which the feelings were conceptualized. I am certain that my white friends did not either. We had not yet grasped the compliment's underlying premise: To be thought of as a Negro is to be thought of as less than human. We were all victims of our culture's racism. We had all grown up on *Little Black Sambo* and *Amos 'n' Andy*.

Another ten years pass. I am thirty-three. My daughter, Maia, is three. I greet a pink-faced, four-year-old boy on the steps of her nursery school. He proudly presents me with a book he has brought for his teacher to read to the class. "It's my favorite," he says. The book is a new edition of *Little Black Sambo*.

INTRODUCTION

THIS article reconsiders the doctrine of discriminatory purpose that was established by the 1976 decision, *Washington v. Davis*.[1] This now well-established doctrine requires plaintiffs challenging the constitutionality of a facially neutral law to prove a racially discriminatory purpose on the part of those responsible for the law's enactment or administration.[2]

Davis has spawned a considerable body of literature treating its merits and failings. Minorities and civil rights advocates have been virtually unanimous in condemning *Davis* and its progeny. They have been joined by a significant number of constitutional scholars who have been equally disapproving, if more restrained, in assessing its damage to the cause of equal opportunity. These critics advance two principal arguments. The first is that a motive-centered doctrine of racial discrimination places a very heavy, and often impossible, burden of persuasion on the wrong side of the dispute. Improper motives are easy to hide. And because behavior results from the interaction of a multitude of motives, governmental officials will always be able to argue that racially neutral considerations prompted their actions. Moreover, where several decisionmakers are involved, proof of racially discriminatory motivation is even more difficult.

The second objection to the *Davis* doctrine is more fundamental. It argues that the injury of racial inequality exists irrespective of the decisionmakers' motives. Does the black child in a segregated school experience less stigma and humiliation because the local school board did not consciously set out to harm her? Are blacks less prisoners of the ghetto because the decision that excludes them from an all-white neighborhood was made with property values and not race in mind? Those who make this second objection reason that the "facts of racial inequality are the real problem."[3] They urge that racially disproportionate harm should trigger heightened judicial scrutiny without consideration of motive.

Supporters of the intent requirement are equally adamant in asserting the doctrine's propriety. They echo the four main arguments that the Court itself set forth in *Davis:* (1) A standard that would subject all governmental action with a racially disproportionate impact to strict judicial scrutiny would cost too much; such a standard, the Court argues, would substantially limit legitimate legislative decisionmaking and would endanger the validity of a "whole range of [existing] tax, welfare, public service, regulatory and licensing statutes;"[4] (2) a disproportionate impact standard would make innocent people bear the costs of remedying a harm in which they played no part; (3) an impact test would be inconsistent with equal protection values, because the judicial decisionmaker would have to explicitly consider race; and (4) it would be inappropriate for the judiciary to choose to remedy the racially disproportionate impact of otherwise neutral governmental actions at the expense of other legitimate social interests.

My own sympathies lie with the critics of the doctrine of discriminatory purpose. The problems posed by a disproportionate impact standard do not seem insurmountable. And none of the current doctrine's proponents explain why it is important to search for bad motives or why such a search is the only alternative to an impact test. But I do not intend to simply add another chapter to the intent/impact debate. Rather, I wish to suggest another way to think about racial discrimination, a way that more accurately describes both its origins and the nature of the injury it inflicts.

Much of one's inability to know racial discrimination when one sees it results from a failure to recognize that racism is both a crime and a disease. This failure is compounded by a reluctance to admit that the illness of racism infects almost everyone. Acknowledging and understanding the malignancy are prerequisites to the discovery of an appropriate cure. But the diagnosis is difficult, because our own contamination with the very illness for which a cure is sought impairs our comprehension of the disorder.

Scholarly and judicial efforts to explain the constitutional significance of disproportionate impact and governmental motive in cases alleging racial discrimination treat these two categories as mutually exclusive. That is, while disproportionate impact may be evidence of racially discriminatory motive, whether impact or motive is the appropriate focus is normally posed in the alternative: Should racially disproportionate impact, standing alone, trigger a heightened level of judicial scrutiny? Or, should the judiciary apply a deferential standard to legislative and administrative decisions absent proof that the decisionmakers intended a racial consequence? Put another way, the Court thinks of facially neutral actions as either intentionally and unconstitutionally or unintentionally and constitutionally discriminatory.

I argue that this is a false dichotomy. Traditional notions of intent do not reflect the fact that decisions about racial matters are influenced in large part by factors that can be characterized as neither intentional—in the sense that certain outcomes are self-consciously sought—nor unintentional—in the sense that the outcomes are random, fortuitous, and uninfluenced by the decisionmaker's beliefs, desires, and wishes.

Americans share a common historical and cultural heritage in which racism has played and still plays a dominant role. Because of this shared experience, we also inevitably share many ideas, attitudes, and beliefs that attach significance to an individual's race and induce negative feelings and opinions about nonwhites. To the extent that this cultural belief system has influenced all of us, we are all racists. At the same time, most of us are unaware of our racism. We do not recognize the ways in which our cultural experience has influenced our beliefs about race or the occasions on which those beliefs affect our actions. In other words, a large part of the behavior that produces racial discrimination is influenced by unconscious racial motivation.

There are two explanations for the unconscious nature of our racially discriminatory beliefs and ideas. First, Freudian theory states that the human mind defends itself against the discomfort of guilt by denying or refusing to recognize those ideas, wishes, and beliefs that conflict with what the individual has learned is good or right. While our historical experience has made racism an integral part of our culture, our society has more recently embraced an ideal that rejects racism as immoral. When an individual experiences conflict between racist ideas and the societal ethic that condemns those ideas, the mind excludes his racism from consciousness.

Second, the theory of cognitive psychology states that the culture—including, for example, the media and an individual's parents, peers, and authority figures—transmits certain beliefs and preferences. Because these beliefs are so much a part of the culture, they are not experienced as explicit lessons. Instead, they seem part of the individual's rational ordering of her perceptions of the world. The individual is unaware, for example, that the ubiquitous presence of a cultural stereotype has influenced her perception that blacks are lazy or unintelligent. Because racism is so deeply ingrained in our culture, it is likely to be transmitted by tacit understandings: Even if a child is not told that blacks are inferior, he learns that lesson by observing the behavior of others. These tacit understandings, because they have never been articulated, are less likely to be experienced at a conscious level.

In short, requiring proof of conscious or intentional motivation as a prerequisite to constitutional recognition that a decision is race-dependent ignores much of what we understand about how the human mind works. It also disregards both the irrationality of racism and the profound effect that the history of American race relations has had on the individual and collective unconscious.[5]

It may often be appropriate for the legal system to disregard the influence of the unconscious on individual or collective behavior. But where the goal is the eradication of invidious racial discrimination, the law must recognize racism's primary source. The equal protection clause requires the elimination of governmental decisions that take race into account without good and important reasons. Therefore, equal

protection doctrine must find a way to come to grips with unconscious racism.

In pursuit of that goal, this article proposes a few test to trigger judicial recognition of race-based behavior. It posits a connection between unconscious racism and the existence of cultural symbols that have racial meaning. It suggests that the "cultural meaning" of an allegedly racially discriminatory act is the best available analogue for, and evidence of, a collective unconscious that we cannot observe directly. This test would thus evaluate governmental conduct to determine whether it conveys a symbolic message to which the culture attaches racial significance. A finding that the culture thinks of an allegedly discriminatory governmental action in racial terms would also constitute a finding regarding the beliefs and motivations of the governmental actors: The actors are themselves part of the culture and presumably could not have acted without being influenced by racial considerations, even if they are unaware of their racist beliefs. Therefore, the court would apply strict scrutiny.

This proposal is relatively modest. It does not abandon the judicial search for unconstitutional motives, nor does it argue that all governmental action with discriminatory impact should be strictly scrutinized. Instead, it urges a more complete understanding of the nature of human motivation. While it is grounded in the Court's present focus on individual responsibility, it seeks to understand individual responsibility in light of modern insights into human personality and collective behavior. In addition, this proposal responds directly to the concern that abandoning the *Washington v. Davis* doctrine will invalidate a broad range of legitimate, race-neutral governmental actions. By identifying those cases where race unconsciously influences governmental action, this new test leaves untouched nonrace-dependent decisions that disproportionately burden blacks only because they are overrepresented the decision's targets or the decision targets or beneficiaries.

This effort to inform the discriminatory intent requirement with the learning of twentieth century psychology is important for at least three reasons. First, the present doctrine, by requiring proof that the defendant was aware of his animus against blacks, severely limits the number of individual cases in which the courts will acknowledge and remedy racial discrimination.

Second, the existing intent requirement's assignment of individualized fault or responsibility for the existence of racial discrimination distorts our perceptions about the causes of discrimination and leads us to think about racism in a way that advances the disease rather than combatting it. By insisting that a blameworthy perpetrator be found before the existence of racial discrimination can be acknowledged, the Court creates an imaginary world where discrimination does not exist unless it was consciously intended. And by acting as if this imaginary world was real and insisting that we participate in this fantasy, the Court and the law it promulgates subtly shape our perceptions of society.[6] The decision to deny relief no longer finds its basis only in raw political power or economic self-interest; it is now justifiable on moral grounds. If there is no discrimination, there is no need for a remedy; if blacks are being treated fairly yet remain at the bottom of the socioeconomic ladder, only their own inferiority can explain their subordinate position.

Finally, the intent doctrine's focus on the narrowest and most unrealistic understanding of individual fault has also engendered much of the resistance to and resentment of affirmative action programs and other race-conscious remedies for past and continuing discrimination. If there can be no discrimination without an identifiable criminal, then "innocent" individuals will resent the burden of remedying an injury for which the law says they are not responsible. Understanding the cultural source of our racism obviates the need for fault, as traditionally conceived, without denying our collective responsibility for racism's eradication. We cannot be individually blamed for unconsciously harboring attitudes that are inescapable in a culture permeated with racism. And without the necessity for blame, our resistance to accepting the need

and responsibility for remedy will be lessened.

Understanding unconscious motivation will also help us comprehend and combat the hegemony of the ideology of equal opportunity. A considerable body of scholarship from the academic left has analyzed the law as a hegemonic tool of domination. According to one theory, domination occurs when the ruling class gains the consent of the dominated classes through a system of ideas that reinforces the morality or inevitability of the existing order. This "interest theory" sees ideology as a consciously wielded weapon, an intellectual tool that a group uses to enhance its political power by institutionalizing a particular view of reality.

Another view of ideology draws upon the theories of unconscious motivation discussed in this article. Under this view, ideology is a defense mechanism against the anxiety felt by those who hold power through means and with motives that they cannot comfortably acknowledge. This "strain theory" explains ideology as a response to the strains that an individual's or a group's social role or position creates. Ideology "provides a 'symbolic outlet' for emotional disturbances generated by social disequilibrium"; it enables privileged individuals to continue practices they would otherwise condemn and in which their own complicity would be painful to admit.

This understanding of ideology provides valuable insight into the seductive powers of the ideology of equal opportunity as well as into our resistance to abandoning one of its most critical conceptual images: the intent requirement. It reconciles the observation that antidiscrimination law has consistently operated not so much in the interests of blacks as in that of white elites with the seemingly conflicting experience that white men in positions of power have often acted and theorized with benign motives. Strain theory recognizes that no ideology of equal opportunity contrived through conscious manipulation can delude its purveyors as powerfully as one that arises by the process of self-mystification. The purveyors of this ideology, unlike charlatans, are themselves deluded.

I. 'THY SPEECH MAKETH THEE MANIFEST': A PRIMER ON THE UNCONSCIOUS AND RACE

WE have found—that is we have been obliged to assume—that very powerful mental processes or ideas exist which can produce all the effects in mental life that ordinary ideas do (including effects that can in their turn become conscious as ideas), though they themselves do not become conscious.

Whatever our preferred theoretical analysis, there is considerable commonsense evidence from our everyday experience to confirm that we all harbor prejudiced attitudes that are kept from our consciousness.

When, for example, a well-known sports broadcaster is carried away by the excitement of a brilliant play by an African American professional football player and refers to the player as a "little monkey" during a nationally televised broadcast,[7] we have witnessed the prototypical parapraxes, or unintentional slip of the tongue. This sportscaster views himself as progressive on issues of race. Many of his most important professional associates are black, and he would no doubt profess that more than a few are close friends. After the incident, he initially claimed no memory of it and then, when confronted with videotaped evidence, apologized and said that no racial slur was intended.[8] There is no reason to doubt the sincerity of his assertion. Why would he intentionally risk antagonizing his audience and damaging his reputation and career? But his inadvertent slip of the tongue was not random.[9] It is evidence of the continuing presence of a derogatory racial stereotype that he has repressed from consciousness and that has momentarily slipped past his ego's censors. Likewise, when Nancy Reagan appeared before a public gathering of then-presidential-candidate Ronald Reagan's political supporters and said that she wished he could be there to "see all these beautiful white people,"[10] one can hardly imagine that it was her self-conscious intent to proclaim publicly her preference for the company of caucasians.

Incidents of this kind are not uncommon, even if only the miscues of the powerful and famous are likely to come to the attention of the press. But because the unconscious also influences selective perceptions, whites are unlikely to hear many of the inadvertent racial slights that are made daily in their presence.

Another manifestation of unconscious racism is akin to the slip of the tongue. One might call it a slip of the mind: While one says what one intends, one fails to grasp the racist implications of one's benignly motivated words or behavior. For example, in the late 1950s and early 1960s, when integration and assimilation were unquestioned ideals among those who consciously rejected the ideology of racism, white liberals often expressed their acceptance of and friendship with blacks by telling them that they "did not think of them as Negroes." Their conscious intent was complimentary. The speaker was saying, "I think of you as normal human beings, just like me." But he was not conscious of the underlying implication of his words. What did this mean about most Negroes? Were they not normal human beings? If the white liberal were asked if this was his inference, he would doubtless have protested that his words were being misconstrued and that he only intended to state that he did not think of anyone in racial terms. But to say that one does not think of a Negro as a Negro is to say that one thinks of him as something else. The statement is made in the context of the real world, and implicit in it is a comparison to some norm. In this case the norm is whiteness. The white liberal's unconscious thought, his slip of the mind, is, "I think of you as different from other Negroes, as more like white people."

One indication of the nonneutrality of the statement, "I don't think of you as a Negro," when spoken as a compliment by a white is the incongruity of the response, "I don't think of you as white." This could also be a complimentary remark coming from a black, conveying the fact that she does not think of her friend in the usual negative terms she associates with whiteness. But this statement does not make sense coming from an individual who would accept as complimentary a statement characterizing her as unlike other Negroes. If anything, the response only makes sense as a lighthearted but cautionary retort. It conveys the following message: "I understand that your conscious intent was benign. But let me tell you something, friend. I think being black is just fine. If anything, our friendship is possible because you are unlike most white folks."

Of course, the statements of both these interlocutors are ethnocentric. But it is the white who has made the slip of the mind. He was unmindful of the ethnocentric premise upon which his "compliment" was based. He would find it painful to know that it is a premise in which he believes. His black friend's ethnocentrism is self-conscious and self-affirming. She is well aware of the impact of her reply. It is a defensive parry against the dominant society's racism.

A crucial factor in the process that produces unconscious racism is the tacitly transmitted cultural stereotype. If an individual has never known a black doctor or lawyer or is exposed to blacks only through a mass media where they are portrayed in the stereotyped roles of comedian, criminal, musician, or athlete, he is likely to deduce that blacks as a group are naturally inclined toward certain behavior and unfit for certain roles. But the lesson is not explicit: It is learned, internalized, and used without an awareness of its source. Thus, an individual may select a white job applicant over an equally qualified black and honestly believe that this decision was based on observed intangibles unrelated to race. The employer perceives the white candidate as "more articulate," "more collegial," "more thoughtful," or "more charismatic." He is unaware of the learned stereotype that influenced his decision. Moreover, he has probably also learned an explicit lesson of which he is very much aware: Good, law-abiding people do not judge others on the basis of race. Even the most thorough investigation of conscious motive will not uncover the race-based stereotype that has influenced his decision.

This same process operates in the case of more far-reaching policy decisions that come to judicial attention because of their discriminatory impact. For example, when an employer or academic administrator discovers that a written examination rejects blacks at a disproportionate rate, she can draw several possible conclusions: that blacks are less qualified than others; that the test is an inaccurate measure of ability; or that the testers have chosen the wrong skills or attributes to measure. When decisionmakers reach the first conclusion, a predisposition to select those data that conform with a racial stereotype may well have influenced them. Because this stereotype has been tacitly transmitted and unconsciously learned, they will be unaware of its influence on their decision.

If the purpose of the law's search for racial animus or discriminatory intent is to identify a morally culpable perpetrator, the existing intent requirement fails to achieve that purpose. There will be no evidence of self-conscious racism where the actors have internalized the relatively new American cultural morality which holds racism wrong or have learned racist attitudes and beliefs through tacit rather than explicit lessons. The actor himself will be unaware that his actions, or the racially neutral feelings and ideas that accompany them, have racist origins.

Of course, one can argue that the law should govern only consciously motivated actions—that societal sanctions can do no more than attempt to require that the individual's ego act as society's agent in censoring out those unconscious drives that society has defined as immoral. Under this view, the law can sanction a defective ego that has not fully internalized current societal morality and has, therefore, allowed illegal racist wishes to reach consciousness and fruition in an illegal act. But the law should not hold an individual responsible for wishes that never reach consciousness, even if they also come to fruition in discriminatory acts.

The problem is that this argument does not tell us why the law should hold the individual responsible for racial injury that results from one form of ego disguise but not the other. I believe the law should be equally concerned when the mind's censor successfully disguises a socially repugnant wish like racism if that motive produces behavior that has a discriminatory result as injurious as if it flowed from a consciously held motive.

II. A Tale of Two Theories

THE second likely challenge to my proposal acknowledges the existence of unconscious racism but questions whether it is important or even useful to take it into account in interpreting and applying the equal protection clause. This question can best be answered by posing a more general question: What is the wrong that the equal protection clause seeks to address? More specifically, what wrong do we seek to address in applying heightened scrutiny to racial classifications? If we can determine the nature of this wrong, we can determine whether identifying the existence of unconscious racial motivation is important to its prevention or remediation.

Two theories have attempted to specify the central function of suspect classification doctrine. The first, the "process defect" theory, sees the judicial intervention occasioned by strict scrutiny of suspect classifications as an appropriate response to distortions in the democratic process. The second theory cites racial stigma as the primary target of suspect classification doctrine. By examining whether and why the determination of self-conscious motive is important to each of these theories, we will be able to determine whether recognizing the presence of unconscious motive furthers the central rationale of each theory.

A. The Process Defect Theory

The chief proponent of the process defect theory has been John Ely.[11] He identifies the systematic exclusion of a group from the normal workings of the political process as the harm that heightened judicial scrutiny for suspect classifications seeks to prevent or remedy. The theory begins with Justice Stone's *Carolene Products* footnote four,[12] which states that "discrete and insular" minorities deserve special constitutional protection. Ely notes that if "minority" referred solely to the fact that the group in question was on the losing side of a particular political battle, or if "discrete and insular" referred only to its position on the wrong side of the statutory line and its inability to gather

enough allies to defeat legislation, then Stone's category would be indeterminate. Justice Stone's reference, argues Ely, was rather to "the sort of 'pluralist' wheeling and dealing" by which minorities in our society typically interact to protect their interests: It denotes those minorities for which "mutual defense pacts will prove recurrently unavailing."

The general idea of this theory is clear enough: Courts should protect those who cannot protect themselves politically. What Ely has added to Justice Stone's hypothesis is an explanation for why the Court should interfere with a political majority's normally legitimate choices in some instances and not in others. It invokes special scrutiny when the minority in question is one that keeps finding itself on the wrong end of legislative classifications because of the distorting effect of prejudice on the judgment of political decisionmakers.

Ely notes that prejudice distorts the political process in two ways: First, it bars groups that are the objects of widespread vilification from the "pluralists bazaar" that Madison believed would allow groups with overlapping interests to create majorities on given issues. The adverse reaction to the vilified minority prevents groups from recognizing and acting upon common interests that would otherwise lead them to form coalitions with the minority on certain issues. Second, prejudice causes the governmental decisionmakers to misapprehend the costs and benefits of their actions, because they seize upon positive myths about the group to which they belong and negative myths about those groups to which they do not. The first defect keeps the political process from giving certain minorities in our nation of minorities a chance to protect themselves within that process. The second defect prevents those who have gained control of the process from rationally and accurately assessing the most efficacious means of achieving even constitutionally legitimate goals.

Motive and intent are at the center of Ely's theory. The function of suspect classification doctrine is to expose unconstitutional motives that may have distorted the process. A statute that classifies by race is strictly scrutinized, because the requirement of "close fit" between end sought and means used will reveal those instances where the actual motive of the legislature was to disadvantage a group simply because of its race.

Under present doctrine, the courts look for Ely's process defect only when the racial classification appears on the face of the statute or when self-conscious racial intent has been proved under the Davis test. But the same process distortions will occur even when the racial prejudice is less apparent. Other groups in the body politic may avoid coalition with blacks without a conscious awareness of their aversion to blacks or of their association of certain characteristics with blacks. They may take stands on issues without realizing that their reasons are, in part, racially oriented. Likewise, the governmental decisionmaker may be unaware that she has devalued the cost of a chosen path, because a group with which she does not identify will bear that cost. Indeed, because of her lack of empathy with the group, she may have never even thought of the cost at all.

Process distortion exists where the unconstitutional motive of racial prejudice has influenced the decision. It matters not that the decisionmaker's motive may lie outside her awareness. For example, in *Village of Arlington Heights v. Metropolitan Housing Development Corp.,*[13] a predominantly white, upper-middle-class Chicago suburb prevented the construction of a proposed housing development for low- and moderate-income families by refusing to rezone the projected site to allow multifamily units. The Supreme Court agreed that the decision not to rezone had racially discriminatory effects, but it rejected the black plaintiffs' equal protection claim on the ground that they had "simply failed to carry their burden of proving that discriminatory purpose was a motivating factor in the Village's decision."[14] The Court focused on the lack of any evidence of conscious intent to discriminate on the part of either the city council in enacting the zoning ordinance that restricted use to single family homes or the planning commission in administering the ordinance.

We can envision several possible scenarios that demonstrate the possible process-distorting effects of unconscious racism on a governmental decision like that in Arlington Heights:

(1) The city council refused to rezone for the sole purpose of stigmatizing and denying housing to blacks. This case resembles *Plessy v. Ferguson*[15] and *Gomillion v. Lightfoot,*[16] in which the only motives were unconstitutional, and the ordinances were, therefore, per se unconstitutional.[17]

(2) The city claims a legitimate economic or environmental purpose, but evidence shows that it sought to exclude blacks in order to achieve that purpose. This case is the same as a classification by race on the face of a statute for which a legitimate goal is claimed. It is the case Ely describes where blacks are consciously excluded from the political process and devalued in the assessment of costs and benefits. When this self-conscious motive can be proved, the resulting classification is subject to strict scrutiny under existing doctrine.

(3) The purpose of the ordinance was economic—i.e., to keep property values up by keeping poor people out—but the decisionmakers associated poverty with blacks and would have weighed the costs and benefits differently if the poor people they envisioned excluding were elderly white people on social security. This "selective sympathy or indifference" could have occurred at a conscious or unconscious level. It is more than likely that the decisionmakers knew that the poor people they were excluding were black, but they would not be likely to have known that they undervalued the cost to poor people because they thought of them as black rather than white.

(4) A constituency within Arlington Heights—for example, elderly whites—did not actively campaign for the rezoning because of aversion to blacks who might have benefited from it. This occurred despite the fact that this constituency's interest in low income housing would otherwise have outweighed its interest in property values. This inability or unwillingness to apprehend and act upon an overlapping interest is precisely the kind of process distortion

through group vilification that Ely describes. It is as likely as not that these elderly voters are largely unaware of the vilification and resulting aversion that preempted their potential coalition with blacks.

(5) No one in Arlington Heights thought about blacks one way or the other—i.e., it was a fight between environmentalists and developers—but an inadvertent devaluing of black interests caused inattention to the costs blacks would have to bear. If one asked the decisionmakers how they had valued the cost to blacks of the exclusionary zoning, they might have responded, "I never thought of that." This is an example of selective indifference or misapprehension of costs that occurs entirely outside of consciousness.

The process defect theory sees suspect classification doctrine as a roundabout way of uncovering unconstitutional motive by suspecting those classifications that disadvantage groups we know to be the object of widespread vilification. But by only suspecting laws that classify by race on their face or are the result of overtly self-conscious racial motivation, the theory stops an important step short of locating and eliminating the defect it has identified. Where a society has recently adopted a moral ethic that repudiates racial disadvantaging for its own sake, governmental decisionmakers are as likely to repress their racial motives as they are to lie to courts or to attempt after-the-fact rationalizations of classifications that are not recial on their face but that do have disproportionate racial impact. Unconscious aversion to a group that has historically been vilified distorts the political process no less than a conscious decision to place race hatred before politically legitimate goals.

Moreover, unconscious prejudice presents an additional problem in that it is not subject to self-correction within the political process. When racism operates at a conscious level, opposing forces can attempt to prevail upon the rationality and moral sensibility of racism's proponents; the self-professed racist may even find religion on the road to Damascus and correct his own ways. But when the discriminator is not aware of his prejudice and is convinced that

he already walks in the path of righteousness, neither reason nor moral persuasion is likely to succeed. The process defect is all the more intractable, and judicial scrutiny becomes imperative.

B. The Stigma Theory

A second theory posits elimination of racially stigmatizing actions as the central concern of the equal protection clause.[18] Under this theory, racial classifications should be strictly scrutinized when they operate to shame and degrade a class of persons by labeling it as inferior. Stigmatization is the process by which the dominant group in society differentiates itself from others by setting them apart, treating them as less than fully human, denying them acceptance by the organized community, and excluding them from participating in that community as equals. If the equal protection clause guarantees the right to be treated as an equal, "the constitutional claim in question can be reduced to a claim to be free from stigma."[19] This theory acknowledges a historical experience in which the dominant group has systematically used stigmatizing labels against blacks and other nonwhites and has developed a social system of laws, practices, and cultural mores that looks down upon these groups, treating them as different from, and inferior to, the norm.

The prevention of stigma was at the core of the Supreme Court's unanimous declaration in *Brown v. Board of Education*[20] that segregated public schools are inherently unequal.[21] In observing that the segregation of black pupils "generates a feeling of inferiority as to their status in the community,"[22] Chief Justice Warren recognized what a majority of the Court had ignored almost sixty years earlier in *Plessy v. Ferguson:*[23] The social meaning of racial segregation in the United States is the designation of a superior and an inferior caste, and segregation proceeds "on the ground that colored citizens are . . . inferior and degraded."[24]

Stigmatizing actions harm the individual in two ways: They inflict psychological injury by assaulting a person's self-respect and human dignity, and they brand the individual with a sign that signals her inferior status to others and designates her as an outcast. The stigma theory recognizes the importance of both self-esteem and the respect of others for participating in society's benefits and responsibilities.

Proponents of this theory have also observed that racial stigma is self-perpetuating. Labeling blacks as inferior denies them access to societal opportunities; as a result, inadequate educational preparation, poverty of experience, and insufficient basic necessities limit their ability to contribute to society, and the prophecy of their inferiority is fulfilled. Furthermore, separate incidents of racial stigmatization do not inflict isolated injuries but are part of a mutually reinforcing and pervasive pattern of stigmatizing actions that cumulate to compose an injurious whole that is greater than the sum of its parts.

The injury of stigmatization consists of forcing the injured individual to wear a badge or symbol that degrades him in the eyes of society. But in most cases the symbol is not inherently pejorative. Rather, the message obtains its shameful meaning from the historical and cultural context in which it is used and, ultimately, from the way it is interpreted by those who witness it. Thus the woman who is asked to use a separate public bathroom from her husband is unlikely to be stigmatized by that action: Our society does not ordinarily interpret sex-segregated toilet facilities as designating the inferiority of women. By contrast, the black who is asked to use a different public bathroom from that of a white companion of the same gender is stigmatized. As Richard Wasserstrom has noted, racially segregated bathrooms were an important part of the system of segregation. That system's ideology held not only that blacks were less than fully human but also that they were dirty and impure. Racially segregated bathrooms ensured that blacks would not contaminate the facilities used by whites.

If stigmatizing actions injure by virtue of the meaning society gives them, then it should be apparent that the evil intent of their authors, while perhaps sufficient, is not necessary to the infliction of the injury. For example, a well-meaning if misguided white employer, having observed that her black employees usually sat together at lunch, might build a separate dining room for them with the intent of making them more comfortable. This action would stigmatize her black employees despite her best intentions. Similarly, when the city of Jackson, Mississippi, closed its public pools after a federal court ordered it to integrate them,[25] the action stigmatized blacks regardless of whether the government's purpose was racial or economic.

Given that stigma occurs whether there is racial animus or not, the answer to our initial question, "Is knowledge about the intent of the governmental actor significant to the achievement of the equal protection clause's purpose?" would seem an obvious "No." But many of the stigma theory's advocates find themselves in a quandary when faced with the question of how the Court should approach laws that are not apparently "race-dependent" but that result in disparate and stigmatizing effects. Kenneth Karst, for example, notes the Supreme Court's recent inhospitality to constitutional claims of disproportionate effect[26] and argues that "[s]urely it is still a responsible form of advocacy to argue that some racially disproportionate effects of governmental action ought to be subjected to judicial scrutiny at a level higher than minimum rationality."[27] He does not, however, elaborate on how the Court should determine which cases to include among that "some." Moreover, the origin of his reluctance to advocate increased scrutiny of all racially discriminatory impact lies in the disproportionate presence of blacks among the poor. He argues that, because the persistence of a racially identifiable economic underclass is probably beyond the capacity of courts to remedy, it is unrealistic to expect the Supreme Court to endorse this increased use of strict scrutiny in the near future.

Similarly, Paul Brest, having persuasively argued the need to eliminate racially disproportionate impact that stigmatizes, cautions that the impact doctrine "cannot reasonably be applied across the board" and urges that the doctrine be used "selectively."[28] He warns that "remedies for disproportionate impact may impose heavy costs on institutions and individuals, and cannot be tailored narrowly to compensate all those and only those whose present situation is the result of past discrimination."[29] Brest's reference to the overbreadth of remedies for disproportionate impact adds to the general concern about unduly limiting legislative discretion and the particular concern about the legitimacy of courts imposing costs on "blameless" individuals and conferring benefits on those who have not been directly harmed.

The consideration of unconscious intent responds to both of these concerns. Identifying stigmatizing actions that were affected by the actor's unconscious racial attitudes achieves two benefits. First, it significantly decreases the absolute number of impact cases subject to heightened scrutiny without eviscerating the substantive content of the equal protection clause. The bridge toll, the sales tax, and the filing fee can no longer be numbered among the parade of horribles that Justice White suggested in *Davis*. At the same time, cases where racially discriminatory impact results directly from past intentional discrimination or from current but unprovable racial animus will be well within judicial reach. A law does not stigmatize blacks simply because exclusion itself is stigmatizing, and, in this instance, they are disproportionately represented among the excluded group. Instead, the stigma stems at least in part from society's predisposition to exclude blacks. The fact that unconscious racial attitudes affected a governmental action is evidence that the racially stigmatizing symbolism preexisted the present impact.

Second, consideration of unconscious motivation provides a neutral principle for judicial intervention—i.e., the identification of a process defect. This counters the argument made against the impact test that the judiciary has no principled basis for imposing a priority for the removal of racial stigma over other social goods to which the political branch might choose to give preeminence. In short, stigma often occurs regardless of the intent of those who have engaged in the stigmatizing action. Thus, it is arguable that under the stigma theory neither conscious nor unconscious intent should be considered, and heightened judicial scrutiny should apply in all cases when governmental

action produces a stigmatizing effect. Nonetheless, recognizing unconscious racism provides a mechanism for effectively responding to continuing race-based inequalities while minimizing the costs of judicial overreaching.

While the cultural meaning test identifies the same elements of the injury of racial discrimination as does the stigma theory, it differs from that theory in two regards. First, it identifies the injury at a different point in the constitutional analysis. The stigma theory explains why recognized racial classifications—i.e., laws whose racial classification is apparent on their face or laws whose racial motive has been proved—should be subject to heightened judicial scrutiny. In nothing that the harm of stigma occurs irrespective of the presence of conscious motive, the cultural meaning test refocuses the stigma theory's inquiry to a different point in time. The presence of racial stigma is viewed as evidence of the existence of a racial classification, not simply as a justification for the heightened scrutiny of such classifications.

Second, the cultural meaning test adds content to the stigma theory's analysis. It locates the origin of racial stigma in the accumulation of the individual unconscious and finds the origin of unconscious racism in the presence of widely shared, tacitly transmitted cultural values. The recognition of these mutually reciprocal origins joins the theoretical description of human action as arising out of autonomous individual choice with the view that such action is socially determined. The cultural meaning theory thus describes a dialectic rather than a dichotomy. It demonstrates that ultimately the proponents of the process defect theory and the stigma theory have identified different manifestations of the same cultural phenomenon.

III. READING THE MIND'S SYMBOLS: HOW DO WE IDENTIFY UNCONSCIOUS RACISM IN SPECIFIC CASES?

A. The "Cultural Meaning" Test

This article's discussion of the stigma theory has anticipated the third likely challenge to my thesis that equal protection doctrine must address the unconscious racism that underlies much of the racially disproportionate impact of governmental policy. This challenge questions how a court would identify those cases where unconscious racism operated in order to determine whether to subject an allegedly discriminatory act to strict scrutiny.

I propose a test that would look to the "cultural meaning" of an allegedly racially discriminatory act as the best available analogue for and evidence of the collective unconscious that we cannot observe directly. This test would evaluate governmental conduct to see if it conveys a symbolic message to which the culture attaches racial significance. The court would analyze governmental behavior much like a cultural anthropologist might: by considering evidence regarding the historical and social context in which the decision was made and effectuated. If the court determined by a preponderance of the evidence that a significant portion of the population thinks of the governmental action in racial terms, then it would presume that socially shared, unconscious racial attitudes made evident by the action's meaning had influenced the decisionmakers. As a result, it would apply heightened scrutiny.

The unconscious racial attitudes of individuals manifest themselves in the cultural meaning that society gives their actions in the following way: In a society that no longer condones overt racist attitudes and behavior, many of these attitudes will be repressed and prevented from reaching awareness in an undisguised form. But as psychologists have found, repressed wishes, fears, anger, and aggression continue to seek expression, most often by attaching themselves to certain symbols in the external world. Repressed feelings and attitudes that are commonly experienced are likely to find common symbols particularly fruitful or productive as a vehicle for their expression. Thus, certain actions, words, or signs may take on meaning within a particular culture as a result of the collective use of those actions, words, or signs to represent or express shared but repressed attitudes. The process is cyclical: The expression of shared attitudes through certain symbols

gives those symbols cultural meaning, and once a symbol becomes an enduring part of the culture, it in turn becomes the most natural vehicle for the expression of those attitudes and feelings that caused it to become an identifiable part of the culture.

Cognitive theory provides an alternative explanation of why the racial meaning the culture gives an action will be evidence of the actor's unconscious racial motivation. According to cognitive theory, those meanings or values that are most deeply ingrained in the culture are commonly acquired early in life through tacit lessons. They are, therefore, less recognizable and less available to the individual's consciousness than other forms of knowledge. Looked at another way, if the action has cultural meaning, this meaning must have been transmitted to an individual who is a member of that culture. If he professes to be unaware of the cultural meaning or attitude, it will almost surely be operating at an unconscious level.

Thus, an action such as the construction of a wall between white and black communities in Memphis[30] would have a cultural meaning growing out of a long history of whites' need to separate themselves from blacks as a symbol of their superiority. Individual members of the city council might well have been unaware that their continuing need to maintain their superiority over blacks, or their failure to empathize with how construction of the wall would make blacks feel, influenced their decision. But if one were to ask even the most self-deluded among them what the residents of Memphis would take the existence of the wall to mean, the obvious answer would be difficult to avoid. If one told the story leading to the wall's construction while omitting one vital fact—the race of those whose vehicular traffic the barrier excluded—and then asked Memphis citizens to describe the residents of the community claiming injury, few, if any, would not guess that they were black.

The current racial meanings of governmental actions are strong evidence that the process defects of group vilification and misapprehension of costs and benefits have occurred whether or not the decisionmakers were conscious that race played a part in their decisionmaking. Moreover, actions that have racial meaning within the culture are also those actions that carry a stigma for which we should have special concern. This is not the stigma that occurs only because of a coincidental congruence between race and poverty. The association of a symbol with race is a residuum of overtly racist practices in the past: The wall conjures up racial inferiority, not the inferiority of the poor or the undesirability of vehicular traffic. And stigma that has racial meaning burdens all blacks and adds to the pervasive, cumulative, and mutually reinforcing system of racial discrimination.

B. Some Easy Cases

Applying the cultural meaning test to a series of cases is the best way to examine its operative effect. These first cases are "easy" in that there will be little disagreement about whether the governmental action in question has racial meaning in our culture. They are cases like the segregated beach, which clearly has racial meaning, and the increased bridge toll, which clearly does not. These cases are instructive for two reasons: The lack of ambiguity in the meaning that will attach to the governmental action allows us to see more clearly the relationship between cultural meaning and unconscious intent; furthermore, these cases demonstrate the usefulness of a test that distinguishes governmental actions that have racial meaning in addition to racially disparate impact from those that have only racially disparate impact.

I. BROWN V. BOARD OF EDUCATION[31]

Charles Black first discussed the "social meaning" of segregation in his brilliantly simple and succinct defense of *Brown*, "The Lawfulness of the Segregation Decisions."[32] He begins with history, and notes that segregation was the direct descendant of slavery and the black codes and an "integral part of the movement to maintain white supremacy."[33] Segregation was not a case of mutual separation but a system that one group imposed on another. Black points to its contextual association with other "indisputably

and grossly" discriminatory practices, such as exclusion from the vote, and to the manner in which segregation as a pattern of law often combined with extralegal patterns of discrimination.[34] That "separate but equal" facilities were almost never really equal is evidence not just of the material inequality they imposed but also of the meaning of segregation to the people who imposed it. He cites the facts that it was actionable defamation in the South to call a white man a Negro and that "a small proportion of Negro 'blood' put one in the inferior race for segregation's purposes" as further evidence of segregation's meaning.[35]

Professor Black closes his catalogue of particulars with the observation that the points he has made "are matters of common knowledge, matters not so much for judicial notice as for the background knowledge of educated men who live in the world."[36] Given this common knowledge, it is difficult, if not impossible, to envision how a governmental decisionmaker might issue an order to segregate without intending, consciously or unconsciously, to injure blacks. Could the defendants in *Brown* have escaped this meaning? Could anyone who grew up in the system Charles Black describes have made a decision to put black and white children in separate schools without that decision being influenced by race?

The "common knowledge," or clear meaning, Black describes is evidence of shared cultural attitudes that have expressed themselves in cultural symbols. The actions involved could have nothing other than a racial meaning within our society. But for purposes of our present analysis, the most important thing to recognize is that an action's meaning derives from a long-term and pervasive association of certain feelings or thoughts with that action. Feelings and thoughts that have become sufficiently widespread and internalized to express themselves in a system of social symbols or meanings do not disappear with the enactment of civil rights legislation. The feelings may be repressed from consciousness, but so long as the symbols they have created retain their meaning, the feelings continue to exist and to shape behavior.

2. NONRACIAL ACTIONS

At the opposite end of the spectrum is a hypothetical increase in the municipal railway fare in a racially and economically diverse municipality. It may be more burdensome on the relatively poor person who must use that transportation than on the relatively rich individual. It may also be true that nonwhites are disproportionately represented among the poor and that, therefore, the increase has a racially disparate impact.[37] But there is no history of using bus or train fares as a way to designate nonwhites as inferior, and, most importantly, we do not think of fare increases in racial terms.

The same would be true of an increase in the sales tax, the fee for obtaining a driver's license, or the cost of a building permit. These are all cases where the impact on blacks in a particular instance may be greater than it is on whites. They are also cases where some stigma may attach to those who are excluded by the governmental action. But we are likely to think of the in-group and out-group in economic rather than racial terms. These actions do not contribute directly to the system of beliefs that labels blacks as inferior. Where the culture as a whole does not think of an action in racial terms, it is also unlikely that unconscious attitudes about race influenced the governmental decision-maker.

The easy cases at this end of the spectrum are precisely the kind of cases to which Justice White alluded in *Davis* when he warned that a discriminatory impact standard might invalidate "a whole range of tax, welfare, public service, regulatory, and licensing statutes that may be more burdensome to the poor and to the average black than to the more affluent white."[38] The cultural meaning test, by distinguishing racially stigmatizing statutes from those that only stigmatize indirectly through their economic impact, would go a long way toward obviating Justice White's concern.

C. Some Harder Cases

Where there is less agreement about the social meaning of allegedly discriminatory governmental action, the application of the cultural

meaning test will, of course, be more difficult. But the process of applying the test and its underlying rationale will be the same. By looking at how the test might be applied to several more difficult cases, this section explores in greater detail how a court might gather and interpret evidence of cultural meaning.

1. ARLINGTON HEIGHTS [39]

In Arlington Heights, a nonprofit development corporation obtained a purchase option on fifteen acres of land on which it planned to develop a federally subsidized, racially integrated, low and moderate income townhouse project. The proposed site of the project was in the Village of Arlington Heights, a Chicago suburb of over 64,000 residents of whom, as of 1970, twenty-seven were black. Because the site was zoned for single family dwellings, the development corporation petitioned the village to rezone the property for multiple family use. When the village board of trustees, following the recommendation of the planning commission, denied the rezoning request, the developer and three blacks who were prospective tenants of the proposed project filed suit in federal district court.

Several kinds of evidence would be available to demonstrate that denying the zoning variance in these circumstances has a cultural meaning that demeans blacks. Initially, plaintiffs could present evidence of the historical and contemporaneous meaning of residential segregation in the culture as a whole. This would include the history of statutorily mandated housing segregation as well as the use of restrictive covenants among private parties that aim to prevent blacks from purchasing property in white neighborhoods. Studies of racially segregated housing patterns throughout the United States and in the areas surrounding Arlington Heights as well as data and attitudinal surveys on residential segregation and "white flight" would also be relevant. Such studies have indicated that collective and individual tolerances for black neighbors vary from community to community. While they ascribe the intolerance to different causes, they agree substantially on the prominence of race in the minds of both those who flee and those who stay. They also note whites' continuing aversion to housing integration.

The body of evidence that documents our culture's frequent attachment of racial meaning to the very existence of segregated housing is extensive and should be more than sufficient to establish the cultural meaning of the Arlington Heights city officials' action. We have rarely come to live in racially segregated enclaves as the result of happenstance or out of mutual choice. We live in segregated neighborhoods because whites have believed that living with or close to blacks lowers their own status. Where one lives is an important index of one's status in our culture, and to live in proximity to those who are looked down upon is to be looked down upon oneself.

This evidence of what racially segregated housing patterns mean in our culture would not be the only evidence available to the court. There is also direct evidence of the meaning Arlington Heights residents attached to the city's decision denying the zoning variance. The planning commission considered the proposal at a series of three public meetings which drew large crowds. Many of those in attendance were quite vocal and demonstrative in their opposition to the project, although some spoke in support of rezoning. But both opponents and supporters referred to the "social issue"—the desirability or undesirability of introducing low and moderate income housing that would probably be racially integrated into this area of Arlington Heights.

The Supreme Court in Arlington Heights noted this evidence and observed that some opponents of the housing project "might have been motivated by opposition to minority groups."[40] But the Court went on to affirm the trial court's holding that the evidence "[did] not warrant the conclusion that this [racial opposition] motivated the defendants."[41] If, however, this same evidence is considered for the purpose of determining the cultural meaning of the city's action, it is far more probative. Even the court's terse description of the public meetings makes clear that race was prominent in the minds of

both opponents and proponents of the project. The trial court, in its search for discriminatory purpose, found that the obvious prominence of the race issue did not warrant a finding of racial motivation. But, if the court's inquiry had focused on the meaning this community attached to the decision to exclude the project, this evidence of heated debate on the question of race would necessarily carry a great deal more weight.

A final source of evidence regarding the racial meaning of the city's action is the unreasonableness of the nonracial criteria upon which the zoning board relied. Single family residences constituted the dominant and preferred land use in the village; the board invoked a "buffer policy" that restricted multiple family residences to areas between single family zones and commercial or industrial zones as its reason for denying the rezoning request. But the proposed multiple family residences were not high-density apartments. The project would have consisted of twenty two-story buildings on fifteen acres of land, 60 percent of which would have remained open space; a screen of trees and shrubs would have separated the project from neighboring houses. There would have been little to distinguish the project from the tracts of small lot, single family dwellings in the area. Applying the "buffer policy" in this case, where none of the legitimate purposes underlying the policy existed, should cast some doubt on whether these "normal criteria" were applied for "normal"—that is, nonracial—reasons. Alternatively, it may indicate the decisionmakers' unconscious, stereotyped view of housing occupied by nonwhites: Their image of what the project would look like may have been influenced as much by their expectations about housing occupied by blacks as by the actual plan and drawings presented.

Our culture attaches racial meaning to residential segregation. When we see an all-white neighborhood in close proximity to an all-black one, we do not imagine that it is white because its inhabitants' forebears settled there generations ago or that blacks have chosen not to live there. Our initial thought is that it is white because nonwhites have been excluded. This cultural meaning is evidence that no one who is a part of this culture could have made a decision like that made in Arlington Heights without race on his mind, the effectiveness of our psychodynamic censors notwithstanding. Furthermore, this cultural meaning is considerably more relevant to the stigmatizing injury that blacks suffer than is the conscious intent of the decisionmakers. If our culture interprets a decision to exclude blacks from a neighborhood as evidence of blacks' continued untouchability, that decision becomes part of the system of mutually reinforcing racial stigma that denies blacks the status of full humanity.

2. *WASHINGTON V. DAVIS*[42]

Davis presents a more difficult case than Arlington Heights. Two unsuccessful black candidates for positions in the District of Columbia Metropolitan Police Department alleged that some of the Department's hiring practices—particularly "Test 21," a written test that blacks failed at a rate roughly four times that of whites—discriminated against blacks and violated the guarantee of equal protection implicit in the fifth amendment's due process clause. "Test 21," which was used throughout the federal civil service, was designed to test verbal ability, vocabulary, reading, and comprehension. While the Court found that the test was a useful indicator of success in police training school, there was no proof that either the test scores or the school's examination scores predicted job performance or measured success in job-related training.

What evidence might the plaintiffs have presented to establish that the government's action in this case had racial meaning? Unlike segregated housing, we do not ordinarily associate the use of civil service exams with race. But an action that has no racial meaning in one context may have significant racial meaning in another. We have seen that human behavior must be examined in context, as it may well derive its meaning from the specific historical and cultural milieu in which it takes place. Despite the race-neutral origins of civil service exams as a generic entity, one has an intuitive sense that their use in this case has racial connotations—that this

case is more like the Memphis wall than it is like an increased bus fare or a regressive tax. It is important to pay heed to one's intuitions at this juncture. One individual's gut feeling is hardly conclusive evidence of cultural meaning, but such feelings often derive from feelings that are more widely shared, and they may well indicate that more substantial testimony is available.

At this point, it is helpful to consider the setting in which "Test 21" was employed. Can one identify the contextual elements that have attracted the attention of our intuition? Are there elements not present in other civil service cases, elements that speak in terms of race? The most obvious racial element is the exam's racially disproportionate impact. One can argue that the government's action racially stigmatizes because blacks fail the exam in larger numbers than whites. But not every case of racially disparate impact has racial meaning. An increased bus fare may burden a larger percentage of blacks than whites, but we do not think of the fare increase as a direct stigmatization of blacks. It does not convey a message of racial inferiority. Thus, if the governmental action in *Davis* conveys a racial message, it must derive that meaning from something other than, or in addition to, its racial impact. Like the traffic barrier in *Memphis v. Greene*, there must be something in the particulars of its historical and cultural context that causes us to interpret this action—at least intuitively—in racial terms.

I suggest that there are two such elements. The first involves the nature of the work or activity from which blacks have been excluded: the job of police officer in a predominantly but not entirely black community. The second relates to the reason given for their exclusion: that they failed to demonstrate sufficient proficiency in verbal and written language skills.

It is significant that the challenged action in *Davis* excluded blacks from working as police officers and not as mail carriers or bus drivers. The occupation of police officer has symbolic meaning within our culture. Police officers represent the law as well as enforce it. They are armed and have discretionary authority to use violence. They are charged with protecting the lives and property of some individuals within society and controlling the violent and unlawful behavior of others. If history—the accumulated meaningful behavior of our culture—has taught us to attach significance to race in considering these elements of the job of police officer— authority, control, protection, and sanctioned violence—then an action that determines the racial composition of a police force also has racial meaning.

Furthermore, throughout American history police forces have had a different relationship to black communities than to white communities. In white communities, the police officer is viewed as a public servant. His job is to protect the lives and property of those in the community where he works. But the job of the law enforcement officer in black communities has been to control the communities' inhabitants and to protect the lives and property of whites who perceive blacks as the primary potential source of violence and crime.

For blacks, those entrusted with law enforcement and the firepower that gives them authority have always been servants of the white men in power who exploit blacks economically and demean them socially.[43] Slaves were forbidden to bear arms and a white police force of overseers and sheriffs' posses enforced the master's law. With the abolition of slavery, the use of organized, socially sanctioned violence against blacks increased, and the authority of the sheriff's office was often indistinguishable from that of the Ku Klux Klan. As recently as 1967, there were nearly a dozen major American cities where blacks accounted for over 25 percent of the population that were patrolled by police forces with only a token minority representation. It is not surprising that many black communities continue to view the police as an occupying army.

The fact that police officers are authority figures to white as well as black citizens is also significant in determining the cultural meaning of excluding large numbers of blacks from the D.C. police force. To the extent that our culture attaches specific meaning to the assignment of racial groups to certain occupational and hierarchical roles, behavior that maintains those role assignments will have racial meaning. For example, whites are accustomed to seeing blacks as servants performing menial tasks. Thus, whites are generally neither surprised nor threatened when they see black porters, maids, and janitors. This is not simply a reflection of the fact that many blacks have performed these jobs. It is also indicative of a historical and culturally ingrained system of beliefs that leads us to think of blacks as suited to these jobs, to associate the jobs with blacks.

By contrast, whites are not accustomed to seeing blacks in positions of authority or power. Black managers, black professors, and black doctors are confronted with reactions ranging from disbelief to resistance to concern about their competence. The historical exclusion of blacks from these jobs has been rationalized by a belief in their unsuitability for these roles. What is at issue here is not just occupational stereotypes born out of habit. These stereotypes manifest a larger and more complex ideology that has legitimized the white-over-black authority relationship. Stereotypes are cultural symbols. They constitute our contemporary interpretation of past and present meaningful behavior.

The argument in defense of all-male police forces provides a useful analogue for understanding our less readily apparent attitudes about authority and race. In suits alleging discrimination against women in the selection of patrol officers, police department defendants have argued that women would not make good officers because the job requires an individual who can command respect from the man on the street. Men, they have argued, would not take orders from women, and, therefore, women would be less effective patrol persons. In other words, the departments' discriminatory hiring practices have been defended as a necessary adaptation to the sexist beliefs and practices of the culture.

Whites would be less likely to verbalize the same argument regarding blacks, but the fact remains that many individuals in our culture continue to resist and resent taking orders from blacks. If the court were convinced that the absence or presence of substantial numbers of black police officers on the D.C. force would be interpreted as the maintenance or disestablishment of culturally instilled beliefs about the need to control blacks and the appropriate roles for blacks and whites in authority relationships, then the Civil Service Commission's decision to rely on "Test 21" would have racial meaning.

There is another reason why a significant segment of the culture is likely to view the exclusionary impact of "Test 21" in racially stigmatizing terms. "Test 21" was primarily a test of verbal and written skills. The Civil Service Commission justified its use of the test by noting its desire to upgrade the communication skills of the city's police officers. Our society has increasingly sought to measure intelligence through the use of written tests, and we have come to believe that performance on such tests accurately reflects the whole of our intelligence. Thus, most people are likely to think of those who performed poorly on "Test 21" not simply as lacking in communication skills but as unintelligent. The average person is likely to see the city's use of the test as an admirable and reasonable attempt to insure that the city has smart police officers. If larger numbers of blacks than whites fail the test, this will be seen as proof that blacks are not smart enough for the job.

But evidence of cultural meaning must include more than disproportionate impact. Some whites also performed poorly on the test. Observers of the test's results would not necessarily conclude that, because blacks performed less well on this test, they are intellectually inferior as a group. They might think instead that the blacks who took this test just happened to be a less intelligent group, that less well-educated people performed less well on the test and the blacks who took this test had not on the whole received as good an education as the whites, or that poor people are less intelligent and blacks had done less well because a higher percentage of them were poor.

The cultural meaning test would require the plaintiffs to produce evidence that a substantial part of the population will interpret the disproportionate results of "Test 21" not as the product of random selection or the differential educational background or socioeconomic status of the test takers but as testimony to the inherent intellectual abilities of the racial groups to which the test takers belong. In other words, the government's use of the test has racial meaning if our culture has taught us to believe that blacks that fail the test have done so because they are black. Plaintiffs trying *Davis* under the test proposed in this article would present evidence detailing both the history and the contemporary manifestations of this myth. They would seek to convince the court that most people in our culture believe that the average white person is inherently smarter than the average black person and that whites will interpret the racially selective impact of "Test 21" as a confirmation of that belief. If the culture gives the governmental action this kind of racial meaning, the action constitutes a direct racial stigmatization. Like the segregated beach and the Memphis wall, it conveys a message that has its origins in a pervasive and mutually reinforcing pattern of racially stigmatizing actions, and it adds one more stigmatizing action to that pattern. Presumably, the decisionmakers who chose to use "Test 21" were aware of that message and were influenced by it, whether consciously or unconsciously.

Ely's process defect analysis helps explain why proof that governmental action will be interpreted in racial terms should lead a court to closely scrutinize that action. In selecting "Test 21" to screen police applicants, the Civil Service Commission weighed a number of benefits and costs. The fact that the test helps select candidates with good communication skills is, presumably, a benefit. Yet the test may also exclude many of those who are best able to establish rapport with the residents of the communities in which they work and best able to inspire their trust and confidence. The test may save time and money by making it unnecessary to offer additional training in communication skills in the police academy. But it may also create costs by selecting those candidates who will most need sensitivity training and community relations workshops. Likewise, the less tangible benefits of maintaining a work force with which the predominantly white residents of Capitol Hill, visiting tourists, and upper level bureaucrats will be comfortable must be weighed against the costs of failing to create more employment opportunities for the city's predominantly nonwhite, low income residents.

This is but a small sampling of the kind of political prioritizing that must take place when any decision is made. Much of this weighing of costs and benefits is implicit. Some considerations receive the lowest priority because they are never considered. The Court in *Davis* tells us that the government's purpose in adopting "Test 21" was to "modestly upgrade the communicative abilities of its employees."[44] We do not know whether this benefit was considered so important that it outweighed all of the costs listed above, or whether those costs were never even considered. An unconscious belief in the intellectual inferiority of blacks may have led the decisionmakers to put more stock in the test's ability to measure relevant skills than was justified. An inarticulate discomfort when confronted by blacks in positions of authority may not have led a commissioner to intentionally exclude blacks from the force, but it may have caused him to respond to the test's potential for discriminatory impact with relief rather than concern. His insensitivity to the importance the city's blacks would attach to more black faces on the beat might mean that this consideration was never even weighed in the balance.

These are the very "racially selective sympath[ies] and indifference[s]"[45] that create misapprehensions of process defects. These sympathies overestimate the validity of generalizations that are self-flattering—for example, that written tests accurately measure an important kind of intelligence. And they undervalue the benefits of alternatives—for example, a test that measures judgment in real life situations or empathy with community residents—that would enhance the fortunes of others.

CONCLUSION

ULTIMATELY, the greatest stumbling block to any proposal to modify the intent requirement will not be its lack of jurisprudential efficacy but the perception among those who give substance to our jurisprudence that it will operate against their self-interest. Derrick Bell has noted that the interests of blacks in achieving racial equality have been accommodated only when they have converged with the interests of powerful whites: The legal establishment has not responded to civil rights claims that threaten the superior societal status of upper and middle class whites.[46] Alan Freeman has argued persuasively for the more radical proposition that antidiscrimination law has affirmatively advanced racism by promoting an ideology that justifies the continued economic subjugation of blacks.[47] The intent requirement is a centerpiece in an ideology of equal opportunity that legitimizes the continued existence of racially and economically discriminatory conditions and rationalizes the superordinate status of privileged whites.

The workings of the unconscious make this dissonance between efforts to achieve full civil rights for blacks and the self-interest of those who are most able to effect change even more difficult to overcome. The ideology of which Freeman speaks is more than a consciously wielded hegemonic tool of domination. It is also an unconscious defense mechanism against the guilt and anxiety of those who hold power and privilege through means and with motives that they cannot acknowledge. Racism continues to be aided and abetted by self-conscious bigots and well-meaning liberals alike.

I do not anticipate that either the Supreme Court or the academic establishment will rush to embrace and incorporate the approach this article proposes. It has not been my purpose to advance an analysis that is attractive for its ease of application or for its failure to challenge accepted and comfortable ways of thinking about equal protection and race. Rather, it is my hope that the preliminary thoughts expressed in the preceding pages will stimulate others to think about racism in a new way and will provoke a discussion of how equal protection doctrine can best incorporate this understanding of racism.

This article has argued that judicial exploration of the cultural meaning of governmental actions with racially discriminatory impact is the best way to discover the unconscious racism of governmental actors. This exploration will be beset by the complexities and inadequacies of social interpretation and buffeted by the head winds of political resistance. Perhaps I am overly optimistic in believing that in the process of this difficult exploration we may discover and understand a collective self-interest that overshadows the multitude of parochial self-interests the unconscious seeks to disguise and shield. But of one thing I am certain. A difficult and painful exploration beats death at the hands of the disease.

NOTES

1. 426 U.S. at 229 (1976).

2. For example, *Hunter v. Underwood,* 471 U.S. 222 (1985). In Hunter, the Court determined that a provision in the Alabama Constitution disenfranchising persons convicted of crimes involving moral turpitude violated the equal protection clause. Even though the provision was racially neutral on its face, its original enactment was motivated by a desire to discriminate against blacks, and it had had a racially discriminatory impact since its adoption. The Court reaffirmed the doctrine that "[p]roof of racially discriminatory intent or purpose is required to show a violation of the Equal Protection Clause." *Id.* at 226 (citing *Village of Arlington Heights v. Metropolitan Hous. Dev. Corp.,* 429 U.S. at 252, 264–65 (1977)). A LEXIS search in October of 1986 found thirty-eight cases that cite *Davis* for the principle that proof of discriminatory intent is necessary when disproportionate impact results from facially neutral governmental action.

3. Karst, "The Costs of Motive-Centered Inquiry," 15 *San Diego L. Rev.* 1163, 1165 (1978).

4. *Washington v. Davis,* 426 U.S. 229, 248 & n.14 (1976) (citing Goodman, "De Facto School Segregation: A Constitutional and Empirical Analysis," 60 *Calif. L. Rev.* 275, 300 (1972))

5. In using the term "collective unconscious," I refer to the collection of widely shared individual memories, beliefs, and understandings that exist in the mind at a nonreporting level. This nonreporting mental activity is widely shared

because individuals who live within the same culture share common developmental experiences. This use of the term "collective unconscious" is to be distinguished from Jung's "collective unconscious," which he described as that part of the psyche that retains and transmits the common psychological inheritance of humankind. Henderson, "Ancient Myths and Modern Man," in *Man and His Symbols* 104, 107 (C. Jung ed. 1964). It should also be distinguished from Freud's "archaic remnants," which Jung described as "mental forms whose presence cannot be explained by anything in the individual's own life [and] which seem to be aboriginal, innate, and inherited shapes of the human mind." Jung, "Approaching the Unconscious," in *Man and His Symbols, supra,* at 18, 67.

6. Several critical commentators have described the process by which law transmits ideological imagery that helps to preserve and legitimize existing power relationships. Those in power use the legal system to achieve results in individual legal disputes that maintain the status quo. What is less obvious, but perhaps more important, is the use of legal ideas to create and transmit utopian images that serve to justify that status quo. By representing reality in ideal terms, the law validates the socioeconomic setting in which legal decisions are made. The ideological imagery masks or denies the reality of oppressive or alienating social and economic relations and persuades us that they are fair. See, for example, D. Hay, P. Linebaugh, J. Rule, E. Thompson & C. Winslow, *Albion's Fatal Tree* (1975); Delgado, "The Imperial Scholar: Reflections on a Review of Civil Rights Literature" [in this collection]; ... Kennedy, "The Structure of Blackstone's Commentaries," 28 *Buffalo L. Rev.* 205 (1979). ...

7. Shapiro, "Cosell's Remark Raises Ire," *Wash. Post,* Sept. 6, 1983, at D6, col. 1.

8. "No man respects Alvin Garrett more than I do. I talked about that man's ability to be so elusive despite the smallness of his size." *Id.*

9. Why, for instance, did Cosell use the word "monkey," an animal long associated with caricatures and stereotypes of blacks, rather than "rabbit" or "deer" or "jet"?

10. Mrs. Reagan made the comment at a reception in Chicago. The manager of Reagan's Illinois campaign defended Mrs. Reagan by pointing out that "she was talking to her husband about the white snow and that's how she got mixed up." *Wash. Post,* Feb. 18, 1980, at A2, col. 1; see also R. Dugger, *On Reagan: The Man and His Presidency* 202 (1983).

11. See J. Ely, *Democracy and Distrust* 135–79 (1980). ...

12. *Carolene Prods.,* 304 U.S. at 152 n.4.

13. 429 U.S. at 252 (1977).

14. *Id.* at 270.

15. 163 U.S. at 537 (1896).

16. 364 U.S. at 339 (1960).

17. In Gomillion, the Court set aside the Alabama legislature's action changing the shape of Tuskegee from a square to a "strangely irregular twenty-eight-sided figure," thereby removing from the city all but a handful of black voters but not one white. The Court found these facts "[t]antamount for all practical purposes to a mathematical demonstration, that the legislation is solely concerned with . . . fencing Negro citizens out of the town." *Id.* at 341.

18. See *Strauder v. West Virginia*, 100 U.S. 303 (1880) (striking down a state law excluding blacks from juries). In that case, Justice Strong, writing for the court, held that the fourteenth amendment protects blacks "from legal discriminations, implying inferiority in civil society," and that the West Virginia statute was "practically a brand upon them" and "an assertion of their inferiority." *Id.* at 308; see also *Plessy v. Ferguson*, 163 U.S. 537, 560, 562 (1896) (Harlan, J., dissenting) (referring to the segregation of railway passengers as a "badge of servitude" which proceeded "on the ground that colored citizens are . . . inferior and degraded").

19. Karst, "Why Equality Matters", 17 *Ga. L. Rev.* 245, 249 (1983).

20. 347 U.S. at 483 (1954).

21. "We conclude that in the field of public education the doctrine of 'separate but equal' has no place. Separate educational facilities are inherently unequal." *Id.* at 495.

22. *Id.* at 494.

23. 163 U.S. at 537 (1896).

24. *Id.* at 560 (Harlan, J., dissenting).

25. See *Palmer v. Thompson*, 403 U.S. at 217 (1971).

26. Karst, *supra* note 19, at 275.

27. *Id.*

28. *Id.* at 29. Brest argues that the disproportionate impact doctrine sometimes serves the antidiscrimination principle by creating a rebuttable presumption of intentional discrimination. But he stops short of applying a pure uneven impact test "for the reasons suggested by Mr. Justice White's parade of horribles in *Washington v. Davis.*" *Id.* Instead, he expressly applies the presumption only in school desegregation and employment discrimination cases. *Id.* at 29–30.

29. *Id.* at 36.

30. *City of Memphis v. Greene*, 451 U.S. at 100 (1981).

31. 347 U.S. at 483 (1954).

32. Black, "The Lawfulness of the Segregated Decisions," 69 *Yale L. J.* 421 (1960).

33. *Id.* at 424–25.

34. *Id.* at 425. Although these extralegal patterns of discrimination are generally not state actions, they can nevertheless assist us in understanding the meaning and assessing the impact of state actions.

35. Black, *supra* note 32, at 425–26.

36. *Id.* at 426.

37. "Disparate impact" is a term of art which the Supreme Court has adopted in decisions interpreting Title VII of the 1964 Civil Rights Act, 42 U.S.C. s 2000e (1982). Disparate impact cases "involve employment practices that are facially neutral . . . but that in fact fall more harshly on one group than another and cannot be justified by business necessity." *International Bhd. of Teamsters v. United States*, 431 U.S. 324, 336 n.15 (1977).

38. *Davis*, 426 U.S. at 248.

39. *Village of Arlington Heights v. Metropolitan Hous. Dev. Corp.*, 429 U.S. at 252 (1977).

40. *Id.* at 269.

41. *Id.* at 269.

42. 426 U.S. at 229 (1976).

43. [T]here is no "American dilemma" because black people in this country form a colony, and it is not in the interest of the colonial power to liberate them. Black people are legal citizens of the United States with, for the most part, the same legal rights as other citizens. Yet they stand as colonial subjects in relation to the white society. Thus institutional racism has another name: colonialism . . . . The black community perceives the "white power structure" in very concrete terms. The man in the ghetto sees his white landlord come only to collect exorbitant rants and fail to make necessary repairs, while both know that the white-dominated city building inspection department will wink at violations or impose only slight fines. The man in the ghetto sees the white policeman on the corner brutally manhandle a black drunkard in a doorway, and at the same time accept a pay-off from one of the agents of the white-controlled rackets. . . . He is not about to listen to intellectual discourses on the pluralistic and fragmented nature of political power. He is faced with a "white power structure" as monolithic as Europe's colonial offices have been to African and Asian colonies. S. Carmichael & C. Hamilton, *Black Power: The Politics of Liberation in America* 5–10 (1967); see also F. Fanon, *The Wretched of the Earth* 38 (1963) ("The colonial world is a world cut in two. The dividing line, the frontiers are shown by barracks and police stations. In the colonies it is the policeman and the soldier who are the official, instituted go-betweens, the spokesmen of the settler and his rule of oppression."); Delgado, " 'Rotten Social Background': Should the Criminal Law Recognize a Defense of Severe Environmental Deprivation?," 3 *L. & Inequality* 9, 29–30 (1985).

44. *Davis*, 426 U.S. at 246.

45. Brest, "Forward in Defense of the Antidiscrimination Principle," 90 *Harv. L. Rev.* 1, 14 (1976).

46. Bell, "Brown v. Board of Education and the Interest-Convergence Dilemma," 93 *Harv. L. Rev.* 518, 523–24 (1980). . . .

47. Freeman, "Legitimating Racial Discrimination Through Antidiscrimination Law: A Critical Review of Supreme Court Doctrine" [in this collection].

č

A CRITIQUE OF "OUR CONSTITUTION IS COLOR-BLIND"
Neil Gotanda

I. INTRODUCTION

THIS article examines the ideological content of the claim that "our Constitution is color-blind"[1] and argues that the U.S. Supreme Court's use of color-blind constitutionalism—a collection of legal themes functioning as a racial ideology—fosters white racial domination. Though aspects of color-blind constitutionalism can be traced to pre–Civil War debates, the modern concept developed after the passage of the Thirteenth, Fourteenth, and Fifteenth Amendments, and it matured in 1955, in *Brown v. Board of Education.*[2] A color-blind interpretation of the Constitution legitimates and thereby maintains the social, economic, and political advantages that whites hold over other Americans. . . .

The Supreme Court's color-blind constitutionalism uses race to cover four distinct ideas: status-race, formal-race, historical-race, and culture-race. Status-race is the traditional notion of race as an indicator of social status. While traditional status-race is now largely discredited, it remains important as the racial model for efforts aimed at eradicating intentional forms of racial subordination, with their implication of racial inferiority.

The second use of race, formal-race, refers to socially constructed formal categories. Black and white are seen as neutral, apolitical descriptions, reflecting merely "skin color" or region of ancestral origin. Formal-race is unrelated to ability, disadvantage, or moral culpability. Moreover, formal-race categories are unconnected to social attributes such as culture, education, wealth, or language; this "unconnectedness" is the defining characteristic of formal-race, and no other usage of "race" incorporates the concept.

Historical-race, however, does assign substance to racial categories. Historical-race embodies past and continuing racial subordination, and is the meaning of race which the court contemplates when it applies "strict scrutiny" to racially disadvantaging government conduct. The state's use of racial categories is regarded as so closely linked to illegitimate racial subordination that it is automatically judicially suspect.

Finally, culture-race uses "black" to refer to African-American culture, community, and consciousness. Culture refers to broadly shared beliefs and social practices; community refers to both the physical and spiritual senses of the term; and African-American consciousness refers to black nationalist and other traditions of self-awareness, as well as to action based on that self-awareness. Culture-race is the basis for the developing concept of cultural diversity. . . .

II. Racial Categories

BOTH in constitutional discourse and in larger society, race is considered a legitimate and proper means of classifying Americans. Its frequent use suggests that there is a consensus about what the "races" are. . . . While the social content of race has varied throughout American history, the practice of using race as a commonly recognized social divider has remained almost constant. In this section, the term "racial category" refers to this distinct, consistent practice of classifying people in a socially determined and socially determinative way. The American racial classification practice has included a particular rule for defining the racial categories black and white. That rule, which has been termed "hypodescent," is the starting point for this analysis.

A. American Racial Classification: Hypodescent
One way to begin a critique of the American system of racial classification is to ask "Who is black?" This question rarely provokes analysis; its answer is seen as so self-evident that challenges are novel and noteworthy. Americans no longer have need of a system of judicial screening to decide a person's race; the rules are simply absorbed without explicit articulation.

1. THE RULE OF HYPODESCENT
American racial classifications follow two formal rules: The *rule of recognition* holds that any

person whose black-African ancestry is visible is black. The *rule of descent* holds that any person with a known trace of African ancestry is black, notwithstanding that person's visual appearance, or, stated differently, that the offspring of a black and a white is black.

Historians and social scientists have noted the existence of these rules, often summarized as the "one drop of blood" rule, in their analysis of the American system of racial classification. Anthropologist Marvin Harris has suggested a name for the American system of social reproduction: "hypodescent."

2. ALTERNATIVES TO HYPODESCENT
The American legal system today lacks intermediate or "mixed-race" classifications. While the establishment of self-contained black or white racial categories may seem obvious, an examination of other classification schemes reveals that the American categories are not exhaustive.

Let us posit the two original races—one a "pure black," the other a "pure white." As interracial reproduction occurs, a multiracial society emerges. Four historically documented examples of nonbinary schemes to categorize mixed-race offspring have evolved: mulatto, named fractions, majoritarian, and social continuum. All of these schemes are logically symmetrical, so, at least in theory, neither "pure race" is privileged over the other. Consider each of the schemes in detail:

a. Mulatto. All mixed offspring are called mulattoes, irrespective of the percentages or fractions of their black or white ancestry.

b. Named fractions. Individuals are assigned labels according to the fractional composition of their racial ancestry. Thus, a mulatto is one-half white and one-half black; a quadroon is one-fourth black and three-fourths white, a sambo one-fourth white and three-fourths black, etc.[3]

c. Majoritarian. The higher percentage of either white or black ancestry determines the white or black label.

d. Social continuum. This is a variation on the named fractions scheme: labels generally correspond to the proportion of white or black ancestry, but social status is also an important factor in determining which label applies. The result is a much less rigid system of racial classification.[4]

It is worth repeating two observations that apply to all four schemes. First, the use of racial categories presumes that at some time "pure" races existed. Second, because these schemes are symmetrical, nothing in them suggests inequality or subordination between races.

3. SUPPORT FOR RACIAL SUBORDINATION

The hypodescent rule, when combined with color-blind constitutionalism, conveys a complex and powerful ideology that supports racial subordination. Briefly, hypodescent imposes racial subordination through its implied validation of white racial purity. Subordination occurs in the very act of a white person recognizing a black person's race. Much of constitutional discourse disguises that subordination by treating racial categories as if they were stable and immutable. Finally, the treatment of racial categories as functionally objective devalues the socioeconomic and political history of those placed within them. Through this complex process of assertion, disguise, and devaluation, racial categorization based on hypodescent advances white interests.

B. Assertion of Racial Subordination

I. EQUALITY AND THE SOCIAL METAPHOR OF RACIAL PURITY

Looking at the lack of symmetry between racial categories provides a means of further understanding hypodescent. Under hypodescent, black parentage is recognized through the generations. The metaphor is one of purity and contamination: white is unblemished and pure, so one drop of ancestral black blood renders one black. Black ancestry is a contaminant that overwhelms white ancestry.[5] Thus, under the American system of racial classification, claiming a white racial identity is a declaration of racial purity and an implicit assertion of racial domination. The symmetry of racial categorization systems other than hypodescent brings a sense of objectivity and neutrality to these

schemes, and a comparison of hypodescent to symmetrical systems exposes its nonneutral assumptions.

2. SUBORDINATION IN RECOGNITION

Under hypodescent, the moment of racial recognition is the moment in which is *reproduced* the inherent asymmetry of the metaphor of racial contamination and the implicit impossibility of racial equality. The situation that bares most fully the subordinating aspect of the moment of racial classification arises when a black person is at first mistaken for white and then recognized as black.

Before the moment of recognition, white acquaintances may let down their guard, betraying attitudes consistent with racial subordination, but which whites have learned to hide in the presence of nonwhites. Their meeting and initial conversation were based on the unsubordinated equality of a white-white relationship, but at the moment of racial recognition the exchange is transformed into a white-black relationship of subordination. In that moment of recognition lies the hidden assertion of white racial purity. The moment of racial recognition is thus characterized by an unconscious assertion of the racial hierarchy implied by hypodescent.

C. Disguising the Mutability of Racial Categorization

One persistent dimension of racial categorization is its treatment of race as a fixed trait. This belief in the immutable quality of race flows from two traditions. One tradition studies race as a phenomenon appropriate to the natural sciences. This tradition initially studied race to "prove" primarily the inferiority of the negro race, and is now largely discredited. The second tradition emphasizes physiognomy; it characterizes race as biological, thereby suggesting that race is unchangeable. Both traditions contribute to a societal view of race as a neutral, objective, and apolitical characteristic.

This section argues that race is anything but immutable. Neither tradition can claim true objectivity. Further, the American racial categorization scheme is not only historically contin-

gent, but, to some extent, legislatively determined.

I. THE SCIENTIFIC LEGITIMATION OF RACE

Historically, scientific discourse has played a
central role in legitimating status-based racial
classifications. For example, the racial "science"
of the eighteenth and nineteenth centuries justified slavery by asserting the inferiority of African-Americans. The work of Blumenbach, a
German comparative anatomist of the late eighteenth century, who classified humans into five
principal races—Caucasian, Mongolian, Malay,
American, and Ethiopian—was particularly influential. While no longer cited in scientific
journals, Blumenbach's racial classifications
have remained embedded in popular notions of
race. Even after a century of efforts to discredit
scientific theories asserting the "natural" superiority of the white race, race continues to be
accepted as a scientific concept.

The Supreme Court's modern discussions of
race purport to be disengaged from the older
scientific tradition.[6] In a 1987 case, *Saint Francis
College v. Al-Khazraji,*[7] the court examined
whether an Arab could seek damages for race
discrimination under 42 U.S.C. s 1981. Answering in the affirmative, the court's unanimous
opinion disavowed the traditional anthropologi-
cal categories of race. Justice Byron White
wrote, "such discrimination is racial discrimination that Congress intended s 1981 to forbid,
whether or not it would be classified as racial in
terms of modern scientific theory."[8] Moreover,
in dicta, the court expressed sympathy for the
position that race is a sociopolitical rather than
scientific characteristic.

However, the court was not ready to back
away entirely from the idea that racial categories
were based in natural science. Justice White
continued, "[t]he Court of Appeals was thus
quite right in holding that s 1981, 'at a minimum,' reaches discrimination against an individual 'because he or she is genetically part of
an ethnically and physiognomically distinctive
sub-grouping of homo sapiens.' " [...] The
court's equivocating in *Saint Francis College* suggests that the justices are not yet comfortable
with abandoning entirely the security of immutable racial categories.

2. THE TRADITION OF PHYSIOGNOMY

The immutability of racial classifications can be
seen in our everyday understanding of the terms
"black" and "white." Generally speaking, these
classifications are fixed; we cannot change our
race to suit a personal preference. One does not
arise in the morning and say, "I think that today
is my 'white' day and tomorrow will be my
'black' day." These racial classifications are "objective" and "immutable" in the sense that they
are external to subjective preferences, and therefore unchanging. The links between racial categorization and skin color, physiognomy, and
ancestry reinforce the belief that racial identity
is immutable.

By contrast, other societies—including racially stratified Western societies—do not insist
that their racial labels are "objective"; accordingly, their definitions of race are much more
fluid. For example, "[i]n Brazil one can pass to
another racial category regardless of how dark
one may be. . . . Brazilians say 'Money whitens,'
meaning that the richer a dark man gets the
lighter will be the racial category to which he
will be assigned by his friends, relatives and
business associates."[9] The Brazilian experience
highlights the arbitrariness of the American
classification system's assertion that race is a
fixed and objective feature.

Justice Stewart's dissent in *Fullilove v. Klutznick* illustrates how racial categories are linked
to physiognomy or ancestry and then described
as immutable: "Under our Constitution, the
government may never act to the detriment of a
person solely because of that person's race. The
color of a person's skin and the country of
his origin are immutable facts. . . ."[10] Stewart's
reference to skin color invokes "science"; this
"scientific fact" is then transferred to the racial
category to assert the immutability of the racial
category. This process results in a racial classification that looks like a fact.

Facts are commonly thought to be objective
and neutral—devoid of normative social significance. However, a distinction must be drawn
between the objectivity of scientific facts and
the subjectivity of legal facts. Justice Stewart's
qualifier "immutable" suggests a higher level of
objectivity than is traditionally accorded legal
facts. While Justice Stewart may have been

justified in deeming a person's skin color immutable, the implicit link of skin color to race is a social and legal assertion, not a scientific fact.

A more recent example of the court confusing racial classifications with scientific fact occurred during oral argument in *Metro Broadcasting, Inc. v. FCC*.[11] Justice Antonin Scalia engaged in a widely reported exchange with counsel defending the FCC's policy of "qualitative enhancement" for minority and women seeking broadcast station licenses. Attacking the argument that minorities and women would encourage diversity in programming, Justice Scalia repeatedly asked whether the policy was a matter of "blood," at one point charging that the policy reduced to a question of "blood . . . blood, not background and environment."

The context of Justice Scalia's insistence upon "blood" suggests he was referring metaphorically to ancestry as determining racial classification. "Blood" is a rich metaphor and includes, in this context, the suggestion of biological lines of descent. Justice Scalia's implication is that race, as a category of biology and science, has no relation to "background and environment"; in his view, race and its metaphor, blood, are neutral and without social content and, therefore, inappropriate criteria to be used in granting broadcast licenses.

The modern use of the physiognomic tradition has ironic implications when considered in light of the goals of the scientists who originally studied physiognomy. Nineteenth-century racial scientists hoped to prove that the African race was inherently inferior. The modern tradition links racial categories to science in order to show that race is a neutral and apolitical term without social content. However, both traditions support racial subordination.

3. THE HISTORICAL CONTINGENCY OF RACIAL CATEGORIES

Modern ways of thinking about racial categories evolved throughout American history. In the early colonial period, racial classifications were highly fluid. Social status often depended as much on the labor status of the individual as on his or her place of origin. Typically, Africans were brought to the colonies as captives, and Europeans as contractual or indentured servants. Winthrop Jordan has described the individual political dimensions of labor in seventeenth-century Virginia and Maryland as "states of unfreedom." There was a hierarchy among those who were not slaves but were also not free; the labels for such labor varied. In Virginia and Maryland, where the English colonists were the dominant group, the various "unfree" were also described as "un-English"; the term included French, Africans, and Scots. There were additional labels specific to the African laborers. While the early records are incomplete, there is clear evidence that by the middle of the seventeenth century, English colonists maintained some Africans in a status distinguishable from European indentured labor.

Sources from that century variously describe Africans as "heathen," "infidel," and "negro." These terms were attempts to justify the political status of the Africans. The racial classifications differentiated Europeans from the natives of colonized and imperially exploited parts of the world, but the classifications did not indicate a clearly developed belief that slavery was an appropriate condition for Africans.

English colonists gradually came to prefer enslaved African labor over indentured Europeans. By the end of the seventeenth century, the number of slaves had increased dramatically. As slavery became entrenched as the primary source of agricultural labor, slaveholders developed a complementary ideological structure of racial categories that served to legitimate slavery. The formal legal system was tailored to reflect these categories and enforce slave labor. In 1705, the Virginia Assembly created the first recognizable slave code. Besides codifying punishment for slaves who stole or ran away, the slave code contained specific rules of descent for classifying offspring. Punishments for blacks and mulattoes differed from those for indentured servants. This institutionalization of racial classifications linked to disparate treatment marked the first formal establishment of racial categories in colonial America.

The new racial classifications offered a basis for legitimating subordination which was unlike the justifications previously employed. By keying official rules of descent to national origin, the classification scheme differentiated those who were "enslaveable" from those who were not. Membership in the new social category of "Negro" became itself sufficient justification for enslaveability.

One can, therefore, do more than assert generally that race is not scientific, or that race is socially constructed. One can say that our particular system of classification, with its metaphorical construction of racial purity for whites, has a specific history as a badge of enslaveability. As such, the metaphor of purity is not a logical oddity but, rather, an integral part of the construction of the system of racial subordination embedded in American society. Under color-blind constitutionalism, when race is characterized as objective and apolitical, this history is disguised and discounted.

4. LEGISLATIVE DETERMINATION OF RACIAL CATEGORIES

An examination of past American law provides additional support for the assertion that racial classifications are not immutable. Before the Civil War, almost every state had statutes or judicial decisions defining race; indeed, until World War II, such statutes were common and not limited to the South. Likewise, antimiscegenation statutes were widespread, even where Jim Crow segregation was not mandated. These statutes demonstrate the variations possible in a scheme of racial classification; often the race of the offspring of a racially mixed couple was determined by a statutory formula.

A widely publicized example of statutory classification of race occurred in Louisiana in the early eighties. While most jurisdictions had abolished mandatory classifications by the seventies, Louisiana's birth certificate statute required a statutorily defined racial identification. A Louisiana woman, Susie Guillory Phipps, on applying for a passport, was "sick for three days" when she discovered that her birth certificate listed both her parents as colored; she challenged the statute in court. At trial and on appeal, the Louisiana courts upheld the constitutionality of the fractional classification statute, and Phipps's birth certificate was not changed.

The statutory histories of state racial classification schemes emphasize the role of govern-

ment in defining racial categories. Government's role has been less obvious since the civil rights movement's focused attention on the rights of individuals already classified as black. Color-blind constitutionalism implicitly adopts a particular understanding of race as objective and immutable, which may be less obvious than legislative enactments, but is no less significant.

III. FORMAL-RACE AND UNCONNECTEDNESS

THE Supreme Court has used words such as "race," "black," and "white" without explanation or qualification. In doing so, it has disguised its own role in perpetuating racial subordination. The modern court has moved away from the two notions of race which recognize the diverging historical experiences of black and white Americans—status-race and historical-race. In place of these concepts, the court relies increasingly on the formal-race concept of race, a vision of race as unconnected to the historical reality of black oppression. As this section shows, formal-race is a concept of limited power analytically and politically. By relying on it, the court denies the experience of oppression and limits the range of remedies available for redress.

A. Status-Race, Formal-Race, and Historical-Race
I. STATUS-RACE: *DRED SCOTT*
In the antebellum era, the inferior status of blacks was an accepted legal standard. The most famous court decision to embrace this status-race concept was Chief Justice Roger Taney's opinion in *Dred Scott v. Sandford*. Chief Justice Taney wrote that, at the time of the founding of the Republic, the "negro African race" had been "regarded as beings . . . so far inferior, that they had no rights which the white man was bound to respect."[12] For Chief Justice Taney, the distinct, inferior status of blacks was implicit in the Constitution and overrode any congressional pronouncements to the contrary. The court's modern opinions tolerate the legacy of status-race in the private sphere only. Private citizens are free to make contracts, form associations, speak, write, and worship in a manner predicated on the belief that blacks are inher-

ently and biologically inferior to whites. These broad-based individual freedoms protecting status-race beliefs significantly aid the legitimation of racist conduct.

2. FORMAL-RACE: *PLESSY V. FERGUSON*

The well-known "separate but equal" case, *Plessy v. Ferguson*,[13] epitomizes formal-race analysis. In upholding a Louisiana statute requiring separate seating for blacks and whites in public carriers, the *Plessy* court used race in a manner that sharply differed from the older status-race notion in *Dred Scott.* The Plessy Court found:

> the underlying fallacy of the plaintiff's argument to consist in the assumption that the enforced separation of the two races stamps the colored race with a badge of inferiority. If this be so, it is not by reason of anything found in the act, but solely because the colored race chooses to put that construction upon it.[14]

Turning a blind eye to history, the court maintained that the segregation statute said nothing about the status of blacks, indeed, that the statute was racially "neutral." Besides presuming that racial classifications are unconnected to social status or historical experience, the court's formal-race analysis fails to recognize ties between the classification scheme of one statute and the treatment of race in other legislation. The court did not see statutes segregating railroad service, schools, and housing as inherently connected to each other or to a legal and social system that perpetuated the stigma of inferiority based on race.

Formal-race and status-race offer two differing interpretations of Jim Crow segregation. Under the status-race approach, which assumes the subordinated status of blacks, racial segregation by custom or statute reflects a "commonsense" understanding of the "natural" racial hierarchy; in contrast, the formal-race, color-blind approach assumes "equal protection of the law" based on common "citizenship." Given these assumptions, racial segregation is simply a legislative differentiation that must be considered to have no inherent social meaning. Even with formal-race's rejection of the inferior status of blacks, *Plessy* makes clear that formal-race unconnectedness often renders harsh results.

3. HISTORICAL-RACE

In contrast to the majority opinion in *Plessy*, Justice John Harlan's oft-quoted dissent argued vigorously against the neutrality of race-based segregation:

> Every one knows that the statute in question had its origin in the purpose, not so much to exclude white persons from railroad cars occupied by blacks, as to exclude colored people from coaches occupied by or assigned to white persons. . . . The thing to accomplish was, under the guise of giving equal accommodation for whites and blacks, to compel the latter to keep to themselves while travelling in railroad passenger coaches.[15]

Justice Harlan recognized that segregation based on race is inherently subordinating. By rejecting the majority's view that racial segregation is unconnected to oppression and by refusing to adopt the rigid legalism of formal-race Justice Harlan anticipated by a half century the spirit of *Brown v. Board of Education*.[16]

Justice Harlan was advocating a peculiar mix of historical-race and formal-race. Government acts were required to be genuinely neutral; therefore judicial review of race-based legislation should recognize the historical content of race. However, formal-race dictated Justice Harlan's vision of the private sphere:

> The white race deems itself to be the dominant race in this country. And so it is, in prestige, in achievements, in education, in wealth and in power. So, I doubt not, it will continue to be for all time, if it remains true to its great heritage and holds fast to the principles of constitutional liberty.[17]

More recently, Justice Thurgood Marshall used historical-race in his *Bakke v. Regents of University of California* dissent.[18] Marshall argued that:

> It is unnecessary in 20th-century America to have individual Negroes demonstrate that they have been victims of racial discrimination; the racism of our society has been so pervasive that none, regardless of wealth or position, has managed to escape its impact. The experience of Negroes in America has been different in kind, not just in degree, from that of other ethnic groups. It is not merely the history of slavery alone but also that a whole people were marked as inferior by the law. And that mark has endured.[19]

Marshall's comments emphasize that in historical-race usage, racial categories describe relations of oppression and unequal power. Historical-race usage of "black" does not have the same meaning as usage of "white": black is the reification of subordination, whereas white is the reification of privilege and superordination. This asymmetry of white and black corresponds to the asymmetry of hypodescent and its metaphor of racial purity and racial contamination.

B. Formal-Race and Unconnectedness in Racial Discourse

Current Supreme Court cases use race most commonly to mean formal-race. Racial classification has lost its connection to social reality. This trend is demonstrated by the voting rights, affirmative action, and jury selection cases, as well as the works of two prominent academics discussed below. This section reveals the pervasiveness and the dangers of the formal-race approach.

I. VOTING RIGHTS

Unconnectedness can be seen in cases concerning the electoral franchise and political power. It appears most clearly in the dissent in *Rome v. United States*,[20] a case upholding the constitutionality of amendments to the Voting Rights Act of 1965.[21] The amendments shifted to local jurisdictions the burden of proving that a proposed change in voting arrangements would not adversely affect black voters. Justices Potter Stewart and William Rehnquist, the dissenters, objected to the premise underlying the amendments: "The need to prevent this disparate impact is premised on the assumption that white candidates will not represent black interests, and that States should devise a system encouraging blacks to vote in a block for black candidates."[22] For Justices Stewart and Rehnquist, the "assumption" that race and voting patterns were or ought to be linked was constitutionally impermissible. They objected also to "the notion that Congress could empower a later generation of blacks to 'get even' for wrongs inflicted on their forebears."[23]

Chief Justice Rehnquist's and Justice Stewart's opposition to Congress's effort to consider the political character of blackness and whiteness stemmed from their belief that "white" and "black" are devoid of political content, an assumption negated by any study of the interplay between voters' decisions and race. This presumption of unconnectedness has led Chief Justice Rehnquist and Justice Stewart to argue in other cases that the evidentiary burden should be on plaintiffs to establish both the unfair results of a redistricting plan, and that the intent of the boundary drawers was to be unfair. These justices would make formal-race unconnectedness an axiom of constitutional interpretation of voting rights, nullifying any present or future congressional attempts to account for the link between race and political power. Their theory would pose a substantial barrier to race-conscious legislative efforts to halt discrimination against black voters.

2. AFFIRMATIVE ACTION

In many discussions of affirmative action, advocates of a color-blind position equate race with formal-race. An example of this is Justice William Douglas's dissent in *DeFunis v. Odegaard*.[24] DeFunis was a white applicant to the University of Washington Law School who charged that less qualified minority applicants had been accepted while he had been denied admission. Justice Douglas stated unequivocally that race is an impermissible consideration in the context of college admissions: "A DeFunis who is white is entitled to no advantage by reason of that fact; nor is he subject to any disability, no matter what his race or color. Whatever his race, he had a constitutional right to have his application considered on its individual merits in a racially neutral manner."[25] Consideration of past segregation by the University of Washington—indeed, any consideration of this country's history of oppression at all—is impermissible. Justice Douglas's philosophy remains alive on the court today; Justice Scalia quoted Douglas's dissent with approval in his *City of Richmond v. J. A. Croson Co.* concurrence.[26]

3. JURY SELECTION

In *Batson v. Kentucky*[27] the Supreme Court liberalized the evidentiary requirements for proving that a prosecutor's peremptory jury challenges were racially discriminatory in violation of the Equal Protection Clause. Justice Powell argued that "[c]ompetence to serve as a juror ultimately depends on an assessment of individual qualifications and ability impartially to consider evidence presented at a trial. . . . A person's race simply 'is unrelated to his fitness as a juror.' "[28]

The *Batson* decision redressed the historical-race problem of blacks being barred from serving on juries and, therefore, was a significant step forward. However, Justice Powell's statement that race is "unrelated" invokes that unconnectedness of a juror's formal-race classification to any other personal attributes that might relate to jury duty. This reliance upon unconnectedness was unnecessary and unfortunate: use of unconnectedness separates the decision from the context of Justice Powell's otherwise substantial reliance on historical-race analysis.

4. ECONOMIC ANALYSIS

Richard Posner, in *The Economics of Justice*, uses the term "[r]ace per se—that is, race completely divorced from certain characteristics that may be strongly correlated with . . . it" to analyze "reverse discrimination."[29] Posner would object to the argument that diversity in a student body is a proper basis for preferential treatment of minorities. He argues that "[t]here are black people . . . who have the same tastes, manners, experiences, aptitudes and aspirations as the whites with whom one might compare them."[30] Consequently, if "race per se" may be used as a proxy for those characteristics in the diversity context, then "race per se" may also be legitimately employed in more sinister ways. For example, if race and an undesirable employment characteristic are correlated, then race may be used to justify employment discrimination.

Posner's "race per se" is, of course, identical to formal-race. His analysis, like many formal-race analyses, overlooks social reality: the presence of a black—any black, notwithstanding his or her correlative factors—will likely alter the reactions of whites in a given setting, so "per se" integration is itself a positive good.

The economist Thomas Sowell provides another example of unconnectedness in his writings on the significance of race.[31] Himself black, Sowell illustrates the multiple uses of the word "discrimination" by discussing the hypothetical treatment of an unnamed "group." For example, one typical usage of discrimination is when "[m]embers of a particular group are accorded fewer and poorer opportunities than members of the general population with the same current capabilities."[32] Racial groups are fungible under all of Sowell's definitions; while he does discuss discrimination against specific minorities, the basis for his discussion is an abstract framework, devoid of historical-race content. There is nothing inherent in "black" or "white" which renders it unamenable to analysis as just any "group."

C. Support for Racial Subordination

I. UNCONNECTEDNESS LIMITS RACISM TO SUBJECTIVE PREJUDICE

Formal-race unconnectedness is linked to a particular conceptualization of racism. Race, as formal-race, is seen as an attribute of individuality unrelated to social relations. Unconnectedness limits the concept of racism and the label "racist" to those individuals who maintain irrational personal prejudices against persons who "happen" to be in the racial category black. Racism is irrational because race is seen as unconnected from social reality, a concept that describes nothing more than a person's physical appearance.

Under this view, racism is thought of only as an individual prejudice. Despite the fact that personal racial prejudices have social origins, racism is considered to be an individual and personal trait. Society's racism is then viewed as merely the collection, or extension, of personal prejudices. In the extreme, racism could come to be defined as a mental illness. These extremely individualized views of racism exclude an understanding of the fact that race has institutional or structural dimensions beyond the formal racial classification. However, individual irrationality and mental illness simply do not adequately explain racism and racial subordination.

Furthermore, the view that racism is merely an irrational prejudice suggests that the types of remedies available to address racial subordination and oppression are limited. For example, programs providing economic aid would be thought of as an ineffective weapon against racism, because such programs address individual prejudicial attitudes only indirectly. A minority set-aside program such as that proposed by the City of Richmond directly addresses the present effects of past racial exclusion from the building trades as well as the continuing de facto exclusion of nonwhites. Yet such a program attacks prejudicial attitudes only indirectly: by demonstrating the capabilities of black contractors (thus denying the validity of status-race inferiority) and providing common workplace interactions (thus breaking down irrational prejudice).

The Supreme Court's use of formal-race unconnectedness is consistent with its view that the particular manifestations of racial subordination—substandard housing, education, employment, and income for large portions of the black community—are better interpreted as isolated phenomena than as aspects of the broader, more complex phenomenon called "race." This disaggregated treatment veils the continuing oppression of institutional racism. It whittles racism down to the point at which racism can be understood as an attitude problem amenable to formal-race solutions. However, formal-race legalism hinders this country's ability to address the clear correlation between racial minority populations and the concentrations of these various, supposedly distinct problems. Even if one admits that large numbers of the unemployed and undereducated youth in the inner cities are black, unconnectedness hinders the government's ability to use that correlation as a basis for attacking social ills.

This hindrance occurs in two ways. First, because each social problem is considered to be independent of its racial component, any proposed government program is analyzed as though it addresses a nonracial issue. Even in cases where the problems are obviously related

to dysfunctional interracial relations—problems such as housing and employment—the issues are discussed as though they have no history or context at all.

Second, the court often invokes the metaphor of the "equal starting point" when analyzing social problems. This metaphor ignores historical-race and the cumulative disadvantages that are the starting point for so many black citizens. The metaphor implies that if blacks are underrepresented in a particular employment situation, it must be a result of market forces; any statistical correlation is either coincidental or beyond the control of the employer, and is, in any case, unrelated to the employer's past practices.

In short, color-blind constitutionalists live in an ideological world where racial subordination is ubiquitous yet disregarded—unless it takes the form of individual, intended, and irrational prejudice. Perhaps formal-race analysis would be a useful tool for fighting racism if it recognized that racism is complex and systemic. However, as presently used, formal-race unconnectedness helps to maintain white privilege by limiting discussion or consideration of racial subordination.

2. STRICT SCRUTINY AND AFFIRMATIVE ACTION
Invocation of strict scrutiny, the strongest form of equal protection judicial review, is generally fatal to the race-based government action. The doctrine of strict scrutiny has proved a powerful legal weapon and has regularly been used to strike down Jim Crow segregation throughout public facilities.

The distinction among the different uses of race developed in this article suggests two interpretations of strict scrutiny. The first is the interpretation used in *Brown v. Board of Education*,[33] which considered race a classification that subordinates blacks. This is historical-race, and against this background, the court rightly employed strict scrutiny to review government activity.

The second interpretation of race in strict scrutiny cases is that of *City of Richmond v. J.A. Croson Co.*,[34] in which race is seen as formal-race. In this interpretation, it is the arbitrary character of racial classifications that requires strict judicial scrutiny. Because formal-race is a misapprehension of the nature of race in America, the appropriateness of analytically combining formal-race with strict scrutiny is open to criticism. Both interpretations of strict scrutiny are further examined below, and used as the basis for a discussion of affirmative action programs.

Historical-race and strict scrutiny. The historical-race rationale for strict scrutiny derives from *Brown v. Board of Education,* in which the court ruled that segregated education was inherently unequal. The decision rejected the formal-race doctrine of *Plessy* in favor of the theory that race, as used in the context of education, was both intended to, and had the effect of, subordinating black school children. The cases immediately following *Brown* continued its approach: they recognized that the use of racial classifications to segregate was inherently subordinating and struck down the vast majority of Jim Crow laws as unconstitutional.

Under the *Brown* interpretation of strict scrutiny, heightened judicial review should be applied to all restrictions that curtail the civil rights of a racial group. In the context of the racial subordination of blacks, the implied rationale for such heightened review has been the past and continuing racial subordination of the group as a whole. If one summarizes these cases by stating that "race triggers strict scrutiny," then one is using "race" to mean historical-race.

Formal-race and strict scrutiny. A different racial usage is involved if one argues that the government's use of any racial classification triggers strict scrutiny. This strong version of color-blind constitutionalism has not yet been adopted by a majority of the Supreme Court, although Justice O'Connor has provided a clear description of the position: "the Constitution requires that the Court apply a strict standard of scrutiny to evaluate racial classifications. . . . 'Strict scrutiny' requires that, to be upheld, racial classifications must be determined to be necessary and narrowly tailored to achieve a compelling state interest."[35]

This version of racial strict scrutiny—that use of any racial classification is subject to strict scrutiny without reference to historical or social context—is best interpreted as a use of formal-race. Strict scrutiny is triggered whether the classification is designed to remedy the effects of past subordination or designed to further oppress a traditionally subordinated racial group.

This shift from the use of strict scrutiny to review governmental oppression of blacks to review of any use of race has never been explicitly addressed by the court; the underlying justification for the change remains undiscussed.

Judicial review of affirmative action. The court's decision in *City of Richmond v. J.A. Croson Co.*[36] demonstrates clearly that formal-race strict scrutiny can severely limit the range of constitutionally permissible governmental remedies for racial subordination. To see how the strong formal-race interpretation of strict scrutiny differs from the historical-race interpretation, consider how the Richmond affirmative action program might be analyzed under both interpretations.

Under the historical-race interpretation, the City of Richmond would explain that its affirmative action program was designed to help blacks by redressing past and continuing racial subordination. Richmond's use of historical-race explicitly considers the legacy of racial discrimination in Richmond: because historical-race includes continuing racial subordination, its use provides a rationale for race-conscious remedial governmental action today. In other words, historical-race usage is the shorthand summary of the historical and social justifications for race-conscious affirmative action programs. Assuming that the program is well designed, there would be a reasonable fit between the use of racial categories and the goals of the remedial program.

Obviously, historical-race is not the same for whites as for blacks. The history of segregation is not the history of blacks creating racial categories to legitimate slavery, nor is it a history of segregated institutions aimed at subordinating whites. Indeed, racial categories themselves, with their metaphorical themes of white racial purity and nonwhite contamination, have different meanings for blacks and whites. If judicial review is to consider the past and continuing character of racial subordination, then an affirmative action program aimed at alleviating the effects of racial subordination should not automatically be subject to the same standard of review as Jim Crow segregation laws. Judicial review using historical-race should be asymmetric because of the fundamentally different histories of whites and blacks.

Contrast this with the formal-race approach—strict scrutiny to evaluate any racial classification. This symmetrical standard of review cannot be justified by racial history, because racial history is skewed. Nor can it mean that the seriousness of past and continuing racial subordination is no longer important. If racial subordination did not pervade society, then heightened judicial review would be unnecessary, and rational basis review would be appropriate for all formal-race categorizations.

The choice, then, to ignore racial history and existing racial subordination in applying strict scrutiny to all racial classifications is essentially a decision to use only formal-race. But what justifies the court's election of formal-race strict scrutiny? The strict scrutiny that developed originally in an atmosphere of governmental attempts to curtail blacks' civil rights has been transformed into formal-race scrutiny. The result is that government programs designed to assist blacks are being struck down. This is perverse.[37] Historically, racial subordination has been the privileging of whites over nonwhites, and a proper remedial program would work to redress that history. Instead, the use of formal-race strict scrutiny is applied to proposed remedies and results in their being declared unconstitutional, thereby perpetuating societal advantages for whites.

Justice Scalia's cramped argument at the close of his *Croson* concurrence demonstrates how formal-race fails to account for our nation's history of subordination in the context of remedies. Justice Scalia maintains that "a race-neutral remedial program" will be constitutionally permissible and will also provide advantages to blacks. He concedes that there has been a history of racial subordination, but he nevertheless advocates a remedy aimed only at the "disadvantaged as such." Justice Scalia claims that such a program would have the desirable incidental effect of helping black individuals, but he insists on ignoring any historical connection between harm and race discrimination. The notion of systematic racial subordination—of the relevance of the group—is totally absent.

IV. Color-Blind Constitutionalism and Social Change

THIS section critiques color-blind constitutionalism as a means and as an end for American society. As a means, color-blind constitutionalism is meant to educate the American public by demonstrating the "proper" attitude toward race: the end of color-blind constitutionalism is a racially assimilated society in which race is irrelevant. However, taken too far, this goal of a color-blind society has disturbing implications for cultural and racial diversity. Other goals, less drastic than complete racial assimilation, are tolerance and diversity. This section defines tolerance as the view that multiculturalism and multiracialism are necessary evils that should be tolerated within American society. Diversity, on the other hand, is defined as the view that racial and cultural pluralism is a positive good.[38]

A. Means: The Public Nonrecognition Model and Its Limits

In his *Minnick v. California Department of Corrections* dissent, Justice Stewart explains that government nonrecognition of race is implicitly intended to provide a model for private-sphere behavior. The model functions both negatively and positively. The negative model suggests that social progress is most effectively achieved by judging people according to their ability, and, therefore, that race-based decision-making seduces citizens away from a more legitimate merit-based system.[39]

There are two problems with the negative model. The first is its unquestioned assumption that meritocratic systems are valid; the second is its implicit denial of any possible positive values to race. In particular, the negative model devalues black culture—culture-race in this article—and unjustifiably assumes the social superiority of mainstream white culture.

The positive behavior model—government nonrecognition serving as an example for private conduct—also has problems. First, there is the practical impossibility of nonrecognition as a standard for either public or private conduct. Second, the implicit social goal of assimilation degrades positive aspects of blackness.

Color-blind constitutionalism not only offers a flawed behavioral model for private citizens, but its effectiveness in promoting social change is limited. Color-blindness strikes down Jim Crow segregation but offers no vision for attacking less overt forms of racial subordination. The color-blind ideal of the future society has been exhausted since the implementation of *Brown v. Board of Education* and its progeny.

One example of how limited the color-blind approach is as a weapon against discrimination can be seen in the area of voting rights, a core area of public life. Color-blind constitutionalists, filing dissents in *Rome v. United States* and *Rogers v. Lodge,* argued that Congress had unconstitutionally abandoned a formal-race, individual-remedy approach in favor of more sweeping, race-conscious remedies for racial discrimination.

As Justice Scalia's concurrence in *City of Richmond v. J. A. Croson Co.* and the dissent in *Metro Broadcasting, Inc. v. FCC* make clear, a strong version of public-sphere nonrecognition would not permit governmental consideration of race, except in an extremely narrow set of court-mandated remedies. Were such a formula adopted, color-blind constitutionalism would limit the abilities of states and Congress to pursue broad remedial legislation aimed at racial disparities.

A final example of color-blind nonrecognition as limiting racial social change inheres in the public/private distinction. The combination of the view that nonrecognition limits government action with the belief that there exists a private-sphere right to discriminate constitutes a seductive and consistent ideology—one declaring that the continuance of white racial

dominance is a constitutionally protected norm. The end result of this combination is that racial social change—remediation for centuries of subordination—must take place outside of legal discourse and the sphere of government action.

B. Ends: Assimilation, Tolerance, and Diversity

The examination of color-blind constitutionalism as means leaves open the question of what the color-blind society of the future would look like. This subsection asks that very question.
[...]

The color-blind assimilationist ideal seeks homogeneity in society rather than diversity. Such an ideal neglects the positive aspects of race, particularly the cultural components that distinguish us from one another. It may not be a desirable result for those cultural components to be subsumed into a society that recognizes commonalities.

I. CULTURE-RACE

The assimilationist color-blind society ignores and thereby devalues culture-race. Culture-race includes all aspects of culture, community, and consciousness. The term includes, for example, the customs, beliefs, and intellectual and artistic traditions of black America, as well as institutions such as black churches and colleges.

With two notable exceptions, the court has devalued or ignored black culture, community, and consciousness. Its opinions use the same categorical name—black—to designate reified systemic subordination (what I have termed historical-race) as well as the cultural richness that defines culture-race. Only by treating culture-race as analytically distinct from other usages of race can one begin to address the link between the cultural practices of blacks and the subordination of blacks—elements that are, in fact, inseparable in the lived experience of race.

The two exceptions, where the court appropriately recognized culture-race, are *Metro Broadcasting, Inc. v. FCC*[40] and *Bakke v. Regents of University of California.*[41] In *Metro Broadcasting,* his last opinion for the court, Justice Brennan applied an intermediate standard of review, arguing that Congress's desire to promote broadcast opportunities for racial minority viewpoints was a legitimate and important government interest. Drawing heavily on *Bakke*, the court's landmark case on affirmative action in university admissions decisions, Justice Brennan wrote:

[E]nhancing broadcast diversity is, at the very least, an important governmental objective and is therefore a sufficient basis for the Commission's minority ownership policies. Just as a "diverse student body" contributing to a "robust exchange of ideas" is a "constitutionally permissible goal" on which a race-conscious university admissions program may be predicated, the diversity of views and information on the airwaves serves important First Amendment values. The benefits of such diversity are not limited to the members of minority groups who gain access to the broadcasting industry by virtue of the ownership policies; rather, the benefits redound to all members of the viewing and listening audience. As Congress found, "the American public will benefit by having access to a wider diversity of information sources."[42]

Justice John Paul Stevens, in his concurrence, distinguished more explicitly the remedial dimension from the diversity consideration:

Today, the Court squarely rejects the proposition that a governmental decision that rests on a racial classification is never permissible except as a remedy for a past wrong.... I endorse this focus on the future benefit, rather than the remedial justification, of such decisions.

I remain convinced, of course, that racial or ethnic characteristics provide a relevant basis for disparate treatment only in extremely rare situations and that it is therefore "especially important that the reasons for any such classification be clearly identified and unquestionably legitimate." ... The public interest in broadcast diversity—like the interest in an integrated police force, diversity in the composition of a public school faculty or diversity in the student body of a professional school—is in my view unquestionably legitimate.[43]

Essentially, Justice Stevens was distinguishing historical-race (remedial justification) and culture-race (future benefit).

Bakke and *Metro Broadcasting* notwithstanding, the court usually fails to include the positive aspects of black culture in its deliberations. *Palmore v. Sidoti*[44] is typical. In that case, the court unanimously rejected a Florida trial court's

decision to modify a white mother's custody of her child after the mother married a black man. The court acknowledged that there was "a risk that a child living with a stepparent of a different race may be subject to a variety of pressures and stresses not present if the child were living with parents of the same racial or ethnic origin,"[45] but nevertheless concluded that a court could not constitutionally consider such private biases.

What the court (and most of the subsequent commentary on the decision) failed to consider was the possibility that a black stepfather might offer a positive value to the child beyond a caring home.[46] The child was to be raised in a bicultural environment. In that environment, the child had the possibility of being exposed not only to her mother's background but also to black culture in a way that the child could never have experienced in her biological father's home—within her family environment. The child would have access to a rich life experience, one completely inaccessible in her father's household. The court simply lacked the imagination to consider and separate the subordination dimension of race—the historical-race element that accounted for prejudice outside the home—from the positive concept of culture-race. Such analysis is a difficult social enterprise and deserves case-by-case review, not a blanket rule that a court may never consider the effects of racism. . . .

2. ASSIMILATION AND CULTURAL GENOCIDE

Implicit in the color-blind assimilationist vision is a belief that, ultimately, race should have no real significance; instead, it should be limited to the formal categories of white and black, unconnected to any social, economic, or cultural practice. However, if the underlying social reality of race is understood as encompassing one's social being, then an assimilationist goal that would abolish the significance of minority social categories has far-reaching repercussions. The successful abolition of "black" as a meaningful concept would require abolishing the distinctiveness that we attribute to black community, culture, and consciousness.

The abolition of a people's culture is, by

definition, cultural genocide. In short, assimilation as a societal goal has grave potential consequences for blacks and other nonwhites. However utopian it appears, the color-blind assimilationist program implies the hegemony of white culture.

3. COLOR-BLIND TOLERANCE AND DIVERSITY

As a social ideal, tolerance is the acceptance of race as a necessary evil. Diversity, on the other hand, considers race to be a positive good. Tolerance seems closest to the approach of color-blind advocates such as Justice Scalia. However, Justice Scalia's comments seem more limited in scope and cynical in tone: he strongly asserts the constitutional limitations on those seeking an end to racism but offers nothing substantive as an alternative. In his *City of Richmond v. J. A. Croson Co.* concurrence, Justice Scalia suggests that one should address the specifics of past discrimination in nonracial terms. He proposes the use of "race-neutral remedial programs" but offers no explanation as to how such a program would avoid the very problem to which it is addressed—the concentrations of black poverty and political powerlessness. Such programs either would be doomed to be ineffective solutions for blacks, or else would violate the intent standard of *Washington v. Davis.*[47]

In short, as a goal, tolerance fails to suggest a better society or improved social relations. Under the goal of racial diversity, racial distinctions would be maintained, but would lose their negative connotations: each group would make a positive and unique contribution to the overall social good.

The vision of diversity has significant, subtle limits. As normally articulated, diversity is premised on the existence of race as it now exists, as a conflation of subordination, black culture, and color-blind unconnectedness. Without more, diversity accepts the prevailing limits and social practices of race, including the hypodescent rule. The assumption that it is possible to identify racial classifications of black and white, to consider them apart from their social setting, and then to make those same racial categories the basis for positive social

practice is unfounded. Without a clear social commitment to rethink the nature of racial categories and abolish their underlying structure of subordination, the politics of diversity will remain incomplete.

The difficulty of transforming traditional racial categories into a positive construct can be seen in the construct of whiteness. A crucial dimension of whiteness is white racial privilege. Whiteness becomes a political issue where an entrenched position of dominance is challenged.

A different dimension of "whiteness" is ethnic or national heritage. The immigrant origins of ethnic white European-Americans are accepted and often embraced, though not always denominated as racial; whiteness as racial dominance substantially overlaps, and sometimes supersedes, the ethnic experience. Indeed, some of the most deeply embedded explicit racial violence and assertions of racial inferiority have come from "white ethnic" enclaves. European ethnicity has a social existence apart from racial domination, but the separation of racial subordination from such ethnicity can be a complex political and social enterprise.

Aside from European ethnicity, there are other cultural aspects of whiteness as racial domination. The Confederate flag is a complex symbol, but whiteness as domination is clearly a significant aspect of its symbolism. As representative of a southern culture, the Confederate flag has provided a point of symbolic controversy as it flies over southern statehouses or is worn in schools or displayed in public.

An unstated problem in these debates is that of cultural self-identification when one does not claim a particular ethnic identity. If one identifies oneself simply as a "white American" without any particular ethnic or racial identity, my suggested model of whiteness as reified racial privilege does not make available any particularized identity.

A goal of public-sphere diversity has its social price. Diversity in its narrow sense does not truly challenge existing racial practice but, rather, seeks to accommodate present racial divisions by casting them in a positive light. All too often, discussions of diversity do not address its central problem, the transformation of existing categories of domination into an altogether different, positive social formation.

V. An Alternative to Color-Blind Constitutionalism

A. Minimal Requirements for a Revised Approach to Race

This article's central claim is that modern color-blind constitutionalism supports the supremacy of white interests and must therefore be regarded as racist. There is no legitimate rationale for the automatic rejection of all governmental consideration of race. However, strict scrutiny should not be abandoned altogether, given its efficacy as a weapon against segregation in years past. In particular, we shall see that a rhetoric of rights remains vital to the antiracist struggle. This section, therefore, suggests some minimal requirements for an alternative constitutional approach to race.

First, any revised approach to race and the Constitution must explicitly recognize that race is not a simple, unitary phenomenon. Rather, as discussed above, race is a unique social formation with its own meanings, understandings, discourses, and interpretive frameworks. As a socially constructed category with multiple meanings, race cannot be easily isolated from lived social experience. Moreover, race cannot legitimately be described and understood according to legal discourse. Any effort to understand its nature must go beyond legal formalism.

Second, constitutional jurisprudence on race must accommodate legitimate governmental efforts to address white racial privilege. The Supreme Court must not only acknowledge the multiple dimensions of race in the abstract but also expressly permit the different aspects of race to be considered in judicial and legislative decisions. Further, any constitutional program must recognize the cultural genocide implicit in the development of a color-blind society and acknowledge the importance of black culture, community, and consciousness.

Because of a genuine concern that any change in doctrine may weaken the struggle against racial oppression, the court must maintain all existing constitutional protection for racial minorities against a resurgence of the white supremacist movement. Equal protection and due process should be buttressed as ideological and political barriers against Jim Crow and segregationist variations of white supremacy rather than transformed into barriers against legitimate government efforts to address racial subordination.

Finally, a revised approach to race must recognize the systemic nature of subordination in American society. The Supreme Court's efforts to interpret the equal protection and due process clauses have addressed race, gender, sexuality, and class. To date, the court has regarded these phenomena as distinct, but racial subordination is inherently connected to other forms of subordination. The deep social context in which they are interwoven has begun to draw increasing attention. . . .

1. THE FREE EXERCISE AND ANTI-ESTABLISHMENT OF RELIGION: RELIGION-BLINDNESS AND COLOR-BLINDNESS

There is a body of constitutional doctrine that suggests a more subtle approach to constitutional review. The First Amendment religion clauses—the free exercise and establishment clauses—provide a possible analogy accommodating some of the criteria outlined above when applied to race. The court's recent decisions on religion betray a qualitative difference between the court's attitudes toward religion and toward race.

In church-state questions, the court has rejected a "religion-blind" standard for governmental activity. That is, the court recognizes the importance of religious affiliation to many Americans and does not see its goal as diminishing or eradicating the institution of religion in American life. While some have argued that religion-blindness is the appropriate role for government, their arguments have not prevailed either in the public imagination or with the court.

The court has instead proceeded along the two related lines dictated by the Constitution—promoting the free exercise of religion and preventing the establishment of any one religion.

These two approaches, while doctrinally distinct and separately discussed in judicial opinions, are logically linked as theoretical opposites. For example, where religious "establishment" is alleged, such as when Christian prayers are said in public schools, a corresponding "free exercise" problem exists—students of other religions are prevented from exercising their own faiths during prayer time.[48] Similarly, a free exercise issue such as the use of peyote in ceremonies of the Native American Church, involves the "establishment" of traditional religion, where the use of peyote warrants criminal penalties.

The free exercise cases are informed by the attitude that religion and religious practice are important and valuable aspects of human experience.

B. Religion Jurisprudence as a Model for Race Jurisprudence

The free exercise and establishment clause decisions provide a model for constitutional adjudication in the area of race to supplant the color-blind model. The race jurisprudence of the Supreme Court contains only an inkling of the deference found in its religion jurisprudence. Once we appreciate the complex and socially embedded character of race, however, we may view the concerns and considerations involved in judicial review of racial decision-making as being similar to those involved in interpreting the religion clauses. If the religion cases are intellectually or emotionally unsatisfying, they at least represent a serious effort by the court to address a complex of social issues with nuanced, historically grounded legal distinctions.

Once the historical context of racial subordination has been acknowledged, remedies that explicitly consider race become constitutionally possible. Instead of a constricted discourse on the legitimacy of the use of "race," a more measured discussion of the proper standard of review becomes possible. Issues of racial remedies, like decisions about the relationship between church and state, can then be discussed as policy decisions rather than as complex studies of judicial review of the democratic process.

Culture-race, with its wide range of social and cultural references, makes possible a form of free exercise of the positive aspects of race—recognizing black and white cultures as legitimate aspects of the American social fabric. Further, free exercise of race would allow, within appropriate limits, open discussion and implementation of governmental remedies to address the historical legacy of racial discrimination. Also protected will be the culture, community, and consciousness of American racial minorities. European-American cultures would also be recognized and respected, of course, even though their existence has not been challenged in the same manner as black culture. Just as permitting the free exercise of religion is, in theory, not an endorsement of any one religion but, rather, only a recognition of respect for the practice of religion, so the free exercise of culture-race would not be an endorsement of racism.

There is also an "establishment" analog for race. What is impermissible—what the government may not "establish"—is racial subordination and white supremacy: the use of either status-race or formal-race to establish domination, hierarchy, and exploitation.

The paired considerations of racial establishment and free exercise are mixed in our social existence. The free exercise of some aspects of a white culture may overlap or coincide with racial domination, as with the attachment of many white southerners to the Confederate flag. Efforts to abolish domination will, therefore, interfere with the free exercise of race in such instances. The suggestion from the religion cases about how to approach this conflict is that the two discussions—of racial subordination and of black culture—can be considered together. Any problem should be addressed in its particular context, without the doctrinal compulsion to satisfy all aspects of either racial subordination or respect for racial-ethnic culture.

VI. CONCLUSION

BY returning to strict scrutiny as the sole equal protection principle for racial judicial review, the color-blind constitutionalists would have the Supreme Court risk perpetuating racism and undermining its own legitimacy. This article invokes a parallel between the modern civil rights movement and the "first" Reconstruction; the Supreme Court's civil rights decisions of 1989 are the equivalent of the Compromise of 1877, which ended the first Reconstruction. By fixating on formal-race and ignoring the reality of racial subordination, the court, in this second post-Reconstruction era, risks establishing a new equivalent of *Plessy v. Ferguson*.[49] There is, however, a second parallel for the court. The greater danger for the current court is that it will face the loss of legitimacy which confronted the Taney Court after *Dred Scott*.

The United States is entering a period of cultural diversity more extensive than any in its history. In the past, white racial hegemony went essentially unchallenged. The court today faces a far more complex set of issues. Whatever the validity in 1896 of Justice Harlan's comment in *Plessy*—that "our Constitution is . . . color-blind"—the concept is inadequate to deal with today's racially stratified, culturally diverse, and economically divided nation. The court must either develop new perspectives on race and culture, or run the risk of losing legitimacy and relevance in a crucial arena of social concern.

NOTES

1. *Plessy v. Ferguson*, 163 U.S. 537, 559 (1896) (Harlan, J., dissenting).

2. 349 U.S. 294 (1955).

3. This type of classification arrangement evolved in parts of the West Indies and Latin America, with additional labels for those with Indian blood. One classification scheme proceeded thus: mulatto (Negro and white); quadroon (mulatto and white); octoroon (quadroon and white); cascos (mulatto and mulatto); sambo (mulatto and Negro); mango (sambo and Negro); mustifee (octoroon and white); and mustifino (mustifee and white); C. B. Davenport, *Heredity of Skin Color in Negro-White Crosses*, 27 (1913).

4. This is the prevailing classification scheme in several Latin American societies; Brazil's system is probably the most widely described. At least one well-known author has claimed that Brazilian society is largely free of racial prejudice; G. Freyre, *The Masters and the Slaves: A Study in the Development of Brazilian Civilization*, at xii–xiv (2nd ed. 1956). Others have contested that claim; see, for example,

C. N. Degler, *Neither Black Nor White: Slavery and Race Relations in Brazil and the United States*, 110–11 (1971) (distinguishing the "color prejudice" found in Brazil from genetically based "racial prejudice" in the U.S.). [. . .]

5. Writer and poet Langston Hughes observed in 1953: " 'It's powerful,' [Simple] said . . .
'That one drop of Negro blood—because just one drop of black blood makes a man colored. *One* drop—you are a Negro! Now, why is that? Why is Negro blood so much more powerful than any other kind of blood in the world? If a man has Irish blood in him, people will say, "He's *part* Irish." If he has a little Jewish blood, they'll say, "He's *half* Jewish." But if he has just a small bit of colored blood in him bam!—*"He's a Negro!"* Not, "He's *part* Negro." No, be it ever so little, if that blood is black, *"He's a Negro!"* Now, that is what I do not understand—why our *one* drop is so powerful. . . . Black is powerful. You can have ninety-nine drops of white blood in your veins down South—but if that other *one* drop is black, shame on you! Even if you look white, you're black. That drop is powerful' "; L. Hughes, *Simple Takes a Wife*, 85 (1953).

6. *U.S. v. Thind*, 261 U.S. 204 (1922), was an early attempt by the Supreme Court to distance itself from the scientific discourse. . . .

7. 481 U.S. 604 (1987).

8. *Id.* at 613.

9. M. Harris, *Patterns of Race in the Americas*, 59 (1964).

10. *Fullilove v. Klutznick*, 448 U.S. 448, 524 (1980) (Stewart, J., dissenting).

11. *Metro Broadcasting, v. FCC*, 110 S. Ct. 2997 (1990).

12. *Dred Scott v. Sandford*, 60 U.S. (19 How.) 393, 407 (1857).

13. 163 U.S. 537 (1896).

14. *Plessy*, 163 U.S. at 551.

15. *Id.* at 556–57 (Harlan, J., dissenting).

16. 347 U.S. 483 (1954).

17. *Plessy*, 163 U.S. at 559 (Harlan, J., dissenting).

18. 438 U.S. 265 (1977).

19. *Id.* at 400 (Marshall, J., dissenting).

20. 446 U.S. 156 (1980).

21. 42 U.S.C. s 1973 (1988).

22. *Rome*, 446 U.S. at 218 (Rehnquist, J., dissenting).

23. *Id.*

24. *DeFunis v. Odegaard*, 416 U.S. 312, 320 (1974) (Douglas, J., dissenting).

25. *Id.* at 337.

26. 488 U.S. 469, 527 (1988) (Scalia, J., concurring).

27. 476 U.S. 79 (1986).

28. *Id.* at 87 (citation omitted).

29. R. A. Posner, *The Economics of Justice,* 367 (1981); see also *id.* at 351–401; R. A. Posner, *Economic Analysis of Law,* 615–25 (3d ed. 1986).

30. Posner, *The Economics of Justice, supra* note 29, at 367.

31. T. Sowell, *Race and Economics,* 159 (1975).

32. *Id.* at 160.

33. 347 U.S. 483 (1954).

34. 488 U.S. 469 (1988).

35. *Metro Broadcasting, Inc. v. FCC,* 110 S. Ct. 2997, 3029 (1990) (O'Connor, J., dissenting).

36. 488 U.S. 469 (1989).

37. As Justice Scalia explains formal-race strict scrutiny: "The difficulty of overcoming the effects of past discrimination is as nothing compared with the difficulty of eradicating from our society the source of those effects, which is the tendency—fatal to a Nation such as ours—to classify and judge men and women on the basis of their country of origin or the color of their skin. A solution to the first problem that aggravates the second is no solution at all"; *Croson,* 488 U.S. at 520–21 (Scalia, J., concurring).
Scalia's analysis misses entirely the character of racial subordination. It is not racial classification in the abstract that is problematic. Rather, it is the assymetry of the American classification scheme that is the starting point for understanding racial subordination. Furthermore, even after having adopted hypodescent's metaphorical assertion of racial purity, Scalia would deny that the content of American hypodescent is white racial purity. In his view, it is the subordination of blacks and other nonwhites by whites which underlies racism, not the abstract nature of classification. Even his suggestion of how to "judge men and women" makes no differentiation between white and black. The problem has not historically been black judgment of whites. It has been white judgment of blacks.

38. These definitions are from Robert Paul Wolff's discussion of democratic pluralism: "The first defense of pluralism views it as a distasteful but unavoidable evil; the second portrays it as a useful means for preserving some measure of democracy under the unpromising conditions of mass industrial society. The last defense goes far beyond these in its enthusiasm for pluralism; it holds that a pluralistic society is natural and good and an end to be sought in itself." R. P. Wolff, "Beyond Tolerance," in R. P. Wolff, B. Moore, Jr., and H. Marcuse, eds., *A Critique of Pure Tolerance,* 4, 17 (1965).

39. *Minnick v. California Department of Corrections,* 452 U.S. 105, 129 (1981) (Stewart, J., dissenting). . . .

40. 110 S. Ct. 2997 (1990).

41. 438 U.S. 265 (1978).

42. 110 S. Ct. at 3010–11 (citations omitted).

43. *Id.* at 3028 (Stevens, J., concurring).

44. 466 U.S. 429 (1984).

45. *Id.* at 433.

46. David Strauss has argued that the Court was telling the trial judge that his custody decision was incorrect *because* he did *not* take race into account, thus holding, "in an important sense, that race-conscious action was constitutionally required"; D. Strauss, "The Myth of Colorblindness," *1986 Sup. Ct. Rev.,* 99, 105.

47. 426 U.S. 229 (1975).

48. *Wallace v. Jaffree,* 472 U.S. 38 (1985).

49. 163 U.S. 537 (1896).

❦

WHITENESS AS PROPERTY
Cheryl I. Harris

she walked into forbidden worlds
impaled on the weapon of her own pale skin
she was a sentinel
at impromptu planning sessions
of her own destruction. . . .

—Cheryl I. Harris, "Poem for Alma"

[P]etitioner was a citizen of the United States and a resident of the state of Louisiana of mixed descent, in the proportion of seven eighths Caucasian and one eighth African blood; that the mixture of colored blood was not discernible in him, and that he was entitled to every recognition, right, privilege and immunity secured to the citizens of the United States of the white race by its Constitution and laws . . . and thereupon entered a passenger train and took possession of a vacant seat in a coach where passengers of the white race were accommodated.

—*Plessy v. Ferguson*[1]

I. Introduction

IN the thirties, some years after my mother's family became part of the great river of black migration that flowed north, my Mississippi-born grandmother was confronted with the harsh matter of economic survival for herself and her two daughters. Having separated from my grandfather, who himself was trapped on the fringes of economic marginality, she took one long hard look at her choices and presented herself for employment at a major retail store in Chicago's central business district. This decision would have been unremarkable for a white woman in similar circumstances, but for my grandmother it was an act of both great daring and self-denial—for in so doing she was presenting herself as a white woman. In the parlance of racist America, she was "passing."

Her fair skin, straight hair, and aquiline features had not spared her from the life of sharecropping into which she had been born in anywhere/nowhere, Mississippi—the outskirts of Yazoo City. In the burgeoning landscape of urban America, though, anonymity was possible for a black person with "white" features. She was transgressing boundaries, crossing borders, spinning on margins, traveling between dualities of Manichean space, rigidly bifurcated into light/dark, good/bad, white/black. No longer immediately identifiable as "Lula's daughter," she could thus enter the white world, albeit on a false passport, not merely passing but trespassing.

Every day my grandmother rose from her bed in her house in a black enclave on the south side of Chicago, sent her children off to a black school, boarded a bus full of black passengers, and rode to work. No one at her job ever asked if she was black; the question was unthinkable. By virtue of the employment practices of the "fine establishment" in which she worked, she could not have been. Catering to the upper middle class, understated tastes required that blacks not be allowed.

She quietly went about her clerical tasks, not once revealing her true identity. She listened to the women with whom she worked discuss their worries—their children's illnesses, their husband's disappointments, their boyfriends' infidelities—all of the mundane yet critical things that made up their lives. She came to know them but they did not know her, for my grandmother occupied a completely different place. That place—where white supremacy and economic domination meet—was unknown turf to her white co-workers. They remained oblivious to the worlds within worlds that existed just beyond the edge of their awareness and yet were present in their very midst.

Each evening, my grandmother, tired and worn, retraced her steps home, laid aside her mask, and reentered herself. Day in and day out, she made herself invisible, then visible again, for a price too inconsequential to do more than barely sustain her family and at a cost too precious to conceive. She left the job some years later, finding the strain too much to bear.

From time to time, as I later sat with her, she would recollect that period, and the cloud of some painful memory would pass across her face. Her voice would remain subdued, as if to contain the still-remembered tension. On rare occasions, she would wince, recalling some particularly racist comment made in her presence because of her presumed shared group affiliation. Whatever retort might have been called for had been suppressed long before it reached her lips, for the price of her family's well-being was her silence. Accepting the risk of self-annihilation was the only way to survive.

Although she never would have stated it this way, the clear and ringing denunciations of racism she delivered from her chair when advanced arthritis had rendered her unable to work were informed by those experiences. The fact that self-denial had been a logical choice and had made her complicit in her own oppression at times fed the fire in her eyes when she confronted some daily outrage inflicted on black people. Later, these painful memories forged her total identification with the civil rights movement. Learning about the world at her knee as I did, these experiences also came to inform my outlook and my understanding of the world.

My grandmother's story is far from unique. Indeed, there are many who crossed the color line never to return. Passing is well known among black people in the United States; it is a feature of race subordination in all societies structured on white supremacy. Notwithstanding the purported benefits of black heritage in an era of affirmative action, passing is not an obsolete phenomenon that has slipped into history.

The persistence of passing is related to the historical and continuing pattern of white racial domination and economic exploitation, which has invested passing with a certain economic logic. It was a given for my grandmother that being white automatically ensured higher economic returns in the short term and greater economic, political, and social security in the long run. Becoming white meant gaining access to a whole set of public and private privileges that materially and permanently guaranteed basic subsistence needs and, therefore, survival. Becoming white increased the possibility of controlling critical aspects of one's life rather than being the object of others' domination.

My grandmother's story illustrates the valorization of whiteness as treasured property in a society structured on racial caste. In ways so embedded that it is rarely apparent, the set of assumptions, privileges, and benefits that accompany the status of being white have become a valuable asset—one that whites sought to protect and those who passed sought to attain, by fraud if necessary. Whites have come to expect and rely on these benefits, and over time these expectations have been affirmed, legitimated, and protected by the law. Even though the law is neither uniform nor explicit in all instances, in protecting settled expectations based on white privilege, American law has recognized a property interest in whiteness that, although unacknowledged, now forms the background against which legal disputes are framed, argued, and adjudicated.

This article investigates the relationships between concepts of race and property, and it reflects on how rights in property are contingent on, intertwined with, and conflated with race. Through this entangled relationship between race and property, historical forms of domination have evolved to reproduce subordination in the present. [. . .]

II. THE CONSTRUCTION OF RACE AND THE EMERGENCE OF WHITENESS AS PROPERTY

THE racialization of identity and the racial subordination of blacks and Native Americans provided the ideological basis for slavery and conquest. Although the systems of oppression of blacks and Native Americans differed in form—the former involving the seizure and appropriation of labor, the latter entailing the seizure and appropriation of land—undergirding both was a racialized conception of property implemented by force and ratified by law.

The origins of property rights in the United States are rooted in racial domination. Even in the early years of the country, it was not the concept of race alone that operated to oppress blacks and Indians; rather, it was the interaction between conceptions of race and property which played a critical role in establishing and maintaining racial and economic subordination.

The hyperexploitation of black labor was accomplished by treating black people themselves as objects of property. Race and property were thus conflated by establishing a form of property contingent on race: only blacks were subjugated as slaves and treated as property. Similarly, the conquest, removal, and extermination of Native American life and culture were ratified by conferring and acknowledging the property rights of whites in Native American land. Only white possession and occupation of land was validated and therefore privileged as a basis for property rights. These distinct forms of exploitation each contributed in varying ways to the construction of whiteness as property.

A. Forms of Racialized Property: Relationships Between Slavery, Race, and Property

1. THE CONVERGENCE OF RACIAL AND LEGAL STATUS

Although the early colonists were cognizant of race, racial lines were neither consistently nor sharply delineated among or within all social groups. Captured Africans sold in the Americas were distinguished from the population of indentured or bond servants—"unfree" white labor—but it was not an irrebuttable presumption that all Africans were "slaves," or that slavery was the only appropriate status for them. The distinction between African and white indentured labor grew, however, as decreasing terms of service were introduced for white bond servants. Simultaneously, the demand for labor intensified, resulting in a greater reliance on African labor and a rapid increase in the number of Africans imported to the colonies.

The construction of white identity and the ideology of racial hierarchy were intimately tied to the evolution and expansion of the system of chattel slavery. The further entrenchment of plantation slavery was in part an answer to a social crisis produced by the eroding capacity of the landed class to control the white labor population. The dominant paradigm of social relations, however, was that while not all Africans were slaves, virtually all slaves were not white. It was their racial Otherness that came to justify the subordinated status of blacks. The result was a classification system that "key[ed]

official rules of descent to national origin" so that "[m]embership in the new social category of 'Negro' became itself sufficient justification for enslaveability."[2] Although the cause of the increasing gap between the status of African and white labor is contested by historians, it is clear that "[t]he economic and political interests defending Black slavery were far more powerful than those defending indentured servitude."[3]

By the 1660s, the especially degraded status of blacks as chattel slaves was recognized by law. Between 1680 and 1682, the first slave codes appeared, enshrining the extreme deprivations of liberty already existing in social practice. Many laws parceled out differential treatment based on racial categories: blacks were not permitted to travel without permits, to own property, to assemble publicly, or to own weapons— nor were they to be educated. Racial identity was further merged with stratified social and legal status: "black" racial identity marked who was subject to enslavement, whereas "white" racial identity marked who was "free" or, at minimum, not a slave. The ideological and rhetorical move from "slave" and "free" to "black" and "white" as polar constructs marked an important step in the social construction of race.

2. IMPLICATIONS FOR PROPERTY

The social relations that produced racial identity as a justification for slavery also had implications for the conceptualization of property. This result was predictable, as the institution of slavery, lying at the very core of economic relations, was bound up with the idea of property. Through slavery, race and economic domination were fused.[4]

Slavery produced a peculiar, mixed category of property and humanity—a hybrid with inherent instabilities that were reflected in its treatment and ratification by the law. The dual and contradictory character of slaves as property and persons was exemplified in the Representation Clause of the Constitution. Representation in the House of Representatives was apportioned on the basis of population computed by counting all persons and "three-fifths of all other persons"—slaves. Gouveneur Morris's remarks before the Constitutional Convention posed the essential question: "Upon what principle is it that slaves shall be computed in the representation? Are they men? Then make them Citizens & let them vote? Are they property? Why then is no other property included?"[5]

The cruel tension between property and humanity was also reflected in the law's legitimation of the use of blackwomen's bodies as a means of increasing property.[6] In 1662, the Virginia colonial assembly provided that "[c]hildren got by an Englishman upon a Negro woman shall be bond or free according to the condition of the mother. . . ."[7] In reversing the usual common law presumption that the status of the child was determined by the father, the rule facilitated the reproduction of one's own labor force. Because the children of blackwomen assumed the status of their mother, slaves were bred through blackwomen's bodies. The economic significance of this form of exploitation of female slaves should not be underestimated. Despite Thomas Jefferson's belief that slavery should be abolished, like other slaveholders, he viewed slaves as economic assets, noting that their value could be realized more efficiently from breeding than from labor. A letter he wrote in 1805 stated, "I consider the labor of a breeding woman as no object, and that a child raised every 2 years is of more profit than the crop of the best laboring man."[8]

Even though there was some unease in slave law, reflective of the mixed status of slaves as humans and property, the critical nature of social relations under slavery was the commodification of human beings. Productive relations in early American society included varying forms of sale of labor capacity, many of which were highly oppressive; but slavery was distinguished from other forms of labor servitude by its permanency and the total commodification attendant to the status of the slave. Slavery as a legal institution treated slaves as property that could be transferred, assigned, inherited, or posted as collateral.[9] For example, in *Johnson v. Butler*,[10] the plaintiff sued the defendant for failing to pay a debt of $496 on a specified date; because the covenant had called for payment of the debt in "money or negroes," the plaintiff

contended that the defendant's tender of one negro only, although valued by the parties at an amount equivalent to the debt, could not discharge the debt. The court agreed with the plaintiff. This use of Africans as a stand-in for actual currency highlights the degree to which slavery "propertized" human life.

Because the "presumption of freedom [arose] from color [white]" and the "black color of the race [raised] the presumption of slavery," whiteness became a shield from slavery, a highly volatile and unstable form of property. In the form adopted in the United States, slavery made human beings market-alienable and in so doing, subjected human life and personhood—that which is most valuable—to the ultimate devaluation. Because whites could not be enslaved or held as slaves, the racial line between white and black was extremely critical; it became a line of protection and demarcation from the potential threat of commodification, and it determined the allocation of the benefits and burdens of this form of property. White identity and whiteness were sources of privilege and protection; their absence meant being the object of property.

Slavery as a system of property facilitated the merger of white identity and property. Because the system of slavery was contingent on and conflated with racial identity, it became crucial to be "white," to be identified as white, to have the property of being white. Whiteness was the characteristic, the attribute, the property of free human beings. . . .

B. *Critical Characteristics of Property and Whiteness*
1. WHITENESS AS A TRADITIONAL FORM OF PROPERTY

Whiteness fits the broad historical concept of property described by classical theorists. In James Madison's view, for example, property "embraces every thing to which a man may attach a value and have a right," referring to all of a person's legal rights. Property as conceived in the founding era included not only external objects and people's relationships to them, but also all of those human rights, liberties, powers, and immunities that are important for human well-being, including freedom of expression, freedom of conscience, freedom from bodily harm, and free and equal opportunities to use personal faculties.

Whiteness defined the legal status of a person as slave or free. White identity conferred tangible and economically valuable benefits, and it was jealously guarded as a valued possession, allowed only to those who met a strict standard of proof. Whiteness—the right to white identity as embraced by the law—is property if by "property" one means all of a person's legal rights.

Other traditional theories of property emphasize that the "natural" character of property is derivative of custom, contrary to the notion that property is the product of a delegation of sovereign power. This "bottom-up" theory holds that the law of property merely codifies existing customs and social relations. Under that view, government-created rights such as social welfare payments cannot constitute legitimate property interests because they are positivistic in nature. Other theorists have challenged this conception, and argued that even the most basic of "customary" property rights—the rule of first possession, for example—is dependent on its acceptance or rejection in particular instances by the government. Citing custom as a source of property law begs the central question: Whose custom?

Rather than remaining within the bipolar confines of custom or command, it is crucial to recognize the dynamic and multifaceted relationship among custom, command, and law, as well as the extent to which positionality determines how each may be experienced and understood. Indian custom was obliterated by force and replaced with the regimes of common law which embodied the customs of the conquerors. The assumption of American law as it related to Native Americans was that conquest did give rise to sovereignty. Indians experienced the property laws of the colonizers and the emergent American nation as acts of violence perpetuated by the exercise of power and ratified through the rule of law. At the same time, these laws were perceived as custom and "common sense" by the colonizers. The founders, for instance, so thoroughly embraced Lockean labor theory as the basis for a right of acquisition because it affirmed the right of the New World settlers to settle on and acquire the frontier. It confirmed and ratified their experience.

The law's interpretation of those encounters between whites and Native Americans not only inflicted vastly different results on them but also established a pattern—a custom—of valorizing whiteness. As the forms of racialized property were perfected, the value and protection extended to whiteness increased. Regardless of which theory of property one adopts, the concept of whiteness—established by centuries of custom (illegitimate custom, but custom nonetheless) and codified by law—may be understood as a property interest.

2. PROPERTY AND EXPECTATIONS

"Property is nothing but the basis of expectation," according to Jeremy Bentham, "consist[ing] in an established expectation, in the persuasion of being able to draw such and such advantage from the thing possessed."[11] The relationship between expectations and property remains highly significant, as the law "has recognized and protected even the expectation of rights as actual legal property."[12] This theory does not suggest that all values or all expectations give rise to property, but those expectations in tangible or intangible things which are valued and protected by the law are property.

In fact, the difficulty lies not in identifying expectations as a part of property but, rather, in distinguishing which expectations are reasonable and therefore merit the protection of the law as property. Although the existence of certain property rights may seem self-evident, and the protection of certain expectations may seem essential for social stability, property is a legal construct by which selected private interests are protected and upheld. In creating property "rights," the law draws boundaries and enforces or reorders existing regimes of power. The inequalities that are produced and reproduced are not givens or inevitabilities; rather, they are conscious selections regarding the structuring of social relations. In this sense, it is contended that property rights and interests are not "natural" but "creation[s] of law." In a society structured on racial subordination, white privilege became an expectation and, to apply Margaret Radin's concept, whiteness became the quintessential property for personhood. The law constructed "whiteness" as an objective fact, although in reality it is an ideological proposition imposed through subordination. This move is the central feature of "reification": "Its basis is that a relation between people takes on the character of a thing and thus acquires a 'phantom objectivity,' an autonomy that seems so strictly rational and all-embracing as to conceal every trace of its fundamental nature: the relation between people."[13] Whiteness was an "object" over which continued control was—and is—expected. . . .

Because the law recognized and protected expectations grounded in white privilege (albeit not explicitly in all instances), these expectations became tantamount to property that could not permissibly be intruded upon without consent. As the law explicitly ratified those expectations in continued privilege or extended ongoing protection to those illegitimate expectations by failing to expose or to disturb them radically, the dominant and subordinate positions within the racial hierarchy were reified in law. When the law recognizes, either implicitly or explicitly, the settled expectations of whites built on the privileges and benefits produced by white supremacy, it acknowledges and reinforces a property interest in whiteness that reproduces black subordination.

3. THE PROPERTY FUNCTIONS OF WHITENESS

In addition to the theoretical descriptions of property, whiteness also meets the functional criteria of property. Specifically, the law has accorded "holders" of whiteness the same privileges and benefits accorded holders of other types of property. The liberal view of property is that it includes the exclusive rights of possession, use, and disposition. Its attributes are the right to transfer or alienability, the right to use and enjoyment, and the right to exclude others. Even when examined against this limited view,

whiteness conforms to the general contours of property. It may be a "bad" form of property, but it is property nonetheless.

a. Rights of disposition Property rights are traditionally described as fully alienable. Because fundamental personal rights are commonly understood to be inalienable, it is problematic to view them as property interests. However, as Margaret Radin notes, "inalienability" is not a transparent term; it has multiple meanings that refer to interests that are nonsalable, nontransferable, or non-market-alienable. The common core of inalienability is the negation of the possibility of separation of an entitlement, right, or attribute from its holder.

Classical theories of property identified alienability as a requisite aspect of property; thus, that which is inalienable cannot be property. As the major exponent of this view, John Stuart Mill argued that public offices, monopoly privileges, and human beings—all of which were or should have been inalienable—should not be considered property at all. Under this account, if inalienability inheres in the concept of property, then whiteness, incapable of being transferred or alienated either inside or outside the market, would fail to meet a criterion of property.

As Radin notes, however, even under the classical view, alienability of certain property was limited. Mill also advocated certain restraints on alienation in connection with property rights in land and, probably, other natural resources. In fact, the law has recognized various kinds of inalienable property. For example, entitlements of the regulatory and welfare states, such as transfer payments and government licenses, are inalienable; yet they have been conceptualized and treated as property by law. Although this "new property" has been criticized as being improper—that is, not appropriately cast as property—the principal objection has been based on its alleged lack of productive capacity, not on its inalienability.

The law has also acknowledged forms of inalienable property derived from nongovernmental sources. In the context of divorce, courts have held that professional degrees or licenses held by one party and financed by the labor of the other is marital property whose value is subject to allocation by the court. A medical or law degree is not alienable either in the market or by voluntary transfer. Nevertheless, it is included as property when dissolving a legal relationship.

Indeed, Radin argues that as a deterrent to the dehumanization of universal commodification, market-inalienability may be justified to protect property important to the person and to safeguard human flourishing. She suggests that noncommodification or market-inalienability of personal property or those things essential to human flourishing is necessary to guard against the objectification of human beings. To avoid that danger, "we must cease thinking that market alienability is inherent in the concept of property." Following this logic, then, the inalienability of whiteness should not preclude the consideration of whiteness as property. Paradoxically, its inalienability may be more indicative of its perceived enhanced value rather than of its disqualification as property.

b. Right to use and enjoyment Possession of property includes the rights of use and enjoyment. If these rights are essential aspects of property, it is because "the problem of property in political philosophy dissolves into . . . questions of the will and the way in which we use the things of this world."[14] As whiteness is simultaneously an aspect of identity and a property interest, it is something that can both be experienced and deployed as a resource. Whiteness can move from being a passive characteristic as an aspect of identity to an active entity that—like other types of property—is used to fulfill the will and to exercise power. The state's official recognition both of a racial identity that subordinated blacks and of privileged rights in property based on race, elevated whiteness from a passive attribute to an object of law and a resource deployable at the social, political, and institutional level to maintain control. Thus, a white person "used and enjoyed" whiteness whenever she took advantage of the privileges accorded white people simply by virtue of their whiteness—

when she exercised any number of rights reserved for the holders of whiteness. Whiteness as the embodiment of white privilege transcended mere belief or preference; it became usable property, the subject of the law's regard and protection. In this respect, whiteness, as an active property, has been used and enjoyed.

c. . . . The conception of reputation as property found its origins in early concepts of property which encompassed things (such as land and personalty), income (such as revenues from leases, mortgages, and patent monopolies), and one's life, liberty, and labor. . . . The idea of self-ownership, then, was particularly fertile ground for the idea that reputation, as an aspect of identity earned through effort, was similarly property. Moreover, the loss of reputation was capable of being valued in the market.

The direct manifestation of the law's legitimation of whiteness as reputation is revealed in the well-established doctrine that to call a white person "black" is to defame her.[15] Although many of the cases were decided in an era when the social and legal stratification of whites and blacks was more absolute, as late as 1957 the principle was reaffirmed, notwithstanding significant changes in the legal and political status of blacks. As one court noted, "there is still to be considered the social distinction existing between the races," and the allegation was likely to cause injury.[16] A black person, however, could not sue for defamation if she was called "white." Because the law expressed and reinforced the social hierarchy as it existed, it was presumed that no harm could flow from such a reversal.

Private identity based on racial hierarchy was legitimated as public identity in law, even after the end of slavery and the formal end of legal race segregation. Whiteness as interpersonal hierarchy was recognized externally as race reputation. Thus, whiteness as public reputation and personal property was affirmed.

d. The absolute right to exclude Many theorists have traditionally conceptualized property as including the exclusive rights of use, disposition, and possession, with possession embracing the absolute right to exclude. The right to exclude was the central principle, too, of whiteness as identity, for whiteness in large part has been characterized not by an inherent unifying characteristic but by the exclusion of others deemed to be "not white." The possessors of whiteness were granted the legal right to exclude others from the privileges inhering in whiteness; whiteness became an exclusive club whose membership was closely and grudgingly guarded. The courts played an active role in enforcing this right to exclude—determining who was or was not white enough to enjoy the privileges accompanying whiteness. In that sense, the courts protected whiteness as they did any other form of property.

Moreover, as it emerged, the concept of whiteness was premised on white supremacy rather than on mere difference. "White" was defined and constructed in ways that increased its value by reinforcing its exclusivity. Indeed, just as whiteness as property embraced the right to exclude, whiteness as a theoretical construct evolved for the very purpose of racial exclusion. Thus, the concept of whiteness is built on exclusion and racial subjugation. This fact was particularly evident during the period of the most rigid racial exclusion, for whiteness signified racial privilege and took the form of status property.

At the individual level, recognizing oneself as "white" necessarily assumes premises based on white supremacy: it assumes that black ancestry in any degree, extending to generations far removed, automatically disqualifies claims to white identity, thereby privileging "white" as unadulterated, exclusive, and rare. Inherent in the concept of "being white" was the right to own or hold whiteness to the exclusion and subordination of blacks. Because "[i]dentity is . . . continuously being constituted through social interactions,"[17] the assigned political, economic, and social inferiority of blacks necessarily shaped white identity. In the commonly held popular view, the presence of black "blood"—including the infamous "one-drop"—consigned a person to being "black" and evoked the "meta-phor . . . of purity and contamination" in which black blood is a contaminant and white racial identity is pure. Recognizing or identifying oneself as white is thus a claim of racial purity, an assertion that one is free of any taint of black blood. The law has played a critical role in legitimating this claim.

C. White Legal Identity: The Law's Acceptance and Legitimation of Whiteness as Property

The law assumed the crucial task of racial classification, and accepted and embraced the then-current theories of race as biological fact. This core precept of race as a physically defined reality allowed the law to fulfill an essential function—to "parcel out social standing according to race" and to facilitate systematic discrimination by articulating "seemingly precise definitions of racial group membership." This allocation of race and rights continued a century after the abolition of slavery.

The law relied on bounded, objective, and scientific definitions of race—what Neil Gotanda has called "historical-race"[18]—to construct whiteness as not merely race, but race plus privilege. By making race determinant and the product of rationality and science, dominant and subordinate positions within the racial hierarchy were disguised as the product of natural law and biology rather than as naked preferences. Whiteness as racialized privilege was then legitimated by science and was embraced in legal doctrine as "objective fact."

Case law that attempted to define race frequently struggled over the precise fractional amount of black "blood"—traceable black ancestry—that would defeat a claim to whiteness. Although the courts applied varying fractional formulas in different jurisdictions to define "black" or, in the terms of the day, "negro" or "colored," the law uniformly accepted the rule of hypodescent[19]—racial identity was governed by blood, and white was preferred.

This legal assumption of race as blood-borne was predicated on the pseudo-sciences of eugenics and craniology, which saw their major development during the eighteenth and nineteenth centuries. The legal definition of race was the "objective" test propounded by racist theorists of the day, who described race to be immutable, scientific, biologically determined—an unsullied fact of the blood rather than a volatile and violently imposed regime of racial hierarchy.

In adjudicating who was "white," courts sometimes noted that, by physical characteristics, the individual whose racial identity was at issue appeared to be white and, in fact, had been regarded as white in the community. Yet if an individual's blood was tainted, she could not claim to be "white" as the law understood, regardless of the fact that phenotypically she may have been completely indistinguishable from a white person, may have lived as a white person, and may have descended from a family that lived as whites. Although socially accepted as white, she could not legally be white. Blood as "objective fact" predominated over appearance and social acceptance, which were socially fluid and subjective measures.

In fact, though, "blood" was no more objective than that which the law dismissed as subjective and unreliable. The acceptance of the fiction that the racial ancestry could be determined with the degree of precision called for by the relevant standards or definitions rested on false assumptions that racial categories of prior ancestors had been accurately reported, that those reporting in the past shared the definitions currently in use, and that racial purity actually existed in the United States.[20] Ignoring these considerations, the law established rules that extended equal treatment to those of the "same blood," albeit of different complexions, because it was acknowledged that, "[t]here are white men as dark as mulattoes, and there are pure-blooded albino Africans as white as the whitest Saxons."[21]

The standards were designed to accomplish what mere observation could not: "That even Blacks who did not look Black were kept in their place."[22] Although the line of demarcation between black and white varied from rules that classified as black a person containing "any drop of Black blood" to more liberal rules that defined persons with a preponderance of white blood to be white,[23] the courts universally accepted the notion that white status was something of value that could be accorded only to those persons whose proofs established their whiteness as defined by the law.[24] Because legal recognition of a person as white carried material benefits, "false" or inadequately supported claims were denied like any other unsubstantiated claim to a property interest. Only those who could lay "legitimate" claims to whiteness could be legally recognized as white, because allowing physical attributes, social acceptance, or self-identification to determine whiteness would diminish its value and destroy the underlying presumption of exclusivity. In effect, the courts erected legal "no trespassing" signs.

In the realm of social relations, racial recognition in the United States is thus an act of race subordination. In the realm of legal relations, judicial definition of racial identity based on white supremacy reproduced that race subordination at the institutional level. In transforming white to whiteness, the law masked the ideological content of racial definition and the exercise of power required to maintain it: "It convert[ed] an] abstract concept into [an] entity."[25]

2. WHITENESS AS RACIALIZED PRIVILEGE

The material benefits of racial exclusion and subjugation functioned, in the labor context, to stifle class tensions among whites. White workers perceived that they had more in common with the bourgeoisie than with fellow workers who were black. Thus, W. E. B. Du Bois's classic historical study of race and class, *Black Reconstruction*,[26] noted that, for the evolving white working class, race identification became crucial to the ways that it thought of itself and conceived its interests. There were, he suggested, obvious material benefits, at least in the short term, to the decision of white workers to define themselves by their whiteness: their wages far exceeded those of blacks and were high even in comparison with world standards. Moreover, even when the white working class did not collect increased pay as part of white privilege, there were real advantages not paid in direct income: whiteness still yielded what Du

Bois termed a "public and psychological wage" vital to white workers.[27] Thus, Du Bois noted that whites

> were given public deference . . . because they were white. They were admitted freely with all classes of white people, to public functions, to public parks. . . . The police were drawn from their ranks, and the courts, dependent on their votes, treated them with . . . leniency. . . . Their vote selected public officials, and while this had small effect upon the economic situation, it had great effect on their personal treatment. . . . White schoolhouses were the best in the community, and conspicuously placed, and they cost anywhere from twice to ten times as much per capita as the colored schools.[28]

The central feature of the convergence of "white" and "worker" lay in the fact that racial status and privilege could ameliorate and assist in "evad[ing] rather than confront[ing class] exploitation."[29] Although not accorded the privileges of the ruling class, in both the North and South, white workers could accept their lower class position in the hierarchy "by fashioning identities as 'not slaves' and as 'not Blacks.'"[30] Whiteness produced—and was reproduced by—the social advantage that accompanied it.

Whiteness was also central to national identity and to the republican project. The amalgamation of various European strains into an American identity was facilitated by an oppositional definition of black as Other. As Andrew Hacker suggests, fundamentally, the question was not so much "who is white" but, rather, "who may be considered white," for the historical pattern was that various immigrant groups of different ethnic origins were accepted into a white identity shaped around Anglo-American norms. Current members then "ponder[ed] whether they want[ed] or need[ed] new members as well as the proper pace of new admissions into this exclusive club."[31] Through minstrel shows in which white actors masquerading in blackface played out racist stereotypes, the popular culture put the black at "'solo spot centerstage, providing a relational model in contrast to which masses of Americans could establish a positive and superior sense of identi-

ty,' . . [one] . . . established by an infinitely manipulable negation comparing whites with a construct of a socially defenseless group."[32]

It is important to note the effect of this hypervaluation of whiteness. Owning white identity as property affirmed the self-identity and liberty of whites and, conversely, denied the self-identity and liberty of blacks. The attempts to lay claim to whiteness through "passing" painfully illustrate the effects of the law's recognition of whiteness. The embrace of a lie, undertaken by my grandmother and the thousands like her, could occur only when oppression makes self-denial and the obliteration of identity rational and, in significant measure, beneficial. The economic coercion of white supremacy on self-definition nullifies any suggestion that passing is a logical exercise of liberty or self-identity. The decision to pass as white was not a choice, if by that word one means voluntariness or lack of compulsion. The fact of race subordination was coercive, and it circumscribed the liberty to define oneself. Self-determination of identity was not a right for all people but a privilege accorded on the basis of race. The effect of protecting whiteness at law was to devalue those who were not white by coercing them to deny their identity in order to survive.

I. WHITENESS, RIGHTS, AND NATIONAL IDENTITY

The concept of whiteness was carefully protected because so much was contingent upon it. Whiteness conferred on its owners aspects of citizenship which were all the more valued because they were denied to others. Indeed, the very fact of citizenship itself was linked to white racial identity. The Naturalization Act of 1790 restricted citizenship to persons who resided in the United States for two years, who could establish their good character in court, and who were "white." Moreover, the trajectory of expanding democratic rights for whites was accompanied by the contraction of the rights of blacks in an ever-deepening cycle of oppression. The franchise, for example, was broadened to extend voting rights to unpropertied white men at the same time that black voters were specifically disenfranchised, arguably shifting the property required for voting from land to whiteness. This racialized version of republicanism—this *Herrenvolk* republicanism—constrained any vision of democracy from addressing the class hierarchies adverse to many who considered themselves white.

The inherent contradiction between the bondage of blacks and republican rhetoric that championed the freedom of "all" men was resolved by positing that blacks were different. The laws did not mandate that blacks be accorded equality under the law because nature—not man, not power, not violence—had determined their degraded status. Rights were for those who had the capacity to exercise them, a capacity denoted by racial identity. This conception of rights was contingent on race, on whether one could claim whiteness—a form of property. This articulation of rights that were contingent on property ownership was a familiar paradigm, as similar requirements had been imposed on the franchise in the early part of the Republic. For the first two hundred years of the country's existence, the system of racialized privilege in the public and private spheres carried through this linkage of rights and inequality, of rights and property. Whiteness as property was the critical core of a system that affirmed the hierarchical relations between white and black. . . .

III. THE PERSISTENCE OF WHITENESS AS PROPERTY

A. The Persistence of Whiteness as Valued Social Identity

Even as the capacity of whiteness to deliver is arguably diminished by the elimination of rigid racial stratifications, whiteness continues to be perceived as materially significant. Because real power and wealth never have been accessible to more than a narrowly defined ruling elite, for many whites the benefits of whiteness as property, in the absence of legislated privilege, may have been reduced to a claim of relative privilege only in comparison to people of color. Nevertheless, whiteness retains its value as a "consola-

tion prize": it does not mean that all whites will win, but simply that they will not lose, if losing is defined as being on the bottom of the social and economic hierarchy—the position to which blacks have been consigned.

Andrew Hacker, in his 1992 book *Two Nations*,[33] recounts the results of a recent exercise that probed the value of whiteness according to the perceptions of whites. The study asked a group of white students how much money they would seek if they were changed from white to black. "Most seemed to feel that it would not be out of place to ask for $50 million, or $1 million for each coming black year." Whether this figure represents an accurate amortization of the societal cost of being black in the United States, it is clear that whiteness is still perceived to be valuable. The wages of whiteness are available to all whites, regardless of class position—even to those whites who are without power, money, or influence. Whiteness, the characteristic that distinguishes them from blacks, serves as compensation even to those who lack material wealth. It is the relative political advantages extended to whites, rather than actual economic gains, that are crucial to white workers. Thus, as Kimberlé Crenshaw points out, whites have an actual stake in racism.[34] Because blacks are held to be inferior, although no longer on the basis of science as antecedent determinant but, rather, by virtue of their position at the bottom, it allows whites—all whites—to "include themselves in the dominant circle. [Although most whites] hold no real power, [all can claim] their privileged racial identity."[35]

White workers often identify themselves primarily as white rather than as workers because it is through their whiteness that they are afforded access to a host of public, private, and psychological benefits. It is through the concept of whiteness that class-consciousness among white workers is subordinated and attention is diverted from class oppression.

Although dominant societal norms have embraced the ideas of fairness and nondiscrimination, removal of privilege and antisubordination principles are actively rejected or at best ambiguously received, because expectations of white privilege are bound up with what is considered essential for self-realization. Among whites, the idea persists that their whiteness is meaningful. Whiteness is an aspect of racial identity surely, but it is much more; it remains a concept based on relations of power, a social construct predicated on white dominance and black subordination.

B. Subordination through Denial of Group Identity

Whiteness as property is also constituted through the reification of expectations in the continued right of white-dominated institutions to control the legal meaning of group identity. This reification manifests itself in the law's dialectical misuse of the concept of group identity as it pertains to racially subordinated peoples. The law has recognized and codified racial group identity as an instrument of exclusion and exploitation; however, it has refused to recognize group identity when asserted by racially oppressed groups as a basis for affirming or claiming rights. The law's approach to group identity reproduces subordination, in the past through "race-ing" a group—that is, by assigning a racial identity that equated with inferior status and, in the present, by erasing racial group identity.

In part, the law's denial of the existence of racial groups is not only predicated on the rejection of the ongoing presence of the past, but it is also grounded on a basic tenet of liberalism—that constitutional protections inhere in individuals, not in groups. As informed by the Lockean notion of the social contract, the autonomous, free will of the individual is central; indeed, it is the individual who, in concert with other individuals, elects to enter into political society and to form a state of limited powers. This philosophical view of society is closely aligned with the antidiscrimination principle—the idea being that equality mandates only the equal treatment of individuals under the law. Within this framework, the idea of the social group has no place.

Although the law's determination of any "fact," including that of group identity, is not infinitely flexible, its studied ignorance of the issue of racial group identity ensures wrong results by assuming a pseudo-objective posture that does not permit it to hear the complex dialogue concerning identity questions, particularly as they pertain to historically dominated groups.

Instead, the law holds to the basic premise that definition from above can be fair to those below, that beneficiaries of racially conferred privilege have the right to establish norms for those who have historically been oppressed pursuant to those norms, and that race is not historically contingent. Although the substance of race definitions has changed, what persists is the expectation of white-controlled institutions in the continued right to determine meaning—the reified privilege of power—that reconstitutes the property interest in whiteness in contemporary form.

. . .

IV. DELEGITIMATING THE PROPERTY INTEREST IN WHITENESS THROUGH AFFIRMATIVE ACTION

WITHIN the worlds of de jure and de facto segregation, whiteness has value, whiteness is valued, and whiteness is expected to be valued in law. The legal affirmation of whiteness and white privilege allowed expectations that originated in injustice to be naturalized and legitimated. The relative economic, political, and social advantages dispensed to whites under systematic white supremacy in the United States were reinforced through patterns of oppression of blacks and Native Americans. Materially, these advantages became institutionalized privileges; ideologically, they became part of the settled expectations of whites—a product of the unalterable original bargain. The law masks as natural what is chosen; it obscures the consequences of social selection as inevitable. The result is that the distortions in social relations are immunized from truly effective intervention, because the existing inequities are obscured and rendered nearly invisible. The existing state of affairs is considered neutral and fair, however unequal and unjust it is in substance. Although the existing state of inequitable distribution is the product of institutionalized white supremacy and economic exploitation, it is seen by whites as part of the natural order of things, something that cannot legitimately be disturbed. Through legal doctrine, expectation of continued privilege based on white domination was reified; whiteness as property was reaffirmed.

The property interest in whiteness has proven to be resilient and adaptive to new conditions. Over time it has changed in form but it has retained its essential exclusionary character and continued to distort outcomes of legal disputes by favoring and protecting settled expectations of white privilege. The law expresses the dominant conception of constructs such as "rights," "equality," "property," "neutrality," and "power": rights mean shields from interference; equality means formal equality; property means the settled expectations that are to be protected; neutrality means the existing distribution, which is natural; and power is the mechanism for guarding all of this. . . .

Affirmative action begins the essential work of rethinking rights, power, equality, race, and property from the perspective of those whose access to each of these has been limited by their oppression. [. . .] From this perspective, affirmative action is required on moral and legal grounds to delegitimate the property interest in whiteness—to dismantle the actual and expected privilege that has attended "white" skin since the founding of the country. Like "passing," affirmative action undermines the property interest in whiteness. Unlike passing, which seeks the shelter of an assumed whiteness as a means of extending protection at the margins of racial boundaries, affirmative action denies the privileges of whiteness and seeks to remove the legal protections of the existing hierarchy spawned by race oppression. What passing attempts to circumvent, affirmative action moves to challenge.

Rereading affirmative action to delegitimate the property interest in whiteness suggests that if, historically, the law has legitimated and protected the settled whites' expectations in white privilege, delegitimation should be accomplished not merely by implementing equal treat-

ment but also by equalizing treatment among the groups that have been illegitimately privileged or unfairly subordinated by racial stratification. Obviously, the meaning of equalizing treatment would vary, because the extent of privilege and subordination is not constant with reference to all societal goods. In some instances, the advantage of race privilege to poorer whites may be materially insignificant when compared to their class disadvantage against more privileged whites. But exposing the critical core of whiteness as property—the unconstrained right to exclude—directs attention toward questions of redistribution and property that are crucial under both race and class analysis. The conceptions of rights, race, property, and affirmative action as currently understood are unsatisfactory and insufficient to facilitate the self-realization of oppressed people. . . .

A. Affirmative Action: A New Form of Status Property?

If whiteness as property is the reification, in law, of expectations of white privilege, then according privilege to blacks through systems of affirmative action might be challenged as performing the same ideological function, but on the other side of the racial line. As evidence of a property interest in blackness, some might point out that, recently, some whites have sought to characterize themselves as belonging to a racial minority. Equating affirmative action with whiteness as property, however, is false and can only be maintained if history is ignored or inverted while the premises inherent in the existing racial hierarchy are retained. Whiteness as property is derived from the deep historical roots of systematic white supremacy which have given rise to definitions of group identity predicated on the racial subordination of the Other, and have reified expectations of continued white privilege. This reification differs in crucial ways from the premises, intent, and objectives of affirmative action.

Fundamentally, affirmative action does not reestablish a property interest in blackness, because black identity is not the functional opposite of whiteness. Even today, whiteness is still intertwined with the degradation of blacks and is still valued because "the artifact of 'whiteness'. . . sets a floor on how far [whites] can fall." Acknowledging black identity does not involve the systematic subordination of whites, nor does it even set up a danger of doing so. Affirmative action is based on principles of antisubordination, not principles of black superiority.

The removal of white privilege pursuant to a program of affirmative action would not be implemented under an ideology of subordination, nor would it be situated in the context of the historical or present exploitation of whites. It is thus not a matter of implementing systematic disadvantage to whites or installing mechanisms of group exploitation. Whites are not an oppressed people and are not at risk of becoming so. Those whites who are disadvantaged in society suffer not because of their race but in spite of it. Refusing to implement affirmative action as a remedy for racial subordination will not alleviate the class oppression of poor whites; indeed, failing to do so will reinforce the existing regime of race and class domination which leaves lower-class whites more vulnerable to class exploitation. Affirmative action does not institute a regime of racialized hierarchy in which all whites, because they are white, are deprived of economic, social, and political benefits. It does not reverse the hierarchy; rather, it levels the racial privilege.

Even if one rejects the notion that properly constructed affirmative action policies cause whites no injustice, affirmative action does not implement a set of permanent, never-ending privileges for blacks. Affirmative action does not distort black expectations because it does not naturalize these expectations. Affirmative action can only be implemented through conscious intervention, and it requires constant monitoring and reevaluation—so it does not function behind a mask of neutrality in the realm beyond scrutiny. Affirmative action for blacks does not reify existing patterns of privilege, nor does it produce subordination of whites as a group. If anything, it might fairly be said that affirmative action creates a property

interest in true equal opportunity—opportunity and means that are equalized.

B. *What Affirmative Action Has Been; What Affirmative Action Might Become*

The truncated application of affirmative action as a policy has obscured affirmative action as a concept. The ferocious and unending debate on affirmative action cannot be understood unless the concept of affirmative action is considered and conceptually disengaged from its application in the United States.

As policy, affirmative action does not have a clearly identifiable pedigree; rather, it was one of the limited concessions offered in official response to demands for justice pressed by black constituencies. Despite uneven implementation in the areas of public employment, higher education, and government contracts, it translated into the attainment by blacks of jobs, admissions to universities, and contractual opportunities. Affirmative action programs did not, however, stem the tide of growing structural unemployment and underemployment among black workers, nor did it prevent the decline in material conditions for blacks as a whole. Such programs did not change the subordinated status of blacks, in part because of structural changes in the economy, and in part because the programs were not designed to do so.

However, affirmative action is more than a program: it is a principle, internationally recognized, based on a theory of rights and equality. Formal equality overlooks structural disadvantage and requires mere nondiscrimination or "equal treatment"; by contrast, affirmative action calls for equalizing treatment by redistributing power and resources in order to rectify inequities and to achieve real equality. The current polarized debate on affirmative action and the intense political and judicial opposition to the concept is thus grounded in the fact that, in its requirement of equalizing treatment, affirmative action implicitly challenges the sanctity of the original and derivative present distribution of property, resources, and entitlements, and it directly confronts the notion that there is a protectable property interest in "whiteness." If affirmative action doctrine were freed from the constraint of protecting the property interest in whiteness—if, indeed, it were conceptualized from the perspective of those on the bottom—it might assist in moving away from a vision of affirmative action as an uncompensated taking and inspire a new perspective on identity as well. The fundamental precept of whiteness, the core of its value, is its exclusivity; but exclusivity is predicated not on any intrinsic characteristic, but on the existence of the symbolic Other, which functions to "create an illusion of unity" among whites. Affirmative action might challenge the notion of property and identity as the unrestricted right to exclude. In challenging the property interest in whiteness, affirmative action could facilitate the destruction of the false premises of legitimacy and exclusivity inherent in whiteness and break the distorting link between white identity and property.

Affirmative action in the South African context offers a point of comparison. It has emerged as one of the democratic movement's central demands, appearing in both the constitutional guidelines and draft Bill of Rights issued by the African National Congress. These documents simultaneously denounce all forms of discrimination and embrace affirmative action as a mechanism for rectifying the gross inequities in South African society.

The South African conception of affirmative action expands the application of affirmative action to a much broader domain than has typically been envisioned in the United States. That is, South Africans consider affirmative action a strategic measure to address directly the distribution of property and power, with particular regard to the maldistribution of land and the need for housing. This policy has not yet been clearly defined, but what is implied by this conception of affirmative action is that existing distributions of property will be modified by rectifying unjust loss and inequality. Property rights will then be respected, but they will not be absolute; rather, they will be considered against a societal requirement of affirmative action. In essence, this conception of affirmative action is moving toward the reallocation of power and the right to have a

say. This conception is in fact consistent with the fundamental principle of affirmative action and effectively removes the constraint imposed in the American model, which strangles affirmative action principles by protecting the property interest in whiteness.

V. Conclusion

WHITENESS as property has carried and produced a heavy legacy. It is a ghost that has haunted the political and legal domains in which claims for justice have been inadequately addressed for far too long. Only rarely declaring its presence, it has warped efforts to remediate racial exploitation. It has blinded society to the systems of domination that work against so many by retaining an unvarying focus on vestiges of systemic racialized privilege which subordinates those perceived as a particularized few—the Others. It has thwarted not only conceptions of racial justice but also conceptions of property which embrace more equitable possibilities. In protecting the property interest in whiteness, property is assumed to be no more than the right to prohibit infringement on settled expectations, ignoring countervailing equitable claims predicated on a right to inclusion. It is long past time to put the property interest in whiteness to rest. Affirmative action can assist in that task. If properly conceived and implemented, it is not only consistent with norms of equality but also essential to shedding the legacy of oppression.

NOTES

1. 163 U.S. 537, 538 (1896).

2. N. Gotanda, "A Critique of 'Our Constitution is ColorBlind,'" 44 *Stan L. Rev,.* 1, 34 (1991) [the essay is included in this volume—ED.].

3. D. Roediger, *The Wages of Whiteness,* at 32 (1991).

4. The system of racial oppression grounded in slavery was driven in large measure (although by no means exclusively) by economic concerns. . . .

5. M. Farrand, ed., 2 *The Records of the Federal Convention of 1787,* at 222 (1911).

6. My use of the term "blackwomen" is an effort to use language that more clearly reflects the unity of identity as "black" and "woman," with neither aspect primary or

subordinate to the other. It is an attempt to realize in practice what has been identified in theory—that, as Kimberlé Crenshaw notes, blackwomen exist "at the crossroads of gender and race hierarchies"; K. Crenshaw, "Whose Story Is It, Anyway? Feminist and Antiracist Appropriations of Anita Hill," in Toni Morrison, ed., *Race-ing Justice, En-gendering Power: Essays on Anita Hill, Clarence Thomas, and the Construction of Social Reality*, 402, 403 (1992). [. . .]

7. A. L. Higginbotham, Jr., *In the Matter of Color: Race and the American Legal Process*, at 43 (1978). [. . .]

8. Letter from Thomas Jefferson to John Jordan (Dec. 21, 1805), cited in R. Takaki, *Iron Cages: Race and Culture in Nineteenth-Century America*, at 44 (1990).

9. By 1705, Virginia had classified slaves as real property; see Higginbotham, *supra* note 7, at 52. In Massachusetts and South Carolina, slaves were identified as chattel; *id.* at 78, 211.

10. 4 Ky. (1 Bibb) 97 (1815).

11. Jeremy Bentham, "Security and Equality in Property," in C. B. Macpherson, ed., *Property: Mainstream and Critical Positions*, at 51–52 (1978). [. . .]

12. *Id.* at 366.

13. G. Lukacs, *History and Class Consciousness*, 83, trans. R. Livingstone (1971).

14. K. R. Minogue, "The Concept of Property and Its Contemporary Significance," in J. R. Pennock and J. W. Chapman, eds., *Nomos XXII: Property*, at 15 (1980).

15. See J. H. Crabb, "Annotation, Libel and Slander: Statements Respecting Race, Color, or Nationality as Actionable," 46 *A. L. R.*, 2d 1287, 1289 (1956) ("The bulk of the cases have arisen from situations in which it was stated erroneously that a white person was a Negro. According to the majority rule, this is libelous per se"). [. . .]

16. *Bowen v. Independent Publishing Co.*, 96 S.E.2d 564, 565 (S.C. 1957).

17. R. C. Post, "The Social Foundations of Defamation Law: Reputation and the Constitution," 74 *Cal. L. Rev.*, 691, 709 (1986). . . .

18. Gotanda defines "historical-race" as socially constructed formal categories predicated on race subordination that included presumed substantive characteristics relating to "ability, disadvantage, or moral culpability" [the essay is included in this volume—ED.].

19. "Hypodescent" is the term used by anthropologist Marvin Harris to describe the American system of racial classification in which the subordinate classification is assigned to the offspring if there is one "superordinate" and one "subordinate" parent. Under this system, the child of a black parent and a white parent is black; M. Harris, *Patterns of Race in the Americas*, 37, 56 (1964).

20. It is not at all clear that even the slaves imported from abroad represented "pure negro races." As Gunner Myrdal noted, many of the tribes imported from Africa had intermingled with peoples of the Mediterranean, among them Portuguese slave traders. Other slaves brought to the United States came via the West Indies, where some Africans had been brought directly, but still others had been brought via Spain and Portugal, countries in which extensive interracial sexual relations had occurred. By the mid-nineteenth century it was, therefore, a virtual fiction to speak of "pure blood" as it relates to racial identification in the United States; see G. Myrdal, *An American Dilemma*, at 123 (1944).

21. *People v. Dean*, 14 Mich. 406, 422 (1866).

22. R. T. Diamond and R. J. Cottrol, "Codifying Caste: Louisiana's Racial Classification Scheme and the Fourteenth Amendment," 29 *Loy. L. Rev.*, 255, 281 (1983).

23. See, for example, *Gray v. Ohio*, 4 Ohio 353, 355 (1831).

24. The courts adopted this standard even as they critiqued the legitimacy of such rules and definitions. For example, in *People v. Dean*, 14 Mich. 406 (1886), the court, in interpreting the meaning of the word "white" for the purpose of determining whether the defendant had voted illegally, criticized as "absurd" the notion that "a preponderance of mixed blood, on one side or the other of any given standard, has the remotest bearing upon personal fitness or unfitness to possess political privileges"; *id.* at 417. Yet it held that the electorate that had voted for racial exclusion had the right to determine voting privileges; see *id.* at 416.

25. S. J. Gould, *The Mismeasure of Man*, 24 (1981).

26. W. E. B. Du Bois, *Black Reconstruction* (1976) [1935].

27. *Id.* at 700.

28. *Id.* at 700-01.

29. Roediger, *supra* note 3, at 13. [. . .]

30. *Id.* at 13.

31. *Id.* at 9.

32. *Id.* at 118 (quoting Alan W. C. Green, " 'Jim Crow,' 'Zip Coon': The Northern Origin of Negro Minstrelsy," 11 *Mass. Rev.*, 385, 395 (1970)).

33. A. Hacker, *Two Nations*, 155 (1992).

34. See K. W. Crenshaw, "Race, Reform, and Retrenchment: Transformation and Legitimation in Antidiscrimination Law," 101 *Harv. L. Rev.*, 1331, 1381 (1988) [the essay is included in this volume—ED.].

35. Roediger, *supra* note 3, at 5.

❦

RACE IN THE TWENTY-FIRST CENTURY:
EQUALITY THROUGH LAW?

Linda Greene

The burden of proof is always upon him. For the interpretation and realization of these rights he is forced to appeal to the Supreme Court.

Thus the Negro has been compelled to substitute the complicated, arduous and expensive processes of litigation for the ballot box. What other groups are able to do for themselves, the Negro hopes the judiciary to do for him. There is more than ample evidence in the decisions of the supreme tribunal of the land on questions involving the rights of the Negro to disprove the possibility of any general relief from this quarter.

—Dr. Ralph Bunche, 1934.[1]

I. INTRODUCTION

DURING 1989 the Supreme Court decided several important civil rights cases[2] to which civil rights leaders responded with dismay. All these decisions concerned discrimination in employment and addressed a wide range of issues: whether white employees collaterally may attack court-approved consent decrees,[3] the proof requirements in *Griggs v. Duke Power*,[4] disparate-impact cases,[5] the applicability of Reconstruction-era civil rights statutes to private discrimination,[6] as well as the constitutionality of a local government program requiring contractors to employ minority subcontractors.[7] In each of these cases, the majority of the court employed formalistic and hypertechnical reasoning to limit the scope of redress for the racial inequities plaguing racial minority groups. In ingenious ways, these decisions explode the post-*Brown*[8] assumptions about racial discrimination's existence, its meaning and importance, and the role of the judiciary in its redress. These decisions contribute to the development of a legal structure in which racial inequities may be immune from legal redress and, perhaps more important, in which racial discrimination plausibly may be denied. In short, the 1989 Supreme Court decisions create barriers to changes in the racial status quo.

The civil rights decisions of the 1989 term

force us to refocus on a question presented time and time again, before and after *Dred Scott*[9]— whether meaningful equality can be obtained for African-Americans through law. I will discuss these decisions by elaborating on several themes embodied in these decisions. These themes include formalism and equality, the tendency to interpret statutes rigidly, narrowly, and hypertechnically, thereby stripping them of transformative content; politics and equality, the tendency to reduce all questions of racial equality to political questions, thereby stripping constitutional legitimacy from racial civil rights; and the rights of whites and equality, the tendency to give legal legitimacy to the efforts of whites, who historically have benefited from racism, to maintain the racial status quo.

II. FORMALISN AND EQUALITY

A. Introduction

One theme embodied in the 1989 civil rights cases is formalism, the tendency to approach the task of interpretation as an enterprise unaffected by either contextual reality or likely result. This tendency is particularly obvious in *Wards Cove Packing Co. v. Atonio*[10] and *Patterson v. McLean Credit Union*.[11] In these cases, the Supreme Court majority uses language that preserves the appearance of proper concern for achieving equality—yet, in both, the reasoning seems indifferent to reality and to the impact of the decisions on the historical victims of racial discrimination.

B. Wards Cove Packing Co. v. Atonio

The *Wards Cove* decision may have the greatest impact on equality law because of the sweeping changes it arguably makes in employment discrimination law. *Wards Cove* does not follow the *Griggs v. Duke Power* tradition of ferreting out policies that perpetuate segregation in employment. Instead, *Wards Cove* treats segregative policies as socially neutral and cautions courts to refrain from interfering with employment policies. This result is accomplished through the use of an often surreal analysis of statistics, as well as through a casual disregard of twenty years of employment discrimination law.

In *Wards Cove,* the court considered whether a cannery company's maintenance of a segregated work force violated Title VII. The record revealed that Wards Cove hired—season after season—predominantly white workers in its skilled positions and predominantly nonwhite (Alaskan natives) workers in its unskilled positions.[12] Nonwhite cannery workers claimed that the employer's method of selecting employees created an illegally segregated work force; they also attacked the employer's maintenance of racially segregated housing and dining facilities. Though the court below considered both disparate impact and disparate treatment claims, the court "granted certiorari for the purpose of addressing these disputed questions of the proper application of Title VII's disparate-impact theory of liability."[13] A majority of the court decided that the lower court's decision had accorded too much weight to statistics that had demonstrated the segregated nature of the employer's workforce.

Justice Byron White, in whose opinion Chief Justice William Rehnquist and Justices Sandra Day O'Connor, Antonin Scalia, and Anthony Kennedy joined, accused the Ninth Circuit of giving too much weight to statistics and to "racial imbalance."[14] The court rejected the statistical comparison of the predominantly white noncannery workforce to the predominantly nonwhite cannery workforce: "[T]he cannery work force in no way reflected 'the pool of qualified job applicants' or the '*qualified* population in the labor force.' "[15] Justice White said that Title VII requires a " 'proper comparison' between the racial composition of the qualified persons in the labor market and the persons holding at-issue jobs."[16] According to Justice White, the racial disparities in skilled positions were just as likely to be "due to a dearth of qualified nonwhite applicants (for reasons that are not petitioners' fault)."[17] Though this reasoning implied that comparisons between the nonskilled cannery positions (predominantly held by nonwhites) and the skilled noncannery positions (predominantly held by whites) might well have been considered appropriate, Justice White rejected this possibility:

> Racial imbalance in one segment of an employer's work force does not, without more, establish a prima facie case rate impact with respect to the selection of workers for the employer's other positions, even where workers for the different positions may have somewhat fungible skills (as is arguably the case for cannery and unskilled noncannery workers).[18]

Justice White advised lower courts that this kind of statistical evidence may be ignored unless challengers show evidence of barriers to application, deterrence, or that the percentage of nonwhites selected is significantly lower than that of nonwhites applying.

It seems counterintuitive that the plantationlike segregation of *Wards Cove* can be maintained under Title VII, but Justice White said that the alternatives were unacceptable. According to him, strict judicial scrutiny of workplace segregation would drive employers to adopt quotas.

> [A]ny employer who had a segment of his work force that was—for some reason—racially imbalanced, could be hauled into court and forced to engage in the expensive and time-consuming task of defending the "business necessity" of the methods used to select the other members of his work force. The only practicable option for many employers will be to adopt racial quotas, insuring that no portion of his work force deviates in racial composition from other portions thereof. . . .[19]

Thus, Justice White suggested that the court's abhorrence for quotas and its reluctance to impose undue burdens on employers required the court to give Wards Cove's statistics of segregation little weight.

These "racial balance" and "employer burden" considerations also may account for some of the questionable logic used to justify the irrelevance of Wards Cove's statistics. For instance, Justice White attempts to demonstrate the irrelevancy of Wards Cove's decision to hire only nonwhites for cannery work and whites for noncannery work by suggesting that the company, at any moment, could cease to use the segregated union it had chosen to supply its cannery jobs with nonwhite workers. If the company did so, Justice White argues, the factual basis of the nonwhite workers' complaints about predominantly white noncannery jobs would disappear, because the company could eliminate the segregated nature of its cannery workforce overnight.[20]

The court gave no weight to the context in which these disparities occurred, one in which the employer exercised complete control over the workforce availability, for both cannery and noncannery work, by choosing where to recruit potential employees. Rather, the court's logic seems driven by an important subtext: glaring racial segregation is more likely to be the result of the employer's innocence. Even if one suspends judgment and concedes the validity of such a principle, the "plantation" facts in *Wards Cove* suggest that innocence was the least likely explanation.

If Justice White had written no more, *Wards Cove* could have been distinguished as a decision limited to the nuances, vagaries, and complexities of workforce statistical analyses. However, his opinion also addressed the evidentiary burden that employers must meet to justify and retain segregative employment policies. Justice White declared that employment practices which produce workplace segregation need not be "essential or indispensable" to the employer;[21] rather, they merely need serve the "legitimate employment goals" of the employer. Moreover, he also explained that the Ninth Circuit had erred in requiring that Wards Cove bear the burden of persuasion on the business justification for its segregative practices. Justice White cited none of the court's decisions that firmly had placed upon the employer the burden of proving the business necessity of segregative policies;[22] nor did he acknowledge that in the two decades since *Griggs,* courts, employers, and Title VII claimants have understood that upon proof of disparate impact, the burden of persuasion would shift to the employer.[23]

In two casual paragraphs, devoid of any discussion on the rationale for disparate impact theory, Justice White may have rewritten the two most important principles in Title VII law. First, "[t]he Act proscribes not only overt discrimination but also practices that are fair in form, but discriminatory in operation."[24] Second, in order to limit the extent to which employment policies create "built in headwinds"

against protected groups, "Congress has placed on the employer the burden of showing that any given requirement must have a manifest relationship to the employment in question."[25]

Whether *Wards Cove* squarely overturns *Griggs* may be open to debate, but the reasoning in *Wards Cove* seriously undermines the policies of Title VII as articulated in *Griggs.*[26] *Wards Cove* treats workplace segregation as a neutral phenomenon free of negative connotation and illegal implication. While *Griggs* followed *Brown's*[27] aspiration to a society free of racial distinctions, *Wards Cove* rejects such aspirations as meddlesome to employers and tainted with the possibility of racial parity.

After *Wards Cove* Title VII remains, but it seems an empty shell where its content matters most—cases in which employment policies prevent whole groups (not merely individuals) from enjoying employment opportunities. Disparate impact theory allowed the notion of equality to have palpable substantive content, not merely formal content, in a new era in which employers no longer advertise "whites only" but still manage to maintain and perpetuate workplace segregation. Disparate impact theory embodied normative notions about the workplace environment, about the positive aspects of interracial association,[28] about the value of employment choices to individuals, about the potential of historically excluded groups to make greater contributions to American society, and about the risks we all incur when race and economic status are linked too closely. *Wards Cove* rejects all this in a decision formally cast in statistical analyses and evidentiary rules.

More than a century ago, Justice John Harlan warned that the Supreme Court was turning the precious rights so recently acquired by the freedmen into "planted baubles" fit for no practical purpose.[29] Then he spoke of the court's creative arguments that amounted to a refusal to give the same force and content to the Civil War amendments as the court had given the slavery clauses of the Constitution. Justice Harlan saw his court creating a legal structure in which consequences of slavery would linger, and in which racism would flourish. *Wards Cove* suggests the development of a trend similar to that prophetically observed by Harlan. By treating segregative practices as neutral, and by rejecting racial pluralism as a positive development, the court is moving to limit the transformative possibilities of Title VII. If this trend continues, the court will guarantee that the unfinished racial business of the twentieth century will be passed down to the next century.

C. Patterson v. McLean Credit Union

Patterson v. McLean Credit Union also employed formalistic reasoning to strip an equality statute of content and importance. In *Patterson*, the court considered whether Section 1981,[30] a Reconstruction-era civil rights statute, applied to the racial discrimination and harassment a black female bank teller suffered after a credit union hired her.[31] Brenda Patterson's supervisor stared at her, assigned her cleaning duty, made racist remarks in her presence, and refused to train or promote her.[32] In *Patterson*, Justice Kennedy, joined by Chief Justice Rehnquist and Justices White, O'Connor, and Scalia, decided that the racial indignities suffered by Brenda Patterson were not actionable under Section 1981: "[N]one of the conduct which petitioner alleges as part of the racial harassment against her involves either a refusal to make a contract with her or the impairment of her ability to enforce her established contract rights. Rather, the conduct which petitioner labels as actionable racial harassment is postformation conduct by the employer relating to the terms and conditions of continuing employment."[33] The court concluded that the language of Section 1981, "all persons shall have the same right . . . To make and enforce contracts . . . As is enjoyed by white citizens,"[34] does not include the right to be free from racial harassment in the performance of a contract.[35]

Justice Kennedy used structural, semantic, and logical arguments to limit the scope of the statute. The crucial structural argument was his treatment of Section 1981 as embodying two rights (rather than a bundle of rights flowing from the elimination of slave status): the right to "make" contracts and the right to "enforce" contracts. Justice Kennedy discussed these two "rights" separately."[36] He invoked the "plain meaning" talisman to limit the meaning of the word "make" to "formation," "refusal to enter into a contract," or "offer[ing] to make a contract only on discriminatory terms."[37]

> [T]he right to make contracts does not extend, as a matter of either logic or semantics, to conduct by the employer after the contract relation has been established, including breach of the terms of the contract or imposition of discriminatory working conditions. Such postformation conduct does not involve the right to make a contract, but rather implicates the performance of established contract obligations and conditions of continuing employment. . . .[38]

Justice Kennedy also relied upon the "plain meaning" approach to conclude that the words " 'the same right . . . To enforce . . . contracts . . . as is enjoyed by white citizens' "[39] were irrelevant to the actual performance of a contract.[40] In this portion of the opinion, he treated the word "enforce" as if it were self-explanatory, while explaining the word nonetheless. His search for authoritative support stopped with his rather curious citation of Justice White's dissent in *Runyon v. McCrary*,[41] the 1976 decision which held that Section 1981 applied to private contracts.[42]

Justice Kennedy also concluded that a limited interpretation of Section 1981 was required because Title VII exists. There is no attempt to suggest that Congress sought to repeal or limit section 1981 when it enacted, and subsequently amended, Title VII; rather, Justice Kennedy simply suggests that matters involving performance and conditions of employment are "matters more naturally governed . . . By Title VII,"[43] and that allowing these matters to be actionable under Section 1981 would "undermine the detailed and well-crafted procedures for conciliation and resolution of Title VII claims."[44] Thus, while he scrupulously avoided the assertion that Congress intended to restrict Section 1981 when it enacted Title VII, he nevertheless decided that Congress's inclusion of the conciliation processes in Title VII may be read to suggest a preference for those processes—however lengthy—prior to the commencement of litigation.

Justice Kennedy also used federalism arguments to limit the rights protected by Section 1981, asserting that endorsing more than minimal coverage would necessarily require the "federalization" of state contract law and remedies." He argued that because Section 1981 covers all contracts, not just employment contracts, any contract breached because of racial animus would be actionable. In this manner, Justice Kennedy limited the scope of Section 1981. He combined federalism and floodgate arguments; as such, his opinion here is reminiscent of those nineteenth-century arguments that rejected, on federalist grounds, the notion that the national government ought to be primarily responsible for guaranteeing the rights of the freedmen or insuring meaningful equality.

Finally, Justice Kennedy rejected and labeled as "bootstrap" the argument that the racial harassment Brenda Patterson experienced after her contract was made suggested that her contract had not been made in a racially neutral manner: "[T]he question under § 1981 remains whether the employer, *at the time of the formation of the contract,* in fact intentionally refused to enter into a contract with the employee on racially neutral terms. . . . We think it clear that the conduct challenged by petitioner relates not to her employer's refusal to enter into a contract with her, but rather to the conditions of her employment."[45]

One striking aspect of Justice Kennedy's opinion was his failure to address the context in which Section 1981 was passed and the intent and values that the Thirty-ninth Congress embodied in that statute. This legislative history was briefly reviewed by Justice William Brennan, who dissented (with Justices Thurgood Marshall and Harry Blackmun) from the court's decision to exclude claims of racial harassment from Section 1981.[46]

Justice Brennan noted that Section 1981 grew out of Congress's realization that former masters and other employers were hiring blacks and then treating them as if the institution of slavery had never been abolished.[47] He noted that whippings and the meting out of harsher punishments to black employees were among the practices brought to the attention of the Thirty-ninth Congress. In short, Justice Brennan said

that the Thirty-ninth Congress had observed the recreation of slave conditions of employment "*even when the relations between employers and laborers had been fixed by contract.*"[48]

A cursory review of the state legislation passed immediately after emancipation provides some insight into how the dream of emancipation became a nightmare for many former slaves. "The [state] legislation in regard to freedmen seemed to have for its object the perpetuation of the spirit of slavery after its body had been decently buried."[49] A Mississippi law passed in 1865 permitted former masters both to obtain the service of their former slaves who were unemployed and to administer corporal punishment.[50] Another 1865 Mississippi law provided that "Negroes" who left their jobs without good cause before the end of their contracts would forfeit all wages.[51] An 1865 South Carolina statute declared that "[a]ll persons of color who make contracts for service or labor shall be known as servants, and those with whom they contract as masters."[52] These are a few of the laws that attempted to dictate the relationships between white employers and the freedmen after contracts had been "made." In addition to these statutes, historians note that despite the recent guarantee of emancipation, blacks were subjected to violence when they attempted to act as free men in their contractual relations. According to Eric Foner: "Freedmen were assaulted and murdered for attempting to leave plantations, disputing contract settlements, not laboring in the manner desired by their employers, attempting to buy or rent land, and resisting whipping. One black who refused to be bound and whipped . . . was shot dead by his employer, a prominent Texas lawyer."[53]

When the Thirty-ninth Congress acted to protect the rights of blacks, the horrors of the postemancipation period did not allow Congress an escape into the distinctions between formation, enforcement, and performance which Justice Kennedy found so intriguing. The issue in 1866 was how to give to blacks what they had been denied since 1619: the dignity and sanctity of contract without its antithesis, the degradation of slavery. No phrase could have better summed up Congress's intent to break with the pat than the "same rights as whites." Justice Kennedy ignored this history.

It is not surprising, then, that his opinions do not dare to venture into the nineteenth century. Had they done so, he would have had to acknowledge that harassment, intimidation, verbal abuse, subjugation, threats of violence, and violence were the conditions of the slave experience. He would also have had to note that after emancipation, and despite some protective laws, former slave masters continued to act as if the master-slave relation had never been dissolved. History shows that the immediate problem was not reluctance to "contract" in the most limited sense of the word; there was as much work to be done after the end of slavery as before. Rather, what the former slavemasters resisted was treating the freedmen as equal persons entitled to the respect accorded whites throughout the course of the contractual relationship. These masters insisted on using the same violence, intimidation, and harassment they had used with impunity before emancipation. In 1866, if having the same right as whites to make and enforce a contract meant anything, it meant the right to be free from slavery conditions during the entire scope of the contractual relationship.

Justice Kennedy's arguments were based on semantics and logical abstractions devoid of nineteenth- and twentieth-century realities. According to his reasoning, as long as a black is permitted to agree to work, the racism that ensues is not a denial of the right to make and enforce a contract. If the employer fails to warn that he expects sexual favors from his black female employee and then asks for them, there is no relief under Section 1981. If an employer puts the black employees out of the sight of customers, refers to them as "n———" in front of co-workers and customers alike, there is no relief under Section 1981. If an employer inflicts corporal punishment, there is no relief either. None of this, according to Justice Kennedy, concerns the right to make and enforce a contract.

At the turn of the twenty-first century, 120 years after the official end of slavery, how unseemly for America, and how tragic for black

Americans, that civil rights advocates must petition Congress to provide immediate and effective judicial relief in racial harassment cases. But, as the historian Foner suggests, our racial past is prologue: "From the enforcement of the rights of citizens to the stubborn problems of economic and racial justice, the issues central to Reconstruction are as old as the American Republic, and as contemporary as the inequalities that still afflict our society."[54]

III. RIGHTS OF WHITES

ANOTHER theme embodied in the 1989 decisions is concern for the "rights of whites." *City of Richmond v. J. A. Croson Co.*[55] surely embodies this theme. Justice O'Connor's decision vigorously protects whites against both the economic aspirations of black contractors and the political effectiveness of black leaders and constituents. *Wards Cove* also respects and facilitates the "rights of whites" in two ways: by offering legitimacy to segregated job categories, thereby benefiting the historical beneficiaries of segregation; and by granting virtual legal immunity to employers using such categories, by stacking the litigation deck in their favor. However, the case most explicit on the "rights of whites" is *Martin v. Wilks*.

In *Martin v. Wilks*, white firefighters sued the city of Birmingham and alleged that the city was promoting "less qualified" blacks on the basis of race.[56] In 1974 blacks had sued the city of Birmingham, alleging that the city's employment policies excluded them from employment, in violation of Title VII. After a trial concerning applicant-screening tests, the district court found a Title VII violation. A second trial was held on the city's promotional practices; after the evidence was presented but before the judge issued his decision, the parties, the blacks and the city, negotiated and agreed to a consent decree. The court required the parties to provide notice of the proposed consent decree to all interested persons. Thereafter, the court held a fairness hearing at which a group of black employees complained that the proposed relief was inadequate, and a group of white employees complained that race-conscious relief was illegal and inappropriate. The district court explicitly considered whether the race-conscious measures of the consent decree were compatible with previous Supreme Court decisions. After the district court approved the consent decree, the white firefighters, who had presented their objections to the decree, sought intervention as well as an injunction against the enforcement of the consent decree. These requests were denied and Birmingham immediately implemented the consent decree by promoting eight whites and five blacks. Immediately thereafter, a new group of white firefighters sued; these firefighters were aware of the original lawsuit but had not asked to intervene. The district court dismissed this lawsuit "as [an] impermissible collateral attack on the consent decree."[57]

In *Martin v. Wilks,* Chief Justice Rehnquist, in an opinion joined by Justices White, O'Connor, Scalia, and Kennedy, held that the collateral attack was not barred. The court candidly acknowledged that the Third, Fourth, Fifth, Sixth, and Ninth Circuits had barred such collateral attacks. Chief Justice Rehnquist then distinguished *Martin v. Wilks* from one of the court's major cases holding nonparties bound to a consent decree, the *Penn-Central Merger & N & W Inclusion Cases.*[58] *Penn-Central* was distinguishable, according to Chief Justice Rehnquist, because of the "extraordinary nature of the proceedings challenging the merger of giant railroads"; this sort of complex lawsuit should not be compared with "ordinary civil actions in a district court."[59] For these "ordinary civil actions," Rule 19 of the Federal Rules of Civil Procedure requires joinder; hence, the collateral attack was not barred.

Chief Justice Rehnquist dismissed the argument that permitting unlimited collateral attacks would be burdensome to civil rights litigation. He acknowledged that the court had a choice between either requiring those who might be affected by a judgment to intervene or requiring plaintiffs to join all parties who might be affected. He simply chose to burden the plaintiffs.

Chief Justice Rehnquist also rejected the argument that permitting these collateral attacks would undermine the "congressional policy fa-

voring voluntary settlement of employment discrimination claims."[60] He ordered the remand of *Martin v. Wilks* for trial on the legality of the consent decree.

The remainder of the court dissented. Justices Marshall, Brennan, and Blackmun joined an opinion written by Justice Stevens.[61] Justice Stevens saw a distinction between legal rights—such as contractual rights, which may not be impaired unless the individuals possessing such rights are parties to a consent decree—and conditions of employment, such as promotions for blacks, which "as a practical matter, may have a serious effect on their opportunities for employment or promotion." Justice Stevens conceded that even those in the latter category might attack a consent decree on limited grounds, but that the circumstances would have to be extraordinary.[62] "Any other conclusion would subject large employers who seek to comply with the law by remedying past discrimination to a never-ending stream of litigation and potential liability. It is unfathomable that either Title VII or the Equal Protection Clause demands such a counter-productive result."[63]

Justice Stevens reminded the majority that the whites who collaterally attack today were and are the "beneficiaries" of past discrimination against blacks. Any remedy that seeks to right these wrongs

> will necessarily have an adverse impact on whites, who must now share their job and promotion opportunities with blacks. Just as white employees in the past were innocent beneficiaries of illegal discriminatory practices, so is it inevitable that some of the same white employees will be innocent victims who must share some of the burdens resulting from the redress of the past wrongs.[64]

While the "rights of whites" dimension of *Martin v. Wilks* is glaring, the same sentiments are present in *Wards Cove* in a less obvious fashion. In *Wards Cove,* the formal question involved the burden of proof applicable in Title VII disparate impact cases, yet the court also considered the interests of whites—in maintaining a system that prefers them—as submerged in the interest of the employer. The employer was treated not as having an interest in the maintenance of the racial status quo but, rather, as having an interest in the preservation of "management prerogatives."[65] In *Martin v. Wilks*, the interests are posed much more directly: May white employees, unhappy with the effect of a consent decree on their prerogatives, attack it, despite the Birmingham Fire Department's historical protection of their group's interests? May they intervene, not to protect contractually acquired rights such as seniority or benefits, but to protect their interest in promotions pursuant to a test that perpetuates a racial hierarchy? *Martin v. Wilks* is also interesting and important because it suggests that the interests of white employees no longer converge with those of employers. *Martin v. Wilks* ignores the historical protection that white employers have accorded white employees, but it implicitly acknowledges the reality that public employers now have new obligations and more diverse constituencies to protect.

The idea of the "rights of whites" is not a new one in American race law. Certainly we can trace it to the unloading of slaves at Annapolis and Jamestown before the eighteenth century, to the slavery compromises of 1789, and to its verbal apogee in *Dred Scott*.[66] The idea was more covert after the passage of the Civil War amendments, though it is ironic that shortly after the Supreme Court's grand pronouncements about the purpose of these amendments in the *Slaughterhouse Cases*,[67] Justice Bradley bitterly and candidly suggested that the time had come for blacks to "cease to be a special favorite of the laws."[68] After *Plessy*[69] sanctioned state racism, the court did not need to speak openly of "white rights"; rather, the discussion centered on "the reasonableness of distinctions" and "customs and usages of the community,"[70] and even on the "benefits" to blacks of disadvantageous treatment.[71] A half century later, *Brown II*'s[72] "all deliberate speed" language arguably invited lower courts to covertly consider the interests of whites in the maintenance of the status quo.

By the late sixties, the courts were beginning to consider what sort of Title VII remedies would be appropriate to remedy the blatant job segregation that still persisted in many companies. These job segregation cases provide an interesting insight into the process by which the rights of whites were incorporated into modern equality law. In cases in which the relationship of white jobs and income to overtly racist policies could not be denied, the courts sought to reconcile the idea of complete relief for blacks against the vested interest of white employees in maintaining the status quo. The competing remedial theories were evaluated openly in terms of their impact on whites and compromises were struck that, assuming economic growth, would permit an eventual change in the status quo without divesting whites of the jobs they held in part because of historic racial discrimination against blacks.

However, it was *DeFunis v. Odegaard*,[73] in which a white student asserted a Fourteenth Amendment challenge to a University of Washington Law School program to admit blacks, that ushered in a new era of legal rhetoric about white rights. Though the *DeFunis* case was dismissed as moot, his cause was taken up by *Bakke*,[74] *Fullilove*,[75] *Croson*, and others. The objective—the invocation of strict legal scrutiny for challenges made by white males against programs designed to provide new opportunity for blacks—was finally achieved in *Croson*.

In *Wards Cove, Croson*, and *Wilks*, the rights of whites find recognition and protection. In each case, the source of protection is different, but the result is the same. It is troubling that none of these cases acknowledges that the interests asserted may be characterized as an interest in the continued racial hegemony of whites, in the subordination of blacks. To be sure, our principles of due process do not permit contractual rights, property rights, or seniority rights to be impaired without notice and opportunity to be heard. But it is quite different—or at least it should be quite different in the post-*Brown* era—to come to the courts with a simple request to maintain the racial status quo. In light of our history, it is not surprising that such claims have been made; it is, however, troubling that the claims have been judicially validated.

IV. CONCLUSION

THE hope that the ideal of racial equality might be made legitimate through law, that racial equality might be achieved through law, has sustained many members of the post-

Brown generation. Charles Hamilton Houston, one of the greatest constitutional lawyers and an architect of twentieth-century constitutional equality, was quite realistic about the possibility of achieving equality through law. He viewed his legal assault on segregation not as an end in itself but, rather, as an opportunity to determine the limits of the system's tolerance for freedom and equality. In late 1949, a few months before his death, Houston spoke these prescient words: "I regard what I am doing and my work as a lawyer not as an end in itself, but simply as the means of a technician probing in the courts, which are products of the existing system, how far the existing system will permit the exercise of freedom before it clamps down."[76]

Another important black American was even more skeptical than Houston about the possibilities of achieving equality through law. In 1934, Ralph Bunche[77] outlined a variety of tactics blacks might employ to improve their status. Bunche stated that the confidence blacks had in the possibilities of civil libertarianism as a basis of struggle for equality was misplaced. The utility of the Thirteenth, Fourteenth, and Fifteenth Amendments as a basis for black equality was limited:

> [T]he Constitution is a very flexible instrument and that, in the nature of things, it cannot be anything more than the controlling elements of the American society wish it to be. . . . And, what [the courts and legislatures] wish it to be can never be more than what American public opinion wishes it to be. . . . It follows, therefore, that the policy of civil libertarianism is circumscribed by the dominant mores of the society. Its success, in the final analysis, must depend upon its ability to create a sympathetic response to its appeals among the influential elements in the controlling population.[78]

Dr. Bunche wrote in 1934, but his warning about the limits of the court are still important. It is no accident that the 1989 decisions reflect a selective activism and restraint, with results usually detrimental to blacks. This result is not surprising: the justices appointed to the court by President Reagan have joined to form a majority that opposes a strong role for the courts in identifying and remedying discrimination. A new legal structure is being erected. It comes complete with reassuring caveats, techni-

cal analyses, and evidentiary nuances. It surrounds, and it legitimizes the racial status quo. In the long run, the new structure may be just as effective as the rationalizations of the *Plessy* era, with one important distinction: the new regime is cloaked in post-*Brown* legitimacy and sustains *Brown*'s myth of a new racial order. Racism is now plausibly deniable.

In a short *Wards Cove* dissent, Justice Blackmun lamented the judicial turn of events represented by *Wards Cove* and other recent decisions. "One wonders whether the majority still believes that race discrimination—or, more accurately, race discrimination against non-whites—is a problem in our society, or even remembers that it ever was."[79]

It is not too early to ask the questions that Houston and Bunche raised. While the efforts that have led to the demise of overt legal racism must be applauded, the creation of a new legal order that legitimates the maintenance of racial subordination and domination must be condemned. In the short run, there may be no choice but to continue to probe "the existing system" for the possibility that it may yield racial justice. In the long run, though, it may be necessary to ask whether the confinement of the movement for racial equality to civil rights litigation exposes the movement to great risk. It is not only possible that if so confined, meaningful equality may not be achieved, but also that the very legitimacy of alternate avenues to racial justice may be compromised. It is perhaps too early to concede the limits of a legal strategy in the twenty-first century. However, given the recent Supreme Court trends, those who seek racial justice must remain prepared to expose more dramatically, as did the students of Greensboro, the manner in which the existing legal framework may immorally and unduly limit and dampen the aspiration of African-Americans for universal freedom.[80]

NOTES

1. R. Bunche, "A Critical Analysis of the Tactics and Programs of Minority Groups," in *Black Protest Thought in the Twentieth Century*, 183, 197 (2d ed. 1971).

2. *Public Employees Retirement Sys. v. Betts*, 109 S. Ct. 2854 (1989); *Independent Federation of Flight Attendants v.*

Zipes, 109 S. Ct. 2732 (1989); *Jett v. Dallas Independent School Dist.,* 109 S. Ct. 2702 (1989); *Patterson v. McLean Credit Union,* 109 S. Ct. 2363 (1989); *Lorance v. AT&T Technologies,* 109 S. Ct. 2261 (1989); *Martin v. Wilks,* 109 S. Ct. 2180 (1989); *Wards Cove Packing Co. v. Atonio,* 109 S. Ct. 2115 (1989).

3. *Wilks,* 109 S. Ct. 2180.

4. 401 U.S. 424 (1971).

5. *Wards Cove,* 109 S. Ct. 2115.

6. *Patterson v. McLean Credit Union,* 109 S. Ct. 2363 (1989).

7. *City of Richmond v. J. A. Croson Co.,* 109 S. Ct. 706, to be published at 488 U.S. 469 (1989).

8. *Brown v. Board of Education.,* 347 U.S. 483 (1954).

9. *Dred Scott v. Sandford,* 60 U.S. (19 How.) 393 (1857).

10. 109 S. Ct. 2115 (1989).

11. 109 S. Ct. 2363 (1989).

12. *Wards Cove,* 109 S. Ct. at 2120.

13. *Id.* at 2121 (citation omitted).

14. *Id.* at 2123.

15. *Id.* at 2122 (emphasis in original).

16. *Id.* at 2121.

17. *Id.* at 2122.

18. *Id.*

19. *Id.* at 2122.

20. *Id.* at 2123.

21. *Id.* at 2126.

22. In his dissent, Justice Stevens cited six Supreme Court cases in which the court allocated to the employer the burden of persuasion on the issue of business necessity; see *id.* at 2130 n. 14 (Stevens, J., dissenting).

23. Justice Stevens's dissent reviewed the Supreme Court and many circuit court decisions affected by Justice White's opinion; *id.* at 2132–33. Justice Stevens's opinion was joined by Justices Brennan, Marshall, and Blackmun.

24. *Griggs v. Duke Power,* 401 U.S. 424, 431 (1971).

25. *Id.* at 432.

26. *Wards Cove,* 109 S. Ct. at 2132.

27. *Brown v. Board of Education,* 347 U.S. 483 (1954).

28. Greene, "Title VII Class Actions: Standing at Its Edge," 58 *U. Det J. Urb. L.,* 645, 665–66 (1981).

29. *The Civil Rights Cases,* 109 U.S. 3, 48 (1883) (Harlan, J., dissenting).

30. 42 U.S.C. §1981 (1982).

31. *Patterson,* 109 S. § Ct. at 2374.

32. *Id.* at 2373. Justice Kennedy accepted as true Brenda Patterson's allegations of racial harassment that her supervisor "periodically stared at her for several minutes at a time; that he gave her too many tasks, causing her to complain that she was under too much pressure; that among the tasks given her were sweeping and dusting, jobs not given to white employees. On one occasion [her supervisor] told [her] that blacks are known to work slower than whites"; *id.* (citation omitted).

33. *Id.* at 2374.

34. *Id.* at 2373 (quoting 42 U.S.C. § 1981).

35. *Id.*

36. *Id.* at 2372.

37. *Id.*

38. *Id.* at 2373.

39. *Id.* (quoting 42 U.S.C. § 1981).

40. *Id.*

41. 427 U.S. 160 (1976).

42. *Patterson,* 109 S. Ct. at 2373. Justice White argued in *Runyon* that whites never had the right to make a contract with an unwilling person. Therefore, § 1981 could not prohibit racially motivated refusals to contract; *Runyon,* 427 U.S. at 193–95 (White, J., dissenting). In addition, Justice White said that § 1981 had been passed pursuant to the Fourteenth Amendment and therefore could not have addressed private racially discriminatory conduct; *id.* at 195–211. It is unclear what Justice Kennedy intended to communicate by citing Justice White. Perhaps Justice Kennedy meant to suggest his general agreement with Justice White's previously expressed skepticism about the scope of § 1981.

43. *Id.*

44. *Id.* at 2374.

45. *Id.* at 2376–77 (emphasis in original).

46. *Id.* at 2388 (Brennan, J., concurring in part and dissenting in part).

47. *Id.*

48. *Id.* (emphasis in original).

49. A. Guernsey and H. Alden, *Harpers Pictorial History of the Civil War,* 804 (1866).

50. 1866 Miss. Laws 862, reprinted in A. Guernsey and H. Alden, *supra* note 49, at 804 n. 2.

51. *Id.* at 804 n. 2.

52. 1865 S. C. Acts 251, reprinted in A. Guernsey and H. Alden, eds., *supranote 49,* at 804 n. 2..

53. E. Foner, *Reconstruction: America's Unfinished Revolution, 1863–1877,* at 121 (1988).

54. *Id.* at xxvii.

55. 109 S. Ct. 706 (to be published at 488 U.S. 469 (1989)).

56. *Patterson,* 109 S. Ct. at 2183.

57. *Id.* at 2183–84.

58. 389 U.S. 486 (1968).

59. *Martin v. Wilks,* 109 S. Ct. at 2186–87.

60. *Id.* at 2187–88.

61. *Id.* (Stevens, J., dissenting).

62. *Id.* at 2195. Among the examples cited by Justice Stevens is *Korematsu v. United States,* 584 F. Supp. 1406 (N.D. Cal. 1984), in which the district court granted a writ of *coram nobis* vacating a conviction based on government concealment of critical contradictory evidence in *Korematsu v. United States,* 323 U.S. 214 (1944).

63. *Martin v. Wilks,* 109 S. Ct. at 2200 (Stevens, J., dissenting).

64. *Id.* (footnote omitted).

65. See *supra* text accompanying notes 14–28.

66. *Dred Scott v. Sandford,* 60 U.S. (19 How.) 393 (1857).

67. 83 U.S. (16 Wall.) 36 (1873).

68. *The Civil Rights Cases,* 109 U.S. 3 (1883).

69. *Plessy v. Ferguson,* 163 U.S. 537 (1896).

70. *Id.* at 550–51.

71. *Cumming v. County Board of Education,* 175 U.S. 528, 544 (1899).

72. *Brown v. Board of Education,* 349 U.S. 294 (1955).

73. 416 U.S. 312 (1974).

74. *Regents of the University of California v. Bakke,* 438 U.S. 265 (1978) (Bakke challenged the medical school's special admissions program which favored certain minority applicants).

75. *Fullilove v. Klutznick,* 448 U.S. 448 (1980) (challenge made against a federal program requiring a minimum amount of the financial assistance provided for building public facilities be awarded to minority businesses).

76. G. McNeil, *Groundwork* at xvii (1983) at 208 (quoting statement of Charles H. Houston (circa Dec. 1949)).

77. Ralph Bunche served as chairman of the Department of Political Science at Howard University in the thirties and eventually served as the under secretary of the United Nations; Bunche, *supra* note 1, at 183.

78. *Id.* at 195.

79. *Wards Cove Packing Co. v. Atonio,* 109 S. Ct. 2115, 2136 (1989) (Blackmun, J., dissenting).

❦

RACIAL REALISM
Derrick A. Bell, Jr.

THE struggle by black people to obtain freedom, justice, and dignity is as old as this nation. At times, great and inspiring leaders rose out of desperate situations to give confidence and feelings of empowerment to the black community. Most of these leaders urged their people to strive for racial equality. They were firmly wedded to the idea that the courts and judiciary were the vehicle to better the social position of blacks. In spite of dramatic civil rights movements and periodic victories in the legislatures, black Americans by no means are equal to whites. Racial equality is, in fact, not a realistic goal. By constantly aiming for a status that is unobtainable in a perilously racist America, black Americans face frustration and despair. Over time, our persistent quest for integration has hardened into self-defeating rigidity.

Black people need reform of our civil rights strategies as badly as those in the law needed a new way to consider American jurisprudence prior to the advent of the Legal Realists.[1] By viewing the law—and, by extension, the courts—as instruments for preserving the status quo and only periodically and unpredictably serving as a refuge of oppressed people, blacks can refine the work of the Realists. Rather than challenging the entire jurisprudential system, as the Realists did, blacks' focus must be much narrower—a challenge to the principle of racial equality. This new movement is appropriately called "Racial Realism," and it is a legal and social mechanism on which blacks can rely to have their voice and outrage heard.

Reliance on rigid application of the law is no less damaging or ineffectual simply because it is done for the sake of ending discriminatory racial practices. Indeed, Racial Realism is to race relations what "Legal Realism" is to jurisprudential thought. The Legal Realists were a group of scholars in the early part of the twentieth century who challenged the classical structure of law as a formal group of common law rules that, if properly applied to any given situation, lead to a right—and therefore just—result.[2]

The Realists comprised a younger generation of scholars—average age forty-two[3]—who were willing to challenge what they viewed as the rigid ways of the past. More than their classical counterparts, they had been influenced by the rapid spread of the scientific outlook and the growth of social sciences. Such influence predisposed them to accept a critical and empirical attitude toward the law,[4] in contrast to the formalists who insisted that law was logically self-evident, objective, a priori valid, and internally consistent. The great majority of the movement's pioneers had practical experience, which strengthened their awareness of the changing and subjective elements in the legal system. This awareness flew in the face of the Langdellian conception of law as unchanging truth and an autonomous system of rules.[5]

The Realists took their cue from Oliver Wendell Holmes, who staged a fifty-year battle against legalistic formalism. According to Holmes's scientific and relativistic lines of attack, judges settled cases not by deductive reasoning, but rather by reliance on value-laden, personal beliefs. To Holmes, such judges engineered socially desirable policies based on these beliefs, which, like all moral values, were wholly relative and determined by one's particular environment.[6] Realist notions also were grounded in the views of the Progressives during the 1890s. Concerned with social welfare legislation and administrative regulation, the Progressives criticized the conceptualization of property rights being expounded by the United States Supreme Court.[7] Creating a remedy based upon the finding of a property right was the court's way of subtly imposing personal and moral beliefs; abstraction was the method it used to accomplish its purpose. The Realists stressed the *function* of law, however, rather than the *abstract conceptualization* of it.[8]

The Realists also had a profound impact by demonstrating the circularity of defining rights as "objective," which definition depended, in large part, on a distinction between formalistically bounded spheres between public and private.[9] Classical judges justified decisions by appealing to these spheres. For example, an opinion would justify finding a defendant liable because she had invaded the (private) property rights of the plaintiff; but such a justification, the Realists pointed out, was inevitably circular because there would be such a private property right if and only if the court found for the plaintiff or declared the statute unconstitutional. The cited reasons for decisions were only results, and as such served to obscure the extent to which the state's enforcement power through the courts lay behind private property and other rights claims.

Closely linked with the Realists' attack on the logic of rights theory was their attack on the logic of precedent. No two cases, the Realists pointed out, are ever exactly alike. Hence, a procedural rule from a former case cannot simply be applied to a new case with a multitude of facts that vary from the former case. Rather, the judge must choose whether or not the ruling in the earlier case should be extended to include the new case. Such a choice basically is about the relevancy of facts, and decisions about relevancy are never logically compelled. Decisions merely are subjective judgments made to reach a particular result. Decisions about the relevance of distinguishing facts are value-laden and dependent upon a judge's own experiences.[10]

The imperatives of this Realist attack were at least two. First, to clear the air of "beguiling but misleading conceptual categories"[11] so that thought could be redirected toward facts (rather than nonexistent spheres of classism) and ethics. If social decision-making was inevitably moral choice, policymakers needed some ethical basis upon which to make their choices.[12] And second, the Realists' critique suggested that the whole liberal worldview of private rights and public sovereignty mediated by the rule of law needed to be exploded. The Realists argued that a worldview premised upon the public and private spheres is an attractive mirage that masks the reality of economic and political power.[13] This two-pronged attack had profoundly threatening consequences: it carried with it the potential collapse of legal liberalism.[14] Realism, in short, changed the face of American jurisprudence by exposing the result-oriented, value-laden nature of legal decision-making. Many divergent philosophies emerged to combat, not a little defensively, the attack on law as instrumental, not self-evidently logical, and "made" by judges, rather than simply derived from transcendent or ultimate principles.[15]

As every civil rights lawyer has reason to know—despite law school indoctrination and belief in the "rule of law"—abstract principles lead to legal results that harm blacks and perpetuate their inferior status. Racism provides a basis for a judge to select one available premise rather than another when incompatible claims arise. A paradigm example presents itself in the case of *Regents of the University of California v. Bakke*.[16] Relying heavily on the formalistic language of the Fourteenth Amendment and utterly ignoring social questions about which race in fact has power and advantages and which race has been denied entry for centuries into academia,[17] the court held that an affirmative action policy may not unseat white candidates on the basis of their race. By introducing an artificial and inappropriate parity in its reasoning, the court effectively made a choice to ignore historical patterns, to ignore contemporary statistics, and to ignore flexible reasoning. Following a Realist approach, the court would have observed the social landscape and noticed the skewed representation of minority medical school students. It would have reflected on the possible reasons for these demographics, including inadequate public school systems in urban ghettos, lack of minority professionals to serve as role models, and the use of standardized tests evaluated according to "white" criteria. Taking these factors into consideration, the court very well may have decided *Bakke* differently.[18]

Bakke serves as an example of how formalists can use abstract concepts, such as equality, to mask policy choices and value judgments. Abstraction, in the place of flexible reasoning, removes a heavy burden from a judge's task; at the same time, her opinion appears to render the "right" result. Thus, cases such as *Bakke* should inspire many civil rights lawyers to reexamine the potential of equality jurisprudence to improve the lives of black Americans.

The protection of whites' race-based privilege, so evident in the *Bakke* decision, has become a common theme in civil rights decisions, particularly in many of those decided by an increasingly conservative Supreme Court. The addition of Judge Clarence Thomas to that court, as the replacement for Justice Thurgood Marshall, is likely to add deep insult to the continuing injury inflicted on civil rights advocates. The cut is particularly unkind because the choice of a black like Clarence Thomas replicates the slave masters' practice of elevating to overseer and other positions of quasi-power those slaves willing to mimic the masters' views, carry out orders, and by their presence provide a perverse legitimacy to the oppression they aided and approved.

For liberals in general, and black people in particular, the appointment of Thomas to the Supreme Court, his confirmation hearings, and the nation's reaction to Professor Anita Hill's sexual harrassment charges, all provide most ominous evidence that we are in a period of racial rejection, a time when many whites can block out their own justified fears about the future through increasingly blatant forms of discrimination against blacks.[19]

The decline of black people is marked by a precipitous collapse in our economic status and the frustration of our political hopes. An ultimate rebuff and symbol of our powerlessness is President Bush's elevation of one of us who is willing to denigrate and disparage all who look like him to gain personal favor, position, and prestige.[20] Here, historical parallels contain a fearful symmetry. In 1895, Booker T. Washington, another black man who had risen from the bottom—in Washington's case, that bottom was slavery itself—gained instant and lasting status in white America by declaring, in his now-famous Atlanta Compromise speech, that black people should eschew racial equality and seek to gain acceptance in the society by becoming useful through trades and work skills developed through hard work, persistence, and sacrifice.

Whites welcomed Washington's conciliatory, nonconfrontational policy and deemed it a sufficient self-acceptance for the society's involuntary subordination of blacks in every area of life.

The historian, Louis R. Harlan, informs us that Booker T. Washington, in his own way, was a double agent.[21] While preaching black humility to whites, Washington privately fought lynching, disenfranchisement, peonage, educational discrimination, and segregation. It is not even a close question, however, that no amount of private support for black rights could undo the damage of Washington's public pronouncements.

The Booker T. Washington speech marked a watershed in race relations at the close of the nineteenth century. There is more than ample reason to believe the Thomas appointment and confirmation proceedings that followed will mark and mar the status of blacks well into the twenty-first century. Certainly, the high and low drama in those hearings contained enough racial symbols to challenge analysts for years to come.[22]

In the first phase of the confirmation hearings, Justice Thomas's testimony provided a definitive illustration of waffling, obfuscation, and disingenuousness. Thomas, and those who prepared him for his appearance, assumed— accurately as it turned out—that his seat on the nation's most prestigious court could be secured by ignoring every politically controversial statement that he had ever said or written, while recalling precisely everything his grandfather did for him.

The hearings also provided further proof that even the most accomplished blacks can be ignored with impunity when they seek to challenge an exercise of white, conservative power. Thus, the opposition to the Thomas appointment by some of the most prestigious black legal academics—including Charles Lawrence of Stanford; Drew Days of Yale; Christopher Edley of Harvard; Dean Haywood Burns of City University of New York at Queens; and Patricia King of Georgetown—easily was neutralized by a collection of Thomas's childhood friends, former staff members, and well-meaning but confused blacks who, unaware of and unconcerned about his record or the antiblack stance of the conservative whites supporting him, nevertheless "hoped for the best" as they supported Thomas because he was a "brother."

The second phase of the confirmation hearings provided further proof that black people, notwithstanding their growing numbers in the middle class, are at risk of remaining in a subordinate status. I consider the nationally televised Senate proceedings an American morality play, conducted under circumstances that forced both Judge Clarence Thomas and Professor Anita Hill to disparage each other's character regarding matters of deeply personal conduct. The battle, fought in front of the upper echelons of the white power structure, was unwinnable from the start and desired by neither combatant. Its proximate causes were the president's hypocrisy in using race to shield his effort to stack the Supreme Court with conservative judges, and the Senate's insensitivity to women's growing awareness and resentment of sexual harassment in the workplace.

The hearings were a reminder of how frequently in American history blacks became the involuntary pawns in defining and resolving society's serious social issues. Recall that blacks' rights were sacrificed when the Framers built slavery into the Constitution in 1787 to enable the forming of a new and stronger government. Their rights were sacrificed again in the Hayes-Tilden Compromise of 1877 to avoid another civil war.[23]

Clarence Thomas, a black man who overcame humble beginnings and gained professional eminence by embracing the self-help ideology of those who have aided his climb, became a symbol of the crumbling of the judicial nomination process, in which conservativism is more important than professional eminence. Anita Hill, a silenced victim of alleged unwanted sexual overtures of a former supervisor and mentor, became the unwilling agent through which opponents of the nominee hoped to block President Bush's plan to stack the court with his followers.[24]

Rather than face repetition of the embarrassing and trauma-filled confirmation process, the administration and the Senate likely will try to avoid another grueling battle if a Supreme Court seat becomes vacant in the future. And as a result of the hearings' focus on the meaning of sexual harassment in the workplace, many men, particularly at the professional level, will speak with considerable thought about matters of sexuality to female colleagues and subordinates. Both reforms are much-needed. As in the Reconstruction era, blacks will serve as the involuntary sacrifices whose victimization helps to point white society and their country in the right direction.

Beyond symbolism though, the message of the Thomas appointment virtually demands that equality advocates reconsider their racial goals. This is not, as some may think, an overreaction to a temporary setback in the long "march to freedom" that blacks have been making since far before the Emancipation Proclamation. Rather, the event is both a reminder and a warning of the vulnerability of black rights and of the willingness of powerful whites to sacrifice and subvert these rights in furtherance of political or economic ends. I speak here not of some new prophetic revelation. Rather, these are frequently stated yet seldom acknowledged truths that we continue to ignore at our peril.

What was it about our reliance on racial remedies that may have prevented us from recognizing that abstract legal rights, such as equality, could do little more than bring about the cessation of one form of discriminatory conduct, which soon appeared in a more subtle though no less discriminatory form? I predict that this examination will require us to redefine goals of racial equality and opportunity to which blacks have adhered with far more simple faith than hardheaded reflection.

I would urge that we begin this review with a statement that many will wish to deny, but none can refute. It is this: Black people will never gain full equality in this country. Even those herculean efforts we hail as successful will produce no more than temporary "peaks of progress," short-lived victories that slide into irrelevance as racial patterns adapt in ways that maintain white dominance. This is a hard-to-accept fact that all history verifies. We must acknowledge it and move on to adopt policies based on what I call "Racial Realism." This mind-set or philosophy requires us to acknowledge the permanence of our subordinate status. That acknowledgement enables us to avoid despair and frees us to imagine and implement

racial strategies that can bring fulfillment and even triumph.

Legal precedents we thought permanent have been overturned, distinguished, or simply ignored. All too many of the black people we sought to lift through law from a subordinate status to equal opportunity are more deeply mired in poverty and despair than they were during the "separate but equal" era.

Despite our successful effort to strip the law's endorsement from the hated Jim Crow signs, contemporary color barriers are less visible but no less real or less oppressive. Today, one can travel for thousands of miles across this country and never come across a public facility designated for "colored" or "white." Indeed, the very absence of visible signs of discrimination creates an atmosphere of racial neutrality which encourages whites to believe that racism is a thing of the past.

Today, blacks experiencing rejection for a job, a home, a promotion anguish over whether race or individual failing prompted their exclusion. Either conclusion breeds frustration and eventually despair. We call ourselves "African Americans," but despite centuries of struggle, none of us—no matter our prestige or position—is more than a few steps away from a racially motivated exclusion, restriction, or affront.

There is little reason to be shocked at my prediction that blacks will not be accepted as equals, a status that has eluded us as a group for more than three hundred years. The current condition of most blacks provides support for this position.[25] It is surely possible to use statistics to distort, and I do wish for revelations showing that any of the dreadful data illustrating the plight of so many black people is false or misleading. Yet there is little effort to discredit the shocking disparities contained in these reports. Even so, the reports have little effect on policymakers or the society in general.

Statistics and studies reflect racial conditions that transformed the "we have a dream" mentality of the sixties into the trial by racial ordeal so many blacks are suffering in the nineties. The adverse psychological effects of nonexistent opportunity are worse than the economic and social loss. As the writer Maya Angelou, put it recently: "In these bloody days and frightful nights when an urban warrior can find no face more despicable than his own, no ammunition more deadly than self-hate and no target more deserving of his true aim than his brother, we must wonder how we came so late and lonely to this place."[26]

As a veteran of a civil rights era that is now over, I regret the need to explain what went wrong. Clearly, we need to examine what it was about our reliance on racial remedies that may have prevented us from recognizing that these legal rights could do little more than bring about the cessation of one form of discriminatory conduct, which soon appeared in a more subtle though no less discriminatory form. The question is whether this examination requires us to redefine goals of racial equality and opportunity to which blacks have adhered for more than a century. The answer, must be a resounding yes.

Traditional civil rights law is highly structured and founded on the belief that the Constitution was intended—at least after the Civil War amendments—to guarantee equal rights to blacks. The belief in eventual racial justice, and the litigation and legislation based on that belief, was always dependent on the ability of believers to remain faithful to their creed of racial equality while rejecting the contrary message of discrimination that survived their best efforts to control or eliminate it.

Despite the Realist challenge that demolished its premises, the basic formalist model of law survives, although in bankrupt form. *Bakke*, as well as numerous other decisions that thwart the use of affirmative action and set-aside programs, illustrates that notions of racial equality fit conveniently into the formalist model of jurisprudence. Thus, a judge may advocate the importance of racial equality while arriving at a decision detrimental to black Americans. In fact, racial equality can be used to keep blacks out of institutions of higher education, such as the one at issue in *Bakke*. By reasoning that race-conscious policies derogate the meaning if racial equality, a judge can manipulate the law and arrive at an outcome based upon her

worldview, to the detriment of blacks seeking enrollment.

The message the formalist model conveys is that existing power relations in the real world are by definition legitimate and must go unchallenged.[27] Equality theory also necessitates such a result. Nearly every critique the Realists launched at the formalists can be hurled at advocates of liberal civil rights theory. Precedent, rights theory, and objectivity merely are formal rules that serve a covert purpose; even in the context of equality theory, they will never vindicate the legal rights of black Americans.

Outside of the formalistic logic in racial equality cases, history should also trigger civil rights advocates to question the efficacy of equality theory. After all, it is an undeniable fact that the Constitution's Framers initially opted to protect property, including enslaved Africans in that category, through the Fifth Amendment. Those committed to racial equality also had to overlook the political motivations for the Civil War amendments—self-interested motivations almost guaranteeing that when political needs changed, the protection provided the former slaves would not be enforced.[28] Analogize this situation with that presented in *Bakke:* arguably the court ruled as it did because of the anti-affirmative action rhetoric sweeping the political landscape. In conformation with past practice, protection of black rights is now predictably episodic. For these reasons, both the historic pattern and its contemporary replication require review and replacement of the now-defunct, racial equality ideology.

Racism translates into a societal vulnerability of black people that few politicians—including our last two presidents—seem able to resist. And why not? The practice of using blacks as scapegoats for failed economic or political policies works every time. The effectiveness of this "racial bonding" by whites requires that blacks seek a new and more realistic goal for our civil rights activism. It is time we concede that a commitment to racial equality merely perpetuates our disempowerment. Rather, we need a mechanism to make life bearable in a society where blacks are a permanent, subordinate class.[29] Our empowerment lies in recognizing that Racial Realism may open the gateway to attaining a more meaningful status.

Some blacks already understand and act on the underlying rationale of Racial Realism. Unhappily, most black spokespersons and civil rights organizations remain committed to the ideology of racial equality. Acceptance of the Racial Realism concept would enable them to understand and respond to recurring aspects of our subordinate status. It would free them to think and plan within a context of reality rather than idealism. The reality is that blacks still suffer disproportionately higher rates of poverty, joblessness, and insufficient health care than other ethnic populations in the United States.[30] The ideal is that law, through racial equality, can lift them out of this trap. I suggest we abandon this ideal and move on to a fresh, realistic approach.

Casting off the burden of equality ideology will lift the sights, providing a bird's-eye view of situations that are distorted by race. From this broadened perspective on events and problems, we can better appreciate and cope with racial subordination.

While implementing Racial Realism we must simultaneously acknowledge that our actions are not likely to lead to transcendent change and, despite our best efforts, may be of more help to the system we despise than to the victims of that system we are trying to help. Nevertheless, our realization, and the dedication based on that realization, can lead to policy positions and campaigns that are less likely to worsen conditions for those we are trying to help and more likely to remind those in power that there are imaginative, unabashed risk-takers who refuse to be trammeled upon. Yet confrontation with our oppressors is not our sole reason for engaging in Racial Realism. Continued struggle can bring about unexpected benefits and gains that in themselves justify continued endeavor. The fight itself has meaning and should give us hope for the future.

I am convinced that there is something real out there in America for black people. It is not, however, the romantic love of integration; it is surely not the long-sought goal of equality under law, though we must maintain the struggle against racism, else the erosion of black rights will become even worse than it is now. The Racial Realism that we must seek is simply a hard-eyed view of racism as it is and our subordinate role in it. We must realize, as our slave forebears did, that the struggle for freedom is, at bottom, a manifestation of our humanity which survives and grows stronger through resistance to oppression, even if that oppression is never overcome.

A final remembrance may help make my point. The year was 1964. It was a quiet, heat-hushed evening in Harmony, a small black community near the Mississippi Delta. Some Harmony residents, in the face of increasing white hostility, were organizing to ensure implementation of a court order mandating desegregation of their schools the next September. Walking with Mrs. Biona MacDonald, one of the organizers, up a dusty, unpaved road toward her modest home, I asked where she found the courage to continue working for civil rights in the face of intimidation that included her son losing his job in town, the local bank trying to foreclose on her mortgage, and shots fired through her living room window. "Derrick," she said slowly, seriously, "I am an old woman. I lives to harass white folks."

Mrs. MacDonald did not say she risked everything because she hoped or expected to win out over the whites who, as she well knew, held all the economic and political power, and the guns as well. Rather, she recognized that—powerless as she was—she had and intended to use courage and determination as weapons "to harass white folks." Her fight, in itself, gave her strength and empowerment in a society that relentlessly attempted to wear her down. Mrs. MacDonald did not even hint that her harassment would topple whites' well-entrenched power; rather, her goal was defiance, and its harassing effect was more potent precisely because she placed herself in confrontation with her oppressors with full knowledge of their power and willingness to use it.

Mrs. MacDonald avoided discouragement and defeat because at the point that she determined to resist her oppression, she was triumphant. Nothing the all-powerful whites could do to her would diminish her triumph. Mrs. MacDonald understood twenty-five years ago the theory that I am espousing in the nineties for black leaders and civil rights lawyers to adopt. If you remember her story, you will understand my message.

NOTES

1. According to one scholar: "[t]he state of American law invited and even necessitated [the Realists'] devastating attacks. The inconsistencies between the practices of a rapidly changing industrial nation and the claims of a mechanical juristic system had grown so acute by the 1920s that in the minds of an increasing number of individuals, the old jurisprudence could no longer justify and explain contemporary practice. It had become clear, Judge Cardozo declared in 1932, that 'the agitations and the promptings of a changing civilization' demanded more flexible legal forms and demanded equally 'a jurisprudence and philosophy adequate to justify the change.'" E. A. Purcell, Jr., "American Jurisprudence between the Wars: Legal Realism and the Crisis of Democratic Theory," in L. M. Friedman and H. N. Scheiber, eds., *American Law and the Constitutional Order*, 359, 362 (enlarged ed. 1988). Purcell calls the pre-Realist jurisprudence "a rigid and formalistic profession" and notes that even stalwart defenders of orthodoxy acknowledged the massive confusion and self-contradiction that case law overload (case law being the centerpiece of the formalists' common law logic) had created; *id.* at 361–62.

2. See E. Mensch, "The History of Mainstream Legal Thought," in D. Kairys, ed. in *The Politics of Law*, 18–20 (1990). A relatively precise characterization of the classical structure is given by Purcell: "The old legal theory claimed that reasoning proceeded syllogistically from [mechanical] rules and precedents through the particular facts of a case to a clear decision"; Purcell, *supra* note 1, at 360. Many historians also refer to the classical structure as formalism. Perhaps not as accurately as Purcell, Richard Posner defines "formalism" as a term that can be used "simply to mean the use of logic in legal reasoning"; R. Posner, "Jurisprudential Responses to Legal Realism," 73 *Cornell L. Rev.*, 326, 326 (1988). Finally, Elizabeth Mensch calls formalism's heavy emphasis on objective rights, rules, processes, and precedents "analogic refinement run rampant"; Mensch, *supra*, at 18.

3. Purcell, *supra* note 1, at 362.

4. Empiricism is a crucial aspect of Racial Realism. By taking into consideration the abysmal statistics regarding the social status of black Americans, their oppressions is validated; see *infra* note 30 and accompanying text.

5. See *id.* at 361–63.

6. At this point it might be helpful to recognize an implicit distinction between the *absence* of values and the *impossibility of empirically demonstrable objective moral stan-*

dards. Holmes's relativism—that values are wholly determined by one's particular environment not existing somewhere "out there" for any impartial judge to discover and apply—has been called "cynical"; see *id.* at 361. Realists also embraced the notion that "there could be no such thing as a *demonstrable* moral standard"; *id.* at 367. This kind of reasoning incurred the wrath of many, particularly as the threat of war and Nazi totalitarianism made the defense of undeniable moral grounds for democracy more urgent; *id.* at 369.

Despite having earlier agreed that formal law overemphasized logical uniformity and often frustrated the workings of justice, see *id.* at 361. Roscoe Pound called the Realists' take on morals a breed of "philosophical nominalism"; *id.* at 365, and at his most vitriolic, called Realism a "give-it-up philosophy"; *id.* at 369. Morris R. Cohen pointed to the antidemocratic implication of a judicial theory which seemed to claim that judges' subjective decisions were the only law; Cohen implied that the Realists were justifying judicial despotism when he declared, "To be ruled by a judge is, to the extent that he is not bound by law, tyranny or despotism;" *id.* at 367. In contemporary law, positivists fearful of unrestrained judicial power have attacked modern strands of Realism, as have committed rights theorists, who reject the notion that enshrined rights are mere interests to be balanced against all other interests; see A. Allen, "Legal Philosophy," in S. Gilles, ed., *Looking at Law School*, 305, 315 (1990).

7. "The Realist movement was part of the general twentieth-century revolt against formalism and conceptualism. . . . More specifically and politically, Realism was also a reaction against Supreme Court decisions like *Coppage*, which had invalidated progressive regulatory legislation favored even by many business leaders"; see Mensch, *supra* note 2, at 21. In *Coppage v. Kansas*, 236 U.S. 1 (1915), the court contracts coerced workers to accept the terms imposed by employers, rendering meaningless the formal law concept of freedom of contract. Although the court did not deny the presence of unequal bargaining power, it reasoned that the employees merely encountered economic coercion. Because the formal common law definition of duress which would have excused nonperformance of the contracts did not include economic coercion, the workers were deemed to have freely exercised their choice. The court would not allow the state to invade the liberty rights of contracting parties; see Mensch, *supra* note 2, at 20.

8. See K. L. Hall, *The Magic Mirror, Law in American History*, 269 (1989); see also Purcell, *supra* note 1, at 361 ("Brandeis and Frankfurter argued that judges must consciously consider the probable social resuls of their decisions. Scientific studies of social needs and problems, rather than syllogistic reasoning, should be the determining factor.").

There were also instrumentalist underpinnings to the Realists' conception of law: "Much of Realist scholarship was . . . devoted to exposing the incoherence of established patterns of reasoning in judicial decisions. By undermining the inexorability of such logic, the Realists hoped to reveal the 'real' question in judicial decisions: why 'the court select[ed] . . . one available premise rather than the other.' This was the point in Realist analysis where social science entered. . . . The 'real' question in liberty of contract cases was, therefore, not, 'is there a liberty to contract in the due process clause?,' but 'do industrial workers in fact have no bargaining power to choose the terms of their employment?' This question was, the Realists believed, susceptible of empirical analysis"; G. E. White, "From Realism to Critical Legal Studies: A Truncated Intellectual History," 40 *Sw. L. J.*, 819, 822–23 (1986) (citation omitted). See also Hall, *supra*, at 270 ("Realists . . . rejected formalistic and deductive logic, which, they argued merely concealed a judge's prejudices and preferences. The Realists indeed believed in general legal principles, but they insisted that the traditional deference accorded to precedent was merely a screen that shielded the inherently conservative biases of most judges").

9. See F. Olsen, "The Myth of State Intervention in the Family," 18 *Mich. J. L. Ref.*, 835 (1985).

10. See Mensch, *supra* note 2, at 22. For example, another judge might have viewed *Regents of the University of California v. Bakke*, 438 U.S. 265 (1978), as similar to *Griggs v. Duke Power*, 401 U.S. 424 (1971), in which blacks were deemed to have suffered discriminatory impact when their employer required all workers to have a high school diploma and to pass a given standardized test. The court in *Griggs* used flexible reasoning in arriving at its decision, considering blacks' dismal access to education. Later decisions, however, prove that victories for blacks in the courts regarding issues of affirmative action are, at best, sporadic.

11. Mensch, *supra* note 2, at 23.

12. See *id.*

13. *Id.* at 23–24. Implicit in the approach taken by the Realists is the notion that courts rendered decisions that were suspect because of their reliance on subjective and abstract concepts. The history of the Realist movement bears out this fact: "Legal scholars who came to call themselves Realists began with the perception that many early twentieth-century judicial decisions were 'wrong.' [The decisions] were wrong as matters of policy in that they promoted antiquated concepts and values and ignored changed social conditions. They were wrong as exercises in logic in that they began with unexamined premises and reasoned syllogistically and artificially to conclusions. They were wrong as efforts in governance in that they refused to include relevant information, such as data about the effects of legal rules on those subject to them, and insisted upon a conception of law as an autonomous entity isolated from nonlegal phenomena. Finally, they were wrong in that they perpetuated a status quo that had fostered rank inequalities of wealth, status, and condition, and was out of touch with the modern world"; White, *supra* note 8, at 821.

14. See Mensch, *supra* note 2, at 23.

15. Process jurisprudence, for example, stressed the reliability and necessity of formal process as a means of reining in what its adherents feared was unrestrained judicial power outlined by the Realist critique; see Hall, *supra* note 8, at 311. Closely allied with the philosophy of "neutral principles," which urged that choices made between conflicting rights be conducted with impartiality and objectivity. In this view, "neutral principles" of jurisprudence transcended the result of any particular case at hand, judicial restraint being paramount; see *id.* at 311–12. Ironically, the legal decisions written during the Warren Court's reign invoked principles antithetical to the Realist's approach. The philosophy of Substantive Liberal Jurisprudence emerged, in which the court believed that it had a positive responsibility to intervene where social injustice was evident. Warren believed that the political process was too often insensitive to the values for which the United States should stand; see *id.* at 312; see also Mensch, *supra* note 2, at 31. Warren sympathized with marginalized populations, believing that the law must progress with changing social conditions, but he too imposed his values in legal decisions to make the result seem inevitable.

Somewhat allied with Substantive Liberal Jurisprudence but attempting to achieve more fidelity to the empiricism of the Realist program was the Law and Society movement, which has asked at least one crucial question: "Does the law in action conform to the law on the books?" Its adherents utilize empirical research to demonstrate the dysfunctional expression of formal law in the real world and to expose how the legal process concealed the power relations embedded in the society that the law was designed to rule; see White, *supra* note 8, at 830–35.

A combination of events led to the decline of Law and Society's influence, and the emergence of the more radical (and self-distinguished) philosophy of the Critical Legal Studies movement; see *id.* at 832–36. One proponent of the latter, Mark Tushnet—who had been a student of Law and Society—claimed that Law and Society ignored the extent to which the law serves *to legitimate* power relations, to persuade both oppressor and oppressed that their conditions or existence were just. Tushnet pointed out that Law and Society's emphasis on "archaic rules" highlighted the maladaptivity or outdatedness of rules. His criticism was grounded in the idea that rules, whether archaic or not, often function to legitimate a calculated unresponsiveness on the part of the legal order; see *id.* at 833. In response to both Realism and Substantive Liberal Jurisprudence, a conservative reaction obsessed with original intent emerged, in part to cement so-called original values, in part because its adherents feared that the Warren Court's operation included the substitution of biased judicial values for that which had supposedly proven inimitable for two centuries; see Hall, *supra* note 8, at 312.

16. 438 U.S. 265 (1978).

17. But see R. L. Kennedy, "Racial Critiques of Legal Academia," 102 *Harv. L. Rev.*, 1745 (1989), in which the

author denies that racism accounts for the significant lack of black law professors in the country. Rather, he asserts that there simply are not enough qualified black candidates to fill these positions; *id.* at 1762. The responses to the Kennedy assertion were prompt and vigorous: see, for example, M. S. Ball, "Colloquy—Responses to Randall Kennedy's Racial Critiques of Legal Academia," 103 *Harv. L. Rev.*, 1855 (1990).

18. Although historians disagree about the historical impact of the Realists' contribution, a few claims can be made about their influence; see Hall, *supra* note 8, at 271. By the forties, American jurisprudence regarded two Realist claims as settled propositions: first, that judges made law when they declared legal rules because the rules were not logically necessary and reflected policy judgments, and second, that the law could not be a static entity, indeed, that its progressive development depended on its rules being responsive to current social conditions; White, *supra* note 8, at 828. *Bakke* implicitly rejects this latter proposition.

19. Thomas played on these fears when he invoked the image of a lynch mob to portray the Senate inquiry. As one commentator has noted, "Any American with a sense of history understood the connotations of Thomas's claim that he was a lynch victim, casting the fourteen white men of the Senate Judiciary Committee as his lynch mob;" N. I. Painters, "Who Was Lynched?," *The Nation*, 577 (1991).

20. One critic of black conservatives states, "These black men tend to be high achievers who may feel diminished by the notion they got where they are because of affirmative action . . . [They] are really trying to affirm that their status is the result of a fair fight;" J. Malveaux, "Why Are the Black Conservatives All Men?," *Ms.* (March/April 1991), 60–61.

21. L. R. Harlan, *Separate and Equal*, 42–43, 99–100 (1968).

22. Clarence Thomas, no less than Booker T. Washington, could prove an unwitting double agent. In his first civil rights decision, Justice Thomas voted with the conservative majority in a voting rights case, *Presley v. Etowah County Commission*, 1992 U.S. LEXIS 554 (Jan. 27, 1992). If this voting pattern continues, Thomas will disappoint those blacks who supported him in the hope that, once on the court, he would drop the anticivil rights views that propelled him there. In addition, he could undermine the dwindling support for law-oriented civil rights groups and cause blacks to turn to more militant leadership. Thus, as I suggested in an op-ed piece, Thomas, seemingly a black conservative, may prove to be a black revolutionary—despite himself; D. Bell, "A Radical Double Agent," *New York Times* (Sept. 9, 1991), A15.

23. D. A. Bell, Jr., *Race, Racism and American Law*, 26–27 (2d ed. 1980).

24. Women's rights groups view the attention Hill's charges received as a much-needed publicizing of a form of sex discrimination recognized only recently and reluctantly by courts and society.

25. In central Harlem, where 96 percent of the inhabitants are black and 41 percent live below the poverty line, the age-adjusted rate of mortality was the highest for New York City—more than double that of U.S. whites, and 50 percent higher than that of U.S. blacks generally. Black men in Harlem are less likely to reach the age of 65 than men in Bangladesh; C. McCord, M.D., and H. P. Freeman, M.D., "Excess Mortality in Harlem," 322 *New Eng. J. Med.*, 173 (1990). While the Harlem phenomenon is extreme, it is not unique: of 353 health areas in New York City, 54 also had twice as many deaths among people under the age of 65 as would be expected if the death rates of U.S. whites applied. All but one of these areas of high mortality were predominantly black or Hispanic.

The economist David Swinton has summarized the income and employment status of black Americans. D. H. Swinton, "The Economic Status of African Americans: 'Permanent' Poverty and Inequality," in *The State of Black America*, 25 (1991). Both in absolute terms, and in comparison to white Americans, blacks have high unemployment rates. As of November 1990, the unemployment rate for black men was 11.5 percent, about 2.5 times the corresponding white male rate of 4.6 percent. The slightly lower rate for black women, at 10.2 percent, was 2.3 times the white rate. Black teenage unemployment was 35.8 percent, 2.6 times the white rate of 13.8 percent; *id.* Again, these disparities have remained steady since 1970, although the degree of inequality generally increased over time. Dr. Swinton cautions that the unemployment indicator "does not take into account the lower participation, part-time workers or discouraged workers. Therefore, this indicator *understates* the black unemployment disadvantage"; *id.* at 62 (emphasis added).

Swinton explains that blacks also have low rates of employment, inferior occupational distributions, and low wages and earnings; *id.* at 29. In 1989, black per capita income was $8,747, only about 59 percent of white per capita income of $14,896. In the aggregate, the income of the African-American population was $186 billion short of the income required for parity. This inequality has been within two percentage points of this figure every year since 1970, suggesting to Dr. Swinton that "this degree of relative inequality appears to be a permanent feature of the American economy"; *id.*

Statistically, blacks have low incomes and high poverty rates. In fact, in 1989, there were about 9.3 million black persons living in poverty. Blacks were three times more likely to have income below the poverty level than whites, a gap that has remained fairly steady since 1970; *id.* at 42.

26. Maya Angelou, "I Dare to Hope," *New York Times* (Aug. 25, 1991), E15.

27. Mensch, *supra* note 2, at 21.

28. Interest in protecting blacks from continued assertions of white domination in the South already had waned by the time of the Hayes-Tilden Compromise of 1877. With an eye toward ensuring the victory of the Republican Rutherford B. Hayes in a disputed presidential election, the North was more than ready to agree to a compromise that ill served blacks. Among other things, it promised Democrats both removal of remaining federal troops from the southern states and freedom from intervention in "political affairs" in those states; see Bell, *supra* note 23, at 26–27.

29. The continuing burdens of discrimination are not limited to the poorest black Americans. A study conducted by black and white testers found that blacks were required to pay more for new cars even when blacks and whites negotiated the car purchases in similar fashion; I. Ayres, "Fair Driving: Gender and Race Discrimination in Retail Car Negotiations," 104 *Harv. L. Rev.*, 817 (1991).

30. Blacks own little wealth and small amounts of business property. No significant progress is being made to improve the status of blacks and to close the gaps. Thus, the disparities in measures of economic status have persisted at roughly the same level for the last two decades, and many indicators of inequality have even drifted upward during this period; Swinton, *supra* note 25, at 29–40.

❦

Part Five

THE SEARCH FOR AN OPPOSITIONAL VOICE

Five

THE SEARCH FOR AN OPPOSITIONAL VOICE

As many essays in the foregoing chapters illustrate, Critical Race scholarship often contends that mainstream claims to racial and cultural neutrality improperly take as a baseline norm white cultural patterns. In this section, several Critical Race Theorists confront the same claim in one of its most traditional domains—the implied objective, neutral, and impersonal voice of mainstream scholarship. Each of the essays in this section exemplifies the possibility of grounding a scholarly voice in the material, aesthetic, emotional, and spiritual experiences of people of color. Each starts from the assumption that the medium of expression necessarily reflects and expresses culture and meaning; all contest the very language of mainstream legal and social analysis.

In addition to providing a systematic description of Critical Race Theory, John Calmore's essay "Critical Race Theory, Archie Shepp, and Fire Music" presents the challenge of authenticity that blacks face when confronted with the feigned impersonality of the conventional scholarly voice. The essay itself is organized to mirror a jazz ensemble piece, as Calmore weaves together riffs on Archie Shepp, the revolutionary idea of "fire music," the aspirations of Critical Race Theory, and the articulation of a social theory of multiculturalism within which African-Americans would retain cultural distinctiveness and thus remain a people.

While Calmore is focused on the voice of the scholar as writer, Taunya Banks and Charles Lawrence each explore the meaning of a distinctive voice in the context of pedagogy. In Banks's narrative description of her experiences as a black woman in law school classrooms, she not only articulates the particular ways that a black woman is constructed by reigning representational frameworks but also subverts those categories, sometimes implicitly and sometimes as part of a self-conscious intervention into manner in which the social structure of legal education distributes power, prestige, and legitimacy. Similarly, in his article Charles Lawrence addresses the ways in which progressive scholars of color can conceive of themselves as liberation workers even within the confines of law school culture. In Lawrence's description, the false objectivity of the conventional scholarly voice is mirrored by the false neutrality assumed by the reigning image of the teacher. Drawing upon the African-American tradition of resistance, he offers an alternative that links the existential grounding of the narrative method with the concrete dynamics of the classroom.

PART FIVE

THE SEARCH FOR AN OPPOSITIONAL VOICE

CRITICAL RACE THEORY, ARCHIE
SHEPP, AND FIRE MUSIC: SECURING AN
AUTHENTIC INTELLECTUAL LIFE IN A
MULTICULTURAL WORLD

John O. Calmore

If you ever find
yourself, some where
lost and surrounded
by enemies
who won't let you
speak in your own language
who destroy your statues
& instruments, who ban
your omm bomm ba boom
then you are in trouble
they ban your
oom boom ba boom
you in deep deep
trouble
humph!
probably take you several hundred years
to get
out!

—Amiri Baraka, *Why's/Wise*

I. Introduction

A. Orientation Principles: Oppositional
Cultural Practice, Fundamental Criticism,
and Border Crossings

This article addresses the matters of race and
culture. It reacts against assumptions similar to
Gunnar Myrdal's that "it is to the advantage of
American Negroes as individuals and as a group
to become assimilated into American culture,
to acquire the traits held in esteem by dominant
Americans."[1] This promise of social mobility is
made in opposition to the idea that blacks and
whites in the United States are inevitably tied
to distinctly separate cultures. While I do not
believe that distinct cultural division is inevitable, it is a persistent fact of life. Moreover,
normatively I do not believe this is necessarily a
bad thing.

As many whites experience competitive advantage and relative prosperity over blacks, they
are encouraged to believe in an imagined cultural superiority that, in turn, reinforces their
conviction—like that of nineteenth-century
missionaries—that our blackness is a condition
from which we must be liberated. In retreat
briefly during the sixties, this conviction is once
again salient. This article examines its underlying assumptions and value judgments against a
background in which the nation's meanings of
race and social justice are being contested within
a context of the increasingly complex dynamics
of an evolving multicultural society, as non-
European outside others press for a reinterpretation of America's common ground, shared
values, and rules of the game.[2] . . .

African-American jazz music relates to my
quest here. Cornel West makes a number of
points about jazz appreciation which I believe
reflect upon how the art form inspires my approach to scholarship to the point that I place
so much jazz stuff in a law review article.
According to West:

One of the reasons jazz is so appealing to large
numbers of white Americans is precisely because
they feel in this black musical tradition, not just
black musicians but black humanity is being asserted by artists who do not look at themselves in
relation to whites or engage in self-pity or white
put-down.

Jazz is the middle road between invisibility and
anger. It is where self-confident creativity resides.
Black music is paradigmatic of how black persons
have best dealt with their humanity, their complexity—their good and bad, negative and positive

aspects, without being excessively preoccupied with whites. Duke Ellington, Louis Armstrong, and Coltrane were just being themselves.[3]

. . .

In the mid-sixties, Archie Shepp took his "fundamentally critical" tenor saxophone and stepped outside the commercially laden mainstream's musical community of assumptions and voiced his dissent beyond the ways it would be tolerated within the constraints of conventional jazz. Twenty-five or so years later, some legal scholars of color, including myself, are voicing our dissent from many of the law's underlying assumptions. It is Critical Race Theory's basic move from bit criticism to fundamental criticism that authenticates us as intellectuals of color and legitimatizes us as exemplars of oppositional cultural practice. We are grounding critical race scholarship in a sense of reality which reflects our distinctive experiences as people of color. Race-conscious experience is a springboard from which we engage in fundamental criticism. . . .

II. Archie Shepp: The Who and Wherefore

A. Archie Shepp—The Creative Intellectual and His Oppositional Cultural Practice

As artistic expression, Archie Shepp's music reflects much of what Critical Race Theory's legal scholarship reflects, for art denotes skill in performance, as acquired through experience and observation as well as through study. Although this is an obsolete use, art once meant learning and scholarship. In its most distinct sense, art implies a personal, unanalyzable creative imagination and power. Art is a direct cultural manifestation that synthesizes and refines a lifestyle and worldview. Critical Race Theory's scholarship, at its best, creates an art style that represents a fulfillment of culture. Not content to imitate white or dominant scholarship's canons, methods, and analyses, people of color are adding our own distinctly stylized dimensions to legal scholarship. As Albert Murray observes, art stylizes experience: "What it objectifies, embodies, abstracts, expresses, and symbolizes is a sense of life. . . . More specifi-

cally, an art style is the assimilation in terms of which a given community, folk, or communion of faith embodies its basic attitudes toward experience."[4]

Archie Shepp was born in Fort Lauderdale, Florida, in 1937, and he grew up in Philadelphia. He graduated from Goddard College in 1959 with a degree in dramatic literature. Shepp first came to popular attention in this country in the early sixties. My "association" with Shepp dates back to my junior year of college at Stanford, in 1966, when the university sponsored a jazz weekend and Shepp presented his music. It was one of the most moving and black-reinforcing experiences of my life. Then as now, black intellect and black culture—black voices, if you will—were greatly misperceived and discounted. In college I was a token representative in what was literally an alien land, and from that position, the psychology of race compelled me to examine how values about differences were formulated and acted upon. Through Archie Shepp's fire music I came to appreciate how the psychology of race forces us to examine behavior at the personal, interpersonal, and societal levels. Prior to college, growing up in the black northwest community of an otherwise white Pasadena, I had never been forced to undertake such an examination, at least not rigorously, because in my small world being black was not the tight fit it proved to be in Palo Alto.

Archie Shepp entered this foreign, sometimes hostile world and stood as an artistic and intellectual giant who, in no more than two or three hours, presented to me (and the predominantly white audience) a counterdominant difference that simply had to be valued. He played his horn brilliantly and he articulated, with words like "transmogrification," what his role and artistry were all about. . . . He personified a positive contrast not only to the musical world of white America but also to the assimilationist ethic that purportedly had to be embraced and represented in order to "succeed." . . .

Amiri Baraka has described Shepp's music as "openly agitational art meant to get people hot and make them do something about the ugliness of what is. It was meant to be a revolutionary art, a people's art, fuel for social transformation."[5] Critical Race Theory, as I see it, finds its finest expression when it, too, serves as "fuel for social transformation." In that sense, our efforts must, while directed by critical theory, extend beyond critique and theory to lend support to the struggle to relieve the extraordinary suffering and racist oppression that is commonplace in the life experiences of too many people of color.

John Coltrane, who died on July 17, 1967, is the exemplar of fire music. Shepp said, after playing with him during the summer of 1965, that Coltrane "taught . . . people to listen beyond the expected, how to hear themselves and their times in jazz."[6] Thus, like Critical Race Theory, fire music represented a distinctly African-American approach to cultural expression, heavily influenced by an experiential perspective. The growling, raspy tenor saxophone of Archie Shepp resembled black voices of life and protest. [. . .] Baraka has claimed: "The most expressive [black] music of any given period will be an exact reflection of what the [African-American] himself is. It will be a portrait of the [black] in America at that particular time. Who he thinks he is, what he thinks America or the world to be, given the circumstances, prejudices and delights of that particular America."[7] Shepp has personified the best of this tradition. If we substitute the words "legal scholarship" for "music" in the above quotation, we begin to appreciate the depth and resonance of the current legal writing by so many people of color.

B. The Bebop Roots of Fire Music

Bebop represented a conscious step toward African and African-American music that could not be commercialized by whites. Beboppers began to see themselves as artists rather than as entertainers. Major innovators of this music include Charlie Parker, Dizzy Gillespie, Thelonious Monk, Bud Powell, Max Roach, Kenney Clarke, and Charlie Christian. Many of these musicians played in the big bands of Billy Eckstein. A second line of bebop was formed by such musicians as Miles Davis, Fats Navarro, and Dexter Gordon.

With origins in the blues and the bop era of the forties, fire music also represented a reformulation of jazz in terms of a deliberate expression of a black aesthetic that was neither effortless nor achieved instantaneously. In *Blues People*, Baraka explains:

> The direction, the initial response, which led to hard bop is more profound than its excesses. It is as much of a "move" within the black psyche as was the move north in the beginning of the [twentieth] century. The idea of the Negro's having "roots" and that they are a valuable possession, rather than the source of ineradicable shame, is perhaps the profoundest change within the Negro consciousness since the early part of the century. It is a re-evaluation that could only be made possible by the conclusions and redress of attitude that took place in the forties. . . . The form and content of Negro music in the forties re-created, or reinforced, the social and historical alienation of the Negro in America, but in the Negro's terms. . . . By the fifties this alienation was seen by many Negro musicians not only as valuable, in the face of whatever ugliness the emptiness of the "general" culture served to emphasize, but as necessary.[8]

Sometime in the seventies (and continuing today) many African-Americans lost sight of this. With this point of view and direction, however, Shepp's saxophone has played the fire music toward which African-American legal scholars must, by analogy, now return. At an earlier time, the oppression of the race was more universal, and, because we were in the same boat together, it was easier to know what we were against and what we were for. Now, we must deliberately stand against racist oppression and class subjugation, even though some of us may have sailed into a relatively safe harbor. . . .

C. Fire Music Contextualized

Frank Kofsky has analyzed the revolutionary music—the fire music—that came out of the sixties, and he demonstrates that developments in that music paralleled the developments in the black community, developments that were characterized by black nationalism, the return to African roots, and increasing expressions of militancy.[9] He argues that this music did not evolve in an aesthetic vacuum but, rather, reflected the social history of urban blacks in

America. At the time, many of the primary jazz innovators were expressing and anticipating black ghetto moods, emotions, and aspirations. He thus introduced his book with the normative assertion of Archie Shepp: "The Negro musician is a reflection of the Negro people as a social phenomenon. His purpose ought to be to liberate America aesthetically and socially from its inhumanity."[10]

Just as some have questioned the distinctive voice of Critical Race Theory, jazz critics sought to devalue the music of Shepp and other blacks who had departed from the mainstream. These critics argued that jazz is not primarily an African-American art form because anyone can learn to play it; jazz has no particular social content—"specifically, it in no way pertains more closely to black experiences, perceptive modes, sensibilities, and so on, than it does to white."[11]

It is of course true that whites play jazz. Indeed, groups led by Archie Shepp often included important white musicians, such as bassist Charlie Haden and trombonist Russell Rudd. Moreover, many of the most famous and commercially successful jazz musicians have been white: Dave Brubeck, Bob James, Stan Getz, David Sanborn, Bill Evans, Gerry Mulligan, Chet Baker, Benny Goodman, and Stan Kenton come to mind. But the jazz that whites play has historically been very different from that played by blacks. Much jazz innovation has been led by black artists whose music was influenced by their experience of living in a black world segregated from white society.[12] For example, a Langston Hughes poem explains bop music's derivation as follows:

"You must not know where Bop comes
    from," said
Simple, astonished at my ignorance.
"I do not know," I said. "Where?"
"From the police," said Simple.
"What do you mean, from the police?"
"From the police beating Negroes' heads,"
    said Simple.
"Every time a cop hits a Negro with his billy
    club, that old club says,
"BOP! BOP! . . . BE-BOP! . . . MOP! . . .
    BOP!'

"That Negro hollers, 'Ooool-ya-koo! Ou-
    o-o!'
"Old Cop just keeps on, 'MOP! MOP! . . .
    BE-BOP! . . . MOP!'"

That's where Be-Bop came from, beaten right out of some Negro's head into them horns and saxophones and piano keys that plays it. . . ."[13]

The contention that the fire music of the sixties was either antijazz or devoid of social content is myopic. As Shepp says: "Some of us [jazz musicians] are more bitter about the way things are going. We are only an extension of that entire civil-rights–Black Muslims–black nationalist movement that is taking place in America. That is fundamental to music." By relying on an identification with urban black America and by rejecting the canons of European culture, Shepp's fire music was distinctively black. And like Critical Race Theory's readership, for many listeners it was an acquired taste. . . .

III. CRITICAL RACE THEORY THEMES, PERSPECTIVES, AND DIRECTIONS

A. An Overview of Critical Race Theory
Critical Race Theory begins with a recognition that "race" is not a fixed term; instead, it is a fluctuating, decentered complex of social meanings that are formed and transformed under the constant pressures of political struggle. The challenge thus presented is to examine how individual and group identities, under broadly disparate circumstances, as well as the racial institutions and social practices linked to those identities, are formed and transformed historically by actors who politically contest the social meanings of race.

As a form of oppositional scholarship, Critical Race Theory challenges the universality of white experience and judgment as the authoritative standard that binds people of color and normatively measures, directs, controls, and regulates the terms of proper thought, expression, presentment, and behavior. As represented by legal scholars, Critical Race Theory challenges the dominant discourses on race and racism as they relate to law. The task is to identify values and norms that have been disguised and subordinated in the law. As critical race scholars, we thus seek to demonstrate that our experiences as people of color are legitimate, appropriate, and effective bases for analyzing the legal system and racial subordination. This process is vital to our transformative vision. This theory-practice approach, a praxis, if you will, finds a variety of emphases among those who follow it, and the concepts are now rather open and still being explored. . . .

John Brenkman provides some insight as to what makes Critical Race Theory "critical."[14] Although he focuses on how literary criticism can foster social criticism, his "critical hermeneutics" can be applied to interpreting texts as I have characterized them here. He sees culture as constituting the forms of symbolization, representation, and expression through which a group secures its identity and solidarity. Culture enables a group to situate reciprocal relationships and mutual understandings while simultaneously differentiating itself from other groups with which it is interdependently linked, whether as a matter of cooperation or of antagonism. Hence, there is a tightly woven interplay between social critique, especially as oppositional cultural practice, and experiential interpretation. One's hermeneutic experience, however, does not automatically lend itself to critique. Instead, Brenkman contends that what determines whether our interpretations are socially critical or uncritical is the set of commitments we develop regarding the symbolic and social struggles between the legitimation and the opposition to domination, oppression, and injustice. So, then, Critical Race Theory can be identified as such not because a random sample of people of color are voicing a position but, rather, because certain people of color have deliberately chosen race-conscious orientations and objectives to resolve conflicts of interpretation in acting on the commitment to social justice and antisubordination.

Drawing again from Brenkman, I contend that Critical Race Theory can be described in part as an expression of critical hermeneutics which reflects what he characterizes as a way of appreciating the dynamics of a "critical-utopian interpretation of cultural practices and tradi-

tions."[15] In grasping the dynamics at play here, he argues that through trying to understand the past while assuming responsibility for the future, we shape our "critical relation" to society as we oppose business as usual. As a result, our orientation moves us in directions both critical and anticipatory: on the one hand, we challenge the forms of domination that structure not only culture's production but also its reception; on the other, we try to identify and clarify progressive social changes whose needs arise from the symbolic world of culture, and whose realization lies in political self-organization and action. Moreover, to advance such a project, we discover the required interpretive procedures—fire music or what have you—at the point where cultural heritages and social critique converge.

In sum, as critical race theorists confront the texts of America's dominant legal, social, and cultural strata, we are critical, fundamentally so, because we engage these texts in a way that counters their oppressive and subordinating features. In this endeavor we are not simply in opposition; we are not rebels without a cause. We are the "new interpreters" who demand of the dominant institutions a new validity, as described in the following passage from Brenkman:

> Insofar as the transmitted text comes to address new interpreters, it occasions or invites a communicative experience that is no longer contained within the horizon of the text's original context or the close circle of its original audience. As soon as the text comes to address interpreters who are differently situated historically and socially, its promise of uncoerced mutual understanding undergoes a change. The text now makes a claim to validity that was not immanent in its original context. The new claim to validity comes from the specific, historically contingent demands for validity on the part of the interpreters—demands shaped by contemporary forms of resistance and opposition to domination and to the systematic distortions of communication which legitimate domination.[16]

Like fire music's oppositional stance, Critical Race Theory presents not only a different methodology and grounding but also a message different from traditional race scholarship, now euphemistically known as "civil rights" or "antidiscrimination" scholarship. Critical Race Theory recombines and extends existing means of legal redress; hence, it is necessarily eclectic, incorporating what seems helpful from various disciplines, doctrines, styles, and methods. The theory attempts to extend the narrow world of traditional legal scholarship without indulging in dysfunctional deviance, instead establishing intellectual credibility, on the one hand, and reconciling the elements of effective theory and practice, on the other. Explanation arises from the particular and the personal. In contrast to traditional scholarship, the focus is much more extralegal and contextual, less restricted by doctrinal analysis as a controlling center. It is concerned with redressing conditions of oppression and subordination which exist beyond their narrow translation into judicially recognizable claims and relief. Historical discrimination and its legacy merge more definitively and symbiotically with the present to provide the temporal context. While not abandoning a faith in rights strategy, Critical Race Theory recognizes that such a strategy cannot be divorced from the larger economics and politics of things. It recognizes that whatever the specific issues of legal cases and controversies may be, the overriding issues of social justice and institutional legitimacy always lurk nearby.

Critical Race Theory recognizes the inadequacy of disaggregating individual plaintiffs and causes of action from the larger context of social conflict which lies at the heart of a racist regime. Hence, formal, individualized equality of opportunity and objective norms of meritocracy can hardly serve as viable opposition to group inequality and subjective bias. Moreover, societal fault and accountability cannot be reduced to actionable claims only when evidenced by individual responsibility for intentional wrong. Finally, many adherents of Critical Race Theory see an interlocking set of oppressions that extend beyond the singular base of race and include the bases of gender, economic class, and sexual orientation.

Critical Race Theory attempts to construct a social reality and direct operation within it. It is a way of finding meaning within legal scholarship through combining language, thought, and experience. Voice is important—how voice is expressed, how voice is informed, how our voice differs from the dominant voice. Hence, Critical Race Theory's linguistics is experiential and pragmatic, focusing on "the nature of language as a social instrument, an instrument through which human beings create or constitute or stipulate a (social) world they may share, and then . . . 'get things done with words' in that world."[17] Our voice, as heard in legal scholarship, recounts our perception, experience, and understanding of law in ways that are primarily colored, if you will, by our own unique biography and history. As people of color, we recognize the centrality of race in a social order that is maintained and perpetuated in significant ways by the rule of law. As scholars, our writing acknowledges this centrality that contextualizes our work.

B. Authenticity and the Existential Grounding of Critical Race Theory

The power to define ourselves and our world is radical per se. However, Critical Race Theory also helps to erect and maintain a sense of authenticity, without which our work will probably fail to connect significantly with our community's agenda of social action. Authenticity implies trustworthiness and good faith in presentment. I associate it quite closely with integrity. According to Robert Terry, by guiding our actions, authenticity characterizes a force in our lives that allows us not only to make sense of our world but also to act purposefully within it. In this way, authenticity connotes being true to both oneself and one's world. Terry explains further: "If I am untrue to the world, I lose my grasp on what is happening around and to me and thus make judgments that lead to behaviors inappropriate to situations in which I find myself. I distort what is happening to me and, because of this false diagnosis of my situation, continually make erroneous judgments."[18]

Terry is analyzing racism as a source of inauthenticity in white people, their organizations, and their institutions. He distinguishes the inauthenticity of whites from the alienation of people of color. Racism, though, particularly in integrated settings (however minimal or token), tends to move people of color from the alienated to the inauthentic. Amatzi Etzioni's distinction is helpful here, for he observes that an inauthentic relation, institution, or society presents the appearance of responsiveness against the backdrop of an underlying alienating condition.[19] While inauthentic and alienating conditions both exclude inauthentic structures, more than alienating ones, they operate to conceal their contours and to generate a feigned flexibility, or mere appearance of responsiveness. . . .

> Authenticity exists where responsiveness exists and is experienced as such. The world responds to the actor's efforts, and its dynamics are comprehensible. . . . [A]uthenticity requires not only that the actor be conscious, committed, and hold a share of the societal power, but also that the three components of the active orientation be balanced and connected. It is the fate of the inauthentic man that what he knows does not fit what he feels, and what he affects is not what he knows or is committed to do. His world has come apart.[20]

Hence, a major theme of Critical Race Theory reflects the colored intellectual's persistent battle to avoid being rendered inauthentic by the pressures of adapting to the white world and, instead, to take an oppositional stance by relying on one's true existential life, which is rooted in a world of color even though not stuck there. . . .

As a reflection of authenticity, critical race scholarship also rejects the traditional dictates that implore one to write and study as a detached observer whose work is purportedly objective, neutral, and balanced. In the classic sense of "professing," critical race scholars advocate and defend positions. Fran Olsen points out that traditional scholarship's appearance of balance presupposes a status quo baseline that hinders both understanding and social change. Critical Race Theory tends, in response, toward very personal expression that allows our experiences and lessons, learned as people of color, to convey the knowledge we possess in a way that is empowering to us and, it is hoped, ultimately empowering to those on whose behalf we act.

Those of us who profess Critical Race Theory are, in simplest terms, trying to be true to ourselves. And in so doing, we quest more for social transformation and self-respect than for social acceptance, scholarly citation, or, in some cases, even tenure. Critical Race Theory, at bottom, is a matter of existential voice. As people of color we recognize the centrality of race and write about law—its operation, its social ordering, its history, its values, and its ideological vectors—in a way that reflects our different experience, insight, and views. . . .

C. Linking Separate African-American Class Interests

Largely as a result of the civil rights movement and the surging economy of the sixties, the black middle class more than doubled in size by 1970 and constituted 27 percent of all black workers. As institutions of business, industry, and higher learning presented new opportunities to African-Americans, class division within the race became more pronounced. Indeed, Morton Wenger argues that dominant America's provision of instant mobility to the black middle class reflected an ideological substitution of the new "petite bourgeoise's" personal achievements for class liberation. This division imposes a risk that the class situation, social orientation, and living space of black intellectuals may remove us from a strong identification with the black poor's values, interests, and needs. Thus, the question becomes: How credible is it for us—as black intellectuals—to speak about the black community, not to mention speaking on its behalf?

Certain facts evidence bridges that enable those of us in white legal academies nonetheless to speak meaningfully about overall community betterment. As recently as 1962, few middle-class children were able to remain in that class during adulthood, and even fewer working-class children succeeded in moving up to the middle class as adults. Bart Landry explains that in the mid-seventies, as a result of increased mobility opportunities, the middle class was "mainly recruited from the sons and daughters of garbage collectors, assembly line workers, domestics, waiters, taxicab drivers, and farmers."[21] Even though during this time the passing of middle-class status from one generation to the next increased, this "recruitment" from the lower classes helps to explain why 80 percent of the present middle class is first generation. Most of us have roots extending into the neighborhoods and homes, the communities and families, where poor and working-class blacks still reside.

Additionally, it is now clear that the black middle class still resides within segregated communities, even though many of its members no longer live in inner-city ghettos. The large majority of black middle-class households are in close proximity to poor blacks, and they share neighborhoods with skilled and unskilled numbers of the working class. . . .

Under these circumstances, intellectual talk of a black community is not necessarily academic. Moreover, the experiential basis of our writing need not defeat our own intragroup diversities; it need not collapse into an absurd essentialism. Generally, the life chances, experiences, and styles of blacks and whites, however, are distinctively separate, sufficiently so—indeed extremely so—to provide very different "data" that support certain generalizations.

Critical Race Theory, though antiessentialist, nonetheless emphasizes the commonalities developed from a race-consciousness that recognizes, in Patricia Williams's words, that "the simple matter of the color of one's skin so profoundly affects the way one is treated, so radically shapes what one is allowed to think and feel about this society, that the decision to generalize from this division is valid."[22] What Critical Race Theory expresses in this way is not a matter of essence, but certainly one of prevalence. It is not a matter of necessary, inevitable expression but, rather, one of deliberate identification and incorporation of data available from colored histories and subjugated narratives, from colored biographies and group identities.

The distinctiveness of colored voices often traces back to an oppositional cultural frame of reference that is shaped by our experiences of racial stratification rather than benign race relations. Of course, African-American culture is rich and extends far beyond reacting to this stratification. However, because of the long history and starkness of black-white stratification, the oppositional cultural frame of reference is a key factor that generates a distinctive voice orientation.

When people of color deemphasize an individuality that tries to transcend color—when we attempt, in other words, to express valid generalizations generated out of race-consciousness—we challenge the underlying inadequacy of dominant legal discourse, what Kimberlé Crenshaw has labeled "perspectivelessness."[23] Such a position holds that legal analysis is possible without taking into account various conflicts of individual values, experiences, and worldviews. According to Crenshaw, by stripping away the analysis of any particular cultural, political, or class characteristic, this perspectivelessness is presented as the objective, neutral legal discourse, with a corollary of "color-blindness," used to reduce conflict and devalue the relevance of our particular perspectives.

D. The Concept of Culture and the Significance of Cultural Analysis

. . . A subordinate group's cultural heritage reflects both internal and external traits and patterns that are mediated through a distinctive institutional life within its subsocietal structure. Internal traits and patterns derive directly from a shared history and value system, going to the core of the culture. External traits and patterns represent the "historical vicissitudes" of a group's adaptation of response to its immediate environment.[24] The evolution of a subordinated culture's external traits and patterns often reflects a reaction to cultural containment.

The issue of cultural containment manifests strange dynamics. Through marginalized experiences and perspectives, people of color who choose to do so can move, literally and figuratively, from one cultural realm to the next. Historically, African-American cultural life has experienced a tension between an emphasis on maintaining and experiencing a unique self-identity, on the one hand, and an emphasis on fully participating in American society by relying on universalistic, rather than racially distinct, orientations, on the other. This dialectical tension is a fundamental duality in African-American life.

Law, of course, is not only an instrument of social control but also a symbolic expression of dominant society. An important aspect of cultural analysis incorporates consideration of how these two characteristics of social control and symbolic expression intersect with symbolic boundaries that separate or integrate diverse peoples and cultures. Without negating the importance of force and fraud as determinants of oppression, or the social structure that supports that oppression, "[s]ymbolic boundaries separate realms, creating the contexts in which meaningful thought and action can take place."[25] The focus on symbolic boundaries, however, should not detract from concrete investigation. Viewing culture as an observable aspect of human behavior emphasizes the realities of symbolic boundaries. Beyond conceptual distinctions in people's minds, these boundaries are publicly visible in discourse, in the way in which social interaction occurs, and in tangible objects. Society expends resources in creating and maintaining them, and its activities may often reflect "efforts to sharpen eroded boundaries, to redefine cultural distinctions, or as symptoms of ambiguous frameworks. Identifying these activities is a concrete task to which cultural analysis can be applied."[26] . . .

E. Cultural Orientation and Liberating Practice

We should use culture to provide different ways of seeing the world as a prelude to socially reconstructing it. My approach here emphasizes the sociology of knowledge itself, the analysis of cultural orientation itself, and the intersection of the two. Thus, my position that culture is extremely important to Critical Race Theory and liberating practice eschews any claim that culture maintains a superautonomy that reduces all facets of social experience to issues of culture, and that cultural change is therefore the key to all other change.

One must avoid the risk that an emphasis on cultural investigation can be misinterpreted as "culturalism," which, according to Arif Dirlik, is that "ensemble of intellectual orientations

that crystallize methods logically around the reduction of social and historical questions to abstract questions of culture."[27] To ignore the issue of culture, however, is to remain locked in a state of cultural unconsciousness, under the control of imposed and conditioned vistas. This likely would defeat the self-conscious critical orientation that is part of the initial preparation for radical activity. . . .

The reciprocal relationship between community and culture grows more tenuous as we recognize that individuals do not belong merely to one discrete community. Marking the multiple, often overlapping communities that a person belongs to are such factors as place of birth, socialization, formal education, church, residence, and work; race, ethnicity, gender, and age; scholarship and readership. Thus, as a product of community, culture can be ambiguously produced and received. One way to militate against negative ambiguity is to emphasize the cultural distinctiveness that stems from our home culture; another way is to commit to relying on that distinctiveness to resist domination and subordination. These efforts, in turn, help to identify the significance of critical race scholars as a unique intelligentsia within the legal academy. To use Duncan Kennedy's characterization, critical race scholars constitute a knowledge class of law professors who, acting individually or within self-organizing groups, "work at defining their community's identity . . . its interests in competition and cooperation with other communities, and its possible strategies."[28]

Because our effectiveness is largely determined by our access to resources that lie within white institutional hands, an emphasis on our distinctiveness is not easily accommodated within the normal arrangements and practices. How people of color adapt to this situation gives rise to conflicts in orientation, as we must emphasize whether we are more directed by assimilation or autonomy, by individual self-fulfillment or collective responsibility, by group accommodation or group resistance. Critical race scholars adopt in each case the latter orientation. To do otherwise is to accept an integrated context that reflects tokenism, gradualism, and paternalism. To do otherwise is to discount too greatly the prevalence of group domination and subordination. . . .

Critical Race Theory is based significantly on culture; its adherents not only recognize this but emphasize it. When we assert that our voices and experiences are distinctively not white, we are also saying that we are inner-directed as to white people because we reflect distinctively colored cultural backgrounds, valuations, and frames of reference. This is so in spite of any number of border crossings that, at any given moment, may situate us more within dominant culture rather than our home cultures. How could it be otherwise unless all of the interested parties were (color) blind and amnesic? . . .

Tying Critical Race Theory so blatantly to ideology may take us involuntarily into deep water, because the term "ideology" is associated with so many negatives. [. . .] The ideology of Critical Race Theory should not scare away people of color. . . . Our ideology maps social reality in an attempt to make "incomprehensible social situations meaningful, to so construe them as to make it possible to act purposefully within them."[29] This is true whether we refer to our intellectual roles within the legal academy or to our activist roles there and outside that rarefied air. As John Broson Childs has argued, culture represents "the keystone upon which the foundation of modern African-American intellectual thought" has developed.[30] Critical Race Theory can mature toward a significant representation of cultural analysis as it bears on legal values and thereby move to destroy the foundations and structures of racial subordination. . . .

IV. CRITICAL RACE THEORY AND FUTURE-SOCIETY RIGHTS

. . .

A. The Attack on Cultural Racism

Racism combines individual, institutional, and cultural aspects. All three facets of racism must continue to be marked as points of attack. It is cultural racism, however, that commands my attention in this writing. Dominant society re-

lies heavily on cultural racism and stereotypes to bias both its interpretation and evaluation of the subordinated group. Cultural bias sets standards for performance in terms of the tendencies, skills, or attributes of white America, and it is against these standards that all other groups are measured. Poor performance by the members of these groups is translated into inferior capacity that represents general group traits. A second and related fundamental cultural bias is dominant society's practice of giving more value and status to areas in which white people excel or find interest than to those areas in which people of color have excelled or demonstrated aptitude or interest.

. . . Take, for example, the ways many whites characterize the "suitable" employee. In a recent study to assess the importance of race as a factor in hiring decisions, one interviewed employer indicated that "the styles of interaction" characteristic of many blacks were inappropriate to the business world:

> I think for most middle-class white people there's a big cultural gap between them and the culture . . . I would call typical of many Chicago black men, and it's not something that a lot of white people are comfortable with. There's a certain type of repartee that goes on between black guys; even in this building you see it. We have a security guard and a couple of his friends that come in, I'm real uncomfortable with that. You know, I do my best to realize it's a cultural thing, but I don't like it, I don't think it's being professional, and I don't think it's the right atmosphere for a building.[31]

Another employer focused on black speech patterns and styles of dress:

> We have a couple of black workers—a friend of mine, one of the black secretaries who's been here several years, said, "Well, they're black but their soul is white" and, because culturally, they're white. They do not have black accents. They do not—I think the accent is a big part of it. If someone—it doesn't matter—if someone is black but they speak with the same accent as a Midwestern white person, it completely changes the perception of them. And then dress is part of it. So, you're dealing with what is almost more socioeconomic prejudice than purely racial prejudice.[32]

A placement director focused not on styles of interaction but on styles of presentation as inappropriate, complaining that "a lot of the blacks still wear their hair in tons and millions of braids all over their heads. They're sort of hostile."[33] In the lower-skilled blue-collar and service job market, trainability rather than experience is often valued and blacks get stereotyped as untrainable and undependable.[34] Again, "it's a cultural thing."

It is through dominant cultural understandings, then, that whites act out and reinforce racism as it is found in social relations, institutional arrangements, and personal behavior. Generated through culture, racism is self-generative, and thus change is difficult because the appearance of change often substitutes for substantive change. I do not want to understate the significance of personal and institutional racism, but I agree strongly with Benjamin Bowser and Raymond Hunt that "[i]f we were somehow able to separate interest-group-manipulated institutions from their cultural hearts, racism would lose its ideological veil, appear as exactly what it is, and thereby lose legitimacy."[35] White racism results, in part, from cultural conditioning that reinforces and in turn is reinforced by the particular actions of interest groups. Institutional arrangements are organized and manipulated by power holders in our political economy with the aim of securing maximum social control and selective privilege. As Bowser and Hunt contend, "Racism . . . is an element of culture which conveniently lends itself to interest group struggles for social power. Success in gaining societal control and securing its benefits reinforces cultural racism by verifying the 'truth' of white supremacy and buttresses its institutional bastions. Institutional racism finally compels personal racism."[36] . . .

Through racialized color-blindness, the core civic ideals advanced today by the new racism are radically individualized opportunity, opportunity based substantially on the operation of a free-market economy, and minimal state intervention, particularly by the federal government. There is no need to be racist in the old sense if the reigning ideology adopts a color-blind orientation that defeats the legitimacy of group rights and the corresponding attempts to establish collective equality by imposing responsibil-

ity on the national government to redress racial subordination and structural inequality, as currently practiced and as a legacy of past state-sanctioned racism. In discussing race and reaction, Michael Omi and Howard Winant correctly point out that the new racism, which is camouflaged in code words and cultural messages, continues to subordinate those historically disadvantaged as a result of overt racism.[37] They contend that

> [t]he forces of racial reaction have seized on the notion of racial equality advanced by the racial minority movements and rearticulated its meaning for the contemporary period. Racial reaction has repackaged the earlier themes—infusing them with new political meaning and linking them to other key elements of conservative ideology.[38]

The discussion of cultural racism indicates that racial identification is a social construction of self-identification and societal determination. In all regions of the United States, black-white relations are still marked by this "we-they" character. Conversely, there is simultaneously at work an external, societally designated racial distinctiveness that raises the "theyness" side of the duality. In this regard, many white Americans see the African-American as a conflicting, contrasting conception of whites. This affects and is affected by such factors as dominant society's nullification of our distinctiveness and the delegitimation of African-Americans as a group, and, at the other, more benevolent extreme, the nullification of our unique group characteristics and absorption of the group into larger society, which often takes form in sociocultural assimilation or biological amalgamation through intermarriage.

The latter route to assimilation or amalgamation has never been successfully traveled by black America at large, although at any given time, in a variety of situations, individual blacks have tokenistically made progress this way. European ethnic groups have done much better; indeed, it is the disparate histories of African-Americans and these white ethnic groups in traveling along this path that argues for a need to distinguish race from ethnicity rather than treating these categories as combined. . . .

As a civil rights promise, integration was

conceived as a reciprocal process whereby white and black Americans would gravitate toward each other, exchanging culture and sharing decision-making power over institutions and communications. This concept of integration was based on an appreciation of American society's culturally pluralistic nature. However, things have gone off track. As viewed by Tony Brown, "the ideal of assimilation replaced the hard-fought-for integration as pluralism" which stemmed from a respect for differences.[39] In theory and fact, African-Americans generally came to pursue social association with whites for its own sake, implying that inferior "blacks must mix with superior whites and emulate them"—a sure-fire formula for black failure.[40] In 1897, W. E. B. Du Bois said that our "destiny is not absorption by the white Americans."[41] Assimilation resembles the attempt to run away from ourselves, with success coming only through the negation of self, history, culture, and community.

Beyond an opposition to assimilation, adherents of Critical Race Theory must act in formally organized and also informal ways to advance a bridging project that will facilitate, among people of color, dialogue, understanding, and collaboration among our own communities. Our community relations must be broadened and deepened. Multiculturalism need not be merely an overly romanticized abstraction; it can be made to serve as a viable organizing concept for valuing diversity. After the recent disturbance in Los Angeles, a group of Asian-Pacific-American leaders offered a perspective on human relations that we should adopt: "Los Angeles must resolve misunderstandings and hate revealed by the riots. We need mechanisms for interactive, multicultural synergy."[42] The notion of "interactive, multicultural synergy" is a call not just to people of color, but to the nation.

Those of us engaged in Critical Race Theory are undertaking an ambitious commitment to personify movement intellectuals rather than established intellectuals. Because we are professionally engaged in the production of ideas or the manipulation of symbols as colored professors of law at established institutions, we must

go out of our way to contribute to the ideological direction of critical social movements for rights and social justice. Critical Race Theory presents the opportunity not simply to carve out space to challenge established intellectuals and to reinterpret established practices: as a growing movement, it can provide opportunities for new types of intellectuals to emerge.

Not only must we confront dominant society and culture's ideological right wing, but also we must contend with a growing segment of colored intellectuals who have joined that camp. These colored intellectuals are prone to suffer a race-image anxiety, rely on a Eurocentric cultural frame of reference, and adopt a model of resolving racial conflict that emphasizes assimilationist and integrationist goals and value orientations. . . .

V. Conclusion

THROUGH a connection with African-American culture, as expressed in the fire music of Archie Shepp, I have tried to illustrate how critical race scholarship provides an oppositional expression that challenges oppression. In the process, white experience and judgment are rejected as paradigms against which people of color must be measured. As reality itself is contested as a culturally directed and socially constructed reference, critical race theorists are insurgents in the effort to undermine dominant, context-setting assumptions and truths. This oppositional grounding is a distinctive, experiential, and subjective orientation, which directs critical race theorists to connect politics and culture insofar as they offer alternative definitions of reality.

The fundamental identity of critical race theorists also is culturally directed and socially constructed so that people of color deliberately emphasize their outside-Other marginality and turn it toward advantageous perspective building, intellectual presentment, ideological commitment, and concrete advocacy on behalf of those oppressed by virtue of race and, perhaps, such other interlocking factors as economic class, gender, and sexual orientation. Authenticity toward oneself and toward the world are reinforced as colored intellectuals reject assimilating absorption and rely instead on cultural autonomy, even while fighting to bring oppressed peoples into the national community as American citizens or members of society who are viably integrated within the nation's structures of opportunity, power, and privilege.

Recognizing oppression as a condition that directs redress, I have explicitly sought to explain oppression in terms of cultural silencing and invasion, exploitation, structured containment and expendability, and the dominant imposition of a prescribed reality. To the extent that rights assertion and exercise are viable, I have contended that, at present, the principal force of a rights strategy lies in its wedgelike rhetorical challenges that attempt to awaken a sense of injustice among both victims and victimizers. Rights are constructed as claims to power, privilege, and resources. These claims also bear on improving viable collective identity and solidarity. In a rights-driven social movement, I have argued, we must take into account not only social relations, but also cultural orientations, not only oppositional social projects, but also contested structures of oppression.

At present, the development of legal doctrine associated with race law unfolds from a stony judiciary largely divorced from the needs and aspirations of people of color—people who do not unquestioningly accept the inevitability and legitimacy of their own continued oppression. To redirect dominant society and its state apparatus, I have urged an all-out attack on cultural racism: We must employ rights and social justice claims like a wedge in order to break free of dominant truths that tell lies about the colored past, present, and future.

I have earnestly thought about how to end this article, rather than just stop writing. I have, however, arrived at no satisfying way to do it. Part of the difficulty, I suspect, is an audience problem. When all is said and done, this writing is probably for my children, ten-year-old Jonathan and six-year-old Canai, and for their rainbow of little friends, associates, and peers, who at this time cannot really appreciate fully what I have struggled to write here. Perhaps the slim hope, however, does indeed lie in "cohort replacement."[43]

The nation's pressing challenge, I think, lies in adults providing good answers to questions such as these: Can this "one nation under God" continue as currently constituted and oriented without burning out or burning up before Jonathan, Canai, and their group can position themselves to improve the situation? When they are able, will they still be willing, as they are now when left to their own devices, to reconcile human differences? Will they properly recognize those differences as culturally and socially constructed determinants of value which place a disproportionately high premium on whiteness, elitism, maleness, high income, or wealth? Will enough of them reject the pursuit of life, liberty, and happiness which is so constricted by a material aggrandizement secured at the expense of social relations that value people, cooperation, inclusive community, and true broad access to the realization, finally, of America's high positive ideals? Can we save the children so that they will have their chance to save the nation?

NOTES

1. Gunnar Myrdal, 2 *The American Dilemma: The Negro Problem and Modern Democracy,* 929 (1944).

2. During the sixties, black nationalism relied on a positive, autonomous African-American culture to counter integrationists who sought to direct the civil rights movement primarily toward increasing significant access to white society and cultural enrichment. Manning Marable has summarized the characteristics of black nationalism to include the following: "a strong personal pride in one's black cultural and ethnic heritage, an advocacy of separate black economic and social institutions within black communities, a rejection of the tactics and principles of integrationist black leaders, a commitment to struggle against white authority, oppression and racism, and an approach to the world from a cultural frame of reference reflecting positively upon the black human experience"; M. Marable, *From the Grassroots: Social and Political Essays Toward Afro-American Liberation,* 2 (1980). While my ideological orientation is rooted in black nationalism, it branches beyond. As Marable has advised, "In the pursuit of an ideological consensus, a new black common sense of liberation, it is crucial that the positive elements of integration be merged with the activist tradition of black nationalism"; *id.* at 15. In this article, I am trying to reflect this critical balance and tension with the objective of contributing to the articulation of this "new common sense of liberation."

3. Cornel West, "Charlie Parker Didn't Give a Damn," 8 New Persp. Q. (Summer 1991), 60, 63.

4. A. Murray, *The Omni-Americans: Some Alternatives to the Folklore of White Supremacy*, 54 (1983). . . .

5. "Interview: Archie Shepp Speaks Frankly on Music," *Nat'l L. Leader* (Oct. 20, 1983), 7. . . .

6. Nat Hentoff, liner notes for J. Coltrane and A. Shepp, *New Things at Newport* (Impulse Records, 1965).

7. F. Kofsky, *Black Nationalism and the Revolution in Music*, 142 (1970).

8. LeRoi Jones, *Blues People: The Negro Experience in White America and the Music That Developed from It* (1963), at 218–19 (emphasis added). Between the bop and hard bop eras, roughly from 1950 to 1954, the jazz style known as "cool jazz" or "West Coast jazz" appeared. Bebop was a nascent movement, killed by the recession following the end of World War II. Cool jazz developed almost completely as a white form of jazz, although the ubiquitous Miles Davis is the salient exception. Those who developed the cool sound include Shelly Manne, Art Rogers, Bud Shank, Bill Evans, Stan Getz, Zoot Sims, Gerry Mulligan, Chet Baker, and Dave Brubeck; Kofsky, *supra* note 7, at 31–33. Cool jazz manifested a severance of jazz from its black roots and its repotting, so to speak, in the world of more "dignified" contemporary Europeanized music; *id.* at 32–33. Usually this entailed making the music more melodic. Hard bop was ushered in by Davis with his 1954 recording "Walkin" (not "Walking"). According to Davis, "That record was a mother . . . man, with Horace [Silver] laying down that funky piano of his and Art playing them bad rhythms behind us on the drums. It was something else. I wanted to take the music back to the fire and improvisations of bebop, that kind of thing that Diz and Bird had started. But also I wanted to take the music forward into a more funky kind of blues, the kind of thing that Horace would take us to"; Davis and Troupe, *Miles: The Autobiography* (1989), at 177. As Davis explained, "Birth of the Cool had . . . mainly come out of what Duke Ellington and Billy Strayhorn had already done; it just made the music 'whiter,' so that white people could digest it better"; *id.* at 219. While bop was a music of engagement, cool was quintessentially a reflection of individual disengagement; Kofsky, *supra* note 7, at 31. Hard bop in large part was a reaction to cool jazz and a response to the fifties civil rights protests; *id.* at 38. It set the stage for the funky soul music that was later popularized in the sixties by Marvin Gaye, Otis Redding, Wilson Pickett, Aretha Franklin, and James Brown.

9. Kofsky, *supra* note 7.

10. *Id.* at 9. . . .

11. *Id.* at 16. . . .

12. Jones, *supra* note 8, at 191; Kofsky, *supra* note 7, at 23.

13. L. Hughes, *The Best of Simple*, 117–18 (1961) (emphasis added). According to Kofsky, "Bebop can . . . be viewed in its social aspect as a manifesto of rebellious black musicians unwilling to submit to further exploitation"; Kofsky, *supra*

note 7, at 57. Beyond jazz the "bebop" tradition of policing (read brutality) remains strong. . . .

14. J. Brenkman, *Culture and Domination* (1987).

15. *Id.* at 229.

16. *Id.* at 233. . . .

17. Jerome Brunner, "Pragmatics of Language and Language of Pragmatics," 51 *Soc. Res.*, 969 (1984) (quoting J. Austin, *How to Do Things with Words* (1962)). [. . .] Richard Delgado contends: "Stories, parables, chronicles, and narratives are powerful means for destroying mindset—the bundle of presuppositions, received wisdoms, and shared understandings against a background of which legal and political discourse takes place. These matters are rarely focused on. They are like eyeglasses we have worn a long time. They are nearly invisible; we use them to scan and interpret the world and only rarely examine them for themselves. Ideology—the received wisdom—makes current social arrangements seem fair and natural. Those in power sleep well at night—their conduct does not seem to them like oppression"; R. Delgado, "When a Story Is Just a Story: Does Voice Really Matter?," 76 *Va. L. Rev.* 95 (1990), 2413–14. For Delgado, stories and counterstories can "stir imagination in ways in which more conventional discourse cannot," in hope of quickening and engaging conscience; *id.* at 2415.

18. R. Terry, "The Negative Impact on White Values," in B. P. Bowser and R. G. Hunt, eds., *Impacts of Racism on White Americans*, 121–122 (1981).

19. A. Etzioni, *The Active Society: A Theory of Societal Political Processes*, 619 (1968).

20. *Id.* at 620. Hear Coltrane and Shepp, "*Call Me By My Rightful Name*," *supra* note 6.

21. L. Bart Landry, *The New Black Middle Class*, 85 (1987).

22. P. J. Williams, *The Alchemy of Race and Rights*, 256 (1991).

23. K. W. Crenshaw, "Forword: Toward a Race-conscious Pedagogy in Legal Education," 11 *Nat'l Black L. J.*, 1 (1989).

24. C. H. Arce, "A Reconsideration of Chicano Culture and Identity," 110 *Daedalus*, 177, 179 (1981). . . .

25. Wuthnow et al., *Cultural Analysis: The Work of Peter L. Berger, Mary Douglas, Michel Foucault and Jürgen Habermas*, 260, 268 (1986).

26. *Id.* at 260–61.

27. A. Dirlik, "Culturalism as Hegemonic Ideology and Liberating Practice," *Cultural Critique* (spring 1987), 13, 17.

28. D. Kennedy, "A Cultural Pluralist Case for Affirmative Action in Legal Academia," *Duke L. J.*, 705 (1990).

29. C. Geertz, *The Interpretation of Cultures*, 220 (1973).

30. J. B. Childs, "Concepts of Culture in Afro-American Political Thought, 1890–1920," 4 *Soc. Text*, 143 (1987).

31. J. Kirschenman and K. M. Neckerman, " 'We'd Love to Hire Them, But . . .': The Meaning of Race for Employers," in C. Jencks and P. E. Peterson, eds., *The Urban Underclass*, 223–24 (1991).

32. *Id.* at 224.

33. *Id.* at 223.

34. *Id.* at 227–28.

35. B. P. Bowser and R. G. Hunt, "Afterthoughts and Reflections," in *Impacts of Racism, supra* note 18, at 245, 251.

36. *Id.*

37. M. Omi and H. Winant, *Racial Formation in the United States: From the 1960s to the 1980s*, 120 (1986).

38. *Id.* at 114.

39. B. Ringer and E. Lawless, *Race-ethnicity and Society*, 18 (1989).

40. *Id.*

41. K. Karst, *Belonging to America: Equal Citizenship and the Constitution*, 117 (1989), citing Philip S. Foner, ed., W. E. B. Du Bois, *Speaker: Speeches and Addresses, 1890–1919* (1970).

42. S. Kwoh et al., "Finding Ways to Salve Intergroup Sore Points," *Los Angeles Times* (June 5, 1992), B7.

43. G. Firebaugh and K. E. Denis, "Trends in Antiblack Prejudice, 1972–1984: Region and Cohort Effects," 94 *Am. J. Soc.* 251 (1988) (attributing a decline in antiblack prejudice to attitudinal changes and cohort replacement—the replacement of older, more prejudiced birth cohorts with younger, less prejudiced ones).

TWO LIFE STORIES: REFLECTIONS OF ONE BLACK WOMAN LAW PROFESSOR
Taunya Lovell Banks

THE dispute at Harvard Law School over the absence of black women from the faculty is disturbing.[1] Particularly distressing is the use of the term "role model" as the articulated rationale for hiring a black woman law professor.[2] The term "role model" seems soft, unlike the word "mentor." A role model is a person whose "behavior in a particular role is imitated by others."[3] Most often a role model is passive, an image to be emulated. On the other hand, a mentor is more aggressively involved with protégé. The word "mentor" has an intellectual connotation that the term "role model" generally lacks. Because mentors provide some intellectual guidance, they also must be respected intellectually.

Good law teacher are intellectually challenging and aggressively involved with students. Thus, the need for black women mentors/intellectuals is a better justification for hiring black women as law teachers than is the need for role models. Law faculties may not take this argument seriously because of the societal bias against all women (and black men) as intellectuals and leaders. Today there still are teachers at prominent colleges and universities who openly espouse the intellectual inferiority of blacks and all women.[4]

Arguments challenging the legitimacy of nonwhite intellectuals suppose the correctness of a cultural imperialism based on male-dominated, Eurocentric norms. This unicultural perspective sees different and complex human experiences as weakening rather than enriching the intellectual community.[5] My argument for the inclusion of more women law teachers to serve as mentors/intellectuals goes beyond modeling arguments, to the very nature of the scholarly dialogue.

In arguing for the inclusion of black women on law faculties, I do not pretend that there is a single set of common experiences that all black people or black women share. Nor do I contend

that a black woman can capture the complexities
or varied lifestyles, and . . . approaching legal
issues of concern to all black women. How . . .
varied life experiences of being black and female
in a white male–dominated society affect our
individual perspectives.[6] Thus, the absence of
black women from the legal landscape—especially as legal academia . . . impoverishes the
imagination of law students and other legal
academicians.

There is, however, an important but subtle
difference between opening the legal landscape
to black women and attempting to discover,
prove, and legitimate their intellectual worth.[7]
In opening the legal landscape to black women,
who are generally perceived as being at the
bottom of the American hierarchy, it becomes
possible to open the legal landscape to all members of American society. However, any attempt
to justify the inclusion of black women law
professors based on some assertion of a special
perspective common to all blacks, or to all black
women, may be both difficult to make and
politically risky—although ultimately right.[8] If
not carefully crafted, these arguments can be
distorted by opponents in order to legitimate
further charges regarding our intellectual inferiority.

As it is, black women academics/intellectuals
already occupy a precarious position in legal
education. We are misfits, not fully accepted by
the black or white community; and as women,
we still are not full members of the feminist
community. We are, as Harold Cruse characterized black intellectuals almost thirty years ago, a
"rootless class of displaced persons"[9]—outsiders
even within our own communities. Thus, my
struggle as an academic is to teach and write
truthfully and accurately, despite feeling that I
fit into no world.

Truth-telling for me is easier with some issues (notably race) than others (especially class).
I still have some discomfort with my own class
background. Only lately have I come to accept
that I am a third-generation college teacher. All
of my grandparents attended college, and both
my parents have doctoral degrees. This part of
my background is unusual, even for most of my
white colleagues. Although not wealthy, I grew

up middle-class in black Washington, D.C., a
community infamous for its class- and color-
(literally, shades of skin color). In these respects,
my background is different from that of many
other black women law teachers.

As with all people, there are degrees of difference among black women academics. We are
part of multiple cultures based on gender, race,
class, region, and for some, ethnicity and sexuality. Unfortunately, the nature of traditional legal
dialogue within law schools and legal education
devalues life experiences; instead, it favors the
notion that bland, "objectively reasoned" arguments, often devoid of any humanistic concern,
are the only way to convey important legal ideas.
This is a one-dimensional scholarly dialogue, a
cerebral discussion of law. The body of legal
scholarship should be more diverse, since the
law, at the very least, is two-dimensional.

This second dimension, the inclusion of multiple life experiences, is missing from the legal
scholarly dialogue. These excluded or devalued
life experiences raise legal, social, and moral
issues that are worthy of discussion and should
be addressed by legal scholars because they
reflect law as it operates. This second dimension
is missing from classroom discussions as well.
For example, my presence in the classroom and
the academic community creates a potentially
richer learning experience: I bring a whole
segment of life experiences related to law
which is missing from the legal landscape. Law
teachers, like scholars, tend to ignore or minimize these experiences because they are unaware of the negative consequences of exclusion.
They are unaware because law faculties are so
homogenized, especially as regards race and
gender.[10]

I will use two stories to illustrate how my life
experiences affect my point of view. The first
story has to do with my perceived position in
American society. The second story shows how
my experiences influence the way I view legal
issues. Recently, I discovered that most of my
conversations with friends are a series of stories
we tell each other. Through these stories we
indirectly learn much about each other's lives,
unhindered by modesty or shame. Sometimes
standard English words just strung together in

logical straightforward sentences are not always the best way to convey important legal ideas.

My first story relates an experience common to almost all black people. It illustrates how black people who are unknown to whites are categorized by them only on the basis of color.

I. THE ELEVATOR

ONE Saturday afternoon I entered an elevator in a luxury condominium in downtown Philadelphia with four other black women law professors; we were leaving the apartment of another black woman law professor. The elevator was large and spacious. A few floors later, the door opened and a white woman in her late fifties peered in, let out a muffled cry of surprise, stepped back and let the door close without getting on. Several floors later the elevator stopped again, and the doors opened to reveal yet another white middle-aged woman, who also decided not to get on.

Following the first incident, we looked at each other somewhat puzzled; after the second incident we laughed in disbelief, belatedly realizing that the two women seemed afraid to get on an elevator in a luxury condominium with five well-dressed black women in their thirties and forties.[11] Our laughter, the nervous laugh blacks often express when faced with the blatant or unconscious racism of white America, masked our shock and hurt.

The elevator incident is yet another reminder that no matter how well-educated, well-dressed, or financially secure we may be, we are black first and thus still undesirable others to too many white Americans. It reminds me that no matter what my accomplishments, I am still perceived as less than equal—and even dangerous!

The elevator incident is a painful reminder that white attitudes about race have not changed, and that too often we "assimilated" blacks buy into these white attitudes. I used to think that whites were afraid only of black men, and I felt safe from that form of racism due to my gender; now, I realize that any black person is threatening. Groups of black women are very threatening even to their white "sisters." We

are threatening even when encountered during the day in a secure building complete with a doorman.

We should not have been surprised by the white women's fear, because of the dominance of fear in women's lives generally. As women we fear rape, assault, and harassment in the street or workplace. Feminist writers point out that the dominance of fear as a part of women's life experience is one way our experiences differ from men's, at least from white men's.[12]

On the other hand, though, we tend to think that only black men's lives are dominated by the experience of "being feared." Yet in this instance, by virtue of color alone, we too were feared. Thus, being feared is not simply a black male experience, it is part of the black experience.[13]

However, I think some of us were surprised that we were not insulated by gender (and perhaps class) from the fear that whites have of blacks. We were instantly categorized, stripped of our individuality, well before those women waiting for the elevator had a chance to know us. We were deprived of our community of gender (and perhaps class) simply because we were classified as black at birth. It is an experience that can happen to any black woman, and in this way black women's experiences are not simply sometimes black and sometimes female. Our experiences as black women fit neither paradigm; in the elevator we were feared, but not because of being black *and male*.[14]

Nevertheless, as a black woman academic in America, I am constantly asked to fit within only one paradigm at a time. I am categorized as being part of a black world, or a white world, or a female world, or a world of poverty and cultural deprivation. Being so variously categorized often causes me to think about all of these worlds collectively when viewing common life experiences.

My second story illustrates how this kind of thinking operates, and how it can operate in a law classroom.

II. THE TRAIN RIDE

I ALWAYS enjoy the train because it is pleasant, reasonably comfortable, usually efficient, and safe. Recently, as the train pulled out of Wilmington, Delaware heading south, I glanced across the aisle and noticed that a man now occupied the window seat. I looked again because there was something about this man which set him apart from the usual train passenger. Finally, I realized that it was his dress. He had a double hood pulled over his head and that hungry and scared look I see on the faces of some homeless people I pass daily on my walk to work. The man glanced furtively at me, smiled, and seemed to relax as he removed his hood, revealing close-cut salt-and-pepper hair and a stubby white hint of a beard.

I resumed reading, still vaguely discomforted by the passenger across the aisle—he had no baggage—and alternately chastising myself for some subconscious class bias. Suddenly, I felt someone staring at me. I looked up and glanced across the aisle—and was sickened when I saw the man smiling at me as he wiggled his bared penis. Determined to stop this man from disturbing other passengers,[15] I started to get up to find a conductor. The man, sensing I was about to betray him, also got up and mumbled something inaudible as he passed me. Like someone in a B movie I shouted, "Stop that man! He just exposed himself." The cashier behind the refreshment counter looked up, and I repeated my alarm. A conductor met the man and escorted him to the rear car.

Feeling relieved, I resumed reading until the conductor approached and asked what had happened. I related the events, and he asked what I wanted him to do with the man. It was an annoying question, since it seemed obvious that the man had committed a criminal offense— indecent exposure.[16] It also was a typical response to a victim of a wrong which society does not take seriously. It was the same question posed to me by colleagues who had heard that a white student told classmates he asked to be transferred to another class because he was too prejudiced to be taught by a black woman. My immediate thought in that case was, "How could a black person understand how to reach a white person who obviously believes and openly espouses an ideology of white supremacy?" I had a similar thought when the train conductor

posed the same question: "How can a woman understand how to stop a man who feels compelled to expose himself to women in public places?" In each instance, the question seemed both inappropriate and insulting, or at the very least, insensitive.

The conductor seemed appropriately indignant. He expressed a desire to beat the man and also offered to scare him. Intellectually, I realized that neither action would solve the problem, because obviously the man was sick, so I asked what options were available. The conductor replied that I could press charges. I was noncommittal, and the conductor left.

Subsequently, the conductor returned with a second conductor who informed me that the man, probably homeless, had no ticket or money. The first conductor apologized and explained that there had never been such an incident on his train. (But was this because no other woman had protested?) Once again they asked me what I wanted done with the man. This time I quickly replied that I would be willing to press charges. There seemed no other way to stop this man from exposing himself to other women. They left only to return shortly with a third conductor; together they explained that the law required them to put a person without a ticket off the train at the next station.[17] No one was listening to what I wanted. When I inquired whether riding on a train without paying the fare was a crime, they responded that it was, but that the police would probably release the man and bar him from the train station. They said that the same thing would happen if I tried to press charges against the man for indecent exposure. As an alternative, they offered to hold the man until I was off the train and safely in a cab, leaving him free to expose himself to other women passengers, who might not openly object.

During the forty-three minute ride from Wilmington to Baltimore, many things went through my mind. Only now do I wonder if the outcome would have been different had I been a white woman. Perhaps not; after all, I am just a woman. From a feminist perspective, I viewed this man's exposed penis directed toward me, a woman unknown to him, as a sexual assault.[18]

However, it would be difficult to argue that the man was attempting sexual battery, and it is doubtful that he intended to create apprehension in my mind of an immediate sexual battery. The man was simply displaying his penis, perhaps as an invitation.

At one level, I have great difficulty viewing the man's action as a simple misdemeanor. Exposing one's naked body in a public setting—nudity per se—is not offensive or threatening. However, the man's conscious sexual actions directed toward me left me shaken and repulsed; they invaded my sense of privacy and safety. At another level, though, a pure feminist analysis does not fully convey my feelings.

The man was old and black, and as a black person I had mixed emotions about filing a complaint against him for a sex offense. Perhaps the conductors, all white men, would have reacted differently had I been a white woman and the man black. I am keenly aware of the historical misuse of sex crimes to oppress black men in the United States.[19] After all, I rationalized, most social science studies indicate that men who expose themselves seldom commit a more serious sex offense such as rape.[20]

People who expose themselves in public are sick, and punishing sick people seems inherently unjust. I questioned the use of criminal sanctions against a mentally ill person who, theoretically, posed no "real" danger to society. Yet my feminist voice whispered, "He does pose a real danger—look at how his actions affected you."

However, I bring still another life experience to this incident which further complicates my analysis. I fear this disclosure will trouble some of my family members, but more perceptive readers might have sensed some connection anyway. My uncle, a quiet and kind man, has been mentally ill for more than twenty-five years; except for a short time at the onset of his illness, he has lived at home with his sister. How different his life might have been had no family member been willing to care for him. His presence in our family has affected us all. But for my family, though, my uncle might be a homeless man.

The analysis of my experience on the train could easily be transferred to my criminal law class. Even raising the issue of indecent exposure in a criminal law class would be novel, since most casebooks omit "minor" sex offenses.[21] I might ask students how society should treat (as opposed to categorize) a man who intentionally exposes his genitals to an unwilling onlooker in public. We could discuss how race and class often affect the ways such a law is enforced against sex offenders, or whether the victim's gender makes a difference in criminalizing conduct and in the seriousness assigned the crime. We might also explore whether women and men differ in their reaction to such conduct, and if so, whether the law recognizes that difference, especially since women are almost exclusively the victims of indecent exposure.[22]

I might ask students whether, even if they believe the act should not be criminalized, it would be kinder to file charges against the man. After all, at least he would get some meals and have a warm place to sleep for a few days. However, students might note that jails and prisons are unsafe places and argue that providing food but unsafe shelter is not a kind act. We might decide that even if jails and prisons were safe, it seems unjust and unconstitutional to deprive an individual of liberty for an act that is not criminal, merely because American society is unwilling to feed and shelter all of its members.[23]

In my seminar on disability law, I might ask students whether, assuming the man is mentally ill, institutionalization and treatment would be an appropriate means of minimizing the problem. We would discuss the constitutional restrictions on involuntary detention and treatment of mentally ill individuals. I would explain that twenty years ago many of today's homeless women and men would have been confined in mental institutions, where they would have been sheltered, fed, and clothed, although not equally. We would learn that a few received treatment, but too many were mistreated or neglected, and that as a result, deinstitutionalization proponents wanted to ensure a more humane and less restrictive environment for nondangerous mentally ill individuals by providing community-based treatment and, where needed, shelter in group homes.

I would ask students why the states failed to provide treatment, and why community residents resisted efforts to place group homes in their neighborhoods. I would note that without either treatment or shelter, the mentally ill, who theoretically pose no danger to themselves or to society (an assumption still open to question),[24] roam American city streets—starving and dying—as an indifferent public walks by wishing they would just disappear. Students would be asked to explore why American society feels no obligation to protect and provide for the mentally ill unless they are institutionalized.

I would ask students whether the presence of this mentally disturbed penniless man reflects society's failure to help all homeless people, approximately one third of whom suffer from serious mental illnesses. Students would be asked to look beyond the numbers to find out more about homeless women and men, look at their age, race, class, and quality of life. We would discuss why mentally ill people are appearing in growing numbers on the streets.

The presence of increasing numbers of homeless families on American streets also reflects the unwillingness of one of the wealthiest countries in the world to include food and shelter among those basic rights guaranteed by the Constitution—surely an issue for my constitutional law class. I would ask whether it matters that a disproportionate number of homeless people are women, people of color, and children who are both female and black, or whether society's indifference here reflects its indifference to important issues of race, gender, and class generally.

It is this frame of reference I bring into my classroom. My life stories influence my perspective, a perspective unable to function within a single paradigm, because I am too many things at one time. My perspective often transcends race and gender and is sometimes fully or partially conscious of the complexities and intersection of race, gender, and class. It is a multiple perspective not represented in our casebooks or legal literature.

NOTES

1. In April, 1990, Harvard Law pofessor Derrick Bell, a black man, announced that he was taking a leave of absence without pay until the law school appointed a tenured black woman to its faculty. Professor Bell said that he could not in "good conscience" continue to serve as a "role model" for both black men and black women. F. Butterfield, "Harvard Law Professor Quits Until Black Woman Is Named," *New York Times* (April 24, 1990), A1.

2. Not only did Professor Bell use the term "role model" but the *New York Times* quoted one black first-year woman student as saying, "We need black women role models"; F. Butterfield, "Harvard Law School Torn by Race Issue," *New York Times* (April 26, 1990), A20. The term "role model" was then used by some detractors to suggest that both Professor Bell and his supporters simply wanted any black woman appointed without regard to her scholarship and teaching; see, for example, J. Yardley, "The Case for Merit at Harvard Law," *Washington Post* (April 30, 1990), B2; George F. Will, "Academic Set-Asides,: *Washington Post* (May 17, 1990), A27. Little attention was paid to the words of another black woman law student quoted in the *New York Times* article as saying the law faculty "have had years to find a black woman, but they just want to keep the status quo, what they call the comfort level of white men. The fact remains that we are getting only a white male corporate view of the law. We need black women *mentors* to tell us what it is like out there when we join a firm and start trying to get clients"; Butterfield, *supra* A20 (emphasis added).

3. *A Supplement to the Oxford English Dictionary,* 1021 (1982).

4. See, for example, "Campus Is Split over Statement by a Professor," *New York Times* (Dec. 23, 1990), 28 (tenured University of California anthropology professor makes statements suggesting that women have smaller brains than men, and that race makes a difference in academic ability). Cornel West writes that the black intellectual is burdened by charges of intellectual inferiority, which then generate anxieties for those intellectuals seeking legitimization through the academy; C. West, "The Black Intellectual," 1 *Cultural Critique*, 109, 116–17 (fall 1985). Stephen Carter's essay "The Best Black, and Other Tales," is the best current example of West's point. Carter's essay graphically illustrates the notion that despite one's achievements, whites, and, too often, black intellectuals, buy into the notion that blacks are intellectually inferior or perceived as such; S. L. Carter, "The Best Black, and Other Tales," 1 *Reconstruction*, 6 (winter 1990).

5. Some scholars are beginning to discuss this concern. See, for example, M. J. Matsuda, "Looking to the Bottom: Critical Legal Studies and Reparations," 22 *Harv. C.R.-C.L. L. Rev.*, 323 (1987) [the essay is included in this volume—Ed.]; "Affirmative Action and Legal Knowledge: Planting Seeds in Plowed-up Ground," 11 *Harv. Women's*

L. J., 1 (1988); "When the First Quail Calls: Multiple Consciousness as Jurisprudential Method," 11 *Women's Rts. L. Rptr.*, 7 (spring 1989). See also K. Crenshaw, "Demarginalizing the Intersection of Race and Sex: A Black Feminist Critique of Antidiscrimination Doctrine, Feminist Theory and Antiracist Politics," *U. Chi. Legal. F.*, 139, 152–60 (1989); R. Delgado, "Storytelling for Oppositionists and Others: A Plea for Narrative," 87 *Mich. L. Rev.*, 2411 (1989); G. Torres and K. Milun, "Translating 'Yonnondio' by Precedent and Evidence: The Mashpee Indian Case," *Duke L. J.*, 625 (1990) [the essay is included in this volume—ED.].

6. For a more complete discussion of this point, see K. Crenshaw, *supra* note 5.

7. Hazel Carby faults black feminist criticism, along with the women's and black studies movements, for accepting in large part the prevailing paradigms of academic scholarship. . . .

8. Patricia Williams captures my feelings when she writes: "I do believe that the simple matter of the color of one's skin so profoundly affects the way one is treated, so radically shapes what one is allowed to think and feel about this society, that the decision to generalize from such a division [between 'black' and 'white'] is valid." P. Williams, *The Alchemy of Race Rights*, 256 (1991).

9. H. Cruse, *The Crisis of the Negro Intellectual*, 454 (1967).

10. Richard Chused's 1987 study of law faculties found that women occupy 15.9 percent and blacks 3.7 percent of all tenured or tenure-track positions at the American Association of Law School member institutions participating in the survey; R. H. Chused, "The Hiring and Retention of Minorities and Women on American Law Faculties," 137 *U. Pa. L. Rev.*, 537, 540 n.19, 548. . . .

11. In all fairness I later learned that the first woman refuses to get on an elevator with *anyone*, but that still does not adequately resolve my feelings about the second incident.

12. For example, Robin West points out that patriarchy as experienced by modern women is profoundly negative and pervasively violent; R. West, "Feminism, Critical Social Theory and Law," *U. Chi. Legal F.*, 59, 61 (1989). She notes that fear, specifically of sexual violence, is a defining role in women's lives; *id.* at 62–63. See also C. Littleton, "Equality and Feminist Legal Theory," 48 *U. Pitt L. Rev.*, 1043–44 (1987); K. Bumiller, "Rape as a Legal Symbol: An Essay on Sexual Violence and Racism," 42 *U. Miami L. Rev.*, 75, 76, 91 (1987).

13. Robin West uses the term "ethical fear" to describe "a fear so pervasive that it forces [those who have it] to adapt continually to its pressures and begins actually to determine their personality and character"; R. West, "The Supreme Court 1989 Term—Foreword: Taking Freedom Seriously," 104 *Harv. L. Rev.*, 43, 91 (1990). West takes the term "ethical fear" from Vaclav Havel, but uses it in a

different context. Havel uses the term to describe "the pervasive threat of official violence engendered by a police state"; *id.* at 91–92 n.209, citing V. Havel, "Letter to Gustáv Husák," in J. Vladislav, ed., *Vaclav Havel, or Living in Truth*, 3, 5 (1986). West, however, uses the term to describe the consequences of living with the threat of violence from other citizens, a fear she characterizes as common to both women (fear of rape) and residents of crime-ridden neighborhoods (fear of violent crime); *id.* However, the black experience in America includes both Havel's and West's "ethical fear." We have adapted to the threat of official violence, and we adapted to the threat of random violence (lynching). Starting with the slave experience, black women have adapted to the fear of sexual violence. In addition, though, black men *and* women are forced to adapt to another "ethical fear," the fear of being feared and the dangers implicit in generating this fear.

14. There is an even more insidious aspect to this story. Its underlying theme is the continuing lack of racial equality, but implicit in this quest for equality is the desire for acceptance. Having lived in America for so many years, we should have realized that black people will never be accepted as equals by many whites. Thus, any quest for an equality based on a notion of acceptance is doomed to failure because acceptance can always be withheld by those from whom we seek it. We must first free ourselves of the need to be accepted before we can create and write about a theory to liberate people of color. Intellectually I know all of this, but it is hard to kill the demon—the need for acceptance in a culture you do not dominate or control. Christine Littleton wrote about this problem, which she termed "equality as acceptance," in the context of gender oppression; C. Littleton, *supra* note 12.

15. This was not the first time that a man had exposed himself to me, and I think that fact caused me to take some action. Twenty-two years earlier, a black man exposed himself as I sat in my car in the parking lot of a Jackson, Mississippi, public library. I remember feeling shocked, scared, and then sickened, but I never told anyone about it for almost fifteen years. However, I never forgot the incident or my feelings.

16. Indecent exposure is defined in section 213.5 of the Model Penal Code, to wit: "Indecent Exposure: A person commits a misdemeanor if, for the purpose of arousing or gratifying sexual desire of himself or of any person other than his spouse, he exposes his genitals under circumstances in which he knows his conduct is likely to cause affront or harm"; 2 *Model Penal Code and Commentary*, §213.5 at 405 (1980).

17. Homeless people know about this law and sneak on trains, gradually working their way up and down the East Coast.

18. A traditional criminal law definition of an assault is either an attempt to commit a battery or an intentional placing of another in apprehension of receiving an immedi-

ate battery; R. M. Perkins and R. N. Boyce, *Criminal Law*, 159 (3d ed. 1982).

19. See G. Lerner, ed., *Black Women in White America: A Documentary History*, 193–215 (1973) (documenting black women's efforts to challenge the myth of the black rapist by proving the falseness of the accusation, the disproportionate punishment for the crime where the defendant is black, and the use of the myth to justify lynching); A. Y. Davis, *Women, Race and Class*, 172–201 (1981) (discussing the unwillingness of white women to help dispel the myth and its connection to the rise of lynching).

20. See, for example, J. W. Mohr, R. E. Turner, and M. B. Jerry, *Pedophilia and Exhibitionism*, 118 (1964) (exposure is the final act, and the exhibitor does not seek any further relationship with the victim); E. F. Berah and R. G. Myers, "The Offense Records of a Sample of Convicted Exhibitionists" 11 *Bull. Am. Acad. Psychiatry Law*, 365 (1983).

21. N. S. Erickson, "Final Report: 'Sex Bias in the Teaching of Criminal Law,'" 42 *Rutg. L. Rev*, 309, 384–86 (1990).

22. Mohr, Turner, and Jerry, *Pedophilia and Exhibitionism*, *supra* note 20, at 115.

23. In *O'Connor v. Donaldson*, the U.S. Supreme Court said in dicta that institutional confinement is rarely, if ever, necessary to ensure a mentally ill person a decent living standard. . . .

24. In castigating New York State for abandoning mentally ill individuals, noted author and neurologist Oliver Sacks writes, "There are 80,000 desperately ill and wretched people on our streets, not only homeless and endangered, and perhaps dangerous to others, but often in a nightmare of their own psychoses"; O. Sacks, "Forsaking the Mentally Ill," *New York Times* (Feb. 13, 1991), A23. In addition, I am not sure that so-called nondangerous mentally ill homeless people do not pose some danger to society in the broader sense of the word. By allowing mentally ill homeless people—or any homeless person—to roam the streets, we cause society to become more desensitized and dehumanized. We must take individual responsibility for all homeless people. Robin West, contrasting Vaclav Havel's "postdemocratic liberalism" to American liberal legalism, writes that individual "responsibility . . . is both a precondition and consequence of individual liberty [and] 'is not just the expression of an introverted, self-contained responsibility that individuals have to and for themselves alone, but responsibility to and for the *world*'"; R. West, *supra* note 13, at 66 (quoting V. Havel, "The Power of the Powerless," in J. Vladislav, ed., *supra* note 13, at 36, 103. (emphasis in original). . . .

THE WORD AND THE RIVER: PEDAGOGY AS SCHOLARSHIP AS STRUGGLE
Charles R. Lawrence, III

I. THE GENESIS OF THE ARTICLE: REFLECTING ON WHAT I/WE THINK ABOUT AND DO

A. Talking to Students about Being a Scholar

What is the role of the word—the spoken word, the preached word, the whispered-in-the-nighttime word, the written word, the published word—in the fight for black freedom?[1]

A group of students at Stanford have asked me to speak on minority scholarship and I have begun my presentation with this quote from *There Is a River*,[2] Vincent Harding's compelling and inspirational history of black radicalism in America. I have told the panel's organizers that I am neither willing nor able to attempt even a cursory description of the multifaceted work of my colleagues of color, but that I would be glad to ruminate on my own work as well as my aspirations for that work. I have recently assigned several chapters from Harding's book to one of my classes, and his portrayal of the tradition of "radical teaching among dominated Africa peoples"[3] has given focus to my reflections concerning my own scholarship.

I feel an immediate kinship with the tradition that Harding describes and names "the Word."[4] It is a tradition of teaching, preaching, and healing; an interdisciplinary tradition wherein healers are concerned with the soul and preachers with the pedagogy of the oppressed;[5] a tradition that eschews hierarchy in the face of the need for all of us who seek liberation to be both teachers and students. The Word is an articulation and validation of our common experience. It is a vocation of struggle against dehumanization, a practice of raising questions about reasons for oppression, an inheritance of passion and hope. . . .

B. Understanding That Preaching and Practice Are One

Within the Word we find two dimensions, reflection and action, in such radical interaction that if one is sacrificed—even in part—the other immediately suffers. There is no true word that is not at the same time a praxis.[6] . . .

It is evident to me that the Word requires a unity of pedagogy and scholarship, and that I cannot, I should not, separate methodology from substance or objective. This was not a new idea to me; I had heard it from others and nodded my head in agreement.[7] I had even been a practitioner of this ideal, probably more so than most. But this was nonetheless a "eureka" type of experience. This was a way of understanding what might enable me to transmit my experience to others.

If the role of the Word includes its use and value as a unifying force, a statement of protest, an expression of courage, an organizing tool, the articulation of utopian dreams or a higher law, then our methodology must inspire and advance those uses and values. If the nature of the Word is that it is subjective, consciously historical, and revisionist; if it is both pragmatic (responding to the immediate necessities of survival and struggle) and poetic (responding to the immediate need of expression of feeling); if it must proceed from the specifics of experience and articulation of that experience toward the abstraction of theory; if it is reflection on action, informed by active struggle and in turn informing that struggle; if it is double voiced, expressing the ambiguity of those who know the experience of belonging and not belonging, then our methodology must be a vehicle designed to carry out these complex and varied tasks. Our way of speaking the Word, of gathering the Word, of spreading the Word, must be open. It must be a form that admits all comers, that does not have a dress code or a requirement that it be filed in triplicate.

One of the ways I have experienced this necessary relationship between substance and methodology, between reflection and action, is through my teaching and the way my teaching informs my scholarship. In fact, my teaching (in the broadest sense, my dialogue with others) is the chief source of nourishment for my scholarship. The Word is praxis, not just in the "more obvious ways the thoughtful work of a scholar provides strategy or frames new conceptual arguments for the activist lawyer or community organizer, but in the ongoing work of the scholar as teacher. By speaking and hearing the Word in our classrooms, in our offices, or in community meetings we transform our own understanding of our relationship with the world and thereby transform the world. In my teaching about law I try to leave space for, to encourage, and to value, the articulation of feeling and experience. This is particularly important in teaching law, where the story that is told within the dominant discourse has systematically excluded the experience of people of color and other outsiders, and where we are trained to believe that the story told by those in power is a universal story.

Every new and important understanding or insight that I have reached and found a way to articulate in my writing has come from dialogue with my students and with teachers. The conversations that produce theory are those which identify and articulate dissonance between existing legal theory and our individual/collective feeling and experience. Articulate descriptions of what we experience and feel must be placed alongside the descriptions produced by dominant theorists. Where there is discourse or where there are notes missing in the law's written score, our conversations must be an improvisational search for notes that are harmonious with the way we experience the world. . . .

II. The Gifts of the Word; A Paradigm for Scholar/Teachers

IN THIS part of the article I address the elements or characteristics of the paradigm I have called the Word and explore how it expresses itself in both scholarship and pedagogy. In so doing, I will refer to the work of exemplary scholars, artists, teachers, and activists, keeping in mind my earlier observation that the Word eschews any segregation of these roles. I begin by focusing on that part of the Word that would be called scholarship in the dominant academic culture. This is that part of our work that manifests itself in a formal written product.

A. The Gift of Identity: Embracing Subjectivity

A self-conscious commitment to a subjective perspective is critical to the work of practitioners of the Word. I will consider three separate though interrelated meanings that may be given to the term "subjective" which enable and are central to our scholarship. These meanings are the following: subjective, indicating the scholars' positioned perspective in viewing and recording social constructs; subjective, indicating nonneutrality of purpose, that the scholar embraces certain values and that her work is avowedly political (read liberationist); subjective, indicating that the scholar places herself in the linguistic position of subject rather than object, a being capable of acting upon the world rather than as one upon whom others act.

I. SUBJECTIVITY AS POSITIONED PERSPECTIVE

Most legal academics aspire to the classical scholarly paradigm of the detached, objective observer/recorder. This model envisions scholars achieving an unbiased and universal perspective by distancing themselves from the social reality they seek to describe. The Word, in stark contrast, embraces positioned perspective. It recognizes the impossibility of distance and impartiality in the observation of a play in which the observers must also be actors. However, championing subjectivity is more than an acknowledgement of the existence and validity of many different and competing perspectives.[8] Practitioners of the Word must learn to privilege their own perspectives and those of other outsiders, understanding that the dominant legal discourse is premised upon the claim to knowledge of objective truths and the existence of neutral principles. We must free ourselves from the mystification produced by this ideology. We must learn to trust our own senses, feelings, and experiences, and to give them authority, even (or especially) in the face of dominant accounts of social reality that claim universality.

"Universal" accounts are particularly pernicious when the assertion of universality is left unstated, as is most often the case.[9] An exchange between two colleagues, one a white male and the other a woman of color, demonstrates both the oppressive power of the unstated, universalized premise and the liberating power of the outsider's ability to give her own positioned perspective authority.

A faculty group to which I had presented my thoughts on teaching and on my race discrimination class was also developing a curriculum for lawyering for social change. We were now in our second semester of regular meetings. Two of my colleagues had taken on the burdensome and thankless task of assembling materials for the group to read and discuss in a seminar format. The third set of readings included a series of articles discussing I.Q. and theories about its relationship to race and poverty. The articles were highly technical "scientific" pieces and, with the exception of a chapter from Stephen Jay Gould's *The Mismeasure of Man*, were all by "neoconservative" authors. The cover memorandum attached to the materials reads as follows: "We thought we'd begin by continuing the discussion on Marxism, focusing on the Reich/Edwards/Gordon material. I've attached a set of readings on 'neoconservative' theory, not because they'd necessarily come next in the actual course, but because they seem to pose a very different (but very powerful) set of pedagogical problems. Unlike the Marxist material (unfamiliar and difficult), these materials may seem quite familiar but quite offensive to a large number of the students. I'd like to discuss that problem, as well as the substantive issues."[10]

Several days before we met to discuss these materials, another member of the working group, a black woman colleague, came by my office. She was upset and concerned about the readings, particularly by their format and the cover memo that accompanied them. I shared many of her concerns and encouraged her to draft a memorandum sharing them with the group. Although the memorandum, an eleven-page effort, is too long to quote in full here, the section that responded to the cover memorandum is most relevant to this discussion in that it demonstrates how outsiders can be liberated by embracing a positioned perspective.

> [T]here is a very small, subtle, perhaps unconscious but devastating frame contained in the cover memo to these materials. I refer to the language that these materials "may seem offensive." This is a laissez-faire, open-ended throw away that implies that the opinions expressed herein are just opinions and that all opinions are valid or equal. While this may be true in some ultimate sense, as reflecting the truth of the speaker's world, I thought we wanted, in this course, to have a more specific political agenda.
>
> It seems to me that an important shift of reference comes about when you assume not that some "might" be offended but that these ARE offensive because there are some who are not just offended, but powerful and visible enough to have that opinion extend itself as an attribute of the materials themselves. I am offended. Therefore, these materials are offensive. It is at this point that we can begin to have a discussion about why I am offended, about what it is in these materials that has the property of "offense-to-me."
>
> Any other stance, I think any other balance, allows the laziness of majoritarian opting out. The materials, because they "might" be offensive to an invisible unnamed some, therefore take on the property of "might-being" a little bit offensive in small part. But because, after all, they only might be offensive, they could just as well take on the character of being for the most part not offensive. It is thus that materials can get manipulated imagistically rather than analytically, as though the topic were something that could be decided by a simple vote. So if a majority of people enter the class feeling that their I.Q. is higher than that of Blacks, these readings, as presently constituted, will allow them to feel OK about that. Black inferiority is just one of several valid interpretations. And if most of the class is authorized to feel that way by the cues in the materials or in the presentation of them, then we have succeeded only in legitimating the status quo and in subordinating the already subordinated.

"I am offended. Therefore, these materials are offensive." It is these words that are revolutionary. The author has done much more than offer a different perspective on the materials. She has given her/our perspective authority, and in doing so she has shown us that we can do the same. The unstated assertion of objectivity and universality in the materials and in their presentation is made explicit and challenged. It is

unmasked and revealed as a perspective that advances values and goals inimical to our own. Thus, by embracing a positioned perspective, this gifted practitioner of the Word reallocated the power to define what is real.

. . .

Mari Matsuda has observed that the jurisprudence of color is "consciously historical and revisionist"[11] and has identified a particularly important function of positioned perspective. Adopting a positioned perspective is to write our histories: to tell the silenced stories, the unrecorded perspectives, of our foremothers and forefathers. Historical revisionism is critical because full personhood is itself defined in part by one's authority to tell one's own story. Historians make history even as they record it. Discovering and rewriting the record reshapes history itself, and our contemporary social context is in turn changed.[12] This becomes important to the liberating task of embracing a positioned perspective. What we see and feel today, our own perspectives and perceptions, appear distorted and unreal when they appear against the background of a history that has excluded the voices of those who have seen the world from positions most like our own. When we hear their stories, our own stories take on a contextual frame that gives them meaning. They become more comprehensible. They are easier to trust.

. . .

2. SUBJECTIVITY AS TAKING SIDES: EMBRACING NONNEUTRALITY

If anything I do, in the way of writing novels or whatever I write, isn't about the village or the community or about you, then it isn't about anything. I am not interested in indulging myself in some private exercise of my imagination . . . which is to say yes, the work must be political.[13]

The Word is also subjective in the sense that it makes no claim to value neutrality. Matsuda describes the jurisprudence of people of color as "pragmatist" and "bottom-line instrumentalist."[14] Freeman contrasts the result-oriented "victim perspective"[15] with a "perpetrator perspective" that claims to seek neutral principles based on shared values but is "ultimately indifferent to the condition of the victim."[16] This is another way of saying that practitioners of the Word evaluate work product (judicial opinions, legislation, organizing tactics, ideas, theory, poetry) according to the degree to which the effort serves the cause of liberation.

Embracing instrumentalism, like owning one's perspective, serves a dual liberatory purpose. By keeping our politics at the forefront and measuring our work and that of others by the bottom line of results, we can be certain that theory is disciplined by purpose and guided by the needs and resulting insight of those for whom change is most urgent.[17] An avowedly political posture also serves as an antidote to the mystifying and oppressive properties of the dominant ideology of shared values and neutral principles. This is particularly important to the scholar concerned with racial equality under circumstances in which the dominant legal ideology of equal opportunity employs the rhetoric of antidiscrimination and equal treatment to disguise the clash in values between those who are burdened by and committed to ending discriminatory conditions and those who are responsible for and benefit from those conditions.

The contrast between the Word's nonneutral commitment to "results and dominant scholarship's professed quest for value neutrality and the identification of shared values, a quest that may well be indifferent to results, is striking in the context of faculty debates over the appropriateness of quotas and set-asides to achieve race and gender diversity on law school faculties. A student paper submitted for my race discrimination class recounts the history of students' efforts to encourage the Stanford faculty to increase the numbers of minorities and women teaching at the law school. These efforts had included several informational forums featuring the dean and members of the appointment committee, informal conversations with individual faculty members, letters to the student paper, a student-sponsored affirmative action proposal (at times referred to as "student demands"), and student demonstrations in the dean's office and the faculty club. The paper

also reports faculty responses to the student hiring proposal, a proposal that was submitted to the faculty by a coalition of student organizations representing minorities, women, and progressive white male students.

. . .

3. SUBJECTIVITY AS STANDING IN THE POSITION OF THE SUBJECT

Stories are important. They keep us alive. In the ships, in the camps, in the quarters, fields, prisons, on the road, on the run, underground, under siege, in the throes, on the verge—the storyteller snatches us back from the edge to hear the next chapter. In which we are the subjects. We, the hero of the tales. Our lives preserved. How it was; how it be. Passing it along in the relay. That is what I work to do— to produce stories that save our lives.

I AM SOMEBODY!

—Jesse Jackson

In this section I use the word "subjectivity" to indicate that as practitioners of the Word we must endeavor to place ourselves in the linguistic position of "subject" rather than "object." That is, we must be actors rather than those upon whom others act. This is, for us, an especially important understanding of subjectivity, for the language we use to describe ourselves is both evidence of how we see ourselves and part of the means whereby our self-image is shaped. Language shapes our reality even as it describes it. This, in part, was the lesson of my discussion of positioned perspective. However, I want to suggest something more than what is learned from the observation that our perceptions of the world are valid, and that the articulation of those perceptions must be privileged in the context of a discourse which objectifies and universalizes the perceptions of those who dominate that discourse. When we use language to refer to ourselves, we do more than offer another possible description of the world around us: we define ourselves and our relationship to that world.

The language of self-description has been a particularly powerful and important weapon in the liberationist struggle by African-Americans. The absence of a collective black voice was central to the ethnocentric ideology of the European Renaissance and the Enlightenment—an ideology that denied Africans their humanity and thereby justified their enslavement. Henry Louis Gates notes that for the Enlightenment philosophers the absence of a self-portrayal, of a written history, meant that Africans had "no true self-consciousness, no power to present or represent the black and terrible self": [18]

"[B]lacks lay veiled in a shroud of silence, invisible not because they had no face, but rather because they had no voice. Voice, after all, presupposes a face. That alone which separates the subject from the object is, for Hegel, the absence or presence of the voice, the phenomenological voice; the blackness of invisibility is the blackness of this silence. Without a voice, the African is absent, or defaced, from history. [19]

Early practitioners of the Word recognized the necessity of self-representation to combat this dehumanizing ideology that determined one's very being by presence (or lack thereof) in history and, in turn, viewed one's absence from history as proof of one's lack of consciousness. Frederick Douglass and others created the genre of slave narratives to render in horrific detail the inhumanity of the slave system, but their purpose was also to break the silence that made them objects. Gates says of the slave narratives, "[T]his written language of the ex-slave signified for someone even before it signified something." [20]

. . .

Postmodern literary theorists have articulated the occurrence of this act of self-identification through language by defining subjectivity as the " 'capacity of the speaker to posit himself as subject.' Subjectivity is viewed as a fundamental property of language. 'It is in and through language that man constitutes himself as subject, because language alone establishes the concept of ego in reality, in its reality.' " [21] Thus, language is important because its use signifies, is symbolic of, the speaker's capacity for creativity; and it is the capacity for creativity that makes us human.

The history of African-American efforts to name ourselves, as the first enunciating act of self-definition, and of the resistance to that effort, is testimony to the importance of the symbolism of language in the political/cultural hegemony of American racism. African slaves were prohibited from using their family, ancestral, and tribal names; instead, they were required to use the "Christian" names by which their masters chose to identify them. After emancipation, the practice of whites naming blacks and denying blacks the power to name themselves remained central to the system of symbols that objectified African-Americans and denied their humanity.

In the twenties, the NAACP launched a hard-fought campaign for the use of the word "Negro" (with a capital "N"). For too long African-Americans had heard themselves called "niggers," "jigs," "dinge," "blackbirds," "crows," and "spooks." "Colored," the word then used by respectable whites and many negroes, was offensive in the main because whites insisted on using it. Whatever its origin, the name was now the white man's property, a word he used to name those who could not name themselves. Our insistence, in the sixties, on being called "black" rather than "negro" was likewise an effort to assume the position of subject.

. . .

Practitioners of the Word must assume the position of subject. We must assert our humanity by making ourselves the heroes and heroines of our tales and by unashamedly employing "I" and "we" in our language. We must describe other subjects in our stories and, by presenting multiple points of view, subvert the closed, coherent, noncontradictory world that makes us objects.

B. The Gift (and Burden) of Second Sight: Embracing Duality

The Universe sends me fabulous dreams! Early this morning I dreamed of a two-headed woman. Literally. . . . Who was giving advice to people. . . . Her knowledge was for everyone and it was all striking. While one head talked the other seemed to doze. I was so astonished! For what I realized in the dream is that two-headedness was at one time an actual physical condition and that two-headed people were considered wise. Perhaps this accounts for the adage "Two heads are better than one."[22]

In 1903, W. E. B. Du Bois, in his small and powerful work *The Souls of Black Folk*, described the gift and burden that are inherent in the dual and conflicting heritage of all African-Americans:

> [T]he Negro is a sort of seventh son, born with a veil, and gifted with second sight in this American world, a world that yields him no true self-consciousness, but only lets him see himself through the revelation of the other world. It is a peculiar sensation, this double consciousness, this sense of always looking at oneself through the eyes of others, of measuring one's soul by the tape of a world that looks on in amused contempt and pity.
>
> One ever feels this twoness in the American Negro. Two souls, two thoughts, two unreconciled strivings; two warring ideals in one dark body, whose dogged strength alone keeps it from being torn asunder.[23]

Du Bois's unconsciousness and understanding of this duality within himself was critical to his work as one of the leading practitioners of the Word. He kept his twoness before him despite the pain and anxiety it caused him. He understood that the gift of second sight was contained within and was nurtured by the burden and the pain.

. . .

The first gift of our inherent duality is its revelation of the inevitability and value of positional perspective. What Du Bois described as "this sense of always looking at oneself through the eyes of others" gives the outsider at least two pictures of the object that is himself.

As nonwhites, we are constantly bombarded with more or less severe caricatures of ourselves as we are seen by whites. We cannot help contrasting these views, these perspectives, of who and what we are with our own experience. Nor can we help understanding that our own view is not universal. Those who stand wholly within the dominant culture seldom if ever hear how others view them, and they often ignore or deny those descriptions on the rare occasions when they are confronted by them.

Duality also engenders empathy. One can put oneself in the shoes of another and share another's experience and feeling only to the extent that one can imagine an experience other than one's own. We who experience the duality of belonging and not belonging know the possibility of different, even conflicting, experience at the same moment in time and space, and our ability to imagine experience other than our own is thus enhanced. This talent for empathy is particularly important for practitioners of the Word whose ultimate task is to liberate. We must strive to understand experiences of oppression that are not our own, we must work in concert with those who experience other forms of oppression, because we cannot achieve freedom while others remain enslaved.

Our duality also allows us to empathize with the oppressor. This is essential to the task of casting out that part of each of us that is a slavemaster.[24] Our ability to recognize the oppressor's experience, to know it within ourselves, is also useful in our efforts to heal and reform others who participate in our oppression. When we have struggled with that part of our duality which identifies with the oppressor, we possess an empathy that helps us explain how our oppression is integrally linked to that of our oppressors.

There are heavy burdens that accompany the gift of second sight, the talent for bridge-building, and the skill of bilingualism. Bearing these burdens is especially stressful for people of color who work in the relative isolation of the white academy, and these burdens can become disabling if they go unrecognized or ignored. Practitioners of the Word must learn to support one another in bearing these burdens, and they must learn how and when to refuse to carry the load. There is a saying among Irish poets that the translator is a traitor. Black scholars work within a tradition and discourse in which the white male voice is dominant; much of our work is necessarily translation. We are either translating the work of our colleagues in the legal establishment for use by our brothers and sisters who seek needed, if temporary, remedies in that establishment's legal institutions, or we are translating the life experience of our broth-

ers and sisters in the hope that broader awareness of that experience will produce new converts to the cause of liberation. However,
translation is a treacherous business. Translation of the colonizer's canon spreads its hegemonic message to ears and minds that it might
not otherwise have reached. I experience a
strong sense of ambivalence as I help black law
students to understand and work with legal
doctrine. As they become fluent in this new
language, I watch them internalize its assumptions and accept its descriptions and meanings.
I see them lose fluency in first and second
languages of understanding that they brought
with them to law school.[25]

I also watch myself struggle to maintain some
fluency in languages that are expressive of liberating themes. This is particularly difficult when
one is submerged in an institutional and professional culture where neither these languages nor
the themes they express are valued or rewarded.
When, for example, I was writing my article on
the intent requirement and unconscious racism,[26] I found myself constantly struggling to
maintain an integrity of both voice and substantive position. I recognized quite early on that it
was my effort to speak to two audiences—the
ambivalent, and potentially treacherous, role of
translator—that was causing me such anxiety
and fueling an always-lurking writer's block. In
order to integrate new insights into existing
theory and case law, I was forced to speak
in terms that accepted by implication certain
assumptions I did not share. Even when I
managed to remain true to my convictions,
professional pressures required that I employ
language and references that threatened to make
my work inaccessible to a large part of the
audience I most hoped to reach.

We must always keep in mind Du Bois's
insight that it is precisely these burdens that
bear the gift of second sight. We must learn
not to flee to the safety of assimilation or
isolationism but, rather, must learn from the
war within us and use the pluralist integration
of our two selves as a guiding star in our pursuit
of liberation. We must strive for a single voice
that does not subvert or subordinate either of
our selves, one which instead demands that

others recognize in our contradictory persona a
paradigm for multidimensionality, for connecting understandings of our reality, understandings that reveal the complexity of social meaning and foster the fight for freedom.

C. The Gift of Storytelling: Embracing Narrative

*We are a tongued folk. A race of singers. Our lips
shape words and rhythms which elevate our spirits
and quicken our blood.*[27]

*What I enjoy most in my work is the laughter and
the outrage and the attention to language. . . .
Forays to the Apollo with my daddy and hanging
tough on Speakers Corner with my mama taught
me the power of the word, the importance of the
resistance tradition, and the high standards our
community has regarding verbal performance.*[28]

If the Word is to validate and legitimate the
experience of those it seeks to serve, its form as
well as its content must say to our brothers and
sisters that what you see, think, and feel, the
way you experience life and your creative articulation of that experience, is "scholarship/art"—
is valid and of value. Storytelling, the articulation of experience and imagination in narrative,
poetry, and song, is an important part of the
tradition of African peoples.

There is also a tradition of storytelling in the
law. Litigation is highly formalized storytelling.
The drafting of a contract tells the story of an
agreement and future expectations. But the
law's tradition of storytelling is very different
from the African tradition. Where our tradition
values rich contextual detail, the law excludes
large parts of the story as irrelevant. Where we
seek to convey the full range and depth of
feeling, the law asks us to disregard emotions.
Where we celebrate the specific and the personal, the law tells stories about disembodied
"reasonable men." Where our tradition is oral,
anticipating that the story will change with each
new teller and listener, the law gives primacy to
the words within the four corners of the contract or evidentiary record, making time stand
still and silencing the storyteller who comes
with news of events or understandings that
preceded or followed the written word.

However, the most important difference in these traditions is that they embody different sets of stories. Our stories have, for the most part, not been told or recorded in the literature that is the law. Accordingly, the first reason for embracing narrative is that more of our stories must be told and heard. We remain invisible and unheard in the literature that is the evidentiary database for legal discourse, and when we are seen, in stories told by others, our images are severely distorted by the lenses of fear, bias, and misunderstanding.

There is great persuasive power in narrative. Sara Lawrence Lightfoot locates the source of this power in the story's ability to inspire feelings of commonality and connectedness among tellers, listeners, and the subjects of stories: "[S]tories express depth and complexity. They allow for ambiguity, multiple interpretation, and refracted images. The reader or listener can be convinced and moved, by intellect and emotion. And stories are not exclusive property. One story invites another as people's words weave the tapestry of human connection." [29]

Consider the insight, the compellingly articulated nonrational knowledge, that is contained in the following student reflection pieces responding to readings I assigned in recent classes on Title II of the 1964 Civil Rights Act and on the First Amendment and racist speech:

Heart of Atlanta Motel (Sometimes, news travels slowly.)
Summer, 1965. Father, mother, brother, me. En route to New York City, by way of Gettysburg, Pennsylvania, Washington, D.C., and Annapolis, Maryland. First stop Annapolis, late, tired from hours of driving, and hungry. Hotel, after hotel, after hotel, we find. Simply no room for a family like mine. Brother to the rescue. Colored bellhop gives directions to the nearest colored inn. Where we find club sandwiches and a good night's sleep.

I could talk about how it felt to see my father go in and out of those red and brown brick buildings, in the rain, wondering how they said what they said to him, but I've promised myself not to get angry this trip. Anyway, my grandfather earned a good living for many years as the proprietor of the two colored hotels in Columbus, Ohio, made profitable by the grace of segregation.

"What factors have made it harder to integrate the schools than to integrate the lunch counters, buses and hotels?"

The white folks at lunch counters
Work the same too long
For the same too little
While we pay, side by side,
For the privilege that is not.
And we pay,
Though the key to the hotel suite
Opens neither minds nor opportunity.
And we pay,
Though the ribs in the bottom are sweet.
White folks never give, only sell
That which is worth less.
And we pay.

Protecting Racist Speech
Last summer, a summer associate and I drove from Memphis to Nashville to see a concert. The next morning, her car broke down just outside of Nashville so we spent the day in a small town waiting to get it fixed. We sat in the convenience store connected to the gas station/repair shop watching customers come and go. One young woman wore a t-shirt saying:
FIFTH AVENUE ANNUAL NIGGER NATIONALS
THE FREE RIDE IS OVER
Between the two lines was a drawing of a black man in chains being pulled in opposite directions by two white men on motorcycles. The black man held a banner saying, GET BACK, JACK. Would Justice Black consider this "addressed to or about individuals?" I don't think she planned on running into me (needless to say, we did not acknowledge each other) or any other blacks on that day. Does that matter? Why should it matter that the depiction was of a cartoonish character and not of someone in specific?

Friday Night Videos, April 15, 1988. Two white comedians host. One describes the Democratic frontrunners as Spanky, Buckwheat, and Alfalfa. Goes on to say that the white voters of Wisconsin finally woke up and realized they couldn't vote for Jackson because, "It is the 'White' House and, after all, rules are rules." Both have a good laugh. I'm not interested in banning books or in monitoring Klan meetings, but those bastards came into my home and burned a cross right in the middle of my living room.

It is this power of narrative to build bridges of validation, understanding, and empathy that makes it so powerful as an intellectual and political tool. We must "flood the market with our stories." [30] Only when these stories are told will we begin to recognize the limitations and distortions of narrowly constructed traditional legal analysis. Only as these rich and varied stories are increasingly heard will we begin to shape a new public discourse.

I. NARRATIVE AS METHODOLOGY FOR CONTEXTUALIZATION

Stories always refer to a particular context, place, and moment. The historical and cultural setting is critical to the reader's interpretation of facts, feelings, and understandings. Much of legal analysis is both ahistorical and acontextual.[31] Human problems considered and resolved in the absence of context are often misperceived, misinterpreted, and mishandled. Yet the hazards and liabilities of noncontextual interpretation and decision-making are not experienced randomly. Blacks and others whose stories have been and are excluded from the dominant discourse are more likely to be injured by the error of noncontextual methodology. This is because the reader considering facts and abstract argument without context will inevitably provide a setting of his or her own. This imaginary, though often unacknowledged, contextualization will be based on his or her experiences or upon stories that he or she has heard. The imagined context often directly contradicts the context that would be described by the stories of individuals who are actually involved.

For example, in the case of *City of Richmond v. J. A. Croson Co.*, Justice Sandra Day O'Connor adopts an ahistorical, noncontextual analysis in finding that there was "no direct evidence of race discrimination on the part of the city in letting contracts or any evidence that the city's prime contractors had discriminated against minority owned subcontractors."[32] In declining to hear the many stories that might describe the experience of pervasive historical and contemporary racism in Richmond, stories that would give the city's set-aside policy a compelling purpose, she substitutes stories of her own, stories told by those who have not been the victims of racism. The unarticulated, perhaps unconscious, thought process underlying her opinion goes as follows: *I have not seen or heard stories of discrimination that have moved me to empathize with the black person who has been denied access to the contracting business. In fact, the stories I have heard are stories about men and women who are able to go as far as their talents and motivations will take them.* Thus, Justice O'Connor is able to speculate that perhaps the dearth of minority contractors can be explained by the small number of blacks who desire to become contractors. Justice O'Connor's substitute context is also shaped by an abstract ideal—the "color-blind" society. Thus, implicitly she treats this ideal as if it had already been achieved. The set-aside program is placed in the setting of a society where discrimination has been eradicated. Consequently, the city must present evidence that Richmond is an aberration, an exception in this society that is free of racism. Furthermore, she warns against the creation of race-consciousness in the future, raising the specter of the destruction of this already achieved ideal.

If we are to bring fairness and justice to legal interpretation and discourse, those processes must be informed by the context of history and culture. Our stories must become a chief source of that contextualization.

2. STORIES AS TEXT: NARRATIVE AS A FORM OF KNOWING

It is not enough for us to tell our stories. We must use them as text for research and interpretation. Giving narrative form to experience creates a rich evidentiary record for analysis and assessment of complex social processes. This text will look quite different from that which has served as a ground of inquiry for research and discourse in an academy dominated by white men. This is so because new stories will be told and heard. Yet it is also essential that narrative be valued as a source of data.[33]

In embracing the use of narrative as cultural text, practitioners of the Word must consider and employ methodologies of research and interpretation which draw upon the wealth of articulated experience and feelings contained in our stories. These methodologies must also serve to give legitimacy and authority to this way of knowing. In the white male academy, narrative is valued primarily as an instrument of private expression and self-actualization. Scientists and politicians may occasionally employ the private sphere of literature as a diversionary escape or they may find, in literary criticism, useful paradigms for the interpretation of legal or cultural text. However, narrative is most often viewed by legal scholars and other social scientists as a source of distortion rather than as a resource for understanding.

Fortunately, we are not without role models in our efforts to give authority to narrative. There is a strong tradition among black scholars of wedding literary narrative to social-political science. Frederick Douglass, W. E. B. Du Bois, Zora Neal Hurston, Paul Robeson, Ira Reid, and Pauli Murray all found artistic expression to be an important source of social-political knowledge as well as an indispensable vehicle for sharing that knowledge. Du Bois's *Souls of Black Folk*[34] is perhaps the paradigmatic example of literature as social science and political theory.[35] Other examples include Du Bois's autobiography, *Dusk of Dawn*,[36] and the autobiographical works of Douglass, Hurston, Hughes, and Murray.

Narrative is valuable as text because it is dense in the detailed and moving articulation of the teller's or subject's life experience and feeling. Paradoxically, its value as a vehicle for cultural interpretation also arises out of its capacity to create space for the reader's imagination. Patricia Williams's work is exemplary in this use of narrative. In applying the insights of critical theory to the jurisprudence of rights, she uses language and style in a self-conscious effort to unearth understandings that the law has buried in arcane vocabulary and abstraction. She says of her work: "It is not my goal merely to simplify; I hope that the result is a text that is multilayered—that encompasses the straightforwardness of real life and that reveals complexity of meaning. I am trying to create a genre of legal writing to fill the gaps of traditional legal scholarship. I would like to write in a way that reveals the intersubjectivity of legal constructions, that forces the reader both to participate in the construction of meaning and to be conscious of that process.[37]

In the form of her argument, Williams presents a paradigm for its substantive themes. She

critiques partializing, constricting social-legal construction in which rights are conceived as islands of employment and where there is no safe haven for those whose life is not described and inscribed by those islands. In making this critique, Williams seeks to practice what she preaches by employing narrative to create framework, setting, and tone that are inclusive, not exclusive. She uses words with multifaceted meanings so that different readers will bring different meanings to the text, and so that the same reader will recognize the many possibilities of meaning. She describes personal experiences, which most of her audience will have shared, to introduce analogous unshared experiences. She leaves thoughts and scenes unfinished and white space on the printed page. Her images are both powerful and muted. Her prose is both spare and dense. If these adjective pairs seem paradoxical, they are. Our own imaginations, our own experiences, provide the density that fills the space she creates.

. . .

In short, narrative text facilitates our knowledge of others by its capacity for rich and complex contextual description of events and emotions. At the same time, stories leave space for interpretive intervention that furthers our ability to know ourselves and discover our interrelationship with others.

3. "POETRY IS NOT A LUXURY": NARRATIVE AS IMAGINATION AS SOCIAL TEXT

The gift of storytelling is especially precious to those who would practice the Word because it is the narrative form that gives license and authority to imagination. Through stories, poems, and dreams we are able to explore inarticulate feelings and experiences and to give them name and form. Imagination is the key to our deepest insights and sympathies. It allows us to create, "in the mind or in an outward form . . . images of things once known but absent, of things never seen in their entirety, of things actually nonexistent, of things created new from diverse old elements, or of things perfected or idealized."[38]

In writing about the life of W. E. B. Du Bois, Arnold Rampersad identifies Du Bois's imagination as the sine qua non of his genius and notes that it was this faculty that compelled and pervaded his life's work as a historian, sociologist, journalist, activist, teacher, and autobiographer. Rampersad presents Du Bois's life as "a paradigm of the place of imagination in the practical world."[39] Du Bois was a sometime poet, dramatist, and novelist, and while this literary work was more avocation than vocation, his work as a social scientist and activist is also suffused with poetry and narrative.

> Du Bois declined to see a separation between science and art, believing that such a distinction violated the integrity of intelligence, which could set no wall between one fundamental form of knowledge and another, since all belonged to the world of nature, of truth. . . . He devoted himself to a knowledge of this world equal to the power of his mind to imagine a better one. Science— social science, historical science, the daily observations of persons, places, events—became the mast to which the sail of the imaginary was lashed.[40]

The use of literature and literary criticism to inform legal analysis remains at the fringes of legal discourse but is sufficiently well represented in legal academia to be called a "movement." I will suggest, however, that there are critical differences in the way the Law and Literature movement has used and valued stories and the paradigm that is presented in the work of Du Bois, Hurston, and Hughes. Most advocates of a literary analysis of the law view law and the humanities as two distinct enterprises distinguished in the main by different goals and purposes.

The Law and Literature movement has advanced a number of arguments for the desirability of informing the legal enterprise with the narrative voice. One such argument is similar to one that I made earlier: Traditional legal discourse is dominated by an abstract, mechanistic, professional, and rationalist voice, a voice that would be well complemented by the concrete, empathetic, passionate, human voice of literary narrative. Thus, Julius Getman argues that legal education and scholarship are impoverished by the "undervaluing of 'human voice.'" Getman stresses the value of "language that uses ordinary concepts and familiar situations" as an

adversarial tool, but also notes the power of such language in undermining the self-serving belief among academicians that their sophistication gives them a special and more authoritative perspective on legal issues. Paul Gerwirtz makes a different but related point by reminding us that passion, intuition, and feeling are inevitable cohabitants with reason in law, and by arguing that literature advances the legal enterprise "because it nourishes the kinds of human understanding not achievable through reason alone."[41] I agree fully with both of these observations. As I have noted earlier, though, blacks and other marginalized persons are doubly disabled by the exclusion of the narrative voice. For those of us whose story has not been told, an expansion of the scope and nature of the text has particularly important, and even revolutionary, implications.

A second important theme of the Law and Literature movement focuses on what the law can learn from literature as a parallel form of cultural interpretation. Ronald Dworkin, the chief proponent of this theme, urges that literary criticism serve as a paradigm for the interpretation of legal texts. If the role of literary criticism is to find the way of reading a text that shows it as the best possible work of art, then by analogy interpreters of legal texts should seek the meaning that enables the text to manifest the soundest principle of social or political philosophy it can embody. This suggested use of literary interpretation as an analogue for legal interpretation rests on Dworkin's vision of the unity of ethics and aesthetics in a larger cultural or social text. It is a vision that he shares with James Boyd White. White urges the integration of law and literature as a way of understanding the contingency in all intellectual, artistic, and political forms and of knowing that writers and readers delineate and define communities and cultures through the creation and interpretation of text.[42]

These insights are valuable, but their value is limited—indeed they may even be counterproductive for those individuals and groups whose life experience has been largely excluded from "the text." Robin West recognizes this danger when she notes that White's vision of a culture shaping its ideals and moral codes through the criticism of shared constitutive texts is "unduly bound by the very text he sets out to criticize."[43] Like the community he criticizes, the critic's morality is the product of the community's texts. "The result is social criticism which is constrained and stunted by the texts it criticizes."[44] The "constraint" to which West refers is caused by the exclusion of outsiders, those whose voice is not heard and who are therefore not part of the community's constitutive and defining text: "[T]hose who are excluded from participation simply do not exist for the Whitean 'moral textualist.' Because they do not participate as subjects in the process of critique and self-transformation, they become literally objectified . . . because they are outside the community, they do not speak; because they do not speak, they are objects."[45] This exclusion and objectification is for West, and for me, the more serious problem. If social criticism is grounded in texts that systematically exclude certain voices, then the critics will never see the excluded. They will be morally invisible.

However, I am not entirely sanguine about West's proposed solution to the oppressive inadequacies of "Whitean moral textualism."[46] For it seems to me that West's "different answer to the questions of 'how we form community' and 'how we might form better ones' "[47] does not promise more inclusion and may well perpetuate the objectification of blacks and other outsiders. West substitutes an "interactive community" for the community that is defined by text. She says that this community will be more inclusive because it will include those with whom we interact in nontextual ways, those we oppress and violate and those with whom we are loving and intimate. She argues that "the way to improve our nontextual interactive community is not to 'transform' our texts, but ourselves."[48]

My uneasiness with West's formulation lies not in her desire to broaden the scope of the interpretive enterprise. Rather, it derives from her reasons for abandoning the textual metaphor. In examining the oppressive objectification of textualism West contrasts two novels,

Mark Twain's *Huckleberry Finn* and Toni Morrison's *Beloved*.

> *Beloved* takes as its explicit subject matter the very problem with "moral textualism" which *Huckleberry Finn* only illustrates: "moral textualism" objectifies by excluding those who do not participate in the production, interpretation, or criticism of a society's texts. *Huckleberry Finn* illustrates the problem with authorial irony, but *Beloved* explores and corrects it. In *Beloved*, the silenced and objectified communicate and become subjects. In *Beloved*, those on the outside of the textual community—the dead, the illiterate, the young, the foreign, the gagged—speak without speech to those on the inside.
>   The illiterate and the linguistically incompetent impose their presence. . . .
>   The gagged, the excluded, and the objectified all become subjects. . . .
>   *Beloved* explores communications to, from, and among the textually excluded. When the textually excluded communicate in *Beloved*, they communicate without texts. They communicate, instead, through imagery. . . .
>   They communicate with color . . . and body language, song, dance, and play. . . .[49]

There is a striking ambivalence in West's language here. She speaks of objects who become subjects, and yet these subjects are "without speech" and "linguistically incompetent" The characters in *Beloved* communicate "without texts." Instead they use color, body language, song, dance, and play. West sees that Morrison has turned Twain's objects into subjects by giving them voice, but their voice is not "text." Indeed, it seems that she has done something more than simply make the observation that Dworkin's, White's, and Twain's community of critics will not hear these voices or know this is text when they see it. For even when the characters in *Beloved* communicate with each other, when they sing and dance for themselves, West sees them communicating "without texts."

West suggests that we adopt the paradigm of "interactive communities" because she abhors and condemns the exclusion of those "without texts,"[50] but I fear that in this description she has inadvertently compounded the objectification, or at best failed to escape what she calls "the unbreakable circle of objectivity."[51]

Why are Morrison's characters "linguistically incompetent"? Their language is rich and moving and conceptually precise. Why are song and dance atextual? I see these characters engaged in a parallel text, a text that constitutes another community in which those who are objectified by the dominant society become subjects. The speakers of this text are surely as linguistically competent as those who objectify them. West herself notes that their language expresses feelings as well as words. In fact, this community's text is broader than that of the excluding community, for while Morrison's character Sethe may not have known of the *Dred Scott* decision, she almost certainly understood white folks better than they understood her.

My insistence that the voices of the excluded be viewed as text is more than a matter of semantics. The ability to produce text, to stand in the position of subject and tell one's own story, is central to one's humanity and one's freedom. It is central to the Word. The fact that our text "has been largely oral does not mean that it is not a text. Morrison becomes an exemplary practitioner of the Word by her own valuing of this oral text in *Beloved.* Historian Blanca Silvestrini, in discussing the use of women's stories in Caribbean historiography, speaks of the exclusion of Puerto Rican women from written texts and of the importance of valuing oral text:

> But most of our women did not have access to the written word. For some publishing was beyond any reasonable expectation; they lacked the power, both of making their stories thinkable in a media controlled by men and of making it appear in print. For others, like my grandmother, a large portion of the written text was inaccessible; they were not given the gift of the written word. Does this mean then that a majority of women in the Caribbean were voiceless, thus ahistorical and without culture, or does it point to the need to revise our conceptions of what makes a voice a historical source?[52]

This understanding of the existence of and the need to validate a parallel text among those who are excluded and objectified by the dominant text is what separates the use of narrative by those who would practice the Word from its

use by the mainstream of the Law and Literature movement. For us, the contextualization of ethical debate, the recognition of the contingency and complexity of textual meaning, and, above all, the assertion of our subjective presence as creators and interpreters of text are political acts.

The practitioner of the Word does not view art and literature as a privatized enterprise. No less than the social-political sciences, the arts and literature are viewed as informing and defining public discourse and morality. The way one is portrayed in literature and the way one's own stories are valued are symbolic of one's status in the culture and in the body politic. Moreover, our literature is a necessary vehicle of our liberation. Audre Lorde rightly insists that

> poetry is not a luxury. It is a vital necessity of our existence. It forms the quality of light within which we predicate our hopes and dreams towards survival and change, first made into language, then into idea, then into more tangible action. Poetry is the way we help give name to the nameless so it can be thought. . . . [A]s they become known to and accepted by us, our feelings and honest exploration of them become sanctuaries and spawning grounds for the most radical and daring of ideas. They become a safe house for that difference so necessary to change and the conceptualization of any meaningful action.[53]

Lord's recognition of storytelling as the birthplace of revolutionary theory reaffirms a tradition that values the transposition of feelings and experience into language as a political discipline.

D. The Gift of the Dream: Embracing Utopia

I heard a loud voice in the heavens, and the spirit instantly appeared to me and said . . . I should arise and prepare myself, and slay my enemies with their own weapons . . . for the time was fast approaching when the first should be last and the last should be first.

—Nat Turner, 1831

I have a dream that one day this nation will rise up and live out the true meaning of its creed. . . .
I have a dream that one day on the red hills of Georgia, the sons of former slaves and the sons of

former slaveowners will be able to sit down to-gether at the table of brotherhood. . . .

I have a dream that my four little children will one day live in a nation where they will not be judged by the color of their skin but by the content of their character.

—Martin Luther King, 1963

Perhaps the greatest gift bestowed upon practitioners of the Word is the gift of the dream. It is also the most elusive gift. It is both difficult to define and infrequently bestowed. Dreams are unconscious and instinctual. They are more closely related to feeling and emotion than to rational thought, more akin to matters of the spirit than to matters of science. Thus, dreaming is thought to be the occupation of religious leaders, poets, and indolents. It is hardly considered a scholarly endeavor. Yet the scholar who would also be a freedom fighter must not be afraid to dream. For dreams are by their nature liberating. Furthermore, those who are gifted with the talent of dreaming are often engaged in some way with the work of liberation. Dreamers, be they prophets, politicians, or philosophers, challenge established understandings with the new and unfamiliar.

Black Americans, as a people and a culture, have been dreamers. We have valued our dreams and respected their power.[54] As a community we have taken seriously the heightened empathy of the child born with a caul.[55] We have listened to the voices of our ancestors even when we did not know where those voices came from.[56] We have venerated those women and men within our communities who knew how to heal psychic wounds through prayer and the laying on of hands.[57] And there has been a special place in our hearts for those with visions of new and better futures. It is the revolutionary dreamer who is most revered in the black community.[58]

Those who have enslaved and oppressed blacks have told a story of a people whose indolence, irrationality, excess of passion, and superstition justified their subordinated status. The black scholar who calls upon his colleagues to dream must be careful to distinguish his position from any that supports this stereotype

of the naive primitive ruled by emotion and belief in the fantastic. In insisting upon the value of inspirational insight I do not intend to imply that rigorous rational analysis is not a critical part of this work. Dreams, sleeping or wakeful, may inspire the breakthrough to a new paradigm, but the work of carefully and critically testing that paradigm is essential.

NOTES

1. Vincent Harding, *There Is a River*, 82 (1981).

2. *Id.*

3. *Id.* at 86.

4. *Id.* at 82.

5. My family history is populated by men and women who were teaching, preaching, and healing activists. For an account of this history, see Sara Lawrence Lightfoot, *Balm in Gilead: Journey of a Healer* (1988).

6. Paulo Freire, *Pedagogy of the Oppressed*, 75 (1982).

7. Renato Rosaldo, *Culture and Truth: The Remaking of Social Analysis* (1989).

8. A chief criticism of Minow's otherwise brilliant piece is that it is not sufficiently explicit about the relationship between power and perspective.

9. M. Minow, "Foreword: Justice Engendered," 101 *Harv. L. Rev. 10* (1987).

10. Memorandum from "Your Conveners" to Lawyering for Social Change Work Group (Oct. 10, 1988) (on file with author).

11. M. J. Matsuda, Address Before the American Association of Law Schools, Minority Section (Jan. 9, 1988), at 7.

12. Joan Scott, *Gender and the Politics of History*, 2–3 (1988).

13. Toni Morrison, "Rootedness: The Ancestor as Foundation," in *Black Women Writers*, 339, 339–45.

14. Matsuda, supra note 11, at 4.

15. This perspective judges the efficacy of theories and remedies by whether using them eliminates objective conditions associated with discrimination. See A. Freeman, "Legitimizing Racism Through Antidiscrimination Law: A Critical Review of Supreme Court Doctrine," 62 *Minn. L. Rev.* 1049 (1978), at 1052–53.

16. *Id.* at 1054.

17. Pragmatism helps the scholar avoid elitism by forcing her always to judge the efficacy of theory by its usefulness in righting the everyday wrongs committed against those who are most oppressed. See M. J. Matsuda, "Looking to

the Bottom," 22 *Harv. C.R.-C.L.L. Rev.* 323 (1987), at 344–45.

18. H. L. Gates, Jr., "Frederick Douglass and the Language of Self," in *Figures in Black: Words, Signs, and the "Racial" Self* 98, 104 (H. L. Gates, ed., 1987).

19. *Id.*

20. *Id.* at 105.

21. L. Hutcheon, A Poetics of Postmodernism: *History, Theory, Action* (1988), at 16n (quoting E. Benveniste, *Subjectivity in Language* (1971)).

22. A. Walker, *Living by the Word* (1981), at 1.

23. W.E.B. Du Bois, *The Souls of Black Folk* (1922), at 16–17.

24. Freire, *supra* note 6, at 32–34.

25. See Catherine Weiss and Louis Melling, "The Legal Education of Twenty Women," 40 *Stan. L. Rev.* 1299, 1313–21 (1988).

26. C. R. Lawrence III, "The Id, the Ego and Equal Protection: Reckoning with Unconscious Racism," 39 *Stan. L. Rev. 317* (1987).

27. M. Angelou, "Shades and Slashes of Light," in *Black Women Writers (1950–1980): A Critical Evaluation* (M. Evans, ed., 1984), at 3–5.

28. T. C. Bambara, "Salvation Is the Issue," in *Black Women Writers,* supra note 27, at 43.

29. S. L. Lightfoot, "Balm in Gilead: On Love, Justice and the Word," speech presented to the Equal Rights Advocates Annual Luncheon (June 15, 1988).

30. Robin West, "Jurisprudence and Gender," 55 *U. Chi. L. Rev.,* 1, 65 (1988).

31. See R. W. Gordon, "Historicism in Legal Scholarship," 90 *Yale L.J.* 1017 (1981).

32. 488 U.S. 469, 480 (1989).

33. See B. G. Silvestrini, *Women and Resistance: Her Story in Contemporary Caribbean History* (1990) (discussing the use of narrative in political and social reform).

34. See Du Bois, *supra* note 23.

35. See *infra* notes 39–40 and accompanying text.

36. W.E.B. Du Bois, *Dusk of Dawn* (1984).

37. P. Williams, *The Alchemy of Race and Rights* 6–8 (1991).

38. See A. Rampersad, "The Art and Imagination of W.E.B. Du Bois 4 (1976) (unpublished manuscript, on file with author).

39. *Id.* at 5.

40. *Id.*

41. P. Gewirtz, "Aeschylus' Law," 101 *Harv. L. Rev.* 1043, 1050 (1988).

42. J. B. White, "Law and Literature: No Manifesto," 39 *Mercer L. Rev.* 739 (1986).

43. R. West, "Communities, Texts and Law: Reflections on the Law and Literature Movement," 1 *Yale J. L. & Human* 129, 138 (1988).

44. *Id.*

45. *Id.* at 140.

46. West, *supra* note 76, at 132.

47. *Id.* at 146.

48. *Id.* at 147.

49. *Id.* at 141–43.

50. *Id.*

51. *Id.* at 140.

52. Silvestrini, *supra* note 61, at 29.

53. A. Lourde, *Sister Outsider* (1984).

54. C. G. Jung, *supra* note 90, at 52–53 (describing a culture whose members did not believe dreams to be important and consequently did not believe they dreamed).

55. See T. Ansa, *Baby of the Family.* See also Lightfoot, supra note 5, for M. Lawerence's description of her family's story of the origin of her special insight and healing talents.

56. See T. Morrison, *Beloved* (1987) (drawing upon that part of black culture that is open to messages from ghosts).

57. T. Morrison's character Baby Juggs in the novel *Beloved* embodies these members of our communities.

58. Nat Turner, Harriet Tubman, Sojourner Truth, Marcus Garvey, W.E.B. Du Bois, Martin Luther King, Jr., Malcolm X.

❦

Part Six

THE INTERSECTION OF RACE AND GENDER

Six

THE INTERSECTION OF RACE AND GENDER

As these articles illustrate, Critical Race Theorists reject the liberal conceptualization of race as a natural category, understanding race instead to be constituted through a social process of meaning attribution in which law has played a central role. People are, as Kendall Thomas frames it, "race-d." A related subtheme is that one is race-d in tandem with other social factors, such that one can say that being race-d as a woman of color may diverge significantly from the means by which those engendered as male are race-d. Yet antidiscrimination law as well as liberal race and gender politics overlook the ways that race-ing and en-gendering are interpolated. Just as race is presumed to be a natural category existing independently and apart from law, so too, other identity componants are regarded as natural and mutually exclusive. The rigidity of this framework and its continued centrality in law, politics, and public policy create a host of problems that Austin, Robert, and Crenshaw explore.

In "Mapping the Margins" Kimberlé Crenshaw presents a broad-scale structural accounting of the ways in which identity movements based on gender and racial liberation have failed to address the "intersectionality" of social domination. Focusing on the manner in which domestic violence has been addressed both in national political discourses and in governmental policy, Crenshaw argues that the realities of black female life have been erased: mainstream civil rights rhetoric is based on the experience of black men, while mainstream feminism has

taken the life experiences of white women as the paradigm. Thus, black women are presented with the double burden of race and gender domination but have no discourse responsive to their specific position in the social landscape; instead, they are constantly forced to divide loyalties as social conflict is presented as a choice between grounds of identity. Crenshaw called for a critical analysis that would account for the intersectional complexity of social power while also comprehending the fluid, dynamic, and contested character of representational categories such as "African-American" and "female."

Regina Austin situates her article "Sapphire Bound!" in the space constituted by the absence of legal scholarship addressing the legal problems of black women, and simultaneously, the presence of developed and often complex stereotypes about black women. Austin calls for a black feminist research agenda that would be grounded in the life circumstances of black women. Rather than reject the negative imagery around Sapphiredom, she contends that black women can and should subvert the imagery by embracing it. As such, "Sapphire Bound!" describes a process of social transformation that connects the struggle for racial liberation with the history of racial subordination as part of a shared communal history. Austin then directs her black feminist critique to *Chambers v. Omaha Girls Club*, a case upholding the dismissal of a black woman from her position as an inner-city youth counselor after becoming pregnant. Austin argues that the decision to fire

Crystal Chambers and the opinion justifying the termination—supposedly due to the message her presence would send to other teen-aged girls—are premised upon notions of role modeling that are as uninformed as they are subordinating. Austin shows that the reigning assumptions about black females tethers the scope of black women's reproductive freedom to white middle-class social values.

Issues of reproductive freedom also serve as the focal point for Dorothy Roberts article, "Punishing Drug Addicts Who Have Babies." Roberts's analysis starts from the fact that rates of fetus-endangering drug abuse are virtually the same between black and white pregnant women, yet black women are significantly more likely to be prosecuted for child abuse. Roberts argues that the disproportionate prosecution of black women reveals the continuing power of stereotypes that cast black women as irresponsible mothers. Roberts argues that the punitive, as opposed to therapeutic or welfare-oriented, measures directed against black mothers who use drugs is part of a larger societal process of dehumanization; in her view, social policy must be based on support for black women's reproductive autonomy.

Part Six

THE INTERSECTION OF RACE AND GENDER

MAPPING THE MARGINS: INTERSECTIONALITY, IDENTITY POLITICS, AND VIOLENCE AGAINST WOMEN OF COLOR
Kimberlé Williams Crenshaw

INTRODUCTION

OVER the last two decades, women have organized against the almost routine violence that shapes their lives.[1] Drawing from the strength of shared experience, women have recognized that the political demands of millions speak more powerfully than do the pleas of a few isolated voices. This politicization in turn has transformed the way we understand violence against women. For example, battering and rape, once seen as private (family matters) and aberrational (errant sexual aggression), are now largely recognized as part of a broad-scale system of domination that affects women as a class.[2] This process of recognizing as social and systemic what was formerly perceived as isolated and individual has also characterized the identity politics of African-Americans, other people of color, and gays and lesbians, among others. For all these groups, identity-based politics has been a source of strength, community, and intellectual development.

The embrace of identity politics, however, has been in tension with dominant conceptions of social justice. Race, gender, and other identity categories are most often treated in mainstream liberal discourse as vestiges of bias or domination—that is, as intrinsically negative frameworks in which social power works to exclude or marginalize those who are different.

According to this understanding, our liberatory objective should be to empty such categories of any social significance. Yet implicit in certain strands of feminist and racial liberation movements, for example, is the view that the social power in delineating difference need not be the power of domination; it can instead be the source of social empowerment and reconstruction.

The problem with identity politics is not that it fails to transcend difference, as some critics charge, but rather the opposite—that it frequently conflates or ignores intragroup differences. In the context of violence against women, this elision of difference in identity politics is problematic, fundamentally because the violence that many women experience is often shaped by other dimensions of their identities, such as race and class. Moreover, ignoring difference *within* groups contributes to tension *among* groups, another problem of identity politics which bears on efforts to politicize violence against women. Feminist efforts to politicize experiences of women and antiracist efforts to politicize experiences of people of color have frequently proceeded as though the issues and experiences they each detail occur on mutually exclusive terrains. Although racism and sexism readily intersect in the lives of real people, they seldom do in feminist and antiracist practices. Thus, when the practices expound identity as "woman" *or* "person of color" as an either/or proposition, they relegate the identity of women of color to a location that resists telling.

My objective in this article is to advance the telling of that location by exploring the race and gender dimensions of violence against women of color. Contemporary feminist and antiracist discourses have failed to consider intersectional identities such as women of color.[3] Focusing on two dimensions of male violence against women—battering and rape—I consider how the experiences of women of color are frequently the product of intersecting patterns of racism and sexism,[4] and how these experiences tend not to be represented within the discourses either of feminism or of antiracism. Because of their intersectional identity as both women *and* of color within discourses shaped to respond to one *or* the other, women of color are marginalized within both.

In an earlier article, I used the concept of intersectionality to denote the various ways in which race and gender interact to shape the multiple dimensions of black women's employment experiences.[5] My objective there was to illustrate that many of the experiences black women face are not subsumed within the traditional boundaries of race or gender discrimination as these boundaries are currently understood, and that the intersection of racism and sexism factors into black women's lives in ways that cannot be captured wholly by looking separately at the race or gender dimensions of those experiences. I build on those observations here by exploring the various ways in which race and gender intersect in shaping structural, political, and representational aspects of violence against women of color.[6]

I should say at the outset that intersectionality is not being offered here as some new, totalizing theory of identity. Nor do I mean to suggest that violence against women of color can be explained only through the specific frameworks of race and gender considered here.[7] Indeed, factors I address only in part or not at all, such as class or sexuality, are often as critical in shaping the experiences of women of color. My focus on the intersections of race and gender only highlights the need to account for multiple grounds of identity when considering how the social world is constructed.

I have divided the issues presented in this article into three categories. In Part I, I discuss structural intersectionality, the ways in which the location of women of color at the intersection of race and gender makes our actual experi-

ence of domestic violence, rape, and remedial reform qualitatively different from that of white women. I shift the focus in Part II to political intersectionality, where I analyze how feminist and antiracist politics have both, paradoxically, often helped to marginalize the issue of violence against women of color. Finally, I address the implications of the intersectional approach within the broader scope of contemporary identity politics.

I. Structural Intersectionality

A. Structural Intersectionality and Battering

I observed the dynamics of structural intersectionality during a brief field study of battered women's shelters located in minority communities in Los Angeles. In most cases, the physical assault that leads women to these shelters is merely the most immediate manifestation of the subordination they experience. Many women who seek protection are unemployed or underemployed, and a good number of them are poor. Shelters serving these women cannot afford to address only the violence inflicted by the batterer; they must also confront the other multilayered and routinized forms of domination that often converge in these women's lives, hindering their ability to create alternatives to the abusive relationships that brought them to shelters in the first place. Many women of color, for example, are burdened by poverty, child care responsibilities, and the lack of job skills. These burdens, largely the consequence of gender and class oppression, are then compounded by the racially discriminatory employment and housing practices often faced by women of color, as well as by the disproportionately high unemployment among people of color that makes battered women of color less able to depend on the support of friends and relatives for temporary shelter.

Where systems of race, gender, and class domination converge, as they do in the experiences of battered women of color, intervention strategies based solely on the experiences of women who do not share the same class or race backgrounds will be of limited help to women who face different obstacles because of race and class. Such was the case in 1990 when Congress amended the marriage fraud provisions of the Immigration and Nationality Act to protect immigrant women who were battered or exposed to extreme cruelty by the U.S. citizens or permanent residents these women immigrated to the United States to marry. Under the marriage fraud provisions of the act, a person who immigrated to the United States in order to marry a U.S. citizen or permanent resident had to remain "properly" married for two years before even applying for permanent resident status,[8] at which time applications for the immigrant's permanent status were required of both spouses.[9] Predictably, under these circumstances, many immigrant women were reluctant to leave even the most abusive of partners for fear of being deported. When faced with the choice between protection from their batterers and protection against deportation, many immigrant women chose the latter. Reports of the tragic consequences of this double subordination put pressure on Congress to include in the Immigration Act of 1990 a provision amending the marriage fraud rules to allow for an explicit waiver for hardship caused by domestic violence.[10] Yet many immigrant women, particularly immigrant women of color, have remained vulnerable to battering because they are unable to meet the conditions established for a waiver. The evidence required to support a waiver "can include, but is not limited to, reports and affidavits from police, medical personnel, psychologists, school officials, and social service agencies."[11] For many immigrant women, limited access to these resources can make it difficult for them to obtain the evidence needed for a waiver. Cultural barriers, too, often further discourage immigrant women from reporting or escaping battering situations. Tina Shum, a family counselor at a social service agency, points out that "[t]his law sounds so easy to apply, but there are cultural complications in the Asian community that make even these requirements difficult. . . . Just to find the opportunity and courage to call us is an accomplishment for many."[12] The typical immigrant spouse, she suggests, may live "[i]n an extended family where several generations live together, there may be no privacy on the telephone, no

opportunity to leave the house and no understanding of public phones."[13] As a consequence, many immigrant women are wholly dependent on their husbands as their link to the world outside their homes.

Immigrant women are also vulnerable to spousal violence because so many of them depend on their husbands for information regarding their legal status. Many women who are now permanent residents continue to suffer abuse under threats of deportation by their husbands. Even if the threats are unfounded, women who have no independent access to information will still be intimidated by such threats. Further, even though the domestic violence waiver focuses on immigrant women whose husbands are U.S. citizens or permanent residents, there are countless women married to undocumented workers (or are themselves undocumented) who suffer in silence for fear that the security of their entire families will be jeopardized should they seek help or otherwise call attention to themselves.

Language barriers present another structural problem that often limits opportunities of non-English-speaking women to take advantage of existing support services. Such barriers limit access not only to information about shelters but also to the security that shelters provide. Some shelters turn non-English-speaking women away for lack of bilingual personnel and resources.

These examples illustrate how patterns of subordination intersect in women's experience of domestic violence. Intersectional subordination need not be intentionally produced; in fact, it is frequently the consequence of the imposition of one burden interacting with pre-existing vulnerabilities to create yet another dimension of disempowerment. In the case of the marriage fraud provisions of the Immigration and Nationality Act, the imposition of a policy specifically designed to burden one class—immigrant spouses seeking permanent resident status—exacerbated the disempowerment of those already subordinated by other structures of domination. By failing to take into account immigrant spouses' vulnerability to domestic violence, Congress positioned these women to absorb the simultaneous impact of its anti-immigration policy and their spouses' abuse.

The enactment of the domestic violence waiver of the marriage fraud provisions similarly illustrates how modest attempts to respond to certain problems can be ineffective when the intersectional location of women of color is not considered in fashioning the remedy. Cultural identity and class both affect the likelihood that a battered spouse could take advantage of the waiver. Although the waiver is formally available to all women, the terms of the waiver make it inaccessible to some. Immigrant women who are socially, culturally, or economically privileged are more likely to be able to marshall the resources needed to satisfy the waiver requirements. Those immigrant women who are least able to take advantage of the waiver—women who are socially or economically the most marginal—are the ones most likely to be women of color.

II. Political Intersectionality

THE concept of political intersectionality highlights the fact that women of color are situated within at least two subordinated groups that frequently pursue conflicting political agendas. The need to split one's political energies between two sometimes-opposing groups is a dimension of intersectional disempowerment which men of color and white women seldom confront. Indeed, their specific raced *and* gendered experiences, although intersectional, often define as well as confine the interests of the entire group. For example, racism as experienced by people of color who are of a particular gender—male—tends to determine the parameters of antiracist strategies, just as sexism as experienced by women who are of a particular race—white—tends to ground the women's movement. The problem is not simply that both discourses fail women of color by not acknowledging the "additional" issue of race or of patriarchy but, rather, that the discourses are often inadequate even to the discrete tasks of articulating the full dimensions of racism and sexism. Because women of color experience racism in ways not always the same as those experienced by men of color and sexism in ways not always parallel to experiences of white women, antiracism and feminism are limited, even on their own terms.

Among the most troubling political consequences of the failure of antiracist and feminist discourses to address the intersections of race and gender is the fact that, to the extent that they can forward the interest of "people of color" and "women," respectively, one analysis often implicitly denies the validity of the other. The failure of feminism to interrogate race means that feminism's resistance strategies will often replicate and reinforce the subordination of people of color; likewise, the failure of antiracism to interrogate patriarchy means that antiracism will frequently reproduce the subordination of women. These mutual elisions present a particularly difficult political dilemma for women of color. Adopting either analysis constitutes a denial of a fundamental dimension of our subordination and precludes the development of a political discourse that more fully empowers women of color.

A. The Politicization of Domestic Violence

That the political interests of women of color are obscured and sometimes jeopardized by political strategies that ignore or suppress intersectional issues is illustrated by my experiences in gathering information for this article. I attempted to review Los Angeles Police Department statistics reflecting the rate of domestic violence interventions by precinct, because such statistics can provide a rough picture of arrests by racial group, given the degree of racial segregation in Los Angeles.[14] The LAPD, however, would not release the statistics. A representative explained that the statistics were not released, in part, because domestic violence activists—both within and outside the LAPD—feared that statistics reflecting the extent of domestic violence in minority communities might be selectively interpreted and publicized in ways that would undermine long-term efforts to force the LAPD to address domestic violence as a serious problem. Activists were worried that the statistics might permit opponents to dismiss domestic violence as a minority problem and, therefore, not deserving of aggressive action.

The informant also claimed that representatives from various minority communities opposed the release of these statistics. They were concerned, apparently, that the data would unfairly represent black and brown communities as unusually violent, potentially reinforcing stereotypes that might be used in attempts to justify oppressive police tactics and other discriminatory practices. These misgivings are based on the familiar and not-unfounded premise that certain minority groups—especially black men—have already been stereotyped as uncontrollably violent. Some worry that attempts to make domestic violence an object of political action may only serve to confirm such stereotypes and undermine efforts to combat negative beliefs about the black community.

This account sharply illustrates how women of color can be erased by the strategic silences of antiracism and feminism. The political priorities of both have been defined in ways that suppress information that could facilitate attempts to confront the problem of domestic violence in communities of color.

I. DOMESTIC VIOLENCE AND ANTIRACIST POLITICS

Within communities of color, efforts to stem the politicization of domestic violence are often grounded in attempts to maintain the integrity of the community. The articulation of this perspective takes different forms. Some critics allege that feminism has no place within communities of color, that the issues are internally divisive, and that they represent the migration of white women's concerns into a context in which they are not merely irrelevant but harmful. At its most extreme, this rhetoric denies that gender violence is a problem in the community and characterizes any effort to politicize gender subordination as itself a community problem. This is the position taken by Shahrazad Ali in her controversial book, *The Blackman's Guide to Understanding the Blackwoman.*[15] In this stridently antifeminist tract, Ali draws a positive correlation between domestic violence and the liberation of African-Americans. Ali blames the deteriorating conditions within the black community on the insubordination of black women and on the failure of black men to

control them.[16] She goes so far as to advise black men to physically chastise black women when they are "disrespectful."[17] While she cautions that black men must use moderation in disciplining "their" women, she argues that they must sometimes resort to physical force to reestablish the authority over black women that racism has disrupted.

Ali's premise is that patriarchy is beneficial for the black community, and that it must be strengthened through coercive means if necessary.[18] Yet the violence that accompanies this will to control is devastating, not just for the black women who are victimized but for the entire black community.[19] The recourse to violence to resolve conflicts establishes a dangerous pattern for children raised in such environments and contributes to many other pressing problems.[20] It has been estimated that nearly 40 percent of all homeless women and children have fled violence in the home,[21] and an estimated 63 percent of young men between the ages of eleven and twenty who are imprisoned for homicide have killed their mothers' batterers.[22] Moreover, while gang violence, homicide, and other forms of black-on-black crime have increasingly been discussed within African-American politics, patriarchal ideas about gender and power preclude the recognition of domestic violence as yet another compelling form of black-on-black crime.

Efforts such as Ali's to justify violence against women in the name of black liberation are indeed extreme.[23] The more common problem is that the political or cultural interests of the community are interpreted in a way that precludes full public recognition of the problem of domestic violence. While it would be misleading to suggest that white Americans have come to terms with the degree of violence in their own homes, it is nonetheless the case that race adds yet another dimension to sources of suppression of the problem of domestic violence within nonwhite communities. People of color often must weigh their interests in avoiding issues that might reinforce distorted public perceptions against the need to acknowledge and address intracommunity problems. Yet the cost of suppression is seldom recognized, in part because the failure to discuss the issue shapes perceptions of how serious the problem is in the first place.

The controversy over Alice Walker's novel *The Color Purple* can be understood as an intra-community debate about the political costs of exposing gender violence within the black community. Some critics chastised Walker for portraying black men as violent brutes. One critic lambasted Walker's portrayal of Celie, the emotionally and physically abused protagonist who finally triumphs in the end; the critic contended that Walker had created in Celie a black woman whom she couldn't imagine existing in any black community she knew or could conceive of.[24]

The claim that Celie was somehow an inauthentic character might be read as a consequence of silencing discussion of intracommunity violence. Celie may be unlike any black woman we know because the real terror experienced daily by minority women is routinely concealed in a misguided (though perhaps understandable) attempt to forestall racial stereotyping. Of course, it is true that representations of black violence—whether statistical or fictional—are often written into a larger script that consistently portrays black and other minority communities as pathologically violent. The problem, however, is not so much the portrayal of violence itself as it is the absence of other narratives and images portraying a fuller range of black experience. Suppression of some of these issues in the name of antiracism imposes real costs: where information about violence in minority communities is not available, domestic violence is unlikely to be addressed as a serious issue.

The political imperatives of a narrowly focused antiracist strategy support other practices that isolate women of color. For example, activists who have attempted to provide support services to Asian- and African-American women report intense resistance from those communities. At other times, cultural and social factors contribute to suppression. Nilda Remonte, director of Everywoman's Shelter in Los Angeles, points out that in the Asian community, saving the honor of the family from shame is a priority. Unfortunately, this priority tends to be interpreted as obliging women not to scream rather than obliging men not to hit.

Race and culture contribute to the suppression of domestic violence in other ways as well. Women of color are often reluctant to call the police, a hesitancy likely due to a general unwillingness among people of color to subject their private lives to the scrutiny and control of a police force that is frequently hostile. There is also a more generalized community ethic against public intervention, the product of a desire to create a private world free from the diverse assaults on the public lives of racially subordinated people. The home is not simply a man's castle in the patriarchal sense: it may also function as a safe haven from the indignities of life in a racist society. However, but for this "safe haven" in many cases, women of color victimized by violence might otherwise seek help.

There is also a general tendency within antiracist discourse to regard the problem of violence against women of color as just another manifestation of racism. In this sense, the relevance of gender domination within the community is reconfigured as a consequence of discrimination against men. Of course, it is probably true that racism contributes to the cycle of violence, given the stress that men of color experience in dominant society; it is therefore more than reasonable to explore the links between racism and domestic violence. Yet the chain of violence is more complex and extends beyond this single link. Racism is linked to patriarchy to the extent that racism denies men of color the power and privilege that dominant men enjoy. When violence is understood as an acting-out of being denied male power in other spheres, it seems counterproductive to embrace constructs that implicitly link the solution to domestic violence to the acquisition of greater male power. The more promising political imperative is to challenge the legitimacy of such power expectations by exposing their dysfunctional and debilitating effect on families and communities of color. Moreover, while understanding links between racism and domestic violence is an important component of any effective intervention strategy, it is also clear that women of color need not await the ultimate triumph over racism before they can expect to live violence-free lives.

2. RACE AND THE DOMESTIC VIOLENCE LOBBY

Not only do race-based priorities function to obscure the problem of violence suffered by women of color; feminist concerns often suppress minority experiences as well. Strategies for increasing awareness of domestic violence within the white community tend to begin by citing the commonly shared assumption that battering is a minority problem. The strategy then focuses on demolishing this straw man, stressing that spousal abuse also occurs in the white community. Countless first-person stories begin with a statement like, "I was not supposed to be a battered wife." That battering occurs in families of all races and all classes seems to be an ever-present theme of antiabuse campaigns. First-person anecdotes and studies, for example, consistently assert that battering cuts across racial, ethnic, economic, educational, and religious lines. Such disclaimers seem relevant only in the presence of an initial, widely held belief that domestic violence occurs primarily in minority or poor families. Indeed, some authorities explicitly renounce the "stereotypical myths" about battered women; a few commentators have even transformed the message that battering is not *exclusively* a problem of the poor or minority communities into a claim that it *equally* affects all races and classes. Yet these comments seem less concerned with exploring domestic abuse within "stereotyped" communities than with removing the stereotype as an obstacle to exposing battering within white middle- and upper-class communities.[25]

Efforts to politicize the issue of violence against women challenge beliefs that violence occurs only in homes of Others. While it is unlikely that advocates and others who adopt this rhetorical strategy intend to exclude or ignore the needs of poor and colored women, the underlying premise of this seemingly univeralistic appeal is to keep the sensibilities of dominant social groups focused on the experiences of those groups. Indeed, as subtly suggested by the opening comments of Senator David Boren (Dem.-Okla.) in support of the Violence Against Women Act of 1991, the displacement of the Other as the presumed victim of domestic violence works primarily as a political appeal to rally white elites. Boren said: "Violent crimes against women are not limited to the streets of the inner cities, but also occur in homes in the urban and rural areas across the country. Violence against women affects not only those who are actually beaten and brutalized, but indirectly affects all women. Today, our wives, mothers, daughters, sisters, and colleagues are held captive by fear generated from these violent crimes—held captive not for what they do or who they are, but solely because of gender."[26] Rather than focusing on and illuminating how violence is disregarded when the home is somehow Other, the strategy implicit in Senator Boren's remarks functions instead to politicize the problem only within the dominant community. This strategy permits white women victims to come into focus, but it does little to disrupt the patterns of neglect that permitted the problem to continue as long as it was imagined to be a minority problem. Minority women's experience of violence is ignored, except to the extent that it gains white support for domestic violence programs in the white community.

Senator Boren and his colleagues no doubt believe that they have provided legislation and resources that will address the problems of all women victimized by domestic violence. Yet despite their universalizing rhetoric of "all" women, they were able to empathize with female victims of domestic violence only by looking past the plight of Other women and by recognizing the familiar faces of their own. The strength of the appeal to "protect our women" must be its race and class specificity. After all, it has always been someone's wife, mother, sister, or daughter who has been abused, even when the violence was stereotypically black or brown, and poor. The point here is not that the Violence Against Women Act is particularistic on its own terms, but that unless the senators and other policymakers ask why violence remained insignificant as long as it was understood as a minority problem, it is unlikely that women of color will share equally in the distribution of resources and concern. It is even more unlikely, however, that those in power will be forced to confront this issue. As long as attempts to politicize domestic violence focus on convincing whites that this is not a "minority" problem but *their* problem, any authentic and sensitive attention to the experiences of black and other minority women probably will continue to be regarded as jeopardizing the movement.

While Senator Boren's statement reflects a self-consciously political presentation of domestic violence, an episode of the CBS news program *48 Hours* shows how similar patterns of othering nonwhite women are apparent in journalistic accounts of domestic violence as well.[27] The program presented seven women who were victims of abuse. Six were interviewed at some length along with their family members, friends, supporters, and even detractors. The viewer got to know something about each of these women. These victims were humanized. Yet the seventh woman, the only nonwhite one, never came into focus. She was literally unrecognizable throughout the segment, first introduced by photographs showing her face badly beaten and later shown with her face electronically altered in the videotape of a hearing at which she was forced to testify. Other images associated with this woman included shots of a bloodstained room and blood-soaked pillows. Her boyfriend was pictured handcuffed while the camera zoomed in for a close-up of his bloodied sneakers. Of all the presentations in the episode, hers was the most graphic and impersonal. The overall point of the segment "featuring" this woman was that battering might not escalate into homicide if battered women would only cooperate with prosecutors. However, in focusing on its own agenda and failing to explore why this woman refused to cooperate, the program diminished this woman, communicating, however subtly, that she was responsible for her own victimization.

Unlike the other women, all of whom, again, were white, this black woman had no name, no family, no context. The viewer sees her only as victimized and uncooperative. She cries when shown pictures; she pleads not to be forced to view the bloodstained room and her disfigured face. The program does not help the viewer to understand her predicament. The possible reasons she did not want to testify—fear, love, or possibly both—are never suggested. Most unfortunately, she, unlike the other six, is given no epilogue. While the fates of the other women are revealed at the end of the episode, we discover nothing about the black woman. She, like the Others she represents, is simply left to herself and soon forgotten.

I offer this description to suggest that Other women are silenced as much by being relegated to the margin of experience as by total exclusion. Tokenistic, objectifying, voyeuristic inclusion is at least as disempowering as complete exclusion. The effort to politicize violence against women will do little to address black and other minority women if their images are retained simply to magnify the problem rather than to humanize their experiences. Similarly, the antiracist agenda will not be advanced significantly by forcibly suppressing the reality of battering in minority communities. As the *48 Hours* episode makes clear, the images and stereotypes we fear are indeed readily available, and they are frequently deployed in ways that do not generate sensitive understanding of the nature of domestic violence in minority communities

3. RACE AND DOMESTIC VIOLENCE SUPPORT SERVICES

Women working in the field of domestic violence have sometimes reproduced the subordination and marginalization of women of color by adopting policies, priorities, or strategies of empowerment that either elide or wholly disregard the particular intersectional needs of women of color. While gender, race, and class intersect to create the particular context in which women of color experience violence, certain choices made by "allies" can reproduce intersectional subordination within the very resistance strategies developed to respond to the problem.

This problem is starkly illustrated by the inaccessibility of domestic violence support services for many non-English-speaking women. In a letter written to the deputy commissioner of the New York State Department of Social Services, Diana Campos, director of Human Services for Programas de Ocupaciones y Desarrollo Económico Real, Inc. (PODER), detailed the case of a Latina in crisis who was repeatedly denied accommodation at a shelter because she could not prove that she was English-proficient. The woman had fled her home with her teenaged son, believing her husband's threats to kill them both. She called the domestic violence hotline administered by PODER, seeking shelter for herself and her son. However, because most shelters would not accommodate the woman with her son, they were forced to live on the streets for two days. The hotline counselor was finally able to find an agency that would take both the mother and her son, but when the counselor told the intake coordinator at the shelter that the woman spoke limited English, the coordinator told her that they could not take anyone who was not English-proficient. When the woman in crisis called back and was told of the shelter's "rule," she replied that she could understand English if spoken to her slowly. As Campos explains, Mildred, the hotline counselor, told Wendy, the intake coordinator

that the woman said that she could communicate a little in English. Wendy told Mildred that they could not provide services to this woman because they have house rules that the woman must agree to follow. Mildred asked her, "What if the woman agrees to follow your rules? Will you still not take her?" Wendy responded that all of the women at the shelter are required to attend [a] support group and they would not be able to have her in the group if she could not communicate. Mildred mentioned the severity of this woman's case. She told Wendy that the woman had been wandering the streets at night while her husband is home, and she had been mugged twice. She also reiterated the fact that this woman was in danger of being killed by either her husband or a mugger. Mildred expressed that the woman's safety was a priority at this point, and that once in a safe place, receiving counseling in a support group could be dealt with.[28]

The intake coordinator restated the shelter's policy of taking only English-speaking women,

and stated further that the woman would have to call the shelter herself for screening. If the woman could communicate with them in English, she might be accepted. When the woman called the PODER hotline later that day, she was in such a state of fear that the hotline counselor who had been working with her had difficulty understanding her in Spanish. The woman had been slipping back into her home during the day when her husband was at work. She remained in a heightened state of anxiety because he was returning shortly, and she would be forced to go back out into the streets for yet another night. Campos directly intervened at this point, calling the executive director of the shelter. A counselor called back from the shelter. As Campos reports, the counselor told her that

they did not want to take the woman in the shelter because they felt that the woman would feel isolated. I explained that the son agreed to translate for his mother during the intake process. Furthermore, that we would assist them in locating a Spanish-speaking battered women's advocate to assist in counseling her. Marie stated that utilizing the son was not an acceptable means of communication for them, *since it further victimized the victim.* In addition, she stated that they had similar experiences with women who were non-English-speaking, and that the women eventually just left because they were not able to communicate with anyone. I expressed my extreme concern for her safety and reiterated that we would assist them in providing her with the necessary services until we could get her placed someplace where they had bilingual staff.[29]

After several more calls, the shelter finally agreed to take the woman. The woman called once more during the negotiation; however, once a plan was in place, the woman never called back. Said Campos, "After so many calls, we are now left to wonder if she is alive and well, and if she will ever have enough faith in our ability to help her to call us again the next time she is in crisis."[30]

Despite this woman's desperate need, she was unable to receive the protection afforded English-speaking women, due to the shelter's rigid commitment to exclusionary policies. Perhaps even more troubling than the shelter's lack of bilingual resources was its refusal to allow a friend or relative to translate for the woman. This story illustrates the absurdity of a feminist approach that makes the ability to attend a support group without a translator a more significant consideration in the distribution of resources than the risk of physical harm on the street. The point is not that the shelter's image of empowerment is empty but, rather, that it was imposed without regard to the disempowering consequences for women who didn't match the kind of client the shelter's administrators imagined. Thus, they failed to accomplish the basic priority of the shelter movement—to get the woman out of danger.

Here the woman in crisis was made to bear the burden of the shelter's refusal to anticipate and provide for the needs of non-English-speaking women. Said Campos, "It is unfair to impose more stress on victims by placing them in the position of having to demonstrate their proficiency in English in order to receive services that are readily available to other battered women."[31] The problem is not easily dismissed as one of well-intentioned ignorance. The specific issue of monolingualism and the monistic view of women's experience that set the stage for this tragedy were not new issues in New York. Indeed, several women of color have reported that they had repeatedly struggled with the New York State Coalition Against Domestic Violence over language exclusion and other practices that marginalized the interests of women of color.[32] Yet despite repeated lobbying, the coalition did not act to incorporate the specific needs of nonwhite women into its central organizing vision.

Some critics have linked the coalition's failure to address these issues to the narrow vision of coalition that animated its interaction with women of color in the first place. The very location of the coalition's headquarters in Woodstock, New York—an area where few people of color live—seemed to guarantee that women of color would play a limited role in formulating policy. Moreover, efforts to include women of color came, it seems, as something of an afterthought. Many were invited to participate only after the coalition was awarded a grant by the state to recruit women of color. However,

as one "recruit" said, "they were not really prepared to deal with us or our issues. They thought that they could simply incorporate us into their organization without rethinking any of their beliefs or priorities and that we would be happy."[33] Even the most formal gestures of inclusion were not to be taken for granted. On one occasion when several women of color attended a meeting to discuss a special task force on women of color, the group debated all day over including the issue on the agenda.[34]

The relationship between the white women and the women of color on the board was a rocky one from beginning to end. Other conflicts developed over differing definitions of feminism. For example, the board decided to hire a Latina staffperson to manage outreach programs to the Latino community, but the white members of the hiring committee rejected candidates favored by Latina committee members who did not have recognized feminist credentials. As Campos pointed out, by measuring Latinas against their own biographies, the white members of the board failed to recognize the different circumstances under which feminist consciousness develops and manifests itself within minority communities. Many of the women who interviewed for the position were established activists and leaders within their own community, a fact in itself suggesting that these women were probably familiar with the specific gender dynamics in their communities and were accordingly better qualified to handle outreach than were other candidates with more conventional feminist credentials.[35]

The coalition ended a few months later, when the women of color walked out.[36] Many of these women returned to community-based organizations, preferring to struggle over women's issues within their communities rather than struggle over race and class issues with white middle-class women. Yet as illustrated by the case of the Latina who could find no shelter, the dominance of a particular perspective and set of priorities within the shelter community continues to marginalize the needs of women of color.

The struggle over which differences matter and which do not is neither abstract nor insignificant. Indeed, these conflicts are about more than difference as such; they raise critical issues of power. The problem is not simply that women who dominate the antiviolence movement are different from women of color but, rather, that they frequently have the power to determine, either through material resources or rhetorical resources, whether the intersectional differences of women of color will be incorporated at all into the basic formulation of policy. Thus, the struggle over incorporating these differences is not a petty or superficial conflict about who gets to sit at the head of the table. In the context of violence, it is sometimes a deadly serious matter of who will survive—and who will not.[37]

B. Political Intersectionalities in Rape

In the previous sections, I have used intersectionality to describe or frame various relationships between race and gender. I have used it as a way to articulate the interaction of racism and patriarchy generally. I have also used intersectionality to describe the location of women of color both within overlapping systems of subordination and at the margins of feminism and antiracism. When race and gender factors are examined in the context of rape, intersectionality can be used to map the ways in which racism and patriarchy have shaped conceptualizations of rape, to describe the unique vulnerability of women of color to these converging systems of domination, and to track the marginalization of women of color within antiracist and antirape discourses.[38]

1. RACISM AND SEXISM IN DOMINANT CONCEPTUALIZATIONS OF RAPE

Generations of critics and activists have criticized dominant conceptualizations of rape as racist and sexist. These efforts have been important in revealing the way in which representations of rape both reflect and reproduce race and gender hierarchies in American society. Black women, at once women and people of color, are situated within both groups, each of which has benefited from challenges to sexism and racism, respectively; yet the particular dynamics of gender and race relating to the

rape of black women have received scant attention. Although antiracist and antisexist assaults on rape have been politically useful to black women, at some level, the monofocal antiracist and feminist critiques have also produced a political discourse that disserves black women.

Historically, the dominant conceptualization of rape as quintessentially involving a black offender and a white victim has left black men subject to legal and extralegal violence. The use of rape to legitimize efforts to control and discipline the black community is well established, and the casting of all black men as potential threats to the sanctity of white womanhood is a familiar construct that antiracists confronted and attempted to dispel over a century ago.

Feminists have attacked other dominant, essentially patriarchal, conceptions of rape, particularly as represented through law. The early emphasis of rape law on the propertylike aspect of women's chastity resulted in less solicitude for rape victims whose chastity had been in some way devalued. Some of the most insidious assumptions were written into the law, including the early common law notion that a woman alleging rape must be able to show that she resisted to the utmost in order to prove that she was raped rather than seduced. Women themselves were put on trial, as judge and jury scrutinized their lives to determine whether they were innocent victims or women who essentially got what they were asking for. Legal rules thus functioned to legitimize a good/bad woman dichotomy, and women who led sexually autonomous lives were usually the least likely to be vindicated if they were raped.

Today, long after the most egregious discriminatory laws have been eradicated, constructions of rape in popular discourse and in criminal law continue to manifest vestiges of these racist and sexist themes. As Valerie Smith notes, "a variety of cultural narratives that historically have linked sexual violence with racial oppression continue to determine the nature of public response" to interracial rapes.[39] Smith reviews the well-publicized case of a jogger who was raped in New York's Central Park to expose how the public discourse on the assault "made the story of sexual victimization inseparable from the rhetoric of racism."[40] Smith contends that in dehumanizing the rapists as "savages," "wolves," and "beasts," the press "shaped the discourse around the event in ways that inflamed pervasive fears about black men."[41] Given the chilling parallels between the media representations of the Central Park rape and the sensationalized coverage of similar allegations that in the past frequently culminated in lynchings, one could hardly be surprised when Donald Trump took out a full-page ad in four New York newspapers demanding that New York "Bring Back the Death Penalty, Bring Back Our Police."[42]

Other media spectacles suggest that traditional gender-based stereotypes that oppress women continue to figure in the popular construction of rape. In Florida, for example, a controversy was sparked by a jury's acquittal of a man accused of a brutal rape because, in the jurors' view, the woman's attire suggested that she was asking for sex. Even the press coverage of William Kennedy Smith's rape trial involved a considerable degree of speculation regarding the sexual history of his accuser.

The racism and sexism written into the social construction of rape are merely contemporary manifestations of rape narratives emanating from a historical period when race and sex hierarchies were more explicitly policed. Yet another is the devaluation of black women and the marginalization of their sexual victimizations. This was dramatically shown in the special attention given to the rape of the Central Park jogger during a week in which twenty-eight other cases of first-degree rape or attempted rape were reported in New York. Many of these rapes were as horrific as the rape in Central Park, yet all were virtually ignored by the media. Some were gang rapes, and in a case that prosecutors described as "one of the most brutal in recent years," a woman was raped, sodomized, and thrown fifty feet off the top of a four-story building in Brooklyn. Witnesses testified that the victim "screamed as she plunged down the air shaft. . . . She suffered fractures of both ankles and legs, her pelvis was shattered and she suffered extensive internal injuries."[43] This rape survivor, like most of the other forgotten victims that week, was a woman of color.

In short, during the period when the Central Park jogger dominated the headlines, many equally horrifying rapes occurred. None, however, elicited the public expressions of horror and outrage that attended the Central Park rape. To account for these different responses, Smith suggests a sexual hierarchy in operation that holds certain female bodies in higher regard than others.[44] Statistics from prosecution of rape cases suggest that this hierarchy is at least one significant, albeit often-overlooked, factor in evaluating attitudes toward rape.[45] A study of rape dispositions in Dallas, for example, showed that the average prison term for a man convicted of raping a black woman was two years,[46] as compared to five years for the rape of a Latina and ten years for the rape of a white woman.[47] A related issue is the fact that African-American victims of rape are the least likely to be believed.[48] The Dallas study and others like it also point to a more subtle problem: neither the antirape nor the antiracist political agenda has focused on the black rape victim. This inattention stems from the way the problem of rape is conceptualized within antiracist and antirape reform discourses. Although the rhetoric of both agendas formally includes black women, racism is generally not problematized in feminism, and sexism is not problematized in antiracist discourses. Consequently, the plight of black women is relegated to a secondary importance: the primary beneficiaries of policies supported by feminists and others concerned about rape tend to be white women, and the primary beneficiaries of the black community's concern over racism and rape tend to be black men. Ultimately, the reformist and rhetorical strategies that have grown out of antiracist and feminist rape reform movements have been ineffective in politicizing the treatment of black women.

2. RACE AND THE ANTIRAPE LOBBY

Feminist critiques of rape have focused on the way that rape law has reflected dominant rules and expectations that tightly regulate the sexuality of women. In the context of the rape trial, the formal definition of rape as well as the evidentiary rules applicable in a rape trial discriminate against women by measuring the rape victim against a narrow norm of acceptable sexual conduct for women. Deviation from that norm tends to turn women into illegitimate rape victims, leading to rejection of their claims.

Historically, legal rules dictated, for example, that rape victims must have resisted their assailants in order for their claims to be accepted. Any abatement of struggle was interpreted as the woman's consent to the intercourse, under the logic that a real rape victim would protect her honor virtually to the death. While utmost resistance is not formally required anymore, rape law continues to weigh the credibility of women against narrow normative standards of female behavior. A woman's sexual history, for example, is frequently explored by defense attorneys as a way of suggesting that a woman who consented to sex on other occasions was likely to have consented in the case at issue. Past sexual conduct as well as the specific circumstances leading up to the rape are often used to distinguish the moral character of the "legitimate" rape victim from women who are regarded as morally debased or in some other way "responsible" for their own victimization.

This type of feminist critique of rape law has informed many of the fundamental reform measures enacted in antirape legislation, including increased penalties for convicted rapists and changes in evidentiary rules to preclude attacks on the woman's moral character. These reforms limit the tactics attorneys might use to tarnish the image of the rape victim, but they operate within preexisting social constructs that distinguish victims from nonvictims on the basis of their sexual character. Thus, these reforms, while beneficial, do not challenge the background cultural narratives that undermine the credibility of black women.

Because black women face subordination based on both race and gender, reforms of rape law and judicial procedures which are premised on narrow conceptions of gender subordination may not address the devaluation of black women. Much of the problem results from the way that certain gender expectations for women intersect with certain sexualized notions of race—notions that are deeply entrenched in American culture. Sexualized images of African-Americans go all the way back to Europeans' first engagement with Africans. Blacks have long been portrayed as more sexual, more earthy, more gratification-oriented; these sexualized images of race intersect with norms of women's sexuality, norms that are used to distinguish good women from bad, madonnas from whores. Thus, black women are essentially prepackaged as bad women in cultural narratives about good women who can be raped and bad women who cannot. The discrediting of black women's claims is the consequence of a complex intersection of a gendered sexual system, one that constructs rules appropriate for good and bad women, and a race code that provides images defining the allegedly essential nature of black women. If these sexual images form even part of the cultural imagery of black women, then the very representation of a black female body at least suggests certain narratives that may make black women's rape either less believable or less important. These narratives may explain why rapes of black women are less likely to result in convictions and long prison terms than are rapes of white women.

Rape law reform measures that do not in some way engage and challenge the narratives that are read onto black women's bodies are unlikely to affect the way that cultural beliefs oppress black women in rape trials. While the degree to which legal reform can directly challenge cultural beliefs that shape rape trials is limited, the very effort to mobilize political resources toward addressing the sexual oppression of black women can be an important first step in drawing greater attention to the problem. One obstacle to such an effort has been the failure of most antirape activists to analyze specifically the consequences of racism in the context of rape. In the absence of a direct attempt to address the racial dimensions of rape, black women are simply presumed to be represented in and benefited by prevailing feminist critiques.

3. ANTIRACISM AND RAPE

Antiracist critiques of rape law focus on how the law operates primarily to condemn rapes of white women by black men. While the heightened concern with protecting white women against black men has been primarily criticized as a form of discrimination against black men, it just as surely reflects devaluation of black women; this disregard for black women results from an exclusive focus on the consequences of the problem for black men.[49] Of course, rape accusations historically have provided a justification for white terrorism against the black community, generating a legitimating power of such strength that it created a veil virtually impenetrable to appeals based on either humanity or fact. Ironically, while the fear of the black rapist was exploited to legitimate the practice of lynching, rape was not even alleged in most cases. The well-developed fear of black sexuality served primarily to increase white tolerance for racial terrorism as a prophylactic measure to keep blacks under control. Within the African-American community, cases involving race-based accusations against black men have stood as hallmarks of racial injustice. The prosecution of the Scottsboro boys and the Emmett Till tragedy, for example, triggered African-American resistance to the rigid social codes of white supremacy. To the extent that rape of black women is thought to dramatize racism, it is usually cast as an assault on black manhood, demonstrating his inability to protect black women. The direct assault on black womanhood is less frequently seen as an assault on the black community.

The sexual politics that this limited reading of racism and rape engenders continues to play out today, as illustrated by the Mike Tyson rape trial. The use of antiracist rhetoric to mobilize support for Tyson represented an ongoing practice of viewing with considerable suspicion rape accusations against black men and interpreting sexual racism through a male-centered frame. The historical experience of black men has so completely occupied the dominant conceptions of racism and rape that there is little room to squeeze in the experiences of black women. Consequently, racial solidarity was continually raised as a rallying point on behalf of Tyson, but never on behalf of Desiree Washington, Tyson's black accuser. Leaders ranging from Benjamin Hooks to Louis Farrakhan expressed their support for Tyson, yet no established black leader voiced any concern for Washington. Thus, the fact that black men have often been falsely accused of raping white women underlies the antiracist defense of black men accused of rape even when the accuser herself is a black woman.

As a result of this continual emphasis on black male sexuality as the core issue in antiracist critiques of rape, black women who raise claims of rape against black men are not only disregarded but also sometimes vilified within the African-American community. One can only imagine the alienation experienced by a black rape survivor such as Desiree Washington when the accused rapist is embraced and defended as a victim of racism while she is, at best, disregarded and, at worst, ostracized and ridiculed. In contrast, Tyson was the beneficiary of the long-standing practice of using antiracist rhetoric to deflect the injury suffered by black women victimized by black men. Some defended the support given to Tyson on the ground that all African-Americans can readily imagine their sons, fathers, brothers, or uncles being wrongly accused of rape; yet daughters, mothers, sisters, and aunts also deserve at least a similar concern, since statistics show that black women are more likely to be raped than black men are to be falsely accused of it. Given the magnitude of black women's vulnerability to sexual violence, it is not unreasonable to expect as much concern for black women who are raped as is expressed for the men who are accused of raping them.

Black leaders are not alone in their failure to empathize with or rally around black rape victims. Indeed, some black women were among Tyson's staunchest supporters and Washington's harshest critics.[50] The media widely noted the lack of sympathy black women had for Washington; Barbara Walters used the observation as a way of challenging Washington's credibility, going so far as to press her for a reaction.[51] The most troubling revelation was that many of the women who did not support Washington also doubted Tyson's story. These women did not sympathize with Washington because they believed that she had no business being in Tyson's hotel room at 2:00 A.M. A typical response was offered by one young black woman who stated, "She asked for it, she got it, it's not fair to cry rape."

Indeed, some of the women who expressed their disdain for Washington acknowledged that they encountered the threat of sexual assault almost daily.[52] Yet it may be precisely this threat—along with the relative absence of rhetorical strategies challenging the sexual subordination of black women—that animated their harsh criticism. In this regard, black women who condemned Washington were quite like all other women who seek to distance themselves from rape victims as a way of denying their own vulnerability. Prosecutors who handle sexual assault cases acknowledge that they often exclude women as potential jurors because women tend to empathize least with the victim.[53] To identify too closely with victimization may reveal their own vulnerability.[54] Consequently, women often look for evidence that the victim brought the rape on herself, usually by breaking social rules that are generally held applicable only to women. And when the rules classify women as dumb, loose, or weak, on the one hand, and smart, discriminating, and strong, on the other, it is not surprising that women who cannot step outside the rules to critique them would attempt to validate themselves within them. The position of most black women on this issue is particularly problematic, first, because of the extent to which they are consistently reminded that they are the group most vulnerable to sexual victimization, and, second, because most black women share the African-American community's general resistance to explicitly feminist analysis when it appears to run up against long-standing narratives that construct black men as the primary victims of sexual racism.

C. Rape and Intersectionality in Social Science

The marginalization of black women's experiences within the antiracist and feminist critiques of rape law are facilitated by social science studies that fail to examine the ways in which racism and sexism converge. Gary LaFree's *Rape and Criminal Justice: The Social Construction of Sexual Assault* is a classic example.[55] Through a study of rape prosecutions in Minneapolis, LaFree attempts to determine the validity of two prevailing claims regarding rape prosecutions. The first claim is that black defendants face significant racial discrimination;[56] the second is that rape laws serve to regulate the sexual conduct of women by withholding from rape victims the ability to invoke sexual assault law when they have engaged in nontraditional behavior.[57] LaFree's compelling study concludes that law constructs rape in ways that continue to manifest both racial and gender domination.[58] Although black women are positioned as victims of both the racism and the sexism that LaFree so persuasively details, his analysis is less illuminating than might be expected, because black women fall through the cracks of his dichotomized theoretical framework.

I. RACIAL DOMINATION AND RAPE

LaFree confirms the findings of earlier studies which show that race is a significant determinant in the ultimate disposition of rape cases. He finds that black men accused of raping white women were treated most harshly, while black offenders accused of raping black women were treated most leniently.[59] These effects held true even after controlling for other factors such as injury to the victim and acquaintance between victim and assailant: "Compared to other defendants, blacks who were suspected of assaulting white women received more serious charges, were more likely to have their cases filed as felonies, were more likely to receive prison sentences if convicted, were more likely to be incarcerated in the state penitentiary (as opposed to a jail or minimum-security facility), and received longer sentences on the average."[60]

LaFree's conclusions that black men are differentially punished depending on the race of the victim do not, however, contribute much to understanding the plight of black rape victims. Part of the problem lies in the author's use of "sexual stratification" theory, which posits both that women are differently valued according to their race and that there are certain "rules of sexual access" governing who may have sexual contact with whom in this sexually stratified market.[61] According to the theory, black men are discriminated against in that their forced "access" to white women is more harshly penalized than their forced "access" to black women.[62] LaFree's analysis focuses on the harsh regulation of access by black men to white women, but is silent about the relative subordination of black women to white women. The emphasis on differential access to women is consistent with analytical perspectives that view racism primarily in terms of the inequality between men. From this prevailing viewpoint, the problem of discrimination is that white men can rape black women with relative impunity while black men cannot do the same with white women.[63] Black women are considered victims of discrimination only to the extent that white men can rape them without fear of significant punishment. Rather than being viewed as victims of discrimination in their own right, they become merely the means by which discrimination against black men can be recognized. The inevitable result of this orientation is that efforts to fight discrimination tend to ignore the particularly vulnerable position of black women, who must both confront racial bias *and* challenge their status as instruments, rather than beneficiaries, of the civil rights struggle.

Where racial discrimination is framed by LaFree primarily in terms of a contest between black and white men over women, the racism experienced by black women will only be seen in terms of white male access to them. When rape of black women by white men is eliminated as a factor in the analysis, whether for statistical or other reasons, racial discrimination against black women no longer matters, since LaFree's analysis involves comparing the "access" of white and black men to white women. Yet discrimination against black women does not result simply from white men raping them with little sanction and being punished less than black men who rape white women, nor from white men raping them but not being punished as white men who rape white women would be. Black women are also discriminated against because intraracial rape of white women is treated more seriously than is intraracial rape of black women. However, the differential protection that black and white women receive against intraracial rape is not seen as racist because intraracial rape does not involve a contest between black and white men. In other words, the way the criminal justice system treats rapes of black women by black men and rapes of white women by white men is not seen as raising issues of racism, because black and white men are not involved with each other's women.

In sum, black women who are raped are racially discriminated against because their rapists, whether black or white, are less likely to be charged with rape; and, when charged and convicted, their rapists are less likely to receive significant jail time than are the rapists of white women. While sexual stratification theory does posit that women are stratified sexually by race, most applications of the theory focus on the inequality of male agents of rape rather than on the inequality of rape victims, thus marginalizing the racist treatment of black women by consistently portraying racism in terms of the relative power of black and white men.

In order to understand and treat the victimization of black women as a consequence of racism and of sexism, it is necessary to shift the analysis away from the differential access of men, and more toward the differential protection of women. Throughout his analysis, LaFree fails to do so. His sexual stratification thesis—in particular, its focus on the comparative power of male agents of rape—illustrates how the marginalization of black women in antiracist politics is replicated in social science research. Indeed, the thesis leaves unproblematized the racist subordination of less valuable objects (black women) to more valuable objects (white women), and it perpetuates the sexist treatment of women as property extensions of "their" men.

2. RAPE AND GENDER SUBORDINATION

Although LaFree does attempt to address gender-related concerns of women in his discussion of rape and the social control of women, his theory of sexual stratification fails to focus sufficiently on the effects of stratification on women.[64] LaFree quite explicitly uses a framework that treats race and gender as separate categories, but he gives no indication that he understands how black women may fall between categories, or within both. The problem with LaFree's analysis lies not in its individual observations, which can be insightful and accurate, but rather in his failure to connect them and to develop a broader, deeper perspective. His two-track framework makes for a narrow interpretation of the data because it leaves untouched the possibility that these two tracks may intersect. Further, it is those who exist at the intersection of gender and race discrimination—black women—who suffer from this fundamental oversight.

LaFree attempts to test the feminist hypothesis that "the application of law to nonconformist women in rape cases may serve to control the behavior of all women."[65] This inquiry is important, he explains, because "if women who violate traditional sex roles and are raped are unable to obtain justice through the legal system, then the law may be interpreted as an institutional arrangement for reinforcing women's gender-role conformity."[66] He finds that "acquittals were more common and final sentences were shorter when nontraditional victim behavior was alleged."[67] Thus, LaFree concludes, the victim's moral character was more important than victim injury—indeed, was second only to the defendant's character. Overall, 82.3 percent of the traditional victim cases resulted in convictions and average sentences of 43.38 months; only 50 percent of nontraditional victim cases led to convictions, with an average term of 27.83 months. The effects of traditional and nontraditional behavior by black women are difficult to determine from the information

given and must be inferred from LaFree's passing comments. For example, he notes that black victims were evenly divided between traditional and nontraditional gender roles. This observation, together with the lower rate of conviction for men accused of raping blacks, suggests that gender-role behavior was not as significant in determining case disposition as it was in cases involving white victims. Indeed, LaFree explicitly notes that "the victim's *race* was . . . [a]n important predictor of jurors' case evaluations."[68]

> Jurors were less likely to believe in a defendant's guilt when the victim was black. Our interviews with jurors suggested that part of the explanation for this effect was that jurors . . . [w]ere influenced by stereotypes of black women as more likely to consent to sex or as more sexually experienced and hence less harmed by the assault. In a case involving the rape of a young black girl, one juror argued for acquittal on the grounds that a girl her age from "that kind of neighborhood" probably wasn't a virgin anyway.[69]

LaFree also notes that "[o]ther jurors were simply less willing to believe the testimony of black complainants."[70] One white juror is quoted as saying: "Negroes have a way of not telling the truth. They've a knack for coloring the story. So you know you can't believe everything they say."[71]

Despite explicit evidence that the race of the victim is significant in determining the disposition of rape cases, LaFree concludes that rape law functions to penalize nontraditional behavior in women. LaFree fails to note that racial identification may in some cases serve as a proxy for nontraditional behavior. That is, rape law serves not only to penalize actual examples of nontraditional behavior but also to diminish and devalue women who belong to groups in which nontraditional behavior is perceived as common. For the black rape victim, the disposition of her case may often turn less on her behavior than on her identity. LaFree misses the point that although white and black women have shared interests in resisting the madonna/whore dichotomy altogether, they nevertheless experience its oppressive power differently. Black women continue to be judged by who they are, not by what they do.

3. COMPOUNDING THE MARGINALIZATIONS OF RAPE

LaFree offers clear evidence that racial and sexual hierarchies subordinate black women to white women, as well as to men—both black and white. However, the different effects of rape law on black women are scarcely mentioned in LaFree's conclusions. In a final section, LaFree treats the devaluation of black women as an aside—one without apparent ramifications for rape law. He concludes: "The more severe treatment of black offenders who rape white women (*or, for that matter, the milder treatment of black offenders who rape black women*) is probably best explained in terms of racial discrimination within a broader context of continuing social and physical segregation between blacks and whites."[72] Implicit throughout LaFree's study is the assumption that blacks who are subjected to social control are black *men*. Moreover, the social control to which he refers is limited to securing the boundaries between black males and white females. His conclusion that race differentials are best understood within the context of social segregation as well as his emphasis on the interracial implications of boundary enforcement overlook the intraracial dynamics of race and gender subordination. When black men are leniently punished for raping black women, the problem is *not* "best explained" in terms of social segregation, but in terms of both the race- and gender-based devaluation of black women. By failing to examine the sexist roots of such lenient punishment, LaFree and other writers sensitive to racism ironically repeat the mistakes of those who ignore race as a factor in such cases. Both groups fail to consider directly the situation of black women.

Studies like LaFree's do little to illuminate how the interaction of race, class, and nontraditional behavior affects the disposition of rape cases involving black women. Such an oversight is especially troubling given evidence that many cases involving black women are dismissed outright. Over 20 percent of rape complaints were recently dismissed as "unfounded" by the Oakland Police Department, which did not even interview many, if not most, of the women involved.[73] Not coincidentally, the vast majority of the complainants were black and poor; many of them were substance abusers or prostitutes. Explaining their failure to pursue these complaints, the police remarked that "those cases were hopelessly tainted by women who are transient, uncooperative, untruthful or not credible as witnesses in court."[74]

The effort to politicize violence against women will do little to address the experiences of black and other nonwhite women until the ramifications of racial stratification among women are acknowledged. At the same time, the antiracist agenda will not be furthered by suppressing the reality of intraracial violence against women of color. The effect of both these marginalizations is that women of color have no ready means to link their experiences with those of other women. This sense of isolation compounds efforts to politicize sexual violence within communities of color and perpetuates the deadly silence surrounding these issues.

D. Implications

With respect to the rape of black women, race and gender converge in ways that are only vaguely understood. Unfortunately, the analytical frameworks that have traditionally informed both antirape and antiracist agendas tend to focus only on single issues. They are thus incapable of developing solutions to the compound marginalization of black women victims, who, yet again, fall into the void between concerns about women's issues and concerns about racism. This dilemma is complicated by the role that cultural images play in the treatment of black women victims. That is, the most critical aspects of these problems may revolve less around the political agendas of separate race- and gender-sensitive groups, and more around the social and cultural devaluation of women of color. The stories our culture tells about the experience of women of color present another challenge—and a further opportunity—to apply and evaluate the usefulness of the intersectional critique.

III. CONCLUSION

THIS article has presented intersectionality as a way of framing the various interactions of race and gender in the context of violence against women of color. Yet intersectionality might be more broadly useful as a way of mediating the tension between assertions of multiple identity and the ongoing necessity of group politics. It is helpful in this regard to distinguish intersectionality from the closely related perspective of antiessentialism, from which women of color have critically engaged white feminism for the absence of women of color, on the one hand, and for speaking for women of color, on the other. One rendition of this antiessentialist critique—that feminism essentializes the category "woman"—owes a great deal to the postmodernist idea that categories we consider natural or merely representational are actually socially constructed in a linguistic economy of difference. While the descriptive project of postmodernism—questioning the ways in which meaning is socially constructed—is generally sound, this critique sometimes misreads the meaning of social construction and distorts its political relevance.

One version of antiessentialism, embodying what might be called the vulgarized social construction thesis, is that since all categories are socially constructed, there is no such thing as, say, blacks or women, and thus it makes no sense to continue reproducing those categories by organizing around them.[75] Even the Supreme Court has gotten into this act. In *Metro Broadcasting, Inc. v. FCC*,[76] the court conservatives, in rhetoric that oozes vulgar constructionist smugness, proclaimed that any set-aside designed to increase the voices of minorities on the airwaves was itself based on a racist assumption that skin color is in some way connected to the likely content of one's broadcast.[77]

To say that a category such as race or gender is socially constructed is not to say that that category has no significance in our world. On the contrary, a large and continuing project for subordinated people—and indeed, one of the projects for which postmodern theories have been very helpful—is thinking about the way in which power has clustered around certain categories and is exercised against others. This project attempts to unveil the processes of subordination and the various ways in which those processes are experienced by people who are subordinated and people who are privileged by

them. It is, then, a project that presumes that categories have meaning and consequences. This project's most pressing problem, in many if not most cases, is not the existence of the categories but, rather, the particular values attached to them and the way those values foster and create social hierarchies.

This is not to deny that the process of categorization is itself an exercise of power; the story is much more complicated and nuanced than that. First, the process of categorizing—or, in identity terms, naming—is not unilateral. Subordinated people can and do participate, sometimes even subverting the naming process in empowering ways. One need only think about the historical subversion of the category "black" or the current transformation of "queer" to understand that categorization is not a one-way street. Clearly, there is unequal power, but there is nonetheless some degree of agency that people can and do exert in the politics of naming. Moreover, it is important to note that identity continues to be a site of resistance for members of different subordinated groups. We all can recognize the distinction between the claims "I am black" and the claim "I am a person who happens to be black." "I am black" takes the socially imposed identity and empowers it as an anchor of subjectivity; "I am black" becomes not simply a statement of resistance but also a positive discourse of self-identification, intimately linked to celebratory statements like the black nationalist "black is beautiful." "I am a person who happens to be black," on the other hand, achieves self-identification by straining for a certain universality (in effect, "I am first a person") and for a concomitant dismissal of the imposed category ("black") as contingent, circumstantial, nondeterminant. There is truth in both characterizations, of course, but they function quite differently, depending on the political context. At this point in history, a strong case can be made that the most critical resistance strategy for disempowered groups is to occupy and defend a politics of social location rather than to vacate and destroy it.

Vulgar constructionism thus distorts the possibilities for meaningful identity politics by conflating at least two separate but closely linked manifestations of power. One is the power exercised simply through the process of categorization; the other, the power to cause that categorization to have social and material consequences. While the former power facilitates the latter, the political implications of challenging one over the other matter greatly. We can look at debates over racial subordination throughout history and see that, in each instance, there was a possibility of challenging either the construction of identity or the system of subordination based on that identity. Consider, for example, the segregation system in *Plessy v. Ferguson.*[78] At issue were multiple dimensions of domination, including categorization, the sign of race, and the subordination of those so labeled. There were at least two targets for Plessy to challenge: the construction of identity ("What is a black?"), and the system of subordination based on that identity ("Can blacks and whites sit together on a train?"). Plessy actually made both arguments, one against the coherence of race as a category, the other against the subordination of those deemed to be black. In his attack on the former, Plessy argued that the segregation statute's application to him, given his mixed race status, was inappropriate. The court refused to see this as an attack on the coherence of the race system and instead responded in a way that simply reproduced the black/white dichotomy that Plessy was challenging. As we know, Plessy's challenge to the segregation system was not successful either. In evaluating various resistance strategies today, it is useful to ask which of Plessy's challenges would have been best for him to have won—the challenge against the coherence of the racial categorization system or the challenge to the practice of segregation?

The same question can be posed for *Brown v. Board of Education.*[79] Which of two possible arguments was politically more empowering— that segregation was unconstitutional because the racial categorization system on which it was based was incoherent, or that segregation was unconstitutional because it was injurious to black children and oppressive to their communities? While it might strike some as a difficult question, for the most part, the dimension of racial domination that has been most vexing to African-Americans has not been the social

categorization as such but, rather, the myriad ways in which those of us so defined have been systematically subordinated. With particular regard to problems confronting women of color, when identity politics fail us, as they frequently do, it is not primarily because those politics take as natural certain categories that are socially constructed—instead, it is because the descriptive content of those categories and the narratives on which they are based have privileged some experiences and excluded others.

Along these lines, consider the controversy involving Clarence Thomas and Anita Hill. During the Senate hearings for the confirmation of Clarence Thomas to the Supreme Court, Anita Hill, in bringing allegations of sexual harassment against Thomas, was rhetorically disempowered in part because she fell between the dominant interpretations of feminism and antiracism. Caught between the competing narrative tropes of rape (advanced by feminists), on the one hand, and lynching (advanced by Thomas and his antiracist supporters), on the other, the race and gender dimensions of her position could not be told. This dilemma could be described as the consequence of antiracism's having essentialized blackness and feminism's having essentialized womanhood. However, recognizing as much does not take us far enough, for the problem is not simply linguistic or philosophical in nature; rather, it is specifically political: the narratives of gender are based on the experience of white, middle-class women, and the narratives of race are based on the experience of black men. The solution does not merely entail arguing for the multiplicity of identities or challenging essentialism generally. Instead, in Hill's case, for example, it would have been necessary to assert those crucial aspects of her location which were erased, even by many of her advocates—that is, to state what difference her difference made.

If, as this analysis asserts, history and context determine the utility of identity politics, how then do we understand identity politics today, especially in light of our recognition of multiple dimensions of identity? More specifically, what does it mean to argue that gender identities have been obscured in antiracist discourses, just as race identities have been obscured in feminist discourses? Does that mean we cannot talk about identity? Or instead, that any discourse about identity has to acknowledge how our identities are constructed through the intersection of multiple dimensions? A beginning response to these questions requires us first to recognize that the organized identity groups in which we find ourselves are in fact coalitions, or at least potential coalitions waiting to be formed.

In the context of antiracism, recognizing the ways in which the intersectional experiences of women of color are marginalized in prevailing conceptions of identity politics does not require that we give up attempts to organize as communities of color. Rather, intersectionality provides a basis for reconceptualizing race as a coalition between men and women of color. For example, in the area of rape, intersectionality provides a way of explaining why women of color must abandon the general argument that the interests of the community require the suppression of any confrontation around intraracial rape. Intersectionality may provide the means for dealing with other marginalizations as well. For example, race can also be a coalition of straight and gay people of color, and thus serve as a basis for critique of churches and other cultural institutions that reproduce heterosexism.

With identity thus reconceptualized, it may be easier to understand the need for—and to summon—the courage to challenge groups that are after all, in one sense, "home" to us, in the name of the parts of us that are not made at home. This takes a great deal of energy and arouses intense anxiety. The most one could expect is that we will dare to speak against internal exclusions and marginalizations, that we might call attention to how the identity of "the group" has been centered on the intersectional identities of a few. Recognizing that identity politics takes place at the site where categories intersect thus seems more fruitful than challenging the possibility of talking about categories at all. Through an awareness of intersectionality, we can better acknowledge and ground the differences among us and negotiate the means by which these differences will find expression in constructing group politics.

NOTES

1. Feminist academics and activists have played a central role in forwarding an ideological and institutional challenge to the practices that condone and perpetuate violence against women. See generally S. Brownmiller, *Against Our Will: Men, Women and Rape* (1975); L. M. G. Clark and D. J. Lewis, *Rape: The Price of Coercive Sexuality* (1977); R. E. Dobash and R. Dobash, *Violence against Wives: A Case against the Patriarchy* (1979); N. Gager and C. Schurr, *Sexual Assault: Confronting Rape in America* (1976); D. E. H. Russell, *The Politics of Rape: The Victim's Perspective* (1974); E. A. Stanko, *Intimate Intrusions: Women's Experience of Male Violence* (1985); L. E. Walker, *Terrifying Love: Why Battered Women Kill and How Society Responds* (1989); L. E. Walker, *The Battered Woman Syndrome* (1984); L. E. Walker, *The Battered Woman* (1979).

2. See, for example, S. Schechter, *Women and Male Violence: The Visions and Struggles of the Battered Women's Movement* (1982) (arguing that battering is a means of maintaining women's subordinate position); S. Brownmiller, *supra* note 1 (arguing that rape is a patriarchal practice that subordinates women to men); E. Schneider, "The Violence of Privacy," 23 *Conn. L. Rev.*, 973, 974 (1991) (discussing how "concepts of privacy permit, encourage and reinforce violence against women"); S. Estrich, "Rape," 95 *Yale L. J.* 1087 (1986) (analyzing rape law as one illustration of sexism in criminal law); see also C. A. Mackinnon, *Sexual Harassment of Working Women: A Case of Sex Discrimination*, 143–213 (1979) (arguing that sexual harassment should be redefined as sexual discrimination actionable under Title VII, rather than viewed as misplaced sexuality in the workplace).

3. Although the objective of this article is to describe the intersectional location of women of color and their marginalization within dominant resistance discourses, I do not mean to imply that the disempowerment of women of color is singularly or even primarily caused by feminist and antiracist theorists or activists. Indeed, I hope to dispel any such simplistic interpretations by capturing, at least in part, the way that prevailing structures of domination shape various discourses of resistance. As I have noted elsewhere, "People can only demand change in ways that reflect the logic of the institutions they are challenging. Demands for change that do not reflect . . . dominant ideology . . . will probably be ineffective"; Crenshaw, *Race, Reform, and Retrenchment: Transformation and Legitimation in Antidiscrimination Law*, at 1367. Although there are significant political and conceptual obstacles to moving against structures of domination with an intersectional sensibility, my point is that the effort to do so should be a central theoretical and political objective of both antiracism and feminism.

4. Although this article deals with violent assault perpetrated by men against women, women are also subject to violent assault by women. Violence among lesbians is a hidden but significant problem. One expert reported in a study of 90 lesbian couples that roughly 46 percent of

lesbians have been physically abused by their partners; J. Garcia, "The Cost of Escaping Domestic Violence: Fear of Treatment in a Largely Homophobic Society May Keep Lesbian Abuse Victims from Calling for Help," *Los Angeles Times* (May 6, 1991), 2; see also K. Lobel, ed., *Naming the Violence: Speaking Out about Lesbian Battering* (1986); R. Robson, "Lavender Bruises: Intralesbian Violence, Law and Lesbian Legal Theory," 20 *Golden Gate U. L. Rev.*, 567 (1990). There are clear parallels between violence against women in the lesbian community and violence against women in communities of color. Lesbian violence is often shrouded in secrecy for reasons similar to those which have suppressed the exposure of heterosexual violence in communities of color—fear of embarrassing other members of the community, which is already stereotyped as deviant, and fear of being ostracized from the community. Despite these similarities, there are nonetheless distinctions between male abuse of women and female abuse of women that, in the context of patriarchy, racism, and homophobia, warrant more focused analysis than is possible here.

5. K. Crenshaw, "Demarginalizing the Intersection of Race and Sex," *U. Chi. Legal F.*, 139 (1989).

6. I explicitly adopt a black feminist stance in this survey of violence against women of color. I do this cognizant of several tensions that such a position entails. The most significant one stems from the criticism that while feminism purports to speak for women of color through its invocation of the term "woman," the feminist perspective excludes women of color because it is based upon the experiences and interests of a certain subset of women. On the other hand, when white feminists attempt to include other women, they often add our experiences into an otherwise unaltered framework. It is important to name the perspective from which one constructs her analysis; and for me, that is as a black feminist. Moreover, it is important to acknowledge that the materials that I incorporate in my analysis are drawn heavily from research on black women. On the other hand, I see my own work as part of a broader collective effort among feminists of color to expand feminism to include analyses of race and other factors such as class, sexuality, and age. I have attempted therefore to offer my sense of the tentative connections between my analysis of the intersectional experiences of black women and the intersectional experiences of other women of color. I stress that this analysis is not intended to include falsely nor to exclude unnecessarily other women of color.

7. I consider intersectionality a provisional concept linking contemporary politics with postmodern theory. In mapping the intersections of race and gender, the concept does engage dominant assumptions that race and gender are essentially separate categories. By tracing the categories to their intersections, I hope to suggest a methodology that will ultimately disrupt the tendencies to see race and gender as exclusive or separable. While the primary intersections that I explore here are between race and gender, the concept can and should be expanded by factoring in issues such as class, sexual orientation, age, and color.

8. 8 U.S.C. § 1186a (1988). The marriage fraud amendments provide that an alien spouse "shall be considered, at the time of obtaining the status of an alien lawfully admitted for permanent residence, to have obtained such status on a conditional basis subject to the provisions of this section"; § 1186a(a)(1). An alien spouse with permanent resident status under this conditional basis may have her status terminated if the attorney general finds that the marriage was "improper" (§ 1186a(b)(1)), or if she fails to file a petition or fails to appear at the personal interview (§ 1186a(c)(2)(A)).

9. The marriage fraud amendments provided that for the conditional resident status to be removed "the alien spouse and the petitioning spouse (if not deceased) *jointly* must submit to the Attorney General . . . a petition which requests the removal of such conditional basis and which states, under penalty of perjury, the facts and information"; § 1186a(b)(1)(A) (emphasis added). The amendments provided for a waiver, at the attorney general's discretion, if the alien spouse was able to demonstrate that deportation would result in extreme hardship, or that the qualifying marriage was terminated for good cause; § 1186a(c)(4). However, the terms of this hardship waiver have not adequately protected battered spouses. For example, the requirement that the marriage be terminated for good cause may be difficult to satisfy in states with no-fault divorces; E. P. Lynsky, "Immigration Marriage Fraud Amendments of 1986: Till Congress Do Us Part," 41 *U. Miami L. Rev.*, 1087, 1095 n. 47 (1987) (student author) (citing J. B. Ingber and R. L. Prischet, "The Marriage Fraud Amendments," in S. Mailman, ed., *The New Simpson-Rodino Immigration Law of 1986*, 564–65 (1986).

10. Immigration Act of 1990, Pub. L. No. 101-649, 104 Stat. 4978. The act, introduced by Rep. Louise Slaughter (Dem.–N.Y.), provides that a battered spouse who has conditional permanent resident status can be granted a waiver for failure to meet the requirements if she can show that "the marriage was entered into in good faith and that after the marriage the alien spouse was battered by or was subjected to extreme mental cruelty by the U.S. citizen or permanent resident spouse"; H.R. Rep. No. 723(I), 101st Cong., 2d Sess. 78 (1990), reprinted in 1990 U.S.C.C.A.N. 6710, 6758; see also 8 C.F.R. § 216.5(3) (1992) (regulations for application for waiver based on claim of having been battered or subjected to extreme mental cruelty).

11. H.R. Rep. No. 723(I), *supra* note 10, at 79, reprinted in 1990 U.S.C.C.A.N. 6710, 6759.

12. D. Hodgin, " 'Mail-Order' Brides Marry Pain to Get Green Cards," *Washington Post*, October 16, 1990, at E5.

13. *Id.*

14. Most crime statistics are classified by sex or race but none are classified by sex and race. Because we know that most rape victims are women, the racial breakdown reveals, at best, rape rates for black women. Yet even given this head start, rates for other nonwhite women are difficult to collect. While there are some statistics for Latinas, statistics for Asian and Native American women are virtually nonex-

istent; cf. G. Chezia Carraway, "Violence Against Women of Color," 43 *Stan. L. Rev.*, 1301 (1993).

15. S. Ali, *The Blackman's Guide to Understanding the Blackwoman* (1989). Ali's book sold quite well for an independently published title, an accomplishment no doubt due in part to her appearances on the Phil Donahue, Oprah Winfrey, and Sally Jesse Raphael television talk shows. For public and press reaction, see D. Gillism, "Sick, Distorted Thinking," *Washington Post*, (Oct. 11, 1990), D3; L. Williams, "Black Woman's Book Starts a Predictable Storm," *New York Times* (Oct. 2, 1990), C11; see also P. Cleacue, *Mad at Miles: A Black Woman's Guide to Truth* (1990). The title clearly styled after Ali's, *Mad at Miles* responds not only to issues raised by Ali's book, but also to Miles Davis's admission in his autobiography, *Miles: The Autobiography* (1989), that he had physically abused, among other women, his former wife, actress Cicely Tyson.

16. Ali suggests that the Blackwoman "certainly does not believe that her disrespect for the Blackman is destructive, nor that her opposition to him has deteriorated the Black nation"; S. Ali, *supra* note 15, at viii. Blaming the problems of the community on the failure of the black woman to accept her "real definition," Ali explains that "[n]o nation can rise when the natural order of the behavior of the male and the female have been altered against their wishes by force. No species can survive if the female of the genus disturbs the balance of her nature by acting other than herself"; *id.* at 76.

17. Ali advises the Blackman to hit the Blackwoman in the mouth, "[b]ecause it is from that hole, in the lower part of her face, that all her rebellion culminates into words. Her unbridled tongue is a main reason she cannot get along with the Blackman. She often needs a reminder"; *id.* at 161. Ali warns that "if [the Blackwoman] ignores the authority and superiority of the Blackman, there is a penalty. When she crosses this line and becomes viciously insulting it is time for the Blackman to soundly slap her in the mouth"; *id.*

18. In this regard, Ali's arguments bear much in common with those of neoconservatives who attribute many of the social ills plaguing black America to the breakdown of patriarchal family values; see, for example, W. Raspberry, "If We Are to Rescue American Families, We Have to Save the Boys," *Chicago Tribune* (July 19, 1989), C15; G. F. Will, "Voting Rights Won't Fix It," *Washington Post* (Jan. 23, 1986), A23; G. F. Will, " 'White Racism' Doesn't Make Blacks Mere Victims of Fate," *Milwaukee Journal* (Feb. 21, 1986), 9. Ali's argument shares remarkable similarities to the controversial "Moynihan Report" on the black family, so called because its principal author was now-Senator Daniel P. Moynihan (Dem.–N.Y.). In the infamous chapter entitled "The Tangle of Pathology," Moynihan argued that "the Negro community has been forced into a matriarchal structure which, because it is so out of line with the rest of American society, seriously retards the progress of the group as a whole, and imposes a crushing burden on the Negro male and, in consequence, on a great many Negro women

as well"; Office of Policy Planning and Research, U.S. Department of Labor, *The Negro Family: The Case for National Action*, 29 (1965), reprinted in L. Rainwater and W. L. Yancey, *The Moynihan Report and the Politics of Controversy* 75 (1967). A storm of controversy developed over the book, although few commentators challenged the patriarchal discourse embedded in the analysis. Bill Moyers, then a young minister and speechwriter for President Lyndon B. Johnson, firmly believed that the criticism directed at Moynihan was unfair. Some twenty years later, Moyers resurrected the Moynihan thesis in a special television program, *The Vanishing Family: Crisis in Black America* (CBS television broadcast, Jan. 25, 1986). The show first aired in January 1986 and featured several African-American men and women who had become parents but were unwilling to marry. See A. Linger, "Hardhitting Special About Black Families," *Christian Science Monitor* (Jan. 23, 1986), 23. Many saw the Moyers show as a vindication of Moynihan. President Reagan took the opportunity to introduce an initiative to revamp the welfare system a week after the program aired; M. Barone, "Poor Children and Politics," *Washington Post* (Feb. 10, 1986), A1. Said one official, "Bill Moyers has made it safe for people to talk about this issue, the disintegrating black family structure"; R. Pear, "President Reported Ready to Propose Overhaul of Social Welfare System," *New York Times* (Feb. 1, 1986), A12. Critics of the Moynihan/Moyers thesis have argued that it scapegoats the black family generally and black women in particular. For a series of responses, see "Scapegoating the Black Family," *The Nation* (July 24, 1989) (special issue, edited by Jewell Handy Gresham and Margaret B. Wilkerson, with contributions from Margaret Burnham, Constance Clayton, Dorothy Height, Faye Wattleton, and Marian Wright Edelman). For an analysis of the media's endorsement of the Moynihan/Moyers thesis, see C. Ginsburg, *Race and Media: The Enduring Life of the Moynihan Report* (1989).

19. Domestic violence relates directly to issues that even those who subscribe to Ali's position must also be concerned about. The socioeconomic condition of black males has been one such central concern. Recent statistics estimate that 25 percent of black males in their twenties are involved in the criminal justice systems; see D. G. Savage, "Young Black Males in Jail or in Court Control Study Says," *Los Angeles Times* (Feb. 27, 1990), A1; *Newsday* (Feb. 27, 1990), 15; "Study Shows Racial Imbalance in Penal System," *New York Times* (Feb. 27, 1990), A18. One would think that the linkages between violence in the home and the violence on the streets would alone persuade those like Ali to conclude that the African-American community cannot afford domestic violence and the patriarchal values that support it.

20. A pressing problem is the way domestic violence reproduces itself in subsequent generations. It is estimated that boys who witness violence against women are ten times more likely to batter female partners as adults; *Women and Violence: Hearings before the Senate Comm. on the Judiciary on Legislation to Reduce the Growing Problem of Violent Crime against Women*, 101st Cong., 2d Sess., pt. 2, at 89

(1991) (testimony of Charlotte Fedders). Other associated problems for boys who witness violence against women include higher rates of suicide, violent assault, sexual assault, and alcohol and drug use; *id.*, pt. 2, at 131 (statement of Sarah M. Buel, assistant district attorney, Massachusetts, and supervisor, Harvard Law School Battered Women's Advocacy Project).

21. *Id.* at 142 (statement of Susan Kelly-Dreiss, discussing several studies in Pennsylvania linking homelessness to domestic violence).

22. *Id.* at 143 (statement of Susan Kelly-Dreiss).

23. Another historical example includes Eldridge Cleaver, who argued that he raped white women as an assault upon the white community. Cleaver "practiced" on black women first; E. Cleaver, *Soul on Ice*, 14–15 (1968). Despite the appearance of misogyny in both works, each professes to worship black women as "queens" of the black community. This "queenly subservience" parallels closely the image of the "woman on a pedestal" against which white feminists have railed. Because black women have been denied pedestal status within dominant society, the image of the African queen has some appeal to many African-American women. Although it is not a feminist position, there are significant ways in which the promulgation of the image directly counters the intersectional effects of racism and sexism that have denied African-American women a perch in the "gilded cage."

24. T. Harris, "On *The Color Purple*, Stereotypes, and Silence," 18 *Black Am. Lit. F.*, 155, (1984).

25. On January 14, 1991, Sen. Joseph Biden (Dem.–Del.) introduced Senate Bill 15, the Violence Against Women Act of 1991, comprehensive legislation addressing violent crime confronting women; S. 15, 102d Cong., 1st Sess. (1991). The bill consists of several measures designed to create safe streets, safe homes, and safe campuses for women. More specifically, Title III of the bill creates a civil rights remedy for crimes of violence motivated by the victim's gender; *id.* § 01. Among the findings supporting the bill were "(1) crimes motivated by the victim's gender constitute bias crimes in violation of the victim's right to be free from discrimination on the basis of gender," and "(2) current law [does not provide a civil rights remedy] for gender crimes committed on the street or in the home"; S. Rep. No. 197, 102d Cong., 1st Sess. 27 (1991).

26. 137 Cong. Rec. S611 (daily ed. Jan. 14, 1991) (statement of Senator Boren). Sen. William Cohen (Dem.–Me.) followed with a similar statement, noting "that rapes and domestic assaults are not limited to the streets of our inner cities or to those few highly publicized cases that we read about in the newspapers or see on the evening news. Women throughout the country, in our nation's urban areas and rural communities, are being beaten and brutalized in the streets and in their homes. It is our mothers, wives, daughters, sisters, friends, neighbors, and coworkers who are being victimized; and in many cases, they are being victimized by family members, friends, and acquaintances"; *id.* (statement of Senator Cohen).

27. *48 Hours*, "Till Death Do Us Part" (CBS television broadcast, Feb. 6, 1991).

28. Letter of Diana M. Campos, director of Human Services, PODER, to Joseph Semidei, deputy commissioner, New York State Department of Social Services (Mar. 26, 1992).

29. *Id.* (emphasis added).

30. *Id.*

31. *Id.*

32. Roundtable Discussion on Racism and the Domestic Violence Movement (April 2, 1992) (transcript on file with the *Stanford Law Review*). The participants in the discussion—Diana Campos, director, Bilingual Outreach Project of the New York State Coalition Against Domestic Violence; Elsa A. Rios, project director, Victim Intervention Project (a community-based project in East Harlem, New York, serving battered women); and Haydee Rosario, a social worker with the East Harlem Council for Human Services and a Victim Intervention Project volunteer—recounted conflicts relating to race and culture during their association with the New York State Coalition Against Domestic Violence, a state oversight group that distributed resources to battered women's shelters throughout the state and generally set policy priorities for the shelters that were part of the coalition.

33. *Id.*

34. *Id.*

35. *Id.*

36. Ironically, the specific dispute that led to the walkout concerned the housing of the Spanish-language domestic violence hotline. The hotline was initially housed at the coalition's headquarters, but languished after a succession of coordinators left the organization. Latinas on the coalition board argued that the hotline should be housed at one of the community service agencies, while the board insisted on maintaining control of it. The hotline is now housed at PODER; *id.*

37. Said Campos, "It would be a shame that in New York state a battered woman's life or death were dependent upon her English language skills"; D. M. Campos, *supra* note 28.

38. The discussion in the following section focuses rather narrowly on the dynamics of a black-white sexual hierarchy. I specify African-Americans in part because, given the centrality of sexuality as a site of racial domination of African-Americans, any generalizations that might be drawn from this history seem least applicable to other racial groups. To be sure, the specific dynamics of racial oppression experienced by other racial groups are likely to have a sexual component as well. Indeed, the repertoire of racist imagery that is commonly associated with different racial groups each contain a sexual stereotype as well. These images probably influence the way that rapes involving other minority groups are perceived both internally and in

society at large, but they are likely to function in different ways.

39. V. Smith, "Split Affinities: The Case of Interracial Rape," in M. Hirsch and E. F. Keller, eds., *Conflicts in Feminism*, 271, 274 (1990).

40. *Id.* at 276–78.

41. Smith cites the use of animal images to characterize the accused black rapists, including descriptions such as: " 'a wolfpack of more than a dozen young teenagers' and '[t]here was a full moon Wednesday night. A suitable backdrop for the howling of wolves. A vicious pack ran rampant through Central Park. . . . This was bestial brutality.' " An editorial in the *New York Times* was entitled "The Jogger and the Wolf Pack"; *id.* at 277 (citations omitted).

Evidence of the ongoing link between rape and racism in American culture is by no means unique to media coverage of the Central Park jogger case. In December 1990, the George Washington University student newspaper, *The Hatchet*, printed a story in which a white student alleged that she had been raped at knifepoint by two black men on or near the campus; the story caused considerable racial tension. Shortly after the report appeared, the woman's attorney informed the campus police that his client had fabricated the attack. After the hoax was uncovered, the woman said that she hoped the story "would highlight the problems of safety for women"; F. Banger, "False Rape Report Upsetting Campus," *New York Times* (Dec. 12, 1990), A2; see also L. Payne, "A Rape Hoax Stirs Up Hate," *New York Newsday* (Dec. 16, 1990), 6.

42. W. C. Troft, "Deadly Donald," UP (Apr. 30 1989). Donald Trump explained that he spent $85,000 to take out these ads because "I want to hate these muggers and murderers. They should be forced to suffer and, when they kill, they should be executed for their crimes"; "Trump Calls for Death to Muggers," *Los Angeles Times* (May 1, 1989), A2. But cf. "Leaders Fear 'Lynch' Hysteria in Response to Trump Ads," UPI (May 6, 1989) (community leaders feared that Trump's ads would fan "the flames of racial polarization and hatred"); C. Fuchs Epstein, "Cost of Full Page Ad Could Help Fight Causes of Urban Violence," *New York Times* (May 15, 1989), A18 ("Mr. Trump's proposal could well lead to further violence").

43. R. D. McFadden, "2 Men Get 6 to 18 Years for Rape in Brooklyn," *New York Times* (Oct. 2, 1990), B2. The woman "lay half naked, moaning and crying for help until a neighbor heard her" in the air shaft; "Community Rallies to Support Victim of Brutal Brooklyn Rape," *New York Daily News* (June 26, 1989), 6. The victim "suffered such extensive injuries that she had to learn to walk again. . . . She faces years of psychological counseling"; McFadden, *supra*.

44. Smith points out that "[t]he relative invisibility of black women victims of rape also reflects the differential value of women's bodies in capitalist societies. To the extent that rape is constructed as a crime against the property of privileged white men, crimes against less valuable women— women of color, working-class women, and lesbians, for example—mean less or mean differently than those against

white women from the middle and upper classes"; Smith, *supra* note 39, at 275–76.

45. "Cases involving black offenders and black victims were treated the least seriously"; G. D. LaFree, *Rape and Criminal Justice: The Social Construction of Sexual Assault* (1989). LaFree also notes, however, that "the race composition of the victim-offender dyad" was not the only predictor of case dispositions; *id.* at 219–20.

46. "Race Tilts the Scales of Justice. Study: Dallas Punishes Attacks on Whites More Harshly," *Dallas Times Herald* (Aug. 19, 1990), A1. A study of 1988 cases in Dallas County's criminal justice system concluded that rapists whose victims were white were punished more severely than those whose victims were black or Hispanic. The *Dallas Times Herald*, which had commissioned the study, reported that "[t]he punishment almost doubled when the attacker and victim were of different races. Except for such interracial crime, sentencing disparities were much less pronounced"; *id.*

47. *Id.* Two criminal law experts, Iowa law professor David Baldus and Carnegie-Mellon University professor Alfred Blumstein "said that the racial inequities might be even worse than the figures suggest"; *id.*

48. See G. LaFree, *supra* note 45, at 219–20 (quoting jurors who doubted the credibility of black rape survivors); see also H. Field and L. Bienen, *Jurors and Rape: A Study in Psychology and Law 141* (1980), at 117–18.

49. The statistic that 89 percent of all men executed for rape in this country were black is a familiar one. *Furman v. Georgia*, 408 U.S. 238, 364 (1972) (Marshall, J., concurring). Unfortunately, the dominant analysis of racial discrimination in rape prosecutions generally does not discuss whether any of the rape *victims* in these cases were black; see J. Wriggins, "Rape, Racism, and the Law," 6 *Harv. Women's L. J.*, 103, 113 (1983) (student author).

50. See M. Rosenfeld, "After the Verdict, the Doubts: Black Women Show Little Sympathy for Tyson's Accuser," *Washington Post* (Feb. 13, 1992), D1; A. Johnson, "Tyson Rape Case Strikes a Nerve Among Blacks," *Chicago Tribune* (Mar. 29, 1992), C1; S. P. Kelly, "Black Women Wrestle with Abuse Issue: Many Say Choosing Racial over Gender Loyalty Is Too Great a Sacrifice," *Chicago Star Tribune* (Feb. 18, 1992), A1.

51. *20/20* (ABC television broadcast, Feb. 21, 1992).

52. According to a study by the Bureau of Justice, black women are significantly more likely to be raped than white women, and women in the 16–24 age group are two to three times more likely to be victims of rape or attempted rape than women in any other age group; see R. J. Ostrow, "Typical Rape Victim Called Poor, Young," *Los Angeles Times* (Mar. 25, 1985), 8.

53. See P. Tyre, "What Experts Say About Rape Jurors," *New York Newsday* (May 19, 1991), 10 (reporting that "researchers had determined that jurors in criminal trials side with the complainant or defendant whose ethnic, economic and religious background most closely resembles their own.

The exception to the rule . . . is the way women jurors judge victims of rape and sexual assault"). Linda Fairstein, a Manhattan prosecutor, states, "too often women tend to be very critical of the conduct of other women, and they often are not good jurors in acquaintance-rape cases"; M. Carlson, "The Trials of Convicting Rapists," *Time* (Oct. 14, 1991), 11.

54. As sex crimes prosecutor Barbara Eganhauser notes, even young women with contemporary lifestyles often reject a woman's rape accusation out of fear. "To call another woman the victim of rape is to acknowledge the vulnerability in yourself. They go out at night, they date, they go to bars, and walk alone. To deny it is to say at the trial that women are not victims"; Tyre, *supra* note 53.

55. G. LaFree, *supra* note 45.

56. *Id.* at 49–50.

57. *Id.* at 50–51.

58. *Id.* at 237–40.

59. LaFree concludes that recent studies finding no discriminatory effect were inconclusive because they analyzed the effects of the defendant's race independently of the race of victim. The differential race effects in sentencing are often concealed by combining the harsher sentences given to black men accused of raping white women with the more lenient treatment of black men accused of raping black women; *id.* at 117, 140. Similar results were found in another study: see A. Walsh, "The Sexual Stratification Hypothesis and Sexual Assault in Light of the Changing Conceptions of Race," 25 *Criminology*, 153, 170 (1987) ("sentence severity mean for blacks who assaulted whites, which was significantly in excess of mean for whites who assaulted whites, was masked by the lenient sentence severity mean for blacks who assaulted blacks").

60. G. LaFree, *supra* note 45, at 139–40.

61. Sexual stratification, according to LaFree, refers to the differential valuation of women according to their race and to the creation of "rules of sexual access" governing who may have contact with whom. Sexual stratification also dictates what the penalty will be for breaking these rules: the rape of a white woman by a black man is seen as a trespass on the valuable property rights of white men and is punished most severely; *id.* at 48–49. The fundamental propositions of the sexual stratification thesis have been summarized as follows: (1) Women are viewed as the valued and scarce property of the men of their own race. (2) White women, by virtue of membership in the dominant race, are more valuable than black women. (3) The sexual assault of a white by a black threatens both the white man's "property rights" and his dominant social position. This dual threat accounts for the strength of the taboo attached to interracial sexual assault. (4) A sexual assault by a male of any race upon members of the less valued black race is perceived as nonthreatening to the status quo and therefore less serious. (5) White men predominate as agents of social control. Therefore, they have the power to sanction differentially

according to the perceived threat to their favored social position; Walsh, *supra* note 59, at 155.

62. I use the term "access" guardedly because it is an inapt euphemism for rape. On the other hand, rape is conceptualized differently depending on whether certain race-specific rules of sexual access are violated. Although violence is not explicitly written into the sexual stratification theory, it does work itself into the rules, in that sexual intercourse which violates the racial access rules is presumed to be coercive rather than voluntary; see, for example, *Sims v. Balkam*, 136 S.E. 2d 766, 769 (Ga. 1964) (describing the rape of a white woman by a black man as "a crime more horrible than death"); *Story v. State*, 59 So. 480 (Ala. 1912) ("The consensus of public opinion, unrestricted to either race, is that a white woman prostitute is yet, though lost of virtue, above the even greater sacrifice of the voluntary submission of her person to the embraces of the other race"); Wriggins, *supra* note 49, at 125, 127.

63. This traditional approach places black women in a position of denying their own victimization, requiring them to argue that it is racist to punish black men more harshly for raping white women than for raping black women. However, in the wake of the Mike Tyson trial, it seems that many black women are prepared to do just that; see notes 50–52 *supra* and accompanying text.

64. G. LaFree, *supra* note 45, at 148. LaFree's transition between race and gender suggests that the shift might not loosen the frame enough to permit discussion of the combined effects of race and gender subordination on black women. LaFree repeatedly separates race from gender, treating them as wholly distinguishable issues; see, for example, *id.* at 147.

65. *Id.*

66. *Id.* at 151. LaFree interprets nontraditional behavior to include drinking, drug use, extramarital sex, illegitimate children, and "having a reputation as a 'partier,' a 'pleasure seeker' or someone who stays out late at night"; *id.* at 201.

67. *Id.* at 204.

68. *Id.* at 219 (emphasis added). While there is little direct evidence that prosecutors are influenced by the race of the victim, it is not unreasonable to assume that since race is an important predictor of conviction, prosecutors determined to maintain a high conviction rate might be less likely to pursue a case involving a black victim than a white one. This calculus is probably reinforced when juries fail to convict in strong cases involving black victims. For example, the acquittal of three white St. John's University athletes for the gang rape of a Jamaican schoolmate was interpreted by many as racially influenced. Witnesses testified that the woman was incapacitated during much of the ordeal, having ingested a mixture of alcohol given to her by a classmate who subsequently initiated the assault. The jurors insisted that race played no role in their decision to acquit. "There was no race, we all agreed to it," said one juror; "They were trying to make it racial but it wasn't," said another; "Jurors:

'It Wasn't Racial,'" *New York Newsday* (July 25, 1991), at 4. Yet it is possible that race did influence on some level their belief that the woman consented to what by all accounts, amounted to dehumanizing conduct; see, for example, C. Agus, "Whatever Happened to 'The Rules,'" *New York Newsday* (July 28, 1991), 11 (citing testimony that at least two of the assailants hit the victim in the head with their penises). The jury nonetheless thought, in the words of its foreman, that the defendants' behavior was "obnoxious" but not criminal; see S. H. Schanberg, "Those 'Obnoxious' St. John's Athletes," *New York Newsday* (July 30, 1991), 79. One can imagine a different outcome had the races of the parties only been reversed. Rep. Charles Rangel (Dem.–N.Y.) called the verdict "a rerun of what used to happen in the South"; J. M. Brodie, "The St. John's Rape Acquittal: Old Wounds That Just Won't Go Away," *Black Issues in Higher Educ.* (Aug. 15, 1991), 18. Denise Snyder, executive director of the D.C. Rape Crisis Center, commented: "It's a historical precedent that white men can assault black women and get away with it. Woe be to the black man who assaults white women. All the prejudices that existed a hundred years ago are dormant and not so dormant, and they rear their ugly heads in situations like this. Contrast this with the Central Park jogger who was an upper-class white woman"; J. Mann, "New Age, Old Myths," *Washington Post* (July 26, 1991) C3 (quoting Snyder); see K. Bumiller, "Rape as a Legal Symbol: An Essay on Sexual Violence and Racism," 42 *U. Miami L. Rev.*, 75, 88 ("The cultural meaning of rape is rooted in a symbiosis of racism and sexism that has tolerated the acting out of male aggression against women and, in particular, black women").

69. *Id.* at 219–20 (citations omitted). Anecdotal evidence suggests that this attitude exists among some who are responsible for processing rape cases. Fran Weinman, a student in my seminar on race, gender, and the law, conducted a field study at the Rosa Parks Rape Crisis Center. During her study, she counseled and accompanied a twelve-year-old black rape survivor who became pregnant as a result of the rape. The girl was afraid to tell her parents, who discovered the rape after she became depressed and began to slip in school. Police were initially reluctant to interview the girl. Only after the girl's father threatened to take matters into his own hands did the police department send an investigator to the girl's house. The city prosecutor indicated that the case wasn't a serious one, and was reluctant to prosecute the defendant for statutory rape even though the girl was underage; the prosecutor reasoned, "After all, she looks sixteen." After many frustrations, the girl's family ultimately decided not to pressure the prosecutor any further and the case was dropped; see F. Weinman, "Racism and the Enforcement of Rape Law," 13–30 (1990) (unpublished manuscript) (on file with the *Stanford Law Review*).

70. G. LaFree, *supra* note 45, at 220.

71. *Id.*

72. *Id.* at 239 (emphasis added). The lower conviction rates for those who rape black women may be analogous to the low conviction rates for acquaintance rape. The central issue in many rape cases is proving that the victim did not consent. The basic presumption in the absence of explicit evidence of lack of consent is that consent exists. Certain evidence is sufficient to disprove that presumption, and the quantum of evidence necessary to prove nonconsent increases as the presumptions warranting an inference of consent increases. Some women—based on their character, identity, or dress—are viewed as more likely to consent than other women. Perhaps it is the combination of the sexual stereotypes about black people along with the greater degree of familiarity presumed to exist between black men and black women that leads to the conceptualization of such rapes as existing somewhere between acquaintance rape and stranger rape.

73. C. Cooper, Nowhere to Turn for Rape Victims: High Proportion of Cases Tossed Aside by Oakland Police, *S. F. Examiner*, Sept. 16, 1990, at A10.

74. *Id.* Advocates point out that because investigators work from a profile of the kind of case likely to get a conviction, people left out of that profile are people of color, prostitutes, drug users, and people raped by acquaintances. This exclusion results in "a whole class of women . . . systematically being denied justice. Poor women suffer the most"; *id.*

75. I do not mean to imply that all theorists who have made antiessentialist critiques have lapsed into vulgar constructionism. Indeed, antiessentialists avoid making these troubling moves and would no doubt be receptive to much of the critique set forth herein. I use the phrase "vulgar constructionism" to distinguish between those antiessentialist critiques that leave room for identity politics and those that do not.

76. 110 S. Ct. 2997 (1990).

77. The FCC's choice to employ a racial criterion embodies the related notions that a particular and distinct viewpoint inheres in certain racial groups and that a particular applicant, by virtue of race or ethnicity alone, is more valued than other applicants because the applicant is "likely to provide [that] distinct perspective." The policies directly equate race with belief and behavior, for they establish race as a necessary and sufficient condition of securing the preference. . . . The policies impermissibly value individuals because they presume that persons think in a manner associated with their race; *id.* at 3037 (O'Connor, J., joined by Rehnquist, C. J., and Scalia and Kennedy, J. J., dissenting) (internal citations omitted).

78. 163 U.S. 537 (1896).

79. 397 U.S. 483 (1954).

❧

PUNISHING DRUG ADDICTS WHO HAVE BABIES: WOMEN OF COLOR, EQUALITY, AND THE RIGHT OF PRIVACY

Dorothy E. Roberts

PROLOGUE

A former slave named Lizzie Williams recounted the beating of pregnant slave women on a Mississippi cotton plantation: "I[']s seen nigger women dat was fixin' to be confined do somethin' de white folks didn't like. Dey [the white folks] would dig a hole in de ground just big 'nuff fo' her stomach, make her lie face down an whip her on de back to keep from hurtin' de child."[1]

In July 1989, Jennifer Clarise Johnson, a twenty-three-year-old crack addict, became the first woman in the United States to be criminally convicted for exposing her baby to drugs while pregnant.[2] Florida law enforcement officials charged Johnson with two counts of delivering a controlled substance to a minor after her two children tested positive for cocaine at birth. Because the relevant Florida drug law did not apply to fetuses,[3] the prosecution invented a novel interpretation of the statute. The prosecution obtained Johnson's conviction for passing a cocaine metabolite from her body to her newborn infants during the sixty-second period after birth and before the umbilical cord was cut.[4]

I. INTRODUCTION

A growing number of women across the country have been charged with criminal offenses after giving birth to babies who test positive for drugs.[5] The majority of these women, like Jennifer Johnson, are poor and black.[6] Most are addicted to crack cocaine.[7] The prosecution of drug-addicted mothers is part of an alarming trend toward greater state intervention into the lives of pregnant women under the rationale of protecting the fetuses from harm.[8] This intervention has included compulsory medical treatment, greater restrictions on abortion, and increased supervision of pregnant women's conduct.

Such government intrusion is particularly harsh for poor women of color.[9] They are the least likely to obtain adequate prenatal care, the most vulnerable to government monitoring, and the least able to conform to the white, middle-class standard of motherhood. They are therefore the primary targets of government control.

The prosecution of drug-addicted mothers involves two fundamental tensions. First, punishing a woman for using drugs during pregnancy pits the state's interest in protecting the future health of a child against the mother's interest in autonomy over her reproductive life—interests that until recently had not been thought to be in conflict. Second, such prosecutions represent one of two possible responses to the problem of drug-exposed babies. The government may choose either to help women have healthy pregnancies or to punish women for their prenatal conduct.[10] Although it might seem that the state could pursue both of these avenues at once, the two responses are ultimately irreconcilable. Far from deterring injurious drug use, prosecution of drug-addicted mothers in fact deters pregnant women from using available health and counseling services, because it causes women to fear that, if they seek help, they could be reported to government authorities and charged with a crime.[11] Moreover, prosecution blinds the public to the possibility of nonpunitive solutions and to the inadequacy of the nonpunitive solutions that are currently available.[12]

The debate between those who favor protecting the rights of the fetus and those who favor protecting the rights of the mother has been extensively waged in the literature.[13] This article does not repeat the theoretical arguments for and against state intervention. Rather, it suggests that both sides of the debate have largely overlooked a critical aspect of government prosecution of drug-addicted mothers. Can we determine the legality of the prosecutions simply by weighing the state's abstract interest in the fetus against the mother's abstract interest in autonomy? Can we determine whether the prosecutions are fair simply by deciding the duties a pregnant woman owes to her fetus and then assessing whether the defendant has met them? Can we determine the constitutionality of the government's actions without considering the race of the women being singled out for prosecution?

Before deciding whether the state's interest in preventing harm to the fetus justifies criminal sanctions against the mother, we must first understand the mother's competing perspective and the reasons for the state's choice of a punitive response. This article seeks to illuminate the current debate by examining the experiences of the class of women who are primarily affected—poor black women.

Providing the perspective of poor black women offers two advantages. First, examining legal issues from the viewpoint of those whom they affect most[14] helps to uncover the real reasons for state action and to explain the real harms that it causes. It exposes the way in which the prosecutions deny poor black women a facet of their humanity by punishing their reproductive choices. The government's choice of a punitive response perpetuates the historical devaluation of black women as mothers. Viewing the legal issues from the experiential standpoint of the defendants enhances our understanding of the constitutional dimensions of the state's conduct.[15]

Second, examining the constraints on poor black women's reproductive choices expands our understanding of reproductive freedom in particular and of the right of privacy in general. Much of the literature discussing reproductive freedom has adopted a white middle-class perspective, which focuses narrowly on abortion rights. The feminist critique of privacy doctrine has also neglected many of the concerns of poor women of color.[16]

My analysis presumes that black women experience various forms of oppression simultaneously,[17] as a complex interaction of race, gender, and class that is more than the sum of its parts.[18] It is impossible to isolate any one of the components of this oppression or to separate the experiences that are attributable to one component from experiences attributable to the others. The prosecution of drug-addicted mothers cannot be explained as simply an issue of gender inequality. Poor black women have been selected for punishment as a result of an inseparable combination of their gender, race, and economic status. Their devaluation as mothers, which underlies the prosecutions, has its roots in the unique experience of slavery and has been perpetuated by complex social forces.

Thus, for example, the focus of mainstream feminist legal thought on gender as the primary locus of oppression often forces women of color to fragment their experience in a way that does not reflect the reality of their lives.[19] Angela Harris and others have presented a racial critique of this gender essentialism in feminist legal theory.[20] By introducing the voices of black women, these critics have begun to reconstruct a feminist jurisprudence based on the historical, economic, and social diversity of women's experiences.[21] This new jurisprudence must be used to reconsider the more particular discourse of reproductive rights.

This article advances an account of the constitutionality of prosecutions of drug-addicted mothers which explicitly considers the experiences of poor black women. The constitutional arguments are based on theories both of racial equality and of the right of privacy. I argue that punishing drug addicts who choose to carry their pregnancies to term unconstitutionally burdens the right to autonomy over reproductive decisions. Violation of poor black women's reproductive rights helps to perpetuate a racist hierarchy in our society. The prosecutions thus impose a standard of motherhood that is offensive to principles of both equality and privacy. This article provides insight into the particular and urgent struggle of women of color for reproductive freedom. Further, I intend my constitutional critique of the prosecutions to demonstrate the advantages of a discourse that combines elements of racial equality and privacy theories in advocating the reproductive rights of women of color.

Although women accused of prenatal crimes can present their defenses only in court, judges are not the only government officials charged with a duty to uphold the Constitution.[22]

Given the Supreme Court's current hostility to claims of substantive equality[23] and reproductive rights,[24] my arguments might be directed more fruitfully to legislatures than to the courts.[25] Robin West, among others, has persuasively recharacterized the progressive interpretation of the constitutional guarantees of liberty and equality—such as the redistributive directive embodied in the Fourteenth Amendment[26]—as "political ideals to guide legislation, rather than as legal restraints on legislation."[27]

Legislatures may be more receptive than courts to the claim that punitive policies contribute to the subordinate status of black women. They can serve as a forum for presenting both a vision of a community free from racist standards imposed upon motherhood and as a means of collectively implementing that vision. This article translates the dehumanization that black women experience so that lawmakers may understand and reverse—or at least must confront—the injustice of the prosecutions.[28]

Part II of this article presents background information about the recent prosecutions of drug-addicted mothers and explains why most of the defendants are poor and black. Part III sets out the context in which the prosecutions must be understood—the historical devaluation of black women as mothers. I discuss three aspects of this social phenomenon: the control of black women's reproductive lives during slavery, the abusive sterilization of black women and other women of color during this century, and the disproportionate removal of black children from their families. I also describe how a popular mythology denigrating black motherhood has reinforced and legitimated this devaluation. Part IV characterizes the prosecutions as punishing drug-addicted women for leaving babies. This approach exposes the impact that the government's punitive policy has on the devaluation of black women as mothers. Part V argues that the prosecutions violate the equal protection clause because they are rooted in and perpetuate black subordination. Part VI examines the legal scholarship opposing state intervention in the lives of pregnant women. I show that the typical arguments advanced

against intervention are inadequate to explain or challenge the criminal charges brought against drug-addicted mothers.

Finally, Part VII argues that punishing women for having babies violates their constitutional right of privacy for two reasons: it violates the right of autonomy of women over their reproductive decisions, and it creates an invidious government standard for childbearing. I discuss two benefits of privacy doctrine for advocating the reproductive rights of women of color—its emphasis on the value of personhood, and its protection against the abuse of government power. I argue, however, that the liberal interpretation of privacy is inadequate to eliminate the subordination of black women. I therefore suggest that a progressive understanding of privacy must acknowledge government's affirmative obligation to guarantee the rights of personhood and must recognize the connection between the right of privacy and racial equality.

II. BACKGROUND: THE STATE'S PUNITIVE RESPONSE TO DRUG-ADDICTED MOTHERS

A. The Crack Epidemic and the State's Response

Crack cocaine appeared in America in the early eighties, and its abuse has grown to epidemic proportions.[29] Crack is especially popular among inner-city women.[30] Indeed, evidence shows that, in several urban areas in the United States, more women than men now smoke crack.[31] Most crack-addicted women are of childbearing age, and many are pregnant.[32] This phenomenon has contributed to an explosion in the number of newborns affected by maternal drug use; some experts estimate that as many as 375,000 drug-exposed infants are born every year.[33] In many urban hospitals, the number of these newborns has quadrupled in the last five years.[34] A widely cited 1988 study conducted by the National Association for Perinatal Addiction Research and Education (NAPARE) found that 11 percent of newborns in thirty-six hospitals surveyed were affected by their mothers' illegal drug use during pregnancy.[35] In several hospitals, the proportion of drug-exposed infants was as high as 15 and 25 percent.[36]

Babies born to drug-addicted mothers may suffer a variety of medical, developmental, and behavioral problems, depending on the nature of their mother's substance abuse. Immediate effects of cocaine exposure can include premature birth,[37] low birth weight,[38] and withdrawal symptoms.[39] Cocaine-exposed children have also exhibited neurobehavioral problems, such as mood dysfunction, organizational deficits, poor attention, and impaired human interaction, although it has not been determined whether these conditions are permanent.[40] Congenital disorders and deformities have also been associated with cocaine use during pregnancy.[41] According to NAPARE, babies exposed to cocaine have a tenfold greater risk of suffering Sudden Infant Death Syndrome (SIDS).[42]

Data on the extent and potential severity of the adverse effects of maternal cocaine use are controversial.[43] The interpretation of studies of cocaine-exposed infants is often clouded by the presence of other fetal risk factors, such as the mother's use of additional drugs, cigarettes, or alcohol, and her socioeconomic status.[44] For example, the health prospects of an infant are significantly threatened because pregnant addicts often receive little or no prenatal care and may be malnourished.[45] Moreover, because the medical community has given more attention to studies showing adverse effects of cocaine exposure than to those that deny these effects, the public has a distorted perception of the risks of maternal cocaine use.[46] Researchers have not yet authoritatively determined the percentage of infants exposed to cocaine who actually experience adverse consequences.[47]

The response of state prosecutors, legislators, and judges to the problem of drug-exposed babies has been punitive. They have punished women who use drugs during pregnancy by depriving these mothers of custody of their children, by jailing them during their pregnancy, and by prosecuting them after their babies are born.

The most common penalty for a mother's prenatal drug use is the permanent or temporary removal of her baby.[48] Hospitals in a number of states now screen newborns for evidence of drugs in their urine and report positive results to child welfare authorities.[49] Some child protection agencies institute neglect proceedings to obtain custody of babies with positive toxicologies based solely on these tests.[50] More and more government authorities are also removing drug-exposed newborns from their mothers immediately after birth pending an investigation of parental fitness.[51] In these investigations, positive neonatal toxicologies often raise a strong presumption of parental unfitness,[52] circumventing the inquiry into the mother's ability to care for her child, which is customarily necessary to deprive a parent of custody.[53]

A second form of punishment is the "protective" incarceration of pregnant drug addicts charged with unrelated crimes. In 1988, a Washington, D.C., judge sentenced to jail for the duration of her pregnancy a thirty-year-old woman named Brenda Vaughn, who pleaded guilty to forging $700 worth of checks.[54] The judge stated at sentencing that he wanted to ensure that the baby would be born in jail to protect it from its mother's drug abuse.[55] Although the Vaughn case has received the most attention, anecdotal evidence suggests that defendants' drug use during pregnancy often affects judges' sentencing decisions.[56]

Finally, women have been prosecuted after the birth of their children for having exposed the fetuses to drugs or alcohol.[57] Creative statutory interpretations that once seemed little more than the outlandish concoctions of conservative scholars[58] are now used to punish women. Mothers of children affected by prenatal substance abuse have been charged with crimes such as distributing drugs to a minor, child abuse and neglect, manslaughter, and assault with a deadly weapon.

This article considers the constitutional implications of criminal prosecution of drug-addicted mothers because, as Part IV explains, this penalty most directly punishes poor black women for having babies. When the government prosecutes, its intervention is not designed to protect babies from the irresponsible actions of their mothers (as is arguably the case when the state takes custody of a pregnant addict or her child); rather, the government criminalizes the mother as a consequence of her decision to bear a child.

B. The Disproportionate Impact on Poor Black Women

Poor black women bear the brunt of prosecutors' punitive approach.[59] These women are the primary targets of prosecutors, not because they are more likely to be guilty of fetal abuse, but because they are black and poor. Poor women, who are disproportionately black,[60] are in closer contact with government agencies, and their drug use is therefore more likely to be detected. Black women are also more likely to be reported to government authorities, in part because of the racist attitudes of health care professionals.[61] Finally, their failure to meet society's image of the ideal mother makes their prosecution more acceptable.

To charge drug-addicted mothers with crimes, the state must be able to identify those who use drugs during pregnancy. Because poor women are generally under greater government supervision—through their associations with public hospitals, welfare agencies, and probation officers—their drug use is more likely to be detected and reported.[62] Hospital screening practices result in disproportionate reporting of poor black women.[63] The government's main source of information about prenatal drug use is hospitals' reporting of positive infant toxicologies to child welfare authorities. This testing is implemented almost exclusively by hospitals serving poor minority communities.[64] Private physicians who serve more affluent women perform less of this screening for two reasons: they have a financial stake both in retaining their patients' business and securing referrals from them, and they are socially more like their patients.[65]

Hospitals administer drug tests in a manner that further discriminates against poor black women. One common criterion triggering an infant toxicology screen is the mother's failure to obtain prenatal care,[66] a factor that correlates strongly with race and income.[67] Worse still, many hospitals have no formal screening procedures, relying solely on the suspicions of health

care professionals.[68] This discretion allows doctors and hospital staff to perform tests based on their stereotyped assumptions about drug addicts.[69]

Health care professionals are much more likely to report black women's drug use to government authorities than they are similar drug use by their wealthy white patients.[70] A study recently reported in the *New England Journal of Medicine* demonstrated this racial bias in the reporting of maternal drug use.[71] Researchers studied the results of toxicologic tests of pregnant women who received prenatal care in public health clinics and in private obstetrical offices in Pinellas County, Florida.[72] Substance abuse by pregnant women did not correlate substantively with racial or economic categories,[73] nor was there any significant difference between public clinics and private offices.[74] Despite similar rates of substance abuse, however, black women were ten times more likely than whites to be reported to public health authorities[75] for substance abuse during pregnancy.[76] Although several possible explanations can account for this disparate reporting,[77] both public health facilities and private doctors are more inclined to turn in pregnant black women who use drugs than pregnant white women who use drugs.[78]

It is also significant that, out of the universe of material conduct that can injure a fetus,[79] prosecutors have focused on crack use. The selection of crack addition for punishment can be justified neither by the number of addicts nor the extent of the harm to the fetuses. Excessive alcohol consumption during pregnancy, for example, can cause severe fetal injury,[80] and marijuana use may also adversely affect the unborn.[81] The incidence of both these types of substance abuse is high as well.[82] In addition, prosecutors do not always base their claims on actual harm to the child; rather, they base it on the mere delivery of crack by the mother.[83] Although different forms of substance abuse prevail among pregnant women of various socioeconomic levels and racial and ethnic backgrounds,[84] inner-city black communities have the highest concentrations of crack addicts.[85] Therefore, selecting crack abuse as the primary fetal harm to be punished has a discriminatory impact that cannot be medically justified.

Focusing on black crack addicts rather than on other perpetrators of fetal harms serves two broader social purposes.[86] First, prosecution of these pregnant women serves to degrade women whom society views as undeserving to be mothers and to discourage them from having children. If prosecutors had instead chosen to prosecute affluent women addicted to alcohol or prescription medication, the policy of criminalizing prenatal conduct very likely would have suffered a hasty demise. Society is much more willing to condone the punishment of poor women of color who fail to meet the middle-class ideal of motherhood.

In addition to legitimizing fetal rights enforcement, the prosecution of crack-addicted mothers diverts public attention from social ills such as poverty, racism, and a misguided national health policy—implying instead that shamefully high black infant death rates[87] are caused by the bad acts of individual mothers. Poor black mothers thus become the scapegoats for the black community's ill health. Punishing them assuages any guilt the nation might feel at the plight of an underclass with infant mortality at rates higher than those in some less developed countries.[88] Making criminals of black mothers apparently helps to relieve the nation of the burden of creating a health care system that ensures healthy babies for all its citizens.[89]

For a variety of reasons, then, an informed appraisal of the competing interests involved in the prosecutions must take account of the race of the women affected. Part III examines a significant aspect of black women's experience that underlies the punishment of crack-addicted mothers.

III. The Devaluation of Black Motherhood

THE systematic, institutionalized denial of reproductive freedom has uniquely marked black women's history in America. An important part of this denial has been the devaluation of black women as mothers. A popular mythology that degrades black women and por-

trays them as less deserving of motherhood reinforces this subordination. This mythology is one aspect of a complex set of images that deny black humanity in order to rationalize the oppression of blacks.[90]

In this part, I will discuss three manifestations of the devaluation of black motherhood: the original exploitation of black women during slavery; the more contemporary, disproportionate removal of black children from their mothers' custody; and sterilization abuse. Throughout this part, I will also show how several popular images denigrating black mothers—the licentious Jezebel; the careless, incompetent mother; the domineering matriarch; and the lazy welfare mother—have reinforced and legitimated their devaluation.

A. The Slavery Experience

The essence of black women's experience during slavery was the brutal denial of autonomy over reproduction. Female slaves were commercially valuable to their masters not only for their labor but also for their capacity to produce more slaves.[91] Henry Louis Gates, Jr., writing about the autobiography of a slave named Harriet A. Jacobs, observes that it "charts in vivid detail precisely how the shape of her life and the choices she makes are defined by her reduction to a sexual object, an object to be raped, bred or abused."[92] Black women's childbearing during slavery was thus largely a product of oppression rather than an expression of self-definition and personhood.

The method of whipping pregnant slaves that was used throughout the South vividly illustrates the slaveowners' dual interest in black women as workers and childbearers. Slaveowners forced women to lie face down in a depression in the ground while they were whipped,[93] thus allowing the masters to protect the fetus while abusing the mother. It serves as a powerful metaphor for the evils of a fetal protection policy that denies the humanity of the mother. It is also a forceful symbol of the convergent oppressions inflicted on slave women: they were subjugated at once both as blacks and as females.

From slavery on, black women have fallen

outside the scope of the American ideal of womanhood.[94] Slaveowners forced slave women to perform strenuous labor, which contravened the Victorian female roles prevalent in the dominant white society. Angela Davis has observed: "Judged by the evolving nineteenth-century ideology of femininity, which emphasized women's roles as nurturing mothers and gentle companions and housekeepers for their husbands, Black women were practically anomalies."[95] Black women's historical deviation from traditional female roles has engendered a mythology that denies their womanhood.

One of the most prevalent images of slave women was the character of Jezebel, a woman governed by her sexual desires.[96] As early as 1736, the *South Carolina Gazette* described "African Ladies" as women "of 'strong robust constitution' who were 'not easily jaded out' but able to serve their lovers 'by Night as well as Day.'"[97] This ideological construct of the licentious Jezebel legitimated white men's sexual abuse of black women.[98] The stereotype of black women as sexually promiscuous helped to perpetuate their devaluation as mothers.

The myth of the "bad" black woman was deliberately and systematically perpetuated after slavery ended.[99] For example, historian Philip A. Bruce's book *The Plantation Negro as a Freeman*, published in 1889, strengthened popular views of black degeneracy, male and female.[100] Bruce traced the alleged propensity of the black man to rape white women to the "wantonness of the women of his own race" and "the sexual laxness of plantation women as a class."[101] This image of the sexually loose, impure black woman, which originated in slavery, persists in modern American culture.[102]

Under slavery, black women were also systematically denied the rights of motherhood. Slave mothers had no legal claim to their children;[103] slave masters owned not only black women but also their children. They alienated slave women from their children by selling them to other slaveowners and by controlling childrearing.[104] In 1851, Sojourner Truth reminded the audience at a women's rights convention that society denied black women even the lim-

ited dignity of Victorian womanhood accorded white women of the time, including the right of mothering:

> Dat man ober dar say dat women needs to be helped into carriages, and lifted ober ditches, and to have de best place every whar. Nobody eber heap me into carriages, or ober mud puddles, or gives me any best place . . . and ar'n't I a woman? Look at me! Look at my arm! . . . I have plowed, and planted, and gathered into barns, and no man could head me—and ar'n't I a woman? I could work as much and eat as much as a man (when I could get it), and bear de lash as well—and ar'n't I a woman? I have borne thirteen children and seen em mos' all sold off into slavery, and when I cried out with a mother's grief, none but Jesus heard—and ar'n't I a woman?[105]

Black women struggled in many ways to resist the efforts of slave masters to control their reproductive lives. They used contraceptives and abortifacients, escaped from plantations, feigned illness, endured severe punishment, and fought back rather than submit to slave masters' sexual domination.[106] Free black women with the means to do so purchased freedom for their daughters and sisters.[107] Black women, along with black men, succeeded remarkably often in maintaining the integrity of their family life despite slavery's disrupting effects.[108]

B. The Disproportionate Removal of Black Children

The disproportionate number of black mothers who lose custody of their children through the child welfare system is a contemporary manifestation of the devaluation of black motherhood.[109] This disparate impact of state intervention results in part from black families' higher rate of reliance on government welfare.[110] Because welfare families are subject to supervision by social workers, instances of perceived neglect are more likely to be reported to governmental authorities than neglect on the part of more affluent parents.[111] Black children are also removed from their homes in part because of the child welfare system's cultural bias and application of the nuclear family pattern to black families.[112] Black childrearing patterns that diverge from the norm of the nuclear family have been misinterpreted by government bureaucrats as child neglect.[113] For example, child welfare workers have often failed to respect the long-standing cultural tradition in the black community of shared parenting responsibility among blood-related and nonblood kin.[114] The state has thus been more willing to intrude upon the autonomy of poor black families, and in particular of black mothers, while protecting the integrity of white, middle-class homes.[115]

This devaluation of black motherhood has been reinforced by stereotypes that blame black mothers for the problems of the black family. This scapegoating dates back to slavery, when black mothers were blamed for the devastating effects on their children of both poverty and the abuse of black women. When a one-month-old slave girl named Harriet died in the Abbeville District of South Carolina on December 9, 1849, the census marshal reported the cause of death as "[s]mothered by carelessness of [her] mother."[116] This report was typical of the U. S. census mortality schedules for the southern states in its attribution of a black infant death to accidental suffocation by the mother.[117] Census marshal Charles M. Pelot explained: "I wish it to be distinctly understood that nearly all the accidents occur in the negro population, which goes clearly to prove their great carelessness and total inability to take care of themselves."[118] It now appears that the true cause of these suffocation deaths was Sudden Infant Death Syndrome.[119] Black children died at a dramatically higher rate because of the hard physical work, poor nutrition, and abuse that their slave mothers endured during pregnancy.[120]

The scapegoating of black mothers has manifested itself more recently in the myth of the black matriarch, the domineering female head of the black family. White sociologists have held black matriarchs responsible for the disintegration of the black family and the consequent failure of black people to achieve success in America.[121] Daniel Patrick Moynihan popularized this theory in his 1965 report, *The Negro Family: The Case for National Action*.[122] According to Moynihan: "At the heart of the deterioration of the fabric of the Negro society is the deterioration of the Negro family. It is

the fundamental cause of the weakness of the Negro community. . . . In essence, the Negro community has been forced into a matriarchal structure which, because it is so out of line with the rest of the American society, seriously retards the progress of the group as a whole."[123] Thus, Moynihan attributed the cause of black people's inability to overcome the effects of racism largely to the dominance of black mothers.

C. The Sterilization of Women of Color

Coerced sterilization is one of the most extreme forms of control over a woman's reproductive life. By permanently denying her the right to bear children, sterilization enforces society's determination that a woman does not deserve to be a mother. Unlike white women, poor women of color have been subjected to sterilization abuse[124] for decades.[125] The disproportionate sterilization of black women is yet another manifestation of the dominant society's devaluation of black women as mothers.

Sterilization abuse has taken the form both of blatant coercion and trickery and of subtle influences on women's decisions to be sterilized.[126] In the seventies, some doctors conditioned delivering babies and performing abortions on black women's consent to sterilization.[127] In a 1974 case brought by poor teenage black women in Alabama, a federal district court found that an estimated 100,000 to 150,000 poor women were sterilized annually under federally funded programs.[128] Some of these women were coerced into agreeing to sterilization under the threat that their welfare benefits would be withdrawn unless they submitted to the operation.[129] Despite federal and state regulations intended to prevent involuntary sterilization, physicians and other health care providers continue to urge women of color to consent to sterilization because they view these women's family sizes as excessive and believe these women are incapable of effectively using other methods of birth control.[130]

Current government funding policy perpetuates the encouragement of sterilization of poor, and thus of mainly black, women. The federal government pays for sterilization services under the Medicaid program,[131] while it often does not provide or encourage information about or access to other contraceptive techniques and abortion.[132] In effect, sterilization is the only publicly funded birth control method readily available to poor women of color.

Popular images of the undeserving black mother serve to legitimate government policy as well as the practices of health care providers. The myth of the black Jezebel has been supplemented by the contemporary image of the lazy welfare mother who breeds children at the expense of taxpayers in order to increase the amount of her welfare check.[133] This view of black motherhood provides the rationale for society's restrictions on black female fertility.[134] It is this image of the undeserving black mother that ultimately underlies the government's choice to punish crack-addicted women.

IV. Prosecuting Drug Addicts as Punishment for Having Babies

INFORMED by the historical and present devaluation of black motherhood, we can better understand prosecutors' reasons for punishing drug-addicted mothers. This article views such prosecutions as punishing these women, in essence, for having babies; judges such as the one who convicted Jennifer Johnson are pronouncing not so much "I care about your baby" as "You don't deserve to be a mother."

It is important to recognize at the outset that the prosecutions are based in part on a woman's pregnancy and not on her illegal drug use alone.[135] Prosecutors charge these defendants not with drug use but with child abuse or drug distribution—crimes that relate to their pregnancy. Moreover, pregnant women receive harsher sentences than do drug-addicted men or women who are not pregnant.[136]

The unlawful nature of drug use must not be allowed to confuse the basis of the crimes at issue. The legal rationale underlying the prosecutions does not depend on the illegality of drug use. Harm to the fetus is the crux of the government's legal theory. Criminal charges have been brought against women for conduct that is legal but is alleged to have harmed the fetus.[137]

When a drug-addicted woman becomes pregnant, she has only one realistic avenue to escape criminal charges—abortion.[138] Thus, she is penalized for choosing to have the baby rather than choosing to have an abortion. In this way, the state's punitive action may coerce women to have abortions rather than risk being charged with a crime. Thus, it is the choice of carrying a pregnancy to term that is being penalized.[139]

There is also good reason to question the government's justification for the prosecutions—the concern for the welfare of potential children. I have already discussed the selectivity of the prosecutions with respect to poor black women.[140] This focus on the conduct of one group of women weakens the state's rationale for the prosecutions.

The history of overwhelming state neglect of black children casts further doubt on its professed concern for the welfare of the fetus. When a society has always closed its eyes to the inadequacy of prenatal care available to poor black women, its current expression of interest in the health of unborn black children must be viewed with suspicion. The most telling evidence of the state's disregard of black children is the high rate of infant death in the black community. In 1987, the mortality rate for black infants in the United States was 17.9 deaths per thousand births—more than twice the figure of 8.6 for white infants.[141] In New York City, while infant mortality rates in upper- and middle-income areas were generally less than 9 per thousand in 1986, the rates exceeded 19 in the poor black communities of the South Bronx and Bedford-Stuyvesant and reached 27.6 in Central Harlem.[142]

The main reason for these high mortality rates is inadequate prenatal care.[143] Most poor black women face financial and other barriers to receiving proper care during pregnancy.[144] In 1986, only half of all pregnant black women in the United States received adequate prenatal care.[145] It appears that in the eighties, black women's access to prenatal care has actually declined.[146] The government has chosen to punish poor black women rather than to provide the means for them to have healthy children.

The cruelty of this punitive response is

heightened by the lack of available drug treatment services for pregnant drug addicts.[147] Protecting the welfare of drug addicts' children requires, among other things, adequate facilities for the mother's drug treatment. Yet a drug addict's pregnancy serves as an obstacle to obtaining this treatment. Treatment centers either refuse to treat pregnant women or are effectively closed to them, because the centers are ill-equipped to meet the needs of pregnant addicts.[148] Most hospitals and programs that treat addiction exclude pregnant women because their babies are more likely to be born with health problems requiring expensive care.[149] Program directors also feel that treating pregnant addicts is worth neither the increased cost nor the risk of tort liability.[150]

Moreover, there are several barriers to pregnant women who seek to use centers that will accept them. Drug treatment programs are generally based on male-oriented models that are not geared to the needs of women.[151] The lack of accommodations for children is perhaps the most significant obstacle to treatment. Most outpatient clinics do not provide child care, and many residential treatment programs do not admit children.[152] Furthermore, treatment programs have traditionally failed to provide the comprehensive services that women need, including prenatal and gynecological care, contraceptive counseling, appropriate job training, and counseling for sexual and physical abuse.[153] Predominantly male staffs and clients are often hostile to female clients and employ a confrontational style of therapy that makes many women uncomfortable.[154] Moreover, long waiting lists make treatment useless for women who need help during the limited duration of their pregnancies.[155]

Finally, and perhaps most important, ample evidence reveals that prosecuting addicted mothers may not achieve the government's asserted goal of healthier pregnancies; indeed, such prosecutions will probably lead to the opposite result. Pregnant addicts who seek help from public hospitals and clinics are the ones most often reported to government authorities.[156] The threat of prosecution based on this reporting forces women to remain anonymous

and thus has the reverse effect of deterring pregnant drug addicts from seeking treatment.[157] For this reason, the government's decision to punish drug-addicted mothers is irreconcilable with the goal of helping them.

Pregnancy may be a time when women are most motivated to seek treatment for drug addiction and to make positive lifestyle changes.[158] The government should capitalize on this opportunity by encouraging drug-addicted women to seek help and by providing them with comprehensive treatment. Punishing pregnant women who use drugs only exacerbates the causes of addiction—poverty, lack of self-esteem, and hopelessness.[159] Perversely, this makes it more likely that poor black women's children—the asserted beneficiaries of the prosecutions—will suffer from the same hardships.

V. Punishing Black Mothers and the Perpetuation of Racial Hierarchy

THE previous part showed how recent prosecutions have penalized black women for their reproductive choices based in part on society's devaluation of black motherhood. This analysis implicates two constitutional protections: the equal protection clause of the Fourteenth Amendment and the right of privacy. These two constitutional challenges appeal to different but related values. They are related[160] in the sense that underlying the protection of the individual's autonomy is the principle that all individuals are entitled to equal dignity.[161] A basic premise of equality doctrine is that certain fundamental aspects of the human personality, including decisional autonomy, must be respected in all persons.[162] Theories of racial equality and privacy can be used as related means to achieve a common end of eliminating the legacy of racial discrimination which has devalued black motherhood. Both aim to create a society in which black women's reproductive choices, including the decision to bear children, are given full respect and protection.

The equal protection clause embodies the Constitution's ideal of racial equality.[163] State action that violates this ideal by creating classifications based on race must be subjected to strict judicial scrutiny.[164] The equal protection clause, however, does not explicitly define the meaning of equality or delineate the nature of prohibited government conduct. As a result, equal protection analyses generally have divided into two visions of equality: one that is informed by an antidiscrimination principle, the other by an antisubordination principle.[165]

The antidiscrimination approach identifies the primary threat to equality as the government's "failure to treat Black people as individuals without regard to race."[166] The goal of the antidiscrimination principle is to ensure that all members of society are treated in a color-blind or race-neutral fashion. Under this view of equality, the function of the equal protection clause is to outlaw specific acts committed by individual government officials which discriminate against individual black complainants because of their race. Thus, this approach judges the legitimacy of government action from the perpetrator's perspective.[167] The analysis focuses on the process by which government decisions are made and seeks to purge racial classifications from that process.

The Supreme Court's current understanding of the equal protection clause is based on a narrow interpretation of the antidiscrimination principle.[168] The court has confined discrimination prohibited by the Constitution to state conduct performed with a discriminatory intent.[169] State conduct that disproportionately affects blacks violates the Constitution only if it is accompanied by a purposeful desire to produce this outcome.[170] Although recognized violations are not limited to explicit racial classifications, an invidious purpose cannot be inferred solely from the adverse consequences of racially neutral policies.[171] A black complainant, therefore, need not produce a law that expressly differentiates between whites and blacks; but neither can she simply demonstrate that a color-blind law has a clearly disproportionate impact on blacks. As one commentator has noted, "the Justices have demanded proof . . . that officials were 'out to get' a person or group on account of race."[172]

Black women prosecuted for drug use during

pregnancy nevertheless may be able to make out a prima facie case of discriminatory purpose.[173] The court has recognized that a selection process characterized by broad government discretion that produces unexplained racial disparities may support the presumption of discriminatory purpose.[174] In *Castaneda v. Partida*,[175] for example, the court held that the defendant demonstrated a prima facie case of intentional discrimination in grand jury selection by showing a sufficiently large statistical disparity between the percentage of Mexican-Americans in the population (79 percent) and the percentage of those summoned (39 percent), combined with a selection procedure that relied on the discretion of jury commissioners.[176]

Similarly, a black mother arrested in Pinellas County, Florida, could make out a prima facie case of unconstitutional racial discrimination by showing that a disproportionate number of those chosen for prosecution for exposing newborns to drugs are black. In particular, she could point out the disparity between the percentage of defendants who are black and the percentage of pregnant substance abusers who are black.[177] The above-mentioned *New England Journal of Medicine* study of pregnant women in Pinellas County found that only about 26 percent of those who used drugs were black,[178] yet over 90 percent of Florida prosecutions for drug abuse during pregnancy have been brought against black women.[179] The defendant could buttress her case with the study's finding that, despite similar rates of substance abuse, black women were ten times more likely than white women to be reported to public health authorities for substance abuse during pregnancy.[180] In addition, the defendant could show that health care professionals and prosecutors wield a great deal of discretion in selecting women to be subjected to the criminal justice system.[181] The burden would then shift to the state "to dispel the inference of intentional discrimination" by justifying the racial discrepancy in its prosecutions.[182]

The antisubordination approach to equality would not require black defendants to prove that the prosecutions are motivated by racial bias. Rather than requiring victims to prove distinct instances of discriminating behavior in the administrative process,[183] the antisubordination approach considers the concrete effects of government policy on the substantive condition of the disadvantaged.[184] This perspective recognizes that racial subjugation is not maintained solely through the racially antagonistic acts of individual officials;[185] instead, it views social patterns and institutions that perpetuate the inferior status of blacks as the primary threats to equality. The goal of antisubordination law is a society in which each member is guaranteed equal respect as a human being. Under this conception of equality, the function of the equal protection clause is to dismantle racial hierarchy by eliminating state action or inaction that effectively preserves black subordination.[186]

The prosecution of drug-addicted mothers demonstrates the inadequacy of antidiscrimination analysis and the superiority of the antisubordination approach. Rather than conform black women's experiences to the intent standard, we can use those experiences to reveal the narrowmindedness of the Supreme Court's view of equality. First, the antidiscrimination approach may not adequately protect black women from prosecutions' infringement of equality, because it is difficult to identify individual guilty actors: Who are the government officials motivated by racial bias to punish black women? The hospital staff who test and report mothers to child welfare agencies? The prosecutors who develop and implement policies to charge women who use drugs during pregnancy? Legislators who enact laws protecting the unborn?

It is unlikely that any of these individual actors intentionally singled out black women for punishment based on a conscious devaluation of their motherhood; the disproportionate impact of the prosecutions on poor black women does not result from such isolated, individualized decisions. Rather, it is a result of two centuries of systematic exclusion of black women from tangible and intangible benefits enjoyed by white society. Their exclusion is reflected in black women's reliance on public hospitals and public drug treatment centers, in their failure to obtain adequate prenatal care, in the more frequent reporting of black drug users by health care professionals, and in society's acquiescence in the government's punitive response to the problem of crack-addicted babies.

More generally, the antidiscrimination principle mischaracterizes the role of social norms in perpetuating inequality. This view of equality perceives racism as disconnected acts by individuals who operate outside of the social fabric.[187] The goal of the equal protection clause under this world view is "to separate from the masses of society those blameworthy individuals who are violating the otherwise shared norm."[188]

The prosecutions of drug-addicted mothers demonstrate how dramatically this perspective departs from reality. It is precisely a shared societal norm—the devaluation of black motherhood—that perpetuates the social conditions discussed above and explains why black women are particularly susceptible to prosecution. The court's vision of equality acquiesces in racist norms and institutions by exempting them from a standard that requires proof of illicit motive on the part of an individual governmental actor. The inability to identify and blame an individual government actor allows society to rationalize the disparate impact of the prosecutions as the result of the mothers' own irresponsible actions. Formal equality theory thus legitimates the subordination of black women.

In contrast to the antidiscrimination approach, antisubordination theory mandates that equal protection law concern itself with the concrete ways in which government policy perpetuates the inferior status of black women. The law should listen to the voices of poor black mothers and seek to eliminate their experiences of subordination. From this perspective, the prosecutions of crack-addicted mothers are unconstitutional because they reinforce the myth of the undeserving black mother by singling out—intentionally or not—black women for punishment. The government's punitive policy reflects a long history of denigration of black mothers dating back to slavery, and it serves to perpetuate that legacy of unequal respect. The prosecutions should therefore be upheld only if the state can demonstrate that they serve a compelling interest that could not be achieved through less discriminatory means.[189]

Although the state's asserted interest in ensuring the health of babies is substantial, prosecution does not advance that interest in a sufficiently narrow fashion. First, as I have noted, the government's punitive course of action is inimical to the goal of healthier pregnancies because it deters women from seeking help.[190] In addition, even if the prosecutions could be proved to further the state's interest in children's welfare, they would not survive the "least restrictive alternative" standard, which requires that "even though the governmental purpose be legitimate and substantial, that purpose cannot be pursued by means that broadly stifle fundamental personal liberties when the end can be more narrowly achieved."[191] A public commitment to providing adequate prenatal care for poor women and drug treatment programs that meet the needs of pregnant addicts would be a more effective means for the state to address the problem of drug-exposed babies.[192]

By prosecuting crack-addicted mothers, the government helps to perpetuate the dominant society's devaluation of black motherhood. The antisubordination analysis better uncovers this institutional (rather than individualistic) mechanism for maintaining racial inequality. The government's policy cannot withstand the scrutiny of an equality jurisprudence dedicated to eradicating hierarchies of racial privilege. Still, the focus purely on equality does not address the unique significance of punishing the decision to bear a child. The remainder of this article examines how the prosecutions violate black women's right of privacy and the relationship between that privacy analysis and the goal of racial equality.

VI. A CRITICAL ASSESSMENT OF ARGUMENTS AGAINST INTERVENTION

THERE is now a substantial body of scholarship challenging state intervention in pregnant women's conduct.[193] Yet much of the literature has not sufficiently taken into account the experience of poor black women, the very women who are most affected. In addition, the literature has failed to address adequately the arguments on behalf of fetal protection. In this part, I will critique various reproductive rights theories that have been used to challenge the control of pregnant women and show why they are not helpful in addressing the prosecution of drug-addicted mothers. In Part VII, I will present a privacy argument that more effectively confronts the government's policy. That analysis better explains the constitutional injury caused by the prosecutions because it recognizes race as a critical factor.

A. Bodily Autonomy and Integrity

Much of the discourse challenging state intervention in the decisions of pregnant women has occurred in the context of forced medical treatment.[194] Many commentators have argued that judicial decisions which allow doctors to perform surgery and other procedures on a pregnant woman without her consent violate women's right to bodily autonomy and integrity.[195] It is difficult, however, to transfer the scholarship addressing compulsory medical procedures to the issue of drug-addicted mothers.

The interests of the drug-addicted mother appear to be weaker for three reasons. First, unlike forced medical treatment, punishing the pregnant drug addict does not require her to take affirmative steps to benefit the fetus. She is not asked to be a good samaritan; rather, she is punished for affirmatively doing harm to the fetus. Second, the prosecution of drug-addicted mothers involves no direct physical intrusion. Nor do prosecutions deprive women of control over their bodies by directly compelling them to undergo an unwanted biological process, as is the case with the prohibition of abortion. On this level, punishing drug-addicted mothers does not seem to implicate a mother's right to bodily integrity at all.

Third, the mother's drug use has potentially devastating effects on the fetus and lacks any social justification. Indeed, forcing a woman to refrain from using harmful drugs through incarceration or court order may be seen as a benefit to the woman herself, whereas forced medical procedures often aid the fetus only at the expense of the mother's health or her deeply held religious beliefs. It is therefore harder to identify how the government's action infringes on a constitutionally protected interest. Consequently, some commentators who oppose the regulation of some potentially harmful conduct during pregnancy also justify punishment of pregnant drug users.[196] We must therefore draw on another principle of autonomy to describe the infringement caused by these prosecutions—the right to make decisions about reproduction. In this context, this is the choice of carrying a pregnancy to term.

In addition, many of the issues raised by forced medical treatment seem disconnected from the experiences of poor women of color.[197] For example, much of the literature focuses on ethical issues arising from treating the fetus as a patient and its impact on the relationship between the pregnant woman and her physician.[198] This debate is largely irrelevant to poor black women, the majority of whom receive inadequate prenatal care.[199] Their major concern is not an ethical conflict with their doctor but, rather, affording or finding a doctor in the first place. The issue of whether intricate fetal surgery may be performed against a mother's will is far removed from the urgent needs of poor women who may not have available to them the most rudimentary means to ensure the health of the fetus.[200]

Forced treatment decisions equate women with inert vessels, disregard their own choices, and value them solely for their capacity to nurture a fetus.[201] Although this view of women is reflected as well in the prosecution of drug-addicted mothers, it does not grasp the full indignity of the state's treatment of poor black women. Government control of pregnancy perpetuates stereotypes that value women solely for their procreative capacity; but the prosecutions of crack addicts deny poor black women even this modicum of value. By punishing them for having babies, they are deemed not even worthy of the dignity of childbearing. Thus, the prosecutions debase black women even more than does forced medical treatment's general devaluation of women.[202]

B. The Right to Make Medical and Lifestyle Decisions

A second approach challenges restrictions on maternal conduct during pregnancy by advocating a woman's right to make medical and lifestyle decisions.[203] Rather than focus on a woman's right to protect her body from physical intrusion, this approach focuses on a woman's right to engage in activities of her choice free from government interference. This argument also loses its force in the context of maternal drug addiction. While the danger of government restrictions on a pregnant woman's normal conduct may be apparent, drug use during pregnancy arguably belongs in a separate category. The pregnant drug addict is not asked to refrain from generally acceptable behavior, such as sexual intercourse, work, or exercise. Rather, society demands only that she cease conduct that it already deems illegal and reprehensible.

Arguments based on a woman's right to make decisions about her pregnancy and her fetus also appear weak in the context of maternal drug addiction. Unlike healthy mothers,[204] pregnant drug addicts are not better able to make lifestyle and medical decisions that affect the fetus than is the state or a physician. Nor can we say that a decision to carry a fetus to term automatically demonstrates that a drug-addicted mother cares deeply for it and is in a better position than is the state to monitor her own conduct during pregnancy than is the state. Most would agree that the pregnant drug addict has exercised poor judgment in caring for herself and her fetus. The state should not substitute its judgment for that of the "normal" mother, but intervention in the case of the drug addict seems more justified.

Although the government is arguably better able to make decisions about the care of the fetus than is the drug-addicted mother, it is quite a different matter to allow the government to determine who is entitled to be a mother. State interference in the decision to bear a child is constitutionally more significant than is state control of lifestyle decisions.

The approach advocating interference in women's lifestyles also neglects the concerns of poor women of color. A common criticism of the prosecution of drug-addicted mothers is that the imposition of maternal duties will, over time, lead to punishment for less egregious conduct; commentators have predicted government penalties for cigarette smoking, consumption of alcohol, strenuous physical activity, and failure to follow a doctor's orders.[205] Although valid, this argument ignores the reality of poor black women who are currently being arrested. The reference to a parade of future horribles to criticize the fetal rights doctrine belittles the significance of current government action: it seems to imply that the prosecution of black crack addicts is not enough to generate concern, and that we must postulate the prosecution of white middle-class women in order for the challenge to be meaningful.[206]

C. The Focus on Abortion

Another aspect of the reproductive rights literature that limits our understanding of reproductive choice is its focus on abortion rights. One problem is that this focus provides an inadequate response to a central argument in support of the regulation of pregnancy. John Robertson, for example, has contended that if a woman forgoes her right to an abortion, she forfeits her right to autonomy and choice.[207] If abortion lies at the heart of women's reproductive rights, then state policies that do not interfere with that right are acceptable.[208] Similarly, if the full extent of reproductive freedom is the right to have an abortion, then a policy that encourages abortion[209]—such as the prosecution of crack-addicted mothers—does not interfere with that freedom.[210]

As in the previous approaches, the emphasis on abortion fails to incorporate the needs of poor women of color. The primary concerns of white middle-class women are laws that restrict choices otherwise available to them, such as statutes that make it more difficult to obtain an abortion; however, the main concerns of poor women of color are the material conditions of poverty and oppression that restrict their choices.[211] The reproductive freedom of poor women of color, for example, is limited significantly not only by the denial of access to safe abortions but also by the lack of resources necessary for a healthy pregnancy and parenting relationship.[212] Their choices are limited not only by direct government interference with their decisions, but also by government's failure to facilitate them. The focus of reproductive rights discourse on abortion neglects this broader range of reproductive health issues that affect poor women of color.[213] Addressing the concerns of women of color will expand our vision of reproductive freedom to include the full scope of what it means to have control over one's reproductive life.[214]

VII. Claiming the Right of Privacy for Women of Color

A. Identifying the Constitutional Issue

In deciding which of the competing interests involved in the prosecution of drug-addicted mothers prevails—the state's interest in protecting the health of the fetus or the woman's interest in preventing state intervention—it is essential as a matter of constitutional law to identify the precise nature of the woman's right at stake. In the Johnson case, the prosecutor framed the constitutional issue as follows: "What constitutionally protected freedom did Jennifer engage in when she smoked cocaine?"[215] That was the wrong question: Johnson was not convicted of using drugs. Her "constitutional right" to smoke cocaine was never at issue. Johnson was prosecuted because she chose to carry her pregnancy to term while she was addicted to crack. Had she smoked cocaine during her pregnancy and then had an abortion, she would not have been charged with such a serious crime. Thus, the proper question is, "What constitutionally protected freedom did Jennifer engage in when she decided to have a baby even though she was a drug addict?"

Understanding the prosecution of drug-addicted mothers as punishment for having babies clarifies the constitutional right at stake. The woman's right at issue is not the right to abuse drugs or to cause the fetus to be born with defects.[216] It is the right to choose to be a mother which is burdened by the criminalization of conduct during pregnancy.[217] This view of the constitutional issue reveals the relevance of race to the resolution of the competing interests. Race has historically determined the value society places on an individual's right to choose motherhood; because of the devaluation of black motherhood, protecting the right of black women to choose to bear a child has unique significance. In the following section, I argue that the prosecutions of addicted mothers violate traditional liberal notions of privacy. I also demonstrate how the issue of race informs the traditional analysis and calls for a reassessment of the use of privacy doctrine in the struggle to eliminate gender and racial subordination.

B. Overview of Privacy Arguments

Prosecutions of drug-addicted mothers infringe on two aspects of the right to individual choice in reproductive decision-making. First, they infringe on the freedom to continue a pregnancy that is essential to an individual's personhood and autonomy. This freedom implies that state control of the decision to carry a pregnancy to term can be as pernicious as state control of the decision to terminate a pregnancy. Second, the prosecutions infringe on choice by imposing an invidious government standard for the entitlement to procreate. Such imposition of a government standard for childbearing is one way that society denies the humanity of those who are different. The first approach emphasizes a woman's right to autonomy over her reproductive life; the second highlights a woman's right to be valued equally as a human being.[218] In other words, the prosecution of crack-addicted mothers infringes upon both a mother's right to make decisions that determine her individual identity and her right to be respected equally as a human being by recognizing the value of her motherhood.

Inherent in the thesis of this article is a tension between the reliance on the liberal rhetoric of choice and an acknowledgment of the fallacy of choice for poor women of color. This article also seeks to incorporate liberal notions of individual autonomy while acknowledging the collective injury perpetrated by racism.[219] This tension may be an example of what Mari Matsuda calls "multiple consciousness."[220] Matsuda observes that "outsider" lawyers and scholars must often adopt a "dualist approach"

that incorporates an elitist legal system and the concept of legal rights while seeing the world from the standpoint of the oppressed. "Unlike the postmodern critics of the left . . . outsiders, including feminists and people of color, have embraced legalism as a tool of necessity, making legal consciousness their own in order to attack injustice."[221]

This internal struggle between the embrace of legalism and the recognition of oppression characterizes a process of enlightenment.[222] Working through the privacy analysis from the perspective of poor black women uncovers unexplored benefits to be gained from liberal doctrine while revealing liberalism's inadequacies. This process of putting forth new propositions for challenge and subversion will produce a better understanding of the law and the ways in which it can be used to pursue social justice.

C. The Right to Choose Procreation

Punishing drug-addicted mothers unconstitutionally burdens the right to choose to bear a child. Certain interests of the individual—generally called "rights"—are entitled to heightened protection against government interference under the due process clause of the Fourteenth Amendment.[223] The right of privacy is recognized as one cluster of such interests, implicit in the "liberty" that the Fourteenth Amendment protects.[224] The right of privacy has been interpreted to include the "interest in independence in making certain kinds of important decisions."[225] This concept of decisional privacy seeks[226] to protect intimate or personal affairs that are fundamental to an individual's identity and moral personhood from unjustified government intrusion.[227] At the forefront of the development of the right of privacy has been the freedom of personal choice in matters of marriage and family life.[228] Once an interest has been deemed part of the right of privacy, the government needs a compelling reason to intervene to survive constitutional scrutiny.[229]

There is considerable support for the conclusion that the decision to procreate[230] is part of the right of privacy. The decision to bear children is universally acknowledged in the privacy cases as being "at the very heart" of these consti-tutionally protected choices.[231] In *Eisenstadt v. Baird*,[232] for example, the Supreme Court struck down a Massachusetts statute that pro-hibited the distribution of contraceptives to un-married persons. Although the case was decided on equal protection grounds, the court recog-nized the vital nature of the freedom to choose whether to give birth to a child: "If the right of privacy means anything, it is the right of the individual, married or single, to be free from unwarranted governmental intrusion into mat-ters so fundamentally affecting a person as the decision whether to bear or beget a child."[233]

The right of privacy protects equally the choice to bear children and the choice to refrain from bearing them.[234] The historical experi-ences of black women illustrate the evil of government control over procreative decisions. Their experiences demonstrate that the dual nature of the decisional right recognized in the privacy cases goes beyond the logical implica-tions of making a choice. The exploitation of black women's foremothers during slavery to breed more slaves and the sterilization abuse that they have suffered reveal society's pervasive devaluation of black women as mothers.

Burdening both the right to terminate a preg-nancy and the right to give birth to a child violates a woman's personhood by denying her autonomy over the self-defining decision of whether she will bring another being into the world. Furthermore, criminalizing the choice to give birth imposes tangible burdens on women, as well as the intangible infringement on per-sonhood. Punishing women for having babies is in this sense at least as pernicious as forced maternity at the behest of the state.[235]

If a woman's decision to bear a child is entitled to constitutional protection, it follows that the government may not unduly burden that choice. In *Cleveland Board of Education v. LaFleur*,[236] the court invalidated mandatory maternity leave policies that had the effect of burdening the choice to procreate. The court viewed the school board's policy of forced ma-ternity leave as a form of penalty imposed on pregnant teachers for asserting their right to decide to have children.[237] Although the court

applied a rational basis test to the maternity leave policies in *LaFleur*,[238] the more drastic burden of criminal punishment should warrant strict scrutiny.[239] Even under the court's current analysis, which distinguishes between direct and indirect governmental interference in reproduc-tive decision-making,[240] government intrusion as extreme as criminal prosecution would un-duly infringe on protected autonomy.[241] The court has expressly distinguished, for example, the government's refusal to subsidize the exer-cise of the abortion right from the infliction of criminal penalties on the exercise of that right.[242] Criminal prosecutions of drug-addicted mothers do more than discourage a choice; they exact a severe penalty on the drug user for choosing to complete her pregnancy.

These privacy concepts have two benefits for advocating the reproductive rights of women of color in particular: the right of privacy stresses the value of personhood, and it protects against the totalitarian abuse of government power. First, affirming black women's constitutional claim to personhood is particularly important, because these women historically have been denied the dignity of their full humanity and identity.[243] The principle of self-definition has special significance for black women. Angela Harris recognizes in the writings of Zora Neale Hurston an insistence on a "conception of iden-tity as a construction, not an essence . . . [B]lack women have had to learn to construct them-selves in a society that denied them full selves."[244] Black woman's willful self-definition is an adaptation to a history of social denigra-tion. Rejected from the dominant society's norm of womanhood, black women have been forced to resort to their own internal resources. Harris contrasts this process of affirmative self-definition with the feminist paradigm of women as passive victims. Black women willfully create their own identities out of "fragments of experi-ence, not discovered in one's body or unveiled after male domination is eliminated."[245]

The concept of personhood embodied in the right of privacy can be used to affirm the role of will and creativity in black women's construc-tion of their own identities. Relying on the concept of self-definition celebrates the legacy of black women who have survived and transcended conditions of oppression.[246] The process of defining oneself and declaring one's personhood defies the denial of self-ownership inherent in slavery.[247] Thus, the right of privacy, with its affirmation of personhood, is especially suited for challenging the devaluation of black motherhood underlying the prosecutions of drug-addicted women.

Another important element of the right of privacy is its delineation of the limits of governmental power.[248] The protection from government abuse also makes the right of privacy a useful legal tool for protecting the reproductive rights of women of color.[249] Poor women of color are especially vulnerable to government control over their decisions.[250] The government's pervasive involvement in black women's lives illustrates the inadequacy of the privacy critique presented by some white feminist scholars.[251] Catharine MacKinnon, for example, argues that privacy doctrine is based on the false liberal assumption that government nonintervention into the private sphere promotes women's autonomy.[252] The individual woman's legal right of privacy, according to MacKinnon, functions instead as "a means of subordinating women's collective needs to the imperatives of male supremacy."[253]

This rejection of privacy doctrine does not take into account the contradictory meaning of the private sphere for women of color. Feminist legal theory focuses on the private realm of the family as an institution of violence and subordination.[254] Women of color, however, often experience the family as the site of solace and resistance against racial oppression.[255] For many women of color, the immediate concern in the area of reproductive rights is not abuse in the private sphere but abuse of government power. The prosecution of crack-addicted mothers and coerced sterilization are examples of state intervention which pose a much greater threat for women of color than for white women.

Another telling example is the issue of child custody. The primary concern for white middle-class women with regard to child custody is private custody battles with their husbands following the termination of a marriage.[256] For

women of color, though, the dominant threat is termination of parental rights by the state.[257] Again, the imminent danger faced by poor women of color comes from the public sphere, not the private. Thus, the protection from government interference that privacy doctrine affords may have a different significance for women of color.

D. Unconstitutional Government Standards for Procreation: The Intersection of Privacy and Equality

The equal protection clause and the right of privacy provide the basis for two separate constitutional challenges to the prosecution of drug-addicted mothers. The singling out of black mothers for punishment combines in a single government action several wrongs prohibited by both constitutional doctrines. Black mothers are denied autonomy over procreative decisions because of their race. The government's denial of black women's fundamental right to choose to bear children serves to perpetuate the legacy of racial discrimination embodied in the devaluation of black motherhood. The full scope of the government's violation can better be understood, then, by a constitutional theory that acknowledges the complementary and overlapping qualities of the Constitution's guarantees of equality and privacy.[258] Viewing the prosecutions as imposing a racist government standard for procreation uses this approach.[259]

Poor crack addicts are punished for having babies because they fail to measure up to the state's ideal of motherhood. Prosecutors have brought charges against women who use drugs during pregnancy without demonstrating any harm to the fetus.[260] Moreover, a government policy that has the effect of punishing primarily poor black women for having babies evokes the specter of racial eugenics, especially in light of the history of sterilization abuse of women of color.[261] These factors make clear that these women are not punished simply because they may harm their unborn children; rather, they are punished because the combination of their poverty, race, and drug addiction is seen as making them unworthy of procreating.

This aspect of the prosecutions implicates both equality and privacy interests. The right to bear children goes to the heart of what it means to be human. The value we place on individuals determines whether we see them as entitled to perpetuate themselves in their children. Denying a woman the right to bear children—or punishing her for exercising that right—deprives her of a basic part of her humanity.[262] When this denial is based on race, it also functions to preserve a racial hierarchy that essentially disregards black humanity.

The abuse of sterilization laws designed to effect eugenic policy demonstrates the potential danger of governmental standards for procreation. During the first half of the twentieth century, the eugenics movement[263] embraced the theory[264] that intelligence and other personality traits are genetically determined and therefore inherited. This hereditarian belief, coupled with the reform approach of the Progressive Era, fueled a campaign to remedy America's social problems by stemming biological degeneracy. Eugenicists advocated compulsory sterilization to prevent reproduction by people who were likely to produce allegedly defective offspring. Eugenic sterilization was thought to improve society by eliminating its "socially inadequate" members.[265] Around the turn of the century, many states enacted involuntary sterilization laws directed at those deemed burdens on society, including the mentally retarded, mentally ill, epileptics, and criminals.[266]

In a 1927 decision, *Buck v. Bell*,[267] the Supreme Court upheld the constitutionality[268] of a Virginia involuntary sterilization law.[269] The plaintiff, Carrie Buck, was described in the opinion as "a feeble minded white woman" committed to a state mental institution who was "the daughter of a feeble minded mother in the same institution, and the mother of an illegitimate feeble minded child."[270] The court approved an order of the mental institution that Buck undergo sterilization. Justice Holmes, himself an ardent eugenicist,[271] gave eugenic theory the imprimatur of constitutional law in his infamous declaration: "Three generations of imbeciles are enough."[272]

The salient feature of the eugenic sterilization laws is their brutal imposition of society's restrictive norms of motherhood. Governmental control of reproduction in the name of science masks racist and classist judgments about who deserves to bear children. It is grounded on the premise that people who depart from social norms do not deserve to procreate.[273] Carrie Buck, for example, was punished by sterilization not because of any mental disability, but because of her deviance from society's social and sexual norms.[274]

Explanations of the eugenic rationale reveal this underlying moral standard for procreation. One eugenicist, for example, justified his extreme approach of putting the socially inadequate to death as " 'the surest, the simplest, the kindest, and most humane means for preventing reproduction among those *whom we deem unworthy of the high privilege.*' "[275] Dr. Albert Priddy, the superintendent of the Virginia Colony, similarly explained the necessity of eugenic sterilization in one of his annual reports: the " 'sexual immorality,' of 'anti-social' 'morons' rendered them 'wholly unfit for exercising the *right of motherhood.*' "[276]

Fourteen years after *Buck v. Bell*, the Supreme Court acknowledged the danger of the eugenic rationale. Justice William Douglas recognized both the fundamental quality of the right to procreate and its connection to equality in a later sterilization decision, *Skinner v. Oklahoma*.[277] *Skinner* considered the constitutionality of the Oklahoma Habitual Criminal Sterilization Act[278] authorizing the sterilization of persons convicted two or more times for "felonies involving moral turpitude."[279] An Oklahoma court had ordered Skinner to undergo a vasectomy after he was convicted once of stealing chickens and twice of robbery with firearms.[280] The statute, the court found, treated unequally criminals who had committed intrinsically the same quality of offense. For example, men who had committed grand larceny three times were sterilized, but embezzlers were not. The court struck down the statute as a violation of the equal protection clause. Declaring the right to bear children to be "one of the basic civil rights of man,"[281] the court applied strict scrutiny to the classification[282] and held that the government failed to demonstrate that the statute's classifications were justified by eugenics or the inheritability of criminal traits.[283]

Skinner rested on grounds that linked equal protection doctrine and the right to procreate. Justice Douglas framed the legal question as "a sensitive and important area of human rights."[284] The reason for the court's elevation of the right to procreate was the court's recognition of the significant risk of discriminatory selection inherent in state intervention in reproduction.[285] The court also understood the genocidal implications of a government standard for procreation: "In evil or reckless hands [the government's power to sterilize] can cause races or types which are inimical to the dominant group to wither and disappear."[286] The critical role of procreation to human survival and the invidious potential for government discrimination against disfavored groups makes heightened protection crucial. The court understood the use of the power to sterilize in the government's discrimination against certain types of criminals to be as invidious "as if it had selected a particular race or nationality for oppressive treatment."[287]

Although the reasons advanced for the sterilization of chicken thieves and the prosecution of drug-addicted mothers are different, both practices are dangerous for similar reasons. Both effectuate ethnocentric judgments by the government that certain members of society do not deserve to have children. As the court recognized in *Skinner*, the enforcement of a government standard for childbearing denies the disfavored group a critical aspect of human dignity.[288]

The history of compulsory sterilization demonstrates that society deems women who deviate from its norms of motherhood—in 1941, teenaged delinquent girls like Carrie Buck who bore illegitimate children; today, poor black crack addicts who use drugs during pregnancy—"unworthy of the high privilege" of procreation.[289] The government therefore refuses to affirm their human dignity by helping them to overcome obstacles to good mothering.[290] Rather, it punishes them by sterilization or criminal prosecution and thereby denies them a basic part of their humanity. When this denial

is based on race, the violation is especially serious. Governmental policies that perpetuate racial subordination through the denial of procreative rights, which threaten at once racial equality and privacy, should be subject to the highest scrutiny.

E. Toward a New Privacy Jurisprudence

Imagine that courts and legislatures have accepted the argument that the prosecution of crack-addicted mothers violates their right of privacy. All pending indictments for drug use during pregnancy are dismissed, and bills proposing fetal abuse laws are discarded. Would there be any perceptible change in the inferior status of black women? Pregnant crack addicts would still be denied treatment, and most poor black women would continue to receive inadequate prenatal care. The infant mortality rate for blacks would remain deplorably high. In spite of the benefits of privacy doctrine for women of color, liberal notions of privacy are inadequate to eliminate the subordination of black women. In this section, I will suggest two approaches that I believe are necessary in order for privacy theory to contribute to the eradication of racial hierarchy. First, we need to develop a positive view of the right of privacy. Second, the law must recognize the connection between the right of privacy and racial equality.

The most compelling argument against privacy rhetoric, from the perspective of women of color, is the connection that feminist scholars have drawn between privacy and the abortion funding decisions.[291] Critics of the concept of privacy note that framing the abortion right as a right merely to be shielded from state intrusion into private choices provides no basis for a constitutional claim to public support for abortions. As the court explained in *Harris v. McRae*,[292] "although government may not place obstacles in the path of a woman's exercise of her freedom of choice, it need not remove those not of its own creation."[293] MacKinnon concludes that abortion as a private privilege rather than a public right only serves to perpetuate inequality:

> Privacy conceived as a right from public intervention and disclosure is the opposite of the relief that Harris sought for welfare women. State inter-

vention would have provided a choice women did not have in [the] private [realm]. The women in *Harris,* women whose sexual refusal has counted for particularly little, needed something to make their privacy effective. The logic of the Court's response resembles the logic by which women are supposed to consent to sex. Preclude the alternatives, then call the sole remaining option "her choice." The point is that the alternatives are precluded prior to the reach of the chosen legal doctrine. They are precluded by conditions of sex, race, and class—the very conditions the privacy frame not only leaves tacit but exists to guarantee.[294]

This critique is correct in its observation that the power of privacy doctrine in poor women's lives is constrained by liberal notions of freedom. First, the abstract freedom to choose is of meager value without meaningful options from which to choose and the ability to effectuate one's choice.[295] The traditional concept of privacy makes the false presumption that the right to choose is contained entirely within the individual rather than circumscribed by the material conditions of the individual's life.[296] Second, the abstract freedom of self-definition is of little help to someone who lacks the resources to realize the personality she envisions or whose emergent self is continually beaten down by social forces. Defining the guarantee of personhood as no more than shielding a sphere of personal decisions from the reach of government—merely ensuring the individual's "right to be let alone"—may be inadequate to protect the dignity and autonomy of the poor and oppressed.[297]

The definition of privacy as a purely negative right serves to exempt the state from any obligation to ensure the social conditions and resources necessary for self-determination and autonomous decision-making.[298] Based on this narrow view of liberty, the Supreme Court has denied a variety of claims to government aid.[299] MacKinnon notes that "[i]t is apparently a very short step from that which the government has a duty not to intervene in to that which it has no duty to intervene in."[300] An evolving privacy doctrine need not make the step between these two propositions. Laurence Tribe, for example, has suggested an alternative view of the relationship between the government's negative and

affirmative responsibilities in guaranteeing the rights of personhood: "Ultimately, the affirmative duties of government cannot be severed from its obligations to refrain from certain forms of control; both must respond to a substantive vision of the needs of human personality."[301]

This concept of privacy includes not only the negative proscription against government coercion but also the affirmative duty of government to protect the individual's personhood from degradation and to facilitate the processes of choice and self-determination.[302] This approach shifts the focus of privacy theory from state nonintervention to an affirmative guarantee of personhood and autonomy. Under this postliberal doctrine, the government is not only prohibited from punishing crack-addicted women for choosing to bear children; it is also required to provide drug treatment and prenatal care. Robin West has eloquently captured this progressive understanding of the due process clause in which privacy doctrine is grounded: "The ideal of due process, then, is an individual life free of illegitimate social coercion facilitated by hierarchies of class, gender, or race. The goal is an affirmatively autonomous existence: a meaningfully flourishing, independent, enriched individual life."[303]

This affirmative view of privacy is enhanced by recognizing the connection between privacy and racial equality. The government's duty to guarantee personhood and autonomy stems not only from the needs of the individual but also from the needs of the entire community. The harm caused by the prosecution of crack-addicted mothers is not simply the incursion on each individual crack addict's decision-making; rather, it is the perpetuation of a degraded image that affects the status of an entire race. The devaluation of a poor black addict's decision to bear a child is tied to the dominant society's disregard for the motherhood of all black women. The diminished value placed on black motherhood, in turn, is a badge of racial inferiority worn by all black people. The affirmative view of privacy recognizes the connection between the dehumanization of the individual and the subordination of the group.

Thus, the reason that legislatures should reject laws that punish black women's reproductive choices is not an absolute and isolated notion of individual autonomy. Rather, legislatures should reject these laws as a critical step toward eradicating a racial hierarchy that has historically demeaned black motherhood. Respecting black women's decision to bear children is a necessary ingredient of a community that affirms the personhood of all of its members. The right to reproductive autonomy is in this way linked to the goal of racial equality and the broader pursuit of a just society. This broader dimension of privacy's guarantees provides a stronger claim to government's affirmative responsibilities.

Feminist legal theory, with its emphasis on the law's concrete effect on the condition of women, calls for a reassessment of traditional privacy law. It may be possible, however, to reconstruct a privacy jurisprudence that retains the focus on autonomy and personhood while making privacy doctrine effective.[304] Before dismissing the right of privacy altogether, we should explore ways to give the concepts of choice and personhood more substance.[305] In this way, the continuing process of challenge and subversion [306]—the feminist critique of liberal privacy doctrine, followed by the racial critique of the feminist analysis—will forge a finer legal tool for dismantling institutions of domination.

VIII. Conclusion

OUR understanding of the prosecutions of drug-addicted mothers must include the perspective of the women whom they most directly affect. The prosecutions arise in a particular historical and political context that has constrained reproductive choice for poor women of color. The state's decision to punish drug-addicted mothers rather than to help them stems from the poverty and race of the defendants and from society's denial of their full dignity as human beings. Viewing the issue from their vantage point reveals that the prosecutions punish for having babies women whose motherhood has historically been devalued.

A policy that attempts to protect fetuses by denying the humanity of their mothers will inevitably fail.[307] We must question such a policy's true concern for the dignity of the fetus, just as we question the motives of the slave owner who protected the unborn slave child while whipping his pregnant mother. Although the master attempted to separate the mother and fetus for his commercial ends, their fates were inextricably intertwined. The tragedy of crack babies is initially a tragedy of crack-addicted mothers: both are part of a larger tragedy of a community that is suffering a host of indignities, including, significantly, the denial of equal respect for its women's reproductive decisions.

It is only by affirming the personhood and equality of poor women of color that the survival of their future generations will be ensured. The first principle of the government's response to the crisis of drug-exposed babies should be the recognition of their mothers' worth and entitlement to autonomy over their reproductive lives. A commitment to guaranteeing these fundamental rights of poor women of color, rather than punishing them, is the true solution to the problem of unhealthy babies.

NOTES

1. J. Johnson, "Smothered Slave Infants: Were Slave Mothers at Fault?," 47 *J. S. Hist.*, 493, 513 (1981).

2. See *State v. Johnson*, No. E89-890-CFA, slip op. at 1 (Fla. Cir. Ct. July 13, 1989), aff'd, No. 89-1765, 1991 Fla. App. LEXIS 3583 (Fla. Dist. Ct. App. Apr. 18, 1991); Moss, "Substance Abuse During Pregnancy," 13 *Harv. Women's L. J.* 278, 280–84 (1990); Roberts, "Drug-Addicted Women Who Have Babies," *Trial* (Apr. 1990) 56, 56; Davidson, "Newborn Drug Exposure Conviction a 'Drastic' First," *Los Angeles Times* (July 31, 1989) 1. 1:1. The recent affirmance of the Johnson decision by a Florida appeals court marked the first time that a state appeals court has upheld such a conviction under laws designed to punish the distribution of drugs to children under eighteen; see *New York Times* (Apr. 20, 1991), 6:4.

Since Johnson's conviction, several other women have been charged with crimes for giving birth to crack-exposed infants. See, for example, *State v. Grubbs*, No. 4FA - S89-415 Criminal (Alaska Sup. Ct. Aug. 25, 1989) (sentencing a twenty-three-year-old white woman to six months in jail and five years probation for criminally negligent homicide in the death of her two-week-old son); *State v. Black*, No. 89–5325 (Fla. Cir. Ct. Jan. 3, 1990) (sentencing a thirty-two-year-old black woman to eighteen months in jail and three years' probation for distribution of drugs to a minor); *State v. Welch*, No. 90-CR-006 (Ky. Cir. Ct. March 15, 1990) (sentencing a thirty-three-year-old white woman to jail for child abuse). See, generally, Paltrow and Shende, "State by State Case Summary of Criminal Prosecutions Against Pregnant Women and Appendix of Public Health and Public Interest Groups Opposed to These Prosecutions," Oct. 29, 1990 (unpublished memorandum to ACLU Affiliates and Interested Parties) (on file at the Harvard Law School Library). [hereinafter State Case Summary].

3. See Fla. Stat. Ann. § 893.13(l)(c) (West Supp. 1990).

4. See Trial Transcript at 20–24, 57–60, *State v. Johnson* [hereinafter *Trial Transcript*] (testimony of Drs. Randy Tompkins and Mitchell Perlstein).

5. Since 1987, at least fifty so-called fetal abuse cases have been brought in nineteen states and the District of Columbia; see Hoffman, "Pregnant, Addicted—And Guilty?," *New York Times Magazine* (Aug. 19, 1990), at 32, 35; see also Lewin, "Drug Use in Pregnancy: New Issue for the Courts," *New York Times* (Feb. 5, 1990), A14:1 (reporting that "[p]rosecutors nationwide are putting . . . drug laws to new use to deal with the rapidly growing number of [drug-exposed] babies"); McNamara, "Fetal Endangerment Cases on the Rise," *Boston Globe* (Oct. 3, 1989), 1:2 (noting that ten new "fetal endangerment" cases had been brought nationwide in the three months following the Supreme Court's decision in *Webster v. Reproductive Health Services*, 109 S. Ct. 3040 (1989)).

Several courts have recently dismissed such "fetal abuse" cases; see, for example, *People v. Hardy*, No. 128458, 1991 Mich. App. LEXIS 135 (Mich. Ct. App. Apr. 1, 1991); "Judge Drops Charges of Delivering Drugs to an Unborn Baby," *New York Times* (Feb. 5, 1991), B6:4.

6. According to a memorandum prepared by the ACLU Reproductive Freedom Project, of the 52 defendants, 35 are African-American, 14 are white, 2 are Latina, and 1 is Native American; see "State Case Summary," *supra* note 2; telephone interviews with Joseph Merkin, attorney for Sharon Peters (Jan. 7, 1991), James Shields, North Carolina ACLU (Jan. 7, 1991), and Patrick Young, attorney for Brenda Yurchak (Jan. 7, 1991); see also Kolata, "Bias Seen Against Pregnant Addicts" *New York Times* (July 20, 1990), A13:1 (indicating that of sixty women charged, 80 percent were minorities). The disproportionate prosecution of poor black women can be seen most clearly in the states that have initiated the most cases. In Florida, where two women have been convicted for distributing drugs to a minor, ten out of eleven criminal cases were brought against black women; see "State Case Summary," *supra* note 2, at 3–5. Similarly, of eighteen women in South Carolina charged since August 1989 with either criminal neglect of a child or distribution of drugs to a minor, seventeen have been black; see *id.* at 12.

7. See Hoffman, *supra* note 5, at 35 (noting that "with the exception of a few cases, prosecutors have not gone after pregnant alcoholics").

8. In addition to prosecuting women after the birth of a baby for prenatal crimes, the range of state intrusions on pregnant women's autonomy includes jailing pregnant women, see *infra* notes 54–56 and accompanying text; placing the child in protective custody, see *N. J. Rev. Stat.* § 30:4C-11 (West 1981); allowing tort suits by children against their mothers for negligent conduct during pregnancy, see *Grodin v. Grodin*, 102 Mich. App. 396, 301 N.W.2d 869 (1980); ordering forced medical treatment performed on pregnant women, see In re A.C., 573 A.2d 1235 (D.C. 1990); depriving mothers of child custody based on acts during pregnancy, see *infra* notes 48–53 and accompanying text; upholding employer policies excluding fertile women from the workplace, see *UAW v. Johnson Controls, Inc.*, 886 F. 2d 871 (7th Cir. 1989), rev'd, 111 S. Ct. 1196 (1991) ; and placing greater restrictions on access to abortion, see *Webster v. Reproductive Health Services*, 109 S. Ct. 3040 (1989). For general theoretical treatments of the issues involved in state intervention during pregnancy, see Gallagher, "Prenatal Invasions and Interventions: What's Wrong with Fetal Rights," 10 *Harv. Women's L. J.*, 9 (1987) ; Goldberg, "Medical Choices During Pregnancy: Whose Decision Is It Anyway?," 41 *Rutg. L. Rev.*, 591 (1989); McNulty, "Pregnancy Police: The Health Policy and Legal Implications of Punishing Pregnant Women for Harm to Their Fetuses," 16 *N.Y.U. Rev. L. & Soc. Change*, 277, 279–90 (1988); and Note, "The Creation of Fetal Rights: Conflicts with Women's Constitutional Rights to Liberty, Privacy, and Equal Protection," 95 *Yale L. J.*, 599 (1986).

9. I use the term "women of color" to refer to nonwhite women in America, including black, Latina, Asian, and Native American women. Recognizing the diversity of historical and cultural backgrounds among women of color, this article focuses particularly on the experience of black women in America. When women of color are united in common experience of oppression and poverty, however, I draw more general conclusions about constraints on their reproductive autonomy.

10. In 1990, lawmakers in thirty-four states debated bills concerning prenatal substance abuse; see "Key Battle in War on Drugs: Saving Pregnant Women, Endangered Babies," *State Health Notes* (June 1990), 1:1 (published by the George Washington University Intergovernmental Health Policy Project). In California alone, about twenty different bills relating to the problem of drug use during pregnancy were pending before the legislature as of June 1989; see Marcotte, "Crime and Pregnancy," *A.B.A.J.* (Aug. 1989), 14, 14.

11. See *infra* notes 156–157 and accompanying text.

12. See *infra* notes 87–89 and accompanying text.

13. For arguments supporting the mother's right to autonomy, see sources cited in note 8. For arguments advocating protection of the fetus, see King, "The Juridical Status of the Fetus: A Proposal for Legal Protection of the Unborn," 77 *Mich. L. Rev.*, 1647, 1682–84 (1979); Parness and

Pritchard, "To Be or Not to Be: Protecting the Unborn's Potentiality of Life," 51 *U. Cin. L. Rev.*, 257, 267–86 (1982); Robertson, "Procreative Liberty and the Control of Conception, Pregnancy, and Childbirth," 69 *Va. L. Rev.*, 405, 437–43 (1983); Walker and Puzder, "State Protection of the Unborn after *Roe v. Wade:* A Legislative Proposal," 13 *Stetson L. Rev.*, 237, 253–63 (1984).

14. A growing body of scholarship challenges dominant group scholars' claims to neutrality or universality. This new scholarship is founded on the reality of oppression; see Matsuda, "Public Response to Racist Speech: Considering the Victim's Story," 87 *Mich L. Rev.* 2320, 2323–26 (1989) (describing "outsider jurisprudence"); West, "Progressive and Conservative Constitutionalism," 88 *Mich. L. Rev.* 641, 678–82, 684–86 (1990) (describing "idealistic" and "anti-subordination progressives"). Feminist legal theory is perhaps the most established example of this alternative jurisprudence; see, for example, MacKinnon, "Feminism, Marxism, Method, and the State: Toward Feminist Jurisprudence," 8 *Signs* 635 (1983); Scales, "The Emergence of Feminist Jurisprudence: An Essay," 95 *Yale L. J.*, 1373 (1986); West, "Jurisprudence and Gender," 55 *U. Chi. L. Rev.*, 1 (1988).

The scholarship of people of color is a more recent variety of alternative jurisprudence. See, for example, D. Bell, *And We Are Not Saved* (1987); Cook, "Beyond Critical Legal Studies: The Reconstructive Theology of Dr. Martin Luther King, Jr.," 103 *Harv. L. Rev.*, 985 (1990) [the essay is included in this volume—ED.]; Crenshaw, "Race, Reform, and Retrenchment: Transformation and Legitimation in Antidiscrimination Law," 101 *Harv. L. Rev.* 1331 (1988) [the essay is included in this volume—ED.]. Among this latter group are scholars who, like me, are particularly concerned with the legal problems and concrete experiences of black women; their work has informed and inspired me. See, for example, Austin, "Sapphire Bound!," 1989 *Wis. L. Rev.*, 539 [portions of this essay are included in this volume–ED.]; Harris, "Race and Essentialism in Feminist Legal Theory," 42 *Stan. L. Rev.*, 581 (1990); Scales-Trent, "Black Women and the Constitution: Finding Our Place, Asserting Our Rights," 24 *Harv. C.R.-C.L. L. Rev.*, 9 (1989).

15. For a description and critique of feminist standpoint epistemology, see Bartlett, "Feminist Legal Methods," 103 *Harv. L. Rev.*, 829, 872–7 (1990). Bartlett criticizes feminist standpoint epistemology because it tends to standardize women's characteristics, it denies the significance of the viewpoints of nonvictims, it does not explain differences of perception among women, and it engenders adversarial politics; see *id.* at 873–75. These criticisms have merit. Notwithstanding the problems inherent in adopting a general feminist standpoint epistemology, I believe there is value in the limited project of focusing on the perspective of black women, especially because that perspective has traditionally been ignored.

16. See *infra* notes 197–214, 248–257, and accompanying text.

17. See Harris, *supra* note 14, at 604 ("Far more for black women than for white women, the experience of self is precisely that of being unable to disentangle the web of race and gender—of being enmeshed always in multiple, often contradictory, discourses of sexuality and color"); Kline, "Race, Racism, and Feminist Legal Theory," 12 *Harv. Women's L. J.*, 115, 121 (1989); Scales-Trent, *supra* note 14, at 9. The theme of the simultaneity of multiple forms of oppression is common in black feminist writings: see, for example, Combahee River Collective, "A Black Feminist Statement," in C. Moraga and G. Anzaldua, eds., *This Bridge Called My Back: Writings by Radical Women of Color* 210, 213 (1981); b. hooks, *Ain't I a Woman: Black Women and Feminism,* 12 (1981) ("[A]t the moment of my birth, two factors determined my destiny, my having been born black and my having been born female").

18. See Scales-Trent, *supra* note 14, at 9 and n. 2 (noting that "race and sex interact to magnify the effect of each independently").

19. Angela Harris notes the fragmentation produced by an arithmetic approach to multiple oppression: "The result of essentialism is to reduce the lives of people who experience multiple forms of oppression to addition problems: 'racism + sexism = straight black women's experience' "; Harris, *supra* note 14, at 588.

White feminist scholars do not completely ignore diversity among women. Catharine MacKinnon, for example, acknowledges the experiences of women of color and recognizes that feminist theory must take race into account: see, for example, C. Mackinnon, *Feminism Unmodified,* 2 (1987) ("[G]ender . . . appears partly to comprise the meaning of, as well as bisect, race and class, even as race and class specificities make up, as well as cross-cut, gender").

20. Harris defines gender essentialism as "the notion that a unitary, 'essential' women's experience can be isolated and described independently of race, class, sexual orientation, and other realities of experience"; Harris, *supra* note 14, at 585. She observes that this tendency toward gender essentialism results in the silencing of the very same voices ignored by mainstream legal jurisprudence—including the voices of women of color. See *id.* To claim the existence of a monolithic, universal "woman's voice" is in fact to claim that the voice of white, heterosexual, socioeconomically privileged women can speak for all other women. See *id.* at 588; see also E. SPELMAN, INESSENTIAL WOMEN: PROBLEMS OF EXCLUSION IN FEMINIST THOUGHT 4 (1988) ("[T]he real problem has been how feminist theory has confused the condition of one group of women with the condition of all."); Crenshaw, *Demarginalizing the Intersection of Race and Sex: A Black Feminist Critique of Antidiscrimination Doctrine, Feminist Theory and Racist Politics,* 1989 U. CHI. LEGAL F. 139, 152–60 (arguing that feminist theory has been built only upon the experiences of white women).

21. See A. LORDE, *Age, Race, Class, and Sex: Women Redefining Difference,* in SISTER OUTSIDER 114, 122 (1984)

("Now we must recognize differences among women who are our equals, neither inferior nor superior, and devise ways to see each others' difference to enrich our visions and our joint struggles."); Harris, *supra* note 14, at 585–86; Kline, *supra* note 17, at 150 ("[I]t is imperative that white feminist legal theorists problematize and complicate our analyses by taking into account the real and contradictory differences of interest and power between women that are generated by, and generate, racism."); see also Cain, *Feminist Jurisprudence: Grounding the Theories*, 4 BERKELEY WOMEN'S L. J. 191, 204–05 (1990) ("Good feminist thought ought to reflect the real differences in women's realities, in our lived experiences. These include differences of race, class, age, physical ability and sexual preference." (citation omitted)).

22. The Fourteenth Amendment, for example, explicitly gives Congress the power to enforce the equal protection clause. See U.S. Const. amend. XIV, § 5.

23. See, for example, *Martin v. Wilks*, 490 U.S. 755, 762–63 (1989) (allowing white plaintiffs to challenge affirmative action consent decrees on grounds of reverse discrimination); *Wards Cove Packing Co. v. Atonio*, 490 U.S. 642, 650–52, 659–60 (1989) (limiting the basis for establishing a prima facie case of discrimination and shifting the burden of proving discrimination to employees in Title VII "disparate impact" actions); *City of Richmond v. J. A. Croson Co.*, 488 U.S. 469, 505–06 (1989) (striking down set-aside program for minority contractors as reverse discrimination). But see *Metro Broadcasting, Inc. v. FCC*, 110 S. Ct. 2997, 3009 (1990) (upholding FCC policy designed to achieve more diverse programming by encouraging minority ownership of broadcast licenses).

24. See, for example, *Hodgson v. Minnesota*, 110 S. Ct. 2926, 2969–70 (1990) (upholding state statute requiring notification of two parents before a minor may obtain an abortion unless she secures a court order); *Webster v. Reproductive Health Services*, 109 S. Ct. 3040, 3052 (1989) (permitting state restrictions on abortion, including a ban on the use of public facilities for performing some abortions); *Harris v. McRae*, 448 U.S. 297, 326 (1980) (upholding version of Hyde Amendment that withheld federal Medicaid funds used to reimburse costs of abortion not necessary to save the mother's life); *Maher v. Roe*, 432 U.S. 464, 480 (1977) (permitting states to deny welfare payments for nontherapeutic abortions).

25. West argues that "for both strategic and theoretical reasons, the proper audience for the development of a progressive interpretation of the Constitution is Congress rather than the courts"; West, "Progressive and Conservative Constitutionalism," *supra* note 14, at 650. Alan David Freeman has expressed a similar sentiment in more blunt terms: "If the federal courts are to become, as they were in the past, little more than reactionary apologists for the existing order, we should treat them with the contempt they deserve. One can only hope that other political institutions will be reinvigorated"; Freeman, "Antidiscrimination Law: The View from 1989," 64 *Tul. L. Rev.*, 1407, 1441 (1990). I do not advocate abandoning litigation as at strategy

for challenging government abuses; rather, I am suggesting the exploration of other forums for taking collective action to implement visions of a just society.

State courts and state constitutions may also provide a more progressive understanding of equal protection and privacy rights; see Brennan, "State Constitutions and the Protection of Individual Rights," 90 *Harv. L. Rev.*, 489 (1977); "Developments in the Law—The Interpretation of State Constitutional Rights," 95 *Harv. L. Rev.*, 1324, 1442–43 (1982). State courts, for example, have interpreted the right of teenagers to obtain an abortion without parental consent more broadly under the state constitution's right of privacy than the Supreme Court has under the federal Constitution; compare *American Academy of Pediatrics v. Van de Kamp*, 263 Cal. Rptr. 46, 55 (Cal. Ct. App. 1989) (affirming the issuance of a preliminary injunction of law that prohibited minors from obtaining abortions without parental consent or court order as violating state constitutional right of privacy) and In re T.W., 551 So. 2d 1186, 1194 (Fla. 1989) (holding that a Florida statute requiring minors to obtain parental consent or court order prior to obtaining abortion violated the right of privacy guaranteed by Florida's constitution) with *Hodgson v. Minnesota*, 110 S. Ct. 2926, 2969–70 (1990) (holding that a parental notification requirement with judicially granted exception does not violate the Constitution).

26. See West, "Progressive and Conservative Constitutionalism," *supra* note 14, at 715.

27. *Id.* at 717.

28. Ball argues that some minority scholars are engaged in translating, or making visible, their world so that they may influence and eventually transform the world of conventional academia; see Ball, "The Legal Academy and Minority Scholars," 103 *Harv. L. Rev.*, 1855, 1857–60 (1990).

29. See "Crack: A Disaster of Historic Dimension, Still Growing," *New York Times* (May 28, 1989), 4:1 (editorial).

30. Approximately half of the nation's crack addicts are women; see Alters, "Women and Crack: Equal Addiction, Unequal Care," *Boston Globe* (Nov. 1, 1989), 1:1. Some have theorized that women are attracted to crack because it can be smoked rather than injected; see Teltsch, "In Detroit, a Drug Recovery Center That Welcomes the Pregnant Addict," *New York Times* (Mar. 20, 1990), A14:1. The highest concentrations of crack addicts are found in inner-city neighborhoods; see Malcolm, "Crack, Bane of Inner City, Is Now Gripping Suburbs," *New York Times* (Oct. 1, 1989), 1.1:1.

31. See Kolata, "On Streets Ruled by Crack, Families Die," *New York Times* (Aug. 11, 1989), A13:3.

32. Many crack-addicted women become pregnant as a result of trading sex for crack or turning to prostitution to support their habit; see Alters, *supra* note 30, at 1:1; Kolata, *supra* note 6 at A13:1. Crack seems to encourage sexual activity, in contrast to the passivity induced by heroin addiction; see Alters, *supra* note 30, at 1:1.

33. See Besharov, "Crack Babies: The Worst Threat Is Mom Herself," *Washington Post* (Aug. 6, 1989), B1:1. Approximately ten thousand to one hundred thousand of these newborns are exposed to cocaine or crack cocaine; see Nolan, "Protecting Fetuses from Prenatal Hazards: Whose Crimes? What Punishment?," 9 *Crim. Just. Ethics*, 13, 14 (1990).

34. The number of babies born to cocaine-addicted mothers in New York City, for example, has more than quadrupled since 1985; see "More Births to Cocaine Users," *New York Times* (Apr. 7, 1990), B30:2.

35. See Davidson, "Drug Babies Push Issue of Fetal Rights," *Los Angeles Times* (Apr. 25, 1989), 1.3:3.

36. See *id.*

37. See Chasnoff, Griffith, MacGregor, Dirkes, and Burns, "Temporal Patterns of Cocaine Use in Pregnancy: Perinatal Outcome," 261 *J.A.M.A.*, 1741, 1742 (1989); MacGregor, Keith, Chasnoff, Rosner, Chisum, Shaw, and Minogue, "Cocaine Use During Pregnancy: Adverse Perinatal Outcome," 157 *Am. J. Obstetrics and Gyn.*, 686, 687 (1987); Neerhof, MacGregor, Retzky, and Sullivan, "Cocaine Abuse During Pregnancy: Peripartum Prevalence and Perinatal Outcome," 161 *Am. J. Obstetrics and Gyn.*, 633, 635 (1989).

38. See Petitti and Coleman, "Cocaine and the Risk of Low Birth Weight," 80 *Am. J. Pub. Health*, 25, 25 (1990); Kerr, "Crack Addiction: The Tragic Toll on Women and Their Children," *New York Times* (Feb. 9, 1987), B2:1.

39. See Chasnoff, "Newborn Infants with Drug Withdrawal Symptoms," 9 *Pediatrics Rev.*, 273 (1988).

40. See Chasnoff, "Cocaine, Pregnancy and the Neonate," 15 *Women and Health*, 23, 32–33 (1989); Chasnoff, Burns, Schnoll, and Burns, "Cocaine Use in Pregnancy," 313 *New Eng. J. Med.*, 666, 669 (1985); Howard, "Cocaine and Its Effects on the Newborn," 31 *Dev. Med. and Child Neurology*, 255, 256 (1989).

41. See Chasnoff et al., *supra* note 37, at 1743–44; Revkin, "Crack in the Cradle," *Discover* (Sept. 1989), 62, 63; "Defects Reported in Babies of Cocaine Users," *New York Times* (Aug. 13, 1989), 1.17:1. But see Chasnoff, "Perinatal Effects of Cocaine," *Contemp Ob. Gyn.* (May 1987), 163, 176 ("Cocaine cannot be linked to an increased incidence of congenital malformations").

42. See Marcotte, *supra* note 10, at 14; see also Chasnoff, Burns, and Burns, "Cocaine Use in Pregnancy: Perinatal Morbidity and Mortality," 9 *Neurotoxicology and Teratology*, 291, 292 (1987) (finding 15 percent incidence of Sudden Infant Death Syndrome, "SIDS," in cocaine-exposed infants).

43. See Koren, Graham, Shear, and Einarson, "Bias against the Null Hypothesis: The Reproductive Hazards of Cocaine," *Lancet* (Dec. 16, 1989), 1440; Blakeslee, "Child-Rearing Is Stormy When Drugs Cloud Birth," *New York Times* (May 19, 1990), 1.1:3.

44. See Koren et al., *supra* note 43, at 1441.

45. See Poland, Ager, and Olson, "Barriers to Receiving Adequate Prenatal Care," 157 *Am. J. Obstetrics and Gyn.* 297, 300 (1987); Ryan, Ehrlich, and Finnegan, "Cocaine Abuse in Pregnancy: Effects on the Fetus and Newborn," 9 *Neurotoxicology and Teratology*, 295, 298 (1987). A Northwestern University study of pregnant cocaine addicts found that comprehensive prenatal care may improve the outcome of pregnancies complicated by cocaine abuse. See MacGregor, Keith, Bachicha, and Chasnoff, "Cocaine Abuse During Pregnancy: Correlation between Prenatal Care and Perinatal Outcome," 74 *Obstetrics and Gyn.*, 882, 885 (1989).

46. See Koren et al., *supra* note 43, at 1440–41.

47. See Nolan, *supra* note 33, at 14.

48. See Sherman, "Keeping Babies Free of Drugs," *Nat'l. L. J.* (Oct. 16, 1989), 1:4; Gorman, "Involuntary Drug Testing of New Mothers Gives Birth to Legal Debate," *Los Angeles Times* (Apr. 14, 1988), 2.1:1.

49. Several states have enacted statutes that require the reporting of positive newborn toxicologies to state authorities; see *Mass. Gen. L.* ch. 119, § 51A (Supp. 1990); *Minn. Stat. Ann.* § 626.556 (2) (c) (West Supp. 1991) ; *Okla. Stat. Ann.* tit. 21, § 846 (West Supp. 1991); *Utah Code Ann.* 62A-4-504 (1989). Many hospitals also interpret state child abuse reporting laws to require them to report positive results. For a discussion of the constitutional and ethical issues raised by the drug screening of postpartum women and newborns, see Moss, "Legal Issues: Drug Testing of Postpartum Women and Newborns as the Basis for Civil and Criminal Proceedings," 23 *Clearinghouse Rev.* 1406, 1409–13 (1990); Moss, *supra* note 2, at 292–96.

50. See Moss, *supra* note 2, at 289–90; Sherman, *supra* note 48, at 28:4; Besharov, *supra* note 33, B4:2.
Several states have facilitated this process by expanding the statutory definition of neglected children to include infants who test positive for controlled substances at birth. See *Fla. Stat. Ann.* § 415.503(9)(A)(2) (West. Supp. 1991); Ill. Juvenile Ct. Act, *Ill. Ann. Stat.* ch. 31, para. 802–3, § 2–3 (1) (c) (Smith-Hurd Supp. 1990); *Ind. Code Ann.* § 31-6-4-3.1(1)(b) (West Supp. 1990); *Mass. Gen. L.* ch. 119, § 51A (Supp. 1990); *Nev. Rev. Stat. Ann.* § 432B.330(l)(b) (Michie 1991); *Okla. Stat. Ann.* tit. 10, § 1101(4)(c) (West Supp. 1991).

51. See Note, "The Problem of the Drug-Exposed Newborn: A Return to Principled Intervention," 42 *Stan. L. Rev.*, 745, 749, 752 and n. 25 (1990).

52. See, for example, In re Stefanel Tyesha C., 157 A.D.2d 322, 325–26, 556 N.Y.S.2d 280, 282–83 (N.Y. App. Div. 1990), appeal dismissed, 76 N.Y.2d 1006 (1990) (holding that allegations of a positive infant toxicology, along with the mother's admitted drug use during pregnancy and failure to enroll in a drug rehabilitation program, constituted a cause of action for neglect); In re Baby X, 97 Mich. App. 111, 116, 293 N.W.2d 736, 739 (1980) (holding that a drug-exposed newborn "may properly be considered a

neglected child within the jurisdiction of the probate court").

For a critical analysis of the presumption of parental unfitness, see Note, *supra* note 51, at 755–58.

53. See *Santosky v. Kramer*, 455 U.S. 745, 768 (1982) (holding that proof of neglect by clear and convincing evidence is constitutionally required before state may terminate parental rights). For a general description and critique of state neglect statutes, see Wald, "State Intervention on Behalf of 'Neglected' Children: Standards for Removal of Children from Their Homes, Monitoring the Status of Children in Foster Care, and Termination of Parental Rights," 28 *Stan. L. Rev.* 623, 628–35, 643–48, 665–72 (1976).

54. See *United States v. Vaughn*, Crim. No. F 2172–88 B (D.C. Super. Ct. Aug. 23, 1988); Moss, "Pregnant? Go Directly to Jail," *A.B.A.J.* (Nov. 1, 1988), 20; Cohen, "When a Fetus Has More Rights Than the Mother," *Washington Post* (July 28, 1988), A21:1; see also *Cox v. Court*, 42 Ohio App. 3d 171, 173, 537 N.E.2d 721, 723 (1988) (reversing juvenile court order placing a pregnant woman in a "secure drug facility" to protect the fetus from the woman's cocaine use).

55. At Vaughn's sentencing, Judge Peter Wolf stated: "I'm going to keep her locked up until the baby is born because she's tested positive for cocaine when she came before me. . . . She's apparently an addictive personality, and I'll be darned if I'm going to have a baby born that way"; Moss, *supra* note 54, at 20.

56. See Davidson, *supra* note 35, at 19:1.

57. See *supra* notes 2 and 5.

58. See, for example, Parness, "The Duty to Prevent Handicaps: Laws Promoting the Prevention of Handicaps to Newborns," 5 *W. New Eng. L. Rev.*, 431, 442–52 (1983); Parness and Pritchard, *supra* note 13, at 270 (advocating that states "promote the unborn's potentiality for life by outlawing fetus endangerment, abandonment, neglect and nonsupport") (citations omitted).

59. See *supra* note 6.

60. Black women are five times more likely to live in poverty, five times more likely to be on welfare, and three times more likely to be unemployed than are white women; see *United States Commission on Civil Rights, The Economic Status of Black Women*, 1 (1990).

61. See *infra* notes 70–78 and accompanying text.

62. See McNulty, *supra* note 8, at 319; see also Faller and Ziefert, "Causes of Child Abuse and Neglect," in K. Faller, ed., *Social Work with Abused and Neglected Children*, 32, 46–47 (1981) (providing a similar explanation of why poor parents are more likely to be reported for child neglect).

63. See Note, *supra* note 51, at 753, 782 n. 157; Kolata, *supra* note 31, at A13:3.

64. See Note, *supra* note 51, at 753.

65. See Chasnoff, Landress, and Barrett, "The Prevalence of Illicit Drug or Alcohol Use During Pregnancy and Discrepancies in Mandatory Reporting in Pinellas County, Florida," 322 *New Eng. J. Med.*, 1202, 1205, table 3 (1990); Angel, "Addicted Babies: Legal System's Response Unclear," *Los Angeles Daily J.* (Feb. 29, 1988), 1:6.

66. See Note, *supra* note 51, at 753, 798–99.

67. See Moss, *supra* note 49, at 1412, and *infra* notes 143–146 and accompanying text.

68. See Note, *supra* note 51, at 753.

69. See Chasnoff, Landress, and Barrett, *supra* note 65, at 1206; Note, *supra* note 51, at 754 and n. 36; see also Faller and Ziefert, *supra* note 62, at 47 (noting that professionals are more likely to report child abuse by poor parents because of their disbelief in abuse by their own socioeconomic class).

70. See Note, *supra* note 51, at 754 and n. 36; Chasnoff, Landress, and Barrett, *supra* note 65, at 1205.

71. See Chasnoff, Landress, and Barrett, *supra* note 65, at 1205, Table 3.

72. See *id.* at 1203. The researchers tested urine samples from 715 pregnant women who enrolled for prenatal care in the county during a one-month period. Three hundred eighty women at 5 public health clinics and 335 women at 12 private obstetrical offices were screened for alcohol, opiates, cocaine and its metabolites, and cannabinoids between January 1 and June 30, 1989.

73. See *id.* at 1204. The rate of positive results on toxicologic testing for white women (15.4 percent) was slightly higher than that for black women (14.1 percent); see *id.* 1204, Table 2.

74. "The frequency of a positive result was 16.3 percent for women seen at the public clinics and 13.1 percent for women seen at the private offices"; *id.* at 1203, Table 1.

75. In March 1987, the Florida Department of Health and Rehabilitative Services adopted a policy requiring hospitals to report to local health departments evidence of drug and alcohol use during pregnancy; see *id.* at 1202–03.

76. See *id.* at 1204.

77. The authors of the Pinellas County study suggest several reasons for the discrepancy in reporting. Physicians may have been prompted to test black women and their infants more frequently because the infants displayed more severe symptoms or because black women intoxicated from smoking crack are more readily identified than white women intoxicated from smoking marijuana; see *id.* at 1205. Additionally, the disproportionate reporting of black women may result from socioeconomic factors and the mistaken preconception that substance abuse during pregnancy is predominantly an inner-city, minority group problem; see *id.* at 1206. The second explanation does not negate the racist nature of the rate of reporting and subsequent prosecution of women who use drugs during pregnancy, however. Even if physicians do not consciously decide to report black women rather than white women, their testing and reporting practices unjustifiably discriminate against

black women and thus demonstrate their unconscious racism. See Lawrence, "The Id, the Ego, and Equal Protection: Reckoning with Unconscious Racism," 39 *Stan. L. Rev.,* 316, 328–44 (1987).

78. The striking degree of difference between the reporting rate of drug use by black women and that of white women and the similarity in their rates of substance abuse strongly suggests that racial prejudice and stereotyping must be a factor.

79. Numerous maternal activities are potentially harmful to the developing fetus, including drinking alcohol, taking prescription and nonprescription drugs, smoking cigarettes, failing to eat properly, and residing at high altitudes for prolonged periods; see, for example, *Institute of Med., Preventing Low Birthweight,* 65–72 (1985); Berkowitz, Holford, and Berkowitz, "Effects of Cigarette Smoking, Alcohol, Coffee and Tea Consumption on Preterm Delivery," 7 *Early Hum. Dev.,* 239 (1982); Note, "Parental Liability for Prenatal Injury," 14 *Colum. J. L. and Soc. Probs.* 47, 73–75 (1978). Conduct by people other than the pregnant woman can also threaten the health of the fetus. A pregnant woman's exposure to secondary cigarette smoke, sexually transmitted and other infectious diseases, environmental hazards such as radiation and lead, and physical abuse can harm the fetus; see *Children's Defense Fund, The Health of America's Children,* 35–37 (1989); Note, *supra* note 8, at 606–07.

80. Infants born to mothers who drink heavily during pregnancy may suffer from fetal alcohol syndrome, characterized by physical malformations, small head and body size, poor mental capabilities, and abnormal behavior patterns, including mental retardation; see Clarren and Smith, "The Fetal Alcohol Syndrome," 298 *New Eng. J. Med.,* 1063 (1978); Ouellette, Rosett, Rosman, and Weiner, "Adverse Effects on Offspring of Maternal Alcohol Abuse during Pregnancy," 297 *New Eng. J. Med.,* 528 (1977). Some experts believe that prenatal alcohol exposure is the most common known cause of mental retardation in this country; see Rosenthal, "When a Pregnant Woman Drinks," *New York Times Magazine* (Feb. 4, 1990), 30.

81. Marijuana use during pregnancy has been associated with impaired fetal development and reduced gestational length; see, for example, Fried, Watkinson; and Willan, "Marijuana Use during Pregnancy and Decreased Length of Gestation," 150 *Am. J. Obstetrics and Gyn.,* 23 (1984); Zuckerman, Frank, Hingson, Amaro, Levenson, Kayne, Parker, Vinci, Aboagye, Fried, Cabral, Timperi, and Bauchner, "Effects of Maternal Marijuana and Cocaine Use on Fetal Growth," 320 *New Eng. J. Med.,* 762 (1989).

82. Approximately six thousand to eight thousand newborns each year suffer from fetal alcohol syndrome; see Nolan, *supra* note 33, at 15. An additional thirty-five thousand infants experience less severe effects of maternal drinking; see "Doctors Criticized on Fetal Problem," *New York Times* (Dec. 11, 1990), B10:6. A study of twenty-two hundred women who gave birth at the University of Washing-

ton Hospital in Seattle from March 1989 to March 1990 and who used drugs during or immediately before pregnancy revealed that 20 percent smoked marijuana, 16 percent used cocaine, and 9 percent used either heroin, methadone, or amphetamines; see Blakeslee, "Parents Fight for a Future for Infants Born to Drugs," *New York Times* (May 19, 1990), A1:3; see also Zuckerman et al., *supra* note 81, at 762 (noting that in 1985, 31 percent of American women in their late teens and early twenties reported using marijuana within the past year).

83. See "State Case Summary," *supra* note 2; *infra* note 260.

84. See Chasnoff, Landress, and Barrett, *supra* note 65, at 1204; Malcolm, *supra* note 30, at 1:1. A 1989 study of 2,278 highly educated women found that 30 percent consumed more than one drink per week while pregnant; see Rosenthal, *supra* note 80, at 49. Furthermore, despite the media's depiction of crack addiction as an exclusively inner-city problem, crack use among middle-class and affluent people is on the rise; see Elmer-DeWitt, "A Plague Without Boundaries: Crack, Once a Problem of the Poor, Invades the Middle Class," *Time* (Nov. 6, 1989), 97; Malcolm, *supra* note 30, at 1:1.

85. See Malcolm, *supra* note 30, at 1:1. The Pinellas County study, for example, found that black women tested positive more frequently for cocaine use during pregnancy (7.5 percent versus 1.8 percent for white women), whereas white women tested positive more frequently for the use of marijuana (14.4 percent versus 6.0 percent for black women). See Chasnoff, Landress, and Barrett, *supra* note 65, at 1204, Table 2.

86. See Roberts, "The Bias in Drug Arrests of Pregnant Women," *New York Times* (Aug. 11, 1990), 25:2.

87. In 1987, the mortality rate for black infants was 17.9 deaths per 1000, compared to a rate of 8.6 deaths per 1000 for white infants; see *U.S. Department of Commerce, Bureau of Census, Statistical Abstract of the United States,* 77, Table 110 (1990).

88. In 1986, the black infant mortality rate (18 deaths per 1000 live births) was higher than the infant mortality rate in Bulgaria, Costa Rica, Cuba, and Singapore; see *Children's Defense Fund, supra* note 79, at 14, Table 1.8 (1989). A black infant born in the inner city has an even greater chance of dying before reaching his first birthday; see *id.* at 23, Table 1.10.

89. Descriptions of the degeneracy and disintegration of the black family have played a similar role in explaining poverty, crime, and unemployment in the black community. The self-destructiveness of blacks, rather than racism, is often blamed for their predicament; see Gresham, "The Politics of Family in America," *The Nation* (July 24/31, 1989), 116, 117–19 (discussing how the Moynihan Report on the black family and the CBS Special Report, *The Vanishing Black Family—Crisis in Black America,* made the black family the scapegoat for the condition of black America).

90. See, for example, *id.* at 120 (describing the dominant society's resistance to the concept of black people as "vulnerable human beings"). For a discussion of the hegemonic function of racist ideology, see Crenshaw, *supra* note 14, at 1370–81 (1988). See generally G. Fredrickson, *The Black Image in the White Mind,* 256–82 (1971) (discussing the propagation of theories of black inferiority and degeneracy at the turn of the century); J. Williamson, *The Crucible of Race: Black-White Relations in the American South since Emancipation,* 111–51 (1984) (discussing the prevalence of theories near the turn of the century that blacks, freed from slavery, were returning to their "natural state of bestiality").

91. See A. Davis, *Women, Race, and Class* 7 (1981) ; J. Jones, *Labor of Love, Labor of Sorrow: Black Women and the Family from Slavery to the Present,* 12 (1985). Legislation giving the children of black women and white men the status of slaves left female slaves vulnerable to sexual violation as a means of financial gain; see P. Giddings, *When and Where I Enter: The Impact of Black Women on Race and Sex in America,* 37 (1984). For a discussion of such laws in Virginia and Georgia, see A. Higginbotham, *In the Matter of Color,* 42–45, 252 (1978).

White masters controlled their slaves' reproductive capacity by rewarding pregnancy with relief from work in the field and additions of clothing and food, punishing slave women who did not give birth, manipulating slave marital choices, forcing slave women to breed, and raping them; see J. Jones, *supra,* 34–35; D. Sterling, ed., *We Are Your Sisters: Black Women in the Nineteenth Century,* 24–26 (1984); Clinton, "Caught in the Web of the Big House: Women and Slavery," in W. Raser, R. Saunders, and J. Wakelyn, eds., *The Web of Southern Social Relations,* 19, 23–28 (1985).

92. Gates, "To Be Raped, Bred or Abused," *New York Times Book Rev.* (Nov. 22, 1987), 12 (reviewing H. Jacobs, *Incidents in the Life of a Slave Girl,* J. Yellin ed., (1987)).

93. See J. Jones, *supra* note 91, at 20; Johnson, *supra* note 1, at 513.

94. See A. Davis, *supra* note 91, at 5; D. White, *Ar'n't I a Woman? Female Slaves in the Plantation South,* 16, 27–29 (1985). For a description of gender conventions in the plantation South, see E. Fox-Genovese, *Within the Plantation Household,* 192–241 (1988).

Kimberlé Crenshaw describes how racist ideology reflects an "oppositional dynamic, premised upon maintaining Blacks as an excluded and subordinated 'other' "; Crenshaw, *supra* note 14, at 1381. Under this pattern of oppositional categories, whites are associated with positive characteristics (industrious, intelligent, responsible), while blacks are associated with the opposite, aberrational qualities (lazy, ignorant, shiftless); see *id.* at 1370–71 and n. 151.

95. A. Davis, *supra* note 91, at 7.

96. See D. White, *supra* note 94, at 28–29.

97. *Id.* at 30.

98. See E. Fox-Genovese, *supra* note 94, at 292; D. White, *supra* note 94, at 61.

99. See G. Lerner, ed., *Black Women in White America,* 163–71 (1973); P. Giddings, *supra* note 91, at 85–89; b. hooks, *supra* note 17, at 55–60.

100. See Gresham, *supra* note 89, at 117.

101. P. Bruce, *The Plantation Negro as a Freeman,* 84–85 (1889).

102. See b. hooks, *supra* note 17, at 65–68; Omolade, "Black Women, Black Men and Tawana Brawley: The Shared Condition," 12 *Harv. Women's L. J.,* 12, 16 (1989).

103. See Allen, "Surrogacy, Slavery, and the Ownership of Life," 13 *Harv. J. L. and Pub. Pol'y,* 139, 140 n. 9 (1990). Professor Allen tells the story of Polly, a woman wrongfully held in slavery, who successfully sued a white man in 1842 for the return of her daughter Lucy. Polly used slave law to prove unlawful possession: she argued that because she was not in fact a slave at the time of Lucy's birth, she was the rightful owner of her daughter; see *id.* at 142–44.

104. See *id.* at 140 n. 9; Burnham, "Children of the Slave Community in the United States," 19 *Freedomways,* 75, 75–77 (1979).

105. O. Gilbert, *Narrative of Sojourner Truth,* 133 (1878).

106. See P. Giddings, *supra* note 91, at 46; D. Sterling, ed., *supra* note 91, at 25–26, 58–61; D. White, *supra* note 94, at 76–90.

107. See G. Lerner, ed., *supra* note 99, at 40–42. This practice is poignantly described in the words of a former slave named Anna Julia Cooper in a speech given in 1893 to the Congress of Representative Women: "Yet all through the darkest period of the colored women's oppression in this country her yet unwritten history is full of heroic struggle, a struggle against fearful and overwhelming odds, that often ended in horrible death, to maintain and protect that which woman holds dearer than life. The painful, patient, and silent toil of mothers to gain a fee simple title to the bodies of their daughters, the despairing fight, as of an entrapped tigress, to keep hallowed their own persons, would furnish material for epics"; B. Loewenberg and R. Bogin, eds., *Black Women in Nineteenth-Century American Life,* 329 (1976).

108. See, generally, H. Gutman, *The Black Family in Slavery and Freedom, 1790–1925* (1976) (describing the life of the black family during slavery); Jones, " 'My Mother Was Much of a Woman': Black Women, Work, and the Family Under Slavery," 8 *Feminist Stud.,* 235, 252–61 (1982) (describing the sexual division of labor initiated by slaves within their own communities).

109. See Gray and Nybell, "Issues in African-American Family Preservation," 69 *Child Welfare,* 513, (1990) (noting that about half of the children in foster care are black); Hogan and Sin, "Minority Children and the Child Welfare

System: An Historical Perspective," 33 *Soc. Work*, 493 (1988). Once black children enter foster care, they remain there longer and receive less desirable placements than white children; they are also less likely than white children to be returned home or adopted; see B. Mandell, *Where Are the Children? A Class Analysis of Foster Care and Adoption*, 36 (1973); Gray and Nybell, *supra*, at 513–14; Stehno, "Differential Treatment of Minority Children in Service Systems," 27 *Soc. Work*, 39, 39–41 (1982). These realities have led some blacks to deem foster care a system of legalized slavery; see B. Mandell, *supra*, at 60. Malcolm X described the state's disruption of his own family in these terms:

"Soon the state people were making plans to take over all of my mother's children. . . .

"A Judge . . . in Lansing had authority over me and all of my brothers and sisters. We were 'state children,' court wards; he had the full say-so over us. A white man in charge of a black man's children! Nothing but legal, modern slavery—however kindly intentioned. . . .

"I truly believe that if ever a state social agency destroyed a family, it destroyed ours"; Malcolm X with A. Haley, *The Autobiography of Malcolm X*, 20–21 (1965).

110. See Wald, *supra* note 53, at 629 n. 22.

111. See Faller and Ziefert, *supra* note 62, at 47; Wald, *supra* note 53, at 629 n. 21. For a discussion of the connection between the child welfare system and poverty, see Jenkins, "Child Welfare as a Class System," in A. Schorr, ed., *Children and Decent People*, 3–4 (1974).

112. Cf. *Santosky v. Kramer*, 455 U.S. 745, 763 (1982) (noting that termination proceedings "are often vulnerable to judgments based on cultural or class bias"); Gray and Nybell, *supra* note 109, at 515–17; Stack, "Cultural Perspectives on Child Welfare," 12 *N.Y.U. Rev. L. and Soc. Change*, 539, 541 (1983–84). See, generally, A. Billingsley and J. Giovannoni, *Children of the Storm* (1972) (tracing the history of black children in the American child welfare system).

113. See Gray and Nybell, *supra* note 109, at 515–17; Stack, *supra* note 112, at 541. For descriptions of childrearing patterns in the black community that are considered deviant, such as extended kin networks, see R. Hill, *Informal Adoption among Black Families* (1977); and C. Stack, *All Our Kin: Strategies for Survival in a Black Community*, 62–107 (1974).

114. See Stack, *supra* note 112, at 539–43.

115. See *id.* at 547.

116. Johnson, *supra* note 1, at 493 (quoting S. Carolina Mortality Schedules, 1850, Abbeville District).

117. See *id.* at 493–96.

118. *Id.* at 495 (quoting S. Carolina Mortality Schedules, 1850, Abbeville District).

119. See *id.* at 496–508; Savitt, "Smothering and Overlaying of Virginia Slave Children: A Suggested Explanation," 49 *Bull. Hist. Med.*, 400 (1975).

120. See Johnson, *supra* note 1, at 508–20.

121. See P. Giddings, *supra* note 91, at 325–35; b. hooks, *supra* note 17, at 70–83; R. Staples, *The Black Woman in America*, 10–34 (1976); Gresham, *supra* note 89, at 117–18.

122. Office of Planning and Policy Research, U.S. Department of Labor, *The Negro Family: The Case for National Action* (1965).

123. *Id.* at 5.

124. "Sterilization abuse occurs whenever the sterilization procedure is performed under conditions that . . . pressure an individual into agreeing to be sterilized, or obscure the risks, consequences, and alternatives associated with sterilization"; Petchesky, "Reproduction, Ethics, and Public Policy: The Federal Sterilization Regulations," 9 *Hastings Center Rep.*, 29, 32 (1979); see also Note, "Sterilization Abuse: Current State of the Law and Remedies for Abuse," 10 *Golden Gate U. L. Rev.*, 1147, 1152–53 (1980) (listing many common situations of sterilization abuse).

125. See A. Davis, *supra* note 91, at 215–21 Nsiah-Jefferson, "Reproductive Laws, Women of Color, and Low-Income Women," in S. Cohen and N. Taub, eds., *Reproductive Laws for the 1990s*, at 46–47 (1988). One study found that 43 percent of women sterilized in 1973 under a federally funded program were black, although only 33 percent of the patients were black; see Note, *supra* note 124, at 1153 n. 30. Spanish-speaking women are twice as likely to be sterilized as those who speak English; see Levin and Taub, "Reproductive Rights," in C. Lefcourt, ed., *Women and the Law* § 10A.07 (31[b], at 10A-28 (1989). The racial disparity in sterilization cuts across economic and educational lines, although the frequency of sterilization is generally higher among the poor and uneducated. Another study found that 9.7 percent of college-educated black women had been sterilized, compared to 5.6 percent of college-educated white women. Among women without a high school diploma, 31.6 percent of black women and 14.5 percent of white women had been sterilized; see *id.*

126. See Clarke, "Subtle Forms of Sterilization Abuse: A Reproductive Rights Analysis," in R. Arditti, R. Klein, and S. Minden, eds., *Test-Tube Women*, 120, 120–32 (1984); Nsiah-Jefferson, *supra* note 125, at 44–45; Petchesky, *supra* note 124, at 32.

127. See Nsiah-Jefferson, *supra* note 125, at 46–47.

128. See *Relf v. Weinberger*, 372 F. Supp. 1196, 1199 (D.D.C. 1974), on remand sub nom. *Relf v. Mathews*, 403 F. Supp. 1235 (D.D.C. 1975), vacated sub nom. *Relf v. Weinberger*, 565 F.2d 722 (D.C. Cir. 1977).

129. See *id.*

130. See Nsiah-Jefferson, *supra* note 125, at 47–48; see also Note, *supra* note 124, at 1159–60 (noting the lack of any sanctions for noncompliance with federal sterilization regulations). In contrast to the encouragement of minority

sterilization, our society views childbearing by white women as desirable. Ruth Colker tells the story of a classmate of hers in law school who decided to be sterilized. The university physician refused to allow her to undergo the procedure unless she agreed to attend several sessions with a psychiatrist, presumably to dissuade her from her decision; see Colker, "Feminism, Theology, and Abortion: Toward Love, Compassion, and Wisdom," 77 *Calif. L. Rev.,* 1011, 1067 n. 196 (1989). Colker recognizes that the "physician's actions reflect the dominant social message—that a healthy (white) woman should want to bear a child"; *id.*

131. Subchapters XIX and XX of the Social Security Act provide matching funds for sterilization reimbursement. See 42 U.S.C. §§ 1396a(10)(A), 1397a(a)(2) (1988).

132. See Nsiah-Jefferson, *supra* note 125, at 45–46; Petchesky, *supra* note 124, at 39; Note, *supra* note 124, at 1154.

133. See Harrington, "Introduction" to S. Sheehan, *A Welfare Mother,* at x-xi (1976); Milwaukee County Welfare Rights Org., *Welfare Mothers Speak Out,* 72–92 (1972). In a chapter entitled "Welfare Mythology," the Milwaukee County Welfare Rights organization portrays a common image of welfare mothers: "You give those lazy, shiftless good-for-nothings an inch and they'll take a mile. You have to make it tougher on them. They're getting away with murder now. You have to catch all those cheaters and put them to work or put them in jail. Get them off the welfare rolls. I'm tired of those niggers coming to our state to get on welfare. I'm tired of paying their bills just so they can sit around home having babies, watching their color televisions, and driving Cadillacs"; *id.* at 72. Writers in the eighties claimed that welfare induces poor black women to have babies; see, for example, C. Murray, *Losing Ground,* 154–66 (1984). Other researchers have refuted this claim; see, for example, Darity and Myers, "Does Welfare Dependency Cause Female Headship? The Case of the Black Family," 46 *J. Marriage and Fam.,* 765, 773 (1984) (concluding that "[t]he attractiveness of welfare and welfare dependency exhibits no effects on black female family heads").

134. This thinking was reflected in a newspaper editorial suggesting that black women on welfare should be given incentives to use Norplant, a new contraceptive; see "Poverty and Norplant: Can Contraception Reduce the Underclass?," *Philadelphia Inquirer* (Dec. 12, 1990), A18:1. On January 2, 1991, a California judge ordered a black woman on welfare who was convicted of child abuse to use Norplant for three years as a condition of probation; see Lev, "Judge Is Firm on Forced Contraception, but Welcomes an Appeal," *New York Times* (Jan. 11, 1991), A17:1; see also Lewin, "Implanted Birth Control Device Renews Debate over Forced Contraception," *New York Times* (Jan. 10, 1991), A20:1 (reviewing the debate on forced use of Norplant). The condemnation of single mothers can also be seen as penalizing poor black women for departing from white middle-class norms of motherhood; cf. *Chambers v. Omaha Girls' Club,* 834 F.2d 697 (8th Cir. 1987) (affirming dismissal of Title VII action brought by an unmarried black staff member of a private girls' club who was fired because she

became pregnant). Regina Austin suggests that "young, single, sexually active, fertile, and nurturing black women are being viewed ominously because they have the temerity to attempt to break out of the rigid economic, social, and political categories that a racist, sexist, and class-stratified society would impose upon them"; Austin, *supra* note 14, at 555.

135. At Jennifer Johnson's sentencing, the prosecutor made clear the nature of the charges against her: "About the end of December 1988, our office undertook a policy to begin to deal with mothers like Jennifer Johnson . . . as in the status of a child abuse case, Your Honor. . . . We have never viewed this as a drug case"; Motion for Rehearing and Sentencing at 12, *State v. Johnson,* No. E89–890-CFA (Fla. Cir. Ct. Aug. 25, 1989).

136. The drug user's pregnancy not only greatly increases the likelihood that she will be prosecuted but also greatly enhances the penalty she faces upon conviction. In most states, drug use is a misdemeanor, while distribution of drugs is a felony; see Hoffman, *supra* note 5, at 44.

137. Pamela Rae Stewart, for example, was charged with criminal neglect in part because she failed to follow her doctor's orders to stay off her feet and refrain from sexual intercourse while she was pregnant; see *People v. Stewart,* No. M508197, slip op. at 4 (Cal. Mun. Ct. Feb. 26, 1987); Bonavoglia, "The Ordeal of Pamela Rae Stewart," *Ms.* (July/Aug. 1987), at 92.

138. Seeking drug treatment is not a viable alternative. First, it is likely that the pregnant addict will be unable to find a drug treatment program that will accept her; see *infra* notes 151–155 and accompanying text. Second, even if she successfully completes drug counseling by the end of her pregnancy, she may still be prosecuted for her drug use that occurred during pregnancy before she was able to overcome her addiction.

139. I recognize that both becoming pregnant and continuing a pregnancy to term are not necessarily real "choices" that women—particularly women of color and addicted women—make. Rape, battery, lack of available contraceptives, and prostitution induced by drug addiction may lead a woman to become pregnant without exercising meaningful choice. Similarly, coercion from the father or her family, lack of money to pay for an abortion, or other barriers to access to an abortion may force a woman to continue an unwanted pregnancy; see *infra* note 211.

Nevertheless, these constraints on a woman's choice do not justify the government's punishment of the reproductive course that she ultimately follows. While we work to create the conditions for meaningful reproductive choice, it is important to affirm women's right to be free from unwanted state intrusion in their reproductive decisions.

140. See *supra,* at 1432–36.

141. See U.S. Department of Commerce, Bureau of the Census Statistical Abstract of the United States, 77, Table 110 (1990). This means that in 1987, black children were

2.08 times more likely than white children to die before reaching one year of age. This is the largest gap between black and white infant mortality rates since 1940, when infant mortality data were first reported by race; see *Children's Defense Fund, supra* note 79, at 3.

142. See F. Caro, D. Kalmuss, and I. Lopez, *Barriers to Prenatal Care*, 1 (1988). Another example of the institutionalized devaluation of black life is race-of-the-victim sentencing disparities; see Kennedy, *"McCleskey v. Kemp:* Race, Capital Punishment, and the Supreme Court," 101 *Harv. L. Rev.*, 1388, 1388–90 (1988).

143. See Binsacca, Ellis, Martin, and Petitti, "Factors Associated with Low Birthweight in an Inner-City Population: The Role of Financial Problems," 77 *Am. J. Pub. Health*, 505, 505 (1987); Leveno, Cunningham, Foark, Nelson, and Williams, "Prenatal Care and the Low Birth Weight Infant," 66 *Obstetrics and Gyn.* 599, 602 (1985). Babies born to women who receive no prenatal care are three times more likely to die within the first year than those born to women who receive adequate care; see Hughes, Johnson, Rosenbaum, and Simons, "The Health of America's Mothers and Children: Trends in Access to Care," 20 *Clearinghouse Rev.*, 472, 473 (1986).

144. One of the most significant obstacles to receiving prenatal care is the inability to pay for health care services; see *Children's Defense Fund, supra* note 79, at 43–48; McNulty, *supra* note 8, at 295–97. Most poor women depend on overextended public hospitals for prenatal care because of the scarcity of neighborhood physicians who accept Medicaid; see *id.* Institutional, cultural, and educational barriers also deter poor women of color from using the few available services; see, generally, F. Caro, D. Kalmuss, and I. Lopez, *supra* note 142 (discussing institutional and cultural barriers to prenatal care among low-income women in New York City); Curry, "Nonfinancial Barriers to Prenatal Care," 15 *Women and Health*, 85–87 (1989) (discussing accessibility problems to needed health care sites); Zambrana, "A Research Agenda on Issues Affecting Poor and Minority Women: A Model for Understanding Their Health Needs," 14 *Women and Health*, 137, 148–50 (1988) (discussing cultural barriers to prenatal care). A Haitian woman's explanation of why she discontinued prenatal care illustrates these obstacles to the use of public health facilities: "My friend say go to doctor and get checked. . . . My friend be on the phone much time before they make appointment. They no have space for 30 days.

"When I go to hospital, it confusing. . . . I go early, and see doctor late in the afternoon. . . . I wait on many long lines and take lots of tests. I no understand why so many test every time. No one explain nothing. No one talk my language. I be tired, feel sick from hospital. I go three times, but no more. Too much trouble for nothing"; F. Caro, D. Kalmuss, and I. Lopez, *supra* note 142, at 75–76.

145. See *Children's Defense Fund, supra* note 79, at 4, Table 1.1. The percentage of white women receiving adequate prenatal care was 72.6; see *id.*

146. See Hughes, Johnson, Rosenbaum, and Simons, *supra* note 143, at 473–74; McNulty, *supra* note 8, at 293–94.

The percentage of black women receiving prenatal care in the first three months of pregnancy declined from a high of 62.7 in 1980 to 61.1 in 1988; see Hilts, "Life Expectancy for Blacks in U.S. Shows Sharp Drop," *New York Times* (Nov. 29, 1990), B17:1. The percentage of babies born to black women getting no prenatal care increased from 8.8 in 1980 to 11.0 in 1988; see *id.*

The number of black infant deaths could be reduced significantly by a national commitment to ensuring that all pregnant women receive high-quality prenatal care; see, generally, Leu, "Legislative Research Bureau Report: A Proposal to Strengthen State Measures for the Reduction of Infant Mortality," 23 *Harv. J. Legis.*, 559 (1986) (proposing methods for delivering prenatal care services to poor women). A recently revealed confidential draft of a report by the White House Task Force on Infant Mortality recommends eighteen specific measures costing a total of $480 million per year to reduce infant mortality. "The steps include expansion of Medicaid to cover 120,000 additional pregnant women and children in low-income families, an increase in Federal spending on prenatal care and a requirement for states to provide a uniform set of Medicaid benefits to pregnant women"; Pear, "Study Says U.S. Needs to Attack Infant Mortality," *New York Times* (Aug. 6, 1990), B9:3. Programs specifically designed to provide prenatal care to low-income, high-risk women have succeeded in substantially reducing the rates of low birth weight and high infant mortality; see F. Caro, D. Kalmuss, and I. Lopez, *supra* note 142, at 3–5. For discussions of recommendations of measures to increase the use of prenatal care by poor women, see *id.* at 85–99; and Poland, Ager, and Olson, *supra* note 45, at 303.

147. See Chavkin, "Drug Addiction and Pregnancy: Policy Crossroads," 80 *Am. J. Pub. Health*, 483, 485 (1990); McNulty, *supra* note 8, at 301–02. A 1979 national survey by the National Institute on Drug Abuse found only twenty-five drug treatment programs that described themselves as specifically geared to female addicts; see Chavkin, *supra*, at 485. The lack of facilities for pregnant addicts in two cities illustrates the problem. A recent survey of seventy-eight drug treatment programs in New York City revealed that 54 percent denied treatment to pregnant women, 67 percent refused to treat pregnant addicts on Medicaid, and 87 percent excluded pregnant women on Medicaid addicted specifically to crack. Less than half of those programs that did accept pregnant addicts provided prenatal care, and only two provided child care; see Chavkin, "Help, Don't Jail, Addicted Mothers," *New York Times* (July 18, 1989), A21:2. Similarly, drug-addicted mothers in San Diego must wait up to six months to obtain one of just twenty-six places in residential treatment programs that allow them to live with their children; see Schachter, "Help Is Hard to Find for Addict Mothers: Drug Use 'Epidemic' Overwhelms Services," *Los Angeles Times* (Dec. 12, 1986), 2.1:1; "Substance Abuse Treatment for Women: Crisis in Access," *Health Advoc.* (Spring 1989), 9:1. Furthermore, because Medicaid

covers only seventeen days of a typical twenty-eight-day program, poor women may not be able to afford full treatment even at centers that will accept them; see Hoffman, *supra* note 5, at 44.

148. See Cusky, Berger, and Densen-Gerber, "Issues in the Treatment of Female Addiction: A Review and Critique of the Literature," 6 *Contemp. Drug Probs.* 307, 324–26 (1977); McNulty, *supra* note 8, at 301–02; Suffet, Hutson, and Brotman, "Treatment of the Pregnant Addict: A Historical Overview," in R. Brotman, D. Hutson, and F. Suffet, eds., *Pregnant Addicts and Their Children: A Comprehensive Care Approach*, 13, 21 (1984); Alters, *supra* note 30, 1:1; Freitag, "Hospital Defends Limiting of Drug Program," *New York Times* (Dec. 12, 1989), B9:1.

149. See McNulty, *supra* note 8, at 301; Teltsch, *supra* note 30, A14:1.

150. See Chavkin, "Drug Addiction and Pregnancy: Policy Crossroads," *supra* note 147, at 485; McNulty, "Combatting Pregnancy Discrimination in Access to Substance Abuse Treatment for Low-Income Women," 23 *Clearinghouse Rev.*, 21, 22 (1989).

151. See Cuskey, Berger, and Densen-Gerber, *supra* note 148, at 312–14; Alters, *supra* note 30, 1:1.

152. See McNulty, *supra* note 150, at 22; "Substance Abuse Treatment for Women: Crisis in Access," *supra* note 147, at 9.

153. See Chavkin, "Drug Addiction and Pregnancy: Policy Crossroads," *supra* note 147, at 485; Chavkin, Driver, and Forman, "The Crisis in New York City's Perinatal Services," 89 *N.Y. ST. J. Med.* 658, 661–62 (1989).

154. See Chavkin, "Drug Addiction and Pregnancy: Policy Crossroads," *supra* note 147, at 485; see also National Institute on Drug Abuse, *Drug Dependency in Pregnancy*, 46 (1978) (describing pervasive negative attitudes toward pregnant addicts).

155. The experience of one black pregnant drug addict, whom I will call Mary, exemplifies the barriers to care. Mary needed to find a residential drug treatment program that provided prenatal care and accommodations for her two children, ages three and eight. She tried to get into HUGS (Hope, Unity and Growth), the sole residential treatment program for women with children in Detroit, but there was no vacancy. Mary's only source of public prenatal care was Eleanor Hutzel Hospital, which has a clinic for high-risk pregnancies. She was also able to receive drug counseling on an outpatient basis from the adjacent Eleanore Hutzel Recovery Center. However, Mary encountered an eight-week waiting list at the hospital, and inadequate public transportation made it extremely difficult for her to get there. In the end, she received deficient care for both her addiction and her pregnancy; telephone interview with Adrienne Edmonson-Smith, advocate with the Maternal-Child Health Advocacy Project, Wayne State University (July 25, 1990).

156. See Berrien, "Pregnancy and Drug Use: The Dangerous and Unequal Use of Punitive Measures," 2 *Yale J. L. and Feminism*, 239, 247 (1990). The government learned of Jennifer Johnson's crack addiction only because she confided in the obstetrician who delivered her baby at a public hospital. Her trust in her doctor prompted the hospital to test Johnson and her baby for drugs; see Brief of American Public Health Association and Other Concerned Organizations as Amici Curiae in Support of Appellant at 2, *Johnson v. State*, No. 89-1765 (Fla. Dist. Ct. App. Dec. 28, 1989). Moreover, the state's entire proof of Johnson's criminal intent was based on the theory that her attempts to get help for her addiction showed that she knew that her cocaine use harmed the fetus. The key evidence against her was that, a month before her daughter's birth, Johnson had summoned an ambulance after a crack binge because she was worried about its effect on her unborn child; see *Trial Transcript*, *supra* note 4, at 144.

157. See American Medical Association, "Report of the Board of Trustees on Illegal Interventions During Pregnancy: Court Ordered Medical Treatments and Legal Penalties for Potentially Harmful Behavior by Pregnant Women," 264 *J.A.M.A.*, 2663, 2669 (1990). The reaction of pregnant women in San Diego to the 1987 arrest of Pamela Rae Stewart for harming her unborn child illustrates the deterrent effect of prosecution. Health care professionals reported that their pregnant clients' fear of prosecution for drug use made some of them distrustful and caused others to decline prenatal care altogether; see Moss, *supra* note 49, at 1411–12.

158. See Note, *supra* note 51, at 766 and n. 84; Chavkin, "Help, Don't Jail, Addicted Mothers," *supra* note 147, at A21:2.

159. See Escamilla-Mondanaro, "Women: Pregnancy, Children and Addiction," 9 *J. Psychedelic Drugs*, 59, 59–60 (1977); see also Zuckerman, Amaro, Bauchner, and Cabral, "Depressive Symptoms during Pregnancy: Relationship to Poor Health Behaviors," 160 *Am. J. Obstetrics and Gyn.*, 1107, 1109 (1989) (stating that poor health behavior in pregnancy correlates with such characteristics as "being single, older, unemployed, and having a lower income").

160. See A. Allen, *Uneasy Access: Privacy for Women in a Free Society*, 57–81 (1988) (noting similarity between benefits of privacy and equality for women). But see Sunstein, "Sexual Orientation and the Constitution: A Note on the Relationship Between Due Process and Equal Protection," 55 *U. Chi. L. Rev.*, 1161, 1170–79 (1988) (discussing differences between due process liberty and equal protection). Laurence Tribe and Michael Dorf criticize Sunstein for failing to "take greater account of the inseparability of liberty and equality"; Tribe and Dorf, "Levels of Generality in the Definition of Rights," 57 *U. Chi. L. Rev.*, 1057, 1095 (1990).

161. See Karst, "The Supreme Court, 1976 Term—Foreword: Equal Citizenship under the Fourteenth Amendment, 91 *Harv. L. Rev.* 1, 32 (1977).

162. See R. Dworkin, *Taking Rights Seriously,* 272–78 (1977).

163. The Fourteenth Amendment provides, in relevant part, that "[n]o State shall make or enforce any law which shall . . . deny to any person within its jurisdiction the equal protection of the laws"; U.S. Const. amend. XIV, § 1.

164. Racial classifications are held unconstitutional absent a compelling governmental justification; see *Wygant v. Jackson Board of Education,* 476 U.S. 267, 274 (1986) (plurality opinion); *Palmore v. Sidoti,* 466 U.S. 429, 432 (1984); *Korematsu v. United States,* 323 U.S. 214, 216 (1944). See, generally, L. Tribe, *American Constitutional Law,* § 16–6, at 1451–54 (2d ed. 1988) (explaining the strict scrutiny standard).

165. These competing views of equal protection law have been variously characterized by commentators; see, for example, L. Tribe, *supra* note 164, § 16–21, at 1514–21 (describing the "antidiscrimination" and "antisubjugation" principles); Brest, "The Supreme Court, 1975 Term—Foreword: In Defense of the Antidiscrimination Principle," 90 *Harv. L. Rev.,* 1, 5 (1976) (advocating the antidiscrimination principle as a theory of racial justice); Colker, "Anti-Subordination above All: Sex, Race, and Equal Protection," 61 *N.Y.U. L. Rev.,* 1003, 1005–13 (1986) (comparing the "antidifferentiation" principle with the "anti-subordination" approach).

166. Dimond, "The Anti-Caste Principle—Toward a Constitutional Standard for Review of Race Cases," 30 *Wayne L. Rev.,* 1, 1 (1983).

167. See Freeman, "Legitimizing Racial Discrimination through Antidiscrimination Law: A Critical Review of Supreme Court Doctrine," 62 *Minn. L. Rev.,* 1049, 1052–57 (1978).

168. See Strauss, "Discriminatory Intent and the Taming of *Brown,*" 56 *U. Chi. L. Rev.,* 935, 953–54 (1989). For an analysis of the development of Supreme Court antidiscrimination doctrine, see Dimond, *supra* note 166, at 16–42; and Freeman, *supra* note 167, at 1057–1118.

169. See, for example, *Village of Arlington Heights v. Metropolitan Hous. Dev. Corp.,* 429 U.S. 252, 265 (1977); *Washington v. Davis,* 426 U.S. 229, 239–45 (1976). Commentators have noted that the court adopted the discriminatory intent rule not because this standard is inherently required by the equal protection clause, but because it feared the remedies a discriminatory impact rule would entail; see, for example, Binion, "Intent and Equal Protection: A Reconsideration," 1983 *Sup. Ct. Rev.,* 397, 404–08; Kennedy, *supra* note 142, at 1414 (noting Justice Brennan's derision of the court's "fear of too much justice"); Schwemm, "From Washington to Arlington Heights and Beyond: Discriminatory Purpose in Equal Protection Litigation," 1977 *U. Ill. L.F.,* 961, 1050.

170. Freeman recognizes in the Supreme Court's discriminatory intent standard the twin notions of "fault" and "causation": proof of an equal protection violation requires identification of a blameworthy perpetrator whose actions can be linked to the victim's injury. See Freeman, *supra* note 167, at 1054–56; see also Sullivan, "The Supreme Court, 1985 Term—Comment: Sins of Discrimination: Last Term's Affirmative Action Cases," 100 *Harv. L. Rev.,* 78, 80 (1986) (arguing that "the Court has approved affirmative action only as precise penance for the specific sins of racism a government, union, or employer has committed in the past").

171. See *Personnel Administrator v. Feeney,* 442 U.S. 256, 279 (1979); Kennedy, *supra* note 142, at 1404.

172. Kennedy, *supra* note 142, at 1405.

173. For a discussion of equal protection challenges to racially selective prosecutions, see "Developments in the Law—Race and the Criminal Process," 101 *Harv. L. Rev.,* 1472, 1532–49 (1988).

174. See Kennedy, *supra* note 142, at 1425–27; see, generally, Note, "To Infer or Not to Infer a Discriminatory Purpose: Rethinking Equal Protection Doctrine," 61 *N.Y.U. L. Rev.,* 334, 351–62 (1986) (discussing the impact-inference standard as applied to jury selection and advocating its extension to death penalty cases and other contexts). The cases in which the Supreme Court has applied this reasoning involve challenges to the racial composition of juries; see, for example, *Castaneda v. Partida,* 430 U.S. 482, 500–01 (1977); *Turner v. Fouche,* 396 U.S. 346, 360–61 (1970). The court has not been willing to extend this reasoning to other claims of racial discrimination in the administration of criminal justice; see Cardinale and Feldman, "The Federal Courts and the Right to Nondiscriminatory Administration of the Criminal Law: A Critical View," 29 *Syracuse L. Rev.,* 659, 662–64 (1978); Kennedy, *supra* note 142, at 1402 (observing that "no defendant in state or federal court has ever successfully challenged his punishment on grounds of racial discrimination in sentencing").

175. 430 V.S. 482 (1977).

176. See *id.* at 494–97.

177. See *McCleskey v. Kemp,* 481 U.S. 279, 349–61 (1987) (Blackmun, J., dissenting) (applying the Castaneda test to a claim of discriminatory prosecution); "Developments in the Law," *supra* note 173, at 1552–54 (advocating use of an impact inference standard in the racial prosecution context).

178. See Chasnoff, Landress, and Barrett, *supra* note 65, at 1204, Table 2.

179. See "State Case Summary," *supra* note 2, at 3–5.

180. See *supra* p1434.

181. See *supra* p1433.

182. *Castaneda v. Partida,* 430 U.S. 482, 497–98 (1977).

183. See Binion, *supra* note 169, at 407–08.

184. See Kennedy, *supra* note 142, at 1424–25.

185. See L. Tribe, *supra* at; 164, s 16–21, at 1518, 1520–21.

186. See West, "Progressive and Conservative Constitutionalism," *supra* note 14, at 693–94. Tribe and others have argued that the antisubordination view of equality is more faithful to the historical origins of the Civil War amendments, which were drafted specifically to eradicate racial hierarchy; see L. Tribe, *supra* note 164, s 16–21, at 1516; Freeman, *supra* note 167, at 1061. In the Civil Rights Cases, 109 U.S. 3 (1883), for example, the court asserted that the Thirteenth Amendment abolishes "all badges and incidents of slavery"; *id.* at 20. In the Slaughter-House Cases, 83 U.S. (16 Wall.) 36 (1873), the court identified as the "one pervading purpose" of the amendments "the freedom of the slave race, the security and firm establishment of that freedom, and the protection of the newly-made freeman and citizen from the oppressions of those who had formerly exercised unlimited dominion over him"; *id.* at 71.

187. See Freeman, *supra* note 167, at 1054. K. Crenshaw similarly demonstrates how the "restrictive view" of antidiscrimination law assumes that a racially equitable society already exists; Crenshaw, *supra* note 14, at 1344.

188. Freeman, *supra* note 167, at 1054.

189. See Binion, *supra* note 169, at 447–48.

190. See *supra* notes 156–157 and accompanying text.

191. *Shelton v. Tucker,* 364 U.S. 479, 488 (1960).

192. See *supra* notes 143–155 and accompanying text.

193. See sources cited *supra* note 8.

194. See, for example, Gallagher, *supra* note 8, at 46–58; Nelson, Buggy, and Weil, "Forced Medical Treatment of Pregnant Women: 'Compelling Each to Live as Seems Good to the Rest,'" 37 *Hastings L. J.,* 703 (1986); Rhoden, "The Judge in the Delivery Room: The Emergence of Court-Ordered Caesareans," 74 *Calif. L. Rev.,* 1951 (1986).

195. See, for example, Goldberg, *supra* note 8, at 618–23; Nelson, Buggy, and Weil, *supra* note 194, at 750–57; Rhoden, *supra* note 194, at 1967–75, 1995–99.

196. See, for example, Stearns, "Maternal Duties during Pregnancy: Toward a Conceptual Framework," 21 *New Eng. L. Rev.,* 595, 629–33 (1985–86); Note, "Maternal Rights and Fetal Wrongs: The Case against the Criminalization of 'Fetal Abuse,'" 101 *Harv. L. Rev.,* 994, 1007 (1988).

197. This is not to say that forced medical treatment has no relevance to the lives of poor women of color. In fact, court-ordered medical procedures are performed disproportionately on pregnant minority women. A study of fifteen court-ordered cesarians published in 1987 found that 80 percent involved women of color, and 27 percent of the women were not native English speakers; see Kolder, Gallagher, and Parsons, "Court-Ordered Obstetrical Interventions," 316 *New Eng. J. Med.,* 1192, 1193 (1987); see also Daniels, "Court-Ordered Cesareans: A Growing Concern for Indigent Women," 21 *Clearinghouse Rev.,* 1064 (1988) (comparing the general distribution of cesarian sections with that of cesarians performed pursuant to court order); Gallagher, "Fetus as Patient," in S. Cohen and N. Taub,

eds., *supra* note 125, at 157, 183–84 (discussing the discriminatory impact of forced medical treatment).

198. See, for example, Fletcher, "The Fetus as Patient: Ethical Issues," 246 *J.A.M.A.,* 772 (1981); "Comment, The Fetal Patient and the Unwilling Mother: A Standard for Judicial Intervention," 14 *Pac. L. J.,* 1065, 1065–79 (1983).

199. See *supra* notes 147 and 148.

200. The punishment of drug-addicted mothers raises ethical issues affecting poor women of color, because drug-addicted mothers are often reported to government authorities by their own physicians. In the Johnson trial, for example, Johnson's obstetricians provided the most damaging evidence against her by testifying that she had admitted to them that she had smoked crack soon before both of her children were delivered; see *Trial Transcript, supra* note 4, at 15, 70. Punishing pregnant women based on information from their doctors undermines the confidential doctor-patient relationship and deters women from sharing important information with health care providers or even from obtaining prenatal care; see Berrien, *supra* note 156, at 247; Moss, *supra* note 49, at 1411–12; Roberts, *supra* note 2, at 60–61.

201. See, for example, Annas, "Predicting the Future of Privacy in Pregnancy: How Medical Technology Affects the Legal Rights of Pregnant Women," 13 *Nova L. Rev.,* 329, 345 (1989) ("Treating the fetus against the will of the mother requires us to degrade and dehumanize the mother and treat her as an inert container"); Gallagher, *supra* note 8, at 27 ("The individual women themselves become invisible or viewed only as vessels—carriers of an infinitely more valuable being").

202. See *supra* notes 94–95 and accompanying text.

203. See, for example, Goldberg, *supra* note 8, at 601–04; King, "Should Mom Be Constrained in the Best Interests of the Fetus?," 13 *Nova L. Rev.,* 393, 397 (1989); Note, *supra* note 8, at 613; Note, *supra* note 196, at 998–1002.

204. See, for example, Note, *supra* note 8, at 613 ("[B]ecause the decisions a woman makes throughout her pregnancy depend on her individual values and preferences, complicated sets of life circumstances, and uncertain probabilities of daily risk, the woman herself is best situated to make these complex evaluations"); Note, "Rethinking (M)otherhood: Feminist Theory and State Regulation of Pregnancy," 103 *Harv. L. Rev.,* 1325, 1339–41 (1990) (arguing that "the pregnant woman's physical and psychological position with respect to the fetus makes her a uniquely appropriate decisionmaker").

205. See, for example, Moss, *supra* note 2, at 288–89; Note, *supra* note 8, at 606–07.

206. I recognize, however, the tactical benefit of demonstrating that the prosecution of pregnant crack addicts should be the concern of all women. It may be more effective politically to convince affluent women that such government policies also jeopardize their lifestyles.

207. See Robertson, *supra* note 13, at 437–38, 445–47 ("[The woman] waived her right to resist bodily intrusions made for the sake of the fetus when she chose to continue the pregnancy"); Robertson, "The Right to Procreate and In Utero Fetal Therapy," 3 *J. Legal Med.*, 333, 359 (1982); see also Shaw, "Conditional Prospective Rights of the Fetus," 5 *J. Legal Med.*, 63, 88 (1984) (arguing that the mother's duty to protect the fetus from harm increases after viability "because she has forgone her right to choose abortion").

208. See, for example, Mathieu, "Respecting Liberty and Preventing Harm: Limits of State Intervention in Prenatal Choice," 8 *Harv. J. L. and Pub. Pol'y*, 19, 32–37 (1985) (arguing that the right to an abortion is not inconsistent with the duty to prevent or not cause harm to the fetus); Walker and Puzder, "State Protection of the Unborn After *Roe v. Wade:* A Legislative Proposal," 13 *Stetson L. Rev.*, 237, 241, 253 (1984) (arguing that extending the Fourteenth Amendment's protection to unborn children would not impair women's right to abortion).

209. The prosecution of drug-addicted mothers can be seen as encouraging abortion because pregnant drug addicts may feel pressure to abort the fetus rather than risk being charged with a crime.

210. See Stearns, *supra* note 196, at 604 ("It is inconsistent to argue that a [prenatal duty] rule unconstitutionally removes the right to abort if in fact the rule actually encourages women to exercise that very right").

211. If the facilities necessary to effectuate a reproductive decision cost money, poor women may not be able to afford to take advantage of them. Prenatal care, abortion services, artificial insemination, fetal surgery, contraceptives, and family-planning counseling are some examples of the means to realize a reproductive choice that may be financially inaccessible to low-income women; see, generally, Gertner, "Interference with Reproductive Choice," in S. Cohen and N. Taub, eds., *supra* note 125, at 307, 307–12 (discussing economic and legal obstacles to reproductive choice); Nsiah-Jefferson, *supra* note 125, at 20–23, 50–51 (discussing limitations on access to abortion service and new reproductive technology).

In Roberts, "The Future of Reproductive Choice for Poor Women and Women of Color," 12 *Women's Rts. L. Rep.*, 59 (1990), I describe the constraints on the reproductive choices available to a hypothetical pregnant young woman in the inner city; see *id.* at 62–64.

212. See *supra* note 144.

213. An example of how the unilateral focus on abortion has neglected—even contradicted—the interests of poor women of color is the prochoice opposition to sterilization reform in the seventies. In 1977, the Committee to End Sterilization Abuse introduced in the New York City Council guidelines to prevent sterilization abuse, an important issue for women of color; see *supra* notes 124–130. In 1979, the Department of Health, Education, and Welfare also considered the guidelines, which had two key provisions: they required informed consent in the preferred language of the patient and a thirty-day waiting period between the signing of the consent form and the sterilization procedure. Representatives of the National Abortion Rights Action League and Planned Parenthood testified against the New York and national guidelines as restrictions on women's access to sterilization; see "Tax, Tax Replies," *The Nation* (July 24/31, 1989), at 110, 148 (letter to the editor); see also Petchesky, *supra* note 124, at 35–39 (discussing arguments asserted by opponents of the federal sterilization regulations).

The abortion rights of women of color have also been overlooked. One example is the belated political mobilization on the part of the prochoice movement triggered by the Supreme Court's decision in *Webster v. Reproductive Health Services*, 109 S. Ct. 3040 (1989). There was no similar response to the court's decisions in *Maher v. Roe*, 432 U.S. 464 (1977) and *Harris v. McRae*, 448 U.S. 297 (1980), which allowed the government to deny poor women public funding for abortions. The prochoice movement was relatively complacent about the court's effective denial of access to abortions for poor women until the reproductive rights of affluent women were also threatened; see Stearns, "*Roe v. Wade:* Our Struggle Continues," 4 *Berkeley Women's L. J.*, 1, 7 (1989).

214. The struggle for abortion rights nevertheless continues to play a critical role in advancing women's reproductive autonomy. Expanding the scope of reproductive rights beyond abortion to include the right to bear healthy children may also help prochoice advocates in the abortion debate. One of the tactics of the right-to-life movement is to characterize the prochoice movement as people who do not care about children. I participated in a panel discussion in which the right-to-life participants brought along a contingent of supporters—all with young children on their laps. A more complete view of reproductive choice may help to dispel this image; see Colker, "Reply to Sarah Burns," 13 *Harv. Women's L. J.*, 207, 212 n. 31 (1990). I do not, however, advocate transforming reproductive freedom from a women's rights issue into a children's rights issue; see Burns, "Notes from the Field: A Reply to Professor Colker," 13 *Harv. Women's L. J.*, 189, 205–06 (1990).

215. *Trial Transcript, supra* note 4, at 364.

216. Supreme Court privacy analysis has similarly mischaracterized the fundamental right at issue in other contexts. The court has typically identified the constitutional question as whether there is a fundamental right to engage in the conduct forbidden by the law at issue (for example, abortion, adultery, contraception, or homosexual activity); see, for example, *Michael H. v. Gerald D.*, 109 S.Ct. 2333, 2343 (1989) (identifying the right at issue as "specifically the power of the natural father to assert parental rights over a child born into a woman's existing marriage with another man"); *Bowers v. Hardwick*, 478 U.S. 186, 190 (1986) ("The issue presented is whether the Federal Constitution confers a fundamental right upon homosexuals to engage in sodomy"). Jed Rubenfeld has observed that this approach obscures the real danger of laws that abridge the right of

privacy—their use as a means for government to control critical aspects of our lives and identity; see Rubenfeld, "The Right of Privacy," 102 *Harv. L. Rev.*, 737, 739 (1989). Rubenfeld writes that "[t]he fundament of the right to privacy is not to be found in the supposed fundamentality of what that law proscribes. It is to be found in what the law imposes"; *id.;* see also Tribe and Dorf, *supra* note 160, at 1065–71 (describing the enterprise of designating fundamental rights as a question of the proper level of abstraction at which to portray those rights).

217. Ohio Senate Bill No. 324, which would create a new crime of "prenatal child neglect," forces drug-addicted mothers to choose between going to jail and giving up their right to bear children; see S.B. No. 324, § 2919.221(B), 118th Ohio General Assembly, Regular Session 1989–90. A repeat offender must elect either to undergo tubal ligation or to participate in a five-year contraception program. If she fails to remain drug-free during the five-year program, the judge must sentence her to be sterilized; see S.B. No. 324 § 2919.221(B)(2)(c). If she refuses to make the required election, she will be held guilty of "aggravated prenatal child neglect," a first-degree felony carrying a possible twenty-five-year prison sentence; S.B. No. 324, §§ 2919.221(E), 2929.11(B).

218. Both aspects of the constitutional protection of the individual's personhood satisfy Martin Luther King, Jr.'s test for the legitimacy of man-made laws: "Any law that uplifts human personality is just. Any law that degrades human personality is unjust"; M. L. King, Jr., "Letter from Birmingham Jail," in *Why We Can't Wait*, 85 (1963); West, "Progressive and Conservative Constitutionalism," *supra* note 14, at 686–87.

219. Kimberlé Crenshaw has argued that although liberal legal ideology has served important functions in blacks' struggle against racial domination, it is important to develop strategies that minimize the costs of engaging in legitimating liberal discourse; see Crenshaw, *supra* note 14, at 1384–87. She suggests that such strategies must have a community perspective: "History has shown that the most valuable political asset of the Black community has been its ability to assert a collective identity and to name its collective political reality. Liberal reform discourse must not be allowed to undermine the Black collective identity"; *id.* at 1336.

220. Matsuda, "When the First Quail Calls: Multiple Consciousness as Jurisprudential Method," 2 *Women's Rts. L. Rep.*, 7, 8 (1989).

221. *Id.*

222. See Harris, *supra* note 14, at 584 (discussing the complex dialogue between the aspirational voices of liberalism and the voices of real people). For a discussion of the importance of aspirational thinking, see Colker, *supra* note 130, at 1018–19.

223. See cases cited *infra* note 228.

224. See *Roe v. Wade*, 410 U.S. 113, 152–56 (1973). For a description of the history of privacy jurisprudence, see Rubenfeld, *supra* note 216, at 740–52.

225. *Whalen v. Roe*, 429 U.S. 589, 599–600 (1977).

226. For a discussion of the distinction between decisional privacy and privacy in the sense of restricted access, see Allen, "Taking Liberties: Privacy, Private Choice, and Social Contract Theory," 56 *U. Cin. L. Rev.*, 461, 463–66 (1987). See, generally, Note, "*Roe* and *Paris*: Does Privacy Have a Principle?," 26 *Stan. L. Rev.*, 1161 (1974) (analyzing and defining the concept of privacy).

227. See L. Tribe, *supra* note 164, § 15-1, at 1302–04; Feinberg, "Autonomy, Sovereignty, and Privacy: Moral Ideals in the Constitution?," 58 *Notre Dame L. Rev.*, 445, 446–67 (1983); Gerety, "Redefining Privacy," 12 *Harv. C.R.-C.L. L. Rev.*, 233, 236 (1977) (defining privacy as "an autonomy or control over the intimacies of personal identity"); Henkin, "Privacy and Autonomy," 74 *Colum. L. Rev.*, 1410, 1412–29 (1974). For the classic liberal defense of personal autonomy, see J. S. Mill, *On Liberty*, 77–79 G. Himmelfarb, ed., (1974) [1859].

228. See, for example, *Roe v. Wade*, 410 U.S. 113 (1973) (right to choose whether to terminate a pregnancy); *Loving v. Virginia*, 388 U.S. 1 (1967) (right to choose one's spouse); *Griswold v. Connecticut*, 381 U.S. 479, 485 (1965) (right to decide whether to use contraceptives); *Skinner v. Oklahoma*, 316 U.S. 535 (1942) (right to procreate); *Pierce v. Society of Sisters*, 268 U.S. 510 (1925) (right to select the schooling of children under one's control); *Meyer v. Nebraska*, 262 U.S. 390 (1923) (right to determine the language taught to one's children).

229. See *Roe v. Wade*, 410 U.S. at 155.

230. Exploring the contours of the right to procreate is beyond the scope of this article. I focus on the aspect of the right of privacy that guarantees the choice to carry a pregnancy to term. I want to protect the individual from punishment for making a reproductive decision rather than to fulfill the individual's desire to have children. The value at the heart of my argument is not procreation but autonomy; see L. Tribe, *supra* note 164, § 15-23, at 1423 ("As the Court itself stressed in *Carey*, the constitutional principle of 'individual autonomy' affirmed in these cases protected not procreation, but the individual's 'right of decision' about procreation"; quoting *Carey v. Population Services International*, 431 U.S. 678, 687–89 (1977); emphasis in original).

Delineating the right to procreate is difficult indeed. It involves defining the procreative activities encompassed by the right, as well as the limits on government interference with those activities. New developments in reproductive technology have complicated the problem by allowing people to procreate in ways current law does not contemplate; see, for example, Andrews, "Alternative Modes of Reproduction," in S. Cohen and N. Taub, eds., *supra* note 125, at 259; "Developments in the Law—Medical Technology and the Law," 103 *Harv. L. Rev.*, 1519, 1525–56 (1990); "Special Project: Legal Rights and Issues Surrounding Conception, Pregnancy, and Birth," 39 *Vand. L. Rev.*, 597, 602–52 (1986). For discussions of the right to procreate, see Binion, "Reproductive Freedom and the Constitution: The Limits on Choice," 4 *Berkeley Women's L. J.*, 12, 24–39 (1989); Robertson, *supra* note 13, at 405–20; and Scott, "Sterilization of Mentally Retarded Persons: Reproductive Rights and Family Privacy," *Duke L. J.*, 806, 827–33 (1986).

231. *Carey v. Population Services International,* 431 U.S. 678, 685 (1977). Although dicta in many of the privacy decisions include the decision to bear a child among those protected by the right of privacy, the holdings of the cases concern the freedom not to procreate—the right to avoid unwanted pregnancy through contraception or abortion; see *Carey,* 431 U.S., at 694 (holding that a state law limiting minors' access to contraceptives violated the Fourteenth Amendment); *Roe v. Wade,* 410 U.S. 113, 153 (1973); *Eisenstadt v. Baird,* 405 U.S. 438, 443 (1972) (striking down a state law limiting unmarried people's access to contraceptives); *Griswold v. Connecticut,* 381 U.S. 479, 485 (1965). By contrast, the Supreme Court has hardly addressed the right to bear a child. Its only decision upholding the right to procreate is *Skinner v. Oklahoma,* 316 U.S. 535 (1942); see *infra* pp. 1475–76.

232. 405 U.S. 438 (1972).

233. *Id.* at 453 (emphasis omitted).

234. Support for the right to procreate can be found in the language of *Roe v. Wade,* in which the court held that the constitutional "right of privacy . . . is broad enough to encompass a woman's decision whether or not to terminate her pregnancy"; 410 U.S. at 153. The court made the woman's choice—either to terminate her pregnancy or complete it—the crux of the privacy right it recognized. Because it is the woman's choice that is guaranteed, the alternative to the abortion decision—the decision to carry the fetus to term—must also be protected; see *Thornburgh v. American College of Obstetricians and Gynecologists,* 476 U.S. 747, 778 n. 6 (1986) (Stevens, J., concurring); L. Tribe, *supra* note 164, § 15–10, at 1340 (arguing that the meaning of the privacy cases is that "whether one person's body shall be the source of another life must be left to that person and that person alone to decide"; emphasis omitted); cf. Tribe, "The Curvature of Constitutional Space: What Lawyers Can Learn from Modern Physics," 103 *Harv. L. Rev.*, 1, 14 (1989) (noting the difficulty in justifying any constitutional distinction between "the state's power to require an abortion in certain circumstances and the state's power to forbid one").

235. But see Rubenfeld, *supra* note 216, at 796–97 (arguing that laws limiting family size and laws prohibiting abortion are "enormously different in their real, material effect on individuals' lives" and cautioning against being "misled by their formal similarities"). Rubenfeld finds that although both laws impinge on the childbearing decision, a law that in effect requires women to bear children takes

over women's lives far more than a law that forbids them from having more than a prescribed number of children; see *id.* at 797; see also R. Petchesky, *Abortion and a Woman's Choice,* 387–90 (1984) (criticizing the assumption of "a mistaken symmetry between 'the right to have children' and 'the right . . . not to have them' "). Petchesky postulates that in a society where gender, class, and racial equality have been achieved, the state might be justified in denying individuals a right to procreate. Unlike Petchesky, I have endeavored to analyze the political implications of the punishment of drug-addicted mothers only in the context of the current and historical conditions of gender, class, and racial inequality. Petchesky presents just such an analysis of abortion; see *id.* at 12–13. Rubenfeld also may have reached a different conclusion if he had considered the real, material effects on women of color created by the state's interference in the decision to procreate. Of course, the consequences of compelling childbirth and of prohibiting it are not identical, and the government's asserted justifications for intervention are not always of equal weight.

236. 414 U.S. 632 (1974).

237. See McNulty, *supra* note 8, at 315; Note, *supra* note 8, at 618.

238. LaFleur, 414 U.S. at 639–48.

239. Under *Roe v. Wade,* laws allowing the prosecution of drug-addicted mothers would have to meet a strict scrutiny test. As the Court stated in *Roe,* "where certain 'fundamental rights,' are involved, the Court has held that regulation limiting these rights may be justified only by a 'compelling state interest,' and that legislative enactments must be narrowly drawn to express only the legitimate state interests at stake"; 410 U.S. at 113 (citations omitted). I have already demonstrated that laws punishing drug-addicted mothers do not meet this test; see *supra* notes 190–192 and accompanying text.

240. In upholding the denial of public funding for abortions, the court distinguished between a direct governmental burden on the exercise of reproductive choice and the government's refusal to subsidize one choice, abortion, while subsidizing the alternative, childbirth; see *Webster v. Reproductive Health Services.,* 109 S. Ct. 3040, 3051–53 (1989); *Harris v. McRae,* 448 U.S. 297, 314–18 (1980); *Maher v. Roe,* 432 U.S. 464, 475–77 (1977). See, generally, Appleton, "Beyond the Limits of Reproductive Choice: The Contributions of the Abortion-Funding Cases to Fundamental-Rights Analysis and to the Welfare-Rights Thesis," 81 *Colum. L. Rev.*, 721, 724–45 (1981) (arguing that after *Maher,* state action will only face strict scrutiny if it is an "impingement" on a fundamental right).

241. The court has struck down state regulations of abortion that so restricted women's access to abortion that they effectively denied women a choice; see, for example, *Thornburgh v. American College of Obstetricians and Gynecologists,* 476 U.S. 747, 759–71 (1986) (striking down informed

consent, reporting, and standard of care requirements for postviability abortions); *City of Akron v. Akron Center for Reproductive Health, Inc.*, 462 U.S. 416, 431–52 (1983) (striking down provisions of ordinance requiring parental consent, informed consent, twenty-four-hour waiting period, performance of all second-trimester abortions in a hospital, and "humane and sanitary" disposal of fetal remains); *Colautti v. Franklin*, 439 U.S. 379, 389–401 (1979) (striking down viability-determination and standard-of-care requirements as vague); *Planned Parenthood v. Danforth*, 428 U.S. 52, 69–75 (1976) (striking down, inter alia, spousal and parental consent requirements).

242. See *Colautti*, 439 U.S. at 386 n.7 (describing criminal penalties as a "direct obstacle" to reproductive choice to be distinguished from denial of funding); *Maher*, 432 U.S. at 474 n. 8.

243. Patricia Williams has explored the differing perspectives on "rights" held by blacks and whites—in this case the predominantly white Critical Legal Studies movement. She explains that, for blacks, the stereotyping of human experience created by rights discourse (the focus of the critical legal studies critique) is a lesser historical evil than having been ignored altogether; see Williams, "Alchemical Notes: Reconstructing Ideals from Deconstructed Rights," 22 *Harv. C.R.-C.L. L. Rev.*, 401, 414 (1987) ("The black experience of anonymity, the estrangement of being without a name, has been one of living in the oblivion of society's inverse, beyond the dimension of any consideration at all. Thus, the experience of rights-assertion . . . has been a process of finding the self"). Similarly, Kimberlé Crenshaw observes that dispossessed people use rights rhetoric "to redeem some of the rhetorical promises" of popular political discourse by forcing society to live up to its deepest commitments; see Crenshaw, *supra* note 14, at 1366.

244. Harris, *supra* note 14, at 613 (citing Hurston, "How It Feels to Be Colored Me," in A. Walker, ed., *I Love Myself When I Am Laughing . . . and Then Again When I Am Looking Mean and Impressive*, 152, 155 (1979).

245. *Id.*

246. For examples of black women who have transcended conditions of oppression, see L. Hutchinson, *Anna J. Cooper: A Voice from the South* (1981); and J. Robinson, *The Montgomery Bus Boycott and the Women Who Started It: The Memoir of Jo Ann Gibson Robinson* (1987). The fictional writings of black women also express this tradition; see, for example, T. Morrison, *Beloved* (1987); A. Walker, *The Color Purple* (1982).

247. See Allen, *supra* note 103, at 141.

248. Rubenfeld, for example, proposes an interpretation of the right of privacy which focuses on the affirmative consequences of laws challenged on the basis of privacy claims; see Rubenfeld, *supra* note 216, at 782–84. It is the "totalitarian" intervention of government into a person's life that the right of privacy protects against; *id.* at 787. The right of privacy, then, means "the right not to have the course of one's life dictated by the state"; *id.* at 807.

249. Protection from government power need not be the full extent of the Constitution's guarantee of autonomy and personhood; see *infra* pp. 1478–80. Recognizing that "[a]s long as a state exists and enforces any laws at all, it makes political choices," Frances Olsen argues that the distinction between state intervention and nonintervention is a myth; Olsen, "The Myth of State Intervention in the Family," 18 *U. Mich. J. L. Ref.*, 835, 836 (1985). Olsen further argues that the poor have the least to gain from the rhetoric of nonintervention: "The attempt to criticize state 'intervention' instead of criticizing the particular policies pursued may be especially limiting for poor people, who often have to rely on various government programs and are thus less likely to benefit from any political strategy based on the myth of nonintervention"; *id.* at 863.

250. See *supra* pp. 1432–34.

251. Some feminist scholars have argued that a gender equality approach to reproductive freedom advances women's rights better than a privacy rationale; see, for example, Copelon, "Unpacking Patriarchy: Reproduction, Sexuality, Originalism, and Constitutional Change," in J. Lobel, ed., *A Less Than Perfect Union: Alternative Perspectives on the U.S. Constitution*, 303, 322–26 (1988); Law, "Rethinking Sex and the Constitution," 132 *U. Pa. L. Rev.*, 955, 1016–28 (1984); MacKinnon, "*Roe v. Wade*: A Study in Male Ideology," in J. Garfield and P. Hennessey, eds., *Abortion: Moral and Legal Perspectives*, 45 (1984).

For a dialogue concerning the use of equality doctrine versus privacy doctrine to advocate abortion rights, see Colker, "Feminist Litigation: An Oxymoron?—A Study of the Briefs Filed in *William L. Webster v. Reproductive Health Services*," 13 *Harv. Women's L. J.*, 137 (1990); Burns, "Notes from the Field: A Reply to Professor Colker," 13 *Harv. Women's L. J.*, 189 (1990); and Colker, "Reply to Sarah Burns," 13 *Harv. Women's L. J.*, 207 (1990). In her response to Ruth Colker's criticism of the emphasis on privacy doctrine in feminist litigation, Sarah Burns raises several important questions: "Why should we not insist that the question whether to have an abortion is a woman's private moral decision outside the public realm and beyond public interference? Why is arguing for equality necessarily more 'radical' and less 'liberally co-opted' than arguing for fundamental liberty and autonomy for women? Are not equality concepts co-opted by liberal interpretation? Can equality work as a concept without the concepts of liberty and autonomy?" Burns, *supra* at 193. I attempt to answer some of these questions in this article, especially as they relate to women of color. For a defense of privacy which responds to the feminist critique, see A. Allen, *supra* note 160, at 57 (arguing that the "solution to the privacy problem women face begins with promoting greater emphasis on opportunities for individual forms of privacy, rather than in rejecting privacy"); and Olsen, "The Supreme Court, 1988 Term—Comment: Unraveling Compromise," 103 *Harv. L. Rev.*, 105, 117 (1989) (arguing the importance of extending privacy doctrine equally to women and men, "even as we pursue efforts to dismantle the false dichotomies underlying it").

252. See MacKinnon, *supra* note 251, at 51–53.

253. *Id.* at 49.

254. "[T]he legal concept of privacy can and has shielded the place of battery, marital rape, and women's exploited labor; has preserved the central institutions whereby women are deprived of identity, autonomy, control and self-definition; and has protected the primary activity through which male supremacy is expressed and enforced"; *id.* at 53.

255. See Jones, *supra* note 108, at 237; Kline, *supra* note 17, at 122–23. Patricia Cain observes that lesbians' experiences of the private sphere may also differ from MacKinnon's description: "Lesbians who live our private lives removed from the intimate presence of men do indeed experience time free from male domination. When we leave the male-dominated public sphere, we come home to a woman-identified private sphere"; Cain, *supra* note 21, at 212.

256. See Kline, *supra* note 17, at 129.

257. See *id.* at 128–31 (criticizing a feminist analysis of child custody law that neglects the experiences of black and Native American women); see also *supra* notes 109–115 and accompanying text.

258. See L. Tribe, *supra* note 164, § 16-9, at 1458–60 (discussing the intersection of "preferred rights" and "equality of rights").

259. The issue of the constitutionality of a government standard for procreation raises the question of whether the right to procreate is limited and therefore implies certain requirements for entitlement. Elizabeth Scott, for example, defines the right to procreate as "the right to produce one's own children to rear"; Scott, *supra* note 230, at 329. She argues that constitutional protection extends only to the reproductive interests of prospective rearing parents, because it is the objective of rearing the child that elevates the interest in procreation to the status of a fundamental right. The right to procreate, therefore, "requires an intention as well as an ability to assume the role of parent"; *id.* Thus, a retarded person who is "so severely and irremediably impaired that she could never provide a child with minimally adequate care . . . has no [constitutionally] protectable interest in procreation"; *id.* at 833. The irremediable nature of the retarded person's impairment distinguishes her from a drug addict who is judged to be an unfit parent; cf. *id.* at 833 n. 91 (distinguishing on the basis of irremediability retarded people from those who have previously failed at parenting).

260. In the Johnson trial, for example, the prosecution introduced no evidence that Johnson's children were adversely affected by their mother's crack use. Indeed, there was testimony that the children were healthy and developing normally; see *Trial Transcript, supra* note 4, at 146–47, 120 (testimony of Dr. Randy Tompkin and Clarice Johnson, Jennifer's mother). A law proposed in Ohio makes drug use during pregnancy grounds for sterilization. See

supra note 217. Similarly, several states have enacted statutes that make a woman's drug use during pregnancy by itself grounds to deprive her of custody of her child; see *supra* note 50.

261. See *supra* pp. 1442–43.

262. See Karst, *supra* note 161, at 32; Stefan, "Whose Egg Is It Anyway? Reproductive Rights of Incarcerated, Institutionalized and Incompetent Women," 13 *Nova L. Rev.*, 405, 454 (1989) (discussing the systematic barriers to motherhood imposed on incarcerated women as a part of the process of dehumanization); see also Asch, "Reproductive Technology and Disability," in *Reproductive Laws for the 1990s, supra* note 125, at 106–07 (discussing the importance of the right to choose childbearing for disabled women).

I recognize that there are women who choose not to have children or are incapable of having children, and that this choice or inability does not make them any less human; see Cain, *supra* note 21, at 201, 205 n. 96 (criticizing feminist discourse that privileges the experience of motherhood over other experiences of female connection). It is not the act of having children that makes an individual fully human; it is society's view of whether she deserves to have children.

263. For a discussion of the eugenic sterilization movement in the early twentieth century, see Burgdorf and Burgdorf, "The Wicked Witch Is Almost Dead: *Buck v. Bell* and the Sterilization of Handicapped Persons," 50 *Temp. L. Q.*, 995, 997–1005 (1977); and Cynkar, *Buck v. Bell:* "Felt Necessities" v. Fundamental Values?," 81 *Colum. L. Rev.* 1418, 1425–35 (1981). George P. Smith II has presented a contemporary justification of eugenic sterilization of the mentally handicapped; see Smith, "Limitations on Reproductive Autonomy for the Mentally Handicapped," 4 *J. Contemp. Health L. and Pol'y,* 71, 72, 88–89 (1988).

The discrediting of eugenic theory, the development of the constitutional doctrine of reproductive autonomy, and the changing view of mental retardation have all spurred a major reform of sterilization law in the last two decades. Reports of Nazi Germany's program of racial eugenics achieved through widespread sterilization precipitated the modern rejection of these laws; see Scott, *supra* note 230, at 811–12.

264. For a description of the origins of eugenic theory, see Cynkar, *supra* note 263, at 1420–25.

265. One report written by a leading scholar of the eugenic movement defined the "socially inadequate" as: "(1) feeble-minded; (2) insane (including the psychopathic); (3) criminalistic (including the delinquent and wayward); (4) epileptic; (5) inebriate (including drug-habitués); (6) diseased (including the tuberculous, the syphilitic, the leprous, and others with chronic, infectious and legally segregable diseases); (7) blind (including those with seriously impaired vision); (8) deaf (including those with seriously impaired hearing); (9) deformed (including the crippled); and (10) dependent (including orphans, ne'er-do-wells, the homeless, tramps and paupers)"; Cynkar, *supra* note 263, at

1428, quoting H. Laughlin, *The Legal Status of Eugenical Sterilization*, 65 (1929).

266. As late as 1966, twenty-six states still had eugenic sterilization laws; see Scott, *supra* note 230, at 809 n. 11. It has been estimated that over seventy thousand persons were involuntarily sterilized under these statutes; see Smith, *supra* note 263, at 77 n. 35. For a discussion of the eugenic sterilization statutes, see Ferster, "Eliminating the Unfit— Is Sterilization the Answer?," 27 *Ohio St. L. J.*, 591 (1966).

267. 274 U.S. 200 (1927).

268. The court rejected arguments that the Virginia sterilization law violated the equal protection clause because it applied only to institutionalized persons and that it violated the due process clause because it exceeded the legitimate power of the state; see *id.* at 207–08.

The continued authority of *Buck v. Bell* is highly doubtful in light of the development of reproductive privacy doctrine in the last thirty years. Because sterilization laws infringe what is now acknowledged as a fundamental right, they are subject to strict scrutiny rather than the rational-basis analysis applied in *Bell*; see Murdock, "Sterilization of the Retarded: A Problem or a Solution?," 62 *Calif. L. Rev.*, 917, 921–24 (1974); Sherlock and Sherlock, "Sterilizing the Retarded: Constitutional, Statutory and Policy Alternatives," 60 *N.C.L. Rev.* 943, 953–54 (1982).

269. 1924 Va. Acts 394. For a discussion of the history of the Virginia sterilization law's enactment, see Lombards, "Three Generations, No Imbeciles: New Light on *Buck v. Bell*," 60 *N.Y.U. L. Rev.*, 30, 34–48 (1985).

270. *Bell*, 274 U.S. at 205. Subsequent research has revealed that the court's factual statement was erroneous. Although Carrie Buck became pregnant out of wedlock, the finding that she was "feeble minded" was based on insubstantial testimony; see Gould, "Carrie Buck's Daughter," 2 *Const. Commentary*, 331, 336 (1985); Lombards, *supra* note 269, at 52.

271. See Holmes, "Ideals and Doubts," 10 *Ill. L. Rev.*, 1, 3 (1915) ("I believe that the wholesale social regeneration . . . cannot be affected appreciably by tinkering with the institution of property, but only by taking in hand life and trying to build a race"); Rogat, "Mr. Justice Holmes: A Dissenting Opinion," 15 *Stan. L. Rev.*, 254, 282 (1963) (referring to *Buck v. Bell* as "a judicial manifestation of [Holmes's] intense eugenicist views").

272. *Bell*, 274 U.S. at 207.

273. The distinction I make between punitive and eugenic motive depends not on the specific provisions of the statute but, rather, on the moralistic versus biological impulse underlying the statute. Compulsory sterilization laws—whether criminal or therapeutic—were often based on punitive motivations disguised as a eugenic rationale; see R. Petchesky, *supra* note 235, at 85. Petchesky asserts that the sterilization laws were punitive because "[t]heir aim was not only to reduce lumbers or root out 'defective genes' but also to attack and punish sexual 'promiscuity,' and the sexual

danger thought to emanate from the lower classes, especially lower-class women"; *id.* at 88. My focus is on the statutes' punishment of deviance from the standard for motherhood rather than for sexual deviance alone.

274. Apparently, Carrie was sterilized because she was poor and had been pregnant out of wedlock; see Lombards, *supra* note 269, at 51. The deposition testimony of the state mental institution's trial expert, the famed eugenicist Harry Laughlin, implies this underlying motivation: "These people belong to the shiftless, ignorant, and worthless class of anti-social whites of the South"; *id.* After reviewing the record of the case, Professor Gould concluded: "Her case never was about mental deficiency; it was always a matter of sexual morality and social deviance. . . . Two generations of bastards are enough"; Gould, *supra* note 270, at 336.

275. M. Haller, *Eugenics: Hereditarian Attitudes in American Thought*, 42 (1963) (quoting eugenicist W. Duncan McKim; emphasis added).

276. Lombardo, *supra* notes 269, at 46 (quoting *Report of the Virginia State Epileptic Colony*, 27 (1922–23); emphasis added).

277. 316 U.S. 535 (1942).

278. *Okla. Stat. Ann.* tit. 57, §§ 171–195 (West 1935).

279. *Id.* § 173.

280. See *Skinner*, 316 U.S. at 537.

281. *Id.* at 541.

282. See *id.* at 541.

283. See *id.* at 542.

284. *Id.* at 536. The right of procreation is also considered a human right under international law; see Universal Declaration of Human Rights, art. 16 s 1, G.A. Res. 217 (III), at 74, U.N. Doc. 28. 22 A/810 (1948) ("Men and women of full age, without any limitation due to race, nationality or religion, have the right to marry and to found a family").

285. See L. Tribe, *supra* note 164, § 15–10, at 1339, § 16–12, at 1464.

286. *Skinner*, 316 U.S. at 541.

287. *Id.*

288. See *id.*

289. See *supra* note 275 and accompanying text.

290. See *supra* notes pp. 0000–00.

291. See *supra* notes 213 and 240.

292. 448 U.S. 297 (1980).

293. *Id.* at 316.

294. C. MacKinnon, *supra* note 19, at 101. Rhonda Copelon and Rosalind Petchesky draw similar conclusions about the limits of liberal privacy theory in the abortion funding context; see R. Petchesky, *supra* note 235, at 295–302; Copelon, *supra* note 251, at 322–25.

295. See *supra* note 211. Dependence on public largesse, for example, means that the government can determine which reproductive decisions indigent women may carry out. The Supreme Court erroneously reasoned in the abortion funding decisions that the denial of public funding imposes no new obstacle to reproductive choice: if an indigent woman is unable to effectuate her decision to have an abortion, the court argued, her inability is due to her poverty and not the government's funding policy; see *Maher v. Roe*, 432 U.S. 464, 474 (1977); *Harris*, 448 U.S. at 314–15. Yet the court's reasoning ignores the real-life effect of the government's funding choices on poor women. An indigent woman who is unable to pay for either childbirth or abortion has no choice but to accept the government's determination. By funding only one option, the government has really made the woman's choice for her; see Binion, *supra* note 230, at 19; Goldstein, "A Critique of the Abortion Funding Decisions: On Private Rights in the Public Sector," 8 *Hastings Const. L. Q.*, 313, 315–17 (1981); Tribe, "The Abortion Funding Conundrum: Inalienable Rights, Affirmative Duties, and the Dilemma of Dependence," 99 *Harv. L. Rev.*, 330, 33637 (1985).

296. See R. Petchesky, *supra* note 235, at 295–302; Copelon, *supra* note 251, at 322–23.

297. Thomas Grey notes the distinction between the civil rights and civil liberties perceptions of the personality: "The former tend to see the personality as more socially-constructed, hence socially destructible; the latter see it as more naturally self-reliant and autonomous"; T. Grey, "Civil Rights vs. Civil Liberties: The Case of Discriminatory Verbal Harassment," 1–2 (Mar. 1990; unpublished manuscript on file at the Harvard Law School Library); see also Colker, *supra* note 130, at 1019–21 (describing a group-based and individual-based concept of the "authentic self"). While relying on the right to individual autonomy, I am suggesting that the legal doctrine that protects it should adopt what Grey calls the civil rights perspective of personhood. This concept of autonomy protects the right to make certain choices but recognizes that choices are made in the context of a community and in relation to others; see T. Grey, *supra* at 1. I also recognize that the individual's personhood may be denied as a means of attacking the community as a whole and that the community's support may be necessary for nurturing the individual's personhood. I do not believe that the recognition of these connections between the individual and the community are inherently inconsistent with the notion of autonomy.

298. See Copelon, *supra* note 251, at 323. For a thorough critique of the prevailing conception of the Constitution as solely a charter of negative liberties, see Bandes, "The Negative Constitution: A Critique," 88 *Mich. L. Rev.*, 2271 (1990).

299. See, for example, *DeShaney v. Winnebago County Department of Social Services*, 489 U.S. 189, 196 (1989) ("[O]ur cases have recognized that the Due Process Clauses generally confer no affirmative right to governmental aid, even where such aid may be necessary to secure life, liberty, or property interests of which the government itself may not deprive the individual").

300. C. MacKinnon, *supra* note 19, at 96; see also Copelon, *supra* note 251, at 316 (observing the "sharp tension between the liberal idea of privacy as the negative and qualified right to be let alone as long as nothing too significant is at stake and the more radical idea of privacy as an affirmative liberty of self-determination and an aspect of equal personhood"); West, "Progressive and Conservative Constitutionalism," *supra* note 14, at 646–47 ("[P]rogressives tend to support an 'affirmative' understanding of the liberty protected by the due process clause of the fourteenth amendment . . . while conservatives read the clause as protecting 'negative liberty' only, i.e., the right to be free from certain defined interferences").

301. L. Tribe, *supra* note 164, § 15–2, at 1305.

302. Clearly, the affirmative guarantee of personhood and autonomy must have boundaries. We cannot expect the government to provide every means necessary to fulfill each individual's sense of identity. Moreover, increased government involvement in the processes of individual choice and self-determination may create new dangers. Finally, there may be advantages to using privacy doctrine to protect against the government's abuse of power and using other concepts, such as equality, to achieve more affirmative goals. It is beyond the scope of this article to explore all of the questions raised by the new privacy jurisprudence. My point here is to acknowledge the limitations of current privacy doctrine and to suggest the ingredients of a doctrine that overcomes them. Others have explored the scope of the positive role of government in correcting material inequalities; see, for example, Michelman, "The Supreme Court, 1968 Term—Foreword: On Protecting the Poor Through the Fourteenth Amendment," 83 *Harv. L. Rev.*, 7, 9–13 (1969) (proposing a vision of social justice in which citizens are entitled to "minimum protection against economic hazard"); Tribe, "Unraveling National League of Cities: The New Federalism and ffirmative Rights to Essential Government Services," 90 *Harv. L. Rev.*, 1065, 1090–96 (1977) (interpreting National League of Cities as a recognition of affirmative rights).

303. West, "Progressive and Conservative Constitutionalism," *supra* note 14, at 707.

304. The word "privacy" may be too imbued with limiting liberal interpretation to be a useful descriptive term. "Privacy" connotes shielding from intrusion and thus may be suitable to describe solely the negative proscription against government action. Moreover, the word conjures up the public-private dichotomy. "Liberty," on the other hand, has more potential to include the affirmative duty of government to ensure the conditions necessary for autonomy and self-definition. In reconstructing the constitutional guarantees I have been discussing, it may be more appropriate to rely on the broader concept of "liberty"; see A. Allen, *supra* note 160, at 98–101 (discussing the differences between "liberty" and "privacy").

305. In answering the Critical Legal Studies' critique of rights, Patricia Williams notes that oppression is the result not of "rights-assertion" but, rather, of a failure of "rights-commitment"; Williams, *supra* note 243, at 424. In the same way, the concepts of choice, personhood, and autonomy, which are central to privacy doctrine, are not inherently oppressive, any more than is the concept of equality (which has also been interpreted in ways that perpetuate hierarchy and domination). It is the "constricted referential universe" (*Id.* at 424) of liberal notions—such as negative rights, neutral principles, the public-private dichotomy, and formal equality—that have limited privacy's usefulness for attaining reproductive freedom; see Matsuda, "Looking to the Bottom: Critical Legal Studies and Reparations," 22 *Harv. C.R.-C.L. L. Rev.,* 323, 334–35 (1987) (demonstrating how women and people of color can adopt and transform constitutional text for radical objectives) [the essay is included in this volume—ED.].

306. See *supra* p. 1464.

307. I hear this false dichotomy in the words of Muskegon, Michigan, narcotics officer Al Van Hemert: "If the mother wants to smoke crack and kill herself, I don't care. . . . Let her die, but don't take that poor baby with her"; Hoffman, *supra* note 5, at 34.

꘠

SAPPHIRE BOUND!
Regina Austin

I. "WRITE-OUS" RESISTANCE

I GREW up thinking that "Sapphire" was merely a character on *Amos 'n' Andy,* a figment of a white man's racist, sexist comic imagination.[1] Little did I suspect that Sapphire was a more generally employed appellation for the stereotypical *Black Bitch*—tough, domineering, emasculating, strident, and shrill.[2] Sapphire is the sort of person you look at and wonder how she can possibly stand herself. All she does is complain. Why doesn't that woman shut up?

Black bitch hunts are alive and well in the territory where minority female law faculty labor. There are so many things to get riled about that keeping quiet is impossible. We really cannot function effectively without coming to terms with Sapphire. Should we renounce her, rehabilitate her, or embrace her and proclaim her our own?

I think the time has come for us to get truly hysterical, to take on the role of "professional Sapphires" in a forthright way, to declare that we are serious about ourselves, and to capture some of the intellectual power and resources that are necessary to combat the systematic denigration of minority women. It is time for Sapphire to testify on her own behalf, in writing, complete with footnotes.

"To testify" means several different things in this context: to present the facts, to attest to their accuracy, and to profess a personal belief or conviction. The minority feminist legal scholar must be a witness in each of these senses. She must document the material legal existences of minority women. Her work should explore their concrete problems and needs, many of which are invisible even to minority lawyers because of gender and class differences. Moreover, a synthesis of the values, traditions, and codes that bind women of the same minority group to one another and fuel their collective struggle is crucial to the enterprise. The intellectual product of the minority feminist scholar should incorporate in a formal fashion the ethical and moral consciousnesses of minority women, their aspirations, and their quest for liberation. Her partisanship and advocacy of a minority feminist jurisprudence should be frankly acknowledged and energetically defended. Because her scholarship is to be grounded in the material and ideological realities of minority women and in their cultural and political responses, its operative premises must necessarily be dynamic and primarily immanent; as the lives of minority women change, so too should the analysis.

Finally, the experiential is not to be abandoned by the minority female legal scholar. She must be guided by her life, instincts, sensibility, and politics. The voice and vision reflected in her work should contain something of the essence of the culture she has lived and learned; imagine, if you can, writing a law review article embodying the spontaneity of jazz, the earthiness of the blues, or the vibrancy of salsa.

I have given some thought to the tenets that a black feminist or "womanish" legal jurisprudence might pursue or embrace. We must write with an empowered and empowering voice. The chief sources of our theory should be black women's critiques of a society that is dominated by and structured to favor white men of wealth and power. We should also find inspiration in the modes of resistance which black women mount, individually and collectively, on a daily basis in response to discrimination and exploitation. Our jurisprudence should amplify the criticism and lend clarity and visibility to the positive, transformative cultural parries that are overlooked unless close attention is given to the actual struggles of black women. In addition, our jurisprudence should create enough static to interfere with the transmission of the dominant ideology and jam the messages that reduce our indignation, limit our activism, misdirect our energies, and otherwise make us the (re)producers of our own subordination. By way of an alternative, a black feminist jurisprudence should preach the justness of the direct, participatory, grassroots opposition black women undertake despite enormous material and structural constraints.

The mechanics of undertaking a research project based on the concrete material and legal problems of black women are daunting.

The problems these projects involve are difficult because they do not begin with a case and will not necessarily end with a new rule. The world with which many legal scholars deal is that found within the four corners of judicial opinions. If the decisions and the rubrics they apply pay no attention to race, sex, and class—and insurance and malpractice cases generally do not—then the material conditions of minority females are nowhere to be found, and the legal aspects of the difficulties these conditions cause are nearly impossible to address as a matter of scholarly inquiry. It is thus imperative that we find a way to portray, almost construct for a legal audience, the contemporary reality of the disparate groups of minority women about whom we write. We really cannot do this without undertaking field research or adopting an interdisciplinary approach, relying on the empirical and ethnographic research of others. The latter route is the one that I have taken in this article and elsewhere.[3]

Implementation of an agenda for black feminist legal scholarship, and the expanded study of the legal status of minority women in general, will require the right sort of environmental conditions, such as receptive or at least tolerant nonminority publishers and a network of established academics engaged in similar pursuits. We minority female scholars must devote a bit of our sass to touting the importance of the perspective of minority women and the significance of their concerns to any list of acceptable law review topics. If anyone asks you to talk or write about anything related to your race or your sex, turn the opportunity into one for exploring the legal concerns of women of color.

II. A Sapphire Named Crystal

THE task of articulating and advancing distinctive minority feminist jurisprudential stances will become easier as those of us interested in the status of minority women be-

gin to analyze concrete cases and legal problems. To substantiate my point that a black
feminist perspective can and must be manifest,
I have attempted to apply the rough, tentative
thesis I advance above to the examination of a
particular decision, *Chambers v. Omaha Girls
Club.*[4]

The plaintiff, Crystal Chambers, was employed by the defendant Girls Club of Omaha
as an arts and crafts instructor at a facility
where approximately 90 percent of the program
participants were black. Two years later, Chambers, an unmarried black woman in her early
twenties, was discharged from her job when she
became pregnant. Her dismissal was justified by
the club's so-called "negative role model rule,"
which provided for the immediate discharge of
staff guilty of "[n]egative role modeling for
Girls Club Members" including "such things as
single parent pregnancies."[5]

In her lawsuit, Chambers attacked the role
model rule on several grounds. In her Title VII
claims, for example, she maintained that the
rule would have a disparate impact on black
women because of their significantly higher fertility rate. She further asserted that her discharge constituted per se sex discrimination
barred by the Pregnancy Discrimination Act of
1978. Although soundness of these arguments
was acknowledged, they were effectively countered by the business necessity[6] and the bona
fide occupational qualification of defenses.[7]

The district court ruled against Crystal
Chambers because it concluded that the club's
role model rule was the product of its dedication
to the goal of "helping young girls reach their
fullest potential."[8] Programmatic concerns provided adequate support for the rule. According
to the findings, the club's activities were characterized by a "high staff to member ratio," "extensive contact" and "close relationships" between the staff and members, and an "open,
comfortable atmosphere." Thus, "model" behavior by the staff and imitation by the members were essential to the club's agenda:

> Those closely associated with the Girls Club con-
> tend that because of the unique nature of the
> Girls Club's operations, each activity, formal or
> informal, is premised upon the belief that the girls

will or do emulate, at least in part, the behavior of
staff personnel. Each staff member is trained and
expected to act as a role model and is required, as
a matter of policy, to be committed to the Girls
Club philosophies so that the messages of the
Girls Club can be conveyed with credibility.

The club's goal was to expose its members
"to the greatest number of available positive
options in life"; "teenage pregnancy [was] contrary to this purpose and philosophy," because
it "severely limit[s] the available opportunities
for teenage girls." Citing plaintiff's expert, the
court stated that "[t]eenage pregnancy often
deprives young women of educational, social
and occupational opportunities, creating serious
problems for both the family and society."[9]
The club had several programs that related to
pregnancy prevention.

In the opinion of the district court, the club
"established that it honestly believed that to
permit single pregnant staff members to work
with the girls would convey the impression that
the Girls Club condoned pregnancy for the
girls in the age group it serves."[10] Furthermore,
"[w]hile a single pregnant working woman may,
indeed, provide a good example of hard work
and independence, the same person may be a
negative role model with respect to the Girls
Club objective of diminishing the number of
teenage pregnancies."[11] The club pointed to
the reaction of two members to the earlier
pregnancies of other single staffers in accounting for the genesis of the rule. In one case, a
member who stated "that she wanted to have a
baby as cute" as that of a staff member became
pregnant shortly thereafter; in the second, a
member became upset upon hearing of the
pregnancy of an unmarried staff member.

As painted by the court, there were numerous
indications that the operative animus behind
the role model rule was paternalistic, not racist
or sexist. The North Omaha facility was "purposefully located to better serve a primarily
black population."[12] Although the club's principal administrators were white, the girls served
were black, the staff was black, and Crystal
Chamber's replacements were black; "sensitivity" was shown to the problems of the staff
members, including those who were black,

pregnant, and unmarried. Plaintiff was even offered help in finding other employment after she was fired.

The district court concluded its opinion as follows:

> This Court believes that the policy is a legitimate attempt by a private service organization to attack a significant problem within our society. The evidence has shown that the Girls Club did not intentionally discriminate against the plaintiff and that the policy is related to the Girls Club's central purpose of fostering growth and maturity of young girls. . . . The Court emphasizes, however, that this decision is based upon the unique mission of the Girls Club of Omaha, the age group of the young women served, the geographic locations of the Girls Club facilities, and the comprehensive and historical methods the organization has employed in addressing the problem of teenage pregnancy.[13]

There were dissenting views among the Eighth Circuit judges who considered the case. In opposing the judgment in the club's favor, Judge McMillian demanded hard evidence to support the legality of the negative role model rule:

> Neither an employer's sincere belief, without more, nor a district court's belief, that a discriminatory employment practice is related to and necessary for the accomplishments of the employer's goals is sufficient to establish a (BFOQ) or business necessity defense. The fact that the goals are laudable and the beliefs sincerely held does not substitute for data that demonstrate a relationship between the discriminatory practice and the goals.

A.

For those who have no understanding of the historical oppression of black women and no appreciation of the diversity of their contemporary cultural practices, the outcome of *Chambers* might have a certain policy appeal, one born of sympathy for poor black youngsters and desperation about stemming "the epidemic" of teenage pregnancy that plagues them. According to such an assessment, the club's hope that its members could be influenced by committed counselors who, by example, would prove that life offers more attractive alternatives than early pregnancy and single parenthood was at worst benign, if it was not benevolent.

However, for better informed, more critical evaluators, the opinions are profoundly disturbing. Firing a young, unmarried, pregnant black worker in the name of protecting other young black females from the limited options associated with early and unwed motherhood is ironic, to say the least. The club managed to replicate the very economic hardships and social biases that, according to the district court, made the role model rule necessary in the first place. Crystal Chambers was not much older than some of the club members, and her financial and social status after being fired was probably not that much different from what the members would face if they became pregnant at an early age, without the benefit of a job or the assistance of a fully employed helpmate. On the other hand, she was in many respects better off than many teen mothers: she was in her early twenties and had a decent job. Chambers's condition became problematic because of the enforcement of the role model rule.

The material consequences that befell Chambers—which plague other black women who have children despite their supposed role modeling responsibilities—are not inherent byproducts of single pregnancy and motherhood. The condemnation and the economic hardships that follow in its wake are politically and socially contingent. Furthermore, they are not the product of a consensus that holds across race, sex, and class boundaries.

Implicit in the *Chambers* decision is an assumption that the actual cultural practices and articulated moral positions of the black females who know the struggles of early and single motherhood firsthand are both misguided and destructive. The older women are apparently so outrageous that they represent a grave threat to their own daughters. Yet, for some of us, their portrayal in the *Chambers* opinions is more flattering than the authors intended. Grounded in a culture that turns "bad" (pronounced "baaad") on its head and declares as wily, audacious, and good all conduct that offends the white, male, and middle-class establishments, a black feminist scholar has to wonder whether the villainous black women one discerns lurking in the interstices of the opinions are not doing

something right. A black feminist jurisprudential analysis of *Chambers* must seriously consider
the possibility that young, single, sexually active,
fertile, and nurturing black women are being
viewed ominously because they have the temerity to attempt to break out of the rigid economic, social, and political categories that a
racist, sexist, and the class-stratified society
would impose upon them.

Although the outcome hinged upon it, the
opinions are awfully vague about the adverse
effect that continued employment of an unmarried pregnant arts and crafts instructor would
have had in promoting teenage pregnancy
among the young black club members. I want
to suggest a few possible relationships whose
plausibility is attributable to a deep suspicion of
black women's sexuality and an intense desire
to control their "excessive" promiscuity and fe-
cundity. The first is reminiscent of a bad joke.
The club and the courts conceivably subscribe
to a theory of reproduction—one that can only
be termed "primitive"—which posits that simply seeing an unmarried pregnant woman can
have such a powerful impact on adolescent
females that they will be moved to imitate her
by becoming pregnant themselves.[14] If the girls
are poor, and they and the woman are black,
such a hypothesis might be given credence in
some quarters. Under it, Crystal Chambers's
mere pregnant presence at the club would be
considered a corrupting influence in light of the
club's goals. Surely, the club and the courts do
not believe that black teenage pregnancy is the
product of social voyeurism or a female variant
of "reckless eyeballing."[15]

It is more likely that unmarried, pregnant
Crystal was thought to be a problem because
she functioned as an icon, a reminder of a
powerful culture from which the club members
had to be rescued. The club was supposed to be
a wholesome haven where young black girls
would be introduced to an alternative array of
positive life choices. Crystal Chambers tainted
the environment by introducing into it the
messy, corrupting cultural orientations that
were the target of the club's "repress and replace" mission.

There is a widespread belief that poor black

women who raise children alone in socially
and economically isolated enclaves encourage
teenage pregnancy by example, subsidize it
through informal friendship and extended
family networks, and justify it by prizing motherhood, devaluing marriage, and condoning
welfare dependency. Operating on similar assumptions, the club set about exposing (literally,
it seems) its young members to counterimages
that would act as antidotes to the messages
they absorbed at home. In a newspaper story
concerning Chambers's lawsuit, the attorney for
the club stated that while there was no intent
"to condemn any parent of these girls or any of
the parent's life decisions," the club did undertake to introduce the young members to alternatives that were different from those of the
"girl's home life."[16] The attorney continued,
"We're trying to say that at age 14, girls aren't
necessarily emotionally mature enough to make
the decision to voluntarily get pregnant. Their
parents may have been."[17] The *Omaha World-
Herald* ran an editorial in support of the firing
which continued the theme. The editorial
states: "The absence of strong family structures
among many poor blacks has long been identified as a major obstacle to blacks' entering
the mainstream. A high rate of out-of-wedlock
pregnancies among poor blacks contributes
both to the perpetuation of the poverty cycle
and to the weakness of families caught in that
cycle."

The editorial further argues that if, as Crystal
Chambers asserted, "half the girls at the club
have mothers who aren't married," then that is
"one of the reasons the dismissal policy makes
sense."[18]

This assessment of the danger posed by the
ranks of mothers which Crystal was about to
join attributes to black teenagers a level of
passivity not often associated with adolescence.
Looking to their parent's cultural orientations
to explain teenage pregnancy may be giving the
teens too little credit for attempting to shape
the course of their own lives. It also attributes
too much power to parents whose economic and
social standing renders them impotent to control
either their children's life chances or lives.

Furthermore, the club's conduct is indicative

of the way in which the battle to curb black teenage pregnancy via the use of role models has become a pretext for continuing and expanding the economic and ideological war on unwed black mothers. This emphasis on the impact on teenage pregnancy of single middle-class role models who opt to have children furnishes continued opportunity to add a new twist to the historical efforts to ridicule and control black women's sexuality and reproduction.

Although Crystal Chambers's firing was publicly justified on the ground that she would have an adverse impact on the young club members, it is likely that the club sacked her in part because she resisted its effort to model her in conformity with white and middle-class morality. In its struggles against the culture of the girls' mothers, Chambers, employee and instructor, was supposed to be on the club's side. Like a treasonous recruit, though, she turned up unmarried and pregnant: as such, she embodied the enemy. If the club could not succeed in shaping and restraining the workers whose economic welfare it controlled, how could it expect to win over the young members and supplant their mothers' cultural legacy. The requirement that one allow oneself to be modeled in order to keep one's job is not limited to blacks who are young fertile females. To a certain extent, the trouble that Crystal Chambers encountered is a generic infliction suffered by black role models of both sexes and all ages who reject the part and become rebellious renegades or traitors to the cause of black cultural containment. In sum, then, faulty conceptions of "role modeling" lie at the heart of the policy basis of the *Chambers* decision.

In this article, I explore the contemporary effort to control the sexual and reproductive freedom of those single black mothers who are said to be role models by blaming them for increased black teenage pregnancy. I explore parallels between the parts that "model" black women are supposed to play and historical stereotypes of black females as workers and sexual beings. I then go on to question the propriety of blacks' accepting the guise of model assimilationists.

Aside from the occasional piece that accuses black adolescents of absolute perversity,[19] news accounts and academic literature generally portray black teens who are pregnant or already parents as pursuing private, ad hoc solutions to pervasive systemic economic and political powerlessness. Teenage pregnancy is the product of the complex interaction not only of culture and individual adjustment but also of material conditions that present black teens with formidable obstacles to survival and success. Black adolescents whose families are of low socioeconomic status are at greater risk of becoming teenage mothers than their middle- and upper-class peers.[20] Teenage pregnancy is correlated with the lack of success these black adolescents experience in dealing with institutions that should provide them with an entrée to the society beyond the confines of their communities. Blame for black teenage pregnancy must be shared by an educational system that fails to provide black youngsters with either the desire or the chance to attend college,[21] a labor market that denies them employment that will supply the economic indicia of adulthood,[22] and a health care system that does not deliver adequate birth control, abortion, or family planning services.[23]

The impact of these structural factors does not make the problems constricting the lives of black adolescents entirely beyond their locus of control, however. The cultures of poor young blacks play a role in the reproduction of their material hardship; their cultures also have strengths and virtues. Yet even persons sympathetic to black females like the club members, their mothers, and Crystal Chambers may have a hard time identifying anything positive and liberating about the modes and mores that produce black teen pregnancy and single motherhood. The need to highlight the affirmative while conceding the negative is quite pressing. "Strong and complex identification with one's culture and community is necessary not only for survival but for a positive sense of self, and for the making of an involved and active community member."[24] To be efficacious, that identification must be critical of all the elements that prevent black teens from improving their economic, social, and political circumstances. To the extent that it is, it deserves affirmation from sympathetic supporters. In addition, it is imperative that those who broadly denigrate poor young black mothers be engaged in debate. A critical perspective held by the mothers themselves would provide the strongest possible basis for a counterattack.

The condemnation of black unwed motherhood is so deeply embedded in mainstream thought that its invocation in connection with teenage pregnancy may be considered uncontroversial. Single black mothers get blamed for so much that there is little reason not to blame them for teenage pregnancy as well.

At bottom, unmarried black women workers who have babies are being accused of carrying on like modern-day Jezebels when they should be acting like good revisionist Mammies. Though not totally divorced from reality, Jezebel and Mammy were largely ideological constructs that supported slavery. Each pertained to black female slaves' intertwined roles as sexual beings and workers. Each justified the economic and sexual exploitation of black female slaves by reference to their character traits rather than to the purposes of the masters. Jezebel was the wanton, libidinous black woman whose easy ways excused white men's abuse of their slaves as sexual "partners" and bearers of mulatto offspring.[25] Jezebel was both "free of the social constraints that surrounded the sexuality of white women," to whom she represented a threat, and "isolated from the men of her own community."[26]

In contrast, Mammy was "asexual," "maternal," and "deeply religious."[27] Her principal tasks were caring for the master's children and running the household.[28] Mammy was said to be so enamored of her white charges that she placed their welfare above that of her own children.[29] She was "the perfect slave—a loyal, faithful, contented, efficient, conscientious member of the family who always knew her place; and she gave the slaves a white-approved standard of black behavior."[30] She was "the personification of the ideal slave, and the ideal woman. . . . An ideal symbol of the patriarchal tradition. She was not just a product of the

'cultural uplift' theory," which touted slavery as a means of civilizing blacks, "but she was also a product of the forces that in the South raised motherhood to sainthood."[31]

Commentators have emphasized the negative implications of the Mammy stereotype. Elizabeth Fox-Genovese writes:

> If implicitly the idea of the Mammy referred to motherhood and reproduction, it also claimed those privileges for the masters rather than for the slaves themselves. Just as Buck signaled the threat [to] master-slave relations, Mammy signaled the wish for organic harmony and projected a woman who suckled and reared white masters. The image displaced sexuality into nurture and transformed potential hostility into sustenance and love. It claimed for the white family the ultimate devotion of black women, who reared the children of others as if they were their own. Although the image of the Mammy echoed the importance that black slaves attached to women's roles as mothers, it derived more from the concerns of the master than from those of the slave.[32]

bell hooks sounds a similar theme:

> The mammy image was portrayed with affection by whites because it epitomized the ultimate sexist-racist vision of ideal black womanhood—complete submission to the will of whites. In a sense whites created in the mammy figure a black woman who embodied solely those characteristics they as colonizers wished to exploit. They saw her as the embodiment of woman as passive nurturer, a mother figure who gave all without expectation of return, who not only acknowledged her inferiority to whites but who loved them.[33]

The critique of the images of black women which whites have historically promoted is relevant to the assessment of the treatment accorded contemporary role models. Role models are supposed to forgo the vices of Jezebel and exhibit the many virtues of Mammy. The case of Crystal Chambers illustrates this quite well: when she refused to subordinate her interest in motherhood to the supposed welfare of the club girls, she essentially rejected the club's attempt to impose upon her the "positive" stereotype of the black female as a repressed, self-sacrificing, nurturing woman whose heart extends to other people's children because she cannot (or should not) have kids of her own. Instead, like a Jezebel, Crystal Chambers "flaunted" her sexuality and reproductive capacity, but, unlike her counterpart in slavery, she did so in furtherance of her own ends, in defiance of her white employers, and in disregard of a rule that forbade her from connecting with a man outside of the marriage relationship.

As if to resemble the role model that Fox-Genovese says Mammy could have been, Chambers was supposed to expose the young club members, the beneficiaries of white benevolence, to images congruent with traditional notions of patriarchy which were not entirely consistent with the norms of the black community. She was supposed to be an accomplice in regulating the sexuality of other young black females, in much the same way that she was expected to tolerate the regulation of her own. The courts would have us believe that the club acted for the good of the girls who would miss out on a host of opportunities if they became teen mothers—yet the distinction between paternalism and oppression is hardly crisper now than it was during slavery. It may be that the young women of the club set are not fully informed that there is an increasing demand for their labor and are misreading the material landscape. On the other hand, they could be well informed and reaching more negative assessments of their actual economic prospects. If their options are indeed no greater than they imagine, the effort to repress their fertility may stem from its being dysfunctional for the larger society. Declining to live out the myth of the modern Mammy, Crystal Chambers refused to accept the yoke of paternalism or of oppression for herself and thereby freed the club girls, to a small extent, from manipulation of their productive and reproductive capacities. She then became valueless to her employers and was, in essence, expelled from the big house and returned to the field.

Breaking the hold of ideological shackles that have restricted black women's sexuality and fertility will not be easy. Hortense Spillers, a black female literary critic, has argued that "sexual experience among black people . . . is so boundlessly imagined that it loses meaning and becomes, quite simply, a medium through which the individual is suspended."[34] Jezebel and Mammy, harlot and nun, "whore" and "eunuch" have "acquire[d] mystical attribution . . . divested of specific reference and dispersed over time and space in blind disregard for the particular agents on which it lands."[35] Spillers likens this process to a mugging.[36] She challenges feminist literary critics to find words that embody "differentiated responsiveness,"[37] words that enable us "to imagine women in their living and pluralistic confrontation with experience."[38] Her charge is equally relevant to black feminist jurisprudes.

Some of the black women who are not married yet have babies may be young and wise; others may be poor and brave; and yet a third group may be rich and selfish. Whether they confirm or confound the stereotypes, all of them deserve a measure of freedom with regard to their sexuality that the dominant culture withholds. All of them have the potential for being guerrilla fighters in a war that is being waged on three fronts. Struggles to control sexual expression and reproduction pit the combined hegemonic power of whites, males, and the middle class against overlapping constituencies of women, people of color, and ordinary working folks. Black values regarding individual family formation and parenthood decisions, as befits a community under siege, should facilitate, not interfere with, the critical vision that promotes the "seeing that negotiates at every point a space for living."[39] In other words, black women who attempt to express their sexuality and control their reproduction should not have to travel through a minefield of stereotypes, clichés, and material hardships with the handicap of a restriction that they keep to the right. Black women must be permitted to exercise their judgments without fear of reprisals from patriarchal, bourgeois, and culturally repressive elements within the black community.

There are significant norms that bind and cage a basis for a community of concern among black men and women of various classes and outlooks. They support an agenda of systemic changes to strengthen minority families. Thus, economic resources should be available to both black men and black women who want to maintain families with children. Black teenagers of both sexes should be given the means and the support required to delay parenthood until the time is best for them. Everybody else should be allowed to do what they want to do, with the admonition that they give their offspring the advantages of the prenatal care, schools, and health programs that an ethical society would make available to assure its future.

B.

It is hard to think of Crystal Chambers, arts and crafts instructor, as a role model, as powerless and vulnerable as she ultimately proved to be. Her skills and natural behavior were not particularly valued by the people running the club. Rather than being a role model by virtue of doing her job and living her own life, Chambers was supposed to perform the role of model, play a part that was not of her own design. She was a model in the sense that a model is "something made in a pliable material ([such] as clay or wax) [that is] intended to serve as a pattern of an object or figure to be made in a more permanent material."[40] When she deviated from the club's philosophy and engaged in a practice that was common to the community of black women from which she and the members came, she was fired.

Chambers's experience is emblematic of the political significance of the professional "black role model" (including many of us lawyers and law professors) in this, the post–civil rights, post–black power era.[41] Blacks are deluged with role models. Our attention is constantly being directed to some black person who is, should, or wants to be a role model for others.[42] Many of these role models are black people who have achieved stature and power in the white world because they supposedly represent the interests of the entire black community. Such role models gain capital (literally and figuratively) to the extent that they project an assimilated persona that is as unthreatening to white people as it is (supposed to be) intriguing to our young. They become embodiments of the liberal image of "the successful Negro" with perhaps a bit of "cutup"[43] thrown in to keep them credible. By their sheer visibility, they are of service to those left behind: they are functionally useful in pro-

viding images for emulation, and their legitimacy should be unquestioned. Because the emphasis on role modeling suggests that motivation and aspirations are the cure for the problems of poor minority people, those who accept the appellation "role model" help to contain demands from below for further structural changes and thereby assist in the management of other blacks. Insofar as doing more for the poor is concerned, the service that role models perform is regrettably distinguishable from mentoring or power brokering: role models really do not have very much clout to wield on behalf of other blacks, racial and sexual discrimination and exploitation being what they are.

There are conceptions of "role modeling" that are not quite so alien to the political and cultural heritage of African-American women.[44] As far as I am concerned, Crystal Chambers became more nearly a role model when she fought back, when she became a Sapphire. Her legal protest brought the club's contempt for the values of the population it served into the open. Her behavior and her lawsuit challenged the hegemony of the club's white, patriarchal, and middle-class orientation. Her single motherhood represented an alternative social form that one might choose deliberately, rationally, and proudly. She made manifest the critique that is "life as it is lived" by ordinary black single mothers. Refusing to go along with the program, she joined the host of nonelite black women who every day mount local, small-scale resistance grounded in indigenous cultural values—values whose real political potential is often hidden even from those whose lives they govern.

Nonetheless, there are times when low-volume defiance must give way to all-out "mouthing off." Crystal Chambers's rebellion was ended not because Title VII doctrine could not be manipulated in her favor but because the presiding judges did not respect her normative framework. Her position should have been "out there," vocalized affirmatively, coherently, and vehemently by black women and others before she got to court. History suggests that black people's recourse to conventional warfare on the legal terrain proceeds more smoothly when the positions underlying their claims of entitlement have achieved some positive visibility via skirmishes in the cultural and political domains. Of course, concrete legal cases that prove to be losing efforts may nonetheless provide an opportunity for lawyers and law professors to get their acts together, to engage the enemy, and to refine their arguments. Although the front line may remain in a distant realm, ideas do percolate from one sphere to another, and those of us who are daring may move about as well. Next time we should all be better prepared.

III. FOR KANTI AND ASIA AND FATIMA ... AND RUTH [45] (Which Is to Say, Sapphires by Another Name)

BACK in the sixties, when Aretha Franklin demanded respect ("R-E-S-P-E-C-T") [46] and admonished her listeners to "think about what you're trying to do me," [47] black people knew she was talking to white America. Times have changed. In 1988, vocal innovator Bobby McFerrin ambiguously sings "Don't Worry, Be Happy" with a Caribbean lilt, [48] and the Bush-Quayle campaign tries to steal the song for its anthem. [49] Somewhere along the line, we lost confidence in the political efficacy of cultural critique as a basis for the continuing struggle for black liberation. Perhaps we came to doubt the propriety of our distinctive cultural production, [50] or we foolishly thought that we would be better off if we dispensed with social protest for a while and just relied on the law.

Poor black women have especially suffered as a result. Their enemies have entrapped them in a quagmire of soft variables by challenging their morals and chiding them for looking to the government for relief from economic hardship instead of relying on individual initiative and self-help. The nonsense has deflected attention from the fact that their material circumstances have eroded. [51]

The reign of President Reagan was blessed with unusual legal and political quiescence among black women, but the signs of dissent are there. I have often wondered why black women give their daughters the names they do. Names like Kanti, Asia, Fatima, Rashiah,

Tamika, Latoya, Chauntel, Ebony, and DaJuvetta (for David). [52] The mothers, in naming them, and the girls, in being so named, share a bond with other distinctively named black women—a bond that extends backward in time to slavery. Desperation born of material and political powerlessness may be operating here. Perhaps the mothers are trying to give to their daughters a mark of distinction that will otherwise be denied them because they are black and female. Uncommon names can generate hostility that can be a severe handicap. I like to think that the names are in part an expression of group solidarity and self-affirmation, and not the by-product of the mothers' unfamiliarity with and isolation from the dominant culture. Whether the naming practices represent a tactic of opposition, a critique of a society that typically chooses to call its female children Ashley, Jessica, Amanda, and the like, and a form of cultural resistance, I do not know. The possibility should be fully explored. It is my fondest hope, however, that whatever their mothers' motivations, the little black girls will grow up to see the positive potential of what their mothers did and relish being Sapphires by another name.

NOTES

1. R. Chapman, ed., *New Dictionary of American Slang*, 368 (1986). *Amos 'n' Andy* originated as a radio comedy program about two black males; B. Andrews and A. Juilliard, *Holy Mackerel! The* Amos 'n' Andy *Story*, 15–16 (1986). It was first broadcast in 1928, and the characters were played by the program's white originators; *id. Amos 'n' Andy* came to CBS television in 1951 (*id.* at 60–61) with a cast of carefully chosen black actors; *id.* at 45–59. Various black civil rights organizations condemned the television version as "insulting to blacks" and as portraying blacks "in a stereotyped and derogatory manner." The sponsor withdrew from the show, and it was dropped by the network in 1953; *id.* at 61, 101. It lived on in syndication until 1966; *id.* at 118, 121–22.

Several of my contemporaries who watched *Amos 'n' Andy* have told me that they considered Sapphire a sympathetic character, the justifiably exasperated spouse of a trifling husband. Their comments suggest the potential for subversive interpretations of mass cultural forms.

2. b. hooks, *Ain't I a Woman: Black Women and Feminism*, 85–86 (1981); Scott, "Debunking Sapphire: Toward a Nonracist and Non-sexist Social Science," in G. Hull, P. Scott,

and B. Smith, eds., *All the Women Are White, All the Blacks Are Men, but Some of Us Are Brave,* 85 (1982).

3. See Austin, "Employer Abuse, Worker Resistance, and the Tort of Intentional Infliction of Emotional Distress," 41 *Stan L. Rev.,* 1 (1988).

4. 629 F. Supp. 925 (D.Neb. 1986), aff'd, 834 F.2d 697 (8th Cir. 1987), reh'g denied, 840 F.2d 583 (1988).

5. 834 F.2d at 699 n. 2.

6. 834 F.2nd at 701–3. The burden of persuasion with regard to this defense is now clearly on the Title VII claimant; *Wards Cove Packing Co. v. Atonio,* 57 U.S.L.W. 4583 (U.S. June 5, 1989).

7. 834 F.2d at 703–5.

8. 629 F. Supp. at 943.

9. *Id.* at 928–29.

10. *Id.* at 950.

11. *Id.* at 951.

12. *Id.* at 934.

13. *Id.* at 951–52.

14. See *supra* text accompanying note 11.

15. I. Reed, *Reckless Eyeballing* (1986). In Reed's novel, the term refers to the offense committed by a black man who "stares at a white woman too long"; *id.* at 25. In *Ponton v. Newport News School Board,* 632 F.Supp. 1056 (E.D. Va. 1986), the court rejected the notion that "the mere sight of an unmarried, pregnant teacher would have a sufficiently undesirable influence on schoolchildren to justify excluding the teacher from the classroom"; *id.* at 1062. The court in *Ponton,* however, assumed that the plaintiff's students would not be close enough to her to know her marital status and that her single pregnancy would not interfere with her ability to teach the prescribed curriculum; *id.* at 1062–63.

16. "Unwed Mothers Challenge Firing at Omaha Girls Club," *Omaha World-Herald* (Dec. 1, 1982), 1:1.

17. *Id.*

18. "Dismissal of Two Girls Club Staffers Was Logical", *Omaha World-Herald,* Dec. 11, 1982, at 20, col. 1.

19. See Read, "For Poor Teen-agers, Pregnancies Become New Rite of Passage," *Wall Street J.* (Mar. 17, 1988), 1.1:1.

20. See Hogan and Kitagawa, "The Impact of Social Status, Family Structure, and Neighborhood on the Fertility of Black Adolescents," 90 *Am. J. Soc.,* 825, 846 (1985); A. Abrahamse, P. Morrison, and L. Waite, *Beyond Stereotypes: Who Becomes a Single Teenage Mother,* 57–60 (1988).

21. A study conducted by the Rand Corporation found that "the presence of college plans inhibits single childbearing for blacks by nearly 10 percentage points . . . the strong-

est [effect] . . . measured"; A. Abrahmase, P. Morrison, and L. Waite, *supra* note 20, at 62. See also K. Moore, M. Simms, and C. Betsey, *Choice and Circumstance: Racial Differences in Adolescent Sexuality and Fertility,* xii-xiii, 67–86 (1986) (suggesting that desperately low educational goals are not a significant factor affecting black fertility, although frustration in fulfilling them might be).

22. There is little statistical data concerning the correlation between unemployment and rates of black teenage pregnancy; see K. Moore, M. Simms, and C. Betsey, *supra* note 21, at 87–101. Interview accounts, however, suggest that the inability to procure employment motivates teens, particularly males, to prove their maturity through the conception of children; see *id.* at 90; D. Frank, *Deep Blue Funk and Other Stories: Portraits of Teenage Parents,* 11, 158 (1983); Anderson, "Sex Codes and Family Life among Poor Inner-City Youths," *Annals* (Jan. 1989), 59, 77.

23. See K. Moore, M. Simms, and C. Betsey, *supra* note 21, at 58–59, 62–64; L. Schorr, *Within Our Reach: Breaking the Cycle of Disadvantage,* 40–55 (1988).

24. Fine and Zane, "Bein' Wrapped Too Tight: When Low Income Women Drop Out of High School," in L. Weis, ed., *Dropouts from Schools: Issues, Dilemmas and Solutions* (forthcoming 1989).

25. D. White, *Ar'n't I a Woman? Female Slaves in the Plantation South,* 46, 61 (1985).

26. E. Fox-Genovese, *Within the Plantation Household: Black and White Women of the Old South,* 292 (1988).

27. D. White, *supra* note 25, at 46.

28. E. Genovese, *Roll, Jordan, Roll: The World the Slaves Made,* 353–56 (1972).

29. See *id.* at 356–57 (suggesting that mammies' regard for their masters' children was of strategic significance to their own families).

30. *Id.* at 356.

31. D. White, *supra* note 25, at 58.

32. E. Fox-Genovese, *supra* note 26, at 291–92.

33. b. hooks, *supra* note 2, at 84–85.

34. Spillers, "Interstices: A Small Drama of Words," in *Pleasure and Danger: Exploring Female Sexuality* 73, 85 (C. Vance ed. 1984).

35. *Id.* at 94–95.

36. *Id.* at 95.

37. *Id.*

38. *Id.* at 94.

39. *Id.* at 84.

40. WEBSTER'S THIRD NEW INTERNATIONAL DICTIONARY 1451 (1981).

41. *See generally* Reed, "The 'Black Revolution' and the Reconstitution of Domination", in *Race, Politics, and Culture: Critical Essays on the Radicalism of the 1960's* at 61 (A. Reed ed. 1986).

42. *See, e.g.,* B. REYNOLDS, AND STILL WE RISE: INTERVIEWS WITH 50 BLACKS ROLE MODELS (1988); Raspberry, *"No-Choice" Role-Models Can Be Countered,* Chic. Trib., Oct. 27, 1987, § 1, at 21, col. 2; Arnold & Pristin, *The Rise and Fall of Maxine Thomas,* L.A. Times, May 6, 1988, § 2, at 1, col. 2; Hofman, *Ebony Fashion Fair Raises $15,000 for Black Actors Theatre,* L.A. Times, Apr. 14, 1988, § 9, at 4, col. 2 (Orange Cty, ed.) (theatre group and fashion show "gives audiences a chance to see more blakc role models").

43. "Outspolen" and "militant" are the terms usually employed to described vocal elite champions of the causes of the black masses.

44. *See* Gilkes, *Successful Rebellious Professionals: The Black Woman's Professional Identity and Community Commitment,* 6 PSYCHOLOGY OF WOMEN Q. 289 (1982).

45. Kanti is graduating from high school in Washington, D.C. Asia and Fatima are among the apples of their grandmother's eye. Ruth is the daughter of Crystal Chambers, 629 F.Supp. at 929 n.6.

46. A. Franklin, "Respect," on *Aretha's Gold* slide 1, track 3 (1969).

47. A. FRANKLIN, *Think, on* ARETHA'S GOLD, *supra* note 46, at side 2, track 3; *see also A.* FRANKLIN, *Think (1989),* on THROUGH THE STORM side 2, track 2 (1989).

48. B. McFERRIN, *Don't Worry, Be Happy,* on SIMPLE PLEASURES side 1, track 1 (1988).

49. Philadelphia Inquirer, Oct. 23, 1988, at 3A, col. 3.

50. I use the term expansively. It includes "the collective, creative use of discourses, meanings, materials, practices and group processes to explore, understand and creatively occupy particular positions, relations and sets of material possibilities." Willis, *supra* note 107, at 114.

51. See Simms, "Black Women Who Head Families: An Economic Struggle"; in *Slipping Through the Cracks: The Status of Black Women 141,* 143–148 (M. Simms and J. Malveaux eds. 1986).

52. *See* J. McGregory, Aareck to Zsaneka: African American Names in an Urban Community, 1945–1980 (1985) (master's thesis, Cornell University).

Part Seven

RACE AND POSTMODERNISM

Seven

RACE AND POSTMODERNISM

The essays in this concluding chapter are linked by a shared, explicit engagement with strands of the intellectual movement commonly called "postmodernism." One of the important characteristics of postmodern thought has been its emphasis on the contingent, indeterminate, and socially constructed nature of the categories with which we perceive and converse about the world. Jayne Chong-Soo Lee's essay "Navigating the Topology of Race" is built around such a sensibility. Her essay challenges the argument of Anthony Appiah that the concept of race, of racial difference, has no ground to give it meaning except in racist motivation. Lee counters that Appiah himself has essentialized the idea of race; like all linguistic constructs, race has no fixed meaning but instead meaning changes with social context. She argues for progressive, antiracist deployments of the idea of race rather than its abolition.

In "The Boundaries of Race: Political Geography in Legal Analysis," Richard Ford uses similar critical tools in service of his argument for a form of cultural pluralism that would focus on the character of the space that we occupy socially. Ford deconstructs the conventional understandings of local government and racial justice; in each discussion, Ford shows the seemingly stable dominant forms of thought actually rests on contradictory premises. In each

context, Ford argues for a way out of the contradictions through a new cultural pluralist paradigm for understanding political space and racial justice, a political and social framework built upon the acknowledgement that communities are never homogenous and readymade but, rather, always in the process of being created.

We close the chapter and this collection with Kendall Thomas's "A Popular History of the Angelo Herndon Case." Thomas's essay reflects many of the main Critical Race Theory themes in the context of a close and careful study of Angelo Herndon, a black communist who was convicted in the 1930s of inciting insurrection against the state. As Thomas demonstrates, the dominant legal and historical discourse has reduced the complex story of Herndon's engagement with the legal system to a few abstract and formal legal doctrines. Thomas proposes to recover the neglected cultural history of the case through what he calls "popular memory," a critical historical method that would recover the social, cultural, and ideological struggle suppressed by the dominant focus in legal scholarship on institutional concerns. He then demonstrates these theoretical and methodological convictions through his own, alternative reading of the Herndon case and recovery of the suppressed story of his struggle.

Part Seven

RACE AND POSTMODERNISM

NAVIGATING THE TOPOLOGY OF RACE

Jayne Chong-Soon Lee

[...]

A. Appiah's Motifs

Kwame Anthony Appiah is a prominent participant in the debate over the definitions of race
and the significance of racial difference. A professor of African-American studies and philosophy at Harvard University, Appiah has written
extensively on African and African-American
literary criticism. In a recent collection of his
essays, *In My Father's House*, Appiah addresses
the construction and mapping of race.[1] in his
usual comprehensive and controversial manner.
For the first time, Appiah gathers several
themes that have suffused his writings and presents them as a collection. Layered upon each
other, the essays reveal an even greater intricacy
than each demonstrates individually. Appiah's
discussion of the ontology of race, when considered with his analysis of the universal/particular
dichotomy, evolves into a rich argument about
the politics of racial particularity.[2] Similarly, his
discussion of the legacy of racism and racialism
develops an added urgency when seen together
with his critique of the premises of the African
Nativist movement.[3]

Often brilliant, sometimes contentious, but
always absorbing, Appiah's book elevates the
dialogue on race to a new level. Appiah departs
from the familiar landscape of statistical and
empirical accounts of racial discrimination, and
of historical[4] and economic accounts of racial

ideology, to probe the very definitions of race
itself. He bypasses the empirical question of
whether racism exists to ask the theoretical
question of what race and racism are. Similarly,
he avoids the historical question of who did
what, preferring to ask how the "who" and the
"what" are constituted. By circumventing the
typical questions we ask about race, Appiah
opens up the impasses that currently constrain
the dialogue. By analyzing how racial difference
is constructed, he charts the ways in which
certain groups are designated as racially distinct.
And by asking how racial identity is constructed, Appiah investigates the relationship
between racial category and racial subjectivity.

Taken as a whole, Appiah's argument does
not threaten the possibility of African-American identity, as some commentators have argued.[5] Rather, he questions the uncritical use of
biological and essential conceptions of race as
premises of antiracist struggles.[6] His point is
that we cannot analyze racial difference from
within frameworks that already assume biological difference. These efforts fail to question the
naturalized frameworks or to consider alternatives (for example, the potential of cultural
identities). Further, these attempts fail to take
seriously the legacy of racist domination. The
term "race" may be so historically and socially
overdetermined that it is beyond rehabilitation.
Rather than presume biological and essential
definitions of race to be solutions to racism,
Appiah suggests that we approach these presumptions as problems for antiracism. He
thereby challenges the fundamental tenets of
current antiracist practice.

. . .

II. THE (IM)POSSIBILITY OF RACIAL RESISTANCE

A. Race versus Culture

Not only does Appiah conclude that biological and essential conceptions of race are falsehoods, but he also determines that they are useless at best and dangerous at worst:

> The truth is that there are no races: there is nothing in the world that can do all we ask race to do for us. As we have seen, even the biologist's notion has only limited uses, and the notion that [W. E. B.] Du Bois required, and that underlies the more hateful racisms of the modern era, refers to nothing in the world at all. The evil that is done is done by the concept, and by easy—yet impossible—assumptions as to its application.[7]

Appiah asserts that "[t]alk of 'race' is particularly distressing for those of us who take culture seriously. For where race works—in places where 'gross differences' of morphology are correlated with 'subtle differences' of temperament, belief, and intention," it succeeds only "as an attempt at metonym for culture, and it does so only at the price of biologizing what is culture, ideology."[8] In other words, any conception of race that is significant is really just culture in disguise.

Just what is this culture that Appiah urges us to substitute for race? It is "[w]hat exists 'out there' in the world—communities of meaning, shading variously into each other in the rich structure of the social world. . . ."[9] One of Appiah's earlier essays suggests that these "communities of meaning" are groups of people anchored by ethnic identities. Appiah maintains that in a truly nonracist world, ethnic identities based on racial differences would "entirely wither away."[10] On the other hand, ethnic identities described as "something an African-American identity could become" seem to Appiah "likely to persist."[11] In an ideal world, what we now call a racial identity would become an ethnic identity. Appiah suggests that this notion of ethnic or cultural identity already underlies a progressive view of ostensibly "racial" identity. He points out, for example, that for those who identify themselves as African-American, "what matters . . . is almost always not the unqualified fact of that descent, but rather something that they suppose to go with it: the experience of a life a member of a group of people who experience themselves as—and are held by others to be—a community in virtue of their mutual recognition—and their recognition by others—as people of a common descent."[12] Since any meaningful notion of racial community is really one of cultural community, Appiah believes that culture can and should substitute for race.

The benefits of substituting the notions of an ethnic or cultural identity for a racial one are many. First, we can move away from the notion that race is a biological attribute possessed only by people of color. Second, we can undermine the racialist premise that moral and intellectual characteristics, like physical traits, are inherited. Third, we can counter the belief that nature, not effort, binds together members of a race. Fourth, we can rebut the idea that the ways in which we act, think, and play are inherited, rather than learned. As Henry Louis Gates, Jr., has instructed us, "[o]ne must learn to be 'black' in this society, precisely because 'blackness' is a socially produced category."[13]

However, the problem with this ethnic or cultural identity is precisely what Appiah cites as its advantage—its independence from race. As Michael Omi and Howard Winant have noted, theories that reduce racial identities to ethnic ones fail to account for the centrality of race in the histories of oppressed groups. Such theories also underestimate the degree to which traditional notions of race have shaped, and continue to shape, the societies in which we live. In doing so, these reconceptualizations of race as ethnicity may actually hinder our ability to resist entrenched forms of racism.[14] Although this criticism of ethnicity may apply more to the particularities of American society, it is also pertinent to African societies: after all, the history of colonialism in Africa cannot be mapped simply through cultural identities. We need race to fully understand what happened. Racial domination, not simply cultural oppression, explains imperialism.

Returning to the American context, when race becomes just another ethnic identity, and African-Americans, Latinos, Asian-Americans, and Native Americans become ethnic groups, there is a real danger that the oppression faced historically by these groups will not be fully understood or appreciated. The racial experience is not just quantitatively different from the ethnic one, as Ronald Takaki explains; the racial experience is qualitatively different.[15] For example, the "immigration experience" was dramatically distinct for white ethnics and African-Americans: the majority of the latter group were brought to this country in chains and enslaved for two hundred years. Analogously, during World War II, German-Americans and Italian-Americans were not interned, as were Japanese-Americans. To the extent that ethnicity models take the white ethnic experience as the norm, these theories "blame the victim" when they fail to measure up to this norm.[16] For example, conservative observers wonder why African-Americans have not progressed socially and economically in the United States as have "similarly situated" white ethnic groups, such as Italians and Irish.[17] Most seriously, ethnicity theories fail to account for the ways in which race has already been formalized in our institutions, particularly the law.

B. Races

The most important weakness of Appiah's dismissal of race is that in declaring biological and essential conceptions of race useless and dangerous, he fails to recognize that race is defined not by its inherent content, but by the social relations that construct it. If race is always dangerous, regardless of its meaning within a specific historical and social context, the result is an abstract and unitary conception of race. Basically, Appiah's conception of race fails to acknowledge that meanings change dramatically with social context. For Appiah, once a conception of race is constructed, the possibility of contesting, redefining, and reappropriating it is limited. Because the meaning of race is so constrained, resistance on racial terms becomes difficult. Our best hope is to abandon "race" for "culture."

Whether extrinsic or intrinsic, to Appiah these attitudes are both labeled "racism." In designating all uses of race variants of racism, rather than recognizing their potential to be altogether different phenomena, Appiah may presuppose his conclusion—that all uses of race are hazardous. Paradoxically, by casting both uses of race as racisms, Appiah's conception of race fails to reflect the changing social contexts that produce race, and through which race can be redeployed as a tool of antiracist struggle. While whites have historically used conceptions of "race" to subordinate people of color, some communities of color have successfully reappropriated the categorizations and united around them. They have redeployed "race" as an affirmative category around which people have organized to assert the power of their group and its identity. To deny the term "race" any content, as Appiah would have it, is to deny a powerful metaphor to "racial" groups and to preclude valuable modes of resistance.

Focusing on the different ways in which race is defined is more fruitful than concentrating on the common ways in which race is used. Since the meaning of race depends on the specific social contexts in which it is embedded, we will find as many definitions of race as there are social contexts.[18] With this in mind, we can navigate among different definitions of race simultaneously: biological, social, cultural, essential, and political.[19] Rather than determining whether a definition is oppressive based solely on its content, we can instead examine its effects. In perhaps the most penetrating account of the history of race, Michael Omi and Howard Winant explore the construction of racial identities, and trace how race has changed over time. They investigate the ways in which the sign of race has been appropriated and reappropriated, and how contests over definitions of race have shaped, and been shaped by, American social life and history. Omi and Winant argue that we should stop thinking of race "as an essence, as something fixed, concrete and objective."[20] They suggest that we instead think of "race as an unstable and 'decentered' complex of social meanings constantly being transformed by political struggle."[21] They highlight the contingent and changing nature of race and racism while recognizing its pervasive and systematic effect on our history. They trace the historical development of the category of race, labeling this process "racialization" to signify "the extension of racial meaning to a previously racially unclassified relationship, social practice or group."[22] Similarly, they discuss "racial formation," or "the process by which social, economic and political forces determine the content and importance of racial categories, and by which they are in turn shaped by racial meanings."[23] This theory of racial formation captures the concept of race both as a means of analyzing and ordering the world and as a process of historical and social transformation. In this way, Omi and Winant acknowledge that many definitions of race are possible, and acknowledge heterogeneous terrains of the racial landscape.

However, current discursive frameworks for analyzing race constrain us to either/or binary structures. We are forced to select biological or social conceptions of race; between supporting all versions of race or no versions of race; between implementing race-neutral or race-specific policies. If, like Appiah, we argue that race is socially constructed, then we often lose any chance to account for biology in defining race. While the argument that physical differences alone do not define race is vitally important, it should not preclude us from investigating how race has morphological features. We can explore how racial categories are created and organized around physical characteristics; how biology and the social contexts interrelate to give meaning to these physical traits.[24] In short, race can explain why, in the real world, differences of "color, hair, and bone" still matter.

III. THE LEGAL CONTEXT

A. Judicial Constructions of Race

Racial characterization in the law demonstrates the dangers of continuing to examine solely the content of race, and to endorse unitary definitions of race. In legal discourse, singular notions of race and an either/or binary framework seriously limit the potential of antiracist struggles, exposing them to racist appropriation. The need to stress how race is constructed in social contexts, and how race has a multiplicity of meanings, is urgent for two reasons. First, courts construct definitions of race and racial difference every day, even as they claim to merely reflect preexisting scientific and social facts; second, legal discourse tends to formalize definitions within the framework of the law, magnifying their effect. Criteria that we use loosely in daily life can become rigid tests in the courtroom. A recent controversial Supreme Court decision that interpreted racial definitions demonstrates these tendencies. In *Shaw v. Reno*,[25] the court applied strict scrutiny in evaluating the constitutionality of an electoral reapportionment plan. *Shaw* marked the first time that the court chose to apply identical legal tests to government action designed to benefit historically disadvantaged racial groups and to measures designed to burden these groups in the voting rights arena. The decision, along with an earlier case striking down an affirmative action program,[26] has stirred considerable criticism.[27]

Appiah's critique of the use of unquestioned racial assumptions aptly applies to the Supreme Court's decisions involving racial issues.[28] Despite the frequency of Supreme Court cases dealing with race, the court has not precisely identified the role of race in its decisions. The court purports merely to recognize, not to construct, definitions of race.[29] It has shifted between biological and social definitions of race. In *Shaw*, the court described race in physical terms such as skin color; in other cases, it has characterized race as a social construct, the product of past and present racial discrimination.[30] A survey of the court's varying definitions of race, however, reveals that focus on content, unitary definitions, and either/or frameworks prevail in judicial attempts to determine the significance of racial difference. This singular framework of these definitions has facilitated the court's invalidation of remedial programs vital to antiracist efforts.

B. Shaw v. Reno: *Manipulating the Biological and the Racial*

In *Shaw*, five white voters in North Carolina brought a constitutional challenge to a state-enacted reapportionment plan, alleging that the plan was an unconstitutional racial gerrymander.[31] The court held that the plaintiffs could make a cognizable claim under the equal protection clause of the Fourteenth Amendment "by alleging that the legislation, although race-neutral on its face, rationally cannot be understood as anything other than an effort to separate voters into different districts on the basis of race."[32] The level of review on remand was to be strict scrutiny; the lower court was instructed to determine "whether the North Carolina plan is narrowly tailored to further a compelling governmental interest."[33]

Writing for the majority, Justice Sandra Day O'Connor constructs a biological conception of race. She points out that the main purpose of the equal protection clause is to prevent states "from purposefully discriminating between individuals on the basis of race,"[34] and that "the individual is important, not his race, his creed, or his color."[35] While these references to race do not embody a specific definition, when Justice O'Connor says "race," she clearly means "skin color": "Racial classifications of any sort pose the risk of lasting harm to our society. They reinforce the belief, held by too many for too much of our history, that individuals should be judged by the color of their skin";[36] a "reapportionment plan that includes in one district individuals who belong to the same race, but who are otherwise widely separated by geographical and political boundaries, and who may have little in common with one another but the color of their skin, bears an uncomfortable resemblance to political apartheid."[37]

In defining race, however, Justice O'Connor exploits the rhetorical power of unitary definitions of race and an either/or binary framework of biological and social definitions of race. She depends on a biological notion of race to argue that the law should not recognize race. Tautologically, she defines race as skin color in order to prove that we should not recognize race, since it means nothing more than skin color. For Justice O'Connor, to acknowledge the significance of "skin color" is to attribute an array of character traits on the basis of physical features that bear no relevance to those traits. In

the *Shaw* majority's conception, recognizing the relevance of mere "skin color" is as irrational and insidious as assuming that all members of a racial group share certain moral and cultural traits. For the majority, skin color represents racial essence and negative stereotypes, the racist's assertion that the races possess different natures and moral characteristics and therefore should be valued differently. In its critique of biological race, the majority legitimately objects to the notion that our skin color predicts who we are and what we can be.

The problem, however, is that the court does not simply reject this narrowly biological notion of race as a basis for disparate treatment; rather, it assumes that the invalidity of race so characterized leaves no alternative but to reject the political significance of race altogether:

Classifications of citizens solely on the basis of race "are by their very nature odious to a free people whose institutions are founded upon the doctrine of equality." They threaten to stigmatize individuals by reason of their membership in a racial group and to incite racial hostility. ("[E]ven in the pursuit of remedial objectives, an explicit policy of assignment by race may serve to stimulate our society's latent race-consciousness, suggesting the utility and propriety of basing decisions on a factor that ideally bears no relationship to an individual's worth or needs.")[38]

The court limits race to a biological definition and evokes the opposition between the biological and the social to undermine the validity of race-consciousness, and thus of race-conscious remedies. It accomplishes this by recognizing that biological definitions of race lead to racism; acknowledging only a unitary definition of race, it then concludes that recognizing race leads to racism. While I agree with the assertion that recognizing skin color has in some contexts caused stigmatic harm, I cannot agree with the conclusion that recognizing race must also cause injury.

The majority's argument that all racial classifications cause harm depends on the conflation of biology and race, as well as the use of only one definition of race; further, it invites us to view every acknowledgment of race as racism.

One way to undercut this presumption is to assert, as Appiah has done, that race is not simply biology. The two concepts are analytically unconnected and unconnectable. We might also argue that the attribution of race to skin color is always an act of interpretation. Skin color does not "equal" race unless society recognizes that it does. For example, in *Drylongso: A Self-Portrait of Black America,* John Langston Gwaltney's collection of African-American narratives, Jackson Jordan, Jr., a ninety-year-old African-American man, discusses how people are identified as black:

> Now, you must understand that this is just a name we have. I am not black and you are not black either, if you go by the evidence of your eyes. . . . Anyway, black people are all colors. White people don't all look the same way, but there are many more different kinds of us than there are of them. Then too, there is a certain stage at which you cannot tell who is white and who is black. Many of the people I see who are thought of as black could just as well be white in their appearance. Many of the white people I see are black as far as I can tell by the way they look.[39]

Race cannot be self-evident on the basis of skin color, for skin color alone has no inherent meaning.

Shaw epitomizes the gap between the court's professed "color-blindness" and its undeniable role in the construction of race. The opinion seems to rebuke the district court for taking judicial notice of the appellants' white race, "a fact omitted from [their] complaint,"[40] and emphasizes that the appellants "did not even claim to be white" in their pleading.[41] Even in disclaiming the significance of race, however, the majority writes its biologistic conception of race into the law. Because it does not recognize the nonbiological dimensions of race, the majority must reject the possibility of a nonstigmatic use of "race." Ironically, by doing this, the court adopts a stigmatic biologistic definition of race and does not see its own power to recast the meaning of race into an affirmative use. The court fails to recognize that it does—hence, how it can—shape the terrain of racial difference. . . .

Shaw makes clear the inadequacy of unitary and either/or binary models of racial difference,

and it suggests their potential to cause affirmative harm. Race and racism are fluid: in contrast to the sixties, the concept of liberal "color-blindness" now undermines antiracist efforts. Therefore, rejecting all conceptions of biological race and embracing those of social race leaves open the possibility of racist appropriation and precludes the potential for antiracist struggle. Similarly, rejecting all notions of essential race may dismantle the grounds for affirmative racial solidarity. Because the meaning of race is constructed by the social contexts in which it is located, there can be no consistent content to race. It can always be defined in many different ways, often simultaneously. Because we cannot predict a racist practice from its definition of race, we can never determine beforehand whether a practice will be racist or antiracist solely from its content. We can only examine the way race is being used and what it is being used to say. Only after examining the context and the effect can we determine whether the practice is racist or antiracist. If the practice reinforces the subordination of a historically oppressed group, we can label that practice racist. In *Shaw,* the notion of color-blindness was used to undermine an electoral plan designed to benefit a racial group that had historically been deprived of their right to vote. On the other hand, if the practice alleviates subordination, we can label that practice antiracist. The constantly shifting topology of race requires us to acknowledge that "race" can be defined in many different ways, and that all of these ways—even biological and essential conceptions of race—have their place in antiracist struggles. The best that we can do is to navigate this terrain.

IV. Conclusion

RETURNING to the themes that motivated this review, I pose the following questions again: How can we recognize racial difference without reinscribing racial stereotypes and subordination? How can we trace the historical construction of race without denying groups the power to define themselves racially? How can we critique dominant norms for excluding racial experiences, without ghettoizing people of color by the very particularity that we have invoked? I argue that we can start by recognizing that race is always defined by its social context, and never solely by its content. Additionally, we can recognize that race is always multiplicitous because social contexts are multiplicitous. The use of race to stereotype and discriminate against people differs from the use of race as a basis for racial solidarity. Finally, we can refuse to adhere to the unitary, either/or framework that has constrained race discourse. We can have both biological and social definitions of race, we can have both essential and historical notions of race, we can have both race-neutral and race-conscious remedies, we can have both race and culture. Abandoning one set of definitions entirely may deprive us of useful tools in the struggle against racism.

. . .

Imagine a physical landscape with various distinguishable features—trees, mountains, valleys, and quicksand. An observer on a satellite can see the people below but not the features of the terrain. When she sees people climbing over hills, moving around obstacles, or diving into tunnels, the observer might assume that certain people's "attitudes" prompt certain kinds of actions, while others might have attitudes that encourage other types of movements. However, if the observer were to move closer, she would be able to see that understanding the people's actions entails analyzing the terrain. And the observer would realize that changing people's behavior would entail contouring the terrain differently. By analogy, race continues to exist as it does because we create and recreate it to fit our own social terrain, even as it becomes a part of that terrain.

I end with this image to suggest that the notion of race is not so overdetermined by past and current racial domination that we cannot revive it. Instead of abandoning a terrain twisted by oppression and discrimination, we can try to reshape it with other tools. Instead of referring to a single definition of race, we can refer to multiple definitions of race; instead of talking about racism, we can talk about racisms. Instead of abandoning certain definitions of race, we can employ each of them when necessary. Bio-logical and essential definitions of race may have their place in this topography. Perhaps Appiah's greatest insight is that we must always self-consciously analyze the tools that we use. Whether these tools harm or heal depends on what we do with them. The choice is always ours.

NOTES

1. Kwame Anthony Appiah, *In My Father's House: Africa in the Philosophy of Culture* (1992). Although Appiah's book addresses an array of questions and issues, I will focus on these two specific topics of construction and mapping. I primarily concentrate on two chapters, "The Invention of Africa," and "Illusions of Race."

2. *Id.* at 28–72.

3. *Id.* at 3–27, 47–72.

4. See, for example, George M. Fredrickson, *The Black Image in the White Mind: The Debate on Afro-American Character and Destiny, 1817–1914* (1971); E. D. Genovese, *Roll, Jordan, Roll: The World The Slaves Made* (1974); T. F. Gossett, *Race: The History of An Idea in America* (1963); R. Horsman, *Race and Manifest Destiny: The Origins of American Racial Anglo-Saxonism* (1981); W. D. Jordon, *White Over Black: American Attitudes Toward The Negro, 1550–1812* (1968); A. Saxton, *The Rise and Fall of the White Republic: Class Politics and Mass Culture in Nineteenth-Century America* (1990); A. A. Smedley, *Race in North America: Origin and Evolution of a Worldview* (1993).

5. See, for example, H. A. Baker, Jr., "Caliban's Triple Play," in H. L. Gates, ed., *Race, Writing, and Difference*, at 381, 385 (1986) (arguing that Appiah believes that once science shows that race is not biologically determined, "all talk of 'race' must cease"); J. A. Joyce, "Who the Cap Fit: Unconsciousness and Unconscionableness in the Criticism of Houghton A. Baker, Jr., and Henry Louis Gates, Jr." 18 *New Literary Hist*, at 378–81 (stating that Appiah's argument attacks the very possibility of African-American identity).

6. I suggest that Appiah's work is greatly misunderstood because analytically he separates theory from politics. However, racial theory and racial politics have become so entwined that when he questions the former he inevitably appears to question the latter.

7. Cornell West, "Black Leadership and the Pitfalls of Racial Reasoning," in Toni Morrison, ed., *Race-ing Justice, Engendering Power*, at 45 (1992).

8. *Id.*

9. *Id.*

10. A. Appiah, " 'But Would That Still Be Me?': Notes On Gender, 'Race', Ethnicity, as Sources of 'Identity,' " 87 *J. Phil.*, 493, 499 (1990).

11. *Id.*

12. *Id.* at 497.

13. H. Gates, Jr., *Loose Canons: Notes on the Culture Wars*, at 101 (1992).

14. M. Omi and H. Winant, *Racial Formation in the United States: From the 1960s to the 1980s*, 11, at 10, 21–24 (1986).

15. R. Takaki, "Reflections on Racial Patterns in America," in R. Takaki, ed., *From Different Shores: Perspectives on Race and Ethnicity in America*, 29 (1987).

16. Omi and Winant, *supra* note 14, at 21.

17. *Id.* at 21–24.

18. David Theo Goldberg points out that "[u]nderlying the views both of those who might openly or privately have found racist views compelling and those who clearly considered them troubling was the assumption that racism is singular and monolithic, simply the same attitude manifested in varying circumstances"; D. T. Goldberg, "Introduction," in D. T. Goldberg, ed., *Anatomy of Racism*, at xi (1990).

19. Unlike Appiah, who separates race and culture, Neil Gotanda joins race and culture in what he calls "culture-race"—"all aspects of culture, community, and consciousness"; Gotanda, "A Critique of 'Our Constitution Is Color-Blind,'" 44 *Stan. L. Rev.*, at 56 [the essay is included in this volume-ED.]. On African-Americans, Gotanda writes, "[c]ulture refers to broadly shared beliefs and social practices; community refers to both the physical and spiritual senses of the term; and African-American consciousness refers to Black Nationalist and other traditions of self-awareness and to action based on that self-awareness"; *id.* at 4. Gotanda's article is an excellent example of a more complex and politically empowering theory of race. Recognizing that race takes on many distinct meanings depending on social context, he identifies four ways that the Supreme Court has constructed race: status-race, formal-race, historical-race, and culture-race; *id.*

20. Omi and Winant, *supra* note 14, at 68.

21. *Id.*

22. *Id.* at 64.

23. *Id.* at 61.

24. Paul Gilroy argues that morphology is important to our understanding of race: "[B]iology cannot be wholly dismissed as a factor in the formation and reproduction of 'race.' It is better to confine phenotypes to a relatively autonomous realm of biological determinations which can ascribe a variety of social effects. Accepting that skin 'colour,' however meaningless we know it to be, has a strictly limited material basis in biology, opens up the possibility of engaging with theories of signification which can highlight the elasticity and the emptiness of 'racial' signifiers as well

as the ideological work which has to be done in order to turn them into signifiers in the first place"; P. Gilroy, *"There Ain't No Black in the Union Jack": The Cultural Politics of Race and Nation*, 38–39 (1987).

25. 113 S. Ct. 2816 (1993).

26. *City of Richmond v. J. A. Croson Co.*, 488 U.S. 469 (1989).

27. See, for example, Lynne Duke, "Advocates Say Justices Muddy Voting Rights; Decision in North Carolina Congressional Redistricting Case Criticized as 'Utopianism,'" *Washington Post* (June 30, 1993), A8; see also K. M. Sullivan, "*City of Richmond v. J. A. Croson Co.*: The Backlash against Affirmative Action," 64 *Tul. L. Rev.*, 1609 (1990).

28. I include cases in which race has been addressed directly or in dicta.

29. See text accompanying note 25 *supra*. See generally Jacques Derrida, *Writing and Difference* (Alan Bass trans., 1978) (explaining how discourse determines "reality"); H. L. Gates, *Loose Canons: Notes on the Culture Wars* 37 (1992).

30. See, for example, *Brown v. Board of Education.*, 347 U.S. 483 (1954).

31. 113 S. Ct. at 2819–20.

32. *Id.* at 2828.

33. *Id.* at 2832. According to the court, a districting plan triggers strict scrutiny when a district is "so extremely irregular on its face" that it unequivocally reflects an effort to separate citizens on the basis of race; *id.* at 2824. In *Shaw*, the triggering factors were: (1) that one district was "somewhat hook shaped," tapering to "a narrow band," with "finger-like extensions," resembling a "bug splattered on a windshield," and (2) that the second district wound "in snake-like fashion through tobacco country, financial centers, and manufacturing areas 'until it gobbles in enough enclaves of black neighborhoods,'" becoming so narrow in parts that "[i]f you drove down the interstate with both car doors open, you'd kill most of the people in the district"; *id.* at 2820–21 (quoting state representative Mickey Michaux, in John Biskupic, "N.C. Case to Pose Test of Racial Redistricting," *Washington Post* (Apr. 20, 1993), A4).

34. *Id.* at 2824.

35. *Id.* at 2827 (quoting *Wright v. Rockefeller*, 376 U.S. 52, 66 (1964) (Douglas, J., dissenting)).

36. *Id.* at 2832.

37. *Id.* at 2827.

38. *Id.* at 2824 (quoting *Hirabayashi v. United States*, 320 U.S. 81, 100 (1943)); *United Jewish Orgs. of Williamsburgh, Inc. v. Carey*, 430 U.S. 144, 173 (1977) (citations omitted).

39. J. Langston Gwaltney, *Drylongso: A Self-Portrait of Black America*, 96 (1980).

40. 113 S. Ct. at 2822.

41. *Id.* at 2824.

42. Barbara Jeanne Fields, "Slavery, Race, and Ideology in The United States of America", 181 *New Life Rev.* 113–14 (1990).

43. *Id.* at 114.

ỡ

THE BOUNDARIES OF RACE: POLITICAL GEOGRAPHY IN LEGAL ANALYSIS
Richard Thompson Ford

DURING the seventies and eighties a word disappeared from the American vocabulary—the word was "segregation." It is now passé to speak of racial segregation. In an America that is facing the identity crisis of multiculturalism, where racial diversity seems to challenge the norms and values of the nation's most fundamental institutions, to speak of segregation seems almost quaint. The physical segregation of the races would seem to be a relatively simple matter to address; indeed, many believe it has already been addressed. Discrimination in housing, in the workplace, and in schools is illegal. Thus, it is perhaps understandable that we have turned our attention to other problems, on the assumption that any segregation that remains is either vestigial or freely chosen. However, even as racial segregation has fallen from the national agenda, it has persisted. Even as racial segregation is described as a natural expression of racial and cultural solidarity, a chosen and desirable condition for which government is not responsible and one that government should not oppose, segregation continues to play the same role it always has in American race relations—to isolate, disempower, and oppress.

Segregation is oppressive and disempowering rather than desirable or inconsequential because it involves more than simply the relationship of individuals to other individuals; it also involves the relationship of groups of individuals to political influence and economic resources. Residence is more than a personal choice; it is also a primary source of political identity and economic security.[1] Likewise, residential segregation is more than a matter of social distance; it is a matter of political fragmentation and economic stratification along racial lines, enforced by public policy and the rule of law.

Segregated minority communities have been historically impoverished and politically powerless. Today's laws and institutions need not be explicitly racist to ensure that this state of affairs continues; they need only to perpetuate historical conditions. In this article, I assert that political geography—the position and function of jurisdictional and quasi-jurisdictional boundaries[2]—helps to promote a racially separate and unequal distribution of political influence and economic resources. Moreover, these inequalities fuel the segregative effect of political boundaries in a vicious cycle of causation: each condition contributes to and strengthens the others. Thus, racial segregation persists in the absence of explicit, legally enforceable racial restrictions. Race-neutral policies, set against a historical backdrop of state action in the service of racial segregation and thus against a contemporary backdrop of racially identified space— physical space primarily associated with and occupied by a particular racial group—predictably reproduce and entrench racial segregation and the racial caste system that accompanies it. Thus, the persistence of racial segregation, even in the face of civil rights reform, is not mysterious.

This article employs two lines of analysis in its examination of political space. The first demonstrates that racially identified space both creates and perpetuates racial segregation. The second demonstrates that racially identified space results from public policy and legal sanctions—in short, from state action—rather than from the unfortunate but irremediable consequence of purely private or individual choices. This dual analysis has important legal and moral consequences: if racial segregation is a collective social responsibility rather than exclusively the result of private transgressions, then it must either be accepted as official policy or remedied through collective action.

Part 1 argues that public policy and private actors operate together to create and promote racially identified space and thus racial segregation. In support of this assertion, I offer a hypothetical model to demonstrate that even in the absence of individual racial animus and de jure segregation, historical patterns of racial segregation would be perpetuated by facially race-neutral legal rules and institutions. I conclude the discussion in Part 1 by arguing that the significance of racially identified political geography escapes the notice of judges, poli-

cymakers, and scholars because of two widely held yet contradictory misconceptions: one assumes that political boundaries have no effect on the distribution of persons, political influence, or economic resources, while the other assumes that political boundaries define quasinatural and prepolitical associations of individuals. As we shall see, these two assumptions lead jurists and policymakers to believe that segregated residential patterns are unimportant to the political influence and economic wellbeing of communities, and that such residential patterns are beyond the proper purview of legal and policy reform. These beliefs are often unstated, but they inform judicial decisions and the political and sociological analyses underlying those decisions.

Part 2 demonstrates how racially identified space interacts with facially race-neutral legal doctrine and public policy to reinforce racial segregation rather than to eliminate it gradually. Legal analysis oscillates between two contradictory conceptions of local political space, which correspond to the two misconceptions of space described in Part 1. One conceives of local jurisdictions as geographically defined delegates of centralized power, administrative conveniences without autonomous political significance; the other treats local jurisdictions as autonomous entities that deserve deference because they are manifestations of an unmediated democratic sovereignty. Both accounts avoid examination of the potentially segregated character of local jurisdictions—the first by denying them any legal significance, the second by reference to their democratic origins, or by tacit analogy to private property rights, or both. Thus, legal authorities that subscribe to either of these accounts never confront the problems posed by the many jurisdictions that are segregated or promote racial segregation and inequality.

Two competing normative analyses mirror the doctrinal oscillation between the conception of local governments as agents of state power and the conception of local governments as self-validating political communities. One holds that local governments are powerless creatures of the state and prescribes greater autonomy for local governments; the other, which insists that local governments are powerful, autonomous associations, advocates bringing the "crazy quilt" of parochial localities under centralized control.

Part 3 also returns to our original focus on race relations and suggests that the characteristic oscillation in local government doctrine informed by democratic theory is related to a particularly American conflict between the goals of racial and cultural assimilation, on the one hand, and separatism, on the other. Neither assimilation nor separatism is fully acceptable, and race-relations theorists tend to waver between the two. The reification of political space thus mirrors a reification of race in American thought: race is assumed either to be irrelevant, merely the unfortunate by-product of an ignoble American past and a retrograde mentality, or to be natural and primordial, a genetic or biological identity that simply is unamenable to examination or change.

Finally, Part 3 attempts to mediate the characteristic conflicts between local parochialism and centralized bureaucracy, pluralist competition and republican dialogue, and racial assimilation and racial separatism. In Part III I argue that the location of the politics of difference must be the metropolis, the political space in which the majority of Americans now reside, work, and enjoy recreation, and in which individuals confront racial, cultural, and economic differences. Against the nostalgia of the whole and the one, the "pure" homogeneous community, we should strive for the achievable ideal of the diverse democratic city.

I. CONCEPTIONS AND CONSEQUENCES OF SPACE

A. *The Construction of Racially Identified Space*

Segregation is the missing link in prior attempts to understand the plight of the urban poor. As long as blacks continue to be segregated in American cities, the United States cannot be called a race-blind society.

—Douglas S. Massey and Nancy A. Denton, *American Apartheid*[3]

This article focuses primarily on residential segregation and on the geographic boundaries that define local governments. Although these are not the only examples of racially identified space, they are so intimately linked to issues of political and economic access that they are among the most important. Residence in a municipality or membership in a homeowners association involves more than simply the location of one's domicile; it also involves the right to act as a citizen, to influence the character and direction of a jurisdiction or association through the exercise of the franchise, and to share in public resources. "Housing, after all, is much more than shelter: it provides social status, access to jobs, education and other services...."[4] Residential segregation is self-perpetuating, for in segregated neighborhoods "[t]he damaging social consequences that follow from increased poverty are spatially concentrated ... creating uniquely disadvantaged environments that become progressively isolated—geographically, socially and economically—from the rest of society."[5] Local boundaries drive this cycle of poverty.

Actors public and private laid the groundwork for the construction of racially identified spaces and, therefore, for racial segregation as well. Explicit governmental policy at the local, state, and federal levels has encouraged and facilitated racial segregation. The role of state and local policies in promoting the use of racially restrictive covenants is well known; less well known is the responsibility of federal policy for the pervasiveness of racially restrictive covenants. The federal government continued to promote the use of such covenants until they were declared unconstitutional in the landmark decision *Shelley v. Kraemer*.[6] Federally subsidized mortgages often *required* that property owners incorporate restrictive covenants into their deeds. The federal government consistently gave black neighborhoods the lowest rating for purposes of distributing federally subsidized mortgages. The Federal Housing Administration, which insured private mortgages, advocated the use of zoning and deed restrictions to bar undesirable people and classified black neighbors as nuisances to be avoided along with "stables" and "pig pens."[7]

Not surprisingly, "[b]uilders ... adopted the [racially restrictive] covenant so their property would be eligible for [federal] insurance,"[8] and "private banks relied heavily on the [federal] system to make their own loan decisions. . . . [T]hus [the federal government] not only channeled federal funds away from black neighborhoods but was also responsible for a much larger and more significant disinvestment in black areas by private institutions."[9] Although the federal government ended these discriminatory practices after 1950, only much later did it do anything to remedy the damage it had done or to prevent private actors from perpetuating segregation.[10]

Racial segregation was also maintained by private associations of white homeowners who "lobbied city councils for zoning restrictions and for the closing of hotels and rooming houses . . . threatened boycotts of real estate agents who sold homes to blacks . . . [and] withdrew their patronage from white businesses that catered to black clients."[11] These associations shaped the racial and economic landscape and implemented by private fiat what might well be described as public policies. Thus, private associations as well as governments defined political space.

B. The Perpetuation of Racially Identified Spaces: An Economic-Structural Analysis

The history of public policy and private action in the service of racism reveals the context in which racially identified spaces were created. Much traditional social and legal theory imagines that the elimination of public policies designed to promote segregation will eliminate segregation itself, or will at least eliminate any segregation that can be attributed to public policy and leave only the aggregate effects of individual biases (which are beyond the authority of government to remedy). This view fails, however, to acknowledge that racial segregation is embedded in and perpetuated by the social and political construction of racially identified political space.

I. TROUBLE IN PARADISE: AN ECONOMIC MODEL

Imagine a society with only two groups, blacks and whites,[12] differentiated only by morphology (visible physical differences). Blacks, as a result of historical discrimination, tend on average to earn significantly less than whites. Imagine also that this society has recently (during the past twenty or thirty years) come to see the error of its discriminatory ways. It has enacted a program of reform which has totally eliminated legal support for racial discrimination and, through a concentrated program of public education, has also succeeded in eliminating any vestige of racism from its citizenry. In short, the society has become color-blind. Such a society may feel itself well on its way to the ideal of racial justice and equality, if not already there.

Imagine also that, in our hypothetical society, small, decentralized, and geographically defined governments exercise significant power to tax citizens, and they use the revenues to provide certain public services (such as police and fire protection), public utilities (such as sewage, water, and garbage collection), infrastructure development, and public education.

Finally, imagine that, before the period of racial reform, our society had in place a policy of fairly strict segregation of the races, such that every municipality consisted of two enclaves, one almost entirely white and one almost entirely black. In some cases, whites even reincorporated their enclaves as separate municipalities to ensure the separation of the races. Thus, the now color-blind society confronts a situation of almost complete segregation of the races—a segregation that also fairly neatly tracks a class segregation, because blacks on average earn far less than whites (in part because of their historical isolation from the resources and job opportunities available in the wealthier and socially privileged white communities).

We can assume that all members of this society are indifferent to the race of their neighbors, co-workers, social acquaintances, and so forth. However, we must also assume that most members of this society care a great deal about their economic well-being and are unlikely to make decisions that will adversely affect their financial situation.

Our hypothetical society might feel that, over time, racial segregation would dissipate in the absence of de jure discrimination and racial prejudice. Yet let us examine the likely outcome under these circumstances. Higher incomes in the white neighborhoods would result in larger homes and more privately financed amenities, although public expenditures would be equally distributed among white and black neighborhoods within a single municipality. However, in those municipalities which incorporated along racial lines, white cities would have substantially superior public services (or lower taxes and the same level of services) than the "mixed" cities, due to a higher average tax base. The all-black cities would, it follows, have substantially inferior public services or higher taxes as compared to the mixed cities. Consequently, the wealthier white citizens of mixed cities would have a real economic incentive to depart, or even secede, from the mixed cities, and whites in unincorporated areas would be spurred to form their own jurisdictions and to resist consolidation with the larger mixed cities or all-black cities. Note that this pattern can be explained without reference to "racism": whites might be color-blind yet nevertheless prefer predominantly or all-white neighborhoods on purely economic grounds, as long as the condition of substantial income differentiation obtains.

Of course, simply because municipalities begin as racially segregated enclaves does not mean that they will remain segregated. Presumably, blacks would also prefer the superior public service amenities or lower tax burdens of white neighborhoods, and those with sufficient wealth would move in; remember, in this world there is no racism and there are no cultural differences between the races—people behave as purely rational economic actors. One might imagine that, over time, income levels would even out between the races, and blacks would move into the wealthier neighborhoods, while less fortunate whites would be outbid and would move to the formerly all-black neighborhoods. Hence, racial segregation might eventually be transformed into purely economic segregation.

This conclusion rests, however, on the assumption that residential segregation would not itself affect employment opportunities and economic status. However, because the education

system is financed through local taxes, segregated localities would offer significantly different levels of educational opportunity; the poor, black cities would have poorer educational facilities than would the wealthy, white cities. Thus, whites would, on average, be better equipped to obtain high-income employment than would blacks. Moreover, residential segregation would result in a pattern of segregated informal social networks: neighbors would work and play together in community organizations such as schools, PTAs, Little Leagues, Rotary Clubs, neighborhood-watch groups, cultural associations, and religious organizations. These social networks would form the basis of the ties and the communities of trust that open the doors of opportunity in the business world. All other things being equal, employers would hire people they know and like over people of whom they have no personal knowledge, good or bad; they would hire someone who comes with a personal recommendation from a close friend over someone without such a recommendation. Residential segregation would substantially decrease the likelihood that such connections would be formed between members of different races. Finally, economic segregation would mean that the market value of black homes would be significantly lower than would that of white homes; thus, blacks attempting to move into white neighborhoods would on average have less collateral with which to obtain new mortgages, or less equity to convert into cash.[13]

Inequalities in both educational opportunity and the networking dynamic would result in fewer and less remunerative employment opportunities, and hence lower incomes, for blacks. Poorer blacks, unable to move into the more privileged neighborhoods and cities, would remain segregated; and few, if any, whites would forgo the benefits of their white neighborhoods to move into poorer black neighborhoods, which would be burdened by higher taxes or provided with inferior public services. This does not necessarily mean that income polarization and segregation would constantly increase (although at times they would) but, rather, that they would not decrease over time through a process of osmosis. Instead, every successive generation of blacks and whites would find itself in much the same situation as the previous generation, and in the absence of some intervening factor, the cycle would likely perpetuate itself. At some point an equilibrium might be achieved: generally better-connected and better-educated whites would secure the better, higher-income jobs and disadvantaged blacks would occupy the lower-status and lower-wage jobs.

Even in the absence of racism, then, race-neutral policy could be expected to entrench segregation and socioeconomic stratification in a society with a history of racism. Political space plays a central role in this process. Spatially and racially defined communities perform the "work" of segregation silently. There is no racist actor or racist policy in this model, and yet a racially stratified society is the inevitable result. Although political space seems to be the inert context in which individuals make rational choices, it is in fact a controlling structure in which seemingly innocuous actions lead to racially detrimental consequences.

2. STRANGERS IN PARADISE: A COMPLICATED MODEL

> [Even u]nder the best of circumstances, segregation undermines the ability of blacks to advance their interests because it provides ... whites with no immediate self-interest in their welfare. [Furthermore,] a significant share [of whites] must be assumed to be racially prejudiced and supportive of policies injurious to blacks.
>
> —Douglas S. Massey and Nancy A. Denton, *American Apartheid*[14]

If we now introduce a few real-world complications into our model, we can see just how potent the race-space dynamic is. Suppose that half—only half—of all whites in our society are in some measure racist or harbor some racial fear or concern. These might range from the open-minded liberal who remains somewhat resistant, if only for pragmatic reasons, to mixed-race relations (Spencer Tracy's character in *Guess Who's Coming to Dinner*) to the avowed racial separatist and member of the Ku Klux Klan.

Further suppose that the existence of racism produces a degree of racial fear and animosity of blacks, such that half—only half—of blacks fear or distrust whites to some degree. These might range from a pragmatic belief that blacks need to "keep to their own kind," if only to avoid unnecessary confrontation and strife (Sidney Poitier's father in the same film) to strident nationalist separatism. Let us also assume that significant cultural differences generally exist between whites and blacks.

In this model, cultural differences and socialization would further entrench racial segregation. Even assuming that a few blacks would be able to attain the income necessary to move into white neighborhoods, it is less likely that they would wish to do so. Many blacks would fear and distrust whites and would be reluctant to live among them, especially in the absence of a significant number of other blacks. Likewise, many whites would resent the presence of black neighbors and would try to discourage them, in ways both subtle and overt, from entering white neighborhoods. The result would be an effective "tax" on integration. The additional amenities and lower taxes of the white neighborhood would often be outweighed by the intangible but real costs of living as an isolated minority in an alien and sometimes hostile environment. Many blacks would undoubtedly choose to remain in black neighborhoods.

Moreover, this dynamic would produce racially *identified* spaces. Because our hypothetical society is now somewhat racist, segregated neighborhoods would become identified by the race of their inhabitants; race would be seen as intimately related to the economic and social condition of political space. The creation of racially identified political spaces would make possible a number of regulatory activities and private practices that would further entrench the segregation of the races. For example, because some whites would resent the introduction of blacks into their neighborhoods, real estate brokers would be unlikely to show property in white neighborhoods to blacks for fear that disgruntled white homeowners would boycott them.

Even within mixed cities, localities might decline to provide adequate services in black neighborhoods, and might divert funds to white neighborhoods in order to encourage whites with higher incomes to enter or remain in the jurisdiction. Thus, although our discussion has focused primarily on racially homogeneous jurisdictions with autonomous taxing power, the existence of such jurisdictions might affect the policy of racially heterogeneous jurisdictions, which would have to compete for wealthier residents with the low-tax and superior-service homogeneous cities. This outcome would be especially likely if the mixed jurisdictions were characterized by governmental structures that were either resistant to participation by grass-roots community groups or were otherwise unresponsive to the citizenry as a whole. A dynamic similar to what I have posited for the homogeneous jurisdictions would occur *within* such racially mixed jurisdictions, with neighborhoods taking the place of separate jurisdictions.

Each of these phenomena would exacerbate the others, in a vicious circle of causation. The lack of public services would create a general negative image of poor, black neighborhoods; inadequate police protection would lead to a perception of the neighborhoods as unsafe; uncollected trash would lead to a perception of the neighborhoods as dirty, and so forth. Financial institutions would redline black neighborhoods—refuse to lend to property owners in these areas—because they would be likely to perceive them as financially risky. As a result, both real estate improvement and sale would often become unfeasible.

I. CONCLUSION: THE IMPLICATIONS FOR RACIAL HARMONY

EMPIRICAL study confirms the existence of racially identified space. The foregoing economic model demonstrates that race and class are inextricably linked in American society, and that both are linked to segregation and to the creation of racially identified political spaces. Even if racism could magically be eliminated, racial segregation would be likely to continue as long as we begin with significant income polarization and segregation of the races. Furthermore, even a relatively slight, residual racism severely complicates any effort to eliminate racial segregation that does not directly address political space and class-based segregation.

One might imagine that racism could be overcome by education and rational persuasion alone: because racism is irrational, it seems to follow that, over time, one can argue or educate it away. The model shows that even if such a project were entirely successful, in the absence of any further interventions, racial segregation would remain indefinitely.

Contemporary society imposes significant economic costs on nonsegregated living arrangements. In the absence of a conscious effort to eliminate it, segregation will persist in this atmosphere (although it may appear to be the product of individual choices). The structure of racially identified space is more than the mere vestigial effect of historical racism: it is a structure that continues to exist today with nearly as much force as when policies of segregation were explicitly backed by the force of law. This structure will not gradually atrophy, because it is constantly used and constantly reinforced.

A. Toward a Legal Conception of Space

A whole history remains to be written of spaces— which would at the same time be the history of powers (both these terms in the plural)—from the great strategies of geo-politics to the little tactics of the habitat, . . . passing via economic and political installations.

—Michel Foucault, "The Eye of Power" [15]

There is no self-conscious legal conception of political space. Most legal and political theory focuses almost exclusively on the relationship between individuals and the state. Judges, policymakers, and scholars analogize decentralized governments and associations either to individuals, when considered vis-à-vis centralized government, or to the state, when considered vis-à-vis their own members—yet they consider the development, population and demarcation of space to be irrelevant. Space is *implicitly* understood to be the inert context *in* which, or the deadened material *over* which, legal disputes take place.

Legal boundaries are often ignored because they are imagined to be either the product of aggravated individual choices or the administratively necessary segmentation of centralized governmental power. This representation of boundaries, and hence, of politically created space, allows us to imagine that spatially defined entities are not autonomous associations that wield power. At the same time, space also serves to ground governmental and associational entities. We imagine that the boundaries defining local governments and private concentrations of real property are a natural and inevitable function of geography and of a commitment to self-government or private property. These two views of political geography justify judicial failures to consider the effect of boundaries and space on racial segregation.

However, the development, population, and demarcation of space—those characteristics which must be considered irrelevant in order for space to be seen as merely the aggregation of individual choices or the organizing medium of centralized power—are precisely the characteristics that distinguish spaces politically and economically. Localities define spaces as industrial, commercial, or residential; homeowners' associations define spaces according to density and type of development; zoning and covenanting prescribe who can occupy certain spaces. This spatial differentiation is what I mean by the "political geography of space." Features such as these—features that are not primordial or natural but *are* inherently spatial because they distinguish one space from another—are the product of collective action structured by law.

1. THE TAUTOLOGY OF COMMUNITY SELF-DEFINITION

Space is a salient characteristic of political entities even as it entrenches that segregation. In order to understand why this is so, consider an association that is not spatially defined. Such an association must be defined by particular criteria that can be examined, criticized, and challenged. These criteria also distinguish the asso-

ciation from the mere aggregation of individual member preferences. Even if members are empowered to alter the criteria through a democratic process, the initial selection of membership will affect the outcome of subsequent elections. Thus, although the governance of such an association may be democratic in form, it may well not be democratic ("of the people") in substance if the initial selection of members was highly exclusive. If those excluded from the association claim a right to join, the association cannot justify their exclusion on the basis of democratic rule. Nor can the justification for such an association be that it has a right to self-definition, because the "self" that seeks to define is precisely the subject of dispute.

This tautology of community self-definition is masked when a group can be spatially defined: "We are simply the people who live in area X." Space does the initial work of defining the community or association and imbues the latter with an air of objectivity—indeed, of primordiality. But the tautology is only *masked,* it is not resolved: why should area X be the relevant community, when area X plus area Y might provide an equally or more valid definition of community? The answer cannot appeal to the right of community self-determination: if the people in area Y claim to be part of the larger community X plus Y, then should not their opinion be considered as well as that of the people in area X? It is the question of how communities are and should be defined that concerns us here. Close attention to spatial construction will help us to break free of established but untenable definitions of political community and thereby to open new avenues for combating entrenched structures of residential segregation. I begin by examining the construction of political space and the consequent construction of racially identified space in both public and private law.

2. EXCLUSIONARY ZONING AND LOCAL DEMOCRACY: THE RACIAL POLITICS OF COMMUNITY SELF-DEFINITION

Along with historical de jure segregation, racially exclusionary zoning introduces the racial element into local political geography and thereby creates a structure of racially identified space. The zoning power is justified by reference to an internal local political process: hence the polis that votes on local zoning policy is defined and legitimated by an opaque local geography. At the same time, the effect of this political exclusion for the excluded racial group is considered insignificant: the very local geography in question in the challenged zoning policy is rendered transparent.

Exclusionary zoning is a generic term for zoning restrictions that effectively exclude a particular class of persons from a locality by restricting the land uses they are likely to require. Today, exclusionary zoning takes the form both of restrictions on multifamily housing and of minimum acreage requirements for the construction of single-family home "large-lot" zoning. Exclusionary zoning is a mechanism of the social construction of space. Local space is defined by zoning ordinances as suburban, family-oriented, pastoral, or even equestrian. The ordinances are justified in terms of the types of political spaces they seek to create: a community that wishes to define itself as equestrian may enact an ordinance forbidding the construction of a home on any lot too small to accommodate stables and trotting grounds, or may even ban automobiles from the jurisdiction. The desire to maintain an equestrian community is then offered as the justification for the ordinance. Courts have generally deferred to the internal political processes of the locality and upheld such exclusionary ordinances.

Such a construction of space has a broader political impact than the immediate consequence of the ordinance. By excluding non-equestrians from the community, a locality constructs a political space in which it is unlikely that an electoral challenge to the equestrian ordinance will ever succeed.[16] The "democratic process" that produces and legitimates exclusionary zoning is thus very questionable: in many cases, the only significant vote that will be taken on the exclusionary ordinance is the first vote. After it is enacted, exclusionary zoning has a self-perpetuating quality.[17]

When local policies are challenged as *racially* discriminatory, local boundaries may do the discriminatory work. Because these boundaries are left unexamined, it is impossible for plaintiffs to demonstrate discriminatory intent: the discrimination appears to be the result of aggregated-but-unconnected individual choices or merely a function of economic inequality, and therefore beyond the power of the courts to remedy. In *Village of Arlington Heights v. Metropolitan Housing Development Corp.*,[18] the Supreme Court upheld a village's prohibition of multifamily housing despite demonstrable racially restrictive effects.[19] The court accepted the locality's professed neutral motivation of a commitment to single-family housing and rejected the contention that this commitment could be inextricably bound up with racial and class prejudices.[20]

Most important for our purposes, the court tacitly accepted the zoning policy as the legitimate product of the local democratic process. It relied on the same conception of space that held sway in *Euclid, and accepted local boundaries as the demarcation of an autonomous political unit. But the boundaries,* combined with the zoning policy, exclude "outsiders" from the political processes of the locality.[21] Because it may be the homogeneity of the local political process that is responsible for the racially exclusionary policy, the court's deference to the locality's internal political process is unjustified: it is this very political process (as well as the boundaries that shape that process) that is at issue.[22]

Indeed, racial minorities with significant cultural particularities present an especially strong claim for political inclusion in a jurisdiction: if racial minorities are to enjoy equality in an otherwise racially homogeneous jurisdiction, they must have the opportunity to change the character of the political community, and not merely the right to enter on condition of conformity. Furthermore, even if minorities were willing to conform to a homogeneous community's norms, when exclusionary zoning takes on an economic character, the option may simply be unavailable. According to our economic model, the impoverished condition of segregated minorities is, at least in part, a function of their exclusion from the communities that control wealth and employment opportunities.

3. THE DISTRIBUTIVE CONSEQUENCES OF
SPATIAL EDUCATION: *Milliken* AND *Rodriguez*
Racially identified spaces demarcated by local boundaries have distributive as well as political consequences. Our economic model demonstrates that, because localities administer many taxing and spending functions, boundaries that segregate on the basis of wealth or race ensure that taxes are higher and quality of services lower in some jurisdictions than in others. Moreover, because local boundaries are regarded as sacrosanct in the implementation of desegregation remedies, if interlocal rather than intralocal segregation is more prevalent, the remedies will be of little consequence.

In *Milliken v. Bradley*,[23] the Supreme Court held that court-ordered school busing designed to remedy de jure racial segregation in the Detroit schools could not include predominantly white *suburban* school districts. The court found that because there was no evidence that the suburban districts that would be included under the court-ordered plan had themselves engaged in de jure discrimination, they could not be forced to participate in the busing remedy. This rationale is puzzling unless one views cities not as mere agents of state power but as autonomous entities. If cities were mere agents of state power, the state as a whole would be ultimately responsible for their discriminatory actions. Thus, the state as a whole would bear responsibility for remedying the discriminatory practices: an apportionment of blame and responsibility within the state would be arbitrary, and any such apportionment that hindered effective desegregation would be unacceptable.

One may object that because Michigan had allocated power and authority to cities, the court correctly allocated blame and responsibility in the same manner. However, the court failed to examine the motivation for the position of local jurisdictional boundaries; and by conceiving of local political space as opaque—as defining a singular entity—the court failed to consider the facts that Detroit's racial composition had changed, and that responsibility for historical segregation could no more be confined within

Detroit's city limits than could its white former residents.

By accepting the municipal boundaries as given, the *Milliken* court ironically segregated the scope of the remedy to racial segregation and, thereby, may have allowed the historical segregation to become entrenched rather than remedied. "The plaintiffs were to be trapped within the city's boundaries, without even an opportunity to demand that those boundary lines be justified as either rational or innocently irrational."

A similar pattern and misconception of space prevailed in *San Antonio Independent School District v. Rodriguez*,[24] in which the court held that a school-financing system that was based on local property taxes and produced large disparities in tax-burden-to-expenditure ratios among districts did not violate the equal protection clause. The court reasoned that a commitment to local control obliged it to uphold the Texas school-financing scheme. The court also rejected the argument that the Texas system of local funding was unconstitutionally arbitrary, and it asserted that "any scheme of local taxation—indeed the very existence of identifiable local governmental units—requires the establishment of jurisdictional boundaries that are inevitably arbitrary." The court's argument here is essentially circular. The appellees began by *challenging* as arbitrary the use of local boundaries as a means of determining the distribution of educational funds. The court's response asserts that arbitrariness is inevitable *if* local boundaries are to be respected. This is precisely what was at issue: Are local boundaries to be used to determine school finance levels or not?

The court's circular reasoning reflects another level of incongruence in its logic. While the court based its refusal to overturn the Texas system on respect for local autonomy and local boundaries, at the same time it justified the arbitrariness of Texas's local boundaries on the grounds that local boundaries are irrelevant. If respect for local government were as important as the court claimed, it seems strange that the court would so casually dismiss the fact that the boundaries defining these governments are arbitrary. However, if arbitrariness is inevitable, it seems illogical to accord arbitrarily defined subdivisions such respect.

The court's decision rests on two conflicting conceptions of local government and the political space it occupies. On the one hand, the court conceived of local space as transparent and thus viewed localities as mere subdivisions, the inconsequential and administratively necessary agents of centralized power; on the other, it conceived of local space as opaque and thus viewed localities as deserving of respect as autonomous political entities.

4. CONCLUSION: AUTONOMY AND ASSOCIATION

My thesis in this section has been that political space does the work of maintaining racially identified spaces, while reified political boundaries obscure the role of political space, representing it either as the delegation of state power, and therefore inconsequential, or as natural, and therefore inevitable. Doctrine insists that local governments are merely the geographically defined agents of centralized government. Although such delegation is viewed with great suspicion when the delegate is not geographically defined, courts have shown extreme deference to local political processes. For example, local boundaries become a talisman for purposes of voting rights, even when those denied the right to vote are directly affected by the policies of the jurisdiction. Local boundaries are regarded as sacrosanct even when doing so prevents an equitable distribution of public resources for *state* purposes or interferes with the constitutionally mandated desegregation of *state* schools. Thus, the decisions of the court in the foregoing cases rest on a shifting foundation of local sovereignty and local irrelevance.

One caveat is in order. My discussion has posed the issue as one that involves localities excluding outsiders with possible rights to inclusion. However, we must remember that local government law reflects a *conflict* between democratic inclusiveness and the exclusiveness that makes community possible. Indeed, because our focus is on racial minority groups, the related

tension between integration and separatism warrants consideration. We must not forget that in order to reject segregation, we need not unreservedly accept integration; indeed, especially for racial minorities, some degree of separatism may represent the best or only avenue of empowerment and fulfillment. In the cases I have examined, the reification of political space ensured that the conflict between integration and separatism, inclusion and exclusion, was never even addressed. In some cases, however, there may be good reasons to grant a locality the power to exclude. What are we to make, for example, of cases such as *Belle Terre*,[25] in which one set of associational rights clashes with another, or associational rights clash with rights to political participation?

I have no formula for resolving these issues, but I do submit that we must recognize these conflicts for what they are. If we do so, we may find that often the true conflict is falsely framed in terms of a generic "local sovereignty." As Laurence Tribe notes, the justification of *associational* autonomy is often unpersuasive—many localities are merely spaces where atomistic individuals sleep and occasionally eat. Hence, our desire for local autonomy is often less an impulse to preserve something that is already there than it is a desire to realize an ideal. In realizing this ideal, we must attend to issues of racial segregation and discrimination—in short, to issues of racially identified space—not only because constitutional principles so guide us, but also because the ideal is debased if we do not. As Iris M. Young has written: "The aggregate model . . . reduces the social group to a mere set of attributes attached to individuals. The association model also implicitly conceives the individual as ontologically prior to the collective, as making up, or constituting, groups."[26]

Just as I criticized a *typical* interest group pluralism and republicanism, I have also criticized a liberal *type* of political thought above. There are articulations of liberal political theory which are potentially more hospitable to racial-group identification and to a recognition of the salience of political geography. Many liberals would argue that racial groups are not inconsistent with but, rather, are assimilable to the general liberal typology that conceives of individuals as ontologically prior to groups. On such a view, liberal pluralists should support racial group identification because it is a precondition to meaningful individual choice.[27] Similarly, liberal republicans argue that individually based rights to privacy and association *are* important, though primarily as a means of facilitating the group identification that allows individual citizens to develop views relatively independent of the state.[28]

I disagree with the critics who insist that such attempts to combine insights about the necessity of group and cultural membership with pluralist and republican thought are hopelessly self-contradictory.[29] Such a criticism misses the point that *all* political thought deals in tensions that are an unavoidable feature of the political.[30] The best of political thought recognizes such conflicts and attempts to mediate them. I believe that my proposals and the analysis herein are largely consistent with these more sophisticated forms of liberalism, pluralism, and republicanism.

B. Seeing through but Not Overlooking Space: Statutory and Doctrinal Recognition of the Role of Political Space

Thus far, we have focused on the general tendency in legal analysis both to overlook the consequences of political space in geographically defined entities and to cede talisman significance to politically created boundaries, thereby at once ignoring and reifying political space.

C. Cultural Desegregation: Toward a Legal Practice of Culturally Plural Political Space

I. DESEGREGATION V. INTEGRATION

My discussion of racially identified spaces has been critical of the political boundaries that define these spaces. I have argued that contemporary society, through the mechanism of law, creates and perpetuates racially identified spaces without doing so explicitly. Thus, no attempt is made to justify the political spaces that are so perpetuated. Many readers may take my critique of racialized space as a call for a planned pro-

gram of spatial integration, such as the systematic dispersal of inner-city minority populations to the suburbs with mandatory busing to maintain public school integration. But this type of integration assumes the *existence* of racialized space, space that needs to be integrated. Through the elimination of racially identified space, we may find that some of the classic centralized methods of racial integration are no longer necessary or desirable.

If one accepts the importance of political geography, one might nevertheless object that the reforms proposed in this article will disrupt established communities and introduce elements of uncertainty and instability by removing the system that allowed these communities to come into existence. Political spaces create cultural communities; an implicit part of my thesis is that space, at least as much as time, is responsible for racial and/or cultural identity. Even for those members of a racial group who do not live in a racially identified space, the existence of such a space is central to their identity.[31] Hence, to decenter racially identified space is to some extent to decenter racial identity.

The foregoing analysis should make clear that no political system, including the current one, can remain neutral in the face of the social construction of geography; no system can simply reflect or accommodate "individual choice" as to residence and geographic association; no system is without some systematic bias. Because a truly neutral system is impossible, we must rewrite the laws to *favor*, rather than to obstruct, racial and class desegregation.[32]

A system of desegregated spaces would certainly result in fewer homogeneous spaces and more numerous integrated ones, but such a system is different from the classic model of integration in two important respects. First, it does not impose a particular pattern of integration; rather, it removes the impediments to a more fluid movement of persons and groups within and between political spaces. Second, this model does not accept the current manifestation of political space and simply attempt to "shuffle the demographic deck" to produce a statistical integration; rather, it challenges the mechanism by which political spaces are created and maintained, and by extension, it challenges one of the mechanisms by which racial and cultural hierarchies are maintained.

Thus, cultural desegregation is both more mild and more radical than classic integrationism. It is more mild because it does not mandate integration as an end: group cohesion may exist even in the absence of spatially enforced racial segregation, such that no significant increase in statistical integration will occur. Indeed, I imagine that spatially defined cultural communities that have experienced the exodus of many of their wealthier members (many of whom exit not due to a desire to assimilate but for economic reasons) would experience an increase in group cohesiveness, either because the middle and upper classes would return to culturally defined neighborhoods in the absence of economic and political disincentives, or because, as spatial boundaries become more permeable, geography would become a less important part of community definition. Individuals could be part of a political community that is geographically dispersed, even as many are now a part of dispersed cultural committees. Desegregated space would encourage cultural cohesion by rendering racialized political boundaries more permeable, and thus allowing members of culturally distinct communities to act on their cultural connections regardless of where they happen to reside.

In this latter sense, though, cultural desegregation is also more radical than integration. Cultural desegregation insists that cultural associations may be respected and encouraged regardless of the spatial dispersal of their members. It rejects both the assimilationist notion that individuals should aspire to become members of some imperial master culture, and leave their cultural identity behind in order to gain acceptance by "society-at-large,"[33] and the separatist notion that only through geographic consolidation and cultural anarchy can people of color hope to avoid cultural genocide (or suicide).

2. DESEGREGATED CULTURAL IDENTITY

Cultural desegregation aspires to a society in which cultural identity is dynamic in its definition and cultural communities are fluid but not amorphous. These two ideals are linked in a paradox: because cultural identity is established only in the context of a community or association, the position of cultural associations is critical to the formation of cultural identity; there is no individual cultural identity, for culture implies a community. At the same time, though, cultural specificity must imply an interaction with other cultures: a culture has a specific character only in that it is unlike other cultures with which it compares itself through interaction. However, interaction with other cultures will change a cultural community, and in some sense reduce its specificity. This paradox gives rise to fear of assimilation and inspires some to advocate cultural autarchy.

The solution to this paradox lies in understanding culture as a context, a community of meaning, rather than as a static entity or identity. A cultural community exists in a symbiotic relationship both with its members and with "outsiders." It can neither totally shape its members nor completely exclude outsiders. Yet this does not mean that the community is nothing more than the aggregation of its individual members; a cultural community has autonomy in that it can exert influence over individual members, construct morality, values, and desires, and provide an epistemological framework for its members. One may understand culture "to refer to the cultural community, or cultural structure, itself. On this view, the cultural community continues to exist even when its members are free to modify the character of the culture. . . ."[34]

If this understanding is correct, then culture is not threatened by internal dissent, outside influences, eventual transformation, nor even by the exit of certain members, just as the character of a democratic government is not threatened by changes in administration. To be sure, some changes are for the better and some for the worse, and some changes may indeed threaten the very structure of the culture, just as McCarthyism and the imperial presidency were thought to threaten the very structure of American democracy. However, the process of change itself is not to be feared—in fact, it is to be welcomed, for it is a part of the life of a culture. Although there are certainly distinct cultural communities, the boundaries between them often are a good deal more permeable than most discussions of cultural pluralism and cultural membership would suggest.

3. CULTURAL IDENTITY IN DESEGREGATED SPACE

Cultural associations are among the groups that exercise power, both formally and informally, through their control of physical spaces. Although the link between race and culture is not direct or unproblematic (and is beyond the scope of this article), we can identity this link in the creation and maintenance of racially identified spaces, occupied by racial and cultural communities.

As the tautology of community self-definition demonstrates, it is impossible for any community truly to determine its own identity. Thus, the desegregation of political space cannot provide an atmosphere of unmediated "free choice" for racial and cultural identity formation. What desegregation can do is level the hierarchies of racial and cultural identity so that presently disempowered and subordinated communities are no longer systematically deprived of the political and economic resources that would allow them to thrive rather than merely to survive, and so that such communities could more readily interact with American society as a whole.

Desegregation will undoubtedly alter the character of all racial communities: white communities are defined in part by their position of privilege, while minority communities are defined in part by their subordination and isolation. However, it is unclear exactly what the result of desegregation will be for established racial and cultural groups. Some groups may experience dispersal and disintegration, as ethnic white communities have in many parts of the nation. Some groups may grow stronger and more cohesive as their members gain greater resources and feel less economic pressure to leave racially identified neighborhoods and cities, while those who do leave will be able to experience group solidarity that does not depend on geographic proximity. New but distinct

cultural communities may form as permeable political borders allow social, political, artistic, and educational alliances between previously isolated communities to develop. Whatever the result, it will reflect a form of cultural association and pluralism that is more consistent with the best of American democratic ideals.

III. CONCLUSION: THE BOUNDARIES OF RACE

THIS article has attempted to bring several distinct discourses to bear on the persistent issue of race relations and racial segregation in the United States. I have employed political economy and political geography, Legal Realist analytics, ideal and nonideal normative political and social theory, Critical Legal Theory and Critical Race Theory, and a light dash of postmodernist social theory as well as urbanist theory. My focus herein has been necessarily sweeping and has, I fear, often sacrificed detail for breadth. Every discourse I have employed has a long academic tradition in which countless scholars have probed many of these issues in much greater depth than this article could allow. My goal here is to bring the insights of these various conversations together in order to demonstrate that racial segregation is a consequence of law and policy, that it can be changed by law and policy, and that there is ample precedent in American legal and political thought for the types of changes that would dramatically decrease the degree of segregation in America and the cities.

This article is the beginning of what I hope will be an ongoing project. It probably raises more questions than it answers. I would like to have discussed in much greater detail such questions as the role of political space in the social construction of racial identity and the consequences of political space for identity politics and identity communitarianism, the complexities of all the policy proposals I have advanced, and the importance of changes in the economic structure and cultural logic of late-twentieth-century America for contemporary racial and spatial relations. However, these questions are for another space.

A note on methodology may now be in order. One objection to the relentlessly structural analysis that I have employed is that it devalues human agency and individual morality—that, by focusing on structures, one downplays the personal responsibility of flesh-and-blood people for social inequity. Some may well object that I let racists off the hook by proposing that political and economic institutions make racism inevitable. It is not my intention to supplant a strictly moral argument against racist practices but, instead, to augment such an argument. I do not know what evil lurks in the hearts of men and women; but I do believe that the existing structure of what I have dubbed "racially identified political space" is likely to encourage even good men and women to perpetuate racial hierarchy. We need moral condemnation of racism, but we also need viable solutions. I do not intend this article to in any way stifle the former; I hope it may contribute to identifying the latter.

We need solutions now. The threat of a racially fragmented metropolis and nation looms large on the horizon. The United States is rapidly fulfilling the grim prophesy of the Kerner Commission and becoming *at least* "two societies, one black, one white—separate and unequal."[35] Race relations are at a low ebb, a circumstance that contributes to the declining desirability of life in racially diverse urban areas. At the same time, though, the 1990 census shows for the first time that more than half of all Americans live in megacities—metropolitan areas of more than one million inhabitants. To survive and thrive in the metropolis that is America, we must attend to matters of race and of political space; it is not only space as much as time that hides consequences from us, but it is also location as much as history that defines us. If, as Douglas Massey and Nancy Denton assert, segregation is the missing link in previous attempts to explain the conditions of the underclass, then political geography is the missing element in attempts to reconcile the ideals of majoritarian democracy and private property with those of racial equality and cultural autonomy. The question of political space is not one of narrow concern, the province of cartographers and surveyors; it is also the domain of the "democratic idealist," the activist lawyer, and the scholar of jurisprudence. Most of all it is

the domain of every citizen who believes in the experiment of self-government. The study of political space reveals that "we the people" is not a given but, rather, a contested community in a democratic society. The recognition that political spaces are often racially identified reveals that the boundaries of a democracy share territory with the boundaries of race.

NOTES

1. "Housing denotes an enormously complicated idea. It refers to ... a specific location in relation to work and services, neighbors and neighborhood, property rights and privacy provisions, income and investment opportunities...." R. Montgomery and D. R. Mandelker, eds., *Housing in America: Problems and Perspectives*, 3 (2d ed. 1979).

2. By "quasi-jurisdictional boundaries" I mean the boundaries that define private entities that perform "governmental" functions. These entities, which exercise all the relevant power of governments, constitute an important part of political geography.

3. D. S. Massey and N. A. Denton, *American Apartheid: Segregation and the Making of the Underclass I*, at 3 (1993).

4. R. G. Bratt, C. Hartman, and A. Meyerson, "Editor's Introduction," in R. G. Bratt, C. Hartman and A. Meyerson, eds.,*Critical Perspectives on Housing*, at xi, xviii (1986) (quoting E. P. Achtenburg and P. Marcuse, "Towards the Decommodification of Housing: A Political Analysis and a Progressive Program," in C. Hartman, ed., *America's Housing Crisis*, 202, 207 (1983)).

5. Massey and Denton, *supra* note 3, at 2.

6. 334 U.S. I (1948).

7. See Charles Abrams, *Forbidden Neighbors: A Study of Prejudice in Housing* 231 (1955); see also Massey and Denton, *supra* note 3, at 50–53 (describing the practice of redlining).

8. M. Mahoney, "Note, Law and Racial Geography: Public Housing and the Economy in New Orleans," 42 *Stan. L. Rev.*, 1251, 1258 (1990).

9. Massey and Denton, *supra* note 3, at 52.

10. *Id.* at 36.

11. Massey and Denton, *supra* note 3.

12. Although this article's primary focus is on the position of blacks within a racially segregated political geography, much of the analysis herein will also be applicable to other racial minority groups. Nonetheless, black segregation is far more pronounced than that of any other racial group; see D. Massey and N. Denton, "Trends in Residential Segregation of Blacks, Hispanics, and Asians, 1970–1980," 52 *Am. Soc. Rev.*, 802, 823 (1987). Moreover, racial segregation is an especially important factor in contributing to the concentration of poverty among blacks in particular; see

D. S. Massey and M. L. Eggers, "The Ecology of Inequality: Minorities and the Concentration of Poverty, 1970–1980," 95 *Am. J. Soc.*, 1153, 1185–86 (1990). Therefore my analysis will be of the greatest significance to black segregation.

This article will use terms such as "racial minority" or "people of color" when its analysis has broader applicability, and will use more limiting terminology when the empirical or historical context is limited to a particular group. The goal throughout is to limit the object of the analysis whenever necessary and to leave open the possibility of broad applicability whenever possible.

13. See Robert Staples, *The Urban Plantation: Racism and Colonialism in the Post Civil Rights Era*, 204–05 ("[A] house in a predominantly black neighborhood is devalued by thousands of dollars. . . . [B]lacks receive 1.2 percent of their income from property, compared with seven percent for whites"); S. Minerbrook, "Blacks Locked out of The American Dream," *Bus. and Soc'y. Rev.* (Sept. 22, 1993) 3 ("In 1988, the U.S. Census Bureau concluded that white families had 10 times the wealth of blacks in America. Crucially, 40 percent of that difference was the lack of home equity between black and white families").

14. D. S. Massey and N. A. Denton, *supra* note 3, at 160.

15. M. Foucault, "The Eye of Power," in C. Gordon, ed., *Power, Knowledge*, 146, 149, C. Gordon et al., trans., (1980).

16. Moreover, because most state constitutions provide for local home rule, there is frequently no basis upon which to challenge such an ordinance in state courts.

17. This is merely one example of the tautology of community self-definition. One must decide who is a member of the community before one can inquire as to the community's opinion of itself, whether that inquiry takes the form of a judicial determination, an election or a referendum.

18. 429 U.S. 252 (1977).

19. See *id.* at 268–71.

20. See *id.*

21. Laurence H. Tribe, *American Constitutional Law* § 13-11 to 13, at 1086–91.

22. It is true that the plantiffs did not raise the issue of voting rights in *Arlington Heights*. Of course, their failure to do so is no objection to the thesis that a misconception of political space obscured the tension between local autonomy and centralized power. Indeed, it is further proof: the plantiffs neglected a potentially powerful argument against the zoning restriction because they did not imagine challenging the boundaries that separated them from the political process if Arlington Heights.

23. 418 U.S. 717 (1974).

24. 411 U.S. 1 (1973). *Rodriguez* does not explicitly involve race, although racial overtones shade its discussion of school

districts with vastly disparate tax bases. The *Rodriguez* appellees would have been hard pressed to state a race-based claim without evidence of intentional discrimination. Even if the plaintiff could have shown an overrepresentation of Mexican-Americans in poorer districts, such a showing could be easily dismissed as coincidential unless one were to examine the interaction of race and the structure of political geography in a comprehensive way. Because this Article does that, *Rodriguez* provides a useful supplement to *Milliken* by demonstrating the distributive consequences of local boundaries: segregated localities with unequal tax bases promote a racially disparate distribution of public funds.

25. 416 U.S. 1 (1974).

26. Iris M. Young, *Justice and the Politics of Difference* 44 (1990). I would add to Young's conception that the "authentic self" stands apart from, and outside of, political space.

27. See, for example, W. Kymlicka, *Liberalism, Community, and Culture*, 197 (1989) (arguing that group-based rights are consistent with liberal political thought).

28. See, for example, Frank I. Michelman, "Law's Republic," 97 *Yale L. J.* 1534–36 (1988).

29. See, for example, C. Kukathas, "Are There Any Cultural Rights?" 20 *Pol. Theory*, 105, 115–24 (1992) (criticizing Will Kymlicka's liberal defense of cultural rights); Cynthia V. Ward, "The Limits of 'Liberal Republicanism': Why Group-Based Remedies and Republican Citizenship Don't Mix," 91 *Colum. L. Rev.* 583–84, 589–96, 603–06 (1991) (criticizing Michelman's and Sunstein's republican defenses of group-based rights for oppressed minorities).

30. See generally B. Honig, *Political Theory and the Displacement of Politics*, 200–11 (1993) (arguing that "the perpetuity of contest" is the essential, and most valuable, quality of democratic politics); D. Kennedy, "The Structure of Blackstone's Commentaries," 28 *Buff. L. Rev.*, 205 (1979) (arguing that legal and political analysis is characterized by a "fundamental contradiction" between the need for individual autonomy and the need for affirmation and solidarity in groups).

31. Anyone who doubts the importance of a geographical base need only look to the immigrant and racially identified communities who reconstruct a racionational space within their new home country and who look toward their ancestral homeland long after any tangible connections have disintegrated. Consider the emotional bond of Miami Cubans to a Cuba that is unlikely to accept them within this century and is undoubtedly far less familiar to many of them than Southern Florida; see generally, D. Rieff, *The Exile* (1993). Or consider the ties that bind American Jews to Israel despite, in many cases, the lack of any personal familial connection or any plans to relocate there. Consider also the creation of mythical or quasi-mythical homelands where no real world racial space is available, such as Atzlan for Launos and the mythologized Africa of much "Afrocentric" thought, which bears little resemblance to any part of Africa that exists or has ever existed in history. Racially identified

urban spaces are in this sense, a microcosm of the nationalist homeland ideology projected onto the geography of the metropolis; see R. T. Ford, "Urban Space and the Color Line: The Consequences, Demarcation and Disorientation in the Postmodern Metropolis," 9 *Harv. Black Letter J.*, 117, 132–33 (1992).

32. The loss of the elements of racial identity that are a function of segregation may be a partially positive development. I reject the "culture of poverty" thesis, which often attempts to explain the conditions of the underclass without acknowledging the role of the structural bias and inequity of which residential segregation is the linchpin; see D. P. Moynihan, U. S. Dep't. of Labor, The Negro Family: The Case for National Action 29–30 (1965), in L. Reinwater and W. L. Yancey, *The Moynihan Report and the Politics of Controversy*, 75 (1967). The idea of a harmful and debilitating "culture of segregation," by contrast, has much to recommend it. As Massey and Denton argue: "residential segregation has been instrumental in creating a structural niche within which a deleterious set of attitudes and behaviors . . . has arisen and flourished. . . . [These] attitudes and behaviors . . . are antiethical and often hostile to success in the larger economy"; Massey and Denton, *supra* note 3, at 8. To the extent that racial identity reflects the debilitating and desperate conditions of segregation that have been imposed on the urban poor, it is nothing to celebrate. The sort of loss of cultural cohesion that might occur due to desegregation would only be a loss of mutual shackles and chains.

33. I am always troubled by my loss of eloquence when I attempt to describe what I and many others clumsily refer to as the "dominant culture," "the broader society" (as if the culture of most of the world is somehow narrow), or, worst of all, "white culture." I am most certainly referring to something by way of these terms, something I vaguely imagine resides in windowless rooms in oak-paneled estates near New Haven or Cambridge (Massachusetts or England, you decide). Still, I know of few people of any race who truly belong to this "dominant" culture. It seems to me that this dominant culture is dominant only in that it dominates our collective psyche as a nation—it is a phantasm that haunts American social life, it goes "bump" in the night even as Americans listen to the blues and jazz, mambo and mariachi, eat kimchi and tapas, read Amy Tan and James Baldwin. It is time we exorcise this phantasmal dominant culture once and for all and embrace the multicultural mosaic that has always been America.

34. Kymlicka, *supra* note 27, at 167.

35. U.S. Advisory Commission on Civil Disorders, Report I (1968).

❧

ROUGE ET NOIR REREAD: A POPULAR CONSTITUTIONAl HISTORY OF THE ANGELO HERNDON CASE
Kendall Thomas

I. INTRODUCTION

If the ruling and the oppressed elements in a population, if those who wish to maintain the status quo and those concerned to make changes, had, when they became articulate, the same philosophy, one might well be skeptical of its intellectual integrity.

—John Dewey[1]

IN 1932, Eugene Angelo Braxton Herndon, a young Afro-American member of the Communist Party, U.S.A. (CPUSA), was arrested in Atlanta and charged with an attempt to incite insurrection against that state's lawful authority. Some five years later, in *Herndon v. Lowry*, Herndon filed a writ of habeas corpus asking the U.S. Supreme Court to consider the constitutionality of the Georgia statute under which he had been convicted. Two weeks before his twenty-fourth birthday, the court, voting 5–4, declared the use of the Georgia political crimes statute against him unconstitutional on the grounds that it deprived Herndon of his rights to freedom of speech and assembly, and because the statute failed to furnish a reasonably ascertainable standard of guilt.

Herndon v. Lowry is generally acknowledged as one of the great civil liberties decisions of the thirties, one of the notable "success stories" of the Supreme Court's First Amendment jurisprudence. It marked the first time the Supreme Court had mentioned the Holmes-Brandeis "clear and present danger" formula in the ten years since its decision in *Whitney v. California*.[2] It was also the first case in which the court used the test to uphold the civil liberties claims of an individual against censorial state action, the first time the court reviewed a sedition conviction from the South, and the first political crimes conviction reviewed by the court that involved an African-American defendant.

One of the first critical commentaries on the

case appeared in the 1941 edition of *Free Speech in the United States*, Zechariah Chafee, Jr.'s classic study of First Amendment case law.[3] In an essay entitled *"Rouge et Noir,"* Professor Chafee noted that in *Herndon v. Lowry* "the Supreme Court was faced for the first time with the possibility that American citizens might be hanged or electrocuted for nothing except expressing objectionable opinions or owning objectionable books."[4] Chafee approached the arrest, trial, and conviction of Angelo Herndon as a case study in American political justice. Herndon's real crime, argued Chafee, was that he sought "to put the Fifteenth Amendment into wider effect."[5] Those in power in Georgia, Chafee ironically observed, were "afraid, not that the United States Constitution would be overthrown, but that it might be enforced."[6]

For Chafee, two features of *Herndon v. Lowry* were especially significant. First, the opinion stressed "the importance of the procedure in a sedition prosecution."[7] Second, the case had forced the court to take notice (albeit implicitly) of the political use to which southern states could put their criminal justice systems, crushing not only radical political activity but also moderate dissent and protest as well.

Curiously, Chafee attached little significance to the fact that the 1937 decision marked the third time in as many years that the Supreme Court had been called upon to decide whether the conviction of Angelo Herndon violated the First Amendment. *Free Speech in the United States* merely points out—in a footnote and without comment—that "the Supreme Court at first refused to consider the case at all."[8] Chafee does not discuss the court's 1935 decision not to take appellate jurisdiction on the ground that the federal questions raised on appeal had not been "properly presented";[9] nor does he mention the court's decision later that year refusing (without a written explanation) to grant Herndon's petition for rehearing.[10]

An interesting and revealing separation and categorization of the Supreme Court's three dispositions of the Angelo Herndon case has followed in the legal literature. On the one hand, the favorable opinion in *Herndon v. Lowry* has been included and discussed in any number of casebooks on constitutional law[11] and political and civil rights.[12] Discussion of the first adverse decision, *Herndon v. Georgia* on the other hand, has been confined for the most part to casebooks on federal court jurisdiction and procedure.[13] The court's decision to reject Herndon's petition for rehearing has been ignored altogether. Thus, what is essentially one case has been doctrinally dissected by scholars as though it were made up of three severable, marginally related or even unrelated parts. This conceptual dismemberment of the Angelo Herndon case has handicapped serious historical examination of one of its central themes— the intersection of race, culture, and politics in American constitutional law.

I do not mean to deny the validity of an orthodox doctrinal treatment of the Angelo Herndon case; but I am persuaded that this procedure does not, indeed cannot, allow for more than a partial account of its larger historical meaning. Without a cultural anatomy of the Angelo Herndon case, one cannot hope to attain more than a skeletal picture of its significance as an episode in the history of American constitutionalism during the interwar years.

This article, then, offers a "remembrance" of the case in the form of a cultural history of the political events that led to the court's first response to the case. I believe that the concept of a "popular memory" can offer us great insight into constitutional history, both as object and as method, and I have made the concept central to this article, not simply at the level of accent and emphasis but also in terms of epistemology and interpretation. [. . .]

American constitutional history remains one of the few disciplines in which the call for the rigorous reconstruction of our national past from the bottom up has for the most part been ignored. The historical treatment of constitutional law and politics in America is, in short, still largely an institutional history. We have yet to move beyond magisterial accounts of "great" advocates arguing "great" cases involving "great" issues decided by "great" judges sitting on "great" courts. I believe that American legal scholarship has paid insufficient attention to the cultural history of constitutionalism in America. The chief task of a cultural history of American constitutionalism is to identify and interpret the records left by those who have experienced the American constitutional order from its underside. A cultural history of constitutionalism from below diverges from institutional history in its object of study as well as in its method and procedures. Its project thus differs from the institutionalist enterprise in at least two respects. First, a cultural history of constitutionalism from the bottom up recognizes the right of "un- or misrepresented human groups to speak for and represent themselves in domains defined, politically and intellectually, as normally excluding them, usurping their signifying and representing functions, overriding their historical reality."[14]

More is at stake, however, than "adding one part of a population, that which has been neglected, to another, that which has provided the traditional information base."[15] Constitutional history from the bottom up also seeks to challenge the conceptual order or hierarchy that subtends the exclusion of the common run of human beings and their concerns from the historical study of constitutional law. This project, then, is not directed simply at reversing the long-standing bias against the record of the subaltern in American constitutional history. It also represents an effort "to broaden the basis of history, to enlarge its subject matter, make use of new raw materials and offer new maps of knowledge."[16]

One might anticipate that a popular memory of American constitutionalism will force us to rethink the very terms of constitutional history. The rereading offered here of the Angelo Herndon case should be taken as an illustration of the type of contribution that the quest for the recovery of a popular memory can make. [...]

The perspective of popular historical method permits us to see the extent to which the history of constitutionalism in America, viewed from its underside, can be plotted as a story of a body of law born of sustained struggle, the outcome of painful and passionate political and ideologi-cal contests between subordinate groups and dominant institutions. This is a story that the optic of institutional historiography is by definition unable to see, much less able to view empathetically. In my alternative account and interpretation of the Angelo Herndon case, I hope to show that it is only through the lens of popular memory that we can begin to reach a critical understanding of this and other chapters in the history of American constitutionalism. The method of popular constitutional history does not just re-create a legal case; it recalls a larger, largely forgotten political culture. It permits us to see Angelo Herndon not simply as an issue or problem for constitutional discourse but as a conscious agent in shaping this discourse.[17] In short, popular constitutional historiography refuses to view constitutionalism in American culture as the exclusive preserve of elites and institutions.

I begin with a reading of Angelo Herndon's political autobiography, *Let Me Live*.[18] After placing it within the popular tradition of Afro-American resistance literature, I use it and other contemporaneous texts to offer an alternative account of the Angelo Herndon case from the bottom up. I shall, of course, take up the specific legal issues that were raised, argued, and decided during the course of the case; thus, much of what I have to say will necessarily be cast in the familiar terms of orthodox constitutional history. However, in my reading of these texts of thirties' institutional legal consciousness, I search for traces of popular memory: my central focus is on discovering what the official statements of constitutional doctrine in the Angelo Herndon case tell us about insurgent political consciousness among African-Americans at one key moment in our national past. My purpose in this part, as in the rest of this article, is most emphatically not to offer a revisionist "doctrinal" history of the Angelo Herndon case. Rather, my main interest is in the larger lessons that this episode in our constitutional history conveys about a people's search for political literacy and the obstacles thrown in their way. This lesson is a broad one, of which the doctrinal dimensions of the case are merely one component. [...]

II. The Struggle for an Effective Political Language

[A]nd carmade Hall next he read a piece in The Atlanta Georgian that they was 6,000 dollars raze for the unployed releaf after the Demestrahun at the Cort house on Thirday morning. . . .

—Anonymous, handwritten "minutes" of July 1, 1932, meeting of the Ford and Foster Clubs[19]

A. Popular Culture and Political Consciousness

The Angelo Herndon case powerfully underscores the extent to which the history of the struggle of Afro-American people against an oppressive cultural (social, political, and economic) order has also always been the history of a struggle against an oppressive discursive or symbolic order. Lucius Outlaw describes this struggle as a collective effort

> to embrace where available, to construct where unavailable, those productions and expressions of meaning which serve to reflect the self-affirmations of black people, our views of the world, in concepts and forms which we have projected for these purposes.
> . . . [G]iven the history of enslavement, subjugation, subordination, discrimination, oppressions . . . which have been (and are) directed against us, [the struggle for cultural and political integrity] involves . . . "a counter-movement away from subordination to independence, from alienation through refutation, to self-affirmation," via a process of "reflection" which . . . "creates a different (and opposing) constellation of symbols and assumptions."[20]

One decisive dimension of the African-American struggle for political self-determination has been the practice of symbolic reversal. This term designates a process "whereby one moves on the level of symbolic meaning (and, it is hoped), the level of existence, from imposed determination of one's (a people's) existence to those generated [by] oneself (by the people themselves) in the process of living as affirmations of that existence in its authenticity."[21] Although one may question the adequacy of the larger framework in which it is embedded, Outlaw's basic point is surely correct: the strategic manipulation and reversal of the dominant culture's political symbols is, and has long been, a central feature of African-American resistance movements, in both their reformist and their radical incarnations.

[. . .] African-Americans have lived by and fought through symbols: we cannot hope to comprehend the history of their collective encounter with the ideology and institutions of American constitutionalism unless we carefully attend to its symbolic aspects, conceived both as an arena and as an arsenal of struggle. This is to acknowledge the centrality of culture as the site in which African-Americans have historically sought to make sense of and respond to their experience in the United States.

By culture, I mean a broad range of practices, rituals, attitudes, beliefs, doctrines, images, and ideas that traverse or "saturate"[22] the entire social formation. From this perspective, culture does not "stand above or apart from the many other activities and relationships that make up a society, including the socially organized forms of domination, exploitation, and power pervasive in our own society and its history."[23] To note the significance of cultural practices in the history of American constitutionalism is to view culture as formed by, contributing to, and embedded in law and politics.[24] . . .

Shortly before the Supreme Court rendered its decision in *Herndon v. Lowry*, Random House published *Let Me Live*.[25] The book articulates the cultural foundations of the political struggles waged by African-Americans during the Depression. On one level, Herndon's book is an extended meditation, in autobiographical form, on the relationships between language and power and between cultural and political consciousness.

The cultural tradition within which Herndon comes to grasp the nature of politics is the religion of the black Christian church. Early on in *Let Me Live*, Herndon describes his childhood religious conversion by an old uncle at a revival meeting. As Herndon tells it, this experience shaped and at the same time circumscribed his perception of the problem of race relations in America.

Years after the event, he compares and contrasts the emancipatory potential of religious belief with that of political radicalism after he is introduced to the work of the Unemployed Councils, a national organization for jobless workers of all colors which had formed in the winter of 1929–30.[26] At his first meeting, the unemployed black teenager listens to an old black steelworker explain why he has joined the Unemployed Council.[27] By the end of the meeting, Herndon decides to become one of the "reds," whom the black church had taught him were "wicked people blaspheming against God."[28] In a passage that evokes the tradition of spiritual autobiography, Herndon describes his entry into radical politics and consciousness as a second conversion experience:

> Strange, only once before had I walked up to a speaker who had moved me so deeply and been converted. That was the time when my Uncle Jeremiah preached his first sermon. . . . The emotional motivation in both cases was identical, but what a difference in their nature and in their aim! The change of my viewpoint was almost fabulous, emerging from the urge to escape the cruelties of life in religious abstractions into a healthy, vigorous and realistic recognition that life on earth, which was so full of struggle and tears for the poor, could be changed by the intelligent and organized will of the workers.[29]

For the first time, writes Herndon, he comes to see the promise and necessity for the political program of the CPUSA, which aimed to forge class alliances across the color line. This recognition entails nothing less than a complete reworking of Herndon's worldview:

> That night when I went to bed, I couldn't fall asleep. My mind was too excited by the events of the evening to calm down. Something very important had happened to me, I knew, and I lay with wide open eyes staring into the darkness of my room and thinking that it was at last necessary for me to revise my attitude toward white people. I had discovered at last the truth that not all white people were enemies and exploiters of the Negro people. In fact, the same vicious interests that were oppressing Negro workers were doing the same thing to white workers, that both black and white workers could solve their problems only by a united effort against the common enemy: the rich white people, they who owned the mines, the mills, the factories, the banks.[30]

Herndon's initiation into a new political language—Marxism—brings him to consciousness of the power of language itself. He writes:

My education, as I have made clear in this narrative, was practically nil. Throughout all my struggles and vicissitudes I hungered for learning. . . . But a new force now entered into my life. It created a revolution in it. The education I longed for in the world I had expected to find it [*sic*], I surprisingly began to receive in my new Communist circles. To the everlasting glory of the Communist movement may it be said that wherever it is active, it brings enlightenment and culture. . . . Every meeting of the Unemployment [*sic*] Council became a classroom for me. I never left one of them without bearing away with me the discovery of [a] new idea. Of course, I did not always understand everything that I heard or read, but what of it? It was enough that I understood that they were on the right track.[31]

Throughout *Let Me Live*, Herndon stresses the centrality of education to his political development. At one point, he notes the "painful concentration" with which he read a copy of the *Communist Manifesto* which a white worker had given him. To test his understanding of Marx and Engels, Herndon writes a "simple account"[32] of the text "in my own words":[33]

> The worker has no power. All he possesses is the power of his hands and his brains. It is his ability to produce things. It is only natural, therefore, that he should try and get as much as he can for his labor. To make his demands more effective he is obliged to band together with other workers into powerful labor organizations, for there is strength in numbers. The capitalists, on the other hand, own all the factories, the mines and the government. Their only interest is to make as much profit as they can. They are not concerned with the well-being of those who work for them. We see, therefore, that the interests of the capitalists and the workers are not the same. In fact, they are opposed to each other. What happens? A desperate fight takes place between the two. This is known as the class struggle.[34]

"The idea," says Herndon, "seemed so self-evident that I scolded myself for having been so stupid as not to have recognized it before."[35] In this moment, Herndon appropriates the grammar and categories of Marxist theory for use as a discursive means and an analytic tool with which to explain his condition and that of people like him. His effort to rewrite the *Communist Manifesto* in his own language is an attempt to rewrite his own life experience. Herndon's discovery of the language of class is the beginning of a decisive transformation of his thoughts and feelings about race in America.

The chief theoretical interest of these passages from *Let Me Live,* from the perspective of popular constitutional history, lies less in the substance of Herndon's Marxist politics than in what they indicate about the cultural process and forms through which Herndon's political consciousness was fashioned. Despite its flaws (and there were many),[36] the political culture of American Marxism enabled Angelo Herndon to acquire what so many young African-American men in our time find in the institution of the American prison: a political education providing a basic set of terms—a language—with which to interpret their place in society and try to change it.

It is easy to say in hindsight that Herndon and his black contemporaries were unwitting pawns in a cynical political game waged by the Soviet Union against the United States (and locally by the American Communist Party against the NAACP). It is equally easy to show that, as a theoretical and practical matter, the CPUSA was unwilling or unable to acknowledge that race and culture in American politics could not be subsumed under the language of class struggle. There is some truth in both these claims. In a sense, however, these criticisms are beside the point. We are still left with the task of explaining why blacks like Angelo Herndon chose to join and stay in the CPUSA and why, given all its theoretical and practical shortcomings, an organization like the CPUSA was still able to become such an "important force within the black community during the first years of the depression."[37] More fundamentally, these interpretations run the risk of refusing to see Angelo Herndon and those like him as historical actors in their own right and not merely objects or "instruments of some other will."[38] Nothing could be more elitist than blithely to dismiss Herndon's narrative of his trial and conviction, whether the dismissal takes the form of a weak claim that *Let Me Live* is a layman's legal history with which we need not be concerned, or whether it rests instead on a stronger assertion that the book is merely a piece of audacious Communist Party propaganda. The

belief that Herndon's purported ignorance makes *Let Me Live* irrelevant, or that his perceived insolence makes it unreliable, derives from premises that are more ideological than intellectual. [. . .]

For the popular constitutional historian, one of the most interesting aspects of *Let Me Live* is the fact that it offers an exemplary instance of the way law, politics, and culture articulate at the level of individual consciousness and sensibility. At one point in *Let Me Live,* Herndon acknowledges that "[s]ome people may, perhaps, accuse me of preaching or making unnecessary propaganda for the Communist cause. After all, they might say, this is only the story of my life and does not call for evangelical outbursts."[39] Herndon offers the following response: "To this I will answer in all earnestness that the story of my life without my reactions to my own problems and to the problems of the world with the Communistic viewpoint as its key and guide, without my fervors and indignations, without my hatreds and without my loves, would remain an untrue and distorted narrative, without blood and entrails."[40] These words provide a concrete illustration of the more abstract points I have made concerning the relationship among law, culture, and politics. Consider the cultural content and connotations of the expressive form in which Herndon defends his reliance on the political language of Marxism. His references to his "fervors and indignations," his "hatreds" and "loves," disclose a distinctive "structure of feeling"—a set of "meanings and values as they are actually lived or felt," as opposed to formal ideologies or worldviews. As Herndon tells it, he cannot not make use of the "enlightenment and culture"[41] he has acquired through his involvement with the CPUSA, because they have been woven into his very sensibility. It is only through the template of his cultural and political encounter with Marxism that Herndon can give meaning to his personal experiences in the courtrooms and jailhouses of Georgia. The passage above registers the degree to which Herndon's grasp of legal ideology and institutions emerged from and was embedded in practices and perspectives that were at the same time cultural and political.

Let Me Live resists the disciplinary and discursive encroachments of an institutionalist constitutional orientation. The story it tells is an episode in our constitutional history whose symbolic significance cannot be captured by the instrumental language of law. While an interpretation concerned solely with the legal "issues," "questions," "rules," "holdings," and "principles" raised by the Angelo Herndon case is important, it cannot begin to address the case's deeper cultural and political foundations. Of course, to say that the account of the Angelo Herndon case offered in *Let Me Live* eludes the language of conventional constitutional history does not mean that it cannot be told at all. The story of the role that black political insurgency has played in American constitutionalism—the story of which the Herndon case is a part—can indeed be told, so long as we give due regard to the cultural sources from which that insurgent consciousness emerged and to the cultural forms through which it was expressed. Herndon's account of what his experience with the law meant to him in political and cultural terms is a story that a constitutional history of the case from the bottom up holds itself bound to respect. By using *Let Me Live* as the starting point for my discussion of *Herndon v. Georgia*, I aim to enact at the level of method something similar to the symbolic reversal that Lucius Outlaw has identified as a defining characteristic of African-American political history, and thus to bring the cultural dimensions of the Angelo Herndon case from the margins to the interpretive center of our historical concerns.

B. *"A Scrap of Paper": The Trials of Angelo Herndon*

Let Me Live is a textual record of the inextricable links among law, politics, and culture in the history of Afro-American insurgency. What E. P. Thompson has observed of the literary record left by eighteenth-century English Puritans is equally true of *Let Me Live*. Herndon's account may be read as a "sign of how men felt and hoped, loved and hated, and of how they preserved certain values in the very texture of their language."[42] *Let Me Live* may be interpreted as a product of, and a meditation on, one of the central themes in the history of African people in America: the struggle of a people for political literacy and against the political resistance mobilized to frustrate that collective endeavor. Seen in this light, the Herndon case is an important episode in the historical effort of African-Americans to find a political language with which to understand their past aspirations and to articulate their future aspirations. Against this thematic backdrop, I turn to an account of the "discursive events" that brought Angelo Herndon before the bar of the U.S. Supreme Court.

I. WRITING AND RESISTANCE

An anonymous letter set the events in motion. On the night of June 29, 1932, hundreds of copies of a leaflet were distributed in the poor white and black neighborhoods of Atlanta. It read:

> WORKERS OF ATLANTA! EMPLOYED AND UNEMPLOYED—NEGRO AND WHITE—ATTENTION!
>
> MEN AND WOMEN OF ATLANTA
>
> Thousands of us, together with our families, are at this time facing starvation and misery and are about to be thrown out of our houses because the miserable charity hand-out that some of us were getting has been stopped! Hundreds of thousands of dollars have been collected from workers in this city for relief for the unemployed, and most of it has been squandered in high salaries for the heads of these relief agencies. Mr. T. K. Glenn, president of the Community Chest, is reported to be getting a salary of $10,000 a year. Mr. Frank Neely, executive director of the Community Chest, told the County Commission Saturday that he gets $6,500 a year, while at the same time no worker, no matter how big his family, gets more than two dollars and a half to live on. If we count the salaries paid the secretaries and the investigators working in the thirty-eight relief stations in this city, it should not surprise us that the money for relief was used up and there is no more left to keep us from starvation. If we allow ourselves to starve while these fakers grow fat off our misery, it will be our own fault.
>
> The bosses want us to starve peacefully and by this method save the money they have accumulated off our sweat and blood. We must force them to continue our relief and give more help. We must not allow them to stall us any longer with fake promises. The city and county authorities from the money they have already collected

from us in taxes, and by taking the incomes of the bankers and other rich capitalists, can take care of every unemployed family in Atlanta. We must make them do it.

At a meeting of the County Commissioners last Saturday, it was proposed by Walter S. McNeal, Jr., to have the police round up all unemployed workers and their families and ship them back to the farms and make them work for just board and no wages, while just a few months ago these hypocrites were talking about forced labor in Soviet Russia, a county where there is no starvation and where the workers rule! Are we going to let them force us into slavery?

At this meeting Mr. Hendrix said that there were no starving families in Atlanta, that if there is he has not seen any. Let's all of us, white and Negroes, together, with our women folk and children, go to his office in the country court house on Pryor and Hunter streets Thursday morning at 10:00 o'clock and show this faker that there is plenty of suffering in the city of Atlanta and demand that he give us immediate relief! Organize and fight for unemployment insurance at the expense of the government and the bosses! Demand immediate payment of the bonus to the ex-servicemen. Don't forget Thursday morning at the county court house.

Issued by the
UNEMPLOYMENT COMMITTEE OF ATLANTA
P.O. Box 339.[43]

The following morning Angelo Herndon, a nineteen-year-old black organizer for the CPUSA in Atlanta, was among the leaders of a peaceful march to the Fulton County court building.[44] More than a thousand people, black and white, participated in the protest. The march was reportedly the largest biracial demonstration the South had seen in decades. County officials called in a group of white marchers to discuss their concerns but refused altogether to talk to any of the black demonstrators. The day after the rally, the Fulton County Commission approved a six-thousand-dollar emergency appropriation to buy food for the twenty-three thousand people who had been solely or largely supported by the relief system.

The importance of this demonstration lies in the fact that it served both an instrumental and an expressive function: the gathering at the Fulton County courthouse was simultaneously a political and cultural event. Using forms of popular protest, these hungry and homeless men and women were able to force material

concessions from government officials who had ignored their plight. Equally significant, however, was the symbolic challenge this collective action posed to the racial status quo. In refusing to respect the racial boundaries that had separated them for so long, the poor blacks and whites who participated in the demonstration had taken tentative steps toward the creation of a new political and cultural community. For a brief moment, class consciousness trumped color consciousness, creating possibilities for an effective political coalition and collective self-identification across the color line. This extraordinary fact was not lost on the organizers of the gathering. In a leaflet announcing the government's concession, the Unemployed Council boasted of having "crammed the lie down the throat" of the commissioner who had denied that starving people existed in Atlanta, and it encouraged participants in the rally to help the council "force these fakers" to give more and regular support to the unemployed.[45]

The circular also pointed out that the county commissioners had attempted to divide the demonstrators along racial lines, warning that "[if] we allow the bosses to divide us they will keep us both starving." The pamphlet urged black and white workers to "stick together because that is the only way we can win. The bosses know this: that is why they work so hard to separate us. The privilege of starving separately don't mean anything to any sensible worker these days."[46] The leaflet called on the unemployed to resist any attempt by landlords to try to evict people in their neighborhoods, and it urged "the workers of every neighborhood to get together, organize your committees and see that no worker is evicted because he can't pay the rent."[47] The leaflet ended with a threat that was also a rallying cry: "We refuse to starve!"[48]

The Atlanta Police Department immediately assigned a squad of detectives to shadow the suspected leaders of the Unemployed Council. The department instructed detectives to put the city's post office under special surveillance, because both of the leaflets had listed a post office box there as the Unemployed Council's mailing address.

On the evening of July 11, 1932, two Atlanta policemen arrested Angelo Herndon as he was taking mail from P.O. Box 339. Herndon was taken to his apartment, where the policemen seized all of his books as well as bundles of pamphlets published by the CPUSA. Herndon was then taken to the Fulton County jail, where he was held for eleven days without bail "on suspicion." On July 21, a local white lawyer and two black lawyers filed a petition seeking the release of Herndon, who still had not been formally charged with any crime. A judge for the Fulton County Superior Court denied the request, but he did order the Fulton County Solicitor General's Office to secure an indictment within twenty-four hours or let Herndon go.

The next day, the Fulton County grand jury issued a formal indictment against Herndon.

[S]aid accused, in the County of Fulton and State of Georgia, on the 16th day of July, 1932 [a date on which Herndon was in the custody of the Atlanta police], with force and arms, did make an attempt to join in combined resistance to the lawful authority of the State of Georgia with intent to the denial of the lawful authority of the State of Georgia and with intent to defeat and overthrow the lawful authority of the State of Georgia by violent means and unlawful acts. . . .[49]

To support these charges, the indictment recited a long list of criminal acts that Herndon had allegedly committed. The indictment reads like a register of forbidden speech and transgressive discourse, an index of all the ideas that Georgia authorities feared a disaffected citizen of any class or color might think, hear, utter, read, or write. Herndon, the indictment charged, had called "public assemblies and mass meetings in the homes of various persons names and addresses are to the Grand Jurors unknown and did make speeches to various persons to the Grand Jurors unknown,"[50] allegedly to establish a group of persons "white and colored" under the banner of the courts and to provoke "combined opposition and resistance" to the state.[51]

The indictment further accused Herndon of soliciting persons "whose names are to the Grand Jurors unknown" to join the Communist Party and the Young Communist League.[52]

Despite the fact that the CPUSA and its subsidiary organizations had not been banned by law in Georgia, the indictment stated that Herndon's organizing work was animated by a criminal purpose to create "by acts of violence, by unlawful means and by revolution" a new government "known as the United Soviets Soviet Russia (sic)," sometimes called and known as the "the dictatorship of the Propertyless People."[53] The indictment also charged Herndon with circulating a number of books and pamphlets that called for insurrection, riots, and armed uprisings against the state. The writings cited included *The Life and Struggles of Negro Toilers*, which stated that in "no other so-called civilized country in the world are human beings treated as badly as these 15 million Negroes. They live under perpetual regime of white terror, which expressed itself in lynchings, peonage, racial segregation and other pronounced forms of white chauvinism. . . ."[54] Other writings listed in the indictment included a book called *Communism and Christianism*, which exhorted its readers to "[b]anish the Gods from the Skies and Capitalists from the Earth and Make the World Safe for Industrial Communism,"[55] and the *Southern Worker* and *The Daily Worker*, both CPUSA publications.[56]

Given the language and history of the statute that formed the basis of the indictment, the Herndon case would likely have been politicized even if the defendant had not been a Communist Party member. Angelo Herndon was indicted under Section 56 of the Georgia Penal Code, which read: "Any attempt, by persuasion or otherwise, to induce others to join in any combined resistance to the lawful authority of the State shall constitute an attempt to incite insurrection."[57] Anyone who reads this provision in the context of its long and infamous history is able to see the fear of racial unrest and radical politics that is reflected in every word.

During the 1830s a number of southern state legislatures, shaken by the Nat Turner rebellion and frightened by the increasingly militant posture of the abolitionist movement, enacted criminal laws against insurrection. The purpose of these laws was to guarantee that the full coercive power of the state would suppress not only attempted or actual slave revolts but any public opposition whatsoever to the institution of slavery and its ideology. The Georgia legislature revised its criminal calendar in 1833 to read: "Exciting an insurrection or revolt of slaves, or any attempt by writing, speaking, or otherwise, to excite an insurrection or revolt of slaves, shall be punished with death."[58] The next section of the penal code, which was intended to stop the flow of abolitionist literature into the South, made into a capital offense the introduction or circulation within the state of any written text aimed at inciting resistance, revolt, or insurrection among slaves or free blacks.

After the Civil War, the southern states were forced to revise their statutes to acknowledge the new status of their former slave population. Accordingly, in 1866 the Georgia legislature redrafted many of its laws, including the slave revolt provisions. Specific references to slaves were deleted from the text of these laws, but the concept of insurrection remained central. Insurrection was defined as combined resistance to the lawful authority of the state. The Georgia Penal Code was then amended to read that any "attempt, by persuasion or otherwise, to induce others to join in any combined resistance to the lawful authority of the State, shall constitute an attempt to incite insurrection."[59] Unless a jury recommended mercy, the statutory punishment for insurrection or attempted insurrection was death. The revised statute set no specific punishment for an attempt to incite insurrection (the crime of which Angelo Herndon was accused many years later); presumably, the legislature thought that an attempt to incite insurrection would fall within the language of the amended code. The state legislature also changed the accompanying section of the code dealing with insurrectionary texts, substituting a five- to twenty-year prison term for capital punishment.

There were two recorded prosecutions under the Georgia insurrection laws between 1866 and 1932. The first took place in 1868. John T. Gibson, described in the record as a preacher and a "free person of color,"[60] was charged with inciting one hundred blacks to break into a

Georgia jail to rescue a local black man being held there. Under Gibson's alleged direction, armed blacks attempted to enter the jail but retreated after a guard fired a shot into the crowd. No other violence followed. Gibson was sentenced to death following his conviction for attempting to incite insurrection.

In 1869, Gibson's attorneys appealed his conviction to the Georgia Supreme Court. They argued that the state's penal code failed to expressly include attempts to incite insurrection, as distinguished from insurrection itself and attempted insurrection. The court found for the defense and ordered Gibson's release, reasoning that the rule that required strict construction of penal statutes rendered the Gibson conviction void because the statute had not specifically included attempts to incite insurrection. The opinion called the attention of the legislature to the omission and expressed a hope that this defect would be cured. The Georgia legislature obliged in 1871, making an attempt to incite insurrection a capital crime. The statute remained unused for nearly sixty years, until Fulton County authorities turned to it in the early thirties.

The second recorded use of Georgia's insurrection laws came in the case of the "Atlanta Six." The Atlanta Six were four men and two women, all members of the CPUSA, who were accused of attempting to incite insurrection and circulating insurrectionary literature. It was clear from the beginning that the prosecution of the Atlanta Six was based on the group's political ideology, and not on any alleged criminal acts. Through the efforts of Walter Wilson, a member of the ACLU, several state newspapers published a statement during the summer of 1930, signed by sixty-one prominent Georgians, condemning the political prosecution of the Atlanta Six. Although the statement did not go so far as to endorse Communism, it did argue that members of the CPUSA, like all Americans, should be protected in their constitutional rights of free speech and assembly.

2. WAR OF WORDS

William L. Patterson, the black secretary of the International Labor Defense (the CPUSA's equivalent of today's NAACP Legal Defense and Education Fund), arrived in Atlanta shortly after Herndon's arrest to organize Herndon's legal defense. Patterson promptly denounced the case as a "frame-up" and charged that almost "every bit of so-called 'Red' literature found in [Herndon's] room after this arrest may be found in books, magazines and pamphlets at the public library. Why not arrest the librarian?"[61] John H. Hudson, the prosecutor who later argued the state's case against Herndon, had already made Fulton County's position toward the young black radical, and others like him, emphatically clear: "You well know that this country cannot survive if people are allowed to go from one end to another of this country preaching, teaching, and working for its destruction," Hudson warned. "The Communists must be put down or civilization will fail."

These remarks were the opening shots in a rhetorical battle that was to escalate rapidly in the months before Herndon's trial, in early January 1933. Viewed in the context in which it was fought, this war of words for control over the political interpretation of the Angelo Herndon case was not at all surprising. At the time, there were mounting racial tensions in Atlanta; growing discontent among the city's unemployed in the worst year of the longest, deepest economic depression in modern American history; a perceived need among those in power to crush any and all signs of political insurgency among poor white and black communities; and a single-minded determination on the part of the CPUSA and the International Labor Defense to make the Angelo Herndon case a symbol of racial injustice in America. All this, together with the fact that the arrest and conviction of Angelo Herndon followed closely upon the success of the Unemployment Council's June 1932 demonstration, made for a classic "political" trial.

A publication from the period shows the degree to which the intertwined issues of race, radical politics, and political repression had come to occupy an important place in mainstream political discourse in America. The *Crisis*, a publication of the NAACP, "ask[ed] fourteen editors of leading black newspapers their opinion of Communism"[62] and printed their responses in its April and May issues. The editor of a Maryland newspaper, the *Afro-American*, wrote, "The Communists appear to be the only party going our way. They are as radical as the N.A.A.C.P. were [*sic*] twenty years ago. Since the abolitionists passed off the scene, no white group of national prominence has openly advocated the economic, political and social equality of the black folks."[63]

Although the editor of Virginia's *Norfolk Journal and Guide* did not think communism offered "the way out for the Negro which shall be most beneficial and lasting in the long run," he predicted that the CPUSA would continue to gain adherents in the black community because "traditional American conditions with their race prejudice, economic semi-enslavement, lack of equal opportunity, and discrimination of all sorts have made the Negro susceptible to any doctrine which promises a brighter future, where race and color will not be a penalty."[64] The editor of the *New York Amsterdam News* noted that "[s]ince America's twelve million Negro population is so largely identified with the working class, the wonder is not that the Negro is beginning, at least, to think along Communistic lines, but that he did not embrace that doctrine en masse long ago."[65] The editor of the *Philadelphia Tribune* argued that while

> [t]houghtful Negroes may reason that the philosophy and economic theories of Communism are unsound and will not obtain for them a more equitable distribution of the products of their labor, or a larger degree of justice . . . a drowning man will grab at a straw. When it is considered that equality is the theory of Communism, and that inequality is the result of the present system, it is amazing that millions of Negroes have not joined the followers of the red flag, instead of a few thousands.[66]

The editor of the *Atlanta World* argued that "the Negro as a whole fears Communism—probably because white America has not accepted it. Some frankly believe Red promises would be forgotten were they in power, for aren't they white men too?"[67] The editor did admit, however, that if "enough of us would go

Red," twelve million black communists "would be too big a group to deal with by force."[68] Ten years before, such openly positive views on the Communist Party from leading figures in the black establishment press would have been unthinkable.

The year 1932 also saw the publication of *Georgia Nigger*, a thinly fictionalized account of life in a Georgia prison camp, written by a white journalist named John Spivak.[69] Spivak had been given permission from the state prison commissioner to tour the Georgia convict camps in preparation for a "study" of the state's penal system. Spivak's study turned out to be a scathing expose of the state's brutal prison system, complete with powerful documentary photographs. Although Spivak took care to note that "Georgia does not stand alone as a state lost to fundamental justice and humanity,"[70] this did little to mollify state officials when they learned that a resolution had been introduced in the U.S. Senate calling for an immediate and thorough investigation of the charges that Spivak had made. Although *Georgia Nigger* never directly addressed the political ramifications of a penal system dominated by a largely black population, the CPUSA and the International Labor Defense took full advantage of the propaganda value of Spivak's book and used its image of racial injustice to bring the Angelo Herndon case into the national political consciousness.

3. RACE, RADICALISM, AND RIGHTS

Such was the complex political backdrop against which the trial of Angelo Herndon took place. Although the trial lasted a mere three days, during its course issues were raised and argued that went far beyond the technical legal question of whether Herndon was guilty beyond a reasonable doubt of attempting to incite insurrection. These issues opened onto the whole history of the black experience in the American South: the exclusion of blacks from petit and grand juries in Georgia; the treatment of black prisoners in Georgia jails; the long-standing taboo against black lawyers arguing cases as politically charged as Herndon's; the ideology of southern law and order (laid bare when death threats were made against Herndon, his

attorneys, and anyone else who was bold enough publicly to support or participate in the effort to build a defense movement around the case); the myth of white supremacy, which trumpeted the racial superiority of even the poorest, most illiterate white worker and demonized the class-color alliance of the Unemployed Council as an offense against God and nature; and the meaning of the Marxist theory of revolution generally and the theoretical platform of the CPUSA in particular. By the time the case reached the U.S. Supreme Court, these explosive issues of race, class, and radicalism would be submerged from view. At the trial stage, however, each of these issues provided a site of fierce ideological contestation.

It was the issue of race, though, that served as the most potent conductor for white Georgians' fear of Angelo Herndon and what they took him to represent. Two characteristic passages from the trial record provide an index of the centrality of racial ideology in the Herndon case.

One hotly contested question had to do with how Herndon's race would be referred to during the trial proceedings. At one point, T. J. Stephens, an assistant in the Fulton County Solicitor General's Office and the prosecution's main witness, referred to Herndon as "this darkey." The following exchange ensued between Lee B. Wyatt, the trial court judge, and Ben Davis, the black lawyer and recent Harvard Law School graduate who represented Herndon:

ATTORNEY DAVIS: Mr. Stephens refers to the defendant as "darkey." Your Honor, we wish to remind the prosecution if they insist on using such opprobrious terms to the defendant, we will have to ask for a mistrial, because it is prejudicial to our case.

THE COURT: I don't know whether it is or not; but suppose you refer to him as the defendant.

WITNESS: Your honor, I wish to state that "negro" is the name this man referred to his race by in his conversation with me—these are captious objections.

ATTORNEY DAVIS: But he says "darkey."

THE COURT: Well, refer to him as the defendant then.

WITNESS: I will refer to him as "negro" which is better; he gave the name of Alonzo Herndon—Angelo Herndon; he is the darkey with the glasses on. . . . [71]

A second heated exchange took place during the prosecution's cross-examination of T. J. Corley, an assistant professor of economics at Emory University, whom the defense sought to have qualified as an expert witness on the Marxist theory of the state. The subject under exploration was the "Black Belt" doctrine of the CPUSA, which called for black self-determination and political control over areas of the South in which African-Americans constituted a majority. After trying unsuccessfully to paint the witness as a communist sympathizer, if not an outright member of the CPUSA, the prosecution introduced a motif that it was to play upon throughout the trial.

Q. "Equal rights for the negroes; self-determination in the black belt"; you're able to tell us what that means, aren't you, Doctor?

A. No sir. I did not testify that I understand the planks in the communist platform, I said I was familiar with the party platform. As to whether I will now swear that I understand it, the question which you raise, I should say, is a question of opinion and not of fact, there are some questions of opinion, I could give you my opinion of what it means. As to whether it takes an opinion to tell the court and jury the ordinary Decatur Street meaning of self-determination, I think it is a matter of opinion, there are several techniques by which self-determination might be expressed, for instance, there might be a plebiscite vote, or there might be an election for representatives to a body—there are a number of ways in which self-determination would assert itself, and I think it is a matter of opinion. I have not read this little pamphlet entitled *The Communist Position on the Negro Question*. I would be glad to give the court and jury my understanding of the expression "Equal Rights for Negroes," the meaning of the phrase, as I see it, it is these: These rights are equal rights, are equal rights under the law.

Q. You understand that to mean the right of a colored boy to marry your daughter, if you have one?

ATTORNEY DAVIS: We object to that question on the ground that it is irrelevant and immaterial and calls for a conclusion of the witness.

THE COURT: He has him on cross-examination and that's a part of the language in the platform.

ATTORNEY DAVIS: There is nothing whatever in the platform about intermarriage.

THE COURT: The same quotation he is reading there is in the platform, as I understand.

ATTORNEY DAVIS: You overrule my objection, Your Honor?

THE COURT: I overrule the objection; go ahead.

A. A negro doesn't happen to have the right to marry my daughter, under the laws of this State. I don't know how many States there are in the Union where they do have that right.

Q. Did you know there are twenty States in the United States where the two races can intermarry?

A. No, I didn't know that, I knew there was a number, I didn't know how many.

ATTORNEY DAVIS: I don't see what that has to do with this particular case, Your Honor, we object to it as irrelevant and immaterial.

THE COURT: He has the witness on cross-examination, and he has testified that he knows what that phrase means, and he has a right to determine how much he knows about it, on cross-examination—it isn't his witness. [72]

From our contemporary perspective, it is tempting to laugh at these dialogues, which seem at times to parody themselves. Yet a proper historical reading of the trial record must remain mindful of the fact that these comic exchanges might well have had a tragic, deadly denouement: Herndon's life hung in the balance. If we viewed *Herndon v. Georgia* through the optic of an institutionally oriented constitutional history, we might well be tempted to discount these portions of the trial record on the ground that they have no bearing on the way the procedural and substantive issues raised by the case were discussed before the Supreme Court. As I shall argue presently, however, when viewed through the lens of popular memory, these apparently marginal moments from the Herndon trial record present cultural images and arguments the impact of which was decisive to the outcome of the Herndon prosecution.

My interest at this juncture is in the content of these interrogative exchanges. These ques-

tions and answers, and the ensuing verbal vol-
leys between the prosecution and defense counsel, carry a twofold significance. First and most
obviously, they indicate that the legal issues
raised in the Herndon prosecution were immediately translated into questions of race and
cultural power. The cultural meanings attached
to the fact that Herndon was black quickly and
definitively eclipsed the issues of free speech
and radical politics raised by the case, quite
literally coloring each and every aspect of the
trial proceeding. A second and more complicated issue is the degree to which the Herndon
case was invested with a sexual dimension. The
intersected histories of race and sex in America
tell an unseemly story beyond the scope of the
present discussion. Nonetheless, some attention
to the ideology of "sexual racism"[73] is indispensable in order to understand the precise
cultural inflections of the Angelo Herndon case.
This is so because "at the core of the heart of
the race problem is the sex problem."[74]

One prominent and recurrent theme in the
black American experience is whites' defensive
resort to sexual mythology as a source of ideological resistance to demands for racial justice.
The ideology of white supremacy has rarely
failed to find a dark and dangerous sexual motive behind the assertion of black political and
civil rights. This almost reflexive ascription of
sexual meanings to black political militancy is
surely one of the most constant and curious
features of our national history. In this respect,
the Herndon trial record provides a historical
case study of the effects of sexual racism on
the administration of law generally and the
protection of black political speech in particular.
From the outset, the legal and political issues
raised by the Herndon case were distorted by
the sexual fears and fantasies projected onto
Herndon by a cultural mentality in which power
and dominance were shot through with passion
and desire. For the men who controlled the
government of Fulton County, the most effective way to control, if not crush, the emerging
political discontent that Herndon and the local
CPUSA had successfully tapped was to evoke
the racist mythologies of rapacious black male
sexuality.

The language I have quoted from the Herndon trial record thus provides a vivid textual
instance of how deeply the cultural norms, practices, and protocols of the racially stratified
society in which Herndon lived were inscribed
in the workings of the law. At base, the legal
question of Herndon's guilt or innocence could
not be separated from either the cultural meanings attached to the idea of race or from the
political relations of white supremacy and black
subordination of which those cultural meanings
were both a cause and consequence. Once
drawn, the connection between race and radicalism meant that contested notions of cultural
identity and ideology would constitute the chief
terms in which the legal questions raised in the
Herndon case would be described, discussed,
debated, and decided during the trial proceedings. No one doubted that the outcome of
the case would thus depend as much on who
Herndon was as—if not more than—on what
he had done.

Prosecutor Hudson sought to make the perceived threat that Herndon posed to the local
racial order the pivotal issue in the case. He
made every effort during the trial to ensure that
the racial implications of the events leading up
to Herndon's arrest would be brought to the
attention of the all-white jury. As the passages
from the trial record indicate, the prosecution
lost no opportunity to exploit the symbolism
of Herndon's race. During the course of the
proceedings, the language of race was used both
to degrade Herndon (as in the dispute about
what to call him) and to demonize him (as in
the exchanges about the CPUSA position on
interracial marriage). Given the prosecution's
mobilization of racial meanings and metaphor,
Herndon's lawyer had to choose between two
equally untenable options. Benjamin Davis
could either admit that Herndon's race was in
fact a central issue in the case and respond
directly to the prosecution's race-baiting, or he
could downplay the racial aspects of the case
and address the issue only when the racist tactics
of the prosecution forced him to do so. He took
the latter, defensive posture.

Davis's defense of Angelo Herndon had two
components. First, Davis tried to establish the

technical insufficiency of the evidence introduced by the prosecution. During his cross-examination of Stephens, the assistant solicitor general, Davis successfully pressed the prosecution's key witness to admit that he had no personal knowledge of "any of the acts that have been alleged to be committed in the indictment by the defendant."[77] In addition to Professor T. J. Corley, whose cross-examination allowed the prosecution to raise the specter of interracial marriage, Davis called Mercer G. Evans, a professor of economics at Emory University. Although Judge Wyatt refused to qualify Evans as an expert witness, Davis did use Evans's testimony to show that the same Marxist literature found in Herndon's possession could be read at the Emory University library.

The second component of Herndon's defense was more straightforwardly political. The prosecution had sought to shape the meaning of the events leading to Herndon's arrest by resorting to racial rhetoric. Davis sought to transcend the issue of race by depicting the charges against Herndon as a campaign against the working class. This counterstrategy became clear when Angelo Herndon took the stand in his own behalf. Under Georgia criminal procedure, a defendant could make only an unsworn statement. This statement was not subject to questions by either prosecution or defense lawyers; it was a direct address from the defendant to a jury made up of his peers (in this case, Herndon's "peers" were all white). Herndon began by describing the closing of Fulton County relief agencies in June 1932 and explained the purpose behind the public rally that was organized by the Unemployed Council a few days after the termination of relief was announced. He stressed the power and potential of a class coalition such as that symbolized by the biracial demonstration at the Fulton County courthouse, ending his statement with a prediction that the alliance between poor whites and blacks forged by the Unemployed Council would not be destroyed by silencing its leaders.

> The capitalist class teaches race hatred to Negro and white workers and keeps it going all the time, tit for tat, the white worker running after the Negro worker and the Negro worker running after the white worker, and the capitalist becomes the exploiter and robber of them both. . . . It is in the interest of the capitalist to play one race against the other, so greater profits can be realized from the working people of all races. . . . [A]t the present time there are millions of workers in the United States without work, and the capitalist class, the state government, city government and all other governments, have taken no steps to provide relief for those unemployed. And it seems that this question is left up to the Negro and white workers to solve, and they will solve it by organizing and demanding the right to live, a right that they are entitled to some of the things that they have produced. Not only are they entitled to such things, but it is their right to demand them. When the State of Georgia and the City of Atlanta raised the question of inciting to insurrection and attempting to incite insurrection, or attempting to overthrow the government, all I can say is, that no matter what you do with the Angelo Herndons in the future, this question of unemployment, the question of unity between Negro and white workers cannot be solved with hands that are stained with the blood of an innocent individual.
>
> You may send me to my death, as far as I know. I expect you to do that anyway, so that's beside the point. But no one can deny these facts.[76]

One student of the case has suggested that Herndon's "undiplomatic and inexpedient speech, with its simplistic Marxist interpretations, did little to aid his cause."[77] As one reporter who covered the case wrote, Herndon had "really talked himself into jail. It seemed to me that he wanted to make a martyr of himself, and he did."[78] These observations are undoubtedly true. The position Herndon took in his courtroom address to "the unseen jury of the working class the world over"[79] provides ample evidence of his willingness to be enlisted as a "sacrificial goat" (to use the words of W. E. B. Du Bois[80]) on the altar of international Communism. The immediate goal, however, was clear: Herndon hoped to awaken the class consciousness of the jurors.

The closing statements continued the strategies that the prosecution and defense had followed throughout the trial. The prosecutor predictably played on the jurors' racial solidarity, arguing that they were duty bound as white men to crush Herndon's plan to "attack homes, take our property, rape our women, and murder our children."[81] The final words of Herndon's attorney to the jury were that anything short of Herndon's acquittal would be "making a scrap of paper out of the Bill of Rights, the Constitution of the United States and the State of Georgia."[82] Taking Herndon's lead, however, he spent the greater portion of his summary of the evidence trying to discredit Hudson's use of the race card as a cynical diversion from the real issues in the case. Davis accused the prosecution of seeking to "conjure up" the "basest passion of race prejudice"[83] in the jury. He appealed to the jurors not to let the prosecution's racist tactics blind them to the class interests that they shared with Herndon: "Gentlemen of the Jury, just as starvation, want and suffering knows [sic] no color or race line, neither does injustice and exploitation. What happens to Herndon today as you ponder his fate in the jury room is going to determine what is going to happen to you when the sharp pains of hunger tug at the helpless emaciated forms of your loved ones tomorrow.[84]

By the time the case went to the jury, the ideological battle lines between defense and prosecution could not have been more starkly drawn: at base, the choice between the two competing characterizations of Herndon's political activities would turn on the jurors' choice between competing claims of class and color.

Although Judge Wyatt had not hidden his hostility toward Herndon during the trial, his instructions to the jury were remarkably restrained and, from Herndon's perspective, generally favorable. Wyatt's charge to the jury was based on a much more generous interpretation of Section 56 than the interpretation placed on it when the case was appealed to the Georgia Supreme Court. After reminding the jury that Herndon was entitled to a legal presumption of innocence until proven guilty beyond a reasonable doubt, Judge Wyatt went on to read the indictment. He noted that mere advocacy of insurrection, "however reprehensible morally," would not warrant a guilty verdict unless the state had met its burden of proving that the advocacy was intended to be acted upon immediately: "In order to convict the defendant, gen-

tlemen, it must appear clearly by the evidence that immediate serious violence against the State of Georgia was to be expected or was advocated."[85] Judge Wyatt added that "the mere possession of radical literature . . . alone is not sufficient to constitute the crime of attempting to incite insurrection."[86] After admonishing the jury that the "object of all legal investigations is the discovery of the truth,"[87] the judge sent the twelve white men off to decide the fate of Angelo Herndon.

After deliberating just two hours, the jury returned to announce its verdict. It found Angelo Herndon guilty of attempting to incite insurrection but also "recommended" that the state grant him "mercy," as the jury had the power statutorily to do. This meant that instead of being sentenced to die, Angelo Herndon would be condemned to eighteen to twenty years of what John Spivak had described in *Georgia Nigger* as the living death of a chain gang.

A review of the record leaves little doubt that the prosecution of Angelo Herndon was a classic political trial. Politics figured in the Herndon case in at least two discrete senses. First, the Herndon trial can be called political because of the nature of the formal charges against him. As the language of the Georgia Penal Code and the indictment made clear, the attempt to incite insurrection was deemed a political crime against the "lawful authority of the State of Georgia."

However, the Herndon prosecution discloses a second political aspect that is best understood in cultural rather than legal terms. Attention to the language used at Herndon's trial indicates the degree to which the courtroom struggle over the legality of Herndon's political activities took place within a larger field of cultural contestation over racial meanings. It is not simply that the ideological disputes over race and culture that took place during the Herndon trial were intimately linked to ideological arguments about the legal control of political dissent. Rather, the legal debates at the Herndon trial about the competing claims of state power and individual rights were at the same time debates about the cultural politics—and the political culture—of white racism. To state the point in slightly different terms, it was in the language of race that the courtroom clashes about the proper legal interpretation of Herndon's CPUSA activities found their most potent "cultural signifiers," to use a term of G. Edward White:[88] racial rhetoric inscribed itself alongside and within legal argument. The language of race served as an instrument and a symbol of cultural contention over radical politics and state power.

When the U.S. Supreme Court was asked to review the constitutional issues raised by the Angelo Herndon case, its response betrayed no sign that this had been what one contemporary observer termed "one of the most spectacular trials in the annals of Fulton Superior Court." By that time, the heated disputes over race, culture, and power which had figured so prominently at the trial had apparently disappeared without a trace. With the passage of time and the change of judicial venue, the political passions and prejudices that had led to the trial and conviction of Angelo Herndon were obscured, though not utterly erased, by the cool logic and language of the law. . . .

III. That Court of History: Herndon and the Constitutional Historians

A rationale of history is the first step whereby the dispossessed repossess the world.

—Kenneth Burke[89]

A. Herndon and the Escape from History
This section considers the fate of the Angelo Herndon case in American constitutional historiography. My intention in what follows is not to offer an exhaustive descriptive account and analysis of mainstream American legal scholarship on the case. Rather, my goals are decidedly selective and critical. I want to review three typical historical views of the Angelo Herndon case, developed in the work of Wallace Mendelson,[90] Paul Murphy,[91] and David Currie.[92] More precisely, I want to advance an argument about the rhetorical forms in which these inter-

pretations are cast. I begin with a brief description of the main outlines of what each of these authors has to say about the Angelo Herndon case.

I. HERNDON AND THE HISTORY OF AN IDEAL
In an article entitled "Clear and Present Danger—From Schenck to Dennis,"[93] Wallace Mendelson traces the evolution of the clear and present danger doctrine from its initial use by Justice Holmes. Although Mendelson concedes that the doctrine "has embodied a deeply democratic instinct favoring the free expression of ideas,"[94] he suggests that it "has been more significant as a pervasive atmospheric pressure, than as a reliable standard for the decision of a specific case or as a rationale for a line of cases."[95] The burden of the article is to show how and why clear and present danger has remained more of a "great ideal" than an effective "guide to decision."[96]

Mendelson's main reference to the Angelo Herndon case appears in a brief discussion of the use of the clear and present danger doctrine between 1930 and 1940. According to Mendelson, the "decade of the thirties far surpasses all prior decades in the number of Supreme Court decisions vindicating civil liberties."[97] And yet, he observes, "[t]he danger rule . . . was mentioned only twice—once as an oblique underpinning for the Court's position and once in a dissent by Mr. Justice Cardozo."[98] Both references (we find in Mendelson's footnotes) involve judgments by the court on the issues raised in the Angelo Herndon case.[99]

In charting the fortunes of the clear and present danger test during the thirties, Mendelson aims to paint a picture in which the Hughes Court, unlike its predecessors, courageously assumed the role of guardian and protector against efforts by state and federal authorities to make inroads on the freedom of expression guaranteed under the First Amendment. "The chief justiceship of Mr. Hughes," writes Mendelson, "clearly marks a new dispensation."[100] He concludes that the primary contribution of the Hughes Court is that it kept Holmes's "great ideal"[101] alive (albeit "obliquely") until it could be "revived by a virtually unanimous Court"[102] in the next decade.

2. HERNDON AND THE HISTORY
OF AN AGENDA

Another discussion of the history of the Herndon case is found in Paul Murphy's *The Constitution in Crisis Times, 1918-1969.*[103] For Murphy, the Herndon case is most profitably understood as a product of a decisive ideological shift on the Supreme Court. Under Murphy's interpretation, the social and economic dislocation of the Depression engendered a corresponding crisis in predominant conceptions of the nature of the judicial function in particular as well as in the relationship of law to society in general.[104]

For Murphy, Herndon must be set against the backdrop of this fundamental ideological transformation. Murphy thinks of the First Amendment decisions of the Hughes Court as part of "a new judicial campaign that sought to undermine irresponsible state or state-sanctioned action."[105] These decisions reflected the Supreme Court's acceptance of the increasingly influential idea advanced by the legal realists that government "had an obligation to eliminate legal strictures that prevented the constructive use of personal liberty."[106] In Murphy's reading, however, the Herndon case also demonstrated that the court's new commitment to the protection of individual freedom did not represent a complete break with old understandings. For Murphy, the clearest evidence of this underlying continuity is the fact that the court did not rush to judgment in the Herndon case:

> The Court, on the other hand, clearly had no intention of upholding every vague challenge to local authority simply because local citizens felt that their rights were in one way or another being abrogated. It rejected, in 1935, the plea of a Negro Communist organizer in Georgia that an ancient insurrection statute under which he had been arrested deprived him of his constitutional rights. Its denial was based on the fact that he failed to specify which rights were being violated. Only when, in subsequent appeal, specific charges of free speech violation were leveled did the justices consider the issue. Then, speaking through Justice Roberts, they held that the statute as construed

and applied was repugnant to the Fourteenth Amendment in that it furnished no sufficiently ascertainable standard of guilt and that it interfered unduly with speech and assembly not demonstrably creating a clear and present danger of the use of force against the state.[107]

In Murphy's account, the court's refusal to disregard its procedural requirements was an attempt to reconcile its respect for established principles of constitutional federalism with its increased receptivity to First Amendment claims against the states.

3. HERNDON AND THE HISTORY
OF AN INSTITUTION

A third and more recent historical treatment of the Herndon case appears in David Currie's *The Constitution in the Supreme Court: Civil Rights and Liberties, 1930-1941.*[108] Like Mendelson and Murphy, Currie characterizes the thirties as a period in which the decisions of the court evidenced its increasing inclination "toward stricter scrutiny of punishment for allegedly subversive expression."[109]

Of the court's three considerations of the Herndon case, Currie mentions only *Herndon v. Lowry.*[110] That case stands out because it is the "least revolutionary"[111] of the court's three main decisions regarding the federal constitutional protection against state invasions of civil liberties. In Currie's analysis, the constitutional significance of *Herndon v. Lowry* lies in the fact that it evinced the court's willingness to examine and assess the nature of the evidence on which a challenged conviction for subversive speech was based. For Currie, the court's "new spirit of aggressiveness in reviewing . . . judicial findings affecting expression"[112] in *Herndon v. Lowry* was a sign that a majority of the court had come to accept the orientation toward First Amendment analysis that Justices Oliver Wendell Holmes and Louis Brandeis had staked out in earlier decades.

. . .

C. Making History

The indifference exhibited by Mendelson, Murphy, and Currie to other texts and other narratives—materials from which they might have derived a very different account of the Angelo Herndon case—appears to be driven by largely unacknowledged investments. I do not mean to suggest that the relationship between their interpretations and the ideological investments that inform them is indefensible. Rather, I believe that the combined force of their interpretive models and ideological affiliations forecloses lines of historical inquiry that might call their approaches and results into question. More fundamentally, what Murphy, Mendelson, and Currie have to say about the Angelo Herndon case reflects something more than mere intellectual interest. Ultimately, the belief that the case and the court's First Amendment jurisprudence as a whole reflect "a striving for fidelity to a true line of progress"[113] is just that—a belief. It is this article of faith more than any other feature of their work that forces the recognition that their accounts of Herndon are not disinterested scholarly analyses but rather interested interventions in a contested ideological field. In short, each of these works resonates with ideological affiliations and implications that a popular countermemory of the Herndon case aims (in the strongest sense of the term) to expose. There is a sense that the belief "in the inexorable laws of development" driving the historical work we have examined actually reflects "a certain contempt for ordinary people," such as Herndon.[114]

A popular constitutional history of the Herndon case is skeptical of any historical practice that forces the events that led to *Herndon v. Georgia* and *Herndon v. Lowry* into the interpretive model of foreordained progress. A popular constitutional history is unwilling to impose a teleological framework on the raw material that constitutes its object of study. The source of this agnosticism is a realization that the progressivist vision of constitutional history is both an interpretive structure of "memory and remembering" and, at the same time, an ideological strategy of "organized forgetting":[115] what is forgotten, though, is the lived experience of those whose stories disrupt the ordered image that the historical narrative of constitutional progress imposes on an unruly past.

It is precisely this aspect of organized forget-

ting that I have aimed to identify and interrogate in my critical readings of the rhetorical and narrative dimensions of the accounts of Mendelson, Currie, and Murphy. History does not always have a happy ending. When one considers the cultural context in which *Herndon v. Georgia* arose and was adjudicated, it was at the time far from obvious that the defeat in that case would become the "success story" of *Herndon v. Lowry*. This is probably the main reason for the doctrinal and historical segregation of the two cases from each other, for the events leading up to the court's decision in *Herndon v. Georgia* tell a story of repression and resistance, a story that is crucial to an understanding of the case from the bottom up. A subaltern perspective on the Angelo Herndon case discloses an alternative historical vision of the thirties, in which First Amendment law was a contested terrain, scarred and cracked by a bleak and often bloody political past. In my view, *Let Me Live* and the decision in *Herndon v. Georgia* are important textual sources for recounting this countermemory of repression and resistance. As such, they should not be cordoned off in a separate historical field. . . .

The heart of my argument is that the questions of race, power, and culture are no less central to Herndon's significance in our constitutional history than the aspects of the case around which institutional histories have revolved. I believe, with W. E. B. Du Bois, that the subaltern's view of *Herndon v. Georgia* tells a story of which constitutional history "has saved all too little of authentic record and tried to forget or ignore even the little saved."[116] In reading the record of the case left by Herndon himself, I have sought to highlight features of the case which seem to be outside the interpretive horizon of institutional history. The themes of resistance and repression sounded in *Let Me Live* must be accorded their rightful place, alongside the theme of progress which has so captured the institutionalist's historical imagination. A history of the Angelo Herndon case that ignores his subaltern account of its significance is a history, in Herndon's words, "without blood and entrails."[117] Herndon's account is valuable because it provides a perspective on the case from below—from the point of view of those for whom "[h]istory is what hurts."[118]

I am not endorsing a historical practice that uncritically siphons off Herndon's subaltern experience from the larger historical current of which it was a part. The two are inextricably related; their separation is neither possible nor desirable. However, I do contend that Herndon's subaltern experience (or, more precisely, the recorded remains of it) is as fundamental and significant an index of American constitutionalism as that found in official legal texts. My insistence on reckoning the constitutional meanings into the cultural record left by the historically dispossessed is not merely an effort to replace the current hegemony of institutional history with that of a hegemonic popular memory. It is an attempt, rather, to retrieve the "buried" and "subjugated knowledges"[119] bequeathed to us by Americans who lived out their lives at the bottom of our constitutional order.

My discussion has been guided by three main concerns. First, I have tried to show that the complex ebb and flow of the events that make up American constitutional history is likely to remain obscure unless the experiences of individuals like this young black coal miner are brought to its surface. Second, I have tried to indicate why, when those experiences are brought to the surface of constitutional history, they expand like a ripple in a pond. What Herndon has to say about his experience sheds light on the cultural foundations of legal ideology and institutions—and, thus, it calls our attention to the ways that law and culture have intersected in American constitutional history. Third, in urging that the subaltern record of the Herndon case left in *Let Me Live* must be taken seriously, I have tried to clear the ground for a fresh reading of the text of *Herndon v. Georgia* itself. The interpretive model I have developed for reading Herndon's nonofficial account of the case also provides a framework for rereading official legal texts. The historiographical interest of such an undertaking, as I presently show, is that it permits us to see traces of subaltern political consciousness inscribed in the very terms and texture of the judicial discourse

through which the court tried to avoid both the constitutional issues raised in *Herndon v. Georgia* and the broader conflicts regarding race, culture, and power for which these issues were a site of intersection.

. . .

D. The Rhetoric of Resistance

. . . A rhetorical reading of *Herndon v. Georgia* might most profitably proceed by attending to the "politics of discourse" that informs the court's analysis of when, how, and to whom it may "speak the law." Viewed in these terms, the court's opinion reveals itself to be an instance of the very power that it claims merely to address.

I take the conception of rhetoric as the politics of discourse from Paolo Valesio,[120] who argues that "it is no more possible to speak without being rhetorical than it is to live without breathing."[121] All communication is in this sense rhetorical. Valesio maintains that even discourses like the discourse of law, which pretend a plain, forthright opposition to rhetorical ornament, embody a subtle and deceitful form of rhetoric—what he calls the "rhetoric of antirhetoric."[122] Valesio argues for a technique of "political" reading that delves beneath a discourse's apparent subject matter to reveal the rhetorical structures that are its "bones and sinews," indeed its very "biological structure."[123] Rhetoric, in this perspective, "constitutes the real politics of the text—the only kind of politics that is really relevant to its interpretation."[124]

Few would disagree that the judicial opinion can be placed squarely within the tradition of the "literature of legal persuasion"[125] and conviction. As Anthony Kronman puts it, legal discourse represents, "in essence, the construction of a convincing or persuasive argument."[126] Similarly, Mark Tushnet has broadly defined judicial opinions as "structures of thought . . . [fixed in] documents designed to convince by linking specific results to general assumptions."[127]

What is most striking about the opinion in *Herndon v. Georgia*, however, is the degree to which the suasive work of the text relies on silence and strategic omission. The structured absences in the text of the court's opinion can nonetheless be forced to yield up their meaning. A group of contemporaneous Supreme Court decisions (whose connections to Herndon seem to have eluded most students of the case) help to show that while the court's opinion in *Herndon v. Georgia* claims to be and appears to be about radical politics, it is in fact best understood as a case about the politics of race.

The starting point for such a reading is the very first line of Justice Sutherland's opinion for the court:

> Appellant was sentenced to a term of imprisonment upon conviction by a jury in a Georgia court of first instance of an attempt to incite insurrection by endeavoring to induce others to join in combined resistance to the authority of the state to be accomplished by acts of violence, in violation of Section 56 of the Penal Code of Georgia. The supreme court of the state affirmed the judgment.... On this appeal, the statute is assailed as contravening the due process clause of the Fourteenth Amendment in certain designated particulars. We find it unnecessary to review the points made, since this court is without jurisdiction for the reason that no federal question was seasonably raised in the court below or passed upon by that court.[128]

This opening passage serves a double function. One commentator has suggested that a "substantial part of legal discourse is not even particularly legal ... but is merely descriptive of the facts to be dealt with."[129] This suggests that the "mere description" of the facts in legal discourse cannot be said to be part of its ideological composition; it is, rather, a neutral statement of "what happened." [...]

In my view, it is precisely the conservatism of this statement of the facts—what it does not say—that alerts us to the form of the discursive politics of *Herndon v. Georgia*. The opening passage provides an exemplary instance of the rhetoric of anti-rhetoric.[130] Its substantive function is to limit the scope of the questions which the court will address to its narrowest possible range. Note how little information is given about the "appellant" or about the substantive constitutional issues the court is being asked to address: "We find it unnecessary to review the

points made" to support the appeal. Note, too, the passivity of the language of the final sentence of the paragraph: the problem of jurisdiction, the power of the court to "speak law," is rhetorically framed as something that is "found" or "vested" or "conferred"—not something that is "taken." In Sutherland's view, the court, through no fault of its own, is "without jurisdiction." This presumption of powerlessness shapes the court's subsequent discussion and guides us toward the political core of the text.

Let us compare the passive language of Justice Sutherland with the statement of the facts in Justice Benjamin Cardozo's dissent.[131] Cardozo begins by noting that "[t]he appellant has been convicted of an attempt to incite insurrection in violation of the Penal Code of Georgia."[132] Although the language in which Cardozo frames his statement of the facts is, like Sutherland's opinion, rigorously technical, it stands in subtle but significant contrast to Sutherland's opening lines. Cardozo approaches the facts of the case in terms of the events that led to Herndon's conviction. Sutherland, on the other hand, begins by noting that the "appellant" was "sentenced" to a prison term. By itself, Sutherland's focus on the consequences of the conviction, as opposed to the legal processes that led to the conviction, may not mean much. However, Sutherland's emphasis on punishment is resonant with political meaning, especially when one remembers just who the "appellant" was—a fact that the opinion very carefully avoids mentioning.

The exclusionary force of the bloodless factual language Sutherland uses to set up his legal analysis becomes clear when one compares it to the opening lines of Sutherland's opinion in Powell v. Alabama, the 1932 decision in which the court first took up the constitutional issues presented in the Scottsboro Cases:

> The petitioners, hereinafter referred to as defendants, are negroes charged with the crime of rape, committed upon the persons of two white girls. The crime is said to have been committed on March 25, 1931. The indictment was returned in a state court of first instance on March 31, and the record recites that on the same day the defendants were arraigned and entered pleas of not guilty ... no counsel had been employed, and aside from a

statement made by the trial judge several days later . . . the record does not disclose when . . . or who was appointed. . . . It is perfectly apparent that the proceedings, from beginning to end, took place in an atmosphere of tense, hostile and excited public sentiment. During the entire time, the defendants were closely confined or were under military guard. The record does not disclose their ages, except that one of them was nineteen; but the record clearly indicates that most, if not all, of them were youthful, and they are constantly referred to as "the boys." They were ignorant and illiterate. . . .[133]

This passage is also a statement of the "facts" of a case; but the differences between the two texts, written by the same author, are remarkable. In *Powell*, Sutherland is keenly aware of the concrete circumstances in which the court is intervening. His rhetoric captures the sociopolitical drama behind the legal questions to which the court's judgment is addressed: it notes the convergence of race, gender, age, and class, and it uses the statement of facts to presage the outcome.

The stark contrast between the rhetorical politics of *Powell* and the textual strategy of *Herndon* is startling. In *Herndon*, Sutherland does not note even once that Angelo Herndon, the "appellant" (never even the "defendant"), was black, or that he was only nineteen at the time of his arrest and conviction. But for the pronoun "he," the reader would have no clue even as to Herndon's gender. Nor does Sutherland discuss at all the extent to which Herndon's trial, like that of the Scottsboro defendants, took place in a "tense, hostile" atmosphere. The court cannot have been unmindful of these omitted facts. The constitutional relevance of race in *Herndon* is underscored in the evidentiary record and in Herndon's brief, which describes Sutherland's "accused" as "a Negro."[134] The marked exclusion from Sutherland's opinion of the "language of race"[135] is the most significant textual indication of the court's determination to avoid the constitutional issues in *Herndon v. Georgia*, and with them the political realities in which these issues were lodged.

To make the point another way: The court's silence on the politics of race must be read symptomatically. My choice of that term is

deliberate. Sigmund Freud identified the essence of repression as "simply . . . turning something away, and keeping it at a distance, from the conscious."[136] The court's omission of the fact that Herndon was an African-American criminal defendant appealing a conviction from a southern court is a textualized instance of such a psychic gesture. I shall consider in more depth the meaning of the court's silence on Herndon's race, because it highlights the need to pay close attention to the "political unconscious"[137] of the judicial discourse in *Herndon*. However, first I will discuss Sutherland's other rhetorical silences so that we may consider his silence on Herndon's race against this broader constellation.

We have seen that the inaugural gesture of Sutherland's opinion is one of exclusion, omission, and silence. This rhetorical strategy sets the analytic itinerary of the rest of the opinion:

It is true that there was a preliminary attack upon the indictment in the trial court on the ground, among others, that the statute was in violation "of the Constitution of the United States," and that this contention was overruled. But, in addition to the insufficiency of the specification, the adverse action of the trial court was not preserved by exceptions *pendente lite* or assigned as error in due time in the bill of exceptions, as the settled rules of the state practice require. In that situation, the state supreme court declined to review any of the rulings of the trial court in respect of that and other preliminary issues; and this determination of the state court is conclusive here. *John v. Paullin*, 231 U.S. 583, 585; *Atlantic Coast Line R. Co. v. Mims*, 242 U.S. 532, 535; *Nevada-California-Oregon Ry. v. Burrus*, 244 U.S. 103, 105; *Brooks v. Missouri*, 124 U.S. 394, 400; *Central Union Telephone Co. v. Edwardsville*, 269 U.S. 190, 194–195; *Erie R.R. Co. v. Purdy*, 185 U.S. 148, 154; *Mutual Life Ins. Co. v. McGrew*, 188 U.S. 291, 308.

The federal question was never properly presented to the state supreme court unless upon motion for rehearing; and that court then refused to consider it. The long-established general rule is that the attempt to raise a federal question after judgment, upon a petition for rehearing, comes too late, unless the court actually entertains the question and decides it. *Texas & Pacific C. Ry. Co. v. Southern Pacific Co.*, 137 U.S. 48, 54; *Loeber v. Schroeder*, 149 U.S. 580, 585; *Godchaux Co. v. Estopinal*, 251 U.S. 179, 181; *Rooker v. Fidelity Trust Co.*, 261 U.S. 114, 117; *Tidal Oil Co. v. Flanagan*, 263 U.S. 444, 454–455, and cases cited.[138]

The conceptual infrastructure of this passage argues that a judicial decision can be justified only if it is authorized by an already-existing rule of law—that is, by "precedent." I need not enter here into a full-fledged discussion of theories of legal precedent; rather, I want to approach the dialectical relay between assertion and appeal to authority set up in this passage in terms of what might be called the "politics of spatialization." As law, the thrust of the passage is clear enough: the Supreme Court cannot reach the merits of *Herndon v. Georgia* because the case's constitutional question was not raised in the trial court and because the state supreme court declined to consider it. As discourse, the passage links the past and the present in space, on the page, joining them in a conceptual and doctrinal identity. The unstated assumption behind the citations is that the court is only doing here what it has done many times before, that this case is the same as the past cases cited in the text. The court has no choice but to decline jurisdiction, because like cases must be treated alike. Thus, the discussion of Angelo Herndon's unsuccessful attack on his conviction is situated in an appeal to the authority of the past. "[T]he settled rules of state practice" and a "long-established general rule" dictate the result. Yet this passage is no less ideological than the omission of all information that would have humanized "the accused" or brought to light the social and political circumstances of his case. This becomes clearer in the next paragraph of the opinion:

> Petitioner, however, contends that the present case falls within an exception to the rule—namely, that the question respecting the validity of the statute as applied by the lower court first arose from its unanticipated act in giving to the statute a new construction which threatened rights under the Constitution. There is no doubt that the federal claim was timely if the ruling of the state court could not have been anticipated and a petition for rehearing presented the first opportunity for raising it. *Saunders v. Shaw*, 244 U.S. 317, 320; *Ohio v. Akron Park District*, 281 U.S. 74, 79; *Missouri v. Gehner*, 281 U.S. 313, 320; *Brinkerhoff-Faris Co. v. Hill*, 281 U.S. 673, 677-678; *American Surety Co. v. Baldwin*, 287 U.S. 156, 164; *Great Northern Ry. v. Sunburst Oil Co.*, 287 U.S. 358, 367. The whole point, therefore, is whether the ruling here assailed

[that is, that of the Georgia Supreme Court] should have been anticipated.[139]

In the discussion of the trial proceedings, I note that Judge Wyatt instructed the jury that mere advocacy of insurrection, "however reprehensible morally," would not justify a guilty verdict unless the jury found that Herndon had intended his advocacy to be acted upon immediately: "In order to convict the defendant, gentlemen, it must appear clearly by the evidence that immediate serious violence against the State of Georgia was to be expected or was advocated."[140] Although Herndon's counsel objected to this charge, it *was* in fact stricter than the test they argued should be applied—the clear and present danger test. The Supreme Court had applied the clear and present danger test to statutes, such as Section 56 of the Georgia Penal Code, that did not criminalize specific language but merely prohibited certain acts. When the acts were verbal, the court had held that a conviction could stand only when "the words used are used in such circumstances and are of such a nature as to create a clear and present danger that they will bring about the substantive evils" that Congress and the state legislatures had a "right to prevent."

From Herndon's point of view, then, the critical question on appeal to the Georgia Supreme Court was not whether the trial court had given an unfavorable jury charge—it had not—but whether the evidence warranted a conviction under the jury instruction the trial court had given. However, the state supreme court ruled that the trial court had been wrong in its charge: Section 56, the court said, did not require that violence should follow Herndon's words immediately, or even at all (nor, presumably, that the violent consequences be "serious" or "widespread"); rather, it "would be sufficient that [Herndon] intended [violence] to happen at any time, as a result of his influence, by those whom he sought to incite."[141] On that reading, the court refused to overturn Herndon's conviction. This expansive (to say the least) reading smacks of the old "bad tendency" test the Supreme Court had (apparently) rejected in favor of the clear and present danger test.[142] As Chafee points out in *Free Speech in the United*

States, the state supreme court's test was "so wide as to be fatal to open discussion"[143] or even moderate disagreement and dissent.[144] It was this radically open-ended "bad tendency" interpretation that Herndon's counsel challenged for the first time on a motion for rehearing (a motion the state court rejected on the rather capricious ground that it had not literally meant at any time, but only any reasonable time).[145] Similarly, it was this unanticipated interpretation of Section 56 that was the basis of the argument made on Herndon's behalf before the Supreme Court: that Herndon's case fell within the recognized exception to the rule that the Supreme Court could not take jurisdiction of cases in which the constitutional issues the court was being asked to decide had been raised for the first time on a motion for rehearing in the highest state court after that court had heard and decided the case upon appeal.[146]

As Sutherland analyzes the case, the "whole point" in *Herndon v. Georgia* is not that the state court rejected the trial court's jury charge but rather that Herndon's counsel should have known that the trial court's charge was wrong:

> The verdict of the jury was returned on January 18, 1933, and judgment immediately followed. On July 5, 1933, the trial court overruled a motion for new trial. The original opinion was handed down and the judgment of the state supreme court entered on May 24, 1934, the case having been in that court since the preceding July.
>
> On March 18, 1933, several months prior to the action of the trial court on the motion for new trial, the state supreme court had decided *Carr v. State,* 176 Ga. 747; 169 S. E. 201. In that case Section 56 of the Penal Code, under which it arose, was challenged as contravening the Fourteenth Amendment. The court in substance construed the statute as it did in the present case. In the course of the opinion it said (p. 750): " 'It [the state] cannot reasonably be required to defer the adoption of measures for its own peace and safety until the revolutionary utterances lead to actual disturbances of the public peace of imminent and immediate danger of its own destruction; but it may, in the exercise of its judgment, suppress the threatened danger in its incipiency.... Manifestly, the legislature has authority to forbid the advocacy of a doctrine designed and intended to overthrow the government without waiting until there is a present and imminent danger of the success of the plan advocated. If the State were

compelled to wait until the apprehended danger became certain, then its right to protect itself would come into being simultaneously with the overthrow of the government, when there would be neither prosecuting officers nor courts for the enforcement of the law.' " The language contained in the subquotation is taken from *People v. Lloyd,* 304 Ill. 23, 35; 136 N. E. 505, and is quoted with approval by this court in *Gitlow v. New York,* 268 U.S. 652, 669.

> In the present case, following the language quoted at an earlier point in this opinion to the effect that it was sufficient if the defendant intended an insurrection to follow at any time, etc., the court below, in its original opinion, (178 Ga. 855) added—"It was the intention of this law to arrest at its incipiency any effort to overthrow the State government, where it takes the form of an actual attempt to incite insurrection."[147]

. . .

Earlier in my discussion, I contrasted the texture and tone of Justice Sutherland's statement of the facts in Herndon with his statement of the facts in *Powell v. Alabama.* In *Herndon,* Sutherland recites an antiseptic procedural account; but in *Powell,* he painstakingly situates his discussion of the constitutional issues in a concrete social and political context. What is interesting is that *Powell,* not *Herndon,* is the norm. Of the court's decisions from this period that invalidated the convictions of African-American defendants on constitutional grounds, all except *Herndon* follow *Powell's* rhetorical strategy with respect to the politics of race.

Consider, for example, the language of the court's opinions in *Norris v. Alabama*[148] and *Patterson v. Alabama,*[149] decided a bare month before *Herndon v. Georgia.* Writing for the court in Norris, Chief Justice Hughes begins by noting that the "[p]etitioner, Clarence Norris, is one of nine negro boys who were indicted in March, 1931, in Jackson County Alabama, for the crime of rape."[150] In *Patterson,* another opinion by the chief justice, the race of the defendant and the location of his alleged crime also introduce the court's analysis of the relevant constitutional issues.[151]

A year after *Herndon,* in *Brown v. Mississippi,*[152] the court invalidated several murder convictions because they were based solely on confessions procured by physical torture. Chief Justice Hughes again wrote the opinion, quoting extensively from the Alabama Supreme Court's opinion in the case. The quoted passages refer to the defendants as "all ignorant negroes"[153] and describe in meticulous detail the torture of these "helpless prisoners"[154] at the hands of a white "mob."[155]

In each of these cases, the court placed the brute facts of racism and power in the foreground of its constitutional analysis. The opinions in *Brown, Norris, Powell,* and *Patterson* emphasize these realities of race and region even though, on the face of it, none of the cases required it. Indeed, in *Patterson,* sensitivity to racial politics led the Chief Justice to address the substantive constitutional issues even though the State of Alabama claimed that the court could not properly take jurisdiction.[156] Significantly, the jurisdictional question in *Patterson* was whether the defendant had lost his right to Supreme Court review by failing to take timely action in the state courts to preserve his federal claim. In *Herndon,* Hughes agreed with Sutherland that Angelo Herndon had forfeited his right to Supreme Court jurisdiction; but here, he had no time for too fastidious a concern for the procedural difficulties of the case, given what he describes in constitutional terms as a "serious situation." . . .

In *Brown, Norris, Powell,* and *Patterson,* the Supreme Court acted to protect African-Americans against the most egregious uses of the criminal process as an instrument of racial domination. I believe that the court was able to justify these interventions to the country and to itself by showing that the defendants in those cases fit contemporary cultural images of African-Americans. These defendants, as Justice Sutherland writes in *Powell,* were "ignorant and illiterate Negroes" and thus fit objects for a jurisprudence of "mercy."[157]

Herndon confronted the court with an altogether different sort of black defendant. The Angelo Herndon case marked the first occasion on which the Supreme Court was forced to come to terms so directly with the concept of political crime in a case in which the alleged criminal was a black American. If Angelo

Herndon was a political criminal, what of the white southerners who, if the court upheld his conviction, stood ready to punish him? The court had to face harsh historical and contemporary realities that it could neither ignore nor openly acknowledge. If it intervened, it would have to decisively condemn the racial and political culture that Herndon too had fought. This was a step that ideology and cultural experience did not yet allow the court to take. Indeed, shortly before it decided *Herndon v. Georgia,* it also declared that the Texas Democratic Party's exclusion of blacks was not state action,[158] showing its willingness to tolerate all but the most visible, formal exclusions of black Americans from the political process.

In 1937, two years after *Herndon v. Georgia* and one year after its denial of a motion for a rehearing in the case, the Supreme Court issued its third, final, favorable judgment on Angelo Herndon's constitutional claim.[159] The court's ultimate vindication of Angelo Herndon's First Amendment rights marks an important moment in the history of free speech jurisprudence. As a doctrinal matter, it can and should be viewed as a landmark First Amendment decision. What I have tried to show here, however, is that the history of the Herndon case is more than a story about the constitutional politics of the First Amendment.

There is another story behind the case, and that story is about the constitutional politics of race. Properly understood, the Herndon case must be placed at the intersection of two jurisprudential axes. The Herndon case marks the beginnings of the modern Supreme Court's hesitant and halting efforts to address the dissonance in American legal and political consciousness between two competing images of the African-American community generally and of the black male in particular—as an ignorant and helpless victim, on one hand, and a dangerous insurgent, on the other. In the thirties, these two contradictory images of the black American still weighed like a nightmare on the white American mind. In *Herndon v. Georgia,* the Supreme Court found itself caught between these two warring cultural images, which held decidedly different political and constitutional implications. Rather than choose between them, the court decided not to decide.

V. Conclusion

DAVID Luban has recently argued that legal discourse is "neither analytic nor empirical, but rather historical. The life of the law is not a vision of the future but a vision of the past. . . ." [160] Legal argument may thus be understood as "a struggle for the privilege of recounting the past. To the victor goes the right to infuse a constitutional clause, or a statute, or a series of prior decisions with the meaning that it will henceforth bear. . . ." [161]

What Professor Luban says of legal argument and its outcome holds equally true for argument and interpretation in legal history. This article has undertaken a historical rereading of the Angelo Herndon case from below. I have focused on the events leading up to the Supreme Court's decision in *Herndon v. Georgia*. I have done this not because I believe that *Herndon v. Lowry* was not an important constitutional victory, but rather because the story of the constitutional failure in *Herndon v. Georgia* is an equally important part of the historical record. As we have seen, the great weight of historical scholarship has focused on the court's decision in *Herndon v. Lowry*. The absence of *Herndon v. Georgia* in most histories of the case suggests that some fifty years later, the Angelo Herndon story is still not a fully citable episode in our constitutional history. Revisiting that history from the bottom up, I have aimed to show that we cannot remember only one part of that story without forgetting them both.

NOTES

1. J. Dewey, *Philosophy and Civilization*, 9 (2d ed. 1968) [1931].

2. 274 U.S. 357, 374 (1957). See M. Shapiro, *Freedom of Speech: The Supreme Court and Judicial Review*, 58 (1966).

3. Z. Chafee, Jr., *Free Speech in the United States* (1941). An earlier version of *Free Speech in the United States* was cited by the lawyers who wrote the first Supreme Court brief on Herndon's behalf; see Brief for Appellant at 20, *Herndon v. Georgia*, 295 U.S. 441 (1935) (No. 665).

4. *Id.* at 393.

5. *Id.* at 392. The Fifteenth Amendment states, "The right of citizens of the United States to vote shall not be denied or abridged by the United States or by any State on account of race, color, or previous condition of servitude"; U.S. Const. amend. XV, § 1.

6. Chafee, *supra* note 3, at 392.

7. *Id.* at 393.

8. *Id.* at 390 n. 45.

9. *Herndon v. Georgia*, 295 U.S. 441, 443 (1935).

10. *Id.*, 296 U.S. 661 (1935).

11. See, for example, P. A. Freund et al., *Constitutional Law: Cases And Other Problems*, 1158–62 (4th ed. 1977); G. Gunther, *Constitutional Law*, 1013–15 (11th ed. 1985); G. R. Stone et al., *Constitutional Law*, 966–68 (1986).

12. See, for example, N. Dorsen et al., *Political and Civil Rights in the United States* (4th ed. 1976).

13. See, for example, P. M. Bator et al., *Hart and Wechsler's The Federal Courts and the Federal System* (3d ed. 1988).

14. E. W. Said, "Orientalism Reconsidered," in Francis Barker et al., eds., *Literature, Politics and Theory*, 210, 212 (1986).

15. M. Brown, "History and History's Problem," 16 *Soc. Text*, 136 (1986–87).

16. R. Samuel, "People's History," in *People's History and Socialist Theory*, xvi (1981).

17. This is an appropriate point at which to emphasize that this article is not an exercise in "black" or "Afro-American" historical studies. Stated bluntly, I reject the notion that such a compartmentalization, such an exile to a subdisciplinary ghetto, is either possible or desirable. I believe the late C. L. R. James was right when he remarked on the limitations of black studies as such: "[To] talk to me about black studies as if it's something that concerned [only] black people is an utter denial. This is the history of Western Civilization. I can't see it otherwise. . . . I only know the struggle of people against tyranny and oppression in a certain social and political setting, and, particularly, during the last two hundred years, it's impossible to me to separate black studies from white studies in any theoretical point of view"; C. L. R. James, *At The Rendezvous of Victory*, 194, 201 (1984). This article should be read as an attempt to move the African-American constitutional experience from the margins to the center of American constitutional history.

18. A. Herndon, *Let Me Live* (1937).

19. Transcript of Record, at 76, *Herndon v. State*, 174 S.E. 597 (Ga. 1934). James W. Ford, a trade unionist, was a leading black member of the Communist Party and its vice presidential candidate during the national election of 1932; see H. Klehr, *The Heyday of American Communism: The Depression Decade*, 330–31 (1984). William Z. Foster, of

Irish-immigrant background, was for many years the best-known American Communist and the party's perennial presidential candidate; see *id.* at 19–20. While one might assume that the name Ford and Foster Clubs was used to conceal the fact that the persons mentioned in the minutes were attending a meeting of the Communist Party, it should be noted that in 1932 several prominent nonradical blacks (among them the poet Countee Cullen and the intellectual Kelley Miller) were recruited as members of the Ford-Foster Committee for Equal Negro Rights, led by William Jones, the managing editor of the *Baltimore Afro-American;* see *id.* at 469 n. 16.

20. L. Outlaw, "Language and Consciousness: Toward a Hermeneutic of Black Culture," 1 *Cultural Hermeneutics,* 403 (1974) (quoting J. Turner, "The Sociology of Black Nationalism," in 1 *Black Scholar,* 18 (1969)).

21. Outlaw, *supra* note 20.

22. See E. W. Said, *The World, The Text, and the Critic,* 9 (1983).

23. J. Brenkman, *Culture and Domination,* vii (1987). In "A Dialectical Approach to Culture," the Guinean leader and political theorist Sekou Touré sets forth a definition of culture for continental Africa that parallels the conception of culture central to an understanding of political practice among the people of the African diaspora in the United States: "[Culture embraces] all the material and immaterial works of art and science, plus knowledge, manners, education, a mode of thought, behavior and attitudes accumulated by the people both through and by virtue of their struggle from the hold and domination of nature. . . . [Culture also] stands revealed as both an exclusive creation of the people and a source of creation, as an instrument of socioeconomic liberation and as one of domination. Culture implies our struggle—it is our struggle"; S. Touré, "A Dialectical Approach to Culture," in R. Chrisman and N. Hare, eds., *Contemporary Black Thought,* 5 (1973). For a discussion of the importance of cultural practice for critical race theory, see A. Dirlik, "Culturalism as Hegemonic Ideology and Liberating Practice," 6 *Cultural Critique,* 13 (1987).

24. My point is most emphatically not that culture and power politics are identical. What I do mean to suggest is that cultural products and practices, including legal culture, are part of a "large intellectual endeavor—systems and currents of thought connected in complex ways to doing things, to accomplishing certain things, to force, to social class and economic production, to diffusing ideas, values and world pictures"; Said, *supra* note 22, at 170.

25. Herndon, *supra* note 18.

26. The Communist Party's Unemployed Council (which Herndon refers to in *Let Me Live* as the Unemployment Council) successfully forced important concessions from local relief authorities and landlords, through both advocacy on behalf of the unemployed and direct action—such as eviction protests and demonstrations at relief offices, city halls, and state capitals. The council was particularly effective during the early years of the Depression, when local relief programs were singularly incompetent in dealing with mass unemployment. According to historians of the period, the Unemployed Council played an important role in the "breaking down of barriers" that had frustrated the political coalition between poor whites and blacks, particularly in the South; R. Rozensweig, " 'Organizing the Unemployed': The Early Years of the Depression," 10 *Radical Am.* 37, 42 (1976). The CPUSA has maintained that the council was the "tactical key" to its work during the thirties; *id.* at 40. For a history and analysis of the rise and fall of this movement, see F. F. Pivens and R. A. Cloward, *Poor People's Movements,* 41–95 (1977).

27. Herndon, *supra* note 18, at 77–78.

28. *Id.* at 80.

29. *Id.* at 78.

30. *Id.* at 79–80.

31. *Id.* at 87–88.

32. *Id.* at 82.

33. *Id.*

34. *Id.*

35. *Id.*

36. The Communist Party line on the "negro question" was based on an analysis by Soviet communists that African-Americans were an oppressed nation whose only hope lay in the creation of a sovereign state in the southern "Black Belt." The historical record clearly shows that the theoreticians in Moscow completely misread the aspirations of black people in the United States. The Soviet elite was unable to understand that African-Americans were less interested in being separate from American society than in being fully part of it. Further, the Soviet Union attempted to fit the historical experience of black Americans into the conceptual framework of its policy toward its own ethnic and racial minorities, refusing to acknowledge the particularity of black Americans' experience. Nevertheless, the fact remains that during the thirties, the CPUSA was the only political party in the United States seriously committed to the struggle for racial equality in America (and committed in a sustained way), as well as the only political party in which African-Americans had a leadership role; see generally H. Klehr, *supra* note 19; M. Naison, *Communists in Harlem during the Depression* (1983). For a discussion of the specific question of black American self-determination, see H. Haywood, *Black Bolshevik* (1978). For an interesting contemporary debate on the "black nation" thesis and the CPUSA program to establish an independent, black-controlled political entity in the southern "Black Belt", see G. Breitman, ed., *Leon Trotsky on Black Nationalism and Self-Determination* (1978).

37. F. M. Ottanelli, *The Communist Party of the United States: From the Depression to World War II,* 42 (1991).

38. R. Guha, *Elementary Aspects of Peasant Insurgency in Colonial India*, 38 (1983).

39. Herndon, *supra* note 18, at 89.

40. *Id.*

41. *Id.*. at 87.

42. E. P. Thompson, *Whigs and Hunters*, 49 (1975).

43. Transcript of Record, *supra* note 19, at 123–24. The pamphlet is the first of several texts in the documentary dossier at the end of *Let Me Live*. I give it pride of place in my narrative in the belief that its insurgent consciousness will enhance our epistemic point of view.

44. C. H. Martin, *The Angelo Herndon Case and Southern Justice*, 6 (1976).

45. Transcript of Record, *supra* note 19, at 124–25.

46. *Id.* at 125.

47. *Id.*

48. *Id.* at 126.

49. *Id.* at 5.

50. *Id.* at 9.

51. *Id.* at 8.

52. *Id.*

53. *Id.* at 6.

54. *Id.* at 7.

55. *Id.*

56. *Id.*

57. *Id.*

58. *Id.*

59. *Id.*

60. *Id.* at 21.

61. Martin, *supra* note 44, at 11 (quoting *Daily Worker*, Aug. 3, 1932).

62. H. Aptheker, *A Documentary History of the Negro People in the United States*, 700 (1973).

63. *Id.*

64. *Id.* at 701.

65. *Id.* at 702.

66. *Id.* at 703.

67. *Id.* at 706.

68. *Id.* at 706–07.

69. J. Spivak, *Georgia Nigger* (1932). For a discussion of Spivak's work in the context of the larger documentary movement of which it was a part, see W. Stott, *Documentary Expression and Thirties America* (1973).

70. Spivak, *supra* note 69, at ii.

71. Transcript of Record, *supra* note 19, at 60–61.

72. *Id.* at 80–81.

73. I take this term from C. H. Stember, *Sexual Racism* (1976).

74. *Id.* at ix (quoting James Weldon Johnson). Joel Kovel has described the psychosexual roots of white racism in the following terms: "In the classic South—and, as the fantasies generated there were diffused, throughout America—the sex fantasy has been incorporated into the white assumption of superiority and the demand for black submission. Whenever a black man bowed and scraped, whenever a white man called a black man 'boy,' or in other ways infantilized him, just below the surface of the white man's consciousness, a sexual fantasy would be found yoked to the symbol of power and status. These sex fantasies erupted whenever the power relationships were threatened. In the colonies, the slightest rumor of a slave revolt was accompanied by wild stories of blacks wreaking their ultimate revenge in wholesale rape of white women. Nor should anyone think that, below the surface of reasonable concern, the fears aroused in whites by the current black rebellion are different. The specter of omnipotent black sexuality has obsessed whites from their first glimpse of an African until this very day"; J. Kovel, *White Racism: A Psychohistory* 68 (1970). For another overview of this history, see C. C. Hernton, *Sex and Racism in America* (1965). The most publicized recent chapter in the history of the vexed relationship between sexuality and race in American political culture is the Senate judiciary committee hearings on the charges of sexual harassment leveled at Clarence Thomas. For a treatment of these issues, see Kendall Thomas, "Strange Fruit," in Toni Morrison, ed., *Race-ing Justice, En-gendering Power*, 364 (1992).

75. Transcript of Record, *supra* note 19, at 64.

76. *Id.* at 76–78.

77. Martin, *supra* note 44, at 53–54.

78. *Id.* at 54 (quoting J. H. Street, *Look Away!: A Dixie Notebook*, 149 (1936)).

79. E. Lawson, *Twenty Years on the Chain Gang?* 8 (1935).

80. W. E. B. Du Bois, *W. E. B. Du Bois* 92 (W. M. Tuttle ed., 1972), quoted in B. Boxill, "The Race-Class Questions," in L. Harris, ed., *Philosophy Born of Struggle*, 107 (1983).

81. Martin, *supra* note 44, at 60.

82. Herndon, *supra* note 18, at 354.

83. *Id.* at 353.

84. *Id.*

85. *Id.*

86. *Id.*

87. *Id.* at 135.

88. G. E. White, *The Marshall Court and Cultural Change, 1815–1835,* at 4 (1988) (arguing that cultural signifiers are "words intended to convey a bundle of associations and thereby to invoke an appeal to values perceived to be of great importance in the culture").

89. K. Burke, *Attitudes Toward History,* 315 (1937).

90. W. Mendelson, "Clear and Present Danger—From *Schenck to Dennis,*" 52 Colum. L. Rev., 313 (1952).

91. P. J. Murphy, *The Constitution in Crisis Times, 1918–69* (1972).

92. See D. P. Currie, "The Constitution in the Supreme Court: Civil Rights and Liberties, 1930–1941," 1987 Duke L. J. 800 [hereinafter Currie, "Civil Rights"].

93. Mendelson, *supra* note 90.

94. *Id.* at 313.

95. *Id.*

96. *Id.* at 333.

97. *Id.* at 317.

98. *Id.* (citations omitted).

99. *Id.* at 317 and nn. 20 (citing *Herndon v. Lowry,* 301 U.S. 242 (1937)) and 21 (citing *Herndon v. Georgia,* 295 U.S. 441 (1935)). Note that Mendelson gives citational pride of place to *Herndon v. Lowry,* even though it followed the adverse decision in *Herndon v. Georgia* by some two years. Note too that Mendelson does no more than cite the two decisions, even though they marked the only instances during the entire tenure of the Hughes Court in which the doctrine that is his subject figured in the court's First Amendment jurisprudence.

100. *Id.* at 317.

101. *Id.* at 333.

102. *Id.* at 332.

103. Murphy, *supra* note 91.

104. *Id.* at 99–101, 107–08.

105. *Id.* at 121.

106. *Id.* at 119.

107. *Id.* at 122.

108. D. P. Currie, "The Constitution in the Supreme Court: Civil Rights and Liberties, 1930–1941," 1987 *Duke L. J.,* 800, 811.

109. *Id.* at 811.

110. 301 U.S. 242 (1937).

111. Currie, "Civil Rights," *supra* note 92, at 811.

112. *Id.* at 813.

113. A. Bickel, *The Supreme Court and the Idea of Progress,* 13 (1970).

114. C. Lasch, *The True and Only Heaven: Progress and Its Critics,* 220 (1991).

115. R. Bromley, *Lost Narratives,* 7 (1988). Bromley describes the contested terrain of history as a dialectical unity of anamnesis and amnesia in which "[f]orgetting is as important as remembering. Part of the struggle against cultural power is the challenge to forgetting posed by memory. What is 'forgotten' may represent more threatening aspects of popular 'memory' and have been carefully and consciously, not casually and unconsciously, omitted from the narrative economy of remembering"; *id.* at 12.

116. Herbert Aptheker, Afro-American History: The Modern Era 51 (1971) (quoting W. E. B. Du Bois).

117. Herndon, *supra* note 18, at 89.

118. F. Jameson, *The Political Unconscious,* 102 (1981).

119. M. Foucault, "Two Lectures," in C. Gordon, ed., *Power/Knowledge,* 83, trans. C. Gordon et al. (1980).

120. P. Valesio, *Novantiqua,* 44–45 (1980).

121. *Id.* at 60.

122. *Id.* at 44.

123. *Id.* at 57.

124. *Id.*

125. *Id.*

126. A. T. Kronman, "Foreword: Legal Scholarship and Moral Education," 90 *Yale L. J.,* 955, 961 (1981).

127. M. V. Tushnet, *The American Law of Slavery, 1810–1860: Considerations of Humanity and Interest,* 30 (1981).

128. *Herndon v. Georgia,* 295 U.S. 441, 442 (1935) (footnote omitted).

129. C. Sumner, *Reading Ideologies: An Investigation into the Marxist Theory of Ideology and Law,* 273 (1979). [. . .]

130. Valesio, *supra* note 120, at 44.

131. 295 U.S. at 448 (Cardozo, J., dissenting). Of course, given their opposing arguments, one can see that the rhetorical strategies of these two opinions should be directly opposite.

132. *Id.* at 446 (Cardozo, J., dissenting).

133. *Powell v. Alabama,* 287 U.S. 45, 49–52 (1932).

134. Brief for Appellant at 5, *Herndon v. Georgia,* 295 U.S. 441 (1935) (Nos. 474 & 475).

135. C. Miller, "Constitutional Law and the Rhetoric of Race," in D. Fleming and B. Bailyn, eds., *Law in American History,* 147 (1971).

136. S. Freud, "Repression," in J. Strzchey, ed. and trans., 14 *The Standard Edition of the Complete Psychological Works of Sigmund Freud,* 141, 147 (1957).

137. Fredric Jameson, *Marxism and Historicism*, 11 New Literary Hist. 41, 42 (1979).

138. *Herndon*, 295 U.S. at 442–43.

139. *Id.* at 443–44.

140. Transcript of Record, *supra* note 19, at 133.

141. *Herndon v. State*, 174 S.E. 597, 610 (Ga. Ct. App. 1934).

142. G. Gunther, *Constitutional Law*, 1009 (12th ed. 1991).

143. Chafee, *supra* note 3, at 394.

144. As Justice Owen Roberts pointed out two years after the court's decision, in *Herndon v. Lowry:* "Within what time might one reasonably expect that an attempted organization of the Communist Party in the United States would result in violent action by that party? If a jury returned a special verdict saying twenty years or even fifty years the verdict could not be shown to be wrong"; 301 U.S. 242, 263 (1937).

145. Transcript of Record, *supra* note 19, at 195.

146. *Herndon v. Georgia*, 295 U.S. 441, 443–44 (1935).

147. *Id.* at 444–45.

148. 294 U.S. 587 (1935).

149. 294 U.S. 600 (1935).

150. 294 U.S. at 588.

151. 294 U.S. at 601.

152. 297 U.S. 278 (1936).

153. *Id.* at 281.

154. *Id.* at 282.

155. *Id.*

156. 294 U.S. at 602.

157. *Powell v. Alabama*, 287 U.S. 45, 52 (1932).

158. *Grovey v. Townsend*, 295 U.S. 45 (1935), overruled by *Smith v. Allwright*, 321 U.S. 649 (1944).

159. *Herndon v. Lowry*, 301 U.S. 242 (1937).

160. D. Luban, "Difference Made Legal: The Court and Dr. King," 87 *Mich. L. Rev.*, 2152, 2154 (1989).

161. *Id.* at 2152.

❦